SELECTED STATUTES, RULES AND STANDARDS ON THE LEGAL PROFESSION

1992 Edition

DR7 102
MR 3.3, 3.4

Selected and Edited

By

John S. Dzienkowski
Professor of Law, University of Texas

WEST PUBLISHING CO.
ST. PAUL, MINN., 1992

PREFACE

In the past decade, the ABA, the states, and other entities have been active in the promulgation of standards, rules, and statutes that regulate lawyers' conduct. These sources of the law of professional responsibility have significantly affected the manner in which lawyers analyze problems in this area. Similarly, the existence of different formal sources of professional responsibility have altered the way in which lawyers and law students are taught about ethical problems. This pamphlet of Selected Statutes, Rules and Standards on the Legal Profession is designed to provide teachers and students with easy access to the important sources of professional responsibility.

The 1992 edition of Selected Statutes, Rules and Standards on the Legal Profession varies considerably from the early editions of this work. First, the increase in the number of sources of professional responsibility has necessitated a reorganization of the materials into six different parts: (1) Codes Regulating Lawyers' Conduct; (2) Statutes and Rules of Evidence and Procedure that Affect the Legal Profession; (3) Standards for Specialized Areas of Practice; (4) Standards for the Organized Regulation of Lawyers; (5) Codes of Judicial Conduct; and (6) Selected State Standards, Rules, and Statutes. This reorganization should make the material more accessible and more logical to analyze from the students' perspective. Second, in light of the fact that the American Bar Association has amended the Model Rules of Professional Conduct several times since 1983, it has become necessary to annotate the current version of the Model Rules with indication of the original version of the amended provisions. The annotated version of the Model Rules contained in this pamphlet allows students to compare the current version with the prior version, which appears in a footnote on the same page with the current version. This change should also facilitate the study of cases and ethics opinions that are based upon prior versions of the Model Rules.

Third, in light of the fact that the states have made significant modifications to the ABA's version of the Model Rules, it has become desirable to include a section on selected significant state modifications to the Model Rules. Such a section will allow teachers and students to examine how various states have chosen to modify specific provisions of the Model Rules. Fourth, the reorganization of this pamphlet has highlighted the need to expand the section on standards for specialized areas of practice. As the sources of professional responsibility begin to affect all areas of practice, certain well organized groups of practitioners have sought to enact codes of conduct which recognize unique problems within an area of practice. The future impact of such codes is still uncertain; yet, members of the legal profession must deal with this trend. Fifth, this pamphlet includes the 1990 Model Code of Judicial Conduct, which significantly departs from the prior 1972 Model Code of Judicial Conduct. The 1990 Model Code will undoubtedly cause state and federal judiciaries to begin to examine and to adopt modifications to their codes of judicial conduct. Finally, this edition contains the complete California Code of Professional Conduct and the Disciplinary Rules of the New York Code of Professional Responsibility. These states illustrate two prominent examples of jurisdictions that have rejected the format and structure of the ABA Model Rules.

I sincerely acknowledge the excellent expertise and assistance of David Gunn of the Tarlton Law Library in locating the various state codes of professional responsibility. I welcome comments and suggestions on the materials contained in this edition.

The materials are current through March 1992, and this supplement will be updated periodically to reflect new and amended statutes and rules.

JOHN S. DZIENKOWSKI

Austin, Texas
April 1992

TABLE OF CONTENTS

PART ONE: CODES REGULATING LAWYERS' CONDUCT

PART TWO: STATUTES AND RULES OF EVIDENCE AND PROCEDURE THAT AFFECT THE LEGAL PROFESSION

TABLE OF CONTENTS

PART THREE: STANDARDS FOR SPECIALIZED AREAS OF PRACTICE

PART FOUR: STANDARDS FOR THE ORGANIZED REGULATION OF LAWYERS

PART FIVE: CODES OF JUDICIAL CONDUCT

PART SIX: SELECTED STATE STANDARDS, RULES, AND STATUTES

VI

SELECTED STATUTES, RULES AND STANDARDS ON THE LEGAL PROFESSION

1992 Edition

PART ONE

CODES AND STANDARDS REGULATING LAWYERS' CONDUCT

Table of Contents

Introduction

One of the traditional characteristics of a profession is the attempt to achieve self regulation. Throughout history, professions have enacted codes of conduct to assert control over their members. Various groups within the legal profession have similarly sought to exercise a degree of self regulation by enacting codes of conduct. This part includes several codes and standards which have attempted to regulate the conduct of all lawyers in their practice of law.

The first three codes contained in this section were promulgated by the American Bar Association (ABA), a national voluntary organization of lawyers. The ABA has assumed the primary responsibility for promulgating national ethical standards for the legal profession. In 1908, the ABA enacted 32 Canons of Professional Ethics. In 1969, it replaced the Canons with the Model Code of Professional Responsibility. In 1983, the Model Code was replaced with the Model Rules of Professional Conduct.

Although the ABA's codes of conduct have been influential in shaping the law of professional responsibility, they only have force as a body of rules with its voluntary members. However, the various states

1

and the federal courts have looked to the ABA versions as a basis for regulating lawyers within the jurisdiction. Thus, the ABA's codes have been used as the basis for state and federal codes. With the Model Code, many states adopted the ABA version without many significant changes. However, with the ABA's promulgation of the Model Rules, the states have been less deferential. Many states have made significant modifications to the ABA version. Thus, this part includes a section on significant state modifications to the Model Rules.

The lack of deference to the ABA Model Rules could have been predicted in light of the significant controversy that occurred during the debates over the Model Rules. One very important component of the debate was the effort of the American Trial Lawyer's Foundation to draft an alternative code of conduct for lawyers. The resulting document, The American Lawyers' Code of Conduct, is included in this part as it illustrates the choices that could have been made at the time the ABA enacted the Model Rules.

A final series of documents in this part reflect a recent trend on the part of the ABA and the states to focus on lawyer professionalism as a basis for regulating lawyers' conduct. The origin of this movement was a study on professionalism commissioned by the ABA. The results of the study identified several reasons for the decline in lawyer professionalism and offered several suggestions to address this problem. The ABA Creed of Professionalism and the ABA Pledge of Professionalism illustrate attempts to implement the suggestions of the Commission on Professionalism. The Texas Creed on Professionalism provides a similar example of a state effort to address this problem. The ABA's Aspirational Goals on Lawyer Advertising provide a more concrete example of urging standards of professionalism in the communication of advertising to the general public.

AMERICAN BAR ASSOCIATION MODEL RULES OF PROFESSIONAL CONDUCT

Annotated to Reflect Amendments and Prior Text of the Model Rules in Footnotes.

Adopted August 1983, as Amended to August, 1991.

———

[Less than a decade after the Model Code of Professional Responsibility was promulgated in 1969, the ABA established a commission to create another code of ethics for the legal profession. Between 1977 to 1983 the Kutak Commission, named after its chairman Robert Kutak, proceeded to write several drafts of a new code of conduct for lawyers. In 1983, the ABA enacted the Model Rules of Professional Conduct based upon the work of the Kutak Commission. The Model Rules were a response to criticisms about the Model Code's focus on litigation and its three tier structure of canons, ethical considerations, and disciplinary rules. The Model Rules follow a UCC or restatement-like approach by placing the rule of professional responsibility in text and including elaborative material in the comments. Since its adoption in 1983, the ABA has amended the Model Rules several times, and thus this version of the Model Rules is annotated to indicate in footnotes the manner in which the ABA has amended the Model Rules since the original adoption in 1983. Although the current ABA version is important, the original version of the Model Rules is more likely to form the basis for the state adoptions of the Model Rules. When studying a case or an ethics opinion in the various states, one should examine whether the decision is based upon the current version of the Model Rules or a prior version. Additionally, the comments to the Model Rules are numbered sequentially under each Model Rule provision to facilitate citation of a particular comment. Ed.]

———

CONTENTS

Preamble, Scope, and Terminology

CLIENT–LAWYER RELATIONSHIP

3

ABA MODEL RULES

PREAMBLE, SCOPE, AND TERMINOLOGY

Preamble: A Lawyer's Responsibilities

[1]   A lawyer is a representative of clients, an officer of the legal system and a public citizen having special responsibility for the quality of justice.

[2]   As a representative of clients, a lawyer performs various functions.   As advisor, a lawyer provides a client with an informed understanding of the client's legal rights and obligations and explains their practical implications.   As advocate, a lawyer zealously asserts the client's position under the rules of the adversary system.   As negotiator, a lawyer seeks a result advantageous to the client but consistent with requirements of honest dealing with others.   As intermediary between clients, a lawyer seeks to reconcile their divergent interests as an advisor and, to a limited extent, as a spokesperson for each client.   A lawyer acts as evaluator by examining a client's legal affairs and reporting about them to the client or to others.

[3]   In all professional functions a lawyer should be competent, prompt and diligent.   A lawyer should maintain communication with a client concerning the representation.   A lawyer should keep in confidence information relating to representation of a client except so far as disclosure is required or permitted by the Rules of Professional Conduct or other law.

5

[4] A lawyer's conduct should conform to the requirements of the law, both in professional service to clients and in the lawyer's business and personal affairs. A lawyer should use the law's procedures only for legitimate purposes and not to harass or intimidate others. A lawyer should demonstrate respect for the legal system and for those who serve it, including judges, other lawyers and public officials. While it is a lawyer's duty, when necessary, to challenge the rectitude of official action, it is also a lawyer's duty to uphold legal process.

[5] As a public citizen, a lawyer should seek improvement of the law, the administration of justice and the quality of service rendered by the legal profession. As a member of a learned profession, a lawyer should cultivate knowledge of the law beyond its use for clients, employ that knowledge in reform of the law and work to strengthen legal education. A lawyer should be mindful of deficiencies in the administration of justice and of the fact that the poor, and sometimes persons who are not poor, cannot afford adequate legal assistance, and should therefore devote professional time and civic influence in their behalf. A lawyer should aid the legal profession in pursuing these objectives and should help the bar regulate itself in the public interest.

[6] Many of a lawyer's professional responsibilities are prescribed in the Rules of Professional Conduct, as well as substantive and procedural law. However, a lawyer is also guided by personal conscience and the approbation of professional peers. A lawyer should strive to attain the highest level of skill, to improve the law and the legal profession and to exemplify the legal profession's ideals of public service.

[7] A lawyer's responsibilities as a representative of clients, an officer of the legal system and a public citizen are usually harmonious. Thus, when an opposing party is well represented, a lawyer can be a zealous advocate on behalf of a client and at the same time assume that justice is being done. So also, a lawyer can be sure that preserving client confidences ordinarily serves the public interest because people are more likely to seek legal advice, and thereby heed their legal obligations, when they know their communications will be private.

[8] In the nature of law practice, however, conflicting responsibilities are encountered. Virtually all difficult ethical problems arise from conflict between a lawyer's responsibilities to clients, to the legal system and to the lawyer's own interest in remaining an upright person while earning a satisfactory living. The Rules of Professional Conduct prescribe terms for resolving such conflicts. Within the framework of these Rules many difficult issues of professional discretion can arise. Such issues must be resolved through the exercise of sensitive professional and moral judgment guided by the basic principles underlying the Rules.

[9] The legal profession is largely self-governing. Although other professions also have been granted powers of self-government, the legal

profession is unique in this respect because of the close relationship between the profession and the processes of government and law enforcement. This connection is manifested in the fact that ultimate authority over the legal profession is vested largely in the courts.

[10] To the extent that lawyers meet the obligations of their professional calling, the occasion for government regulation is obviated. Self-regulation also helps maintain the legal profession's independence from government domination. An independent legal profession is an important force in preserving government under law, for abuse of legal authority is more readily challenged by a profession whose members are not dependent on government for the right to practice.

[11] The legal profession's relative autonomy carries with it special responsibilities of self-government. The profession has a responsibility to assure that its regulations are conceived in the public interest and not in furtherance of parochial or self-interested concerns of the bar. Every lawyer is responsible for observance of the Rules of Professional Conduct. A lawyer should also aid in securing their observance by other lawyers. Neglect of these responsibilities compromises the independence of the profession and the public interest which it serves.

[12] Lawyers play a vital role in the preservation of society. The fulfillment of this role requires an understanding by lawyers of their relationship to our legal system. The Rules of Professional Conduct, when properly applied, serve to define that relationship.

Scope

[1] The Rules of Professional Conduct are rules of reason. They should be interpreted with reference to the purposes of legal representation and of the law itself. Some of the Rules are imperatives, cast in the terms "shall" or "shall not." These define proper conduct for purposes of professional discipline. Others, generally cast in the term "may," are permissive and define areas under the Rules in which the lawyer has professional discretion. No disciplinary action should be taken when the lawyer chooses not to act or acts within the bounds of such discretion. Other Rules define the nature of relationships between the lawyer and others. The Rules are thus partly obligatory and disciplinary and partly constitutive and descriptive in that they define a lawyer's professional role. Many of the Comments use the term "should." Comments do not add obligations to the Rules but provide guidance for practicing in compliance with the Rules.

[2] The Rules presuppose a larger legal context shaping the lawyer's role. That context includes court rules and statutes relating to matters of licensure, laws defining specific obligations of lawyers and substantive and procedural law in general. Compliance with the Rules, as with all law in an open society, depends primarily upon understanding and voluntary compliance, secondarily upon reinforcement by peer and public opinion and finally, when necessary, upon enforcement

through disciplinary proceedings. The Rules do not, however, exhaust the moral and ethical considerations that should inform a lawyer, for no worthwhile human activity can be completely defined by legal rules. The Rules simply provide a framework for the ethical practice of law.

[3] Furthermore, for purposes of determining the lawyer's authority and responsibility, principles of substantive law external to these Rules determine whether a client-lawyer relationship exists. Most of the duties flowing from the client-lawyer relationship attach only after the client has requested the lawyer to render legal services and the lawyer has agreed to do so. But there are some duties, such as that of confidentiality under Rule 1.6, that may attach when the lawyer agrees to consider whether a client-lawyer relationship shall be established. Whether a client-lawyer relationship exists for any specific purpose can depend on the circumstances and may be a question of fact.

[4] Under various legal provisions, including constitutional, statutory and common law, the responsibilities of government lawyers may include authority concerning legal matters that ordinarily reposes in the client in private client-lawyer relationships. For example, a lawyer for a government agency may have authority on behalf of the government to decide upon settlement or whether to appeal from an adverse judgment. Such authority in various respects is generally vested in the attorney general and the state's attorney in state government, and their federal counterparts, and the same may be true of other government law officers. Also, lawyers under the supervision of these officers may be authorized to represent several government agencies in intragovernmental legal controversies in circumstances where a private lawyer could not represent multiple private clients. They also may have authority to represent the "public interest" in circumstances where a private lawyer would not be authorized to do so. These Rules do not abrogate any such authority.

[5] Failure to comply with an obligation or prohibition imposed by a Rule is a basis for invoking the disciplinary process. The Rules presuppose that disciplinary assessment of a lawyer's conduct will be made on the basis of the facts and circumstances as they existed at the time of the conduct in question and in recognition of the fact that a lawyer often has to act upon uncertain or incomplete evidence of the situation. Moreover, the Rules presuppose that whether or not discipline should be imposed for a violation, and the severity of a sanction, depend on all the circumstances, such as the willfulness and seriousness of the violation, extenuating factors and whether there have been previous violations.

[6] Violation of a Rule should not give rise to a cause of action nor should it create any presumption that a legal duty has been breached. The Rules are designed to provide guidance to lawyers and to provide a structure for regulating conduct through disciplinary agencies. They are not designed to be a basis for civil liability. Furthermore, the

8

purpose of the Rules can be subverted when they are invoked by opposing parties as procedural weapons. The fact that a Rule is a just basis for a lawyer's self-assessment, or for sanctioning a lawyer under the administration of a disciplinary authority, does not imply that an antagonist in a collateral proceeding or transaction has standing to seek enforcement of the Rule. Accordingly, nothing in the Rules should be deemed to augment any substantive legal duty of lawyers or the extra-disciplinary consequences of violating such a duty.

[7] Moreover, these Rules are not intended to govern or affect judicial application of either the attorney-client or work product privilege. Those privileges were developed to promote compliance with law and fairness in litigation. In reliance on the attorney-client privilege, clients are entitled to expect that communications within the scope of the privilege will be protected against compelled disclosure. The attorney-client privilege is that of the client and not of the lawyer. The fact that in exceptional situations the lawyer under the Rules has a limited discretion to disclose a client confidence does not vitiate the proposition that, as a general matter, the client has a reasonable expectation that information relating to the client will not be voluntarily disclosed and that disclosure of such information may be judicially compelled only in accordance with recognized exceptions to the attorney-client and work product privileges.

[8] The lawyer's exercise of discretion not to disclose information under Rule 1.6 should not be subject to reexamination. Permitting such reexamination would be incompatible with the general policy of promoting compliance with law through assurances that communications will be protected against disclosure.

[9] The Comment accompanying each Rule explains and illustrates the meaning and purpose of the Rule. The Preamble and this note on Scope provide general orientation. The Comments are intended as guides to interpretation, but the text of each Rule is authoritative. Research notes were prepared to compare counterparts in the ABA Model Code of Professional Responsibility (adopted 1969, as amended) and to provide selected references to other authorities. The notes have not been adopted, do not constitute part of the Model Rules, and are not intended to affect the application or interpretation of the Rules and Comments.

Terminology

[1] "Belief" or "Believes" denotes that the person involved actually supposed the fact in question to be true. A person's belief may be inferred from circumstances.

[2] "Consult" or "Consultation" denotes communication of information reasonably sufficient to permit the client to appreciate the significance of the matter in question.

[3] "Firm" or "Law firm" denotes a lawyer or lawyers in a private firm, lawyers employed in the legal department of a corporation or other organization and lawyers employed in a legal services organization. See Comment, Rule 1.10.

[4] "Fraud" or "Fraudulent" denotes conduct having a purpose to deceive and not merely negligent misrepresentation or failure to apprise another of relevant information.

[5] "Knowingly," "Known," or "Knows" denotes actual knowledge of the fact in question. A person's knowledge may be inferred from circumstances.

[6] "Partner" denotes a member of a partnership and a shareholder in a law firm organized as a professional corporation.

[7] "Reasonable" or "Reasonably" when used in relation to conduct by a lawyer denotes the conduct of a reasonably prudent and competent lawyer.

[8] "Reasonable belief" or "Reasonably believes" when used in reference to a lawyer denotes that the lawyer believes the matter in question and that the circumstances are such that the belief is reasonable.

[9] "Reasonably should know" when used in reference to a lawyer denotes that a lawyer of reasonable prudence and competence would ascertain the matter in question.

[10] "Substantial" when used in reference to degree or extent denotes a material matter of clear and weighty importance.

MODEL RULES OF PROFESSIONAL CONDUCT

CLIENT–LAWYER RELATIONSHIP

RULE 1.1 Competence

A Lawyer shall provide competent representation to a client. Competent representation requires the legal knowledge, skill, thoroughness and preparation reasonably necessary for the representation.

COMMENT:

Legal Knowledge and Skill

[1] In determining whether a lawyer employs the requisite knowledge and skill in a particular matter, relevant factors include the relative complexity and specialized nature of the matter, the lawyer's general experience, the lawyer's training and experience in the field in question, the preparation and study the lawyer is able to give the matter and whether it is feasible to refer the matter to, or associate or consult with, a lawyer of established competence in the field in question. In many instances, the required proficiency is that of a general

practitioner. Expertise in a particular field of law may be required in some circumstances.

[2] A lawyer need not necessarily have special training or prior experience to handle legal problems of a type with which the lawyer is unfamiliar. A newly admitted lawyer can be as competent as a practitioner with long experience. Some important legal skills, such as the analysis of precedent, the evaluation of evidence and legal drafting, are required in all legal problems. Perhaps the most fundamental legal skill consists of determining what kind of legal problems a situation may involve, a skill that necessarily transcends any particular specialized knowledge. A lawyer can provide adequate representation in a wholly novel field through necessary study. Competent representation can also be provided through the association of a lawyer of established competence in the field in question.

[3] In an emergency a lawyer may give advice or assistance in a matter in which the lawyer does not have the skill ordinarily required where referral to or consultation or association with another lawyer would be impractical. Even in an emergency, however, assistance should be limited to that reasonably necessary in the circumstances, for ill considered action under emergency conditions can jeopardize the client's interest.

[4] A lawyer may accept representation where the requisite level of competence can be achieved by reasonable preparation. This applies as well to a lawyer who is appointed as counsel for an unrepresented person. See also Rule 6.2.

Thoroughness and Preparation

[5] Competent handling of a particular matter includes inquiry into and analysis of the factual and legal elements of the problem, and use of methods and procedures meeting the standards of competent practitioners. It also includes adequate preparation. The required attention and preparation are determined in part by what is at stake; major litigation and complex transactions ordinarily require more elaborate treatment than matters of lesser consequence.

Maintaining Competence

[6] To maintain the requisite knowledge and skill, a lawyer should engage in continuing study and education. If a system of peer review has been established, the lawyer should consider making use of it in appropriate circumstances.

MODEL CODE COMPARISON:

DR 6–101(A)(1) provided that a lawyer shall not handle a matter "which he knows or should know that he is not competent to handle, without associating himself with a lawyer who is competent to handle it"; DR 6–101(A)(2) requires "preparation adequate in the circum-

11

stances." Rule 1.1 more fully particularizes the elements of competence. Whereas DR 6–101(A)(3) prohibited the "[N]eglect of a legal matter," Rule 1.1 does not contain such a prohibition. Instead, Rule 1.1 affirmatively requires the lawyer to be competent.

RULE 1.2 Scope of Representation

(a) A lawyer shall abide by a client's decisions concerning the objectives of representation, subject to paragraphs (c), (d) and (e), and shall consult with the client as to the means by which they are to be pursued. A lawyer shall abide by a client's decision whether to accept an offer of settlement of a matter. In a criminal case, the lawyer shall abide by the client's decision, after consultation with the lawyer, as to a plea to be entered, whether to waive jury trial and whether the client will testify.

(b) A lawyer's representation of a client, including representation by appointment, does not constitute an endorsement of the client's political, economic, social or moral views or activities.

(c) A lawyer may limit the objectives of the representation if the client consents after consultation.

(d) A lawyer shall not counsel a client to engage, or assist a client, in conduct that the lawyer knows is criminal or fraudulent, but a lawyer may discuss the legal consequences of any proposed course of conduct with a client and may counsel or assist a client to make a good faith effort to determine the validity, scope, meaning or application of the law.

(e) When a lawyer knows that a client expects assistance not permitted by the rules of professional conduct or other law, the lawyer shall consult with the client regarding the relevant limitations on the lawyer's conduct.

COMMENT:

Scope of Representation

[1] Both lawyer and client have authority and responsibility in the objectives and means of representation. The client has ultimate authority to determine the purposes to be served by legal representation, within the limits imposed by law and the lawyer's professional obligations. Within those limits, a client also has a right to consult with the lawyer about the means to be used in pursuing those objectives. At the same time, a lawyer is not required to pursue objectives or employ means simply because a client may wish that the lawyer do so. A clear distinction between objectives and means sometimes cannot be drawn, and in many cases the client-lawyer relationship partakes of a joint undertaking. In questions of means, the lawyer should assume responsibility for technical and legal tactical issues, but should defer to the client regarding such questions as the expense to be incurred and concern for third persons who might be adversely affected. Law

defining the lawyer's scope of authority in litigation varies among jurisdictions.

[2] In a case in which the client appears to be suffering mental disability, the lawyer's duty to abide by the client's decisions is to be guided by reference to Rule 1.14.

Independence from Client's Views or Activities

[3] Legal representation should not be denied to people who are unable to afford legal services, or whose cause is controversial or the subject of popular disapproval. By the same token, representing a client does not constitute approval of the client's views or activities.

Services Limited in Objectives or Means

[4] The objectives or scope of services provided by a lawyer may be limited by agreement with the client or by the terms under which the lawyer's services are made available to the client. For example, a retainer may be for a specifically defined purpose. Representation provided through a legal aid agency may be subject to limitations on the types of cases the agency handles. When a lawyer has been retained by an insurer to represent an insured, the representation may be limited to matters related to the insurance coverage. The terms upon which representation is undertaken may exclude specific objectives or means. Such limitations may exclude objectives or means that the lawyer regards as repugnant or imprudent.

[5] An agreement concerning the scope of representation must accord with the Rules of Professional Conduct and other law. Thus, the client may not be asked to agree to representation so limited in scope as to violate Rule 1.1, or to surrender the right to terminate the lawyer's services or the right to settle litigation that the lawyer might wish to continue.

Criminal, Fraudulent and Prohibited Transactions

[6] A lawyer is required to give an honest opinion about the actual consequences that appear likely to result from a client's conduct. The fact that a client uses advice in a course of action that is criminal or fraudulent does not, of itself, make a lawyer a party to the course of action. However, a lawyer may not knowingly assist a client in criminal or fraudulent conduct. There is a critical distinction between presenting an analysis of legal aspects of questionable conduct and recommending the means by which a crime or fraud might be committed with impunity.

[7] When the client's course of action has already begun and is continuing, the lawyer's responsibility is especially delicate. The lawyer is not permitted to reveal the client's wrongdoing, except where permitted by Rule 1.6. However, the lawyer is required to avoid furthering the purpose, for example, by suggesting how it might be

concealed. A lawyer may not continue assisting a client in conduct that the lawyer originally supposes is legally proper but then discovers is criminal or fraudulent. Withdrawal from the representation, therefore, may be required.

[8] Where the client is a fiduciary, the lawyer may be charged with special obligations in dealings with a beneficiary.

[9] Paragraph (d) applies whether or not the defrauded party is a party to the transaction. Hence, a lawyer should not participate in a sham transaction; for example, a transaction to effectuate criminal or fraudulent escape of tax liability. Paragraph (d) does not preclude undertaking a criminal defense incident to a general retainer for legal services to a lawful enterprise. The last clause of paragraph (d) recognizes that determining the validity or interpretation of a statute or regulation may require a course of action involving disobedience of the statute or regulation or of the interpretation placed upon it by governmental authorities.

MODEL CODE COMPARISON

Paragraph (a) has no counterpart in the Disciplinary Rules of the Model Code. EC 7-7 stated: "In certain areas of legal representation not affecting the merits of the cause or substantially prejudicing the rights of a client, a lawyer is entitled to make decisions on his own. But otherwise the authority to make decisions is exclusively that of the client. . . ." EC 7-8 stated that "[I]n the final analysis, however, the . . . decision whether to forego legally available objectives or methods because of nonlegal factors is ultimately for the client. . . . In the event that the client in a nonadjudicatory matter insists upon a course of conduct that is contrary to the judgment and advice of the lawyer but not prohibited by Disciplinary Rules, the lawyer may withdraw from the employment." DR 7-101(A)(1) provided that a lawyer "shall not intentionally . . . fail to seek the lawful objectives of his client through reasonably available means permitted by law. . . . A lawyer does not violate this Disciplinary Rule, however, by . . . avoiding offensive tactics. . . ."

Paragraph (b) has no counterpart in the Model Code.

With regard to paragraph (c), DR 7-101(B)(1) provided that a lawyer may, "where permissible, exercise his professional judgment to waive or fail to assert a right or position of his client."

With regard to paragraph (d), DR 7-102(A)(7) provided that a lawyer shall not "counsel or assist his client in conduct that the lawyer knows to be illegal or fraudulent." DR 7-102(A)(6) provided that a lawyer shall not "participate in the creation or preservation of evidence when he knows or it is obvious that the evidence is false." DR 7-106 provided that a lawyer shall not "advise his client to disregard a standing rule of a tribunal or a ruling of a tribunal . . . but he may take appropriate steps in good faith to test the validity of such rule or ruling." EC 7–5 stated that a lawyer "should never encourage or aid his client to commit criminal acts or counsel his client on how to violate the law and avoid punishment therefor."

With regard to Rule 1.2(e), DR 2–110(C)(1)(c) provided that a lawyer may withdraw from representation if a client "insists" that the lawyer engage in "conduct that is illegal or that is prohibited under the Disciplinary Rules." DR 9–101(C) provided that "a lawyer shall not state or imply that he is able to influence improperly . . . any tribunal, legislative body or public official."

RULE 1.3 Diligence

A lawyer shall act with reasonable diligence and promptness in representing a client.

COMMENT:

[1] A lawyer should pursue a matter on behalf of a client despite opposition, obstruction or personal inconvenience to the lawyer, and may take whatever lawful and ethical measures are required to vindicate a client's cause or endeavor. A lawyer should act with commitment and dedication to the interests of the client and with zeal in advocacy upon the client's behalf. However, a lawyer is not bound to press for every advantage that might be realized for a client. A lawyer has professional discretion in determining the means by which a matter should be pursued. See Rule 1.2. A lawyer's workload should be controlled so that each matter can be handled adequately.

[2] Perhaps no professional shortcoming is more widely resented than procrastination. A client's interests often can be adversely affected by the passage of time or the change of conditions; in extreme instances, as when a lawyer overlooks a statute of limitations, the client's legal position may be destroyed. Even when the client's interests are not affected in substance, however, unreasonable delay can cause a client needless anxiety and undermine confidence in the lawyer's trustworthiness.

[3] Unless the relationship is terminated as provided in Rule 1.16, a lawyer should carry through to conclusion all matters undertaken for a client. If a lawyer's employment is limited to a specific matter, the relationship terminates when the matter has been resolved. If a lawyer has served a client over a substantial period in a variety of matters, the client sometimes may assume that the lawyer will continue to serve on a continuing basis unless the lawyer gives notice of withdrawal. Doubt about whether a client-lawyer relationship still exists should be clarified by the lawyer, preferably in writing, so that the client will not mistakenly suppose the lawyer is looking after the client's affairs when the lawyer has ceased to do so. For example, if a lawyer has handled a judicial or administrative proceeding that produced a result adverse to the client but has not been specifically instructed concerning pursuit of an appeal, the lawyer should advise

the client of the possibility of appeal before relinquishing responsibility for the matter.

MODEL CODE COMPARISON:

DR 6–101(A)(3) required that a lawyer not "[n]eglect a legal matter entrusted to him." EC 6–4 stated that a lawyer should "give appropriate attention to his legal work." Canon 7 stated that "a lawyer should represent a client zealously within the bounds of the law." DR 7–101(A)(1) provided that a lawyer "shall not intentionally . . . fail to seek the lawful objectives of his client through reasonably available means permitted by law and the Disciplinary Rules. . . ." DR 7–101(A)(3) provided that a lawyer "shall not intentionally . . . [p]rejudice or damage his client during the course of the relationship. . . ."

RULE 1.4 Communication

(a) A lawyer shall keep a client reasonably informed about the status of a matter and promptly comply with reasonable requests for information.

(b) A lawyer shall explain a matter to the extent reasonably necessary to permit the client to make informed decisions regarding the representation.

COMMENT:

[1] The client should have sufficient information to participate intelligently in decisions concerning the objectives of the representation and the means by which they are to be pursued, to the extent the client is willing and able to do so. For example, a lawyer negotiating on behalf of a client should provide the client with facts relevant to the matter, inform the client of communications from another party and take other reasonable steps that permit the client to make a decision regarding a serious offer from another party. A lawyer who receives from opposing counsel an offer of settlement in a civil controversy or a proffered plea bargain in a criminal case should promptly inform the client of its substance unless prior discussions with the client have left it clear that the proposal will be unacceptable. See Rule 1.2(a). Even when a client delegates authority to the lawyer, the client should be kept advised of the status of the matter.

[2] Adequacy of communication depends in part on the kind of advice or assistance involved. For example, in negotiations where there is time to explain a proposal the lawyer should review all important provisions with the client before proceeding to an agreement. In litigation a lawyer should explain the general strategy and prospects of success and ordinarily should consult the client on tactics that might injure or coerce others. On the other hand, a lawyer ordinarily cannot be expected to describe trial or negotiation strategy in detail. The guiding principle is that the lawyer should fulfill reasonable client

expectations for information consistent with the duty to act in the client's best interests, and the client's overall requirements as to the character of representation.

[3] Ordinarily, the information to be provided is that appropriate for a client who is a comprehending and responsible adult. However, fully informing the client according to this standard may be impracticable, for example, where the client is a child or suffers from mental disability. See Rule 1.14. When the client is an organization or group, it is often impossible or inappropriate to inform every one of its members about its legal affairs; ordinarily, the lawyer should address communications to the appropriate officials of the organization. See Rule 1.13. Where many routine matters are involved, a system of limited or occasional reporting may be arranged with the client. Practical exigency may also require a lawyer to act for a client without prior consultation.

Withholding Information

[4] In some circumstances, a lawyer may be justified in delaying transmission of information when the client would be likely to react imprudently to an immediate communication. Thus, a lawyer might withhold a psychiatric diagnosis of a client when the examining psychiatrist indicates that disclosure would harm the client. A lawyer may not withhold information to serve the lawyer's own interest or convenience. Rules or court orders governing litigation may provide that information supplied to a lawyer may not be disclosed to the client. Rule 3.4(c) directs compliance with such rules or orders.

MODEL CODE COMPARISON:

Rule 1.4 has no direct counterpart in the Disciplinary Rules of the Model Code. DR 6–101(A)(3) provided that a lawyer shall not "[n]eglect a legal matter entrusted to him." DR 9–102(B)(1) provided that a lawyer shall "[p]romptly notify a client of the receipt of his funds, securities, or other properties." EC 7–8 stated that a lawyer "should exert his best efforts to insure that decisions of his client are made only after the client has been informed of relevant considerations." EC 9–2 stated that "a lawyer should fully and promptly inform his client of material developments in the matters being handled for the client."

RULE 1.5 Fees

(a) A lawyer's fee shall be reasonable. The factors to be considered in determining the reasonableness of a fee include the following:

(1) the time and labor required, the novelty and difficulty of the questions involved, and the skill requisite to perform the legal service properly;

(2) the likelihood, if apparent to the client, that the acceptance of the particular employment will preclude other employment by the lawyer;

(3) the fee customarily charged in the locality for similar legal services;

(4) the amount involved and the results obtained;

(5) the time limitations imposed by the client or by the circumstances;

(6) the nature and length of the professional relationship with the client;

(7) the experience, reputation, and ability of the lawyer or lawyers performing the services; and

(8) whether the fee is fixed or contingent.

(b) When the lawyer has not regularly represented the client, the basis or rate of the fee shall be communicated to the client, preferably in writing, before or within a reasonable time after commencing the representation.

(c) A fee may be contingent on the outcome of the matter for which the service is rendered, except in a matter in which a contingent fee is prohibited by paragraph (d) or other law. A contingent fee agreement shall be in writing and shall state the method by which the fee is to be determined, including the percentage or percentages that shall accrue to the lawyer in the event of settlement, trial or appeal, litigation and other expenses to be deducted from the recovery, and whether such expenses are to be deducted before or after the contingent fee is calculated. Upon conclusion of a contingent fee matter, the lawyer shall provide the client with a written statement stating the outcome of the matter and, if there is a recovery, showing the remittance to the client and the method of its determination.

(d) A lawyer shall not enter into an arrangement for, charge, or collect:

(1) any fee in a domestic relations matter, the payment or amount of which is contingent upon the securing of a divorce or upon the amount of alimony or support, or property settlement in lieu thereof; or

(2) a contingent fee for representing a defendant in a criminal case.

(e) a division of fee between lawyers who are not in the same firm may be made only if:

(1) the division is in proportion to the services performed by each lawyer or, by written agreement with the client, each lawyer assumes joint responsibility for the representation;

(2) **the client is advised of and does not object to the participation of all the lawyers involved; and**

(3) **the total fee is reasonable.**

COMMENT:

Basis or Rate of Fee

[1] When the lawyer has regularly represented a client, they ordinarily will have evolved an understanding concerning the basis or rate of the fee. In a new client-lawyer relationship, however, an understanding as to the fee should be promptly established. It is not necessary to recite all the factors that underlie the basis of the fee, but only those that are directly involved in its computation. It is sufficient, for example, to state that the basic rate is an hourly charge or a fixed amount or an estimated amount, or to identify the factors that may be taken into account in finally fixing the fee. When developments occur during the representation that render an earlier estimate substantially inaccurate, a revised estimate should be provided to the client. A written statement concerning the fee reduces the possibility of misunderstanding. Furnishing the client with a simple memorandum or a copy of the lawyer's customary fee schedule is sufficient if the basis or rate of the fee is set forth.

Terms of Payment

[2] A lawyer may require advance payment of a fee, but is obliged to return any unearned portion. See Rule 1.16(d). A lawyer may accept property in payment for services, such as an ownership interest in an enterprise, providing this does not involve acquisition of a proprietary interest in the cause of action or subject matter of the litigation contrary to Rule 1.8(j).* However, a fee paid in property instead of money may be subject to special scrutiny because it involves questions concerning both the value of the services and the lawyer's special knowledge of the value of the property.

[3] An agreement may not be made whose terms might induce the lawyer improperly to curtail services for the client or perform them in a way contrary to the client's interest. For example, a lawyer should not enter into an agreement whereby services are to be provided only up to a stated amount when it is foreseeable that more extensive services probably will be required, unless the situation is adequately explained to the client. Otherwise, the client might have to bargain for further assistance in the midst of a proceeding or transaction. However, it is proper to define the extent of services in light of the client's ability to pay. A lawyer should not exploit a fee arrangement based primarily on hourly charges by using wasteful procedures. When there

---

* In 1987, the ABA added the following clause to the 1983 version of the Model Rules: "providing this does not involve ac-quisition of a proprietary interest in the cause of action or subject matter of the litigation contrary to Rule 1.8(j)."

is doubt whether a contingent fee is consistent with the client's best interest, the lawyer should offer the client alternative bases for the fee and explain their implications. Applicable law may impose limitations on contingent fees, such as a ceiling on the percentage.

Division of Fee

[4] A division of fee is a single billing to a client covering the fee of two or more lawyers who are not in the same firm. A division of fee facilitates association of more than one lawyer in a matter in which neither alone could serve the client as well, and most often is used when the fee is contingent and the division is between a referring lawyer and a trial specialist. Paragraph (e) permits the lawyers to divide a fee on either the basis of the proportion of services they render or by agreement between the participating lawyers if all assume responsibility for the representation as a whole and the client is advised and does not object. It does not require disclosure to the client of the share that each lawyer is to receive. Joint responsibility for the representation entails the obligations stated in Rule 5.1 for purposes of the matter involved.

Disputes Over Fees

[5] If a procedure has been established for resolution of fee disputes, such as an arbitration or mediation procedure established by the bar, the lawyer should conscientiously consider submitting to it. Law may prescribe a procedure for determining a lawyer's fee, for example, in representation of an executor or administrator, a class or a person entitled to a reasonable fee as part of the measure of damages. The lawyer entitled to such a fee and a lawyer representing another party concerned with the fee should comply with the prescribed procedure.

MODEL CODE COMPARISON:

DR 2–106(A) provided that a lawyer "shall not enter into an agreeement for, charge, or collect an illegal or clearly excessive fee." DR 2–106(B) provided that a fee is "clearly excessive when, after a review of the facts, a lawyer of ordinary prudence would be left with a definite and firm conviction that the fee is in excess of a reasonable fee." The factors of a reasonable fee in Rule 1.5(a) are substantially identical to those listed in DR 2–106(B). EC 2–17 states that a lawyer "should not charge more than a reasonable fee . . . ."

There was no counterpart to Rule 1.5(b) in the Disciplinary Rules of the Model Code. EC 2–19 stated that it is "usually beneficial to reduce to writing the understanding of the parties regarding the fee, particularly when it is contingent."

There was no counterpart to paragraph (c) in the Disciplinary Rules of the Model Code. EC 2–20 provided that "[c]ontingent fee arrangements in civil cases have long been commonly accepted in the United States," but that "a lawyer generally should decline to accept employment on a contingent fee basis by one who is able to pay a reasonable fixed fee . . . ."

With regard to paragraph (d), DR 2–106(C) prohibited "a contingent fee in a criminal case." EC 2–20 provided that "contingent fee arrangements in domestic relation cases are rarely justified."

With regard to paragraph (e), DR 2–107(A) permitted division of fees only if: "(1) The client consents to employment of the other lawyer after a full disclosure that a division of fees will be made. (2) The division is in proportion to the services performed and responsibility assumed by each. (3) The total fee does not exceed clearly reasonable compensation . . . ." Paragraph (e) permits division without regard to the services rendered by each lawyer if they assume joint responsibility for the representation.

RULE 1.6 Confidentiality of Information*

(a) A lawyer shall not reveal information relating to representation of a client unless the client consents after consultation, except for disclosures that are impliedly authorized in order to carry out the representation, and except as stated in paragraph (b).

(b) A lawyer may reveal such information to the extent the lawyer reasonably believes necessary:

(1) to prevent the client from committing a criminal act that the lawyer believes is likely to result in imminent death or substantial bodily harm; or

(2) to establish a claim or defense on behalf of the lawyer in a controversy between the lawyer and the client, to establish a defense to a criminal charge or civil claim against the lawyer based upon conduct in which the client was involved, or to respond to allegations in any proceeding concerning the lawyer's representation of the client.

COMMENT:

[1] The lawyer is part of a judicial system charged with upholding the law. One of the lawyer's functions is to advise clients so that they avoid any violation of the law in the proper exercise of their rights.

[2] The observance of the ethical obligation of a lawyer to hold inviolate confidential information of the client not only facilitates the full development of facts essential to proper representation of the client but also encourages people to seek early legal assistance.

* In 1991, The ABA House of Delegates rejected the ethics committee recommendation that it modify Model Rule 1.6. The rejected language would have inserted the following exception to the general rule of confidentiality under Model Rule 1.6(b): "to rectify the consequences of a client's criminal or fraudulent act in the furtherance of which the lawyer's services had been used."

[3]   Almost without exception, clients come to lawyers in order to determine what their rights are and what is, in the maze of laws and regulations, deemed to be legal and correct.   The common law recognizes that the client's confidences must be protected from disclosure. Based upon experience, lawyers know that almost all clients follow the advice given, and the law is upheld.

[4]   A fundamental principle in the client-lawyer relationship is that the lawyer maintain confidentiality of information relating to the representation.   The client is thereby encouraged to communicate fully and frankly with the lawyer even as to embarrassing or legally damaging subject matter.

[5]   The principle of confidentiality is given effect in two related bodies of law, the attorney-client privilege (which includes the work product doctrine) in the law of evidence and the rule of confidentiality established in professional ethics.   The attorney-client privilege applies in judicial and other proceedings in which a lawyer may be called as a witness or otherwise required to produce evidence concerning a client. The rule of client-lawyer confidentiality applies in situations other than those where evidence is sought from the lawyer through compulsion of law.   The confidentiality rule applies not merely to matters communicated in confidence by the client but also to all information relating to the representation, whatever its source.   A lawyer may not disclose such information except as authorized or required by the Rules of Professional Conduct or other law.   See also Scope.

[6]   The requirement of maintaining confidentiality of information relating to representation applies to government lawyers who may disagree with the policy goals that their representation is designed to advance.

Authorized Disclosure

[7]   A lawyer is impliedly authorized to make disclosures about a client when appropriate in carrying out the representation, except to the extent that the client's instructions or special circumstances limit that authority.   In litigation, for example, a lawyer may disclose information by admitting a fact that cannot properly be disputed, or in negotiation by making a disclosure that facilitates a satisfactory conclusion.

[8]   Lawyers in a firm may, in the course of the firm's practice, disclose to each other information relating to a client of the firm, unless the client has instructed that particular information be confined to specified lawyers.

Disclosure Adverse to Client

[9]   The confidentiality rule is subject to limited exceptions.   In becoming privy to information about a client, a lawyer may foresee that the client intends serious harm to another person.   However, to the

22

extent a lawyer is required or permitted to disclose a client's purposes, the client will be inhibited from revealing facts which would enable the lawyer to counsel against a wrongful course of action. The public is better protected if full and open communication by the client is encouraged than if it is inhibited.

Several situations must be distinguished.

[10] First, the lawyer may not counsel or assist a client in conduct that is criminal or fraudulent. See Rule 1.2(d). Similarly, a lawyer has a duty under Rule 3.3(a)(4) not to use false evidence. This duty is essentially a special instance of the duty prescribed in Rule 1.2(d) to avoid assisting a client in criminal or fraudulent conduct.

[11] Second, the lawyer may have been innocently involved in past conduct by the client that was criminal or fraudulent. In such a situation the lawyer has not violated Rule 1.2(d), because to "counsel or assist" criminal or fraudulent conduct requires knowing that the conduct is of that character.

[12] Third, the lawyer may learn that a client intends prospective conduct that is criminal and likely to result in imminent death or substantial bodily harm. As stated in paragraph (b)(1), the lawyer has professional discretion to reveal information in order to prevent such consequences. The lawyer may make a disclosure in order to prevent homicide or serious bodily injury which the lawyer reasonable believes is intended by a client. It is very difficult for a lawyer to "know" when such a heinous purpose will actually be carried out, for the client may have a change of mind.

[13] The lawyer's exercise of discretion requires consideration of such factors as the nature of the lawyer's relationship with the client and with those who might be injured by the client, the lawyer's own involvement in the transaction and factors that may extenuate the conduct in question. Where practical, the lawyer should seek to persuade the client to take suitable action. In any case, a disclosure adverse to the client's interest should be no greater than the lawyer reasonably believes necessary to the purpose. A lawyer's decision not to take preventive action permitted by paragraph (b)(1) does not violate this Rule.

Withdrawal

[14] If the lawyer's services will be used by the client in materially furthering a course of criminal or fraudulent conduct, the lawyer must withdraw, as stated in Rule 1.16(a)(1).

[15] After withdrawal the lawyer is required to refrain from making disclosure of the clients' confidences, except as otherwise provided in Rule 1.6. Neither this Rule nor Rule 1.8(b) nor Rule 1.16(d) prevents the lawyer from giving notice of the fact of withdrawal, and

the lawyer may also withdraw or disaffirm any opinion, document, affirmation, or the like.

[16] Where the client is an organization, the lawyer may be in doubt whether contemplated conduct will actually be carried out by the organization. Where necessary to guide conduct in connection with this Rule, the lawyer may make inquiry within the organization as indicated in Rule 1.13(b).

Dispute Concerning Lawyer's Conduct

[17] Where a legal claim or disciplinary charge alleges complicity of the lawyer in a client's conduct or other misconduct of the lawyer involving representation of the client, the lawyer may respond to the extent the lawyer reasonably believes necessary to establish a defense. The same is true with respect to a claim involving the conduct or representation of a former client. The lawyer's right to respond arises when an assertion of such complicity has been made. Paragraph (b)(2) does not require the lawyer to await the commencement of an action or proceeding that charges such complicity, so that the defense may be established by responding directly to a third party who has made such an assertion. The right to defend, of course, applies where a proceeding has been commenced. Where practicable and not prejudicial to the lawyer's ability to establish the defense, the lawyer should advise the client of the third party's assertion and request that the client respond appropriately. In any event, disclosure should be no greater than the lawyer reasonably believes is necessary to vindicate innocence, the disclosure should be made in a manner which limits access to the information to the tribunal or other persons having a need to know it, and appropriate protective orders or other arrangements should be sought by the lawyer to the fullest extent practicable.

[18] If the lawyer is charged with wrongdoing in which the client's conduct is implicated, the rule of confidentiality should not prevent the lawyer from defending against the charge. Such a charge can arise in a civil, criminal or professional disciplinary proceeding, and can be based on a wrong allegedly committed by the lawyer against the client, or on a wrong alleged by a third person; for example, a person claiming to have been defrauded by the lawyer and client acting together. A lawyer entitled to a fee is permitted by paragraph (b)(2) to prove the services rendered in an action to collect it. This aspect of the rule expresses the principle that the beneficiary of a fiduciary relationship may not exploit it to the detriment of the fiduciary. As stated above, the lawyer must make every effort practicable to avoid unnecessary disclosure of information relating to a representation, to limit disclosure to those having the need to know it, and to obtain protective orders or make other arrangements minimizing the risk of disclosure.

Disclosures Otherwise Required or Authorized

[19]   The attorney-client privilege is differently defined in various jurisdictions.   If a lawyer is called as a witness to give testimony concerning a client, absent waiver by the client, Rule 1.6(a) requires the lawyer to invoke the privilege when it is applicable.   The lawyer must comply with the final orders of a court or other tribunal of competent jurisdiction requiring the lawyer to give information about the client.

[20]   The Rules of Professional Conduct in various circumstances permit or require a lawyer to disclose information relating to the representation.   See Rules 2.2, 2.3, 3.3 and 4.1.   In addition to these provisions, a lawyer may be obligated or permitted by other provisions of law to give information about a client.   Whether another provision of law supersedes Rule 1.6 is a matter of interpretation beyond the scope of these Rules, but a presumption should exist against such a supersession.

Former Client

[21]   The duty of confidentiality continues after the client-lawyer relationship has terminated.

MODEL CODE COMPARISON:

Rule 1.6 eliminates the two-pronged duty under the Model Code in favor of a single standard protecting all information about a client "relating to the representation."   Under DR 4–101, the requirement applied only to information protected by the attorney-client privilege and to information "gained in" the professional relationship that "the client has requested be held inviolate or the disclosure of which would be embarrassing or would be likely to be detrimental to the client."   EC 4–4 added that the duty differed from the evidentiary privilege in that it existed "without regard to the nature or source of information or the fact that others share the knowledge."   Rule 1.6 imposes confidentiality on information relating to the representation even if it is acquired before or after the relationship existed.   It does not require the client to indicate information that is to be confidential, or permit the lawyer to speculate whether particular information might be embarrassing or detrimental.

Paragraph (a) permits a lawyer to disclose information where impliedly authorized to do so in order to carry out the representation.   Under DR 4–101(B) and (C), a lawyer was not permitted to reveal "confidences" unless the client first consented after disclosure.

Paragraph (b) redefines the exceptions to the requirement of confidentiality.   Regarding paragraph (b)(1), DR 4–101(C)(3) provided that a lawyer "may reveal . . . [t]he intention of his client to commit a crime and the information necessary to prevent the crime."   This option existed regardless of the seriousness of the proposed crime.

With regard to paragraph (b)(2), DR 4–101(C)(4) provided that a lawyer may reveal "[c]onfidences or secrets necessary to establish or collect his fee or to defend himself or his employers or associates against an accusation of wrongful conduct." Paragraph (b)(2) enlarges the exception to include disclosure of information relating to claims by the lawyer other than for the lawyer's fee; for example, recovery of property from the client.

RULE 1.7 Conflict of Interest: General Rule

(a) A lawyer shall not represent a client if the representation of that client will be directly adverse to another client, unless:

(1) the lawyer reasonably believes the representation will not adversely affect the relationship with the other client; and

(2) each client consents after consultation.

(b) A lawyer shall not represent a client if the representation of that client may be materially limited by the lawyer's responsibilities to another client or to a third person, or by the lawyer's own interests, unless:

(1) the lawyer reasonably believes the representation will not be adversely affected; and

(2) the client consents after consultation. When representation of multiple clients in a single matter is undertaken, the consultation shall include explanation of the implications of the common representation and the advantages and risks involved.

COMMENT:

Loyalty to a Client

[1] Loyalty is an essential element in the lawyer's relationship to a client. An impermissible conflict of interest may exist before representation is undertaken, in which event the representation should be declined. The lawyer should adopt reasonable procedures, appropriate for the size and type of firm and practice, to determine in both litigation and non-litigation matters the parties and issues involved and to determine whether there are actual or potential conflicts of interest.*

[2] If such a conflict arises after representation has been undertaken, the lawyer should withdraw from the representation. See Rule 1.16. Where more than one client is involved and the lawyer withdraws because a conflict arises after representation, whether the lawyer may continue to represent any of the clients is determined by Rule

* The ABA added this sentence in the comments to the Model Rules in 1987. The remainder of paragraph 1 in the origi- nal version of this comment now appears in the current paragraph 2.

1.9. See also Rule 2.2(c). As to whether a client-lawyer relationship exists or, having once been established, is continuing, see Comment to Rule 1.3 and Scope.

[3] As a general proposition, loyalty to a client prohibits undertaking representation directly adverse to that client without that client's consent. Paragraph (a) expresses that general rule. Thus, a lawyer ordinarily may not act as advocate against a person the lawyer represents in some other matter, even if it is wholly unrelated. On the other hand, simultaneous representation in unrelated matters of clients whose interests are only generally adverse, such as competing economic enterprises, does not require consent of the respective clients. Paragraph (a) applies only when the representation of one client would be directly adverse to the other.

[4] Loyalty to a client is also impaired when a lawyer cannot consider, recommend or carry out an appropriate course of action for the client because of the lawyer's other responsibilities or interests. The conflict in effect forecloses alternatives that would otherwise be available to the client. Paragraph (b) addresses such situations. A possible conflict does not itself preclude the representation. The critical questions are the likelihood that a conflict will eventuate and, if it does, whether it will materially interfere with the lawyer's independent professional judgment in considering alternatives or foreclose courses of action that reasonably should be pursued on behalf of the client. Consideration should be given to whether the client wishes to accommodate the other interest involved.

Consultation and Consent

[5] A client may consent to representation notwithstanding a conflict. However, as indicated in paragraph (a)(1) with respect to representation directly adverse to a client, and paragraph (b)(1) with respect to material limitations on representation of a client, when a disinterested lawyer would conclude that the client should not agree to the representation under the circumstances, the lawyer involved cannot properly ask for such agreement or provide representation on the basis of the client's consent. When more than once client is involved, the question of conflict must be resolved as to each client. Moreover, there may be circumstances where it is impossible to make the disclosure necessary to obtain consent. For example, when the lawyer represents different clients in related matters and one of the clients refuses to consent to the dislcosure necessary to permit the other client to make an informed decision, the lawyer cannot properly ask the latter to consent.

Lawyer's Interests

[6] The lawyer's own interests should not be permitted to have adverse effect on representation of a client. For example, a lawyer's

27

need for income should not lead the lawyer to undertake matters that cannot be handled competently and at a reasonable fee. See Rules 1.1 and 1.5. If the probity of a lawyer's own conduct in a transaction is in serious question, it may be difficult or impossible for the lawyer to give a client detached advice. A lawyer may not allow related business interests to affect representation, for example, by referring clients to an enterprise in which the lawyer has an undisclosed interest.

Conflicts in Litigation

[7] Paragraph (a) prohibits representation of opposing parties in litigation. Simultaneous representation of parties whose interests in litigation may conflict, such as co-plaintiffs or co-defendants, is governed by paragraph (b). An impermissible conflict may exist by reason of substantial discrepancy in the parties' testimony, incompatibility in positions in relation to an opposing party or the fact that there are substantially different possibilities of settlement of the claims or liabilities in question. Such conflicts can arise in criminal cases as well as civil. The potential for conflict of interest in representing multiple defendants in a criminal case is so grave that ordinarily a lawyer should decline to represent more than one codefendant. On the other hand, common representation of persons having similar interests is proper if the risk of adverse effect is minimal and the requirements of paragraph (b) are met. Compare Rule 2.2 involving intermediation between clients.

[8] Ordinarily, a lawyer may not act as advocate against a client the lawyer represents in some other matter, even if the other matter is wholly unrelated. However, there are circumstances in which a lawyer may act as advocate against a client. For example, a lawyer representing an enterprise with diverse operations may accept employment as an advocate against the enterprise in an unrelated matter if doing so will not adversely affect the lawyer's relationship with the enterprise or conduct of the suit and if both clients consent upon consultation. By the same token, government lawyers in some circumstances may represent government employees in proceedings in which a government agency is the opposing party. The propriety of concurrent representation can depend on the nature of the litigation. For example, a suit charging fraud entails conflict to a degree not involved in a suit for a declaratory judgment concerning statutory interpretation.

[9] A lawyer may represent parties having antagonistic positions on a legal question that has arisen in different cases, unless representation of either client would be adversely affected. Thus, it is ordinarily not improper to assert such positions in cases pending in different trial courts, but it may be improper to do so in cases pending at the same time in an appellate court.

Interest of Person Paying for a Lawyer's Service

[10]   A lawyer may be paid from a source other than the client, if the client is informed of that fact and consents and the arrangement does not compromise the lawyer's duty of loyalty to the client. See Rule 1.8(f). For example, when an insurer and its insured have conflicting interests in a matter arising from a liability insurance agreement, and the insurer is required to provide special counsel for the insured, the arrangement should assure the special counsel's professional independence. So also, when a corporation and its directors or employees are involved in a controversy in which they have conflicting interests, the corporation may provide funds for separate legal representation of the directors or employees, if the clients consent after consultation and the arrangement ensures the lawyer's professional independence.

Other Conflict Situations

[11]   Conflicts of interest in contexts other than litigation sometimes may be difficult to assess. Relevant factors in determining whether there is potential for adverse effect include the duration and intimacy of the lawyer's relationship with the client or clients involved, the functions being performed by the lawyer, the likelihood that actual conflict will arise and the likely prejudice to the client from the conflict if it does arise. The question is often one of proximity and degree.

[12]   For example, a lawyer may not represent multiple parties to a negotiation whose interests are fundamentally antagonistic to each other, but common representation is permissible where the clients are generally aligned in interest even though there is some difference of interest among them.

[13]   Conflict questions may also arise in estate planning and estate administration. A lawyer may be called upon to prepare wills for several family members, such as husband and wife, and, depending upon the circumstances, a conflict of interest may arise. In estate administration the identity of the client may be unclear under the law of a particular jurisdiction. Under one view, the client is the fiduciary; under another view the client is the estate or trust, including its beneficiaries. The lawyer should make clear the relationship to the parties involved.

[14]   A lawyer for a corporation or other organization who is also a member of its board of directors should determine whether the responsibilities of the two roles may conflict. The lawyer may be called on to advise the corporation in matters involving actions of the directors. Consideration should be given to the frequency with which such situations may arise, the potential intensity of the conflict, the effect of the lawyer's resignation from the board and the possibility of the corporation's obtaining legal advice from another lawyer in such situations. If there is material risk that the dual role will compromise the lawyer's

independence of professional judgment, the lawyer should not serve as a director.

Conflict Charged by an Opposing Party

[15] Resolving questions of conflict of interest is primarily the responsibility of the lawyer undertaking the representation. In litigation, a court may raise the question when there is reason to infer that the lawyer has neglected the responsibility. In a criminal case, inquiry by the court is generally required when a lawyer represents multiple defendants. Where the conflict is such as clearly to call in question the fair or efficient administration of justice, opposing counsel may properly raise the question. Such an objection should be viewed with caution, however, for it can be misused as a technique of harassment. See Scope.

MODEL CODE COMPARISON:

DR 5–101(A) provided that "[e]xcept with the consent of his client after full disclosure, a lawyer shall not accept employment if the exercise of his professional judgment on behalf of the client will be or reasonably may be affected by his own financial, business, property, or personal interests." DR 5–105(A) provided that a lawyer "shall decline proffered employment if the exercise of his independent professional judgment in behalf of a client will be or is likely to be adversely affected by the acceptance of the proffered employment, or if it would be likely to involve him in representing differing interests, except to the extent permitted under DR 5–105(C)." DR 5–105(C) provided that "a lawyer may represent multiple clients if it is obvious that he can adequately represent the interest of each and if each consents to the representation after full disclosure of the possible effect of such representation on the exercise of his independent professional judgment on behalf of each." DR 5–107(B) provided that a lawyer "shall not permit a person who recommends, employs, or pays him to render legal services for another to direct or regulate his professional judgment in rendering such services."

Rule 1.7 clarifies DR 5–105(A) by requiring that, when the lawyer's other interests are involved, not only must the client consent after consultation but also that, independent of such consent, the representation reasonably appears not to be adversely affected by the lawyer's other interests. This requirement appears to be the intended meaning of the provision in DR 5–105(C) that "it is obvious that he can adequately represent" the client, and was implicit in EC 5–2, which stated that a lawyer "should not accept proffered employment if his personal interests or desires will, or there is a reasonable probability that they will, affect adversely the advice to be given or services to be rendered the prospective client."

RULE 1.8 Conflict of Interest: Prohibited Transactions

(a) A lawyer shall not enter into a business transaction with a client or knowingly acquire an ownership, possessory, security or other pecuniary interest adverse to a client unless:

    (1) the transaction and terms on which the lawyer acquires the interest are fair and reasonable to the client and are fully disclosed and transmitted in writing to the client in a manner which can be reasonably understood by the client;

    (2) the client is given a reasonable opportunity to seek the advice of independent counsel in the transaction; and

    (3) the client consents in writing thereto.

(b) A lawyer shall not use information relating to representation of a client to the disadvantage of the client unless the client consents after consultation, except as permitted or required by Rule 1.6 or Rule 3.3.

(c) A lawyer shall not prepare an instrument giving the lawyer or a person related to the lawyer as parent, child, sibling, or spouse any substantial gift from a client, including a testamentary gift, except where the client is related to the donee.

(d) Prior to the conclusion of representation of a client, a lawyer shall not make or negotiate an agreement giving the lawyer literary or media rights to a portrayal or account based in substantial part on information relating to the representation.

(e) A lawyer shall not provide financial assistance to a client in connection with pending or contemplated litigation, except that:

    (1) a lawyer may advance court costs and expenses of litigation, the repayment of which may be contingent on the outcome of the matter; and

    (2) a lawyer representing an indigent client may pay court costs and expenses of litigation on behalf of the client.

(f) A lawyer shall not accept compensation for representing a client from one other than the client unless:

    (1) the client consents after consultation;

    (2) there is no interference with the lawyer's independence of professional judgment or with the client–lawyer relationship; and

    (3) Information relating to representation of a client is protected as required by rule 1.6.

(g) A lawyer who represents two or more clients shall not participate in making an aggregate settlement of the claims of or against the clients, or in a criminal case an aggregated agreement as to guilty or nolo contendere pleas, unless each client consents after consultation, including disclosure of the existence and nature of all the claims or pleas involved and of the participation of each person in the settlement.

(h) A lawyer shall not make an agreement prospectively limiting the lawyer's liability to a client for malpractice unless permitted by law and the client is independently represented in making the agreement, or settle a claim for such liability with an unrepresented client or former client without first advising that person in writing that independent representation is appropriate in connection therewith.

(i) A lawyer related to another lawyer as parent, child, sibling or spouse shall not represent a client in a representation directly adverse to a person who the lawyer knows is represented by the other lawyer except upon consent by the client after consultation regarding the relationship.

(j) A lawyer shall not acquire a proprietary interest in the cause of action or subject matter of litigation the lawyer is conducting for a client, except that the lawyer may:

(1) acquire a lien granted by law to secure the lawyer's fee or expenses; and

(2) contract with a client for a reasonable contingent fee in a civil case.

COMMENT:

Transactions Between Client and Lawyer

[1] As a general principle, all transactions between client and lawyer should be fair and reasonable to the client. In such transactions a review by independent counsel on behalf of the client is often advisable. Furthermore, a lawyer may not exploit information relating to the representation to the client's disadvantage. For example, a lawyer who has learned that the client is investing in specific real estate may not, without the client's consent, seek to acquire nearby property where doing so would adversely affect the client's plan for investment. Paragraph (a) does not, however, apply to standard commercial transactions between the lawyer and the client for products or services that the client generally markets to others, for example, banking or brokerage services, medical services, products manufactured or distributed by the client, and utilities services. In such transactions, the lawyer has no advantage in dealing with the client, and the restrictions in paragraph (a) are unnecessary and impracticable.

[2] A lawyer may accept a gift from a client, if the transaction meets general standards of fairness. For example, a simple gift such as a present given at a holiday or as a token of appreciation is permitted. If effectuation of a substantial gift requires preparing a legal instrument such as a will or conveyance, however, the client should have the detached advice that another lawyer can provide. Paragraph (c) recog-

nizes an exception where the client is a relative of the donee or the gift is not substantial.

Literary Rights

[3] An agreement by which a lawyer acquires literary or media rights concerning the conduct of the representation creates a conflict between the interests of the client and the personal interests of the lawyer. Measures suitable in the representation of the client may detract from the publication value of an account of the representation. Paragraph (d) does not prohibit a lawyer representing a client in a transaction concerning literary property from agreeing that the lawyer's fee shall consist of a share in ownership in the property, if the arrangement conforms to Rule 1.5 and paragraph (j).

Person Paying for Lawyer's Services

[4] Rule 1.8(f) requires disclosure of the fact that the lawyer's services are being paid for by a third party. Such an arrangement must also conform to the requirements of Rule 1.6 concerning confidentiality and Rule 1.7 concerning conflict of interest. Where the client is a class, consent may be obtained on behalf of the class by court-supervised procedure.

Family Relationships Between Lawyers

[5] Rule 1.8(i) applies to related lawyers who are in different firms. Related lawyers in the same firm are governed by Rules 1.7, 1.9, and 1.10. The disqualification stated in Rule 1.8(i) is personal and is not imputed to members of firms with whom the lawyers are associated.

Acquisition of Interest in Litigation

[6] Paragaph (j) states the traditional general rule that lawyers are prohibited from acquiring a proprietary interest in litigation. This general rule, which has its basis in common law champerty and maintenance, is subject to specific exceptions developed in decisional law and continued in these Rules, such as the exception for reasonable contingent fees set forth in Rule 1.5 and the exception for certain advances of the costs of litigation set forth in paragraph (e).

[7] This Rule is not intended to apply to customary qualification and limitations in legal opinions and memoranda.

MODEL CODE COMPARISON:

With regard to paragraph (a), DR 5–104(A) provided that a lawyer "shall not enter into a business transaction with a client if they have differing interests therein and if the client expects the lawyer to exercise his professional judgment therein for the protection of the client, unless the client has consented after full disclosure." EC 5–3 stated that a lawyer "should not seek to persuade his client to permit him to invest in an undertaking of his client nor make improper use of his professional relationship to influence his client to invest in an enterprise in which the lawyer is interested."

With regard to paragraph (b), DR 4–101(B)(3) provided that a lawyer should not use "a confidence or secret of his client for the advantage of himself, or of a third person, unless the client consents after full disclosure."

There was no counterpart to paragraph (c) in the Disciplinary Rules of the Model Code. EC 5–5 stated that a lawyer "should not suggest to his client that a gift be made to himself or for his benefit. If a lawyer accepts a gift from his client, he is peculiarly susceptible to the charge that he unduly influenced or overreached the client. If a client voluntarily offers to make a gift to his lawyer, the lawyer may accept the gift, but before doing so, he should urge that the client secure disinterested advice from an independent, competent person who is cognizant of all the circumstances. Other than in exceptional circumstances, a lawyer should insist that an instrument in which his client desires to name him beneficially be prepared by another lawyer selected by the client."

Paragraph (d) is substantially similar to DR 5–104(B), but refers to "literary or media" rights, a more generally inclusive term than "publication" rights.

Paragraph (e)(1) is similar to DR 5–103(B), but eliminates the requirement that "the client remains ultimately liable for such expenses."

Paragraph (e)(2) has no counterpart in the Model Code.

Paragraph (f) is substantially identical to DR 5–107(A)(1).

Paragraph (g) is substantially identical to DR 5–106.

The first clause of paragraph (h) is similar to DR 6–102(A). There was no counterpart in the Model Code to the second clause of paragraph (h).

Paragraph (i) has no counterpart in the Model Code.

Paragraph (j) is substantially identical to DR 5–103(A).

RULE 1.9 Conflict of Interest: Former Client *

(a) A lawyer who has formerly represented a client in a matter shall not thereafter represent another person in the same or a substantially related matter in which that person's interests

---

* In 1989, the ABA amended Model Rule 1.9 by moving some of the text in original Model Rule 1.10(b) into current Model Rule 1.9(b). The original Model Rule 1.9(b) was moved to Model Rule 1.9(c). The impetus behind this change was to clarify an overlap between Model Rule 1.9 and 1.10 and to address the question of duties to former clients when a lawyer changes firms and did not represent the former client but may have acquired confidential information about a former client of the old firm. The following represents Model Rule 1.9 as adopted in 1983:

are materially adverse to the interests of the former client unless the former client consents after consultation.

(b) A lawyer shall not knowingly represent a person in the same or a substantially related matter in which a firm with which the lawyer formerly was associated had previously represented a client,

(1) whose interests are materially adverse to that person; and

(2) about whom the lawyer had acquired information protected by Rules 1.6 and 1.9(c) that is material to the matter;

unless the former client consents after consultation.

(c) A lawyer who has formerly represented a client in a matter or whose present or former firm has formerly represented a client in a matter shall not thereafter:

(1) use information relating to the representation to the disadvantage of the former client except as Rule 1.6 or Rule 3.3 would permit or require with respect to a client, or when the information has become generally known; or

(2) reveal information relating to the representation except as Rule 1.6 or Rule 3.3 would permit or require with respect to a client.

COMMENT:

[1] After termination of a client-lawyer relationship, a lawyer may not represent another client except in conformity with this Rule. The principles in Rule 1.7 determine whether the interests of the present and former client are adverse. Thus, a lawyer could not properly seek to rescind on behalf of a new client a contract drafted on behalf of the former client. So also a lawyer who has prosecuted an accused person could not properly represent the accused in a subsequent civil action against the government concerning the same transaction.

[2] The scope of a "matter" for purposes of this Rule may depend on the facts of a particular situation or transaction. The lawyer's involvement in a matter can also be a question of degree. When a lawyer has been directly involved in a specific transaction, subsequent representation of other clients with materially adverse interests clearly

---

RULE 1.9 Conflict of Interest: For-
mer Client

A Lawyer who has formerly represented a client in a matter shall not thereafter:

(a) Represent another person in the same or a substantially related matter in which that person's interests are materially adverse to the interests of the former client unless the former client consents after consultation; or

(b) Use information relating to the representation to the disadvantage of the former client except as Rule 1.6 would permit with respect to a client or when the information has become generally known.

is prohibited. On the other hand, a lawyer who recurrently handled a type of problem for a former client is not precluded from later representing another client in a wholly distinct problem of that type even though the subsequent representation involves a position adverse to the prior client. Similar considerations can apply to the reassignment of military lawyers between defense and prosecution functions within the same military jurisdiction. The underlying question is whether the lawyer was so involved in the matter that the subsequent representation can be justly regarded as a changing of sides in the matter in question.

*Lawyers Moving Between Firms**

[3] When lawyers have been associated within a firm but then end their association, the question of whether a lawyer should undertake representation is more complicated. There are several competing considerations. First, the client previously represented by the former firm must be reasonably assured that the principle of loyalty to the client is not compromised. Second, the rule should not be so broadly cast as to preclude other persons from having reasonable choice of legal counsel. Third, the rule should not unreasonably hamper lawyers from forming new associations and taking on new clients after having left a previous association. In this connection, it should be recognized that today many lawyers practice in firms, that many lawyers to some degree limit their practice to one field or another, and that many move from one association to another several times in their careers. If the concept of imputation were applied with unqualified rigor, the result would be radical curtailment of the opportunity of lawyers to move from one practice setting to another and of the opportunity of clients to change counsel.

[4] Reconciliation of these competing principles in the past has been attempted under two rubrics. One approach has been to seek per se rules of disqualification. For example, it has been held that a partner in a law firm is conclusively presumed to have access to all confidences concerning all clients of the firm. Under this analysis, if a lawyer has been a partner in one law firm and then becomes a partner in another law firm, there may be a presumption that all confidences known by the partner in the first firm are known to all partners in the second firm. This presumption might properly be applied in some circumstances, especially where the client has been extensively represented, but may be unrealistic where the client was represented only for limited purposes. Furthermore, such a rigid rule exaggerates the difference between a partner and an associate in modern law firms.

* The comments under this topic originally appeared under Model Rule 1.10. With the modification of Model Rule 1.9, the ABA moved these comments under Model Rule 1.9 without significant change.

[5] The other rubric formerly used for dealing with disqualification is the appearance of impropriety proscribed in Canon 9 of the ABA Model Code of Professional Responsibility. This rubric has a two fold problem. First, the appearance of impropriety can be taken to include any new client-lawyer relationship that might make a former client feel anxious. If that meaning were adopted, disqualification would become little more than a question of subjective judgment by the former client. Second, since "impropriety" is undefined, the term "appearance of impropriety" is question-begging. It therefore has to be recognized that the problem of disqualification cannot be properly resolved either by simple analogy to a lawyer practicing alone or by the very general concept of appearance of impropriety.

*Confidentiality**

[6] Preserving confidentiality is a question of access to information. Access to information, in turn, is essentially a question of fact in particular circumstances, aided by inferences, deductions or working presumptions that reasonably may be made about the way in which lawyers work together. A lawyer may have general access to files of all clients of a law firm and may regularly participate in discussions of their affairs; it should be inferred that such a lawyer in fact is privy to all information about all the firm's clients. In contrast, another lawyer may have access to the files of only a limited number of clients and participate in discussions of the affairs of no other clients; in the absence of information to the contrary, it should be inferred that such a lawyer in fact is privy to information about the clients actually served but not those of other clients.

[7] Application of paragraph (b) depends on a situation's particular facts. In such an inquiry, the burden of proof should rest upon the firm whose disqualification is sought.

[8] Paragraph (b) operates to disqualify the lawyer only when the lawyer involved has actual knowledge of information protected by Rules 1.6 and 1.9(b). Thus, if a lawyer while with one firm acquired no knowledge or information relating to a particular client of the firm, and that lawyer later joined another firm, neither the lawyer individually nor the second firm is disqualified from representing another client in the same or a related matter even though the interests of the two clients conflict. See Rule 1.10(b) for the restrictions on a firm once a lawyer has terminated association with the firm.

[9] Independent of the question of disqualification of a firm, a lawyer changing professional association has a continuing duty to preserve confidentiality of information about a client formerly represented. See Rules 1.6 and 1.9.

* The comments under this topic originally appeared under Model Rule 1.10. With the modification of Model Rule 1.9, the ABA moved these comments under Model Rule 1.9 without significant change.

*Adverse Positions**

[10] The second aspect of loyalty to a client is the lawyer's obligation to decline subsequent representations involving positions adverse to a former client arising in substantially related matters. This obligation requires abstention from adverse representation by the individual lawyer involved, but does not properly entail abstention of other lawyers through imputed disqualification. Hence, this aspect of the problem is governed by Rule 1.9(a). Thus, if a lawyer left one firm for another, the new affiliation would not preclude the firms involved from continuing to represent clients with adverse interests in the same or related matters, so long as the conditions of paragraphs (b) and (c) concerning confidentiality have been met.

[11] Information acquired by the lawyer in the course of representing a client may not subsequently be used or revealed by the lawyer to the disadvantage of the client. However, the fact that a lawyer has once served a client does not preclude the lawyer from using generally known information about that client when later representing another client.

[12] Disqualification from subsequent representation is for the protection of former clients and can be waived by them. A waiver is effective only if there is disclosure of the circumstances, including the lawyer's intended role in behalf of the new client.

[13] With regard to an opposing party's raising a question of conflict of interest, see Comment to Rule 1.7. With regard to disqualification of a firm with which a lawyer is or was formerly associated, see Rule 1.10.

MODEL CODE COMPARISON: **

There was no counterpart to this Rule in the Disciplinary Rules of the Model Code. Representation adverse to a former client was sometimes dealt with under the rubric of Canon 9 of the Model Code, which provided: "A lawyer should avoid even the appearance of impropriety." Also applicable were EC 4–6 which stated that the "obligation of a lawyer to preserve the confidences and secrets of his client continues after the termination of his employment" and Canon 5 which stated that "[a] lawyer should exercise independent professional judgment on behalf of a client."

---

* The comments under this topic originally appeared under Model Rule 1.10. With the modification of Model Rule 1.9, the ABA moved these comments under Model Rule 1.9 without significant change.

** When ABA modified Model Rule 1.9 in 1989, it did not change the text of the Model Code Comparison. Thus, the current Model Code Comparison only refers to the Model Rule 1.9 as originally enacted.

To understand the amended Model Rule 1.9, one must read the following text quoted from the Code Comparison to Model Rule 1.10: "DR 5–105(D) provided that '[i]f a lawyer is required to decline or to withdraw from employment under a Disciplinary Rule, no partner, or associate, or any other lawyer affiliated with him or his firm, may accept or continue such employment.' "

The provision in paragraph (a) for waiver by the former client is similar to DR 5–105(C).

The exception in the last clause of paragraph (c)(1) permits a lawyer to use information relating to a former client that is in the "public domain," a use that was also not prohibited by the Model Code, which protected only "confidences and secrets." Since the scope of paragraph (a) is much broader than "confidences and secrets," it is necessary to define when a lawyer may make use of information about a client after the client-lawyer relationship has terminated.

RULE 1.10 Imputed Disqualification: General Rule**

(a) While lawyers are associated in a firm, none of them shall knowingly represent a client when any one of them practicing alone would be prohibited from doing so by Rules 1.7, 1.8(c), 1.9 or 2.2.

(b) When a lawyer has terminated an association with a firm, the firm is not prohibited from thereafter representing a person with interests materially adverse to those of a client represented

** In 1989, the ABA amended Model Rule 1.10 to remove original Rule 1.10(b) and move it to Model Rule 1.9(b). The ABA thus renumbered original Model Rule 1.10(c) and 1.10(d) as new Model Rule 1.10(b) and 1.10(c). The impetus behind this change was to clarify an overlap between Model Rule 1.9 and 1.10 and to address the question of duties to former clients when a lawyer changes firms and did not represent the former client but may have acquired confidential information about a former client of the old firm. Also, the ABA added the words "and, not currently represented by the firm" to current Model Rule 1.10(b). This was added to clarify the problem that when a lawyer leaves a firm, Model Rule 1.7's general prohibition of a directly adverse conflict still applies to the situation. The original version of Model Rule 1.10 is reproduced below:

RULE 1.10 Imputed Disqualification: General Rule

(a) While lawyers are associated in a firm, none of them shall knowingly represent a client when any one of them practicing alone would be prohibited from doing so by Rules 1.7, 1.8(c), 1.9 or 2.2.

(b) When a lawyer becomes associated with a firm, the firm may not knowingly represent a person in the same or a substantially related matter in which that lawyer, or a firm with which the lawyer was associated, had previously represented a client whose interests are materially adverse to that person and about whom the lawyer had acquired information protected by Rules 1.6 and 1.9(b) that is material to the matter.

(c) When a lawyer has terminated an association with a firm, the firm is not prohibited from thereafter representing a person with interests materially adverse to those of a client represented by the formerly associated lawyer unless:

(1) the matter is the same or substantially related to that in which the formerly associated lawyer represented the client; and

(2) any lawyer remaining in the firm has information protected by Rules 1.6 and 1.9(b) that is material to the matter.

(d) A disqualification prescribed by this rule may be waived by the affected client under the conditions stated in Rule 1.7.

by the formerly associated lawyer and not currently represented by the firm, unless:

(1) the matter is the same or substantially related to that in which the formerly associated lawyer represented the client; and

(2) any lawyer remaining in the firm has information protected by Rules 1.6 and 1.9(c) that is material to the matter.

(c) A disqualification prescribed by this rule may be waived by the affected client under the conditions stated in Rule 1.7.

COMMENT: *

Definition of "Firm"

[1] For purposes of the Rules of Professional Conduct, the term "firm" includes lawyers in a private firm, and lawyers in the legal

---

* When the ABA amended Model Rule 1.10 in 1989, it moved several paragraphs of comments from Model Rule 1.10 to Model Rule 1.9. The paragraphs which appeared in the original version of the Model Rules are reproduced below:

Lawyers Moving Between Firms

When lawyers have been associated in a firm but then end their association, however, the problem is more complicated. The fiction that the law firm is the same as a single lawyer is no longer wholly realistic. There are several competing considerations. First, the client previously represented must be reasonably assured that the principle of loyalty to the client is not compromised. Second, the rule of disqualification should not be so broadly cast as to preclude other persons from having reasonable choice of legal counsel. Third, the rule of disqualification should not unreasonably hamper lawyers from forming new associations and taking on new clients after having left a previous association. In this connection, it should be recognized that today many lawyers practice in firms, that many to some degree limit their practice to one field or another, and that many move from one association to another several times in their careers. If the concept of imputed disqualification were defined with unqualified rigor, the result would be radical curtailment of the opportunity of lawyers to move from one practice setting to

another and of the opportunity of clients to change counsel.

Reconciliation of these competing principles in the past has been attempted under two rubrics. One approach has been to seek per se rules of disqualification. For example, it has been held that a partner in a law firm is conclusively presumed to have access to all confidences concerning all clients of the firm. Under this analysis, if a lawyer has been a partner in one law firm and then becomes a partner in another law firm, there is a presumption that all confidences known by a partner in the first firm are known to all partners in the second firm. This presumption might properly be applied in some circumstances, especially where the client has been extensively represented, but may be unrealistic where the client was represented only for limited purposes. Furthermore, such a rigid rule exaggerates the difference between a partner and an associate in modern law firms.

The other rubric formerly used for dealing with vicarious disqualification is the appearance of impropriety proscribed in Canon 9 of the ABA Model Code of Professional Responsibility. This rubric has a twofold problem. First, the appearance of impropriety can be taken to include any new client-lawyer relationship that might make a former client feel anxious. If that meaning were adopted, disqualification would become little more than a question of subdepartment of a corporation or other organization, or in a legal services organization. Whether two or more lawyers constitute a firm within this definition can depend on the specific facts. For example, two practitioners who share office space and occasionally consult or assist each other ordinarily would not be regarded as constituting a firm. However, if they present themselves to the public in a way suggesting that they are a firm or conduct themselves as a firm, they should be regarded as a firm for the purposes of the Rules. The terms of any formal agreement between associated lawyers are relevant in determining whether they are a firm, as is the fact that they have mutual access

jective judgment by the former client. Second, since "impropriety" is undefined, the term "appearance of impropriety" is question-begging. It therefore has to be recognized that the problem of imputed disqualification cannot be properly resolved either by simple analogy to a lawyer practicing alone or by the very general concept of appearance of impropriety.

A rule based on a functional analysis is more appropriate for determining the question of vicarious disqualification. Two functions are involved: preserving confidentiality and avoiding positions adverse to a client.

Confidentiality

Preserving confidentiality is a question of access to information. Access to information, in turn, is essentially a question of fact in particular circumstances, aided by inferences, deductions or working presumptions that reasonably may be made about the way in which lawyers work together. A lawyer may have general access to files of all clients of a law firm and may regularly participate in discussions of their affairs; it should be inferred that such a lawyer in fact is privy to all information about all the firm's clients. In contrast, another lawyer may have access to the files of only a limited number of clients and participate in discussion of the affairs of no other clients; in the absence of information to the contrary, it should be inferred that such a lawyer in fact is privy to information about the clients actually served but not those of other clients.

Application of paragraphs (b) and (c) depends on a situation's particular facts. In any such inquiry, the burden of proof

should rest upon the firm whose disqualification is sought.

Paragraphs (b) and (c) operate to disqualify the firm only when the lawyer involved has actual knowledge of information protected by Rules 1.6 and 1.9(b). Thus, if a lawyer while with one firm acquired no knowledge of information relating to a particular client of the firm, and that lawyer later joined another firm, neither the lawyer individually nor the second firm is disqualified from representing another client in the same or a related matter even though the interests of the two clients conflict.

Independent of the question of disqualification of a firm, a lawyer changing professional association has a continuing duty to preserve confidentiality of information about a client formerly represented. See Rules 1.6 and 1.9.

Adverse Positions

The second aspect of loyalty to client is the lawyer's obligation to decline subsequent representations involving positions adverse to a former client arising in substantially related matters. This obligation requires abstention from adverse representation by the individual lawyer involved, but does not properly entail abstention of other lawyers through imputed disqualification. Hence, this aspect of the problem is governed by Rule 1.9(a). Thus, if a lawyer left one firm for another, the new affiliation would not preclude the firms involved from continuing to represent clients with adverse interests in the same or related matters, so long as the conditions of Rule 1.10(b) and (c) concerning confidentiality have been met.

to information concerning the clients they serve. Furthermore, it is relevant in doubtful cases to consider the underlying purpose of the Rule that is involved. A group of lawyers could be regarded as a firm for purposes of the rule that the same lawyer should not represent opposing parties in litigation, while it might not be so regarded for purposes of the rule that information acquired by one lawyer is attributed to the other.

[2] With respect to the law department of an organization, there is ordinarily no question that the members of the department constitute a firm within the meaning of the Rules of Professional Conduct. However, there can be uncertainty as to the identity of the client. For example, it may not be clear whether the law department of a corporation represents a subsidiary or an affiliated corporation, as well as the corporation by which the members of the department are directly employed. A similar question can arise concerning an unincorporated association and its local affiliates.

[3] Similar questions can also arise with respect to lawyers in legal aid. Lawyers employed in the same unit of a legal service organization constitute a firm, but not necessarily those employed in separate units. As in the case of independent practitioners, whether the lawyers should be treated as associated with each other can depend on the particular rule that is involved, and on the specific facts of the situation.

[4] Where a lawyer has joined a private firm after having represented the government, the situation is governed by Rule 1.11(a) and (b); where a lawyer represents the government after having served private clients, the situation is governed by Rule 1.11(c)(1). The individual lawyer involved is bound by the Rules generally, including Rules 1.6, 1.7 and 1.9.

[5] Different provisions are thus made for movement of a lawyer from one private firm to another and for movement of a lawyer between a private firm and the government. The government is entitled to protection of its client confidences and, therefore, to the protections provided in Rules 1.6, 1.9 and 1.11. However, if the more extensive disqualification in Rule 1.10 were applied to former government lawyers, the potential effect on the government would be unduly burdensome. The government deals with all private citizens and organizations and, thus, has a much wider circle of adverse legal interests than does any private law firm. In these circumstances, the government's recruitment of lawyers would be seriously impaired if Rule 1.10 were applied to the government. On balance, therefore, the government is better served in the long run by the protections stated in Rule 1.11.

Principles of Imputed Disqualification

[6] The rule of imputed disqualification stated in paragraph (a) gives effect to the principle of loyalty to the client as it applies to

lawyers who practice in a law firm. Such situations can be considered from the premise that a firm of lawyers is essentially one lawyer for purposes of the rules governing loyalty to the client, or from the premise that each lawyer is vicariously bound by the obligation of loyalty owed by each lawyer with whom the lawyer is associated. Paragraph (a) operates only among the lawyers currently associated in a firm. When a lawyer moves from one firm to another, the situation is governed by Rules 1.9(b) and 1.10(b).

[7] * Rule 1.10(b) operates to permit a law firm, under certain circumstances, to represent a person with interests directly adverse to those of a client represented by a lawyer who formerly was associated with the firm. The Rule applies regardless of when the formerly associated lawyer represented the client. However, the law firm may not represent a person with interests adverse to those of a present client of the firm, which would violate Rule 1.7. Moreover, the firm may not represent the person where the matter is the same or substantially related to that in which the formerly associated lawyer represented the client and any other lawyer currently in the firm has material information protected by Rules 1.6 and 1.9(c).

MODEL CODE COMPARISON:

DR 5–105(D) provided that "[i]f a lawyer is required to decline or to withdraw from employment under a Disciplinary Rule, no partner, or associate, or any other lawyer affiliated with him or his firm, may accept or continue such employment."

RULE 1.11 Successive Government and Private Employment

(a) **Except as law may otherwise expressly permit, a lawyer shall not represent a private client in connection with a matter in which the lawyer participated personally and substantially as a public officer or employee, unless the appropriate government agency consents after consultation. No lawyer in a firm with which that lawyer is associated may knowingly undertake or continue representation in such a matter unless:**

(1) **the disqualified lawyer is screened from any participation in the matter and is apportioned no part of the fee therefrom; and**

(2) **written notice is promptly given to the appropriate government agency to enable it to ascertain compliance with the provisions of this rule.**

(b) **Except as law may otherwise expressly permit, a lawyer having information that the lawyer knows is confidential government information about a person acquired when the lawyer was a public officer or employee, may not represent a private client**

* The ABA added this entire paragraph to the comments to Model Rule 1.10 in 1989. Thus, this language does not appear in the original version of the Model Rules.

whose interests are adverse to that person in a matter in which the information could be used to the material disadvantage of that person. A firm with which that lawyer is associated may undertake or continue representation in the matter only if the disqualified lawyer is screened from any participation in the matter and is apportioned no part of the fee therefrom.

(c) Except as law may otherwise expressly permit, a lawyer serving as a public officer or employee shall not:

(1) participate in a matter in which the lawyer participated personally and substantially while in private practice or nongovernmental employment, unless under applicable law no one is, or by lawful delegation may be, authorized to act in the lawyer's stead in the matter; or

(2) negotiate for private employment with any person who is involved as a party or as attorney for a party in a matter in which the lawyer is participating personally and substantially, except that a lawyer serving as a law clerk to a judge, other adjudicative officer or arbitrator may negotiate for private employment as permitted by Rule 1.12(b) and subject to the conditions stated in Rule 1.12(b).

(d) As used in this rule, the term "matter" includes:

(1) any judicial or other proceeding, application, request for a ruling or other determination, contract, claim, controversy, investigation, charge, accusation, arrest or other particular matter involving a specific party or parties; and

(2) any other matter covered by the conflict of interest rules of the appropriate government agency.

(e) As used in this rule, the term "confidential government information" means information which has been obtained under governmental authority and which, at the time this rule is applied, the government is prohibited by law from disclosing to the public or has a legal privilege not to disclose, and which is not otherwise available to the public.

COMMENT:

[1] This Rule prevents a lawyer from exploiting public office for the advantage of a private client. It is a counterpart of Rule 1.10(b), which applies to lawyers moving from one firm to another.

[2] A lawyer representing a government agency, whether employed or specially retained by the government, is subject to the Rules of Professional Conduct, including the prohibition against representing adverse interests stated in Rule 1.7 and the protections afforded former clients in Rule 1.9. In addition, such a lawyer is subject to Rule 1.11 and to statutes and government regulations regarding conflict of interest. Such statutes and regulations may circumscribe the extent to which the government agency may give consent under this Rule.

[3]   Where the successive clients are a public agency and a private client, the risk exists that power or discretion vested in public authority might be used for the special benefit of a private client. A lawyer should not be in a position where benefit to a private client might affect performance of the lawyer's professional functions on behalf of public authority. Also, unfair advantage could accrue to the private client by reason of access to confidential government information about the client's adversary obtainable only through the lawyer's government service. However, the rules governing lawyers presently or formerly employed by a government agency should not be so restrictive as to inhibit transfer of employment to and from the government. The government has a legitimate need to attract qualified lawyers as well as to maintain high ethical standards. The provisions for screening and waiver are necessary to prevent the disqualification rule from inposing too severe a deterrent against entering public service.

[4]   When the client is an agency of one government, that agency should be treated as a private client for purposes of this Rule if the lawyer thereafter represents an agency of another government, as when a lawyer represents a city and subsequently is employed by a federal agency.

[5]   Paragraphs (a)(1) and (b) do not prohibit a lawyer from receiving a salary or partnership share established by prior independent agreement. They prohibit directly relating the attorney's compensation to the fee in the matter in which the lawyer is disqualified.

[6]   Paragraph (a)(2) does not require that a lawyer give notice to the government agency at a time when premature disclosure would injure the client; a requirement for premature disclosure might preclude engagement of the lawyer. Such notice is, however, required to be given as soon as practicable in order that the government agency will have a reasonable opportunity to ascertain that the lawyer is complying with Rule 1.11 and to take appropriate action if it believes the lawyer is not complying.

[7]   Paragaph (b) operates only when the lawyer in question has knowledge of the information, which means actual knowledge; it does not operate with respect to information that merely could be imputed to the lawyer.

[8]   Paragraphs (a) and (c) do not prohibit a lawyer from jointly representing a private party and a government agency when doing so is permitted by Rule 1.7 and is not otherwise prohibited by law.

[9]   Paragraph (c) does not disqualify other lawyers in the agency with which the lawyer in question has become associated.

MODEL CODE COMPARISON:

Paragraph (a) is similar to DR 9–101(B), except that the latter used the terms "in which he had substantial responsibility while he was a public employee."

Paragraphs (b), (c), (d) and (e) have no counterparts in the Model Code.

RULE 1.12 Former Judge or Arbitrator

(a) Except as stated in paragraph (d), a lawyer shall not represent anyone in connection with a matter in which the lawyer participated personally and substantially as a judge or other adjudicative officer, arbitrator or law clerk to such a person, unless all parties to the proceeding consent after consultation.

(b) A lawyer shall not negotiate for employment with any person who is involved as a party or as attorney for a party in a matter in which the lawyer is participating personally and substantially as a judge or other adjudicative officer, or arbitrator. A lawyer serving as a law clerk to a judge, other adjudicative officer or arbitrator may negotiate for employment with a party or attorney involved in a matter in which the clerk is participating personally and substantially, but only after the lawyer has notified the judge, other adjudicative officer or arbitrator.

(c) If a lawyer is disqualified by paragraph (a), no lawyer in a firm with which that lawyer is associated may knowingly undertake or continue representation in the matter unless:

(1) the disqualified lawyer is screened from any participation in the matter and is apportioned no part of the fee therefrom; and

(2) written notice is promptly given to the appropriate tribunal to enable it to ascertain compliance with the provisions of this rule.

(d) An arbitrator selected as a partisan of a party in a multi-member arbitration panel is not prohibited from subsequently representing that party.

COMMENT:

This Rule generally parallels Rule 1.11. The term "personally and substantially" signifies that a judge who was a member of a multi-member court, and thereafter left judicial office to practice law, is not prohibited from representing a client in a matter pending in the court, but in which the former judge did not participate. So also the fact that a former judge exercised administrative responsibility in a court does not prevent the former judge from acting as a lawyer in a matter where the judge had previously exercised remote or incidental administrative responsibility that did not affect the merits. Compare the Comment to Rule 1.11. The term "adjudicative officer" includes such officials as judges pro tempore, referees, special masters, hearing officers and other parajudicial officers, and also lawyers who serve as part-time judges. Compliance Canons A(2), B(2) and C of the Model Code of Judicial Conduct provide that a part-time judge, judge pro tempore or retired judge recalled to active service, may not "act as a lawyer in any proceeding in which he served as a judge or in any other proceeding related thereto." Although phrased differently from this Rule, those Rules correspond in meaning.

MODEL CODE COMPARISON:

Paragaph (a) is substantially similar to DR 9–101(A), which provided that a lawyer "shall not accept private employment in a matter upon the merits of which he has acted in a judicial capacity." Paragraph (a) differs, however, in that it is broader in scope and states more specifically the persons to whom it applies. There was no counterpart in the Model Code to paragraphs (b), (c) or (d).

With regard to arbitrators, EC 5–20 stated that "a lawyer [who] has undertaken to act as an impartial arbitrator or mediator, . . . should not thereafter represent in the dispute any of the parties involved." DR 9–101(A) did not permit a waiver of the disqualification applied to former judges by consent of the parties. However, DR 5–105(C) was similar in effect and could be construed to permit waiver.

RULE 1.13 Organization as Client

(a) A lawyer employed or retained by an organization represents the organization acting through its duly authorized constituents.

(b) If a lawyer for an organization knows that an officer, employee or other person associated with the organization is engaged in action, intends to act or refuses to act in a matter related to the representation that is a violation of a legal obligation to the organization, or a violation of law which reasonably might be imputed to the organization, and is likely to result in substantial injury to the organization, the lawyer shall proceed as is reasonably necessary in the best interest of the organization. In determining how to proceed, the lawyer shall give due consideration to the seriousness of the violation and its consequences, the scope and nature of the lawyer's representation, the responsibility in the organization and the apparent motivation of the person involved, the policies of the organization concerning such matters and any other relevant considerations. Any measures taken shall be designed to minimize disruption of the organization and the risk of revealing information relating to the representation to persons outside the organization. Such measures may include among others:

(1) asking reconsideration of the matter;

(2) advising that a separate legal opinion on the matter be sought for presentation to appropriate authority in the organization; and

(3) referring the matter to higher authority in the organization, including, if warranted by the seriousness of the matter, referral to the highest authority that can act in behalf of the organization as determined by applicable law.

(c) If, despite the lawyer's efforts in accordance with paragraph (b), the highest authority that can act on behalf of the organization insists upon action, or a refusal to act, that is clearly a violation of law and is likely to result in substantial injury to the organization, the lawyer may resign in accordance with rule 1.16.

(d) In dealing with an organization's directors, officers, employees, members, shareholders or other constituents, a lawyer shall explain the identity of the client when it is apparent that the organization's interests are adverse to those of the constituents with whom the lawyer is dealing.

(e) A lawyer representing an organization may also represent any of its directors, officers, employees, members, shareholders or other constituents, subject to the provisions of rule 1.7. If the organization's consent to the dual representation is required by rule 1.7, the consent shall be given by an appropriate official of the organization other than the individual who is to be represented, or by the shareholders.

COMMENT:

The Entity as the Client

[1] An organizational client is a legal entity, but it cannot act except through its officers, directors, employees, shareholders and other constituents.

[2] Officers, directors, employees and shareholders are the constituents of the corporate organizational client. The duties defined in this Comment apply equally to unincorporated associations. "Other constituents" as used in this Comment means the positions equivalent to officers, directors, employees and shareholders held by persons acting for organizational clients that are not corporations.

[3] When one of the constituents of an organizational client communicates with the organization's lawyer in that person's organizational capacity, the communication is protected by Rule 1.6. Thus, by way of example, if an organizational client requests its lawyer to investigate allegations of wrongdoing, interviews made in the course of that investigation between the lawyer and the client's employees or other constituents are covered by Rule 1.6. This does not mean, however, that constituents of an organizational client are the clients of the lawyer. The lawyer may not disclose to such constituents information relating to the representation except for disclosures explicitly or impliedly authorized by the organizational client in order to carry out the representation or as otherwise permitted by Rule 1.6.

48

[4] When constituents of the organization make decisions for it, the decisions ordinarily must be accepted by the lawyer even if their utility or prudence is doubtful. Decisions concerning policy and operations, including ones entailing serious risk, are not as such in the lawyer's province. However, different considerations arise when the lawyer knows that the organization may be substantially injured by action of [a] constituent that is in violation of law. In such a circumstance, it may be reasonably necessary for the lawyer to ask the constituent to reconsider the matter. If that fails, or if the matter is of sufficient seriousness and importance to the organization, it may be reasonably necessary for the lawyer to take steps to have the matter reviewed by a higher authority in the organization. Clear justification should exist for seeking review over the head of the constituent normally responsible for it. The stated policy of the organization may define circumstances and prescribe channels for such review, and a lawyer should encourage the formulation of such a policy. Even in the absence of organization policy, however, the lawyer may have an obligation to refer a matter to higher authority, depending on the seriousness of the matter and whether the constituent in question has apparent motives to act at variance with the organization's interest. Review by the chief executive officer or by the board of directors may be required when the matter is of importance commensurate with their authority. At some point it may be useful or essential to obtain an independent legal opinion.

[5] In an extreme case, it may be reasonably necessary for the lawyer to refer the matter to the organization's highest authority. Ordinarily, that is the board of directors or similar governing body. However, applicable law may prescribe that under certain conditions highest authority reposes elsewhere; for example, in the independent directors of a corporation.

Relation to Other Rules

[6] The authority and responsibility provided in paragraph (b) are concurrent with the authority and responsibility provided in other Rules. In particular, this Rule does not limit or expand the lawyer's responsibility under Rules 1.6, 1.8, and 1.16, 3.3 or 4.1. If the lawyer's services are being used by an organization to further a crime or fraud by the organization, Rule 1.2(d) can be applicable.

Government Agency

[7] The duty defined in this Rule applies to governmental organizations. However, when the client is a governmental organization, a different balance may be appropriate between maintaining confidentiality and assuring that the wrongful official act is prevented or rectified, for public business is involved. In addition, duties of lawyers employed by the government or lawyers in military service may be defined by statutes and regulation. Therefore, defining precisely the identity of

the client and prescribing the resulting obligations of such lawyers may be more difficult in the government context. Although in some circmstances the client may be a specific agency, it is generally the government as a whole. For example, if the action or failure to act involves the head of a bureau, either the department of which the bureau is a part or the government as a whole may be the client for purpose of this Rule. Moreover, in a matter involving the conduct of government officials, a government lawyer may have authority to question such conduct more extensively than that of a lawyer for a private organization in similar circumstances. This Rule does not limit that authority. See note on Scope.

Clarifying the Lawyer's Role

[8] There are times when the organization's interest may be or become adverse to those of one or more of its constituents. In such circumstances the lawyer should advise any constituent, whose interest the lawyer finds adverse to that of the organization of the conflict or potential conflict of interest, that the lawyer cannot represent such constituent, and that such person may wish to obtain independent representation. Care must be taken to assure that the individual understands that, when there is such adversity of interest, the lawyer for the organization cannot provide legal representation for that constituent individual, and that discussions between the lawyer for the organization and the individual may not be privileged.

[9] Whether such a warning should be given by the lawyer for the organization to any constituent individual may turn on the facts of each case.

Dual Representation

[10] Paragraph (e) recognizes that a lawyer for an organization may also represent a principal officer or major shareholder.

Derivative Actions

[11] Under generally prevailing law, the shareholders or members of a corporation may bring suit to compel the directors to perform their legal obligations in the supervision of the organization. Members of unincorporated associations have essentially the same right. Such an action may be brought nominally by the organization, but usually is, in fact, a legal controversy over management of the organization.

[12] The question can arise whether counsel for the organization may defend such an action. The proposition that the organization is the lawyer's client does not alone resolve the issue. Most derivative actions are a normal incident of an organization's affairs, to be defended by the organization's lawyer like any other suit. However, if the claim involves serious charges of wrongdoing by those in control of the organization, a conflict may arise between the lawyer's duty to the

organization and the lawyer's relationship with the board. In those circumstances, Rule 1.7 governs who should represent the directors and the organization.

MODEL CODE COMPARISON:

There was no counterpart to this Rule in the Disciplinary Rules of the Model Code. EC 5–18 stated that a "lawyer employed or retained by a corporation or similar entity owes his allegiance to the entity and not to a stockholder, director, officer, employee, representative, or other person connected with the entity. In advising the entity, a lawyer should keep paramount its interests and his professional judgment should not be influenced by the personal desires of any person or organization. Occasionally, a lawyer for an entity is requested by a stockholder, director, officer, employee, representative, or other person connected with the entity to represent him in an individual capacity; in such case the lawyer may serve the individual only if the lawyer is convinced that differing interests are not present." EC 5–24 stated that although a lawyer "may be employed by a business corporation with non-lawyers serving as directors or officers, and they necessarily have the right to make decisions of business policy, a lawyer must decline to accept direction of his professional judgment from any layman." DR 5–107(B) provided that a lawyer "shall not permit a person who . . . employs . . . him to render legal services for another to direct or regulate his professional judgment in rendering such legal services."

RULE 1.14 Client Under a Disability

(a) **When a client's ability to make adequately considered decisions in connection with the representation is impaired, whether because of minority, mental disability or for some other reason, the lawyer shall, as far as reasonably possible, maintain a normal client–lawyer relationship with the client.**

(b) **A lawyer may seek the appointment of a guardian or take other protective action with respect to a client, only when the lawyer reasonably believes that the client cannot adequately act in the client's own interest.**

COMMENT:

[1] The normal client-lawyer relationship is based on the assumption that the client, when properly advised and assisted, is capable of making decisions about important matters. When the client is a minor or suffers from a mental disorder or disability, however, maintaining the ordinary client-lawyer relationship may not be possible in all respects. In particular, an incapacitated person may have no power to make legally binding decisions. Nevertheless, a client lacking legal competence often has the ability to understand, deliberate upon, and reach conclusions about matters affecting the client's own well-being.

51

Furthermore, to an increasing extent the law recognizes intermediate degrees of competence. For example, children as young as five or six years of age, and certainly those of ten or twelve, are regarded as having opinions that are entitled to weight in legal proceedings concerning their custody. So also, it is recognized that some persons of advanced age can be quite capable of handling routine financial matters while needing special legal protection concerning major transactions.

[2] The fact that a client suffers a disability does not diminish the lawyer's obligation to treat the client with attention and respect. If the person has no guardian or legal representative, the lawyer often must act as de facto guardian. Even if the person does have a legal representative, the lawyer should as far as possible accord the represented person the status of client, particularly in maintaining communication.

[3] If a legal representative has already been appointed for the client, the lawyer should ordinarily look to the representative for decisions on behalf of the client. If a legal representative has not been appointed, the lawyer should see to such an appointment where it would serve the client's best interests. Thus, if a disabled client has substantial property that should be sold for the client's benefit, effective completion of the transaction ordinarily requires appointment of a legal representative. In many circumstances, however, appointment of a legal representative may be expensive or traumatic for the client. Evaluation of these considerations is a matter of professional judgment on the lawyer's part.

[4] If the lawyer represents the guardian as distinct from the ward, and is aware that the guardian is acting adversely to the ward's interest, the lawyer may have an obligation to prevent or rectify the guardian's misconduct. See Rule 1.2(d).

Disclosure of the Client's Condition

[5] Rules of procedure in litigation generally provide that minors or persons suffering mental disability shall be represented by a guardian or next friend if they do not have a general guardian. However, disclosure of the client's disability can adversely affect the client's interests. For example, raising the question of disability could, in some circumstances, lead to proceedings for involuntary commitment. The lawyer's position in such cases is an unavoidably difficult one. The lawyer may seek guidance from an appropriate diagnostician.

MODEL CODE COMPARISON:

There was no counterpart to this Rule in the Disciplinary Rules of the Model Code. EC 7-11 stated that the "responsibilities of a lawyer may vary according to the intelligence, experience, mental condition or age of a client. . . . Examples include the representation of an illiterate or an incompetent." EC 7-12 stated that "[a]ny mental or physical condition of a client that renders him incapable of making a considered judgment on his own behalf casts additional responsibilities upon his lawyer. Where an incompetent is acting through a guardian or other legal representative, a lawyer must look to such representative for those decisions which are normally the prerogative of the client to make. If a client under disability has no legal representative, his lawyer may be compelled in court proceedings to make decisions on behalf of the client. If the client is capable of understanding the matter in question or of contributing to the advancement of his interests, regardless of whether he is legally disqualified from performing certain acts, the lawyer should obtain from him all possible aid. If the disability of a client and the lack of a legal representative compel the lawyer to make decisions for his client, the lawyer should consider all circumstances then prevailing and act with care to safeguard and advance the interests of his client. But obviously a lawyer cannot perform any act or make any decision which the law requires his client to perform or make, either acting for himself if competent, or by a duly constituted representative if legally incompetent."

RULE 1.15 Safekeeping Property

(a) **A lawyer shall hold property of clients or third persons that is in a lawyer's possession in connection with a representation separate from the lawyer's own property. Funds shall be kept in a separate account maintained in the state where the lawyer's office is situated, or elsewhere with the consent of the client or third person. Other property shall be identified as such and appropriately safeguarded. Complete records of such account funds and other property shall be kept by the lawyer and shall be preserved for a period of [five years] after termination of the representation.**

(b) **Upon receiving funds or other property in which a client or third person has an interest, a lawyer shall promptly notify the client or third person. Except as stated in this rule or otherwise permitted by law or by agreement with the client, a lawyer shall promptly deliver to the client or third person any funds or other property that the client or third person is entitled to receive and, upon request by the client or third person, shall promptly render a full accounting regarding such property.**

(c) **When in the course of representation a lawyer is in possession of property in which both the lawyer and another person claim interests, the property shall be kept separate by the lawyer until there is an accounting and severance of their interest. If a dispute arises concerning their respective interests, the portion in dispute shall be kept separate by the lawyer until the dispute is resolved.**

53

COMMENT:

[1] A lawyer should hold property of others with the care required of a professional fiduciary. Securities should be kept in a safe deposit box, except when some other form of safekeeping is warranted by special circumstances. All property which is the property of clients or third persons should be kept separate from the lawyer's business and personal property and, if monies, in one or more trust accounts. Separate trust accounts may be warranted when administering estate monies or acting in similar fiduciary capacities.

[2] Lawyers often receive funds from third parties from which the lawyer's fee will be paid. If there is risk that the client may divert the funds without paying the fee, the lawyer is not required to remit the portion from which the fee is to be paid. However, a lawyer may not hold funds to coerce a client into accepting the lawyer's contention. The disputed portion of the funds should be kept in trust and the lawyer should suggest means for prompt resolution of the dispute, such as arbitration. The undisputed portion of the funds shall be promptly distributed.

[3] Third parties, such as a client's creditors, may have just claims against funds or other property in a lawyer's custody. A lawyer may have a duty under applicable law to protect such third-party claims against wrongful interference by the client, and accordingly may refuse to surrender the property to the client. However, a lawyer should not unilaterally assume to arbitrate a dispute between the client and the third party.

[4] The obligations of a lawyer under this Rule are independent of those arising from activity other than rendering legal services. For example, a lawyer who serves as an escrow agent is governed by the applicable law relating to fiduciaries even though the lawyer does not render legal services in the transaction.

[5] A "client's security fund" provides a means through the collective efforts of the bar to reimburse persons who have lost money or property as a result of dishonest conduct of a lawyer. Where such a fund has been established, a lawyer should participate.

MODEL CODE COMPARISON:

With regard to paragraph (a), DR 9–102(A) provided that "funds of clients" are to be kept in an identifiable bank account in the state in which the lawyer's office is situated. DR 9–102(B)(2) provided that a lawyer shall "identify and label securities and properties of a client . . . and place them in . . . safekeeping. . . ." DR 9–102(B)(3) required that a lawyer "[m]aintain complete records of all funds, securities, and other properties of a client. . . ." Paragraph (a) extends these requirements to property of a third person that is in the lawyer's possession in connection with the representation.

Paragraph (b) is substantially similar to DR 9–102(B)(1), (3) and (4).

Paragraph (c) is similar to DR 9–102(A)(2), except that the requirement regarding disputes applies to property concerning which an interest is claimed by a third person as well as by a client.

RULE 1.16 Declining or Terminating Representation

(a) Except as stated in paragraph (c), a lawyer shall not represent a client or, where representation has commenced, shall withdraw from the representation of a client if:

(1) the representation will result in violation of the rules of professional conduct or other law;

(2) the lawyer's physical or mental condition materially impairs the lawyer's ability to represent the client; or

(3) the lawyer is discharged.

(b) Except as stated in paragraph (c), a lawyer may withdraw from representing a client if withdrawal can be accomplished without material adverse effect on the interests of the client, or if:

(1) the client persists in a course of action involving the lawyer's services that the lawyer reasonably believes is criminal or fraudulent;

(2) the client has used the lawyer's services to perpetrate a crime or fraud;

(3) a client insists upon pursuing an objective that the lawyer considers repugnant or imprudent;

(4) the client fails substantially to fulfill an obligation to the lawyer regarding the lawyer's services and has been given reasonable warning that the lawyer will withdraw unless the obligation is fulfilled;

(5) the representation will result in an unreasonable financial burden on the lawyer or has been rendered unreasonably difficult by the client; or

(6) other good cause for withdrawal exists.

(c) When ordered to do so by a tribunal, a lawyer shall continue representation notwithstanding good cause for terminating the representation.

(d) Upon termination of representation, a lawyer shall take steps to the extent reasonably practicable to protect a client's interests, such as giving reasonable notice to the client, allowing time for employment of other counsel, surrendering papers and property to which the client is entitled and refunding any advance payment of fee that has not been earned. The lawyer may retain papers relating to the client to the extent permitted by other law.

COMMENT:

[1] A lawyer should not accept representation in a matter unless it can be performed competently, promptly, without improper conflict of interest and to completion.

Mandatory Withdrawal

[2] A lawyer ordinarily must decline or withdraw from representation if the client demands that the lawyer engage in conduct that is illegal or violates the Rules of Professional Conduct or other law. The lawyer is not obliged to decline or withdraw simply because the client suggests such a course of conduct; a client may make such a suggestion in the hope that a lawyer will not be constrained by a professional obligation.

[3] When a lawyer has been appointed to represent a client, withdrawal ordinarily requires approval of the appointing authority. See also Rule 6.2. Difficulty may be encountered if withdrawal is based on the client's demand that the lawyer engage in unprofessional conduct. The court may wish an explanation for the withdrawal, while the lawyer may be bound to keep confidential the facts that would constitute such an explanation. The lawyer's statement that professional considerations require termination of the representation ordinarily should be accepted as sufficient.

Discharge

[4] A client has a right to discharge a lawyer at any time, with or without cause, subject to liability for payment for the lawyer's services. Where future dispute about the withdrawal may be anticipated, it may be advisable to prepare a written statement reciting the circumstances.

[5] Whether a client can discharge appointed counsel may depend on applicable law. A client seeking to do so should be given a full explanation of the consequences. These consequences may include a decision by the appointing authority that appointment of successor counsel is unjustified, thus requiring the client to represent himself.

[6] If the client is mentally incompetent, the client may lack the legal capacity to discharge the lawyer, and in any event the discharge may be seriously adverse to the client's interests. The lawyer should make special effort to help the client consider the consequences and, in an extreme case, may initiate proceedings for a conservatorship or similar protection of the client. See Rule 1.14.

Optional Withdrawal

[7] A lawyer may withdraw from representation in some circumstances. The lawyer has the option to withdraw if it can be accomplished without material adverse effect on the client's interests. Withdrawal is also justified if the client persists in a course of action that the lawyer reasonably believes is criminal or fraudulent, for a lawyer is

not required to be associated with such conduct even if the lawyer does not further it. Withdrawal is also permitted if the lawyer's services were misused in the past even if that would materially prejudice the client. The lawyer also may withdraw where the client insists on a repugnant or imprudent objective.

[8] A lawyer may withdraw if the client refuses to abide by the terms of an agreement relating to the representation, such as an agreement concerning fees or court costs or an agreement limiting the objectives of the representation.

Assisting the Client Upon Withdrawal

[9] Even if the lawyer has been unfairly discharged by the client, a lawyer must take all reasonable steps to mitigate the consequences to the client. The lawyer may retain papers as security for a fee only to the extent permitted by law.

[10] Whether or not a lawyer for an organization may under certain unusual circumstances have a legal obligation to the organization after withdrawing or being discharged by the organization's highest authority is beyond the scope of these Rules.

MODEL CODE COMPARISON:

With regard to paragraph (a), DR 2–109(A) provided that a lawyer "shall not accept employment . . . if he knows or it is obvious that [the prospective client] wishes to . . . [b]ring a legal action . . . or otherwise have steps taken for him, merely for the purpose of harassing or maliciously injuring any person. . . ." Nor may a lawyer accept employment if the lawyer is aware that the prospective client wishes to "[p]resent a claim or defense . . . that is not warranted under existing law, unless it can be supported by good faith argument for an extension, modification, or reversal of existing law." DR 2–110(B) provided that a lawyer "shall withdraw from employment . . . if:

"(1) He knows or it is obvious that his client is bringing the legal action . . . or is otherwise having steps taken for him, merely for the purpose of harassing or maliciously injuring any person.

"(2) He knows or it is obvious that his continued employment will result in violation of a Disciplinary Rule.

"(3) His mental or physical condition renders it unreasonably difficult for him to carry out the employment effectively.

"(4) He is discharged by his client."

With regard to paragraph (b), DR 2–110(C) permitted withdrawal regardless of the effect on the client if:

"(1) His client: (a) Insists upon presenting a claim or defense that is not warranted under existing law and cannot be supported by good faith argument for an extension, modification, or reversal of existing law; (b) Personally seeks to pursue an illegal course of conduct; (c)

Insists that the lawyer pursue a course of conduct that is illegal or that is prohibited under the Disciplinary Rules; (d) By other conduct renders it unreasonably difficult for the lawyer to carry out his employment effectively; (e) Insists, in a matter not pending before a tribunal, that the lawyer engage in conduct that is contrary to the judgment and advice of the lawyer but not prohibited under the Disciplinary Rules; (f) Deliberately disregards an agreement or obligation to the lawyer as to expenses and fees.

"(2) His continued employment is likely to result in a violation of a Disciplinary Rule.

"(3) His inability to work with co-counsel indicates that the best interest of the client likely will be served by withdrawal.

"(4) His mental or physical condition renders it difficult for him to carry out the employment effectively.

"(5) His client knowingly and freely assents to termination of his employment.

"(6) He believes in good faith, in a proceeding pending before a tribunal, that the tribunal will find the existence of other good cause for withdrawal."

With regard to paragraph (c), DR 2–110(A)(1) provided: "If permission for withdrawal from employment is required by the rules of a tribunal, the lawyer shall not withdraw . . . without its permission."

RULE 1.17 Sale of Law Practice*

A lawyer or a law firm may sell or purchase a law practice, including good will, if the following conditions are satisfied:

(a) The seller ceases to engage in the private practice of law [in the geographic area] [in the jurisdiction] (a jurisdiction may elect either version) in which the practice has been conducted;

(b) The practice is sold as an entirety to another lawyer or law firm;

(c) Actual written notice is given to each of the seller's clients regarding:

(1) the proposed sale;

(2) the terms of any proposed change in the fee arrangement authorized by paragraph (d);

(3) the client's right to retain other counsel or to take possession of the file; and

(4) the fact that the client's consent to the sale will be presumed if the client does not take any action or does not

---

* Model Rule 1.17 did not appear in the original version of the Model Rules. This provision and its comments were added by the ABA in 1990.

otherwise object within niney (90) days of receipt of the notice.

If a client cannot be given notice, the representation of that client may be transferred to the purchaser only upon entry of an order so authorizing by a court having jurisdiction. The seller may disclose to the court *in camera* information relating to the representation only to the extent necessary to obtain an order authorizing the transfer of a file.

(d) The fees charged clients shall not be increased by reason of the sale. The purchaser may, however, refuse to undertake the representation unless the client consents to pay the purchaser fees at a rate not exceeding the fees charged by the purchaser for rendering substantially similar services prior to the initiation of the purchase negotiations.

COMMENT:

[1] The practice of law is a profession, not merely a business. Clients are not commodities that can be purchased and sold at will. Pursuant to this Rule, when a lawyer or an entire firm ceases to practice and another lawyer or firm takes over the representation, the selling lawyer or firm may obtain compensation for the reasonable value of the practice as may withdrawing partners of law firms. See Rules 5.4 and 5.6.

Termination of Practice by the Seller

[2] The requirement that all of the private practice be sold is satisfied if the seller in good faith makes the entire practice available for sale to the purchaser. The fact that a number of the seller's clients decide not to be represented by the purchaser but take their matters elsewhere, therefore, does not result in a violation. Neither does a return to private practice as a result of an unanticipated change in circumstances result in a violation. For example, a lawyer who has sold the practice to accept an appointment to judicial office does not violate the requirement that the sale be attendant to cessation of practice if the lawyer later resumes private practice upon being defeated in a contested or a retention election for the office.

[3] The requirement that the seller cease to engage in the private practice of law does not prohibit employment as a lawyer on the staff of a public agency or a legal services entity which provides legal services to the poor, or as in-house counsel to a business.

[4] The Rule permits a sale attendant upon retirement from the private practice of law within the jurisdiction. Its provisions, therefore, accommodate the lawyer who sells the practice upon the occasion of moving to another state. Some states are so large that a move from one locale therein to another is tantamount to leaving the jurisdiction in which the lawyer has engaged in the practice of law. To also accommodate lawyers so situated, states may permit the sale of the

practice when the lawyer leaves the geographic area rather than the jurisdiction. The alternative desired should be indicated by selecting one of the two provided for in Rule 1.17(a).

Single Purchaser

[5] The Rule requires a single purchaser. The prohibition against piecemeal sale of a practice protects those clients whose matters are less lucrative and who might find it difficult to secure other counsel if a sale could be limited to substantial fee-generating matters. The purchaser is required to undertake all client matters in the practice, subject to client consent. If, however, the purchaser is unable to undertake all client matters because of a conflict of interest in a specific matter respecting which the purchaser is not permitted by Rule 1.7 or another rule to represent the client, the requirement that there be a single purchaser is nevertheless satisfied.

Client Confidences, Consent and Notice

[6] Negotiations between seller and prospective purchaser prior to disclosure of information relating to a specific representation of an identifiable client no more violate the confidentiality provisions of Model Rule 1.6 than do preliminary discussions concerning the possible association of another lawyer or mergers between firms, with respect to which client consent is not required. Providing the purchaser access to client-specific information relating to the representation and to the file, however, requires client consent. The Rule provides that before such information can be disclosed by the seller to the purchaser the client must be given actual written notice of the contemplated sale, including the identity of the purchaser and any proposed change in the terms of future representation, and must be told that the decision to consent or make other arrangements must be made within 90 days. If nothing is heard from the client within that time, consent to the sale is presumed.

[7] A lawyer or law firm ceasing to practice cannot be required to remain in practice because some clients cannot be given actual notice of the proposed purchase. Since these clients cannot themselves consent to the purchase or direct any other disposition of their files, the Rule requires an order from a court having jurisdiction authorizing their transfer or other disposition. The Court can be expected to determine whether reasonable efforts to locate the client have been exhausted, and whether the absent client's legitimate interests will be served by authorizing the transfer of the file so that the purchaser may continue the representation. Preservation of client confidences requires that the petition for a court order be considered *in camera.* (A procedure by which such an order can be obtained needs to be established in jurisdictions in which it presently does not exist.)

[8] All the elements of client autonomy, including the client's absolute right to discharge a lawyer and transfer the representation to another, survive the sale of the practice.

Fee Arrangements Between Client and Purchaser

[9]   The sale may not be financed by increases in fees charged the clients of the practice. Existing agreements between the seller and the client as to fees and the scope of the work must be honored by the purchaser, unless the client consents after consultation. The purchaser may, however, advise the client that the purchaser will not undertake the representation unless the client consents to pay the higher fees the purchaser usually charges. To prevent client financing of the sale, the higher fee the purchaser may charge must not exceed the fees charged by the purchaser for substantially similar service rendered prior to the initiation of the purchase negotiations.

[10]   The purchaser may not intentionally fragment the practice which is the subject of the sale by charging significantly different fees in substantially similar matters. Doing so would make it possible for the purchaser to avoid the obligation to take over the entire practice by charging arbitrarily higher fees for less lucrative matters, thereby increasing the likelihood that those clients would not consent to the new representation.

Other Applicable Ethical Standards

[11]   Lawyers participating in the sale of a law practice are subject to the ethical standards applicable to involving another lawyer in the representation of a client. These include, for example, the seller's obligation to exercise competence in identifying a purchaser qualified to assume the practice and the purchaser's obligation to undertake the representation competently (see Rule 1.1); the obligation to avoid disqualifying conflicts, and to secure client consent after consultation for those conflicts which can be agreed to (see Rule 1.7); and the obligation to protect information relating to the representation (see Rules 1.6 and 1.9).

[12]   If approval of the substitution of the purchasing attorney for the selling attorney is required by the rules of any tribunal in which a matter is pending, such approval must be obtained before the matter can be included in the sale (see Rule 1.16).

Applicability of the Rule

[13]   This Rule applies to the sale of a law practice by representatives of a deceased, disabled or disappeared lawyer. Thus, the seller may be represented by a non-lawyer representative not subject to these Rules. Since, however, no lawyer may participate in a sale of a law practice which does not conform to the requirements of this Rule, the representatives of the seller as well as the purchasing lawyer can be expected to see to it that they are met.

[14]   Admission to or retirement from a law partnership or professional association, retirement plans and similar arrangements, and a sale of tangible assets of a law practice, do not constitute a sale or purchase governed by this Rule.

[15] This Rule does not apply to the transfers of legal representation between lawyers when such transfers are unrelated to the sale of a practice.

MODEL CODE COMPARISON:

There was no counterpart to this Rule in the Model Code.

COUNSELOR

RULE 2.1 Advisor

In representing a client, a lawyer shall exercise independent professional judgment and render candid advice. In rendering advice, a lawyer may refer not only to law but to other considerations such as moral, economic, social and political factors, that may be relevant to the client's situation.

COMMENT:

Scope of Advice

[1] A client is entitled to straightforward advice expressing the lawyer's honest assessment. Legal advice often involves unpleasant facts and alternatives that a client may be disinclined to confront. In presenting advice, a lawyer endeavors to sustain the client's morale and may put advice in as acceptable a form as honesty permits. However, a lawyer should not be deterred from giving candid advice by the prospect that the advice will be unpalatable to the client.

[2] Advice couched in narrowly legal terms may be of little value to a client, especially where practical considerations, such as cost or effects on other people, are predominant. Purely technical legal advice, therefore, can sometimes be inadequate. It is proper for a lawyer to refer to relevant moral and ethical considerations in giving advice. Although a lawyer is not a moral advisor as such, moral and ethical considerations impinge upon most legal questions and may decisively influence how the law will be applied.

[3] A client may expressly or impliedly ask the lawyer for purely technical advice. When such a request is made by a client experienced in legal matters, the lawyer may accept it at face value. When such a request is made by a client inexperienced in legal matters, however, the lawyer's responsibility as advisor may include indicating that more may be involved than strictly legal considerations.

[4] Matters that go beyond strictly legal questions may also be in the domain of another profession. Family matters can involve problems within the professional competence of psychiatry, clinical psychology or social work; business matters can involve problems within the competence of the accounting profession or of financial specialists. Where consultation with a professional in another field is itself something a competent lawyer would recommend, the lawyer should make such a recommendation. At the same time, a lawyer's advice at its best

often consists of recommending a course of action in the face of conflicting recommendations of experts.

Offering Advice

[5] In general, a lawyer is not expected to give advice until asked by the client. However, when a lawyer knows that a client proposes a course of action that is likely to result in substantial adverse legal consequences to the client, duty to the client under Rule 1.4 may require that the lawyer act if the client's course of action is related to the representation. A lawyer ordinarily has no duty to initiate investigation of a client's affairs or to give advice that the client has indicated is unwanted, but a lawyer may initiate advice to a client when doing so appears to be in the client's interest.

MODEL CODE COMPARISON:

There was no direct counterpart to this Rule in the Disciplinary Rules of the Model Code. DR 5–107(B) provided that a lawyer "shall not permit a person who recommends, employs, or pays him to render legal services for another to direct or regulate his professional judgment in rendering such legal services." EC 7–8 stated that "[a]dvice of a lawyer to his client need not be confined to purely legal considerations. . . . In assisting his client to reach a proper decision, it is often desirable for a lawyer to point out those factors which may lead to a decision that is morally just as well as legally permissible. . . . In the final analysis, however, . . . the decision whether to forego legally available objectives or methods because of nonlegal factors is ultimately for the client. . . ."

RULE 2.2 Intermediary

(a) A lawyer may act as intermediary between clients if:

(1) the lawyer consults with each client concerning the implications of the common representation, including the advantages and risks involved, and the effect on the attorney–client privileges, and obtains each client's consent to the common representation;

(2) the lawyer reasonably believes that the matter can be resolved on terms compatible with the clients' best interests, that each client will be able to make adequately informed decisions in the matter and that there is little risk of material prejudice to the interest of any of the clients if the contemplated resolution is unsuccessful; and

(3) the lawyer reasonably believes that the common representation can be undertaken impartially and without improper effect on other responsibilities the lawyer has to any of the clients.

(b) While acting as intermediary, the lawyer shall consult with each client concerning the decisions to be made and the considerations relevant in making them, so that each client can make adequately informed decisions.

(c) A lawyer shall withdraw as intermediary if any of the clients so request, or if any of the conditions stated in paragraph (a) is no longer satisfied. Upon withdrawal, the lawyer shall not continue to represent any of the clients in the matter that was the subject of the intermediation.

COMMENT:

[1] A lawyer acts as intermediary under this Rule when the lawyer represents two or more parties with potentially conflicting interests. A key factor in defining the relationship is whether the parties share responsibility for the lawyer's fee, but the common representation may be inferred from other circumstances. Because confusion can arise as to the lawyer's role where each party is not separately represented, it is important that the lawyer make clear the relationship.

[2] The Rule does not apply to a lawyer acting as arbitrator or mediator between or among parties who are not clients of the lawyer, even where the lawyer has been appointed with the concurrence of the parties. In performing such a role the lawyer may be subject to applicable codes of ethics, such as the Code of Ethics for Arbitration in Commercial Disputes prepared by a joint Committee of the American Bar Association and the American Arbitration Association.

[3] A lawyer acts as intermediary in seeking to establish or adjust a relationship between clients on an amicable and mutually advantageous basis; for example, in helping to organize a business in which two or more clients are entrepreneurs, working out the financial reorganization of an enterprise in which two or more clients have an interest, arranging a property distribution in settlement of an estate or mediating a dispute between clients. The lawyer seeks to resolve potentially conflicting interests by developing the parties' mutual interests. The alternative can be that each party may have to obtain separate representation, with the possibility in some situations of incurring additional cost, complication or even litigation. Given these and other relevant factors, all the clients may prefer that the lawyer act as intermediary.

[4] In considering whether to act as intermediary between clients, a lawyer should be mindful that if the intermediation fails the result can be additional cost, embarrassment and recrimination. In some situations the risk of failure is so great that intermediation is plainly impossible. For example, a lawyer cannot undertake common representation of clients between whom contentious litigation is imminent or who contemplate contentious negotiations. More generally, if the relationship between the parties has already assumed definite antagonism, the possibility that the clients' interests can be adjusted by intermediation ordinarily is not very good.

[5] The appropriateness of intermediation can depend on its form. Forms of intermediation range from informal arbitration, where each client's case is presented by the respective client and the lawyer decides the outcome, to mediation, to common representation where the clients' interests are substantially though not entirely compatible. One form may be appropriate in circumstances where another would not. Other relevant factors are whether the lawyer subsequently will represent both parties on a continuing basis and whether the situation involves creating a relationship between the parties or terminating one.

Confidentiality and Privilege

[6] A particularly important factor in determining the appropriateness of intermediation is the effect on client-lawyer confidentiality and the attorney-client privilege. In a common representation, the lawyer is still required both to keep each client adequately informed and to maintain confidentiality of information relating to the representation. See Rules 1.4 and 1.6. Complying with both requirements while acting as intermediary requires a delicate balance. If the balance cannot be maintained, the common representation is improper. With regard to the attorney-client privilege, the prevailing rule is that as between commonly represented clients the privilege does not attach. Hence, it must be assumed that if litigation eventuates between the clients, the privilege will not protect any such communications, and the clients should be so advised.

[7] Since the lawyer is required to be impartial between commonly represented clients, intermediation is improper when that impartiality cannot be maintained. For example, a lawyer who has represented one of the clients for a long period and in a variety of matters might have diffculty being impartial between that client and one to whom the lawyer has only recently been introduced.

Consultation

[8] In acting as intermediary between clients, the lawyer is required to consult with the clients on the implications of doing so, and proceed only upon consent based on such a consultation. The consultation should make clear that the lawyer's role is not that of partisanship normally expected in other circumstances.

[9] Paragraph (b) is an application of the principle expressed in Rule 1.4. Where the lawyer is intermediary, the clients ordinarily must assume greater responsibility for decisions than when each client is independently represented.

Withdrawal

[10] Common representation does not diminish the rights of each client in the client-lawyer relationship. Each has the right to loyal and diligent representation, the right to discharge the lawyer as stated in

Rule 1.16, and the protection of Rule 1.9 concerning obligations to a former client.

MODEL CODE COMPARISON:

There was no direct counterpart to this Rule in the Disciplinary Rules of the Model Code. EC 5–20 stated that a "lawyer is often asked to serve as an impartial arbitrator or mediator in matters which involve present or former clients. He may serve in either capacity if he first discloses such present or former relationships." DR 5–105(B) provided that a lawyer "shall not continue multiple employment if the exercise of his independent judgment in behalf of a client will be or is likely to be adversely affected by his representation of another client, or if it would be likely to involve him in representation of differing interests, except to the extent permitted under DR 5–105(C)." DR 5–105(C) provided that "a lawyer may represent multiple clients if it is obvious that he can adequately represent the interests of each and if each consents to the representation after full disclosure of the possible effect of such representation on the exercise of his independent professional judgment on behalf of each."

RULE 2.3 Evaluation for Use by Third Persons

(a) A lawyer may undertake an evaluation of a matter affecting a client for the use of someone other than the client if:

(1) the lawyer reasonably believes that making the evaluation is compatible with other aspects of the lawyer's relationship with the client; and

(2) the client consents after consultation.

(b) Except as disclosure is required in connection with a report of an evaluation, information relating to the evaluation is otherwise protected by rule 1.6.

COMMENT:

Definition

[1] An evaluation may be performed at the client's direction but for the primary purpose of establishing information for the benefit of third parties; for example, an opinion concerning the title of property rendered at the behest of a vendor for the information of a prospective purchaser, or at the behest of a borrower for the information of a prospective lender. In some situations, the evaluation may be required by a government agency; for example, an opinion concerning the legality of the securities registered for sale under the securities laws. In other instances, the evaluation may be required by a third person, such as a purchaser of a business.

[2] Lawyers for the government may be called upon to give a formal opinion on the legality of contemplated government agency action. In making such an evaluation, the government lawyer acts at

the behest of the government as the client but for the purpose of establishing the limits of the agency's authorized activity. Such an opinion is to be distinguished from confidential legal advice given agency officials. The critical question is whether the opinion is to be made public.

[3] A legal evaluation should be distinguished from an investigation of a person with whom the lawyer does not have a client-lawyer relationship. For example, a lawyer retained by a purchaser to analyze a vendor's title to property does not have a client-lawyer relationship with the vendor. So also, an investigation into a person's affairs by a government lawyer, or by special counsel employed by the government, is not an evaluation as that term is used in this Rule. The question is whether the lawyer is retained by the person whose affairs are being examined. When the lawyer is retained by that person, the general rules concerning loyalty to client and preservation of confidences apply, which is not the case if the lawyer is retained by someone else. For this reason, it is essential to identify the person by whom the lawyer is retained. This should be made clear not only to the person under examination, but also to others to whom the results are to be made available.

Duty to Third Person

[4] When the evaluation is intended for the information or use of a third person, a legal duty to that person may or may not arise. That legal question is beyond the scope of this Rule. However, since such an evaluation involves a departure from the normal client-lawyer relationship, careful analysis of the situation is required. The lawyer must be satisfied as a matter of professional judgment that making the evaluation is compatible with other functions undertaken in behalf of the client. For example, if the lawyer is acting as advocate in defending the client against charges of fraud, it would normally be incompatible with that responsibility for the lawyer to perform an evaluation for others concerning the same or a related transaction. Assuming no such impediment is apparent, however, the lawyer should advise the client of the implications of the evaluation, particularly the lawyer's responsibilities to third persons and the duty to disseminate the findings.

Access to and Disclosure of Information

[5] The quality of an evaluation depends on the freedom and extent of the investigation upon which it is based. Ordinarily a lawyer should have whatever latitude of investigation seems necessary as a matter of professional judgment. Under some circumstances, however, the terms of the evaluation may be limited. For example, certain issues or sources may be categorically excluded, or the scope of search may be limited by time constraints or the noncooperation of persons having relevant information. Any such limitations which are material

to the evaluation should be described in the report. If after a lawyer
has commenced an evaluation, the client refuses to comply with the
terms upon which it was understood the evaluation was to have been
made, the lawyer's obligations are determined by law, having reference
to the terms of the client's agreement and the surrounding circumstances.

Financial Auditors' Requests for Information

[6] When a question concerning the legal situation of a client
arises at the instance of the client's financial auditor and the question
is referred to the lawyer, the lawyer's response may be made in
accordance with procedures recognized in the legal profession. Such a
procedure is set forth in the American Bar Association Statement of
Policy Regarding Lawyers' Responses to Auditors' Requests for Information, adopted in 1975.

MODEL CODE COMPARISON:

There was no counterpart to this Rule in the Model Code.

ADVOCATE

RULE 3.1 Meritorious Claims and Contentions

**A lawyer shall not bring or defend a proceeding, or assert or
controvert an issue therein, unless there is a basis for doing so
that is not frivolous, which includes a good faith argument for an
extension, modification or reversal of existing law. A lawyer for
the defendant in a criminal proceeding, or the respondent in a
proceeding that could result in incarceration, may nevertheless so
defend the proceeding as to require that every element of the case
be established.**

COMMENT:

[1] The advocate has a duty to use legal procedure for the fullest
benefit of the client's cause, but also a duty not to abuse legal procedure. The law, both procedural and substantive, establishes the limits
within which an advocate may proceed. However, the law is not
always clear and never is static. Accordingly, in determining the
proper scope of advocacy, account must be taken of the law's ambiguities and potential for change.

[2] The filing of an action or defense or similar action taken for a
client is not frivolous merely because the facts have not first been fully
substantiated or because the lawyer expects to develop vital evidence
only by discovery. Such action is not frivolous even though the lawyer
believes that the client's position ultimately will not prevail. The
action is frivolous, however, if the client desires to have the action
taken primarily for the purpose of harassing or maliciously injuring a
person or if the lawyer is unable either to make a good faith argument

on the merits of the action taken or to support the action taken by a good faith argument for an extension, modification or reversal of existing law.

MODEL CODE COMPARISON:

DR 7–102(A)(1) provided that a lawyer may not "[f]ile a suit, assert a position, conduct a defense, delay a trial, or take other action on behalf of his client when he knows or when it is obvious that such action would serve merely to harass or maliciously injure another." Rule 3.1 is to the same general effect as DR 7–102(A)(1), with three qualifications. First, the test of improper conduct is changed from "merely to harass or maliciously injure another" to the requirement that there be a basis for the litigation measure involved that is "not frivolous." This includes the concept stated in DR 7–102(A)(2) that a lawyer may advance a claim or defense unwarranted by existing law if "it can be supported by good faith argument for an extension, modification, or reversal of existing law." Second, the test in Rule 3.1 is an objective test, whereas DR 7–102(A)(1) applied only if the lawyer "knows or when it is obvious" that the litigation is frivolous. Third, Rule 3.1 has an exception that in a criminal case, or a case in which incarceration of the client may result (for example, certain juvenile proceedings), the lawyer may put the prosecution to its proof even if there is no nonfrivolous basis for defense.

RULE 3.2 Expediting Litigation

A lawyer shall make reasonable efforts to expedite litigation consistent with the interests of the client.

COMMENT:

Dilatory practices bring the administration of justice into disrepute. Delay should not be indulged merely for the convenience of the advocates, or for the purpose of frustrating an opposing party's attempt to obtain rightful redress or repose. It is not a justification that similar conduct is often tolerated by the bench and bar. The question is whether a competent lawyer acting in good faith would regard the course of action as having some substantial purpose other than delay. Realizing financial or other benefit from otherwise improper delay in litigation it not a legitimate interest of the client.

MODEL CODE COMPARISON:

DR 7–101(A)(1) stated that a lawyer does not violate the duty to represent a client zealously "by being punctual in fulfilling all professional commitments." DR 7–102(A)(1) provided that a lawyer "shall not . . . file a suit, assert a position, conduct a defense [or] delay a trial . . . when he knows or when it is obvious that such action would serve merely to harass or maliciously injure another."

RULE 3.3   Candor Toward the Tribunal

(a) A lawyer shall not knowingly:

(1) make a false statement of material fact or law to a tribunal;

(2) fail to disclose a material fact to a tribunal when disclosure is necessary to avoid assisting a criminal or fraudulent act by the client;

(3) fail to disclose to the tribunal legal authority in the controlling jurisdiction known to the lawyer to be directly adverse to the position of the client and not disclosed by opposing counsel; or

(4) offer evidence that the lawyer knows to be false. If a lawyer has offered material evidence and comes to know of its falsity, the lawyer shall take reasonable remedial measures.

(b) The duties stated in paragraph (a) continue to the conclusion of the proceeding, and apply even if compliance requires disclosure of information otherwise protected by rule 1.6.

(c) A lawyer may refuse to offer evidence that the lawyer reasonably believes is false.

(d) In an ex parte proceeding, a lawyer shall inform the tribunal of all material facts known to the lawyer which will enable the tribunal to make an informed decision, whether or not the facts are adverse.

COMMENT:

[1] The advocate's task is to present the client's case with persuasive force. Performance of that duty while maintaining confidences of the client is qualified by the advocate's duty of candor to the tribunal. However, an advocate does not vouch for the evidence submitted in a cause; the tribunal is responsible for assessing its probative value.

Representations by a Lawyer

[2] An advocate is responsible for pleadings and other documents prepared for litigation, but is usually not required to have personal knowledge of matters asserted therein, for litigation documents ordinarily present assertions by the client, or by someone on the client's behalf, and not assertions by the lawyer. Compare Rule 3.1. However, an assertion purporting to be on the lawyer's own knowledge, as in an affidavit by the lawyer or in a statement in open court, may properly be made only when the lawyer knows the assertion is true or believes it to be true on the basis of a reasonably diligent inquiry. There are circumstances where failure to make a disclosure is the equivalent of an affirmative misrepresentation. The obligation prescribed in Rule 1.2(d) not to counsel a client to commit or assist the client in commit-

ting a fraud applies in litigation. Regarding compliance with Rule 1.2(d), see the Comment to that Rule. See also the Comment to Rule 8.4(b).

Misleading Legal Argument

[3] Legal argument based on a knowingly false representation of law constitutes dishonesty toward the tribunal. A lawyer is not required to make a disinterested exposition of the law, but must recognize the existence of pertinent legal authorities. Furthermore, as stated in paragraph (a)(3), an advocate has a duty to disclose directly adverse authority in the controlling jurisdiction which has not been disclosed by the opposing party. The underlying concept is that legal argument is a discussion seeking to determine the legal premises properly applicable to the case.

False Evidence

[4] When evidence that a lawyer knows to be false is provided by a person who is not the client, the lawyer must refuse to offer it regardless of the client's wishes.

[5] When false evidence is offered by the client, however, a conflict may arise between the lawyer's duty to keep the client's revelations confidential and the duty of candor to the court. Upon ascertaining that material evidence is false, the lawyer should seek to persuade the client that the evidence should not be offered or, if it has been offered, that its false character should immediately be disclosed. If the persuasion is ineffective, the lawyer must take reasonable remedial measures.

[6] Except in the defense of a criminal accused, the rule generally recognized is that, if necessary to rectify the situation, an advocate must disclose the existence of the client's deception to the court or to the other party. Such a disclosure can result in grave consequences to the client, including not only a sense of betrayal but also loss of the case and perhaps a prosecution for perjury. But the alternative is that the lawyer cooperate in deceiving the court, thereby subverting the truth-finding process which the adversary system is designed to implement. See Rule 1.2(d). Furthermore, unless it is clearly understood that the lawyer will act upon the duty to disclose the existence of false evidence, the client can simply reject the lawyer's advice to reveal the false evidence and insist that the lawyer keep silent. Thus the client could in effect coerce the lawyer into being a party to fraud on the court.

Perjury by a Criminal Defendant

[7] Whether an advocate for a criminally accused has the same duty of disclosure has been intensely debated. While it is agreed that the lawyer should seek to persuade the client to refrain from perjurious

testimony, there has been dispute concerning the lawyer's duty when that persuasion fails. If the confrontation with the client occurs before trial, the lawyer ordinarily can withdraw. Withdrawal before trial may not be possible, however, either because trial is imminent, or because the confrontation with the client does not take place until the trial itself, or because no other counsel is available.

[8] The most difficult situation, therefore, arises in a criminal case where the accused insists on testifying when the lawyer knows that the testimony is perjurious. The lawyer's effort to rectify the situation can increase the likelihood of the client's being convicted as well as opening the possibility of a prosecution for perjury. On the other hand, if the lawyer does not exercise control over the proof, the lawyer participates, although in a merely passive way, in deception of the court.

[9] Three resolutions of this dilemma have been proposed. One is to permit the accused to testify by a narrative without guidance through the lawyer's questioning. This compromises both contending principles; it exempts the lawyer from the duty to disclose false evidence but subjects the client to an implicit disclosure of information imparted to counsel. Another suggested resolution, of relatively recent origin, is that the advocate be entirely excused from the duty to reveal perjury if the perjury is that of the client. This is a coherent solution but makes the advocate a knowing instrument of perjury.

[10] The other resolution of the dilemma is that the lawyer must reveal the client's perjury if necessary to rectify the situation. A criminal accused has a right to the assistance of an advocate, a right to testify and a right of confidential communication with counsel. However, an accused should not have a right to assistance of counsel in committing perjury. Furthermore, an advocate has an obligation, not only in professional ethics but under the law as well, to avoid implication in the commission of perjury or other falsification of evidence. See Rule 1.2(d).

Remedial Measures

[11] If perjured testimony or false evidence has been offered, the advocate's proper course ordinarily is to remonstrate with the client confidentially. If that fails, the advocate should seek to withdraw if that will remedy the situation. If withdrawal will not remedy the situation or is impossible, the advocate should make disclosure to the court. It is for the court then to determine what should be done—making a statement about the matter to the trier of fact, ordering a mistrial or perhaps nothing. If the false testimony was that of the client, the client may controvert the lawyer's version of their communication when the lawyer discloses the situation to the court. If there is an issue whether the client has committed perjury, the lawyer cannot represent the client in resolution of the issue and a mistrial may be unavoidable. An unscrupulous client might in this way attempt to

produce a series of mistrials and thus escape prosecution. However, a second such encounter could be construed as a deliberate abuse of the right to counsel and as such a waiver of the right to further representation.

Constitutional Requirements

[12] The general rule—that an advocate must disclose the existence of perjury with respect to a material fact, even that of a client— applies to defense counsel in criminal cases, as well as in other instances. However, the definition of the lawyer's ethical duty in such a situation may be qualified by constitutional provisions for due process and the right to counsel in criminal cases. In some jurisdictions these provisions have been construed to require that counsel present an accused as a witness if the accused wishes to testify, even if counsel knows the testimony will be false. The obligation of the advocate under these Rules is subordinate to such a constitutional requirement.

Duration of Obligation

[13] A practical time limit on the obligation to rectify the presentation of false evidence has to be established. The conclusion of the proceeding is a reasonably definite point for the termination of the obligation.

Refusing to Offer Proof Believed to be False

[14] Generally speaking, a lawyer has authority to refuse to offer testimony or other proof that the lawyer believes is untrustworthy. Offering such proof may reflect adversely on the lawyer's ability to discriminate in the quality of evidence and thus impair the lawyer's effectiveness as an advocate. In criminal cases, however, a lawyer may, in some jurisdictions, be denied this authority by constitutional requirements governing the right to counsel.

Ex Parte Proceedings

[15] Ordinarily, an advocate has the limited responsibility of presenting one side of the matters that a tribunal should consider in reaching a decision; the conflicting position is expected to be presented by the opposing party. However, in an ex parte proceeding, such as an application for a temporary restraining order, there is no balance of presentation by opposing advocates. The object of an ex parte proceeding is nevertheless to yield a substantially just result. The judge has an affirmative responsibility to accord the absent party just consideration. The lawyer for the represented party has the correlative duty to make disclosures of material facts known to the lawyer and that the lawyer reasonably believes are necessary to an informed decision.

MODEL CODE COMPARISON:

Paragraph (a)(1) is substantially identical to DR 7–102(A)(5), which provided that a lawyer shall not "knowingly make a false statement of law or fact."

Paragraph (a)(2) is implicit in DR 7–102(A)(3), which provided that "a lawyer shall not . . . knowingly fail to disclose that which he is required by law to reveal."

Paragraph (a)(3) is substantially identical to DR 7–106(B)(1).

With regard to paragraph (a)(4), the first sentence of this subparagraph is similar to DR 7–102(A)(4), which provided that a lawyer shall not "knowingly use" perjured testimony or false evidence. The second sentence of paragraph (a)(4) resolves an ambiguity in the Model Code concerning the action required of a lawyer who discovers that the lawyer has offered perjured testimony or false evidence. DR 7–102(A) (4), quoted above, did not expressly deal with this situation, but the prohibition against "use" of false evidence can be construed to preclude carrying through with a case based on such evidence when that fact has become known during the trial. DR 7–102(B)(1), also noted in connection with Rule 1.6, provided that a lawyer "who receives information clearly establishing that . . . [h]is client has . . . perpetrated a fraud upon . . . a tribunal shall [if the client does not rectify the situation] . . . reveal the fraud to the . . . tribunal. . . ." Since use of perjured testimony or false evidence is usually regarded as "fraud" upon the court, DR 7–102(B)(1) apparently required disclosure by the lawyer in such circumstances. However, some states have amended DR 7–102(B)(1) in conformity with an ABA-recommended amendment to provide that the duty of disclosure does not apply when the "information is protected as a privileged communication." This qualification may be empty, for the rule of attorney-client privilege has been construed to exclude communications that further a crime, including the crime of perjury. On this interpretation of DR 7–102(B)(1), the lawyer has a duty to disclose the perjury.

Paragraph (c) confers discretion on the lawyer to refuse to offer evidence that the lawyer "reasonably believes" is false. This gives the lawyer more latitude than DR 7–102(A)(4), which prohibited the lawyer from offering evidence the lawyer "knows" is false.

There was no counterpart in the Model Code to paragraph (d).

RULE 3.4 Fairness to Opposing Party and Counsel

A lawyer shall not:

(a) unlawfully obstruct another party's access to evidence or unlawfully alter, destroy or conceal a document or other material having potential evidentiary value. A lawyer shall not counsel or assist another person to do any such act;

74

(b) falsify evidence, counsel or assist a witness to testify falsely, or offer an inducement to a witness that is prohibited by law;

(c) knowingly disobey an obligation under the rules of a tribunal except for an open refusal based on an assertion that no valid obligation exists;

(d) in pretrial procedure, make a frivolous discovery request or fail to make reasonably diligent effort to comply with a legally proper discovery request by an opposing party;

(e) in trial, allude to any matter that the lawyer does not reasonably believe is relevant or that will not be supported by admissible evidence, assert personal knowledge of facts in issue except when testifying as a witness, or state a personal opinion as to the justness of a cause, the credibility of a witness, the culpability of a civil litigant or the guilt or innocence of an accused; or

(f) request a person other than a client to refrain from voluntarily giving relevant information to another party unless:

(1) the person is a relative or an employee or other agent of a client; and

(2) the lawyer reasonably believes that the person's interests will not be adversely affected by refraining from giving such information.

COMMENT:

[1] The procedure of the adversary system contemplates that the evidence in a case is to be marshalled competitively by the contending parties. Fair competition in the adversary system is secured by prohibitions against destruction or concealment of evidence, improperly influencing witnesses, obstructive tactics in discovery procedure, and the like.

[2] Documents and other items of evidence are often essential to establish a claim or defense. Subject to evidentiary privileges, the right of an opposing party, including the government, to obtain evidence through discovery or subpoena is an important procedural right. The exercise of that right can be frustrated if relevant material is altered, concealed or destroyed. Applicable law in many jurisdictions makes it an offense to destroy material for purpose of impairing its availability in a pending proceeding or one whose commencement can be foreseen. Falsifying evidence is also generally a criminal offense. Paragraph (a) applies to evidentiary material generally, including computerized information.

[3] With regard to paragrah (b), it is not improper to pay a witness's expenses or to compensate an expert witness on terms permitted by law. The common law rule in most jurisdictions is that it is

improper to pay an occurrence witness any fee for testifying and that it is improper to pay an expert witness a contingent fee.

[4] Paragraph (f) permits a lawyer to advise employees of a client to refrain from giving information to another party, for the employees may identify their interests with those of the client. See also Rule 4.2.

MODEL CODE COMPARISON:

With regard to paragraph (a), DR 7-109(A) provided that a lawyer "shall not suppress any evidence that he or his client has a legal obligation to reveal." DR 7-109(B) provided that a lawyer "shall not advise or cause a person to secrete himself . . . for the purpose of making him unavailable as a witness. . . ." DR 7-106(C)(7) provided that a lawyer shall not "[i]ntentionally or habitually violate any established rule of procedure or of evidence."

With regard to paragraph (b), DR 7-102(A)(6) provided that a lawyer shall not participate "in the creation or preservation of evidence when he knows or it is obvious that the evidence is false." DR 7-109(C) provided that a lawyer "shall not pay, offer to pay, or acquiesce in the payment of compensation to a witness contingent upon the content of his testimony or the outcome of the case. But a lawyer may advance, guarantee or acquiesce in the payment of: (1) Expenses reasonably incurred by a witness in attending or testifying; (2) Reasonable compensation to a witness for his loss of time in attending or testifying; [or] (3) A reasonable fee for the professional services of an expert witness." EC 7-28 stated that witnesses "should always testify truthfully and should be free from any financial inducements that might tempt them to do otherwise."

Paragraph (c) is substantially similar to DR 7-106(A), which provided that "A lawyer shall not disregard . . . a standing rule of a tribunal or a ruling of a tribunal made in the course of a proceeding, but he may take appropriate steps in good faith to test the validity of such rule or ruling."

Paragraph (d) has no counterpart in the Model Code.

Paragraph (e) substantially incorporates DR 7-106(C)(1), (2), (3) and (4). DR 7-106(C)(2) proscribed asking a question "intended to degrade a witness or other person," a matter dealt with in Rule 4.4. DR 7-106(C) (5), providing that a lawyer shall not "fail to comply with known local customs of courtesy or practice," was too vague to be a rule of conduct enforceable as law.

With regard to paragraph (f), DR 7-104(A)(2) provided that a lawyer shall not "give advice to a person who is not represented . . . other than the advice to secure counsel, if the interests of such person are or have a reasonable possibility of being in conflict with the interests of his client."

RULE 3.5 Impartiality and Decorum of the Tribunal

A lawyer shall not:

(a) seek to influence a judge, juror, prospective juror or other official by means prohibited by law;

(b) communicate ex parte with such a person except as permitted by law; or

(c) engage in conduct intended to disrupt a tribunal.

COMMENT:

[1] Many forms of improper influence upon a tribunal are proscribed by criminal law. Others are specified in the ABA Model Code of Judicial Conduct, with which an advocate should be familiar. A lawyer is required to avoid contributing to a violation of such provisions.

[2] The advocate's function is to present evidence and argument so that the cause may be decided according to law. Refraining from abusive or obstreperous conduct is a corollary of the advocate's right to speak on behalf of litigants. A lawyer may stand firm against abuse by a judge but should avoid reciprocation; the judge's default is no justification for similar dereliction by an advocate. An advocate can present the cause, protect the record for subsequent review and preserve professional integrity by patient firmness no less effectively than by belligerence or theatrics.

MODEL CODE COMPARISON:

With regard to paragraphs (a) and (b), DR 7–108(A) provided that "[b]efore the trial of a case a lawyer . . . shall not communicate with . . . anyone he knows to be a member of the venire. . . ." DR 7–108(B) provided that during the trial of a case a lawyer "shall not communicate with . . . any member of the jury." DR 7–110(B) provided that a lawyer shall not "communicate . . . as to the merits of the cause with a judge or an official before whom the proceeding is pending, except . . . upon adequate notice to opposing counsel," or as "otherwise authorized by law."

With regard to paragraph (c), DR 7–106(C)(6) provided that a lawyer shall not engage in "undignified or discourteous conduct which is degrading to a tribunal."

RULE 3.6 Trial Publicity

(a) A lawyer shall not make an extrajudicial statement that a reasonable person would expect to be disseminated by means of public communication if the lawyer knows or reasonably should know that it will have a substantial likelihood of materially prejudicing an adjudicative proceeding.

(b) A statement referred to in paragraph (a) ordinarily is likely to have such an effect when it refers to a civil matter triable to a jury, a criminal matter, or any other proceeding that could result in incarceration, and the statement relates to:

(1) the character, credibility, reputation or criminal record of a party, suspect in a criminal investigation or witness, or the identity of a witness, or the expected testimony of a party or witness;

(2) in a criminal case or proceeding that could result in incarceration, the possibility of a plea of guilty to the offense or the existence or contents of any confession, admission, or statement given by a defendant or suspect or that person's refusal or failure to make a statement;

(3) the performance or results of any examination or test or the refusal or failure of a person to submit to an examination or test, or the identity or nature of physical evidence expected to be presented;

(4) any opinion as to the guilt or innocence of a defendant or suspect in a criminal case or proceeding that could result in incarceration;

(5) information the lawyer knows or reasonably should know is likely to be inadmissible as evidence in a trial and would if disclosed create a substantial risk of prejudicing an impartial trial; or

(6) the fact that a defendant has been charged with a crime, unless there is included therein a statement explaining that the charge is merely an accusation and that the defendant is presumed innocent until and unless proven guilty.

(c) Notwithstanding paragraph (a) and (b)(1–5), a lawyer involved in the investigation or litigation of a matter may state without elaboration:

(1) the general nature of the claim or defense;

(2) the information contained in a public record;

(3) that an investigation of the matter is in progress, including the general scope of the investigation, the offense or claim or defense involved and, except when prohibited by law, the identity of the persons involved;

(4) the scheduling or result of any step in litigation;

(5) a request for assistance in obtaining evidence and information necessary thereto;

(6) a warning of danger concerning the behavior of a person involved, when there is reason to believe that there exists the likelihood of substantial harm to an individual or to the public interest; and

(7) in a criminal case:

    (i) the identity, residence, occupation and family status of the accused;

    (ii) if the accused has not been apprehended, information necessary to aid in apprehension of that person;

    (iii) the fact, time and place of arrest; and

    (iv) the identity of investigating and arresting officers or agencies and the length of the investigation.

COMMENT:

[1] It is difficult to strike a balance between protecting the right to a fair trial and safeguarding the right of free expression. Preserving the right to a fair trial necessarily entails some curtailment of the information that may be disseminated about a party prior to trial, particularly where trial by jury is involved. If there were no such limits, the result would be the practical nullification of the protective effect of the rules of forensic decorum and the exclusionary rules of evidence. On the other hand, there are vital social interests served by the free dissemination of information about events having legal consequences and about legal proceedings themselves. The public has a right to know about threats to its safety and measures aimed at assuring its security. It also has a legitimate interest in the conduct of judicial proceedings, particularly in matters of general public concern. Furthermore, the subject matter of legal proceedings is often of direct significance in debate and deliberation over questions of public policy.

[2] No body of rules can simultaneously satisfy all interests of fair trial and all those of free expression. The formula in this Rule is based upon the ABA Model Code of Professional Responsibility and the ABA Standards Relating to Fair Trial and Free Press, as amended in 1978.

[3] Special rules of confidentiality may validly govern proceedings in juvenile, domestic relations and mental disability proceedings, and perhaps other types of litigation. Rule 3.4(c) requires compliance with such Rules.

MODEL CODE COMPARISON:

Rule 3.6 is similar to DR 7–107, except as follows: First, Rule 3.6 adopts the general criteria of "substantial likelihood of materially prejudicing an adjudicative proceeding" to describe impermissible conduct. Second, Rule 3.6 transforms the particulars in DR 7–107 into an illustrative compilation that gives fair notice of conduct ordinarily posing unacceptable dangers to the fair administration of justice. Finally, Rule 3.6 omits DR 7–107(C)(7), which provided that a lawyer may reveal "[a]t the time of seizure, a description of the physical evidence seized, other than a confession, admission or statement." Such revelations may be substantially prejudicial and are frequently the subject of pretrial suppression motions, which, if successful, may be circumvented by prior disclosure to the press.

RULE 3.7 Lawyer as Witness

(a) A lawyer shall not act as advocate at a trial in which the lawyer is likely to be a necessary witness except where:

(1) the testimony relates to an uncontested issue;

(2) the testimony relates to the nature and value of legal services rendered in the case; or

(3) disqualification of the lawyer would work substantial hardship on the client.

(b) A lawyer may act as advocate in a trial in which another lawyer in the lawyer's firm is likely to be called as a witness unless precluded from doing so by rule 1.7 or rule 1.9.

COMMENT:

[1] Combining the roles of advocate and witness can prejudice the opposing party and can involve a conflict of interest between the lawyer and client.

[2] The opposing party has proper objection where the combination of roles may prejudice that party's rights in the litigation. A witness is required to testify on the basis of personal knowledge, while an advocate is expected to explain and comment on evidence given by others. It may not be clear whether a statement by an advocate-witness should be taken as proof or as an analysis of the proof.

[3] Paragraph (a)(1) recognizes that if the testimony will be uncontested, the ambiguities in the dual role are purely theoretical. Paragraph (a)(2) recognizes that where the testimony concerns the extent and value of legal services rendered in the action in which the testimony is offered, permitting the lawyers to testify avoids the need for a second trial with new counsel to resolve that issue. Moreover, in such a situation the judge has first hand knowledge of the matter in issue; hence, there is less dependence on the adversary process to test the credibility of the testimony.

[4] Apart from these two exceptions, paragraph (a)(3) recognizes that a balancing is required between the interests of the client and those of the opposing party. Whether the opposing party is likely to suffer prejudice depends on the nature of the case, the importance and probable tenor of the lawyer's testimony, and the probability that the lawyer's testimony will conflict with that of other witnesses. Even if there is risk of such prejudice, in determining whether the lawyer should be disqualified due regard must be given to the effect of disqualification on the lawyer's client. It is relevant that one or both parties could reasonably foresee that the lawyer would probably be a witness. The principle of imputed disqualification stated in Rule 1.10 has no application to this aspect of the problem.

[5] Whether the combination of roles involves an improper conflict of interest with respect to the client is determined by Rule 1.7 or 1.9. For example, if there is likely to be substantial conflict between the testimony of the client and that of the lawyer or a member of the lawyer's firm, the representation is improper. The problem can arise whether the lawyer is called as a witness on behalf of the client or is called by the opposing party. Determining whether or not such a conflict exists is primarily the responsibility of the lawyer involved. See Comment to Rule 1.7. If a lawyer who is a member of a firm may not act as both advocate and witness by reason of conflict of interest, Rule 1.10 disqualifies the firm also.

MODEL CODE COMPARISON:

DR 5–102(A) prohibited a lawyer, or the lawyer's firm, from serving as advocate if the lawyer "learns or it is obvious that he or a lawyer in his firm ought to be called as a witness on behalf of his client." DR 5–102(B) provided that a lawyer, and the lawyer's firm, may continue representation if the "lawyer learns or it is obvious that he or a lawyer in his firm may be called as a witness other than on behalf of his client . . . until it is apparent that his testimony is or may be prejudicial to his client." DR 5–101(B) permitted a lawyer to testify while representing a client: "(1) If the testimony will relate solely to an uncontested matter; (2) If the testimony will relate solely to a matter of formality and there is no reason to believe that substantial evidence will be offered in opposition to the testimony; (3) If the testimony will relate solely to the nature and value of legal services rendered in the case by the lawyer or his firm to the client; (4) As to any matter if refusal would work a substantial hardship on the client because of the distinctive value of the lawyer or his firm as counsel in the particular case."

The exception stated in paragraph (a)(1) consolidates provisions of DR 5–101(B)(1) and (2). Testimony relating to a formality, referred to in DR 5–101(B)(2), in effect defines the phrase "uncontested issue," and is redundant.

RULE 3.8 Special Responsibilities of a Prosecutor*

The prosecutor in a criminal case shall:

(a) refrain from prosecuting a charge that the prosecutor knows is not supported by probable cause;

(b) make reasonable efforts to assure that the accused has been advised of the right to, and the procedure for obtaining, counsel and has been given reasonable opportunity to obtain counsel;

* In 1990, the ABA added the text in subparagraph (f) to original Model Rule 3.8. This amendment seeks to address the profession's concerns over the increased use of subpoenas that are directed towards attorneys for information about their clients. The adopted rule seeks to limit the use of such subpoenas because of their potential to disrupt the attorney-client relationship.

(c) not seek to obtain from an unrepresented accused a waiver of important pretrial rights, such as the right to a preliminary hearing;

(d) make timely disclosure to the defense of all evidence or information known to the prosecutor that tends to negate the guilt of the accused or mitigates the offense, and, in connection with sentencing, disclose to the defense and to the tribunal all unprivileged mitigating information known to the prosecutor, except when the prosecutor is relieved of this responsibility by a protective order of the tribunal; and

(e) exercise reasonable care to prevent investigators, law enforcement personnel, employees or other persons assisting or associated with the prosecutor in a criminal case from making an extrajudicial statement that the prosecutor would be prohibited from making under rule 3.6.

(f) not subpoena a lawyer in a grand jury or other criminal proceeding to present evidence about a past or present client unless:

(1) the prosecutor reasonably believes:

(i) the information sought is not protected from disclosure by any applicable privilege;

(ii) the evidence sought is essential to the successful completion of an ongoing investigation or prosecution;

(iii) there is no other feasible alternative to obtain the information; and

(2) the prosecutor obtains prior judicial approval after an opportunity for an adversarial proceeding.

COMMENT:

[1] A prosecutor has the responsibility of a minister of justice and not simply that of an advocate. This responsibility carries with it specific obligations to see that the defendant is accorded procedural justice and that guilt is decided upon the basis of sufficient evidence. Precisely how far the prosecutor is required to go in this direction is a matter of debate and varies in different jurisdictions. Many jurisdictions have adopted the ABA Standards of Criminal Justice Relating to Prosecution Function, which in turn are the product of prolonged and careful deliberation by lawyers experienced in both criminal prosecution and defense. See also Rule 3.3(d), governing ex parte proceedings, among which grand jury proceedings are included. Applicable law may require other measures by the prosecutor and knowing disregard of those obligations or a systematic abuse of prosecutorial discretion could constitute a violation of Rule 8.4.

[2] Paragraph (c) does not apply to an accused appearing pro se with the approval of the tribunal. Nor does it forbid the lawful

questioning of a suspect who has knowingly waived the rights to counsel and silence.

[3] The exception in paragraph (d) recognizes that a prosecutor may seek an appropriate protective order from the tribunal if disclosure of information to the defense could result in substantial harm to an individual or to the public interest.

[4] * Paragraph (f) is intended to limit the issuance of lawyer subpoenas in grand jury and other criminal proceedings to those situations in which there is a genuine need to intrude into the client-lawyer relationship. The prosecutor is required to obtain court approval for the issuance of the subpoena after an opportunity for an adversarial hearing is afforded in order to assure an independent determination that the applicable standards are met.

MODEL CODE COMPARISON:

DR 7–103(A) provided that a "public prosecutor . . . shall not institute . . . criminal charges when he knows or it is obvious that the charges are not supported by probable cause." DR 7–103(B) provided that "[a] public prosecutor . . . shall make timely disclosure . . . of the existence of evidence, known to the prosecutor . . . that tends to negate the guilt of the accused, mitigate the degree of the offense, or reduce the punishment."

RULE 3.9 Advocate in Nonadjudicative Proceedings

A lawyer representing a client before a legislative or administrative tribunal in a nonadjudicative proceeding shall disclose that the appearance is in a representative capacity and shall conform to the provisions of rules 3.3(a) through (c), 3.4(a) through (c), and 3.5.

COMMENT:

[1] In representation before bodies such as legislatures, municipal councils, and executive and administrative agencies acting in a rule-making or policy-making capacity, lawyers present facts, formulate issues and advance argument in the matters under consideration. The decision-making body, like a court, should be able to rely on the integrity of the submissions made to it. A lawyer appearing before such a body should deal with the tribunal honestly and in conformity with applicable rules of procedure.

[2] Lawyers have no exclusive right to appear before nonadjudicative bodies, as they do before a court. The requirements of this Rule therefore may subject lawyers to regulations inapplicable to advocates who are not lawyers. However, legislatures and administrative agen-

* The ABA added this paragraph in 1990
when it amended Model Rule 3.8 by adding
subparagraph (f).

83

cies have a right to expect lawyers to deal with them as they deal with courts.

[3] This Rule does not apply to representation of a client in a negotiation or other bilateral transaction with a governmental agency; representation in such a transaction is governed by Rules 4.1 through 4.4.

MODEL CODE COMPARISON:

EC 7–15 stated that a lawyer "appearing before an administrative agency, regardless of the nature of the proceeding it is conducting, has the continuing duty to advance the cause of his client within the bounds of the law." EC 7–16 stated that "[w]hen a lawyer appears in connection with proposed legislation, he . . . should comply with applicable laws and legislative rules." EC 8–5 stated that "[f]raudulent, deceptive, or otherwise illegal conduct by a participant in a proceeding before a . . . legislative body . . . should never be participated in . . . by lawyers." DR 7–106(B)(1) provided that "[i]n presenting a matter to a tribunal, a lawyer shall disclose . . . [u]nless privileged or irrelevant, the identity of the clients he represents and of the persons who employed him."

TRANSACTIONS WITH PERSONS OTHER THAN CLIENTS

RULE 4.1 Truthfulness in Statements to Others

In the course of representing a client a lawyer shall not knowingly:

(a) make a false statement of material fact or law to a third person; or

(b) fail to disclose a material fact to a third person when disclosure is necessary to avoid assisting a criminal or fraudulent act by a client, unless disclosure is prohibited by rule 1.6.

COMMENT:

Misrepresentation

[1] A lawyer is required to be truthful when dealing with others on a client's behalf, but generally has no affirmative duty to inform an opposing party of relevant facts. A misrepresentation can occur if the lawyer incorporates or affirms a statement of another person that the lawyer knows is false. Misrepresentations can also occur by failure to act.

Statements of Fact

[2] This Rule refers to statements of fact. Whether a particular statement should be regarded as one of fact can depend on the circumstances. Under generally accepted conventions in negotiation, certain types of statements ordinarily are not taken as statements of material fact. Estimates of price or value placed on the subject of a transaction

and a party's intentions as to an acceptable settlement of a claim are in this category, and so is the existence of an undisclosed principal except where nondisclosure of the principal would constitute fraud.

Fraud by Client

[3] Paragraph (b) recognizes that substantive law may require a lawyer to disclose certain information to avoid being deemed to have assisted the client's crime or fraud. The requirement of disclosure created by this paragraph is, however, subject to the obligations created by Rule 1.6.

MODEL CODE COMPARISON:

Paragraph (a) is substantially similar to DR 7–102(A)(5), which stated that "[i]n his representation of a client, a lawyer shall not . . . [k]nowingly make a false statement of law or fact."

With regard to paragraph (b), DR 7–102(A)(3) provided that a lawyer shall not "[c]onceal or knowingly fail to disclose that which he is required by law to reveal."

RULE 4.2 Communication With Person Represented by Counsel

In representing a client, a lawyer shall not communicate about the subject of the representation with a party the lawyer knows to be represented by another lawyer in the matter, unless the lawyer has the consent of the other lawyer or is authorized by law to do so.

COMMENT:

[1] This Rule does not prohibit communication with a party, or an employee or agent of a party, concerning matters outside the representation. For example, the existence of a controversy between a government agency and a private party, or between two organizations, does not prohibit a lawyer for either from communicating with nonlawyer representatives of the other regarding a separate matter. Also, parties to a matter may communicate directly with each other and a lawyer having independent justification for communicating with the other party is permitted to do so. Communications authorized by law include, for example, the right of a party to a controversy with a government agency to speak with government officials about the matter.

[2] In the case of an organization, this Rule prohibits communications by a lawyer for one party concerning the matter in representation with persons having a managerial responsibility on behalf of the organization, and with any other person whose act or omission in connection with that matter may be imputed to the organization for purposes of civil or criminal liability or whose statement may constitute an admission on the part of the organization. If an agent or employee of the organization is represented in the matter by his or her own

counsel, the consent by that counsel to a communication will be sufficient for purposes of this Rule. Compare Rule 3.4(f).

[3] This Rule also covers any person, whether or not a party to a formal proceeding, who is represented by counsel concerning the matter in question.

MODEL CODE COMPARISON:

This Rule is substantially identical to DR 7–104(A)(1).

RULE 4.3 Dealing With Unrepresented Person

In dealing on behalf of a client with a person who is not represented by counsel, a lawyer shall not state or imply that the lawyer is disinterested. When the lawyer knows or reasonably should know that the unrepresented person misunderstands the lawyer's role in the matter, the lawyer shall make reasonable efforts to correct the misunderstanding.

COMMENT:

An unrepresented person, particularly one not experienced in dealing with legal matters, might assume that a lawyer is disinterested in loyalties or is a disinterested authority on the law even when the lawyer represents a client. During the course of a lawyer's representation of a client, the lawyer should not give advice to an unrepresented person other than the advice to obtain counsel.

MODEL CODE COMPARISON:

There was no direct counterpart to this Rule in the Model Code. DR 7–104(A)(2) provided that a lawyer shall not "[g]ive advice to a person who is not represented by a lawyer, other than the advice to secure counsel. . . . ."

RULE 4.4 Respect for Rights of Third Persons

In representing a client, a lawyer shall not use means that have no substantial purpose other than to embarrass, delay, or burden a third person, or use methods of obtaining evidence that violate the legal rights of such a person.

COMMENT:

Responsibility to a client requires a lawyer to subordinate the interests of others to those of the client, but that responsibility does not imply that a lawyer may disregard the rights of third persons. It is impractical to catalogue all such rights, but they include legal restrictions on methods of obtaining evidence from third persons.

MODEL CODE COMPARISON:

DR 7–106(C)(2) provided that a lawyer shall not "[a]sk any question that he has no reasonable basis to believe is relevant to the case and that is intended to degrade a witness or other person." DR 7–102(A)(1) provided that a lawyer shall not "take . . . action on behalf of his client when he knows or when it is obvious that such action would serve merely to harass or maliciously injure another." DR 7–108(D) provided that "[a]fter discharge of the jury . . . the lawyer shall not ask questions or make comments to a member of that jury that are calculated merely to harass or embarrass the juror. . . ." DR 7–108(E) provided that a lawyer "shall not conduct . . . a vexatious or harassing investigation of either a venireman or a juror."

LAW FIRMS AND ASSOCIATIONS

RULE 5.1 Responsibilities of a Partner or Supervisory Lawyer

(a) **A partner in a law firm shall make reasonable efforts to ensure that the firm has in effect measures giving reasonable assurance that all lawyers in the firm conform to the rules of professional conduct.**

(b) **A lawyer having direct supervisory authority over another lawyer shall make reasonable efforts to ensure that the other lawyer conforms to the rules of professional conduct.**

(c) **A lawyer shall be responsible for another lawyer's violation of the rules of professional conduct if:**

(1) **the lawyer orders or, with knowledge of the specific conduct, ratifies the conduct involved; or**

(2) **the lawyer is a partner in the law firm in which the other lawyer practices, or has direct supervisory authority over the other lawyer, and knows of the conduct at a time when its consequences can be avoided or mitigated but fails to take reasonable remedial action.**

COMMENT:

[1] Paragraphs (a) and (b) refer to lawyers who have supervisory authority over the professional work of a firm or legal department of a government agency. This includes members of a partnership and the shareholders in a law firm organized as a professional corporation; lawyers having supervisory authority in the law department of an enterprise or government agency; and lawyers who have intermediate managerial responsibilities in a firm.

[2] The measures required to fulfill the responsibility prescribed in paragraphs (a) and (b) can depend on the firm's structure and the nature of its practice. In a small firm, informal supervision and occasional admonition ordinarily might be sufficient. In a large firm, or in practice situations in which intensely difficult ethical problems frequently arise, more elaborate procedures may be necessary. Some firms, for example, have a procedure whereby junior lawyers can make confidential referral of ethical problems directly to a designated senior partner or special committee. See Rule 5.2. Firms, whether large or small, may also rely on continuing legal education in professional

ethics. In any event, the ethical atmosphere of a firm can influence the conduct of all its members and a lawyer having authority over the work of another may not assume that the subordinate lawyer will inevitably conform to the Rules.

[3] Paragraph (c)(1) expresses a general principle of responsibility for acts of another. See also Rule 8.4(a).

[4] Paragraph (c)(2) defines the duty of a lawyer having direct supervisory authority over performance of specific legal work by another lawyer. Whether a lawyer has such supervisory authority in particular circumstances is a question of fact. Partners of a private firm have at least indirect responsibility for all work being done by the firm, while a partner in charge of a particular matter ordinarily has direct authority over other firm lawyers engaged in the matter. Appropriate remedial action by a partner would depend on the immediacy of the partner's involvement and the seriousness of the misconduct. The supervisor is required to intervene to prevent avoidable consequences of misconduct if the supervisor knows that the misconduct occurred. Thus, if a supervising lawyer knows that a subordinate misrepresented a matter to an opposing party in negotiation, the supervisor as well as the subordinate has a duty to correct the resulting misapprehension.

[5] Professional misconduct by a lawyer under supervision could reveal a violation of paragraph (b) on the part of the supervisory lawyer even though it does not entail a violation of paragraph (c) because there was no direction, ratification or knowledge or the violation.

[6] Apart from this Rule and Rule 8.4(a), a lawyer does not have disciplinary liability for the conduct of a partner, associate or subordinate. Whether a lawyer may be liable civilly or criminally for another lawyer's conduct is a question of law beyond the scope of these Rules.

MODEL CODE COMPARISON:

There was no direct counterpart to this Rule in the Model Code. DR 1–103(A) provided that a lawyer "possessing unprivileged knowledge of a violation of DR 1–102 shall report such knowledge to . . . authority empowered to investigate or act upon such violation."

RULE 5.2 Responsibilities of a Subordinate Lawyer

(a) A lawyer is bound by the rules of professional conduct notwithstanding that the lawyer acted at the direction of another person.

(b) A subordinate lawyer does not violate the rules of professional conduct if that lawyer acts in accordance with a supervisory lawyer's reasonable resolution of an arguable question of professional duty.

COMMENT:

[1] Although a lawyer is not relieved of responsibility for a violation by the fact that the lawyer acted at the direction of a supervisor, that fact may be relevant in determining whether a lawyer had the knowledge required to render conduct a violation of the Rules. For example, if a subordinate filed a frivolous pleading at the direction of a supervisor, the subordinate would not be guilty of a professional violation unless the subordinate knew of the document's frivolous character.

[2] When lawyers in a supervisor-subordinate relationship encounter a matter involving professional judgment as to ethical duty, the supervisor may assume responsibility for making the judgment. Otherwise a consistent course of action or position could not be taken. If the question can reasonably be answered only one way, the duty of both lawyers is clear and they are equally responsible for fulfilling it. However, if the question is reasonably arguable, someone has to decide upon the course of action. That authority ordinarily reposes in the supervisor, and a subordinate may be guided accordingly. For example, if a question arises whether the interests of two clients conflict under Rule 1.7, the supervisor's reasonable resolution of the question should protect the subordinate professionally if the resolution is subsequently challenged.

MODEL CODE COMPARISON:

There was no counterpart to this Rule in the Model Code.

RULE 5.3   Responsibilities Regarding Nonlawyer Assistants

With respect to a nonlawyer employed or retained by or associated with a lawyer:

(a) a partner in a law firm shall make reasonable efforts to ensure that the firm has in effect measures giving reasonable assurance that the person's conduct is compatible with the professional obligations of the lawyer;

(b) a lawyer having direct supervisory authority over the nonlawyer shall make reasonable efforts to ensure that the person's conduct is compatible with the professional obligations of the lawyer; and

(c) a lawyer shall be responsible for conduct of such a person that would be a violation of the rules of professional conduct if engaged in by a lawyer if:

(1) the lawyer orders or, with the knowledge of the specific conduct, ratifies the conduct involved; or

(2) the lawyer is a partner in the law firm in which the person is employed, or has direct supervisory authority over the person, and knows of the conduct at a time when its consequences can be avoided or mitigated but fails to take reasonable remedial action.

COMMENT:

Lawyers generally employ assistants in their practice, including secretaries, investigators, law student interns, and paraprofessionals. Such assistants, whether employees or independent contractors, act for the lawyer in rendition of the lawyer's professional services. A lawyer should give such assistants appropriate instruction and supervision concerning the ethical aspects of their employment, particularly regarding the obligation not to disclose information relating to representation of the client, and should be responsible for their work product. The measures employed in supervising nonlawyers should take account of the fact that they do not have legal training and are not subject to professional discipline.

MODEL CODE COMPARISON:

There was no direct counterpart to this Rule in the Model Code. DR 4–101(D) provided that a lawyer "shall exercise reasonable care to prevent his employees, associates, and others whose services are utilized by him from disclosing or using confidences or secrets of a client. . . ." DR 7–107(J) provided that "[a] lawyer shall exercise reasonable care to prevent his employees and associates from making an extrajudicial statement that he would be prohibited from making under DR 7–107."

RULE 5.4 Professional Independence of a Lawyer*

(a) A lawyer or law firm shall not share legal fees with a nonlawyer, except that:

(1) an agreement by a lawyer with the lawyer's firm, partner, or associate may provide for the payment of money, over a reasonable period of time after the lawyer's death, to the lawyer's estate or to one or more specified persons;

(2) a lawyer who purchases the practice of a deceased, disabled, or disappeared lawyer may, pursuant to the provisions of Rule 1.17, pay to the estate or other representative of that lawyer the agreed-upon purchase price; and

(3) a lawyer or law firm may include nonlawyer employees in a compensation or retirement plan, even though the

* In 1990, the ABA amended the text of Model Rule 5.4(a)(2) to recognize the addition of Model Rule 1.17 on the sale of a law practice. The original Model Rule 5.4(a)(2) read as follows:

RULE 5.4 Professional Independence of a Lawyer

(a) A lawyer or law firm shall not share legal fees with a nonlawyer, except that:

* * *

(2) a lawyer who undertakes to complete unfinished legal business of a deceased lawyer may pay to the estate of the deceased lawyer that proportion of the total compensation which fairly represents the services rendered by the deceased lawyer; and

* * *

plan is based in whole or in part on a profit-sharing arrangement.

(b) A lawyer shall not form a partnership with a nonlawyer if any of the activities of the partnership consist of the practice of law.

(c) A lawyer shall not permit a person who recommends, employs, or pays the lawyer to render legal services for another to direct or regulate the lawyer's professional judgment in rendering such legal services.

(d) A lawyer shall not practice with or in the form of a professional corporation or association authorized to practice law for a profit, if:

(1) a nonlawyer owns any interest therein, except that a fiduciary representative of the estate of a lawyer may hold the stock or interest of the lawyer for a reasonable time during administration;

(2) a nonlawyer is a corporate director or officer thereof; or

(3) a nonlawyer has the right to direct or control the professional judgment of a lawyer.

COMMENT:

The provisions of this Rule express traditional limitations on sharing fees. These limitations are to protect the lawyer's professional independence of judgment. Where someone other than the client pays the lawyer's fee or salary, or recommends employment of the lawyer, that arrangement does not modify the lawyer's obligation to the client. As stated in paragraph (c), such arrangements should not interfere with the lawyer's professional judgment.

MODEL CODE COMPARISON:

Paragraph (a) is substantially identical to DR 3-102(A).

Paragraph (b) is substantially identical to DR 3-103(A).

Paragraph (c) is substantially identical to DR 5-107(B).

Paragraph (d) is substantially identical to DR 5-107(C).

RULE 5.5 Unauthorized Practice of Law

A lawyer shall not:

(a) practice law in a jurisdiction where doing so violates the regulation of the legal profession in that jurisdiction; or

(b) assist a person who is not a member of the bar in the performance of activity that constitutes the unauthorized practice of law.

COMMENT:

The definition of the practice of law is established by law and varies from one jurisdiction to another. Whatever the definition, limiting the practice of law to members of the bar protects the public against rendition of legal services by unqualified persons. Paragraph (b) does not prohibit a lawyer from employing the services of paraprofessionals and delegating functions to them, so long as the lawyer supervises the delegated work and retains responsibility for their work. See Rule 5.3. Likewise, it does not prohibit lawyers from providing professional advice and instruction to nonlawyers whose employment requires knowledge of law; for example, claims adjusters, employees of financial or commercial institutions, social workers, accountants and persons employed in government agencies. In addition, a lawyer may counsel nonlawyers who wish to proceed pro se.

MODEL CODE COMPARISON:

With regard to paragraph (a), DR 3–101(B) of the Model Code provided that "[a] lawyer shall not practice law in a jurisdiction where to do so would be in violation of regulations of the profession in that jurisdiction."

With regard to paragraph (b), DR 3–101(A) of the Model Code provided that "[a] lawyer shall not aid a non-lawyer in the unauthorized practice of law."

RULE 5.6 Restrictions on Right to Practice

A lawyer shall not participate in offering or making:

(a) a partnership or employment agreement that restricts the rights of a lawyer to practice after termination of the relationship, except an agreement concerning benefits upon retirement; or

(b) an agreement in which a restriction on the lawyer's right to practice is part of the settlement of a controversy between private parties.

COMMENT:

[1] An agreement restricting the right of partners or associates to practice after leaving a firm not only limits their professional autonomy but also limits the freedom of clients to choose a lawyer. Paragraph (a) prohibits such agreements except for restrictions incident to provisions concerning retirement benefits for service with the firm.

[2] Paragraph (b) prohibits a lawyer from agreeing not to represent other persons in connection with settling a claim on behalf of a client.

[3] * This Rule does not apply to prohibit restrictions that may be included in the terms of the sale of a law practice pursuant to Rule 1.17.

MODEL CODE COMPARISON:

This Rule is substantially similar to DR 2–108.

RULE 5.7 Provision of Ancillary Services **

(a) **A lawyer shall not practice law in a law firm which owns a controlling interest in, or operates, an entity which provides non-legal services which are ancillary to the practice of law, or otherwise provides such ancillary non-legal services, except as provided in paragraph (b).**

(b) **A lawyer may practice law in a law firm which provides non-legal services which are ancillary to the practice of law if:**

(1) **The ancillary services are provided solely to clients of the law firm and are incidental to, in connection with and concurrent to, the provision of legal services by the law firm to such clients;**

(2) **Such ancillary services are provided solely by employees of the law firm itself and not by a subsidiary or other affiliate of the law firm;**

(3) **The law firm makes appropriate disclosure in writing to its clients; and**

(4) **The law firm does not hold itself out as engaging in any non-legal activities except in conjunction with the provision of legal services, as provided in this rule.**

(c) **One or more lawyers who engage in the practice of law in a law firm shall neither own a controlling interest in, nor operate, an entity which provides non-legal services which are ancillary to the practice of law, nor otherwise provide such ancillary non-legal services, except that their firms may provide such services as provided in paragraph (b).**

(d) **Two or more lawyers who engage in the practice of law in separate law firms shall neither own a controlling interest in, nor operate, an entity which provides non-legal services which are**

---

* This paragraph was added by the ABA in 1990 to resolve the potential overlap between this provision and the restrictions placed in Model Rule 1.17 regarding the sale of a law practice.

** Model Rule 5.7 did not appear in the original version of the Model Rules. In 1991, the ABA added this provision and its comments in response to the debate creat-ed by the adoption of the District of Columbia rule that allows lawyers and non-lawyers to practice together in the same law firm. D.C. Rule 5.4 is contained on pages 192–195. Model Rule 5.7 was passed by a vote of 197 to 186 in the House of Delegates and the August 1992 meeting will consider a recommendation to rescind the rule.

ancillary to the practice of law, nor otherwise provide such ancillary non-legal services.

COMMENT:

General

[1] For many years, lawyers have provided to their clients non-legal services which are ancillary to the practice of law. Such services included title insurance, trust services and patent consulting. In most instances, these ancillary nonlegal services were provided to law firm clients in connection with, and concurrent to, the provision of legal services by the lawyer or law firm. The provision of such services afforded benefits to clients, including making available a greater range of services from one source and maintaining technical expertise in various fields within a law firm. However, the provision of both legal and ancillary nonlegal services raises ethical concerns, including conflicts of interest, confusion on the part of clients and possible loss (or inapplicability) of the attorney-client privilege, which may not have been addressed adequately by the other Model Rules of Professional Conduct.

[2] Eventually, law firms began to form affiliates, largely staffed by nonlawyers, to provide ancillary nonlegal services to both clients and customers who were not clients for legal services. In addition to exacerbating the ethical problems of conflicts of interest, confusion and threats to confidentiality, the large-scale movement of law firms into ancillary nonlegal businesses raised serious professionalism concerns, including compromising lawyers' independent judgment, the loss of the bar's right to self-regulation and the provision of legal services by entities controlled by nonlawyers.

[3] Rule 5.7 addresses both the ethical and professionalism concerns implicated by the provision of ancillary nonlegal services by lawyers and law firms. It preserves the ability of lawyers to provide additional services to their clients and maintain within the law firm a broad range of technical expertise. However, Rule 5.7 restricts the ability of law firms to provide ancillary nonlegal services through affiliates to nonclient customers and clients alike, the rendition of which raises serious ethical and professionalism concerns.

Limitations on the Provision of Nonlegal Services Which Are Ancillary to the Practice of Law

[4] Paragraph (a) attempts to forestall the ethical and professional concerns which are raised when law firms own or operate nonlegal businesses which are ancillary to the practice of law or otherwise provide such services. The provision of such ancillary services by law firms has the potential of compromising a lawyer's independent professional judgment and otherwise causing harm to law firm clients (*e.g.,* creating conflicts of interest, jeopardizing clients' expectations of confi-

dentiality and causing confusion on the part of clients). Additionally, serious threats to lawyers' professionalism are also posed when law firms own or operate ancillary businesses which provide services to persons who are not concurrently seeking legal services from the law firm.

[5] Paragraph (a) prohibits lawyers from practicing in a law firm which owns a controlling interest in, or operates, an entity which provides nonlegal services which are ancillary to the practice of law, or which provides such ancillary services from within the law firm, unless such services are incidental to the law firm's provision of legal services as set forth in Paragraph (b).

[6] The term "nonlegal services which are ancillary to the practice of law" refers to those services which satisfy all or most of the following indicia: (1) are provided to clients of a law firm (or customers of a business owned or controlled by a law firm); (2) clearly do not constitute the practice of law; (3) are readily available from those not licensed to practice law; (4) are functionally connected to the provision of legal services, i.e., services which are often sought or needed in connection with (and in addition to) legal services; (5) involve intellectual ability or learning; and (6) have the potential for creating serious ethical problems in the lawyer-client relationship, such as compromising the independent professional judgment of lawyers; creating conflicts of interest; threatening the clients' (or customers') expectations of confidentiality and/or causing confusion on the part of clients or customers.

[7] Among those activities which are not included in the term "nonlegal services which are ancillary to the practice of law" because they do not pose serious ethical problems in the lawyer-client relationship are:

(1) law firms or lawyers owning, for example, restaurants, shops or taxi services (since these services are not functionally connected to the practice of law);

(2) law firms providing copying services or other clerical services incidental to the practice of law;

(3) law firms owning and managing the buildings in which their offices are located or other property (since owning and managing property—even through a subsidiary or affiliate—is not functionally connected to the provision of legal services to clients);

(4) a law firm providing services or products intended for use by other lawyers, such as publications, software programs, or legal malpractice insurance (since such services or products are not functionally connected to the provision of legal services to clients);

(5) lawyers serving as fiduciaries of trusts or corporate directors or lawyers serving in quasi-judicial positions such as mediators or arbitrators.

[8] When services provided by a law firm are performed by non-lawyers, there should be an initial presumption that the services do not constitute the practice of law and may be a "nonlegal service which is ancillary to the practice of law." In addition, a presumption that a service is "ancillary to the practice of law" should exist if the service is normally provided by nonlawyers in discrete professions or occupations, e.g., doctors, architects, engineers, real estate brokers, investment bankers or financial consultants.

[9] Note that Paragraph (a) does not prohibit a lawyer from practicing in a law firm which acquires a passive financial interest in an entity which provides nonlegal ancillary services (i.e., purchasing shares of an investment banking firm or a consulting company), provided that the interest is not a controlling one. This rule does not define the concept of control, which is generally a fact-based inquiry dependent on the particular facts and circumstances. However, the existence of an ownership interest by lawyers in other entities (especially clients) may implicate conflict of interest concerns (see Model Rules of Professional Conduct 1.7 and 1.8) and may require disclosure by the lawyers pursuant to these rules.

Connection Between the Provision of Legal and Ancillary Nonlegal Services

[10] Paragraph (b) preserves the ability of law firms to provide nonlegal services which are ancillary to the practice of law, but under conditions designed to ensure that such services are closely related to the firms' provision of legal services and not independent of, and unrelated to, such legal services.

[11] Subsection (1) of Paragraph (b) requires that ancillary nonlegal services be provided solely to law firm clients (as opposed to persons who are not currently seeking legal services from a law firm) and be incidental to, in connection with, and concurrent to, the provision of legal services by the law firm. The requirement that ancillary services be "incidental to" and "in connection with" the firm's provision of legal services seeks to ensure that any nonlegal services be secondary to, strictly related to, and under the supervision of those responsible for, the provision of legal services.

[12] Paragraph (b) permits law firms to employ the services of other professionals if their services are connected to the firm's provision of legal services. For example, an architect on staff at a law firm would be permitted to help clients and lawyers understand the technical issues in a construction contract negotiation, a building accident litigation or the like. However, the requirement in Paragraph (b) that such services be "incidental to" and "in connection with" the provision of legal services would proscribe a law firm from employing architects to design buildings for law firm clients or for nonclient customers who do not use the law firm's legal services. Similarly, an investment

banker on staff at a law firm would be permitted to assist lawyers in the negotiation of a transaction or the litigation of valuation issues or the like, as well as to consult with law firm clients when the firm is providing legal services to them, but a law firm would be prohibited from employing investment bankers to seek out acquisitions, sell securities (or otherwise secure financing) or perform other investment banking services unrelated to a pending legal representation. Likewise, a corporation pursuing an acquisition might need the assistance of nonlawyer lobbyists before a state legislature considering anti-takeover legislation. Such lobbying designed to forestall (or attain) a change in the law, if provided by nonlawyers within a law firm, could reasonably be construed to be incidental to the firm's provision of legal services.

[13] Paragraph (b) also requires that the provision of nonlegal services be concurrent with the provision of legal services. In essence, law firm clients (like nonlegal services customers generally) may not obtain ancillary nonlegal services from the law firm (e.g., investment banking services or medical tests), and the firm may not provide them, at a time when the client is not obtaining legal services from the law firm on a related matter.

Provision of Ancillary Nonlegal Services by Employees of Law Firms

[14] Subsection (2) of Paragraph (b), in an effort to vitiate risks of compromise to lawyers' professional judgment, conflicts of interest, client confusion and potential loss of confidentiality, provides that any ancillary services provided by a law firm must be performed within the law firm by employees of the law firm itself (who work together with, and are supervised by, the firm's lawyers), and not through a subsidiary or affiliate of the law firm. This requirement closely unites the provision of legal and nonlegal services under the supervision of lawyers and thereby affords lawyers the opportunity to ensure that their nonlawyer employees are acting responsibly and in accordance with the rules of legal ethics. Such a requirement minimizes the risks of nonlegal employees either providing advice with which the firm's lawyers will disagree and/or engaging in improper behavior for which the firm's lawyers would be responsible. In addition, structuring the provision of nonlegal services in such a way forestalls confusion on the part of clients as to whether the nonlegal services are provided subject to the limitations of the Model Rules (and will prevent lawyers from seeking to provide services outside of the protections afforded to clients by the Model Rules). Finally, if lawyers are present (or otherwise involved) in the provision of nonlegal services ancillary to the practice of law, there is a greater likelihood that client confidences will be protected and a client will be able to maintain evidentiary privileges with respect to communications made by the client to the providers of nonlegal ancillary services. Paragraph (b)(2) is not designed to limit the ability of lawyers to retain outside (*i.e.,* nonaffiliated) consultants

such as experts, private investigators or accountants to help them provide legal services to clients.

Disclosure Requirements Relating to the Provision of Ancillary Nonlegal Services

[15] Subsection (3) of Paragraph (b) requires that before providing ancillary services to a client, a law firm must comply with appropriate disclosure requirements (as mandated in Model Rule of Professional Conduct 1.8, relevant case law and other authorities) and fully disclose in writing the firm's interest in the providers of nonlegal services employed by the firm and the potential conflicts of interest inherent in the provision of such services. The law firm should also consider, in appropriate circumstances, recommending that the client seek the advice of independent counsel (or independent providers of nonlegal services) before obtaining nonlegal services from the firm.

Representations Concerning Ancillary and Nonlegal Services

[16] Subsection (4) of Paragraph (b) ensures that when law firms deal with clients (whether prospective or actual) or the public, they do not represent themselves as providing any ancillary nonlegal services independent of the firm's provision of legal services. This proscription attempts to obviate the risks of confusion on the part of clients and the public, actual or apparent overreaching by attorneys and improper solicitation. It ensures that clients and the public are aware that they are dealing with a law firm and can therefore assume that representatives of the firm are bound by the rules of legal ethics; prospective or actual clients do not feel compelled to use the firm's ancillary services; and law firms do not engage in improper solicitation by seeking business for the firm's nonlegal services with an expectation that these nonlegal services will serve as a "feeder" for the firm's legal services. Paragraph (b)(4) also seeks to preserve the unique and independent status of the legal profession in the public's perception by preventing law firms from representing themselves to clients and the public as multidisciplinary conglomerates or otherwise emphasizing their nonlegal activities.

[17] Paragraph (b)(4) is not intended to preclude law firms from making the existence of their nonlegal business known to clients who have retained the firm for legal services, and who, in the attorney's opinion, might have a need for the firm's ancillary services in addition to legal services (subject to appropriate disclosure requirements). In addition, Paragraph (b)(4) is not intended to prevent individual lawyers from indicating that they are qualified or licensed in other professions, e.g., accounting, where relevant jurisdictions so permit.

Provision of Ancillary Nonlegal Services By One or More Lawyers in a Law Firm

[18] Paragraph (c) prevents one or more lawyers in a single law firm from owning or operating an entity which provides nonlegal services which are ancillary to the practice of law. Paragraph (c) attempts to prevent lawyers or law firms from circumventing the restrictions on law firm ownership and operation of ancillary businesses by vesting ownership not in the entire law firm, but in one or more of the attorneys in a law firm. The ethical and professional concerns inherent in the ownership of ancillary businesses are not vitiated when ownership or operation is vested in several partners in a law firm (as opposed to an entire law firm). However, a law firm itself may provide such ancillary nonlegal services in accordance with Paragraph (b).

Provision of Ancillary Nonlegal Services by Lawyers from Different Law Firms

[19] Paragraph (d) addresses the concerns which may result when lawyers in separate law firms own or operate an entity which provides nonlegal services which are ancillary to the practice of law. The ethical and professional concerns inherent in the ownership and operation of such ancillary businesses by law firms (or one or more lawyers in a firm) are also present (or may be exacerbated) when lawyers in different firms own or operate such businesses.

MODEL CODE COMPARISON

There was no counterpart to this Rule in the Model Code.

PUBLIC SERVICE

RULE 6.1 Pro Bono Publico Service

A lawyer should render public interest legal service. A lawyer may discharge this responsibility by providing professional services at no fee or a reduced fee to persons of limited means or to public service or charitable groups or organizations, by service in activities for improving the law, the legal system or the legal profession, and by financial support for organizations that provide legal services to persons of limited means.

COMMENT:

[1] The ABA House of Delegates has formally acknowledged "the basic responsibility of each lawyer engaged in the practice of law to provide public interest legal services" without fee, or at a substantially reduced fee, in one or more of the following areas: poverty law, civil rights law, public rights law, charitable organization representation and the administration of justice. This Rule expresses that policy but is not intended to be enforced through disciplinary process.

[2] The rights and responsibilities of individuals and organizations in the United States are increasingly defined in legal terms. As a consequence, legal assistance in coping with the web of statutes, rules and regulations is imperative for persons of modest and limited means, as well as for the relatively well-to-do.

[3] The basic responsibility for providing legal services for those unable to pay ultimately rests upon the individual lawyer, and personal involvement in the problems of the disadvantaged can be one of the most rewarding experiences in the life of a lawyer. Every lawyer, regardless of professional prominence or professional workload, should find time to participate in or otherwise support the provision of legal services to the disadvantaged. The provision of free legal services to those unable to pay reasonable fees continues to be an obligation of each lawyer as well as the profession generally, but the efforts of individual lawyers are often not enough to meet the need. Thus, it has been necessary for the profession and government to institute additional programs to provide legal services. Accordingly, legal aid offices, lawyer referral services and other related programs have been developed, and others will be developed by the profession and government. Every lawyer should support all proper efforts to meet this need for legal services.

MODEL CODE COMPARISON:

There was no counterpart of this Rule in the Disciplinary Rules of the Model Code. EC 2-25 stated that the "basic responsibility for providing legal services for those unable to pay ultimately rests upon the individual lawyer. . . . Every lawyer, regardless of professional prominence or professional work load, should find time to participate in serving the disadvantaged." EC 8-9 stated that "[t]he advancement of our legal system is of vital importance in maintaining the rule of law . . . [and] lawyers should encourage, and should aid in making, needed changes and improvements." EC 8-3 stated that "[t]hose persons unable to pay for legal services should be provided needed services."

RULE 6.2 Accepting Appointments

A lawyer shall not seek to avoid appointment by a tribunal to represent a person except for good cause, such as:

(a) representing the client is likely to result in violation of the rules of professional conduct or other law;

(b) representing the client is likely to result in an unreasonable financial burden on the lawyer; or

(c) the client or the cause is so repugnant to the lawyer as to be likely to impair the client-lawyer relationship or the lawyer's ability to represent the client.

COMMENT:

[1]   A lawyer ordinarily is not obliged to accept a client whose character or cause the lawyer regards as repugnant. The lawyer's freedom to select clients is, however, qualified. All lawyers have a responsibility to assist in providing pro bono publico service. See Rule 6.1. An individual lawyer fulfills this responsibility by accepting a fair share of unpopular matters or indigent or unpopular clients. A lawyer may also be subject to appointment by a court to serve unpopular clients or persons unable to afford legal services.

Appointed Counsel

[2]   For good cause a lawyer may seek to decline an appointment to represent a person who cannot afford to retain counsel or whose cause is unpopular. Good cause exists if the lawyer could not handle the matter competently, see Rule 1.1, or if undertaking the representation would result in an improper conflict of interest, for example, when the client or the cause is so repugnant to the lawyer as to be likely to impair the client-lawyer relationship or the lawyer's ability to represent the client. A lawyer may also seek to decline an appointment if acceptance would be unreasonably burdensome, for example, when it would impose a financial sacrifice so great as to be unjust.

[3]   An appointed lawyer has the same obligations to the client as retained counsel, including the obligations of loyalty and confidentiality, and is subject to the same limitations on the client-lawyer relationship, such as the obligation to refrain from assisting the client in violation of the Rules.

MODEL CODE COMPARISON:

There was no counterpart to this Rule in the Disciplinary Rules of the Model Code. EC 2–29 stated that when a lawyer is "appointed by a court or requested by a bar association to undertake representation of a person unable to obtain counsel, whether for financial or other reasons, he should not seek to be excused from undertaking the representation except for compelling reasons. Compelling reasons do not include such factors as the repugnance of the subject matter of the proceeding, the identity or position of a person involved in the case, the belief of the lawyer that the defendant in a criminal proceeding is guilty, or the belief of the lawyer regarding the merits of the civil case." EC 2–30 stated that "a lawyer should decline employment if the intensity of his personal feelings, as distinguished from a community attitude, may impair his effective representation of a prospective client."

RULE 6.3 Membership in Legal Services Organization

A lawyer may serve as a director, officer or member of a legal services organization, apart from the law firm in which the lawyer practices, notwithstanding that the organization serves persons having interests adverse to a client of the lawyer. The lawyer shall not knowingly participate in a decision or action of the organization:

(a) if participating in the decision or action would be incompatible with the lawyer's obligations to a client under rule 1.7; or

(b) where the decision or action could have a material adverse effect on the representation of a client of the organization whose interests are adverse to a client of the lawyer.

COMMENT:

[1] Lawyers should be encouraged to support and participate in legal service organizations. A lawyer who is an officer or a member of such an organization does not thereby have a client-lawyer relationship with persons served by the organization. However, there is potential conflict between the interests of such persons and the interests of the lawyer's clients. If the possibility of such conflict disqualified a lawyer from serving on the board of a legal services organization, the profession's involvement in such organizations would be severely curtailed.

[2] It may be necessary in appropriate cases to reassure a client of the organization that the representation will not be affected by conflicting loyalties of a member of the board. Established, written policies in this respect can enhance the credibility of such assurances.

MODEL CODE COMPARISON:

There was no counterpart to this Rule in the Model Code.

RULE 6.4 Law Reform Activities Affecting Client Interests

A lawyer may serve as a director, officer or member of an organization involved in reform of the law or its administration notwithstanding that the reform may affect the interests of a client of the lawyer. When the lawyer knows that the interests of a client may be materially benefitted by a decision in which the lawyer participates, the lawyer shall disclose that fact but need not identify the client.

COMMENT:

Lawyers involved in organizations seeking law reform generally do not have a client-lawyer relationship with the organization. Otherwise, it might follow that a lawyer could not be involved in a bar association law reform program that might indirectly affect a client. See also Rule 1.2(b). For example, a lawyer specializing in antitrust litigation might be regarded as disqualified from participating in drafting revisions of rules governing that subject. In determining the nature and scope of participation in such activities, a lawyer should be mindful of obligations to clients under other Rules, particularly Rule 1.7. A lawyer is professionally obligated to protect the integrity of the program by making an appropriate disclosure within the organization when the lawyer knows a private client might be materially benefitted.

102

MODEL CODE COMPARISON:

There was no counterpart to this Rule in the Model Code.

INFORMATION ABOUT LEGAL SERVICES

RULE 7.1 Communications Concerning a Lawyer's Services

A lawyer shall not make a false or misleading communication about the lawyer or the lawyer's services. A communication is false or misleading if it:

(a) contains a material misrepresentation of fact or law, or omits a fact necessary to make the statement considered as a whole not materially misleading;

(b) is likely to create an unjustified expectation about results the lawyer can achieve, or states or implies that the lawyer can achieve results by means that violate the rules of professional conduct or other law; or

(c) compares the lawyer's services with other lawyers' services, unless the comparison can be factually substantiated.

COMMENT:

This Rule governs all communications about a lawyer's services, including advertising permitted by Rule 7.2. Whatever means are used to make known a lawyer's services, statements about them should be truthful. The prohibition in paragraph (b) of statements that may create "unjustified expectations" would ordinarily preclude advertisements about results obtained on behalf of a client, such as the amount of a damage award or the lawyer's record in obtaining favorable verdicts, and advertisements containing client endorsements. Such information may create the unjustified expectation that similar results can be obtained for others without reference to the specific factual and legal circumstances.

MODEL CODE COMPARISON:

DR 2–101 provided that "[a] lawyer shall not . . . use . . . any form of public communication containing a false, fraudulent, misleading, deceptive, self-laudatory or unfair statement or claim." DR 2–101(B) provided that a lawyer "may publish or broadcast . . . the following information . . . in the geographic area or areas in which the lawyer resides or maintains offices or in which a significant part of the lawyer's clientele resides, provided that the information . . . complies with DR 2–101(A), and is presented in a dignified manner. . . ." DR 2–101(B) then specified twenty-five categories of information that may be disseminated. DR 2–101(C) provided that "[a]ny person desiring to expand the information authorized for disclosure in DR 2–101(B), or to provide for its dissemination through other forums may apply to [the agency having jurisdiction under state law]. . . . The relief granted in response to any such application shall be promulgated as an amendment to DR 2–101(B), universally applicable to all lawyers."

RULE 7.2 Advertising*

(a) Subject to the requirements of rule 7.1 and 7.3, a lawyer may advertise services through public media, such as a telephone directory, legal directory, newspaper or other periodical, outdoor advertising, radio or television, or through written or recorded communication.

(b) A copy or recording of an advertisement or written communication shall be kept for two years after its last dissemination along with a record of when and where it was used.

(c) A lawyer shall not give anything of value to a person for recommending the lawyer's services, except that a lawyer may

(1) pay the reasonable costs of advertisements or communications permitted by this Rule;

(2) pay the usual charges of a not-for-profit lawyer referral service or legal service organization; and

(3) pay for a law practice in accordance with Rule 1.17.

(d) Any communication made pursuant to this rule shall include the name of at least one lawyer responsible for its content.

COMMENT:

[1] To assist the public in obtaining legal services, lawyers should be allowed to make known their services not only through reputation but also through organized information campaigns in the form of advertising. Advertising involves an active quest for clients, contrary to the tradition that a lawyer should not seek clientele. However, the public's need to know about legal services can be fulfilled in part

---

* The ABA amended Model Rule 7.2 in 1989 to conform to the holding in Shapero v. Kentucky Bar Ass'n, 486 U.S. 466 (1988) and in 1990 to reflect the addition of Model Rule 1.17 on the sale of a law practice. The original version of Model Rule 7.2 read as follows:

RULE 7.2 Advertising

(a) Subject to the requirements of Rules 7.1, a lawyer may advertise services through public media, such as a telephone directory, legal directory, newspaper or other periodical, outdoor, radio or television, or through written communication not involving solicitation as defined in Rule 7.3.

(b) A copy or recording of an advertisement or written communica-

tion shall be kept for two years after its last dissemination along with a record of when and where it was used.

(c) A lawyer shall not give anything of value to a person for recommending the lawyer's services, except that a lawyer may pay the reasonable cost of advertising or written communication permitted by this rule and may pay the usual charges of a not-for-profit lawyer referral service or other legal service organization.

(d) Any communication made pursuant to this rule shall include the name of at least one lawyer responsible for its content.

through advertising. This need is particularly acute in the case of persons of moderate means who have not made extensive use of legal services. The interest in expanding public information about legal services ought to prevail over considerations of tradition. Nevertheless, advertising by lawyers entails the risk of practices that are misleading or overreaching.

[2] This Rule permits public dissemination of information concerning a lawyer's name or firm name, address and telephone number; the kinds of services the lawyer will undertake; the basis on which the lawyer's fees are determined, including prices for specific services and payment and credit arrangements; a lawyer's foreign language ability; names of references and, with their consent, names of clients regularly represented; and other information that might invite the attention of those seeking legal assistance.

[3] Questions of effectiveness and taste in advertising are matters of speculation and subjective judgment. Some jurisdictions have had extensive prohibitions against television advertising, against advertising going beyond specified facts about a lawyer, or against "undignified" advertising. Television is now one of the most powerful media for getting information to the public, particularly persons of low and moderate income; prohibiting television advertising, therefore, would impede the flow of information about legal services to many sectors of the public. Limiting the information that may be advertised has a similar effect and assumes that the bar can accurately forecast the kind of information that the public would regard as relevant.

[4] Neither this Rule nor Rule 7.3 prohibits communications authorized by law, such as notice to members of a class in class action litigation.

Record of Advertising

[5] Paragraph (b) requires that a record of the content and use of advertising be kept in order to facilitate enforcement of this Rule. It does not require that advertising be subject to review prior to dissemination. Such a requirement would be burdensome and expensive relative to its possible benefits, and may be of doubtful constitutionality.

Paying Others to Recommend a Lawyer*

[6] A lawyer is allowed to pay for advertising permitted by this Rule and for the purchase of a law practice in accordance with the provisions of Rule 1.17, but otherwise is not permitted to pay another person for channeling professional work. This restriction does not prevent an organization or person other than the lawyer from advertis-

---

* In 1990, the ABA added the clause "and for the purchase of a law practice in accordance with the provisions of Rule 1.17" to reflect to addition of this provision to the Model Rules.

ing or recommending the lawyer's services. Thus, a legal aid agency or prepaid legal services plan may pay to advertise legal services provided under its auspices. Likewise, a lawyer may participate in not-for-profit lawyer referral programs and pay the usual fees charged by such programs. Paragraph (c) does not prohibit paying regular compensation to an assistant, such as a secretary, to prepare communications permitted by this Rule.

MODEL CODE COMPARISON:

With regard to paragraph (a), DR 2–101(B) provided that a lawyer "may publish or broadcast, subject to DR 2–103, . . . in print media . . . or television or radio. . . ."

With regard to paragraph (b), DR 2–101(D) provided that if the advertisement is "communicated to the public over television or radio, . . . a recording of the actual transmission shall be retained by the lawyer."

With regard to paragraph (c), DR 2–103(B) provided that a lawyer "shall not compensate or give anything of value to a person or organization to recommend or secure his employment . . . except that he may pay the usual and reasonable fees or dues charged by any of the organizations listed in DR 2–103(D)." (DR 2–103(D) referred to legal aid and other legal services organizations.) DR 2–101(I) provided that a lawyer "shall not compensate or give anything of value to representatives of the press, radio, television, or other communication medium in anticipation of or in return for professional publicity in a news item."

There was no counterpart to paragraph (d) in the Model Code.

RULE 7.3 Direct Contact With Prospective Clients**

(a) A lawyer shall not by in-person or live telephone contact solicit professional employment from a prospective client with whom the lawyer has no family or prior professional relationship

** The ABA amended the original version of Model Rule 7.3 in 1989 because in 1988 the Supreme Court had declared a blanket restriction on targeted mailings unconstitutional under the First Amendment. See Shapero v. Kentucky Bar Ass'n, 486 U.S. 466 (1988). The Kentucky rule which was the subject of the Supreme Court decision was identical to the original Model Rule 7.3. This provision read as follows:

RULE 7.3 Direct Contact With Prospective Clients

A lawyer may not solicit professional employment from a prospective client with whom the lawyer has

no family or prior professional relationship, by mail, in-person or otherwise, when a significant motive for the lawyer's doing so is the lawyer's pecuniary gain. The term "solicit" includes contact in person, by telephone or telegraph, by letter or other writing or by other communication directed to a specific recipient, but does not include letters addressed or advertising circulars distributed generally to persons not known to need legal services of the kind provided by the lawyer in a particular matter, but who are so situated that they might in general find such services useful.

when a significant motive for the lawyer's doing so is the lawyer's pecuniary gain.

(b) A lawyer shall not solicit professional employment from a prospective client by written or recorded communication or by in-person or telephone contact even when not otherwise prohibited by paragraph (a), if:

(1) the prospective client has made known to the lawyer a desire not to be solicited by the lawyer; or

(2) the solicitation involves coercion, duress or harassment.

(c) Every written or recorded communication from a lawyer soliciting professional employment from a prospective client known to be in need of legal services in a particular matter, and with whom the lawyer has no family or prior professional relationship, shall include the words "Advertising Material" on the outside envelope and at the beginning and ending of any recorded communication.

(d) Notwithstanding the prohibitions in paragraph (a), a lawyer may participate with a prepaid or group legal service plan operated by an organization not owned or directed by the lawyer which uses in-person or telephone contact to solicit memberships or subscriptions for the plan from persons who are not known to need legal services in a particular matter covered by the plan.

COMMENT: *

[1] There is a potential for abuse inherent in direct in-person or live telephone contact by a lawyer with a prospective client known

* The ABA amended the comments to Model Rule 7.3 in 1989 to reflect changes made in the text of the Rule brought about by the *Shapero* decision. The text of the original comment reads as follows:

COMMENT:

There is a potential for abuse inherent in direct solicitation by a lawyer of prospective clients known to need legal services. It subjects the lay person to the private importuning of a trained advocate, in a direct interpersonal encounter. A prospective client often feels overwhelmed by the situation giving rise to the need for legal services, and may have an impaired capacity for reason, judgment and protective self-interest. Furthermore, the lawyer seeking the retainer is faced with a conflict stemming from the lawyer's own interest, which may color the advice and representation offered the vulnerable prospect.

The situation is therefore fraught with the possibility of undue influence, intimidation, and over-reaching. This potential for abuse inherent in direct solicitation of prospective clients justifies its prohibition, particularly since lawyer advertising permitted under Rule 7.2 offers an alternative means of communicating necessary information to those who may be in need of legal services.

Advertising makes it possible for a prospective client to be informed about the need for legal services, and about the qualifications of available lawyers and law firms, without subjecting the prospective client to direct personal persuasion that may overwhelm the client's judgment.

The use of general advertising to transmit information from lawyer to prospective client, rather than direct private contact, will help to assure that the

107

to need legal services. These forms of contact between a lawyer and a prospective client subject the layperson to the private importuning of the trained advocate in a direct interpersonal encounter. The prospective client, who may already feel overwhelmed by the circumstances giving rise to the need for legal services, may find it difficult fully to evaluate all available alternatives with reasoned judgment and appropriate self-interest in the face of the lawyer's presence and insistence upon being retained immediately. The situation is fraught with the possibility of undue influence, intimidation, and over-reaching.

information flows cleanly as well as freely. Advertising is out in public view, thus subject to scrutiny by those who know the lawyer. This informal review is itself likely to help guard against statements and claims that might constitute false or misleading communications, in violation of Rule 7.1. Direct, private communications from a lawyer to a prospective client are not subject to such third-scrutiny and consequently are much more likely to approach (and occasionally cross) the dividing line between accurate representations and those that are false and misleading.

These dangers attend direct solicitation whether in-person or by mail. Direct mail solicitation cannot be effectively regulated by means less drastic than outright prohibition. One proposed safeguard is to require that the designation "Advertising" be stamped on any envelope containing a solicitation letter. This would do nothing to assure the accuracy and reliability of the contents. Another suggestion is that solicitation letters be filed with a state regulatory agency. This would be ineffective as a practical matter. State lawyer discipline agencies struggle for resources to investigate specific complaints, much less for those necessary to screen lawyers' mail solicitation material. Even if they could examine such materials, agency staff members are unlikely to know anything about the lawyer or about the prospective client's underlying problem. Without such knowledge they cannot determine whether the lawyer's representations are misleading. In any event, such review would be after the fact, potentially too late to avert the undesirable

consequences of disseminating false and misleading material.

General mailings not speaking to a specific matter do not pose the same danger of abuse as targeted mailings, and therefore are not prohibited by this Rule. The representations made in such mailings are necessarily general rather than tailored, less importuning than informative. They are addressed to recipients unlikely to be specially vulnerable at the time, hence who are likely to be more skeptical about unsubstantiated claims. General mailings not addressed to recipients involved in a specific legal matter or incident, therefore, more closely resemble permissible advertising rather than prohibited solicitation.

Similarly, this Rule would not prohibit a lawyer from contacting representatives of organizations or groups that may be interested in establishing a group or prepaid legal plan for its members, insureds, beneficiaries or other third parties for the purpose of informing such entities of the availability of and details concerning the plan or arrangement which he or his firm is willing to offer. This form of communication is not directed to a specific prospective client known to need legal services related to a particular matter. Rather, it is usually addressed to an individual acting in a fiduciary capacity seeking a supplier of legal services for others who may, if they choose, become prospective clients of the lawyer. Under these circumstances, the activity which the lawyer undertakes in communicating with such representatives and the type of information transmitted to the individual are functionally similar to and serve the same purpose as advertising permitted under Rule 7.2.

[2] This potential for abuse inherent in direct in-person or live telephone solicitation of prospective clients justifies its prohibition, particularly since lawyer advertising and written and recorded communication permitted under Rule 7.2 offer alternative means of conveying necessary information to those who may be in need of legal services. Advertising and written and recorded communications which may be mailed or autodialed make it possible for a prospective client to be informed about the need for legal services, and about the qualifications of available lawyers and law firms, without subjecting the prospective client to direct in-person or telephone persuasion that may overwhelm the client's judgment.

[3] The use of general advertising and written and recorded communications to transmit information from lawyer to prospective client, rather than direct in-person or live telephone contact, will help to assure that the information flows cleanly as well as freely. The contents of advertisements and communications permitted under Rule 7.2 are permanently recorded so that they cannot be disputed and may be shared with others who know the lawyer. This potential for informal review is itself likely to help guard against statements and claims that might constitute false and misleading communications, in violation of Rule 7.1. The contents of direct in-person or live telephone conversations between a lawyer to a prospective client can be disputed and are not subject to third-party scrutiny. Consequently, they are much more likely to approach (and occasionally cross) the dividing line between accurate representations and those that are false and misleading.

[4] There is far less likelihood that a lawyer would engage in abusive practices against an individual with whom the lawyer has a prior personal or professional relationship or where the lawyer is motivated by considerations other than the lawyer's pecuniary gain. Consequently, the general prohibition in Rule 7.3(a) and the requirements of Rule 7.3(c) are not applicable in those situations.

[5] But even permitted forms of solicitation can be abused. Thus, any solicitation which contains information which is false or misleading within the meaning of Rule 7.1, which involves coercion, duress or harassment within the meaning of Rule 7.3(b)(2), or which involves contact with a prospective client who has made known to the lawyer a desire not to be solicited by the lawyer within the meaning of Rule 7.3(b)(1) is prohibited. Moreover, if after sending a letter or other communication to a client as permitted by Rule 7.2 the lawyer receives no response, any further effort to communicate with the prospective client may violate the provisions of Rule 7.3(b).

[6] This Rule is not intended to prohibit a lawyer from contacting representatives of organizations or groups that may be interested in establishing a group or prepaid legal plan for their members, insureds, beneficiaries or other third parties for the purpose of informing such entities of the availability of and details concerning the plan or ar-

rangement which the lawyer or lawyer's firm is willing to offer. This form of communication is not directed to a prospective client. Rather, it is usually addressed to an individual acting in a fudiciary capacity seeking a supplier of legal services for others who may, if they choose, become prospective clients of the lawyer. Under these circumstances, the activity which the lawyer undertakes in communicating with such representatives and the type of information transmitted to the individual are functionally similar to and serve the same purpose as advertising permitted under Rule 7.2.

[7] The requirement in Rule 7.3(c) that certain communications be marked "Advertising Material" does not apply to communications sent in response to requests of potential clients or their spokespersons or sponsors. General announcements by lawyers, including changes in personnel or office location, do not constitute communications soliciting professional employment from a client known to be in need of legal services within the meaning of this Rule.

[8] Paragraph (d) of this Rule would permit an attorney to participate with an organization which uses personal contact to solicit members for its group or prepaid legal service plan, provided that the personal contact is not undertaken by any lawyer who would be a provider of legal services through the plan. The organization referred to in paragraph (d) must not be owned by or directed (whether as manager or otherwise) by any lawyer or law firm that participates in the plan. For example, paragraph (d) would not permit a lawyer to create an organization controlled directly or indirectly by the lawyer and use the organization for the in-person or telephone solicitation of legal employment of the lawyer through memberships in the plan or otherwise. The communication permitted by these organizations also must not be directed to a person known to need legal services in a particular matter, but is to be designed to inform potential plan members gnerally of another means of affordable legal services. Lawyers who participate in a legal service plan must reasonably assure that the plan sponsors are in compliance with Rules 7.1, 7.2 and 7.3(a). See 8.4(a).

MODEL CODE COMPARISON:

DR 2–104(A) provided with certain exceptions that "[a] lawyer who has given in-person unsolicited advice to a layperson that he should obtain counsel or take legal action shall not accept employment resulting from that advice. . . ." The exceptions include DR 2–104(A)(1), which provided that a lawyer "may accept employment by a close friend, relative, former client (if the advice is germane to the former employment), or one whom the lawyer reasonably believes to be a client." DR 2–104(A)(2) through DR 2–104(A)(5) provided other exceptions relating, respectively, to employment resulting from public educational programs, recommendation by a legal assistance organization, public speaking or writing and representing members of a class in class action litigation.

RULE 7.4   Communication of Fields of Practice

A lawyer may communicate the fact that the lawyer does or does not practice in particular fields of law. A lawyer shall not state or imply that the lawyer is a specialist except as follows:

(a) a lawyer admitted to engage in patent practice before the united states patent and trademark office may use the designation "Patent Attorney" or a substantially similar designation;

(b) a lawyer engaged in admiralty practice may use the designation "Admiralty," "Proctor in Admiralty" or a substantially similar designation; and

(c) (provisions on designation of specialization of the particular state).

COMMENT: *

[1] This Rule permits a lawyer to indicate areas of practice in communications about the lawyer's services; for example, in a telephone directory or other advertising. If a lawyer practices only in certain fields, or will not accept matters except in such fields, the lawyer is permitted so to indicate. However, a lawyer is not permitted to state that the lawyer is a "specialist," practices a "specialty," or "specializes in" particular fields. These terms have acquired a secondary meaning implying formal recognition as a specialist and therefore, use of these terms is misleading. [An exception would apply in those states which provide procedures for certification or recognition of specialization and the lawyer has complied with such procedures.]

[2] Recognition of specialization in patent matters is a matter of long-established policy of the Patent and Trademark Office. Designation of admiralty practice has a long historical tradition associated with maritime commerce and the federal courts.

* In 1989, the ABA amended the comment to Model Rule 7.3 to reflect concerns that the language in the original comment may violate the Supreme Court's legal advertising decisions. The original language read as follows:

COMMENT:

This Rule permits a lawyer to indicate areas of practice in communications about the lawyer's services; for example, in a telephone directory or other advertising. If a lawyer practices only in certain fields, or will not accept matters except in such fields, the lawyer is permitted so to indicate. However, stating that the lawyer is a "specialist" or that the lawyer's practice "is limited to" or "concentrated in" particular fields is not permitted. These terms have acquired a secondary meaning implying formal recognition as a specialist. Hence, use of these terms may be misleading unless the lawyer is certified or recognized in accordance with procedures in the state where the lawyer is licensed to practice.

MODEL CODE COMPARISON:

DR 2–105(A) provided that a lawyer "shall not hold himself out publicly as a specialist, as practicing in certain areas of law or as limiting his practice . . . except as follows:

"(1) A lawyer admitted to practice before the United States Patent and Trademark Office may use the designation 'Patents,' 'Patent Attorney,' 'Patent Lawyer,' or 'Registered Patent Attorney' or any combination of those terms, on his letterhead and office sign.

"(2) A lawyer who publicly discloses fields of law in which the lawyer . . . practices or states that his practice is limited to one or more fields of law shall do so by using designations and definitions authorized and approved by [the agency having jurisdiction of the subject under state law].

"(3) A lawyer who is certified as a specialist in a particular field of law or law practice by [the authority having jurisdiction under state law over the subject of specialization by lawyers] may hold himself out as such, but only in accordance with the rules prescribed by that authority."

EC 2–14 stated that "In the absence of state controls to insure the existence of special competence, a lawyer should not be permitted to hold himself out as a specialist, . . . other than in the fields of admiralty, trademark, and patent law where a holding out as a specialist historically has been permitted."

RULE 7.5 Firm Names and Letterheads

(a) A lawyer shall not use a firm name, letterhead or other professional designation that violates rule 7.1. A trade name may be used by a lawyer in private practice if it does not imply a connection with a government agency or with a public or charitable legal services organization and is not otherwise in violation of rule 7.1.

(b) A law firm with offices in more than one jurisdiction may use the same name in each jurisdiction, but identification of the lawyers in an office of the firm shall indicate the jurisdictional limitations on those not licensed to practice in the jurisdiction where the office is located.

(c) The name of a lawyer holding a public office shall not be used in the name of a law firm, or in communications on its behalf, during any substantial period in which the lawyer is not actively and regularly practicing with the firm.

(d) Lawyers may state or imply that they practice in a partnership or other organization only when that is the fact.

COMMENT:

[1] A firm may be designated by the names of all or some of its members, by the names of deceased members where there has been a continuing succession in the firm's identity or by a trade name such as the "ABC Legal Clinic." Although the United States Supreme Court has held that legislation may prohibit the use of trade names in professional practice, use of such names in law practice is acceptable so long as it is not misleading. If a private firm uses a trade name that includes a geographical name such as "Springfield Legal Clinic," an express disclaimer that it is a public legal aid agency may be required to avoid a misleading implication. It may be observed that any firm name including the name of a deceased partner is, strictly speaking, a trade name. The use of such names to designate law firms has proven a useful means of identification. However, it is misleading to use the name of a lawyer not associated with the firm or a predecessor of the firm.

[2] With regard to paragraph (d), lawyers sharing office facilities, but who are not in fact partners, may not denominate themselves as, for example, "Smith and Jones," for that title suggests partnership in the practice of law.

MODEL CODE COMPARISON:

With regard to paragraph (a), DR 2–102(A) provided that "[a] lawyer . . . shall not use . . . professional announcement cards . . . letterheads, or similar professional notices or devices, except . . . if they are in dignified form. . . ." DR 2–102(B) provided that "[a] lawyer in private practice shall not practice under a trade name, a name that is misleading as to the identity of the lawyer or lawyers practicing under such name, or a firm name containing names other than those of one or more of the lawyers in the firm, except that . . . a firm may use as . . . its name the name or names of one or more deceased or retired members of the firm or of a predecessor firm in a continuing line of succession."

With regard to paragraph (b), DR 2–102(D) provided that a partnership "shall not be formed or continued between or among lawyers licensed in different jurisdictions unless all enumerations of the members and associates of the firm on its letterhead and in other permissible listings make clear the jurisdictional limitations on those members and associates of the firm not licensed to practice in all listed jurisdictions; however, the same firm name may be used in each jurisdiction."

With regard to paragraph (c), DR 2–102(B) provided that "[a] lawyer who assumes a judicial, legislative, or public executive or administrative post or office shall not permit his name to remain in the name of a law firm . . . during any significant period in which he is not actively and regularly practicing law as a member of the firm. . . ."

Paragraph (d) is substantially identical to DR 2–102(C).

MAINTAINING THE INTEGRITY OF THE PROFESSION

RULE 8.1 Bar Admission and Disciplinary Matters

An applicant for admission to the bar, or a lawyer in connection with a bar admission application or in connection with a disciplinary matter, shall not:

(a) knowingly make a false statement of material fact; or

(b) fail to disclose a fact necessary to correct a misapprehension known by the person to have arisen in the matter, or knowingly fail to respond to a lawful demand for information from an admission or disciplinary authority, except that this rule does not require disclosure of information otherwise protected by rule 1.6.

COMMENT:

[1] The duty imposed by this Rule extends to persons seeking admission to the bar as well as to lawyers. Hence, if a person makes a material false statement in connection with an application for admission, it may be the basis for subsequent disciplinary action if the person is admitted, and in any event may be relevant in a subsequent admission application. The duty imposed by this Rule applies to a lawyer's own admission or discipline as well as that of others. Thus, it is a separate professional offense for a lawyer to knowingly make a misrepresentation or omission in connection with a disciplinary investigation of the lawyer's own conduct. This Rule also requires affirmative clarification of any misunderstanding on the part of the admissions or disciplinary authority of which the person involved becomes aware.

[2] This Rule is subject to the provisions of the Fifth Amendment of the United States Constitution and corresponding provisions of state constitutions. A person relying on such a provision in response to a question, however, should do so openly and not use the right of nondisclosure as a justification for failure to comply with this Rule.

[3] A lawyer representing an applicant for admission to the bar, or representing a lawyer who is the subject of a disciplinary inquiry or proceeding, is governed by the rules applicable to the client-lawyer relationship.

MODEL CODE COMPARISON:

DR 1–101(A) provided that a lawyer is "subject to discipline if he has made a materially false statement in, or if he has deliberately failed to disclose a material fact requested in connection with, his application for admission to the bar." DR 1–101(B) provided that a lawyer "shall not further the application for admission to the bar of another person known by him to be unqualified in respect to character, education, or other relevant attribute." With respect to paragraph (b),

DR 1–102(A)(5) provided that a lawyer shall not engage in "conduct that is prejudicial to the administration of justice."

RULE 8.2 Judicial and Legal Officials

(a) A lawyer shall not make a statement that the lawyer knows to be false or with reckless disregard as to its truth or falsity concerning the qualifications or integrity of a judge, adjudicatory officer or public legal officer, or of a candidate for election or appointment to judicial or legal office.

(b) A lawyer who is a candidate for judicial office shall comply with the applicable provisions of the code of judicial conduct.

COMMENT:

[1] Assessments by lawyers are relied on in evaluating the professional or personal fitness of persons being considered for election or appointment to judicial office and to public legal offices, such as attorney general, prosecuting attorney and public defender. Expressing honest and candid opinions on such matters contributes to improving the administration of justice. Conversely, false statements by a lawyer can unfairly undermine public confidence in the administration of justice.

[2] When a lawyer seeks judicial office, the lawyer should be bound by applicable limitations on political activity.

[3] To maintain the fair and independent administration of justice, lawyers are encouraged to continue traditional efforts to defend judges and courts unjustly criticized.

MODEL CODE COMPARISON:

With regard to paragraph (a), DR 8–102(A) provided that a lawyer "shall not knowingly make false statements of fact concerning the qualifications of a candidate for election or appointment to a judicial office." DR 8–102(B) provided that a lawyer "shall not knowingly make false accusations against a judge or other adjudicatory officer."

Paragraph (b) is substantially identical to DR 8–103.

RULE 8.3 Reporting Professional Misconduct*

(a) A lawyer having knowledge that another lawyer has committed a violation of the rules of professional conduct that raises a substantial question as to that lawyer's honesty, trustworthiness or fitness as a lawyer in other respects, shall inform the appropriate professional authority.

* In 1991, the ABA amended Model Rule 8.3(c) to include the reference to the protection of certain information obtained in lawyer assistance programs. The original version of 8.3(c) read as follows: "This rule does not require disclosure of information otherwise protected by Rule 1.6."

115

(b) **A lawyer having knowledge that a judge has committed a violation of applicable rules of judicial conduct that raises a substantial question as to the judge's fitness for office shall inform the appropriate authority.**

(c) **This rule does not require disclosure of information otherwise protected by Rule 1.6 or information gained by a lawyer or judge while serving as a member of an approved lawyers assistance program to the extent that such information would be confidential if it were communicated subject to the attorney-client privilege.**

COMMENT:

[1] Self-regulation of the legal profession requires that members of the profession initiate disciplinary investigation when they know of a violation of the Rules of Professional Conduct. Lawyers have a similar obligation with respect to judicial misconduct. An apparently isolated violation may indicate a pattern of misconduct that only a disciplinary investigation can uncover. Reporting a violation is especially important where the victim is unlikely to discover the offense.

[2] A report about misconduct is not required where it would involve violation of Rule 1.6. However, a lawyer should encourage a client to consent to disclosure where prosecution would not substantially prejudice the client's interests.

[3] If a lawyer were obliged to report every violation of the Rules, the failure to report any violation would itself be a professional offense. Such a requirement existed in many jurisdictions but proved to be unenforceable. This Rule limits the reporting obligation to those offenses that a self-regulating profession must vigorously endeavor to prevent. A measure of judgment is, therefore, required in complying with the provisions of this Rule. The term "substantial" refers to the seriousness of the possible offense and not the quantum of evidence of which the lawyer is aware. A report should be made to the bar disciplinary agency unless some other agency, such as a peer review agency, is more appropriate in the circumstances. Similar considerations apply to the reporting of judicial misconduct.

[4] The duty to report professional misconduct does not apply to a lawyer retained to represent a lawyer whose professional conduct is in question. Such a situation is governed by the rules applicable to the client-lawyer relationship.

[5] Information about a lawyer's or judge's misconduct or fitness may be received by a lawyer in the course of that lawyer's participation in an approved lawyers' or judges' assistance program. In that circumstance, providing for the confidentiality of such information encourages lawyers and judges to seek treatment through such program. Conversely, without such confidentiality, lawyers and judges may hesitate to seek assistance from these programs, which may then result in

additional harm to their professional careers and additional injury to the welfare of clients and the public. The Rule therefore exempts the lawyer from the reporting requirements of paragraphs (a) and (b) with respect to information that would be privileged if the relationship between the impaired lawyer or judge and the recipient of the information were that of a client and a lawyer. On the other hand, a lawyer who receives such information would nevertheless be required to comply with the Rule 8.3 reporting provisions to report misconduct if the impaired lawyer or judge indicates an intent to engage in illegal activity, for example, the conversion of client funds to his or her use.

MODEL CODE COMPARISON:

DR 1–103(A) provided that "[a] lawyer possessing unprivileged knowledge of a violation of [a Disciplinary Rule] shall report such knowledge to . . . authority empowered to investigate or act upon such violation."

RULE 8.4 Misconduct

It is professional misconduct for a lawyer to:

(a) violate or attempt to violate the rules of professional conduct, knowingly assist or induce another to do so, or do so through the acts of another;

(b) commit a criminal act that reflects adversely on the lawyer's honesty, trustworthiness or fitness as a lawyer in other respects;

(c) engage in conduct involving dishonesty, fraud, deceit or misrepresentation;

(d) engage in conduct that is prejudicial to the administration of justice;

(e) state or imply an ability to influence improperly a government agency or official; or

(f) knowingly assist a judge or judicial officer in conduct that is a violation of applicable rules of judicial conduct or other law.

COMMENT:

[1] Many kinds of illegal conduct reflect adversely on fitness to practice law, such as offenses involving fraud and the offense of willful failure to file an income tax return. However, some kinds of offense carry no such implication. Traditionally, the distinction was drawn in terms of offenses involving "moral turpitude." That concept can be construed to include offenses concerning some matters of personal morality, such as adultery and comparable offenses, that have no specific connection to fitness for the practice of law. Although a lawyer is personally answerable to the entire criminal law, a lawyer should be professionally answerable only for offenses that indicate lack of those characteristics relevant to law practice. Offenses involving violence,

117

dishonesty or breach of trust, or serious interference with the administration of justice are in that category. A pattern of repeated offenses, even ones of minor significance when considered separately, can indicate indifference to legal obligation.

[2] A lawyer may refuse to comply with an obligation imposed by law upon a good faith belief that no valid obligation exists. The provisions of Rule 1.2(d) concerning a good faith challenge to the validity, scope, meaning or application of the law apply to challenges of legal regulation of the practice of law.

[3] Lawyers holding public office assume legal responsibilities going beyond those of other citizens. A lawyer's abuse of public office can suggest an inability to fulfill the professional role of attorney. The same is true of abuse of positions of private trust such as trustee, executor, administrator, guardian, agent and officer, director or manager of a corporation or other organization.

MODEL CODE COMPARISON:

With regard to paragraphs (a) through (d) DR 1–102(A) provided that a lawyer shall not:

"(1) Violate a Disciplinary Rule.

"(2) Circumvent a Disciplinary Rule through actions of another.

"(3) Engage in illegal conduct involving moral turpitude.

"(4) Engage in conduct involving dishonesty, fraud, deceit, or misrepresentation.

"(5) Engage in conduct that is prejudicial to the administration of justice.

"(6) Engage in any other conduct that adversely reflects on his fitness to practice law."

Paragraph (e) is substantially similar to DR 9–101(C).

There was no direct counterpart to paragraph (f) in the Disciplinary Rules of the Model Code. EC 7–34 stated in part that "[a] lawyer . . . is never justified in making a gift or a loan to a [judicial officer] except as permitted by . . . the Code of Judicial Conduct." EC 9–1 stated that a lawyer "should promote public confidence in our [legal] system and in the legal profession."

RULE 8.5 Jurisdiction

A lawyer admitted to practice in this jurisdiction is subject to the disciplinary authority of this jurisdiction although engaged in practice elsewhere.

COMMENT:

[1] In modern practice lawyers frequently act outside the territorial limits of the jurisdiction in which they are licensed to practice, either

in another state or outside the United States. In doing so, they remain subject to the governing authority of the jurisdiction in which they are licensed to practice. If their activity in another jurisdiction is substantial and continuous, it may constitute practice of law in that jurisdiction. See Rule 5.5.

[2] If the rules of professional conduct in the two jurisdictions differ, principles of conflict of laws may apply. Similar problems can arise when a lawyer is licensed to practice in more than one jurisdiction.

[3] Where the lawyer is licensed to practice law in two jurisdictions which impose conflicting obligations, applicable rules of choice of law may govern the situation. A related problem arises with respect to practice before a federal tribunal, where the general authority of the states to regulate the practice of law must be reconciled with such authority as federal tribunals may have to regulate practice before them.

MODEL CODE COMPARISON:

There was no counterpart to this Rule in the Model Code.

TABLES A AND B: RELATED SECTIONS IN THE ABA MODEL CODE OF PROFESSIONAL RESPONSIBILITY

TABLE A *

ABA Model Rules	ABA Model Code
Competence	
Rule 1.1	EC 1–1, EC 1–2, EC 6–1, EC 6–2, EC 6–3, EC 6–4, EC 6–5, DR 6–101(A)
Scope of Representation	
Rule 1.2(a)	EC 5–12, EC 7–7, EC 7–8, DR 7–101 (A)(1)
Rule 1.2(b)	EC 7–17
Rule 1.2(c)	EC 7–8, EC 7–9, DR 7–101(B)(1)
Rule 1.2(d)	EC 7–1, EC 7–2, EC 7–5, EC 7–22, DR 7–102(A)(6), (7) & (8), DR 7–106
Rule 1.2(e)	DR 2–110(C)(1)(c), DR 9–101(C)
Diligence	
Rule 1.3	EC 2–31, EC 6–4, EC 7–1, EC 7–38, DR 6–101(A)(3), DR 7–101(A)(1) & (3)
Communication	
Rule 1.4(a)	EC 7–8, EC 9–2, DR 6–101(A)(3), DR 9–102(B)(1)
Rule 1.4(b)	EC 7–8
Fees	
Rule 1.5(a)	EC 2–16, EC 2–17, EC 2–18, DR 2–106 (A) & (B)
Rule 1.5(b)	EC 2–19
Rule 1.5(c)	EC 2–20, EC 5–7
Rule 1.5(d)	EC 2–20, DR 2–106 (C)
Rule 1.5(e)	EC 2–22, DR 2–107 (A)
Confidentiality of Information	
Rule 1.6(a)	EC 4–1, EC 4–2, EC 4–3, EC 4–4, DR 4–101(A), (B) & (C)
Rule 1.6(b)(1)	EC 4–2, DR 4–101 (C)(3), DR 7–102(B)
Rule 1.6(b)(2)	DR 4–101(C)(4)

ABA Model Rules	ABA Model Code
Conflict of Interest	
Rule 1.7(a)	EC 5–1, EC 5–14, EC 5–15, EC 5–17, EC 5–21, EC 5–22, DR 5–101(A), DR 5–105(A) & (B), DR 5–107(B)
Rule 1.7(b) & (b) (1)	EC 2–21, EC 5–1, EC 5–2, EC 5–3, EC 5–9, EC 5–11, EC 5–13, EC 5–14, EC 5–15, EC 5–16, EC 5–17, EC 5–19, EC 5–21, EC 5–22, EC 5–23, DR 5–101(A) & (B), DR 5–102, DR 5–104(A), DR 5–105(A), (B) & (C), DR 5–107(A)
Rule 1.7(b)(2)	EC 5–16, EC 5–17, DR 7–106(B)(2)
Prohibited Transactions	
Rule 1.8(a)	EC 5–3, EC 5–5, DR 5–104(A)
Rule 1.8(b)	EC 4–5, DR 4–101 (B)
Rule 1.8(c)	EC 5–1, EC 5–2, EC 5–5, EC 5–6
Rule 1.8(d)	EC 5–1, EC 5–3, EC 5–4, DR 5–104(B)
Rule 1.8(e)	EC 5–1, EC 5–3, EC 5–7, EC 5–8, DR 5–103(B)
Rule 1.8(f)	EC 2–21, EC 5–1, DR 5–107(A) & (B)
Rule 1.8(g)	EC 5–1, DR 5–106 (A)
Rule 1.8(h)	EC 6–6, DR 6–102 (A)
Rule 1.8(i)	None
Rule 1.8(j)	EC 5–1, EC 5–7, DR 5–101(A), DR 5–103(A)
Former Client	
Rule 1.9(a)	DR 5–105(C)
Rule 1.9(b)	EC 4–5, EC 4–6

* Table A provides cross-references to related provisions, but only in the sense that the provisions consider substantially similar subject matter or reflect similar concerns. A cross-reference does not indicate that a provision of the ABA Model Code of Professional Responsibility has been incorporated by the provision of a Model Rule. The Canons of the Code are not cross-referenced.

TABLES

ABA Model Rules	ABA Model Code
Imputed Disqualification	
Rule 1.10(a)	EC 4–5, DR 5–105 (D)
Rule 1.10(b)	EC 4–5, DR 5–105 (D)
Rule 1.10(c)	DR 5–105(A)
Rule 1.10(d)	EC 5–16
Successive Government and Private Employment	
Rule 1.11(a)	EC 9–3, DR 9–101 (B)
Rule 1.11(b)	None
Rule 1.11(c)	EC 8–8
Rule 1.11(d)	None
Rule 1.11(e)	None
Former Judge or Arbitrator	
Rule 1.12(a) & (b)	EC 5–20, EC 9–3, DR 9–101(A) & (B)
Rule 1.12(c)	DR 5–105(D)
Rule 1.12(d)	None
Organization as Client	
Rule 1.13(a)	EC 5–18, EC 5–24
Rule 1.13(b)	EC 5–18, EC 5–24, DR 5–107(B)
Rule 1.13(c)	EC 5–18, EC 5–24, DR 5–105(D), DR 5–107(B)
Rule 1.13(d)	EC 5–16
Rule 1.13(e)	EC 4–4, EC 5–16, DR 5–105(B) & (C)
Disabled Client	
Rule 1.14(a)	EC 7–11, EC 7–12
Rule 1.14(b)	EC 7–12
Safekeeping Property	
Rule 1.15	EC 5–7, EC 9–5, EC 9–7, DR 5–103(A) (1), DR 9–102
Declining or Terminating Representation	
Rule 1.16(a)(1)	EC 2–30, EC 2–31, EC 2–32, DR 2–103 (E), DR 2–104(A), DR 2–109(A), DR 2–110(B)(1) & (2)
Rule 1.16(a)(2)	EC 1–6, EC 2–30, EC 2–31, EC 2–32, DR 2–110(B)(3), DR 2–110(C)(4)
Rule 1.16(a)(3)	EC 2–31, EC 2–32, DR 2–110(B)(4)
Rule 1.16(b)(1)	EC 2–31, EC 2–32, DR 2–110(C)(1)(b) & (c), DR 2–110(C)(2)
Rule 1.16(b)(2)	EC 2–31, EC 2–32, DR 2–110(C)(2)
Rule 1.16(b)(3)	EC 2–30, EC 2–31, EC 2–32, DR 2–110 (C)(1)(d)
Rule 1.16(b)(4)	EC 2–31, EC 2–32, DR 2–110(C)(1)(f)(i) (j)

ABA Model Rules	ABA Model Code
Declining or Terminating Representation (C't'd)	
Rule 1.16(b)(5)	EC 2–32, DR 2–110 (C)(1)(d) & (e)
Rule 1.16(b)(6)	EC 2–32, DR 2–110 (C)(6)
Rule 1.16(c)	EC 2–32, DR 2–110 (A)(1)
Rule 1.16(d)	EC 2–32, DR 2–110 (A)(2) & (3)
Advisor	
Rule 2.1	EC 5–11, EC 7–3, EC 7–8, DR 5–107 (B)
Intermediary	
Rule 2.2(a)(1)	EC 4–2, EC 5–14, EC 5–15, EC 5–16, EC 5–20, DR 5–105 (A) & (C)
Rule 2.2(a)(2) & (3)	EC 5–14, EC 5–15, DR 5–105(A) & (C)
Rule 2.2(b)	EC 5–16
Rule 2.2(c)	EC 5–15, EC 5–19, DR 5–105(B) & (C)
Evaluation for Use by Third Persons	
Rule 2.3	None
Meritorious Claims and Contentions	
Rule 3.1	EC 7–1, EC 7–4, EC 7–5, EC 7–14, EC 7–25, DR 1–102(A) (5), DR 2–109(A)(B) (1), DR 7–102(A)(1) & (2)
Expediting Litigation	
Rule 3.2	EC 7–20, DR 1–102 (A)(5), DR 7–101(A) (1) & (2)
Candor Toward the Tribunal	
Rule 3.3(a)(1)	EC 7–4, EC 7–32, EC 8–5, DR 1–102 (A)(4) & (5), DR 7–102(A)(4) & (5)
Rule 3.3(a)(2)	EC 8–5, DR 1–102 (A)(4) & (5), DR 7–102(A)(3), DR 7–102(B)(1), DR 7–109 (A)
Rule 3.3(a)(3)	EC 7–23, DR 1–102 (A)(5), DR 7–106(B) (1)
Rule 3.3(a)(4)	EC 7–5, EC 7–26, EC 8–5, DR 1–102 (A)(4) & (5), DR 7–102(A)(7), DR 7–102(B)(1)
Rule 3.3(b)	EC 8–5, DR 7–102 (B)
Rule 3.3(c)	EC 7–24, EC 7–25
Rule 3.3(d)	EC 7–24, EC 7–27

121

ABA Model Rules	ABA Model Code
Fairness to Opposing Party and Counsel	
Rule 3.4(a)	EC 7–6, EC 7–27, DR 1–102(A)(4) & (5), DR 7–106(C)(7), DR 7–109(A) & (B)
Rule 3.4(b)	EC 7–6, EC 7–28, DR 1–102(A)(4), (5) & (6), DR 7–102(A)(6), DR 7–109(C)
Rule 3.4(c)	EC 7–22, EC 7–25, EC 7–38, DR 1–102 (A)(5), DR 7–106 (A), DR 7–106(C)(5) & (7)
Rule 3.4(d)	DR 1–102(A)(5), DR 7–106(A), DR 7–106 (C)(7)
Rule 3.4(e)	EC 7–24, EC 7–25, DR 1–102(A)(5), DR 7–106(C)(1), (2), (3) & (4)
Rule 3.4(f)	EC 7–27, DR 1–102 (A)(5), DR 7–104(A) (2), DR 7–109(B)
Impartiality and Decorum	
Rule 3.5(a)	EC 7–20, EC 7–29, EC 7–31, EC 7–32, EC 7–34, DR 7–106, DR 7–108, DR 7–109, DR 7–110, DR 8–101(A)
Rule 3.5(b)	EC 7–35, DR 7–108, DR 7–110(A) & (B)
Rule 3.5(c)	EC 7–20, EC 7–25, EC 7–36, EC 7–37, DR 7–101(A)(1), DR 7–106(C)(6)
Trial Publicity	
Rule 3.6	EC 7–25, EC 7–33, DR 7–107
Lawyer as Witness	
Rule 3.7(a)	EC 5–9, EC 5–10, DR 5–101(B)(1) & (2), DR 5–102
Rule 3.7(b)	EC 5–9, DR 5–101 (B), DR 5–102
Special Responsibilities of a Prosecutor	
Rule 3.8(a)	EC 7–11, EC 7–13, EC 7–14, DR 7–103 (A)
Rule 3.8(b)	EC 7–11, EC 7–13
Rule 3.8(c)	EC 7–11, EC 7–13, EC 7–18
Rule 3.8(d)	EC 7–11, EC 7–13, DR 7–103(B)
Rule 3.8(e)	None

ABA Model Rules	ABA Model Code
Advocate in Nonadjudicative Proceedings	
Rule 3.9	EC 7–11, EC 7–15, EC 7–16, EC 8–4, EC 8–5, DR 7–106 (B)(2), DR 9–101(C)
Truthfulness to Others	
Rule 4.1	EC 7–5, DR 7–102 (A)(3), (4), (5) & (7), DR 7–102(B)
Communication With Represented Persons	
Rule 4.2	EC 2–30, EC 7–18, DR 7–104(A)(1)
Dealing With Unrepresented Persons	
Rule 4.3	EC 2–3, EC 7–18, DR 7–104(A)(2)
Respect for Rights of Third Persons	
Rule 4.4	EC 7–10, EC 7–14, EC 7–21, EC 7–25, EC 7–29, EC 7–30, EC 7–37, DR 2–110 (B)(1), DR 7–101(A) (1), DR 7–102(A)(1), DR 7–106(C)(2), DR 7–107(D), (E) & (F), DR 7–108(D), (E) & (F)
Responsibilities of a Partner or Supervisory Lawyer	
Rule 5.1(a) & (b)	EC 4–5, DR 4–101 (D), DR 7–107(J)
Rule 5.1(c)	DR 1–102(A)(2), DR 1–103(A), DR 7–108 (E)
Responsibilities of a Subordinate Lawyer	
Rule 5.2	None
Responsibilities Regarding Nonlawyer Assistants	
Rule 5.3(a)	EC 3–6, EC 4–2, EC 4–5, EC 7–28, DR 4–101(D), DR 7–107 (J)
Rule 5.3(b)	DR 1–102(A)(2), DR 7–107(J), DR 7–108 (B), DR 7–108(E)
Rule 5.3(c)	None
Professional Independence of Lawyer	
Rule 5.4(a)	EC 2–33, EC 3–8, EC 5–24, DR 2–103 (D)(4)(d), (e) & (f), DR 3–102(A), DR 5–107(C)(3)
Rule 5.4(b)	EC 2–33, EC 3–8, DR 3–103(A)
Rule 5.4(c)	EC 2–33, EC 5–23, DR 2–103(C), DR 5–107(B)
Rule 5.4(d)	EC 2–33, EC 3–8, DR 5–107(C)

ABA Model Rules	ABA Model Code
Unauthorized Practice of Law	
Rule 5.5	DR 3–101(A) & (B)
Restrictions on Right to Practice	
Rule 5.6	DR 2–108
Pro Bono Publico Service	
Rule 6.1	EC 1–2, EC 1–4, EC 2–1, EC 2–2, EC 2–16, EC 2–24, EC 2–25, EC 6–2, EC 8–1, EC 8–2, EC 8–3, EC 8–7, EC 8–9
Accepting Appointments	
Rule 6.2(a)	EC 2–1, EC 2–25, EC 2–27, EC 2–28, EC 2–29, EC 8–3
Rule 6.2(b)	EC 2–16, EC 2–25, EC 2–29, EC 2–30
Rule 6.2(c)	EC 2–25, EC 2–27, EC 2–29, EC 2–30
Membership in Legal Services Organization	
Rule 6.3	EC 2–33, DR 5–101 (A)
Law Reform Activities Affecting Client Interests	
Rule 6.4	EC 2–33, DR 5–101 (A), DR 8–101
Communication Concerning Lawyer's Services	
Rule 7.1(a)	EC 2–8, EC 2–9, EC 2–10, DR 2–101(A), (B), (C), (E), (F) & (G), DR 2–102(E)
Rule 7.1(b)	EC 2–5, EC 2–8, EC 2–9, EC 9–4, DR 2–101(A), (B), (C), (E), (F) & (G), DR 9–101 (C)
Rule 7.1(c)	EC 2–8, EC 2–9, EC 2–10, DR 2–101(A), (B), (C), (E), (F) & (G)
Advertising	
Rule 7.2(a)	EC 2–1, EC 2–2, EC 2–6, EC 2–7, EC 2–8, EC 2–15, DR 2–101(B) & (H), DR 2–102(A) & (B), DR 2–103(B), DR 2–104 (A)(4) & (5)
Rule 7.2(b)	DR 2–101(D)
Rule 7.2(c)	EC 2–8, EC 2–15, DR 2–101(I), DR 2–103(B), (C) & (D)
Rule 7.2(d)	None

ABA Model Rules	ABA Model Code
Direct Contact With Prospective Clients	
Rule 7.3	EC 2–3, EC 2–4, EC 5–6, DR 2–103(A), DR 2–103(C)(1), DR 2–103(D)(4)(b) & (c), DR 2–104(A)(1), (2), (3) & (5)
Communication of Fields of Practice	
Rule 7.4	EC 2–1, EC 2–7, EC 2–8, EC 2–14, DR 2–101(B)(2), DR 2–102(A)(3), DR 2–102(E), DR 2–105 (A)
Rule 7.4(a)	DR 2–105(A)(1)
Rule 7.4(b)	EC 2–14
Rule 7.4(c)	DR 2–105(A)(2) & (3)
Firm Names and Letterheads	
Rule 7.5(a)	EC 2–11, EC 2–13, DR 2–102(A)(4), DR 2–102(B), (D) & (E), DR 2–105
Rule 7.5(b)	EC 2–11, DR 2–102 (D)
Rule 7.5(c)	EC 2–11, EC 2–12, DR 2–102(B)
Rule 7.5(d)	EC 2–11, EC 2–13, DR 2–102(C)
Bar Admission and Disciplinary Matters	
Rule 8.1(a)	EC 1–1, EC 1–2, EC 1–3, DR 1–101(A) & (B)
Rule 8.1(b)	DR 1–102(A)(5), DR 1–103(B)
Judges and Legal Officials	
Rule 8.2(a)	EC 8–6, DR 8–102
Rule 8.2(b)	DR 8–103
Reporting Professional Misconduct	
Rule 8.3	EC 1–3, DR 1–103 (A)
Misconduct	
Rule 8.4(a)	EC 1–5, EC 1–6, EC 9–6, DR 1–102(A) (1) & (2), DR 2–103 (E), DR 7–102(A) & (B)
Rule 8.4(b)	EC 1–5, DR 1–102 (A)(3) & (6), DR 7–102(A)(8), DR 8–101(A)(3)
Rule 8.4(c)	EC 1–5, EC 9–4, DR 1–102(A)(4), DR 8–101(A)(3)
Rule 8.4(d)	EC 3–9, EC 8–3, DR 1–102(A)(5), DR 3–101(B)
Rule 8.4(e)	EC 1–5, EC 9–2, EC 9–4, EC 9–6, DR 9–101(C)

ABA Model Rules	ABA Model Code
Misconduct (C't'd)	
Rule 8.4(f)	EC 1–5, EC 7–34, EC 9–1, DR 1–102 (A)(3), (4), (5) & (6), DR 7–110(A), DR 8–101(A)(2)
Jurisdiction	
Rule 8.5	None

TABLE B *

ABA Model Code	ABA Model Rules
Canon 1: Integrity of Profession	
EC 1–1	Rules 1.1, 8.1(a)
EC 1–2	Rules 1.1, 6.1, 8.1 (a)
EC 1–3	Rules 8.1(a), 8.3
EC 1–4	Rule 6.1
EC 1–5	Rule 8.4(a), (b), (c), (e) & (f)
EC 1–6	Rules 1.16(a)(2), 8.4 (a)
DR 1–101	Rule 8.1(a)
DR 1–102(A)(1)	Rule 8.4(a)
DR 1–102(A)(2)	Rules 5.1(c), 5.3(b), 8.4(a)
DR 1–102(A)(3)	Rule 8.4(b) & (f)
DR 1–102(A)(4)	Rules 3.3(a)(1), (2) & (4), 3.4(a) & (b), 8.4(c) & (f)
DR 1–102(A)(5)	Rules 3.1, 3.2, 3.3 (a)(1), (2) & (4), 3.4, 8.4(d) & (f)
DR 1–102(A)(6)	Rules 3.4(b), 8.4(b) & (f)
DR 1–103(A)	Rules 5.1(c), 8.3
DR 1–103(B)	Rule 8.1(b)
Canon 2: Making Counsel Available	
EC 2–1	Rules 6.1, 6.2(a), 7.2(a), 7.4
EC 2–2	Rules 6.1, 7.2(a)
EC 2–3	Rules 4.3, 7.3
EC 2–4	Rule 7.3
EC 2–5	Rule 7.1(b)
EC 2–6	Rule 7.2(a)
EC 2–7	Rules 7.2(a), 7.4
EC 2–8	Rules 7.1, 7.2(a) & (c), 7.4
EC 2–9	Rule 7.1
EC 2–10	Rule 7.1(a) & (c)
EC 2–11	Rule 7.5
EC 2–12	Rule 7.5(c)
EC 2–13	Rule 7.5(a) & (d)
EC 2–14	Rule 7.4
EC 2–15	Rule 7.2(a) & (c)

ABA Model Code	ABA Model Rules
Canon 2: Making Counsel Available (C't'd)	
EC 2–16	Rules 1.5(a), 6.1, 6.2(b)
EC 2–17	Rule 1.5(a)
EC 2–18	Rule 1.5(a)
EC 2–19	Rule 1.5(b)
EC 2–20	Rule 1.5(c) & (d)
EC 2–21	Rules 1.7(b), 1.8(f)
EC 2–22	Rule 1.5(e)
EC 2–23	None
EC 2–24	Rule 6.1
EC 2–25	Rules 6.1, 6.2
EC 2–26	None
EC 2–27	Rule 6.2(a) & (c)
EC 2–28	Rule 6.2(a)
EC 2–29	Rule 6.2
EC 2–30	Rules 1.16(a)(1) & (2), 1.16(b)(3), 4.2, 6.2(b) & (c)
EC 2–31	Rules 1.3, 1.16(a) & (b)
EC 2–32	Rule 1.16(a), (b), (c) & (d)
EC 2–33	Rules 5.4, 6.3, 6.4
DR 2–101(A)	Rule 7.1
DR 2–101(B)	Rules 7.1, 7.2(a)
DR 2–101(C)	Rule 7.1
DR 2–101(D)	Rule 7.2(b)
DR 2–101(E)	Rule 7.1
DR 2–101(F)	Rule 7.1
DR 2–101(G)	Rule 7.1
DR 2–101(H)	Rule 7.2
DR 2–101(I)	Rule 7.2(c)
DR 2–102(A)	Rules 7.2(a), 7.4
DR 2–102(B)	Rules 7.2(a), 7.5(a) & (c)
DR 2–102(C)	Rule 7.5(d)
DR 2–102(D)	Rule 7.5(a) & (b)
DR 2–102(E)	Rules 7.1(a), 7.4, 7.5(a)
DR 2–103(A)	Rule 7.3
DR 2–103(B)	Rule 7.2(a) & (c)
DR 2–103(C)	Rules 5.4(a), 7.2(c), 7.3
DR 2–103(D)	Rules 1.16(a)(1), 5.4 (a), 7.2(c), 7.3
DR 2–103(E)	Rules 1.16(a), 7.2 (a), 7.3
DR 2–104	Rules 1.16(a), 7.3
DR 2–105	Rule 7.4
DR 2–106(A)	Rule 1.5(a)
DR 2–106(B)	Rule 1.5(a)
DR 2–106(C)	Rule 1.5(d)
DR 2–107(A)	Rule 1.5(e)

* Table B provides cross-references to related provisions, but only in the sense that the provisions consider substantially similar subject matter or reflect similar concerns. A cross-reference does not indicate that a provision of the ABA Model Code of Professional Responsibility has been incorporated by the provision of a Model Rule. The Canons of the Code are not cross-referenced.

TABLES

ABA Model Code	ABA Model Rules	ABA Model Code	ABA Model Rules
Canon 2: Making Counsel Available (C't'd)		*Canon 5: Independent Judgment* (C't'd)	
		EC 5–15	Rules 1.7, 2.2(a) & (c)
DR 2–107(B)	Rule 5.4(a)(1)		
DR 2–108(A)	Rule 5.6	EC 5–16	Rules 1.7(b), 1.10 (d), 1.13(d) & (e), 2.2(a)(1) & (b)
DR 2–108(B)	Rule 5.6		
DR 2–109(A)	Rules 1.16(a)(1), 3.1		
DR 2–110(A)	Rule 1.16(c) & (d)		
DR 2–110(B)	Rules 1.16(a), 3.1, 4.4	EC 5–17	Rule 1.7
		EC 5–18	Rule 1.13(a), (b) & (c)
DR 2–110(C)	Rules 1.2(e), 1.16(a) & (b)	EC 5–19	Rules 1.7(b), 2.2(c)
Canon 3: Unauthorized Practice		EC 5–20	Rules 1.12(a) & (b), 2.2(a)(1)
EC 3–1	None	EC 5–21	Rule 1.7
EC 3–2	None	EC 5–22	Rule 1.7
EC 3–3	Rule 8.4(e)	EC 5–23	Rules 1.7(b), 5.4(c)
EC 3–4	None	EC 5–24	Rules 1.13(a), (b) & (c), 5.4(a)
EC 3–5	None		
EC 3–6	Rule 5.3(a)		
EC 3–7	None	DR 5–101(A)	Rules 1.7, 1.8(j), 6.3, 6.4
EC 3–8	Rule 5.49(a), (b) & (d)		
EC 3–9	Rule 8.4(d)	DR 5–101(B)	Rules 1.7(b), 3.7
DR 3–101(A)	Rule 5.5	DR 5–102(A)	Rules 1.7(b), 3.7
DR 3–101(B)	Rules 5.5, 8.4(d)	DR 5–102(B)	Rules 1.7(b), 3.7
DR 3–102	Rule 5.4(a)	DR 5–103(A)	Rules 1.8(j), 1.15
DR 3–103	Rule 5.4(b)	DR 5–103(B)	Rule 1.8(e)
Canon 4: Confidences and Secrets		DR 5–104(A)	Rules 1.7(b), 1.8(a)
EC 4–1	Rule 1.6(a)	DR 5–104(B)	Rule 1.8(d)
EC 4–2	Rules 1.6(a) & (b) (1), 2.2(a)(1), 5.3(a)	DR 5–105(A)	Rules 1.7, 1.10(c), 2.2(a)
EC 4–3	Rule 1.6(a)	DR 5–105(B)	Rules 1.7, 1.13(e), 2.2(c)
EC 4–4	Rules 1.6(a), 1.13(e)		
EC 4–5	Rules 1.8(b), 1.9(b), 1.10(a) & (b), 5.1(a) & (c), 5.3(a)	DR 5–105(C)	Rules 1.7(b), 1.13 (e), 1.9(a), 2.2
		DR 5–105(D)	Rules 1.10(a), 1.12 (c), 1.13(c)
EC 4–6	Rule 1.9(b)	DR 5–106	Rule 1.8(g)
DR 4–101(A)	Rule 1.6(a)	DR 5–107(A)	Rules 1.7(b), 1.8(f)
DR 4–101(B)	Rules 1.6(a), 1.8(b), 1.9(b)	DR 5–107(B)	Rules 1.7(a), 1.8(f), 1.13(b) & (c), 2.1, 5.4(c)
DR 4–101(C)	Rules 1.6(a) & (b)		
DR 4–101(D)	Rules 5.1(a) & (b), 5.3(a) & (b)	DR 5–107(C)	Rule 5.4(a) & (d)
Canon 5: Independent Judgment		*Canon 6: Competence*	
EC 5–1	Rules 1.7(a) & (b), 1.8(c), (d), (e), (f), (g) & (j)	EC 6–1	Rule 1.1
		EC 6–2	Rules 1.1, 5.1(a) & (b), 6.1
EC 5–2	Rules 1.7(b), 1.8(c)	EC 6–3	Rule 1.1
EC 5–3	Rules 1.7(b), 1.8(a), (d) & (e)	EC 6–4	Rules 1.1, 1.3
		EC 6–5	Rule 1.1
EC 5–4	Rule 1.8(d)	EC 6–6	Rule 1.8(h)
EC 5–5	Rule 1.8(a) & (c)	DR 6–101	Rules 1.1, 1.3, 1.4 (a)
EC 5–6	Rules 1.8(c), 7.3		
EC 5–7	Rules 1.5(c), 1.8(e) & (j), 1.15	DR 6–102	Rule 1.8(h)
		Canon 7: Zeal Within the Law	
EC 5–8	Rule 1.8(e)	EC 7–1	Rules 1.2(d), 1.3, 3.1
EC 5–9	Rules 1.7(b), 3.7	EC 7–2	Rule 1.2(d)
EC 5–10	Rule 3.7(a)	EC 7–3	Rule 2.1
EC 5–11	Rules 1.7(b), 2.1	EC 7–4	Rules 3.1, 3.3(a)(1)
EC 5–12	Rule 1.2(a)	EC 7–5	Rules 1.2(d), 3.1, 3.3(a)(4), 4.1
EC 5–13	Rule 1.7(b)		
EC 5–14	Rules 1.7(a), 2.2(a)	EC 7–6	Rule 3.4(a) & (b)
		EC 7–7	Rule 1.2(a)

ABA Model Code	ABA Model Rules	ABA Model Code	ABA Model Rules
Canon 7: Zeal Within the Law (C't'd)		*Canon 7: Zeal Within the Law* (C't'd)	
EC 7–8	Rules 1.2(a) & (c), 1.4, 2.1	DR 7–104	Rules 3.4(f), 4.2, 4.3
EC 7–9	Rule 1.2(c)	DR 7–105	None
EC 7–10	Rule 4.4	DR 7–106(A)	Rules 1.2(d), 3.4(c) & (d), 3.5(a)
EC 7–11	Rules 1.14(a), 3.8 (a), (b), (c) & (d), 3.9	DR 7–106(B)	Rules 1.7(b)(2), 3.3 (a)(3), 3.9
EC 7–12	Rule 1.14	DR 7–106(C)	Rules 3.4(a), (c), (d) & (e), 3.5(c), 4.4
EC 7–13	Rule 3.8		
EC 7–14	Rules 3.1, 3.8(a), 4.4	DR 7–107(A)–(I)	Rule 3.6
		DR 7–107(D)–(F)	Rule 4.4
EC 7–15	Rule 3.9	DR 7–107(J)	Rules 5.1(a) & (b), 5.3(a) & (b)
EC 7–16	Rule 3.9		
EC 7–17	Rule 1.2(b)	DR 7–108(A)	Rule 3.5(a) & (b)
EC 7–18	Rules 3.8(c), 4.2, 4.3	DR 7–108(B)	Rules 3.5(a), (b), (c), (d) & (f), 5.3(b)
EC 7–19	None	DR 7–108(C)	Rule 3.5(a) & (b)
EC 7–20	Rules 3.2, 3.5(a) & (c)	DR 7–108(D)	Rule 4.4
		DR 7–108(E)	Rules 4.4, 5.1(c), 5.3(b)
EC 7–21	Rule 4.4		
EC 7–22	Rules 1.2(d), 3.4(c)	DR 7–108(F)	Rule 4.4
EC 7–23	Rule 3.3(a)(3)	DR 7–108(G)	None
EC 7–24	Rules 3.3(c) & (d), 3.4(e)	DR 7–109(A)	Rules 3.3(a)(2), 3.4 (a)
EC 7–25	Rules 3.1, 3.3(c), 3.4(c) & (e), 3.5(c), 3.6, 4.4	DR 7–109(B)	Rule 3.4(a) & (f)
		DR 7–109(C)	Rule 3.4(b)
		DR 7–110(A)	Rules 3.5(a), 8.4(f)
EC 7–26	Rule 3.3(a)(4)	DR 7–110(B)	Rule 3.5(a) & (b)
EC 7–27	Rules 3.3(d), 3.4(a) & (f)	*Canon 8: Improving Legal System*	
EC 7–28	Rules 3.4(b), 5.3(a)	EC 8–1	Rule 6.1
EC 7–29	Rules 3.5(a), 4.4	EC 8–2	Rule 6.1
EC 7–30	Rule 4.4	EC 8–3	Rules 6.1, 6.2(a), 8.4(d)
EC 7–31	Rule 3.5(a)	EC 8–4	Rule 3.9
EC 7–32	Rules 3.3(a)(1), 3.5 (a)	EC 8–5	Rules 3.3(a)(1), (2) & (4), 3.3(b), 3.9
EC 7–33	Rule 3.6	EC 8–6	Rule 8.2(a)
EC 7–34	Rules 3.5(a), 8.4(f)	EC 8–7	Rule 6.1
EC 7–35	Rule 3.5(b)	EC 8–8	Rule 1.11(c)
EC 7–36	Rule 3.5(c)	EC 8–9	Rule 6.1
EC 7–37	Rules 3.5(c), 4.4	DR 8–101	Rules 3.5, 8.4(b), (c) & (f)
EC 7–38	Rules 1.3, 3.4(c)		
EC 7–39	None	DR 8–102	Rule 8.2(a)
DR 7–101(A)	Rules 1.2(a), 1.3, 3.2, 3.5(c), 4.4	DR 8–103	Rule 8.2(b)
		Canon 9: Appearance of Impropriety	
DR 7–101(B)	Rules 1.2, 1.16(b)	EC 9–1	Rule 8.4(f)
DR 7–102(A)(1)	Rules 3.1, 4.4	EC 9–2	Rules 1.4(a), 8.4(e)
DR 7–102(A)(2)	Rule 3.1	EC 9–3	Rules 1.11(a), 1.12 (a) & (b)
DR 7–102(A)(3)	Rules 3.3(a)(2), 4.1		
DR 7–102(A)(4)	Rules 3.3(a) & (c), 4.1	EC 9–4	Rules 7.1(b), 8.4(c) & (e)
DR 7–102(A)(5)	Rules 3.3(a)(1), 4.1	EC 9–5	Rule 1.15
DR 7–102(A)(6)	Rules 1.2(d), 3.4(b)	EC 9–6	Preamble, Rule 8.4 (e)
DR 7–102(A)(7)	Rules 1.2(d), 3.3(a) (4), 4.1		
		EC 9–7	Rule 1.15
DR 7–102(A)(8)	Rules 1.2(d), 8.4(a) & (b)	DR 9–101(A)	Rule 1.12(a) & (b)
DR 7–102(B)	Rules 1.6(b)(1), 3.3 (b), 4.1	DR 9–101(B)	Rules 1.11(a), 1.12 (a) & (b)
DR 7–103(A)	Rule 3.8(a)	DR 9–101(C)	Rules 1.2(e), 3.9, 7.1(b), 8.4(e)
DR 7–103(B)	Rule 3.8(d)	DR 9–102	Rules 1.4(a), 1.15

INDEX TO ABA MODEL RULES

A

Acquiring interest in litigation, Rule 1.8(j)
 contingent fee, Rule 1.8(j)(2)
Administration of justice,
 lawyer's duty to seek, Preamble
Administrative agencies and tribunals,
 appearance before, Rule 3.9 (Comment)
Admiralty practice,
 advertising, Rule 7.4(b)
Admission to practice, Rule 8.1
Advance fee payments,
 propriety of, Rule 1.5 (Comment)
Adversary system,
 duty of lawyer to, Preamble
Adverse legal authority,
 lawyer's duty to disclose, Rule 3.3(a)(3)
Advertising,
  See also Solicitation, Letterheads,
   Firm names, Specialization.
 by mail, Rule 7.3
 class action members, to notify, Rule 7.2
  (Comment)
 communications concerning a lawyer's
  services, generally, Rule 7.1
 comparisons with services of other lawyers, Rule 7.1(c)
 endorsements by clients, Rule 7.1 (Comment)
 fields of practice, Rule 7.4
 permitted forms, Rule 7.2
 prior results, Rule 7.1 (Comment)
 specialization Rule 7.5
Advice to client,
 candor, duty of, Rule 2.1
 used to engage in criminal or fraudulent
  conduct, Rule 1.2 (Comment)
 when lawyer not competent in area,
  Rule 1.1
Advisor,
 lawyer as, Preamble
Advocate,
 in nonadjudicative proceedings, Rule 3.9
 lawyer as, Preamble
Appeal,
 advising client of possibility, Rule 1.3
  (Comment)
Appearance of impropriety, Rule 1.10
  (Comment)
Appointed counsel,
 accepting appointments, Rule 6.2
 endorsement of client's views, Rule 1.2(b)
 requirement of competence, Rule 1.1
 withdrawal by, Rule 1.16 (Comment)
Arbitrator,
 former arbitrator negotiating for private
  employment, Rule 1.12(b)

B

Attorney-client privilege,
 distinguished from confidentiality rule,
  Rule 1.6 (Comment)
 intermediation, effect on, Rule 2.2(a)(1)
Attorney general,
 authority of, Scope
Authority of lawyer,
 decisionmaking authority, Rule 1.2(a)
 government lawyer, Scope
Autonomy of legal profession, Preamble

B

Belief,
 defined, Terminology
Believes,
 defined, Terminology
Business affairs of lawyer,
 duty to conduct in compliance with law,
  Preamble

C

Candor toward the tribunal,
 requirements of, Rule 3.3
Cause of action,
 violation of Rules as basis for, Scope
Civil disobedience,
 to test validity of statute, Rule 1.2 (Comment)
Civil liability,
 violation of Rules as basis for, Scope
Class actions,
 notice to members, Rule 7.2 (Comment)
Client-lawyer relationship,
 existence of defined by substantive law,
  Scope
Client's security fund,
 participation in, Rule 1.15 (Comment)
Comments,
 do not expand lawyer's responsibilities,
  Scope
Communication,
 duty to maintain with client, Preamble,
  Rule 1.4 (Comment)
 with represented party, Rule 4.2
 with third persons, Rule 4.1
 with unrepresented persons, Rule 4.3
 withholding information from client,
  Rule 1.4 (Comment)
Competence,
 duty of, Preamble
Competent representation,
 requirements of, Rule 1.1
Confidences of client,
 corporate client, Rule 1.13 (Comment)
 disclosure of, generally, Preamble, Rule
  1.6(b)

INDEX

W

Waiver,
    prosecutor obtaining from criminal defendant, Rule 3.8(c)
Withdrawal,
    conflict of interest, Rule 1.7 (Comment)
    discharge, Rule 1.16(a)(3)
    from intermediation, Rule 2.2(c)
    giving notice of fact of, Rule 1.6 (Comment)
    incapacity, Rule 1.16(a)(2)
    property of client, Rule 1.16(d)
    when client persists in criminal or fraudulent conduct, Rule 1.2 (Comment);
        Rule 1.6 (Comment); Rule 1.16(b)(1);
        Rule 1.13(c)
Witness,
    bribing, Rule 3.4(b)

Witness—Cont'd
    client's right to decide whether to testify,
        Rule 1.2(a)
    expenses, payment of, Rule 3.4 (Comment)
    expert, payment of, Rule 3.4 (Comment)
    lawyer as, Rule 3.7
Work product privilege,
    Rules do not affect application of, Scope

Z

Zealous representation,
    opposing party well-represented, Preamble
    requirement of, Rule 1.3 (Comment)

132

SELECTED SIGNIFICANT STATE MODIFICATIONS TO THE ABA MODEL RULES

The ABA Model Rules are designed to serve as a model for the states to consider and adopt. The enactment of the Model Rules caused most of the states to at least reconsider their local codes of ethics. As of the date of this publication, thirty-five states replaced codes based upon the Model Code and enacted codes based upon the structure and content of the Model Rules. Every one of these states has in some way amended the Model Rules provisions. Three states (New York, Oregon, and Virginia) have amended their version of the Model Code to reflect certain Model Rules' provisions. One state, California, did not base its code on the Model Code originally and refused to base a 1989 revision on the Model Rules.

In light of the many state modifications to the Model Rules, it is useful to examine selected significant state amendments. Some of these amendments illustrate substantive disagreements with the position adopted by the ABA in the Model Rules. Other modifications reflect local practices that the states have chosen to memorialize in the local code. Still other changes illustrate the desire to be more elaborative with respect to the language in the text. The selected state variations presented in this section fall within each of these categories.

The selected significant state modifications to the ABA Model Rules are presented under the order of the rules and within this framework by alphabetical order of the states. This chapter is intended to be illustrative and not exhaustive of the many state modifications. The comments to the state rule are included only if they are relevant to the difference that is illustrated.

TABLE OF CONTENTS

Indiana Rule 1.8(k).
Minnesota Rule 1.8(e)(3).
Texas Rule 1.09 (Modification of Model Rule 1.9).
Utah Rule 1.9(a).
District of Columbia Rule 1.11.
New Hampshire Rule 1.11A.
Montana Rule 1.17.

Counsellor

Oregon Rule DR 5–106 (Modification to Model Rule 2.2).

Advocate

Wyoming Rule 3.1.
Kansas Rule 3.5.

Transactions With Persons Other Than Clients

Louisiana Rule 4.2.
New Mexico Rule 16–402 (Modification of Model Rule 4.2).
Texas Rule 4.02 (Modification of Model Rule 4.2).
Minnesota Rule 4.3.
Texas Rule 4.04 (Modification of Model Rule 4.4).

Law Firms and Associations

Texas Rule 5.01 (Modification of Model Rule 5.1).
Texas Rule 5.02 (Modification of Model Rule 5.2).
District of Columbia Rule 5.4.

Public Service

South Dakota Rule 6.1.

Information About Legal Services

Delaware Rule 7.1.
Arizona Rule 7.2.
Delaware Rule 7.2.
Connecticut Rule 7.3.
Delaware Rule 7.3.
Delaware Rule 7.4.

Maintaining the Integrity of the Profession

Kansas Rule 8.3.
Louisiana Rule 8.4.
District of Columbia Rule 9.1.
Appendix: States That Have Adopted a Version of the Model Rules.

_____

CLIENT–LAWYER RELATIONSHIP

Texas Rule 1.01 (Modification of Model Rules 1.1 and 1.3)

[Texas has combined Model Rule 1.1 (competence) and 1.3 (diligence) into one rule.]

RULE 1.01 Competent and Diligent Representation

(a) A lawyer shall not accept or continue employment in a legal matter which the lawyer knows or should know is beyond the lawyer's competence, unless:

(1) another lawyer who is competent to handle the matter is, with the prior informed consent of the client, associated in the matter; or

(2) the advice or assistance of the lawyer is reasonably required in an emergency and the lawyer limits the advice and assistance to that which is reasonably necessary in the circumstances.

(b) In representing a client, a lawyer shall not:

(1) neglect a legal matter entrusted to the lawyer; or

(2) frequently fail to carry out completely the obligations that the lawyer owes to a client or clients.

(c) As used in this Rule, "neglect" signifies inattentiveness involving a conscious disregard for the responsibilities owed to a client or clients.

COMMENT:

Accepting Employment

[1] A lawyer generally should not accept or continue employment in any area of the law in which the lawyer is not and will not be prepared to render competent legal services. "Competence" is defined in Terminology as possession of the legal knowledge, skill, and training reasonably necessary for the representation. Competent representation contemplates appropriate application by the lawyer of that legal knowledge, skill and training, reasonable thoroughness in the study and analysis of the law and facts, and reasonable attentiveness to the responsibilities owed to the client.

[2] In determining whether a matter is beyond a lawyer's competence, relevant factors include the relative complexity and specialized nature of the matter, the lawyer's general experience in the field in question, the preparation and study the lawyer will be able to give the matter, and whether it is feasible either to refer the matter to or associate a lawyer of established competence in the field in question. The required attention and preparation are determined in part by what

135

is at stake; major litigation and complex transactions ordinarily require more elaborate treatment than matters of lesser consequences.

[3] A lawyer may not need to have special training or prior experience to accept employment to handle legal problems of a type with which the lawyer is unfamiliar. Although expertise in a particular field of law may be useful in some circumstances, the appropriate proficiency in many instances is that of a general practitioner. A newly admitted lawyer can be as competent in some matters as a practitioner with long experience. Some important legal skills, such as the analysis of precedent, the evaluation of evidence and legal drafting, are required in all legal problems. Perhaps the most fundamental legal skill consists of determining what kind of legal problems a situation may involve, a skill that necessarily transcends any particular specialized knowledge.

[4] A lawyer possessing the normal skill and training reasonably necessary for the representation of a client in an area of law is not subject to discipline for accepting employment in a matter in which, in order to represent the client properly, the lawyer must become more competent in regard to relevant legal knowledge by additional study and investigation. If the additional study and preparation will result in unusual delay or expense to the client, the lawyer should not accept employment except with the informed consent of the client.

[5] A lawyer offered employment or employed in a matter beyond the lawyer's competence generally must decline or withdraw from the employment or, with the prior informed consent of the client, associate a lawyer who is competent in the matter. Paragraph (a)(2) permits a lawyer, however, to give advice or assistance in an emergency in a matter even though the lawyer does not have the skill ordinarily required if referral to or consultation with another lawyer would be impractical and if the assistance is limited to that which is reasonably necessary in the circumstances.

Competent and Diligent Representation

[6] Having accepted employment, a lawyer should act with competence, commitment and dedication to the interest of the client and with zeal in advocacy upon the client's behalf. A lawyer should feel a moral or professional obligation to pursue a matter on behalf of a client with reasonable diligence and promptness despite opposition, obstruction or personal inconvenience to the lawyer. A lawyer's workload should be controlled so that each matter can be handled with diligence and competence. As provided in paragraph (a), an incompetent lawyer is subject to discipline.

Neglect

[7] Perhaps no professional shortcoming is more widely resented than procrastination. A client's interests often can be adversely affect-

136

ed by the passage of time or the change of conditions; in extreme instances, as when a lawyer overlooks a statute of limitations, the client's legal position may be destroyed. Under paragraph (b), a lawyer is subject to professional discipline for neglecting a particular legal matter as well as for frequent failures to carry out fully the obligations owed to one or more clients. A lawyer who acts in good faith is not subject to discipline, under those provisions for an isolated inadvertent or unskilled act or omission, tactical error, or error of judgment. Because delay can cause a client needless anxiety and undermine confidence in the lawyer's trustworthiness, there is a duty to communicate reasonably with clients; see Rule 1.03.

Maintaining Competence

[8] Because of the vital role of lawyers in the legal process, each lawyer should strive to become and remain proficient and competent in the practice of law. To maintain the requisite knowledge and skill of a competent practitioner, a lawyer should engage in continuing study and education. If a system of peer review has been established, the lawyer should consider making use of it in appropriate circumstances. Isolated instances of faulty conduct or decision should be identified for purposes of additional study or instruction.

Michigan Rule 1.2

[Michigan has amended Model Rule 1.2(a) to read as follows:]

RULE 1.2   Scope of Representation

(a) A lawyer shall seek the lawful objectives of a client through reasonably available means permitted by law and these rules. A lawyer does not violate this rule by acceding to reasonable requests of opposing counsel which do not prejudice the rights of the client, by being punctual in fulfilling all professional commitments, by avoiding offensive tactics, or by treating with courtesy and consideration all persons involved in the legal process. A lawyer shall abide by a client's decision whether to accept an offer of settlement or mediation evaluation of a matter. In a criminal case, the lawyer shall abide by the client's decision, after consultation with the lawyer, as to a plea to be entered, whether to waive jury trial, and whether the client will testify. In representing a client, a lawyer may, where permissible, exercise professional judgment to waive or fail to assert a right or position of the client.

* * *

Florida Rule 4–1.5 (modification of Model Rule 1.5)

[Florida has amended Model Rule 1.5 to read as follows:]

RULE 4–1.5. Fees for Legal Services

(A) An attorney shall not enter into an agreement for, charge, or collect an illegal, prohibited, or clearly excessive fee. A fee is clearly excessive when:

(1) After a review of the facts, a lawyer of ordinary prudence would be left with a definite and firm conviction that the fee exceeds a reasonable fee for services provided to such a degree as to constitute clear overreaching or an unconscionable demand by the attorney; or

(2) The fee is sought or secured by the attorney by means of intentional misrepresentation or fraud upon the client, a nonclient party, or any court, as to either entitlement to, or amount of, the fee.

(B) Factors to be considered as guides in determining a reasonable fee include the following:

(1) The time and labor required, the novelty, complexity, and difficulty of the questions involved, and the skill requisite to perform the legal service properly;

(2) The likelihood that the acceptance of the particular employment will preclude other employment by the lawyer;

(3) The fee, or rate of fee, customarily charged in the locality for legal services of a comparable or similar nature;

(4) The significance of, or amount involved in, the subject matter of the representation, the responsibility involved in the representation, and the results obtained;

(5) The time limitations imposed by the client or by the circumstances and, as between attorney and client, any additional or special time demands or requests of the attorney by the client;

(6) The nature and length of the professional relationship with the client;

(7) The experience, reputation, diligence, and ability of the lawyer or lawyers performing the service and the skill, expertise, or efficiency of effort reflected in the actual providing of such services; and

(8) Whether the fee is fixed or contingent, and, if fixed as to amount or rate, then whether the client's ability to pay rested to any significant degree on the outcome of the representation.

(C) In determining a reasonable fee, the time devoted to the representation and customary rate of fee need not be the sole or controlling factors. All factors set forth in this rule should be considered, and may be applied, in justification of a fee higher or lower than that which would result from application of only the time and rate factors.

(D) Contracts or agreements for attorney's fees between attorney and client will ordinarily be enforceable according to the terms of such contracts or agreement, unless found to be illegal, prohibited by this rule, or clearly excessive as defined by this rule.

(E) When the lawyer has not regularly represented the client, the basis or rate of the fee shall be communicated to the client, preferably in writing, before or within a reasonable time after commencing the representation.

(F) As to contingent fees:

(1) A fee may be contingent on the outcome of the matter for which the service is rendered, except in a matter in which a contingent fee is prohibited by paragraph (F)(3) or by law. A contingent fee agreement shall be in writing and shall state the method by which the fee is to be determined, including the percentage or percentages that shall accrue to the lawyer in the event of settlement, trial, or appeal, litigation and other expenses to be deducted from the recovery, and whether such expenses are to be deducted before or after the contingent fee is calculated. Upon conclusion of a contingent fee matter, the lawyer shall provide the client with a written statement stating the outcome of the matter and, if there is a recovery, showing the remittance to the client and the method of its determination.

(2) Every lawyer who accepts a retainer or enters into an agreement, express or implied, for compensation for services rendered or to be rendered in any action, claim, or proceeding whereby the lawyer's compensation is to be dependent or contingent in whole or in part upon the successful prosecution or settlement thereof shall do so only where such fee arrangement is reduced to a written contract, signed by the client, and by a lawyer for the lawyer or for the law firm representing the client. No lawyer or firm may participate in the fee without the consent of the client in writing. Each participating lawyer or law firm shall sign the contract with the client and shall agree to assume joint legal responsibility to the client for the performance of the services in question as if each were partners of the other lawyer or law firm involved. The client shall be furnished with a copy of the signed contract and any subsequent notices or consents. All provisions of this rule shall apply to such fee contracts.

(3) A lawyer shall not enter into an arrangement for, charge, or collect:

(a) Any fee in a domestic relations matter, the payment or amount of which is contingent upon the securing of a divorce or upon the amount of alimony or support, or property settlement in lieu thereof; or

(b) A contingent fee for representing a defendant in a criminal case.

(4) A lawyer who enters into an arrangement for, charges, or collects any fee in an action or claim for personal injury or for property damages or for death or loss of services resulting from personal injuries based upon tortious conduct of another, including products liability claims, whereby the compensation is to be dependent or contingent in whole or in part upon the successful prosecution or settlement thereof shall do so only under the following requirements:

(a) The contract shall contain the following provisions:

1. "The undersigned client has, before signing this contract, received and read the statement of client's rights and understands each of the rights set forth therein. The undersigned client has signed the statement and received a signed copy to refer to while being represented by the undersigned attorney(s)."

2. "This contract may be cancelled by written notification to the attorney at any time within three (3) business days of the date the contract was signed, as shown below, and if cancelled the client shall not be obligated to pay any fees to the attorney(s) for the work performed during that time. If the attorney(s) have advanced funds to others in representation of the client, the attorney(s) are entitled to be reimbursed for such amounts as they have reasonably advanced on behalf of the client."

(b) The contract for representation of a client in a matter set forth in paragraph (F)(4) may provide for a contingent fee arrangement as agreed upon by the client and the lawyer, except as limited by the following provisions:

1. Without prior court approval as specified below, any contingent fee which exceeds the following standards shall be presumed, unless rebutted, to be clearly excessive:

a. 33⅓% of any recovery up to $1 million through the time of filing of an answer or the demand for appointment of arbitrators;

140

b. 40% of any recovery up to $1 million from the time of filing an answer or the demand for appointment of arbitrators through the entry of judgment;

c. 30% of any recovery between $1 and $2 million;

d. 20% of any recovery in excess of $2 million;

e. If all defendants admit liability at the time of filing their answers and request a trial only on damages:

(i) 33⅓% of any recovery up to $1 million through trial;

(ii) 20% of any recovery between $1 and $2 million;

(iii) 15% of any recovery in excess of $2 million;

f. An additional 5% of any recovery after notice of appeal is filed or post-judgment relief or action is required for recovery on the judgment.

2. If any client is unable to obtain an attorney of the client's choice because of the limitations set forth in (F)(4) (b)1, the client may petition the circuit court for approval of any fee contract between the client and an attorney of the client's choosing. Such authorization shall be given if the court determines the client has a complete understanding of his or her rights and the terms of the proposed contract. The application for authorization of such a contract can be filed as a separate proceeding before suit or simultaneously with the filing of a complaint. Proceedings thereon may occur before service on the defendant and this aspect of the file may be sealed. Authorization of such a contract shall not bar subsequent inquiry as to whether the fee actually claimed or charged is clearly excessive under paragraphs (A) and (B).

3. In cases where the client is to receive a recovery which will be paid to the client on a future structured or periodic basis, the contingent fee percentage shall only be calculated on the cost of the structured verdict or settlement or, if the cost is unknown, on the present money value of the structured verdict or settlement, whichever is less. If the damages and the fee are to be paid out over the long term future schedule, then this limitation does not apply. No attorney may separately negotiate with the defendant for that attorney's fees in a structured verdict or settlement where such separate negotiations would place the attorney in a position of conflict.

(c) Before a lawyer enters into a contingent fee contract for representation of a client in a matter set forth in this rule, the lawyer shall provide the client with a copy of the statement of client's rights and shall afford the client a full and complete opportunity to understand each of the rights as set forth therein. A copy of the statement, signed by both the client and the lawyer, shall be given to the client to retain and the lawyer shall keep a copy in the client's file. The statement shall be retained by the lawyer with the written fee contract and closing statement under the same conditions and requirements as paragraph (F)(5).

(d) As to lawyers not in the same firm, a division of any fee within paragraph (F)(4) shall be on the following basis:

1. To the lawyer assuming primary responsibility for the legal services on behalf of the client, a minimum of 75% of the total fee.

2. To the lawyer assuming secondary responsibility for the legal services on behalf of the client, a maximum of 25% of the total fee. Any fee in excess of 25% shall be presumed to be clearly excessive.

3. The 25% limitation shall not apply to those cases in which two (2) or more lawyers or firms accept substantially equal active participation in the providing of legal services. In such circumstances counsel shall apply for circuit court authorization of the fee division in excess of 25%, based upon a sworn petition signed by all counsel which shall disclose in detail those services to be performed. The application for authorization of such a contract may be filed as a separate proceeding before suit or simultaneously with the filing of a complaint. Proceedings thereon may occur before service of process on any party and this aspect of the file may be sealed. Authorization of such contract shall not bar subsequent inquiry as to whether the fee actually claimed or charged is clearly excessive. An application under this section shall contain a certificate showing service on the client and the Florida Bar. Counsel may proceed with representation of the client pending court approval.

4. The percentages required by this section shall be applicable after deduction of any fee payable to separate counsel retained especially for appellate purposes.

(5) In the event there is a recovery, upon the conclusion of the representation, the lawyer shall prepare a closing

statement reflecting an itemization of all costs and expenses, together with the amount of fee received by each participating lawyer or law firm. A copy of the closing statement shall be executed by all participating lawyers, as well as the client, and each shall receive a copy. Each participating lawyer shall retain a copy of the written fee contract and closing statement for six (6) years after execution of the closing statement. Any contingent fee contract and closing statement shall be available for inspection at reasonable times by the client, by any other person upon judicial order, or by the appropriate disciplinary agency.

(G) Subject to the provisions of paragraph (F)(4)(d), a division of fee between lawyers who are not in the same firm may be made only if the total fee is reasonable and:

(1) The division is in proportion to the services performed by each lawyer; or

(2) By written agreement with the client:

(a) Each lawyer assumes joint legal responsibility for the representation and agrees to be available for consultation with the client; and

(b) The agreement fully discloses that a division of fees will be made and the basis upon which the division of fees will be made.

(H) Charges made by any lawyer or law firm under an approved credit plan shall be only for services actually rendered or cash actually paid on behalf of the client. No higher fee shall be charged and no additional charge shall be imposed by reason of a lawyer's or law firm's participation in an approved credit plan.

STATEMENT OF CLIENT'S RIGHTS

Before you, the prospective client, arrange a contingent fee agreement with a lawyer, you should understand this statement of your rights as a client. This statement is not a part of the actual contract between you and your lawyer, but, as a prospective client, you should be aware of these rights:

1. There is no legal requirement that a lawyer charge a client a set fee or a percentage of money recovered in a case. You, the client, have the right to talk with your lawyer about the proposed fee and to bargain about the rate or percentage as in any other contract. If you do not reach an agreement with one lawyer you may talk with other lawyers.

2. Any contingent fee contract must be in writing and you have three (3) business days to reconsider the contract. You may cancel the contract without any reason if you notify your lawyer in writing within three (3) business days of signing the contract. If you withdraw from

143

the contract within the first three (3) business days, you do not owe the lawyer a fee although you may be responsible for the lawyer's actual costs during that time. If your lawyer begins to represent you, your lawyer may not withdraw from the case without giving you notice, delivering necessary papers to you, and allowing you time to employ another lawyer. Often, your lawyer must obtain court approval before withdrawing from a case. If you discharge your lawyer without good cause after the three-day period, you may have to pay a fee for work the lawyer has done.

3. Before hiring a lawyer, you, the client, have the right to know about the lawyer's education, training, and experience. If you ask, the lawyer should tell you specifically about his or her actual experience dealing with cases similar to yours. If you ask, the lawyer should provide information about special training or knowledge and give you this information in writing if you request it.

4. Before signing a contingent fee contract with you, a lawyer must advise you whether he or she intends to handle your case alone or whether other lawyers will be helping with the case. If your lawyer intends to refer the case to other lawyers he or she should tell you what kind of fee sharing arrangement will be made with the other lawyers. If lawyers from different law firms will represent you, at least one lawyer from each law firm must sign the contingent fee contract.

5. If your lawyer intends to refer your case to another lawyer or counsel with other lawyers, your lawyer should tell you about that at the beginning. If your lawyer takes the case and later decides to refer it to another lawyer or to associate with other lawyers, you should sign a new contract which includes the new lawyers. You, the client, also have the right to consult with each lawyer working on your case and each lawyer is legally responsible to represent your interests and is legally responsible for the acts of the other lawyers involved in the case.

6. You, the client, have the right to know in advance how you will need to pay the expenses and the legal fees at the end of the case. If you pay a deposit in advance for costs, you may ask reasonable questions about how the money will be or has been spent and how much of it remains unspent. Your lawyer should give a reasonable estimate about future necessary costs. If your lawyer agrees to lend or advance you money to prepare or research the case, you have the right to know periodically how much money your lawyer has spent on your behalf. You also have the right to decide, after consulting with your lawyer, how much money is to be spent to prepare a case. If you pay the expenses, you have the right to decide how much to spend. Your lawyer should also inform you whether the fee will be based on the gross amount recovered or on the amount recovered minus the costs.

7. You, the client, have the right to be told by your lawyer about possible adverse consequences if you lose the case. Those adverse

consequences might include money which you might have to pay to your lawyer for costs and liability you might have for attorney's fees to the other side.

8. You, the client, have the right to receive and approve a closing statement at the end of the case before you pay any money. The statement must list all of the financial details of the entire case, including the amount recovered, all expenses, and a precise statement of your lawyer's fee. Until you approve the closing statement you need not pay any money to anyone, including your lawyer. You also have the right to have every lawyer or law firm working on your case sign this closing statement.

9. You, the client, have the right to ask your lawyer at reasonable intervals how the case is progressing and to have these questions answered to the best of your lawyer's ability.

10. You, the client, have the right to make the final decision regarding settlement of a case. Your lawyer must notify you of all offers of settlement before and after the trial. Offers during the trial must be immediately communicated and you should consult with your lawyer regarding whether to accept a settlement. However, you must make the final decision to accept or reject a settlement.

11. If at any time, you, the client, believe that your lawyer has charged an excessive or illegal fee, you, the client, have the right to report the matter to The Florida Bar, the agency that oversees the practice and behavior of all lawyers in Florida. For information on how to reach The Florida Bar, call 904-222-5286, or contact the local bar association. Any disagreement between you and your lawyer about a fee can be taken to court and you may wish to hire another lawyer to help you resolve this disagreement. Usually fee disputes must be handled in a separate lawsuit.

_____   _____
Client Signature   Attorney Signature

_____   _____
Date   Date

COMMENT

Basis or rate of fee

When the lawyer has regularly represented a client, they ordinarily will have evolved an understanding concerning the basis or rate of the fee. In a new client-lawyer relationship, however, an understanding as to the fee should be promptly established. It is not necessary to recite all the factors that underlie the basis of the fee, but only those that are directly involved in its computation. It is sufficient, for example, to state the basic rate is an hourly charge or a fixed amount or an estimated amount, or to identify the factors that may be taken into account in finally fixing the fee. When developments occur during the representation that render an earlier estimate substantially inaccurate, a revised estimate should be provided to the client. A written statement concerning the fee reduces the possibility of misunderstanding. Furnishing the client with a simple memorandum or a copy of the lawyer's customary fee schedule is sufficient if the basis or rate of the fee is set forth.

Rule 4–1.8(e) should be consulted regarding a lawyer's providing financial assistance to a client in connection with litigation.

Terms of payment

A lawyer may require advance payment of a fee, but is obliged to return any unearned portion. See rule 4–1.16(d). A lawyer is not, however, required to return retainers which, pursuant to an agreement with a client, are not refundable. A lawyer may accept property in payment for services, such as an ownership interest in an enterprise, providing this does not involve acquisition of a proprietary interest in the cause of action or subject matter of the litigation contrary to rule 4–1.8(i). However, a fee paid in property instead of money may be subject to special scrutiny because it involves questions concerning both the value of the services and the lawyer's special knowledge of the value of the property.

An agreement may not be made whose terms might induce the lawyer improperly to curtail services for the client or perform them in a way contrary to the client's interest. For example, a lawyer should not enter into an agreement whereby services are to be provided only up to a stated amount when it is foreseeable that more extensive services probably will be required, unless the situation is adequately explained to the client. Otherwise, the client might have to bargain for further assistance in the midst of a proceeding or transaction. However, it is proper to define the extent of services in light of the client's ability to pay. A lawyer should not exploit a fee arrangement based primarily on hourly charges by using wasteful procedures. When there is doubt whether a contingent fee is consistent with the client's best interest, the lawyer should offer the client alternative bases for the fee and explain their implications. Applicable law may impose limitations on contingent fees, such as a ceiling on the percentage.

Rule 4–1.5(F)(3) does not apply to lawyers seeking to obtain or enforce judgments for arrearages.

Contingent fee regulation

Rule 4–1.5(F)(4) should not be construed to apply to actions or claims seeking property or other damages arising in the commercial litigation context.

Rule 4–1.5(F)(4)(b) is intended to apply only to contingent aspects of fee agreements. In the situation where a lawyer and client enter a contract for part noncontingent and part contingent attorney's fees, rule 4–1.5(F)(4)(b) should not be construed to apply to and prohibit or limit the noncontingent portion of the fee agreement. An attorney could properly charge and retain the noncontingent portion of the fee even if the matter was not successfully prosecuted or if the noncontingent portion of the fee exceeded the schedule set forth in rule 4–1.5(F) (4)(b). Rule 4–1.5(F)(4)(b) should, however, be construed to apply to any additional contingent portion of such a contract when considered together with earned noncontingent fees. Thus, under such a contract a lawyer may demand or collect only such additional contingent fees as would not cause the total fees to exceed the schedule set forth in rule 4–1.5(F)(4)(b).

The limitations in rule 4–1.5(F)(4)(b)1.d. are only to be applied in the case where all the defendants admit liability at the time they file their initial answer and the trial is only on the issue of the amount or extent of the loss or the extent of injury suffered by the client. If the trial involves not only the issue of damages but such questions as proximate cause, affirmative defenses, seat belt defense, or other similar matters, the limitations are not to be applied because of the contingent nature of the case being left for resolution by the trier of fact.

Rule 4–1.5(F)(4)(b)2. provides the limitations set forth in paragraph (F)(4)(b)1. may be waived by the client upon approval by a circuit court judge. This waiver provision may not be used to authorize a lawyer to charge a client a fee which would exceed rule 4–1.5(A) or (B). It is contemplated that this waiver provision will not be necessary except where the client wants to retain a particular lawyer to represent him or her or the case involves complex, difficult, or novel questions of law or fact which would justify a contingent fee greater than the schedule but not a contingent fee which would exceed rule 4–1.5(B).

Upon a petition by a client, the trial court reviewing the waiver request must grant that request if the trial court finds the client: (a) understands his or her right to have the limitations in rule 4–1.5(F)(4) (b) applied in the specific matter; and (b) understands and approves the terms of the proposed contract. The consideration by the trial court of the waiver petition is not to be used as an opportunity for the court to inquire into the merits or details of the particular action or claim which is the subject of the contract.

The proceedings before the trial court and the trial court's decision on a waiver request are to be confidential and not subject to discovery by any of the parties to the action or by any other individual or entity except The Florida Bar. However, terms of the contract approved by the trial court may be subject to discovery if the contract (without court approval) was subject to discovery under applicable case law or rules of evidence.

Rule 4–1.5(F)(4)(b)3. prohibits a lawyer from charging the contingent fee percentage on the total, future value of a recovery being paid on a structured or periodic basis. This prohibition does not apply if the lawyer's fee is being paid over the same length of time as the schedule of payments to the client.

Division of fee

A division of fee is a single billing to a client covering the fee of two or more lawyers who are not in the same firm. A division of fee facilitates association of more than one lawyer in a matter in which neither alone could serve the client as well, and most often is used when the fee is contingent and the division is between a referring lawyer and a trial specialist. Subject to the provisions of paragraph (F)(4)(d), paragraph (G) permits the lawyers to divide a fee on either the basis of the proportion of services they render or by agreement between the participating lawyers if all assume responsibility for the representation as a whole and the client is advised and does not object. It does require disclosure to the client of the share that each lawyer is to receive. Joint responsibility for the representation entails the obligations stated in rule 4–5.1 for purposes of the matter involved.

Disputes over fees

If a procedure has been established for resolution of fee disputes, such as an arbitration or mediation procedure established by the bar, the lawyer should conscientiously consider submitting to it. Law may prescribe a procedure for determining a lawyer's fee, for example, in representation of an executor or administrator, a class, or a person entitled to a reasonable fee as part of the measure of damages. The lawyer entitled to such a fee and a lawyer representing another party concerned with the fee should comply with the prescribed procedure.

Referral fees and practices

A secondary lawyer shall not be entitled to a fee greater than the limitation set forth in rule 4–1.5(F)(4)(d)2. merely because the lawyer agrees to do some or all of the following: (a) consults with the client; (b) answers interrogatories; (c) attends depositions; (d) reviews pleadings; (e) attends the trial; or (f) assumes joint legal responsibility to the client. However, the provisions do not contemplate that a secondary lawyer who does more than the above is necessarily entitled to a larger percentage of the fee than that allowed by the limitation.

The provisions of rule 4–1.5(F)(4)(d)3. only apply where the participating lawyers have for purposes of the specific case established a co-counsel relationship. The need for court approval of a referral fee arrangement under rule 4–1.5(F)(4)(d)3. should only occur in a small percentage of cases arising under rule 4–1.5(F)(4).

In determining if a co-counsel relationship exists, the court should look to see if the lawyers have established a special partnership agreement for the purpose of the specific case or matter. If such an agreement does exist, it must provide for a sharing of services or responsibility and the fee division is based upon a division of the services to be rendered or the responsibility assumed. It is contemplated that a co-counsel situation would exist where a division of responsibility is based upon, but not limited to, the following: (a) based upon geographic considerations, the lawyers agree to divide the legal work, responsibility and representation in a convenient fashion. Such a situation would occur when different aspects of a case must be handled in different locations; (b) where the lawyers agree to divide the legal work and representation based upon their particular expertise in the substantive areas of law involved in the litigation; or (c) where the lawyers agree to divide the legal work and representation along established lines of division, such as liability and damages, causation and damages or other similar factors.

The trial court's responsibility when reviewing an application for authorization of a fee division under rule 4–1.5(F)(4)(d)3. is to determine if a co-counsel relationship exists in that particular case. If the court determines a co-counsel relationship exists and authorizes the fee division requested, the court does not have any responsibility to review or approve the specific amount of the fee division agreed upon by the lawyers and the client.

Rule 4–1.5(F)(4)(d)4. applies to the situation where appellate counsel is retained during the trial of the case to assist with the appeal of the case. The percentages set forth in paragraph (F)(4)(d) are to be applicable after appellate counsel's fee is established. However, the effect should not be to impose an unreasonable fee on the client.

Illinois Rule 1.5

[Illinois has added subsections (g) through (j) to Model Rule 1.5]

RULE 1.5 Fees

* * *

(g) A division of fees shall be made in proportion to the services performed and responsibility assumed by each lawyer, except where the primary service performed by one lawyer is the referral of the client to another lawyer and

(1) the receiving lawyer discloses that the referring lawyer has received or will receive economic benefit from the referral and the extent and basis of such economic benefit, and

(2) the referring lawyer agrees to assume the same legal responsibility for the performance of the services in question as would a partner of the receiving lawyer.

(h) The total fee of the lawyers shall be reasonable.

(i) For purposes of Rule 1.5 "economic benefit" shall include:

(1) the amount of participation in the fee received with regard to the particular matter;

(2) any other form of remuneration passing to the referring lawyer from the receiving lawyer, whether or not with regard to the particular matter; and

(3) an established practice of referrals to and from or from and to the receiving lawyer and the referring lawyer.

(j) Notwithstanding Rule 1.5(f), a payment may be made to a lawyer formerly in the firm, pursuant to a separation or retirement agreement.

Kansas Rule 1.5

[Kansas has substituted the following provisions for Model Rule 1.5(c) through (e):]

RULE 1.5

(c) A lawyer's fee shall be reasonable but a court determination that a fee is not reasonable shall not be presumptive evidence of a violation that requires discipline of the attorney.

(d) A fee may be contingent on the outcome of the matter for which the service is rendered, except in a matter in which a contingent fee is prohibited by paragraph (f) or other law. A contingent fee agreement shall be in writing and shall state the method by which the fee is to be determined, including the percentage or percentages that shall accrue to the lawyer in the event of settlement, trial or appeal, and the litigation and other expenses to be deducted from the recovery. All such expenses shall be deducted before the contingent fee is calculated. Upon conclusion of a contingent fee matter, the lawyer shall provide the client with a written statement stating the outcome of the matter and, if there is a recovery, showing the client's share and amount and the method of its determination. The statement shall advise the client of the right to have the fee reviewed as provided in subsection (e).

(e) Upon application by the client, all fee contracts shall be subject to review and approval by the appropriate court having jurisdiction of the matter and the court shall have the authority to determine whether the contract is reasonable. If the court finds the contract is not reasonable, it shall set and allow a reasonable fee.

Texas Rule 1.04 (modification of Model Rule 1.5)

[Texas has modified several subsections of Model Rule 1.5 (fees) to read as follows:]

RULE 1.04.   Fees

(a) **A lawyer shall not enter into an arrangement for, charge, or collect an illegal fee or unconscionable fee. A fee is unconscionable if a competent lawyer could not form a reasonable belief that the fee is reasonable.**

* * *

(f) **A division or agreement for division of a fee between lawyers who are not in the same firm shall not be made unless:**

    (1) **the division is:**

        (i) **in proportion to the professional services performed by each lawyer;**

        (ii) **made with a forwarding lawyer; or**

        (iii) **made, by written agreement with the client, with a lawyer who assumes joint responsibility for the representation;**

    (2) **the client is advised of, and does not object to, the participation of all the lawyers involved; and**

    (3) **the aggregate fee does not violate paragraph (a).**

* * *

COMMENT:

1. A lawyer in good conscience should not charge or collect more than a reasonable fee, although he may charge less or no fee at all. The determination of the reasonableness of a fee, or of the range of reasonableness, can be a difficult question, and a standard of "reasonableness" is too vague and uncertain to be an appropriate standard in a disciplinary action. For this reason, paragraph (a) adopts, for disciplinary purposes only, a clearer standard: the lawyer is subject to discipline for an illegal fee or an unconscionable fee. Paragraph (a) defines an unconscionable fee in terms of the reasonableness of the fee but in a way to eliminate factual disputes as to the fee's reasonableness. The Rule's "unconscionable" standard, however, does not preclude use of the "reasonableness" standard of paragraph (b) in other settings.

Basis or Rate of Fee

2. When the lawyer has regularly represented a client, they ordinarily will have evolved an understanding concerning the basis or rate of the fee. If, however, the basis or rate of fee being charged to a regularly represented client differs from the understanding that has evolved, the lawyer should so advise the client. In a new client-lawyer relationship, an understanding as to the fee should be promptly estab-

lished. It is not necessary to recite all the factors that underlie the basis of the fee, but only those that are directly involved in its computation. It is sufficient, for example, to state that the basic rate is an hourly charge or a fixed amount or an estimated amount, in order to identify the factors that may be taken into account in finally fixing the fee. When developments occur during the representation that render an earlier estimate substantially inaccurate, a revised estimate should be provided to the client. A written statement concerning the fee reduces the possibility of misunderstanding, and when the lawyer has not regularly represented the client it is preferable for the basis or rate of the fee to be communicated to the client in writing. Furnishing the client with a simple memorandum or a copy of the lawyer's customary fee schedule is sufficient if the basis or rate of the fee is set forth. In the case of a contingent fee, a written agreement is mandatory.

* * *

Unconscionable Fees

7. Two principal circumstances combine to make it difficult to determine whether a particular fee is unconscionable within the disciplinary test provided by paragraph (a) of this Rule. The first is the subjectivity of a number of the factors relied on to determine the reasonableness of fees under paragraph (b). Because those factors do not permit more than an approximation of a range of fees that might be found reasonable in any given case, there is a corresponding degree of uncertainty in determining whether a given fee is unconscionable. Secondly, fee arrangements normally are made at the outset of representation, a time when many uncertainties and contingencies exist, while claims of unconscionability are made in hindsight when the contingencies have been resolved. The "unconscionability" standard adopts that difference in perspective and requires that a lawyer be given the benefit of any such uncertainties for disciplinary purposes only. Except in very unusual situations, therefore, the circumstances at the time a fee arrangement is made should control in determining a question of unconscionability.

8. Two factors in otherwise borderline cases might indicate a fee may be unconscionable. The first is overreaching by a lawyer, particularly of a client who was unusually susceptible to such overreaching. The second is a failure of the lawyer to give at the outset a clear and accurate explanation of how a fee was to be calculated. For example, a fee arrangement negotiated at arm's length with an experienced business client would rarely be subject to question. On the other hand, a fee arrangement with an uneducated or unsophisticated individual having no prior experience in such matters should be more carefully scrutinized for overreaching. While the fact that a client was at a marked disadvantage in bargaining with a lawyer over fees will not make a fee unconscionable, application of the disciplinary test may

require some consideration of the personal circumstances of the individuals involved.

* * *

Division of Fees

10.   A division of fees is a sharing of a single billing to a client between two or more lawyers who are not in the same firm.   A division of fees facilitates association of more than one lawyer in a matter in which neither alone could serve the client as well, and most often is used when the fee is contingent and the division is between a referring lawyer and a trial specialist.   Because the association of additional counsel normally will result in a further disclosure of client confidences and have a financial impact on a client, advance disclosure of the existence of that proposed association and client consent generally are required.   Where those consequences will not arise, however, disclosure is not mandated by this Rule.   For example, if a lawyer hires a second lawyer for consultation and advice on a specialized aspect of a matter and that consultation will not necessitate the disclosure of confidential information and the hiring lawyer both absorbs the entire cost of the second lawyer's fees and assumes all responsibility for the advice ultimately given the client, a division of fees within the meaning of this Rule is not involved.   See also Comment 3 to Rule 5.04.

11.   Paragraph (f) permits lawyers to divide a fee on one of three bases.   The first is in proportion to the professional services performed by each.   The second continues the Texas practice of permitting a division of fees with a forwarding attorney.   The third permits fees to be divided with a lawyer who, by written agreement with the client, assumes joint responsibility for the representation.   The second and the third methods permit the fees to be divided in any mutually agreeable proportion.   If the third method is used, a lawyer may satisfy his or her obligations of "joint responsibility" for the representation either by being an attorney of record in the matter or by discharging the responsibilities imposed on a "supervised lawyer" under these rules.   See Rule 5.02.   Paragraph (f) does not require disclosure to the client of the share that each lawyer is to receive.

Fee Disputes and Determinations

12.   If a procedure has been established for resolution of fee disputes, such as an arbitration or mediation procedure established by a bar association, the lawyer should conscientiously consider submitting to it.   Law may prescribe a procedure for determining a lawyer's fee, for example, in representation of an executor or administrator, or when a class or a person is entitled to recover a reasonable attorney's fee as part of the measure of damages.   All involved lawyers should comply with any prescribed procedures.

Michigan Rule 1.6

[Michigan has modified Model Rule 1.6 to read as follows:]

RULE 1.6 Confidentiality of Information

(a) "Confidence" refers to information protected by the client-lawyer privilege under applicable law, and "secret" refers to other information gained in the professional relationship that the client has requested be held inviolate or the disclosure of which would be embarrassing or would be likely to be detrimental to the client.

(b) Except when permitted under paragraph (c), a lawyer shall not knowingly:

(1) reveal a confidence or secret of a client;

(2) use a confidence or secret of a client to the disadvantage of the client; or

(3) use a confidence or secret of a client for the advantage of the lawyer or of a third person, unless the client consents after full disclosure.

(c) A lawyer may reveal:

(1) confidences or secrets with the consent of the client or clients affected, but only after full disclosure to them;

(2) confidences or secrets when permitted or required by these rules, or when required by law or by court order;

(3) confidences and secrets to the extent reasonably necessary to rectify the consequences of a client's illegal or fraudulent act in the furtherance of which the lawyer's services have been used;

(4) the intention of a client to commit a crime and the information necessary to prevent the crime; and

(5) confidences or secrets necessary to establish or collect a fee, or to defend the lawyer or the lawyer's employees or associates against an accusation of wrongful conduct.

(d) A lawyer shall exercise reasonable care to prevent employees, associates, and others whose services are utilized by the lawyer from disclosing or using confidences or secrets of a client, except that a lawyer may reveal the information allowed by paragraph (c) through an employee.

COMMENT

The lawyer is part of a judicial system charged with upholding the law. One of the lawyer's functions is to advise clients so that they avoid any violation of the law in the proper exercise of their rights.

The observance of the ethical obligation of a lawyer to hold inviolate confidential information of the client not only facilitates the full

154

development of facts essential to proper representation of the client, but also encourages people to seek early legal assistance.

Almost without exception, clients come to lawyers in order to determine what their rights are and what is, in the maze of laws and regulations, deemed to be legal and correct. The common law recognizes that the client's confidences must be protected from disclosure. Upon the basis of experience, lawyers know that almost all clients follow the advice given and that the law is upheld.

A fundamental principle in the client-lawyer relationship is that the lawyer maintain confidentiality of information relating to the representation. The client is thereby encouraged to communicate fully and frankly with the lawyer even as to embarrassing or legally damaging subject matter.

The principle of confidentiality is given effect in two related bodies of law, the client-lawyer privilege (which includes the work-product doctrine) in the law of evidence and the rule of confidentiality established in professional ethics. The client-lawyer privilege applies in judicial and other proceedings in which a lawyer may be called as a witness or otherwise required to produce evidence concerning a client. The rule of client-lawyer confidentiality applies in situations other than those where evidence is sought from the lawyer through compulsion of law. The confidentiality rule applies to confidences and secrets as defined in the rule. A lawyer may not disclose such information except as authorized or required by the Rules of Professional Conduct or other law. See also Scope, ante.

The requirement of maintaining confidentiality of information relating to representation applies to government lawyers who may disagree with the policy goals that their representation is designed to advance.

Authorized Disclosure. A lawyer is impliedly authorized to make disclosures about a client when appropriate in carrying out the representation, except to the extent that the client's instructions or special circumstances limit that authority. In litigation, for example, a lawyer may disclose information by admitting a fact that cannot properly be disputed, or, in negotiation, by making a disclosure that facilitates a satisfactory conclusion.

Lawyers in a firm may, in the course of the firm's practice, disclose to each other information relating to a client of the firm, unless the client has instructed that particular information be confined to specified lawyers, or unless the disclosure would breach a screen erected within the firm in accordance with Rules 1.10(b), 1.11(a), or 1.12(c).

Disclosure Adverse to Client. The confidentiality rule is subject to limited exceptions. In becoming privy to information about a client, a lawyer may foresee that the client intends to commit a crime. To the extent a lawyer is prohibited from making disclosure, the interests of the potential victim are sacrificed in favor of preserving the client's confidences even though the client's purpose is wrongful. To the extent a lawyer is required or permitted to disclose a client's purposes, the client may be inhibited from revealing facts which would enable the lawyer to counsel against a wrongful course of action. A rule governing disclosure of threatened harm thus involves balancing the interests of one group of potential victims against those of another. On the assumption that lawyers generally fulfill their duty to advise against the commission of deliberately wrongful acts, the public is better protected if full and open communication by the client is encouraged than if it is inhibited.

Generally speaking, information relating to the representation must be kept confidential as stated in paragraph (b). However, when the client is or will be engaged in criminal conduct or the integrity of the lawyer's own conduct is involved, the principle of confidentiality may appropriately yield, depending on the lawyer's knowledge about and relationship to the conduct in question, and the seriousness of that conduct. Several situations must be distinguished.

First, the lawyer may not counsel or assist a client in conduct that is illegal or fraudulent. See Rule 1.2(c). Similarly, a lawyer has a duty under Rule 3.3(a)(4) not to use false evidence. This duty is essentially a special instance of the duty prescribed in Rule 1.2(c) to avoid assisting a client in illegal or fraudulent conduct. The same is true of compliance with Rule 4.1 concerning truthfulness of a lawyer's own representations.

Second, the lawyer may have been innocently involved in past conduct by the client that was criminal or fraudulent. In such a situation the lawyer has not violated Rule 1.2(c), because to "counsel or assist" criminal or fraudulent conduct requires knowing that the conduct is of that character. Even if the involvement was innocent, however, the fact remains that the lawyer's professional services were made the instrument of the client's crime or fraud. The lawyer, therefore, has a legitimate interest in being able to rectify the consequences of such conduct, and has the professional right, although not a professional duty, to rectify the situation. Exercising that right may require revealing information relating to the representation. Paragraph (c)(3) gives the lawyer professional discretion to reveal such information to the extent necessary to accomplish rectification. However, the constitutional rights of defendants in criminal cases may limit the extent to which counsel for a defendant may correct a misrepresentation that is based on information provided by the client. See comment to Rule 3.3.

Third, the lawyer may learn that a client intends prospective conduct that is criminal. Inaction by the lawyer is not a violation of Rule 1.2(c), except in the limited circumstances where failure to act constitutes assisting the client. See comment to Rule 1.2(c). However, the lawyer's knowledge of the client's purpose may enable the lawyer to prevent commission of the prospective crime. If the prospective crime is likely to result in substantial injury, the lawyer may feel a moral obligation to take preventive action. When the threatened injury is grave, such as homicide or serious bodily injury, a lawyer may have an obligation under tort or criminal law to take reasonable preventive measures. Whether the lawyer's concern is based on moral or legal considerations, the interest in preventing the harm may be more compelling than the interest in preserving confidentiality of information relating to the client. As stated in paragraph (c)(4), the lawyer has professional discretion to reveal information in order to prevent a client's criminal act.

It is arguable that the lawyer should have a professional obligation to make a disclosure in order to prevent homicide or serious bodily injury which the lawyer knows is intended by the client. However, it is very difficult for a lawyer to "know" when such a heinous purpose will actually be carried out, for the client may have a change of mind. To require disclosure when the client intends such an act, at the risk of professional discipline if the assessment of the client's purpose turns out to be wrong, would be to impose a penal risk that might interfere with the lawyer's resolution of an inherently difficult moral dilemma.

The lawyer's exercise of discretion requires consideration of such factors as magnitude, proximity, and likelihood of the contemplated wrong; the nature of the lawyer's relationship with the client and with those who might be injured by the client; the lawyer's own involvement in the transaction; and factors that may extenuate the conduct in question. Where practical, the lawyer should seek to persuade the client to take suitable action. In any case, a disclosure adverse to the client's interest should be no greater than the lawyer reasonably believes necessary to the purpose. A lawyer's decision not to make a disclosure permitted by paragraph (c) does not violate this rule.

Where the client is an organization, the lawyer may be in doubt whether contemplated conduct will actually be carried out by the organization. Where necessary to guide conduct in connection with this rule, the lawyer should make an inquiry within the organization as indicated in Rule 1.13(b).

Paragraph (c)(3) does not apply where a lawyer is employed after a crime or fraud has been committed to represent the client in matters ensuing therefrom.

Withdrawal. If the lawyer's services will be used by the client in materially furthering a course of criminal or fraudulent conduct, the lawyer must withdraw, as stated in Rule 1.16(a)(1).

After withdrawal the lawyer is required to refrain from making disclosure of the client's confidences, except as otherwise provided in Rule 1.6. Neither this rule nor Rule 1.8(b) nor Rule 1.16(d) prevents the lawyer from giving notice of the fact of withdrawal, and the lawyer may also withdraw or disaffirm any opinion, document, affirmation, or the like.

Dispute Concerning Lawyer's Conduct. Where a legal claim or disciplinary charge alleges complicity of the lawyer in a client's conduct or other misconduct of the lawyer involving representation of the client, the lawyer may respond to the extent the lawyer reasonably believes necessary to establish a defense. The same is true with respect to a claim involving the conduct or representation of a former client. The lawyer's right to respond arises when an assertion of complicity or other misconduct has been made. Paragraph (c)(5) does not require the lawyer to await the commencement of an action or proceeding that charges complicity or other misconduct, so that the defense may be established by responding directly to a third party who has made such an assertion. The right to defend, of course, applies where a proceeding has been commenced. Where practicable and not prejudicial to the lawyer's ability to establish the defense, the lawyer should advise the client of the third party's assertion and request that the client respond appropriately. In any event, disclosure should be no greater than the lawyer reasonably believes is necessary to vindicate innocence, the disclosure should be made in a manner which limits access to the information to the tribunal or other persons having a need to know it, and appropriate protective orders or other arrangements should be sought by the lawyer to the fullest extent practicable.

If the lawyer is charged with wrongdoing in which the client's conduct is implicated, the rule of confidentiality should not prevent the lawyer from defending against the charge. Such a charge can arise in a civil, criminal, or professional disciplinary proceeding, and can be based on a wrong allegedly committed by the lawyer against the client, or on a wrong alleged by a third person, for example, a person claiming to have been defrauded by the lawyer and client acting together.

A lawyer entitled to a fee is permitted by paragraph (c)(5) to prove the services rendered in an action to collect it. This aspect of the rule expresses the principle that the beneficiary of a fiduciary relationship may not exploit it to the detriment of the fiduciary. As stated above, the lawyer must make every effort practicable to avoid unnecessary disclosure of information relating to a representation, to limit disclosure to those having the need to know it, and to obtain protective orders or make other arrangements minimizing the risk of disclosure.

Disclosures Otherwise Required or Authorized. The scope of the client-lawyer privilege is a question of law. If a lawyer is called as a witness to give testimony concerning a client, absent waiver by the client, paragraph (b)(1) requires the lawyer to invoke the privilege when it is applicable. The lawyer must comply with the final orders of a court or other tribunal of competent jurisdiction requiring the lawyer to give information about the client.

The Rules of Professional Conduct in various circumstances permit or require a lawyer to disclose information relating to the representation. See Rules 2.2, 2.3, 3.3 and 4.1. In addition to these provisions, a lawyer may be obligated or permitted by other provisions of law to give information about a client. Whether another provision of law supersedes Rule 1.6 is a matter of interpretation beyond the scope of these rules, but a presumption should exist against such a supersession.

Former Client. The duty of confidentiality continues after the client-lawyer relationship has terminated. See Rule 1.9.

Minnesota Rule 1.6

[Minnesota has modified Model Rule 1.6 to read as follows:]

RULE 1.6. Confidentiality of Information

(a) Except when permitted under paragraph (b), a lawyer shall not knowingly:

(1) reveal a confidence or secret of a client;

(2) use a confidence or secret of a client to the disadvantage of the client;

(3) use a confidence or secret of a client for the advantage of the lawyer or a third person, unless the client consents after consultation.

(b) A lawyer may reveal:

(1) confidences or secrets with the consent of the client or clients affected, but only after consultation with them;

(2) confidences or secrets when permitted under the Rules of Professional Conduct or required by law or court order;

(3) the intention of a client to commit a crime and the information necessary to prevent a crime;

(4) confidences and secrets necessary to rectify the consequences of a client's criminal or fraudulent act in the furtherance of which the lawyer's services were used;

(5) confidences or secrets necessary to establish or collect a fee or to defend the lawyer or employees or associates against an accusation of wrongful conduct.

(c) A lawyer shall exercise reasonable care to prevent employees, associates and others whose services the lawyer utilizes from disclosing or using confidences or secrets of a client, except that a lawyer may reveal the information allowed by paragraph (b) through an employee.

(d) "Confidence" refers to information protected by the attorney-client privilege under applicable law, and "secret" refers to other information gained in the professional relationship that the

159

client has requested be held inviolate or the disclosure of which would be embarrassing or would be likely to be detrimental to the client.

COMMENT—1989

General

Both the fiduciary relationship existing between lawyer and client and the proper functioning of the legal system require the lawyer to preserve confidences and secrets of one who has employed or sought to employ the lawyer. A client must feel free to discuss whatever the client wishes with the lawyer and a lawyer must be equally free to obtain information beyond what the client volunteers. A lawyer should be fully informed of all the facts of the matter the lawyer is handling in order for the client to obtain the full advantage of our legal system. It is for the lawyer in the exercise of independent professional judgment to separate the relevant and important from the irrelevant and unimportant.

Observance of the lawyer's ethical obligation to hold inviolate the client's confidences and secrets not only facilitates the full development of facts essential to proper representation of the client but also encourages people to seek early legal assistance.

Authorized Disclosure

The obligation to protect confidences and secrets obviously does not preclude a lawyer from revealing information when the client consents after consultation, when necessary to perform professional employment, when permitted by the Rules of Professional Conduct or when required by law.

The confidentiality required under this rule should not allow a client to utilize the lawyer's services in committing a criminal or fraudulent act. A lawyer is permitted to reveal the intention of a client to commit a crime and the information necessary to prevent the crime. In addition, where the lawyer finds out, after the fact, that the lawyer's services were used by the client to commit a criminal or fraudulent act, the lawyer has discretion to reveal information necessary to rectify the consequences of the client's crime or fraud. A lawyer is not permitted, however, to disclose a client's criminal or fraudulent act committed prior to the client's retention of the lawyer's services.

Unless the client otherwise directs, a lawyer may disclose the client's affairs to partners or associates.

It is a matter of common knowledge that the normal operation of a law office exposes confidential professional information to non-lawyer employees of the office, particularly secretaries and those having access to the files; and this obligates a lawyer to exercise care in selecting and training employees so that the sanctity of all confidences and secrets of clients may be preserved.

If the obligation extends to two or more clients as to the same information, a lawyer should obtain the permission of all before revealing the information.

A lawyer must always be sensitive to the client's rights and wishes and act scrupulously in making decisions which may involve disclosure of information obtained in the professional relationship. Thus, in the absence of the client's consent after consultation, a lawyer should not associate another lawyer in handling a matter; nor, in the absence of consent, seek counsel from another lawyer if there is a reasonable possibility that the client's identity or confidences or secrets would be revealed to that lawyer. Both social amenities and professional duty should cause a lawyer to shun indiscreet conversations concerning clients.

Unless the client otherwise directs, it is not improper for a lawyer to give limited information from the lawyer's files to an outside agency necessary for statistical, bookkeeping, accounting, data processing, banking, printing, or other legitimate purposes, provided the lawyer exercises due care in selecting the agency and warns the agency that the information must be kept confidential.

Protecting Confidences

The attorney-client privilege is more limited than the lawyer's ethical obligation to guard the client's confidences and secrets. The ethical obligation, unlike the evidentiary privilege, exists without regard to the nature or source of information or the fact that others share the knowledge.

A lawyer should endeavor to act in a manner which preserves the evidentiary privilege; for example, the lawyer should avoid professional discussions in the presence of persons to whom the privilege does not extend. A lawyer owes an obligation to advise the client of the attorney-client privilege and timely to assert the privilege unless it is waived by the client.

Using Confidences or Secrets

A lawyer should not use information acquired in the course of the representation of a client to the client's disadvantage and a lawyer should not use, except with the client's consent after full disclosure, such information for the lawyer's own purposes.

Likewise, a lawyer should be diligent in efforts to prevent misuse of such information by employees and associates.

A lawyer should exercise care to prevent disclosure of confidences and secrets of one client to another and should accept no employment that might require such disclosure.

Former Client

The lawyer's obligation to preserve the client's confidences and secrets continues after termination of the employment. Thus, a lawyer should not attempt to sell a law practice as a going business because, among other reasons, to do so would involve disclosure of confidences and secrets.

A lawyer should also provide for the protection of the client's confidences and secrets following the termination of the practice of the lawyer, whether termination is due to death, disability or retirement. For example, a lawyer might provide for the client's personal papers to be returned to the client and for the lawyer's papers to be delivered to another lawyer or to be destroyed. In determining the method of disposition, the client's instructions and wishes should be a dominant consideration.

Texas Rule 1.05 *(modification of Model Rule 1.6)*

[Texas has modified Model Rule 1.6 (Confidentiality) to read as follows:]

RULE 1.05. Confidentiality of Information

(a) "Confidential information" includes both "privileged information" and "unprivileged client information." "Privileged information" refers to the information of a client protected by the lawyer-client privilege of Rule 503 of the Texas Rules of Evidence or of Rule 503 of the Texas Rules of Criminal Evidence or by the principles of attorney-client privilege governed by Rule 501 of the Federal Rules of Evidence for United States Courts and Magistrates. "Unprivileged client information" means all information relating to a client or furnished by the client, other than privileged information, acquired by the lawyer during the course of or by reason of the representation of the client.

(b) Except as permitted by paragraphs (c) and (d), or as required by paragraphs (e) and (h), a lawyer shall not knowingly:

(1) Reveal confidential information of a client or a former client to:

(i) a person that the client has instructed is not to receive the information; or

(ii) anyone else, other than the client, the client's representatives, or the members, associates, or employees of the lawyer's law firm.

(2) Use confidential information of a client to the disadvantage of the client unless the client consents after consultation.

(3) Use confidential information of a former client to the disadvantage of the former client after the representation is

162

concluded unless the former client consents after consultation or the confidential information has become generally known.

(4) Use privileged information of a client for the advantage of the lawyer or of a third person, unless the client consents after consultation.

(c) A lawyer may reveal confidential information:

(1) When the lawyer has been expressly authorized to do so in order to carry out the representation.

(2) When the client consents after consultation.

(3) To the client, the client's representatives, or the members, associates, and employees of the lawyer's firm, except when otherwise instructed by the client.

(4) When the lawyer has reason to believe it is necessary to do so in order to comply with a court order, a Texas Rule of Professional Conduct, or other law.

(5) To the extent reasonably necessary to enforce a claim or establish a defense on behalf of the lawyer in a controversy between the lawyer and the client.

(6) To establish a defense to a criminal charge, civil claim or disciplinary complaint against the lawyer or the lawyer's associates based upon conduct involving the client or the representation of the client.

(7) When the lawyer has reason to believe it is necessary to do so in order to prevent the client from committing a criminal or fraudulent act.

(8) To the extent revelation reasonably appears necessary to rectify the consequences of a client's criminal or fraudulent act in the commission of which the lawyer's services had been used.

(d) A lawyer also may reveal unprivileged client information:

(1) When impliedly authorized to do so in order to carry out the representation.

(2) When the lawyer has reason to believe it is necessary to do so in order to:

(i) carry out the representation effectively;

(ii) defend the lawyer or the lawyer's employees or associates against a claim of wrongful conduct;

(iii) respond to allegations in any proceeding concerning the lawyer's representation of the client; or

(iv) prove the services rendered to a client, or the reasonable value thereof, or both, in an action against another person or organization responsible for the payment of the fee for services rendered to the client.

(e) **When a lawyer has confidential information clearly establishing that a client is likely to commit a criminal or fraudulent act that is likely to result in death or substantial bodily harm to a person, the lawyer shall reveal confidential information to the extent revelation reasonably appears necessary to prevent the client from committing the criminal or fraudulent act.**

(f) **A lawyer shall reveal confidential information when required to do so by Rule 3.03(a)(2), 3.03(b), or by Rule 4.01(b).**

COMMENT

Confidentiality Generally

1.   Both the fiduciary relationship existing between lawyer and client and the proper functioning of the legal system require the preservation by the lawyer of confidential information of one who has employed or sought to employ the lawyer. Free discussion should prevail between lawyer and client in order for the lawyer to be fully informed and for the client to obtain the full benefit of the legal system. The ethical obligation of the lawyer to protect the confidential information of the client not only facilitates the proper representation of the client but also encourages potential clients to seek early legal assistance.

2.   Subject to the mandatory disclosure requirements of paragraphs (e) and (f) the lawyer generally should be required to maintain confidentiality of information acquired by the lawyer during the course of or by reason of the representation of the client. This principle involves an ethical obligation not to use the information to the detriment of the client or for the benefit of the lawyer or a third person. In regard to an evaluation of a matter affecting a client for use by a third person, see Rule 2.02.

3.   The principle of confidentiality is given effect not only in the Texas Rules of Professional Conduct but also in the law of evidence regarding the attorney-client privilege and in the law of agency. The attorney-client privilege, developed through many decades, provides the client a right to prevent certain confidential communications from being revealed by compulsion of law. Several sound exceptions to confidentiality have been developed in the evidence law of privilege. Exceptions exist in evidence law where the services of the lawyer were sought or used by a client in planning or committing a crime or fraud as well as where issues have arisen as to breach of duty by the lawyer or by the client to the other.

4.   Rule 1.05 reinforces the principles of evidence law relating to the attorney-client privilege. Rule 1.05 also furnishes considerable protection to other information falling outside the scope of the privilege. Rule 1.05 extends ethical protection generally to unprivileged information relating to the client or furnished by the client during the

course of or by reason of the representation of the client. In this respect Rule 1.05 accords with general fiduciary principles of agency.

5.   The requirement of confidentiality applies to government lawyers who may disagree with the policy goals that their representation is designed to advance.

Disclosure for Benefit of Client

6.   A lawyer may be expressly authorized to make disclosures to carry out the representation and generally is recognized as having implied-in-fact authority to make disclosures about a client when appropriate in carrying out the representation to the extent that the client's instructions do not limit that authority. In litigation, for example, a lawyer may disclose information by admitting a fact that cannot properly be disputed, or in negotiation by making a disclosure that facilitates a satisfactory conclusion. The effect of Rule 1.05 is to require the lawyer to invoke, for the client, the attorney-client privilege when applicable; but if the court improperly denies the privilege, under paragraph (c)(4) the lawyer may testify as ordered by the court or may test the ruling as permitted by Rule 3.04(d).

7.   In the course of a firm's practice, lawyers may disclose to each other and to appropriate employees information relating to a client, unless the client has instructed that particular information be confined to specified lawyers. Subparagraphs (b)(1) and (c)(3) continue these practices concerning disclosure of confidential information within the firm.

Use of Information

8.   Following sound principles of agency law, subparagraphs (b)(2) and (4) subject a lawyer to discipline for using information relating to the representation in a manner disadvantageous to the client or beneficial to the lawyer or a third person, absent the informed consent of the client. The duty not to misuse client information continues after the client-lawyer relationship has terminated. Therefore, the lawyer is forbidden by subparagraph (b)(3) to use, in absence of the client's informed consent, confidential information of the former client to the client's disadvantage, unless the information is generally known.

Discretionary Disclosure Adverse to Client

9.   In becoming privy to information about a client, a lawyer may foresee that the client intends serious and perhaps irreparable harm. To the extent a lawyer is prohibited from making disclosure, the interests of the potential victim are sacrificed in favor of preserving the client's information—usually unprivileged information—even though the client's purpose is wrongful. On the other hand, a client who knows or believes that a lawyer is required or permitted to disclose a client's wrongful purposes may be inhibited from revealing facts which

would enable the lawyer to counsel effectively against wrongful action. Rule 1.05 thus involves balancing the interests of one group of potential victims against those of another. The criteria provided by the Rule are discussed below.

10.   Rule 503(d)(1), Texas Rules of Civil Evidence (Tex.R.Civ.Evid.), and Rule 503(d)(1), Texas Rules of Criminal Evidence (Tex.R.Crim. Evid.), indicate the underlying public policy of furnishing no protection to client information where the client seeks or uses the services of the lawyer to aid in the commission of a crime or fraud. That public policy governs the dictates of Rule 1.05. Where the client is planning or engaging in criminal or fraudulent conduct or where the culpability of the lawyer's conduct is involved, full protection of client information is not justified.

11.   Several other situations must be distinguished. First, the lawyer may not counsel or assist a client in conduct that is criminal or fraudulent. See Rule 1.02(c). As noted in the Comment to that Rule, there can be situations where the lawyer may have to reveal information relating to the representation in order to avoid assisting a client's criminal or fraudulent conduct, and sub-paragraph (c)(4) permits doing so. A lawyer's duty under Rule 3.03(a) not to use false or fabricated evidence is a special instance of the duty prescribed in Rule 1.02(c) to avoid assisting a client in criminal or fraudulent conduct, and sub-paragraph (c)(4) permits revealing information necessary to comply with Rule 3.03(a) or (b). The same is true of compliance with Rule 4.01. See also paragraph (f).

12.   Second, the lawyer may have been innocently involved in past conduct by the client that was criminal or fraudulent. In such a situation the lawyer has not violated Rule 1.02(c), because to "counsel or assist" criminal or fraudulent conduct requires knowing that the conduct is of that character. Since the lawyer's services were made an instrument of the client's crime or fraud, the lawyer has a legitimate interest both in rectifying the consequences of such conduct and in avoiding charges that the lawyer's participation was culpable. Sub-paragraph (c)(6) and (8) give the lawyer professional discretion to reveal both unprivileged and privileged information in order to serve those interests. See paragraph (g). In view of Tex.R.Civ.Evid. Rule 503(d)(1), and Tex.R.Crim.Evid. 503(d)(1), however, rarely will such information be privileged.

13.   Third, the lawyer may learn that a client intends prospective conduct that is criminal or fraudulent. The lawyer's knowledge of the client's purpose may enable the lawyer to prevent commission of the prospective crime or fraud. When the threatened injury is grave, the lawyer's interest in preventing the harm may be more compelling than the interest in preserving confidentiality of information. As stated in subparagraph (c)(7), the lawyer has professional discretion, based on reasonable appearances, to reveal both privileged and unprivileged

information in order to prevent the client's commission of any criminal or fraudulent act. In some situations of this sort, disclosure is mandatory. See paragraph (e) and Comments 18–20.

14. The lawyer's exercise of discretion under paragraphs (c) and (d) involves consideration of such factors as the magnitude, proximity, and likelihood of the contemplated wrong, the nature of the lawyer's relationship with the client and with those who might be injured by the client, the lawyer's own involvement in the transaction, and factors that may extenuate the client's conduct in question. In any case, a disclosure adverse to the client's interest should be no greater than the lawyer believes necessary to the purpose. Although preventive action is permitted by paragraphs (c) and (d), failure to take preventive action does not violate those paragraphs. But see paragraphs (e) and (f). *Because these rules do not define standards of civil liability of lawyers for professional conduct, paragraphs (c) and (d) do not create a duty on the lawyer to make any disclosure and no civil liability is intended to arise from the failure to make such disclosure.*

15. A lawyer entitled to a fee necessarily must be permitted to prove the services rendered in an action to collect it, and this necessity is recognized by sub-paragraphs (c)(5) and (d)(2)(iv). This aspect of the rule, in regard to privileged information, expresses the principle that the beneficiary of a fiduciary relationship may not exploit the relationship to the detriment of the fiduciary. Any disclosure by the lawyer, however, should be as protective of the client's interests as possible.

16. If the client is an organization, a lawyer also should refer to Rule 1.12 in order to determine the appropriate conduct in connection with this Rule.

Client Under a Disability

17. In some situations, Rule 1.02(g) requires a lawyer representing a client under a disability to seek the appointment of a legal representative for the client or to seek other orders for the protection of the client. The client may or may not, in a particular matter, effectively consent to the lawyer's revealing to the court confidential information and facts reasonably necessary to secure the desired appointment or order. Nevertheless, the lawyer is authorized by paragraph (c)(4) to reveal such information in order to comply with Rule 1.02(g). See also paragraph 5, Comment to Rule 1.03.

Mandatory Disclosure Adverse to Client

18. Rule 1.05(e) and (f) place upon a lawyer professional obligations in certain situations to make disclosure in order to prevent certain serious crimes by a client or to prevent involvement by the lawyer in a client's crimes or frauds. Except when death or serious bodily harm is likely to result, a lawyer's obligation is to dissuade the

167

client from committing the crime or fraud or to persuade the client to take corrective action; see Rule 1.02(d) and (e).

19.   Because it is very difficult for a lawyer to know when a client's criminal or fraudulent purpose actually will be carried out, the lawyer is required by paragraph (e) to act only if the lawyer has information "clearly establishing" the likelihood of such acts and consequences.   If the information shows clearly that the client's contemplated crime or fraud is likely to result in death or serious injury, the lawyer must seek to avoid those lamentable results by revealing information necessary to prevent the criminal or fraudulent act.   When the threatened crime or fraud is likely to have the less serious result of substantial injury to the financial interests or property of another, the lawyer is not required to reveal preventive information but may do so in conformity to paragraph (c)(7).   See also paragraph (f); Rule 1.02(d) and (e);   and Rule 3.03(b) and (c).

20.   Although a violation of paragraph (e) will subject a lawyer to disciplinary action, the lawyer's decisions whether or how to act should not constitute grounds for discipline unless the lawyer's conduct in the light of those decisions was unreasonable under all existing circumstances as they reasonably appeared to the lawyer.   This construction necessarily follows from the fact that paragraph (e) bases the lawyer's affirmative duty to act on how the situation "reasonably appears" to the lawyer, while that imposed by paragraph (f) arises only when a lawyer "knows" that the lawyer's services have been misused by the client.   See also Rule 3.03(b).

Withdrawal

21.   If the lawyer's services will be used by the client in materially furthering a course of criminal or fraudulent conduct, the lawyer must withdraw, as stated in Rule 1.15(a)(1).   After withdrawal, a lawyer's conduct continues to be governed by Rule 1.05.   However, the lawyer's duties of disclosure under paragraph (e) of the Rule, insofar as such duties are mandatory, do not survive the end of the relationship even though disclosure remains permissible under paragraphs (6), (7), and (8) if the further requirements of such paragraph are met.   Neither this Rule nor Rule 1.15 prevents the lawyer from giving notice of the fact of withdrawal, and no rule forbids the lawyer to withdraw or disaffirm any opinion, document, affirmation, or the like.

22.   [Blank]

Other Rules

23.   Various other Texas Rules of Professional Conduct permit or require a lawyer to disclose information relating to the representation. See Rules 1.07, 1.12, 2.02, 3.03 and 4.01.   In addition to these provisions, a lawyer may be obligated by other provisions of statutes or other law to give information about a client.   Whether another provision of

law supersedes Rule 1.05 is a matter of interpretation beyond the scope of these Rules, but sub-paragraph (c)(4) protects the lawyer from discipline who acts on reasonable belief as to the effect of such laws.

Texas Rule 1.06 (modification of Model Rule 1.7)

[Texas has modified Model Rule 1.7 (Conflict of Interest) as follows:]

RULE 1.06. Conflict of Interest: General Rule

(a) A lawyer shall not represent opposing parties to the same litigation.

(b) In other situations and except to the extent permitted by paragraph (c), a lawyer shall not represent a person if the representation of that person:

(1) involves a substantially related matter in which that person's interests are materially and directly adverse to the interests of another client of the lawyer or the lawyer's firm; or

(2) reasonably appears to be or become adversely limited by the lawyer's or law firm's responsibilities to another client or to a third person or by the lawyer's or law firm's own interests.

(c) A lawyer may represent a client in the circumstances described in (b) if:

(1) the lawyer reasonably believes the representation of each client will not be materially affected; and

(2) each affected or potentially affected client consents to such representation after full disclosure of the existence, nature, implications, and possible adverse consequences of the common representation and the advantages involved, if any.

(d) A lawyer who has represented multiple parties in a matter shall not thereafter represent any of such parties in a dispute among the parties arising out of the matter, unless prior consent is obtained from all such parties to the dispute.

(e) If a lawyer has accepted representation in violation of this Rule, or if multiple representation properly accepted becomes improper under this Rule, the lawyer shall promptly withdraw from one or more representations to the extent necessary for any remaining representation not to be in violation of these Rules.

(f) If a lawyer would be prohibited by this Rule from engaging in particular conduct, no other lawyer while a member or associated with that lawyer's firm may engage in that conduct.

COMMENT:

Loyalty to a Client

1. Loyalty is an essential element in the lawyer's relationship to a client. An impermissible conflict of interest may exist before representation is undertaken, in which event the representation should be declined. If such a conflict arises after representation has been undertaken, the lawyer must take effective action to eliminate the conflict, including withdrawal if necessary to rectify the situation. See also Rule 1.16. When more than one client is involved and the lawyer withdraws because a conflict arises after representation, whether the lawyer may continue to represent any of the clients is determined by this Rule and Rules 1.05 and 1.09. See also Rule 1.07(c). Under this Rule, any conflict that prevents a particular lawyer from undertaking or continuing a representation of a client also prevents any other lawyer who is or becomes a member of or an associate with that lawyer's firm from doing so. See paragraph (f).

2. A fundamental principle recognized by paragraph (a) is that a lawyer may not represent opposing parties in litigation. The term "opposing parties" as used in this Rule contemplates a situation where a judgment favorable to one of the parties will directly impact unfavorably upon the other party. Moreover, as a general proposition loyalty to a client prohibits undertaking representation directly adverse to the representation of that client in a substantially related matter unless that client's fully informed consent is obtained and unless the lawyer reasonably believes that the lawyer's representation will be reasonably protective of that client's interests. Paragraphs (b) and (c) express that general concept.

Conflicts in Litigation

3. Paragraph (a) prohibits representation of opposing parties in litigation. Simultaneous representation of parties whose interests in litigation are not actually directly adverse but where the potential for conflict exists, such as co-plaintiffs or co-defendants, is governed by paragraph (b). An impermissible conflict may exist or develop by reason of substantial discrepancy in the parties' testimony, incompatibility in positions in relation to an opposing party or the fact that there are substantially different possibilities of settlement of the claims or liabilities in question. Such conflicts can arise in criminal cases as well as civil. The potential for conflict of interest in representing multiple defendants in a criminal case is so grave that ordinarily a lawyer should decline to represent more than one co-defendant. On the other hand, common representation of persons having similar interests is proper if the risk of adverse effect is minimal and the requirements of paragraph (b) are met. Compare Rule 1.07 involving intermediation between clients.

Conflict with Lawyer's Own Interests

4.   Loyalty to a client is impaired not only by the representation of opposing parties in situations within paragraphs (a) and (b)(1) but also in any situation when a lawyer may not be able to consider, recommend or carry out an appropriate course of action for one client because of the lawyer's own interests or responsibilities to others.   The conflict in effect forecloses alternatives that would otherwise be available to the client.   Paragraph (b)(2) addresses such situations.   A potential possible conflict does not itself necessarily preclude the representation.   The critical questions are the likelihood that a conflict exists or will eventuate and, if it does, whether it will materially and adversely affect the lawyer's independent professional judgment in considering alternatives or foreclose courses of action that reasonably should be pursued on behalf of the client.   It is for the client to decide whether the client wishes to accommodate the other interest involved.   However, the client's consent to the representation by the lawyer of another whose interests are directly adverse is insufficient unless the lawyer also believes that there will be no materially adverse effect upon the interests of either client.   See paragraph (c).

5.   The lawyer's own interests should not be permitted to have adverse effect on representation of a client, even where paragraph (b)(2) is not violated.   For example, a lawyer's need for income should not lead the lawyer to undertake matters that cannot be handled competently and at a reasonable fee.   See Rules 1.01 and 1.04.   If the probity of a lawyer's own conduct in a transaction is in question, it may be difficult for the lawyer to give a client detached advice.   A lawyer should not allow related business interests to affect representation, for example, by referring clients to an enterprise in which the lawyer has an undisclosed interest.

Meaning of Directly Adverse

6.   Within the meaning of Rule 1.06(b), the representation of one client is "directly adverse" to the representation of another client if the lawyer's independent judgment on behalf of a client or the lawyer's ability or willingness to consider, recommend or carry out a course of action will be or is reasonably likely to be adversely affected by the lawyer's representation of, or responsibilities to, the other client.   The dual representation also is directly adverse if the lawyer reasonably appears to be called upon to espouse adverse positions in the same matter or a related matter.   On the other hand, simultaneous representation in unrelated matters of clients whose interests are only generally adverse, such as competing economic enterprises, does not constitute the representation of directly adverse interests.   Even when neither paragraph (a) nor (b) is applicable, a lawyer should realize that a business rivalry or personal differences between two clients or potential clients may be so important to one or both that one or the other would

consider it contrary to its interests to have the same lawyer as its rival even in unrelated matters; and in those situations a wise lawyer would forego the dual representation.

Full Disclosure and Informed Consent

7. A client under some circumstances may consent to representation notwithstanding a conflict or potential conflict. However, as indicated in paragraph (c)(1), when a disinterested lawyer would conclude that the client should not agree to the representation under the circumstances, the lawyer involved should not ask for such agreement or provide representation on the basis of the client's consent. When more than one client is involved, the question of conflict must be resolved as to each client. Moreover, there may be circumstances where it is impossible to make the full disclosure necessary to obtain informed consent. For example, when the lawyer represents different clients in related matters and one of the clients refuses to consent to the disclosure necessary to permit the other client to make an informed decision, the lawyer cannot properly ask the latter to consent.

8. Disclosure and consent are not formalities. Disclosure sufficient for sophisticated clients may not be sufficient to permit less sophisticated clients to provide fully informed consent. While it is not required that the disclosure and consent be in writing, it would be prudent for the lawyer to provide potential dual clients with at least a written summary of the considerations disclosed.

9. In certain situations, such as in the preparation of loan papers or the preparation of a partnership agreement, a lawyer might have properly undertaken multiple representation and be confronted subsequently by a dispute among those clients in regard to that matter. Paragraph (d) forbids the representation of any of those parties in regard to that dispute unless informed consent is obtained from all of the parties to the dispute who had been represented by the lawyer in that matter.

10. A lawyer may represent parties having antagonistic positions on a legal question that has arisen in different cases, unless representation of either client would be adversely affected. Thus, it is ordinarily not improper to assert such positions in cases pending in different trial courts, but it may be improper to do so in cases pending at the same time in an appellate court.

11. Ordinarily, it is not advisable for a lawyer to act as advocate against a client the lawyer represents in some other matter, even if the other matter is wholly unrelated and even if paragraphs (a), (b), and (d) are not applicable. However, there are circumstances in which a lawyer may act as advocate against a client, for a lawyer is free to do so unless this Rule or another rule of the Texas Rules of Professional Conduct would be violated. For example, a lawyer representing an enterprise with diverse operations may accept employment as an advo-

cate against the enterprise in a matter unrelated to any matter being handled for the enterprise if the representation of one client is not directly adverse to the representation of the other client. The propriety of concurrent representation can depend on the nature of the litigation. For example, a suit charging fraud entails conflict to a degree not involved in a suit for declaratory judgment concerning statutory interpretation.

Interest of Person Paying for a Lawyer's Service

12. A lawyer may be paid from a source other than the client, if the client is informed of that fact and consents and the arrangement does not compromise the lawyer's duty of loyalty to the client. See Rule 1.08(e). For example, when an insurer and its insured have conflicting interests in a matter arising from a liability insurance agreement, and the insurer is required to provide special counsel for the insured, the arrangement should assure the special counsel's professional independence. So also, when a corporation and its directors or employees are involved in a controversy in which they have conflicting interests, the corporation may provide funds for separate legal representation of the directors or employees, if the clients consent after consultation and the arrangement ensures the lawyer's professional independence.

Non-litigation Conflict Situations

13. Conflicts of interest in contexts other than litigation sometimes may be difficult to assess. Relevant factors in determining whether there is potential for adverse effect include the duration and intimacy of the lawyer's relationship with the client or clients involved, the functions being performed by the lawyer, the likelihood that actual conflict will arise and the likely prejudice to the client from the conflict if it does arise. The question is often one of proximity and degree.

14. For example, a lawyer may not represent multiple parties to a negotiation whose interests are fundamentally antagonistic to each other, but common representation may be permissible where the clients are generally aligned in interest even though there is some difference of interest among them.

15. Conflict questions may also arise in estate planning and estate administration. A lawyer may be called upon to prepare wills for several family members, such as husband and wife, and, depending upon the circumstances, a conflict of interest may arise. In estate administration it may be unclear whether the client is the fiduciary or is the estate or trust, including its beneficiaries. The lawyer should make clear the relationship to the parties involved.

16. A lawyer for a corporation or other organization who is also a member of its board of directors should determine whether the responsibilities of the two roles may conflict. The lawyer may be called on to

advise the corporation in matters involving actions of the directors. Consideration should be given to the frequency with which such situations may arise, the potential intensity of the conflict, the effect of the lawyer's resignation from the board and the possibility of the corporation's obtaining legal advice from another lawyer in such situations. If there is material risk that the dual role will compromise the lawyer's independence of professional judgment, the lawyer should not serve as a director.

Conflict Charged by an Opposing Party

17. Raising questions of conflict of interest is primarily the responsibility of the lawyer undertaking the representation. In litigation, a court may raise the question when there is reason to infer that the lawyer has neglected the responsibility. In a criminal case, inquiry by the court is generally required when a lawyer represents multiple defendants. Where the conflict is such as clearly to call in question the fair or efficient administration of justice, opposing counsel may properly raise the question. Such an objection should be viewed with great caution, however, for it can be misused as a technique of harassment. See Preamble: Scope.

18. Except when the absolute prohibition of this rule applies or in litigation when a court passes upon issues of conflicting interests in determining a question of disqualification of counsel, resolving questions of conflict of interests may require decisions by all affected clients as well as by the lawyer.

Utah Rule 1.7(c)

[Utah has added section (c) to Model Rule 1.7]

RULE 1.7. Conflict of Interest: General Rule

(c) A lawyer shall not simultaneously represent the interests of adverse parties in separate matters, unless:

(1) The lawyer reasonably believes the representation of each will not be adversely affected; and

(2) Each client consents after consultation.

District of Columbia Rule 1.8

[The District of Columbia has added subsection (i) to Model Rule 1.8]

RULE 1.8 Conflict of Interest: Prohibited Transactions

* * *

(i) A lawyer shall not impose a lien upon any part of a client's files, except upon the lawyer's own work product, and then only to the extent that the work product has not been paid for. This work product exception shall not apply when the client has become unable to pay, or when withholding the lawyer's work

174

product would present a significant risk to the client of irreparable harm.

COMMENT:

* * *

Liens on Lawyer's Work Product

[8]   Rule 1.16(d) requires a lawyer to surrender papers and property to which the client is entitled when representation of the client terminates.   Paragraph (i) of this Rule states a narrow exception to Rule 1.16(d): a lawyer may retain the lawyer's own work product if the client has not paid for the work.   However, if the client has paid for the work product, the client is entitled to receive it, even if the client has not previously seen or received a copy of the work product.   Furthermore, the lawyer may not retain the work product for which the client has not paid, if the client has become unable to pay or if withholding the work product might irreparably harm the client's interest.

[9]   Under Rule 1.16(d), for example, a lawyer would be required to return all papers received from a client, such as birth certificates, wills, tax returns, or "green cards."   Rule 1.8(i) does not permit retention of such papers to secure payment of any fee due.   Only the lawyer's own work product—results of factual investigations, legal research and analysis, and similar materials generated by the lawyer's own effort—could be retained.   (The term "work product" as used in paragraph (i) is not limited to materials falling within the "work product doctrine," but includes any material generated by the lawyer whether or not in connection with pending or anticipated litigation.)   And a lawyer could not withhold all of the work product merely because a portion of the lawyer's fees had not been paid.

[10]   There are situations in which withholding the work product would not be permissible because of irreparable harm to the client. The possibility of involuntary incarceration or criminal conviction constitutes one category of irreparable harm.   The realistic possibility that a client might irretrievably lose a significant right or become subject to a significant liability because of the withholding of the work product constitutes another category of irreparable harm.   On the other hand, the mere fact that the client might have to pay another lawyer to replicate the work product does not, standing alone, constitute irreparable harm.   These examples are merely indicative of the meaning of the term "irreparable harm," and are not exhaustive.

Illinois Rule 1.5

[Illinois has added the following provision to Model Rule 1.8]

RULE 1.5   Conflict of Interest: Prohibited Transactions

* * *

(h) A lawyer shall not enter into an agreement with a client or former client limiting or purporting to limit the right of the client or former client to file or pursue any complaint before the Attorney Registration and Disciplinary Commission.

Indiana Rule 1.8(k)

[Indiana has added the following provision to Model Rule 1.8.]

RULE 1.8　Conflict of Interest: Prohibited Transactions

* * *

(k) A part-time prosecutor or deputy prosecutor authorized by statute to otherwise engage in the practice of law shall refrain from representing a private client in any matter wherein exists an issue upon which said prosecutor has statutory prosecutorial authority or responsibilities. This restriction is not intended to prohibit representation in tort cases in which investigation and any prosecution of infractions has terminated, nor to prohibit representation in family law matters involving no issue subject to prosecutorial authority or responsibilities. Upon a prior, express written limitation of responsibility to exclude prosecutorial authority in matters related to family law, a part-time deputy prosecutor may fully represent private clients in cases involving family law.

Minnesota Rule 1.8(e)(3)

[Minnesota has added the following provision to Model Rule 1.8(e):]

RULE 1.8　Conflict of Interest: Prohibited Transactions

* * *

(e) A lawyer shall not provide financial assistance to a client in connection with pending or contemplated litigation, except that:

* * *

(3) a lawyer may guarantee a loan reasonably needed to enable the client to withstand delay in litigation that would otherwise put substantial pressure on the client to settle a case because of financial hardship rather than on the merits, provided the client remains ultimately liable for repayment of the loan without regard to the outcome of the litigation and, further provided, that no promise of such financial assistance was made to the client by the lawyer, or by another in the lawyer's behalf, prior to the employment of that lawyer by that client.

Texas Rule 1.09 (Modification of Model Rule 1.9)

[Texas has modified Rule 1.9 (Former Client Conflicts) as follows:]

RULE 1.09   Conflict of Interest: Former Client

(a) Without prior consent, a lawyer who personally has formerly represented a client in a matter shall not thereafter represent another person in a matter adverse to the former client:

(1) if it is the same or a substantially related matter;

(2) in which such other person questions the validity of the lawyer's services or work product for the former client; or

(3) if the representation in reasonable probability will involve a violation of Rule 1.05.

(b) Except to the extent authorized by Rule 1.10, when lawyers are or have become members of or associated with a firm, none of them shall knowingly represent a client if any one of them practicing alone would be prohibited from doing so by paragraph (a).

(c) When the association of a lawyer with a firm has terminated, the lawyers who were then associated with that lawyer shall not knowingly represent a client if the lawyer whose association with that firm has terminated would be prohibited from doing so by paragraph (a)(1) or if the representation in reasonable probability will involve a violation of Rule 1.05.

COMMENT:

1. Rule 1.09 addresses the circumstances in which a lawyer in private practice, and other lawyers who were, are or become members of or associated with a firm in which that lawyer practiced or practices, may represent a client against a former client of that lawyer or the lawyer's former firm. Whether a lawyer, or that lawyer's present or former firm, is prohibited from representing a client in a matter by reason of the lawyer's successive government and private employment is governed by Rule 1.10 rather than by this Rule.

2. Paragraph (a) concerns the situation where a lawyer once personally represented a client and now wishes to represent a second client against that former client. Whether such a personal attorney-client relationship existed involves questions of both fact and law that are beyond the scope of these Rules. See Preamble: Scope. Among the relevant factors, however, would be how the former representation actually was conducted within the firm; the nature and scope of the former client's contacts with the firm (including any restrictions the client may have placed on the dissemination of confidential information within the firm); and the size of the firm.

177

3.   Although paragraph (a) does not absolutely prohibit a lawyer from representing a client against a former client, it does provide that the latter representation is improper if any of three circumstances exists, except with prior consent. The first prohibition is against representation adverse to a former client if it is the same or a substantially related matter. The second circumstance is that the lawyer may not represent a client who questions the validity of the lawyer's services or work product for the former client. Thus, for example, a lawyer who drew a will leaving a substantial portion of the testator's property to a designated beneficiary would violate paragraph (a) by representing the testator's heirs at law in an action seeking to overturn the will.

4.   Paragraph (a)'s third limitation on undertaking a representation against a former client is that it may not be done if there is a "reasonable probability" that the representation would cause the lawyer to violate the obligations owed the former client under Rule 1.05. Thus, for example, if there were a reasonable probability that the subsequent representation would involve either an unauthorized disclosure of confidential information under Rule 1.05(b)(1) or an improper use of such information to the disadvantage of the former client under Rule 1.05(b)(3), that representation would be improper under paragraph (a). Whether such a reasonable probability exists in any given case will be a question of fact.

5.   Paragraph (b) extends paragraph (a)'s limitations on an individual lawyer's freedom to undertake a representation against that lawyer's former client to all other lawyers who are or become members of or associated with the firm in which that lawyer is practicing. Thus, for example, if a client severs the attorney-client relationship with a lawyer who remains in a firm, the entitlement of that individual lawyer to undertake a representation against that former client is governed by paragraph (a); and all other lawyers who are or become members of or associated with that lawyer's firm are treated in the same manner by paragraph (b). Similarly, if a lawyer severs his or her association with a firm and that firm retains as a client a person whom the lawyer personally represented while with the firm, that lawyer's ability thereafter to undertake a representation against that client is governed by paragraph (a); and all other lawyers who are or become members of or associates with that lawyer's new firm are treated in the same manner by paragraph (b).

6.   Paragraph (c) addresses the situation of former partners or associates of a lawyer who once had represented a client when the relationship between the former partners or associates and the lawyer has been terminated. In that situation, the former partners or associates are prohibited from questioning the validity of such lawyer's work product and from undertaking representation which in reasonable probability will involve a violation of Rule 1.05. Such a violation could occur, for example, when the former partners or associates retained

materials in their files from the earlier representation of the client that, if disclosed or used in connection with the subsequent representation, would violate Rule 1.05(b)(1) or (b)(3).

7. Thus, the effect of paragraphs (b) and (c) is to extend any inability of a particular lawyer under paragraph (a) to undertake a representation against a former client to all other lawyers who are or become members of or associated with any firm in which that lawyer is practicing. Should those other lawyers cease to be members of the same firm as the lawyer affected by paragraph (a) without themselves coming within its restrictions, they thereafter may undertake the representation against the lawyer's former client unless prevented from doing so by some other of these Rules.

8. Although not required to do so by Rule 1.05 or this Rule, some courts, as a procedural decision, disqualify a lawyer for representing a present client against a former client when the subject matter of the present representation is so closely related to the subject matter of the prior representation that confidences obtained from the former client might be useful in the representation of the present client. See Comment 17 to Rule 1.06. This so-called "substantial relationship" test is defended by asserting that to require a showing that confidences of the first client were in fact used for the benefit of the subsequent client as a condition to procedural disqualification would cause disclosure of the confidences that the court seeks to protect. A lawyer is not subject to discipline under Rule 1.05(b)(1), (3), or (4), however, unless the protected information is actually used. Likewise, a lawyer is not subject to discipline under this Rule unless the new representation by the lawyer in reasonable probability would result in a violation of those provisions.

9. Whether the "substantial relationship" test will continue to be employed as a standard for procedural disqualification is a matter beyond the scope of these Rules. See Preamble: Scope. The possibility that such a disqualification might be sought by the former client or granted by a court, however, is a matter that could be of substantial importance to the present client in deciding whether or not to retain or continue to employ a particular lawyer or law firm as its counsel. Consequently, a lawyer should disclose those possibilities, as well as their potential consequences for the representation, to the present client as soon as the lawyer becomes aware of them; and the client then should be allowed to decide whether or not to obtain new counsel. See Rules 1.03(b) and 1.06(b).

10. This Rule is primarily for the protection of clients and its protections can be waived by them. A waiver is effective only if there is consent after disclosure of the relevant circumstances, including the lawyer's past or intended role on behalf of each client, as appropriate. See Comments 7 and 8 to Rule 1.06.

Utah Rule 1.9(a)

[Utah has modified Model Rule 1.9(a) as follows:]

RULE 1.9   Conflict of Interest: Former Client

A lawyer who has formerly represented a client in a matter shall not thereafter:

(a) Represent another person in the same or a substantially factually related matter in which that person's interests are materially adverse to the interests of the former client unless the former client consents after consultation; or

(b) Use information relating to the representation to the disadvantage of the former client except as Rule 1.6 would permit with respect to a client or when the information has become generally known.

COMMENT:

After termination of a client-lawyer relationship, a lawyer may not represent another client except in conformity with this Rule. The principles in Rule 1.7 determine whether the interests of the present and former client are adverse. Thus, a lawyer could not properly seek to rescind on behalf of a new client a contract drafted on behalf of the former client. So also a lawyer who has prosecuted an accused person could not properly represent the accused in a subsequent civil action against the government concerning the same transaction.

The scope of a "matter" for purposes of Rule 1.9(a) may depend on the facts of a particular situation or transaction. The lawyer's involvement in a matter can also be a question of degree. When a lawyer has been directly involved in a specific transaction, subsequent representation of other clients with materially adverse interests clearly is prohibited. On the other hand, a lawyer who recurrently handled a type of problem for a former client is not precluded from later representing another client in a wholly distinct problem of that type even though the subsequent representation involves a position adverse to the prior client. Similar considerations can apply to the reassignment of military lawyers between defense and prosecution functions within the same military jurisdiction. The underlying question is whether the lawyer was so involved in the matter that the subsequent representation can be justly regarded as a changing of sides in the matter in question.

Information acquired by the lawyer in the course of representing a client may not subsequently be used by the lawyer to the disadvantage of the client. However, the fact that a lawyer has once served a client does not preclude the lawyer from using generally known information about the client when later representing another client.

Disqualification from subsequent representation is for the protection of clients and can be waived by them. A waiver is effective only if there is disclosure of the circumstances, including the lawyer's intended role in behalf of the new client.

With regard to an opposing party's raising a question of conflict of interest, see Comment to Rule 1.7. With regard to disqualification of a firm with which a lawyer is associated, see Rule 1.10.

District of Columbia Rule 1.11

[The District of Columbia has added the following provisions to Model Rule 1.11]

RULE 1.11 Successive Government and Private Employment

* * * *

(d) Except as provided in paragraph (e), when any of counsel, lawyer, partner, or associate of a lawyer personally disqualified under paragraph (a) accepts employment in connection with a matter giving rise to the personal disqualification, the following notifications shall be required:

(1) The personally disqualified lawyer shall submit to the public department or agency by which the lawyer was formerly employed and serve on each other party to any pertinent proceeding a signed document attesting that during the period of disqualification the personally disqualified lawyer will not participate in any manner in the matter or the representation, will not discuss the matter or the representation with any partner, associate, or of counsel lawyer, and will not share in any fees for the matter or the representation.

(2) At least one affiliated lawyer shall submit to the same department or agency and serve on the same parties a signed document attesting that all affiliated lawyers are aware of the requirement that the personally disqualified lawyer be screened from participating in or discussing the matter or the representation and describing the procedures being taken to screen the personally disqualified lawyer.

(e) If a client requests in writing that the fact and subject matter of a representation subject to paragraph (d) not be disclosed by submitting the signed statements referred to in paragraph (d), such statements shall be prepared concurrently with undertaking the representation and filed with bar counsel under seal. If at any time thereafter the fact and subject matter of the representation are disclosed to the public or become a part of the public record, the signed statements previously prepared shall be promptly submitted as required by paragraph (d).

(f) Signed documents filed pursuant to paragraph (d) shall be available to the public, except to the extent that a lawyer submitting a signed document demonstrates to the satisfaction of the public department or agency upon which such documents are

served that public disclosure is inconsistent with Rule 1.6 or provisions of law.

New Hampshire Rule 1.11A

[New Hampshire has added the following provision to address the conduct of lawyer officials:]

RULE 1.11A   Conduct of Lawyer–Officials

(a) **Definitions.** As used in this rule:

(1) lawyer-official means a lawyer actively engaged in the practice of law, who is a member of the governmental body;

(2) government body means any state or local governmental agency, board, body, council or commission; and

(3) interest means a direct, personal and pecuniary interest, individually or on a client's behalf, in a matter which is under consideration by the governmental body of which the lawyer-official is a member.

(b) No lawyer-official shall:

(1) participate in any hearing, debate, discussion or vote, or in any manner otherwise attempt to influence the outcome of a matter in which he or she has an interest;

(2) utilize information obtained in such capacity for his or her own personal benefit or that of his or her clients or the clients of the firm with which the lawyer-official is associated;

(3) appear on behalf of a client before any governmental body of which the lawyer-official is a member or whose members have been appointed by the governmental body of which the lawyer-official is a member;

(4) accept anything of value from any person or organization when the lawyer-official knows or reasonably should know that the offer is for the purpose of influencing the lawyer-official's actions or decisions;

(5) use his or her official position to influence or to attempt to influence any governmental body to act in favor of the lawyer-official or the lawyer-official's clients or clients of the firm with which the lawyer-official is associated.

(c) Other lawyers in the firm with which the lawyer-official is associated may not appear on behalf of clients before the governmental body of which the lawyer-official is a member, or any governmental body whose members have been appointed by the body of which the lawyer-official is a member, unless the lawyer-official publicly disqualifies himself or herself and refrains from participation in the matter in accordance with paragraph (b)(1) of this Rule, and otherwise conducts himself or herself with respect to the matter in accordance with paragraph (b) of this Rule.

Montana Rule 1.17

[Montana has added Rule 1.17 which has no counterpart in the Model Rules]

RULE 1.17 Government Employment

An attorney employed by a department of the State of Montana or municipality on a part-time or fee basis shall not accept other employment during the course of which it would be possible to use or otherwise rely on information obtained by reason of government employment that is injurious, confidential or privileged and not otherwise discoverable.

COUNSELLOR

Oregon Rule DR 5–106 *(Modification to Model Rule 2.2)*

[Oregon has modified Model Rule 2.2 to read as follows:]

DR 5–106. Mediation

(A) A lawyer may act as a mediator for multiple parties in any matter if:

(1) The lawyer clearly informs the parties of the lawyer's role and they consent to this arrangement; and

(2) The lawyer gives advice to a party only in the presence of all parties in the matter.

(B) A lawyer serving as a mediator may draft a settlement agreement but must advise and encourage the parties to seek independent legal advice before executing it.

(C) A lawyer serving as a mediator may not act on behalf of any party in court nor represent one party against the other in any related legal proceeding.

(D) A lawyer shall withdraw as mediator if any of the parties so request, or if any of the conditions stated in DR 5–106(A) are no longer satisfied. Upon withdrawal, the lawyer shall not continue to act on behalf of any of the parties in the matter that was the subject of the mediation.

ADVOCATE

Wyoming Rule 3.1

[Wyoming has modified Model Rule 3.1 to read as follows:]

RULE 3.1 Meritorious Claims and Contentions

A lawyer shall not bring or defend a proceeding, or assert or controvert an issue therein, unless there is a basis for doing so that is not frivolous, which includes a good faith argument for an extension, modification or reversal of existing law. A lawyer for the defendant in a criminal proceeding, or the respondent in a proceeding that could result in incarceration, may nevertheless so defend the proceeding as to require that every element of the case be established. The signature of an attorney constitutes a certificate by him that he has read the pleading, motion, or other court document; that to the best of his knowledge, information, and belief, formed after reasonable inquiry, it is well grounded in fact and is warranted by existing law or a good faith argument for the extension, modification, or reversal of existing law; and that it is not interposed for any improper purpose such as to harass or to cause unnecessary delay or needless increase in the cost of litigation.

COMMENT:

[1] The advocate has a duty to use legal procedure for the fullest benefit of the client's cause, but also a duty not to abuse legal procedure. The law, both procedural and substantive, establishes the limits within which an advocate may proceed. However, the law is not always clear and never is static. Accordingly, in determining the proper scope of advocacy, account must be taken of the law's ambiguities and potential for change.

[2] The filing of an action, defense or other document in court is not frivolous merely because the facts have not first been fully substantiated or because the lawyer expects to develop vital evidence by discovery. Such action is not frivolous even though the lawyer believes that the client's position ultimately will not prevail. The action is frivolous, however, if the client or attorney desires to have the action taken primarily for the purpose of harassing, delaying or causing unnecessary expense or if the lawyer is unable either to make a good faith argument on the merits of the action taken or to support the action taken by a good faith argument for an extension, modification or reversal of existing law. The last sentence of Rule 3.1 is based on Rule 11 of the Federal Rules of Civil Procedure. It imposes an affirmative duty on an advocate to make reasonable inquiry, both as to the facts and law, before filing a pleading or other court document. A violation subjects the lawyer to discipline.

Kansas Rule 3.5

[Kansas has modified Model Rule 3.5 to read as follows:]

RULE 3.5 Impartiality and Decorum of the Tribunal

A lawyer shall not:

(a) give or lend anything of value to a judge, official, or employee of a tribunal except as permitted by Section C(4) of Canon 5 of the Code of Judicial Conduct as it may, from time to time be adopted in Kansas, nor may a lawyer attempt to improperly influence a judge, official or employee of a tribunal, but a lawyer may make a contribution to the campaign fund of a candidate for judicial office in conformity with Section B(2) under Canon 7 of the Code of Judicial Conduct;

(b) communicate or cause another to communicate with a member of a jury or the venire from which the jury will be selected about the matters under consideration other than in the course of official proceedings until after the discharge of the jury from further consideration of the case;

(c) communicate or cause another to communicate as to the merits of a cause with a judge or official before whom an adversary proceeding is pending except:

(1) in the course of official proceedings in the cause;

(2) in writing, if the lawyer promptly delivers a copy of the writing to opposing counsel or to the adverse party if unrepresented;

(3) orally upon adequate notice to opposing counsel or the adverse party if unrepresented;

(4) as otherwise authorized by law or court rule;

(d) engage in undignified or discourteous conduct degrading to a tribunal.

KANSAS COMMENT:

Rule 3.5 in the proposed Model Rules as adopted by the ABA has been substantially modified to include more specific guidelines and prohibitions such as were included in the Model Code. The reason for this is that the Kansas committee felt that existing disciplinary rules, 7.106(C)(6), 7.108, 7.109, 7.110 were more specific and preferable in many respects to the proposed model rule. Model Rule 3.5 prohibits a lawyer from seeking to influence a judge, juror, prospective juror or other official by means prohibited by law. The Kansas committee felt that this is too narrow a prohibition and would permit some things that should not be permitted. The committee has reimposed the absolute prohibition of DR 7–110(A) upon a lawyer giving or lending anything of value to a judge or official; except as permitted by the Canons of Judicial Ethics. In other words, a lawyer may ethically give what a judge may ethically receive. It was felt that such a *per se* rule is preferable to one that would require proof that the gift or loan was prompted by an attempt to influence the official.

Similarly, it was felt by the Kansas committee that the more specific provisions found in DR 7–108 regarding communication with jurors was preferable in that they give more guidance to the lawyer as to what communications are permitted and what communications are not permitted and further would give more guidance to the disciplinary authority as to when a violation had been committed.

Section (c) of the Model Rule prohibited conduct intended to disrupt a tribunal and, therefore, impliedly would authorize undignified or discourteous conduct degrading to a tribunal, prohibited under DR 7–106(C)(6), unless the intent to disrupt is established. The Kansas committee is of the opinion that standards of lawyer conduct in the courtroom should not be lowered as the model rule would appear to do.

TRANSACTIONS WITH PERSONS OTHER THAN CLIENTS

Louisiana Rule 4.2

[Louisiana has modified Model Rule 4.2 to read as follows:]

RULE 4.2 Communication With Person Represented by Counsel

In representing a client, a lawyer shall not communicate about the subject of the representation with a party the lawyer knows to be represented by another lawyer in the matter, unless the lawyer has the consent of the other lawyer or is authorized by law to do so. A lawyer shall not effect the prohibited communication through a third person, including the lawyer's client.

New Mexico Rule 16–402 (Modification of Model Rule 4.2)

[New Mexico has modified Model Rule 4.2 to read as follows:]

RULE 16–402. Communication With Person Represented by Counsel

In representing a client, a lawyer shall not communicate about the subject of the representation with a party the lawyer knows to be represented by another lawyer in the matter, unless the lawyer has the consent of the other lawyer or is authorized by law to do so. Except for persons having a managerial responsibility on behalf of the organization, an attorney is not prohibited from communicating directly with employees of a corporation, partnership or other entity about the subject matter of the representation even though the corporation, partnership or entity itself is represented by counsel.

Texas Rule 4.02 (Modification of Model Rule 4.2)

[Texas has modified Model Rule 4.2 as follows:]

RULE 4.02. Communication With One Represented by Counsel

(a) In representing a client, a lawyer shall not communicate or cause or encourage another to communicate about the subject of the representation with a person, organization or entity of government the lawyer knows to be represented by another lawyer regarding that subject, unless the lawyer has the consent of the other lawyer or is authorized by law to do so.

(b) In representing a client a lawyer shall not communicate or cause another to communicate about the subject of representation with a person or organization a lawyer knows to be employed or retained for the purpose of conferring with or advising another lawyer about the subject of the representation, unless the lawyer has the consent of the other lawyer or is authorized by law to do so.

(c) For the purpose of this rule, "organization or entity of government" includes: (1) those persons presently having a managerial responsibility with an organization or entity of government that relates to the subject of the representation, or (2) those persons presently employed by such organization or entity and whose act or omission in connection with the subject of representation may make the organization or entity of government vicariously liable for such act or omission.

(d) When a person, organization, or entity of government that is represented by a lawyer in a matter seeks advice regarding that matter from another lawyer, the second lawyer is not prohibited by paragraph (a) from giving such advice without notifying or seeking consent of the first lawyer.

COMMENT:

1. Paragraph (a) of this Rule is directed at efforts to circumvent the lawyer-client relationship existing between other persons, organizations or entities of government and their respective counsel. It prohibits communications that in form are between a lawyer's client and another person, organization or entity of government represented by counsel where, because of the lawyer's involvement in devising and controlling their content, such communications in substance are between the lawyer and the represented person, organization or entity of government.

2. Paragraph (a) does not, however, prohibit communication between a lawyer's client and persons, organizations, or entities of government represented by counsel, as long as the lawyer does not cause or encourage the communication without the consent of the lawyer for the other party. Consent may be implied as well as expressed, as, for example, where the communication occurs in the form of a private placement memorandum or similar document that obviously is intended for multiple recipients and that normally is furnished directly to persons, even if known to be represented by counsel. Similarly, that paragraph does not impose a duty on a lawyer to affirmatively discourage communication between the lawyer's client and other represented persons, organizations or entities of government. Furthermore, it does not prohibit client communications concerning matters outside the subject of the representation with any such person, organization, or entity of government. Finally, it does not prohibit a lawyer from

187

furnishing a "second opinion" in a matter to one requesting such opinion, nor from discussing employment in the matter if requested to do so.   But see Rule 7.02.

3.   Paragraph (b) of this Rule provides that unless authorized by law, experts employed or retained by a lawyer for a particular matter should not be contacted by opposing counsel regarding that matter without the consent of the lawyer who retained them.   However, certain governmental agents or employees such as police may be contacted due to their obligations to the public at large.

4.   In the case of an organization or entity of government, this Rule prohibits communications by a lawyer for one party concerning the subject of the representation with persons having a managerial responsibility on behalf of the organization that relates to the subject of the representation and with those persons presently employed by such organization or entity whose act or omission may make the organization or entity vicariously liable for the matter at issue, without the consent of the lawyer for the organization or entity of government involved.   This Rule is based on the presumption that such persons are so closely identified with the interests of the organization or entity of government that its lawyers will represent them as well.   If, however, such an agent or employee is represented in the matter by his or her own counsel that presumption is inapplicable.   In such cases, the consent by that counsel to communicate will be sufficient for purposes of this Rule.   Compare Rule 3.04(f).   Moreover, this Rule does not prohibit a lawyer from contacting a former employee of a represented organization or entity of a government, nor from contacting a person presently employed by such an organization or entity whose conduct is not a matter at issue but who might possess knowledge concerning the matter at issue.

Minnesota Rule 4.3

[Minnesota has modified Model Rule 4.3 to read as follows:]

RULE 4.3.   Dealing With Unrepresented Person

(a) **In dealing on behalf of a client with a person who is not represented by counsel, a lawyer shall clearly disclose whether the client's interests are adverse to the interests of such person and shall not state or imply that the lawyer is disinterested.**

(b) **When the lawyer knows or reasonably should know that the unrepresented person misunderstands the lawyer's role in the matter, the lawyer shall make reasonable efforts to correct the misunderstanding.**

(c) **During the course of representation of a client a lawyer shall not give advice to a person who is not represented by a lawyer, other than the advice to secure counsel, on those issues as** to which the interests of each person are or have a reasonable possibility of being in conflict with the interests of the client.

COMMENT—1985:

An unrepresented person, particularly one not experienced in dealing with legal matters, might assume that a lawyer is disinterested in loyalties or is a disinterested authority on the law even when the lawyer represents a client.

Texas Rule 4.04 *(Modification of Model Rule 4.4)*

[Texas has modified Model Rule 4.4 as follows:]

RULE 4.04   Respect for Rights of Third Persons

* * *

(b) A lawyer shall not present, participate in presenting, or threaten to present:

(1) criminal or disciplinary charges solely to gain an advantage in a civil matter; or

(2) civil, criminal or disciplinary charges against a complainant, a witness, or a potential witness in a bar disciplinary proceeding solely to prevent participation by the complainant, witness or potential witness therein.

LAW FIRMS AND ASSOCIATIONS

Texas Rule 5.01 *(Modification of Model Rule 5.1)*

[Texas has modified Model Rule 5.1 as follows:]

RULE 5.01   Responsibilities of a Partner or Supervisory Lawyer

A lawyer shall be subject to discipline because of another lawyer's violation of these rules of professional conduct if:

(a) The lawyer is a partner or supervising lawyer and orders, encourages, or knowingly permits the conduct involved; or

(b) The lawyer is a partner in the law firm in which the other lawyer practices, is the general counsel of a government agency's legal department in which the other lawyer is employed, or has direct supervisory authority over the other lawyer, and with knowledge of the other lawyer's violation of these rules knowingly fails to take reasonable remedial action to avoid or mitigate the consequences of the other lawyer's violation.

COMMENT:

1. Rule 5.01 conforms to the general principle that a lawyer is not vicariously subjected to discipline for the misconduct of another person, under Rule 8.04, a lawyer is subject to discipline if the lawyer knowingly assists or induces another to violate these rules. Rule 5.01(a)

189

additionally provides that a partner or supervising lawyer is subject to discipline for ordering or encouraging another lawyer's violation of these rules. Moreover, a partner or supervising lawyer is in a position of authority over the work of other lawyers and the partner or supervising lawyer may be disciplined for permitting another lawyer to violate these rules.

2. Rule 5.01(b) likewise is concerned with the lawyer who is in a position of authority over another lawyer and who knows that the other lawyer has committed a violation of a rule of professional conduct. A partner in a law firm, the general counsel of a government agency's legal department, or a lawyer having direct supervisory authority over specific legal work by another lawyer, occupies the position of authority contemplated by Rule 5.01(b).

3. Whether a lawyer has "direct supervisory authority over the other lawyer" in particular circumstances is a question of fact. In some instances, a senior associate may be a supervising attorney.

4. The duty imposed upon the partner or other authoritative lawyer by Rule 5.01(b) is to take reasonable remedial action to avoid or mitigate the consequences of the other lawyer's known violation. Appropriate remedial action by a partner or other supervisory lawyer would depend on may factors, such as the immediacy of the partner's or supervisory lawyer's knowledge and involvement, the nature of the action that can reasonably be expected to avoid or mitigate injurious consequences, and the seriousness of the anticipated consequences. In some circumstances, it may be sufficient for a junior partner to refer the ethical problem directly to a designated senior partner or a management committee. A lawyer supervising a specific legal matter may be required to intervene more directly. For example if a supervising lawyer knows that a supervised lawyer misrepresented a matter to an opposing party in negotiation, the supervisor as well as the other lawyer may be required by Rule 5.01(b) to correct the resulting misapprehension.

5. Thus, neither Rule 5.01(a) nor Rule 5.01(b) visits vicarious disciplinary liability upon the lawyer in a position of authority. Rather, the lawyer in such authoritative position is exposed to discipline only for his or her own knowing actions or failures to act. Whether a lawyer may be liable civilly or criminally for another lawyer's conduct is a question of law beyond the scope of these rules.

6. Wholly aside from the dictates of these rules for discipline, a lawyer in a position of authority in a firm or government agency or over another lawyer should feel a moral compunction to make reasonable efforts to ensure that the office, firm, or agency has in effect appropriate procedural measures giving reasonable assurance that all lawyers in the office conform to these rules. This moral obligation, although not required by these rules, should fall also upon lawyers who

have intermediate managerial responsibilities in the law department of an organization or government agency.

7.   The measures that should be undertaken to give such reasonable assurance may depend on the structure of the firm or organization and upon the nature of the legal work performed.   In a small firm, informal supervision and an occasional admonition ordinarily will suffice.   In a large firm, or in practice situations where intensely difficult ethical problems frequently arise, more elaborate procedures may be called for in order to give such assurance.   Obviously, the ethical atmosphere of a firm influences the conduct of all of its lawyers. Lawyers may rely also on continuing legal education in professional ethics to guard against unintentional misconduct by members of their firm or organization.

Texas Rule 5.02 (Modification of Model Rule 5.2)

[Texas has modified Model Rule 5.2 as follows:]

RULE 5.02   Responsibilities of a Supervised Lawyer

A lawyer is bound by these rules notwithstanding that the lawyer acted under the supervision of another person, except that a supervised lawyer does not violate these rules if that lawyer acts in accordance with a supervisory lawyer's reasonable resolution of an arguable question of professional conduct.

COMMENT:

1.   Rule 5.02 embodies the fundamental concept that every lawyer is a trained, mature, licensed professional who has sworn to uphold ethical standards and who is responsible for the lawyer's own conduct. Accordingly, a lawyer is not relieved from compliance with these rules because the lawyer acted under the supervision of an employer or other person.   In some situations, the fact that a lawyer acted at the direction or order of another person may be relevant in determining whether the lawyer had the knowledge required to render the conduct a violation of these rules.   The fact of supervision may also, of course, be a circumstance to be considered by a grievance committee or court in mitigation of the penalty to be imposed for violation of a rule.

2.   In many law firms and organizations, the relatively inexperienced lawyer works as an assistant to a more experienced lawyer or is directed, supervised or given guidance by an experienced lawyer in the firm.   In the normal course of practice the senior lawyer has the responsibility for making the decisions involving professional judgment as to procedures to be taken, the status of the law, and the propriety of actions to be taken by the lawyers.   Otherwise a consistent course of action could not be taken on behalf of clients.   The junior lawyer reasonably can be expected to acquiesce in the decisions made by the senior lawyer unless the decision is clearly wrong.

191

3. Rule 5.02 take a realistic attitude toward those prevailing modes of practice by lawyers not engaged in solo practice. Accordingly, Rule 5.02 provides the supervised lawyer with a special defense in a disciplinary proceeding in which the lawyer is charged with having violated a rule of professional conduct. The supervised lawyer is entitled to this defense only if it appears that an arguable question of professional conduct was resolved by a supervising lawyer and that a resolution made by the supervising lawyer was a reasonable resolution. The resolution is a reasonable one, even if it is ultimately found to be officially unacceptable, provided it would have appeared reasonable to a disinterested, competent lawyer based on the information reasonably available to the supervising lawyer at the time the resolution was made. "Supervisory lawyer" as used in Rule 5.02 should be construed in conformity with prevailing modes of practice in firms and other groups and, therefore, should include a senior lawyer who undertakes to resolve the question of professional propriety as well as a lawyer who more directly supervises the supervised lawyer.

4. By providing such a defense to the supervised lawyer, Rule 5.02 recognizes that the inexperienced lawyer working under the direction or supervision of an employer or senior attorney is not in a favorable position to disagree with reasonable decisions made by the experienced lawyer. Often, the only choices available to the supervised lawyer would be to accept the decision made by the senior lawyer or to resign or otherwise lose the employment. This provision of Rule 5.02 also recognizes that it is not necessarily improper for the inexperienced lawyer to rely, reasonably and in good faith, upon decisions made in unclear matters by senior lawyers in the organization.

5. The defense provided by this Rule is available without regard to whether the conduct in question was originally proposed by the supervised lawyer or another person. Nevertheless, the supervised lawyer is not permitted to accept an unreasonable decision as to the propriety of professional conduct. The Rule obviously provides no defense to the supervised lawyer who participates in clearly wrongful conduct. Reliance can be placed only upon a reasonable resolution made by the supervisory lawyer.

6. The protection afforded by Rule 5.02 to a supervised lawyer relates only to professional disciplinary proceedings. Whether a similar defense may exist in actions in tort or for breach of contract is a question beyond the scope of the Texas Rules of Professional Conduct.

District of Columbia Rule 5.4

RULE 5.4 Professional Independence of a Lawyer

(a) A lawyer or law firm shall not share legal fees with a nonlawyer, except that:

192

(1) an agreement by a lawyer with the lawyer's firm, partner, or associate may provide for the payment of money, over a reasonable period of time after the lawyer's death, to the lawyer's estate or to one or more specified persons;

(2) a lawyer who undertakes to complete unfinished legal business of a deceased lawyer may pay to the estate of the deceased lawyer that proportion of the total compensation which fairly represents the services rendered by the deceased lawyer;

(3) a lawyer or law firm may include nonlawyer employees in a compensation or retirement plan, even though the plan is based in whole or in part on a profit-sharing arrangement; and

(4) sharing of fees is permitted in a partnership or other form of organization which meets the requirements of paragraph (b).

(b) A lawyer may practice law in a partnership or other form of organization in which a financial interest is held or managerial authority is exercised by an individual nonlawyer who performs professional services which assist the organization in providing legal services to clients, but only if:

(1) the partnership or organization has as its sole purpose providing legal services to clients;

(2) all persons having such managerial authority or holding a financial interest undertake to abide by these rules of professional conduct;

(3) the lawyers who have a financial interest or managerial authority in the partnership or organization undertake to be responsible for the nonlawyer participants to the same extent as if nonlawyer participants were lawyers under rule 5.1;

(4) the foregoing conditions are set forth in writing.

(c) A lawyer shall not permit a person who recommends, employs, or pays the lawyer to render legal services for another to direct or regulate the lawyer's professional judgment in rendering such legal services.

COMMENT:

[1] The provisions of this Rule express traditional limitations on sharing fees with nonlawyers. (On sharing fees among lawyers not in the same firm, see Rule 1.5(e).) These limitations are to protect the lawyer's professional independence of judgment. Where someone other than the client pays the lawyer's fee or salary, or recommends employment of the lawyer, that arrangement does not modify the lawyer's

obligation to the client. As stated in paragraph (c), such arrangements should not interfere with the lawyer's professional judgment.

[2] Traditionally, the canons of legal ethics and disciplinary rules prohibited lawyers from practicing law in a partnership that includes nonlawyers or in any other organization where a nonlawyer is a shareholder, director, or officer. Notwithstanding these strictures, the profession implicitly recognized exceptions for lawyers who work for corporate law departments, insurance companies, and legal service organizations.

[3] As the demand increased for a broad range of professional services from a single source, lawyers employed professionals from other disciplines to work for them. So long as the nonlawyers remained employees of the lawyers, these relationships did not violate the disciplinary rules. However, when lawyers and nonlawyers considered forming partnerships and professional corporations to provide a combination of legal and other services to the public, they faced serious obstacles under the former rules.

[4] This Rule rejects an absolute prohibition against lawyers and nonlawyers joining together to provide collaborative services, but continues to impose traditional ethical requirements with respect to the organization thus created. Thus, a lawyer may practice law in an organization where nonlawyers hold a financial interest or exercise managerial authority, but only if the conditions set forth in subparagraphs (b)(1), (b)(2), and (b)(3) are satisfied, and, pursuant to subparagraph (b)(4), satisfaction of these conditions is set forth in a written instrument. The requirement of a writing helps ensure that these important conditions are not overlooked in establishing the organizational structure of entities in which nonlawyers enjoy an ownership or managerial role equivalent to that of a partner in a traditional law firm.

[5] Nonlawyer participants under Rule 5.4 ought not be confused with nonlawyer assistants under Rule 5.3. Nonlawyer participants are persons having managerial authority or financial interests in organizations which provide legal services. Within such organizations, lawyers with financial interests or managerial authority are held responsible for ethical misconduct by nonlawyer participants about which the lawyers know or reasonably should know. This is the same standard of liability contemplated by Rule 5.1, regarding the responsibilities of lawyers with direct supervisory authority over other lawyers.

[6] Nonlawyer assistants under Rule 5.3 do not have managerial authority or financial interests in the organization. Lawyers having direct supervisory authority over nonlawyer assistants are held responsible only for ethical misconduct by assistants about which the lawyers actually know.

[7]   As the introductory portion of Subparagraph (b) makes clear, the purpose of liberalizing the rules regarding the possession of a financial interest or the exercise of management authority by a nonlawyer is to permit nonlawyer professionals to work with lawyers in the delivery of legal services without being relegated to the role of an employee.   For example, the Rule permits economists to work in a firm with antitrust or public utility practitioners, psychologists or psychiatric social workers to work with family law practitioners to assist in counseling clients, nonlawyer lobbyists to work with lawyers who perform legislative services, certified public accountants to work in conjunction with tax lawyers or others who use accountants' services in performing legal services, and professional managers to serve as office managers, executive directors, or in similar positions.   In all of these situations, the professionals may be given financial interests or managerial responsibility, so long as all of the requirements of subparagraph (c) are met.

[8]   Subparagraph (b) does not permit an individual or entity to acquire all or any part of the ownership of a law partnership or other form of law practice organization for investment or other purposes.   It thus does not permit a corporation, an investment banking firm, an investor, or any other person or entity to entitle itself to all or any portion of the income or profits of a law firm or other similar organization.   Since such an investor would not be an individual performing professional services within the law firm or other organization, the requirements of subparagraph (b) would not be met.

[9]   The term "individual" in subparagraph (b) is not intended to preclude the participation in a law firm or other organization by an individual professional corporation in the same manner as lawyers who have incorporated as a professional corporation currently participate in partnerships which include professional corporations.

[10]   Some sharing of fees is likely to occur in the kinds of organizations permitted by paragraph (b).   Subparagraph (a)(4) makes it clear that such fee-sharing is not prohibited.

* * *

PUBLIC SERVICE

South Dakota Rule 6.1

[South Dakota has modified Model Rule 6.1 to read as follows:]

RULE 6.1 Pro Bono Publico Service

A lawyer should render public interest legal service.

A lawyer may discharge this responsibility by:

(a) providing professional services at no fee or a reduced fee to persons of limited means or to public service or charitable groups or organizations; or

195

(b) by service without compensation in public interest activities that improve the law, the legal system or the legal profession; or

(c) by financial support for organizations that provide legal services to persons of limited means.

COMMENT:

Each lawyer engaged in the practice of law has a responsibility to provide public interest legal services without fee, or at a substantially reduced fee, in one or more of the following areas: poverty law, civil rights law, public rights law, charitable organization representation and the administration of justice. This Rule expresses that policy but is not intended to be enforced through disciplinary process.

The rights and responsibilities of individuals and organizations in the United States are increasingly defined in legal terms. As a consequence, legal assistance in coping with the web of statutes, rules and regulations is imperative for all persons.

The basic responsibility for providing legal services for those unable to pay ultimately rests upon the individual lawyer, and personal involvement in the problems of the disadvantaged can be one of the most rewarding experiences in the life of a lawyer. Every lawyer, regardless of professional prominence or professional workload, should find time to participate in or otherwise support the provision of legal services to the disadvantaged. The provision of free legal services to those unable to pay reasonable fees continues to be an obligation of each lawyer as well as the profession generally, but the efforts of individual lawyers are often not enough to meet the need. Thus, it has been necessary for the profession and government to institute additional programs to provide legal services. Accordingly, legal aid offices, lawyer referral services and other related programs have been developed, and others will be developed by the profession and government. Every lawyer should support all proper efforts to meet this need for legal services.

The Rule has been restructured to make it clear that the "pro bono publico" obligation can also be discharged by uncompensated service in public interest activities and by financial support for legal service organizations.

INFORMATION ABOUT LEGAL SERVICES

Delaware Rule 7.1

[Delaware has amended Model Rule 7.1 to read as follows:]

RULE 7.1. Advertising

  (a) Advertising by a lawyer shall not:

    (1) Contain any untrue statement; or,

(2) Contain any matter or present or arrange any matter in a manner or format which is false, deceptive or which tends to confuse, deceive or mislead the public; or

(3) Contain any statement concerning the quality of any legal services offered (best, excellent, better, experienced and the like); or

(4) Contain any statements characterizing the size of the advertiser's fees or directly or indirectly comparing the size of the advertiser's fees (lowest, low, modest, reasonable, affordable and the like) to fees of other attorneys for like services unless such advertising lawyer has substantial evidence that such a statement is correct; or,

(5) Omit to state any fact necessary to make the statements made, in light of the circumstances under which they are made, not misleading to the public.

(b) Disclosures.

(1) A lawyer who advertises areas of practice shall either comply with Rule 7.5 or include the following disclaimer: "Listing of areas of practice does not represent official certification as a specialist in those areas."

(2) A lawyer who advertises contingent fee services shall state that a client must pay the expenses of litigation regardless of its outcome unless the lawyer intends to absorb those expenses pursuant to Rule 1.8(e).

(3) When a specific fee, magnitude of fee or range of fees is advertised by a lawyer the advertisement shall:

    (a) Identify with particularity the specific service or services to which the fee information applies.

    (b) State that: "The extent of legal services required depends upon the facts in each case. If additional services are required, full information on additional charges will be provided at the first consultation."

    (c) If the lawyer's costs and disbursements are not included in the advertised fee, this fact must be disclosed.

(c) Prominence of disclosures.

(1) In written or printed advertising, the required disclaimers and disclosures shall be in type size at least as large as the language qualified.

(2) In broadcast advertising, required disclaimers and disclosures shall be articulated at least as slowly and loudly as the remainder of the message.

(3) The advertising lawyer shall maintain a copy of each advertisement, or in the case of broadcast advertising, a recording capable of producing a replica, for at least one year after its last dissemination.

(d) Adherence to advertised fees.

(1) Unless otherwise stated in the advertisement: (a) in the case of advertised fees, a lawyer shall be bound, for two months after the fee information is last made public, to undertake and complete all services advertised for the fee advertised; provided, however, that, (b) if the advertisement occurs in a periodical which occurs less frequently than once every two months, the lawyer is so bound until the publication of the next succeeding issue of the periodical, and (c) if the advertisement occurs in a format which is not periodical, the lawyer shall be so bound for one year after the last publication.

(2) If legal services required by a client whose representation arose either in whole or in part in response to the advertisement shall exceed those for which fee information was advertised, the client shall be charged no greater fee without prior written consent.

(e) Conduct not permitted.

(1) No lawyer shall advertise by personal, telephonic or direct mail contact.

(2) Except as consideration for advertising permitted by this Rule, a lawyer shall not, directly or indirectly, compensate or give anything of value to any representative of the radio, television or print media in anticipation of, in return for, or in reasonable expectation of professional publicity.

(f) Definition of advertisement. "Advertise" and "Advertisement", as used in this Rule, (1) shall include any broadcast, publication, direct mail or other public communication on behalf of a lawyer intended or reasonably to be anticipated to lead to professional employment, (2) without limitation, shall include any sign, writing or other display visible to potential clients, and (3) but shall not include advertising which contains only the information permitted in professional notices or devices regulated by Rule 7.2.

(g) Certain applications of the Rule.

(1) The provisions of this Rule, insofar as they apply to a lawyer, apply, as well, to any law firm, including without limitation, a partnership, association or professional corporation, with which a lawyer practices.

(2) The provisions of this Rule with the exception of 7.1(a) (1), (2), (5) do not apply to communications by a lawyer to clients, former clients, and personal friends.

(h) Direct mail advertising.

(1) **Notwithstanding paragraph (e)(1) of this Rule, direct written communication, as for example direct mail, may be used for the distribution of such information as is permitted by this Rule; provided, however, that such communications (a) shall include on the face of the envelope or sheet containing the address and on each page of the advertisement in type at least as large as the largest in the advertisement the words: "Advertising Material" and (b) shall not be distributed at a time calculated to relate to events in the personal life of any recipient.**

(2) **One copy of each direct written communication and the names and addresses of those to whom it was sent shall be sent simultaneously to the Chairman of the Board on Professional Responsibility of the Delaware Supreme Court.**

COMMITTEE COMMENT:

Rule 7 has been completely revised to utilize the Delaware Supreme Court Committee on Advertising suggestions, which became a part of the Delaware Lawyer's Code of Professional Responsibility. However, the reference in Rule 7.2(a)(6) to law lists "certified by the American Bar Association as being in compliance with its Rules and Standards" has been deleted since the ABA no longer promulgates rules for standards of this type.

This Rule has been enacted in the context of developing law on lawyer advertising. Bates v. State Bar of Arizona, 433 U.S. 350 (1977) ("Bates"), and In re RMJ, 102 S.Ct. 929 (1982), the leading cases, establish that although a ban on lawyer advertising violates a lawyer's first amendment right to freedom of commercial speech, regulation of advertising which is not more extensive than is necessary to serve a substantial public interest is permitted. The Rule balances these competing considerations.

The primary interest served by lawyer advertising is improved informed public access to the Bar through a free flow of accurate information relating to the qualification of lawyers. See, e.g., Bates, 433 U.S. at 364. Certain other subsidiary benefits may also be served, such as reduced legal costs and improved access to practice by new attorneys. Unregulated advertising, however, creates a risk of misleading and overreaching practices. It may lead the public to believe that legal costs are predictable, or that the advertising lawyer is officially certified as to skill in an area of specialty. Certain types of advertising may invade privacy, encourage needless litigation or, in extreme forms, debase the profession and thereby make it less able to effectively represent the public.

Bates, as construed by the Court in RMJ, establishes that:

A. Since legal services are not capable of standardization, and since the public is not knowledgeable in the field, regulation of advertising is legitimate;

B. Deceptive advertising may be banned altogether;

C. In preventing deception, a requirement for fuller disclosure is to be preferred to restrictions on disclosure;

D. Warnings or disclaimers may be appropriate to avoid deception even in the context of advertising as to price;

E. Interference with commercial speech must exist only in proportion to the substantial public interest the interference serves.

See 102 S.Ct. at 935–37.

The Rule, in putting these principles into effect, may be seen as containing three basic divisions. Sections (a) through (c) deal with disclosure. Sections (d) and (e) regulate conduct and Sections (f) and (g) contain definitions and general standards of application.

(a) Anti-fraud provisions.—Subsections (a)(1), (2) and (5) are general anti-fraud provisions derived from the California Code of Professional Responsibility and comport with the mandates of Bates and RMJ. Subsection (3) prohibits advertising attorneys from making representations regarding the quality of service. Such statements are prohibited because, as pointed out in the Bates decision, they are not capable of measurement or verification and thus are potentially misleading. Bates, 433 U.S. at 383–84. See also Mezrano v. Alabama State Bar, No. 81–1069, slip op, at 3–4 (Ala. April 8, 1983). Subsection (4) prohibits unsubstantiated claims regarding an attorney's fees. Comparative information with respect to fees may imply a comparison as to quality of services rendered, a comparison which the Supreme Court in Bates deemed inherently suspect. See Bates, 433 U.S. at 383–84. If the advertisement is challenged, the rule places on the advertising lawyer the burden of establishing that the claim made regarding the fee is accurate. The Bates court recognized that the standard for regulating false or misleading advertising by attorneys is higher because of the lack of sophistication of the public about legal services. Bates, 433 U.S. at 383. The rule seeks to prevent the public from being misled into concluding that the advertising lawyer's service is cheaper, more expert or more likely to achieve success than is reasonably justified by the facts.

(b) Disclosures.—Section (b) contains the disclaimers that must be included in attorney advertising. Lawyers who advertise special areas of practice must advise that they have no official certification of expertise in such areas. Information regarding an attorney's areas of practice helps the public identify and retain legal counsel appropriate to the particular situation. Such advertising, however, bears a strong

likelihood of misleading the public that a given lawyer is an expert or specialist in a particular field of law. The RMJ Court recognized this potential when it referred to lists of areas of practice as an example of "potentially misleading information" which may be in need of a disclaimer or explanation. In re RMJ, 102 S.Ct. at 937. So as to permit consumers of legal services to choose an attorney who will be able to provide them with the necessary legal representation, the rule allows attorneys to list their areas of practice. This is balanced, however, by inclusion of the required disclaimer so to protect consumers from being misled. This rule is not intended to apply to an attorney who advertises a specific service unless the context of the advertisement indicates an area of practice.

The Bates court expressly provided that the bar has power to "correct omissions that have the effect of presenting an inaccurate picture." Bates, 433 U.S. at 375. So as to prevent a consumer of legal services on a contingent fee basis from inaccurately concluding that he will pay nothing unless the litigation is successful, subsection (2) requires the advertiser to explain that the client must pay the expenses regardless of the outcome, unless the lawyer intends to absorb the expenses pursuant to Rule 1.8(e).

Since legal problems are often not resolved simply, the resulting costs, delays and, in the case of adversary matters, adverse results, frequently take the client unfairly unaware. Subsection (3), therefore, requires lawyers who advertise to advise the public that legal problems may not be subject to simple inexpensive solutions and to put prospective clients on notice that, should the matter go beyond the services advertised, additional fees and costs may be incurred. This disclosure is in keeping with the Supreme Court's recognition that disclaimers with respect to fee advertising may be necessary to prevent an advertisement from being misleading. See In re RMJ, 102 S.Ct. at 936.

(c) Prominence of disclosures.—In Bates, the Supreme Court stated that "it is the bar's role to assure that the populace is sufficiently informed as to enable it to place advertising in its proper perspective." Bates, 433 U.S. at 375. So as to permit the public to receive all advertised information with equal emphasis, section (c) requires disclaimers to be in type as large as the language qualified. In the case of broadcast advertising, pace and volume are used as the measures of emphasis.

(d) Adherence to advertised fees.—So as to keep unanticipated charges to a minimum, section (d) requires lawyers to either warn that their fees may change, obtain prior consent to such changes or complete the advertised services for the fees advertised.

(e) Conduct not permitted.—Section (e) prohibits in-person solicitation, purchased publicity and direct mail advertising. There is a split of authority as to whether direct mail advertising is protected speech. In the Matter of Frank, 440 N.E.2d 676 (Ind.Supr.1982), Dayton Bar

Assoc. v. Herzog, 70 Ohio St.2d 261 (1982) and Kansas v. Moses, 642 P.2d 1004 (Kan.Supr.1982), have all upheld bans on direct mail advertising. Koffler v. Joint Bar Assoc., 412 N.E.2d 927 (N.Y.1980) and Kentucky Bar Assoc. v. Stuart, 568 S.W.2d 933 (Ky.Supr.1978), have struck them down. The ABA House of Delegates, after debate, recently amended proposed Model Rules 7.3 to ban all direct mail solicitation, where there exists significant motive for pecuniary gain.

In Central Hudson Gas & Electric Corp. v. Public Service Commission, 447 U.S. 557 (1980), the Supreme Court required any ban on commercial speech to satisfy certain requirements including, as one such requirement, the advancement of a substantial state interest which cannot be protected in a less restrictive way.

Direct mail communications are shielded from public scrutiny, comparison and evaluation and are particularly subject to abuse as solicitation. Solicitation for pecuniary gain is not protected by the First Amendment. In re Primus, 436 U.S. 412 (1978); Ohralik v. Ohio State Bar Assoc., 436 U.S. 445 (1978). In addition, direct mail intrudes uninvited into homes of private persons.

The decision to permit a free flow of information from more general advertising while banning advertising by direct mail seeks to facilitate informed decisions through openly available public information which can be used for comparative purposes. The importance of insuring that advertising remain open, public information was recognized by the Supreme Court in Bates. The Court stated that "advertising will permit the comparison of rates among competitors, thus revealing if the rates are reasonable." Bates, 433 U.S. at 382. Such a comparison is not possible if advertising is conducted by private mailings. At the same time, prohibition of direct mail advertising avoids both intrusions on privacy and the grave risk of misinformation or solicitation for pecuniary gain.

Proscribing direct mail advertising is the least restrictive method of advancing the state's interest in facilitating informed decision making and preventing misinformation or solicitation. It is impractical to rely on the advertiser to insure that the recipient is neither solicited nor misinformed. With the limited financial resources available to a small bar such as Delaware's, effective regulation of direct mail advertising is simply not feasible. Any partial limitation or restriction on direct mail advertising does not cure or protect the consumer from the potential abuses resulting from the in-person solicitation described by Justice Powell in Ohralik v. Ohio State Bar Association, 436 U.S. 445 (1978). After-the-fact review of solicitation letters will not protect consumers from the impact of a mass-mailing of misleading advertisements. As stated by the Supreme Court of Tennessee, "such advertising poses insurmountable problems in enforcement and is unnecessary to a proper enjoyment of the constitutional right of commercial speech." In re Petition for Rule of Court Governing Lawyer Advertising, 564 S.W.2d 638, 644 (Tenn.1978).

(f) Definition of advertisement.—Section (f) defines advertising broadly and makes the Rule applicable to law firms and other organizations making legal services available to the public.

(g) Certain applications of the Rule.—Section (g) makes it clear that communications to clients and personal friends, as contrasted with communications with the public at large, are not restricted by the Rule.

(h) Direct mail advertising.—Section (h) modifies paragraph (e)(1) to take into account the recent case of Spencer v. The Honorable Justices of the Supreme Court of Pennsylvania, E.D.Pa. 2/1/84, No. 82–4704.

Arizona Rule 7.2

[Arizona has modified Model Rule 7.2 to read as follows:]

ER 7.2   Advertising

(a) Subject to the requirements of ER 7.1 and ER 7.3, a lawyer may advertise services through public media, such as a telephone directory, legal directory, newspaper or other periodical, outdoor, radio or television, or through written communication.

(b) A copy or recording of an advertisement or written communication shall be kept for three years after its last dissemination along with a record of when and where it was used.

(c) A lawyer shall not give anything of value to a person for recommending the lawyer's services, except that a lawyer may pay the reasonable cost of advertising or written communication permitted by this rule and may pay the usual charges of a not-for-profit lawyer referral service or other legal service organization.

(d) Any communication made pursuant to this rule shall include the name of at least one lawyer responsible for its content.

(e) Written communications to prospective clients for the purpose of obtaining professional employment are subject to the following requirements:

(1) Such written communications shall be plainly marked "Advertisement" on the face of the envelope and at the top of each page of the written communication in type no smaller than the largest type used in the written communication; and

(2) A copy of each such written communication shall be retained by the lawyer for three years. If written communications identical in content are sent to two or more prospective clients, the lawyer may comply with this requirement by retaining a single copy together with a list of the names and addresses of persons to whom the written communication was sent.

(f) A lawyer shall not send, or knowingly permit to be sent, on behalf of himself, his firm, his partner, an associate, or any other lawyer affiliated with him or his firm, a written communication to a prospective client for the purpose of obtaining professional employment if:

(1) The written communication concerns a specific matter and the lawyer knows or reasonably should know that the person to whom the communication is directed is represented by a lawyer in the matter;

(2) It has been made known to the lawyer that the person does not want to receive such communications from the lawyer;

(3) The communication includes coercion, duress, fraud, overreaching, harassment, intimidation, or undue influence; or

(4) The communication is otherwise improper under ER 7.1.

(g) A lawyer or his partner or associate or any other lawyer affiliated with him or his firm may be recommended, employed or paid by, or may cooperate with, one of the following offices or organizations that promote the use of his services or those of his partner or associate or any other lawyer affiliated with him or his firm if there is no interference with the exercise of independent professional judgment in behalf of his client:

(1) A legal aid office or public defender office which is operated or sponsored by a duly accredited law school, by a bona fide non-profit community organization, or by a governmental agency; or which is operated, sponsored, or approved by a bar association;

(2) A military legal assistance office;

(3) A lawyer referral service operated, sponsored, or approved by a bar association;

(4) Any bona fide organization that recommends, furnishes or pays for legal services to its members or beneficiaries, provided the following conditions are satisfied:

(A) Such organization, including any affiliate, is so organized and operated that no profit is derived by it from the rendition of legal services by lawyers, and that, if the organization is organized for profit, the legal services are not rendered by lawyers employed, directed, supervised or selected by it, except in connection with matters where such organization bears ultimate liability of its members or beneficiary;

(B) Neither the lawyer, nor his partner or associate, nor any other lawyer affiliated with him or his firm, nor any non-lawyer, shall have initiated or promoted such organization for the primary purpose of providing financial or other benefit to such lawyer, partner, associate or affiliated lawyer;

(C) Such organization is not operated for the purpose of procuring legal work or financial benefit for any lawyer as a private practitioner outside of the legal services program of the organization;

(D) The member or beneficiary to whom the legal services are furnished, and not such organization, is recognized as the client of the lawyer in the matter;

(E) Any member or beneficiary who is entitled to have legal services furnished or paid for by the organization may, if such member or beneficiary so desires, select counsel other than that furnished, selected or approved by the organization for the particular matter involved; and the legal service plan of such organization provides appropriate relief for any member or beneficiary who asserts a claim that representation by counsel furnished, selected or approved would be unethical, improper or inadequate under the circumstances of the matter involved and the plan provides an appropriate procedure for seeking such relief;

(F) The lawyer does not know or have cause to know that such organization is in violation of applicable laws, rules of court and other legal requirements that govern its legal service operations; and

(G) Such organization has filed with the appropriate disciplinary authority at least annually a report with respect to its legal service plan, if any, showing its terms, schedule of benefits, subscription charges, agreements with counsel, and financial results of its legal service activities, or if it has failed to do so, the lawyer does not know or have cause to know of such failure.

(5) A public interest law firm, which is defined as: A nonprofit firm which provides, without cost or at a substantially reduced fee, legal services which would not be provided by a governmental agency or by any other means, and has been recognized and approved as such by the Board of Governors of the State Bar of Arizona, and which falls exclusively into one or more of the following areas:

(A) Poverty Law. Legal services in civil and criminal matters of importance to a client who does not have the financial resources to compensate counsel.

(B) Individual Civil Rights Law. Legal representation of an important right of an individual which society has a special interest in protecting, but which the client would not otherwise seek to vindicate.

(C) Public Rights Law. Legal representation involving an important right belonging to the public at large, where those asserting the right would not otherwise seek its vindication.

(D) Charitable Organization Representation. Legal service to charitable, religious, civic and educational institutions in matters in furtherance of their organizational purpose where the payment of customary legal fees would significantly deplete the organization's economic resources.

(h) A lawyer shall not accept employment when he knows or it is obvious that the person who seeks his services does so as a result of conduct prohibited under this rule.

COMMENT:

To assist the public in obtaining legal services, lawyers should be allowed to make known their services not only through reputation but also through organized information campaigns in the form of advertising. Advertising involves an active quest for clients, contrary to the tradition that a lawyer should not seek clientele. However, the public's need to know about legal services can be fulfilled in part through advertising. This need is particularly acute in the case of persons of moderate means who have not made extensive use of legal services. The interest in expanding public information about legal services ought to prevail over considerations of tradition. Nevertheless, advertising by lawyers entails the risk of practices that are misleading or overreaching.

This rule permits public dissemination of information concerning a lawyer's name or firm name, address and telephone number; the kinds of services the lawyer will undertake; the basis on which the lawyer's fees are determined, including prices for specific services and payment and credit arrangements; a lawyer's foreign language ability; names of references and, with their consent, names of clients regularly represented; and other information that might invite the attention of those seeking legal assistance.

Questions of effectiveness and taste in advertising are matters of speculation and subjective judgment. Some jurisdictions have had extensive prohibitions against television advertising or against advertising going beyond specified facts about a lawyer. Television is now one of the most powerful media for getting information to the public, particularly persons of low and moderate income; prohibiting television advertising, therefore, would impede the flow of information about legal services to many sectors of the public. Limiting the information that may be advertised has a similar effect and assumes that the bar can accurately forecast the kind of information that the public would regard as relevant.

Neither this rule nor ER 7.3 prohibits communications authorized by law, such as notice to members of a class in class action litigation.

Records of Advertising

Paragraph (b) requires that a record of the content and use of advertising be kept in order to facilitate enforcement of this rule. It does not require that advertising be subject to review prior to dissemination. Such a requirement would be burdensome and expensive relative to its possible benefits, and may be of doubtful constitutionality.

Paying Others to Recommend a Lawyer

A lawyer is allowed to pay for advertising permitted by this Rule, but otherwise is not permitted to pay another person for channeling professional work. This restriction does not prevent an organization or person other than the lawyer from advertising or recommending the lawyer's services. Thus, a legal aid agency or prepaid legal services plan may pay to advertise legal services provided under its auspices. Likewise, a lawyer may participate in not-for-profit lawyer referral programs and pay the usual fees charged by such programs. Paragraph (c) does not prohibit paying regular compensation to an assistant, such as a secretary, to prepare communications permitted by this rule.

Delaware Rule 7.2

[Delaware has modified Model Rule 7.2 to read as follows:]

RULE 7.2. Professional Notices, Letterheads and Offices

(a) Unless the provisions of Rule 7.1 are satisfied, a lawyer or law firm shall not use or participate in the use of professional cards, professional announcement cards, office signs, letterheads or similar professional notices or devices, except that the following may be used if in a dignified form:

(1) A professional card of a lawyer identifying him by name and as a lawyer, and giving his addresses, telephone numbers, the name of his law firm and any information permitted under Rule 7.5. A professional card of a law firm may also give the names of members and associates. Such cards may be used for identification.

(2) A brief professional announcement card stating new or changed associations or addresses, change of firm name or similar matters pertaining to the professional offices of a lawyer or law firm, which may be mailed to friends and relatives. It shall not state biographical data except to the extent reasonably necessary to identify the lawyer or to explain the change in his association, but it may state the immediate past position of the lawyer. It may give the names and dates of predecessor firms in a continuing line of succession. It shall not state the nature of the practice, except as permitted under Rule 7.5.

(3) A sign on or near the door of the office and in the building directory identifying the law office. The sign shall not state the nature of the practice, except as permitted under Rule 7.5.

(4) A letterhead of a lawyer identifying him by name and as a lawyer, and giving his addresses, telephone numbers, the name of his law firm, associates and any information permitted under Rule 7.5. A letterhead of a law firm may also give the names of members and associates, and names and dates relating to deceased and retired members. A lawyer may be designated "Of Counsel" on a letterhead if he has a continuing relationship with a lawyer or law firm, other than as a partner or associate. A lawyer or law firm may be designated as "General Counsel" or by similar professional reference on stationery of a client if he or the firm devotes a substantial amount of professional time in the representation of that client. The letterhead of a law firm may give the names and dates of predecessor firms in a continuing line of succession.

(5) A listing of the office of a lawyer or law firm in the alphabetical and classified sections of a telephone directory, but the listing may give only the name of the lawyer or law firm, the fact he is a lawyer, addresses, and telephone numbers. The listing shall not be in distinctive form or type. A law firm may have a listing in the firm name separate from that of its members and associates. The listing in the classified section shall not be under a heading or classification other than "Attorneys" or "Lawyers," except that additional headings or classifications descriptive of the types of practice referred to in Rule 7.5 are permitted.

(6) A listing in a reputable law list or legal directory giving brief biographical and other informative data. A law list or directory is not reputable if its management or contents are likely to be misleading or injurious to the public or to the profession. The published data may include only the following: Name, including name of law firm and names of

professional associates; addresses and telephone numbers; one or more fields of law in which the lawyer or law firm concentrates; a statement that practice is limited to one or more fields of law; a statement that the lawyer or law firm specializes in a particular field of law or law practice but only if authorized under Rule 7.5(a)(4); date and place of birth; date and place of admission to the bar of state and federal courts; schools attended, with dates of graduation, degrees, and other scholastic distinctions; public or quasi-public offices; military service; posts of honor; legal authorships; legal teaching positions; memberships, offices, committee assignments, and section memberships in bar associations; memberships and offices in legal fraternities and legal societies; technical and professional licenses; memberships in scientific, technical and professional associations and societies, foreign language ability; names and addresses of references, and, with their consent, names of clients regularly represented.

(b) A lawyer in private practice shall not practice under a trade name, a name that is misleading as to the identity of the lawyer or lawyers practicing under such name or a firm name containing names other than those of 1 or more of the lawyers in the firm; except that the name of a professional corporation or professional association may contain "P.C." or "P.A." or similar symbols indicating the name of the organization, and, if otherwise lawful, a firm may use as, or continue to include in, its name the name or names of 1 or more deceased or retired members of the firm or of a predecessor firm in a continuing line of succession. A lawyer who assumes a judicial, legislative or public executive or administrative post or office shall not permit his name to remain in the name of a law firm or to be used in professional notices of the firm during any significant period in which he is not actively and regularly practicing law as a member of the firm, and during such period other members of the firm shall not use his name in the firm name or in professional notices of the firm.

(c) A lawyer shall not hold himself out as having a partnership with 1 or more lawyers unless they are in fact partners.

(d) A partnership shall not be formed or continued between or among lawyers licensed in different jurisdictions unless all enumerations of the members and associates of the firm on its letterhead, and in other permissible listings, make clear the jurisdictional limitations on those members and associates of the firm not licensed to practice in all listed jurisdictions; however, the same firm name may be used in each jurisdiction.

(e) Nothing contained herein shall prohibit a lawyer from using or permitting the use of, in connection with his name, an earned degree or title derived therefrom indicating his training in the law.

Connecticut Rule 7.3

[Connecticut has amended Model Rule 7.3(a) to read as follows:]

RULE 7.3 Personal Contact With Prospective Clients

(a) Subject to the requirements of paragraph (b), a lawyer may initiate personal contact with a prospective client for the purpose of obtaining professional employment only in the following circumstances:

(1) If the prospective client is a close friend, relative, former client or one whom the lawyer reasonably believes to be a client;

(2) Under the auspices of a public or charitable legal services organization;

(3) Under the auspices of a bona fide political, social, civic, fraternal, employee or trade organization whose purposes include but are not limited to providing or recommending legal services, if the legal services are related to the principal purposes of the organization.

(b) A lawyer shall not contact, or send a written communication to, a prospective client for the purpose of obtaining professional employment if:

(1) The lawyer knows or reasonably should know that the physical, emotional or mental health of the person is such that the person could not exercise reasonable judgment in employing a lawyer,

(2) The person has made known to the lawyer a desire not to receive communications from the lawyer, or

(3) The communication involves coercion, duress, or harassment.

COMMENT:

Unrestricted solicitation involves definite social harms. Among these are harassment, overreaching, provocation of nuisance litigation and schemes for systematic fabrication of claims, all of which were experienced prior to adoption of restrictions on solicitation. Measures reasonably designed to suppress these harms are constitutionally legitimate. At the same time, measures going beyond realization of such objectives would appear to be invalid under relevant decisions of the United States Supreme Court.

In determining whether a contact is permissible under Rule 7.3(b), it is relevant to consider the time and circumstances under which the contact is initiated. For example, a person undergoing active medical treatment for traumatic injury is unlikely to be in an emotional state in which reasonable judgment about employing a lawyer can be exercised.

Delaware Rule 7.3

[Delaware has modified Model Rule 7.3 to read as follows:]

RULE 7.3. Recommendation of Professional Employment

(a) A lawyer shall not, except as authorized in Rule 7.1, recommend employment as a private practitioner, of himself, his partner or associate to a lay person who has not sought his advice regarding employment of a lawyer.

(b) A lawyer shall not compensate or give anything of value to a person or organization to recommend or secure his employment by a client, or as a reward for having made a recommendation resulting in his employment by a client, except that he may pay the usual and reasonable fees or dues charged by any of the organizations listed in Rule 7.3.

(c) A lawyer shall not request a person or organization to recommend or promote the use of his services or those of his partner or associates, or any other lawyer affiliated with him or his firm, as a private practitioner, except as authorized in Rule 7.1, and expect that:

(1) He may request referrals from a lawyer referral service operated, sponsored or approved by a bar association and may pay its fees incident thereto.

(2) He may cooperate with the legal service activities of any of the offices or organizations enumerated in Rule 7.3(d) (1) through (4) and may perform legal services for those to whom he was recommended by it to do such work if:

(a) The person to whom the recommendation is made is a member or beneficiary of such office or organization; and

(b) The lawyer remains free to exercise his independent professional judgment on behalf of his client.

(d) A lawyer or his partner or associates or any other lawyer affiliated with him or his firm may be recommended, employed or paid by, or may cooperate with, 1 of the following offices or organizations that promote the use of his services or those of his partner or associate or any other lawyer affiliated with him or his firm, if there is no interference with the exercise of independent professional judgment in behalf of his client.

(1) A legal office or public defender office:

(a) Operated or sponsored by a duly accredited law school.

(b) Operated or sponsored by a bona fide nonprofit community organization.

(c) Operated or sponsored by a governmental agency.

(d) Operated, sponsored or approved by a bar association.

(2) A military legal assistance office.

(3) A lawyer referral service operated, sponsored or approved by a bar association.

(4) Any bona fide organization that recommends, furnishes or pays for legal services to its members or beneficiaries provided the following conditions are satisfied:

(a) Such organization, including any affiliate, is so organized and operated that no profit is derived by it from the rendition of legal services by lawyers, and that, if the organization is organized for profit, the legal services are not rendered by lawyers employed, directed, supervised or selected by it, except in connection with matters where such organization bears ultimate liability of its member or beneficiary.

(b) Neither the lawyer, nor his partner, nor associate, nor any other lawyer affiliated with him or his firm, nor any nonlawyer, shall have initiated or promoted such organization for the primary purpose of providing financial or other benefit to such lawyer, partner, associate or affiliated lawyer.

(c) Such organization is not operated for the purpose of procuring legal work or financial benefit for any lawyer as a private practitioner outside of the legal services program of the organization.

(d) The member or beneficiary to whom the legal services are furnished, and not such organization, is recognized as the client of the lawyer in the matter.

(e) Any member or beneficiary who is entitled to have legal services furnished or paid for by the organization may, if such member or beneficiary so desires, select counsel other than that furnished, selected or approved by the organization for the particular matter involved; and the legal service plan of such organization provides appropriate relief for any member or beneficiary who asserts a claim that representation by counsel furnished, selected or approved would be unethical, improper or inadequate under the circumstances of the matter involved and the plan provides an appropriate procedure for seeking such relief.

(f) The lawyer does not know or have cause to know that such organization is in violation of applicable laws, rules of court or other legal requirements that govern its legal service operations.

(g) Such organization has filed with the Board on Professional Responsibility of the Supreme Court, at least annually, a report with respect to its legal service plan, showing its terms, its schedule of benefits, its subscription charges, agreements with counsel and financial results of its legal service activities.

(5) Any other nonprofit organization that recommends, furnishes, or pays for legal services to its members or beneficiaries, but only in those instances and to the extent that controlling constitutional interpretation at the time of the rendition of the services requires the allowance of such legal service activities, and only if the following conditions, unless prohibited by such interpretation, are met:

(a) The primary purposes of such organization do not include the rendition of legal services.

(b) The recommending, furnishing, or paying for legal services to its members is incidental and reasonably related to the primary purpose of such organization.

(c) Such organization does not derive a financial benefit from the rendition of legal services by the lawyer.

(d) The member or beneficiary for whom the legal services are rendered, and not such organization, is recognized as the client of the lawyer in that matter.

(e) A lawyer shall not accept employment when he knows or should know that the person who seeks his services does so as a result of conduct prohibited under this Rule.

INTERPRETIVE GUIDELINE NO. 1—Re: RESIDENTIAL REAL ESTATE TRANSACTIONS

The following statements of principles are promulgated as interpretive guidelines in the application to residential real estate transactions in The Delaware Lawyers' Rules of Professional Conduct:

(a) Before accepting representation of a buyer or mortgagor of residential property (including condominiums under the Unit Property Act of the State of Delaware), upon referral by the seller, lender, real estate agent, or other person having an interest in the transaction, it is the ethical duty of a lawyer to inform the buyer or mortgagor in writing at the earliest practicable time:

(1) That the buyer or mortgagor has the absolute right (regardless of any preference that the seller, real estate agent,

lender, or other person may have and regardless of who is to pay attorney's fees) to retain a lawyer of his own choice to represent him throughout the transaction, including the examination and certification of title, the preparation of documents, and the holding of settlement; and

(2) As to the identity of any other party having an interest in the transaction whom the lawyer may represent, including a statement that such other representation may be possibly conflicting and may adversely affect the exercise of the lawyer's professional judgment on behalf of the buyer or mortgagor in case of a dispute between the parties. For the purpose of this Guideline, a lawyer shall be deemed to have a "possibly conflicting" representation if he represents the seller or has represented the seller on a continuing basis in the past; or if he represents the real estate agent or has represented the real estate agent on a continuing basis in the past; or if he represents the lender or has represented the lender on a continuing basis in the past.

(b) Unless a lawyer has been freely and voluntarily selected by the buyer or mortgagor after he has made to the buyer or mortgagor the statements and disclosures hereinabove required, the lawyer may not ethically:

(1) Certify, report, or represent for any purpose that the buyer or mortgagor is his client, or that the buyer or mortgagor is or was obligated for any legal service rendered by him in the transaction; or

(2) Participate in causing the buyer or mortgagor, directly or indirectly, to bear any charge for his legal service; except that the lawyer for a lender may receive from the buyer or mortgagor, directly or indirectly, payment of the lender's reasonable and necessary legal expenses for preparation of documents at the request of the buyer's or mortgagor's lawyer, for attendance at settlement, and for title insurance properly specified by the lender (within the provisions of 18 Del.C. § 2305(a)(1)) but unobtainable by the buyer's or mortgagor's lawyer, provided that the buyer's or mortgagor's obligation to pay each such legal expense is particularized as a term and condition of the loan; or

(3) Participate as the buyer's or mortgagor's lawyer in any transaction in which his representation of the buyer or mortgagor has been made a term or condition of the transaction, directly or indirectly.

(c) The information supplied to the buyer or mortgagor in writing shall contain a description of the attorney's interest or

214

interests sufficient to enable the buyer or mortgagor to determine whether he should obtain a different attorney.

Delaware Rule 7.4

[Delaware has modified Model Rule 7.4 to read as follows:]

RULE 7.4   Suggestion of Need of Legal Services

(a) A lawyer who has given in-person unsolicited advice to a lay person that he should obtain counsel or take action shall not accept employment resulting from that advice, except that:

(1) A lawyer may accept employment by a close friend, relative, former client (if the advice is germane to the former employment), or one whom the lawyer reasonably believes to be a client.

(2) A lawyer may accept employment that results from his participation in activities designed to educate lay persons to recognize legal problems, to make intelligent selection of counsel or to utilize available legal services if such activities are conducted or sponsored by a qualified assistance organization.

(3) A lawyer who is recommended, furnished or paid by a qualified legal assistance organization enumerated in Rule 7.3(d)(1) through (4) may represent a member or beneficiary thereof, to the extent and under the conditions prescribed therein.

(4) Without affecting his right to accept employment, a lawyer may speak publicly or write for publication on legal topics so long as he does not emphasize his own professional experience or reputation and does not undertake to give individual advice.

(5) If success in asserting rights or defenses of his client in litigation in the nature of a class action is dependent upon the joinder of others, a lawyer may accept, but shall not seek, employment from those contacted for the purpose of obtaining their joinder.

MAINTAINING THE INTEGRITY OF THE PROFESSION

Kansas Rule 8.3

[Kansas amended Model Rule 8.3 as follows:]

RULE 8.3   Reporting Professional Misconduct

(a) A lawyer having knowledge that another lawyer has committed a violation of the Rules of Professional Conduct that raises a substantial question as to that lawyer's honesty, trustworthiness or fitness as a lawyer in other respects, shall inform the appropriate professional authority.

(b) A lawyer having knowledge that a judge has committed a violation of applicable rules of judicial conduct that raises a substantial question as to the judge's fitness for office shall inform the appropriate authority.

(c) This rule does not require disclosure of information otherwise protected by Rule 1.6. In addition, a lawyer is not required to disclose information concerning any such violation which is discovered through participation in a Substance Abuse Committee, Service to the Bar Committee or similar committee sponsored by a state or local bar association, or by participation in a self-help organization such as Alcoholics Anonymous, through which aid is rendered to another lawyer who may be impaired in the practice of law.

* * *

KANSAS COMMENT:

Substance Abuse Committees have earned an important position in the organization of bar association activities and render a valuable and important service to the profession and the public. As such, these committees and other recognized self-help organizations, and the lawyers who serve on them should be allowed to function without fear of the requirement to report every violation which might be uncovered during the course of their service. To provide otherwise might inhibit free and open communication by the incapacitated lawyer and result in neglected matters remaining so. In this instance, the Kansas Committee feels that the public is better served by providing a measure of confidentiality to the incapacitated lawyer's communications with those who would help the lawyer in serving clients.

Louisiana Rule 8.4

[Louisiana has amended Model Rule 8.4 to add the following:]

RULE 8.4 Misconduct

It is professional misconduct for a lawyer to:

* * *

(g) Except upon the expressed assertion of a constitutional privilege, to fail to cooperate with the Committee on Professional Responsibility in its investigation of alleged misconduct.

(h) Present, participate in presenting, or threaten to present criminal charges solely to obtain an advantage in a civil matter.

District of Columbia Rule 9.1

[The District of Columbia has added the following provision which has no counterpart in the Model Rules]

NONDISCRIMINATION BY MEMBERS OF THE BAR

RULE 9.1 Discrimination in Employment

A lawyer shall not discriminate against any individual in conditions of employment because of the individual's race, color, religion, national origin, sex, age, marital status, sexual orientation, family responsibility, or physical handicap.

COMMENT:

[1] This provision is modeled after the D.C. Human Rights Act, D.C. Code § 1–2512 (1981), though in some respects more limited in scope. There are also provisions of federal law that contain certain prohibitions on discrimination in employment. The rule is not intended to create ethical obligations that exceed those imposed on a lawyer by applicable law.

[2] A similar rule has been adopted by the highest court in Vermont. A similar rule is also under consideration for adoption by the courts in New York based on the recommendations of the New York State Bar Association.

[3] The investigation and adjudication of discrimination claims may involve particular expertise of the kind found within the D.C. Office of Human Rights and the federal Equal Employment Opportunity Commission. Such experience may involve, among other things, methods of analysis of statistical data regarding discrimination claims. These agencies also have, in appropriate circumstances, the power to award remedies to the victims of discrimination, such as reinstatement or back pay, which extend beyond the remedies that are available through the disciplinary process. Remedies available through the disciplinary process include such sanctions as disbarment, suspension, censure, and admonition, but do not extend to monetary awards or other remedies that could alter the employment status to take into account the impact of prior acts of discrimination.

[4] If proceedings are pending before other organizations, such as the D.C. Office of Human Rights or the Equal Employment Opportunity Commission, the processing of complaints by Bar Counsel may be deferred or abated where there is substantial similarity between the complaint filed with Bar Counsel and material allegations involved in such other proceedings. See § 19(d) of Rule XI of the Rules Governing the Bar of the District of Columbia.

Appendix:

States That Have Adopted a Version of the Model Rules *

Alabama
Arizona
Arkansas
Connecticut
Delaware
District of Columbia
Florida
Idaho
Illinois
Indiana
Kansas
Kentucky
Louisiana
Maryland
Michigan
Minnesota
Mississippi
Missouri
Montana
Nevada
New Hampshire
New Jersey
New Mexico
North Carolina (structure of Rules and Comment but organized under
    the Canons of the Model Code)
North Dakota
Oklahoma
Pennsylvania
Rhode Island
South Carolina
South Dakota
Texas
Utah
Washington
West Virginia
Wisconsin
Wyoming

* Source: ABA/BNA Manual on Professional Conduct 01:3 (1991) (State Ethics
Rules).

AMERICAN BAR ASSOCIATION MODEL CODE OF PROFESSIONAL RESPONSIBILITY

As Amended and in Effect as of 1983.

[The Model Code of Professional Responsibility was the product of the Wright Committee's efforts to replace the Canons of Professional Ethics, which had grown from 32 canons in 1908 to 47 canons in 1964. The Model Code was enacted by the ABA in 1969, and subsequently, most states adopted codes of professional responsibility based upon the Model Code. The distinctive feature of the Model Code is its organization into canons, ethical considerations, and disciplinary rules. The canons provided the Model Code with a theoretical structure. Each canon was a general directive to lawyers about the law of professional responsibility. The ethical considerations were more detailed in that they discussed actual fact situations that arose under each canon. Each ethical consideration, however, was only aspirational in nature. Lawyers were supposed to strive to follow the ethical considerations, but they were not considered binding. The disciplinary rules were the provisions that lawyers needed to follow to avoid disciplinary liability. These rules established minimum standards that lawyers were required to follow and standards that were enforced by the disciplinary committees. The ABA replaced the Model Code with the Model Rules of Professional Responsibility in 1983. Ed.]

TABLE OF CONTENTS *

* Prepared by Editor.

PREAMBLE AND PRELIMINARY STATEMENT

Preamble [1]

The continued existence of a free and democratic society depends upon recognition of the concept that justice is based upon the rule of law grounded in respect for the dignity of the individual and his capacity through reason for enlightened self-government.[2] Law so grounded makes justice possible, for only through such law does the dignity of the individual attain respect and protection. Without it, individual rights become subject to unrestrained power, respect for law is destroyed, and rational self-government is impossible.

Lawyers as guardians of the law, play a vital role in the preservation of society. The fulfillment of this role requires an understanding by lawyers of their relationship with and function in our legal system.[3] A consequent obligation of lawyers is to maintain the highest standards of ethical conduct.

In fulfilling his professional responsibilities, a lawyer necessarily assumes various roles that require the performance of many difficult tasks. Not every situation which he may encounter can be foreseen,[4]

1. The footnotes are intended merely to enable the reader to relate the provisions of this Code to the ABA Canons of Professional Ethics adopted in 1908, as amended, the Opinions of the ABA Committee on Professional Ethics, and a limited number of other sources; they are not intended to be an annotation of the views taken by the ABA Special Committee on Evaluation of Ethical Standards. Footnotes citing ABA Canons refer to the ABA Canons of Professional Ethics, adopted in 1908, as amended.

2. Cf. ABA Canons, Preamble.

3. "[T]he lawyer stands today in special need of a clear undertstanding of his obligations and of the vital connection between these obligations and the role his profession plays in society." *Professional Responsibility: Report of the Joint Conference,* 44 A.B.A.J. 1159, 1160 (1958).

4. "No general statement of the responsibilities of the legal profession can encompass all the situations in which the lawyer

but fundamental ethical principles are always present to guide him. Within the framework of these principles, a lawyer must with courage and foresight be able and ready to shape the body of the law to the ever-changing relationships of society.[5]

The Code of Professional Responsibility points the way to the aspiring and provides standards by which to judge the transgressor. Each lawyer must find within his own conscience the touchstone against which to test the extent to which his actions should rise above minimum standards. But in the last analysis it is the desire for the respect and confidence of the members of his profession and of the society which he serves that should provide to a lawyer the incentive for the highest possible degree of ethical conduct. The possible loss of that respect and confidence is the ultimate sanction. So long as its practitioners are guided by these principles, the law will continue to be a noble profession. This is its greatness and its strength, which permit of no compromise.

Preliminary Statement

In furtherance of the principles stated in the Preamble, the American Bar Association has promulgated this Code of Professional Responsibility, consisting of three separate but interrelated parts: Canons, Ethical Considerations, and Disciplinary Rules.[6] The Code is designed to be adopted by appropriate agencies both as an inspirational guide to the members of the profession and as a basis for disciplinary action when the conduct of a lawyer falls below the required minimum standards stated in the Disciplinary Rules.

may be placed. Each position held by him makes its own peculiar demands. These demands the lawyer must clarify for himself in the light of the particular role in which he serves." *Professional Responsibility: Report of the Joint Conference*, 44 A.B.A.J. 1159, 1218 (1958).

5. "The law and its institutions change as social conditions change. They must change if they are to preserve, much less advance, the political and social values from which they derive their purposes and their life. This is true of the most important of legal institutions, the profession of law. The profession, too, must change when conditions change in order to preserve and advance the social values that are its reasons for being." Cheatham, *Availability of Legal Services: The Responsibility of the Individual Lawyer and the Organized Bar*, 12 U.C.L.A.L.Rev. 438, 440 (1965).

6. The Supreme Court of Wisconsin adopted a Code of Judicial Ethics in 1967. "The code is divided into standards and rules, the standards being statements of what the general desirable level of conduct should be, the rules being particular canons, the violation of which shall subject an individual judge to sanctions." In re Promulgation of a Code of Judicial Ethics, 36 Wis.2d 252, 255, 153 N.W.2d 873, 874 (1967).

The portion of the Wisconsin Code of Judicial Ethics entitled "Standards" states that "[t]he following standards set forth the significant qualities of the ideal judge . . . ." Id., 36 Wis.2d at 256, 153 N.W.2d at 875. The portion entitled "Rules" states that "[t]he court promulgates the following rules because the requirements of judicial conduct embodied therein are of sufficient gravity to warrant sanctions if they are not obeyed . . . ." Id., 36 Wis.2d at 259, 153 N.W.2d at 876.

Obviously the Canons, Ethical Considerations, and Disciplinary Rules cannot apply to non-lawyers; however, they do define the type of ethical conduct that the public has a right to expect not only of lawyers but also of their non-professional employees and associates in all matters pertaining to professional employment. A lawyer should ultimately be responsible for the conduct of his employees and associates in the course of the professional representation of the client.

The Canons are statements of axiomatic norms, expressing in general terms the standards of professional conduct expected of lawyers in their relationships with the public, with the legal system, and with the legal profession. They embody the general concepts from which the Ethical Considerations and the Disciplinary Rules are derived.

The Ethical Considerations are aspirational in character and represent the objectives toward which every member of the profession should strive. They constitute a body of principles upon which the lawyer can rely for guidance in many specific situations.[7]

The Disciplinary Rules, unlike the Ethical Considerations, are mandatory in character. The Disciplinary Rules state the minimum level of conduct below which no lawyer can fall without being subject to disciplinary action. Within the framework of fair trial,[8] the Disciplina-

7. "Under the conditions of modern practice is it peculiarly necessary that the lawyer should understand, not merely the established standards of professional conduct, but the reasons underlying these standards. Today the lawyer plays a changing and increasingly varied role. In many developing fields the precise contribution of the legal profession is as yet undefined." *Professional Responsibility: Report of the Joint Conference*, 44 A.B.A.J. 1159 (1958).

"A true sense of professional responsibility must derive from an understanding of the reasons that lie back of specific restraints, such as those embodied in the Canons. The grounds for the lawyer's peculiar obligations are to be found in the nature of his calling. The lawyer who seeks a clear understanding of his duties will be led to reflect on the special services his profession renders to society and the services it might render if its full capacities were realized. When the lawyer fully understands the nature of his office, he will then discern what restraints are necessary to keep that office wholesome and effective." *Id.*

8. "Disbarment, designed to protect the public, is a punishment or penalty imposed on the lawyer. * * * He is accordingly entitled to procedural due process, which includes fair notice of the charge." In re Ruffalo, 390 U.S. 544, 550, 20 L.Ed.2d 117, 122, 88 S.Ct. 1222, 1226 (1968), rehearing denied, 391 U.S. 961, 20 L.Ed.2d 874, 88 S.Ct. 1833 (1968).

"A State cannot exclude a person from the practice of law or from any other occupation in a manner or for reasons that contravene the Due Process or Equal Protection Clause of the Fourteenth Amendment. . . . A State can require high standards of qualification . . . but any qualification must have a rational connection with the applicant's fitness or capacity to practice law." Schware v. Bd. of Bar Examiners, 353 U.S. 232, 239, 1 L.Ed.2d 796, 801–02, 77 S.Ct. 752, 756 (1957).

"[A]n accused lawyer may expect that he will not be condemned out of a capricious self-righteousness or denied the essentials of a fair hearing." Kingsland v. Dorsey, 338 U.S. 318, 320, 94 L.Ed. 123, 126, 70 S.Ct. 123, 124–25 (1949).

"The attorney and counsellor being, by the solemn judicial act of the court, clothed with his office, does not hold it as a matter of grace and favor. The right which it

ry Rules should be uniformly applied to all lawyers,[9] regardless of the nature of their professional activities.[10] The Code makes no attempt to prescribe either disciplinary procedures or penalties [11] for violation of a Disciplinary Rule,[12] nor does it undertake to define standards for civil liability of lawyers for professional conduct. The severity of judgment against one found guilty of violating a Disciplinary Rule should be determined by the character of the offense and the attendant circumstances.[13] An enforcing agency, in applying the Disciplinary Rules, may find interpretive guidance in the basic principles embodied in the Canons and in the objectives reflected in the Ethical Considerations.

confers upon him to appear for suitors, and to argue causes is something more than a mere indulgence, revocable at the pleasure of the court, or at the command of the legislature. It is a right of which he can only be deprived by the judgment of the court, for moral or professional delinquency." Ex parte Garland, 71 U.S. (4 Wall.) 333, 378–79, 18 L.Ed. 366, 370 (1866).

See generally Comment, *Procedural Due Process and Character Hearings for Bar Applicants,* 15 Stan.L.Rev. 500 (1963).

9. "The canons of professional ethics must be enforced by the Courts and must be respected by members of the Bar if we are to maintain public confidence in the integrity and impartiality of the administration of justice." In re Meeker, 76 N.M. 354, 357, 414 P.2d 862, 864 (1966), appeal dismissed, 385 U.S. 449 (1967).

10. See ABA Canon 45.

"The Canons of this Association govern all its members, irrespective of the nature of their practice, and the application of the Canons is not affected by statutes or regulations governing certain activities of lawyers which may prescribe less stringent standards." ABA Comm. on Professional Ethics, Opinions, No. 203 (1940) [hereinafter each Opinion is cited as "ABA Opinion"].

Cf. *ABA Opinion* 152 (1936).

11. "There is generally no prescribed discipline for any particular type of improper conduct. The disciplinary measures taken are discretionary with the courts, which may disbar, suspend, or merely censure the attorney as the nature of the offense and past indicia of character

may warrant." Note, 43 Cornell L.Q. 489, 495 (1958).

12. The Code seeks only to specify conduct for which a lawyer should be disciplined. Recommendations as to the procedures to be used in disciplinary actions and the gravity of disciplinary measures appropriate for violations of the Code are within the jurisdiction of the American Bar Association Special Committee on Evaluation of Disciplinary Enforcement.

13. "The severity of the judgment of this court should be in proportion to the gravity of the offenses, the moral turpitude involved, and the extent that the defendant's acts and conduct affect his professional qualifications to practice law." Louisiana State Bar Ass'n v. Steiner, 204 La. 1073, 1092–93, 16 So.2d 843, 850 (1944) (Higgins, J., concurring in decree).

"Certainly an erring lawyer who has been disciplined and who having paid the penalty has given satisfactory evidence of repentance and has been rehabilitated and restored to his place at the bar by the court which knows him best ought not to have what amounts to an order of permanent disbarment entered against him by a federal court solely on the basis of an earlier criminal record and without regard to his subsequent rehabilitation and present good character . . . . We think, therefore, that the district court should reconsider the appellant's application for admission and grant it unless the court finds it to be a fact that the appellant is not presently of good moral or professional character." In re Dreier, 258 F.2d 68, 69–70 (3d Cir.1958).

CANON 1

A Lawyer Should Assist in Maintaining the Integrity and Competence of the Legal Profession

ETHICAL CONSIDERATIONS

EC 1–1 A basic tenet of the professional responsibility of lawyers is that every person in our society should have ready access to the independent professional services of a lawyer of integrity and competence. Maintaining the integrity and improving the competence of the bar to meet the highest standards is the ethical responsibility of every lawyer.

EC 1–2 The public should be protected from those who are not qualified to be lawyers by reason of a deficiency in education [1] or moral standards [2] or of other relevant factors [3] but who nevertheless seek to

1. "[W]e cannot conclude that all educational restrictions [on bar admission] are unlawful. We assume that few would deny that a grammar school education requirement, before taking the bar examination, was reasonable. Or that an applicant had to be able to read or write. Once we conclude that *some* restriction is proper, then it becomes a matter of degree—the problem of drawing the line.

. . . .

"We conclude the fundamental question here is whether Rule IV, Section 6 of the Rules Pertaining to Admission of Applicants to the State Bar of Arizona is 'arbitrary, capricious and unreasonable.' We conclude an educational requirement of graduation from an accredited law school is not." Hackin v. Lockwood, 361 F.2d 499, 503–04 (9th Cir.1966), cert. denied, 385 U.S. 960, 17 L.Ed.2d 305, 87 S.Ct. 396 (1966).

2. "Every state in the United States, as a prerequisite for admission to the practice of law, requires that applicants possess 'good moral character.' Although the requirement is of judicial origin, it is now embodied in legislation in most states." Comment, *Procedural Due Process and Character Hearings for Bar Applicants,* 15 Stan.L.Rev. 500 (1963).

"Good character in the members of the bar is essential to the preservation of the integrity of the courts. The duty and power of the court to guard its portals against intrusion by men and women who are mentally and morally dishonest, unfit because

of bad character, evidenced by their course of conduct, to participate in the administrative law, would seem to be unquestioned in the matter of preservation of judicial dignity and integrity." In re Monaghan, 126 Vt. 53, 222 A.2d 665, 670 (1966).

"Fundamentally, the question involved in both situations [i.e. admission and disciplinary proceedings] is the same—is the applicant for admission or the attorney sought to be disciplined a fit and proper person to be permitted to practice law, and that usually turns upon whether he has committed or is likely to continue to commit acts of moral turpitude. At the time of oral argument the attorney for respondent frankly conceded that the test for admission and for discipline is and should be the same. We agree with this concession." Hallinan v. Comm. of Bar Examiners, 65 Cal.2d 447, 453, 421 P.2d 76, 81, 55 Cal.Rptr. 228, 233 (1966).

3. "Proceedings to gain admission to the bar are for the purpose of protecting the public and the courts from the ministrations of persons unfit to practice the profession. Attorneys are officers of the court appointed to assist the court in the administration of justice. Into their hands are committed the property, the liberty and sometimes the lives of their clients. This commitment demands a high degree of intelligence, knowledge of the law, respect for its function in society, sound and faithful judgment and, above all else, integrity of character in private and profession-

practice law. To assure the maintenance of high moral and educational standards of the legal profession, lawyers should affirmatively assist courts and other appropriate bodies in promulgating, enforcing, and improving requirements for admission to the bar.[4] In like manner, the bar has a positive obligation to aid in the continued improvement of all phases of pre-admission and post-admission legal education.

EC 1-3 Before recommending an applicant for admission, a lawyer should satisfy himself that the applicant is of good moral character. Although a lawyer should not become a self-appointed investigator or judge of applicants for admission, he should report to proper officials all unfavorable information he possesses relating to the character or other qualifications of an applicant.[5]

EC 1-4 The integrity of the profession can be maintained only if conduct of lawyers in violation of the Disciplinary Rules is brought to the attention of the proper officials. A lawyer should reveal voluntarily to those officials all unprivileged knowledge of conduct of lawyers which he believes clearly to be in violation of the Disciplinary Rules.[6] A lawyer should, upon request, serve on and assist committees and boards having responsibility for the administration of the Disciplinary Rules.[7]

EC 1-5 A lawyer should maintain high standards of professional conduct and should encourage fellow lawyers to do likewise. He should be temperate and dignified, and he should refrain from all illegal and morally reprehensible conduct.[8] Because of his position in society, even minor violations of law by a lawyer may tend to lessen public confidence in the legal profession. Obedience to law exemplifies respect for law. To lawyers especially, respect for the law should be more than a platitude.

EC 1-6 An applicant for admission to the bar or a lawyer may be unqualified, temporarily or permanently, for other than moral and

al conduct." In re Monaghan, 126 Vt. 53, 222 A.2d 665, 676 (1966) (Holden, C.J., dissenting).

4. "A bar composed of lawyers of good moral character is a worthy objective but it is unnecessary to sacrifice vital freedoms in order to obtain that goal. It is also important both to society and the bar itself that lawyers be unintimidated—free to think, speak, and act as members of an Independent Bar." Konigsberg v. State Bar, 353 U.S. 252, 273, 1 L.Ed.2d 810, 825, 77 S.Ct. 722, 733 (1957).

5. *See* ABA Canon 29.

6. ABA Canon 28 designates certain conduct as unprofessional and then states that: "A duty to the public and to the profession devolves upon every member of the Bar having knowledge of such practices upon the part of any practitioner immediately to inform thereof, to the end that the offender may be disbarred." ABA Canon 29 states a broader admonition: "Lawyers should expose without fear or favor before the proper tribunals corrupt or dishonest conduct in the profession."

7. "It is the obligation of the organized Bar and the individual lawyer to give unstinted cooperation and assistance to the highest court of the state in discharging its function and duty with respect to discipline and in purging the profession of the unworthy." *Report of the Special Committee on Disciplinary Procedures,* 80 A.B.A. Rep. 463, 470 (1955).

8. Cf. ABA Canon 32.

educational reasons, such as mental or emotional instability. Lawyers should be diligent in taking steps to see that during a period of disqualification such person is not granted a license or, if licensed, is not permitted to practice.[9] In like manner, when the disqualification has terminated, members of the bar should assist such person in being licensed, or, if licensed, in being restored to his full right to practice.

DISCIPLINARY RULES

DR 1-101 Maintaining Integrity and Competence of the Legal Profession.

(A) A lawyer is subject to discipline if he has made a materially false statement in, or if he has deliberately failed to disclose a material fact requested in connection with, his application for admission to the bar.[10]

(B) A lawyer shall not further the application for admission to the bar of another person known by him to be unqualified in respect to character, education, or other relevant attribute.[11]

DR 1-102 Misconduct.

(A) A lawyer shall not:

(1) Violate a Disciplinary Rule.

9. "We decline, on the present record, to disbar Mr. Sherman or to reprimand him—not because we condone his actions, but because, as heretofore indicated, we are concerned with whether he is mentally responsible for what he has done.

"The logic of the situation would seem to dictate the conclusion that, if he was mentally responsible for the conduct we have outlined, he should be disbarred; and, if he was not mentally responsible, he should not be permitted to practice law.

"However, the flaw in the logic is that he may have been mentally irresponsible [at the time of his offensive conduct] . . ., and, yet, have sufficiently improved in the almost two and one-half years intervening to be able to capably and competently represent his clients. . . .

. . .

"We would make clear that we are satisfied that a case has been made against Mr. Sherman, warranting a refusal to permit him to further practice law in this state unless he can establish his mental irre-

sponsibility at the time of the offenses charged. The burden of proof is upon him.

"If he establishes such mental irresponsibility, the burden is then upon him to establish his present capability to practice law." In re Sherman, 58 Wash.2d 1, 6–7, 354 P.2d 888, 890 (1960), cert. denied, 371 U.S. 951, 9 L.Ed.2d 499, 83 S.Ct. 506 (1963).

10. "This Court has the inherent power to revoke a license to practice law in this State, where such license was issued by this Court, and its issuance was procured by the fraudulent concealment, or by the false and fraudulent representation by the applicant of a fact which was manifestly material to the issuance of the license." North Carolina ex rel. Attorney General v. Gorson, 209 N.C. 320, 326, 183 S.E. 392, 395 (1936), cert. denied, 298 U.S. 662, 80 L.Ed. 1387, 56 S.Ct. 752 (1936).

See also Application of Patterson, 318 P.2d 907, 913 (Or.1957), cert. denied, 356 U.S. 947, 2 L.Ed.2d 822, 78 S.Ct. 795 (1958).

11. See ABA Canon 29.

(2) **Circumvent a Disciplinary Rule through actions of another.**[12]

(3) **Engage in illegal conduct involving moral turpitude.**[13]

(4) **Engage in conduct involving dishonesty, fraud, deceit, or misrepresentation.**

(5) **Engage in conduct that is prejudicial to the administration of justice.**

12. In *ABA Opinion* 95 (1933), which held that a municipal attorney could not permit police officers to interview persons with claims against the municipality when the attorney knew the claimants to be represented by counsel, the Committee on Professional Ethics said:

"The law officer is, of course, responsible for the acts of those in his department who are under his supervision and control." *Opinion 85.* In re Robinson, 136 N.Y.S. 548 (affirmed 209 N.Y. 354–1912) held that it was a matter of disbarment for an attorney to adopt a general course of approving the unethical conduct of employees of his client, even though he did not actively participate therein.

" '. . . The attorney should not advise or sanction acts by his client which he himself should not do.' *Opinion 75.*"

13. "The most obvious non-professional ground for disbarment is conviction for a felony. Most states make conviction for a felony grounds for automatic disbarment. Some of these states, including New York, make disbarment mandatory upon conviction for *any* felony, while others require disbarment only for those felonies which involve moral turpitude. There are strong arguments that some felonies, such as involuntary manslaughter, reflect neither on an attorney's fitness, trustworthiness, nor competence and, therefore, should not be grounds for disbarment, but most states tend to disregard these arguments and, following the common law rule, make disbarment mandatory on conviction for any felony." Note, 43 Cornell L.Q. 489, 490 (1958).

"Some states treat conviction for misdemeanors as grounds for automatic disbarment . . . . However, the vast majority, accepting the common law rule, require

that the misdemeanor involve moral turpitude. While the definition of moral turpitude may prove difficult, it seems only proper that those minor offenses which do not affect the attorney's fitness to continue in the profession should not be grounds for disbarment. A good example is an assault and battery conviction which would not involve moral turpitude unless done with malice and deliberation." Id. at 491.

"The term 'moral turpitude' has been used in the law for centuries. It has been the subject of many decisions by the courts but has never been clearly defined because of the nature of the term. Perhaps the best general definition of the term 'moral turpitude' is that it imports an act of baseness, vileness or depravity in the duties which one person owes to another or to society in general, which is contrary to the usual, accepted and customary rule of right and duty which a person should follow. 58 C.J.S. at page 1201. Although offenses against revenue laws have been held to be crimes of moral turpitude, it has also been held that the attempt to evade the payment of taxes due to the government or any subdivision thereof, while wrong and unlawful, does not involve moral turpitude. 58 C.J.S. at page 1205." Comm. on Legal Ethics v. Scheer, 149 W.Va. 721, 726–27, 143 S.E.2d 141, 145 (1965).

"The right and power to discipline an attorney, as one of its officers, is inherent in the court. . . . This power is not limited to those instances of misconduct wherein he has been employed, or has acted, in a professional capacity; but, on the contrary, this power may be exercised where his misconduct outside the scope of his professional relations shows him to be an unfit person to practice law." In re Wilson, 391 S.W.2d 914, 917–18 (Mo.1965).

(6) **Engage in any other conduct that adversely reflects on his fitness to practice law.[14]**

DR 1–103 Disclosure of Information to Authorities.

(A) **A lawyer possessing unprivileged knowledge of a violation of DR 1–102 shall report such knowledge to a tribunal or other authority empowered to investigate or act upon such violation.[15]**

(B) **A lawyer possessing unprivileged knowledge or evidence concerning another lawyer or a judge shall reveal fully such knowledge or evidence upon proper request of a tribunal or other authority empowered to investigate or act upon the conduct of lawyers or judges.[16]**

CANON 2

A Lawyer Should Assist the Legal Profession in Fulfilling Its Duty to Make Legal Counsel Available

ETHICAL CONSIDERATIONS

EC 2–1 The need of members of the public for legal services [1] is met only if they recognize their legal problems, appreciate the importance of seeking assistance,[2] and are able to obtain the services of acceptable

---

14. "It is a fair characterization of the lawyer's responsibility in our society that he stands 'as a shield,' to quote Devlin, J., in defense of right and to ward off wrong. From a profession charged with these responsibilities there must be exacted those qualities of truth-speaking, of a high sense of honor, of granite discretion, of the strictest observance of fiduciary responsibility, that have, throughout the centuries, been compendiously described as 'moral character.'" Schware v. Bd. of Bar Examiners, 353 U.S. 232, 247 L.Ed.2d 796, 806, 77 S.Ct. 752, 761 (1957) (Frankfurter, J., concurring).

"Particularly applicable here is Rule 4.47 providing that 'A lawyer should always maintain his integrity; and shall not willfully commit any act against the interest of the public; nor shall he violate his duty to the courts or his clients; *nor shall he, by any misconduct, commit any offense against the laws of Missouri or the United States of America, which amounts to a crime involving acts done by him contrary to justice, honesty, modesty or good morals;* nor shall he be guilty of any other misconduct whereby, for the protection of the

public and those charged with the administration of justice, he should no longer be entrusted with the duties and responsibilities belonging to the office of an attorney.'" In re Wilson, 391 S.W.2d 914, 917 (Mo.1965).

15. See ABA Canon 29; cf. ABA Canon 28.

16. Cf. ABA Canons 28 and 29.

1. "Men have need for more than a system of law; they have need for a system of law which functions, and that means they have need for lawyers." Cheatham, *The Lawyer's Role and Surroundings,* 25 Rocky Mt.L.Rev. 405 (1953).

2. "Law is not self-applying; men must apply and utilize it in concrete cases. But the ordinary man is incapable. He cannot know the principles of law or the rules guiding the machinery of law administration; he does not know how to formulate his desires with precision and to put them into writing; he is ineffective in the presentation of his claims." Cheatham, *The Lawyer's Role and Surroundings,* 25 Rocky Mt.L.Rev. 405 (1953).

legal counsel.[3] Hence, important functions of the legal profession are to educate laymen to recognize their problems, to facilitate the process of intelligent selection of lawyers, and to assist in making legal services fully available.[4]

Recognition of Legal Problems

EC 2-2 The legal profession should assist lay-persons to recognize legal problems because such problems may not be self-revealing and often are not timely noticed. Therefore, lawyers should encourage and participate in educational and public relations programs concerning our legal system with particular reference to legal problems that frequently arise. Preparation of advertisements and professional articles for lay publications [5] and participation in seminars, lectures, and civic programs should be motivated by a desire to educate the public to an awareness of legal needs and to provide information relevant to the selection of the most appropriate counsel rather than to obtain publicity for particular lawyers. The problems of advertising on television

3. "This need [to provide legal services] was recognized by . . . Mr. [Lewis F.] Powell [Jr., President, American Bar Association, 1963–64], who said: 'Looking at contemporary America realistically, we must admit that despite all our efforts to date (and these have not been insignificant), far too many persons are not able to obtain equal justice under law. This usually results because their poverty or their ignorance has prevented them from obtaining legal counsel.'" Address by E. Clinton Bamberger, Association of American Law Schools 1965 Annual Meeting, Dec. 28, 1965, in Proceedings, Part II, 1965, 61, 63–64 (1965).

"A wide gap separates the need for legal services and its satisfaction, as numerous studies reveal. Looked at from the side of the layman, one reason for the gap is poverty and the consequent inability to pay legal fees. Another set of reasons is ignorance of the need for and the value of legal services, and ignorance of where to find a dependable lawyer. There is fear of the mysterious processes and delays of the law, and there is fear of overreaching and overcharging by lawyers, a fear stimulated by the occasional exposure of shysters." Cheatham, *Availability of Legal Services: The Responsibility of the Individual Lawyer and of the Organized Bar,* 12 U.C.L.A.L. Rev. 438 (1965).

4. "It is not only the right but the duty of the profession as a whole to utilize such

methods as may be developed to bring the services of its members to those who need them, so long as this can be done ethically and with dignity." *ABA Opinion* 320 (1968).

"[T]here is a responsibility on the bar to make legal services available to those who need them. The maxim, 'privilege brings responsibilities,' can be expanded to read, exclusive privilege to render public service brings responsibility to assure that the service is available to those in need of it." Cheatham, *Availability of Legal Services: The Responsibility of the Individual Lawyer and of the Organized Bar,* 12 U.C.L.A.L. Rev. 438, 443 (1965).

"The obligation to provide legal services for those actually caught up in litigation carries with it the obligation to make preventive legal advice accessible to all. It is among those unaccustomed to business affairs and fearful of the ways of the law that such advice is often most needed. If it is not received in time, the most valiant and skillful representation in court may come too late." *Professional Responsibility: Report of the Joint Conference,* 44 A.B. A.J. 1159, 1216 (1958).

5. "A lawyer may with propriety write articles for publications in which he gives information upon the law. . . ." A.B.A. Canon 40.

require special consideration, due to the style, cost, and transitory nature of such media. If the interests of laypersons in receiving relevant lawyer advertising are not adequately served by print media and radio advertising, and if adequate safeguards to protect the public can reasonably be formulated, television advertising may serve a public interest.

As amended in 1977.

EC 2-3 Whether a lawyer acts properly in volunteering in-person advice to a layperson to seek legal services depends upon the circumstances.[6] The giving of advice that one should take legal action could well be in fulfillment of the duty of the legal profession to assist laypersons in recognizing legal problems.[7] The advice is proper only if motivated by a desire to protect one who does not recognize that he may have legal problems or who is ignorant of his legal rights or obligations. It is improper if motivated by a desire to obtain personal benefit, secure personal publicity, or cause legal action to be taken merely to harass or injure another. A lawyer should not initiate an in-person contact with a non-client, personally or through a representative, for the purpose of being retained to represent him for compensation.

As amended in 1977.

EC 2-4 Since motivation is subjective and often difficult to judge, the motives of a lawyer who volunteers in-person advice likely to produce legal controversy may well be suspect if he receives professional employment or other benefits as a result.[8] A lawyer who volunteers in-

---

6. See ABA Canon 28.

7. This question can assume constitutional dimensions: "We meet at the outset the contention that 'solicitation' is wholly outside the area of freedoms protected by the First Amendment. To this contention there are two answers. The first is that a State cannot foreclose the exercise of constitutional rights by mere labels. The second is that abstract discussion is not the only species of communication which the Constitution protects; the First Amendment also protects vigorous advocacy, certainly of lawful ends, against governmental intrusion. . . .

. . . .

"However valid may be Virginia's interest in regulating the traditionally illegal practice of barratry, maintenance and champerty, that interest does not justify the prohibition of the NAACP activities disclosed by this record. Malicious intent was of the essence of the common-law offenses of fomenting or stirring up litiga-

tion. And whatever may be or may have been true of suits against governments in other countries, the exercise in our own, as in this case of First Amendment rights to enforce Constitutional rights through litigation, as a matter of law, cannot be deemed malicious." NAACP v. Button, 371 U.S. 415, 429, 439-40, 9 L.Ed.2d 405, 415-16, 422, 83 S.Ct. 328, 336, 341 (1963).

8. It is disreputable for an attorney to breed litigation by seeking out those who have claims for personal injuries or other grounds of action in order to secure them as clients, or to employ agents or runners, or to reward those who bring or influence the bringing of business to his office. . . . Moreover, it tends quite easily to the institution of baseless litigation and the manufacture of perjured testimony. From early times, this danger has been recognized in the law by the condemnation of the crime of common barratry, or the stirring up of suits or quarrels between

person advice that one should obtain the services of a lawyer generally should not himself accept employment, compensation, or other benefit in connection with that matter. However, it is not improper for a lawyer to volunteer such advice and render resulting legal services to close friends, relatives, former clients (in regard to matters germane to former employment), and regular clients.[9]

As amended in 1977.

EC 2–5 A lawyer who writes or speaks for the purpose of educating members of the public to recognize their legal problems should carefully refrain from giving or appearing to give a general solution applicable to all apparently similar individual problems,[10] since slight changes in fact situations may require a material variance in the applicable advice; otherwise, the public may be mislead and misadvised. Talks and writings by lawyers for laypersons should caution them not to attempt to solve individual problems upon the basis of the information contained therein.[11]

As amended in 1977.

Selection of a Lawyer

EC 2–6 Formerly a potential client usually knew the reputations of local lawyers for competency and integrity and therefore could select a practitioner in whom he had confidence. This traditional selection process worked well because it was initiated by the client and the choice was an informed one.

EC 2–7 Changed conditions, however, have seriously restricted the effectiveness of the traditional selection process. Often the reputations of lawyers are not sufficiently known to enable laypersons to make intelligent choices.[12] The law has become increasingly complex and

individuals at law or otherwise." In re Ades, 6 F.Supp. 467, 474–75 (D.Mary.1934).

9. "*Rule 2.*

"§ a. . . . .

"[A] member of the State Bar shall not solicit professional employment by

"(1) Volunteering counsel or advice except where ties of blood relationship or trust make it appropriate." Cal.Business and Professions Code § 6076 (West 1962).

10. "*Rule 18* . . . A member of the State Bar shall not advise inquirers or render opinions to them through or in connection with a newspaper, radio or other publicity medium of any kind in respect to their specific legal problems, whether or not such attorney shall be compensated for his services." Cal.Business and Professions Code § 6076 (West 1962).

11. "In any case where a member might well apply the advice given in the opinion to his individual affairs, the lawyer rendering the opinion [concerning problems common to members of an association and distributed to the members through a periodic bulletin] should specifically state that this opinion should not be relied on by any member as a basis for handling his individual affairs, but that in every case he should consult his counsel. In the publication of the opinion the association should make a similar statement." *ABA Opinion* 273 (1946).

12. "A group of recent interrelated changes bears directly on the availability of legal services. . . . [One] change is the constantly accelerating urbanization of the country and the decline of personal and neighborhood knowledge of whom to retain as a professional man." Cheatham,

specialized. Few lawyers are willing and competent to deal with every kind of legal matter, and many laypersons have difficulty in determining the competence of lawyers to render different types of legal services. The selection of legal counsel is particularly difficult for transients, persons moving into new areas, persons of limited education or means, and others who have little or no contact with lawyers.[13] Lack of information about the availability of lawyers, the qualifications of particular lawyers, and the expense of legal representation leads laypersons to avoid seeking legal advice.

As amended in 1977.

EC 2-8 Selection of a lawyer by a layperson should be made on an informed basis. Advice and recommendation of third parties—relatives, friends, acquaintances, business associates, or other lawyers—and disclosure of relevant information about the lawyer and his practice may be helpful. A layperson is best served if the recommendation is disinterested and informed. In order that the recommendation be disinterested, a lawyer should not seek to influence another to recommend his employment. A lawyer should not compensate another person for recommending him, for influencing a prospective client to employ him, or to encourage future recommendations.[14] Advertisements and public communications, whether in law lists, telephone directories, newspapers, other forms of print media, television or radio, should be formulated to convey only information that is necessary to make an appropriate selection. Such information includes: (1) office information, such as, name, including name of law firm and names of professional associates; addresses; telephone numbers; credit card acceptability; fluency in foreign languages; and office hours; (2) relevant biographical information; (3) description of the practice, but only by using designations and definitions authorized by [the agency having jurisdiction of the subject under state law], for example, one or more fields of law in which the lawyer or law firm practices; a statement that practice is limited to one or more fields of law; and/or a statement that the lawyer or law firm specializes in a particular field of law practice, but only by using designations, definitions and standards authorized by [the agency having jurisdiction of the subject under state law]; and (4) permitted fee information. Self-laudation should be avoided.

As amended in 1978.

Selection of a Lawyer: Lawyer Advertising

EC 2-9 The lack of sophistication on the part of many members of the public concerning legal services, the importance of the interests affected by the choice of a lawyer and prior experience with unrestricted

---

Availability of Legal Services: The Responsibility of the Individual Lawyer and of the Organized Bar, 12 U.C.L.A.L.Rev. 438, 440 (1965).

13. Cf. Cheatham, *A Lawyer When Needed: Legal Services for the Middle Classes,* 63 Colum.L.Rev. 973, 974 (1963).

14. See ABA Canon 28.

lawyer advertising, require that special care be taken by lawyers to avoid misleading the public and to assure that the information set forth in any advertising is relevant to the selection of a lawyer. The lawyer must be mindful that the benefits of lawyer advertising depend upon its reliability and accuracy. Examples of information in lawyer advertising that would be deceptive include misstatements of fact, suggestions that the ingenuity or prior record of a lawyer rather than the justice of the claim are the principal factors likely to determine the result, inclusion of information irrelevant to selecting a lawyer, and representations concerning the quality of service, which cannot be measured or verified. Since lawyer advertising is calculated and not spontaneous, reasonable regulation of lawyer advertising designed to foster compliance with appropriate standards serves the public interest without impeding the flow of useful, meaningful, and relevant information to the public.

As amended in 1977.

EC 2-10 A lawyer should ensure that the information contained in any advertising which the lawyer publishes, broadcasts or causes to be published or broadcast is relevant, is disseminated in an objective and understandable fashion, and would facilitate the prospective client's ability to compare the qualifications of the lawyers available to represent him. A lawyer should strive to communicate such information without undue emphasis upon style and advertising strategems which serve to hinder rather than to facilitate intelligent selection of counsel. Because technological change is a recurrent feature of communications forms, and because perceptions of what is relevant in lawyer selection may change, lawyer advertising regulations should not be cast in rigid, unchangeable terms. Machinery is therefore available to advertisers and consumers for prompt consideration of proposals to change the rules governing lawyer advertising. The determination of any request for such change should depend upon whether the proposal is necessary in light of existing Code provisions, whether the proposal accords with standards of accuracy, reliability and truthfulness, and whether the proposal would facilitate informed selection of lawyers by potential consumers of legal services. Representatives of lawyers and consumers should be heard in addition to the applicant concerning any proposed change. Any change which is approved should be promulgated in the form of an amendment to the Code so that all lawyers practicing in the jurisdiction may avail themselves of its provisions.

As amended in 1977.

EC 2-11 The name under which a lawyer conducts his practice may be a factor in the selection process.[15] The use of a trade name or an assumed name could mislead laypersons concerning the identity, responsibility, and status of those practicing thereunder.[16] Accordingly, a

---

15. *Cf. ABA Opinion* 303 (1961).   16. *See* ABA Canon 33.

lawyer in private practice should practice only under a designation containing his own name, the name of a lawyer employing him, the name of one or more of the lawyers practicing in a partnership, or, if permitted by law, the name of a professional legal corporation, which should be clearly designated as such. For many years some law firms have used a firm name retaining one or more names of deceased or retired partners and such practice is not improper if the firm is a bona fide successor of a firm in which the deceased or retired person was a member, if the use of the name is authorized by law or by contract, and if the public is not misled thereby.[17] However, the name of a partner who withdraws from a firm but continues to practice law should be omitted from the firm name in order to avoid misleading the public.

As amended in 1977.

EC 2–12 A lawyer occupying a judicial, legislative, or public executive or administrative position who has the right to practice law concurrently may allow his name to remain in the name of the firm if he actively continues to practice law as a member thereof. Otherwise, his name should be removed from the firm name,[18] and he should not be identified as a past or present member of the firm; and he should not hold himself out as being a practicing lawyer.

EC 2–13 In order to avoid the possibility of misleading persons with whom he deals, a lawyer should be scrupulous in the representation of his professional status.[19] He should not hold himself out as being a partner or associate of a law firm if he is not one in fact,[20] and thus should not hold himself out as partner or associate if he only shares offices with another lawyer.[21]

17. Id.

"The continued use of a firm name by one or more surviving partners after the death of a member of the firm whose name is in the firm title is expressly permitted by the Canons of Ethics. The reason for this is that all of the partners have by their joint and several efforts over a period of years contributed to the good will attached to the firm name. In the case of a firm having widespread connections, this good will is disturbed by a change in firm name every time a name partner dies, and that reflects a loss in some degree of the good will to the building up of which the surviving partners have contributed their time, skill and labor through a period of years. To avoid this loss the firm name is continued, and to meet the requirements of the Canon the individuals constituting the firm from time to time are listed." *ABA Opinion* 267 (1945).

"Accepted local custom in New York recognizes that the name of a law firm does not necessarily identify the individual members of the firm, and hence the continued use of a firm name after the death of one or more partners is not a deception and is permissible. . . . The continued use of a deceased partner's name in the firm title is not affected by the fact that another partner withdraws from the firm and his name is dropped, or the name of the new partner is added to the firm name." *Opinion* No. 45, Committee on Professional Ethics, New York State Bar Ass'n, 39 N.Y.St.B.J. 455 (1967).

18. Cf. ABA Canon 33 and *ABA Opinion* 315 (1965).

19. Cf. *ABA Opinions* 283 (1950) and 81 (1932).

20. See *ABA Opinion* 316 (1967).

21. "The word 'associates' has a variety of meanings. Principally through custom

EC 2-14 In some instances a lawyer confines his practice to a particular field of law.[22] In the absence of state controls to insure the existence of special competence, a lawyer should not be permitted to hold himself out as a specialist or as having official recognition as a specialist, other than in the fields of admiralty, trademark, and patent law where a holding out as a specialist historically has been permitted. A lawyer may, however, indicate in permitted advertising, if it is factual, a limitation of his practice or one or more particular areas or fields of law in which he practices using designations and definitions authorized for that purpose by [the state agency having jurisdiction]. A lawyer practicing in a jurisdiction which certifies specialists must also be careful not to confuse laypersons as to his status. If a lawyer discloses areas of law in which he practices or to which he limits his practice, but is not certified in [the jurisdiction], he, and the designation authorized in [the jurisdiction], should avoid any implication that he is in fact certified.

As amended in 1977.

EC 2-15 The legal profession has developed lawyer referral systems designed to aid individuals who are able to pay fees but need assistance in locating lawyers competent to handle their particular problems. Use of a lawyer referral system enables a layman to avoid an uninformed selection of a lawyer because such a system makes possible the employment of competent lawyers who have indicated an interest in the subject matter involved. Lawyers should support the principle of lawyer referral systems and should encourage the evolution of other ethical plans which aid in the selection of qualified counsel.

Financial Ability to Employ Counsel: Generally

EC 2-16 The legal profession cannot remain a viable force in fulfilling its role in our society unless its members receive adequate compensation for services rendered, and reasonable fees [23] should be charged in appropriate cases to clients able to pay them. Nevertheless, persons unable to pay all or a portion of a reasonable fee should be able to

the word when used on the letterheads of law firms has come to be regarded as describing those who are employees of the firm. Because the word has acquired this special significance in connection with the practice of the law the use of the word to describe lawyer relationships other than employer-employee is likely to be misleading." In re Sussman and Tanner, 241 Ore. 246, 248, 405 P.2d 355, 356 (1965).

According to *ABA Opinion* 310 (1963), use of the term "associates" would be misleading in two situations: (1) where two lawyers are partners and they share both responsibility and liability for the partnership; and (2) where two lawyers practice separately, sharing no responsibility or liability, and only share a suite of offices and some costs.

22. "For a long time, many lawyers have, of necessity, limited their practice to certain branches of law. The increasing complexity of the law and the demand of the public for more expertness on the part of the lawyer has, in the past few years— particularly in the last ten years—brought about specialization on an increasing scale." *Report of the Special Committee on Specialization and Specialized Legal Services,* 79 A.B.A.Rep. 582, 584 (1954).

23. See ABA Canon 12.

obtain necessary legal services,[24] and lawyers should support and participate in ethical activities designed to achieve that objective.[25]

Financial Ability to Employ Counsel: Persons Able to Pay Reasonable Fees

EC 2–17 The determination of a proper fee requires consideration of the interests of both client and lawyer.[26] A lawyer should not charge more than a reasonable fee,[27] for excessive cost of legal service would deter laymen from utilizing the legal system in protection of their rights. Furthermore, an excessive charge abuses the professional relationship between lawyer and client. On the other hand, adequate compensation is necessary in order to enable the lawyer to serve his client effectively and to preserve the integrity and independence of the profession.[28]

EC 2–18 The determination of the reasonableness of a fee requires consideration of all relevant circumstances,[29] including those stated in the Disciplinary Rules. The fees of a lawyer will vary according to many factors, including the time required, his experience, ability, and reputation, the nature of the employment, the responsibility involved, and the results obtained. It is a commendable and long-standing tradition of the bar that special consideration is given in the fixing of any fee for services rendered a brother lawyer or a member of his immediate family.

As amended in 1974.

EC 2–19 As soon as feasible after a lawyer has been employed, it is desirable that he reach a clear agreement with his client as to the basis of the fee charges to be made. Such a course will not only prevent later misunderstanding but will also work for good relations between the lawyer and the client. It is usually beneficial to reduce to writing the understanding of the parties regarding the fee, particularly when it is contingent. A lawyer should be mindful that many persons who desire to employ him may have had little or no experience with fee charges of lawyers, and for this reason he should explain fully to such persons the reasons for the particular fee arrangement he proposes.

24. Cf. ABA Canon 12.

25. "If there is any fundamental proposition of government on which all would agree, it is that one of the highest goals of society must be to achieve and maintain equality before the law. Yet this ideal remains an empty form of words unless the legal profession is ready to provide adequate representation for those unable to pay the usual fees." *Professional Representation: Report of the Joint Conference,* 44 A.B.A.J. 1159, 1216 (1958).

26. See ABA Canon 12.

27. Cf. ABA Canon 12.

28. "When members of the Bar are induced to render legal services for inadequate compensation as a consequence the quality of the service rendered may be lowered, the welfare of the profession injured and the administration of justice made less efficient." *ABA Opinion* 302 (1961).

Cf. *ABA Opinion* 307 (1962).

29. See ABA Canon 12.

EC 2–20 Contingent fee arrangements [30] in civil cases have long been commonly accepted in the United States in proceedings to enforce claims. The historical bases of their acceptance are that (1) they often, and in a variety of circumstances, provide the only practical means by which one having a claim against another can economically afford, finance, and obtain the services of a competent lawyer to prosecute his claim, and (2) a successful prosecution of the claim produces a *res* out of which the fee can be paid.[31] Although a lawyer generally should decline to accept employment on a contingent fee basis by one who is able to pay a reasonable fixed fee, it is not necessarily improper for a lawyer, where justified by the particular circumstances of a case, to enter into a contingent fee contract in a civil case with any client who, after being fully informed of all relevant factors, desires that arrangement. Because of the human relationships involved and the unique character of the proceedings, contingent fee arrangements in domestic relation cases are rarely justified. In administrative agency proceedings contingent fee contracts should be governed by the same consideration as in other civil cases. Public policy properly condemns contingent fee arrangements in criminal cases, largely on the ground that legal services in criminal cases do not produce a *res* with which to pay the fee.

EC 2–21 A lawyer should not accept compensation or any thing of value incident to his employment or services from one other than his client without the knowledge and consent of his client after full disclosure.[32]

EC 2–22 Without the consent of his client, a lawyer should not associate in a particular matter another lawyer outside his firm. A fee may properly be divided between lawyers [33] properly associated if the division is in proportion to the services performed and the responsibility assumed by each lawyer [34] and if the total fee is reasonable.

30. See ABA Canon 13; see also MacKinnon, Contingent Fees for Legal Services (1964) (A report of the American Bar Foundation).

"A contract for a reasonable contingent fee where sanctioned by law is permitted by *Canon 13*, but the client must remain responsible to the lawyer for expenses advanced by the latter. 'There is to be no barter of the privilege of prosecuting a cause for gain in exchange for the promise of the attorney to prosecute at his own expense.' (Cardozo, C.J. In Matter of Gilman, 251 N.Y. 265, 270–271.)" *ABA Opinion* 246 (1942).

31. See Comment, *Providing Legal Services for the Middle Class in Civil Matters: The Problem, the Duty and a Solution,* 26 U.Pitt.L.Rev. 811, 829 (1965).

32. See ABA Canon 38.

"Of course, as . . . [Informal Opinion 679] points out, there must be full disclosure of the arrangement [that an entity other than the client pays the attorney's fee] by the attorney to the client. . . ." *ABA Opinion* 320 (1968).

33. "Only lawyers may share in . . . a division of fees, but . . . it is not necessary that both lawyers be admitted to practice in the same state, so long as the division was based on the division of services or responsibility." *ABA Opinion* 316 (1967).

34. See ABA Canon 34.

"We adhere to our previous rulings that where a lawyer merely brings about the employment of another lawyer *but renders*

EC 2–23 A lawyer should be zealous in his efforts to avoid controversies over fees with clients [35] and should attempt to resolve amicably any differences on the subject.[36] He should not sue a client for a fee unless necessary to prevent fraud or gross imposition by the client.[37]

Financial Ability to Employ Counsel: Persons Unable to Pay Reasonable Fees

EC 2–24 A layman whose financial ability is not sufficient to permit payment of any fee cannot obtain legal services, other than in cases where a contingent fee is appropriate, unless the services are provided for him. Even a person of moderate means may be unable to pay a reasonable fee which is large because of the complexity, novelty, or difficulty of the problem or similar factors.[38]

no service and assumes no responsibility in the matter, a division of the latter's fee is improper. *(Opinions 18 and 153).*

"It is assumed that the bar, generally, understands what acts or conduct of a lawyer may constitute 'services' to a client within the intendment of *Canon 12.* Such acts or conduct invariably, if not always involve 'responsibility' on the part of the lawyer, whether the word 'responsibility' be construed to denote the possible resultant legal or moral liability on the part of the lawyer to the client or to others, or the onus of deciding what should or should not be done in behalf of the client. The word 'services' in *Canon 12* must be construed in this broad sense and may apply to the selection and retainer of associate counsel as well as to others acts or conduct in the client's behalf." *ABA Opinion* 204 (1940).

35. See ABA Canon 14.

36. Cf. *ABA Opinion* 320 (1968).

37. See ABA Canon 14.

"Ours is a learned profession, not a mere money-getting trade. . . . Suits to collect fees should be avoided. Only where the circumstances imperatively require, should resort be had to a suit to compel payment. And where a lawyer does resort to a suit to enforce payment of fees which involves a disclosure, he should carefully avoid any disclosure not clearly necessary to obtaining or defending his rights." *ABA Opinion* 250 (1943).

But cf. *ABA Opinion* 320 (1968).

38. "As a society increases in size, sophistication and technology, the body of laws which is required to control that soci-

ety also increases in size, scope and complexity. With this growth, the law directly affects more and more facets of individual behavior, creating an expanding need for legal services on the part of the individual members of the society. . . . As legal guidance in social and commercial behavior increasingly becomes necessary, there will come a concurrent demand from the layman that such guidance be made available to him. This demand will not come from those who are able to employ the best legal talent, nor from those who can obtain legal assistance at little or no cost. It will come from the large 'forgotten middle income class,' who can neither afford to pay proportionately large fees nor qualify for ultra-low-cost services. The legal profession must recognize this inevitable demand and consider methods whereby it can be satisfied. If the profession fails to provide such methods, the laity will." Comment, *Providing Legal Services for the Middle Class in Civil Matters: The Problem, the Duty and a Solution,* 26 U.Pitt.L.Rev. 811, 811–12 (1965).

"The issue is not whether we shall do something or do nothing. The demand for ordinary everyday legal justice is so great and the moral nature of the demand is so strong that the issue has become whether we devise, maintain, and support suitable agencies able to satisfy the demand, or by our own default, force the government to take over the job, supplant us, and ultimately dominate us." Smith, *Legal Service Offices for Persons of Moderate Means,* 1949 Wis.L.Rev. 416, 418 (1949).

EC 2–25 Historically, the need for legal services of those unable to pay reasonable fees has been met in part by lawyers who donated their services or accepted court appointments on behalf of such individuals. The basic responsibility for providing legal services for those unable to pay ultimately rests upon the individual lawyer, and personal involvement in the problems of the disadvantaged can be one of the most rewarding experiences in the life of a lawyer. Every lawyer, regardless of professional prominence or professional workload, should find time to participate in serving the disadvantaged. The rendition of free legal services to those unable to pay reasonable fees continues to be an obligation of each lawyer, but the efforts of individual lawyers are often not enough to meet the need.[39] Thus it has been necessary for the profession to institute additional programs to provide legal services.[40] Accordingly, legal aid offices,[41] lawyer referral services, and other related programs have been developed, and others will be developed, by the profession.[42] Every lawyer should support all proper efforts to meet this need for legal services.[43]

39. "Lawyers have peculiar responsibilities for the just administration of the law, and these responsibilities include providing advice and representation for needy persons. To a degree not always appreciated by the public at large, the bar has performed these obligations with zeal and devotion. The Committee is persuaded, however, that a system of justice that attempts, in mid-twentieth century America, to meet the needs of the financially incapacitated accused through primary or exclusive reliance on the uncompensated services of counsel will prove unsuccessful and inadequate. . . . A system of adequate representation, therefore, should be structured and financed in a manner reflecting its public importance. . . . We believe that fees for private appointed counsel should be set by the court within maximum limits established by the statute." Report of the Att'y Gen's Comm. on Poverty and the Administration of Criminal Justice 41–43 (1963).

40. "At present this representation [of those unable to pay usual fees] is being supplied in some measure through the spontaneous generosity of individual lawyers, through legal aid societies, and—increasingly—through the organized efforts of the Bar. If those who stand in need of this service know of its availability and their need is in fact adequately met, the precise mechanism by which this service is provided becomes of secondary importance.

It is of great importance, however, that both the impulse to render this service and the plan for making that impulse effective, should arise within the legal profession itself." *Professional Responsibility: Report of the Joint Conference,* 44 A.B.A.J. 1159, 1216 (1958).

41. "Free legal clinics carried on by the organized bar are not ethically objectionable. On the contrary, they serve a very worthwhile purpose and should be encouraged." *ABA Opinion* 191 (1939).

42. "Whereas the American Bar Association believes that it is a fundamental duty of the bar to see to it that all persons requiring legal advice be able to attain it, irrespective of their economic status . . . .

"Resolved, that the Association approves and sponsors the setting up by state and local bar associations of lawyer referral plans and low-cost legal service methods for the purpose of dealing with cases of persons who might not otherwise have the benefit of legal advice . . . ." *Proceedings of the House of Delegates of the American Bar Association,* Oct. 30, 1946, 71 A.B.A. Rep. 103, 109–10 (1946).

43. "The defense of indigent citizens, without compensation, is carried on throughout the country by lawyers representing legal aid societies, not only with the approval, but with the commendation of those acquainted with the work. Not

Acceptance and Retention of Employment

EC 2–26 A lawyer is under no obligation to act as advisor or advocate for every person who may wish to become his client; but in furtherance of the objective of the bar to make legal services fully available, a lawyer should not lightly decline proffered employment. The fulfillment of this objective requires acceptance by a lawyer of his share of tendered employment which may be unattractive both to him and the bar generally.[44]

EC 2–27 History is replete with instances of distinguished and sacrificial services by lawyers who have represented unpopular clients and causes. Regardless of his personal feelings, a lawyer should not decline representation because a client or a cause is unpopular or community reaction is adverse.[45]

EC 2–28 The personal preference of a lawyer to avoid adversary alignment against judges, other lawyers,[46] public officials, or influential members of the community does not justify his rejection of tendered employment.

EC 2–29 When a lawyer is appointed by a court or requested by a bar association to undertake representation of a person unable to obtain

infrequently services are rendered out of sympathy or for other philanthropic reasons, by individual lawyers who do not represent legal aid societies. There is nothing whatever in the Canons to prevent a lawyer from performing such an act, nor should there be." *ABA Opinion* 148 (1935).

44. But cf. ABA Canon 31.

45. "One of the highest services the lawyer can render to society is to appear in court on behalf of clients whose causes are in disfavor with the general public." *Professional Responsibility: Report of the Joint Conference*, 44 A.B.A.J. 1159, 1216 (1958).

One author proposes the following proposition to be included in "A Proper Oath for Advocates": "I recognize that it is sometimes difficult for clients with unpopular causes to obtain proper legal representation. I will do all that I can to assure that the client with the unpopular cause is properly represented, and that the lawyer representing such a client receives credit from and support of the bar for handling such a matter." Thode, *The Ethical Standard for the Advocate*, 39 Texas L.Rev. 575, 592 (1961).

"§ 6068. . . . It is the duty of an attorney.

. . .

"(h) Never to reject, for any consideration personal to himself, the cause of the defenseless or the oppressed." Cal.Business and Professions Code § 6068 (West 1962). Virtually the same language is found in the Oregon statutes at Ore.Rev. Stats. Ch. 9, § 9.460(8).

See Rostow, *The Lawyer and His Client*, 48 A.B.A.J. 25 and 146 (1962).

46. See ABA Canons 7 and 29.

"We are of the opinion that it is not professionally improper for a lawyer to accept employment to compel another lawyer to honor the just claim of a layman. On the contrary, it is highly proper that he do so. Unfortunately, there appears to be a widespread feeling among laymen that it is difficult, if not impossible, to obtain justice when they have claims against members of the Bar because other lawyers will not accept employment to proceed against them. The honor of the profession, whose members proudly style themselves officers of the court, must surely be sullied if its members bind themselves by custom to refrain from enforcing just claims of laymen against lawyers." *ABA Opinion* 144 (1935).

counsel, whether for financial or other reasons, he should not seek to be excused from undertaking the representation except for compelling reasons.[47] Compelling reasons do not include such factors as the repugnance of the subject matter of the proceeding, the identity [48] or position of a person involved in the case, the belief of the lawyer that the defendant in a criminal proceeding is guilty,[49] or the belief of the lawyer regarding the merits of the civil case.[50]

EC 2-30 Employment should not be accepted by a lawyer when he is unable to render competent service [51] or when he knows or it is obvious that the person seeking to employ him desires to institute or maintain an action merely for the purpose of harassing or maliciously injuring another.[52] Likewise, a lawyer should decline employment if the intensity of his personal feeling, as distinguished from a community attitude, may impair his effective representation of a prospective client. If a lawyer knows a client has previously obtained counsel, he should not accept employment in the matter unless the other counsel approves [53] or withdraws, or the client terminates the prior employment.[54]

EC 2-31 Full availability of legal counsel requires both that persons be able to obtain counsel and that lawyers who undertake representation complete the work involved. Trial counsel for a convicted defendant should continue to represent his client by advising whether to take an appeal and, if the appeal is prosecuted, by representing him through the appeal unless new counsel is substituted or withdrawal is permitted by the appropriate court.

47. ABA Canon 4 uses a slightly different test, saying, "A lawyer assigned as counsel for an indigent prisoner ought not to ask to be excused for any trivial reason. . . ."

48. Cf. ABA Canon 7.

49. See ABA Canon 5.

50. Dr. Johnson's reply to Boswell upon being asked what he thought of "supporting a cause which you know to be bad" was: "Sir, you do not know it to be good or bad till the Judge determines it. I have said that you are to state facts fairly; so that your thinking, or what you call knowing, a cause to be bad, must be from reasoning, must be from supposing your arguments to be weak and inconclusive. But, Sir, that is not enough. An argument which does not convince yourself, may convince the Judge to whom you urge it; and if it does convince him, why, then, Sir, you are wrong, and he is right." 2 Boswell, The Life of Johnson 47–48 (Hill ed. 1887).

51. "The lawyer deciding whether to undertake a case must be able to judge objectively whether he is capable of handling it and whether he can assume its burdens without prejudice to previous commitments. . . ." *Professional Responsibility: Report of the Joint Conference*, 44 A.B.A.J. 1158, 1218 (1958).

52. "The lawyer must decline to conduct a civil cause or to make a defense when convinced that it is intended merely to harass or to injure the opposite party or to work oppression or wrong." ABA Canon 30.

53. See ABA Canon 7.

54. Id.

"From the facts stated we assume that the client has discharged the first attorney and given notice of the discharge. Such being the case, the second attorney may properly accept employment. *Canon 7; Opinions 10, 130, 149*." *ABA Opinion* 209 (1941).

EC 2–32   A decision by a lawyer to withdraw should be made only on the basis of compelling circumstances,[55] and in a matter pending before a tribunal he must comply with the rules of the tribunal regarding withdrawal. A lawyer should not withdraw without considering carefully and endeavoring to minimize the possible adverse effect on the rights of his client and the possibility of prejudice to his client [56] as a result of his withdrawal. Even when he justifiably withdraws, a lawyer should protect the welfare of his client by giving due notice of his withdrawal,[57] suggesting employment of other counsel, delivering to the client all papers and property to which the client is entitled, cooperating with counsel subsequently employed, and otherwise endeavoring to minimize the possibility of harm. Further, he should refund to the client any compensation not earned during the employment.[58]

EC 2–33   As a part of the legal profession's commitment to the principle that high quality legal services should be available to all, attorneys are encouraged to cooperate with qualified legal assistance organizations providing prepaid legal services. Such participation should at all times be in accordance with the basic tenets of the profession: independence, integrity, competence and devotion to the interests of individual clients. An attorney so participating should make certain that his relationship with a qualified legal assistance organization in no way interferes with his independent, professional representation of the interests of the individual client. An attorney should avoid situations in which officials of the organization who are not lawyers attempt to direct attorneys concerning the manner in which legal services are performed for individual members, and should also avoid situations in which considerations of economy are given undue weight in determining the attorneys employed by an organization or the legal services to be performed for the member or beneficiary rather than competence and quality of service. An attorney interested in maintaining the historic traditions of the profession and preserving the function of a lawyer as a trusted and independent advisor to individual members of society should carefully assess such factors when accepting employment by, or otherwise participating in, a particular qualified legal assistance organization,

---

55.   See ABA Canon 44.

"I will carefully consider, before taking a case, whether it appears that I can fully represent the client within the framework of law. If the decision is in the affirmative, then it will take extreme circumstances to cause me to decide later that I cannot so represent him." Thode, *The Ethical Standard for the Advocate*, 39 Texas L.Rev. 575, 592 (1961) (from "A Proper Oath for Advocates").

56.   *ABA Opinion* 314 (1965) held that a lawyer should not disassociate himself from a cause when "it is obvious that the very act of disassociation would have the effect of violating *Canon 37*."

57.   ABA Canon 44 enumerates instances in which ". . . the lawyer may be warranted in withdrawing on due notice to the client, allowing him time to employ another lawyer."

58.   *See* ABA Canon 44.

and while so participating should adhere to the highest professional standards of effort and competence.

Added in 1974; amended in 1975.

DISCIPLINARY RULES

DR 2-101 Publicity.

(A) A lawyer shall not, on behalf of himself, his partner, associate or any other lawyer affiliated with him or his firm, use or participate in the use of any form of public communication containing a false, fraudulent, misleading, deceptive, self-laudatory or unfair statement or claim.

(B) In order to facilitate the process of informed selection of a lawyer by potential consumers of legal services, a lawyer may publish or broadcast, subject to DR 2-103, the following information in print media distributed or over television or radio broadcast in the geographic area or areas in which the lawyer resides or maintains offices or in which a significant part of the lawyer's clientele resides, provided that the information disclosed by the lawyer in such publication or broadcast complies with DR 2-101(A), and is presented in a dignified manner:

   (1) Name, including name of law firm and names of professional associates; addresses and telephone numbers;

   (2) One or more fields of law in which the lawyer or law firm practices, a statement that practice is limited to one or more fields of law, or a statement that the lawyer or law firm specializes in a particular field of law practice, to the extent authorized under DR 2-105;

   (3) Date and place of birth;

   (4) Date and place of admission to the bar of state and federal courts;

   (5) Schools attended, with dates of graduation, degrees and other scholastic distinctions;

   (6) Public or quasi-public offices;

   (7) Military service;

   (8) Legal authorships;

   (9) Legal teaching positions;

   (10) Memberships, offices, and committee assignments, in bar associations;

   (11) Membership and offices in legal fraternities and legal societies;

   (12) Technical and professional licenses;

(13) Memberships in scientific, technical and professional associations and societies;

(14) Foreign language ability;

(15) Names and addresses of bank references;

(16) With their written consent, names of clients regularly represented;

(17) Prepaid or group legal services programs in which the lawyer participates;

(18) Whether credit cards or other credit arrangements are accepted;

(19) Office and telephone answering service hours;

(20) Fee for an initial consultation;

(21) Availability upon request of a written schedule of fees and/or an estimate of the fee to be charged for specific services;

(22) Contingent fee rates subject to DR 2–106(C), provided that the statement discloses whether percentages are computed before or after deduction of costs;

(23) Range of fees for services, provided that the statement discloses that the specific fee within the range which will be charged will vary depending upon the particular matter to be handled for each client and the client is entitled without obligation to an estimate of the fee within the range likely to be charged. In print size equivalent to the largest print used in setting forth the fee information;

(24) Hourly rate, provided that the statement discloses that the total fee charged will depend upon the number of hours which must be devoted to the particular matter to be handled for each client and the client is entitled to without obligation an estimate of the fee likely to be charged, in print size at least equivalent to the largest print used in setting forth the fee information;

(25) Fixed fees for specific legal services,* the description of which would not be misunderstood or be deceptive, provided that the statement discloses that the quoted fee will be available only to clients whose matters fall into the services described and that the client is entitled without obligation to a specific estimate of the fee likely to be charged in print size at least equivalent to the largest print used in setting forth the fee information.

* The agency having jurisdiction under state law may desire to issue appropriate guidelines defining "specific legal services."

(C) Any person desiring to expand the information authorized for disclosure in DR 2-101(B), or to provide for its dissemination through other forums may apply to [the agency having jurisdiction under state law]. Any such application shall be served upon [the agencies having jurisdiction under state law over the regulation of the legal profession and consumer matters] who shall be heard, together with the applicant, on the issue of whether the proposal is necessary in light of the existing provisions of the Code, accords with standards of accuracy, reliability and truthfulness, and would facilitate the process of informed selection of lawyers by potential consumers of legal services. The relief granted in response to any such application shall be promulgated as an amendment to DR 2-101(B), universally applicable to all lawyers.*

(D) If the advertisement is communicated to the public over television or radio, it shall be prerecorded, approved for broadcast by the lawyer, and a recording of the actual transmission shall be retained by the lawyer.

(E) If a lawyer advertises a fee for a service, the lawyer must render that service for no more than the fee advertised.

(F) Unless otherwise specified in the advertisement if a lawyer publishes any fee information authorized under DR 2-101(B) in a publication that is published more frequently than one time per month, the lawyer shall be bound by any representation made therein for a period of not less than 30 days after such publication. If a lawyer publishes any fee information authorized under DR 2-101(B) in a publication that is published once a month or less frequently, he shall be bound by any representation made therein until the publication of the succeeding issue. If a lawyer publishes any fee information authorized under DR 2-101(B) in a publication which has no fixed date for publication of a succeeding issue, the lawyer shall be bound by any representation made therein for a reasonable period of time after publication but in no event less than one year.

(G) Unless otherwise specified, if a lawyer broadcasts any fee information authorized under DR 2-101(B), the lawyer shall be bound by any representation made therein for a period of not less than 30 days after such broadcast.

(H) This rule does not prohibit limited and dignified identification of a lawyer as a lawyer as well as by name:

(1) In political advertisements when his professional status is germane to the political campaign or to a political issue.

---

* The agency having jurisdiction under state law should establish orderly and expeditious procedures for ruling on such applications.

   (2) In public notices when the name and profession of a lawyer are required or authorized by law or are reasonably pertinent for a purpose other than the attraction of potential clients.

   (3) In routine reports and announcements of a bona fide business, civic, professional, or political organization in which he serves as a director or officer.

   (4) In and on legal documents prepared by him.

   (5) In and on legal textbooks, treatises, and other legal publications, and in dignified advertisements thereof.

(I) A lawyer shall not compensate or give any thing of value to representatives of the press, radio, television, or other communication medium in anticipation of or in return for professional publicity in a news item.

As amended in 1974, 1975, 1977 and 1978.

DR 2-102   Professional Notices, Letterheads and Offices.

(A) A lawyer or law firm shall not use or participate in the use of professional cards, professional announcement cards, office signs, letterheads, or similar professional notices or devices, except that the following may be used if they are in dignified form:

   (1) A professional card of a lawyer identifying him by name and as a lawyer, and giving his addresses, telephone numbers, the name of his law firm, and any information permitted under DR 2-105. A professional card of a law firm may also give the names of members and associates. Such cards may be used for identification.

   (2) A brief professional announcement card stating new or changed associations or addresses, change of firm name, or similar matters pertaining to the professional offices of a lawyer or law firm, which may be mailed to lawyers, clients, former clients, personal friends, and relatives.[59] It shall not state biographical data except to the extent reasonably necessary to identify the lawyer or to explain the change in his association, but it may state the immediate past position of the lawyer.[60] It may give the names

---

59. See *ABA Opinion* 301 (1961).

60. "[I]t has become commonplace for many lawyers to participate in government service; to deny them the right, upon their return to private practice, to refer to their prior employment in a brief and dignified manner, would place an undue limitation upon a large element of our profession. It is entirely proper for a member of the profession to explain his absence from private practice, where such is the primary purpose of the announcement, by a brief and dignified reference to the prior employment.

". . . [A]ny such announcement should be limited to the immediate past connection of the lawyer with the government, made upon his leaving that position

and dates of predecessor firms in a continuing line of succession. It shall not state the nature of the practice except as permitted under DR 2-105.[61]

(3) A sign on or near the door of the office and in the building directory identifying the law office. The sign shall not state the nature of the practice, except as permitted under DR 2-105.

(4) A letter head of a lawyer identifying him by name and as a lawyer, and giving his addresses, telephone numbers, the name of his law firm, associates and any information permitted under DR 2-105. A letterhead of a law firm may also give the names of members and associates,[62] and names and dates relating to deceased and retired members.[63] A lawyer may be designated "Of Counsel" on a letterhead if he has a continuing relationship with a lawyer or law firm, other than as a partner or associate. A lawyer or law firm may be designated as "General Counsel" or by similar professional reference on stationary of a client if he or the firm devotes a substantial amount of professional time in the representation of that client.[64] The letterhead of a law firm may give the names and dates of predecessor firms in a continuing line of succession.

(B) A lawyer in private practice shall not practice under a trade name, a name that is misleading as to the identity of the lawyer or lawyers practicing under such name, or a firm name containing names other than those of one or more of the lawyers in the firm, except that the name of a professional corporation or professional association may contain "P.C." or "P.A." or similar symbols indicating the nature of the organization, and if otherwise lawful a firm may use as, or continue to include in, its name the name or names of one or more deceased or retired members of the firm or of a predecessor firm in a continuing line of succession.[65] A lawyer who assumes a judicial, legislative, or public executive or administrative post or office shall not permit his name to remain in the name of a law firm or to be used in professional notices of the firm during any significant period in which he is not actively and regularly practicing law as a member of the

---

to enter private practice." *ABA Opinion* 301 (1961).

61. See *ABA Opinion* 251 (1943).

62. "Those lawyers who are working for an individual lawyer or a law firm may be designated on the letterhead and in other

appropriate places as 'associates'." *ABA Opinion* 310 (1963).

63. See ABA Canon 33.

64. But see *ABA Opinion* 285 (1951).

65. See ABA Canon 33; cf. *ABA Opinions* 318 (1967), 267 (1945), 219 (1941), 208 (1940), 192 (1939), 97 (1933), and 6 (1925).

firm,[66] and during such period other members of the firm shall not use his name in the firm name or in professional notices of the firm.[67]

(C) A lawyer shall not hold himself out as having a partnership with one or more other lawyers or professional corporations unless they are in fact partners.[68]

(D) A partnership shall not be formed or continued between or among lawyers licensed in different jurisdictions unless all enumerations of the members and associates of the firm on its letterhead and in other permissible listings make clear the jurisdictional limitations on those members and associates of the firm not licensed to practice in all listed jurisdictions; [69] however, the same firm name may be used in each jurisdiction.

(E) Nothing contained herein shall prohibit a lawyer from using or permitting the use of, in connection with his name, an earned degree or title derived therefrom indicating his training in the law.

As amended in 1976, 1977, 1979 and 1980.

DR 2-103 Recommendation of Professional Employment.[70]

(A) A lawyer shall not, except as authorized in DR 2-101(B), recommend employment as a private practitioner,[71] of himself, his partner, or associate to a layperson who has not sought his advice regarding employment of a lawyer.[72]

66. *ABA Opinion* 318 (1967) held, anything to the contrary in Formal Opinion 315 or in the other opinions cited notwithstanding that: Where a partner whose name appears in the name of a law firm is elected or appointed to high local, state or federal office, which office he intends to occupy only temporarily, at the end of which time he intends to return to his position with the firm, and procided that he is not precluded by holding such office from engaging in the practice of law and does not in fact sever his relationship with the firm but only takes a leave of absence, and provided that there is no local law, statute or custom to the contrary, his name may be retained in the firm name during his term or terms of office, but only if proper precautions are taken not to mislead the public as to his degree of participation in the firm's affairs.

Cf. *ABA Opinion* 143 (1935). New York County Opinion 67, and New York City Opinions 36 and 798; but cf. *ABA Opinion* 192 (1939) and Michigan Opinion 164.

67. Cf. ABA Canon 33.

68. See *ABA Opinion* 277 (1948); cf. ABA Canon 33 and *ABA Opinions* 318 (1967), 126 (1935), 115 (1934), and 106 (1934).

69. See *ABA Opinions* 318 (1967) and 316 (1967); cf. ABA Canon 33.

70. Cf. ABA Canon 28.

71. "We think it clear that a lawyer's seeking employment in an ordinary law office, or appointment to a civil service position, is not prohibited by . . . [Canon 27]." *ABA Opinion* 197 (1939).

72. "[A] lawyer may not seek from persons not his clients the opportunity to perform . . . a [legal] checkup." *ABA Opinion* 307 (1962).

(B) A lawyer shall not compensate or give anything of value to a person or organization to recommend or secure his employment [73] by a client, or as a reward for having made a recommendation resulting in his employment [74] by a client, except that he may pay the usual and reasonable fees or dues charged by any of the organizations listed in DR 2-103(D).

(C) A lawyer shall not request a person or organization to recommend or promote the use of his services or those of his partner or associate, or any other lawyer affiliated with him or his firm, as a private practitioner, [75] except as authorized in DR 2-101, and except that

(1) He may request referrals from a lawyer referral service operated, sponsored, or approved by a bar association and may pay its fees incident thereto. [76]

(2) He may cooperate with the legal service activities of any of the offices or organizations enumerated in DR 2-103(D) (1) through (4) and may perform legal services for those to whom he was recommended by it to do such work if:

(a) The person to whom the recommendation is made is a member or beneficiary of such office or organization; and

(b) The lawyer remains free to exercise his independent professional judgment on behalf of his client.

(D) A lawyer or his partner or associate or any other lawyer affiliated with him or his firm may be recommended, employed or paid by, or may cooperate with, one of the following offices or organizations that promote the use of his services or those of his partner or associate or any other lawyer affiliated with him or his firm if there is no interference with

---

73. Cf. *ABA Opinion* 78 (1932).

74. "'No financial connection of any kind between the Brotherhood and any lawyer is permissible. No lawyer can properly pay any amount whatsoever to the Brotherhood or any of its departments, officers or members as compensation, reimbursement of expenses or gratuity in connection with the procurement of a case.'" In re Brotherhood of R.R. Trainmen, 13 Ill. 2d 391, 398, 150 N.E.2d 163, 167 (1958), quoted in In re Ratner, 194 Kan. 362, 372, 399 P.2d 865, 873 (1956).

See *ABA Opinion* 147 (1935).

75. "This Court has condemned the practice of ambulance chasing through the media of runners and touters. In similar fashion we have with equal emphasis condemned the practice of direct solicitation by a lawyer. We have classified both offenses as serious breaches of the Canons of Ethics demanding severe treatment of the offending lawyer." State v. Dawson, 111 So.2d 427, 431 (Fla.1959).

76. "Registrants [of a lawyer referral plan] may be required to contribute to the expense of operating it by a reasonable registration charge or by a reasonable percentage of fees collected by them." *ABA Opinion* 291 (1956).

Cf. *ABA Opinion* 227 (1941).

the exercise of independent professional judgment in behalf of his client:

(1) A legal aid office or public defender office:

   (a) Operated or sponsored by a duly accredited law school.

   (b) Operated or sponsored by a bona fide nonprofit community organization.

   (c) Operated or sponsored by a governmental agency.

   (d) Operated, sponsored, or approved by a bar association.[77]

(2) A military legal assistance office.

(3) A lawyer referral service operated, sponsored, or approved by a bar association.

(4) Any bona fide organization that recommends, furnishes or pays for legal services to its members or beneficiaries [78] provided the following conditions are satisfied:

   (a) Such organization, including any affiliate, is so organized and operated that no profit is derived by it from the rendition of legal services by lawyers, and that, if the organization is organized for profit, the legal services are not rendered by lawyers employed, directed, supervised or selected by it except in connection with matters where such organization bears ultimate liability of its member or beneficiary.

   (b) Neither the lawyer, nor his partner, nor associate, nor any other lawyer affiliated with him or his firm, nor any non-lawyer, shall have initiated or promoted such organization for the primary purpose of providing financial or other benefit to such lawyer, partner, associate or affiliated lawyer.

   (c) Such organization is not operated for the purpose of procuring legal work or financial benefit for any lawyer as a private practitioner outside of the legal services program of the organization.

   (d) The member or beneficiary to whom the legal services are furnished, and not such organization, is recognized as the client of the lawyer in the matter.

   (e) Any member or beneficiary who is entitled to have legal services furnished or paid for by the organiza-

77. Cf. *ABA Opinion* 148 (1935).

78. United Mine Workers v. Ill. State Bar Ass'n., 389 U.S. 217, 19 L.Ed.2d 426, 88 S.Ct. 353 (1967); Brotherhood of R.R. Trainmen v. Virginia, 371 U.S. 1, 12 L.Ed. 2d 89, 84 S.Ct. 1113 (1964); NAACP v. Button, 371 U.S. 415, 9 L.Ed.2d 405, 83 S.Ct. 328 (1963).

tion may, if such member or beneficiary so desires, select counsel other than that furnished, selected or approved by the organization for the particular matter involved; and the legal service plan of such organization provides appropriate relief for any member or beneficiary who asserts a claim that representation by counsel furnished, selected or approved would be unethical, improper or inadequate under the circumstances of the matter involved and the plan provides an appropriate procedure for seeking such relief.

(f) The lawyer does not know or have cause to know that such organization is in violation of applicable laws, rules of court and other legal requirements that govern its legal service operations.

(g) Such organization has filed with the appropriate disciplinary authority at least annually a report with respect to its legal service plan, if any, showing its terms, its schedule of benefits, its subscription charges, agreements with counsel, and financial results of its legal service activities or, if it has failed to do so, the lawyer does not know or have cause to know of such failure.

(E) A lawyer shall not accept employment when he knows or it is obvious that the person who seeks his services does so as a result of conduct prohibited under this Disciplinary Rule.

As amended in 1974, 1975 and 1977.

DR 2-104   Suggestion of Need of Legal Services.[79, 80]

(A) A lawyer who has given in-person unsolicited advice to a layperson that he should obtain counsel or take legal action shall not accept employment resulting from that advice,[81] except that:

(1) A lawyer may accept employment by a close friend, relative, former client (if the advice is germane to the former employment), or one whom the lawyer reasonably believes to be a client.[82]

---

79. "If a bar association has embarked on a program of institutional advertising for an annual legal check-up and provides brochures and reprints, it is not improper to have these available in the lawyer's office for persons to read and take." *ABA Opinion* 307 (1962).

Cf. *ABA Opinion* 121 (1934).

80. ABA Canon 28.

81. Cf. *ABA Opinions* 229 (1941) and 173 (1937).

82. "It certainly is not improper for a lawyer to advise his regular clients of new statutes, court decisions, and administrative rulings, which may affect the client's interests, provided the communication is strictly limited to such information. . . .

"When such communications go to concerns or individuals other than regular cli-

(2) A lawyer may accept employment that results from his participation in activities designed to educate laypersons to recognize legal problems, to make intelligent selection of counsel, or to utilize available legal services if such activities are conducted or sponsored by a qualified legal assistance organization.

(3) A lawyer who is recommended, furnished or paid by a qualified legal assistance organization enumerated in DR 2-103(D)(1) through (4) may represent a member or beneficiary thereof, to the extent and under the conditions prescribed therein.

(4) Without affecting his right to accept employment, a lawyer may speak publicly or write for publication on legal topics [83] so long as he does not emphasize his own professional experience or reputation and does not undertake to give individual advice.

(5) If success in asserting rights or defenses of his client in litigation in the nature of a class action is dependent upon the joinder of others, a lawyer may accept, but shall not seek, employment from those contacted for the purpose of obtaining their joinder.[84]

As amended in 1974, 1975 and 1977.

DR 2-105 Limitation of Practice.[85]

(A) A lawyer shall not hold himself out publicly as a specialist, as practicing in certain areas of law or as limiting his practice permitted under DR 2-101(B), except as follows:

(1) A lawyer admitted to practice before the United States Patent and Trademark Office may use the designation "Patents," "Patent Attorney," "Patent Lawyer," or "Registered Patent Attorney" or any combination of those terms, on his letterhead and office sign.

(2) A lawyer who publicly discloses fields of law in which the lawyer or the law firm practices or states that his practice

ents of the lawyer, they are thinly disguised advertisements for professional employment, and are obviously improper." *ABA Opinion* 213 (1941).

"It is our opinion that where the lawyer has no reason to believe that he has been supplanted by another lawyer, it is not only his right, but it might even be his duty to advise his client of any change of fact or law which might defeat the client's testamentary purpose as expressed in the will.

"Periodic notices might be sent to the client for whom a lawyer has drawn a will, suggesting that it might be wise for the client to reexamine his will to determine whether or not there has been any change in his situation requiring a modification of his will." *ABA Opinion* 210 (1941).

Cf. ABA Canon 28.

83. Cf. *ABA Opinion* 168 (1937).

84. But cf. *ABA Opinion* 111 (1934).

85. See ABA Canon 45; cf. ABA Canons 43, and 46.

is limited to one or more fields of law shall do so by using designations and definitions authorized and approved by [the agency having jurisdiction of the subject under state law].

(3) A lawyer who is certified as a specialist in a particular field of law or law practice by [the authority having jurisdiction under state law over the subject of specialization by lawyers] may hold himself out as such, but only in accordance with the rules prescribed by that authority.[86]

As amended in 1977.

DR 2–106   Fees for Legal Services.[87]

(A) A lawyer shall not enter into an agreement for, charge, or collect an illegal or clearly excessive fee.[88]

(B) A fee is clearly excessive when, after a review of the facts, a lawyer of ordinary prudence would be left with a definite and firm conviction that the fee is in excess of a reasonable fee. Factors to be considered as guides in determining the reasonableness of a fee include the following:

(1) The time and labor required, the novelty and difficulty of the questions involved, and the skill requisite to perform the legal service properly.

(2) The likelihood, if apparent to the client, that the acceptance of the particular employment will preclude other employment by the lawyer.

(3) The fee customarily charged in the locality for similar legal services.

(4) The amount involved and the results obtained.

(5) The time limitations imposed by the client or by the circumstances.

(6) The nature and length of the professional relationship with the client.

(7) The experience, reputation, and ability of the lawyer or lawyers performing the services.

---

86. This provision is included to conform to action taken by the ABA House of Delegates at the Mid-Winter Meeting, January, 1969.

87. See ABA Canon 12.

88. The charging of a "clearly excessive fee" is a ground for discipline. State ex rel. Nebraska State Bar Ass'n. v. Richards, 165 Neb. 80, 90, 84 N.W.2d 136, 143 (1957).

"An attorney has the right to contract for any fee he chooses so long as it is not excessive (see Opinion 190), and this Committee is not concerned with the amount of such fees unless so excessive as to constitute a misappropriation of the client's funds (see Opinion 27)." *ABA Opinion* 320 (1968).

Cf. *ABA Opinions* 209 (1940), 190 (1939), and 27 (1930) and State ex rel. Lee v. Buchanan, 191 So.2d 33 (Fla.1966).

(8) **Whether the fee is fixed or contingent.**[89]

(C) **A lawyer shall not enter into an arrangement for, charge, or collect a contingent fee for representing a defendant in a criminal case.**[90]

DR 2-107   Division of Fees Among Lawyers.

(A) **A lawyer shall not divide a fee for legal services with another lawyer who is not a partner in or associate of his law firm or law office, unless:**

(1) **The client consents to employment of the other lawyer after a full disclosure that a division of fees will be made.**

(2) **The division is made in proportion to the services performed and responsibility assumed by each.**[91]

(3) **The total fee of the lawyers does not clearly exceed reasonable compensation for all legal services they rendered the client.**[92]

(B) **This Disciplinary Rule does not prohibit payment to a former partner or associate pursuant to a separation or retirement agreement.**

DR 2-108   Agreements Restricting the Practice of a Lawyer.

(A) **A lawyer shall not be a party to or participate in a partnership or employment agreement with another lawyer that restricts the right of a lawyer to practice law after the termi-**

---

89. Cf. ABA Canon 13; see generally MacKinnon, Contingent Fees for Legal Services (1964) (A Report of the American Bar Foundation).

90. "Contingent fees, whether in civil or criminal cases, are a special concern of the law. . . .

"In criminal cases, the rule is stricter because of the danger of corrupting justice. The second part of Section 542 of the Restatement [of Contracts] reads: 'A bargain to conduct a criminal case . . . in consideration of a promise of a fee contingent on success is illegal. . . .'" Peyton v. Margiotti, 398 Pa. 86, 156 A.2d 865, 967 (1959).

"The third area of practice in which the use of the contingent fee is generally considered to be prohibited is the prosecution and defense of criminal cases. However, there are so few cases, and these are predominantly old, that it is doubtful that there can be said to be any current law on

the subject. . . . In the absence of cases on the validity of contingent fees for defense attorneys, it is necessary to rely on the consensus among commentators that such a fee is void as against public policy. The nature of criminal practice itself makes unlikely the use of contingent fee contracts." MacKinnon, Contingent Fees for Legal Services 52 (1964) (A Report of the American Bar Foundation).

91. See ABA Canon 34 and *ABA Opinions* 316 (1967) and 294 (1958); see generally *ABA Opinions* 265 (1945), 204 (1940), 190 (1939), 171 (1937), 153 (1936), 97 (1933), 63 (1932), 28 (1930), 27 (1930), and 18 (1930).

92. "*Canon 12* contemplates that a lawyer's fee should not exceed *the value of the services* rendered. . . .

"*Canon 12* applies, whether joint or separate fees are charged [by associate attorneys] . . . ." *ABA Opinion* 204 (1940).

nation of a relationship created by the agreement, except as a condition to payment of retirement benefits.[93]

(B) In connection with the settlement of a controversy or suit, a lawyer shall not enter into an agreement that restricts his right to practice law.

DR 2-109 Acceptance of Employment.

(A) A lawyer shall not accept employment on behalf of a person if he knows or it is obvious that such person wishes to:

(1) Bring a legal action, conduct a defense, or assert a position in litigation, or otherwise have steps taken for him, merely for the purpose of harassing or maliciously injuring any person.[94]

(2) Present a claim or defense in litigation that is not warranted under existing law, unless it can be supported by good faith argument for an extension, modification, or reversal of existing law.

DR 2-110 Withdrawal From Employment.[95]

(A) In general.

(1) If permission for withdrawal from employment is required by the rules of a tribunal, a lawyer shall not withdraw from employment in a proceeding before that tribunal without its permission.

(2) In any event, a lawyer shall not withdraw from employment until he has taken reasonable steps to avoid foreseeable prejudice to the rights of his client, including giving due notice to his client, allowing time for employment of other counsel, delivering to the client all papers and property to which the client is entitled, and complying with applicable laws and rules.

(3) A lawyer who withdraws from employment shall refund promptly any part of a fee paid in advance that has not been earned.

(B) Mandatory withdrawal.

---

93. "[A] general covenant restricting an employed lawyer, after leaving the employment, from practicing in the community for a stated period, appears to this Committee to be an unwarranted restriction on the right of a lawyer to choose where he will practice and inconsistent with our professional status. Accordingly, the Committee is of the opinion it would be improper for the employing lawyer to require the covenant and likewise for the employed lawyer to agree to it." *ABA Opinion* 300 (1961).

94. See ABA Canon 30.

"*Rule 13.* . . . A member of the State Bar shall not accept employment to prosecute or defend a case solely out of spite, or solely for the purpose of harassing or delaying another. . . ." Cal.Business and Professions Code § 6067 (West 1962).

95. Cf. ABA Canon 44.

A lawyer representing a client before a tribunal, with its permission if required by its rules, shall withdraw from employment, and a lawyer representing a client in other matters shall withdraw from employment, if:

(1) He knows or it is obvious that his client is bringing the legal action, conducting the defense, or asserting a position in the litigation, or is otherwise having steps taken for him, merely for the purpose of harassing or maliciously injuring any person.

(2) He knows or it is obvious that his continued employment will result in violation of a Disciplinary Rule.[96]

(3) His mental or physical condition renders it unreasonably difficult for him to carry out the employment effectively.

(4) He is discharged by his client.

(C) Permissive withdrawal.[97]

If DR 2–110(B) is not applicable, a lawyer may not request permission to withdraw in matters pending before a tribunal, and may not withdraw in other matters, unless such request or such withdrawal is because:

(1) His client:

(a) Insists upon presenting a claim or defense that is not warranted under existing law and cannot be supported by good faith argument for an extension, modification, or reversal of existing law.[98]

(b) Personally seeks to pursue an illegal course of conduct.

(c) Insists that the lawyer pursue a course of conduct that is illegal or that is prohibited under the Disciplinary Rules.

(d) By other conduct renders it unreasonably difficult for the lawyer to carry out his employment effectively.

(e) Insists, in a matter not pending before a tribunal, that the lawyer engage in conduct that is contrary to the judgment and advice of the lawyer but not prohibited under the Disciplinary Rules.

(f) Deliberately disregards an agreement or obligation to the lawyer as to expenses or fees.

(2) His continued employment is likely to result in a violation of a Disciplinary Rule.

96. See also Code of Professional Responsibility, DR 5–102 and DR 5–105.

97. Cf. ABA Canon 4.

98. Cf. Anders v. California, 386 U.S. 738, 18 L.Ed.2d 493, 87 S.Ct. 1396 (1967), rehearing denied, 388 U.S. 924, 18 L.Ed.2d 1377, 87 S.Ct. 2094 (1967).

(3) His inability to work with co-counsel indicates that the best interests of the client likely will be served by withdrawal.

(4) His mental or physical condition renders it difficult for him to carry out the employment effectively.

(5) His client knowingly and freely assents to termination of his employment.

(6) He believes in good faith, in a proceeding pending before a tribunal, that the tribunal will find the existence of other good cause for withdrawal.

CANON 3

A Lawyer Should Assist in Preventing the Unauthorized Practice of Law

ETHICAL CONSIDERATIONS

EC 3–1 The prohibition against the practice of law by a layman is grounded in the need of the public for integrity and competence of those who undertake to render legal services. Because of the fiduciary and personal character of the lawyer-client relationship and the inherently complex nature of our legal system, the public can better be assured of the requisite responsibility and competence if the practice of law is confined to those who are subject to the requirements and regulations imposed upon members of the legal profession.

EC 3–2 The sensitive variations in the considerations that bear on legal determinations often make it difficult even for a lawyer to exercise appropriate professional judgment, and it is therefore essential that the personal nature of the relationship of client and lawyer be preserved. Competent professional judgment is the product of a trained familiarity with law and legal processes, a disciplined, analytical approach to legal problems, and a firm ethical commitment.

EC 3–3 A non-lawyer who undertakes to handle legal matters is not governed as to integrity or legal competence by the same rules that govern the conduct of a lawyer. A lawyer is not only subject to that regulation but also is committed to high standards of ethical conduct. The public interest is best served in legal matters by a regulated profession committed to such standards.[1] The Disciplinary Rules protect the public in that they prohibit a lawyer from seeking employment by improper overtures, from acting in cases of divided loyalties, and

---

1. "The condemnation of the unauthorized practice of law is designed to protect the public from legal services by persons unskilled in the law. The prohibition of lay intermediaries is intended to insure the loyalty of the lawyer to the client unimpaired by intervening and possibly conflicting interests." Cheatham, *Availability of Legal Services: The Responsibility of the Individual Lawyer and of the Organized Bar,* 12 U.C.L.A.L.Rev. 438, 439 (1965).

from submitting to the control of others in the exercise of his judgment. Moreover, a person who entrusts legal matters to a lawyer is protected by the attorney-client privilege and by the duty of the lawyer to hold inviolate the confidences and secrets of his client.

EC 3–4 A layman who seeks legal services often is not in a position to judge whether he will receive proper professional attention. The entrustment of a legal matter may well involve the confidences, the reputation, the property, the freedom, or even the life of the client. Proper protection of members of the public demands that no person be permitted to act in the confidential and demanding capacity of a lawyer unless he is subject to the regulations of the legal profession.

EC 3–5 It is neither necessary nor desirable to attempt the formulation of a single, specific definition of what constitutes the practice of law.[2] Functionally, the practice of law relates to the rendition of services for others that call for the professional judgment of a lawyer. The essence of the professional judgment of the lawyer is his educated ability to relate the general body and philosophy of law to a specific legal problem of a client; and thus, the public interest will be better served if only lawyers are permitted to act in matters involving professional judgment. Where this professional judgment is not involved, non-lawyers, such as court clerks, police officers, abstracters, and many governmental employees, may engage in occupations that require a special knowledge of law in certain areas. But the services of a lawyer are essential in the public interest whenever the exercise of professional legal judgment is required.

EC 3–6 A lawyer often delegates tasks to clerks, secretaries, and other lay persons. Such delegation is proper if the lawyer maintains a direct relationship with his client, supervises the delegated work, and has complete professional responsibility for the work product.[3] This

2. "What constitutes unauthorized practice of the law in a particular jurisdiction is a matter for determination by the courts of that jurisdiction." *ABA Opinion* 198 (1939).

"In the light of the historical development of the lawyer's functions, it is impossible to lay down an exhaustive definition of 'the practice of law' by attempting to enumerate every conceivable act performed by lawyers in the normal course of their work." State Bar of Arizona v. Arizona Land Title & Trust Co., 90 Ariz. 76, 87, 366 P.2d 1, 8–9 (1961), modified, 91 Ariz. 293, 371 P.2d 1020 (1962).

3. "A lawyer can employ lay secretaries, lay investigators, lay detectives, lay researchers, accountants, lay scriveners, nonlawyer draftsmen or nonlawyer re-

searchers. In fact he may employ nonlawyers to do any task for him except counsel clients about law matters, engage directly in the practice of law, appear in court or appear in formal proceedings a part of the judicial process, so long as it is he who takes the work and vouches for it to the client and becomes responsible to the client." *ABA Opinion* 316 (1967).

ABA Opinion 316 (1967) also stated that if a lawyer practices law as part of a law firm which includes lawyers from several states, he may delegate tasks to firm members in other states so long as he "is the person who, on behalf of the firm, vouched for the work of all of the others and, with the client and in the courts, did the legal acts defined by that state as the practice of law."

delegation enables a lawyer to render legal service more economically and efficiently.

EC 3-7 The prohibition against a non-lawyer practicing law does not prevent a layman from representing himself, for then he is ordinarily exposing only himself to possible injury. The purpose of the legal profession is to make educated legal representation available to the public; but anyone who does not wish to avail himself of such representation is not required to do so. Even so, the legal profession should help members of the public to recognize legal problems and to understand why it may be unwise for them to act for themselves in matters having legal consequences.

EC 3-8 Since a lawyer should not aid or encourage a layman to practice law, he should not practice law in association with a layman or otherwise share legal fees with a layman.[4] This does not mean, however, that the pecuniary value of the interest of a deceased lawyer in his firm or practice may not be paid to his estate or specified persons such as his widow or heirs.[5] In like manner, profit-sharing retirement plans of a lawyer or law firm which include non-lawyer office employ-

"A lawyer cannot delegate his professional responsibility to a law student employed in his office. He may avail himself of the assistance of the student in many of the fields of the lawyer's work, such as examination of case law, finding and interviewing witnesses, making collections of claims, examining court records, delivering papers, conveying important messages, and other similar matters. But the student is not permitted, until he is admitted to the Bar, to perform the professional functions of a lawyer, such as conducting court trials, giving professional advice to clients or drawing legal documents for them. The student in all his work must act as agent for the lawyer employing him, who must supervise his work and be responsible for his good conduct." *ABA Opinion* 85 (1932).

4. "No division of fees for legal services is proper, except with another lawyer . . . ." *ABA Canon* 34. Otherwise, according to *ABA Opinion* 316 (1967), "[t]he Canons of Ethics do not examine into the method by which such persons are remunerated by the lawyer. . . . They may be paid a salary, a per diem charge, a flat fee, a contract price, etc."

See ABA Canons 33 and 47.

5. "Many partnership agreements provide that the active partners, on the death of any one of them, are to make payments to the estate or to the nominee of a deceased partner on a pre-determined formula. It is only where the effect of such an arrangement is to make the estate or nominee a member of the partnership along with the surviving partners that it is prohibited by *Canon 34.* Where the payments are made in accordance with a pre-existing agreement entered into by the deceased partner during his lifetime and providing for a fixed method for determining their amount based upon the value of services rendered during the partner's lifetime and providing for a fixed period over which the payments are to be made, this is not the case. Under these circumstances, whether the payments are considered to be delayed payment of compensation earned but withheld during the partner's lifetime, or whether they are considered to be an approximation of his interest in matters pending at the time of his death, is immaterial. In either event, as Henry S. Drinker says in his book, Legal Ethics, at page 189: 'It would seem, however, that a reasonable agreement to pay the estate a proportion of the receipts for a reasonable period is a proper practical settlement for the lawyer's services to his retirement or death.' " *ABA Opinion* 308 (1963).

ees are not improper.[6] These limited exceptions to the rule against sharing legal fees with laymen are permissible since they do not aid or encourage laymen to practice law.

EC 3–9 Regulation of the practice of law is accomplished principally by the respective states.[7] Authority to engage in the practice of law conferred in any jurisdiction is not per se a grant of the right to practice elsewhere, and it is improper for a lawyer to engage in practice where he is not permitted by law or by court order to do so. However, the demands of business and the mobility of our society pose distinct problems in the regulation of the practice of law by the states.[8] In furtherance of the public interest, the legal profession should discourage regulation that unreasonably imposes territorial limitations upon the right of a lawyer to handle the legal affairs of his client or upon the opportunity of a client to obtain the services of a lawyer of his choice in all matters including the presentation of a contested matter in a tribunal before which the lawyer is not permanently admitted to practice.[9]

DISCIPLINARY RULES

DR 3–101 Aiding Unauthorized Practice of Law.[10]

(A) A lawyer shall not aid a non-lawyer in the unauthorized practice of law.[11]

(B) A lawyer shall not practice law in a jurisdiction where to do so would be in violation of regulations of the profession in that jurisdiction.[12]

6. Cf. ABA Opinion 311 (1964).

7. "That the States have broad power to regulate the practice of law is, of course, beyond question." United Mine Workers v. Ill. State Bar Ass'n, 389 U.S. 217, 222 (1967).

"It is a matter of law, not of ethics, as to where an individual may practice law. Each state has its own rules." *ABA Opinion* 316 (1967).

8. "Much of clients' business crosses state lines. People are mobile, moving from state to state. Many metropolitan areas cross state lines. It is common today to have a single economic and social community involving more than one state. The business of a single client may involve legal problems in several states." *ABA Opinion* 316 (1967).

9. "[W]e reaffirmed the general principle that legal services to New Jersey residents with respect to New Jersey matters may ordinarily be furnished only by New Jersey counsel; but we pointed out that there may be multistate transactions where strict adherence to this thesis would not be in the public interest and that, under the circumstances, it would have been not only more costly to the client but also 'grossly impractical and inefficient' to have had the settlement negotiations conducted by separate lawyers from different states." In re Estate of Waring, 47 N.J. 367, 376, 221 A.2d 193, 197 (1966).

Cf. ABA Opinion 316 (1967).

10. Conduct permitted by the Disciplinary Rules of Canons 2 and 5 does not violate DR 3–101.

11. See ABA Canon 47.

12. It should be noted, however, that a lawyer may engage in conduct, otherwise prohibited by this Disciplinary Rule, where such conduct is authorized by preemptive federal legislation. See Sperry v. Florida, 373 U.S. 379, 10 L.Ed.2d 428, 83 S.Ct. 1322 (1963).

DR 3–102 Dividing Legal Fees With a Non-lawyer.

(A) A lawyer or law firm shall not share legal fees with a non-lawyer,[13] except that:

    (1) An agreement by a lawyer with his firm, partner, or associate may provide for the payment of money, over a reasonable period of time after his death, to his estate or to one or more specified persons.[14]

    (2) A lawyer who undertakes to complete unfinished legal business of a deceased lawyer may pay to the estate of the deceased lawyer that proportion of the total compensation which fairly represents the services rendered by the deceased lawyer.

    (3) A lawyer or law firm may include non-lawyer employees in a compensation or retirement plan, even though the plan is based in whole or in part on a profit-sharing arrangement [15] providing such plan does not circumvent another disciplinary rule.[16]

As amended in 1980.

DR 3–103 Forming a Partnership With a Non-lawyer.

(A) A lawyer shall not form a partnership with a non-lawyer if any of the activities of the partnership consist of the practice of law.[17]

CANON 4

A Lawyer Should Preserve the Confidences and Secrets of a Client

ETHICAL CONSIDERATIONS

EC 4–1 Both the fiduciary relationship existing between lawyer and client and the proper functioning of the legal system require the preservation by the lawyer of confidences and secrets of one who has

---

13. See ABA Canon 34 and *ABA Opinions* 316 (1967), 180 (1938), and 48 (1931).

"The receiving attorney shall not under any guise or form share his fee for legal services with a lay agency, personal or corporate, without prejudice, however, to the right of the lay forwarder to charge and collect from the creditor proper compensation for non-legal services rendered by the law [*sic*] forwarder which are separate and apart from the services performed by the receiving attorney." *ABA Opinion* 294 (1958).

14. See *ABA Opinion* 266 (1945).

15. Cf. *ABA Opinion* 311 (1964).

16. See ABA Informal Opinion 1440 (1979).

17. See ABA Canon 33; cf. *ABA Opinions* 239 (1942) and 201 (1940).

ABA Opinion 316 (1967) states that lawyers licensed in different jurisdictions may, under certain conditions, enter "into an arrangement for the practice of law" and that a lawyer licensed in State A is not, for such purpose a layman in State B.

employed or sought to employ him.[1] A client must feel free to discuss whatever he wishes with his lawyer and a lawyer must be equally free to obtain information beyond that volunteered by his client.[2] A lawyer should be fully informed of all the facts of the matter he is handling in order for his client to obtain the full advantage of our legal system. It is for the lawyer in the exercise of his independent professional judgment to separate the relevant and important from the irrelevant and unimportant. The observance of the ethical obligation of a lawyer to hold inviolate the confidences and secrets of his client not only facilitates the full development of facts essential to proper representation of the client but also encourages laymen to seek early legal assistance.

EC 4–2 The obligation to protect confidences and secrets obviously does not preclude a lawyer from revealing information when his client consents after full disclosure,[3] when necessary to perform his professional employment, when permitted by a Disciplinary Rule, or when required by law. Unless the client otherwise directs, a lawyer may disclose the affairs of his client to partners or associates of his firm. It

1. See ABA Canons 6 and 37 and *ABA Opinions* 287 (1953). "The reason underlying the rule with respect to confidential communications between attorney and client is well stated in Mechem on Agency, 2d Ed., Vol. 2, § 2297, as follows: 'The purposes and necessities of the relation between a client and his attorney require, in many cases on the part of the client, the fullest and freest disclosures to the attorney of the client's objects, motives and acts. This disclosure is made in the strictest confidence, relying upon the attorney's honor and fidelity. To permit the attorney to reveal to others what is so disclosed, would be not only a gross violation of a sacred trust upon his part, but it would utterly destroy and prevent the usefulness and benefits to be derived from professional assistance. Based upon considerations of public policy, therefore, the law wisely declares that all confidential communications and disclosures, made by a client to his legal adviser for the purpose of obtaining his professional aid or advice, shall be strictly privileged:—that the attorney shall not be permitted, without the consent of his client,—and much less will he be compelled—to reveal or disclose communications made to him under such circumstances.' " *ABA Opinion* 250 (1943).

"While it is true that complete revelation of relevant facts should be encouraged for trial purposes, nevertheless an attorney's dealings with his client, if both are sincere, and if the dealings involve more than mere technical matters, should be immune to discovery proceedings. There must be freedom from fear of revealment of matters disclosed to an attorney because of the peculiarly intimate relationship existing." Ellis-Foster Co. v. Union Carbide & Carbon Corp., 159 F.Supp. 917, 919 (D.N.J.1958).

Cf. *ABA Opinions* 314 (1965), 274 (1946) and 268 (1945).

2. "While it is the great purpose of law to ascertain the truth, there is the countervailing necessity of insuring the right of every person to freely and fully confer and confide in one having knowledge of the law, and skilled in its practice, in order that the former may have adequate advice and a proper defense. This assistance can be made safely and readily available only when the client is free from the consequences of apprehension of disclosure by reason of the subsequent statements of the skilled lawyer." Baird v. Koerner, 279 F.2d 623, 629–30 (9th Cir.1960).

Cf. *ABA Opinion* 150 (1936).

3. "Where . . . [a client] knowingly and after full disclosure participates in a [legal fee] financing plan which requires the furnishing of certain information to the bank, clearly by his conduct he has waived any privilege as to that information." *ABA Opinion* 320 (1968).

is a matter of common knowledge that the normal operation of a law office exposes confidential professional information to non-lawyer employees of the office, particularly secretaries and those having access to the files; and this obligates a lawyer to exercise care in selecting and training his employees so that the sanctity of all confidences and secrets of his clients may be preserved. If the obligation extends to two or more clients as to the same information, a lawyer should obtain the permission of all before revealing the information. A lawyer must always be sensitive to the rights and wishes of his client and act scrupulously in the making of decisions which may involve the disclosure of information obtained in his professional relationship.[4] Thus, in the absence of consent of his client after full disclosure, a lawyer should not associate another lawyer in the handling of a matter; nor should he, in the absence of consent, seek counsel from another lawyer if there is a reasonable possibility that the identity of the client or his confidences or secrets would be revealed to such lawyer. Both social amenities and professional duty should cause a lawyer to shun indiscreet conversations concerning his clients.

EC 4-3 Unless the client otherwise directs, it is not improper for a lawyer to give limited information from his files to an outside agency necessary for statistical, bookkeeping, accounting, data processing, banking, printing, or other legitimate purposes, provided he exercises due care in the selection of the agency and warns the agency that the information must be kept confidential.

EC 4-4 The attorney-client privilege is more limited than the ethical obligation of a lawyer to guard the confidence and secrets of his client. This ethical precept, unlike the evidentiary privilege, exists without regard to the nature or source of information or the fact that others share the knowledge. A lawyer should endeavor to act in a manner which preserves the evidentiary privilege; for example, he should avoid professional discussions in the presence of persons to whom the privilege does not extend. A lawyer owes an obligation to advise the client of the attorney-client privilege and timely to assert the privilege unless it is waived by the client.

EC 4-5 A lawyer should not use information acquired in the course of the representation of a client to the disadvantage of the client and a lawyer should not use, except with the consent of his client after full disclosure, such information for his own purposes.[5] Likewise, a lawyer should be diligent in his efforts to prevent the misuse of such informa-

---

4. "The lawyer must decide when he takes a case whether it is a suitable one for him to undertake and after this decision is made, he is not justified in turning against his client by exposing injurious evidence entrusted to him. . . . [D]oing something intrinsically regrettable, because the only alternative involves worse consequences, is a necessity in every profession." Williston, Life and Law 271 (1940).

Cf. *ABA Opinions* 177 (1938) and 83 (1932).

5. See ABA Canon 11.

tion by his employees and associates.[6] Care should be exercised by a lawyer to prevent the disclosure of the confidences and secrets of one client to another,[7] and no employment should be accepted that might require such disclosure.

EC 4-6 The obligation of a lawyer to preserve the confidences and secrets of his client continues after the termination of his employment.[8] Thus a lawyer should not attempt to sell a law practice as a going business because, among other reasons, to do so would involve the disclosure of confidences and secrets.[9] A lawyer should also provide for the protection of the confidences and secrets of his client following the termination of the practice of the lawyer, whether termination is due to death, disability, or retirement. For example, a lawyer might provide for the personal papers of the client to be returned to him and for the papers of the lawyer to be delivered to another lawyer or to be destroyed. In determining the method of disposition, the instructions and wishes of the client should be a dominant consideration.

DISCIPLINARY RULES

DR 4-101 Preservation of Confidences and Secrets of a Client.[10]

(A) "Confidence" refers to information protected by the attorney-client privilege under applicable law, and "secret" refers to other information gained in the professional relationship that the client has requested be held inviolate or the disclosure of which would be embarrassing or would be likely to be detrimental to the client.

(B) Except when permitted under DR 4-101(C), a lawyer shall not knowingly:

(1) Reveal a confidence or secret of his client.[11]

6. See ABA Canon 37.

7. See ABA Canons 6 and 37.

"[A]n attorney must not accept professional employment against a client or a former client which will, or even *may* require him to use confidential information obtained by the attorney in the course of his professional relations with such client regarding the subject matter of the employment . . .." *ABA Opinion* 165 (1936).

8. See ABA Canon 37.

"Confidential communications between an attorney and his client, made because of the relationship and concerning the subject-matter of the attorney's employment, are generally privileged from disclosure without the consent of the client, and this privilege outlasts the attorney's employ-

ment. *Canon 37.*" *ABA Opinion* 154 (1936).

9. Cf. *ABA Opinion* 266 (1945).

10. See ABA Canon 37; cf. ABA Canon 6.

11. "§ 6068 . . . It is the duty of an attorney: . . ..

"(e) To maintain inviolate the confidence, and at every peril to himself to preserve the secrets, of his client." Cal. Business and Professions Code § 6068 (West 1962). Virtually the same provision is found in the Oregon statutes. Ore.Rev. Stat. ch. 9, § 9.460(5).

"Communications between lawyer and client are privileged (Wigmore on Evidence, 3d Ed., Vol. 8, §§ 2290–2329). The modern theory underlying the privilege is

(2) **Use a confidence or secret of his client to the disadvantage of the client.**

(3) **Use a confidence or secret of his client for the advantage of himself**[12] **or of a third person,**[13] **unless the client consents after full disclosure.**

(C) **A lawyer may reveal:**

(1) **Confidences or secrets with the consent of the client or clients affected, but only after a full disclosure to them.**[14]

(2) **Confidences or secrets when permitted under Disciplinary Rules or required by law or court order.**[15]

subjective and is to give the client freedom of apprehension in consulting his legal advisor (ibid., § 2290, p. 548). The privilege applies to communications made in seeking legal advice for any purpose (ibid., § 2294, p. 563). The mere circumstance that the advice is given without charge therefore does not nullify the privilege (ibid., § 2303)." *ABA Opinion* 216 (1941).

"It is the duty of an attorney to maintain the confidence and preserve inviolate the secrets of his client . . . ." *ABA Opinion* 155 (1936).

12. See ABA Canon 11.

"The provision respecting employment is in accord with the general rule announced in the adjudicated cases that a lawyer may not make use of knowledge or information acquired by him through his professional relations with his client, or in the conduct of his client's business, to his own advantage or profit (7 C.J.S., § 125, p. 958; Healy v. Gray, 184 Iowa 111, 168 N.W. 222; Baumgardner v. Hudson, D.C.App., 277 F. 552; Goodrum v. Clement, D.C.App., 277 F. 586)." *ABA Opinion* 250 (1943).

13. See *ABA Opinion* 177 (1938).

14. "[A lawyer] may not divulge confidential communications, information, and secrets imparted to him by the client or acquired during their professional relations, unless he is authorized to do so by the client (People v. Gerold, 265 Ill. 448, 107 N.E. 165, 178; Murphy v. Riggs, 238 Mich. 151, 213 N.W. 110, 112; Opinion of this Committee, No. 91)." *ABA Opinion* 202 (1940).

Cf. *ABA Opinion* 91 (1933).

15. "A defendant in a criminal case when admitted to bail is not only regarded as in the custody of his bail, but he is also in the custody of the law, and admission to bail does not deprive the court of its inherent power to deal with the person of the prisoner. Being in lawful custody, the defendant is guilty of an escape when he gains his liberty before he is delivered in due process of law, and is guilty of a separate offense for which he may be punished. In failing to disclose his client's whereabouts as a fugitive under these circumstances the attorney would not only be aiding his client to escape trial on the charge for which he was indicted, but would likewise be aiding him in evading prosecution for the additional offense of escape.

"It is the opinion of the committee that under such circumstances the attorney's knowledge of his client's whereabouts is not privileged, and that he may be disciplined for failing to disclose that information to the proper authorities. . . ." *ABA Opinion* 155 (1936).

"We held in *Opinion* 155 that a communication by a client to his attorney in respect to the future commission of an unlawful act or to a continuing wrong is not privileged from disclosure. Public policy forbids that the relation of attorney and client should be used to conceal wrongdoing on the part of the client.

. . .

"When an attorney representing a defendant in a criminal case applies on his behalf for probation or suspension of sentence, he represents to the court, by implication at least, that his client will abide by the terms and conditions of the court's order. When that attorney is later

(3) The intention of his client to commit a crime [16] and the information necessary to prevent the crime. [17]

(4) Confidences or secrets necessary to establish or collect his fee [18] or to defend himself or his employees or associates against an accusation of wrongful conduct. [19]

(D) **A lawyer shall exercise reasonable care to prevent his employees, associates, and others whose services are utilized by him from disclosing or using confidences or secrets of a client, except that a lawyer may reveal the information allowed by DR 4-101(C) through an employee.**

advised of a violation of that order, it is his duty to advise his client of the consequences of his act, and endeavor to prevent a continuance of the wrongdoing. If his client thereafter persists in violating the terms and conditions of his probation, it is the duty of the attorney as an officer of the court to advise the proper authorities concerning his client's conduct. Such information, even though coming to the attorney from the client in the course of his professional relations with respect to other matters in which he represents the defendant, is not privileged from disclosure. . . ." *ABA Opinion* 156 (1936).

See *ABA Opinion* 155 (1936).

(16.) *ABA Opinion* 314 (1965) indicates that a lawyer must disclose even the confidences of his clients if "the facts in the attorney's possession indicate beyond reasonable doubt that a crime will be committed."

See *ABA Opinion* 155 (1936).

17. See ABA Canon 37 and *ABA Opinion* 202 (1940).

18. Cf. *ABA Opinion* 250 (1943).

19. See ABA Canon 37 and *ABA Opinions* 202 (1940) and 19 (1930).

"[T]he adjudicated cases recognize an exception to the rule [that a lawyer shall not reveal the confidences of his client], where disclosure is necessary to protect the attorney's interests arising out of the relation of attorney and client in which disclosure was made.

"The exception is stated in Mechem on Agency, 2d Ed., Vol. 2, § 2313, as follows:

'But the attorney may disclose information received from the client when it becomes necessary for his own protection, as if the client should bring an action against the attorney for negligence or misconduct, and it became necessary for the attorney to show what his instructions were, or what was the nature of the duty which the client expected him to perform. So if it became necessary for the attorney to bring an action against the client, the client's privilege could not prevent the attorney from disclosing what was essential as a means of obtaining or defending his own rights.'

"Mr. Jones, in his Commentaries on Evidence, 2d Ed., Vol. 5, § 2165, states the exception thus: 'It has frequently been held that the rule as to privileged communications does not apply when litigation arises between attorney and client to the extent that their communications are relevant to the issue. In such cases, if the disclosure of privileged communications becomes necessary to protect the attorney's rights, he is released from those obligations of secrecy which the law places upon him. He should not, however, disclose more than is necessary for his own protection. It would be a manifest injustice to allow the client to take advantage of the rule of exclusion as to professional confidence to the prejudice of his attorney, or that it should be carried to the extent of depriving the attorney of the means of obtaining or defending his own rights. In such cases the attorney is exempted from the obligations of secrecy.' " *ABA Opinion* 250 (1943).

CANON 5

A Lawyer Should Exercise Independent Professional Judgment on Behalf of a Client

ETHICAL CONSIDERATIONS

EC 5–1 The professional judgment of a lawyer should be exercised, within the bounds of the law, solely for the benefit of his client and free of compromising influences and loyalties.[1] Neither his personal interests, the interests of other clients, nor the desires of third persons should be permitted to dilute his loyalty to his client.

Interests of a Lawyer That May Affect His Judgment

EC 5–2 A lawyer should not accept proffered employment if his personal interests or desires will, or there is a reasonable probability that they will, affect adversely the advice to be given or services to be rendered the prospective client.[2] After accepting employment, a law-

---

1. Cf. ABA Canon 35.

"[A lawyer's] fiduciary duty is of the highest order and he must not represent interests adverse to those of the client. It is true that because of his professional responsibility and the confidence and trust which his client may legitimately repose in him, he must adhere to a high standard of honesty, integrity and good faith in dealing with his client. He is not permitted to take advantage of his position or superior knowledge to impose upon the client; nor to conceal facts or law, nor in any way deceive him without being held responsible therefor." Smoot v. Lund, 13 Utah 2d 168, 172, 369 P.2d 933, 936 (1962).

"When a client engages the services of a lawyer in a given piece of business he is entitled to feel that, until that business is finally disposed of in some manner, he has the undivided loyalty of the one upon whom he looks as his advocate and champion. If, as in this case, he is sued and his home attached by his own attorney, who is representing him in another matter, all feeling of loyalty is necessarily destroyed, and the profession is exposed to the charge that it is interested only in money." Grievance Comm. v. Rattner, 152 Conn. 59, 65, 203 A.2d 82, 84 (1964).

"One of the cardinal principles confronting every attorney in the representation of a client is the requirement of com-

plete loyalty and service in good faith to the best of his ability. In a criminal case the client is entitled to a fair trial, but not a perfect one. These are fundamental requirements of due process under the Fourteenth Amendment. . . . The same principles are applicable in Sixth Amendment cases (not pertinent herein) and suggest that an attorney should have no conflict of interest and that he must devote his full and faithful efforts toward the defense of his client." Johns v. Smyth, 176 F.Supp. 949, 952 (E.D.Va.1959), modified, United States ex rel. Wilkins v. Banmiller, 205 F.Supp. 123, 128 n. 5 (E.D.Pa.1962), aff'd 325 F.2d 514 (3d Cir.1963), cert. denied, 379 U.S. 847, 13 L.Ed.2d 51, 85 S.Ct. 87 (1964).

2. "Attorneys must not allow their private interests to conflict with those of their clients. . . . They owe their entire devotion to the interests of their clients." United States v. Anonymous, 215 F.Supp. 111, 113 (E.D.Tenn.1963).

"[T]he court [below] concluded that a firm may not accept any action against a person whom they are presently representing even though there is no relationship between the two cases. In arriving at this conclusion, the court cites an opinion of the Committee on Professional Ethics of the New York County Lawyers' Association which stated in part: 'While under the circumstances . . . there may be no

yer carefully should refrain from acquiring a property right or assuming a position that would tend to make his judgment less protective of the interests of his client.

EC 5-3   The self-interest of a lawyer resulting from his ownership of property in which his client also has an interest or which may affect property of his client may interfere with the exercise of free judgment on behalf of his client. If such interference would occur with respect to a prospective client, a lawyer should decline employment proffered by him. After accepting employment, a lawyer should not acquire property rights that would adversely affect his professional judgment in the representation of his client. Even if the property interests of a lawyer do not presently interfere with the exercise of his independent judgment, but the likelihood of interference can reasonably be foreseen by him, a lawyer should explain the situation to his client and should decline employment or withdraw unless the client consents to the continuance of the relationship after full disclosure. A lawyer should not seek to persuade his client to permit him to invest in an undertaking of his client nor make improper use of his professional relationship to influence his client to invest in an enterprise in which the lawyer is interested.

EC 5-4   If, in the course of his representation of a client, a lawyer is permitted to receive from his client a beneficial ownership in publication rights relating to the subject matter of the employment, he may be tempted to subordinate the interests of his client to his own anticipated pecuniary gain. For example, a lawyer in a criminal case who obtains from his client television, radio, motion picture, newspaper, magazine, book, or other publication rights with respect to the case may be influenced, consciously or unconsciously, to a course of conduct that will enhance the value of his publication rights to the prejudice of his client. To prevent these potentially differing interests, such arrangements should be scrupulously avoided prior to the termination of all aspects of the matter giving rise to the employment, even though his employment has previously ended.

EC 5-5   A lawyer should not suggest to his client that a gift be made to himself or for his benefit. If a lawyer accepts a gift from his client, he is peculiarly susceptible to the charge that he unduly influenced or over-reached the client. If a client voluntarily offers to make a gift to his lawyer, the lawyer may accept the gift, but before doing so, he should urge that his client secure disinterested advice from an indepen-

actual conflict of interest . . . "maintenance of public confidence in the Bar requires an attorney who has accepted representation of a client to decline, while representing such client, any employment from an adverse party in any matter even though wholly unrelated to the original retainer." See Question and Answer No. 350, N.Y. County L. Ass'n, Questions and Answer No. 450 (June 21, 1956).'" Grievance Comm. v. Rattner, 152 Conn. 59, 65, 203 A.2d 82, 84 (1964).

dent, competent person who is cognizant of all the circumstances.[3] Other than in exceptional circumstances, a lawyer should insist that an instrument in which his client desires to name him beneficially be prepared by another lawyer selected by the client.[4]

EC 5-6 A lawyer should not consciously influence a client to name him as executor, trustee, or lawyer in an instrument. In those cases where a client wishes to name his lawyer as such, care should be taken by the lawyer to avoid even the appearance of impropriety.[5]

EC 5-7 The possibility of an adverse effect upon the exercise of free judgment by a lawyer on behalf of his client during litigation generally makes it undesirable for the lawyer to acquire a proprietary interest in the cause of his client or otherwise to become financially interested in the outcome of the litigation.[6] However, it is not improper for a lawyer to protect his right to collect a fee for his services by the assertion of legally permissible liens, even though by doing so he may acquire an interest in the outcome of litigation. Although a contingent fee arrangement [7] gives a lawyer a financial interest in the outcome of litigation, a reasonable contingent fee is permissible in civil cases because it may be the only means by which a layman can obtain the services of a lawyer of his choice. But a lawyer, because he is in a better position to evaluate a cause of action, should enter into a continent fee arrangement only in those instances where the arrangement will be beneficial to the client.

EC 5-8 A financial interest in the outcome of litigation also results if monetary advances are made by the lawyer to his client.[8] Although this assistance generally is not encouraged, there are instances when it is not improper to make loans to a client. For example, the advancing

3. "Courts of equity will scrutinize with jealous vigilance transactions between parties occupying fiduciary relations toward each other. . . . A deed will not be held invalid, however, if made by the grantor with full knowledge of its nature and effect, and because of the deliberate, voluntary and intelligent desire of the grantor. . . . Where a fiduciary relation exists, the burden of proof is on the grantee or beneficiary of an instrument executed during the existence of such relationship to show the fairness of the transaction, that it was equitable and just and that it did not proceed from undue influence. . . . The same rule has application where an attorney engages in a transaction with a client during the existence of the relation and is benefited thereby. . . . Conversely, an attorney is not prohibited from dealing with his client or buying his property, and such contracts, if open, fair and honest, when deliberately made, are as valid as contracts between other parties. . . . [I]mportant factors in determining whether a transaction is fair include a showing by the fiduciary (1) that he made a full and frank disclosure of all the relevant information that he had: (2) that the consideration was adequate; and (3) that the principal had independent advice before completing the transaction." McFail v. Braden, 19 Ill.2d 108, 117-18, 166 N.E.2d 46, 52 (1960).

4. See State ex rel. Nebraska State Bar Ass'n v. Richards, 165 Neb. 80, 94-95, 84 N.W.2d 136, 146 (1957).

5. See ABA Canon 9.

6. See ABA Canon 10.

7. See Code of Professional Responsibility, EC 2-20.

8. See ABA Canon 42.

or guaranteeing of payment of the costs and expenses of litigation by a lawyer may be the only way a client can enforce his cause of action,[9] but the ultimate liability for such costs and expenses must be that of the client.

EC 5–9 Occasionally a lawyer is called upon to decide in a particular case whether he will be a witness or an advocate. If a lawyer is both counsel and witness, he becomes more easily impeachable for interest and thus may be a less effective witness. Conversely, the opposing counsel may be handicapped in challenging the credibility of the lawyer when the lawyer also appears as an advocate in the case. An advocate who becomes a witness is in the unseemly and ineffective position of arguing his own credibility. The roles of an advocate and of a witness are inconsistent; the function of an advocate is to advance or argue the cause of another, while that of a witness is to state facts objectively.

EC 5–10 Problems incident to the lawyer-witness relationship arise at different stages; they relate either to whether a lawyer should accept employment or should withdraw from employment.[10] Regardless of when the problem arises, his decision is to be governed by the same basic considerations. It is not objectionable for a lawyer who is a potential witness to be an advocate if it is unlikely that he will be called as a witness because his testimony would be merely cumulative or if his testimony will relate only to an uncontested issue.[11] In the exceptional situation where it will be manifestly unfair to the client for the lawyer to refuse employment or to withdraw when he will likely be a witness on a contested issue, he may serve as advocate even though

9. "*Rule 3a.* . . . A member of the State Bar shall not directly or indirectly pay or agree to pay, or represent or sanction the representation that he will pay, medical, hospital or nursing bills or other personal expenses incurred by or for a client, prospective or existing; provided this rule shall not prohibit a member:

"(1) with the consent of the client, from paying or agreeing to pay to third persons such expenses from funds collected or to be collected for the client; or

"(2) after he has been employed, from lending money to his client upon the client's promise in writing to repay such loan; or

"(3) from advancing the costs of prosecuting or defending a claim or action. Such costs within the meaning of this subparagraph (3) include all taxable costs or disbursements, costs or investigation and costs of obtaining and presenting evidence." Cal. Business and Professions Code § 6076 (West Supp.1967).

10. "When a lawyer knows, prior to trial, that he will be a necessary witness, except as to merely formal matters such as identification or custody of a document or the like, neither he nor his firm or associates should conduct the trial. If, during the trial, he discovers that the ends of justice require his testimony, he should, from that point on, if feasible and not prejudicial to his client's case, leave further conduct of the trial to other counsel. If circumstances do not permit withdrawal from the conduct of the trial, the lawyer should not argue the credibility of his own testimony." *A Code of Trial Conduct: Promulgated by the American College of Trial Lawyers*, 43 A.B.A.J. 223, 224–25 (1957).

11. Cf. Canon 19: "When a lawyer is a witness for his client, except as to merely formal matters, such as the attestation or custody of an instrument and the like, he should leave the trial of the case to other counsel."

he may be a witness.[12] In making such decision, he should determine the personal or financial sacrifice of the client that may result from his refusal of employment or withdrawal therefrom, the materiality of his testimony, and the effectiveness of his representation in view of his personal involvement. In weighing these factors, it should be clear that refusal or withdrawal will impose an unreasonable hardship upon the client before the lawyer accepts or continues the employment.[13] Where the question arises, doubts should be resolved in favor of the lawyer testifying and against his becoming or continuing as an advocate.[14]

EC 5–11 A lawyer should not permit his personal interests to influence his advice relative to a suggestion by his client that additional counsel be employed.[15] In like manner, his personal interests should not deter him from suggesting that additional counsel be employed; on the contrary, he should be alert to the desirability of recommending additional counsel when, in his judgment, the proper representation of his client requires it. However, a lawyer should advise his client not to employ additional counsel suggested by the client if the lawyer believes that such employment would be a disservice to the client, and he should disclose the reasons for his belief.

EC 5–12 Inability of co-counsel to agree on a matter vital to the representation of their client requires that their disagreement be submitted by them jointly to their client for his resolution, and the decision of the client shall control the action to be taken.[16]

EC 5–13 A lawyer should not maintain membership in or be influenced by any organization of employees that undertakes to prescribe, direct, or suggest when or how he should fulfill his professional obliga-

12. "It is the general rule that a lawyer may not testify in litigation in which he is an advocate unless circumstances arise which could not be anticipated and it is necessary to prevent a miscarriage of justice. In those rare cases where the testimony of an attorney is needed to protect his client's interests, it is not only proper but mandatory that it be forthcoming." Schwartz v. Wenger, 267 Minn. 40, 43–44, 124 N.W.2d 489, 492 (1963).

13. "The great weight of authority in this country holds that the attorney who acts as counsel and witness, in behalf of his client, in the same cause on a material matter, not of a merely formal character, and not in an emergency, but having knowledge that he would be required to be a witness in ample time to have secured other counsel and given up his service in the case, violates a highly important provision of the Code of Ethics and a rule of

professional conduct, but does not commit a legal error in so testifying, as a result of which a new trial will be granted." Erwin M. Jennings Co. v. DiGenova, 107 Conn. 491, 499, 141 A. 866, 869 (1928).

14. "[C]ases may arise, and in practice often do arise, in which there would be a failure of justice should the attorney withhold his testimony. In such a case it would be a vicious professional sentiment which would deprive the client of the benefit of his attorney's testimony." Connolly v. Straw, 53 Wis. 645, 649, 11 N.W. 17, 19 (1881).

But see canon 19. "Except when essential to the ends of justice, a lawyer should avoid testifying in court in behalf of his client."

15. Cf. ABA Canon 7.

16. See ABA Canon 7.

tions to a person or organization that employs him as a lawyer. Although it is not necessarily improper for a lawyer employed by a corporation or similar entity to be a member of an organization of employees, he should be vigilant to safeguard his fidelity as a lawyer to his employer, free from outside influences.

Interests of Multiple Clients

EC 5–14   Maintaining the independence of professional judgment required of a lawyer precludes his acceptance or continuation of employment that will adversely affect his judgment on behalf of or dilute his loyalty to a client.[17]   This problem arises whenever a lawyer is asked to represent two or more clients who may have differing interests, whether such interests be conflicting, inconsistent, diverse, or otherwise discordant.[18]

EC 5–15   If a lawyer is requested to undertake or to continue representation of multiple clients having potentially differing interests, he must weigh carefully the possibility that his judgment may be impaired or his loyalty divided if he accepts or continues the employment. He should resolve all doubts against the propriety of the representation.   A lawyer should never represent in litigation multiple clients with differing interests; [19] and there are few situations in which he would be justified in representing in litigation multiple clients with potentially differing interests.   If a lawyer accepted such employment and the interests did become actually differing, he would have to withdraw from employment with likelihood of resulting hardship on the clients; and for this reason it is preferable that he refuse the employment

17.   See ABA Canon 6; cf. *ABA Opinions* 261 (1944), 242 (1942), 142 (1935), and 30 (1931).

18.   The ABA Canons speak of "conflicting interests" rather than "differing interests" but make no attempt to define such other than the statement in Canon 6: "Within the meaning of this canon, a lawyer represents conflicting interests when, in behalf of one client, it is his duty to contend for that which duty to another client requires him to oppose."

19.   "Canon 6 of the Canons of Professional Ethics, adopted by the American Bar Association on September 30, 1937, and by the Pennsylvania Bar Association on January 7, 1938, provides in part that 'It is unprofessional to represent conflicting interests, except by express consent of all concerned given after a full disclosure of the facts.   Within the meaning of this Canon, a lawyer represents conflicting interests when, in behalf of one client, it is his duty to contend for that which duty to

another client requires him to oppose.' The full disclosure required by this canon contemplates that the possibly adverse effect of the conflict be fully explained by the attorney to the client to be affected and by him thoroughly understood.   . . .

"The foregoing canon applies to cases where the circumstances are such that possibly conflicting interests may permissibly be represented by the same attorney.   But manifestly, there are instances where the conflicts of interest are so critically adverse as not to admit of one attorney's representing both sides.   Such is the situation which this record presents.   No one could conscionably contend that the same attorney may represent both the plaintiff and defendant in an adversary action. Yet, that is what is being done in this case."   Jedwabny v. Philadelphia Transportation Co., 390 Pa. 231, 235, 135 A.2d 252, 254 (1957), cert. denied, 355 U.S. 966, 2 L.Ed.2d 541, 78 S.Ct. 557 (1958).

initially. On the other hand, there are many instances in which a lawyer may properly serve multiple clients having potentially differing interests in matters not involving litigation. If the interests vary only slightly, it is generally likely that the lawyer will not be subjected to an adverse influence and that he can retain his independent judgment on behalf of each client; and if the interests become differing, withdrawal is less likely to have a disruptive effect upon the causes of his clients.

EC 5–16 In those instances in which a lawyer is justified in representing two or more clients having differing interests, it is nevertheless essential that each client be given the opportunity to evaluate his need for representation free of any potential conflict and to obtain other counsel if he so desires.[20] Thus before a lawyer may represent multiple clients, he should explain fully to each client the implications of the common representation and should accept or continue employment only if the clients consent.[21] If there are present other circumstances that might cause any of the multiple clients to question the undivided loyalty of the lawyer, he should also advise all of the clients of those circumstances.[22]

EC 5–17 Typically recurring situations involving potentially differing interests are those in which a lawyer is asked to represent co-defendants in a criminal case, co-plaintiffs in a personal injury case, an insured and his insurer,[23] and beneficiaries of the estate of a decedent.

20. "Glasser wished the benefit of the undivided assistance of counsel of his own choice. We think that such a desire on the part of an accused should be respected. Irrespective of any conflict of interest, the additional burden of representing another party may conceivably impair counsel's effectiveness.

"To determine the precise degree of prejudice sustained by Glasser as a result of the court's appointment of Stewart as counsel for Kretske is at once difficult and unnecessary. The right to have the assistance of counsel is too fundamental and absolute to allow courts to indulge in nice calculations as to the amount of prejudice arising from its denial." Glasser v. United States, 315 U.S. 60, 75–76, 86 L.Ed. 680, 62 S.Ct. 457, 467 (1942).

21. See ABA Canon 6.

22. Id.

23. Cf. *ABA Opinion* 282 (1950).

"When counsel, although paid by the casualty company, undertakes to represent the policyholder and files his notice of appearance, he owes to his client, the assured, an undeviating and single alle-giance. His fealty embraces the requirement to produce in court all witnesses, fact and expert, who are available and necessary for the proper protection of the rights of his client. . . .

". . . The Canons of Professional Ethics make it pellucid that there are not two standards, one applying to counsel privately retained by a client, and the other to counsel paid by an insurance carrier." American Employers Ins. Co. v. Goble Aircraft Specialties, 205 Misc. 1066, 1075, 131 N.Y.S.2d 393, 401 (1954), motion to withdraw appeal granted, 1 App.Div.2d 1008, 154 N.Y.S.2d 835 (1956).

"[C]ounsel, selected by State Farm to defend Dorothy Walker's suit for $50,000 damages, was apprised by Walker that his earlier version of the accident was untrue and that actually the accident occurred because he lost control of his car in passing a Cadillac just ahead. At that point, Walker's counsel should have refused to participate further in view of the conflict of interest between Walker and State Farm. . . . Instead he participated in the ensuing deposition of the Walkers, even took an

Whether a lawyer can fairly and adequately protect the interests of multiple clients in these and similar situations depends upon an analysis of each case. In certain circumstances, there may exist little chance of the judgment of the lawyer being adversely affected by the slight possibility that the interests will become actually differing; in other circumstances, the chance of adverse effect upon his judgment is not unlikely.

EC 5-18 A lawyer employed or retained by a corporation or similar entity owes his allegiance to the entity and not to a stockholder, director, officer, employee, representative, or other person connected with the entity. In advising the entity, a lawyer should keep paramount its interests and his professional judgment should not be influenced by the personal desires of any person or organization. Occasionally a lawyer for an entity is requested by a stockholder, director, officer, employee, representative, or other person connected with the entity to represent him in an individual capacity; in such case the lawyer may serve the individual only if the lawyer is convinced that differing interests are not present.

EC 5-19 A lawyer may represent several clients whose interests are not actually or potentially differing. Nevertheless, he should explain any circumstances that might cause a client to question his undivided loyalty.[24] Regardless of the belief of a lawyer that he may properly represent multiple clients, he must defer to a client who holds the contrary belief and withdraw from representation of that client.

EC 5-20 A lawyer is often asked to serve as an impartial arbitrator or mediator in matters which involve present or former clients. He may serve in either capacity if he first discloses such present or former relationships. After a lawyer has undertaken to act as an impartial arbitrator or mediator, he should not thereafter represent in the dispute any of the parties involved.

Desires of Third Persons

EC 5-21 The obligation of a lawyer to exercise professional judgment solely on behalf of his client requires that he disregard the desires of others that might impair his free judgment.[25] The desires of a third

---

ex parte sworn statement from Mr. Walker in order to advise State Farm what action it should take, and later used the statement against Walker in the District Court. This action appears to contravene an Indiana attorney's duty 'at every peril to himself, to preserve the secrets of his client' . . .." State Farm Mut. Auto Ins. Co. v. Walker, 382 F.2d 548, 552 (1967), cert. denied, 389 U.S. 1045, 19 L.Ed.2d 837, 88 S.Ct. 789 (1968).

24. See ABA Canon 6.

25. See ABA Canon 35.

"Objection to the intervention of a lay intermediary, who may control litigation or otherwise interfere with the rendering of legal services in a confidential relationship, . . . derives from the element of pecuniary gain. Fearful of dangers thought to arise from that element, the courts of several States have sustained regulations aimed at these activities. We intimate no view one way or the other as to the merits of those decisions with respect to the particular arrangements against which they are directed. It is enough that

person will seldom adversely affect a lawyer unless that person is in a position to exert strong economic, political, or social pressures upon the lawyer. These influences are often subtle, and a lawyer must be alert to their existence. A lawyer subjected to outside pressures should make full disclosure of them to his client; [26] and if he or his client believes that the effectiveness of his representation has been or will be impaired thereby, the lawyer should take proper steps to withdraw from representation of his client.

EC 5-22 Economic, political, or social pressures by third persons are less likely to impinge upon the independent judgment of a lawyer in a matter in which he is compensated directly by his client and his professional work is exclusively with his client. On the other hand, if a lawyer is compensated from a source other than his client, he may feel a sense of responsibility to someone other than his client.

EC 5-23 A person or organization that pays or furnishes lawyers to represent others possesses a potential power to exert strong pressures against the independent judgment of those lawyers. Some employers may be interested in furthering their own economic, political, or social goals without regard to the professional responsibility of the lawyer to his individual client. Others may be far more concerned with establishment or extension of legal principles than in the immediate protection of the rights of the lawyer's individual client. On some occasions, decisions on priority of work may be made by the employer rather than the lawyer with the result that prosecution of work already undertaken for clients is postponed to their detriment. Similarly, an employer may seek, consciously or unconsciously, to further its own economic interests through the action of the lawyers employed by it. Since a lawyer must always be free to exercise his professional judgment without regard to the interests or motives of a third person, the lawyer who is employed by one to represent another must constantly guard against erosion of his professional freedom.[27]

the superficial resemblance in form between those arrangements and that at bar cannot obscure the vital fact that here the entire arrangement employs constitutionally privileged means of expression to secure constitutionally guaranteed civil rights." NAACP v. Button, 371 U.S. 415, 441–42, 9 L.Ed.2d 405, 423–24, 83 S.Ct. 328, 342–43 (1963).

26. Cf. ABA Canon 38.

27. "Certainly it is true that 'the professional relationship between an attorney and his client is highly personal, involving an intimate appreciation of each individual client's particular problem.' And this Committee does not condone practices which interfere with that relationship.

However, the mere fact the lawyer is actually paid by some entity other than the client does not affect that relationship, so long as the lawyer is selected by and is directly responsible to the client. See Informal Opinions 469 and 679. Of course, as the latter decision points out, there must be full disclosure of the arrangement by the attorney to the client. . . ." *ABA Opinion* 320 (1968).

"[A] third party may pay the cost of legal services as long as control remains in the client and the responsibility of the lawyer is solely to the client. Informal Opinions 469 ad [sic] 679. See also *Opinion* 237." Id.

EC 5-24 To assist a lawyer in preserving his professional independence, a number of courses are available to him. For example, a lawyer should not practice with or in the form of a professional legal corporation, even though the corporate form is permitted by law,[28] if any director, officer, or stockholder of it is a non-lawyer. Although a lawyer may be employed by a business corporation with non-lawyers serving as directors or officers, and they necessarily have the right to make decisions of business policy, a lawyer must decline to accept direction of his professional judgment from any layman. Various types of legal aid offices are administered by boards of directors composed of lawyers and laymen. A lawyer should not accept employment from such an organization unless the board sets only broad policies and there is no interference in the relationship of the lawyer and the individual client he serves. Where a lawyer is employed by an organization, a written agreement that defines the relationship between him and the organization and provides for his independence is desirable since it may serve to prevent misunderstanding as to their respective roles. Although other innovations in the means of supplying legal counsel may develop, the responsibility of the lawyer to maintain his professional independence remains constant, and the legal profession must insure that changing circumstances do not result in loss of the professional independence of the lawyer.

DISCIPLINARY RULES

DR 5-101 Refusing Employment When the Interests of the Lawyer May Impair His Independent Professional Judgment.

(A) Except with the consent of his client after full disclosure, a lawyer shall not accept employment if the exercise of his professional judgment on behalf of his client will be or reasonably may be affected by his own financial, business, property, or personal interests.[29]

28. *ABA Opinion* 303 (1961) recognized that "[s]tatutory provisions now exist in several states which are designed to make [the practice of law in a form that will be classified as a corporation for federal income tax purposes] legally possible, either as a result of lawyers incorporating or forming associations with various corporate characteristics."

29. Cf. ABA Canon 6 and *ABA Opinions* 181 (1938), 104 (1934), 103 (1933), 72 (1932), 50 (1931), 49 (1931), and 33 (1931).

"New York County [Opinion] 203. . . . [A lawyer] should not advise a client to employ an investment company in which he is interested, without informing him of this." Drinker, *Legal Ethics* 956 (1953).

"In *Opinions* 72 and 49 this Committee held: The relations of partners in a law firm are such that neither the firm nor any member or associate thereof, may accept any professional employment which any member of the firm cannot properly accept.

"In *Opinion* 16 this Committee held that a member of a law firm could not represent a defendant in a criminal case which was being prosecuted by another member of the firm who was public prosecuting attorney. The Opinion stated that it was

(B) A lawyer shall not accept employment in contemplated or pending litigation if he knows or it is obvious that he or a lawyer in his firm ought to be called as a witness, except that he may undertake the employment and he or a lawyer in his firm may testify:

    (1) If the testimony will relate solely to an uncontested matter.

    (2) If the testimony will relate solely to a matter of formality and there is no reason to believe that substantial evidence will be offered in opposition to the testimony.

    (3) If the testimony will relate solely to the nature and value of legal services rendered in the case by the lawyer or his firm to the client.

    (4) As to any matter, if refusal would work a substantial hardship on the client because of the distinctive value of the lawyer or his firm as counsel in the particular case.

DR 5-102   Withdrawal as Counsel When the Lawyer Becomes a Witness.[30]

(A) If, after undertaking employment in contemplated or pending litigation, a lawyer learns or it is obvious that he or a lawyer in his firm ought to be called as a witness on behalf of his client, he shall withdraw from the conduct of the trial and his firm, if any, shall not continue representation in the trial, except that he may continue the representation and he or a lawyer in his firm may testify in the circumstances enumerated in DR 5-101(B)(1) through (4).

(B) If, after undertaking employment in contemplated or pending litigation, a lawyer learns or it is obvious that he or a lawyer in his firm may be called as a witness other than on behalf of his client, he may continue the representation until it is apparent that his testimony is or may be prejudicial to his client.[31]

clearly unethical for one member of the firm to oppose the interest of the state while another member represented those interests . . .. Since the prosecutor himself could not represent both the public and the defendant, no member of his law firm could either." *ABA Opinion* 296 (1959).

30. Cf. ABA Canon 19 and *ABA Opinions* 220 (1941), 185 (1938), 50 (1931), and 33 (1931); but cf. Erwin M. Jennings Co. v. DiGenova, 107 Conn. 491, 498–99, 141 A. 866, 868 (1928).

31. "This *Canon* [19] *of Ethics* needs no elaboration to be applied to the facts here. Apparently, the object of this precept is to avoid putting a lawyer in the obviously embarrassing predicament of testifying and then having to argue the credibility and effect of his own testimony. It was not designed to permit a lawyer to call opposing counsel as a witness and thereby disqualify him as counsel." Galarowicz v. Ward, 119 Utah 611, 620, 230 P.2d 576, 580 (1951).

DR 5–103 Avoiding Acquisition of Interest in Litigation.

(A) A lawyer shall not acquire a proprietary interest in the cause of action or subject matter of litigation he is conducting for a client,[32] except that he may:

(1) Acquire a lien granted by law to secure his fee or expenses.

(2) Contract with a client for a reasonable contingent fee in a civil case.[33]

(B) While representing a client in connection with contemplated or pending litigation, a lawyer shall not advance or guarantee financial assistance to his client,[34] except that a lawyer may advance or guarantee the expenses of litigation, including court costs, expenses of investigation, expenses of medical examination, and costs of obtaining and presenting evidence, provided the client remains ultimately liable for such expenses.

DR 5–104 Limiting Business Relations With a Client

(A) A lawyer shall not enter into a business transaction with a client if they have differing interests therein and if the client expects the lawyer to exercise his professional judgment therein for the protection of the client, unless the client has consented after full disclosure.

(B) Prior to conclusion of all aspects of the matter giving rise to his employment, a lawyer shall not enter into any arrangement or understanding with a client or a prospective client by which he acquires an interest in publication rights with respect to the subject matter of his employment or proposed employment.

DR 5–105 Refusing to Accept or Continue Employment if the Interests of Another Client May Impair the Independent Professional Judgment of the Lawyer.

(A) A lawyer shall decline proffered employment if the exercise of his independent professional judgment in behalf of a client will be or is likely to be adversely affected by the acceptance of the proffered employment,[35] or if it would be likely to involve him in representing differing interests, except to the extent permitted under DR 5–105(C).[36]

---

32. ABA Canon 10 and *ABA Opinions* 279 (1949), 246 (1942) and 176 (1938).

33. See Code of Professional Responsibility, DR 2–106(C).

34. See ABA Canon 42; cf. *ABA Opinion* 288 (1954).

35. See ABA Canon 6; cf. *ABA Opinions* 167 (1937), 60 (1931), and 40 (1931).

36. *ABA Opinion* 247 (1942) held that an attorney could not investigate a night club shooting on behalf of one of the owner's liability insurers, obtaining the cooperation of the owner, and later represent the

(B) A lawyer shall not continue multiple employment if the exercise of his independent professional judgment in behalf of a client will be or is likely to be adversely affected by his representation of another client, or if it would be likely to involve him in representing differing interests, except to the extent permitted under DR 5–105(C).[37]

(C) In the situations covered by DR 5–105(A) and (B), a lawyer may represent multiple clients if it is obvious that he can adequately represent the interest of each and if each consents to the representation after full disclosure of the possible effect of such representation on the exercise of his independent professional judgment on behalf of each.

(D) If a lawyer is required to decline employment or to withdraw from employment under a Disciplinary Rule, no partner or associate, or any other lawyer affiliated with him or his firm may accept or continue such employment.

As amended in 1974.

DR 5–106   Settling Similar Claims of Clients.[38]

(A) A lawyer who represents two or more clients shall not make or participate in the making of an aggregate settlement of the claims of or against his clients, unless each client has consented to the settlement after being advised of the existence and nature of all the claims involved in the proposed settlement, of the total amount of the settlement, and of the participation of each person in the settlement.

DR 5–107   Avoiding Influence by Others Than the Client.

(A) Except with the consent of his client after full disclosure, a lawyer shall not:

  (1) Accept compensation for his legal services from one other than his client.

  (2) Accept from one other than his client any thing of value related to his representation of or his employment by his client.[39]

injured patron in an action against the owner and a different insurance company unless the attorney obtain the "express consent of all concerned given after a full disclosure of the facts," since to do so would be to represent conflicting interests.

See *ABA Opinions* 247 (1942), 224 (1941), 222 (1941), 218 (1941), 112 (1934), 83 (1932), and 86 (1932).

37. Cf. *ABA Opinions* 231 (1941) and 160 (1936).

38. Cf. *ABA Opinions* 243 (1942) and 235 (1941).

39. See ABA Canon 38.

"A lawyer who receives a commission (whether delayed or not) from a title insurance company or guaranty fund for recommending or selling the insurance to his client, or for work done for the client or the company, without either fully disclosing to the client his financial interest in the transaction, or crediting the client's

(B) **A lawyer shall not permit a person who recommends, employs, or pays him to render legal services for another to direct or regulate his professional judgment in rendering such legal services.**[40]

(C) **A lawyer shall not practice with or in the form of a professional corporation or association authorized to practice law for a profit, if:**

(1) **A non-lawyer owns any interest therein,**[41] **except that a fiduciary representative of the estate of a lawyer may hold the stock or interest of the lawyer for a reasonable time during administration;**

(2) **A non-lawyer is a corporate director or officer thereof;**[42] **or**

(3) **A non-lawyer has the right to direct or control the professional judgment of a lawyer.**[43]

CANON 6

A Lawyer Should Represent a Client Competently

Ethical Considerations

EC 6–1 Because of his vital role in the legal process, a lawyer should act with competence and proper care in representing clients. He should strive to become and remain proficient in his practice [1] and

bill with the amount thus received, is guilty of unethical conduct." *ABA Opinion* 304 (1962).

40. See ABA Canon 35; cf. *ABA Opinion* 237 (1941).

"When the lay forwarder, as agent for the creditor, forwards a claim to an attorney, the direct relationship of attorney and client shall then exist between the attorney and the creditor, and the forwarder shall not interpose itself as an intermediary to control the activities of the attorney." *ABA Opinion* 294 (1958).

41. "Permanent beneficial and voting rights in the organization set up to practice law, whatever its form, must be restricted to lawyers while the organization is engaged in the practice of law." *ABA Opinion* 303 (1961).

42. "*Canon 33* . . . promulgates underlying principles that must be observed no matter in what form of organization lawyers practice law. Its requirement that no person shall be admitted or held out as a practitioner or member who is not a

member of the legal profession duly authorized to practice, and amendable to professional discipline, makes it clear that any centralized management must be in lawyers to avoid a violation of this Canon." *ABA Opinion* 303 (1961).

43. "There is no intervention of any lay agency between lawyer and client when centralized management provided only by lawyers may give guidance or direction to the services being rendered by a lawyer-member of the organization to a client. The language in *Canon 35* that a lawyer should avoid all relations which direct the performance of his duties by or in the interest of an intermediary refers to lay intermediaries and not lawyer intermediaries with whom he is associated in the practice of law." *ABA Opinion* 303 (1961).

1. "[W]hen a citizen is faced with the need for a lawyer, he wants, and is entitled to, the best informed counsel he can obtain. Changing times produce changes in our laws and legal procedures. The natu-

should accept employment only in matters which he is or intends to become competent to handle.

EC 6-2 A lawyer is aided in attaining and maintaining his competence by keeping abreast of current legal literature and developments, participating in continuing legal education programs,[2] concentrating in particular areas of the law, and by utilizing other available means. He has the additional ethical obligation to assist in improving the legal profession, and he may do so by participating in bar activities intended to advance the quality and standards of members of the profession. Of particular importance is the careful training of his younger associates and the giving of sound guidance to all lawyers who consult him. In short, a lawyer should strive at all levels to aid the legal profession in advancing the highest possible standards of integrity and competence and to meet those standards himself.

EC 6-3 While the licensing of a lawyer is evidence that he has met the standards then prevailing for admission to the bar, a lawyer generally should not accept employment in any area of the law in which he is not qualified.[3] However, he may accept such employment if in good faith he expects to become qualified through study and investigation, as long as such preparation would not result in unreasonable delay or expense to his client. Proper preparation and representa-

ral complexities of law require continuing intensive study by a lawyer if he is to render his clients a maximum of efficient service. And, in so doing, he maintains the high standards of the legal profession; and he also increases respect and confidence by the general public." Rochelle & Payne, *The Struggle for Public Understanding*, 25 Texas B.J. 109, 160 (1962).

"We have undergone enormous changes in the last fifty years within the lives of most of the adults living today who may be seeking advice. Most of these changes have been accompanied by changes and developments in the law. . . . Every practicing lawyer encounters these problems and is often perplexed with his own inability to keep up, not only with changes in the law, but also with changes in the lives of his clients and their legal problems.

"To be sure, no client has a right to expect that his lawyer will have all of the answers at the end of his tongue or even in the back of his head at all times. But the client does have the right to expect that the lawyer will have devoted his time and energies to maintaining and improving his competence to know where to look for the

answers, to know how to deal with the problems, and to know how to advise to the best of his legal talents and abilities." Levy & Sprague, *Accounting and Law: Is Dual Practice in the Public Interest?*, 52 A.B.A.J. 1110, 1112 (1966).

2. "The whole purpose of continuing legal education, so enthusiastically supported by the ABA, is to make it possible for lawyers to make themselves better lawyers. But there are no nostrums for proficiency in the law; it must come through the hard work of the lawyer himself. To the extent that that work, whether it be in attending institutes or lecture courses, in studying after hours or in the actual day in and day out practice of his profession, can be concentrated within a limited field, the greater the proficiency and expertness that can be developed." *Report of the Special Committee on Specialization and Specialized Legal Education*, 79 A.B.A.Rep. 582, 588 (1954).

3. "If the attorney is not competent to skillfully and properly perform the work, he should not undertake the service." Degen v. Steinbrink, 202 App.Div. 477, 481, 195 N.Y.S. 810, 814 (1922), aff'd mem., 236 N.Y. 669, 142 N.E. 328 (1923).

tion may require the association by the lawyer of professionals in other disciplines. A lawyer offered employment in a matter in which he is not and does not expect to become so qualified should either decline the employment or, with the consent of his client, accept the employment and associate a lawyer who is competent in the matter.

EC 6–4 Having undertaken representation, a lawyer should use proper care to safeguard the interests of his client. If a lawyer has accepted employment in a matter beyond his competence but in which he expected to become competent, he should diligently undertake the work and study necessary to qualify himself. In addition to being qualified to handle a particular matter, his obligation to his client requires him to prepare adequately for and give appropriate attention to his legal work.

EC 6–5 A lawyer should have pride in his professional endeavors. His obligation to act competently calls for higher motivation than that arising from fear of civil liability or disciplinary penalty.

EC 6–6 A lawyer should not seek, by contract or other means, to limit his individual liability to his client for his malpractice. A lawyer who handles the affairs of his client properly has no need to attempt to limit his liability for his professional activities and one who does not handle the affairs of his client properly should not be permitted to do so. A lawyer who is a stockholder in or is associated with a professional legal corporation may, however, limit his liability for malpractice of his associates in the corporation, but only to the extent permitted by law.[4]

DISCIPLINARY RULES

DR 6–101 Failing to Act Competently.

(A) A lawyer shall not:

> **(1) Handle a legal matter which he knows or should know that he is not competent to handle, without associating with him a lawyer who is competent to handle it.**

> **(2) Handle a legal matter without preparation adequate in the circumstances.**

> **(3) Neglect a legal matter entrusted to him.[5]**

DR 6–102 Limiting Liability to Client.

(A) A lawyer shall not attempt to exonerate himself from or limit his liability to his client for his personal malpractice.

---

4. See *ABA Opinion* 303 (1961); cf. Code of Professional Responsibility EC 2–11.

5. The annual report for 1967–1968 of the Committee on Grievances of the Association of the Bar of the City of New York showed a receipt of 2,232 complaints; of the 828 offenses against clients, 76 involved conversion, 49 involved "overreaching," and 452, or more than half of all such offenses, involved neglect. *Annual Report of the Committee on Grievances of the Association of the Bar of the City of New York,* N.Y.L.J., Sept. 12, 1968, at 4, col. 5.

CANON 7

A Lawyer Should Represent a Client Zealously Within the Bounds of the Law

ETHICAL CONSIDERATIONS

EC 7-1 The duty of a lawyer, both to his client [1] and to the legal system, is to represent his client zealously [2] within the bounds of the law, [3] which includes Disciplinary Rules and enforceable professional

---

1. "The right to be heard would be, in many cases, of little avail if it did not comprehend the right to be heard by counsel. Even the intelligent and educated layman has small and sometimes no skill in the science of law." Powell v. Alabama, 287 U.S. 45, 68–69, 77 L.Ed. 158, 170, 53 S.Ct. 55, 64 (1932).

2. Cf. ABA Canon 4.

"At times . . . [the tax lawyer] will be wise to discard some arguments and he should exercise discretion to emphasize the arguments which in his judgment are most likely to be persuasive. But this process involves legal judgment rather than moral attitudes. The tax lawyer should put aside private disagreements with Congressional and Treasury policies. His own notions of policy, and his personal view of what the law should be, are irrelevant. The job entrusted to him by his client is to use all his learning and ability to protect his client's rights, not to help in the process of promoting a better tax system. The tax lawyer need not accept his client's economic and social opinions, but the client is paying for technical attention and undivided concentration upon his affairs. He is equally entitled to performance unfettered by his attorney's economic and social predilections." Paul, *The Lawyer is a Tax Advisor*, 25 Rocky Mt.L.Rev. 412, 418 (1953).

3. See ABA Canons 15 and 32.

ABA Canon 5, although only speaking of one accused of crime, imposes a similar obligation on the lawyer: "[T]he lawyer is bound, by all fair and honorable means, to present every defense that the law of the land permits, to the end that no person may be deprived of life or liberty, but by due process of law."

"Any persuasion or pressure on the advocate which deters him from planning and carrying out the litigation on the basis of 'what, within the framework of the law, is best for my client's interest?' interferes with the obligation to represent the client fully within the law.

"This obligation, in its fullest sense, is the heart of the adversary process. Each attorney, as an advocate, acts for and seeks that which in his judgment is best for his client, within the bounds authoritatively established. The advocate does not *decide* what is just in this case—he would be usurping the function of the judge and jury—he acts for and seeks for his client that which he is entitled to under the law. He can do no less and properly represent the client." Thode, *The Ethical Standard for the Advocate*, 39 Texas L.Rev. 575, 584 (1961).

"The [Texas public opinion] survey indicates that distrust of the lawyer can be traced directly to certain factors. Foremost of these is a basic misunderstanding of the function of the lawyer as an advocate in an adversary system.

"Lawyers are accused of taking advantage of 'loopholes' and 'technicalities' to win. Persons who make this charge are unaware, or do not understand, that the lawyer is hired to win, and if he does not exercise every legitimate effort in his client's behalf, then he is betraying a sacred trust." Rochelle & Payne, *The Struggle for Public Understanding*, 25 Texas B.J. 109, 159 (1962).

"The importance of the attorney's undivided allegiance and faithful service to one accused of crime, irrespective of the attorney's personal opinion as to the guilt of his client, lies in Canon 5 of the American Bar Association Canon of Ethics.

"The difficulty lies, of course, in ascertaining whether the attorney has been

regulations.[4] The professional responsibility of a lawyer derives from his membership in a profession which has the duty of assisting members of the public to secure and protect available legal rights and benefits. In our government of laws and not of men, each member of our society is entitled to have his conduct judged and regulated in accordance with the law; [5] to seek any lawful objective [6] through legally

guilty of an error of judgment, such as an election with respect to trial tactics, or has otherwise been actuated by his conscience or belief that his client should be convicted in any event. All too frequently courts are called upon to review actions of defense counsel which are, at the most, errors of judgment, not properly reviewable on habeas corpus unless the trial is a farce and a mockery of justice which requires the court to intervene. . . . But when defense counsel, in a truly adverse proceeding, admits that his conscience would not permit him to adopt certain customary trial procedures, this extends beyond the realm of judgment and strongly suggests an invasion of constitutional rights." Johns v. Smyth, 176 F.Supp. 949, 952 (E.D. Va.1959), modified, United States ex rel. Wilkins v. Banmiller, 205 F.Supp. 123, 128, n. 5 (E.D. Pa.1962), aff'd 325 F.2d 514 (3d Cir.1963), cert. denied, 379 U.S. 847, 13 L.Ed.2d 51, 85 S.Ct. 87 (1964).

"The adversary system in law administration bears a striking resemblance to the competitive economic system. In each we assume that the individual through partisanship or through self-interest will strive mightily for his side, and that kind of striving we must have. But neither system would be tolerable without restraints and modifications, and at times without outright departures from the system itself. Since the legal profession is entrusted with the system of law administration, a part of its task is to develop in its members appropriate restraints without impairing the values of partisan striving. An accompanying task is to aid in the modification of the adversary system or departure from it in areas to which the system is unsuited." Cheatham, *The Lawyer's Role and Surroundings*, 25 Rocky Mt.L.Rev. 405, 410 (1953).

4. "Rule 4.15 prohibits, in the pursuit of a client's cause, 'any manner of fraud or chicane'; Rule 4.22 requires 'candor and fairness' in the conduct of the lawyer, and

forbids the making of knowing misquotations; Rule 4.47 provides that a lawyer 'should always maintain his integrity,' and generally forbids all misconduct injurious to the interests of the public, the courts, or his clients, and acts contrary to 'justice, honesty, modesty or good morals.' Our Commissioner has accurately paraphrased these rules as follows: 'An attorney does not have the duty to do all and whatever he can that may enable him to win his client's cause or to further his client's interest. His duty and efforts in these respects, although they should be prompted by his "entire devotion" to the interest of his client, must be within and not without the bounds of the law.' " In re Wines, 370 S.W.2d 328, 333 (Mo.1963).

See Note, 38 Texas L.Rev. 107, 110 (1959).

5. "Under our system of government the process of adjudication is surrounded by safeguards evolved from centuries of experience. These safeguards are not designed merely to lend formality and decorum to the trial of causes. They are predicated on the assumption that to secure for any controversy a truly informed and dispassionate decision is a difficult thing, requiring for its achievement a special summoning and organization of human effort and the adoption of measures to exclude the biases and prejudgments that have free play outside the courtroom. All of this goes for naught if the man with an unpopular cause is unable to find a competent lawyer courageous enough to represent him. His chance to have his day in court loses much of its meaning if his case is handicapped from the outset by the very kind of prejudgment our rules of evidence and procedure are intended to prevent." *Professional Responsibility: Report of the Joint Conference*, 44 A.B.A.J. 1159, 1216 (1958).

6. "[I]t is . . . [the tax lawyer's] positive duty to show the client how to avail

permissible means;[7] and to present for adjudication any lawful claim, issue, or defense.

EC 7-2 The bounds of the law in a given case are often difficult to ascertain.[8] The language of legislative enactments and judicial opinions may be uncertain as applied to varying factual situations. The limits and specific meaning of apparently relevant law may be made doubtful by changing or developing constitutional interpretations, inadequately expressed statutes or judicial opinions, and changing public and judicial attitudes. Certainty of law ranges from well-settled rules through areas of conflicting authority to areas without precedent.

EC 7-3 Where the bounds of law are uncertain, the action of a lawyer may depend on whether he is serving as advocate or adviser. A lawyer may serve simultaneously as both advocate and adviser, but the two roles are essentially different.[9] In asserting a position on behalf of his client, an advocate for the most part deals with past conduct and must take the facts as he finds them. By contrast, a lawyer serving as

himself to the full of what the law permits. He is not the keeper of the Congressional conscience." Paul, *The Lawyer as a Tax Adviser,* 25 Rocky Mt.L.Rev. 412, 418 (1953).

7. See ABA Canons 15 and 30.

8. "The fact that it desired to evade the law, as it is called, is immaterial, because the very meaning of a line in the law is that you intentionally may go as close to it as you can if you do not pass it . . . . It is a matter of proximity and degree as to which minds will differ . . . ." Justice Holmes, in Superior Oil Co. v. Mississippi, 280 U.S. 390, 395–96, 74 L.Ed. 504, 508, 50 S.Ct. 169, 170 (1930).

9. "Today's lawyers perform two distinct types of functions, and our ethical standards should, but in the main do not, recognize these two functions. Judge Philbrick McCoy recently reported to the American Bar Association the need for a reappraisal of the Canons in light of the new and distinct function of counselor, as distinguished from advocate, which today predominates in the legal profession. . . .

". . . In the first place, any revision of the canons must take into account and speak to this new and now predominant function of the lawyer. . . . It is beyond the scope of this paper to discuss the ethical standards to be applied to the counselor except to state that in my opinion such standards should require a greater recogni-

tion and protection for the interest of the public generally than is presently expressed in the canons. Also, the counselor's obligation should extend to requiring him to inform and to impress upon the client a just solution of the problem, considering all interests involved." Thode, *The Ethical Standard for the Advocate,* 39 Texas L.Rev. 575, 578–79 (1961).

"The man who has been called into court to answer for his own actions is entitled to fair hearing. Partisan advocacy plays its essential part in such a hearing, and the lawyer pleading his client's case may properly present it in the most favorable light. A similar resolution of doubts in one direction becomes inappropriate when the lawyer acts as counselor. The reasons that justify and even require partisan advocacy in the trial of a cause do not grant any license to the lawyer to participate as legal advisor in a line of conduct that is immoral, unfair, or of doubtful legality. In saving himself from this unworthy involvement, the lawyer cannot be guided solely by an unreflective inner sense of good faith; he must be at pains to preserve a sufficient detachment from his client's interests so that he remains capable of a sound and objective appraisal of the propriety of what his client proposes to do." *Professional Responsibility: Report of the Joint Conference,* 44 A.B.J. 1159, 1161 (1958).

adviser primarily assists his client in determining the course of future conduct and relationships. While serving as advocate, a lawyer should resolve in favor of his client doubts as to the bounds of the law.[10] In serving a client as adviser, a lawyer in appropriate circumstances should give his professional opinion as to what the ultimate decisions of the courts would likely be as to the applicable law.

Duty of the Lawyer to a Client

EC 7–4 The advocate may urge any permissible construction of the law favorable to his client, without regard to his professional opinion as to the likelihood that the construction will ultimately prevail.[11] His conduct is within the bounds of the law, and therefore permissible, if the position taken is supported by the law or is supportable by a good faith argument for an extension, modification, or reversal of the law. However, a lawyer is not justified in asserting a position in litigation that is frivolous.[12]

10. "[A] lawyer who is asked to advise his client . . . may freely urge the statement of positions most favorable to the client just as long as there is reasonable basis for those positions." *ABA Opinion* 314 (1965).

11. "The lawyer . . . is not an umpire, but an advocate. He is under no duty to refrain from making every proper argument in support of any legal point because he is not convinced of its inherent soundness. . . . His personal belief in the soundness of his cause or of the authorities supporting it, is irrelevant." *ABA Opinion* 280 (1949).

"Counsel apparently misconceived his role. It was his duty to honorably present his client's contentions in the light most favorable to his client. Instead he presumed to advise the court as to the validity and sufficiency of prisoner's motion, by letter. We therefore conclude that the prisoner had no effective assistance of counsel and remand this case to the District Court with instructions to set aside the Judgment, appoint new counsel to represent the prisoner if he makes no objection thereto, and proceed anew." McCartney v. United States, 343 F.2d 471, 472 (9th Cir.1965).

12. "Here the court-appointed counsel had the transcript but refused to proceed with the appeal because he found no merit in it. . . . We cannot say that there was a finding of frivolity by either of the California courts or that counsel acted in any greater capacity than merely as *amicus*

curiae which was condemned in *Ellis,* supra. Hence California's procedure did not furnish petitioner with counsel acting in the role of an advocate nor did it provide that full consideration and resolution of the matter as is obtained when counsel is acting in that capacity. . . .

"The constitutional requirement of substantial equality and fair process can only be attained where counsel acts in the role of an active advocate in behalf of his client, as opposed to that of *amicus curiae.* The no-merit letter and the procedure it triggers do not reach that dignity. Counsel should, and can with honor and without conflict, be of more assistance to his client and to the court. His role as advocate requires that he support his client's appeal to the best of his ability. Of course, if counsel finds his case to be wholly frivolous, after a conscientious examination of it, he should so advise the court and request permission to withdraw. That request must, however, be accompanied by a brief referring to anything in the record that might arguably support the appeal. A copy of counsel's brief should be furnished the indigent and time allowed him to raise any points that he chooses; the court—not counsel—then proceeds, after a full examination of all the proceedings, to decide whether the case is wholly frivolous. If it so finds it may grant counsel's request to withdraw and dismiss the appeal insofar as federal requirements are concerned, or proceed to a decision on the merits, if state

EC 7-5 A lawyer as adviser furthers the interest of his client by giving his professional opinion as to what he believes would likely be the ultimate decision of the courts on the matter at hand and by informing his client of the practical effect of such decision.[13] He may continue in the representation of his client even though his client has elected to pursue a course of conduct contrary to the advice of the lawyer so long as he does not thereby knowingly assist the client to engage in illegal conduct or to take a frivolous legal position. A lawyer should never encourage or aid his client to commit criminal acts or counsel his client on how to violate the law and avoid punishment therefor.[14]

EC 7-6 Whether the proposed action of a lawyer is within the bounds of the law may be a perplexing question when his client is contemplating a course of conduct having legal consequences that vary according to the client's intent, motive, or desires at the time of the action. Often a lawyer is asked to assist his client in developing evidence relevant to the state of mind of the client at a particular time. He may properly assist his client in the development and preservation of evidence of existing motive, intent, or desire; obviously, he may not do anything furthering the creation or preservation of false evidence. In many cases a lawyer may not be certain as to the state of mind of his client, and in those situations he should resolve reasonable doubts in favor of his client.

EC 7-7 In certain areas of legal representation not affecting the merits of the cause or substantially prejudicing the rights of a client, a lawyer is entitled to make decisions on his own. But otherwise the authority to make decisions is exclusively that of the client and, if made within the framework of the law, such decisions are binding on his lawyer. As typical examples in civil cases, it is for the client to decide whether he will accept a settlement offer or whether he will waive his

law so requires. On the other hand, if it finds any of the legal points arguable on their merits (and therefore not frivolous) it must, prior to decision afford the indigent the assistance of counsel to argue the appeal." *Anders v. California,* 386 U.S. 738, 744, 18 L.Ed.2d 493, 498, 87 S.Ct. 1396, 1399–1400 (1967), rehearing denied, 388 U.S. 924, 18 L.Ed.2d 1377, 87 S.Ct. 2094 (1967).

See Paul, *The Lawyer As a Tax Adviser,* 25 Rocky Mt.L.Rev. 412, 432 (1953).

13. See ABA Canon 32.

14. "For a lawyer to represent a syndicate notoriously engaged in the violation of the law for the purpose of advising the members how to break the law and at the same time escape it, is manifestly improp-er. While a lawyer may see to it that anyone accused of crime, no matter how serious and flagrant, has a fair trial, and present all available defenses, he may not co-operate in planning violations of the law. There is a sharp distinction, of course, between advising what can lawfully be done and advising how unlawful acts can be done in a way to avoid conviction. Where a lawyer accepts a retainer from an organization, known to be unlawful, and agrees in advance to defend its members when from time to time they are accused of crime arising out of its unlawful activities, this is equally improper."

"See also *Opinion* 155." *ABA Opinion* 281 (1952).

right to plead an affirmative defense. A defense lawyer in a criminal case has the duty to advise his client fully on whether a particular plea to a charge appears to be desirable and as to the prospects of success on appeal, but it is for the client to decide what plea should be entered and whether an appeal should be taken.[15]

EC 7–8 A lawyer should exert his best efforts to insure that decisions of his client are made only after the client has been informed of relevant considerations. A lawyer ought to initiate this decision-making process if the client does not do so. Advice of a lawyer to his client need not be confined to purely legal considerations.[16] A lawyer should advise his client of the possible effect of each legal alternative.[17] A lawyer should bring to bear upon this decision-making process the fullness of his experience as well as his objective viewpoint.[18] In assisting his client to reach a proper decision, it is often desirable for a lawyer to point out those factors which may lead to a decision that is morally just as well as legally permissible.[19] He may emphasize the possibility of harsh consequences that might result from assertion of legally permissible positions. In the final analysis, however, the lawyer should always remember that the decision whether to forego legally available objectives or methods because of non-legal factors is ultimately for the client and not for himself. In the event that the client in a

15. See ABA Special Committee on Minimum Standards for the Administration of Criminal Justice, *Standards Relating to Pleas of Guilty,* pp. 69–70 (1968).

16. "First of all, a truly great lawyer is a wise counselor to all manner of men in the varied crises of their lives when they most need disinterested advice. Effective counseling necessarily involves a thorough-going knowledge of the principles of the law not merely as they appear in the books but as they actually operate in action." Vanderbilt, *The Five Functions of the Lawyer: Service to Clients and the Public,* 40 A.B.A.J. 31 (1954).

17. "A lawyer should endeavor to obtain full knowledge of his client's cause before advising thereon. . . ." ABA Canon 8.

18. "[I]n devising charters of collaborative effort the lawyer often acts where all of the affected parties are present as participants. But the lawyer also performs a similar function in situations where this is not so, as, for example, in planning estates and drafting wills. Here the instrument defining the terms of collaboration may affect persons not present and often not born. Yet here, too, the good lawyer does not serve merely as a legal conduit for his client's desires, but as a wise counselor, experienced in the art of devising arrangements that will put in workable order the entangled affairs and interests of human beings." *Professional Responsibility: Report of the Joint Conference,* 44 A.B.A.J. 1159, 1162 (1958).

19. See ABA Canon 8.

"Vital as is the lawyer's role in adjudication, it should not be thought that it is only as an advocate pleading in open court that he contributes to the administration of the law. The most effective realization of the law's aims often takes place in the attorney's office, where litigation is forestalled by anticipating its outcome, where the lawyer's quiet counsel takes the place of public force. Contrary to popular belief, the compliance with the law thus brought about is not generally lip-serving and narrow, for by reminding him of its long-run costs the lawyer often deters his client from a course of conduct technically permissible under existing law, though inconsistent with its underlying spirit and purpose." *Professional Responsibility: Report of the Joint Conference,* 44 A.B.A.J. 1159, 1161 (1958).

non-adjudicatory matter insists upon a course of conduct that is contrary to the judgment and advice of the lawyer but not prohibited by Disciplinary Rules, the lawyer may withdraw from the employment.[20]

EC 7–9 In the exercise of his professional judgment on those decisions which are for his determination in the handling of a legal matter,[21] a lawyer should always act in a manner consistent with the best interests of his client.[22] However, when an action in the best interest of his client seems to him to be unjust, he may ask his client for permission to forego such action.[23]

EC 7–10 The duty of a lawyer to represent his client with zeal does not militate against his concurrent obligation to treat with consideration all persons involved in the legal process and to avoid the infliction of needless harm.

EC 7–11 The responsibilities of a lawyer may vary according to the intelligence, experience, mental condition or age of a client, the obligation of a public officer, or the nature of a particular proceeding. Examples include the representation of an illiterate or an incompetent, service as a public prosecutor or other government lawyer, and appearances before administrative and legislative bodies.

EC 7–12 Any mental or physical condition of a client that renders him incapable of making a considered judgment on his own behalf casts additional responsibilities upon his lawyer. Where an incompetent is acting through a guardian or other legal representative, a lawyer must look to such representative for those decisions which are normally the prerogative of the client to make. If a client under disability has no legal representative, his lawyer may be compelled in court proceedings to make decisions on behalf of the client. If the client is capable of understanding the matter in question or of contributing to the advancement of his interests, regardless of whether he is legally disqualified from performing certain acts, the lawyer should obtain from him all possible aid. If the disability of a client and the lack of a legal representative compel the lawyer to make decisions for his client, the lawyer should consider all circumstances then prevailing and act with care to safeguard and advance the interests of his client. But obviously

---

20. "My summation of Judge Sharswood's view of the advocate's duty to the client is that he owes to the client the duty to use all legal means in support of the client's case. However, at the same time Judge Sharswood recognized that many advocates would find this obligation unbearable if applicable without exception. Therefore, the individual lawyer is given the choice of representing his client fully within the bounds set by the law *or of telling his client that he cannot do so,* so that the client may obtain another attorney if he wishes." Thode, *The Ethical Standard for the Advocate,* 39 Texas L.Rev. 575, 582 (1961).

Cf. Code of Professional Responsibility, DR 2–110(C).

21. See ABA Canon 24.

22. Thode, *The Ethical Standard for the Advocate,* 39 Texas L.Rev. 575, 592 (1961).

23. Cf. *ABA Opinions* 253 (1946) and 178 (1938).

a lawyer cannot perform any act or make any decision which the law requires his client to perform or make, either acting for himself if competent, or by a duly constituted representative if legally incompetent.

EC 7–13 The responsibility of a public prosecutor differs from that of the usual advocate; his duty is to seek justice, not merely to convict.[24] This special duty exists because: (1) the prosecutor represents the sovereign and therefore should use restraint in the discretionary exercise of governmental powers, such as in the selection of cases to prosecute; (2) during trial the prosecutor is not only an advocate but he also may make decisions normally made by an individual client, and those affecting the public interest should be fair to all; and (3) in our system of criminal justice the accused is to be given the benefit of all reasonable doubts. With respect to evidence and witnesses, the prosecutor has responsibilities different from those of a lawyer in private practice: the prosecutor should make timely disclosure to the defense of available evidence, known to him, that tends to negate the guilt of the accused, mitigate the degree of the offense, or reduce the punishment. Further, a prosecutor should not intentionally avoid pursuit of evidence merely because he believes it will damage the prosecutor's case or aid the accused.

EC 7–14 A government lawyer who has discretionary power relative to litigation should refrain from instituting or continuing litigation that is obviously unfair. A government lawyer not having such discretionary power who believes there is lack of merit in a controversy submitted to him should so advise his superiors and recommend the avoidance of unfair litigation. A government lawyer in a civil action or administrative proceeding has the responsibility to seek justice and to develop a full and fair record, and he should not use his position or the economic power of the government to harass parties or to bring about unjust settlements or results.

EC 7–15 The nature and purpose of proceedings before administrative agencies vary widely. The proceedings may be legislative or quasi-

24. See ABA Canon 5 and Berger v. United States, 295 U.S. 78, 79 L.Ed. 1314, 55 S.Ct. 629 (1935).

"The public prosecutor cannot take as a guide for the conduct of his office the standards of an attorney appearing on behalf of an individual client. The freedom elsewhere wisely granted to a partisan advocate must be severely curtailed if the prosecutor's duties are to be properly discharged. The public prosecutor must recall that he occupies a dual role, being obligated, on the one hand, to furnish that adversary element essential to the informed decision of any controversy, but being possessed, on the other, of important governmental powers that are pledged to the accomplishment of one objective only, that of impartial justice. Where the prosecutor is recreant to the trust implicit in his office, he undermines confidence, not only in his profession, but in government and the very ideal of justice itself." *Professional Responsibility: Report of the Joint Conference,* 44 A.B.A.J. 1159, 1218 (1958).

"The prosecuting attorney is the attorney for the state, and it is his primary duty not to convict but to see that justice is done." *ABA Opinion* 150 (1936).

judicial, or a combination of both. They may be *ex parte* in character, in which event they may originate either at the instance of the agency or upon motion of an interested party. The scope of an inquiry may be purely investigative or it may be truly adversary looking toward the adjudication of specific rights of a party or of classes of parties. The foregoing are but examples of some of the types of proceedings conducted by administrative agencies. A lawyer appearing before an administrative agency,[25] regardless of the nature of the proceeding it is conducting, has the continuing duty to advance the cause of his client within the bounds of the law.[26] Where the applicable rules of the agency impose specific obligations upon a lawyer, it is his duty to comply therewith, unless the lawyer has a legitimate basis for challenging the validity thereof. In all appearances before administrative agencies, a lawyer should identify himself, his client if identity of his client is not privileged,[27] and the representative nature of his appearance. It is not improper, however, for a lawyer to seek from an agency information available to the public without identifying his client.

EC 7–16 The primary business of a legislative body is to enact laws rather than to adjudicate controversies, although on occasion the activities of a legislative body may take on the characteristics of an adversary proceeding, particularly in investigative and impeachment matters. The role of a lawyer supporting or opposing proposed legislation normally is quite different from his role in representing a person under investigation or on trial by a legislative body. When a lawyer appears in connection with proposed legislation, he seeks to affect the lawmaking process, but when he appears on behalf of a client in investigatory or impeachment proceedings, he is concerned with the protection of the rights of his client. In either event, he should identify himself and his client, if identity of his client is not privileged, and should comply with applicable laws and legislataive rules.[28]

EC 7–17 The obligation of loyalty to his client applies only to a lawyer in the discharge of his professional duties and implies no obligation to adopt a personal viewpoint favorable to the interests or desires of his client.[29] While a lawyer must act always with circum-

---

25. As to appearances before a department of government, Canon 26 provides: "A lawyer openly . . . may render professional services . . . in advocacy of claims before departments of government, upon the same principles of ethics which justify his appearance before the Courts . . . ."

26. "But as an advocate before a service which itself represents the adversary point of view, where his client's case is fairly arguable, a lawyer is under no duty to disclose its weaknesses, any more than he would be to make such a disclosure to a

brother lawyer. The limitations within which he must operate are best expressed in Canon 22 . . . ." *ABA Opinion* 314 (1965).

27. See Baird v. Koerner, 279 F.2d 623 (9th Cir.1960).

28. See ABA Canon 26.

29. "Law should be so practiced that the lawyer remains free to make up his own mind how he will vote, what causes he will support, what economic and political philosophy he will espouse. It is one of the glories of the profession that it admits of

spection in order that his conduct will not adversely affect the rights of a client in a matter he is then handling, he may take positions on public issues and espouse legal reforms he favors without regard to the individual views of any client.

EC 7–18 The legal system in its broadest sense functions best when persons in need of legal advice or assistance are represented by their own counsel. For this reason a lawyer should not communicate on the subject matter of the representation of his client with a person he knows to be represented in the matter by a lawyer, unless pursuant to law or rule of court or unless he has the consent of the lawyer for that person.[30] If one is not represented by counsel, a lawyer representing another may have to deal directly with the unrepresented person; in such an instance, a lawyer should not undertake to give advice to the person who is attempting to represent himself,[31] except that he may advise him to obtain a lawyer.

Duty of the Lawyer to the Adversary System of Justice

EC 7–19 Our legal system provides for the adjudication of disputes governed by the rules of substantive, evidentiary, and procedural law. An adversary presentation counters the natural human tendency to judge too swiftly in terms of the familiar that which is not yet fully known;[32] the advocate, by his zealous preparation and presentation of facts and law, enables the tribunal to come to the hearing with an open and neutral mind and to render impartial judgments.[33] The duty of a

this freedom. Distinguished examples can be cited of lawyers whose views were at variance from those of their clients, lawyers whose skill and wisdom make them valued advisers to those who had little sympathy with their views as citizens." *Professional Responsibility: Report of the Joint Conference,* 44 A.B.A.J. 1159, 1217 (1958).

"No doubt some tax lawyers feel constrained to abstain from activities on behalf of a better tax system because they think that their clients may object. Clients have no right to object if the tax adviser handles their affairs competently and faithfully and independently of his private views as to tax policy. They buy his expert services, not his private opinions or his silence on issues that gravely affect the public interest." Paul, *The Lawyer as a Tax Adviser,* 25 Rocky Mt.L.Rev. 412, 434 (1953).

30. See ABA Canon 9.

31. Id.

32. See *Professional Responsibility: Report of the Joint Conference,* 44 A.B.A.J. 1159, 1160 (1958).

33. "Without the participation of someone who can act responsibly for each of the parties, this essential narrowing of the issues [by exchange of written pleadings or stipulations of counsel] becomes impossible. But here again the true significance of partisan advocacy lies deeper, touching once more the integrity of the adjudicative process itself. It is only through the advocate's participation that the hearing may remain in fact what it purports to be in theory: a public trial of the facts and issues. Each advocate comes to the hearing prepared to present his proofs and arguments, knowing at the same time that his arguments may fail to persuade and that his proof may be rejected as inadequate. . . . The deciding tribunal, on the other hand, comes to the hearing uncommitted. It has not represented to the public that any fact can be proved, that any argument is sound, or that any particular way of stating a litigant's case is the most effective expression of its merits." *Professional*

lawyer to his client and his duty to the legal system are the same: to represent his client zealously within the bounds of the law.[34]

EC 7-20 In order to function properly, our adjudicative process requires an informed, impartial tribunal capable of administering justice promptly and efficiently [35] according to procedures that command public confidence and respect.[36] Not only must there be competent, adverse presentation of evidence and issues, but a tribunal must be aided by rules appropriate to an effective and dignified process. The procedures under which tribunals operate in our adversary system have been prescribed largely by legislative enactments, court rules and decisions, and administrative rules. Through the years certain concepts of proper professional conduct have become rules of law applicable to the adversary adjudicative process. Many of these concepts are the bases for standards of professional conduct set forth in the Disciplinary Rules.

EC 7-21 The civil adjudicative process is primarily designed for the settlement of disputes between parties, while the criminal process is designed for the protection of society as a whole. Threatening to use, or using, the criminal process to coerce adjustment of private civil claims or controversies is a subversion of that process;[37] further, the person against whom the criminal process is so misused may be deterred from asserting his legal rights and thus the usefulness of the civil process in settling private disputes is impaired. As in all cases of abuse of judicial process, the improper use of criminal process tends to diminish public confidence in our legal system.

EC 7-22 Respect for judicial rulings is essential to the proper administration of justice; however, a litigant or his lawyer may, in good faith and within the framework of the law, take steps to test the correctness of a ruling of a tribunal.[38]

Responsibility: Report of the Joint Conference, 44 A.B.A.J. 1159, 1160-61 (1958).

34. Cf. ABA Canons 15 and 32.

35. Cf. ABA Canon 21.

36. See *Professional Responsibility: Report of the Joint Conference,* 44 A.B.A.J. 1159, 1216 (1958).

37. "We are of the opinion that the letter in question was improper, and that in writing and sending it respondent was guilty of unprofessional conduct. This court has heretofore expressed its disapproval of using threats of criminal prosecution as a means of forcing settlement of civil claims. . . .

"Respondent has been guilty of a violation of a principle which condemns any confusion of threats of criminal prosecu-

tion with the enforcement of civil claims. For this misconduct he should be severely censured." Matter of Gelman, 230 App. Div. 524, 527, 245 N.Y.S. 416, 419 (1930).

38. "An attorney has the duty to protect the interests of his client. He has a right to press legitimate argument and to protest an erroneous ruling." Gallagher v. Municipal Court, 31 Cal.2d 784, 796, 192 P.2d 905, 913 (1948).

"There must be protection, however, in the far more frequent case of the attorney who stands on his rights and combats the order in good faith and without disrespect believing with good cause that it is void, for it is here that the independence of the bar becomes valuable." Note, 39 Colum.L. Rev. 433, 438 (1939).

EC 7–23 The complexity of law often makes it difficult for a tribunal to be fully informed unless the pertinent law is presented by the lawyers in the cause. A tribunal that is fully informed on the applicable law is better able to make a fair and accurate determination of the matter before it. The adversary system contemplates that each lawyer will present and argue the existing law in the light most favorable to his client.[39] Where a lawyer knows of legal authority in the controlling jurisdiction directly adverse to the position of his client, he should inform the tribunal of its existence unless his adversary has done so; but, having made such disclosure, he may challenge its soundness in whole or in part.[40]

EC 7–24 In order to bring about just and informed decisions, evidentiary and procedural rules have been established by tribunals to permit the inclusion of relevant evidence and argument and the exclusion of all other considerations. The expression by a lawyer of his personal opinion as to the justness of a cause, as to the credibility of a witness, as to the culpability of a civil litigant, or as to the guilt or innocence of an accused is not a proper subject for argument to the trier of fact.[41] It is improper as to factual matters because admissible evidence possessed by a lawyer should be presented only as sworn testimony. It is improper as to all other matters because, were the rule otherwise, the silence of a lawyer on a given occasion could be construed unfavorably to his client. However, a lawyer may argue, on his analysis of the evidence, for any position or conclusion with respect to any of the foregoing matters.

EC 7–25 Rules of evidence and procedure are designed to lead to just decisions and are part of the framework of the law. Thus while a lawyer may take steps in good faith and within the framework of the law to test the validity of rules, he is not justified in consciously violating such rules and he should be diligent in his efforts to guard against his unintentional violation of them.[42] As examples, a lawyer should subscribe to or verify only those pleadings that he believes are in compliance with applicable law and rules; a lawyer should not make any prefatory statement before a tribunal in regard to the purported

39. "Too many do not understand that accomplishment of the layman's abstract ideas of justice is the function of the judge and jury, and that it is the lawyer's sworn duty to portray his client's case in its most favorable light." Rochelle and Payne, *The Struggle for Public Understanding,* 25 Texas B.J. 109, 159 (1962).

40. "We are of the opinion that this Canon requires the lawyer to disclose such decisions [that are adverse to his client's contentions] to the court. He may, of course, after doing so, challenge the soundness of the decisions or present reasons

which he believes would warrant the court in not following them in the pending case." *ABA Opinion* 146 (1935).

Cf. *ABA Opinion* 280 (1949) and Thode, *The Ethical Standard for the Advocate,* 39 Texas L.Rev. 575, 585–86 (1961).

41. See ABA Canon 15.

"The traditional duty of an advocate is that he honorably uphold the contentions of his client. He should not voluntarily undermine them." Harders v. State of California, 373 F.2d 839, 842 (9th Cir.1967).

42. See ABA Canon 22.

facts of the case on trial unless he believes that his statement will be supported by admissible evidence; a lawyer should not ask a witness a question solely for the purpose of harassing or embarrassing him; and a lawyer should not by subterfuge put before a jury matters which it cannot properly consider.

EC 7–26 The law and Disciplinary Rules prohibit the use of fraudulent, false, or perjured testimony or evidence.[43] A lawyer who knowingly [44] participates in introduction of such testimony or evidence is subject to discipline. A lawyer should, however, present any admissible evidence his client desires to have presented unless he knows, or from facts within his knowledge should know, that such testimony or evidence is false, fraudulent, or perjured.[45]

EC 7–27 Because it interferes with the proper administration of justice, a lawyer should not suppress evidence that he or his client has a legal obligation to reveal or produce. In like manner, a lawyer should not advise or cause a person to secrete himself or to leave the jurisdiction of a tribunal for the purpose of making him unavailable as a witness therein.[46]

EC 7–28 Witnesses should always testify truthfully [47] and should be free from any financial inducements that might tempt them to do otherwise.[48] A lawyer should not pay or agree to pay a non-expert witness an amount in excess of reimbursement for expenses and financial loss incident to his being a witness; however, a lawyer may pay or agree to pay an expert witness a reasonable fee for his services as an expert. But in no event should a lawyer pay or agree to pay a contingent fee to any witness. A lawyer should exercise reasonable

---

43. Id. Cf. ABA Canon 41.

44. See generally *ABA Opinion* 287 (1953) as to a lawyer's duty when he unknowingly participates in introducing perjured testimony.

45. "Under any standard of proper ethical conduct an attorney should not sit by silently and permit his client to commit what may have been perjury, and which certainly would mislead the court and the opposing party on a matter vital to the issue under consideration. . . .

. . .

"Respondent next urges that it was his duty to observe the utmost good faith toward his client, and therefore he could not divulge any confidential information. This duty to the client of course does not extend to the point of authorizing collaboration with him in the commission of fraud." In

re Carroll, 244 S.W.2d 474, 474–75 (Ky. 1951).

46. See ABA Canon 5; cf. *ABA Opinion* 131 (1935).

47. Cf. ABA Canon 39.

48. "The prevalence of perjury is a serious menace to the administration of justice, to prevent which no means have as yet been satisfactorily devised. But there certainly can be no greater incentive to perjury than to allow a party to make payments to its opponents witnesses under any guise or on any excuse, and at least attorneys who are officers of the court to aid it in the administration of justice, must keep themselves clear of any connection which in the slightest degree tends to induce witnesses to testify in favor of their clients." In re Robinson, 151 App.Div. 589, 600, 136 N.Y.S. 548, 556–57 (1912), aff'd, 209 N.Y. 354, 103 N.E. 160 (1913).

diligence to see that his client and lay associates conform to these standards.[49]

EC 7–29   To safeguard the impartiality that is essential to the judicial process, veniremen and jurors should be protected against extraneous influences.[50]   When impartiality is present, public confidence in the judicial system is enhanced.   There should be no extrajudicial communication with veniremen prior to trial or with jurors during trial by or on behalf of a lawyer connected with the case.   Furthermore, a lawyer who is not connected with the case should not communicate with or cause another to communicate with a venireman or a juror about the case.   After the trial, communication by a lawyer with jurors is permitted so long as he refrains from asking questions or making comments that tend to harass or embarrass the juror [51] or to influence actions of the juror in future cases.   Were a lawyer to be prohibited from communicating after a trial with a juror, he could not ascertain if the verdict might be subject to legal challenge, in which event the invalidity of a verdict might go undetected.[52]   When an extrajudicial communication by a lawyer with a juror is permitted by law, it should be made considerately and with deference to the personal feelings of the juror.

EC 7–30   Vexatious or harassing investigations of veniremen or jurors seriously impair the effectiveness of our jury system.   For this reason, a lawyer or anyone on his behalf who conducts an investigation of veniremen or jurors should act with circumspection and restraint.

EC 7–31   Communications with or investigations of members of families of veniremen or jurors by a lawyer or by anyone on his behalf are

49.   "It will not do for an attorney who seeks to justify himself against charges of this kind to show that he has escaped criminal responsibility under the Penal Law, nor can he blindly shut his eyes to a system which tends to suborn witnesses, to produce perjured testimony, and to suppress the truth.   He has an active affirmative duty to protect the administration of justice from perjury and fraud, and that duty is not performed by allowing his subordinates and assistants to attempt to subvert justice and procure results for his clients based upon false testimony and perjured witnesses."   Id., 151 App.Div. at 592, 136 N.Y.S. at 551.

50.   See ABA Canon 23.

51.   "[I]t is unfair to jurors to permit a disappointed litigant to pick over their private associations in search of something to discredit them and their verdict.   And it would be unfair to the public too if jurors should understand that they cannot con-

vict a man of means without risking an inquiry of that kind by paid investigators, with, to boot, the distortions an inquiry of that kind can produce."   State v. LaFera, 42 N.J. 97, 107, 199 A.2d 630, 636 (1964).

52.   *ABA Opinion* 319 (1968) points out that "[m]any courts today, and the trend is in this direction, allow the testimony of jurors as to all irregularities in and out of the courtroom except those irregularities whose existence can be determined only by exploring the consciousness of a single particular juror, New Jersey v. Kociolek, 20 N.J. 92, 118 A.2d 812 (1955).   Model Code of Evidence Rule 301.   Certainly as to states in which the testimony and affidavits of jurors may be received in support of or against a motion for new trial, a lawyer, in his obligation to protect his client, must have the tools for ascertaining whether or not grounds for a new trial exist and it is not unethical for him to talk to and question jurors."

subject to the restrictions imposed upon the lawyer with respect to his communications with or investigations of veniremen and jurors.

EC 7–32 Because of his duty to aid in preserving the integrity of the jury system, a lawyer who learns of improper conduct by or towards a venireman, a juror, or a member of the family of either should make a prompt report to the court regarding such conduct.

EC 7–33 A goal of our legal system is that each party shall have his case, criminal or civil, adjudicated by an impartial tribunal. The attainment of this goal may be defeated by dissemination of news or comments which tend to influence judge or jury.[53] Such news or comments may prevent prospective jurors from being impartial at the outset of the trial [54] and may also interfere with the obligation of jurors

53. Generally see ABA Advisory Committee on Fair Trial and Free Press, Standards Relating to Fair Trial and Free Press (1966).

"[T]he trial court might well have proscribed extrajudicial statements by any lawyer, party, witness, or court official which divulged prejudicial matters . . .. See State v. Van Dwyne, 43 N.J. 369, 389, 204 A.2d 841, 852 (1964), in which the court interpreted Canon 20 of the American Bar Association's Canons of Professional Ethics to prohibit such statements. Being advised of the great public interest in the case, the mass coverage of the press, and the potential prejudicial impact of publicity, the court could also have requested the appropriate city and county officials to promulgate a regulation with respect to dissemination of information about the case by their employees. In addition, reporters who wrote or broadcast prejudicial stories, could have been warned as to the impropriety of publishing material not introduced in the proceedings. . . . In this manner, Sheppard's right to a trial free from outside interference would have been given added protection without corresponding curtailment of the news media. Had the judge, the other officers of the court, and the police placed the interest of justice first, the news media would have soon learned to be content with the task of reporting the case as it unfolded in the courtroom—not pieced together from extrajudicial statements." Sheppard v. Maxwell, 384 U.S. 333, 361–62, 16 L.Ed.2d 600, 619–20, 86 S.Ct. 1507, 1521–22 (1966).

"Court proceedings are held for the solemn purpose of endeavoring to ascertain the truth which is the *sine qua non* of a fair trial. Over the centuries Anglo-American courts have devised careful safeguards by rule and otherwise to protect and facilitate the performance of this high function. As a result, at this time those safeguards do not permit the televising and photographing of a criminal trial, save in two States and there only under restrictions. The federal courts prohibit it by specific rule. This is weighty evidence that our concepts of a fair trial do not tolerate such an indulgence. We have always held that the atmosphere essential to the preservation of a fair trial—the most fundamental of all freedoms—must be maintained at all costs." Estes v. State of Texas, 381 U.S. 532, 540, 14 L.Ed.2d 543, 549, 85 S.Ct. 1628, 1631–32 (1965), rehearing denied, 382 U.S. 875, 15 L.Ed.2d 118, 86 S.Ct. 18 (1965).

54. "Pretrial can create a major problem for the defendant in a criminal case. Indeed, it may be more harmful than publicity during the trial for it may well set the community opinion as to guilt or innocence. . . . The trial witnesses present at the hearing, as well as the original jury panel, were undoubtedly made aware of the peculiar public importance of the case by the press and television coverage being provided, and by the fact that they themselves were televised live and their pictures rebroadcast on the evening show." Id., 381 U.S. at 536–37, 14 L.Ed.2d at 546–47, 85 S.Ct. at 1629–30.

to base their verdict solely upon the evidence admitted in the trial.[55] The release by a lawyer of out-of-court statements regarding an anticipated or pending trial may improperly affect the impartiality of the tribunal.[56] For these reasons, standards for permissible and prohibited conduct of a lawyer with respect to trial publicity have been established.

EC 7–34 The impartiality of a public servant in our legal system may be impaired by the receipt of gifts or loans. A lawyer,[57] therefore, is never justified in making a gift or a loan to a judge, a hearing officer, or an official or employee of a tribunal, except as permitted by Section C(4) of Canon 5 of the Code of Judicial Conduct, but a lawyer may make a contribution to the campaign fund of a candidate for judicial office in

55. "The undeviating rule of this Court was expressed by Mr. Justice Holmes over half a century ago in Patterson v. Colorado, 205 U.S. 454, 462 (1907):

"The theory of our system is that the conclusions to be reached in a case will be induced only by evidence and argument in open court, and not by any outside influence, whether of private talk or public print."

Sheppard v. Maxwell, 384 U.S. 333, 351, 16 L.Ed.2d 600, 614, 86 S.Ct. 1507, 1516 (1966).

"The trial judge has a large discretion in ruling on the issue of prejudice resulting from the reading by jurors of news articles concerning the trial. . . . Generalizations beyond that statement are not profitable, because each case must turn on its special facts. We have here the exposure of jurors to information of a character which the trial judge ruled was so prejudicial it could not be directly offered as evidence. The prejudice to the defendant is almost certain to be as great when that evidence reaches the jury through news accounts as when it is a part of the prosecution's evidence. . . . It may indeed be greater for it is then not tempered by protective procedures." Marshall v. United States, 360 U.S. 310, 312–13, 3 L.Ed.2d 1250, 1252, 79 S.Ct. 1171, 1173 (1959).

"The experienced trial lawyer knows that an adverse public opinion is a tremendous disadvantage to the defense of his client. Although grand jurors conduct their deliberations in secret, they are selected from the body of the public. They are likely to know what the general public knows and to reflect the public attitude.

Trials are open to the public, and aroused public opinion respecting the merits of a legal controversy creates a court room atmosphere which, without any vocal expression in the presence of the petit jury, makes itself felt and has its effect upon the action of the petit jury. Our fundamental concepts of justice and our American sense of fair play requires that the petit jury shall be composed of persons with fair and impartial minds and without preconceived views as to the merits of the controversy, and that it shall determine the issues presented to it solely upon the evidence adduced at the trial and according to the law given in the instructions of the trial judge.

"While we may doubt that the effect of public opinion would sway or bias the judgment of the trial judge in an equity proceeding, the defendant should not be called upon to run that risk and the trial court should not have his work made more difficult by any dissemination of statements to the public that would be calculated to create a public demand for a particular judgment in a prospective or pending case." ABA Opinion 199 (1940).

Cf. Estes v. State of Texas, 381 U.S. 532, 544–45, 14 L.Ed.2d 543, 551, 85 S.Ct. 1628, 1634 (1965), rehearing denied, 381 U.S. 875, 15 L.Ed.2d 118, 86 S.Ct. 18 (1965).

56. See ABA Canon 20.

57. Canon 3 observes that a lawyer "deserves rebuke and denunciation for any device or attempt to gain from a Judge special personal consideration or favor."

See ABA Canon 32.

conformity with Section B(2) under Canon 7 of the Code of Judicial Conduct.[58]

As amended in 1974.

EC 7–35   All litigants and lawyers should have access to tribunals on an equal basis. Generally, in adversary proceedings a lawyer should not communicate with a judge relative to a matter pending before, or which is to be brought before, a tribunal over which he presides in circumstances which might have the effect or give the appearance of granting undue advantage to one party.[59] For example, a lawyer should not communicate with a tribunal by a writing unless a copy thereof is promptly delivered to opposing counsel or to the adverse party if he is not represented by a lawyer. Ordinarily an oral communication by a lawyer with a judge or hearing officer should be made only upon adequate notice to opposing counsel, or, if there is none, to the opposing party. A lawyer should not condone or lend himself to private importunities by another with a judge or hearing officer on behalf of himself or his client.

EC 7–36   Judicial hearings ought to be conducted through dignified and orderly procedures designed to protect the rights of all parties. Although a lawyer has the duty to represent his client zealously, he should not engage in any conduct that offends the dignity and decorum of proceedings.[60] While maintaining his independence, a lawyer should be respectful, courteous, and above-board in his relations with a judge or hearing officer before whom he appears.[61] He should avoid undue solicitude for the comfort or convenience of judge or jury and should avoid any other conduct calculated to gain special consideration.

EC 7–37   In adversary proceedings, clients are litigants and though ill feeling may exist between clients, such ill feeling should not influence a lawyer in his conduct, attitude, and demeanor towards opposing lawyers.[62] A lawyer should not make unfair or derogatory personal reference to opposing counsel. Haranguing and offensive tactics by lawyers interfere with the orderly administration of justice and have no proper place in our legal system.

EC 7–38   A lawyer should be courteous to opposing counsel and should accede to reasonable requests regarding court proceedings, settings,

---

58. "*Judicial Canon 32* provides:

" 'A judge should not accept any presents or favors from litigants, or from lawyers practicing before him or from others whose interests are likely to be submitted to him for judgment.'

"The language of this Canon is perhaps broad enough to prohibit campaign contributions by lawyers, practicing before the court upon which the candidate hopes to sit. However, we do not think it was intended to prohibit such contributions when

the candidate is obligated, by force of circumstances over which he has no control, to conduct a campaign, the expense of which exceeds that which he should reasonably be expected to personally bear!" *ABA Opinion* 226 (1941).

59. See ABA Canons 3 and 32.

60. Cf. ABA Canon 18.

61. See ABA Canons 1 and 3.

62. See ABA Canon 17.

continuances, waiver of procedural formalities, and similar matters which do not prejudice the rights of his client.[63] He should follow local customs of courtesy or practice, unless he gives timely notice to opposing counsel of his intention not to do so.[64] A lawyer should be punctual in fulfilling all professional commitments.[65]

EC 7-39 In the final analysis, proper functioning of the adversary system depends upon cooperation between lawyers and tribunals in utilizing procedures which will preserve the impartiality of tribunals and make their decisional processes prompt and just, without impinging upon the obligation of lawyers to represent their clients zealously within the framework of the law.

DISCIPLINARY RULES

DR 7-101 Representing a Client Zealously.

(A) A lawyer shall not intentionally:[66]

(1) Fail to seek the lawful objectives of his client through reasonably available means[67] permitted by law and the Disciplinary Rules, except as provided by DR 7-101(B). A lawyer does not violate this Disciplinary Rule, however, by acceding to reasonable requests of opposing counsel which do not prejudice the rights of his client, by being punctual in fulfilling all professional commitments, by avoiding offensive tactics, or by treating with courtesy and consideration all persons involved in the legal process.

(2) Fail to carry out a contract of employment entered into with a client for professional services, but he may withdraw as permitted under DR 2-110, DR 5-102, and DR 5-105.

(3) Prejudice or damage his client during the course of the professional relationship[68] except as required under DR 7-102(B).

(B) In his representation of a client, a lawyer may:

(1) Where permissible, exercise his professional judgment to waive or fail to assert a right or position of his client.

(2) Refuse to aid or participate in conduct that he believes to be unlawful, even though there is some support for an argument that the conduct is legal.

---

63. See ABA Canon 24.

64. See ABA Canon 25.

65. See ABA Canon 21.

66. See ABA Canon 15.

67. See ABA Canons 5 and 15; cf. ABA Canons 4 and 32.

68. Cf. ABA Canon 24.

DR 7-102 Representing a Client Within the Bounds of the Law.

(A) In his representation of a client, a lawyer shall not:

    (1) File a suit, assert a position, conduct a defense, delay a trial, or take other action on behalf of his client when he knows or when it is obvious that such action would serve merely to harass or maliciously injure another.[69]

    (2) Knowingly advance a claim or defense that is unwarranted under existing law, except that he may advance such claim or defense it if can be supported by good faith argument for an extension, modification, or reversal of existing law.

    (3) Conceal or knowingly fail to disclose that which he is required by law to reveal.

    (4) Knowingly use perjured testimony or false evidence.[70]

    (5) Knowingly make a false statement of law or fact.

    (6) Participate in the creation or preservation of evidence when he knows or it is obvious that the evidence is false.

    (7) Counsel or assist his client in conduct that the lawyer knows to be illegal or fraudulent.

    (8) Knowingly engage in other illegal conduct or conduct contrary to a Disciplinary Rule.

(B) A lawyer who receives information clearly establishing that:

    (1) His client has, in the course of the representation, perpetrated a fraud upon a person or tribunal shall promptly call upon his client to rectify the same, and if his client refuses or is unable to do so, he shall reveal the fraud to the affected person or tribunal, except when the information is protected as a privileged communication.[71]

    (2) A person other than his client has perpetrated a fraud upon a tribunal shall promptly reveal the fraud to the tribunal.[72]

As amended in 1974.

DR 7-103 Performing the Duty of Public Prosecutor or Other Government Lawyer.[73]

(A) A public prosecutor or other government lawyer shall not institute or cause to be instituted criminal charges when he

69. See ABA Canon 30.

70. Cf. ABA Canons 22 and 29.

71. See ABA Canon 41; cf. Hinds v. State Bar, 19 Cal.2d 87, 92–93, 119 P.2d 134, 137 (1941); but see *ABA Opinion* 287 (1953) and Texas Canon 38. Also see Code of Professional Responsibility. DR 4–101(C)(2).

72. See Precision Inst. Mfg. Co. v. Automotive M.M. Co., 324 U.S. 806, 89 L.Ed. 1381, 65 S.Ct. 993 (1945).

73. Cf. ABA Canon 5.

knows or it is obvious that the charges are not supported by probable cause.

(B) A public prosecutor or other government lawyer in criminal litigation shall make timely disclosure to counsel for the defendant, or to the defendant if he has no counsel, of the existence of evidence, known to the prosecutor or other government lawyer, that tends to negate the guilt of the accused, mitigate the degree of the offense, or reduce the punishment.

DR 7–104 Communicating With One of Adverse Interest.[74]

(A) During the course of his representation of a client a lawyer shall not:

(1) Communicate or cause another to communicate on the subject of the representation with a party he knows to be represented by a lawyer in that matter unless he has the prior consent of the lawyer representing such other party [75] or is authorized by law to do so.

(2) Give advice to a person who is not represented by a lawyer, other than the advice to secure counsel,[76] if the interests of such person are or have a reasonable possibility of being in conflict with the interests of his client.[77]

DR 7–105 Threatening Criminal Prosecution.

(A) A lawyer shall not present, participate in presenting, or threaten to present criminal charges solely to obtain an advantage in a civil matter.

DR 7–106 Trial Conduct.

(A) A lawyer shall not disregard or advise his client to disregard a standing rule of a tribunal or a ruling of a tribunal made in the course of a proceeding, but he may take appropriate steps in good faith to test the validity of such rule or ruling.

(B) In presenting a matter to a tribunal, a lawyer shall disclose:[78]

74. "*Rule 12.* . . . . A member of the State Bar shall not communicate with a party represented by counsel upon a subject of controversy, in the absence and without the consent of such counsel. This rule shall not apply to communications with a public officer, board, committee or body." Cal. Business and Professions Code § 6076 (West 1962).

75. See ABA Canon 9; cf. *ABA Opinions* 124 (1934), 108 (1934), 95 (1933), and 75 (1932); also see In re Schwabe, 242 Or. 169, 174–75, 408 P.2d 922, 924 (1965).

"It is clear from the earlier opinions of this committee that *Canon 9* is to be construed literally and does not allow a communication with an opposing party, without the consent of his counsel, though the purpose merely be to investigate the facts. *Opinions 117, 55, 66,*" ABA Opinion 187 (1938).

76. Cf. *ABA Opinion* 102 (1933).

77. Cf. ABA Canon 9 and *ABA Opinion* 58 (1931).

78. Cf. Note, 38 Texas L.Rev. 107, 108–09 (1959).

    (1) **Legal authority in the controlling jurisdiction known to him to be directly adverse to the position of his client and which is not disclosed by opposing counsel.[79]**

    (2) **Unless privileged or irrelevant, the identities of the clients he represents and of the persons who employed him.[80]**

(C) **In appearing in his professional capacity before a tribunal, a lawyer shall not:**

    (1) **State or allude to any matter that he has no reasonable basis to believe is relevant to the case or that will not be supported by admissible evidence.[81]**

79. "In the brief summary in the 1947 edition of the Committee's decisions (p. 17), *Opinion 146* was thus summarized: *Opinion 146*—A lawyer should disclose to the court a decision directly adverse to his client's case that is unknown to his adversary.

. . .

"We would not confine the Opinion to 'controlling authorities'—i.e., those decisive of the pending case—but, in accordance with the tests hereafter suggested, would apply it to a decision directly adverse to any proposition of law on which the lawyer expressly relies, which would reasonably be considered important by the judge sitting on the case.

. . .

". . . The test in every case should be: Is the decision which opposing counsel has overlooked one which the court should clearly consider in deciding the case? Would a reasonable judge properly feel that a lawyer who advanced, as the law, a proposition adverse to the undisclosed decision, was lacking in candor and fairness to him? Might the judge consider himself misled by an implied representation that the lawyer knew of no adverse authority?" *ABA Opinion* 280 (1949).

80. "The authorities are substantially uniform against any privilege as applied to the fact of retainer or identity of the client. The privilege is limited to confidential communications, and a retainer is not a confidential communication, although it cannot come into existence without some communication between the attorney and the—at that stage prospective—client." United States v. Pape, 144 F.2d 778, 782 (2d Cir. 1944), cert. denied, 323 U.S. 752 89 L.Ed.2d 602, 65 S.Ct. 86 (1944).

"To be sure, there may be circumstances under which the identification of a client may amount to the prejudicial disclosure of a confidential communication, as where the substance of a disclosure has already been revealed but not its source." Colton v. United States, 306 F.2d 633, 637 (2d Cir. 1962).

81. See ABA Canon 22; cf. ABA Canon 17.

"The rule allowing counsel when addressing the jury the widest latitude in discussing the evidence and presenting the client's theories falls far short of authorizing the statement by counsel of matter not in evidence, or indulging in argument founded on no proof, or demanding verdicts for purposes other than the just settlement of the matters at issue between the litigants, or appealing to prejudice or passion. The rule confining counsel to legitimate argument is not based on etiquette, but on justice. Its violation is not merely an overstepping of the bounds of propriety, but a violation of a party's rights. The jurors must determine the issues upon the evidence. Counsel's address should help them do this, not tend to lead them astray." Cherry Creek Nat. Bank v. Fidelity & Cas. Co., 207 App.Div. 787, 790–91, 202 N.Y.S. 611, 614 (1924).

(2) **Ask any question that he has no reasonable basis to believe is relevant to the case and that is intended to degrade a witness or other person.**[82]

(3) **Assert his personal knowledge of the facts in issue, except when testifying as a witness.**

(4) **Assert his personal opinion as to the justness of a cause, as to the credibility of a witness, as to the culpability of a civil litigant, or as to the guilt or innocence of an accused;**[83] **but he may argue, on his analysis of the evidence, for any position or conclusion with respect to the matters stated herein.**

(5) **Fail to comply with known local customs of courtesy or practice of the bar or a particular tribunal without giving to opposing counsel timely notice of his intent not to comply.**[84]

(6) **Engage in undignified or discourteous conduct which is degrading to a tribunal.**

(7) **Intentionally or habitually violate any established rule of procedure or of evidence.**

DR 7-107 Trial Publicity.[85]

(A) **A lawyer participating in or associated with the investigation of a criminal matter shall not make or participate in making**

---

82. Cf. ABA Canon 18.

§ 6068. . . . It is the duty of an attorney:

. . . .

"(f) To abstain from all offensive personality, and to advance no fact prejudicial to the honor or reputation of a party or witness, unless required by the justice of the cause with which he is charged." Cal. Business and Professions Code § 6068 (West 1962).

83. "The record in the case at bar was silent concerning the qualities and character of the deceased. It is especially improper, in addressing the jury in a murder case, for the prosecuting attorney to make reference to his knowledge of the good qualities of the deceased where there is no evidence in the record bearing upon his character. . . . A prosecutor should never inject into his argument evidence not introduced at the trial." People v. Dukes, 12 Ill.2d 334, 341, 146 N.E.2d 14, 17–18 (1957).

84. "A lawyer should not ignore known customs or practice of the Bar or of a particular Court, even when the law permits, without giving timely notice to the opposing counsel." ABA Canon 25.

85. The provisions of Sections (A), (B), (C), and (D) of this Disciplinary Rule incorporate the fair trial-free press standards which apply to lawyers as adopted by the ABA House of Delegates, Feb. 19, 1968, upon the recommendation of the Fair Trial and Free Press Advisory Committee of the ABA Special Committee on Minimum Standards for the Administration of Criminal Justice.

Cf. ABA Canon 20; see generally ABA Advisory Committee on Fair Trial and Free Press, Standards Relating to Fair Trial and Free Press (1966).

"From the cases coming here we note that unfair and prejudicial news comment on pending trials has become increasingly prevalent. Due process requires that the accused receive a trial by an impartial jury free from outside influences. Given the

an extrajudicial statement that a reasonable person would expect to be disseminated by means of public communication and that does more than state without elaboration:

(1) Information contained in a public record.

(2) That the investigation is in progress.

(3) The general scope of the investigation including a description of the offense and, if permitted by law, the identity of the victim.

(4) A request for assistance in apprehending a suspect or assistance in other matters and the information necessary thereto.

(5) A warning to the public of any dangers.

(B) A lawyer or law firm associated with the prosecution or defense of a criminal matter shall not, from the time of the filing of a complaint, information, or indictment, the issuance of an arrest warrant, or arrest until the commencement of the trial or disposition without trial, make or participate in making an extrajudicial statement that a reasonable person would expect to be disseminated by means of public communication and that relates to:

(1) The character, reputation, or prior criminal record (including arrests, indictments, or other charges of crime) of the accused.

(2) The possibility of a plea of guilty to the offense charged or to a lesser offense.

(3) The existence or contents of any confession, admission, or statement given by the accused or his refusal or failure to make a statement.

pervasiveness of modern communications and the difficulty of effacing prejudicial publicity from the minds of the jurors, the trial courts must take strong measures to ensure that the balance is never weighed against the accused. And appellate tribunals have the duty to make an independent evaluation of the circumstances. Of course, there is nothing that prescribes the press from reporting events that transpire in the courtroom. But where there is a reasonable likelihood that prejudicial news prior to trial will prevent a fair trial, the judge should continue the case until the threat abates, or transfer it to another county not so permeated with publicity.

. . . The courts must take such steps by rule and regulation that will protect their processes from prejudicial outside inference. Neither prosecutors, counsel for defense, the accused, witnesses, court staff nor enforcement officers coming under the jurisdiction of the court should be permitted to frustrate its function. Collaboration between counsel and the press as to information affecting the fairness of a criminal trial is not only subject to regulation, but is highly censurable and worthy of disciplinary measures." Sheppard v. Maxwell, 384 U.S. 333, 362–63, 16 L.Ed.2d 600, 620, 86 S.Ct. 1507, 1522 (1966).

(4) The performance or results of any examinations or tests or the refusal or failure of the accused to submit to examinations or tests.

(5) The identity, testimony, or credibility of a prospective witness.

(6) Any opinion as to the guilt or innocence of the accused, the evidence, or the merits of the case.

(C) DR 7-107(B) does not preclude a lawyer during such period from announcing:

(1) The name, age, residence, occupation, and family status of the accused.

(2) If the accused has not been apprehended, any information necessary to aid in his apprehension or to warn the public of any dangers he may present.

(3) A request for assistance in obtaining evidence.

(4) The identity of the victim of the crime.

(5) The fact, time, and place of arrest, resistance, pursuit, and use of weapons.

(6) The identity of investigating and arresting officers or agencies and the length of the investigation.

(7) At the time of seizure, a description of the physical evidence seized, other than a confession, admission, or statement.

(8) The nature, substance, or text of the charge.

(9) Quotations from or references to public records of the court in the case.

(10) The scheduling or result of any step in the judicial proceedings.

(11) That the accused denies the charges made against him.

(D) During the selection of a jury or the trial of a criminal matter, a lawyer or law firm associated with the prosecution or defense of a criminal matter shall not make or participate in making an extra-judicial statement that a reasonable person would expect to be disseminated by means of public communication and that relates to the trial, parties, or issues in the trial or other matters that are reasonably likely to interfere with a fair trial, except that he may quote from or refer without comment to public records of the court in the case.

(E) After the completion of a trial or disposition without trial of a criminal matter and prior to the imposition of sentence, a lawyer or law firm associated with the prosecution or defense shall not make or participate in making an extra-judicial statement that a reasonable person would expect to be disseminated by public communication and that is reasonably likely to affect the imposition of sentence.

(F) The foregoing provisions of DR 7–107 also apply to professional disciplinary proceedings and juvenile disciplinary proceedings when pertinent and consistent with other law applicable to such proceedings.

(G) A lawyer or law firm associated with a civil action shall not during its investigation or litigation make or participate in making an extra-judicial statement, other than a quotation from or reference to public records, that a reasonable person would expect to be disseminated by means of public communication and that relates to:

(1) Evidence regarding the occurrence or transaction involved.

(2) The character, credibility, or criminal record of a party, witness, or prospective witness.

(3) The performance or results of any examinations or tests or the refusal or failure of a party to submit to such.

(4) His opinion as to the merits of the claims or defenses of a party, except as required by law or administrative rule.

(5) Any other matter reasonably likely to interfere with a fair trial of the action.

(H) During the pendency of an administrative proceeding, a lawyer or law firm associated therewith shall not make or participate in making a statement, other than a quotation from or reference to public records, that a reasonable person would expect to be disseminated by means of public communication if it is made outside the official course of the proceeding and relates to:

(1) Evidence regarding the occurrence or transaction involved.

(2) The character, credibility, or criminal record of a party, witness, or prospective witness.

(3) Physical evidence or the performance or results of any examinations or tests or the refusal or failure of a party to submit to such.

(4) His opinion as to the merits of the claims, defenses, or positions of an interested person.

(5) Any other matter reasonably likely to interfere with a fair hearing.

(I) The foregoing provisions of DR 7–107 do not preclude a lawyer from replying to charges of misconduct publicly made against him or from participating in the proceedings of legislative, administrative, or other investigative bodies.

(J) A lawyer shall exercise reasonable care to prevent his employees and associates from making an extra-judicial statement that he would be prohibited from making under DR 7–107.

DR 7–108 Communication With or Investigation of Jurors.

(A) Before the trial of a case a lawyer connected therewith shall not communicate with or cause another to communicate with anyone he knows to be a member of the venire from which the jury will be selected for the trial of the case.

(B) During the trial of a case:

(1) A lawyer connected therewith shall not communicate with or cause another to communicate with any member of the jury.[86]

(2) A lawyer who is not connected therewith shall not communicate with or cause another to communicate with a juror concerning the case.

(C) DR 7–108(A) and (B) do not prohibit a lawyer from communicating with veniremen or jurors in the course of official proceedings.

(D) After discharge of the jury from further consideration of a case with which the lawyer was connected, the lawyer shall not ask questions of or make comments to a member of that jury that are calculated merely to harass or embarrass the juror or to influence his actions in future jury service.[87]

(E) A lawyer shall not conduct or cause, by financial support or otherwise, another to conduct a vexatious or harassing investigation of either a venireman or a juror.

(F) All restrictions imposed by DR 7–108 upon a lawyer also apply to communications with or investigations of members of a family of a venireman or a juror.

(G) A lawyer shall reveal promptly to the court improper conduct by a venireman or a juror, or by another toward a venireman or a juror or a member of his family, of which the lawyer has knowledge.

DR 7–109 Contact With Witnesses.

(A) A lawyer shall not suppress any evidence that he or his client has a legal obligation to reveal or produce.[88]

---

86. See ABA Canon 23.

87. "[I]t would be unethical for a lawyer to harass, entice, induce or exert influence on a juror to obtain his testimony." *ABA Opinion* 319 (1968).

88. See ABA Canon 5.

(B) A lawyer shall not advise or cause a person to secrete himself or to leave the jurisdiction of a tribunal for the purpose of making him unavailable as a witness therein.[89]

(C) A lawyer shall not pay, offer to pay, or acquiesce in the payment of compensation to a witness contingent upon the content of his testimony or the outcome of the case.[90] But a lawyer may advance, guarantee, or acquiesce in the payment of:

    (1) Expenses reasonably incurred by a witness in attending or testifying.

    (2) Reasonable compensation to a witness for his loss of time in attending or testifying.

    (3) A reasonable fee for the professional services of an expert witness.

DR 7-110   Contact With Officials.[91]

(A) A lawyer shall not give or lend any thing of value to a judge, official, or employee of a tribunal, except as permitted by Section C(4) of Canon 5 of the Code of Judicial Conduct, but a lawyer may make a contribution to the campaign fund of a candidate for judicial office in conformity with Section B(2) under Canon 7 of the Code of Judicial Conduct.

(B) In an adversary proceeding, a lawyer shall not communicate, or cause another to communicate, as to the merits of the cause with a judge or an official before whom the proceeding is pending, except:

    (1) In the course of official proceedings in the cause.

    (2) In writing if he promptly delivers a copy of the writing to opposing counsel or to the adverse party if he is not represented by a lawyer.

    (3) Orally upon adequate notice to opposing counsel or to the adverse party if he is not represented by a lawyer.

    (4) As otherwise authorized by law, or by Section A(4) under Canon 3 of the Code of Judicial Conduct.[92]

As amended in 1974.

89. Cf. ABA Canon 5.

"*Rule 15.* . . . A member of the State Bar shall not advise a person, whose testimony could establish or tend to establish a material fact, to avoid service of process, or secrete himself, or otherwise to make his testimony unavailable." Cal.Business and Professions Code § 6076 (West 1962).

90. See In re O'Keefe, 49 Mont. 369, 142 P. 638 (1914).

91. Cf. ABA Canon 3.

92. "*Rule 16.* . . . A member of the State Bar shall not, in the absence of opposing counsel, communicate with or argue to a judge or judicial officer except in open court upon the merits of a contested matter pending before such judge or judicial officer; nor shall he, without furnishing opposing counsel with a copy thereof, address a written communication to a judge

CANON 8

A Lawyer Should Assist in Improving the Legal System

ETHICAL CONSIDERATIONS

EC 8-1   Changes in human affairs and imperfections in human institutions make necessary constant efforts to maintain and improve our legal system.[1]   This system should function in a manner that commands public respect and fosters the use of legal remedies to achieve redress of grievances.   By reason of education and experience, lawyers are especially qualified to recognize deficiencies in the legal system and to initiate corrective measures therein.   Thus they should participate in proposing and supporting legislation and programs to improve the system,[2] without regard to the general interests or desires of clients or former clients.[3]

EC 8-2   Rules of law are deficient if they are not just, understandable, and responsive to the needs of society.   If a lawyer believes that the existence or absence of a rule of law, substantive or procedural, causes or contributes to an unjust result, he should endeavor by lawful means to obtain appropriate change in the law.   He should encourage the simplification of laws and the repeal or amendment of laws that are

or judicial officer concerning the merits of a contested matter pending before such judge or judicial officer.   This rule shall not apply to ex parte matters." Cal.Business and Professions Code § 6076 (West 1962).

1.   ". . . [Another] task of the great lawyer is to do his part individually and as a member of the organized bar to improve his profession, the courts, and the law.   As President Theodore Roosevelt aptly put it, 'Every man owes some of his time to the upbuilding of the profession to which he belongs.'   Indeed, this obligation is one of the great things which distinguishes a profession from a business.   The soundness and the necessity of President Roosevelt's admonition insofar as it relates to the legal profession cannot be doubted.   The advances in natural science and technology are so startling and the velocity of change in business and in social life is so great that the law along with the other social sciences, and even human life itself, is in grave danger of being extinguished by new gods of its own invention if it does not awake from its lethargy. Vanderbilt, *The Five Functions of the Lawyer: Service to Clients and the Public*, 40 A.B.A.J. 31, 31-32 (1954).

2.   See ABA Cannon 29; Cf. Cheatham, *The Lawyer's Role and Surroundings*, 25 Rocky Mt.L.Rev. 405, 406-07 (1953).

"The lawyer tempted by repose should recall the heavy costs paid by his profession when needed legal reform has to be accomplished through the initiative of public-spirited laymen.   Where change must be thrust from without upon an unwilling Bar, the public's least flattering picture of the lawyer seems confirmed.   The lawyer concerned for the standing of his profession will, therefore, interest himself actively in the improvement of the law.   In doing so he will not only help to maintain confidence in the Bar, but will have the satisfaction of meeting a responsibility inhering in the nature of his calling." *Professional Responsibility: Report of the Joint Conference*, 44 A.B.A.J. 1159, 1217 (1958).

3.   See Stayton, *Cum Honore Officium*, 19 Tex.B.J. 765, 766 (1956); *Professional Responsibility: Report of the Joint Conference*, 44 A.B.A.J. 1159, 1162 (1958); and Paul, *The Lawyer as a Tax Adviser*, 25 Rocky Mt.L.Rev. 412, 433-34 (1953).

outmoded.[4] Likewise, legal procedures should be improved whenever experience indicates a change is needed.

EC 8–3 The fair administration of justice requires the availability of competent lawyers. Members of the public should be educated to recognize the existence of legal problems and the resultant need for legal services, and should be provided methods for intelligent selection of counsel. Those persons unable to pay for legal services should be provided needed services. Clients and lawyers should not be penalized by undue geographical restraints upon representation in legal matters, and the bar should address itself to improvements in licensing, reciprocity, and admission procedures consistent with the needs of modern commerce.

EC 8–4 Whenever a lawyer seeks legislative or administrative changes, he should identify the capacity in which he appears, whether on behalf of himself, a client, or the public.[5] A lawyer may advocate such changes on behalf of a client even though he does not agree with them. But when a lawyer purports to act on behalf of the public, he should espouse only those changes which he conscientiously believes to be in the public interest.

EC 8–5 Fraudlent, deceptive, or otherwise illegal conduct by a participant in a proceeding before a tribunal or legislative body is inconsistent with fair administration of justice, and it should never be participated in or condoned by lawyers. Unless constrained by his obligation to preserve the confidences and secrets of his client, a lawyer should reveal to appropriate authorities any knowledge he may have of such improper conduct.

EC 8–6 Judges and administrative officials having adjudicatory powers ought to be persons of integrity, competence, and suitable temperament. Generally, lawyers are qualified, by personal observation or investigation, to evaluate the qualifications of persons seeking or being considered for such public offices, and for this reason they have a special responsibility to aid in the selection of only those who are qualified.[6] It is the duty of lawyers to endeavor to prevent political

4. "There are few great figures in the history of the Bar who have not concerned themselves with the reform and improvement of the law. The special obligation of the profession with respect to legal reform rests on considerations too obvious to require enumeration. Certainly it is the lawyer who has both the best chance to know when the law is working badly and the special competence to put it in order." *Professional Responsibility: Report of the Joint Conference,* 44 A.B.A.J. 1159, 1217 (1958).

5. "*Rule 14.* . . . A member of the State Bar shall not communicate with, or appear before, a public officer, board, committee or body, in his professional capacity, without first disclosing that he is an attorney representing interests that may be affected by action of such officer, board, committee or body." Cal.Business and Professions Code § 6076 (West 1962).

6. See ABA Canon 2.

"Lawyers are better able than laymen to appraise accurately the qualifications of candidates for judicial office. It is proper that they should make that appraisal known to the voters in a proper and dignified manner. A lawyer may with proprie-

considerations from outweighing judicial fitness in the selection of judges. Lawyers should protest earnestly against the appointment or election of those who are unsuited for the bench and should strive to have elected [7] or appointed thereto only those who are willing to forego pursuits, whether of a business, political, or other nature, that may interfere with the free and fair consideration of questions presented for adjudication. Adjudicatory officials, not being wholly free to defend themselves, are entitled to receive the support of the bar against unjust criticism.[8] While a lawyer as a citizen has a right to criticize such officials publicly,[9] he should be certain of the merit of his complaint, use appropriate language, and avoid petty criticisms, for unrestrained and intemperate statements tend to lessen public confidence in our legal system.[10] Criticisms motivated by reasons other than a desire to improve the legal system are not justified.

EC 8–7 Since lawyers are a vital part of the legal system, they should be persons of integrity, of professional skill, and of dedication to the improvement of the system. Thus a lawyer should aid in establishing, as well as enforcing, standards of conduct adequate to protect the public by insuring that those who practice law are qualified to do so.

ty endorse a candidate for judicial office and seek like endorsement from other lawyers. But the lawyer who endorses a judicial candidate or seeks that endorsement from other lawyers should be actuated by a sincere belief in the superior qualifications of the candidate for judicial service and not by personal or selfish motives; and a lawyer should not use or attempt to use the power or prestige of the judicial office to secure such endorsement. On the other hand, the lawyer whose endorsement is sought, if he believes the candidate lacks the essential qualifications for the office or believes the opposing candidate is better qualified, should have the courage and moral stamina to refuse the request for endorsement." *ABA Opinion* 189 (1938).

7. "[W]e are of the opinion that, whenever a candidate for judicial office merits the endorsement and support of lawyers, the lawyers may make financial contributions toward the campaign if its cost, when reasonably conducted, exceeds that which the candidate would be expected to bear personally." *ABA Opinion* 226 (1941).

8. See ABA Canon 1.

9. "Citizens have a right under our constitutional system to criticize governmental officials and agencies. Courts are not, and should not be, immune to such criti-

cism." Konigsberg v. State Bar of California, 353 U.S. 252, 269 (1957).

10. "[E]very lawyer, worthy of respect, realizes that public confidence in our courts is the cornerstone of our governmental structure, and will refrain from unjustified attack on the character of the judges, while recognizing the duty to denounce and expose a corrupt or dishonest judge." Kentucky State Bar Ass'n v. Lewis, 282 S.W.2d 321, 326 (Ky.1955).

"We should be the last to deny that Mr. Meeker has the right to uphold the honor of the profession and to expose without fear or favor corrupt or dishonest conduct in the profession, whether the conduct be that of a judge or not. . . . However, this Canon [29] does not permit one to make charges which are false and untrue and unfounded in fact. When one's fancy leads him to make false charges, attacking the character and integrity of others, he does so at his peril. He should not do so without adequate proof of his charges and he is certainly not authorized to make careless, untruthful and vile charges against his professional brethren." In re Meeker, 76 N.M. 354, 364–65, 414 P.2d 862, 869 (1966), appeal dismissed, 385 U.S. 449, 17 L.Ed.2d 510, 87 S.Ct. 613 (1967).

EC 8–8 Lawyers often serve as legislators or as holders of other public offices. This is highly desirable, as lawyers are uniquely qualified to make significant contributions to the improvement of the legal system. A lawyer who is a public officer, whether full or part-time, should not engage in activities in which his personal or professional interests are or foreseeably may be in conflict with his official duties.[11]

EC 8–9 The advancement of our legal system is of vital importance in maintaining the rule of law and in facilitating orderly changes; therefore, lawyers should encourage, and should aid in making, needed changes and improvements.

DISCIPLINARY RULES

DR 8–101 Action as a Public Official.

(A) A lawyer who holds public office shall not:

    (1) Use his public position to obtain, or attempt to obtain, a special advantage in legislative matters for himself or for a client under circumstances where he knows or it is obvious that such action is not in the public interest.

    (2) Use his public position to influence, or attempt to influence, a tribunal to act in favor of himself or of a client.

    (3) Accept any thing of value from any person when the lawyer knows or it is obvious that the offer is for the purpose of influencing his action as a public official.

11. "*Opinions 16, 30, 34, 77, 118* and *134* relate to *Canon 6,* and pass on questions concerning the propriety of the conduct of an attorney who is a public officer, in representing private interests adverse to those of the public body which he represents. The principle applied in those opinions is that an attorney holding public office should avoid all conduct which might lead the layman to conclude that the attorney is utilizing his public position to further his professional success or personal interests." *ABA Opinion* 192 (1939).

"The next question is whether a lawyer-member of a legislative body may appear as counsel or co-counsel at hearings before a zoning board of appeals, or similar tribunal, created by the legislative group of which he is a member. We are of the opinion that he may practice before fact-finding officers, hearing bodies and commissioners, since under our views he may appear as counsel in the courts where his municipality is a party. Decisions made at such hearings are usually subject to administrative review by the courts upon the record there made. It would be inconsistent to say that a lawyer-member of a legislative body could not participate in a hearing at which the record is made, but could appear thereafter when the cause is heard by the courts on administrative review. This is subject to an important exception. He should not appear as counsel where the matter is subject to review by the legislative body of which he is a member. . . . We are of the opinion that where a lawyer does so appear there would be conflict of interests between his duty as an advocate for his client on the one hand and the obligation to his governmental unit on the other." In re Becker, 16 Ill.2d 488, 494–95, 158 N.E.2d 753, 756–57 (1959).

Cf. *ABA Opinions* 186 (1938), 136 (1935), 118 (1934), and 77 (1932).

DR 8–102 Statements Concerning Judges and Other Adjudicatory Officers.[12]

(A) A lawyer shall not knowingly make false statements of fact concerning the qualifications of a candidate for election or appointment to a judicial office.

(B) A lawyer shall not knowingly make false accusations against a judge or other adjudicatory officer.

DR 8–103 Lawyer Candidate for Judicial Office.

(A) A lawyer who is a candidate for judicial office shall comply with the applicable provisions of Canon 7 of the Code of Judicial Conduct.

Added in 1974.

CANON 9

A Lawyer Should Avoid Even the Appearance of Professional Impropriety

ETHICAL CONSIDERATIONS

EC 9–1 Continuation of the American concept that we are to be governed by rules of law requires that the people have faith that justice can be obtained through our legal system.[1] A lawyer should promote public confidence in our system and in the legal profession.[2]

EC 9–2 Public confidence in law and lawyers may be eroded by irresponsible or improper conduct of a lawyer. On occasion, ethical conduct of a lawyer may appear to laymen to be unethical. In order to avoid misunderstandings and hence to maintain confidence, a lawyer should fully and promptly inform his client of material developments in the matters being handled for the client. While a lawyer should guard against otherwise proper conduct that has a tendency to diminish public confidence in the legal system or in the legal profession, his duty to clients or to the public should never be subordinate merely because the full discharge of his obligation may be misunderstood or may tend to subject him or the legal profession to criticism. When explicit ethical guidance does not exist, a lawyer should determine his conduct

---

12. Cf. ABA Canons 1 and 2.

1. "Integrity is the very breath of justice. Confidence in our law, our courts, and in the administration of justice is our supreme interest. No practice must be permitted to prevail which invites towards the administration of justice a doubt or distrust of its integrity." Erwin M. Jennings Co. v. DiGenova, 107 Conn. 491, 499, 141 A. 866, 868 (1928).

2. "A lawyer should never be reluctant or too proud to answer unjustified criticism of his profession, of himself, or of his brother lawyer. He should guard the reputation of his profession and of his brothers as zealously as he guards his own." Rochelle and Payne, *The Struggle for Public Understanding*, 25 Texas B.J. 109, 162 (1962).

by acting in a manner that promotes public confidence in the integrity and efficiency of the legal system and the legal profession.[3]

EC 9–3 After a lawyer leaves judicial office or other public employment, he should not accept employment in connection with any matter in which he had substantial responsibility prior to his leaving, since to accept employment would give the appearance of impropriety even if none exists.[4]

EC 9–4 Because the very essence of the legal system is to provide procedures by which matters can be presented in an impartial manner so that they may be decided solely upon the merits, any statement or suggestion by a lawyer that he can or would attempt to circumvent those procedures is detrimental to the legal system and tends to undermine public confidence in it.

EC 9–5 Separation of the funds of a client from those of his lawyer not only serves to protect the client but also avoids even the appearance of impropriety, and therefore commingling of such funds should be avoided.

EC 9–6 Every lawyer owes a solemn duty to uphold the integrity and honor of his profession; to encourage respect for the law and for the courts and the judges thereof; to observe the Code of Professional Responsibility; to act as a member of a learned profession, one dedicated to public service; to cooperate with his brother lawyers in supporting the organized bar through the devoting of his time, efforts, and financial support as his professional standing and ability reasonably permit; to conduct himself so as to reflect credit on the legal profession and to inspire the confidence, respect, and trust of his clients and of the public; and to strive to avoid not only professional impropriety but also the appearance of impropriety.[5]

EC 9–7 A lawyer has an obligation to the public to participate in collective efforts of the bar to reimburse persons who have lost money or property as a result of the misappropriation or defalcation of another

---

3. See ABA Canon 29.

4. See ABA Canon 36.

5. "As said in Opinion 49 of the Committee on Professional Ethics and Grievances of the American Bar Association, page 134: 'An attorney should not only avoid impropriety but should avoid the appearance of impropriety.'" State ex rel. Nebraska State Bar Ass'n v. Richards, 165 Neb. 80, 93, 84 N.W.2d 136, 145 (1957).

"It would also be preferable that such contribution [to the campaign of a candidate for judicial office] be made to a campaign committee rather than to the candidate personally. In so doing, possible appearances of impropriety would be re-

duced to a minimum." *ABA Opinion* 226 (1941).

"The lawyer assumes high duties, and has imposed upon him grave responsibilities. He may be the means of much good or much mischief. Interests of vast magnitude are entrusted to him; confidence is reposed in him; life, liberty, character and property should be protected by him. He should guard, wtih jealous watchfulness, his own reputation, as well as that of his profession." People ex rel. Cutler v. Ford, 54 Ill. 520, 522 (1870), and also quoted in State Board of Law Examiners v. Sheldon, 43 Wyo. 522, 526, 7 P.2d 226, 227 (1932).

See *ABA Opinion* 150 (1936).

lawyer, and contribution to a clients' security fund is an acceptable method of meeting this obligation.

DISCIPLINARY RULES

DR 9-101 Avoiding Even the Appearance of Impropriety.[6]

(A) A lawyer shall not accept private employment in a matter upon the merits of which he has acted in a judicial capacity.[7]

(B) A lawyer shall not accept private employment in a matter in which he had substantial responsibility while he was a public employee.[8]

(C) A lawyer shall not state or imply that he is able to influence improperly or upon irrelevant grounds any tribunal, legislative body,[9] or public official.

6. Cf. Code of Professional Responsibility, EC 5-6.

7. See *ABA* Canon 36.

"It is the duty of the judge to rule on questions of law and evidence in misdemeanor cases and examinations in felony cases. That duty calls for impartial and uninfluenced judgment, regardless of the effect on those immediately involved or others who may, directly or indirectly, be affected. Discharge of that duty might be greatly interfered with if the judge, in another capacity, were permitted to hold himself out to employment by those who are to be, or who may be, brought to trial in felony cases, even though he did not conduct the examination. His private interests as a lawyer in building up his clientele, his duty as such zealously to espouse the cause of his private clients and to defend against charges of crime brought by law-enforcement agencies of which he is a part, might prevent, or even destroy, that unbiased judicial judgment which is so essential in the administration of justice.

"In our opinion, acceptance of a judgeship with the duties of conducting misdemeanor trials, and examinations in felony cases to determine whether those accused should be bound over for trial in a higher court, ethically bars the judge from acting as attorney for the defendants upon such trial, whether they were examined by him or by some other judge. Such a practice would not only diminish public confidence in the administration of justice in both courts, but would produce serious conflict between the private interests of the judge as a lawyer, and of his clients, and his duties as a judge in adjudicating important phases of criminal processes in other cases. The public and private duties would be incompatible. The prestige of the judicial office would be diverted to private benefit, and the judicial office would be demeaned thereby." *ABA Opinion* 242 (1942).

"A lawyer, who has previously occupied a judicial position or acted in a judicial capacity, should refrain from accepting employment in any matter involving the same facts as were involved in any specific question which he acted upon in a judicial capacity and, for the same reasons, should also refrain from accepting any employment which might reasonably appear to involve the same facts." *ABA Opinion* 49 (1931).

See *ABA Opinion* 110 (1934).

8. See *ABA Opinions* 135 (1935) and 134 (1935); cf. ABA Canon 36 and *ABA Opinions* 39 (1931) and 26 (1930). But see *ABA Opinion* 37 (1931).

9. "[A statement by a governmental department or agency with regard to a lawyer resigning from its staff that includes a laudation of his legal ability] carries implications, probably not founded in fact, that the lawyer's acquaintance and previous relations with the personnel of the administrative agencies of the government place him in an advantageous position in practicing before such agencies. So to imply would not only represent what probably is

DR 9–102 Preserving Identity of Funds and Property of a Client.[10]

(A) All funds of clients paid to a lawyer or law firm, other than advances for costs and expenses, shall be deposited in one or more identifiable bank accounts maintained in the state in which the law office is situated and no funds belonging to the lawyer or law firm shall be deposited therein except as follows:

(1) Funds reasonably sufficient to pay bank charges may be deposited therein.

(2) Funds belonging in part to a client and in part presently or potentially to the lawyer or law firm must be deposited therein, but the portion belonging to the lawyer or law firm may be withdrawn when due unless the right of the lawyer or law firm to receive it is disputed by the client, in which event the disputed portion shall not be withdrawn until the dispute is finally resolved.

(B) A lawyer shall:

(1) Promptly notify a client of the receipt of his funds, securities, or other properties.

(2) Identify and label securities and properties of a client promptly upon receipt and place them in a safe deposit box or other place of safekeeping as soon as practicable.

(3) Maintain complete records of all funds, securities, and other properties of a client coming into the possession of the lawyer and render appropriate accounts to his client regarding them.

---

untrue, but would be highly reprehensible." *ABA Opinion* 184 (1938).

10. See ABA Canon 11.

"*Rule 9.* . . . A member of the State Bar shall not commingle the money or other property of a client with his own; and he shall promptly report to the client the receipt by him of all money and other property belonging to such client. Unless the client otherwise directs in writing, he shall promptly deposit his client's funds in a bank or trust company . . . in a bank account separate from his own account and clearly designated as 'Clients' Funds Account' or 'Trust Funds Account' or words of similar import. Unless the client otherwise directs in writing, securities of a client in bearer form shall be kept by the attorney in a safe deposit box at a bank or trust company, . . . which safe deposit box shall be clearly designated as 'Client's Account' or 'Trust Account' or words of similar import, and be separate from the attorney's own safe deposit box." Cal.Business and Professions Code § 6076 (West 1962).

"[C]ommingling is committed when a client's money is intermingled with that of his attorney and its separate identity lost so that it may be used for the attorney's personal expenses or subjected to claims of his creditors. . . . The rule against commingling was adopted to provide against the probability in some cases, the possibility in many cases, and the danger in all cases that such commingling will result in the loss of clients' money." Black v. State Bar, 57 Cal.2d 219, 225–26, 368 P.2d 118, 122, 18 Cal.Rptr. 518, 522 (1962).

(4) Promptly pay or deliver to the client as requested by a client the funds, securities, or other properties in the possession of the lawyer which the client is entitled to receive.

DEFINITIONS *

As used in the Disciplinary Rules of the Code of Professional Responsibility:

(1) "Differing interests" include every interest that will adversely affect either the judgment or the loyalty of a lawyer to a client, whether it be a conflicting, inconsistent, diverse, or other interest.

(2) "Law firm" includes a professional legal corporation.

(3) "Person" includes a corporation, an association, a trust, a partnership, and any other organization or legal entity.

(4) "Professional legal corporation" means a corporation, or an association treated as a corporation, authorized by law to practice law for profit.

(5) "State" includes the District of Columbia, Puerto Rico, and other federal territories and possessions.

(6) "Tribunal" includes all courts and all other adjudicatory bodies.

(7) "A Bar association" includes a bar association of specialists as referred to in DR 2–105(A)(1) or (3).

(8) "Qualified legal assistance organization" means an office or organization of one of the four types listed in DR 2–103(D)(1)–(4), inclusive that meets all the requirements thereof.

As amended in 1974.

* "Confidence" and "secret" are defined in DR 4–101(A).

INDEX TO ABA MODEL CODE

A

Acceptance of Employment. *See* Employment, acceptance of.

Acquiring interest in litigation. *See* Adverse effect on professional judgment, interests of lawyer.

Address change, notification of, DR 2–102 (A) (2)

Administrative agencies and tribunals,
former employee, rejection of employment by, DR 9–101 (B)
improper influences on, EC 5–13, EC 5–21, EC 5–24, DR 5–107 (A), (B), EC 8–5, EC 8–6, DR 8–101 (A)
representation of client, generally, Canon 7, EC 7–15, EC 7–16, EC 8–4, EC 8–8, DR 8–101 (A)

Admiralty practitioners, EC 2–14

Admission to practice,
duty of lawyers as to applicants, EC 1–3, DR 1–101 (B)
requirements for, EC 1–2, EC 1–3, EC 1–6, DR 1–101 (A)

Advancing funds to clients, EC 5–8, DR 5–103 (B)
court costs, EC 5–8, DR 5–103 (B)
investigation expenses, EC 5–8, DR 5–103 (B)
litigation expenses, EC 5–7, EC 5–8, DR 5–103 (B)
medical examination, EC 5–8, DR 5–103 (B)
personal expenses, EC 5–8, DR 5–103 (B)

Adversary system, duty of lawyer to, Canon 7

Adverse legal authority, duty to reveal, EC 7–23, DR 7–106 (B) (1)

Adverse effect on professional judgment of lawyer, Canon 5
desires of third persons, EC 5–21 – EC 5–24, DR 5–107
interests of lawyer, EC 5–2 – EC 5–13, DR 5–101, DR 5–104
interests of other clients, EC 5–14 – EC 5–20, DR 5–105, DR 5–106

Advertising,
See also Name, use of. EC 2–6 – EC 2–15, DR 2–101, DR 2–102
announcement of change of association, DR 2–102 (A) (2)
announcement of change of firm name, DR 2–102 (A) (2)
announcement of change of office address, DR 2–102 (A) (2)
announcement of establishment of law office, DR 2–102 (A) (2)

Advertising—Cont'd
announcement of office opening, DR 2–102 (A) (2)
books written by lawyer, DR 2–101 (H) (5)
building directory, DR 2–102 (A) (3)
cards, professional announcement, DR 2–102 (A) (1), (2)
commercial publicity, EC 2–8 – EC 2–10, DR 2–101
compensation for, EC 2–8, DR 2–101 (B), DR 2–101 (I)
jurisdictional limitations of members of firm, required, notice of, DR 2–102 (D)
legal documents, DR 2–101 (H) (4)
letterheads,
of clients, DR 2–102 (A) (4)
of law firm, DR 2–102 (A) (4), DR 2–102 (B)
of lawyer, DR 2–102 (A) (4), DR 2–102 (B)
limited practice, EC 2–14, DR 2–101 (B) (2), DR 2–105
magazine, DR 2–101 (B), DR 2–101 (I)
name, *See* Name, use of newspaper, DR 2–101 (B), DR 2–101 (I)
office, identification of, DR 2–101 (B) (1), DR 2–102 (A)
office address change, DR 2–102 (A) (2)
office building directory, DR 2–102 (A) (3)
office establishment, DR 2–102 (A) (2)
office sign, DR 2–102 (A) (3)
political, DR 2–101 (H) (1)
public notices, DR 2–101 (H) (2)
radio, DR 2–101 (B), DR 2–101 (D), DR 2–101 (I)
reasons for regulating, EC 2–6 – EC 2–10
sign, DR 2–102 (A) (3)
specialization, EC 2–14, DR 2–101 (B) (2), DR 2–105
television, EC 2–8, DR 2–101 (B), (D)
textbook, DR 2–101 (H) (5)
treatises, DR 2–101 (H) (5)

Advice by lawyer to secure legal services, EC 24 – EC 2–5, DR 2–104
client, former or regular, EC 2–4, DR 2–104 (A) (1)
close friend, EC 2–4, DR 2–104 (A) (1)
employment resulting from, EC 2–4, DR 2–104
motivation, effect of, EC 2–4
other laymen parties to class action, DR 2–104 (A) (5)
relative, EC 2–4, DR 2–104 (A) (1)
volunteered, EC 2–4, DR 2–104
within permissible legal service programs, DR 2–104 (A) (3)

320

Advocacy, professional, Canon 7

Aiding unauthorized practice of law, Canon 3

Ambulance chasing. *See* Recommendation of professional employment.

Announcement card. *See* Advertising, cards, professional announcement.

Appearance of impropriety, avoiding, EC 5–6, Canon 9

Appearance of lawyer. *See* Administrative agencies, representation of client before; Courts, representation of client before; Legislature, representation of client before; Witness, lawyer acting as.

Applicant for bar admission. *See* Admission to practice.

Arbitrator, lawyer acting as, EC 5–20

Argument,
   before administrative agency, EC 7–15
   before jury, EC 7–24, EC 7–25, DR 7–106 (C)
   before legislature, EC 7–16
   before tribunal, EC 7–19 – EC 7–25, DR 7–102, DR 7–106

Associates of lawyer, duty to control, EC 1–4, DR 2–103, EC 3–8, EC 3–9, EC 4–2, DR 4–101 (D), DR 7–107

Association of counsel,
   See also Co-counsel; Division of legal fees.
   client's suggestion of, EC 5–10, EC 5–11
   lawyer's suggestion of, EC 5–10, EC 5–11, EC 6–3, DR 6–101 (1)

Assumed name. *See* Name, use of, assumed name.

Attempts to exert personal influence on tribunal, EC 7–24, EC 7–29 – EC 7–33, EC 7–36, DR 7–106 (C), DR 7–108, DR 7–110

Attorney-client privilege. *See also* Confidences of client; Secrets of client. EC 4–4, DR 4–101 (A), DR 7–102 (B) (1)

Attorney's lien. *See* Fee for legal services, collection of. Availability of counsel, EC 2–1, EC 2–7, EC 2–24 – EC 2–33

B

Bank accounts for clients' funds, EC 9–5, DR 9–102

Bank charges on clients' accounts, EC 9–5, DR 9–102

Bar applicant. *See* Admission to practice. bar examiners, assisting, EC 1–2

Bar associations,
   disciplinary authority, assisting, EC 1–4, DR 1–103
   educational activities, EC 6–2
   lawyer referral service, DR 2–103 (C) (1), DR 2–103 (D) (3)
   legal aid office, DR 2–103 (D) (1) (d)

Barratry. *See* Advice by lawyer to secure legal services; Recommendation of professional employment.

Bequest by client to lawyer, EC 5–5

Best efforts. *See* Zeal.

Bounds of law,
   difficulty of ascertaining, EC 7–2, EC 7–3, EC 7–4, EC 7–6
   duty to observe, EC 7–1, DR 7–102
   generally, Canon 7

Bribes. *See* Gifts to tribunal officer or employee by lawyer.

Building directory. *See* Advertising, building directory.

Business card. *See* Advertising, cards, professional.

C

Calling card. *See* Advertising, cards, professional.

Candidate. *See* Political activity.

Canons, purpose and function of, Preamble & Preliminary Statement

Cards. *See* Advertising, cards.

Change of office address. *See* Advertising, announcement of change of office address.

Change of association. *See* Advertising, announcement of change of association.

Change of firm name. *See* Advertising, announcement of change of firm name.

Character requirements, EC 1–3

Class action. *See* Advice by lawyer to secure legal services, parties to legal action.

Clients,
   See also Employment; Adverse effect on professional judgment of lawyer; Fee for legal services; Indigent parties, representation of; Unpopular party, representation of.
   appearance as witness for, EC 5–9, EC 5–10, DR 5–101 (B), DR 5–102
   attorney-client privilege, Canon 4
   commingling of funds of, EC 9–5, DR 9–102
   confidence of, Canon 4
   counselling, EC 7–5, EC 7–7, EC 7–8, EC 7–9, EC 7–12, DR 7–102 (A) (7), (B) (1), DR 7–109 (B)

Clients' security fund, EC 9–7

Co-counsel,
   See also Association of counsel.
   division of fee with, DR 2–107
   inability to work with, DR 2–110 (C) (3)

Commercial publicity. *See* Advertising, commercial publicity.

Commingling of funds, EC 9–5, DR 9–102

E

Fee for legal services—Cont'd
persons able to pay reasonable fee, EC 2–17, EC 2–18
persons only able to pay a partial fee, EC 2–16
persons without means to pay a fee, EC 2–24, EC 2–25
reasonable fee, rational against overcharging, EC 2–17
refund of unearned portion to client, DR 2–110 (A) (3)
Felony. *See* Discipline of lawyer, grounds for, illegal conduct.
Firm name. *See* Name, use of, firm name.
Framework of law. *See* Bounds of law.
Frivolous position, avoiding, EC 7–4, DR 7–102 (A) (1)
Funds of client, protection of, EC 9–5, DR 9–102
Future conduct of client, counseling as to. *See* Clients, counseling.

G

"General counsel" designation, DR 2–102 (A) (4)
Gift to lawyer by client, EC 5–5
Gifts to tribunal officer or employee by lawyer, DR 7–110 (A)
Government legal assistance agencies, working with, DR 2–103 (C) (2), DR 2–103 (D) (1) (C)
Grievance committee. *See* Bar associations, disciplinary authority, assisting.
Guaranteeing payment of client's cost and expenses, EC 5–8, DR 5–103 (B)

H

Harassment, duty to avoid litigation involving, EC 2–30, DR 2–109 (A) (1), DR 7–102 (A) (1)
as limiting practice, EC 2–8, EC 2–14, DR 2–101 (B) (2), DR 2–105
as partnership, EC 2–13, DR 2–102 (C)
as specialist, EC 2–8, EC 2–14, DR 2–101 (B) (2), DR 2–105

I

Identity of client, duty to reveal, EC 7–16, EC 8–5
Illegal conduct, as cause for discipline, EC 1–5, DR 1–102 (A) (3), DR 7–102 (A) (7)
Impartiality of tribunal, aiding in the, Canon 7
Improper influences,
gift or loan to judicial officer, EC 7–34, DR 7–110 (A)
on judgment of lawyer. *See* Adverse effect on professional judgment of lawyer.

Improvement of legal system, EC 8–1, EC 8–2, EC 8–9
Incompetence, mental. *See* Instability, mental or emotional; Mental competence of client.
Incompetence, professional. *See* Competence, professional.
Independent professional judgment, duty to preserve, Canon 5
Indigent parties,
provision of legal services to, EC 2–24, EC 2–25
representation of, EC 2–25
Instability, mental or emotional,
of bar applicant, EC 1–6
of lawyer, EC 1–6, DR 2–110 (B) (3), DR 2–110 (C) (4)
recognition of rehabilitation, EC 1–6
Integrity of legal profession, maintaining, Preamble, EC 1–1, EC 1–4, DR 1–101, EC 8–7
Intent of client, as factor in giving advice, EC 7–5, EC 7–6, DR 7–102
Interests of lawyer. *See* Adverse effect on professional judgment of lawyer, interests of lawyer.
Interests of other client. *See* Adverse effect on professional judgment of lawyer, interests of other clients.
Interests of third person. *See* Adverse effect on professional judgment of lawyer, desires of third persons.
Intermediary, prohibition against use of, EC 5–21, EC 5–23, EC 5–24, DR 5–107 (A), (B)
Interview,
with opposing party, DR 7–104
with news media, EC 7–33, DR 7–107
with witness, EC 7–28, DR 7–109
Investigation expenses, advancing or guaranteeing payment, EC 5–8, DR 5–103 (B)

J

Judges,
false statements concerning, DR 8–102
improper influences on,
gifts to, EC 7–34, DR 7–110 (A)
private communication with, EC 7–39, DR 7–110 (B)
misconduct toward,
criticisms of, EC 8–6
disobedience of orders, EC 7–36, DR 7–106 (A)
false statement regarding, DR 8–102
name in partnership, use of, EC 2–12, DR 2–102 (B)
retirement from bench, EC 9–3
selection of, EC 8–6
Judgment of lawyer. *See* Adverse effect on professional judgment of lawyer.

Q

R

S

Self-interest of lawyer. *See* Adverse effect on professional judgment of lawyer, interests of lawyer.

Self-representation, privilege of, EC 3–7

Settlement agreement, DR 5–106

Solicitation of business. *See* Advertising: Recommendation of professional employment.

Specialist, holding out as, EC 2–14, DR 2–105

Specialization,
admiralty, EC 2–14
holding out as having, EC 2–14, DR 2–105
patents, EC 2–14, DR 2–105 (A) (1)
trademark, EC 2–14, DR 2–105 (A) (1)

Speeches to lay groups, EC 2–2, EC 2–5

State of mind of client, effect of in advising him, EC 7–11, EC 7–12

State's attorney. *See* Prosecuting attorney.

"Stirring up litigation." *See* Advertising: Advice by lawyer to secure legal services; Recommendation of professional employment.

Stockholders of corporation, corporate counsel's allegiance to, EC 5–18

Suit to harass another, duty to avoid, EC 2–30, DR 2–109 (A) (1), EC 7–10, EC 7–14, DR 7–102 (A) (1)

Suit to maliciously harm another, duty to avoid, EC 2–30, DR 2–109 (A) (1), EC 7–10, EC 7–14, DR 7–102 (A) (1)

Suggested fee schedule. *See* Fees for legal services, determination of minimum fee schedule.

Suggestion of need for legal services. *See* Advice by lawyer to secure legal services.

Suppression of evidence, EC 7–27, DR 7–102 (A) (2), DR 7–103 (B), DR 7–106 (C) (7)

T

Technical and professional licenses, DR 2–101 (B) (12), DR 2–102 (E)

Termination of employment. *See* Confidences of client; Employment, withdrawal from.

Third persons, desires of. *See* Adverse effect on professional judgment of lawyer, desires of third persons.

Threatening criminal process, EC 7–21, DR 7–105 (A)

Trademark practitioner, EC 2–14, DR 2–105 (A) (1)

Trade name. *See* Name, use of, trade name.

Trial publicity, EC 7–33, DR 7–107

Trial tactics, Canon 7

Tribunal, representation of client before, Canon 7

Trustee, client naming lawyer as, EC 5–6

U

Unauthorized practice of law,
See also Division of legal fees; Partnership, non-lawyer, with.
aiding a layman in the, prohibited, EC 3–8, DR 3–101 (A)
distinguished from delegation of tasks to subprofessionals, EC 3–5, EC 3–6, DR 3–102 (A) (3)
functional meaning of, EC 3–5, EC 3–9
self-representation by layman not included in, EC 3–7

Undignified conduct, duty to avoid, EC 7–37, EC 7–38

Unlawful conduct, aiding client in, DR 7–102 (A) (6), (7), (B) (1)

Unpopular party, representation of, EC 2–27, EC 2–29, EC 2–30, EC 2–31

Unreasonable fees. *See* Fee for legal services, amount of.

Unsolicited advice. *See* Advice by lawyer to obtain legal services.

V

Varying interests of clients. *See* Adverse effect on professional judgment of a lawyer, interests of other clients.

Violation of disciplinary rule as cause for discipline, DR 1–102 (A) (1), (2)

Violation of law as cause for discipline, EC 1–5, DR 1–102 (3), (4), EC 7–26, DR 7–102 (A) (3)–(8)

Veniremen. *See* Jury.

Voluntary gifts by clients to lawyer, EC 5–5

Volunteered advice to secure legal services. *See* Advice by lawyer to secure legal services.

W

Waiver of position of client, DR 7–101 (B) (1)

Will of client, gift to lawyer in, EC 5–5

Withdrawal. *See* Employment, withdrawal from.

Witness,
communications with, EC 7–27, EC 7–28, DR 7–109
false testimony by, EC 7–26, EC 7–28, DR 7–102 (B) (2)
lawyer acting as, EC 5–9, EC 5–10, DR 5–101 (B), DR 5–102
member of lawyer's firm acting as, DR 5–101 (B), DR 5–102
payment to, EC 7–28, DR 7–109 (C)

AMERICAN BAR ASSOCIATION
CANONS OF PROFESSIONAL ETHICS

As amended until 1969.

[The ABA adopted 32 Canons of Professional Ethics at its thirty-first annual meeting on August 27, 1908. Between 1908 and 1969, the ABA added Canons 33 through 47. Although the Canons were in effect for 61 years, the general aspirational approach of the Canons proved to be outmoded to regulate the conduct of lawyers in the 1950s and 1960s. The Canons were superseded in 1969 by the Model Code of Professional Responsibility. Ed.]

CANONS OF PROFESSIONAL ETHICS

Preamble.

In America, where the stability of Courts and of all departments of government rests upon the approval of the people, it is peculiarly essential that the system for establishing and dispensing Justice be developed to a high point of efficiency and so maintained that the public shall have absolute confidence in the integrity and impartiality of its administration. The future of the Republic, to a great extent, depends upon our maintenance of Justice pure and unsullied. It cannot be so maintained unless the conduct and the motives of the members of our profession are such as to merit the approval of all just men.

No code or set of rules can be framed, which will particularize all the duties of the lawyer in the varying phases of litigation or in all the relations of professional life. The following canons of ethics are adopted by the American Bar Association as a general guide, yet the enumeration of particular duties should not be construed as a denial of the existence of others equally imperative, though not specifically mentioned.

CANON 1

The Duty of the Lawyer to the Courts

It is the duty of the lawyer to maintain towards the Courts a respectful attitude, not for the sake of the temporary incumbent of the judicial office, but for the maintenance of its supreme importance. Judges, not being wholly free to defend themselves, are peculiarly entitled to receive the support of the Bar against unjust criticism and clamor. Whenever there is proper ground for serious complaint of a judicial officer, it is the right and duty of the lawyer to submit his grievances to the proper authorities. In such cases, but not otherwise, such charges should be encouraged and the person making them should be protected.

CANON 2

The Selection of Judges

It is the duty of the Bar to endeavor to prevent political considerations from outweighing judicial fitness in the selections of Judges. It should protest earnestly and actively against the appointment or election of those who are unsuitable for the Bench; and it should strive to have elevated thereto only those willing to forego other employments, whether of a business, political or other character, which may embarrass their free and fair consideration of questions before them for decision. The aspiration of lawyers for judicial position should be governed by an impartial estimate of their ability to add honor to the office and not by a desire for the distinction the position may bring to themselves.

CANON 3

Attempts to Exert Personal Influence on the Court

Marked attention and unusual hospitality on the part of a lawyer to a Judge, uncalled for by the personal relations of the parties, subject both the Judge and the lawyer to misconstructions of motive and should be avoided. A lawyer should not communicate or argue privately with the Judge as to the merits of a pending cause, and he deserves rebuke and denunciation for any device or attempt to gain from a Judge special personal consideration or favor. A self-respecting independence in the discharge of professional duty, without denial or diminution of the courtesy and respect due the Judge's station, is the only proper foundation for cordial personal and official relations between Bench and Bar.

CANON 4

When Counsel for an Indigent Prisoner

A lawyer assigned as counsel for an indigent prisoner ought not to ask to be excused for any trivial reason, and should always exert his best efforts on his behalf.

CANON 5

The Defense or Prosecution of Those Accused of Crime

It is the right of the lawyer to undertake the defense of a person accused of crime, regardless of his personal opinion as to the guilt of the accused; otherwise innocent persons, victims only of suspicious circumstances, might be denied proper defense. Having undertaken such defense, the lawyer is bound, by all fair and honorable means, to present every defense that the law of the land permits, to the end that no person may be deprived of life or liberty, but by due process of law.

The primary duty of a lawyer engaged in public prosecution is not to convict, but to see that justice is done. The suppression of facts or the secreting of witnesses capable of establishing the innocence of the accused is highly reprehensible.

CANON 6

Adverse Influences and Conflicting Interests

It is the duty of a lawyer at the time of retainer to disclose to the client all the circumstances of his relations to the parties, and any interest in or connection with the controversy, which might influence the client in the selection of counsel.

It is unprofessional to represent conflicting interests, except by express consent of all concerned given after a full disclosure of the facts. Within the meaning of this canon, a lawyer represents conflicting interests when, in behalf of one client, it is his duty to contend for that which duty to another client requires him to oppose.

The obligation to represent the client with undivided fidelity and not to divulge his secrets or confidences forbids also the subsequent acceptance of retainers or employment from others in matters adversely affecting any interest of the client with respect to which confidence has been reposed.

CANON 7

Professional Colleagues and Conflicts of Opinion

A client's proffer of assistance of additional counsel should not be regarded as evidence of want of confidence, but the matter should be left to the determination of the client. A lawyer should decline association as colleague if it is objectionable to the original counsel, but if the lawyer first retained is relieved, another may come into the case.

When lawyers jointly associated in a cause cannot agree as to any matter vital to the interest of the client, the conflict of opinion should be frankly stated to him for his final determination. His decision should be accepted unless the nature of the difference makes it impracticable for the lawyer whose judgment has been overruled to cooperate effectively. In this event it is his duty to ask the client to relieve him.

Efforts, direct or indirect, in any way to encroach upon the professional employment of another lawyer, are unworthy of those who should be brethren at the Bar; but, nevertheless, it is the right of any lawyer, without fear or favor, to give proper advice to those seeking relief against unfaithful or neglectful counsel, generally after communication with the lawyer of whom the complaint is made.

CANON 8

Advising Upon the Merits of a Client's Cause

A lawyer should endeavor to obtain full knowledge of his client's cause before advising thereon, and he is bound to give a candid opinion of the merits and probable result of pending or contemplated litigation. The miscarriages to which justice is subject, by reason of surprises and disappointments in evidence and witnesses, and through mistakes of juries and errors of Courts, even though only occasional, admonish lawyers to beware of bold and confident assurances to clients, especially where the employment may depend upon such assurance. Whenever the controversy will admit of fair adjustment, the client should be advised to avoid or to end the litigation.

CANON 9

Negotiations With Opposite Party

A lawyer should not in any way communicate upon the subject of controversy with a party represented by counsel; much less should he undertake to negotiate or compromise the matter with him, but should deal only with his counsel. It is incumbent upon the lawyer most particularly to avoid everything that may tend to mislead a party not represented by counsel, and he should not undertake to advise him as to the law.

CANON 10

Acquiring Interest in Litigation

The lawyer should not purchase any interest in the subject matter of the litigation which he is conducting.

CANON 11

Dealing With Trust Property

The lawyer should refrain from any action whereby for his personal benefit or gain he abuses or takes advantage of the confidence reposed in him by his client.

Money of the client or collected for the client or other trust property coming into the possession of the lawyer should be reported and accounted for promptly, and should not under any circumstances be commingled with his own or be used by him.

CANON 12

Fixing the Amount of the Fee

In fixing fees, lawyers should avoid charges which overestimate their advice and services, as well as those which undervalue them. A client's ability to pay cannot justify a charge in excess of the value of the service, though his poverty may require a less charge, or even none at all. The reasonable requests of brother lawyers, and of their widows and orphans without ample means, should receive special and kindly consideration.

In determining the amount of the fee, it is proper to consider: (1) the time and labor required, the novelty and difficulty of the questions involved and the skill requisite properly to conduct the cause; (2) whether the acceptance of employment in the particular case will preclude the lawyer's appearance for others in cases likely to arise out of the transaction, and in which there is a reasonable expectation that otherwise he would be employed, or will involve the loss of other employment while employed in the particular case or antagonisms with other clients; (3) the customary charges of the Bar for similar services; (4) the amount involved in the controversy and the benefits resulting to the client from the services; (5) the contingency or the certainty of the compensation; and (6) the character of the employment, whether casual or for an established and constant client. No one of these considerations in itself is controlling. They are mere guides in ascertaining the real value of the service.

In determining the customary charges of the Bar for similar services, it is proper for a lawyer to consider a schedule of minimum fees adopted by a Bar Association, but no lawyer should permit himself to be controlled thereby or to follow it as his sole guide in determining the amount of his fee.

In fixing fees it should never be forgotten that the profession is a branch of the administration of justice and not a mere money-getting trade.

CANON 13

Contingent Fees

A contract for a contingent fee, where sanctioned by law, should be reasonable under all the circumstances of the case, including the risk and uncertainty of the compensation, but should always be subject to the supervision of a court, as to its reasonableness.

CANON 14

Suing a Client for a Fee

Controversies with clients concerning compensation are to be avoided by the lawyer so far as shall be compatible with his self-respect and with his right to receive reasonable recompense for his services; and lawsuits with clients should be resorted to only to prevent injustice, imposition or fraud.

CANON 15

How Far a Lawyer May Go in Supporting a Client's Cause

Nothing operates more certainly to create or to foster popular prejudice against lawyers as a class, and to deprive the profession of that full measure of public esteem and confidence which belongs to the proper discharge of its duties than does the false claim, often set up by the unscrupulous in defense of questionable transactions, that it is the duty of the lawyer to do whatever may enable him to succeed in winning his client's cause.

It is improper for a lawyer to assert in argument his personal belief in his client's innocence or in the justice of his cause.

The lawyer owes "entire devotion to the interest of the client, warm zeal in the maintenance and defense of his rights and the exertion of his utmost learning and ability," to the end that nothing be taken or be withheld from him, save by the rules of law, legally applied. No fear of judicial disfavor or public unpopularity should restrain him from the full discharge of his duty. In the judicial forum the client is entitled to the benefit of any and every remedy and defense that is authorized by the law of the land, and he may expect his lawyer to assert every such remedy or defense. But it is steadfastly to be borne in mind that the great trust of the lawyer is to be performed within and not without the bounds of the law. The office of attorney does not permit, much less does it demand of him for any client, violation of law or any manner of fraud or chicane. He must obey his own conscience and not that of his client.

CANON 16

Restraining Clients From Improprieties

A lawyer should use his best efforts to restrain and to prevent his clients from doing those things which the lawyer himself ought not to do, particularly with reference to their conduct towards Courts, judicial officers, jurors, witnesses and suitors. If a client persists in such wrongdoing the lawyer should terminate their relation.

CANON 17

Ill–Feeling and Personalities Between Advocates

Clients, not lawyers, are the litigants. Whatever may be the ill-feeling existing between clients, it should not be allowed to influence counsel in their conduct and demeanor toward each other or toward suitors in the case. All personalities between counsel should be scrupulously avoided. In the trial of a cause it is indecent to allude to the personal history or the personal peculiarities and idiosyncrasies of counsel on the other side. Personal colloquies between counsel which cause delay and promote unseemly wrangling should also be carefully avoided.

CANON 18

Treatment of Witnesses and Litigants

A lawyer should always treat adverse witnesses and suitors with fairness and due consideration, and he should never minister to the malevolence or prejudices of a client in the trial or conduct of a cause. The client cannot be made the keeper of the lawyer's conscience in professional matters. He has no right to demand that his counsel shall abuse the opposite party or indulge in offensive personalities. Improper speech is not excusable on the ground that it is what the client would say if speaking in his own behalf.

CANON 19

Appearance of Lawyer as Witness for His Client

When a lawyer is a witness for his client, except as to merely formal matters, such as the attestation or custody of an instrument and the like, he should leave the trial of the case to other counsel. Except when essential to the ends of justice, a lawyer should avoid testifying in court in behalf of his client.

CANON 20

Newspaper Discussion of Pending Litigation

Newspaper publications by a lawyer as to pending or anticipated litigation may interfere with a fair trial in the Courts and otherwise prejudice the due administration of justice. Generally they are to be condemned. If the extreme circumstances of a particular case justify a statement to the public, it is unprofessional to make it anonymously. An *ex parte* reference to the facts should not go beyond quotation from the records and papers on file in the court; but even in extreme cases it is better to avoid any *ex parte* statement.

CANON 21

Punctuality and Expedition

It is the duty of the lawyer not only to his client, but also to the Courts and to the public to be punctual in attendance, and to be concise and direct in the trial and disposition of causes.

CANON 22

Candor and Fairness

The conduct of the lawyer before the Court and with other lawyers should be characterized by candor and fairness.

It is not candid or fair for the lawyer knowingly to misquote the contents of a paper, the testimony of a witness, the language or the argument of opposing counsel, or the language of a decision of a textbook; or with knowledge of its invalidity, to cite as authority a decision that has been overruled, or a statute that has been repealed; or in argument to assert as a fact that which has not been proved, or in those jurisdictions where a side has the opening and closing arguments to mislead his opponent by concealing or withholding positions in his opening argument upon which his side then intends to rely.

It is unprofessional and dishonorable to deal other than candidly with the facts in taking the statements of witnesses, in drawing affidavits and other documents, and in the presentation of causes.

A lawyer should not offer evidence which he knows the Court should reject, in order to get the same before the jury by argument for its admissibility, nor should he address to the Judge arguments upon any point not properly calling for determination by him. Neither should he introduce into an argument, addressed to the court, remarks or statements intended to influence the jury or bystanders.

These and all kindred practices are unprofessional and unworthy of an officer of the law charged, as is the lawyer, with the duty of aiding in the administration of justice.

CANON 23

Attitude Toward Jury

All attempts to curry favor with juries by fawning, flattery or pretended solicitude for their personal comfort are unprofessional. Suggestions of counsel, looking to the comfort or convenience of jurors, and propositions to dispense with argument, should be made to the Court out of the jury's hearing. A lawyer must never converse privately with jurors about the case; and both before and during the trial he should avoid communicating with them, even as to matters foreign to the cause.

CANON 24

Right of Lawyer to Control the Incidents of the Trial

As to incidental matters pending the trial, not affecting the merits of the cause, or working substantial prejudice to the rights of the client, such as forcing the opposite lawyer to trial when he is under affliction or bereavement; forcing the trial on a particular day to the injury of the opposite lawyer when no harm will result from a trial at a different time; agreeing to an extension of time for signing a bill of exceptions, cross interrogatories and the like, the lawyer must be allowed to judge. In such matters no client has a right to demand that his counsel shall be illiberal, or that he do anything therein repugnant to his own sense of honor and propriety.

CANON 25

Taking Technical Advantage of Opposite Counsel; Agreements With Him

A lawyer should not ignore known customs or practice of the Bar or of a particular Court, even when the law permits, without giving timely notice to the opposing counsel. As far as possible, important agreements, affecting the rights of clients, should be reduced to writing; but it is dishonorable to avoid performance of an agreement fairly made because it is not reduced to writing, as required by rules of Court.

CANON 26

Professional Advocacy Other Than Before Courts

A lawyer openly, and in his true character may render professional services before legislative or other bodies, regarding proposed legislation and in advocacy of claims before departments of government, upon the same principles of ethics which justify his appearance before the Courts; but it is unprofessional for a lawyer so engaged to conceal his attorneyship, or to employ secret personal solicitations, or to use means other than those addressed to the reason and understanding, to influence action.

CANON 27

Advertising, Direct or Indirect

It is unprofessional to solicit professional employment by circulars, advertisements, through toutors or by personal communications or interviews not warranted by personal relations. Indirect advertisements for professional employment such as furnishing or inspiring newspaper comments, or procuring his photograph to be published in connection with causes in which the lawyer has been or is engaged or concerning the manner of their conduct, the magnitude of the interest involved, the importance of the lawyer's position, and all other like self-laudation, offend the traditions and lower the tone of our profession and are reprehensible; but the customary use of simple professional cards is not improper.

Publication in reputable law lists in a manner consistent with the standards of conduct imposed by these canons of brief biographical and informative data is permissible. Such data must not be misleading and may include only a statement of the lawyer's name and the names of his professional associates; addresses, telephone numbers, cable addresses; branches of the profession practiced; date and place of birth and admission to the bar; schools attended; with dates of graduation, degrees and other educational distinctions; public or quasi-public offices; posts of honor; legal authorships; legal teaching positions; memberships and offices in bar associations and committees thereof, in legal and scientific societies and legal fraternities; foreign language ability; the fact of listings in other reputable law lists; the names and addresses of references; and, with their written consent, the names of clients regularly represented. A certificate of compliance with the Rules and Standards issued by the Standing Committee on Law Lists may be treated as evidence that such list is reputable.

It is not improper for a lawyer who is admitted to practice as a proctor in admiralty to use that designation on his letterhead or shingle or for a lawyer who has complied with the statutory requirements of admission to practice before the patent office, to so use the designation "patent attorney" or "patent lawyer" or "trademark attorney" or "trademark lawyer" or any combination of those terms.

CANON 28
Stirring Up Litigation, Directly or Through Agents

It is unprofessional for a lawyer to volunteer advice to bring a lawsuit, except in rare cases where ties of blood, relationship or trust make it his duty to do so. Stirring up strife and litigation is not only unprofessional, but it is indictable at common law. It is disreputable to hunt up defects in titles or other causes of action and inform thereof in order to be employed to bring suit or collect judgment, or to breed litigation by seeking out those with claims for personal injuries or those having any other grounds of action in order to secure them as clients, or to employ agents or runners for like purposes, or to pay or reward, directly or indirectly, those who bring or influence the bringing of such cases to his office, or to remunerate policemen, court or prison officials, physicians, hospital *attachés* or others who may succeed, under the guise of giving disinterested friendly advice, in influencing the criminal, the sick and the injured, the ignorant or others, to seek his professional services. A duty to the public and to the profession devolves upon every member of the Bar having knowledge of such practices upon the part of any practitioner immediately to inform thereof, to the end that the offender may be disbarred.

CANON 29

Upholding the Honor of the Profession

Lawyers should expose without fear or favor before the proper tribunals corrupt or dishonest conduct in the profession, and should accept without hesitation employment against a member of the Bar who has wronged his client. The counsel upon the trial of a cause in which perjury has been committed owe it to the profession and to the public to bring the matter to the knowledge of the prosecuting authorities. The lawyer should aid in guarding the Bar against the admission to the profession of candidates unfit or unqualified because deficient in either moral character or education. He should strive at all times to uphold the honor and to maintain the dignity of the profession and to improve not only the law but the administration of justice.

CANON 30

Justifiable and Unjustifiable Litigations

The lawyer must decline to conduct a civil cause or to make a defense when convinced that it is intended merely to harass or to injure the opposite party or to work oppression or wrong. But otherwise it is his right, and, having accepted retainer, it becomes his duty to insist upon the judgment of the Court as to the legal merits of his client's claim. His appearance in Court should be deemed equivalent to an assertion on his honor that in his opinion his client's case is one proper for judicial determination.

CANON 31

Responsibility for Litigation

No lawyer is obliged to act either as adviser or advocate for every person who may wish to become his client. He has the right to decline employment. Every lawyer upon his own responsibility must decide what employment he will accept as counsel, what causes he will bring into Court for plaintiffs, what cases he will contest in Court for defendants. The responsibility for advising as to questionable transactions, for bringing questionable suits, for urging questionable defenses, is the lawyer's responsibility. He cannot escape it by urging as an excuse that he is only following his client's instructions.

CANON 32

The Lawyer's Duty in Its Last Analysis

No client, corporate or individual, however powerful, nor any cause, civil or political, however important, is entitled to receive nor should any lawyer render any service or advice involving disloyalty to the law whose ministers we are, or disrespect of the judicial office, which we are bound to uphold, or corruption of any person or persons exercising a public office or private trust, or deception or betrayal of the public. When rendering any such improper service or advice, the lawyer invites and merits stern and just condemnation. Correspondingly, he advances the honor of his profession and the best interests of his client when he renders service or gives advice tending to impress upon the client and his undertaking exact compliance with the strictest principles of moral law. He must also observe and advise his client to observe the statute law, though until a statute shall have been construed and interpreted by competent adjudication, he is free and is entitled to advise as to its validity and as to what he conscientiously believes to be its just meaning and extent. But above all a lawyer will find his highest honor in a deserved reputation for fidelity to private trust and to public duty, as an honest man and as a patriotic and loyal citizen.

CANON 33

Partnerships—Names

Partnerships among lawyers for the practice of their profession are very common and are not to be condemned. In the formation of partnerships and the use of partnership names care should be taken not to violate any law, custom, or rule of court locally applicable. Where partnerships are formed between lawyers who are not all admitted to practice in the courts of the state, care should be taken to avoid any misleading name or representation which would create a false impression as to the professional position or privileges of the member not locally admitted. In the formation of partnerships for the practice of law, no person should be admitted or held out as a practitioner or member who is not a member of the legal profession duly authorized to practice, and amenable to professional discipline. In the selection and use of a firm name, no false, misleading, assumed or trade name should be used. The continued use of the name of a deceased or former partner, when permissible by local custom, is not unethical, but care should be taken that no imposition or deception is practiced through this use. When a member of the firm, on becoming a judge, is precluded from practising law, his name should not be continued in the firm name.

Partnerships between lawyers and members of other professions or non-professional persons should not be formed or permitted where any part of the partnership's employment consists of the practice of law.

CANON 34

Division of Fees

No division of fees for legal services is proper, except with another lawyer, based upon a division of service or responsibility.

CANON 35

Intermediaries

The professional services of a lawyer should not be controlled or exploited by any lay agency, personal or corporate, which intervenes between client and lawyer. A lawyer's responsibilities and qualifications are individual. He should avoid all relations which direct the performance of his duties by or in the interest of such intermediary. A lawyer's relation to his client should be personal, and the responsibility should be direct to the client. Charitable societies rendering aid to the indigents are not deemed such intermediaries.

A lawyer may accept employment from any organization, such as an association, club or trade organization, to render legal services in any matter in which the organization, as an entity, is interested, but this employment should not include the rendering of legal services to the members of such an organization in respect to their individual affairs.

CANON 36

Retirement From Judicial Position or Public Employment

A lawyer should not accept employment as an advocate in any matter upon the merits of which he has previously acted in a judicial capacity.

A lawyer, having once held public office or having been in the public employ, should not after his retirement accept employment in connection with any matter which he has investigated or passed upon while in such office or employ.

CANON 37

Confidences of a Client

It is the duty of a lawyer to preserve his client's confidences. This duty outlasts the lawyer's employment, and extends as well to his employees; and neither of them should accept employment which involves or may involve the disclosure or use of these confidences, either for the private advantage of the lawyer or his employees or to the disadvantage of the client, without his knowledge and consent, and even though there are other available sources of such information. A lawyer should not continue employment when he discovers that this obligation prevents the performance of his full duty to his former or to his new client.

If a lawyer is accused by his client, he is not precluded from disclosing the truth in respect to the accusation. The announced intention of a client to commit a crime is not included within the confidences which he is bound to respect. He may properly make such disclosures as may be necessary to prevent the act or protect those against whom it is threatened.

CANON 38

Compensation, Commissions and Rebates

A lawyer should accept no compensation, commissions, rebates or other advantages from others without the knowledge and consent of his client after full disclosure.

CANON 39

Witnesses

A lawyer may properly interview any witness or prospective witness for the opposing side in any civil or criminal action without the consent of opposing counsel or party. In doing so, however, he should scrupulously avoid any suggestion calculated to induce the witness to suppress or deviate from the truth, or in any degree to affect his free and untrammeled conduct when appearing at the trial or on the witness stand.

CANON 40

Newspapers

A lawyer may with propriety write articles for publications in which he gives information upon the law; but he should not accept employment from such publications to advise inquirers in respect to their individual rights.

CANON 41

Discovery of Imposition and Deception

When a lawyer discovers that some fraud or deception has been practiced, which has unjustly imposed upon the court or a party, he should endeavor to rectify it; at first by advising his client, and if his client refuses to forego the advantage thus unjustly gained, he should promptly inform the injured person or his counsel, so that they may take appropriate steps.

CANON 42

Expenses of Litigation

A lawyer may not properly agree with a client that the lawyer shall pay or bear the expenses of litigation; he may in good faith advance expenses as a matter of convenience, but subject to reimbursement.

CANON 43

Approved Law Lists

It shall be improper for a lawyer to permit his name to be published in a law list the conduct, management or contents of which are calculated or likely to deceive or injure the public or the profession, or to lower the dignity or standing of the profession.

CANON 44

Withdrawal From Employment as Attorney or Counsel

The right of an attorney or counsel to withdraw from employment, once assumed, arises only from good cause. Even the desire or consent of the client is not always sufficient. The lawyer should not throw up the unfinished task to the detriment of his client except for reasons of honor or self-respect. If the client insists upon an unjust or immoral course in the conduct of his case, or if he persists over the attorney's remonstrance in presenting frivolous defenses, or if he deliberately disregards an agreement or obligation as to fees or expenses, the lawyer may be warranted in withdrawing on due notice to the client, allowing him time to employ another lawyer. So also when a lawyer discovers that his client has no case and the client is determined to continue it; or even if the lawyer finds himself incapable of conducting the case effectively. Sundry other instances may arise in which withdrawal is to be justified. Upon withdrawing from a case after a retainer has been paid, the attorney should refund such part of the retainer as has not been clearly earned.

CANON 45

Specialists

The canons of the American Bar Association apply to all branches of the legal profession; specialists in particular branches are not to be considered as exempt from the application of these principles.

CANON 46

Notice to Local Lawyers

A lawyer available to act as an associate of other lawyers in a particular branch of the law or legal service may send to local lawyers only and publish in his local legal journal, a brief and dignified announcement of his availability to serve other lawyers in connection therewith. The announcement should be in a form which does not constitute a statement or representation of special experience or expertise.

CANON 47

Aiding the Unauthorized Practice of Law

No lawyer shall permit his professional services, or his name, to be used in aid of, or to make possible, the unauthorized practice of law by any lay agency, personal or corporate.

PARALLEL TABLES BETWEEN THE ABA CANONS OF PROFESSIONAL ETHICS AND THE ABA MODEL CODE OF PROFESSIONAL RESPONSIBILITY *

CANONS OF PROFESSIONAL ETHICS TO CODE OF PROFESSIONAL RESPONSIBILITY

<u>Preamble</u>

Preamble
DR 1–102(A)(5)
EC 7–20
EC 7–39
EC 8–1
EC 9–1
EC 9–2

<u>Canon 1</u>
DR 1–103(B)
EC 7–36
EC 8–6
DR 7–106(C)(6)
DR 8–102(B)

<u>Canon 2</u>
EC 8–6
DR 8–102(A)

<u>Canon 3</u>
EC 7–34
EC 7–35
EC 7–36
DR 7–110

<u>Canon 4</u>
EC 2–29
EC 7–1
EC 7–19
DR 2–110(C)
DR 7–101(A)(1)

<u>Canon 5</u>
EC 1–5
DR 1–102(A)(4)
EC 2–29
EC 7–1
EC 7–4
EC 7–13
EC 7–19
EC 7–27
DR 7–101(A)(1)
DR 7–102(A)(3)–(7)
DR 7–103
DR 7–109(A)–(B)
EC 8–5

<u>Canon 6</u>
EC 4–1
EC 4–5
DR 4–101(B)
EC 5–1
EC 5–3

EC 5–14
EC 5–15
EC 5–16
EC 5–17
EC 5–19
DR 5–101(A)
DR 5–105
DR 5–106
EC 8–8

<u>Canon 7</u>
EC 2–28
EC 2–29
EC 2–30
EC 2–32
DR 2–108
DR 2–110(C)(3)
EC 4–2
EC 5–11
EC 5–12
DR 7–101(A)(2)

<u>Canon 8</u>
EC 2–9
EC 7–5
EC 7–8

<u>Canon 9</u>
EC 7–18
DR 7–104

<u>Canon 10</u>
EC 5–7
DR 5–103(A)

<u>Canon 11</u>
EC 4–5
DR 4–101(B)(3)
EC 9–5
DR 9–102

<u>Canon 12</u>
EC 2–16
EC 2–17
EC 2–18
EC 2–25
DR 2–106

<u>Canon 13</u>
EC 2–20
DR 2–106
EC 5–7
DR 5–103(A)(2)

<u>Canon 14</u>
EC 2–23
EC 5–7
DR 5–103(A)(1)

<u>Canon 15</u>
EC 1–5
DR 1–102(A)(4)
EC 7–1
EC 7–2
EC 7–3
EC 7–4
EC 7–5
EC 7–6
EC 7–19
EC 7–24
EC 7–26
DR 7–101(A)(1)
DR 7–101(B)(2)
DR 7–102(A)(2)
DR 7–102(A)(3)–(7)
DR 7–106(C)(4)
EC 9–2

<u>Canon 16</u>
EC 2–32
DR 2–110(C)(1)(b)
EC 7–28
DR 7–101(A)(2)
EC 8–5

<u>Canon 17</u>
EC 1–5
EC 7–10
EC 7–37
EC 7–38
DR 7–101(A)(1)

<u>Canon 18</u>
EC 1–5
EC 7–10
EC 7–25
EC 7–36
DR 7–101(A)(1)
DR 7–106(C)(2)

<u>Canon 19</u>
EC 5–9
EC 5–10
DR 5–101(B)
DR 5–102

<u>Canon 20</u>
EC 7–33
DR 7–107

<u>Canon 21</u>
EC 6–4
DR 6–101(A)(3)
EC 7–20
EC 7–38
DR 7–101(A)(1)

<u>Canon 22</u>
EC 1–5
DR 1–102(A)(4)
EC 7–6
EC 7–25
EC 7–26
EC 7–27
DR 7–102(A)(3)–(7)
DR 7–106(C)(1)
EC 8–5

<u>Canon 23</u>
EC 7–29
EC 7–31
EC 7–36
DR 7–108

<u>Canon 24</u>
EC 7–7
EC 7–9
EC 7–10
EC 7–38
DR 7–101(A)(1)
DR 7–101(B)(1)

<u>Canon 25</u>
EC 7–38
DR 7–101(A)(1)
DR 7–106(C)(5)

<u>Canon 26</u>
EC 7–15
EC 7–16
EC 7–36
DR 7–106(B)(2)
DR 7–107(F)
DR 7–107(H)
DR 7–107(I)
DR 7–110(B)
EC 8–4

<u>Canon 27</u>
EC 2–2

* Compiled by Olavi Maru, Reference Librarian, William Nelson Cromwell Library, American Bar Foundation.

EC 2-3
EC 2-4
EC 2-8
EC 2-9
EC 2-10
EC 2-14
DR 2-101
DR 2-102(A)
DR 2-102(E)
DR 2-103(A)
DR 2-105(A)

Canon 28
EC 1-4
EC 1-5
EC 2-1
EC 2-2
EC 2-3
EC 2-4
EC 2-8
DR 1-103(A)–(B)
DR 2-103(A)
DR 2-104(A)

Canon 29
EC 1-2
EC 1-3
EC 1-4
DR 1-101(B)
DR 1-103(A)
DR 1-103(B)
EC 2-28
DR 7-102(A)(3)–(7)
DR 7-102(B)(2)
EC 8-1
EC 8-2
EC 8-5
EC 8-7
EC 8-9
EC 9-2
EC 9-6

Canon 30
EC 1-5
DR 1-102(A)(4)

EC 2-3
EC 2-30
DR 2-109(A)(1)
EC 7-1
EC 7-4
EC 7-19
DR 7-101(A)(1)
DR 7-102(A)(1)

Canon 31
EC 2-26
EC 2-27
EC 2-28
EC 2-29
DR 2-109(A)(2)
EC 7-1
EC 7-4
EC 7-5
EC 7-14
EC 7-19
DR 7-101(B)(2)
DR 7-102(A)(2)

Canon 32
EC 1-5
DR 1-102(A)(5)
EC 7-1
EC 7-5
EC 7-19
DR 7-102(A)(3)–(7)
EC 8-5

Canon 33
EC 2-11
EC 2-12
EC 2-13
DR 2-102(B)
DR 2-102(C)
DR 2-102(D)
EC 3-8
DR 3-103
DR 5-107(C)

Canon 34
EC 2-22

DR 2-103(B)
DR 2-107(A)
EC 3-8
DR 3-102

Canon 35
DR 2-103(D)
DR 2-104(A)(2)
DR 2-104(A)(3)
EC 5-1
EC 5-13
EC 5-21
EC 5-22
EC 5-23
EC 5-24
DR 5-107(B)
DR 5-107(C)(3)

Canon 36
EC 9-3
DR 9-101

Canon 37
Canon 4 generally
EC 2-32
DR 2-110
DR 4-101(B)
DR 4-101(B)(2)–(3)
DR 4-101(C)
DR 4-101(D)
DR 7-101(A)(2)

Canon 38
EC 2-21
EC 5-21
DR 5-107(A)(2)

Canon 39
EC 1-5
DR 1-102(A)(4)
EC 7-28
DR 7-102(A)(3)–(7)
DR 7-109(C)

Canon 40
EC 2-2

EC 2-5
DR 2-104(A)(4)

Canon 41
DR 7-102(B)(1)
EC 8-5

Canon 42
EC 5-8
DR 5-103(B)

Canon 43
DR 2-102(A)(6)

Canon 44
EC 1-5
DR 1-102(A)(5)
EC 2-31
EC 2-32
DR 2-110
EC 5-15
EC 5-19
EC 5-21
DR 5-102
DR 5-105(B)
DR 5-105(D)
EC 7-8
DR 7-101(A)(2)

Canon 45
Preliminary statement

Canon 46
EC 2-14
DR 2-105(A)(3)

Canon 47
EC 1-5
DR 1-102(A)(5)
EC 3-1 through
EC 3-9
DR 3-101

PARALLEL TABLES BETWEEN THE ABA MODEL CODE OF PROFESSIONAL RESPONSIBILITY AND THE ABA CANONS OF PROFESSIONAL ETHICS

Code	Canons	Code	Canons
Preamble	Preamble	EC 2–14	27
Preliminary Statement	45		46
		EC 2–16	12
Canon 1		EC 2–17	12
EC 1–2	29	EC 2–18	12
EC 1–3	29	EC 2–20	13
EC 1–4	28	EC 2–21	38
	29	EC 2–22	34
EC 1–5	5	EC 2–23	14
	15	EC 2–25	12
	17	EC 2–26	31
	18	EC 2–27	31
	22	EC 2–28	7
	28		29
	30		31
	32	EC 2–29	4
	39		5
	44		7
	47		31
DR 1–101		EC 2–30	7
(B)	29		30
DR 1–102		EC 2–31	44
(A)(4)	5	EC 2–32	7
	15		16
	22		37
	30		44
	39	DR 2–101	27
(A)(5)	Preamble	DR 2–102	
	32	(A)	27
	44	(A)(6)	43
	47	(B)	33
DR 1–103		(C)	33
(A)	28	(D)	33
	29	(E)	27
(B)	1	DR 2–103	
	28	(A)	27
	29		28
Canon 2		(B)	34
EC 2–1	28	(D)	35
EC 2–2	27	DR 2–104	
	28	(A)	28
	40	(A)(2)	35
EC 2–3	27	(A)(3)	35
	28	DR 2–104	
	30	(A)(4)	40
EC 2–4	27	DR 2–105	
	28	(A)	27
EC 2–5	40	(A)(3)	46
EC 2–8	27	DR 2–106	12
EC 2–8	28		13
EC 2–9	8	DR 2–107	
	27	(A)	34
EC 2–10	27	DR 2–108	7
EC 2–11	33	DR 2–109	
EC 2–12	33	(A)(1)	30
EC 2–13	33	(A)(2)	31
		DR 2–110	37

349

Code	Canons	Code	Canons
EC 7–31	23	(B)(2)	26
EC 7–33	20	(C)(1)	22
EC 7–34	3	(C)(2)	18
EC 7–35	3	(C)(4)	15
EC 7–36	1	(C)(5)	25
	3	(C)(6)	1
	18	DR 7–107	20
	23	(F)	26
	26	(H)	26
EC 7–37	17	(I)	26
EC 7–38	17	DR 7–108	23
	21	DR 7–109	
	24	(A)–(B)	5
	25	(C)	39
EC 7–39	Preamble	DR 7–110	3
DR 7–101	26	(B)	26
(A)(1)	4		
	5	Canon 8	
	15	EC 8–1	Preamble
	17		29
	18	EC 8–2	29
	21	EC 8–4	26
	24	EC 8–5	5
	25		16
	30		22
(A)(2)	7		29
	16		32
	37		41
	44	EC 8–6	1
(B)(1)	24		2
(B)(2)	15	EC 8–7	29
	31	EC 8–8	6
DR 7–102		EC 8–9	29
(A)(1)	30	DR 8–102	
(A)(2)	15	(A)	2
	31	(B)	1
(A)(3)–(7)	5	Canon 9	
	15	EC 9–1	Preamble
	22	EC 9–2	Preamble
	29		15
	32		29
	39	EC 9–3	36
(B)(1)	41	EC 9–5	11
(B)(2)	29	EC 9–6	29
DR 7–103	5	DR 9–101	36
DR 7–104	9	DR 9–102	11
DR 7–106			

THE AMERICAN LAWYER'S CODE OF CONDUCT

This Revised Draft was promulgated in May 1992 by the Commission on Professional Responsibility of the Roscoe Pound—American Trial Lawyers Foundation

---

[During the debate over drafting a replacement for the Model Code, members and leadership from the American Trial Lawyer's Association disagreed with the substantive choice that were made by the Kutak Commission. This group delegated the task of developing an alternative draft to the Commission on Professional Responsibility of the Roscoe Pound—American Trial Lawyers Foundation. This alternative draft sought to influence the members of the ABA in the final drafting and adoption of the Model Rules and the states in the development of the local codes of professional responsibility. This document represents a revised draft which has not been finally approved by the Commission on Professional Responsibility. Ed.]

Contents

Preface
Chairmen's Introduction
Preamble
Terminology

CODE OF CONDUCT

PREFACE
By Theodore I. Koskoff *

On the following pages, we provide you with the text of an important new document: the May 1982 Revised Draft of The American Lawyer's Code of Conduct. This Code was prepared under the auspices of the Roscoe Pound-American Trial Lawyers Foundation, by a Commission on Professional Responsibility of which I am co-chairman. A Public Discussion Draft was issued in June 1980, and published in TRIAL magazine in August of that year.

This Code is quite frankly presented as an alternative to the old Code of Professional Responsibility previously promulgated by the American Bar Association (ABA), and to the new Rules of Professional Conduct that the ABA is apparently about to hawk as the latest thing in legal ethics. It was dissatisfaction with both of these ABA products that both got us going on this Code, and kept us going.

That dissatisfaction was not reduced when the ABA's Kutak Commission published a new draft in mid-1981. It grew. It grew still more when the ABA House of Delegates voted in January 1982 to drop its "old" Code of 1969, and to frame its new Rules only in a new, untried format. Many of us deeply resent the take-it-or-leave-it attitude of the ABA, which seems to be switching codes on us for no better reason than that it has spent so much money on the Kutak Rules that rejecting them would cause it to lose face.

This is not just a squabble over form. It is a serious disagreement over substance. The ABA Commission evidently is trying to win the debate over the substance of legal ethics by side-stepping it. It is trying to make us all not only debate whether and how to amend the present Code, but also debate that question in this very peculiar form: whether and how to amend a code that the Commission has already amended, in ways that even the Commission does not fully understand.

The National Organization of Bar Counsel (NOBC) has demonstrated that the ideas of the Kutak Commission can be integrated into the present Code, so that its proposals can be compared to others, and judged on their merits. NOBC has done this twice, once with each of the Kutak Commission's drafts. The Commission has ignored NOBC's efforts, probably because NOBC rejected some of its proposals. Chairman Kutak and his friends have ramrodded through the ABA a resolution committing the ABA to dropping the present Code.

By publishing this Code in two formats, we are giving notice that we are not going to let the ABA dictate the terms for the debate on lawyer's ethics. We regard the proposed Kutak Rules as fundamental-

* Theodore I. Koskoff was President of ATLA from 1979 to 1980. His practice is in Bridgeport, Connecticut.

ly flawed, and we intend to force Kutak & Co. to debate the issues before the state courts and bar bodies that will really decide what the law of lawyers' ethics is to be.

When you write a new code, you have to be careful not just about what you are putting in, but also about what you are leaving out. For example, the Kutak Commission would drop DR 7–105 of the Code, which forbids threatening criminal prosecution solely to gain an advantage in a civil matter. No provision of the Kutak Rules covers such situations. Does this mean that adopting the Kutak Rules would legitimize blackmail? The Commission gives no explanation.

If you are not careful, you may leave out something whose absence completely changes the context, and thus the meaning, of something you are putting in. One of the purposes of codifying a body of law is to make it clear, and to make clear to everyone just what you are doing when you change it. Amending a code should not be like writing a zero-based budget. You want to keep those portions of existing law that work well, and to change only what needs to be changed. Continuity is not a negligible virtue.

That is why our Commission has taken issue with the ABA's conclusion that the Code of Professional Responsibility is old hat. "With all its serious flaws," my co-chairman Irwin Birnbaum said in the Preface to our June 1980 Draft, "the Code of Professional Responsibility is preferable to the Model Rules" of the Kutak Commission.

We have tried to make it clear just what we think should be changed in today's Code of Professional Responsibility, by including in this Revised Draft a "Proposed Revision" of the CPR. Just what we have changed in our own Code, between the June 1980 Draft and this one, is not quite so clear, and should be spelled out.

The introductory materials, including the preamble, have been substantially pruned, without changing our meaning. Similar trimming may be found in the Comment portions, and in the lengthy "Introductory Comment on Knowing" of the 1980 Draft, replaced by two brief paragraphs of "Terminology." None of these omissions will be missed.

The truly substantive changes are in the Rules, and they are not numerous.

First, and most important, is the Commission's resolution of its ambivalence about the alternative versions of Chapter I, on confidentiality, published in the 1980 Draft. Alternative A was a fairly traditional approach. Alternative B was probably the most thoroughgoing embodiment of the lawyer's "first duty . . . is to keep the secrets of . . . clients," ever included in a draft code of ethics. It would have allowed lawyers to reveal clients' confidences, without client consent, in only two circumstances:

1) where a client impliedly waived confidentiality, or "opened the door," by accusing the lawyer of misconduct; and

2) when the lawyer's lips were pried open by compulsion of law.

We have tried to keep the spirit of that recommendation, although we have tempered it somewhat. Our first principle remains that a client msut be able to confide absolutely in a lawyer, or there may be little point in anyone's having a lawyer. We have rejected one concept that the Kutak Commission apparently espouses, that lawyers have a general duty to do good for society that often overrides their specific duty to serve their clients. Serving clients is the lawyer's basic reason for being a lawyer, and the exceptions to the fundamental rule of absolute loyalty to clients must be minimal, and must be strictly construed.

As revised, Chapter I is closer to the traditional approach of our old Alternative A than it is to the radical position of Alternative B. It is still, however, the strictest set of rules on preserving client confidences in any proposed code of lawyers' conduct. In my view, the Sixth Amendment guarantee of the effective assistance of counsel requires no less.

In Chapter IV, a new Rule 4.2 places a special burden of competence on the lawyer who is held out to a client as having special expertise. This follows the law that has developed in malpractice cases, holding people who call themselves specialists to the standard of care required of such specialists.

A number of other rules have been tightened, but not substantially changed. For example, Rule 2.3 now explicitly requires the client's consent before a lawyer may accept compensation from someone other than the client.

In short, the Commission has refined its product without changing its approach.

We continue to disagree with the Kutak Commission in our basic approach to legal ethics. We believe that a code of lawyers' conduct is important legislation for the entire community, because it affects every person's ability to exercise basic rights. We believe that the basic purpose of such a code should be to enable lawyers to help people—to leave the individual lawyer free to help the individual client.

The Kutak Commission sees lawyers as ombudsmen, who serve the system as much as they serve clients. This is a collectivist, bureaucratic concept. It is the sort of thinking you get from a commission made up of lawyers who work for institutional clients, in institutional firms, and who have lost sight of the lawyer's basic function. Lawyers are not licensed to write prospectuses for giant corporations, or to haggle with federal agencies over regulations and operating rights. We are licensed to represent people in court, which often means people in trouble with the law, and with the government. We are the citizens' champions against official tyranny.

We cannot continue to have a democratic system, as we know it, without a legal profession whose members are free to perform that function. The Kutak Rules contain some useful changes in regulating peripheral aspects of law practice, but they embody a core conviction about the lawyer's role that is fundamentally at odds with the American constitutional system.

That is why we have continued to work on our Code, and why we have issued this Revised Draft. We are not willing to take dictation from the ABA on the standards governing our life's work. We are not willing to allow the Kutak Rules to become the law of legal ethics by default. We intend to fight in the state bar associations, and in the state courts, to preserve the constitutional concept of what a lawyer is, and what a lawyer's duties are.

I invite you to join with us in the fight.

CHAIRMEN'S INTRODUCTION

By Irwin Birnbaum and Theodore I. Koskoff

This Revised Draft of The American Lawyer's Code of Conduct is the second published product of the Commission on Professional Responsibility. It consists of two parts. The primary text is the June, 1980, Public Discussion Draft of the Code, amended to reflect both the comments on that Draft, and the Commission's second thoughts on some matters. The appendix is a reworking of our Code in the form of proposed amended Disciplinary Rules of the Code of Professional Responsibility, now the law of lawyers' conduct in almost every state. The purpose of this second part is to show how the provisions of our Code can be adopted, in whole or in part, as amendments to existing law.

We are presenting the Commission's work in these two formats, because we view the substance of the lawyers' code of conduct as more important than its form. The purpose of our work has been to produce a code that embodies the principles we believe are essential to the effective functioning of the legal profession in a democratic society, and to get such a code adopted, as the law of lawyers' conduct, by the courts. We have no special pride of authorship that compels us to insist that the courts adopt all of our ideas, or none of them, or that our ideas be adopted only in a particular form. The issues involved are too important to play such games with them.

Only the first of these drafts, the American Lawyers' Code of Conduct proper, has been voted upon and approved by the Commission, or bears the stamp of the Commission's original Reporter, Professor Monroe H. Freedman. The reworking of the Code of Professional Responsibility is the work of Professor Freedman's successor as Reporter to the Commission, Mr. Thomas Lumbard of Washington, formerly our Associate Reporter, and a consultant to the Commission since its inception.

This Commission was called the Commission on Professional Responsibility for Trial Practice, when founded in 1979. We quickly found that we could not write a code of conduct solely for trial lawyers. We also found that another Commission, that of the American Bar Association "on Evaluation of Professional Standards," was rewriting the profession's basic code in a way that demanded from us a viable alternative code, applicable to all lawyers.

We obviously believe that our Code is better than the so-called "Model" Rules of Professional Conduct produced by the A.B.A. Commission.[1] Even as amended in 1981, significantly and substantially, and in part reflecting (if not acknowledging) doctrine that we had published, the proposed Model Rules are inferior to the existing Code of Professional Responsibility. With all its flaws, the Code is preferable to the proposed Rules.

Accordingly, we here present our views both in the form we prefer, the *ALCC,* and in the generally accepted form of the *CPR.* This avoids the "take it or leave it" additude expressed by the A.B.A.'s recent endorsement of the proposed Rules drafted by its Commission. It also acknowledges that we, and all other members of today's generation of revisers of the law of lawyers' conduct, are only able to reach higher than our predecessors because we stand upon their shoulders. While flattering ourselves that we are correcting their mistakes, we are neither so blithe as to suggest that we are not introducing errors of our own, nor so foolhardy as not to try to reduce such errors to a minimum.

Our work and our attitude thus stand in stark contrast to those of the A.B.A. Commission. That Commission has refused to build on the wisdom of the past. It has rejected the good faith efforts of others, such as the National Organization of Bar Counsel, to accommodate its ideas to the form of the *CPR.* It has even gone so far as to publish a huge "Alternative Draft" that the New York State Bar Association correctly concluded was not a good faith effort to amend the *CPR.* It was merely an elaborate charade, designed to make the Commission's "Proposed Final Draft" look good by invidious comparison.

The reader will find no such deception in the present document. Unlike the A.B.A. Commission's "Alternative Draft," our Code's Appen-

---

1. The A.B.A. first added the adjective "Model" to the title of its Code to avoid federal charges that its promulgation of The Code was restraint of trade. The A.B.A. Commission now seems to make a virtue of necessity; it always refers to its work-product as the *Model* Rules, although it courts federal displeasure by always calling the CPR "the Code," never the "Model Code."

Refusing to take any A.B.A. product for a model, we consistently refer to existing law as "the Code of Professional Responsibility" and to what the A.B.A. Commission has recommended as "the proposed Rules of Professional Conduct."

dix is a good faith effort to improve upon the *CPR* by preserving and amending it. It was drafted by a Reporter who believes in the wisdom of that approach.[2] It is relatively short, and considerably easier to read than either the elephantine "Alternative Draft" or the "Proposed Final Draft" of the proposed A.B.A. Rules.

We have not called this a "Final Draft," because experience has shown that no draft of such a code is ever "final." The A.B.A. has published amendments to the "Final Draft" of its Code almost annually since 1969. We continue to seek suggestions to improve this Code.

PREAMBLE

This Code of Conduct embodies a traditional and constitutional concept of the role of the American lawyer in our limited form of government, which seeks to maximize individual liberty within a rule of law. The fundamental structure of the role of the American lawyer is fixed by the Bill of Rights of the Constitution; rules of conduct should be designed and interpreted to enhance those rights, not to inhibit them.

The individual rights most relevant to lawyers' duties relate to what we call one's "day in court"—the rights to due process of law, counsel, and trial by jury. Also relevant are rights relating to self-incrimination, confrontation, bail, search and seizure, and cruel and unusual punishment. The right to litigate is also an essential aspect of freedom of speech and of the right to petition for redress of grievances.

As a result of the enormous volume and complexity of our law, ordinary citizens need the assistance of lawyers simply to comprehend and cope with the rules governing their actions. The lawyer therefore serves the most basic individual right, that of personal autonomy: the right to make those decisions that most affect one's own life and values. Without professional assistance, the individual citizen is often unaware of the range of choices available, and of the means to pursue particular choices.

The assistance of counsel is thus essential to justice under law, and to equal protection of the laws. Leaving each person to his or her own resources, without the aid of counsel in comprehending and coping with the complexities of the legal system, would produce gross disparities in justice under law.

All these basic rights, individually and together, express the high value placed by our constitutional democracy on the dignity of the individual. Before any person is significantly affected by society in his or her person, relationships, or property, our system requires that certain processes be duly followed—processes to which competent, independent, and zealous lawyers are essential. And if it be observed that

2. See Lumbard, Setting Standards: The Courts, the Bar, and the Lawyers' Code of Conduct, 30 Cath. Univ. Law Rev. 249 (1981).

the stated ideal is too frequently denied in fact, our response must be that standards for lawyers be so drafted and enforced as to strive to make that ideal a reality.

The legal system that gives context and meaning to basic American rights is the adversary system. It is the adversary system which assures each of us a "champion against a hostile world," and which thereby helps to preserve and enhance our dignity as individuals.

Recognizing that the American attorney functions in an adversary system, and that such a system expresses fundamental American values, helps us to appreciate the emptiness of some cliches of lawyers' ethics. It is said, for example, that the lawyer is an "officer of the court," or an "officer of the legal system." Out of context, such phrases are at best meaningless, and at worst misleading. In the context of the adversary system, it is clear that the lawyer for a private party is and should be an officer of a court only in the sense of serving a court as a zealous, partisan advocate of one side of the case before it, and in the sense of having been licensed by a court to play that very role.

Further, the lawyer who litigates is not the only one who serves in an adversarial role. Lawyers function in an adversary system even when their clients are not actually involved in litigation. Parties to negotiations are usually adversaries, and are always potential adversaries. The lawyer drafting a contract or a will must anticipate and guard against interests adverse to the client's that may exist or that may develop in the course of time. The lawyer who prepares tax returns or other documents for filing with the government can adequately protect a client's interests only by recognizing the possibility of an adverse reaction. Any lawyer who counsels a client about rights, liabilities, and legal choices must be conscious of numerous possible reactions of an adversarial nature.

Unquestionably, there are differences among cases involving litigation, negotiating, drafting, and counseling. Thus, the opportunities to withdraw without prejudicing a client's interests are likely to be greater in counseling than in litigation, and greater in civil litigation than in criminal cases. But the basic principle will remain the same: avoid withdrawal unless significant prejudice to the client can be avoided. We have therefore rejected the idea of writing this Code in separate sections for lawyers in litigation, negotiation, and so forth; at the same time, we have tried throughout to be aware of the variety of services lawyers perform and to make distinctions when they appear appropriate.

In sum, the following American Lawyer's Code of Conduct has been drafted with a recognition that all American lawyers function in an adversary system, and with a commitment to strengthening that system as the embodiment of the constitutional values inherent in the administration of justice in the United States.

The format of this Code embodies an effort to make it as readable and as clear as possible. The Rules are intended to be used for disciplinary purposes; they are written in declarative sentences stating what the lawyer "shall" or "shall not" do. The Rules are followed by Comments, which are not intended to be the basis of disciplinary action, but to enhance understanding of the disciplinary rules. In addition, when useful to avoid ambiguity or to resolved possible conflict between rules, Illustrative Cases are provided.

TERMINOLOGY

Attorney is used as a synonym for "lawyer," but only to distinguish between the lawyer to whom the rule applies and another attorney.

A **client's confidence,** protected by this Code, includes any information obtained by the client's lawyer in the course of and by reason of the lawyer-client relationship.

A lawyer **knows** certain facts, or acts **knowingly** or with **knowledge** of facts, when a person with that lawyer's professional training and experience would be reasonably certain of those facts in view of all the circumstances of which the lawyer is aware. A duty to investigate or inquire is not implied by the use of these words, but may be explicitly required under particular rules. Even in the absence of a duty to investigate, however, a studied rejection of reasonable inferences is inadequate to avoid ethical responsibility.

Reasonable belief, reasonably believes or **reasonable understanding** is the standard used to denote a lawyer's mental state when the lawyer may be required or permitted to act on the basis of incomplete knowledge of relevant facts, as when the lawyer is predicting future events, or is compelled to act on the basis of assumptions or inferences because all the relevant facts cannot be ascertained. The lawyer must understand or suppose the fact or circumstance to be so, and the circumstances must make that understanding or supposition a reasonable one.

CHAPTER I

THE CLIENT'S TRUST AND CONFIDENCES

Rules

1.1. Beginning with the initial interview with a prospective client, a lawyer shall strive to establish and maintain a relationship of trust and confidence with the client. The lawyer shall impress upon the client that the lawyer cannot adequately serve the client without knowing everything that might be relevant to the client's problem, and that the client should not withhold information that the client might think is embarrassing or harmful to the client's interests. The lawyer shall explain to the client the lawyer's obligation of confidentiality.

1.2. Without the client's knowing and voluntary consent, a lawyer shall not directly or indirectly reveal a confidence of a client or former client, or use it in any way detrimental to the interests of the client, except as provided in Rules 1.3 to 1.6, and Rule 6.5. (Rules 1.3 to 1.6 permit divulgence under compulsion of law; to avoid proceeding before a corrupted judge or juror; to defend the lawyer or the lawyer's associates from charges of misconduct; and to prevent imminent danger to human life. Rule 6.5 permits withdrawal in non-criminal cases when the client has induced the lawyer to act through material misrepresentation, even though withdrawal might indirectly divulge a confidence.)

1.3. A lawyer may reveal a client's confidence to the extent required to do so by law, rule of court, or court order, but only after good faith efforts to test the validity of the law, rule, or order have been exhausted.

1.4. A lawyer may reveal a client's confidence when the lawyer knows that a judge or juror in a pending proceeding in which the lawyer is involved has been bribed or subjected to extortion. In such a case, the lawyer shall use all reasonable means to protect the client, consistent with preventing the case from going forward with a corrupted judge or juror.

1.5. A lawyer may reveal a client's confidence to the extent necessary to defend the lawyer or the lawyer's associate or employee against charges of criminal, civil, or professional misconduct asserted by the client, or against formally instituted charges of such conduct in which the client is implicated.

[**1.6.** A lawyer may reveal a client's confidence when and to the extent that the lawyer reasonably believes that divulgence is necessary to prevent imminent danger to human life. The lawyer shall use all reasonable means to protect the client's interests that are consistent with preventing loss of life.]

NOTE: Rule 1.6 was not approved by the Commission, but was supported by so many members that it is included in this Revised Draft as a Supplemental Rule.

Comment

One of the most difficult and delicate responsibilities of the lawyer is to establish and maintain a relationship of trust and confidence with the client. Clients frequently mistrust their lawyers, are embarrassed about the truth, or assume that their lawyers would prefer not to be burdened with knowledge about illegal or immoral conduct. For lawyers to provide effective assistance, however, it is essential that they know everything about the clients' affairs that might be relevant.

If the client were able to distinguish the legally relevant from the legally irrelevant, the useful from the useless, and the incriminatory from the exculpatory, the client would have little need for the lawyer's professional training and skills. And when the lawyer does not have all of the relevant facts, the lawyer's professional abilities are of limited value. Accordingly, the effective functioning of the lawyer-client relationship requires complete candor by the client to the lawyer.

Such candor is in the public interest because only through the counsel and advocacy of a lawyer can each individual fully exercise his or her autonomy and realize other important rights under our Constitution and laws. Further, as every experienced lawyer knows, a substantial part of the lawyer's time is devoted to advising clients that a particular course of conduct should not be followed on grounds of legality or morality. Unless clients asre candid with lawyers, those critical functions cannot be served. The client's sense of trust in the lawyer is therefore vital, and the lawyer's obligation of confidentiality is essential to establishing and maintaining that trust.

The most obvious concern of confidentiality is, of course, with protecting the client's direct communications to the lawyer. But the lawyer must also obtain relevant information from sources other than the client, often through leads provided by the client, and unauthorized divulgence of such information to the client's detriment would seriously impair lawyer-client relationships and could induce clients to limit the scope of their lawyers' investigatory efforts. Accordingly, "confidence," as protected by these rules, is any information obtained by the lawyer in the course of the lawyer-client relationship.

Since candor may be no less important in preliminary interviews, the lawyer-client relationship includes discussions between the lawyer and client to determine whether the lawyer will be retained by the client. Also, the obligation to maintain confidentiality extends beyond the lawyer-client relationship.

It is sometimes suggested that confidentiality is inimical to the truth-seeking function of our system of justice. That is true, however, only in a superficial and short-sighted sense. Certainly, under the adversary system, lawyers frequently have knowledge that the court or other parties would want to have. Most often, however, lawyers have such knowledge precisely because of the established rule of confidentiality. If we were to remove that safeguard, by permitting lawyers to divulge their clients' confidences, lawyers would come to have few truths to divulge.

Nevertheless, in some narrowly circumscribed exceptions, this Code permits lawyers to reveal some confidences. Such exceptions should relfect values of such overriding concern that some minimal systemic risk would be justified. Also, such exceptions should be limited to situations that arise infrequently, to further minimize the risk of impairing lawyer-client trust.

The Rules to this Chapter are more protective of confidentiality that the Code of Professional Responsibility or the A.B.A. Commission's Rules. The exceptions permit divulgence, but do not require it, under compulsion of law; to avoid proceeding before a corrupted judge or juror; to defend the lawyer or the lawyer's associates against formally instituted charges of misconduct, or charges made by the client; and to prevent imminent danger to human life. (Rules 1.3 to 1.6.) Also, withdrawal is permitted in non-criminal cases, even when a confidence might thereby be divulged indirectly, when the client has induced the lawyer to act through material misrepresentation (Rule 6.5; see also Rule 6.6).

The corruption cases are an appropriate exception because the corruption of the impartial judge or jury vitiates the adversary system itself. Since cases of corruption are infrequent, the exception should not have significant impact on the lawyer-client relationship. By contrast, cases of false testimony are more frequent, and the adversary system anticipates and is specifically designed to cope with false testimony through cross-examination, rebuttal, and observation of demeanor during testimony.

These Rules reject the previously recognized exception permitting lawyers to violate confidentiality to collect an unpaid fee. The reason for that exception—the lawyer's financial interest—is not sufficiently weighty to justify impairing confidentiality. On the other hand, a limited exception is permitted, when a lawyer or the lawyer's associate is formally charged with criminal or unprofessional conduct.

Rule 1.2 refers to using a confidence in a way detrimental to "the interests of the client." Here, as elsewhere in this Code, the interests of the client are determined by the client after having been counseled by the lawyer. (See Rules 2.1, 3.1 and 3.2, and the Comment to Chapter II.) If there is inadequate opportunity for consultation, the lawyer should act in accordance with the lawyer's reasonable understanding of what the client would perceive to be in the client's interest.

This Code rejects permitting violation of confidentiality in all cases of "future (or continuing) crimes." First, the category of "crimes" is too broad; it lumps offenses that are openly done and relatively harmless, with those that are clandestine and involve life and death. At the same time, the requirement of a crime may be too narrow; if saving a life, for example, is sufficiently important to justify an exception to confidentiality, then the exception should not turn on technicalities. The exception for 'future or continuing' offenses has also proved unsatisfactory; it is all too easily interpreted to include a failure to relinquish the proceeds of a past crime, or a fugitive's refusal to surrender, thereby permitting or even requiring lawyers to violate confidentiality in situations where their clients are desperately in need of counsel.

Illustrative Cases

1(a). A lawyer representing the wife in a divorce and custody case learns from his client that she had sexual relations with a man other than her husband during the time of separation. The client insists upon not disclosing that fact. The lawyer knows that the judge would want to know it, and would weigh it against the wife in deciding custody. The lawyer would commit a disciplinary violation by informing the judge.

1(b). The same facts as 1(a), and the wife testifies falsely on deposition that she has not had sexual relations with anyone other than her husband during the marriage. The lawyer would commit a disciplinary violation by revealing the perjury.

1(c). A lawyer representing the husband in a divorce case learns that his client's tax returns have understated his income. At deposition, the client produces his tax returns, and testifies that they are complete and accurate. The lawyer would commit a disciplinary violation by revealing knowledge of the false returns to the wife, her lawyer, the judge, or the Internal Revenue Service.

1(d). A lawyer represents a client negotiating the purchase of real estate. During negotiations, the parties and their lawyers discuss the adverse effect of existing zoning restrictions, which prevent commercial development of the property. Just prior to formalizing an agreement of sale, however, the buyer learns that his lawyer has persuaded the zoning board to change the zoning to permit commerical use. The buyer decides not to tell the seller about the imminent zoning change. The buyer's lawyer would commit a disciplinary violation by informing the seller.

1(e). A lawyer representing a client accused of murdering a man learns from his client that the client has killed a young woman and hidden the body in a woods. The lawyer goes to the woods and finds the dead body. Because the client could be implicated through his relationship with the lawyer, or even through circumstantial evidence alone, the lawyer tells no one about the body. The lawyer has not committed a disciplinary violation.

1(f). The same facts as 1(e), but the lawyer, without authorization of the client, tells the young woman's parents. The lawyer has committed a disciplinary violation.

1(g). The same facts as 1(e), but the woman is not dead. However, she is seriously injured and unable to help herself or to get help. The lawyer calls an ambulance for her, but takes care not to be personally indentified. The lawyer has committed a disciplinary violation, if supplementary Rule 1.6 is not adopted as part of the Code.

1(h). A lawyer learns from a client that the latter is hiding out, in violation of bail or probation. The lawyer would commit a disciplinary violation by revealing the client's location to the authorities.

1(i). A lawyer leans from a client during the trial of a civil or criminal case that the client intends to give testimony that the lawyer knows to be false. The lawyer does not present the client's testimony as she otherwise would, but instead simply requests a narrative from the client and returns to her seat at the counsel table. On summation to the jury, the lawyer makes no reference to her client's false testimony, contrary to what she would have done had she not known it to be false. The lawyer has committed disciplinary violations, both in the manner of presenting the client's testimony and in the manner of summation.

1(j). A lawyer learns from a client during the trial of a civil or criminal case that the client intends to give testimony that the lawyer knows to be false. The lawyer reasonably believes that a request for leave to withdraw would be denied and/or would be understood by the judge and by opposing counsel as an indication that the testimony is false. The lawyer does not seek leave to withdraw, presents the client's testimony in the ordinary manner, and refers to it in summation as evidence in the case. The lawyer has not committed a disciplinary violation.

1(k). A lawyer represents a client charged with possessing narcotics. The client is acquitted. In the course of the representation, however, the lawyer has learned from the client that the client is regularly engaged in selling heroin. If the lawyer does not disclose the information about the client to the police, therefore, the client will continue to sell drugs, thereby causing death or serious bodily harm to others. The lawyer would commit a disciplinary violation by revealing the client's confidence.

1(l). A lawyer is retained by an insurance company to represent its insured, who is being sued in a personal injury action. Without the insured client's consent, the lawyer informs the insurance company of possible defenses of the company against the insured client under the policy. The lawyer has committed a disciplinary violation.

CHAPTER II
FIDELITY TO THE CLIENT'S INTERESTS

Rules

2.1. In a matter entrusted to a lawyer by a client, the lawyer shall give undivided fidelity to the cleint's interests as perceived by the client, unaffected by any interest of the lawyer or of any other person, or by the lawyer's perception of the public interest.

2.2. A lawyer may limit the scope of the matter entrusted to the lawyer, subject to Rules 5.1 and 5.2, which relate to the obligation to treat a client fairly and in good faith, and to make clear the scope of the representation.

2.3. With the consent of a client, a lawyer may accept a fee or salary from a person or organization other than the client, subject to Rules 2.1, 2.2, and 2.4.

2.4. A lawyer may serve one or more clients, despite a divided loyalty, if each client who is or may be adversely affected by the divided loyalty is fully informed of the actual or potential adverse effects, and voluntarily consents.

2.5. A lawyer representing a corporation shall, as early as possible in the lawyer-client relationship, inform the board of directors of potential conflicts that might develop among the interests of the board, corporate officers, and shareholders. The lawyer shall receive from the board instructions in advance as to how to resolve such conflicts, and shall take reasonable steps to ensure that officers with whom the lawyer deals, and the shareholders, are made aware of how the lawyer has been instructed to resolve conflicts of interest.

Comment

Because our society places the highest value on the dignity and autonomy of the individual, its lawyers serve the public interest by undivided fidelity to each client's interests as the client perceives them.

That is not to say that lawyers should ignore possible harm to other persons or to public interests, or assume that clients' choices will be made in narrowly selfish terms. On the contrary, in counseling clients, lawyers should advise them fully of all significant potential consequences of particular courses of conduct, and that advice should include moral and public interest concerns along with strictly legal ones. The lawyer's ultimate fidelity, however, is to the client. By maintaining that fidelity, the lawyer acts in the highest public interest.

Just as it would be improper for a lawyer to impose other values upon a client, the lawyer should not impose upon the client an adversarial attitude toward others. For example, if two people seeking a divorce prefer to proceed in an amicable way with a single lawyer, it may be entirely proper for the lawyer to represent both at once. (Whether it would be prudent for the lawyer to do so, and risk subsequent criticism by one party or the other, is a matter of judgment for the lawyer.) Similarly, a lawyer might properly represent two or more partners, or co-defendants in a criminal or civil case, or the driver and the passenger in an automobile negligence action against a third party. In each such case, the clients might well decide that it is in their financial interest and/or in the best interest of their personal relationship to conduct their affairs in a cooperative rather than an adversarial way.

The essential responsibility of the lawyer in such a case is to make sure that each party is fully aware of the actual and potential conflicts of interest, and that each voluntarily consents. One problem that should be addressed particularly is the effect of joint representation on

366

the lawyer-client privilege under applicable law. The clients should also be informed of the likelihood that the lawyer would subsequently be disqualified from representing either party in any dispute that might arise between them.

One of the conundrums of professional ethics has been the responsibility of a corporate lawyer who learns from a corporate official that the official has engaged in illegal conduct, either against or on behalf of the company. In informing the lawyer, the official assumes a confidential relationship. Nevertheless, the lawyer may feel compelled to inform the board of directors, which is generally regarded as the embodiment of the corporate entity. If the board fails to take appropriate action, however, the lawyer may then feel an obligation to inform the shareholders (although the general public will then learn about the problem, to the likely disadvantge of the company). As the question is frequently posed, who is the lawyer's client in such circumstances?

Although it has not been generally recognized, the problem is basically a familiar and relatively simple one of conflict of interest. The lawyer's difficulty is insoluble only because the lawyer has failed to inform the board of readily foreseeable conflicts of interest and to receive guidance in advance. On the basis of the board's instructions, the lawyer can then make sure that each interested party is informed in advance and is thereby in a position to seek adequate protection.

For example, one board might prefer to maximize candor between its officers and the lawyer, and therefore instruct the lawyer to honor the officers' confidences, even in reporting to the board. The shareholders would then be in a position to approve or disapprove that policy, or to relinquish their shares. Another board might prefer to know everything the lawyer knows. In that event the officers would be on notice that they might want to consult with personal counsel before disclosing certain information to corporate counsel. Rule 2.5 requires the lawyer to take the reasonable steps necessary to avoid the situation in which the lawyer has awkward information, and cannot either disclose it or keep it confidential without betraying someone's reasonable expectations of trust.

The requirement is that the lawyer have the issue resolved as early as possible in the lawyer-client relationship. If a conflict arises before the issue is resolved, the lawyer should act in accordance with the lawyer's reasonable belief as to what the board of directors would consider to be in the best interests of the corporation.

Illustrative Cases

2(a). A lawyer represents a defendant charged with tax fraud. It is apparent to the lawyer that the fraud was actually committed by the client's wife, who has not been charged. The client insists that the lawyer conduct the defense without in any way implicating the client's wife. The lawyer would commit a disciplinary violation by violating those instructions.

2(b). A lawyer represents the accused in a criminal case. The lawyer interviews a potential witness whose story strongly supports the defense. Shortly thereafter, however, the lawyer learns that the prosecution has interviewed the same witness and has received a story highly damaging to the defense. At trial, the prosecution does not present the witness. The defendant insists upon calling the witness for the defense. The defense lawyer does not do so, because of concern with the conflicting story the witness has given the prosecution, and the lawyer's judgment that the witness will hurt the defense. The lawyer has committed a disciplinary violation.

2(c). A lawyer represents the driver and passenger of an automobile, who were both injured through the alleged negligence of the driver of another car in an intersection accident. The lawyer has not advised them of potential conflicts in their interests. The lawyer has committed a disciplinary violation.

2(d). A lawyer represents the plaintiff in a civil action. The case is one in which the defendant can be held responsible for the plaintiff's attorney's fees. The lawyer negotiates a settlement for the client, and also negotiates with the defense regarding the lawyer's own fee. The lawyer does not inform the client of the conflict thereby created between the client's interests and the lawyer's. (For example, the client might feel, if fully informed of the circumstances, that the liability settlement should be larger in view of what is available for the lawyer's fee.) Because the client was not in a position to evaluate the settlement with full awareness of the lawyer's conflict, or to consider having additional counsel represent the client's interests in the negotiations, the lawyer has committed a disciplinary violation, even though the ultimate liability settlement and fee were in fact fair.

CHAPTER III

ZEALOUSNESS ON THE CLIENT'S BEHALF

Rules

3.1. A lawyer shall use all legal means that are consistent with the retainer agreement, and reasonably available, to advance a client's interests as the client perceives them.

3.2. A lawyer shall fully inform a client of the client's rights, liabilities, and possible lawful alternatives regarding issues of substantial importance related to the matter for which the lawyer has been retained, except (a) to the extent that the client has instructed the lawyer to exercise the lawyer's judgment without further consultation with the client, or (b) as provided in Rule 3.3.

3.3. A lawyer shall not advise a client about the law when the lawyer knows that the client is requesting the advice for an unlawful purpose likely to cause death or serious physical injury to another person.

3.4. A lawyer shall not knowingly encourage a client to engage in illegal conduct, except in a good faith effort to test the validity or scope of the law.

3.5. A lawyer shall not knowingly participate in unlawfully concealing or destroying evidence, or discourage a witness or potential witness from talking to counsel for another party.

3.6. A lawyer shall not knowingly participate in creating false evidence, or a misrepresentation upon which another person is likely to rely and suffer material detriment.

3.7. A lawyer shall not knowingly file a materially false pleading, present materially false evidence, or make a materially false representation to a court or other tribunal, except as required to do so by Rule 1.2, which proscribes direct or indirect divulgence of a client's confidence.

3.8. A lawyer shall not give legal advice to a person who the lawyer knows is not represented by an attorney, other than the advice to secure counsel, when the lawyer knows that the interests of that person are in conflict or likely to be in conflict with the interests of the lawyer's client.

3.9. A lawyer shall not communicate regarding a legal matter with an adverse party who the lawyer knows is represented in that matter by an attorney, unless the lawyer has been authorized to do so by that party's attorney. However, a lawyer may send a written offer of settlement directly to an adverse party, seven days or more after that party's attorney has received the same offer of settlement in writing.

3.10. A lawyer shall not give a witness money or anything of substantial value, or threaten a witness with harm, in order to induce the witness to testify or dissuade the witness from testifying. However, a lawyer may pay a fee to an expert witness; a lawyer may reimburse a witness' actual, reasonable financial losses and expenses of appearing; a lawyer may give a witness protection against physical harm; and a prosecutor may immunize a witness from prosecution in order to avoid an assertion of the constitutional privilege against self-incrimination.

3.11. Except as permitted by law, a lawyer representing an interested party shall not initiate communication with a judge or hearing officer about the facts or issues in a case that the lawyer knows is pending or likely to be pending before the judge or hearing officer, unless the lawyer has first made a good faith effort to apprise opposing counsel. If a lawyer has an *ex parte* discussion with a judge or hearing officer regarding the issues in a case, the lawyer shall fully inform opposing counsel of the *ex parte* communication at the earliest opportunity, except to the extent prohibited by Rule 1.2, which proscribes unauthorized divulgence of a client's confidences.

Comment

Except when ordered by a court to represent a client, a lawyer has complete discretion whether to accept a particular client. Once a lawyer is committed to represent a client, however, the lawyer has no discretion, short of grounds for withdrawal, to fail to provide the client with every legal recourse that is consistent with the retainer agreement, reasonably available, and in the client's interests as the client perceives them. When there is inadequate opportunity for consultation regarding the client's interests, the lawyer shall act in accordance with the lawyer's reasonable belief as to what the client would perceive to be in the client's interest.

This Code both emphasizes the client's autonomy as a basic value and assumes that the client is competent to make the decisions at issue. Accordingly, the lawyer who represents a person who is incompetent is not bound by the literal terms of those rules. Nor does it appear to be possible to draft disciplinary rules that will adequately deal with the many variations that might arise regarding clients who are altogether or in part incompetent to make decisions in their own interest. Two guidelines can be stated, however. First, the lawyer's controlling concern should be the client's interest as the client would be most likely to perceive it if competent to make the decision. Second, depending upon the circumstances, the lawyer might be well advised to seek guidance from other professionals, such as psychiatrists or social workers, and from members of the client's family.

The phrase "materially false" in Rule 3.7 means false and likely to affect the resolution of one or more issues before the tribunal.

Illustrative Cases

3(a). A lawyer represents the defendant in a bank robbery. The lawyer suggests that the client give the lawyer the gun used in the robbery and the stolen money, so that the lawyer can put them in a place less likely to be searched. The lawyer has committed a disciplinary violation.

3(b). A lawyer represents a client in a murder case. The client leaves the murder weapon with the lawyer. The lawyer fails to advise the client that the weapon might be more accessible to the prosecution in the lawyer's possession than in the client's, and that, if the lawyer retains the weapon, he will produce it if ordered to do so by a valid subpoena. The lawyer has committed a disciplinary violation by failing to fully advise the client.

3(c). The same facts as 3(b). The lawyer would not commit a disciplinary violation by returning the weapon to the client, unless the lawyer also encouraged the client to make it unavailable as evidence.

3(d). The same facts as 3(b). The lawyer would not commit a disciplinary violation by producing the gun in response to a subpoena, unless the lawyer failed first to make a good faith effort to test the validity of the subpoena.

3(e). A lawyer is conducting the defense of a criminal prosecution. The judge calls the lawyer to the bench and asks her whether the defendant is guilty. The lawyer knows that the defendant is guilty, and reasonably believes that an equivocal answer will be taken by the judge as an admission of guilt. The lawyer assures the judge that the defendant is innocent. The lawyer has not committed a disciplinary violation.

3(f). The same facts as in 3(e), but the lawyer replies to the judge, "I'm sorry, Your Honor, but it would be improper for me to answer that question." The lawyer has committed a disciplinary violation.

3(g). The same facts as in 3(e), but the lawyer is an assistant public defender, and the public defender has publicly announced that the office's policy is to refuse to answer such questions and to report every judge who asks such questions to the state Judicial Discipline Commission. For that reason, a refusal to answer would not be taken as an admission of guilt. The lawyer reminds the judge of her office's policy, and asks the judge to withdraw the question. The lawyer has not committed a disciplinary violation.

CHAPTER IV

COMPETENCE

Rules

4.1. At a minimum, a lawyer shall serve a client with skill and care commensurate with that generally afforded to clients by other lawyers in similar matters.

4.2. A lawyer who has held himself or herself out to a client as having special skill and competence relative to a matter in which the client has retained the lawyer shall serve the client with that skill and care generally afforded to clients by lawyers of such skill and competence.

4.3. A lawyer shall take such legal action as is necessary and reasonably available to protect and advance a client's interests in the matter entrusted to the lawyer by the client.

4.4. A lawyer shall seek out all facts and legal authorities that are reasonably available and relevant to a client's interests in the matter entrusted to the lawyer by the client. In so doing, the lawyer shall give due regard not only to established rules of law, but also to developing legal concepts that might affect the client's interests.

4.5. A lawyer shall keep a client currently apprised of all significant developments in the matter entrusted to the lawyer by the client, unless the client has instructed the lawyer to do otherwise.

4.6. A lawyer shall seek out reasonably available resources that are necessary to protect and advance a client's interests, such as experts in specialized areas of the law or experts in non-legal disciplines.

4.7. If a lawyer forms a partnership with a non-lawyer for the purpose of more effectively serving clients' interests, the terms of the partnership shall be consistent with the lawyer's obligations under this Code, with particular reference to Rule 2.1, requiring undivided fidelity to the client.

Comment

It is generally agreed that a lack of competence is unprofessional and that a code of professional conduct should prescribe competence. Drafting rules to that end, however, has proved difficult.

Canon 6 of the Code of Professional Responsibility proscribes the failure to act competently, but defines competence in circular terms as conduct that the lawyer "knows or should know . . . is not competent." The CPR also requires preparation that is "adequate in the circumstances," but adequacy is neither defined nor given a reference point.

This Code requires, at a minimum, a level of skill and care commensurate with that generally provided by other lawyers in similar matters. Recognizing, however, that what is provided by other lawyers may not always amount to an adequate standard of competence, the Rules prescribe specific duties that are defined in terms of what is relevant or necessary to protect and advance the client's interests, and is reasonably available. The client's interests are determined by the client, and delineated by "the matter entrusted to the lawyer." (See Rules 2.2, 5.1, and 5.2, permitting the lawyer to limit the scope of the matter, subject to the requirements of fairness and good faith.)

CHAPTER V
RETAINER AGREEMENTS AND FINANCIAL ARRANGEMENTS WITH CLIENTS

Rules

5.1. A lawyer shall treat a client fairly and in good faith, giving due regard to the client's position of dependence upon the lawyer, the lawyer's special training and experience, and the high degree of trust which a client is entitled to place in a lawyer.

5.2. As soon as practicable after being retained, a lawyer shall make clear to a client, in writing, the material terms of the retainer agreement, including the scope of what the lawyer is undertaking to do for the client, the limits of that undertaking, and the fee and any other obligations the client is assuming.

5.3. A lawyer shall not contract with a client to limit the lawyer's liability to the client for malpractice.

5.4. Lawyers who are not openly associated in the same firm shall not share a fee unless: (a) the division reflects the proportion of work performed by each attorney and the normal billing rate of each; or (b) the client has been informed pursuant to Rule 5.2 of the fact of fee-sharing and the effect on the total fee, and the client consents.

5.5. A lawyer shall not impose a lien upon any part of a client's files, except upon the lawyer's own work product, and then only to the extent that the work product has not been paid for. This work-product exception shall be inapplicable when the client is in fact unable to pay, or when withholding the lawyer's work product would present a significant risk to the client of imprisonment, deportation, destruction of essential evidence, loss of custody of a child, or similar irreparable harm.

5.6. A lawyer shall not give money or anything of substantial value to any person in order to induce that person to become or to remain a client, or to induce that person to retain or to continue the lawyer as counsel on behalf of someone else. However, a lawyer may (a) advance money to a client on any terms that are fair; (b) give money to a client as an act of charity; (c) give money to a client to enable the client to withstand delays in litigation that would otherwise induce the client to settle a case because of financial hardship, rather than on the merits of the client's claim; or (d) charge a fee that is contingent in whole or in part on the outcome of the case.

Comment

Rule 5.4, governing the division of fees by lawyers not openly associated in the same firm, is less restrictive than any other provision or proposal known to the Commission.

First, it allows a fee to be divided, without express client consent, if the division reflects the proportion of each lawyer's contribution to the work of the client, and each lawyer's normal billing rate. (Note that each lawyer would have been retained either by the client, pursuant to Rule 5.2, or by another lawyer pursuant to Rule 4.6, which requires the lawyer to seek out experts in specialized areas of the law to the extent available and necessary, with such notice to the client as is required by Rule 4.5.) Compare DR 2–107 of the Code of Professional Responsibility, and Rule 1.5(d) of the proposed Rules of Professional Conduct.

Second, Rule 5.4 allows any division to which the client consents after being informed of the fact that the lawyers intend to divide the fee, and of the effect of the division on the total fee. In addition, Rule 5.2 requires that this information be provided in writing, including the scope of what each lawyer is to do for the client. That requirement should be sufficient to prevent unfairness to clients.

It must be emphasized that the purpose of allowing fee splitting is to encourage lawyers to refer clients to competent specialists. The proposed Rules of Professional Conduct would continue the existing practice of penalizing such referrals outside one's own firm; even the Massachusetts and California rules prohibit a division that increases the amount of the fee (but only when the two lawyers are not members of the same firm). Such rules exalt the form of association over the substance of client consent and providing better service for the client, particularly in the context of recent increases in the number and size of multi-office firms. It prohibits some lawyers from doing something that other lawyers may do with impunity, and that many lawyers in fact do. It is more realistic to regulate a common practice than to prohibit it on a discriminatory basis, especially when the practice may actually improve the quality of service made available to clients.

Rule 5.6(c) permits a lawyer to give money to a client to enable the client to have access to the legal system or to withstand delay as a form of coercion to settle on unfavorable terms not related to the merits of the case. A not uncommon practice is revealed, for example, in *Abramson v. Kenwood Laboratories, Inc.,* 223 N.Y.S.2d 1005 (1961). There the attorney "frankly stated in the course of the . . . pretrial hearings that he is 'running a business.' He indicated the generally known policy of his insurance carrier to offer payment in settlements of personal injury suits of sums less than what may reasonably be anticipated as the probable recovery upon trial."

Such a practice conflicts most clearly with the fair administration of justice when a plaintiff is in need of immediate funds for food, housing, medical attention, etc., and is therefore under unconscionable pressure to settle for less than a claim is worth. In such a case, the lawyer contributes to the fair administration of justice by giving or lending the funds that are necessary to enable the client to obtain a fair recovery on the merits of the case, uninfluenced by financial pressures resulting from delay.

Rule 5.6(d) permits fees to be contingent in whole or in part on the outcome of any case. Such fees have long been recognized as proper when the client is a plaintiff in civil litigation. The principal reason is that, as a practical matter, most people would not be in a position to seek vindication of their legal rights, however meritorious, if litigating those rights could result in substantial financial loss as well as loss in time and the other burdens of litigation. Since there is little if any incentive to lawyers to take frivolous cases on contingent fees, such cases are screened out through a contingent fee system more effectively than they might be in a system based exclusively upon retainers. Moreover, any concern that contingent fees will induce unethical conduct on the part of lawyers seems fanciful. A lawyer unscrupulous enough to fabricate a case to earn a contingent fee will undoubtedly not hesitate to do so to earn a retainer or to establish a reputation for winning cases.

Similarly, there appears to be no justification, on ethical grounds, to forbid contingent fees to defendants in civil cases. Indeed, the only apparent reason for such a prohibition is that anyone who is worth suing is likely to be able to pay a retainer, and is effectively coerced into doing so because of the pending claim. Thus, a rule against charging contingent fees to defendants has every appearance of being less a matter of ethics than a restraint of trade. If a lawyer considers a complaint to be so lacking in merit as to justify basing the fee in whole or in part on the lawyer's success in defending against it, the lawyer and client should be free to contract on that basis.

There is even more reason for allowing contingent fees for the accused in criminal cases, because the accused who goes to prison, thereby losing any opportunity to earn a living, is far less able to pay a fee than is the accused who is acquitted. Also, lawyers would accept such arrangements only when the defense appeared sufficiently strong to warrant it, and the unscrupulous lawyer would be no more likely to fabricate a defense to earn a contingent fee than to earn a retainer.

When a contingent fee is proposed by an attorney, it is desirable, although it is not required, that a reasonable retainer arrangement be offered to the client in the alternative.

These rules do not preclude any particular mode or terms of payment, such as credit cards or interest on unpaid fees. The lawyer may also accept in payment shares of stock, literary rights, or other property. The only limitation is that the mode and terms of payment be consistent with fairness, good faith, full disclosure, and undivided fidelity to the client's interests, and otherwise be consistent with the provisions of this Code.

Illustrative Cases

5(a). A lawyer represents the widow of a railroad employee killed in a switching accident; the railroad is the defendant. After many months, the case is near trial, but the plaintiff tells the lawyer that she urgently needs money for food and rent, and must therefore settle immediately for whatever she can get. The lawyer reasonably believes that she will receive substantially more in settlement on the eve of the trial or as a result of jury verdict. He therefore gives her money, with the understanding that she will pay it back only if there is a recovery in the case. The lawyer has not committed a disciplinary violation.

5(b). A lawyer advances litigation expenses on behalf of a client on the clear understanding, in writing, that the client will reimburse the lawyer on a monthly basis, and that the client will pay interest at a specified, reasonable rate for any amounts in default. The lawyer has not committed a disciplinary violation.

5(c). A law firm is counsel to a corporation. An officer of the corporation asks a member of the firm to represent him in a divorce. The lawyer does so, without charging the firm's customary fee. The lawyer has committed a disciplinary violation.

CHAPTER VI
WITHDRAWAL FROM REPRESENTATION

Rules

6.1. A lawyer shall withdraw from representing a client when the lawyer is discharged by the client.

6.2. A lawyer may withdraw from representing a client at any time and for any reason if (a) withdrawal will cause no significant harm to the client's interests, (b) the client is fully informed of the consequences of withdrawal and voluntarily assents to it, or (c) withdrawal is pursuant to the terms of the retainer agreement required by Rules 5.1 and 5.2 of this Code.

6.3. A lawyer may withdraw from representing a client if the lawyer reasonably believes that continued employment in the case would be likely to have a seriously adverse effect upon the lawyer's health.

6.4. Unless the lawyer knows that withdrawal would result in significant and irreparable harm to the client, a lawyer may withdraw from representing a client if (a) the client commits a clear and substantial violation of a written agreement regarding fees or expenses, or (b) the lawyer encounters continuing, unavoidable and substantial difficulties in working with co-counsel or with the client.

6.5. In any matter other than criminal litigation, a lawyer may withdraw from representing a client if the lawyer comes to know that the client has knowingly induced the lawyer to take the case or to take action on behalf of the client on the basis of material misrepresentations about the facts of the case, and if withdrawal can be accomplished without a direct violation of confidentiality.

6.6. A lawyer shall decline or withdraw from representing a client when the lawyer knows that such action is necessary to avoid commission by the lawyer of a disciplinary violation, unless such action would result in a violation of Rule 1.2, proscribing direct or indirect divulgence of a client's confidences.

6.7. Whatever the reason for withdrawing from representation, a lawyer shall take reasonable care to avoid foreseeable harm to a client, including giving due notice to the client, allowing reasonable time for substitution of new counsel, cooperating with new counsel, promptly turning over all papers and property to which the client is entitled, and promptly returning any unearned advances.

Comment

Withdrawal from representing a client is the termination of the lawyer's authority to act for the client. What that entails will vary in different situations. Some of the duties that attach at the time of withdrawal are stated by Rule 6.7; others appear in Rule 1.2, relating to continuing confidentiality, and Rule 5.5, limiting the assertion of attorney's liens.

Most of the Rules in this Part state the circumstances under which lawyers are permitted to initiate withdrawal, and the conditions that may circumscribe such withdrawals.

Rule 6.1 is absolute. The lawyer discharged by the client must terminate the representation.

It sometimes appears that this Rule is overridden by a court's refusal to accept the withdrawal of counsel. In such cases, however, the client has the right either to persist in discharging the lawyer, and to go forward without counsel, or to revoke the discharge. Continuing with an unwanted lawyer is a true Hobson's choice, but it is still the client's choice of that course that continues, or revives, the representation.

Rule 6.6 is not absolute, because the duty it embodies, that of avoiding violating the Code, is sometimes subordinate to the paramount duty not to reveal clients' confidences. It should also be noted that Rule 6.5 allows indirect divulgence of confidences by withdrawal from a class of cases also covered by Rule 6.6, those non-criminal matters where the client has knowingly induced the lawyer either to take the case or to take action on the client's behalf, on the basis of material factual misrepresentations.

A lawyer is forbidden by Rule 3.7 to knowingly present false evidence. Therefore, withdrawal from representation would be required by Rule 6.6 when the lawyer knows through a confidence that the client intends to present false evidence, and when withdrawal would not result in violating a confidence. When the lawyer reasonably believes that refusal to present false evidence could result in violating a confidence, however, Rules 1.2, 3.7, and 6.6 require the lawyer to continue in the case.

Rule 6.5 permits withdrawal in a matter, other than criminal litigation, when the lawyer has been induced to take action by misrepresentations by the client, even though withdrawal might result indirectly in divulging a confidence. When the facts of a case fall within Rule 6.5, therefore, Rules 1.2, 3.7, and 6.6 are in part subordinated to it.

Illustrative Cases

6(a). A lawyer representing the accused in a criminal case learns from the client that he intends to present a false alibi. The lawyer knows that he will be required to give an explanation to the judge if he makes motion for leave to withdraw as counsel; he also knows that the judge will take an equivocal explanation as an indication that the client intends to commit perjury. The lawyer nevertheless asks leave to withdraw, telling the judge only, "I have an ethical problem," or, "My client and I do not see eye to eye." The lawyer has commited a disciplinary violation.

6(b). A lawyer represents a client requried to file documents with a government agency. The lawyer comes to know that there are material misrepresentations in documents filed by the lawyer on the client's behalf, and subsequent uncorrected filings would further the misrepresentation. The client insists upon making the subsequent filings. The lawyer's withdrawal would cause no significant harm to the client's interest. The lawyer would commit a disciplinary violation by failing to withdraw.

6(c). The same facts as in 6(b), but the agency has a rule requiring a lawyer to give the agency the reason for any withdrawal. The lawyer would commit a disciplinary violation by withdrawing and thereby directly violating the client's confidences in making the required explanation.

6(d). The same facts as in 6(b). In addition, the lawyer was induced to participate in the earlier filing by knowing misrepresentations by the client to the lawyer; the lawyer's withdrawal would adversely affect the client's ability to meet important deadlines; and the lawyer would not be required to explain his withdrawal to the agency, but the agency would be likely to scrutinize the client's filings more closely. The lawyer would not commit a disciplinary violation either by withdrawing or by going forward with the client.

CHAPTER VII
INFORMING THE PUBLIC ABOUT LEGAL SERVICES

Rules

7.1. A lawyer shall not knowingly make any representation that is materially false or misleading, and that might reasonably be expected to induce reliance by a member of the public in the selection of counsel.

7.2. A lawyer shall not advertise for or solicit clients in a way that violates a valid law imposing reasonable restrictions regarding time or place.

7.3. A lawyer shall not advertise for or solicit clients through another person when the lawyer knows, or could reasonably ascertain, that such conduct violates a contractual or other legal obligation of that other person.

7.4. A lawyer shall not solicit a member of the public when the lawyer has been told by that person or someone acting on that person's behalf that he or she does not want to receive communications from the lawyer.

7.5. A lawyer who advertises for or solicits clients through another person shall be as responsible for that person's representations to and dealings with potential clients as if the lawyer acted personally.

Comment

Access to the legal system is essential to the exercise of fundamental rights, particularly those rights relating to personal autonomy, freedom of expression, counsel, due process, and equal protection of the laws. Yet members of the public are frequently unaware of their need for legal assistance and of its availability. It is thus important for lawyers to provide members of the public with information regarding the availability of lawyers to serve them, the ways in which legal services can be useful, and the costs of legal services. Lawyers are therefore encouraged to advertise and to solicit clients, subject only to restrictions relating to false and misleading representations, harassment, violation of reasonable time and place regulations, and inducing violations by others of contractual or other legal obligations.

Solicitation refers to spoken communication, in person or by telephone, intended to induce the other person to become a client.

Illustrative Cases

7(a). A lawyer advertises truthfully that she has been certified as a specialist in international law by the Trans-World Bar Association, which is a bona fide association of lawyers imposing substantial requirements for such certification. The lawyer has not committed a disciplinary violation.

7(b). A lawyer advertises truthfully that he has been certified as a specialist in Family Law by the State Lawyers Association. The membership of the State Lawyers Association consists only of the lawyer himself, his two partners, and his neighbor. The advertisement is materially misleading, and the lawyer has committed a disciplinary violation.

7(c). A lawyer telephones the fifteen-year-old victim of a recent automobile accident, and is told by her parents that they are arranging for legal represenation for their daughter, that she is in the hospital, and that they do not want him to contact her. The lawyer nevertheless calls upon the girl in the hospital and attempts to induce her to retain him. The lawyer has committed a disciplinary violation.

7(d). A lawyer visits the fifteen-year-old victim of an automobile accident in the hospital, and she retains him on reasonable terms for work he is competent to perform. He has not been instructed not to visit the girl, and the hospital has no regulations against solicitation of patients by lawyers. The lawyer has not committed a disciplinary violation.

Note: A client can discharge a lawyer with or without cause. The liability of the client to the lawyer in that event is a matter of state contract law.

7(e). A lawyer pays a hospital orderly a fee to distribute his professional cards to patients. The hospital has a rule against such conduct by its personnel. The lawyer has committed a disciplinary violation.

CHAPTER VIII

MAINTAINING PROFESSIONAL INTEGRITY AND COMPETENCE

Rules

8.1. A lawyer shall not engage in criminal or otherwise unlawful conduct that creates a substantial doubt that the lawyer will comply with this Code of Conduct.

8.2. Subject to Rule 1.2, proscribing unauthorized divulgence of a client's confidences, a lawyer who knows that an attorney or judge has committed a disciplinary violation, or who has material, adverse information about a candidate for the bar, shall convey that knowledge to the appropriate disciplinary or admission authorities.

8.3. When a lawyer has represented a client, or when, because of the lawyer's association with a law firm, a client of that firm could reasonably believe that the lawyer has had access to the client's confidences, the lawyer shall not thereafter accept employment by any other party whose interests are in any way adverse to the client's and could be materially affected by the lawyer's presumed knowledge of the client's confidences.

8.4. When a lawyer knows that the lawyer's testimony is likely to be offered on a material, disputed issue in a case, the lawyer shall decline or withdraw from representation in the case, unless doing so would cause serious and irreparable injury to the client.

8.5. When a lawyer is disqualified from representing a client under Rule 8.3 no partner or associate of that lawyer, and no one with an of counsel relation to the lawyer, shall represent the client.

8.6. When a lawyer is disqualified by Rule 8.3, 8.4, or 8.5 from representing a client, the disqualification may be waived by the voluntary and informed consent of each person whose interests are protected by the applicable rule.

8.7. A lawyer shall not enter into a commercial transaction or other business relationship with a person who is or was recently a client, unless that person is represented by independent counsel. This Rule does not affect the specific transactions covered by Chapter V of this Code, relating to retainer agreements and financial arrangements with clients.

8.8. A lawyer shall not commence having sexual relations with a client during the lawyer-client relationship.

8.9. A lawyer shall not act as officer or director of a publicly held corporation that is a client of the lawyer, of the lawyer's partner or associate, or of any firm or attorney with whom the lawyer has an of counsel relationship.

8.10. A lawyer serving on the board of a charitable or public organization shall not participate in discussing or voting upon any matter before the board that the lawyer knows might materially affect the interests of a client of the lawyer or of the lawyer's firm.

8.11. A lawyer shall not participate in arranging for a gift from a client to the lawyer, to a member of the lawyer's family, or to one who is a partner, associate, or of counsel to the lawyer.

8.12. When a lawyer holds money or property in whole or in part for the benefit of someone else, the lawyer shall hold it in trust, separate from the lawyer's own money and property, and appropriately identified, recorded, and safeguarded. When another person becomes entitled to receive any part of the money or property, the lawyer shall promptly deliver it to that person. If a dispute develops regarding entitlement to any part of the money or property, the lawyer may take action in accordance with applicable law, such as by depositing with a court the money or property that is in dispute, pending determination of the dispute.

8.13. A lawyer shall not enter into an agreement that unreasonably restricts a lawyer's right to practice law or to communicate with members of the public, and which thereby interferes with the freedom of clients to obtain counsel of their choice. However, lawyers in a partnership or similar professional relationship may make reasonable agreements regarding the allocation of fees among themselves with respect to clients who elect to continue with one or another lawyer upon termination of the professional relationship between the lawyers.

8.14. A lawyer shall not knowingly assist or seek to induce a disciplinary violation by another lawyer.

8.15. A lawyer shall take reasonable care to assure that none of the lawyer's partners, associates, or employees commits an act that would be a disciplinary violation if committed by the lawyer.

Comment

Satisfying each person's sense of justice is a high value in a society that respects the dignity of the individual, and public confidence in the administration of justice is necessary to maintain respect for law. For those reasons, it is a truism that justice must not only be done but that it must be seen to be done.

The role of lawyers is an essential element of the administration of justice, and rules of lawyers' conduct define that role. Thus, lawyers not only must comply with rules of professional conduct; they also must be seen as complying with them. For the profession to promulgate ethical rules, yet appear to wink at violations, can only result in disrespect for the profession and thereby in disrespect for the administration of justice. Thus, the concept that a lawyer should avoid the appearance of impropriety is an extremely important one. Embodying that concept in specific rules is, however, exceedingly difficult.

An early draft of this Code included the following provision:

> A lawyer shall avoid acting in such a way that a fair-minded person, knowing all of the relevant facts that are readily available, would conclude that, in the generality of such cases, disciplinary violations are likely to occur in a significant number of instances.

This views the appearance of impropriety from the perspective of a fair-minded person, not that of either a naif or a cynic. The appearance depends upon the facts readily available. The question is not whether the lawyer has in fact acted improperly, since the issue of appearances ordinarily arises in situations in which the impropriety would be extremely difficult to detect or to prove. The focus is on the generality of cases, and on whether improprieties are likely to occur in a significant number of instances.

Phrased otherwise: lawyers should avoid situations in which temptation and opportunity for wrongdoing are high, and detection or proof of wrongdoing would be difficult—situations, that is, in which common sense and experience inform us that a significant number of people will not be able to resist temptation. An obvious example is the lawyer who puts the client's funds into the lawyer's checking account.

The Commission accepted the proposed Rule as an aspirational guide, but found it too vague to be an acceptable basis for disciplinary action. Instead, this Chapter consists solely of rules proscribing particular conduct that gives rise to reasonable inferences of impropriety.

For example, Rule 8.8 forbids a lawyer to commence having sexual relations with a client during the lawyer-client relationship. This rule, like Rule 5.1, recognizes the dependency of a client upon a lawyer, the high degree of trust that a client is entitled to place in a lawyer, and the potential for unfair advantage in such a relationship. Other professionals, such as psychiatrists, have begun to face up to analogous problems.

Rule 8.1 provides for discipline of a lawyer who, either as a lawyer or as a private citizen, engages in unlawful conduct not specifically covered by other provisions of this Code if that conduct is relevant to one's performance as a lawyer.

Here again, an effort has been made to avoid unfairly vague terms. The elusive concept of moral turpitude is not used, nor is the undefined standard of "fitness to practice law." To warrant professional sanctions, the conduct must be unlawful—a felony, misdemeanor, or violation of rule of court—and must create a substantial doubt that the lawyer will comply with the rules of conduct required of lawyers.

This Code has no rule requiring each lawyer to do a particular amount of uncompensated public interest or *pro bono publico* work, on pain of professional discipline. That does not mean that the attorney members of the Commission are unwilling to perform such services or that the non-lawyer members do not want to share in the benefits of *pro bono* work. Rather, it is apparent to the Commission that such a rule would be inherently so vague as to be unenforceable and unenforced, and therefore hypocritical.

All lawyers should do work in the public interest. But some lawyers should not be telling other lawyers how much *pro bono* work they should be doing, and for whom, and disciplining them if they do not. Nor should codes of conduct purport to impose disciplinary requirements that the codifiers know will not be enforced.

Illustrative Cases

8(a). A lawyer represents the D Company, which is the defendant in an anti-trust action brought by the government. Subsequently, the lawyer represents the P Company, which is suing the D Company in a private anti-trust action involving the same alleged violation. Unless the D Company has knowingly and voluntarily assented to the lawyer's representation of the P Company, the lawyer has committed a disciplinary violation.

8(b). The same facts as in 8(a), but another attorney in the lawyer's firm represents the P Company, and the firm undertakes to "insulate" the lawyer from any involvement in the case. Unless the D Company has knowingly and voluntarily assented to the insulating or screening arrangement, and to the other attorney's representation of the P Company, the other attorney has committed a disciplinary violation.

8(c). A lawyer expects to cross examine a witness who previously was acquitted in a criminal case. The lawyer offers to pay the witness' previous attorney to provide information, learned by representing the witness in the criminal case, that could be used to discredit the witness on cross examination. The lawyer has committed a disciplinary violation.

CHAPTER IX

RESPONSIBILITIES OF GOVERNMENT LAWYERS

Rules

9.1. A lawyer serving as public prosecutor shall not seek evidence to support a prosecution against a particular individual unless that individual is identified as a suspect in the course of a good faith investigation into suspected criminal conduct.

9.2. In exercising discretion to investigate or to prosecute, a lawyer serving as public prosecutor shall not show favoritism for, or invidiously discriminate against, one person among others similarly situated.

9.3. A lawyer serving as public prosecutor shall not seek or sign formal charges, or proceed to trial, unless a fair-minded juror could conclude beyond a reasonable doubt that the accused is guilty, on the basis of all of the facts that are known to the prosecutor and likely to be admissible into evidence.

9.4. A lawyer serving as public prosecutor before a grand jury shall not interfere with the independence of the grand jury, preempt a function of the grand jury, or use the processes of the grand jury for purposes not approved by the grand jury.

9.5. A lawyer serving as public prosecutor shall not use unconscionable pressures in plea bargaining, such as charging an accused in several counts for what is essentially a single offense, or charging an accused with a more serious offense than is warranted under Rule 9.3.

9.6. A lawyer serving as public prosecutor shall not condition a dismissal, nolle prosequi, or similar action on an accused's relinquishment of constitutional rights, or of rights against the government, a public official, or any other person, other than relinquishment of those rights inherent in pleading not guilty and proceeding to trial.

9.7. A lawyer serving as public prosecutor shall promptly make available to defense counsel, without request for it, any information that the prosecutor knows is likely to be useful to the defense.

9.8. A lawyer serving as public prosecutor shall not strike jurors on grounds of race, religion, national or ethnic background, or sex, except to counteract the use of such tactics initiated by the defense.

9.9. A lawyer serving as public prosecutor, who knows that a defendant is not receiving or has not received effective assistance of counsel, shall promptly advise the court, on the record when possible.

9.10. A lawyer representing the government before a court or other tribunal shall inform the tribunal of any facts or legal authorities that might materially affect the decision in the case, and that have not been brought to the attention of the tribunal by other counsel.

9.11. A lawyer in public service shall not engage in publicity regarding a criminal investigation or proceeding, or an administrative investigation or proceeding involving charges of wrongdoing, until after the announcement of a disposition of the case. However, the lawyer may publicize information that is (a) necessary to protect the public from an accused who is at large and reasonably believed to be dangerous; (b) necessary to help in apprehending a suspect; or (c) necessary to rebut publicized allegations of improper conduct on the part of the lawyer or the lawyer's staff.

9.12. A lawyer in public service shall not knowingly violate the rights of any person, or knowingly tolerate the violation of any person's rights by any other public employee.

9.13. A lawyer in public service shall not use the powers of public office for personal advantage, favoritism, or retaliation.

9.14. A lawyer shall not accept private employment relating to any matter in which the lawyer participated personally and substantially while in public service.

9.15. When a lawyer is disqualified from representing a client under Rule 9.14, no partner or associate of the lawyer, and no one with an of counsel relationship to the lawyer, shall represent the client.

9.16. A lawyer in public service shall not participate in any matter in which the lawyer participated personally and substantially in private practice.

9.17. While a lawyer in public service is participating personally and substantially in a matter in which a private attorney's client has a material interest, neither lawyer shall comment to the other about the government lawyer's private employment possibilities.

Supplementary Provisions *

9.18. For one year after leaving public service, a lawyer shall not counsel or otherwise represent a client who was previously involved in any matter in which the lawyer participated personally and substantially within one year prior to leaving public service.

9.19. For one year after leaving public service, a lawyer shall not become a partner or associate of, or have an of counsel relationship with, any law firm that represented an interested party in any matter in which the lawyer participated personally and substantially within one year prior to leaving public service.

9.20. For one year after entering public service, a lawyer shall not participate in any matter in which an interested party was the lawyer's client within one year before the lawyer entered public service, or in which an interested party is represented by a lawyer who was the partner or associate of, or had an of counsel relationship to, the lawyer within one year before the lawyer entered public service, unless (a) the lawyer was appointed to office by the chief executive officer of the jurisdiction, with approval of a legislative body, or (b) the lawyer's participation is approved by a superior who was appointed by the chief executive officer with approval of a legislative body, or (c) the lawyer was elected to office.

* These provisions have not been approved by the Commission, principally because of concern about their effect in smaller communities served by very few lawyers.

9.21. When a lawyer is disqualified from representing a client under Rules 9.18 or 9.19, no partner or associate of the lawyer, and no one of counsel to the lawyer, shall represent the client.

Comment

Government lawyers are, of course, covered by rules that relate to lawyers generally. But government lawyers have significantly different roles and functions from lawyers representing private parties, and their ethical difficulties and the solutions to them must vary accordingly. Those differences stem principally from important distinctions between the government and the individual citizen. One such distinction is the paramount value given the sanctity of the individual in our society. Another is the awesome power of the government, a power that the founders of our nation had good reason to circumscribe in the Bill of Rights and elsewhere in the Constitution. A third difference is the majesty and dignity of our government. Conduct that may be tolerable in individuals may be reprehensible when done under color of law on behalf of the nation or a state.

In addition, the prosecutor has extraordinary powers of a quasi-judicial nature. The discretion to select a person to investigate has been described by Justice Robert Jackson (a former Attorney General) as "the most dangerous power" of the prosecutor. The prosecutor also decides the crime to be charged, affects the punishment, and even decides whether to prosecute at all. In the course of exercising that awesome discretion, the prosecutor is frequently called upon to make decisions which, in private litigation, would be made by a client rather than by the lawyer. Thus, to say that the prosecutor has special responsibilities in wielding the vast discretionary powers of government, is simply to recognize that the prosecutor is the person who has that discretionary power.

Defense counsel has special professional responsibilities deriving from the importance of confidentiality between attorney and client, the presumption of innocence, the constitutional right to counsel, and the constitutional privilege against self-incrimination. The prosecutor, who does not represent a private client, is not affected by those considerations in the same way.

Thus a defense attorney may be professionally bound to withhold evidence. There is nothing unethical in keeping a guilty defendant off the stand and putting the government to its proof; the Constitution guarantees the defendant nothing less. Obviously, however, the prosecutor is not similarly privileged to withhold material evidence; the constitutional command is precisely the contrary.

In recognition of the different roles of defense counsel and prosecutor, the American Bar Association and the Association of American Law Schools, in their Joint Conference Report on Professional Responsibility, concluded: "The public prosecutor cannot take as a guide for the conduct of his office the standards of an attorney appearing on the behalf of an individual client. The freedom elsewhere wisely granted to partisan advocacy must be severely curtailed if the prosecutor's duties are to be properly discharged."

As the Code of Professinoal Responsibility states, the responsibility of a public prosecutor "differs from that of the usual advocate; his duty is to seek justice, not merely to convict." The ABA Standards Relating to the Prosecution and the Defense Function also emphasize the unique role of the prosecutor: "Although the prosecutor operates within the adversary system, it is fundamental that his obligation is to protect the innocent as well as to convict the guilty, to guard the rights of the accused as well as to enforce the rights of the public." Unfortunately, however, neither the Code nor the Standards provides adequate rules governing prosecutorial misconduct, and the proposed Rules of Professional Conduct are similarly deficient.

Rule 9.3 forbids a prosecutor to seek an indictment or proceed to trial unless a fairminded juror could conclude that the accused is guilty beyond a reasonable doubt, on the basis of the facts known to the prosecutor and likely to be admissible at trial. A further ethical obligation is assumed by many conscientious prosecutors; they will not seek an indictment or proceed to trial unless they are satisfied that the accused is guilty beyond a reasonable doubt, on the basis of all the facts known to them, regardless of admissibility. That rule should be followed in all cases, but is not here made the basis of a disciplinary violation, because the subjective nature of the standard makes it impossible to enforce.

Along with other unique powers of office, a prosecutor is privileged, in an indictment, to publish severely defamatory information against a private person. Despite their inherent harmfulness, indictments must be publicly available to prevent the abuses of secret proceedings. There is no similar justification, however, for a prosecutor to engage in press conferences, press releases, and other publicity efforts that have the effect of impairing or destroying the reputation of an accused without the due process of a trial or hearing. Yet, on the other hand, an accused may never be more in need of the First Amendment rights to freedom of speech than when officially labeled a wrongdoer before family, friends, neighbors, and business associates. Many defendants are inarticulate; almost all need the special skills of a lawyer as spokesperson. That is why this Code places restrictions on preconviction publicity by public officials, who act under color of law, but recognizes that the First Amendment precludes such restrictions on the speech of private persons and their attorneys.

The prosecutor working with a grand jury has peculiar responsibilities. The grand jury resembles an adjudicative tribunal, but its procedures are usually not adversary. Suspects who appear before it usually cannot be accompanied by counsel. The entire process is usually conducted *ex parte;* one side, the defense, cannot appear. The prosecutor presents evidence before the grand jury, as an advocate does before other tribunals, but also advises the grand jury, which is the representative of the people, regarding the course of action it should take.

This function is sometimes described as quasi-judicial: the prosecutor has much the same relation to a grand jury as a judge instructing a petit jury on the law. It is also, however, akin to the relationship of a lawyer in private practice to a client, particularly to the board of directors of a corporate client. The prosecutor has much the same obligations to a grand jury as the private lawyer to the private client, particularly the duty to serve the client's interests not as the lawyer perceives them, but as the client perceives them, and therefore to act as the servant, not the master, of the grand jury. Indeed, the grand jury prosecutor is almost the only lawyer for the public who has a real opportunity to consult directly with a duly constituted body, representative of the public, whose members have no conflicting interest (such as the desire to stay in office).

Ironically, however, the American grand jury has been criticized as a "rubber stamp for the prosecutor," because some prosecutors have used it improperly as an investigative tool and as a device for obtaining unwarranted indictments. Prosecutors have had grand juries dissolved because they would not indict, or because they wished to indict, quite properly, persons the prosecutor did not want indicted. Prosecutors have routinely issued "grand jury subpoenas" for documents they wished to examine, without obtaining the consent of "their" grand juries, or even consulting the grand jury.

Rule 9.4 proscribes such abuses by prosecutors of the extraordinary powers of grand juries, when it is read in conjunction with other applicable rules in this Chapter. Particularly applicable are Rule 9.1, which proscribes seeking evidence to prosecute persons not identified as bona fide suspects; Rule 9.2, proscribing discriminating among potential defendants; and Rule 9.3, prohibiting seeking or signing indictments not likely to result in proper convictions. Most significant is Rule 9.10, which requires the prosecutor to inform the grand jury of all facts and legal authorities that might materially affect its decisions, because it is a tribunal before which no other counsel has the right to present facts or argument. Taken together with Rule 9.4, these rules should substantially contribute to returning the grand jury to its constitutional role as a bulwark between the citizen and the power of the state, and reducing its use as a cat's paw for the overzealous prosecutor.

Rule 9.13 forbids a lawyer in public service to use the powers of public office for personal advantage, favoritism, or retaliation. The use of an Enemies List in a prosecutor's office would be a clear violation of that rule. See also Rule 9.1. A lawyer in public service should also take pains to avoid participating in any matter in which members of the public might reasonably, though erroneously, believe that the lawyer is motivated by personal concern, such as a grudge. One way for a prosecutor to attempt to avoid such appearances is to move for the appointment of special prosecutors in cases in which the prosecutor's own motives might reasonably be questioned.

There is a common error of ethical discourse that should be avoided in interpreting the rules in this Code: When an appellate court affirms a conviction, that does not necessarily mean that the prosecutor's conduct has comported with professional ethics. A court might well decide that particular conduct by a prosecutor does not warrant reversal of a conviction on constitutional grounds, yet that same conduct might be a serious disciplinary violation.

Whenever this Chapter imposes special obligations upon lawyers serving as public prosecutors, that category includes enforcement lawyers for regulatory agencies, regardless of whether criminal or civil sanctions are being invoked. Also included are lawyers serving as bar counsel or in a similar disciplinary role.

One of the most controversial areas of appearance of impropriety has been, paradoxically, that in which the public nature of the profession is most obvious—conflicts of interest of the lawyer in (or formerly in) public service. In order to resolve that problem, it is important to note how narrow the area of dispute actually is.

First, there is virtual unanimity that when a lawyer has had substantial, personal participation in a matter while in public service, that lawyer should be disqualified from subsequently participating in the same matter on behalf of a private client.* Also, a lawyer in public service should not negotiate for private employment with a party or law firm whose interests the lawyer is able to affect.

There are several reasons for such rules. The present or former government attorney might be in a position to give one private party an unfair advantage over others through the favored use of confidential government information. There is also the possibility of favoritism to the former colleague on the part of lawyers still involved in the matter. The Association of the Bar of the City of New York has found "inevitable pressure" on government lawyers to show favoritism to private firms with whom they might later seek employment. Cases have also arisen in which there was an appearance of abuse of official power to create subsequent private employment for an attorney, or to give an attorney an advantage against a private party in subsequent private litigation.

---

* The reference to lawyers "in public service" includes judges and their law clerks; "matter" includes any judicial administrative, or other proceeding, application, request for a ruling or other determination, contract negotiation, claim, controversy, charge, accusation, arrest, or other particular matter.

A second principle on which there is general agreement is that of imputed disqualification. That is, when a lawyer is disqualified from representing a private client because of previous public service in the same matter, then that lawyer's partners and associates—those with whom the lawyer shares daily conversation and annual profits—should also be disqualified.

The narrow focus of disagreement has been whether the imputed disqualification of partners and associates should be subject to a waiver. A waiver would be based on a determination by the government agency involved that the disqualified attorney has been "screened" or "insulated" from any participation in the case. There are three major objections to the screening-waiver device, however, and none of them has been successfully answered.

The first unanswered objection is that no adequate standards for screening and granting waivers have been articulated: once we recognize that disqualification is appropriate, it is hardly sufficient to base a waiver on the mere assurance of the disqualified lawyers that they will not do anything improper.

The second unanswered objection is the virtual impossibility of policing violations once a waiver has been given.

Finally, the screening-waiver device compounds the initial conflict of interest by adding another. Agency lawyers who are called upon to grant or deny a waiver on behalf of a former colleague's law firm will have a substantial personal incentive to be generous in granting the waiver, because they will expect to make similar requests when they leave government service.

The principal argument in favor of permitting a screening-waiver device is that the government would find it impossible to hire competent lawyers if the screening-waiver exception is rejected, because lawyers would fear becoming unemployable. But if concern over the denial of waivers would indeed result in the unemployability of former government lawyers, that problem would prevail as long as there were any significant risk that waivers would be denied in particular cases. That is, unless the waiver device were a sham, and waivers were to be granted as a matter of course whenever requested, the asserted risks of hiring former government employees would still discourage law firms from employing them, and would thus discourage lawyers from entering government service.

In fact, however, no instance has ever been given of a government employee who would be rendered unemployable by the rejection of a waiver-screening exception. Unquestionably, a particular lawyer might have to forgo employment with a particular law firm, or even with three or four firms, but that is hardly the sweeping effect that has been projected by opponents of the ethical rule.

It should be emphasized, however, that these rules are not motivated by disapproval of the so-called revolving door between government service and private practice, but by the serious likelihood of professional impropriety inherent in the lawyer's switching from one side to the other.

In addition to dealing with the problem of the lawyer who switches sides in the same matter, these rules seek also to discourage the situation in which a lawyer is representing the government's interests and, at the same time, may be contemplating leaving government service and going to work for a party or a law firm whose interests the government lawyer is able to affect. Because it is easy for understandings of future employment to be reached without any realistic opportunity to discover or to prove that to have been the case, the Supplementary Provisions establish time bars to employment of former government lawyers by some parties and firms in some circumstances.

Illustrative Cases

9(a). A police officer tells a prosecutor that he is sure a cache of contraband can be found in a particular dwelling. The prosecutor learns, in questioning the officer, that the officer cannot substantiate his hunch with evidence sufficient to obtain a search warrant. The prosecutor does not tell the officer to invent a pretext for entering the premises and to seize the contraband, but says nothing when the officer says he is going to do so. The prosecutor has committed a disciplinary violation.

9(b). A lawyer with the Public Contracts Award Board is advising the Board regarding the award of a contract for widgets. The attorney for Multinational Widgets, Inc., discusses his client's proposal with the Board lawyer. During the discussion, the attorney comments to the Board lawyer that his firm is looking for young lawyers with the Board lawyer's background, and that the Board lawyer should be sure to see him if he decides to leave government service. The attorney for Multinational has committed a disciplinary violation.

9(c). The same facts as 9(b). The Board lawyer fails to report the Multinational lawyer's comment to the disciplinary board. The Board lawyer has committed a disciplinary violation.

SELECTED STANDARDS ON PROFESSIONALISM AND COURTESY

Table of Contents

AMERICAN BAR ASSOCIATION REPORT OF COMMISSION ON PROFESSIONALISM (1986)

(Selected sections)

[The report has been approved for distribution by the House of Delegates of the American Bar Association. However, the views expressed are those of the Commission on Professionalism. They have not been approved by the House of Delegates or the Board of Governors and, accordingly, should not be construed as representing the policy of the Association. Ed.]

* * * *

III. THE MEANING OF PROFESSIONALISM

"Professionalism" is an elastic concept the meaning and application of which are hard to pin down. That is perhaps as it should be. The term has a rich, long-standing heritage, and any single definition runs the risk of being too confining.

Yet the term is so important to lawyers that at least a working definition seems essential. Lawyers are proud of being part of one of the "historic" or "learned" professions, along with medicine and the clergy, which have been seen as professions through many centuries.

When he was asked to define a profession, Dean Roscoe Pound of Harvard Law School said:

The term refers to a group . . . pursuing a learned art as a common calling in the spirit of public service—no less a public service because it may incidentally be a means of livelihood.

Pursuit of the learned art in the spirit of a public service is the primary purpose.

The rhetoric may be dated, but the Commission believes the spirit of Dean Pound's definition stands the test of time. The practice of law "in the spirit of a public service" can and ought to be the hallmark of the legal profession.

More recently, others have identified some common elements which distinguish a profession from other occupations. Commission member Professor Eliot Freidson of New York University defines our profession as:

An occupation whose members have special privileges, such as exclusive licensing, that are justified by the following assumptions:

1. That its practice requires substantial intellectual training and the use of complex judgments.

2. That since clients cannot adequately evaluate the quality of the service, they must trust those they consult.

3. That the client's trust presupposes that the practitioner's self-interest is overbalanced by devotion to serving both the client's interest and the public good, and

4. That the occupation is self-regulating—that is, organized in such a way as to assure the public and the courts that its members are competent, do not violate their client's trust, and transcend their own self-interest.

Again, the Commission suggests that this list of elements is useful in thinking through the issues which follow.

Some may argue on the basis of the cases previously discussed that the legal profession is no longer "special." They might say that lawyers should treat their ideals as archaic, construe the rules of professional conduct as narrowly as possible, and try only to maximize their incomes. The Commission disagrees. Moreover, the testimony we have heard and the surveys we have examined indicate that the public wants the legal profession to maintain its long-held professional ideals. Indeed, the public should expect no less.

We have earlier described the diversity of the Bar, both in terms of demographics and areas of practice. One can properly ask whether any common ideas of professionalism can suffice for such a varied institution. We believe they can. While one must always be conscious of the variety within the legal profession, more unites than separates us.

* * *

The suggestions and conclusions which follow are grouped by the role to be played by each segment of the Bar. In discussing the practicing Bar, we want it to be clear that we are including in that category all lawyers—whether litigators or non-litigators, whether sole practitioners, members or employees of firms, government lawyers or lawyers employed by corporations, educational institutions or other entities.

It is our hope that the recommendations which follow will not be unobserved aspirations, but will represent concrete ways in which lawyers can inspire a rebirth of respect and confidence in themselves, in the services they provide and in the legal system itself. We believe that much can be done. Taken individually, the proposals may not appear substantial, but in the aggregate we believe they can have a significant impact. However, to be effective, they must have the support not only of every part of the legal community, but also of the citizens of this country—the public whose interests lawyers are to serve.

We first present a summary of our recommendations, and then a discussion of each.

IV. SUMMARY OF RECOMMENDATIONS

A. LAW SCHOOLS

1. Law schools should give continuing attention to the form and content of their courses in ethics and professionalism. They should weave ethical and professional issues into courses in both substantive and procedural fields. They should give serious consideration to supplementing courses in ethics and professionalism with a required summer reading list for entering students and with a film or videotape on ethics, along the lines discussed later in this report.

2. Law schools should expose students to promising new methods of dealing with legal problems. Thus, for example, consideration should be given to instruction in such matters as alternative methods of dispute resolution and processes of negotiation.

3. Deans and faculties of law schools should keep in mind that the law school experience provides a student's first exposure to the profession, and that professors inevitably serve as important role models for students. Therefore, the highest standards of ethics and professionalism should be adhered to within law schools.

4. Law schools should adopt codes of student conduct, possibly based on the Model Rules of Professional Conduct. They should report convictions of serious infractions of law school rules to the Character and Fitness Committees, or their equivalent, of states in which the student applies for admission to the Bar.

5. Law schools should retain high admission standards in the face of declining applications and should not lower their standards for graduation.

B. PRACTICING BAR AND BAR ASSOCIATIONS

1. Law firms should help their newly-admitted associates to face the practical and ethical issues which inevitably arise in practice. This can be done in a variety of ways, and small firms or sole practitioners should work together to sponsor programs to facilitate such training. Local bar associations and law schools should assist in such efforts.

2. In order to assure greater competence of practicing lawyers, continuing legal education courses should be strengthened and made mandatory. Where practical, some form of examination in courses taken should be required.

3. The Commission recommends that the American Bar Association prepare a series of six to eight films or videotapes dealing with ethical and professional issues. The tapes should effectively present a wide range of such issues and should use the Socratic approach so effectively used in the Columbia University Media & Society Seminar programs. If feasible, at least one such tape should be designed especially for use in law schools. The tapes also should be made available to state and local bar associations for use in mandatory continuing legal education programs.

4. False, fraudulent or misleading advertising is not constitutionally protected and should be referred to disciplinary authorities for action against offending lawyers. Appropriate measures short of disciplinary action should be considered. Such measures could include requiring an advertisement to contain warnings or disclaimers.

5. The Bar should place increasing emphasis on the role of lawyers as officers of the court, or more broadly, as officers of the system of justice. Lawyers should exercise independent judgment as to how to pursue legal matters. They have a duty to make the system of justice work properly. Ideally, clients should recognize this duty and appreciate the importance to society of maintaining the system of justice.

6. The Bar should study the issue of the participation of law firms and individual lawyers in business activities, certainly where either actual or potential conflicts of interest may be involved.

7. When not representing clients before legislative bodies, lawyers should put aside self-interest and should support legislation that is in the public interest. In addition, the Bar should urge legislative bodies to consider the consequences of proposed legislation on the courts. All too frequently, such legislation, when enacted, inundates the courts with cases never contemplated by the drafters.

8. Fees are a source of misunderstanding between many lawyers and their clients. Further, the amount of fees charged by lawyers in some instances results in bitter criticism of the Bar. The Commission suggests:

a. Fee arrangements between lawyers and their clients should be in writing, where feasible.

b. If, at the end of a lawyer's services in any matter, the client believes that the fee charged was inappropriate, the client should be able to have the matter reviewed by an impartial fee review committee, possibly appointed by the state Supreme Court. All such committees or entities should include lay members.

9. Lawyers and judges should report to the appropriate disciplinary committee or prosecuting attorney any serious misconduct on the part of other lawyers and judges which they believe would support a complaint for discipline or criminal charges.

10. Bar associations should be constantly alert to seek improvements in the system of justice. This should embrace such activities as supporting an expanded use of alternative methods of dispute resolution.

C. JUDGES

1. Trial judges should take a more active role in the conduct of litigation. They should see that cases advance promptly, fairly and without abuse. Granting increased authority to judges runs the risk of arbitrary behavior on their part, but reviewing courts should provide whatever counterbalance is needed.

2. Judges should impose sanctions for abuse of the litigation process. Currently, the Federal Rules of Civil Procedure permit the imposition of sanctions for such abuses, and increasing use is being made of the sanctions to penalize the lawyer or the client, or both. In many state systems, the Supreme Courts have not promulgated such rules. State Supreme Courts should adopt rules similar to Rule 11 of the Federal Rules, so that authority to act is clearly given to trial judges.

3. Merit selection should be the means by which judges are chosen. The Commission believes that a bench of the quality that merit selection can provide is essential to improve our system of justice.

4. State disciplinary agencies under the control of state supreme courts are, in general, insufficiently funded and staffed. They now cannot do much more than deal with charges of theft, neglect or the commission of a felony. Adequate funding should be made available to the disciplinary agencies, enabling them to do a thorough and competent job in pursuing the full range of offenses which occur.

5. State supreme courts control admission to the Bar. They often charge character and fitness committees or their equivalent with the responsibility of reviewing the qualifications of applicants. Adequate funding and authority should be provided to such committees so that they can do a thorough job of investigation.

D. IN GENERAL

All segments of the Bar should:

1. Preserve and develop within the profession integrity, competence, fairness, independence, courage and a devotion to the public interest.

2. Resolve to abide by higher standards of conduct than the minimum required by the Code of Professional Responsibility and the Model Rules of Professional Conduct.

3. Increase the participation of lawyers in *pro bono* activities and help lawyers recognize their obligation to participate.

4. Resist the temptation to make the acquisition of wealth a primary goal of law practice.

5. Encourage innovative methods which simplify and make less expensive the rendering of legal services.

6. Educate the public about legal processes and the legal system.

7. Resolve to employ all the organizational resources necessary in order to assure that the legal profession is effectively self-regulating.

* * *

AMERICAN BAR ASSOCIATION
A LAWYER'S CREED OF PROFESSIONALISM

On August 9th, 1988, the American Bar Association House of Delegates adopted the following resolutions regarding so-called "Codes of Courtesy."

BE IT RESOLVED that the American Bar Association recommends to state and local bar associations that they encourage their members to accept as a guide for their individual conduct, and to comply with, a lawyer's creed of professionalism.

BE IT FURTHER RESOLVED that nothing contained in such a creed shall be deemed to supersede or in any way amend the Model Rules of Professional Conduct or other disciplinary codes, alter existing standards of conduct against which lawyer negligence might be judged or become a basis for the imposition of civil penalty of any kind.

Following is a proposed example of "A Lawyer's Creed of Professionalism."

Preamble

As a lawyer I must strive to make our system of justice work fairly and efficiently. In order to carry out that responsibility, not only will I comply with the letter and spirit of the disciplinary standards applicable to all lawyers, but I will also conduct myself in accordance with the following Creed of Professionalism when dealing with my client, opposing parties, their counsel, the courts and the general public.

A. **With respect to my client:**

1. I will be loyal and committed to my client's cause, but I will not permit that loyalty and commitment to interfere with my ability to provide my client with objective and independent advice;

2. I will endeavor to achieve my client's lawful objectives in business transactions and in litigation as expeditiously and economically as possible;

3. In appropriate cases, I will counsel my client with respect to mediation, arbitration and other alternative methods of resolving disputes;

4. I will advise my client against pursuing litigation (or any other course of action) that is without merit and against insisting on tactics which are intended to delay resolution of the matter or to harass or drain the financial resources of the opposing party;

5. I will advise my client that civility and courtesy are not to be equated with weakness;

6. While I must abide by my client's decision concerning the objectives of the representation, I nevertheless will counsel my client that a willingness to initiate or engage in settlement discussions is consistent with zealous and effective representation.

B. **With respect to opposing parties and their counsel:**

1. I will endeavor to be courteous and civil, both in oral and in written communications;

2. I will not knowingly make statements of fact or of law that are untrue;

3. In litigation proceedings I will agree to reasonable requests for extensions of time or for waiver of procedural formalities when the legitimate interests of my client will not be adversely affected;

4. I will endeavor to consult with opposing counsel before scheduling depositions and meetings and before re-scheduling hear-

ings, and I will cooperate with opposing counsel when scheduling changes are requested;

5. I will refrain from utilizing litigation or any other course of conduct to harass the opposing party;

6. I will refrain from engaging in excessive and abusive discovery, and I will comply with all reasonable discovery requests;

7. I will refrain from utilizing delaying tactics;

8. In depositions and other proceedings, and in negotiations, I will conduct myself with dignity, avoid making groundless objections and refrain from engaging in acts of rudeness or disrespect;

9. I will not serve motions and pleadings on the other party, or his counsel, at such a time or in such a manner as will unfairly limit the other party's opportunity to respond;

10. In business transactions I will not quarrel over matters of form or style, but will concentrate on matters of substance and content;

11. I will clearly identify, for other counsel or parties, all changes that I have made in documents submitted to me for review.

C. **With respect to the courts and other tribunals:**

1. I will be a vigorous and zealous advocate on behalf of my client, while recognizing, as an officer of the court, that excessive zeal may be detrimental to my client's interests as well as to the proper functioning of our system of justice;

2. Where consistent with my client's interests, I will communicate with opposing counsel in an effort to avoid litigation and to resolve litigation that has actually commenced;

3. I will voluntarily withdraw claims or defenses when it becomes apparent that they do not have merit or are superfluous;

4. I will refrain from filing frivolous motions;

5. I will make every effort to agree with other counsel, as early as possible, on a voluntary exchange of information and on a plan for discovery;

6. I will attempt to resolve, by agreement, my objections to matters contained in my opponent's pleadings and discovery requests;

7. When scheduled hearings or depositions have to be cancelled, I will notify opposing counsel, and, if appropriate, the court (or other tribunal) as early as possible;

8. Before dates for hearings or trials are set—or, if that is not feasible, immediately after such dates have been set—I will attempt to verify the availability of key participants and wit-

nesses so that I can promptly notify the court (or other tribunal) and opposing counsel of any likely problem in that regard;

9. In civil matters, I will stipulate to facts as to which there is no genuine dispute;

10. I will endeavor to be punctual in attending court hearings, conferences and depositions;

11. I will at all times be candid with the court.

D. With respect to the public and to our system of justice:

1. I will remember that, in addition to commitment to my client's cause, my responsibilities as a lawyer include a devotion to the public good;

2. I will endeavor to keep myself current in the areas in which I practice and, when necessary, will associate with, or refer my client to, counsel knowledgeable in another field of practice;

3. I will be mindful of the fact that, as a member of a self-regulating profession, it is incumbent on me to report violations by fellow lawyers of any disciplinary rule;

4. I will be mindful of the need to protect the image of the legal profession in the eyes of the public and will be so guided when considering methods and contents of advertising;

5. I will be mindful that the law is a learned profession and that among its desirable goals are devotion to public service, improvement of administration of justice, and the contribution of uncompensated time and civic influence on behalf of those persons who cannot afford adequate legal assistance.

AMERICAN BAR ASSOCIATION LAWYER'S PLEDGE OF PROFESSIONALISM

I will remember that the practice of law is first and foremost a profession, and I will subordinate business concerns to professionalism concerns.

I will encourage respect for the law and our legal system through my words and actions.

I will remember my responsibilities to serve as an officer of the court and protector of individual rights.

I will contribute time and resources to public service, public education, charitable, and *pro bono* activities in my community.

I will work with the other participants in the legal system, including judges, opposing counsel and those whose practices are different from mine, to make our legal system more accessible and responsive.

I will resolve matters expeditiously and without unnecessary expense.

I will resolve disputes through negotiation whenever possible.

I will keep my clients well-informed and involved in making the decisions that affect them.

I will continue to expand my knowledge of the law.

I will achieve and maintain proficiency in my practice.

I will be courteous to those with whom I come into contact during the course of my work.

I will honor the spirit and intent, as well as the requirements, of the applicable rules or code of professional conduct for my jurisdiction, and will encourage others to do the same.

AMERICAN BAR ASSOCIATION ASPIRATIONAL GOALS ON LAWYER ADVERTISING

Preamble

During the past decade, the courts have sought to define the nature and extent of permissible advertising by lawyers. In a series of decisions, the U.S. Supreme Court has held that lawyer advertising which is not false or misleading is commercial speech entitled to protection under the First Amendment of the U.S. Constitution.

Pending further clarification by the courts, some advertising practices exist which may be detrimental. Some forms of advertising may adversely affect public perceptions about the justice system itself. For example, empirical evidence suggests that undignified advertising can detract from the public's confidence in the legal profession and respect for the justice system.

Under present case law, the matter of dignity is widely believed to be so subjective as to be beyond the scope of constitutionally permitted regulation. Nevertheless, it seems entirely proper for the organized bar to suggest non-binding aspirational goals urging lawyers who wish to advertise to do so in a dignified manner. Although only aspirational, such goals must be scrupulously sensitive to fundamental constitutional rights of lawyers and the needs of the public.

It is the role and responsibility of lawyers to provide legal services to the public. It has been demonstrated by responsible studies that people sometimes do not receive needed legal services, either because they are unaware of available services, don't understand how they can benefit from those services or don't understand how to obtain them. Therefore, it is also the legal profession's responsibility to inform the public about the availability of legal services and how to obtain and use them.

Advertising is one of many methods by which lawyers can inform the public about legal services. Although most people find a lawyer through word-of-mouth networks of family, friends and work associates, when properly done, advertising can help people to better understand the legal services available to them and how to obtain those services.

When properly done, advertising can also be a productive way for lawyers to build and maintain their client bases. Advertising and other forms of marketing can enable lawyers to attain efficiencies of scale which may help make legal services more affordable. As the Supreme Court pointed out in *Bates v. State Bar of Arizona*, 433 U.S. 350, 377 (1977), it is "entirely possible that advertising will serve to reduce, not advance, the cost of legal services to the consumer."

Lawyers are at all times officers of the court, and as such, they have a special obligation to assure that their conduct conforms to the highest ideals of the legal profession. Thus, lawyers who advertise should be mindful not only of the effect their advertising may have on their own professional image but also of the effect it may have on the public's overall perception of the judicial system.

If lawyer advertising avoids false, misleading or deceptive representations, or coercive or misleading solicitation, it advances the goal of bringing needed legal services to more people than are now being served.

However, when advertising though not false, misleading or deceptive degenerates into undignified and unprofessional presentations, the public is not served, the lawyer who advertised does not benefit and the image of the judicial system may be harmed.

Accordingly, lawyer advertising should exemplify the inherent dignity and professionalism of the legal community. Dignified lawyer advertising tends to inspire public confidence in the professional competence and ability of lawyers and portrays the commitment of lawyers to serve clients' legal needs in accordance with the ethics and public service tradition of a learned profession.

Lawyer advertising is a key facet of the marketing and delivery of legal services to the public. The professional conduct rules for lawyers adopted by the states regulate some aspects of lawyer advertising, but they also leave lawyers much latitude to decide how to advertise. The following Aspirational Goals are presented in an effort to suggest how lawyers can achieve the beneficial goals of advertising while minimizing or eliminating altogether its negative implications.

These aspirational goals are not intended to establish mandatory requirements which might form the basis for disciplinary enforcement. Rules of Professional Conduct and Disciplinary Rules of Codes of Professional Responsibility in effect in all jurisdictions establish the standards which all lawyers who advertise must meet. Rather, these aspirational goals are intended to provide suggested objectives which all lawyers who engage in advertising their services should be encouraged to achieve in order that lawyer advertising may be more effective and reflect the professionalism of the legal community.

Aspirational Goals

1. Lawyer advertising should encourage and support the public's confidence in the individual lawyer's competence and integrity as well as the commitment of the legal profession to serve the public's legal needs in the tradition of the law as a learned profession.

2. Since advertising may be the only contact many people have with lawyers, advertising by lawyers should help the public understand its legal rights and the judicial process and should uphold the dignity of the legal profession.

3. While "dignity" and "good taste" are terms open to subjective interpretation, lawyers should consider that advertising which reflects the ideals stated in these Aspirational Goals is likely to be dignified and suitable to the profession.

4. Since advertising must be truthful and accurate, and not false or misleading, lawyers should realize that ambiguous or confusing advertising can be misleading.

5. Particular care should be taken in describing fees and costs in advertisements. If an advertisement states a specific fee for a particular service, it should make clear whether or not all problems of that type can be handled for that specific fee. Similar care should be taken in describing the lawyer's areas of practice.

6. Lawyers should consider that the use of inappropriately dramatic music, unseemly slogans, hawkish spokespersons, premium offers, slapstick routines or outlandish settings in advertising does not instill confidence in the lawyer or the legal profession and undermines the serious purpose of legal services and the judicial system.

7. Advertising developed with a clear identification of its potential audience is more likely to be understandable, respectful and appropriate to that audience, and, therefore, more effective. Lawyers should consider using advertising and marketing professionals to assist in identifying and reaching an appropriate audience.

8. How advertising conveys its message is as important as the message itself. Again, lawyers should consider using professional consultants to help them develop and present a clear message to the audience in an effective and appropriate way.

9. Lawyers should design their advertising to attract legal matters which they are competent to handle.

10. Lawyers should be concerned with making legal services more affordable to the public. Lawyer advertising may be designed to build

up client bases so that efficiencies of scale may be achieved that will translate into more affordable legal services.

THE TEXAS LAWYER'S CREED—
A MANDATE FOR PROFESSIONALISM

promulgated by the Supreme Court of Texas and the
Texas Court of Criminal Appeals (1989)

I am a lawyer; I am entrusted by the People of Texas to preserve and improve our legal system. I am licensed by the Supreme Court of Texas. I must therefore abide by the Texas Disciplinary Rules of Professional Conduct, but I know that Professionalism requires more than merely avoiding the violation of laws and rules. I am committed to this Creed for no other reason than it is right.

I. OUR LEGAL SYSTEM

A lawyer owes to the administration of justice personal dignity, integrity, and independence. A lawyer should always adhere to the highest principles of professionalism.

1. I am passionately proud of my profession. Therefore, "My word is my bond."

2. I am responsible to assure that all persons have access to competent representation regardless of wealth or position in life.

3. I commit myself to an adequate and effective pro bono program.

4. I am obligated to educate my clients, the public, and other lawyers regarding the spirit and letter of this Creed.

5. I will always be conscious of my duty to the judicial system.

II. LAWYER TO CLIENT

A lawyer owes to a client allegiance, learning, skill, and industry. A lawyer shall employ all appropriate means to protect and advance the client's legitimate rights, claims, and objectives. A lawyer shall not be deterred by any real or imagined fear of judicial disfavor or public unpopularity, nor be influenced by mere self-interest.

1. I will advise my client of the contents of this Creed when undertaking representation.

2. I will endeavor to achieve my client's lawful objectives in legal transactions and in litigation as quickly and economically as possible.

3. I will be loyal and committed to my client's lawful objectives, but I will not permit that loyalty and commitment to interfere with my duty to provide objective and independent advice.

4. I will advise my client that civility and courtesy are expected and are not a sign of weakness.

5. I will advise my client of proper and expected behavior.

6. I will treat adverse parties and witnesses with fairness and due consideration. A client has no right to demand that I abuse anyone or indulge in any offensive conduct.

7. I will advise my client that we will not pursue conduct which is intended primarily to harass or drain the financial resources of the opposing party.

8. I will advise my client that we will not pursue tactics which are intended primarily for delay.

9. I will advise my client that we will not pursue any course of action which is without merit.

10. I will advise my client that I reserve the right to determine whether to grant accommodations to opposing counsel in all matters that do not adversely affect my client's lawful objectives. A client has no right to instruct me to refuse reasonable requests made by other counsel.

11. I will advise my client regarding the availability of mediation, arbitration, and other alternative methods of resolving and settling disputes.

III. LAWYER TO LAWYER

A lawyer owes to opposing counsel, in the conduct of legal transactions and the pursuit of litigation, courtesy, candor, cooperation, and scrupulous observance of all agreements and mutual understandings. Ill feelings between clients shall not influence a lawyer's conduct, attitude, or demeanor toward opposing counsel. A lawyer shall not engage in unprofessional conduct in retaliation against other unprofessional conduct.

1. I will be courteous, civil, and prompt in oral and written communications.

2. I will not quarrel over matters of form or style, but I will concentrate on matters of substance.

3. I will identify for other counsel or parties all changes I have made in documents submitted for review.

4. I will attempt to prepare documents which correctly reflect the agreement of the parties. I will not include provisions which have not been agreed upon or omit provisions which are necessary to reflect the agreement of the parties.

5. I will notify opposing counsel, and, if appropriate, the Court or other persons, as soon as practicable, when hearings, depositions, meetings, conferences or closings are cancelled.

6. I will agree to reasonable requests for extensions of time and for waiver of procedural formalities, provided legitimate objectives of my client will not be adversely affected.

7. I will not serve motions or pleadings in any manner that unfairly limits another party's opportunity to respond.

8. I will attempt to resolve by agreement my objections to matters contained in pleadings and discovery requests and responses.

9. I can disagree without being disagreeable. I recognize that effective representation does not require antagonistic or obnoxious behavior. I will neither encourage nor knowingly permit my client or anyone under my control to do anything which would be unethical or improper if done by me.

10. I will not, without good cause, attribute bad motives or unethical conduct to opposing counsel nor bring the profession into disrepute by unfounded accusations of impropriety. I will avoid disparaging personal remarks or acrimony towards opposing counsel, parties and witnesses. I will not be influenced by any ill feeling between clients. I will abstain from any allusion to personal peculiarities or idiosyncrasies of opposing counsel.

11. I will not take advantage, by causing any default or dismissal to be rendered, when I know the identity of an opposing counsel, without first inquiring about that counsel's intention to proceed.

12. I will promptly submit orders to the Court. I will deliver copies to opposing counsel before or contemporaneously with submission to the Court. I will promptly approve the form of orders which accurately reflect the substance of the rulings of the Court.

13. I will not attempt to gain an unfair advantage by sending the Court or its staff correspondence or copies of correspondence.

14. I will not arbitrarily schedule a deposition, Court appearance, or hearing until a good faith effort has been made to schedule it by agreement.

15. I will readily stipulate to undisputed facts in order to avoid needless costs or inconvenience for any party.

16. I will refrain from excessive and abusive discovery.

17. I will comply with all reasonable discovery requests. I will not resist discovery requests which are not objectionable. I will not make objections nor give instructions to a witness for the purpose of delaying or obstructing the discovery process. I will encourage witnesses to respond to all deposition questions which are reasonably understandable. I will neither encourage nor permit my witness to quibble about words where their meaning is reasonably clear.

18. I will not seek Court intervention to obtain discovery which is clearly improper and not discoverable.

19. I will not seek sanctions or disqualification unless it is necessary for protection of my client's lawful objectives or is fully justified by the circumstances.

IV. LAWYER AND JUDGE

Lawyers and judges owe each other respect, diligence, candor, punctuality, and protection against unjust and improper criticism and attack. Lawyers and judges are equally responsible to protect the dignity and independence of the Court and the profession.

1. I will always recognize that the position of judge is the symbol of both the judicial system and administration of justice. I will refrain from conduct that degrades this symbol.

2. I will conduct myself in Court in a professional manner and demonstrate my respect for the Court and the law.

3. I will treat counsel, opposing parties, the Court, and members of the Court staff with courtesy and civility.

4. I will be punctual.

5. I will not engage in any conduct which offends the dignity and decorum of proceedings.

6. I will not knowingly misrepresent, mischaracterize, misquote or miscite facts or authorities to gain an advantage.

7. I will respect the rulings of the Court.

8. I will give the issues in controversy deliberate, impartial and studied analysis and consideration.

9. I will be considerate of the time constraints and pressures imposed upon the Court, Court staff and counsel in efforts to administer justice and resolve disputes.

*

PART TWO

STATUTES AND RULES OF EVIDENCE AND PROCEDURE THAT AFFECT THE LEGAL PROFESSION

Table of Contents

Introduction

Until recently, most courses and casebooks in professional responsibility focused solely on the ABA's model codes of conduct. However, the law which governs and regulates the conduct of lawyers must go far beyond the ABA's pronouncements. One other source of law which affects lawyers' conduct must include federal statutes, rules of evidence, procedure, and court. This part includes statutes and rules of evidence and procedure which affect the practice of law.

SELECTED FEDERAL STATUTES

5 U.S.C.A.

CHAPTER 73. SUITABILITY, SECURITY, AND CONDUCT

18 U.S.C.A.

CHAPTER 11. BRIBERY AND GRAFT

CHAPTER 21. CONTEMPTS

CHAPTER 49. FUGITIVES FROM JUSTICE

CHAPTER 63. MAIL FRAUD

CHAPTER 73. OBSTRUCTION OF JUSTICE

---

5 U.S.C.A.

CHAPTER 73. SUITABILITY, SECURITY, AND CONDUCT

§ 7301. Presidential Regulations

* * *

Executive Order No. 12674: Principles of Ethical Conduct for Government Officers and Employees

"By virtue of the authority vested in me as President by the Constitution and the laws of the United States of America, and in order to establish fair and exacting standards of ethical conduct for all executive branch employees, it is hereby ordered as follows:

Part I—Principles Of Ethical Conduct

Section 101. Principles of Ethical Conduct. To ensure that every citizen can have complete confidence in the integrity of the Federal Government, each Federal employee shall respect and adhere to the fundamental principles of ethical service as implemented in regulations promulgated under sections 201 and 301 of this order:

"(a) Public service is a public trust, requiring employees to place loyalty to the Constitution, the laws, and ethical principles above private gain.

"(b) Employees shall not hold financial interests that conflict with the conscientious performance of duty.

"(c) Employees shall not engage in financial transactions using nonpublic Government information or allow the improper use of such information to further any private interest.

"(d) An employee shall not, except pursuant to such reasonable exceptions as are provided by regulation, solicit or accept any gift or other item of monetary value from any person or entity seeking official action from, doing business with, or conducting activities regulated by the employee's agency, or whose interests may be substantially affected by the performance or nonperformance of the employee's duties.

"(e) Employees shall put forth honest effort in the performance of their duties.

"(f) Employees shall make no unauthorized commitments or promises of any kind purporting to bind the Government.

"(g) Employees shall not use public office for private gain.

"(h) Employees shall act impartially and not give preferential treatment to any private organization or individual.

"(i) Employees shall protect and conserve Federal property and shall not use it for other than authorized activities.

"(j) Employees shall not engage in outside employment or activities, including seeking or negotiating for employment, that conflict with official Government duties and responsibilities.

"(k) Employees shall disclose waste, fraud, abuse, and corruption to appropriate authorities.

"(l) Employees shall satisfy in good faith their obligations as citizens, including all just financial obligations, especially those—such as Federal, State, or local taxes—that are imposed by law.

"(m) Employees shall adhere to all laws and regulations that provide equal opportunity for all Americans regardless of race, color, religion, sex, national origin, age, or handicap.

"**(n)** Employees shall endeavor to avoid any actions creating the appearance that they are violating the law or the ethical standards promulgated pursuant to this order.

"**Sec. 102. Limitations on Outside Earned Income.**

"**(a)** No employee who is appointed by the President to a full-time noncareer position in the executive branch (including full-time noncareer employees in the White House Office, the Office of Policy Development, and the Office of Cabinet Affairs), shall receive any earned income for any outside employment or activity performed during that Presidential appointment.

"**(b)** The prohibition set forth in subsection (a) shall not apply to any full-time noncareer employees employed pursuant to 3 U.S.C. 105 [section 105 of Title 3, The President] and 3 U.S.C. 107(a) [section 107(a) of Title 3] at salaries below the minimum rate of basic pay then paid for GS–9 of the General Schedule. Any outside employment must comply with relevant agency standards of conduct, including any requirements for approval of outside employment.

"**Part II—Office Of Government Ethics Authority**

"**Sec. 201. The Office of Government Ethics.** The Office of Government Ethics shall be responsible for administering this order by:

"**(a)** Promulgating, in consultation with the Attorney General and the Office of Personnel Management, regulations that establish a single, comprehensive, and clear set of executive-branch standards of conduct that shall be objective, reasonable, and enforceable.

"**(b)** Developing, disseminating, and periodically updating an ethics manual for employees of the executive branch describing the applicable statutes, rules, decisions, and policies.

"**(c)** Promulgating, with the concurrence of the Attorney General, regulations interpreting the provisions of the post-employment statute, section 207 of title 18, United States Code [section 207 of Title 18, Crimes and Criminal Procedure]; the general conflict-of-interest statute, section 208 of title 18, United States Code [section 208 of Title 18]; and the statute prohibiting supplementation of salaries, section 209 of title 18, United States Code [section 209 of Title 18].

"**(d)** Promulgating, in consultation with the Attorney General and the Office of Personnel Management, regulations establishing a system of nonpublic (confidential) financial disclosure by executive branch employees to complement the system of public disclosure under the Ethics in Government Act of 1978. Such regulations shall include criteria to guide agencies in determining which employees shall submit these reports.

"**(e)** Ensuring that any implementing regulations issued by agencies under this order are consistent with and promulgated in accordance with this order.

"**Sec. 202. Executive Office of the President.** In that the agencies within the Executive Office of the President (EOP) currently exercise functions that are not distinct and separate from each other within the meaning and for the purposes of section 207(e) of title 18, United States Code [section 207(e) of Title 18], those agencies shall be treated as one agency under section 207(c) of title 18, United States Code [section 207(c) of Title 18].

"Part III—Agency Responsibilities

"**Sec. 301. Agency Responsibilities.** Each agency head is directed to:

"**(a)** Supplement, as necessary and appropriate, the comprehensive executive branch-wide regulations of the Office of Government Ethics, with regulations of special applicability to the particular functions and activities of that agency. Any supplementary agency regulations shall be prepared as addenda to the branch-wide regulations and promulgated jointly with the Office of Government Ethics, at the agency's expense, for inclusion in Title 5 of the Code of Federal Regulations.

"**(b)** Ensure the review by all employees of this order and regulations promulgated pursuant to the order.

"**(c)** Coordinate with the Office of Government Ethics in developing annual agency ethics training plans. Such training shall include mandatory annual briefings on ethics and standards of conduct for all employees appointed by the President, all employees in the Executive Office of the President, all officials required to file public or nonpublic financial disclosure reports, all employees who are contracting officers and procurement officials, and any other employees designated by the agency head.

"**(d)** Where practicable, consult formally or informally with the Office of Government Ethics prior to granting any exemption under section 208 of title 18, United States Code [section 208 of Title 18], and provide the Director of the Office of Government Ethics a copy of any exemption granted.

"**(e)** Ensure that the rank, responsibilities, authority, staffing, and resources of the Designated Agency Ethics Official are sufficient to ensure the effectiveness of the agency ethics program. Support should include the provision of a separate budget line item for ethics activities, where practicable.

* * *

18 U.S.C.A.

CHAPTER 11. BRIBERY AND GRAFT

§ 201. Bribery of public officials and witnesses

(a) For the purpose of this section—

(1) the term "public official" means Member of Congress, Delegate, or Resident Commissioner, either before or after such official has qualified, or an officer or employee or person acting for or on behalf of the United States, or any department, agency or branch of Government thereof, including the District of Columbia, in any official function, under or by authority of any such department, agency, or branch of Government, or a juror;

(2) the term "person who has been selected to be a public official" means any person who has been nominated or appointed to be a public official, or has been officially informed that such person will be so nominated or appointed; and

(3) the term "official act" means any decision or action on any question, matter, cause, suit, proceeding or controversy, which may at any time be pending, or which may by law be brought before any public official, in such official's official capacity, or in such official's place of trust or profit.

(b) Whoever—

(1) directly or indirectly, corruptly gives, offers or promises anything of value to any public official or person who has been selected to be a public official, or offers or promises any public official or any person who has been selected to be a public official to give anything of value to any other person or entity, with intent—

(A) to influence any official act; or

(B) to influence such public official or person who has been selected to be a public official to commit or aid in committing, or collude in, or allow, any fraud, or make opportunity for the commission of any fraud, on the United States; or

(C) to induce such public official or such person who has been selected to be a public official to do or omit to do any act in violation of the lawful duty of such official or person;

(2) being a public official or person selected to be a public official, directly or indirectly, corruptly demands, seeks, receives, accepts, or agrees to receive or accept anything of value personally or for any other person or entity, in return for:

(A) being influenced in the performance of any official act;

(B) being influenced to commit or aid in committing, or to collude in, or allow, any fraud, or make opportunity for the commission of any fraud, on the United States; or

(C) being induced to do or omit to do any act in violation of the official duty of such official or person;

(3) directly or indirectly, corruptly gives, offers, or promises anything of value to any person, or offers or promises such person to give anything of value to any other person or entity, with intent to influence the testimony under oath or affirmation of such first-mentioned person as a witness upon a trial, hearing, or other proceeding, before any court, any committee of either House or both Houses of Congress, or any agency, commission, or officer authorized by the laws of the United States to hear evidence or take testimony, or with intent to influence such person to absent himself therefrom;

(4) directly or indirectly, corruptly demands, seeks, receives, accepts, or agrees to receive or accept anything of value personally or for any other person or entity in return for being influenced in testimony under oath or affirmation as a witness upon any such trial, hearing, or other proceeding, or in return for absenting himself therefrom;

shall be fined not more than three times the monetary equivalent of the thing of value, or imprisoned for not more than fifteen years, or both, and may be disqualified from holding any office of honor, trust, or profit under the United States.

(c) Whoever—

(1) otherwise than as provided by law for the proper discharge of official duty—

(A) directly or indirectly gives, offers, or promises anything of value to any public official, former public official, or person selected to be a public official, for or because of any official act performed or to be performed by such public official, former public official, or person selected to be a public official; or

(B) being a public official, former public official, or person selected to be a public official, otherwise than as provided by law for the proper discharge of official duty, directly or indirectly demands, seeks, receives, accepts, or agrees to receive or accept anything of value personally for or because of any official act performed or to be performed by such official or person;

(2) directly or indirectly, gives, offers, or promises anything of value to any person, for or because of the testimony under oath or affirmation given or to be given by such person as a witness upon a trial, hearing, or other proceeding, before any court, any committee

of either House or both Houses of Congress, or any agency, commission, or officer authorized by the laws of the United States to hear evidence or take testimony, or for or because of such person's absence therefrom;

(3) directly or indirectly demands, seeks, receives, accepts, or agrees to receive or accept anything of value personally for or because of the testimony under oath or affirmation given or to be given by such person as a witness upon any such trial, hearing, or other proceeding, or for or because of such person's absence therefrom;

shall be fined under this title or imprisoned for not more than two years, or both.

(d) Paragraphs (3) and (4) of subsection (b) and paragraphs (2) and (3) of subsection (c) shall not be construed to prohibit the payment or receipt of witness fees provided by law, or the payment, by the party upon whose behalf a witness is called and receipt by a witness, of the reasonable cost of travel and subsistence incurred and the reasonable value of time lost in attendance at any such trial, hearing, or proceeding, or in the case of expert witnesses, a reasonable fee for time spent in the preparation of such opinion, and in appearing and testifying.

(e) The offenses and penalties prescribed in this section are separate from and in addition to those prescribed in sections 1503, 1504, and 1505 of this title.

§ 202. Definitions

(a) For the purpose of sections 203, 205, 207, 208, and 209 of this title the term "special Government employee" shall mean an officer or employee of the executive or legislative branch of the United States Government, of any independent agency of the United States or of the District of Columbia, who is retained, designated, appointed, or employed to perform, with or without compensation, for not to exceed one hundred and thirty days during any period of three hundred and sixty-five consecutive days, temporary duties either on a full-time or intermittent basis, a part-time United States commissioner, a part-time United States magistrate, or, regardless of the number of days of appointment, an independent counsel appointed under chapter 40 of title 28 and any person appointed by that independent counsel under section 594(c) of title 28. Notwithstanding the next preceding sentence, every person serving as a part-time local representative of a Member of Congress in the Member's home district or State shall be classified as a special Government employee. . . .

(b) For the purposes of sections 205 and 207 of this title, the term "official responsibility" means the direct administrative or operating authority, whether intermediate or final, and either exercisable alone or with others, and either personally or through subordinates, to approve, disapprove, or otherwise direct Government action.

(c) Except as otherwise provided in such sections, the terms "officer" and "employee" in sections 203, 205, 207 through 209 and 218 of this title, mean those individuals defined in sections 2104 and 2105 of title 5. The terms "officer" and "employee" shall not include the President, the Vice President, a Member of Congress, or a Federal judge.

(d) The term "Member of Congress" in sections 204 and 207 means—

(1) a United States Senator; and

(2) a Representative in, or a Delegate or Resident Commissioner to, the House of Representatives.

(e) As used in this chapter, the term—

(1) "executive branch" includes each executive agency as defined in title 5, and any other entity or administrative unit in the executive branch;

(2) "judicial branch" means the Supreme Court of the United States; the United States courts of appeals; the United States district courts; the Court of International Trade; the United States bankruptcy courts; any court created pursuant to article I of the United States Constitution, including the Court of Military Appeals, the United States Claims Court, and the United States Tax Court, but not including a court of a territory or possession of the United States; the Federal Judicial Center; and any other agency, office, or entity in the judicial branch; and

(3) "legislative branch" means—

(A) the Congress; and

(B) the Office of the Architect of the Capitol, the United States Botanic Garden, the General Accounting Office, the Government Printing Office, the Library of Congress, the Office of Technology Assessment, the Congressional Budget Office, the United States Capitol Police, and any other agency, entity, office, or commission established in the legislative branch.

§ 203. Compensation to Members of Congress, officers, and others in matters affecting the Government

(a) Whoever, otherwise than as provided by law for the proper discharge of official duties, directly or indirectly—

(1) demands, seeks, receives, accepts, or agrees to receive or accept any compensation for any representational services, as agent or attorney or otherwise, rendered or to be rendered either personally or by another—

(A) at a time when such person is a Member of Congress, Member of Congress Elect, Delegate, Delegate Elect, Resident Commissioner, or Resident Commissioner Elect; or

(B) at a time when such person is an officer or employee or Federal Judge of the United States in the executive, legislative, or judicial branch of the Government, or

in any agency of the United States, in relation to any proceeding, application, request for a ruling or other determination, contract, claim, controversy, charge, accusation, arrest, or other particular matter in which the United States is a party or has a direct and substantial interest, before any department, agency, court, court-martial, officer, or any civil, military, or naval commission; or

(2) knowingly gives, promises, or offers any compensation for any such representational services rendered or to be rendered at a time when the person to whom the compensation is given, promised, or offered, is or was such a Member, Member Elect, Delegate, Delegate Elect, Commissioner, Commissioner Elect, Federal Judge, officer, or employee;

shall be subject to the penalties set forth in section 216 of this title.

(b) Whoever, otherwise than as provided by law for the proper discharge of official duties, directly or indirectly—

(1) demands, seeks, receives, accepts, or agrees to receive or accept any compensation for any representational services, as agent or attorney or otherwise, rendered or to be rendered either personally or by another, at a time when such person is an officer or employee of the District of Columbia, in relation to any proceeding, application, request for a ruling or other determination, contract, claim, controversy, charge, accusation, arrest, or other particular matter in which the District of Columbia is a party or has a direct and substantial interest, before any department, agency, court, officer, or commission; or

(2) knowingly gives, promises, or offers any compensation for any such representational services rendered or to be rendered at a time when the person to whom the compensation is given, promised, or offered, is or was an officer or employee of the District of Columbia;

shall be subject to the penalties set forth in section 216 of this title; and

(c) A special Government employee shall be subject to subsections (a) and (b) only in relation to a particular matter involving a specific party or parties—

(1) in which such employee has at any time participated personally and substantially as a Government employee or as a special Government employee or as a special Government employee

through decision, approval, disapproval, recommendation, the rendering of advice, investigation or otherwise; or

(2) which is pending in the department or agency of the Government in which such employee is serving except that paragraph (2) of this subsection shall not apply in the case of a special Government employee who has served in such department or agency no more than sixty days during the immediately preceding period of three hundred and sixty-five consecutive days.

(d) Nothing in this section prevents an officer or employee, including a special Government employee, from acting, with or without compensation, as agent or attorney for or otherwise representing his parents, spouse, child, or any person for whom, or for any estate for which, he is serving as guardian, executor, administrator, trustee, or other personal fiduciary except—

(1) in those matters in which he has participated personally and substantially as a Government employee or as a special Government employee through decision, approval, disapproval, recommendation, the rendering of advice, investigation, or otherwise; or

(2) in those matters that are the subject of his official responsibility,

subject to approval by the Government official responsible for appointment to his position.

(e) Nothing in this section prevents a special Government employee from acting as agent or attorney for another person in the performance of work under a grant by, or a contract with or for the benefit of, the United States if the head of the department or agency concerned with the grant or contract certifies in writing that the national interest so requires and publishes such certification in the Federal Register.

(f) Nothing in this section prevents an individual from giving testimony under oath or from making statements required to be made under penalty of perjury.

§ 204. Practice in United States Claims Court or the United States Court of Appeals for the Federal Circuit by Members of Congress

Whoever, being a Member of Congress or Member of Congress Elect, practices in the United States Claims Court or the United States Court of Appeals for the Federal Circuit shall be subject to the penalties set forth in section 216 of this title.

§ 205. Activities of officers and employees in claims against and other matters affecting the Government

(a) Whoever, being an officer or employee of the United States in the executive, legislative, or judicial branch of the Government or in any agency of the United States, otherwise than in the proper discharge of his official duties—

> (1) acts as agent or attorney for prosecuting any claim against the United States, or receives any gratuity, or any share of or interest in any such claim in consideration of assistance in the prosecution of such claim, or

> (2) acts as agent or attorney for anyone before any department, agency, court, court-martial, officer, or civil, military, or naval commission in connection with any covered matter in which the United States is a party or has a direct and substantial interest—

shall be subject to the penalties set forth in section 216 of this title.

(b) Whoever, being an officer or employee of the District of Columbia or an officer or employee of the Office of the United States Attorney for the District of Columbia, otherwise than in the proper discharge of official duties—

> (1) acts as agent or attorney for prosecuting any claim against the District of Columbia, or receives any gratuity, or any share of or interest in any such claim in consideration of assistance in the prosecution of such claim; or

> (2) acts as agent or attorney for anyone before any department, agency, court, officer, or commission in connection with any covered matter in which the District of Columbia is a party or has a direct and substantial interest;

shall be subject to the penalties set forth in section 216 of this title.

(c) A special Government employee shall be subject to subsections (a) and (b) only in relation to a covered matter involving a specific party or parties—

> (1) in which he has at any time participated personally and substantially as a Government employee or special Government employee through decision, approval, disapproval, recommendation, the rendering of advice, investigation, or otherwise; or

> (2) which is pending in the department or agency of the Government in which he is serving.

Paragraph (2) shall not apply in the case of a special Government employee who has served in such department or agency no more than sixty days during the immediately preceding period of three hundred and sixty-five consecutive days.

(d) Nothing in subsection (a) or (b) prevents an officer or employee, if not inconsistent with the faithful performance of his duties, from acting without compensation as agent or attorney for, or otherwise representing, any person who is the subject of disciplinary, loyalty, or other personnel administration proceedings in connection with those proceedings.

(e) Nothing in subsection (a) or (b) prevents an officer or employee, including a special Government employee, from acting, with or without compensation, as agent or attorney for, or otherwise representing, his parents, spouse, child, or any person for whom, or for any estate for which, he is serving as guardian, executor, administrator, trustee, or other personal fiduciary except—

(1) in those matters in which he has participated personally and substantially as a Government employee or special Government employee through decision, approval, disapproval, recommendation, the rendering of advice, investigation, or otherwise, or

(2) in those matters which are the subject of his official responsibility,

subject to approval by the Government official responsible for appointment to his position.

(f) Nothing in subsection (a) or (b) prevents a special Government employee from acting as agent or attorney for another person in the performance of work under a grant by, or a contract with or for the benefit of, the United States if the head of the department or agency concerned with the grant or contract certifies in writing that the national interest so requires and publishes such certification in the Federal Register.

(g) Nothing in this section prevents an officer or employee from giving testimony under oath or from making statements required to be made under penalty for perjury or contempt.

(h) For the purpose of this section, the term "covered matter" means any judicial or other proceeding, application, request for a ruling or other determination, contract, claim, controversy, investigation, charge, accusation, arrest, or other particular matter.

§ 207. Restrictions on former officers, employees, and elected officials of the executive and legislative branches

(a) Restrictions on all officers and employees of the executive branch and certain other agencies.—

(1) Permanent restrictions on representation on particular matters.—Any person who is an officer or employee (including any special Government employee) of the executive branch of the United States (including any independent agency of the United States), or of the District of Columbia, and who, after the termination of his or her service or employment with the United States or the District of Columbia, knowingly makes, with the intent to influence, any communication to or appearance before any officer or employee of any department, agency, court, or court-martial of the United States or the District of Columbia, on behalf of any other person (except the United States or the District of Columbia) in connection with a particular matter—

(A) in which the United States or the District of Columbia is a party or has a direct and substantial interest,

(B) in which the person participated personally and substantially as such officer or employee, and

(C) which involved a specific party or specific parties at the time of such participation,

shall be punished as provided in section 216 of this title.

(2) **Two-year restrictions concerning particular matters under official responsibility.**—Any person subject to the restrictions contained in paragraph (1) who, within 2 years after the termination of his or her service or employment with the United States or the District of Columbia, knowingly makes, with the intent to influence, any communication to or appearance before any officer or employee of any department, agency, court, or court-martial of the United States or the District of Columbia, on behalf of any other person (except the United States or the District of Columbia), in connection with a particular matter—

(A) in which the United States or the District of Columbia is a party or has a direct and substantial interest,

(B) which such person knows or reasonably should know was actually pending under his or her official responsibility as such officer or employee within a period of 1 year before the termination of his or her service or employment with the United States or the District of Columbia, and

(C) which involved a specific party or specific parties at the time it was so pending,

shall be punished as provided in section 216 of this title.

(3) **Clarification of restrictions.**—The restrictions contained in paragraphs (1) and (2) shall apply—

(A) in the case of an officer or employee of the executive branch of the United States (including any independent agency), only with respect to communications to or appearances before any officer or employee of any department, agency, court, or court-martial of the United States on behalf of any other person (except the United States), and only with respect to a matter in which the United States is a party or has a direct and substantial interest; and

(B) in the case of an officer or employee of the District of Columbia, only with respect to communications to or appearances before any officer or employee of any department, agency, or court of the District of Columbia on behalf of any other person (except the District of Columbia), and only with respect to a matter in which the District of Columbia is a party or has a direct and substantial interest.

(b) One-year restrictions on aiding or advising.—

(1) In general.—Any person who is a former officer or employee of the executive branch of the United States (including any independent agency) and is subject to the restrictions contained in subsection (a)(1), or any person who is a former officer or employee of the legislative branch or a former Member of Congress, who personally and substantially participated in any ongoing trade or treaty negotiation on behalf of the United States within the 1–year period preceding the date on which his or her service or employment with the United States terminated, and who had access to information concerning such trade or treaty negotiation which is exempt from disclosure under section 552 of title 5, which is so designated by the appropriate department or agency, and which the person knew or should have known was so designated, shall not, on the basis of that information, knowingly represent, aid, or advise any other person (except the United States) concerning such ongoing trade or treaty negotiation for a period of 1 year after his or her service or employment with the United States terminates. Any person who violates this subsection shall be punished as provided in section 216 of this title.

(2) Definition.—For purposes of this paragraph—

(A) the term "trade negotiation" means negotiations which the President determines to undertake to enter into a trade agreement pursuant to section 1102 of the Omnibus Trade and Competitiveness Act of 1988, and does not include any action taken before that determination is made; and

(B) the term "treaty" means an international agreement made by the President that requires the advice and consent of the Senate.

(c) One-year restrictions on certain senior personnel of the executive branch and independent agencies.—

(1) Restrictions.—In addition to the restrictions set forth in subsections (a) and (b), any person who is an officer or employee (including any special Government employee) of the executive branch of the United States (including an independent agency), who is referred to in paragraph (2), and who, within 1 year after the termination of his or her service or employment as such officer or employee, knowingly makes, with the intent to influence, any communication to or appearance before any officer or employee of the department or agency in which such person served within 1 year before such termination, on behalf of any other person (except the United States), in connection with any matter on which such person seeks official action by any officer or employee of such department or agency, shall be punished as provided in section 216 of this title.

(2) Persons to whom restrictions apply.—(A) Paragraph (1) shall apply to a person (other than a person subject to the restrictions of subsection (d))—

(i) employed at a rate of pay specified in or fixed according to subchapter II of chapter 53 of title 5,

(ii) employed in a position which is not referred to in clause (i) and for which the basic rate of pay, exclusive of any locality-based pay adjustment under section 5302 of title 5 (or any comparable adjustment pursuant to interim authority of the President), is equal to or greater than the rate of basic pay payable for level V of the Executive Schedule;

(iii) appointed by the President to a position under section 105(a)(2)(B) of title 3 or by the Vice President to a position under section 106(a)(1)(B) of title 3, or

(iv) employed in a position which is held by an active duty commissioned officer of the uniformed services who is serving in a grade or rank for which the pay grade (as specified in section 201 of title 37) is pay grade 0–7 or above.

(B) Paragraph (1) shall not apply to a special Government employee who serves less than 60 days in the 1–year period before his or her service or employment as such employee terminates.

(C) At the request of a department or agency, the Director of the Office of Government Ethics may waive the restrictions contained in paragraph (1) with respect to any position, or category of positions, referred to in clause (ii) or (iv) of subparagraph (A), in such department or agency if the Director determines that—

(i) the imposition of the restrictions with respect to such position or positions would create an undue hardship on the department or agency in obtaining qualified personnel to fill such position or positions, and

(ii) granting the waiver would not create the potential for use of undue influence or unfair advantage.

(d) Restrictions on very senior personnel of the executive branch and independent agencies.—

(1) Restrictions.—In addition to the restrictions set forth in subsections (a) and (b), any person who—

(A) serves in the position of Vice President of the United States,

(B) is employed in a position in the executive branch of the United States (including any independent agency) at a rate of pay payable for level I of the Executive Schedule or employed in a position in the Executive Office of the President at a rate of pay payable for level II of the Executive Schedule, or

(C) is appointed by the President to a position under section 105(a)(2)(A) of title 3 or by the Vice President to a position under section 106(a)(1)(A) of title 3,

and who, within 1 year after the termination of that person's service in that position, knowingly makes, with the intent to influence, any communication to or appearance before any person described in paragraph (2), on behalf of any other person (except the United States), in connection with any matter on which such person seeks official action by any officer or employee of the executive branch of the United States, shall be punished as provided in section 216 of this title.

(2) **Persons who may not be contacted.**—The persons referred to in paragraph (1) with respect to appearances or communications by a person in a position described in subparagraph (A), (B), or (C) of paragraph (1) are—

(A) any officer or employee of any department or agency in which such person served in such position within a period of 1 year before such person's service or employment with the United States Government terminated, and

(B) any person appointed to a position in the executive branch which is listed in sections 5312, 5313, 5314, 5315, or 5316 of title 5.

(e) **Restrictions on members of Congress and officers and employees of the legislative branch.**—

(1) **Members of congress and elected officers.**—(A) Any person who is a Member of Congress or an elected officer of either House of Congress and who, within 1 year after that person leaves office, knowingly makes, with the intent to influence, any communication to or appearance before any of the persons described in subparagraph (B) or (C), on behalf of any other person (except the United States) in connection with any matter on which such former Member of Congress or elected officer seeks action by a Member, officer, or employee of either House of Congress, in his or her official capacity, shall be punished as provided in section 216 of this title.

(B) The persons referred to in subparagraph (A) with respect to appearances or communications by a former Member of Congress are any Member, officer, or employee of either House of Congress, and any employee of any other legislative office of the Congress.

(C) The persons referred to in subparagraph (A) with respect to appearances or communications by a former elected officer are any Member, officer, or employee of the House of Congress in which the elected officer served.

(2) **Personal staff.**—(A) Any person who is an employee of a Senator or an employee of a Member of the House of Representatives and who, within 1 year after the termination of that employment, knowingly makes, with the intent to influence, any communication to or appearance before any of the persons described in subparagraph (B), on behalf of any other person (except the United States) in connection with any matter on which such former employee seeks action by a Member, officer, or employee of either House of Congress, in his or her official capacity, shall be punished as provided in section 216 of this title.

(B) The persons referred to in subparagraph (A) with respect to appearances or communications by a person who is a former employee are the following:

(i) the Senator or Member of the House of Representatives for whom that person was an employee; and

(ii) any employee of that Senator or Member of the House of Representatives.

(3) **Committee staff.**—Any person who is an employee of a committee of Congress and who, within 1 year after the termination of that person's employment on such committee, knowingly makes, with the intent to influence, any communication to or appearance before any person who is a Member or an employee of that committee or who was a Member of the committee in the year immediately prior to the termination of such person's employment by the committee, on behalf of any other person (except the United States) in connection with any matter on which such former employee seeks action by a Member, officer, or employee of either House of Congress, in his or her official capacity, shall be punished as provided in section 216 of this title.

(4) **Leadership staff.**—(A) Any person who is an employee on the leadership staff of the House of Representatives or an employee on the leadership staff of the Senate and who, within 1 year after the termination of that person's employment on such staff, knowingly makes, with the intent to influence, any communication to or appearance before any of the persons described in subparagraph (B), on behalf of any other person (except the United States) in connection with any matter on which such former employee seeks action by a Member, officer, or employee of either House of Congress, in his or her official capacity, shall be punished as provided in section 216 of this title.

(B) The persons referred to in subparagraph (A) with respect to appearances or communications by a former employee are the following:

(i) in the case of a former employee on the leadership staff of the House of Representatives, those persons are any Member of the leadership of the House of Representatives and any employee on the leadership staff of the House of Representatives; and

(ii) in the case of a former employee on the leadership staff of the Senate, those persons are any Member of the leadership of the Senate and any employee on the leadership staff of the Senate.

(5) **Other legislative offices.**—(A) Any person who is an employee of any other legislative office of the Congress and who, within 1 year after the termination of that person's employment in such office, knowingly makes, with the intent to influence, any communication to or appearance before any of the persons described in subparagraph (B), on behalf of any other person (except the United States) in connection with any matter on which such former employee seeks action by any officer or employee of such office, in his or her official capacity, shall be punished as provided in section 216 of this title.

(B) The persons referred to in subparagraph (A) with respect to appearances or communications by a former employee are the employees and officers of the former legislative office of the Congress of the former employee.

(6) **Limitation on restrictions.**—(A) The restrictions contained in paragraphs (2), (3), and (4) apply only to acts by a former employee who, for at least 60 days, in the aggregate, during the 1–year period before that former employee's service as such employee terminated, was paid a rate of basic pay equal to or greater than an amount which is 75 percent of the basic rate of pay payable for a Member of the House of Congress in which such employee was employed.

(B) The restrictions contained in paragraph (5) apply only to acts by a former employee who, for at least 60 days, in the aggregate, during the 1–year period before that former employee's service as such employee terminated, was employed in a position for which the rate of basic pay, exclusive of any locality-based pay adjustment under section 5302 of title 5 (or any comparable adjustment pursuant to interim authority of the President), is equal to or greater than the basic rate of pay payable for level V of the Executive Schedule.

(7) **Definitions.**—As used in this subsection—

(A) the term "committee of Congress" includes standing committees, joint committees, and select committees;

(B) a person is an employee of a House of Congress if that person is an employee of the Senate or an employee of the House of Representatives;

(C) the term "employee of the House of Representatives" means an employee of a Member of the House of Representatives, an employee of a committee of the House of Representatives, an employee of a joint committee of the Congress whose pay is disbursed by the Clerk of the House of Representatives, and an employee on the leadership staff of the House of Representatives;

(D) the term "employee of the Senate" means an employee of a Senator, an employee of a committee of the Senate, an employee of a joint committee of the Congress whose pay is disbursed by the Secretary of the Senate, an employee on the leadership staff of the Senate;

(E) a person is an employee of a Member of the House of Representatives if that person is an employee of a Member of the House of Representatives under the clerk hire allowance;

(F) a person is an employee of a Senator if that person is an employee in a position in the office of a Senator;

(G) the term "employee of any other legislative office of the Congress" means an officer or employee of the Architect of the Capitol, the United States Botanic Garden, the General Accounting Office, the Government Printing Office, the Library of Congress, the Office of Technology Assessment, the Congressional Budget Office, the Copyright Royalty Tribunal, the United States Capitol Police, and any other agency, entity, or office in the legislative branch not covered by paragraph (1), (2), (3), or (4) of this subsection;

(H) the term "employee on the leadership staff of the House of Representatives" means an employee of the office of a Member of the leadership of the House of Representatives described in subparagraph (L), and any elected minority employee of the House of Representatives;

(I) the term "employee on the leadership staff of the Senate" means an employee of the office of a Member of the leadership of the Senate described in subparagraph (M);

(J) the term "Member of Congress" means a Senator or a Member of the House of Representatives;

(K) the term "Member of the House of Representatives" means a Representative in, or a Delegate or Resident Commissioner to, the Congress;

(L) the term "Member of the leadership of the House of Representatives" means the Speaker, majority leader, minority leader, majority whip, minority whip, chief deputy majority whip, chief deputy minority whip, chairman of the Democratic Steering Committee, chairman and vice chairman of the Democratic Caucus, chairman, vice chairman, and secretary of the

Republican Conference, chairman of the Republican Research Committee, and chairman of the Republican Policy Committee, of the House of Representatives (or any similar position created on or after the effective date set forth in section 102(a) of the Ethics Reform Act of 1989);

(M) the term "Member of the leadership of the Senate" means the Vice President, and the President pro tempore, Deputy President pro tempore, majority leader, minority leader, majority whip, minority whip, chairman and secretary of the Conference of the Majority, chairman and secretary of the Conference of the Minority, chairman and co-chairman of the Majority Policy Committee, and chairman of the Minority Policy Committee, of the Senate (or any similar position created on or after the effective date set forth in section 102(a) of the Ethics Reform Act of 1989).

(f) Restrictions relating to foreign entities.—

(1) **Restrictions.**—Any person who is subject to the restrictions contained in subsection (c), (d), or (e) and who knowingly, within 1 year after leaving the position, office, or employment referred to in such subsection—

(A) represents a foreign entity before any officer or employee of any department or agency of the United States with the intent to influence a decision of such officer or employee in carrying out his or her official duties, or

(B) aids or advises a foreign entity with the intent to influence a decision of any officer or employee of any department or agency of the United States, in carrying out his or her official duties,

shall be punished as provided in section 216 of this title.

(2) **Definition.**—For purposes of this subsection, the term "foreign entity" means the government of a foreign country as defined in section 1(e) of the Foreign Agents Registration Act of 1938, as amended, or a foreign political party as defined in section 1(f) of that Act.

(g) Special rules for detailees.—

For purposes of this section, a person who is detailed from one department, agency, or other entity to another department, agency, or other entity shall, during the period such person is detailed, be deemed to be an officer or employee of both departments, agencies, or such entities.

(h) Designations of separate statutory agencies and bureaus.—

(1) **Designations.**—For purposes of subsection (c) and except as provided in paragraph (2), whenever the Director of the Office of

Government Ethics determines that an agency or bureau within a department or agency in the executive branch exercises functions which are distinct and separate from the remaining functions of the department or agency and that there exists no potential for use of undue influence or unfair advantage based on past Government service, the Director shall by rule designate such agency or bureau as a separate department or agency. On an annual basis the Director of the Office of Government Ethics shall review the designations and determinations made under this subparagraph and, in consultation with the department or agency concerned, make such additions and deletions as are necessary. Departments and agencies shall cooperate to the fullest extent with the Director of the Office of Government Ethics in the exercise of his or her responsibilities under this paragraph.

(2) **Inapplicability of designations.**—No agency or bureau within the Executive Office of the President may be designated under paragraph (1) as a separate department or agency. No designation under paragraph (1) shall apply to persons referred to in subsection (c)(2)(A)(i) or (iii).

(i) **Definitions.**—

For purposes of this section—

(1) the term "officer or employee", when used to describe the person to whom a communication is made or before whom an appearance is made, with the intent to influence, shall include—

(A) in subsections (a), (c), and (d), the President and the Vice President; and

(B) in subsection (f), the President, the Vice President, and Members of Congress;

(2) the term "participated" means an action taken as an officer or employee through decision, approval, disapproval, recommendation, the rendering of advice, investigation, or other such action; and

(3) the term "particular matter" includes any investigation, application, request for a ruling or determination, rulemaking, contract, controversy, claim, charge, accusation, arrest, or judicial or other proceeding.

(j) **Exceptions.**—

(1) **Official government duties.**—The restrictions contained in this section shall not apply to acts done in carrying out official duties on behalf of the United States or the District of Columbia or as an elected official of a State or local government.

(2) **State and local governments and institutions, hospitals, and organizations.**—The restrictions contained in subsec-

tions (c), (d), and (e) shall not apply to acts done in carrying out official duties as an employee of—

(A) an agency or instrumentality of a State or local government if the appearance, communication, or representation is on behalf of such government, or

(B) an accredited, degree-granting institution of higher education, as defined in section 1201(a) of the Higher Education Act of 1965, or a hospital or medical research organization, exempted and defined under section 501(c)(3) of the Internal Revenue Code of 1986, if the appearance, communication, or representation is on behalf of such institution, hospital, or organization.

(3) **International organizations.**—The restrictions contained in this section shall not apply to an appearance or communication on behalf of, or advice or aid to, an international organization in which the United States participates, if the Secretary of State certifies in advance that such activity is in the interests of the United States.

(4) **Special knowledge.**—The restrictions contained in subsections (c), (d), and (e) shall not prevent an individual from making or providing a statement, which is based on the individual's own special knowledge in the particular area that is the subject of the statement, if no compensation is thereby received.

(5) **Exception for scientific or technological information.**—The restrictions contained in subsections (a), (c), and (d) shall not apply with respect to the making of communications solely for the purpose of furnishing scientific or technological information, if such communications are made under procedures acceptable to the department or agency concerned or if the head of the department or agency concerned with the particular matter, in consultation with the Director of the Office of Government Ethics, makes a certification, published in the Federal Register, that the former officer or employee has outstanding qualifications in a scientific, technological, or other technical discipline, and is acting with respect to a particular matter which requires such qualifications, and that the national interest would be served by the participation of the former officer or employee. For purposes of this paragraph, the term "officer or employee" includes the Vice President.

(6) **Exception for testimony.**—Nothing in this section shall prevent an individual from giving testimony under oath, or from making statements required to be made under penalty of perjury. Notwithstanding the preceding sentence—

(A) a former officer or employee of the executive branch of the United States (including any independent agency) who is subject to the restrictions contained in subsection (a)(1) with respect to a particular matter may not, except pursuant to court order, serve as an expert witness for any other person (except the United States) in that matter; and

(B) a former officer or employee of the District of Columbia who is subject to the restrictions contained in subsection (a) (1) with respect to a particular matter may not, except pursuant to court order, serve as an expert witness for any other person (except the District of Columbia) in that matter.

(k)(1)(A) The President may grant a waiver of a restriction imposed by this section to any officer or employee described in paragraph (2) if the President determines and certifies in writing that it is in the public interest to grant the waiver and that the services of the officer or employee are critically needed for the benefit of the Federal Government. Not more than 25 officers and employees currently employed by the Federal Government at any one time may have been granted waivers under this paragraph.

(B)(i) A waiver granted under this paragraph to any person shall apply only with respect to activities engaged in by that person after that person's Federal Government employment is terminated and only to that person's employment at a Government-owned, contractor operated entity with which the person served as an officer or employee immediately before the person's Federal Government employment began.

(ii) Notwithstanding clause (i), a waiver granted under this paragraph to any person who was an officer or employee of Lawrence Livermore National Laboratory, Los Alamos National Laboratory, or Sandia National Laboratory immediately before the person's Federal Government employment began shall apply to that person's employment by any such national laboratory after the person's employment by the Federal Government is terminated.

(2) Waivers under paragraph (1) may be granted only to civilian officers and employees of the executive branch, other than officers and employees in the Executive Office of the President.

(3) A certification under paragraph (1) shall take effect upon its publication in the Federal Register and shall identify—

(A) the officer or employee covered by the waiver by name and by position, and

(B) the reasons for granting the waiver.

A copy of the certification shall also be provided to the Director of the Office of Government Ethics.

(4) The President may not delegate the authority provided by this subsection.

(5)(A) Each person granted a waiver under this subsection shall prepare reports, in accordance with subparagraph (B), stating whether the person has engaged in activities otherwise prohibited by this section for each six-month period described in subparagraph (B), and if so, what those activities were.

(B) A report under subparagraph (A) shall cover each six-month period beginning on the date of the termination of the person's Federal Government employment (with respect to which the waiver under this subsection was granted) and ending two years after that date. Such report shall be filed with the President and the Director of the Office of Government Ethics not later than 60 days after the end of the six-month period covered by the report. All reports filed with the Director under this paragraph shall be made available for public inspection and copying.

(C) If a person fails to file any report in accordance with subparagraphs (A) and (B), the President shall revoke the waiver and shall notify the person of the revocation. The revocation shall take effect upon the person's receipt of the notification and shall remain in effect until the report is filed.

(D) Any person who is granted a waiver under this subsection shall be ineligible for appointment in the civil service unless all reports required of such person by subparagraphs (A) and (B) have been filed.

(E) As used in this subsection, the term "civil service" has the meaning given that term in section 2101 of title 5.

§ 208. Acts affecting a personal financial interest

(a) Except as permitted by subsection (b) hereof, whoever, being an officer or employee of the executive branch of the United States Government, or of any independent agency of the United States, a Federal Reserve bank director, officer, or employee, or an officer or employee of the District of Columbia, including a special Government employee, participates personally and substantially as a Government officer or employee, through decision, approval, disapproval, recommendation, the rendering of advice, investigation, or otherwise, in a judicial or other proceeding, application, request for a ruling or other determination, contract, claim, controversy, charge, accusation, arrest, or other particular matter in which, to his knowledge, he, his spouse, minor child, general partner, organization in which he is serving as officer, director, trustee, general partner or employee, or any person or organization with whom he is negotiating or has any arrangement concerning prospective employment, has a financial interest—

Shall be subject to the penalties set forth in section 216 of this title.

(b) Subsection (a) shall not apply—

(1) if the officer or employee first advises the Government official responsible for appointment to his or her position of the nature and circumstances of the judicial or other proceeding, application, request for a ruling or other determination, contract, claim, controversy, charge, accusation, arrest, or other particular matter and makes full disclosure of the financial interest and receives in advance a written determination made by such official that the interest is not so substantial as to be deemed likely to affect the integrity of the services which the Government may expect from such officer or employee;

(2) if, by regulation issued by the Director of the Office of Government Ethics, applicable to all or a portion of all officers and employees covered by this section, and published in the Federal Register, the financial interest has been exempted from the requirements of subsection (a) as being too remote or too inconsequential to affect the integrity of the services of the Government officers or employees to which such regulation applies;

(3) in the case of a special Government employee serving on an advisory committee within the meaning of the Federal Advisory Committee Act (including an individual being considered for an appointment to such a position), the official responsible for the employee's appointment, after review of the financial disclosure report filed by the individual pursuant to the Ethics in Government Act of 1978, certifies in writing that the need for the individual's services outweighs the potential for a conflict of interest created by the financial interest involved; or

(4) the financial interest that would be affected by the particular matter involved is that resulting solely from the interest of the officer or employee, or his or her spouse or minor child, in birthrights—

(A) in an Indian tribe, band, nation, or other organized group or community, including any Alaska Native village corporation as defined in or established pursuant to the Alaska Native Claims Settlement Act, which is recognized as eligible for the special programs and services provided by the United States to Indians because of their status as Indians,

(B) in an Indian allotment the title to which is held in trust by the United States or which is inalienable by the allottee without the consent of the United States, or

(C) in an Indian claims fund held in trust or administered by the United States,

if the particular matter does not involve the Indian allotment or claims fund or the Indian tribe, band, nation, organized group or community, or Alaska Native village corporation as a specific party or parties.

(c)(1) For the purpose of paragraph (1) of subsection (b), in the case of class A and B directors of Federal Reserve Banks, the Board of Governors of the Federal Reserve System shall be deemed to be the Government official responsible for appointment.

(2) The potential availability of an exemption under any particular paragraph of subsection (b) does not preclude an exemption being granted pursuant to another paragraph of subsection (b).

(d)(1) Upon request, a copy of any determination granting an exemption under subsection (b)(1) or (b)(3) shall be made available to the public by the agency granting the exemption pursuant to the procedures set forth in section 105 of the Ethics in Government Act of 1978. In making such determination available, the agency may withhold from disclosure any information contained in the determination that would be exempt from disclosure under section 552 of title 5. For purposes of determinations under subsection (b)(3), the information describing each financial interest shall be no more extensive than that required of the individual in his or her financial disclosure report under the Ethics in Government Act of 1978.

(2) The Office of Government Ethics, after consultation with the Attorney General, shall issue uniform regulations for the issuance of waivers and exemptions under subsection (b) which shall—

(A) list and describe exemptions; and

(B) provide guidance with respect to the types of interests that are not so substantial as to be deemed likely to affect the integrity of the services the Government may expect from the employee.

§ 209. Salary of Government officials and employees payable only by United States

(a) Whoever receives any salary, or any contribution to or supplementation of salary, as compensation for his services as an officer or employee of the executive branch of the United States Government, of any independent agency of the United States, or of the District of Columbia, from any source other than the Government of the United States, except as may be contributed out of the treasury of any State, county, or municipality; or

Whoever, whether an individual, partnership, association, corporation, or other organization pays, or makes any contribution to, or in any way supplements the salary of, any such officer or employee under circumstances which would make its receipt a violation of this subsection—

Shall be subject to the penalties set forth in section 216 of this title.

(b) Nothing herein prevents an officer or employee of the executive branch of the United States Government, or of any independent agency of the United States, or of the District of Columbia, from continuing to participate in a bona fide pension, retirement, group life, health or accident insurance, profit-sharing, stock bonus, or other employee welfare or benefit plan maintained by a former employer.

(c) This section does not apply to a special Government employee or to an officer or employee of the Government serving without compensation, whether or not he is a special Government employee, or to any person paying, contributing to, or supplementing his salary as such.

(d) This section does not prohibit payment or acceptance of contributions, awards, or other expenses under the terms of chapter 41 of title 5.

(e) This section does not prohibit the payment of actual relocation expenses incident to participation, or the acceptance of same by a participant in an executive exchange or fellowship program in an executive agency: *Provided*, That such program has been established by statute or Executive order of the President, offers appointments not to exceed three hundred and sixty-five days, and permits no extensions in excess of ninety additional days or, in the case of participants in overseas assignments, in excess of three hundred and sixty-five days.

(f) This section does not prohibit acceptance or receipt, by any officer or employee injured during the commission of an offense described in section 351 or 1751 of this title, of contributions or payments from an organization which is described in section 501(c)(3) of the Internal Revenue Code of 1954 and which is exempt from taxation under section 501(a) of such Code.

§ 216. Penalties and injunctions

(a) The punishment for an offense under sections 203, 204, 205, 207, 208, or 209 of this title is the following:

(1) Whoever engages in the conduct constituting the offense shall be imprisoned for not more than one year or fined in the amount set forth in this title, or both.

(2) Whoever willfully engages in the conduct constituting the offense shall be imprisoned for not more than five years or fined in the amount set forth in this title, or both.

(b) The Attorney General may bring a civil action in the appropriate United States district court against any person who engages in conduct constituting an offense under sections 203, 204, 205, 207, 208, or 209 of this title and, upon proof of such conduct by a preponderance of the evidence, such person shall be subject to a civil penalty of not more than $50,000 for each violation or the amount of compensation which the person received or offered for the prohibited conduct, whichever amount is greater. The imposition of a civil penalty under this subsection does not preclude any other criminal or civil statutory, common law, or administrative remedy, which is available by law to the United States or any other person.

(c) If the Attorney General has reason to believe that a person is engaging in conduct constituting an offense under section 203, 204, 205, 207, 208, or 209 of this title, the Attorney General may petition an appropriate United States district court for an order prohibiting that person from engaging in such conduct. The court may issue an order prohibiting that person from engaging in such conduct if the court finds that the conduct constitutes such an offense. The filing of a petition under this section does not preclude any other remedy which is available by law to the United States or any other person.

§ 218.   Voiding transactions in violation of chapter; recovery by the United States

In addition to any other remedies provided by law the President or, under regulations prescribed by him, the head of any department or agency involved, may declare void and rescind any contract, loan, grant, subsidy, license, right, permit, franchise, use, authority, privilege, benefit, certificate, ruling, decision, opinion, or rate schedule awarded, granted, paid, furnished, or published, or the performance of any service or transfer or delivery of any thing to, by or for any agency of the United States or officer or employee of the United States or person acting on behalf thereof, in relation to which there has been a final conviction for any violation of this chapter, and the United States shall be entitled to recover in addition to any penalty prescribed by law or in a contract the amount expended or the thing transferred or delivered on its behalf, or the reasonable value thereof.

CHAPTER 21.   CONTEMPTS

§ 401.   Power of court

A court of the United States shall have power to punish by fine or imprisonment, at its discretion, such contempt of its authority, and none other, as—

(1) Misbehavior of any person in its presence or so near thereto as to obstruct the administration of justice;

(2) Misbehavior of any of its officers in their official transactions;

(3) Disobedience or resistance to its lawful writ, process, order, rule, decree, or command.

§ 402.   Contempts constituting crimes

Any person, corporation or association willfully disobeying any lawful writ, process, order, rule, decree, or command of any district court of the United States or any court of the District of Columbia, by doing any act or thing therein, or thereby forbidden, if the act or thing so done be of such character as to constitute also a criminal offense under any statute of the United States or under the laws of any State in which the act was committed, shall be prosecuted for such contempt as provided in section 3691 of this title and shall be punished by fine or imprisonment, or both.

Such fine shall be paid to the United States or to the complainant or other party injured by the act constituting the contempt, or may, where more than one is so damaged, be divided or apportioned among them as the court may direct, but in no case shall the fine to be paid to the United States exceed, in case the accused is a natural person, the sum of $1,000, nor shall such imprisonment exceed the term of six months.

This section shall not be construed to relate to contempts committed in the presence of the court, or so near thereto as to obstruct the administration of justice, nor to contempts committed in disobedience of any lawful writ, process, order, rule, decree, or command entered in any suit or action brought or prosecuted in the name of, or on behalf of, the United States, but the same, and all other cases of contempt not specifically embraced in this section may be punished in conformity to the prevailing usages at law.

For purposes of this section, the term "State" includes a State of the United States, the District of Columbia, and any commonwealth, territory, or possession of the United States.

CHAPTER 49. FUGITIVES FROM JUSTICE

§ 1074. Flight to avoid prosecution for damaging or destroying any building or other real or personal property

(a) Whoever moves or travels in interstate or foreign commerce with intent either (1) to avoid prosecution, or custody, or confinement after conviction, under the laws of the place from which he flees, for willfully attempting to or damaging or destroying by fire or explosive any building, structure, facility, vehicle, dwelling house, synagogue, church, religious center or educational institution, public or private, or (2) to avoid giving testimony in any criminal proceeding relating to any such offense shall be fined not more than $5,000 or imprisoned not more than five years, or both.

(b) Violations of this section may be prosecuted in the Federal judicial district in which the original crime was alleged to have been committed or in which the person was held in custody or confinement: *Provided, however,* That this section shall not be construed as indicating an intent on the part of Congress to prevent any State, Territory, Commonwealth, or possession of the United States of any jurisdiction over any offense over which they would have jurisdiction in the absence of such section.

CHAPTER 63.　MAIL FRAUD

§ 1341.　Frauds and swindles

Whoever, having devised or intending to devise any scheme or artifice to defraud, or for obtaining money or property by means of false or fraudulent pretenses, representations, or promises, or to sell, dispose of, loan, exchange, alter, give away, distribute, supply, or furnish or procure for unlawful use any counterfeit or spurious coin, obligation, security, or other article, or anything represented to be or intimated or held out to be such counterfeit or spurious article, for the purpose of executing such scheme or artifice or attempting so to do, places in any post office or authorized depository for mail matter, any matter or thing whatever to be sent or delivered by the Postal Service, or takes or receives therefrom, any such matter or thing, or knowingly causes to be delivered by mail according to the direction thereon, or at the place at which it is directed to be delivered by the person to whom it is addressed, any such matter or thing, shall be fined not more than $1,000 or imprisoned not more than five years, or both. If the violation affects a financial institution, such person shall be fined not more than $1,000,000 or imprisoned not more than 20 years, or both.

CHAPTER 73.　OBSTRUCTION OF JUSTICE

§ 1501.　Assault on process server

Whoever knowingly and willfully obstructs, resists, or opposes any officer of the United States, or other person duly authorized, in serving, or attempting to serve or execute, any legal or judicial writ or process of any court of the United States, or United States commissioner; or

Whoever assaults, beats, or wounds any officer or other person duly authorized, knowing him to be such officer, or other person so duly authorized, in serving or executing any such writ, rule, order, process, warrant, or other legal or judicial writ or process—

Shall, except as otherwise provided by law, be fined not more than $300 or imprisoned not more than one year, or both.

§ 1502.　Resistance to extradition agent

Whoever knowingly and willfully obstructs, resists, or opposes an extradition agent of the United States in the execution of his duties, shall be fined not more than $300 or imprisoned not more than one year, or both.

§ 1503.　Influencing or injuring officer or juror generally

Whoever corruptly, or by threats or force, or by any threatening letter or communication, endeavors to influence, intimidate, or impede any grand or petit juror, or officer in or of any court of the United

440

States, or officer who may be serving at any examination or other proceeding before any United States commissioner or other committing magistrate, in the discharge of his duty, or injures any such grand or petit juror in his person or property on account of any verdict or indictment assented to by him, or on account of his being or having been such juror, or injures any such officer, commissioner, or other committing magistrate in his person or property on account of the performance of his official duties, or corruptly or by threats or force, or by any threatening letter or communication, influences, obstructs, or impedes, or endeavors to influence, obstruct, or impede, the due administration of justice, shall be fined not more than $5,000 or imprisoned not more than five years, or both.

§ 1504. Influencing juror by writing

Whoever attempts to influence the action or decision of any grand or petit juror of any court of the United States upon any issue or matter pending before such juror, or before the jury of which he is a member, or pertaining to his duties, by writing or sending to him any written communication, in relation to such issue or matter, shall be fined not more than $1,000 or imprisoned not more than six months, or both.

Nothing in this section shall be construed to prohibit the communication of a request to appear before the grand jury.

§ 1505. Obstruction of proceedings before departments, agencies, and committees

Whoever, with intent to avoid, evade, prevent, or obstruct compliance, in whole or in part, with any civil investigative demand duly and properly made under the Antitrust Civil Process Act, willfully withholds, misrepresents, removes from any place, conceals, covers up, destroys, mutilates, alters, or by other means falsifies any documentary material, answers to written interrogatories, or oral testimony, which is the subject of such demand; or attempts to do so or solicits another to do so; or

Whoever corruptly, or by threats or force, or by any threatening letter or communication influences, obstructs, or impedes or endeavors to influence, obstruct, or impede the due and proper administration of the law under which any pending proceeding is being had before any department or agency of the United States, or the due and proper exercise of the power of inquiry under which any inquiry or investigation is being had by either House, or any committee of either House or any joint committee of the Congress—

Shall be fined not more than $5,000 or imprisoned not more than five years, or both.

441

§ 1506. Theft or alteration of record or process; false bail

Whoever feloniously steals, takes away, alters, falsifies, or otherwise avoids any record, writ, process, or other proceeding, in any court of the United States, whereby any judgment is reversed, made void, or does not take effect; or

Whoever acknowledges, or procures to be acknowledged in any such court, any recognizance, bail, or judgment, in the name of any other person not privy or consenting to the same—

Shall be fined not more than $5,000 or imprisoned not more than five years, or both.

§ 1507. Picketing or parading

Whoever, with the intent of interfering with, obstructing, or impeding the administration of justice, or with the intent of influencing any judge, juror, witness, or court officer, in the discharge of his duty, pickets or parades in or near a building housing a court of the United States, or in or near a building or residence occupied or used by such judge, juror, witness, or court officer, or with such intent uses any sound-truck or similar device or resorts to any other demonstration in or near any such building or residence, shall be fined not more than $5,000 or imprisoned not more than one year, or both.

Nothing in this section shall interfere with or prevent the exercise by any court of the United States of its power to punish for contempt.

§ 1508. Recording, listening to, or observing proceedings of grand or petit juries while deliberating or voting

Whoever knowingly and willfully, by any means or device whatsoever—

>   (a) records, or attempts to record, the proceedings of any grand or petit jury in any court of the United States while such jury is deliberating or voting; or

>   (b) listens to or observes, or attempts to listen to or observe, the proceedings of any grand or petit jury of which he is not a member in any court of the United States while such jury is deliberating or voting—

shall be fined not more than $1,000 or imprisoned not more than one year, or both.

Nothing in paragraph (a) of this section shall be construed to prohibit the taking of notes by a grand or petit juror in any court of the United States in connection with and solely for the purpose of assisting him in the performance of his duties as such juror.

§ 1509. Obstruction of court orders

Whoever, by threats or force, willfully prevents, obstructs, impedes, or interferes with, or willfully attempts to prevent, obstruct, impede, or interfere with, the due exercise of rights or the performance of duties under any order, judgment, or decree of a court of the United States, shall be fined not more than $1,000 or imprisoned not more than one year, or both.

No injunctive or other civil relief against the conduct made criminal by this section shall be denied on the ground that such conduct is a crime.

§ 1510. Obstruction of criminal investigations

(a) Whoever willfully endeavors by means of bribery to obstruct, delay, or prevent the communication of information relating to a violation of any criminal statute of the United States by any person to a criminal investigator shall be fined not more than $5,000, or imprisoned not more than five years, or both.

(b)(1) Whoever, being an officer of a financial institution, with the intent to obstruct a judicial proceeding, directly or indirectly notifies any other person about the existence or contents of a subpoena for records of that financial institution, or information that has been furnished to the grand jury in response to that subpoena, shall be fined under this title or imprisoned not more than 5 years, or both.

(2) Whoever, being an officer of a financial institution, directly or indirectly notifies—

> (A) a customer of that financial institution whose records are sought by a grand jury subpoena; or

> (B) any other person named in that subpoena;

about the existence or contents of that subpoena or information that has been furnished to the grand jury in response to that subpoena, shall be fined under this title or imprisoned not more than one year, or both.

(3) As used in this subsection—

> (A) the term "an officer of a financial institution" means an officer, director, partner, employee, agent, or attorney of or for a financial institution; and

> (B) the term "subpoena for records" means a Federal grand jury subpoena for customer records that has been served relating to a violation of, or a conspiracy to violate—

>> (i) section 215, 656, 657, 1005, 1006, 1007, 1014, or 1344; or

>> (ii) section 1341 or 1343 affecting a financial institution.

(c) As used in this section, the term "criminal investigator" means any individual duly authorized by a department, agency, or armed force of the United States to conduct or engage in investigations of or prosecutions for violations of the criminal laws of the United States.

§ 1511. Obstruction of State or local law enforcement

(a) It shall be unlawful for two or more persons to conspire to obstruct the enforcement of the criminal laws of a State or political subdivision thereof, with the intent to facilitate an illegal gambling business if—

(1) one or more of such persons does any act to effect the object of such a conspiracy;

(2) one or more of such persons is an official or employee, elected, appointed, or otherwise, of such State or political subdivision; and

(3) one or more of such persons conducts, finances, manages, supervises, directs, or owns all or part of an illegal gambling business.

(b) As used in this section—

(1) "illegal gambling business" means a gambling business which—

(i) is a violation of the law of a State or political subdivision in which it is conducted;

(ii) involves five or more persons who conduct, finance, manage, supervise, direct, or own all or part of such business; and

(iii) has been or remains in substantially continuous operation for a period in excess of thirty days or has a gross revenue of $2,000 in any single day.

(2) "gambling" includes but is not limited to pool-selling, book-making, maintaining slot machines, roulette wheels, or dice tables, and conducting lotteries, policy, bolita or numbers games, or selling chances therein.

(3) "State" means any State of the United States, the District of Columbia, the Commonwealth of Puerto Rico, and any territory or possession of the United States.

(c) This section shall not apply to any bingo game, lottery, or similar game of chance conducted by an organization exempt from tax under paragraph (3) of subsection (c) of section 501 of the Internal Revenue Code of 1954, as amended, if no part of the gross receipts derived from such activity inures to the benefit of any private shareholder, member, or employee of such organization, except as compensation for actual expenses incurred by him in the conduct of such activity.

(d) Whoever violates this section shall be punished by a fine of not more than $20,000 or imprisonment for not more than five years, or both.

§ 1512. Tampering with a witness, victim, or an informant

(a)(1) Whoever kills or attempts to kill another person, with intent to—

(A) prevent the attendance or testimony of any person in an official proceeding;

(B) prevent the production of a record, document, or other object, in an official proceeding; or

(C) prevent the communication by any person to a law enforcement officer or judge of the United States of information relating to the commission or possible commission of a Federal offense or a violation of conditions of probation, parole, or release pending judicial proceedings;

shall be punished as provided in paragraph (2).

(2) The punishment for an offense under this subsection is—

(A) in the case of a killing, the punishment provided in sections 1111 and 1112 of this title; and

(B) in the case of an attempt, imprisonment for not more than twenty years.

(b) Whoever knowingly uses intimidation or physical force, or threatens another person, or attempts to do so, or engages in misleading conduct toward another person, with intent to—

(1) influence, delay, or prevent the testimony of any person in an official proceeding;

(2) cause or induce any person to—

(A) withhold testimony, or withhold a record, document, or other object, from an official proceeding;

(B) alter, destroy, mutilate, or conceal an object with intent to impair the object's integrity or availability for use in an official proceeding;

(C) evade legal process summoning that person to appear as a witness, or to produce a record, document, or other object, in an official proceeding; or

(D) be absent from an official proceeding to which such person has been summoned by legal process; or

(3) hinder, delay, or prevent the communication to a law enforcement officer or judge of the United States of information relating to the commission or possible commission of a Federal offense or a violation of conditions of probation, parole, or release pending judicial proceedings;

shall be fined not more than $250,000 or imprisoned not more than ten years, or both.

(c) Whoever intentionally harasses another person and thereby hinders, delays, prevents, or dissuades any person from—

(1) attending or testifying in an official proceeding;

(2) reporting to a law enforcement officer or judge of the United States the commission or possible commission of a Federal offense or a violation of conditions of probation, parole, or release pending judicial proceedings;

(3) arresting or seeking the arrest of another person in connection with a Federal offense; or

(4) causing a criminal prosecution, or a parole or probation revocation proceeding, to be sought or instituted, or assisting in such prosecution or proceeding;

or attempts to do so, shall be fined not more than $25,000 or imprisoned not more than one year, or both.

(d) In a prosecution for an offense under this section, it is an affirmative defense, as to which the defendant has the burden of proof by a preponderance of the evidence, that the conduct consisted solely of lawful conduct and that the defendant's sole intention was to encourage, induce, or cause the other person to testify truthfully.

(e) For the purposes of this section—

(1) an official proceeding need not be pending or about to be instituted at the time of the offense; and

(2) the testimony, or the record, document, or other object need not be admissible in evidence or free of a claim of privilege.

(f) In a prosecution for an offense under this section, no state of mind need be proved with respect to the circumstance—

(1) that the official proceeding before a judge, court, magistrate, grand jury, or government agency is before a judge or court of the United States, a United States magistrate, a bankruptcy judge, a Federal grand jury, or a Federal Government agency; or

(2) that the judge is a judge of the United States or that the law enforcement officer is an officer or employee of the Federal Government or a person authorized to act for or on behalf of the Federal Government or serving the Federal Government as an adviser or consultant.

(g) There is extraterritorial Federal jurisdiction over an offense under this section.

§ 1905. Disclosure of confidential information generally

Whoever, being an officer or employee of the United States or of any department or agency thereof, or agent of the Department of Justice as defined in the Antitrust Civil Process Act (15 U.S.C. 1311–1314), publishes, divulges, discloses, or makes known in any manner or to any extent not authorized by law any information coming to him in the course of his employment or official duties or by reason of any examination or investigation made by, or return, report or record made to or filed with, such department or agency or officer or employee thereof, which information concerns or relates to the trade secrets, processes, operations, style of work, or apparatus, or to the identity, confidential statistical data, amount or source of any income, profits, losses, or expenditures of any person, firm, partnership, corporation, or association; or permits any income return or copy thereof or any book containing any abstract or particulars thereof to be seen or examined by any person except as provided by law; shall be fined not more than $1,000, or imprisoned not more than one year, or both; and shall be removed from office or employment.

CHAPTER 201. CRIMINAL PROCEDURE—GENERAL PROVISIONS

§ 3004. Decorum in court room—(Rule)

SEE FEDERAL RULES OF CRIMINAL PROCEDURE

Photographing or radio broadcasting prohibited, Rule 53.

§ 3005. Counsel and witnesses in capital cases

Whoever is indicted for treason or other capital crime shall be allowed to make his full defense by counsel learned in the law; and the court before which he is tried, or some judge thereof, shall immediately, upon his request, assign to him such counsel, not exceeding two, as he may desire, who shall have free access to him at all reasonable hours. He shall be allowed, in his defense to make any proof that he can produce by lawful witnesses, and shall have the like process of the court to compel his witnesses to appear at his trial, as is usually granted to compel witnesses to appear on behalf of the prosecution.

§ 3006. Assignment of counsel—(Rule)

SEE FEDERAL RULES OF CRIMINAL PROCEDURE

Appointment by court, Rule 44.

Accused to be informed of right to counsel, Rules 5 and 44.

§ 3006A. Adequate representation of defendants

(a) **Choice of plan.**—Each United States district court, with the approval of the judicial council of the circuit, shall place in operation throughout the district a plan for furnishing representation for any person financially unable to obtain adequate representation in accordance with this section. Representation under each plan shall include counsel and investigative, expert, and other services necessary for adequate representation. Each plan shall provide the following:

(1) Representation shall be provided for any financially eligible person who—

(A) is charged with a felony or a Class A misdemeanor;

(B) is a juvenile alleged to have committed an act of juvenile delinquency as defined in section 5031 of this title;

(C) is charged with a violation of probation;

(D) is under arrest, when such representation is required by law;

(E) is charged with a violation of supervised release or faces modification, reduction, or enlargement of a condition, or extension or revocation of a term of supervised release;

(F) is subject to a mental condition hearing under chapter 313 of this title;

(G) is in custody as a material witness;

(H) is entitled to appointment of counsel under the sixth amendment to the Constitution; or

(I) faces loss of liberty in a case, and Federal law requires the appointment of counsel.

(2) Whenever the United States magistrate or the court determines that the interests of justice so require, representation may be provided for any financially eligible person who—

(A) is charged with a Class B or C misdemeanor, or an infraction for which a sentence to confinement is authorized; or

(B) is seeking relief under section 2241, 2254, or 2255 of title 28.

(3) Private attorneys shall be appointed in a substantial proportion of the cases. Each plan may include, in addition to the provisions for private attorneys, either of the following or both:

(A) Attorneys furnished by a bar association or a legal aid agency.

(B) Attorneys furnished by a defender organization established in accordance with the provisions of subsection (g).

Prior to approving the plan for a district, the judicial council of the circuit shall supplement the plan with provisions for representation on appeal. The district court may modify the plan at any time with the approval of the judicial council of the circuit. It shall modify the plan when directed by the judicial council of the circuit. The district court shall notify the Administrative Office of the United States Courts of any modification of its plan.

(b) **Appointment of counsel.**—Counsel furnishing representation under the plan shall be selected from a panel of attorneys designated or approved by the court, or from a bar association, legal aid agency, or defender organization furnishing representation pursuant to the plan. In every case in which a person entitled to representation under a plan approved under subsection (a) appears without counsel, the United States magistrate or the court shall advise the person that he has the right to be represented by counsel and that counsel will be appointed to represent him if he is financially unable to obtain counsel. Unless the person waives representation by counsel, the United States magistrate or the court, if satisfied after appropriate inquiry that the person is financially unable to obtain counsel, shall appoint counsel to represent him. Such appointment may be made retroactive to include any representation furnished pursuant to the plan prior to appointment. The United States magistrate or the court shall appoint separate counsel for persons having interests that cannot properly be represented by the same counsel, or when other good cause is shown.

(c) **Duration and substitution of appointments.**—A person for whom counsel is appointed shall be represented at every stage of the proceedings from his initial appearance before the United States magistrate or the court through appeal, including ancillary matters appropriate to the proceedings. If at any time after the appointment of counsel the United States magistrate or the court finds that the person is financially able to obtain counsel or to make partial payment for the representation, it may terminate the appointment of counsel or authorize payment as provided in subsection (f), as the interests of justice may dictate. If at any stage of the proceedings, including an appeal, the United States magistrate or the court finds that the person is financially unable to pay counsel whom he had retained, it may appoint counsel as provided in subsection (b) and authorize payment as provided in subsection (d), as the interests of justice may dictate. The United States magistrate or the court may, in the interests of justice, substitute one appointed counsel for another at any stage of the proceedings.

(d) **Payment for representation.**—

(1) **Hourly rate.**—Any attorney appointed pursuant to this section or a bar association or legal aid agency or community defender organization which has provided the appointed attorney shall, at the conclusion of the representation or any segment thereof, be compensated at a rate not exceeding $60 per hour for time expended in court or before a United States magistrate and $40 per hour for time reasonably expended out of court, unless the Judicial Conference determines that a higher rate of not in excess of $75 per hour is justified for a circuit or for particular districts within a circuit, for time expended in court or before a United States magistrate and for time expended out of court. The Judicial Conference shall develop guidelines for determining the maximum hourly rates for each circuit in accordance with the preceding sentence, with variations by district, where appropriate, taking into account such factors as the minimum range of the prevailing

hourly rates for qualified attorneys in the district in which the representation is provided and the recommendations of the judicial councils of the circuits. Not less than 3 years after the effective date of the Criminal Justice Act Revision of 1986, the Judicial Conference is authorized to raise the maximum hourly rates specified in this paragraph up to the aggregate of the overall average percentages of the adjustments in the rates of pay under the General Schedule made pursuant to section 5305 of title 5 on or after such effective date. After the rates are raised under the preceding sentence, such maximum hourly rates may be raised at intervals of not less than 1 year each, up to the aggregate of the overall average percentages of such adjustments made since the last raise was made under this paragraph. Attorneys shall be reimbursed for expenses reasonably incurred, including the costs of transcripts authorized by the United States magistrate or the court.

(2) **Maximum amounts.**—For representation of a defendant before the United States magistrate or the district court, or both, the compensation to be paid to an attorney or to a bar association or legal aid agency or community defender organization shall not exceed $3,500 for each attorney in a case in which one or more felonies are charged, and $1,000 for each attorney in a case in which only misdemeanors are charged. For representation of a defendant in an appellate court, the compensation to be paid to an attorney or to a bar association or legal aid agency or community defender organization shall not exceed $2,500 for each attorney in each court. For any other representation required or authorized by this section, the compensation shall not exceed $750 for each attorney in each proceeding.

(3) **Waiving maximum amounts.**—Payment in excess of any maximum amount provided in paragraph (2) of this subsection may be made for extended or complex representation whenever the court in which the representation was rendered, or the United States magistrate if the representation was furnished exclusively before him, certifies that the amount of the excess payment is necessary to provide fair compensation and the payment is approved by the chief judge of the circuit. The chief judge of the circuit may delegate such approval authority to an active circuit judge.

(4) **Filing claims.**—A separate claim for compensation and reimbursement shall be made to the district court for representation before the United States magistrate and the court, and to each appellate court before which the attorney provided representation to the person involved. Each claim shall be supported by a sworn written statement specifying the time expended, services rendered, and expenses incurred while the case was pending before the

United States magistrate and the court, and the compensation and reimbursement applied for or received in the same case from any other source. The court shall fix the compensation and reimbursement to be paid to the attorney or to the bar association or legal aid agency or community defender organization which provided the appointed attorney. In cases where representation is furnished exclusively before a United States magistrate, the claim shall be submitted to him and he shall fix the compensation and reimbursement to be paid. In cases where representation is furnished other than before the United States magistrate, the district court, or an appellate court, claims shall be submitted to the district court which shall fix the compensation and reimbursement to be paid.

(5) **New trials.**—For purposes of compensation and other payments authorized by this section, an order by a court granting a new trial shall be deemed to initiate a new case.

(6) **Proceedings before appellate courts.**—If a person for whom counsel is appointed under this section appeals to an appellate court or petitions for a writ of certiorari, he may do so without prepayment of fees and costs or security therefor and without filing the affidavit required by section 1915(a) of title 28.

(e) **Services other than counsel.**—

(1) **Upon request.**—Counsel for a person who is financially unable to obtain investigative, expert, or other services necessary for adequate representation may request them in an ex parte application. Upon finding, after appropriate inquiry in an ex parte proceeding, that the services are necessary and that the person is financially unable to obtain them, the court, or the United States magistrate if the services are required in connection with a matter over which he has jurisdiction, shall authorize counsel to obtain the services.

(2) **Without prior request.**—(A) Counsel appointed under this section may obtain, subject to later review, investigative, expert, and other services without prior authorization if necessary for adequate representation. Except as provided in subparagraph (B) of this paragraph, the total cost of services obtained without prior authorization may not exceed $300 and expenses reasonably incurred.

(B) The court, or the United States magistrate (if the services were rendered in a case disposed of entirely before the United States magistrate), may, in the interest of justice, and upon the finding that timely procurement of necessary services could not await prior authorization, approve payment for such services after they have been obtained, even if the cost of such services exceeds $300.

(3) Maximum amounts.—Compensation to be paid to a person for services rendered by him to a person under this subsection, or to be paid to an organization for services rendered by an employee thereof, shall not exceed $1,000, exclusive of reimbursement for expenses reasonably incurred, unless payment in excess of that limit is certified by the court, or by the United States magistrate if the services were rendered in connection with a case disposed of entirely before him, as necessary to provide fair compensation for services of an unusual character or duration, and the amount of the excess payment is approved by the chief judge of the circuit. The chief judge of the circuit may delegate such approval authority to an active circuit judge.

(f) Receipt of other payments.—Whenever the United States magistrate or the court finds that funds are available for payment from or on behalf of a person furnished representation, it may authorize or direct that such funds be paid to the appointed attorney, to the bar association or legal aid agency or community defender organization which provided the appointed attorney, to any person or organization authorized pursuant to subsection (e) to render investigative, expert, or other services, or to the court for deposit in the Treasury as a reimbursement to the appropriation, current at the time of payment, to carry out the provisions of this section. Except as so authorized or directed, no such person or organization may request or accept any payment or promise of payment for representing a defendant.

(g) Defender organization.—

(1) Qualifications.—A district or a part of a district in which at least two hundred persons annually require the appointment of counsel may establish a defender organization as provided for either under subparagraphs (A) or (B) of paragraph (2) of this subsection or both. Two adjacent districts or parts of districts may aggregate the number of persons required to be represented to establish eligibility for a defender organization to serve both areas. In the event that adjacent districts or parts of districts are located in different circuits, the plan for furnishing representation shall be approved by the judicial council of each circuit.

(2) Types of defender organizations.—

(A) Federal Public Defender Organization.—A Federal Public Defender Organization shall consist of one or more full-time salaried attorneys. An organization for a district or part of a district or two adjacent districts or parts of districts shall be supervised by a Federal Public Defender appointed by the court of appeals of the circuit, without regard to the provisions of title 5 governing appointments in the competitive service, after considering recommendations from the district court or courts to be served. Nothing contained herein shall be deemed to authorize more than one Federal Public Defender within a single judicial district. The Federal Public Defender shall be appointed for a term of four years, unless sooner removed by the court of appeals of the circuit for incompetency, misconduct in office, or neglect of duty. Upon the expiration of his term, a Federal Public Defender may, by a majority vote of the judges of the court of appeals, continue to perform the duties of his office until his successor is appointed, or until one year after the expiration of such Defender's term, whichever is earlier. The compensation of the Federal Public Defender shall be fixed by the court of appeals of the circuit at a rate not to exceed the compensation received by the United States attorney for the district where representation is furnished or, if two districts or parts of districts are involved, the compensation of the higher paid United States attorney of the districts. The Federal Public Defender may appoint, without regard to the provisions of title 5 governing appointments in the competitive service, full-time attorneys in such number as may be approved by the court of appeals of the circuit and other personnel in such number as may be approved by the Director of the Administrative Office of the United States Courts. Compensation paid to such attorneys and other personnel of the organization shall be fixed by the Federal Public Defender at a rate not to exceed that paid to attorneys and other personnel of similar qualifications and experience in the Office of the United States attorney in the district where representation is furnished or, if two districts or parts of districts are involved, the higher compensation paid to persons of similar qualifications and experience in the districts. Neither the Federal Public Defender nor any attorney so appointed by him may engage in the private practice of law. Each organization shall submit to the Director of the Administrative Office of the United States Courts, at the time and in the form prescribed by him, reports of its activities and financial position and its proposed budget. The Director of the Administrative Office shall submit, in accordance with section 605 of title 28, a budget for each organization for each fiscal year and shall out of the appropriations therefor make payments to and on behalf of each organization. Payments under this subparagraph to an organization shall be in lieu of payments under subsection (d) or (e).

(B) **Community Defender Organization.**—A Community Defender Organization shall be a non-profit defense counsel service established and administered by any group authorized by the plan to provide representation. The organization shall be eligible to furnish attorneys and receive payments under this section if its bylaws are set forth in the plan of the district or districts in which it will serve. Each organization shall submit to the Judicial Conference of the United States an annual report setting forth its activities and financial position and the anticipated caseload and expenses for the next fiscal year. Upon application an organization may, to the extent approved by the Judicial Conference of the United States:

(i) receive an initial grant for expenses necessary to establish the organization; and

(ii) in lieu of payments under subsection (d) or (e), receive periodic sustaining grants to provide representation and other expenses pursuant to this section.

(3) **Malpractice and negligence suits.**—The Director of the Administrative Office of the United States Courts shall, to the extent the Director considers appropriate, provide representation for and hold harmless, or provide liability insurance for, any person who is an officer or employee of a Federal Public Defender Organization established under this subsection, or a Community Defender Organization established under this subsection which is receiving periodic sustaining grants, for money damages for injury, loss of liberty, loss of property, or personal injury or death arising from malpractice or negligence of any such officer or employee in furnishing representational services under this section while acting within the scope of that person's office or employment.

(h) **Rules and reports.**—Each district court and court of appeals of a circuit shall submit a report on the appointment of counsel within its jurisdiction to the Administrative Office of the United States Courts in such form and at such times as the Judicial Conference of the United States may specify. The Judicial Conference of the United States may, from time to time, issue rules and regulations governing the operation of plans formulated under this section.

(i) **Appropriations.**—There are authorized to be appropriated to the United States courts, out of any money in the Treasury not otherwise appropriated, sums necessary to carry out the provisions of this section, including funds for the continuing education and training of persons providing representational services under this section. When so specified in appropriation acts, such appropriations shall remain available until expended. Payments from such appropriations shall be made under the supervision of the Director of the Administrative Office of the United States Courts.

(j) **Districts included.**—As used in this section, the term "district court" means each district court of the United States created by chapter 5 of title 28, the District Court of the Virgin Islands, the District Court for the Northern Mariana Islands, and the District Court of Guam.

(k) **Applicability in the District of Columbia.**—The provisions of this section shall apply in the United States District Court for the

District of Columbia and the United States Court of Appeals for the District of Columbia Circuit. The provisions of this section shall not apply to the Superior Court of the District of Columbia and the District of Columbia Court of Appeals.

28 U.S.C.A.

CHAPTER 5. DISTRICT COURTS

§ 144. Bias or prejudice of judge

Whenever a party to any proceeding in a district court makes and files a timely and sufficient affidavit that the judge before whom the matter is pending has a personal bias or prejdice either against him or in favor of any adverse party, such judge shall proceed no further therein, but another judge shall be assigned to hear such proceeding.

The affidavit shall state the facts and the reasons for the belief that bias or prejudice exists, and shall be filed not less than ten days before the beginning of the term at which the proceeding is to be heard, or good cause shall be shown for failure to file it within such time. A party may file only one such affidavit in any case. It shall be accompanied by a certificate of counsel of record stating that it is made in good faith.

CHAPTER 17. JUDGES—RESIGNATION—RETIREMENT

§ 372. Retirement for disability; substitute judge on failure to retire; judicial discipline

(a) Any justice or judge of the United States appointed to hold office during good behavior who becomes permanently disabled from performing his duties may retire from regular active service, and the President shall, by and with the advice and consent of the Senate, appoint a successor.

Any justice or judge of the United States desiring to retire under this section shall certify to the President his disability in writing.

Whenever an associate justice of the Supreme Court, a chief judge of a circuit or the chief judge of the Court of International Trade, desires to retire under this section, he shall furnish to the President a certificate of disability signed by the Chief Justice of the United States.

A circuit or district judge, desiring to retire under this section, shall furnish to the President a certificate of disability signed by the chief judge of his circuit.

A judge of the Court of International Trade desiring to retire under this section, shall furnish to the President a certificate of disability signed by the chief judge of his court.

Each justice or judge retiring under this section after serving ten years continuously or otherwise shall, during the remainder of his lifetime, receive the salary of the office. A justice or judge retiring under this section who has served less than ten years in all shall, during the remainder of his lifetime, receive one-half the salary of the office.

(b) Whenever any judge of the United States appointed to hold office during good behavior who is eligible to retire under this section does not do so and a certificate of his disability signed by a majority of the members of the Judicial Council of his circuit in the case of a circuit or district judge, or by the Chief Justice of the United States in the case of the Chief Judge of the Court of International Trade, or by the chief judge of his court in the case of a judge of the Court of International Trade, is presented to the President and the President finds that such judge is unable to discharge efficiently all the duties of his office by reason of permanent mental or physical disability and that the appointment of an additional judge is necessary for the efficient dispatch of business, the President may make such appointment by and with the advice and consent of the Senate. Whenever any such additional judge is appointed, the vacancy subsequently caused by the death, resignation, or retirement of the disabled judge shall not be filled. Any judge whose disability causes the appointment of an additional judge shall, for purpose of precedence, service as chief judge, or temporary performance of the duties of that office, be treated as junior in commission to the other judges of the circuit, district, or court.

(c)(1) Any person alleging that a circuit, district, or bankruptcy judge, or a magistrate, has engaged in conduct prejudicial to the effective and expeditious administration of the business of the courts, or alleging that such a judge or magistrate is unable to discharge all the duties of office by reason of mental or physical disability, may file with the clerk of the court of appeals for the circuit a written complaint containing a brief statement of the facts constituting such conduct.

(2) Upon receipt of a complaint filed under paragraph (1) of this subsection, the clerk shall promptly transmit such complaint to the chief judge of the circuit, or, if the conduct complained of is that of the chief judge, to that circuit judge in regular active service next senior in date of commission (hereafter, for purposes of this subsection only, included in the term "chief judge"). The clerk shall simultaneously transmit a copy of the complaint to the judge or magistrate whose conduct is the subject of the complaint.

(3) After expeditiously reviewing a complaint, the chief judge, by written order stating his reasons, may—

> (A) dismiss the complaint, if he finds it to be (i) not in conformity with paragraph (1) of this subsection, (ii) directly related to the merits of a decision or procedural ruling, or (iii) frivolous; or

(B) conclude the proceeding if he finds that appropriate corrective action has been taken.

The chief judge shall transmit copies of his written order to the complainant and to the judge or magistrate whose conduct is the subject of the complaint.

(4) If the chief judge does not enter an order under paragraph (3) of this subsection, such judge shall promptly—

(A) appoint himself and equal numbers of circuit and district judges of the circuit to a special committee to investigate the facts and allegations contained in the complaint;

(B) certify the complaint and any other documents pertaining thereto to each member of such committee; and

(C) provide written notice to the complainant and the judge or magistrate whose conduct is the subject of the complaint of the action taken under this paragraph.

(5) Each committee appointed under paragraph (4) of this subsection shall conduct an investigation as extensive as it considers necessary, and shall expeditiously file a comprehensive written report thereon with the judicial council of the circuit. Such report shall present both the findings of the investigation and the committee's recommendations for necessary and appropriate action by the judicial council of the circuit.

(6) Upon receipt of a report filed under paragraph (5) of this subsection, the judicial council—

(A) may conduct any additional investigation which it considers to be necessary;

(B) shall take such action as is appropriate to assure the effective and expeditious administration of the business of the courts within the circuit, including, but not limited to, any of the following actions:

(i) directing the chief judge of the district of the magistrate whose conduct is the subject of the complaint to take such action as the judicial council considers appropriate;

(ii) certifying disability of a judge appointed to hold office during good behavior whose conduct is the subject of the complaint, pursuant to the procedures and standards provided under subsection (b) of this section;

(iii) requesting that any such judge appointed to hold office during good behavior voluntarily retire, with the provision that the length of service requirements under section 371 of this title shall not apply;

(iv) ordering that, on a temporary basis for a time certain, no further cases be assigned to any judge or magistrate whose conduct is the subject of a complaint;

    (v) censuring or reprimanding such judge or magistrate by means of private communication;

    (vi) censuring or reprimanding such judge or magistrate by means of public announcement; or

    (vii) ordering such other action as it considers appropriate under the circumstances, except that (I) in no circumstances may the council order removal from office of any judge appointed to hold office during good behavior, and (II) any removal of a magistrate shall be in accordance with section 631 of this title and any removal of a bankruptcy judge shall be in accordance with section 152 of this title; and

    (C) shall immediately provide written notice to the complainant and to such judge or magistrate of the action taken under this paragraph.

    (7)(A) In addition to the authority granted under paragraph (6) of this subsection, the judicial council may, in its discretion, refer any complaint under this subsection, together with the record of any associated proceedings and its recommendations for appropriate action, to the Judicial Conference of the United States.

    (B) In any case in which the judicial council determines, on the basis of a complaint and an investigation under this subsection, or on the basis of information otherwise available to the council, that a judge appointed to hold office during good behavior has engaged in conduct—

    (i) which might constitute one or more grounds for impeachment under article I of the Constitution; or

    (ii) which, in the interest of justice, is not amenable to resolution by the judicial council,

the judicial council shall promptly certify such determination, together with any complaint and a record of any associated proceedings, to the Judicial Conference of the United States.

    (C) A judicial council acting under authority of this paragraph shall, unless contrary to the interests of justice, immediately submit written notice to the complainant and to the judge or magistrate whose conduct is the subject of the action taken under this paragraph.

    (8) Upon referral or certification of any matter under paragraph (7) of this subsection, the Judicial Conference, after consideration of the prior proceedings and such additional investigation as it considers appropriate, shall by majority vote take such action, as described in paragraph (6)(B) of this subsection, as it considers appropriate. If the Judicial Conference concurs in the determination of the council, or makes its own determination, that consideration of impeachment may be warranted, it shall so certify and transmit the determination and the record of proceedings to the House of Representatives for whatever action the House of Representatives considers to be necessary.

(9)(A) In conducting any investigation under this subsection, the judicial council, or a special committee appointed under paragraph (4) of this subsection, shall have full subpoena powers as provided in section 332(d) of this title.

(B) In conducting any investigation under this subsection, the Judicial Conference, or a standing committee appointed by the Chief Justice under section 331 of this title, shall have full subpoena powers as provided in that section.

(10) A complainant, judge, or magistrate aggrieved by a final order of the chief judge under paragraph (3) of this subsection may petition the judicial council for review thereof. A complainant, judge, or magistrate aggrieved by an action of the judicial council under paragraph (6) of this subsection may petition the Judicial Conference of the United States for review thereof. The Judicial Conference, or the standing committee established under section 331 of this title, may grant a petition filed by a complainant, judge, or magistrate under this paragraph. Except as expressly provided in this paragraph, all orders and determinations, including denials of petitions for review, shall be final and conclusive and shall not be judicially reviewable on appeal or otherwise.

(11) Each judicial council and the Judicial Conference may prescribe such rules for the conduct of proceedings under this subsection, including the processing of petitions for review, as each considers to be appropriate. Such rules shall contain provisions requiring that—

(A) adequate prior notice of any investigation be given in writing to the judge or magistrate whose conduct is the subject of the complaint;

(B) the judge or magistrate whose conduct is the subject of the complaint be afforded an opportunity to appear (in person or by counsel) at proceedings conducted by the investigating panel, to present oral and documentary evidence, to compel the attendance of witnesses or the production of documents, to cross-examine witnesses, and to present argument orally or in writing; and

(C) the complainant be afforded an opportunity to appear at proceedings conducted by the investigating panel, if the panel concludes that the complainant could offer substantial information.

Any rule promulgated under this subsection shall be a matter of public record, and any such rule promulgated by a judicial council may be modified by the Judicial Conference. No rule promulgated under this subsection may limit the period of time within which a person may file a complaint under this subsection.

(12) No judge or magistrate whose conduct is the subject of an investigation under this subsection shall serve upon a special committee appointed under paragraph (4) of this subsection, upon a judicial council, upon the Judicial Conference, or upon the standing committee established under section 331 of this title, until all related proceedings under this subsection have been finally terminated.

(13) No person shall be granted the right to intervene or to appear as amicus curiae in any proceeding before a judicial council or the Judicial Conference under this subsection.

(14) All papers, documents, and records of proceedings related to investigations conducted under this subsection shall be confidential and shall not be disclosed by any person in any proceeding unless—

　　(A) the judicial council of the circuit, the Judicial Conference of the United States, or the Senate or the House of Representatives by resolution, releases any such material which is believed necessary to an impeachment investigation or trial of a judge under article I of the Constitution; or

　　(B) authorized in writing by the judge or magistrate who is the subject to the complaint and by the chief judge of the circuit, the Chief Justice, or the chairman of the standing committee established under section 331 of this title.

(15) Each written order to implement any action under paragraph (6)(B) of this subsection, which is issued by a judicial council, the Judicial Conference, or the standing committee established under section 331 of this title, shall be made available to the public through the appropriate clerk's office of the court of appeals for the circuit. Unless contrary to the interests of justice, each such order issued under this paragraph shall be accompanied by written reasons therefor.

(16) Except as expressly provided in this subsection, nothing in this subsection shall be construed to affect any other provision of this title, the Federal Rules of Civil Procedure, the Federal Rules of Criminal Procedure, the Federal Rules of Appellate Procedure, or the Federal Rules of Evidence.

(17) The United States Claims Court, the Court of International Trade, and the Court of Appeals for the Federal Circuit shall each prescribe rules, consistent with the foregoing provisions of this subsection, establishing procedures for the filing of complaints with respect to the conduct of any judge of such court and for the investigation and resolution of such complaints. In investigating and taking action with respect to any such complaint, each such court shall have the powers granted to a judicial council under this subsection.

CHAPTER 21.　COURTS AND JUDGES

§ 454.　Practice of law by justices and judges

Any justice or judge appointed under the authority of the United States who engages in the practice of law is guilty of a high misdemeanor.

§ 455. Disqualification of justice, judge, or magistrate

(a) Any justice, judge, or magistrate of the United States shall disqualify himself in any proceeding in which his impartiality might reasonably be questioned.

(b) He shall also disqualify himself in the following circumstances:

(1) Where he has a personal bias or prejudice concerning a party, or personal knowledge of disputed evidentiary facts concerning the proceeding;

(2) Where in private practice he served as lawyer in the matter in controversy, or a lawyer with whom he previously practiced law served during such association as a lawyer concerning the matter, or the judge or such lawyer has been a material witness concerning it;

(3) Where he has served in governmental employment and in such capacity participated as counsel, adviser or material witness concerning the proceeding or expressed an opinion concerning the merits of the particular case in controversy;

(4) He knows that he, individually or as a fiduciary, or his spouse or minor child residing in his household, has a financial interest in the subject matter in controversy or in a party to the proceeding, or any other interest that could be substantially affected by the outcome of the proceeding;

(5) He or his spouse, or a person within the third degree of relationship to either of them, or the spouse of such a person:

(i) Is a party to the proceeding, or an officer, director, or trustee of a party;

(ii) Is acting as a lawyer in the proceeding;

(iii) Is known by the judge to have an interest that could be substantially affected by the outcome of the proceeding;

(iv) Is to the judge's knowledge likely to be a material witness in the proceeding.

(c) A judge should inform himself about his personal and fiduciary financial interests, and make a reasonable effort to inform himself about the personal financial interests of his spouse and minor children residing in his household.

(d) For the purposes of this section the following words or phrases shall have the meaning indicated:

(1) "proceeding" includes pretrial, trial, appellate review, or other stages of litigation;

(2) the degree of relationship is calculated according to the civil law system;

(3) "fiduciary" includes such relationships as executor, administrator, trustee, and guardian;

461

(4) "financial interest" means ownership of a legal or equitable interest, however small, or a relationship as director, adviser, or other active participant in the affairs of a party, except that:

(i) Ownership in a mutual or common investment fund that holds securities is not a "financial interest" in such securities unless the judge participates in the management of the fund;

(ii) An office in an educational, religious, charitable, fraternal, or civic organization is not a "financial interest" in securities held by the organization;

(iii) The proprietary interest of a policyholder in a mutual insurance company, of a depositor in a mutual savings association, or a similar proprietary interest, is a "financial interest" in the organization only if the outcome of the proceeding could substantially affect the value of the interest;

(iv) Ownership of government securities is a "financial interest" in the issuer only if the outcome of the proceeding could substantially affect the value of the securities.

(e) No justice, judge, or magistrate shall accept from the parties to the proceeding a waiver of any ground for disqualification enumerated in subsection (b). Where the ground for disqualification arises only under subsection (a), waiver may be accepted provided it is preceded by a full disclosure on the record of the basis for disqualification.

(f) Notwithstanding the preceding provisions of this section, if any justice, judge, magistrate, or bankruptcy judge to whom a matter has been assigned would be disqualified, after substantial judicial time has been devoted to the matter, because of the appearance or discovery, after the matter was assigned to him or her, that he or she individually or as a fiduciary, or his or her spouse or minor child residing in his or her household, has a financial interest in a party (other than an interest that could be substantially affected by the outcome), disqualification is not required if the justice, judge, magistrate, bankruptcy judge, spouse or minor child, as the case may be, divests himself or herself of the interest that provides the grounds for the disqualification.

SELECTED RULES OF EVIDENCE AND PROCEDURE

Federal Rules of Evidence for United States Courts and Magistrates

FEDERAL RULES OF EVIDENCE FOR UNITED STATES COURTS AND MAGISTRATES

Rule 501. General Rule

Except as otherwise required by the Constitution of the United States or provided by Act of Congress or in rules prescribed by the Supreme Court pursuant to statutory authority, the privilege of a witness, person, government, State, or political subdivision thereof shall be governed by the principles of common law as they may be interpreted by the courts of the United States in the light of reason and experience. However, in civil actions and proceedings, with respect to

463

an element of a claim or defense as to which State law supplies the rule of decision, the privilege of a witness, person, government, State, or political subdivision thereof shall be determined in accordance with State law.

Rule 605. Competency of Judge as Witness

The judge presiding at the trial may not testify in that trial as a witness. No objection need be made in order to preserve the point.

APPENDIX OF DELETED RULES OF EVIDENCE

Rule 503. Lawyer-Client Privilege [Not enacted.]

(a) Definitions. As used in this rule:

(1) A "client" is a person, public officer, or corporation, association, or other organization or entity, either public or private, who is rendered professional legal services by a lawyer, or who consults a lawyer with a view to obtaining professional legal services from him.

(2) A "lawyer" is a person authorized, or reasonably believed by the client to be authorized, to practice law in any state or nation.

(3) A "representative of the lawyer" is one employed to assist the lawyer in the rendition of professional services.

(4) A communication is "confidential" if not intended to be disclosed to third persons other than those to whom disclosure is in furtherance of the rendition of professional legal services to the client or those reasonably necessary for the transmission of the communication.

(b) General rule of privilege. A client has a privilege to refuse to disclose and to prevent any other person from disclosing confidential communications made for the purpose of facilitating the rendition of professional legal services to the client, (1) between himself or his representative and his lawyer or his lawyer's representative, or (2) between his lawyer and the lawyer's representative, or (3) by him or his lawyer to a lawyer representing another in a matter of common interest, or (4) between representatives of the client or between the client and a representative of the client, or (5) between lawyers representing the client.

(c) Who may claim the privilege. The privilege may be claimed by the client, his guardian or conservator, the personal representative of a deceased client, or the successor, trustee, or similar representative of a corporation, association, or other organization, whether or not in existence. The person who was the lawyer at the time of the communication may claim the privilege but only on behalf of the client. His authority to do so is presumed in the absence of evidence to the contrary.

(d) Exceptions. There is no privilege under this rule:

(1) Furtherance of crime or fraud. If the services of the lawyer were sought or obtained to enable or aid anyone to commit or plan to commit what the client knew or reasonably should have known to be a crime or fraud; or

(2) Claimants through same deceased client. As to a communication relevant to an issue between parties who claim through the same deceased client, regardless of whether the claims are by testate or intestate sucession or by *inter vivos* transaction; or

(3) Breach of duty by lawyer or client. As to a communication relevant to an issue of breach of duty by the lawyer to his client or by the client to his lawyer; or

(4) Document attested by lawyer. As to a communication relevant to an issue concerning an attested document to which the lawyer is an attesting witness; or

(5) Joint clients. As to a communication relevant to a matter of common interest between two or more clients if the communication was made by any of them to a lawyer retained or consulted in common, when offered in an action between any of the clients.

FEDERAL RULES OF CIVIL PROCEDURE
(as amended to May 1, 1988)

Rule 11. Signing of Pleadings, Motions, and Other Papers; Sanctions

Every pleading, motion, and other paper of a party represented by an attorney shall be signed by at least one attorney of record in the attorney's individual name, whose address shall be stated. A party who is not represented by an attorney shall sign the party's pleading, motion, or other paper and state the party's address. Except when otherwise specifically provided by rule or statute, pleadings need not be verified or accompanied by affidavit. The rule in equity that the averments of an answer under oath must be overcome by the testimony of two witnesses or of one witness sustained by corroborating circumstances is abolished. The signature of an attorney or party constitutes a certificate by the signer that the signer has read the pleading, motion, or other paper; that to the best of the signer's knowledge, information, and belief formed after reasonable inquiry it is well grounded in fact and is warranted by existing law or a good faith argument for the extension, modification, or reversal of existing law, and that it is not interposed for any improper purpose, such as to harass or to cause unnecessary delay or needless increase in the cost of litigation. If a pleading, motion, or other paper is not signed, it shall be stricken unless it is signed promptly after the omission is called to the attention of the pleader or movant.　If a pleading, motion, or other paper is signed in violation of this rule, the court, upon motion or upon its own initiative, shall impose upon the person who signed it, a represented party, or both, an appropriate sanction, which may include an order to pay to the other party or parties the amount of the reasonable expenses incurred because of the filing of the pleading, motion, or other paper, including a reasonable attorney's fee.

(As amended Apr. 28, 1983, eff. Aug. 1, 1983; Mar. 2, 1987, eff. Aug. 1, 1987).

1983 Amendment

Since its original promulgation, Rule 11 has provided for the striking of pleadings and the imposition of disciplinary sanctions to check abuses in the signing of pleadings. Its provisions have always applied to motions and other papers by virtue of incorporation by reference in Rule 7(b)(2).　The amendment and the addition of Rule 7(b)(3) expressly confirms this applicability.

Experience shows that in practice Rule 11 has not been effective in deterring abuses. See 6 Wright & Miller, Federal Practice and Procedure: Civil § 1334 (1971).　There has been considerable confusion as to (1) the circumstances that should trigger striking a pleading or motion or taking disciplinary action, (2) the standard of conduct expected of attorneys who sign pleadings and motions, and (3) the range of available and appropriate sanctions.　See Rodes, Ripple & Mooney, Sanctions Imposable for Violations of the Federal Rules of Civil Procedure 64–65, Federal Judicial Center (1981).　The new language is intended to reduce the reluctance of courts to impose sanctions, see Moore, Federal Practice ¶ 7.05, at 1547, by emphasizing the responsibilities of the attorney and reenforcing those obligations by the imposition of sanctions.

The amended rule attempts to deal with the problem by building upon and expanding the equitable doctrine permitting the court to award expenses, including attorney's fees, to a litigant whose opponent acts in bad faith in institutin or conduction litigation.　See, e.g., *Roadway Express, Inc. v. Piper*, 447 U.S. 752, (1980); *Hall v. Cole*, 412 U.S. 1, 5 (1973). Greater attention by the district courts to pleading and motion abuse and the imposition of sanctions when appropriate, should idscourage dilatory or abusive tactics and help to streamline the litigation process by lessening frivolous claims or defenses.

The expanded nature of the lawyer's certification in the fifth sentence of amended Rule 11 recognizes that the litigation process may be abused for purposes other than delay.　See, e.g., *Browning Debenture Holders' Committee v. DASA Corp.*, 560 F.2d 1078 (2d Cir.1977).

The words "good ground to support" the pleading in the original rule were interpreted to have both factual and legal elements.　See, e.g., *Heart Disease Research Foundation v. General Motors Corp.*, 15 Fed.R.Serv.2d 1517, 1519 (S.D.N.Y.1972).　They have been replaced by a standard of conduct that is more focused.

The new language stresses the need for some prefiling inquiry into both the facts and the law to satisfy the affirmative duty imposed by the rule.　The standard is one of reasonableness under the circumstances.　See *Kinee v. Abraham Lincoln Fed. Sav. & Loan Ass'n*, 365 F.Supp. 975 (E.D.Pa.1973).　This standard is more stringent than the original good-faith formula and thus it is expected that a greater range of circumstances will trigger its violation.　See *Nemeroff v. Abelson*, 620 F.2d 339 (2d Cir.1980).

The rule is not intended to chill an attorney's enthusiasm or creativity in pursuing factual or legal theories.　The court is expected to avoid using the wisdom of hindsight and should test the signer's conduct by inquiring what was reasonable to believe at the time the pleading, motion, or other paper was submitted.　Thus, what constitutes a reasonable inquiry may depend on such is expected to avoid using the wisdom of hindsight and should test the signer's conduct by inquiring what was reasonable to believe at the time the pleading, motion, or other paper was submitted.　Thus, what constitutes a reasonable inquiry may depend on such factors as how much time for investigation was available to the signer; whether he had to rely on a client for information as to the facts underlying the pleading, motion, or other paper; whether the pleading, motion, or other paper was based on a plausible view of the law; or whether he depended on forwarding counsel or another member of the bar.

The rule does not require a party or an attorney to disclose privileged communications or work product in order to show that the signing of the pleading, motion, or other paper is substantially justified. The provisions of Rule 26(c), including appropriate orders after in camera inspection by the court, remain available to protect a party claiming privilege or work product protection.

Amended Rule 11 continues to apply to anyone who signs a pleading, motion, or other paper. Although the standard is the same for unrepresented parties, who are obliged themselves to sign the pleadings, the court has sufficient discretion to take account of the special circumstances that often arise in pro se situations. See *Haines v. Kerner*, 404 U.S. 519 (1972).

The provision in the original rule for striking pleadings and motions as sham and false has been deleted. The passage has rarely been utilized, and decisions thereunder have tended to confuse the issue of attorney honesty with the merits of the action. See generally Risinger, Honesty in Pleading and its Enforcement: Some "Striking" Problems with Fed.R.Civ.P. 11, 61 Minn.L.Rev. 1 (1976). Motions under this provision generally present issues better dealt with under Rules 8, 12, or 56. See *Murchison v. Kirby*, 27 F.R.D. 14 (S.D.N.Y.1961); 5 Wright & Miller, Federal Practice and Procedure: Civil § 1334 (1969).

The former reference to the inclusion of scandalous or indecent matter, which is itself strong indication that an improper purpose underlies the pleading, motion, or other paper, also has been deleted as unnecessary. Such matter may be stricken under Rule 12(f) as well as dealt with under the more general language of amended Rule 11.

The text of the amended rule seeks to dispel apprehensions that efforts to obtain enforcement will be fruitless by insuring that the rule will be applied when properly invoked. The word "sanctions" in the caption for example, stresses a deterrent orientation in dealing with improper pleadings, motions or other papers. This corresponds to the approach in imposing sanctions for discovery abuses. See *National Hockey League v. Metropolitan Hockey Club*, 427 U.S. 639 (1976) (per curiam). And the words "shall impose" in the last sentence focus the court's attention on the need to impose sanctions for pleading and motion abuses. The court, however, retains the necessary flexibility to deal appropriately with violations of the rule. It has discretion to tailor sanctions to the particular facts of the case, with which it should be well acquainted.

The reference in the former text to wilfulness as a prerequisite to disciplinary action has been deleted. However, in considering the nature and severity of the sanctions to be imposed, the court should take account of the state of the attorney's or party's actual or presumed knowledge when the pleading or other paper was signed. Thus, for example, when a party is not represented by counsel, the absence of legal advise is an appropriate factor to be considered.

Courts currently appear to believe they may impose sanctions on their own motion. See *North American Trading Corp. v. Zale Corp.*, 73 F.R.D. 293 (S.D.N.Y.1979). Authority to do so has been made explicit in order to overcome the traditional reluctance of courts to intervene unless requested by one of the parties. The detection and punishment of a violation of the signing requirement, encouraged by the amended rule, is part of the court's responsibility for securing the system's effective operation.

If the duty imposed by the rule is violated, the court should have the discretion to impose sanctions on either the attorney, the party the signing attorney represents, or both, or on an unrepresented party who signed the pleading, and the new rule so provides. Although Rule 11 has been silent on the point, courts have claimed the power to impose sanctions on an attorney personally, either by imposing costs or employing the contempt technique. See 5 Wright & Miller, Federal Practice and Procedure: Civil § 1334 (1969); 2A Moore, Federal Practice ¶ 11.02, at 2104 n. 8. This power has been used infrequently. The amended rule should eliminate any doubt as to the propriety of assessing sanctions against the attorney.

Even though it is the attorney whose signature violates the rule, it may be appropriate under the circumstances of the case to impose a sanction on the client. See *Browning Debenture Holders' Committee v. DASA Corp.*, supra. This modification brings Rule 11 in line with practice under Rule 37, which allows sanctions for abuses during discovery to be imposed upon the party, the attorney, or both.

A party seeking sanctions should give notice to the court and the offending party promptly upon discovering a basis for doing so. The time when sanctions are to be imposed rests in the discretion of the trial judge. However, it is anticipated that in the case of pleadings the sanctions issue under Rule 11 normally will be determined at the end of the litigation, and in the case of motions at the time when the motion is decided or shortly thereafter. The procedure obviously must comport with due process requirements. The particular format to be followed should depend on the circumstances of the situation and the severity of the sanction under consideration. In many situations the judge's participation in the proceedings provides him with full knowledge of the relevant facts and little further inquiry will be necessary.

To assure that the efficiencies achieved through more effective operation of the pleading regiment will not be offset by the cost of satellite litigation over the imposition of sanctions, the court must to the extent possible limit the scope of sanction proceedings to the record. Thus, discovery should be conducted only by leave of the court, and then only is extraordinary circumstances.

Although the encompassing reference to "other papers" in new Rule 11 literally includes discovery papers, the certification requirement in that context is governed by proposed new Rule 26(g). Discovery motions, however, fall within the ambit of Rule 11.

Rule 16. Pretrial Conferences; Scheduling; Management

(a) Pretrial Conferences; Objectives. In any action, the court may in its discretion direct the attorneys for the parties and any unrepresented parties to appear before it for a conference or conferences before trial for such purposes as

    (1) expediting the disposition of the action;

    (2) establishing early and continuing control so that the case will not be protracted because of lack of management;

    (3) discouraging wasteful pretrial activities;

    (4) improving the quality of the trial through more thorough preparation, and;

    (5) facilitating the settlement of the case.

(b) Scheduling and Planning. Except in categories of actions exempted by district court rule as inappropriate, the judge, or a magistrate when authorized by district court rule, shall, after consulting with the attorneys for the parties and any unrepresented parties, by a scheduling conference, telephone, mail, or other suitable means, enter a scheduling order that limits the time

    (1) to join other parties and to amend the pleadings;

    (2) to file and hear motions; and

    (3) to complete discovery.

The scheduling order also may include

    (4) the date or dates for conferences before trial, a final pretrial conference, and trial; and

    (5) any other matters appropriate in the circumstances of the case.

The order shall issue as soon as practicable but in no event more than 120 days after filing of the complaint. A schedule shall not be modified except by leave of the judge or a magistrate when authorized by district court rule upon a showing of good cause.

(c) Subjects to Be Discussed at Pretrial Conferences. The participants at any conference under this rule may consider and take action with respect to

(1) the formulation and simplification of the issues, including the elimination of frivolous claims or defenses;

(2) the necessity or desirability of amendments to the pleadings;

(3) the possibility of obtaining admissions of fact and of documents which will avoid unnecessary proof, stipulations regarding the authenticity of documents, and advance rulings from the court on the admissibility of evidence;

(4) the avoidance of unnecessary proof and of cumulative evidence;

(5) the identification of witnesses and documents, the need and schedule for filing and exchanging pretrial briefs, and the date or dates for further conferences and for trial;

(6) the advisability of referring matters to a magistrate or master;

(7) the possibility of settlement or the use of extrajudicial procedures to resolve the dispute;

(8) the form and substance of the pretrial order;

(9) the disposition of pending motions;

(10) the need for adopting special procedures for managing potentially difficult or protracted actions that may involve complex issues, multiple parties, difficult legal questions or unusual proof problems; and

(11) such other matters as may aid in the disposition of the action.

At least one of the attorneys for each party participating in any conference before trial shall have authority to enter into stipulations and to make admissions regarding all matters that the participants may reasonably anticipate may be discussed.

(d) Final Pretrial Conference. Any final pretrial conference shall be held as close to the time of trial as reasonable under the circumstances. The participants at any such conference shall formulate a plan for trial, including a program for facilitating the admission of evidence. The conference shall be attended by at least one of the attorneys who will conduct the trial for each of the parties and by any unrepresented parties.

(e) Pretrial Orders. After any conference held pursuant to this rule, an order shall be entered reciting the action taken. This order shall control the subsequent course of the action unless modified by a subsequent order. The order following a final pretrial conference shall be modified only to prevent manifest injustice.

(f) Sanctions. If a party or party's attorney fails to obey a scheduling or pretrial order, or if no appearance is made on behalf of a party at a scheduling or pretrial conference, or if a party or party's attorney is substantially unprepared to participate in the conference, or if a party or party's attorney fails to participate in good faith, the judge, upon motion or the judge's own initiative, may make such orders with regard hereto as are just, and among others any of the orders provided in Rule 37(b)(2)(B), (C), (D). In lieu of or in addition to any other sanction, the judge shall require the party or the attorney representing the party or both to pay the reasonable expenses incurred because of any noncompliance with this rule, including attorney's fees, unless the judge finds that the noncompliance was substantially justified or that other circumstances make an award of expenses unjust.

(As amended Apr. 28, 1983, eff. Aug. 1, 1983; Mar. 2, 1987, eff. Aug. 1, 1987.)

1983 Amendment

Introduction

Rule 16 has not been amended since the Federal Rules were promulgated in 1938. In many reports, the rule has been a success. For example, there is evidence that pretrial conferences may improve the quality of justice rendered in the federal courts by sharpening the preparation and presentation of cases, tending to eliminate trial surprise, and improving, as well as facilitating, the settlement process. See 6 Wright & Miller, *Federal Practice and Procedure: Civil* § 1522 (1971). However, in other respects particularly with regard to case management, the rule has not always been as helpful as it might have been. Thus there has been a widespread feeling that amendment is necessary to encourage pretrial management that meets the needs of modern litigation. See *Report of the National Commission for the Review of Antitrust Laws and Procedures* (1979).

Major criticism of Rule 16 has centered on the fact that its application can result in over-regulation of some cases and under-regulation of others. In simple, run-of-the-mill cases, attorneys have found pretrial requirements burdensome. It is claimed that over-administration leads to a series of mini-trials that result in a waste of an attorney's time and needless expense to a client. Pollack, *Pretrial Procedures More Effectively Handled*, 65 F.R.D. 475 (1974). This is especially likely to be true when pretrial proceedings occur long before trial. At the other end of the spectrum, the discretionary character of Rule 16 and its orientation toward a single conference late in the pretrial process has led to under-administration of complex or protracted cases. Without judicial guidance beginning shortly after institution, these cases often become mired in discovery.

Four sources of criticism of pretrial have been identified. First, conferences often are seen as a mere exchange of legalistic contentions without any real analysis of the particular case. Second, the result frequently is nothing but a formal agreement on minutiae. Third, the conferences are seen as unnecessary and time-consuming in cases that will be settled before trial. Fourth, the meetings can be ceremonial and ritualistic, having little effect on the trial and being of minimal value, particularly when the attorneys attending the sessions are not the ones who will try the case or lack authority to enter into binding stipulations. See generally *McCargo v. Hedrick*, 545 F.2d 393 (4th Cir.1976); Pollack, *Pretrial Procedures More Efficiently Handled*, 65 F.R.D. 475 (1974); Rosenberg, *The Pretrial Conference and Effective Justice* 45 (1964).

There also have been difficulties with the pretrial orders that issue following Rule 16 conferences. When an order is entered far in advance of trial, some issues may not be properly formulated. Counsel naturally are cautious and often try to preserve as many options as possible. If the judge who tries the case did not conduct the conference, he could find it difficult to determine exactly what was agreed to at the conference. But any insistence on a detailed order may be too burdensome, depending on the nature or posture of the case.

Given the significant changes in federal civil litigation since 1938 that are not reflected in Rule 16, it has been extensively rewritten and expanded to meet the challenges of modern litigation. Empirical studies reveal that when a trial judge intervenes personally at an early stage to assume judicial control over a case and to schedule dates for completion by the parties of the principal pretrial steps, the case is disposed of by settlement or trial more efficiently and with less cost and delay than when the parties are left to their own devices. Flanders, *Case Management and Court Management in United States District Courts* 17, Federal Judicial Center (1977). Thus, the rule mandates a pretrial scheduling order. However, although scheduling and pretrial conferences are encouraged in appropriate cases, they are not mandated.

Discussion

. . . .

Subdivision (f); Sanctions. Original Rule 16 did not mention the sanctions that might be imposed for failing to comply with the rule. However, courts have not hesitated to enforce it by appropriate measures. See, *e.g., Link v. Wabash R. Co.,* 370 U.S. 626 (1962) (district court's dismissal under Rule 41(b) after plaintiff's attorney failed to appear at a pretrial conference upheld); *Admiral Theatre Corp. v. Douglas Theatre,* 585 F.2d 877 (8th Cir.1978) (district court has discretion to exclude exhibits or refuse to permit the testimony of a witness not listed prior to trial in contravention of its pretrial order).

To reflect that existing dependence upon Rule 41(b) or the court's inherent power to regulate litigation, *cf. Societe Internationale Pour Participations Industrielles et Commerciales, S.A. v. Rogers,* 357 U.S. 197 (1958), Rule 16(f) expressly provides for imposing sanctions on disobedient or recalcitrant parties, their attorneys, or both in four types of situations. Rodes, Ripple & Mooney, *Sanctions Imposable for Violations of the Federal Rules of Civil Procedure* 65–67, 80–84, Federal Judicial Center (1981). Furthermore, explicit reference to sanctions reenforces the rule's intention to encourage forceful judicial management.

Rule 16(f) incorporates portions of Rule 37(b)(2), which prescribes sanctions for failing to make discovery. This should facilitate application of Rule 16(f), since courts and lawyers already are familiar with the Rule 37 standards. Among the sanctions authorized by the new subdivision are: preclusion order, striking a pleading, staying the proceeding, default judgment, contempt, and charging a party, his attorney, or both with the expenses, including attorney's fees, caused by noncompliance. The contempt sanction, however, is only available for a violation of a court order. The references in Rule 16(f) are not exhaustive.

As is true under Rule 37(b)(2), the imposition of sanctions may be sought by either the court or a party. In addition, the court has discretion to impose whichever sanction it feels is appropriate under the circumstances. Its action is reviewable under the abuse-of-discretion standard. See *National Hockey League v. Metropolitan Hockey Club, Inc.,* 427 U.S. 639 (1976).

Rule 26. General Provisions Governing Discovery

(a) Discovery Methods. Parties may obtain discovery by one or more of the following methods: depositions upon oral examination or written questions; written interrogatories; production of documents or things or permission to enter upon land or other property, for inspection and other purposes; physical and mental examinations; and requests for admission.

(b) Discovery Scope and Limits. Unless otherwise limited by order of the court in accordance with these rules, the scope of discovery is as follows:

(1) In General. Parties may obtain discovery regarding any matter, not privileged, which is relevant to the subject matter involved in the pending action, whether it relates to the claim or defense of the party seeking discovery or to the claim or defense of any other party, including the existence, description, nature, custody, condition and location of any books, documents, or other tangible things and the identity and location of persons having knowledge of any discoverable matter. It is not ground for objection that the information sought will be inadmissible at the trial if the information sought appears reasonably calculated to lead to the discovery of admissible evidence.

The frequency or extent of use of the discovery methods set forth in subdivision (a) shall be limited by the court if it determines that: (i) the discovery sought is unreasonably cumulative or duplicative, or is obtainable from some other source that is more convenient, less burdensome, or less expensive; (ii) the party seeking discovery has had ample opportunity by discovery in the action to obtain the information sought; or (iii) the discovery is unduly burdensome or expensive, taking into account the needs of the case, the amount in controversy, limitations on the parties' resources, and the importance of the issues at stake in the litigation. The court may act upon its own initiative after reasonable notice or pursuant to a motion under subdivision (c).

(2) Insurance Agreements. A party may obtain discovery of the existence and contents of any insurance agreement under which any person carrying on an insurance business may be liable to satisfy part or all of a judgment which may be entered in the action or to indemnify or reimburse for payments made to satisfy the judgment. Information concerning the insurance agreement is not by reason of disclosure admissible in evidence at trial. For purposes of this paragraph, an application for insurance shall not be treated as part of an insurance agreement.

(3) Trial Preparation; Materials. Subject to the provisions of subdivision (b)(4) of this rule, a party may obtain discovery of documents and tangible things otherwise discoverable under subdivision (b)(1) of this rule and prepared in anticipation of litigation or for trial by or for another party or by or for that other party's representative (including the other party's attorney, consultant, surety, indemnitor, insurer, or agent) only upon a showing that the party seeking discovery has substantial need of the materials in the preparation of the party's case and that the party is unable without undue hardship to obtain the substantial equivalent of the materials by other means. In ordering discovery of such materials when

472

the required showing has been made, the court shall protect against disclosure of the mental impressions, conclusions, opinions, or legal theories of an attorney or other representative of a party concerning the litigation.

A party may obtain without the required showing a statement concerning the action or its subject matter previously made by that party. Upon request, a person not a party may obtain without the required showing a statement concerning the action or its subject matter previously made by that person. If the request is refused, the person may move for a court order. The provisions of Rule 37(a)(4) apply to the award of expenses incurred in relation to the motion. For purposes of this paragraph, a statement previously made is (A) a written statement signed or otherwise adopted or approved by the person making it, or (B) a stenographic, mechanical, electrical, or other recording, or a transcription thereof, which is a substantially verbatim recital of an oral statement by the person making it and contemporaneously recorded.

(4) **Trial Preparation; Experts.** Discovery of facts known and opinions held by experts, otherwise discoverable under the provisions of subdivision (b)(1) of this rule and acquired or developed in anticipation of litigation or for trial, may be obtained only as follows:

(A)(i) A party may through interrogatories require any other party to identify each person whom the other party expects to call as an expert witness at trial, to state the subject matter on which the expert is expected to testify, and to state the substance of the facts and opinions to which the expert is expected to testify and a summary of the grounds for each opinion. (ii) Upon motion, the court may order further discovery by other means, subject to such restrictions as to scope and such provisions, pursuant to subdivision (b)(4)(C) of this rule, concerning fees and expenses as the court may deem appropriate.

(B) A party may discover facts known or opinions held by an expert who has been retained or specially employed by another party in anticipation of litigation or preparation for trial and who is not expected to be called as a witness at trial, only as provided in Rule 35(b) or upon a showing of exceptional circumstances under which it is impracticable for the party seeking discovery to obtain facts or opinions on the same subject by other means.

(C) Unless manifest injustice would result, (i) the court shall require that the party seeking discovery pay the expert a reasonable fee for time spent in responding to discovery under subdivisions (b)(4)(A)(ii) and (b)(4)(B) of this rule; and (ii) with respect to discovery obtained under subdivision (b)(4)(A)(ii) of this rule the court may require, and with respect to discovery obtained under subdivision (b)(4)(B) of this rule the court shall require, the party seeking discovery to pay the other party a fair portion of the fees and expenses reasonably incurred by the latter part in obtaining facts and opinions from the expert.

(c) **Protective Orders.** Upon motion by a party or by the person from whom discovery is sought, and for good cause shown, the court in which the action is pending or alternatively, on matters relating to a deposition, the court in the district where the deposition is to be taken may make any order which justice requires to protect a party or person from annoyance, embarrassment, oppression, or undue burden or expense, including one or more of the following: (1) that the discovery not be had; (2) that the discovery may be had only on specified terms and conditions, including a designation of the time or place; (3) that the discovery may be had only by a method of discovery other than that selected by the party seeking discovery; (4) that certain matters not be inquired into, or that the scope of the discovery be limited to certain matters; (5) that discovery be conducted with no one present except persons designated by the court; (6) that a deposition after being sealed be opened only by order of the court; (7) that a trade secret or other confidential research, development, or commercial information not be disclosed or be disclosed only in a designated way; (8) that the parties simultaneously file specified documents or information enclosed in sealed envelopes to be opened as directed by the court.

If the motion for a protective order is denied in whole or in part, the court may, on such terms and conditions as are just, order that any party or person provide or permit discovery. The provisions of Rule 37(a)(4) apply to the award of expenses incurred in relation to the motion.

(d) **Sequence and Timing of Discovery.** Unless the court upon motion, for the convenience of parties and witnesses and in the interests of justice, orders otherwise, methods of discovery may be used in any sequence and the fact that a party is conducting discovery, whether by deposition or otherwise, shall not operate to delay any other party's discovery.

(e) **Supplementation of Responses.** A party who has responded to a request for discovery with a response that was complete when made is under no duty to supplement the response to include information thereafter acquired, except as follows:

(1) A party is under a duty seasonably to supplement the response with respect to any question directly addressed to (A) the identity and location of persons having knowledge of discoverable matters, and (B) the identity of each person expected to be called as an expert witness at trial, the subject matter on which the person is expected to testify, and the substance of the person's testimony.

(2) A party is under a duty seasonably to amend a prior response if the party obtains information upon the basis of which (A) the party knows that the response was incorrect when made, or (B) the party knows that the response though correct when made is no longer true and the circumstances are such that a failure to amend the response is in substance a knowing concealment.

(3) A duty to supplement responses may be imposed by order of the court, agreement of the parties, or at any time prior to trial through new requests for supplementation of prior responses.

(f) Discovery Conference. At any time after commencement of an action the court may direct the attorneys for the parties to appear before it for a conference on the subject of discovery. The court shall do so upon motion by the attorney for any party if the motion includes:

(1) A statement of the issues as they then appear;

(2) A proposed plan and schedule of discovery;

(3) Any limitations proposed to be placed on discovery;

(4) Any other proposed orders with respect to discovery; and

(5) A statement showing that the attorney making the motion has made a reasonable effort to reach agreement with opposing attorneys on the matters set forth in the motion. Each party and each party's attorney are under a duty to participate in good faith in the framing of a discovery plan if a plan is proposed by the attorney for any party. Notice of the motion shall be served on all parties. Objections or additions to matters set forth in the motion shall be served not later than 10 days after service of the motion.

Following the discovery conference, the court shall enter an order tentatively identifying the issues for discovery purposes, establishing a plan and schedule for discovery, setting limitations on discovery, if any; and determining such other matters, including the allocation of expenses, as are necessary for the proper management of discovery in the action. An order may be altered or amended whenever justice so requires.

Subject to the right of a party who properly moves for a discovery conference to prompt convening of the conference, the court may combine the discovery conference with a pretrial conference authorized by Rule 16.

(g) Signing of Discovery Requests, Responses, and Objections. Every request for discovery or response or objection thereto made by a party represented by an attorney shall be signed by at least one attorney of record in the attorney's individual name, whose address shall be stated. A party who is not represented by an attorney shall sign the request, response, or objection and state the party's address. The signature of the attorney or party constitutes a certification that the signer has read the request, response, or objection, and that to the best of the signer's knowledge, information, and belief formed after a reasonable inquiry it is: (1) consistent with these rules and warranted by existing law or a good faith argument for the extension, modification, or reversal of existing law; (2) not interposed for any improper purpose, such as to harass or to cause unnecessary delay or needless increase in the cost of litigation; and (3) not unreasonable or unduly burdensome or expensive, given the needs of the case, the discovery already had in the case, the amount in controversy, and the importance of the issues at stake in the litigation. If a request, response, or objection is not signed, it shall be stricken unless it is signed promptly after the omission is called to the attention of the party making the request, response, or objection, and a party shall not be obligated to take any action with respect to it until it is signed.

If a certification is made in violation of the rule, the court, upon motion or upon its own initiative, shall impose upon the person who made the certification, the party on whose behalf the request, response, or objection is made, or both, an appropriate sanction, which may include an order to pay the amount of the reasonable expenses incurred because of the violation, including a reasonable attorney's fee.

(As amended Dec. 27, 1946, eff. Mar. 19, 1948; Jan. 21, 1963, eff. July 1, 1963; Feb. 28, 1966, eff. July 1, 1966; Mar. 30, 1970, eff. July 1, 1970; Apr. 29, 1980, eff. Aug. 1, 1980; Apr. 28, 1983, eff. Aug. 1, 1983; Mar. 2, 1987, eff. Aug. 1, 1987.)

Notes of Advisory Committee on Rules

Subdivision (b)(3)—Trial Preparation: Materials.

Some of the most controversial and vexing problems to emerge from the discovery rules have arisen out of requests for the production of documents or things prepared in anticipation of litigation or for trial. The existing rules make no explicit provision for such materials. Yet, two verbally distinct doctrines have developed, each conferring a qualified immunity on these materials—the "good cause" requirement in Rule 34 (now generally held applicable to discovery of documents via deposition under Rule 45 and interrogatories under Rule 33) and the work-product doctrine of *Hickman v. Taylor*, 329 U.S. 495 (1947). Both demand a showing of justification before production can be had, the one of "good cause" and the other variously described in the *Hickman* case: "necessity or justification," "denial * * * would unduly prejudice the preparation of petitioner's case," or "cause hardship or injustice" 329 U.S. at 509–510.

In deciding the *Hickman* case, the Supreme Court appears to have expressed a preference in 1947 for an approach to the problem of trial preparation materials by judicial decision rather than by rule. Sufficient experience has accumulated, however, with lower court applications of the *Hickman* decision to warrant a reappraisal.

The major difficulties visible in the existing case law are (1) confusion and disagreement as to whether "good cause" is made out by a showing of relevance and lack of privilege, or requires an additional showing of necessity, (2) confusion and disagreement as to the scope of the *Hickman* work-product doctrine, particularly whether it extends beyond work actually performed by lawyers, and (3) the resulting difficulty of relating the "good cause" required by Rule 34 and the "necessity or justification" of the work-product doctrine, so that their respective roles and the distinctions between them are understood.

Basic Standard.—Since Rule 34 in terms requires a showing of "good cause" for the production of all documents and things, whether or not trial preparation is involved, courts have felt that a single formula is called for and have differed over whether a showing of relevance and lack of privilege is enough or whether more must be shown. When the facts of the cases are studied, however, a distinction emerges based upon the type of materials. With respect to documents not obtained or prepared with an eye to litigation, the decisions, while not uniform, reflect a strong and increasing tendency to relate "good cause" to a showing that the documents are relevant to the subject matter of the action. E.g., *Connecticut Mutual Life Ins. Co. v. Shields*, 17 F.R.D. 273 (S.D.N.Y. 1955), with cases cited; *Houdry Process Corp. v. Commonwealth Oil Refining Co.*, 24 F.R.D. 58 (S.D.N.Y.1959); see *Bell v. Commercial Ins. Co.*, 280 F.2d 514, 517 (3d Cir.1960). When the party whose documents are sought shows that the request for production is unduly burdensome or oppressive, courts have denied discovery for lack of "good cause" although they might just as easily have based their decision on the protective provisions of existing Rule 30(b) (new Rule 26(c)). E.g., *Lauer v. Tankrederi*, 39 F.R.D. 334 (E.D.Pa. 1966).

As to trial-preparation materials, however, the courts are increasingly interpreting "good cause" as requiring more than relevance. When lawyers have prepared or obtained the materials for trial, all courts require more than relevance; so much is clearly commanded by *Hickman*. But even as to the preparatory work of nonlawyers, while some courts ignore work-product and equate "good cause" with relevance, e.g., *Brown v. New York, N.H. & H.R.R.*, 17 F.R.D. 324 (S.D.N.Y.1955), the more recent trend is to read "good cause" as requiring inquiry into the importance of and need for the materials as well as into alternative sources for securing the same information. In *Guilford Nat'l Bank v. Southern Ry.*, 297 F.2d 921 (4th Cir.1962), statements of witnesses obtained by claim agents were held not discoverable because both parties had had equal access to the witnesses at about the same time, shortly after the collision in question. The decision was based solely on Rule 34 and "good cause"; the court declined to rule on whether the statements were work-products. The court's treatment of "good cause" is quoted at length and with approval in *Schlagenhauf v. Holder*, 379 U.S. 104, 117–118 (1964). See also *Mitchell v. Bass*, 252 F.2d 513 (8th Cir.1958); *Hauger v. Chicago, R.I. & Pac. R.R.*, 216 F.2d 501 (7th Cir.1954); *Burke v. United States*, 32 F.R.D. 213 (E.D.N.Y. 1963). While the opinions dealing with "good cause" do not often draw an explicit distinction between trial preparation materials and other materials, in fact an overwhelming proportion of the cases in which a special showing is required are cases involving trial preparation materials.

The rules are amended by eliminating the general requirement of "good cause" from Rule 34 but retaining a requirement of a special showing for trial preparation materials in this subdivision. The required showing is expressed, not in terms of "good cause" whose generality has tended to encourage confusion and controversy, but in terms of the elements of the special showing to be made: substantial need of the materials in the preparation of the case and inability without undue hardship to obtain the substantial equivalent of the materials by other means.

These changes conform to the holdings of the cases, when viewed in light of their facts. Apart from trial preparation, the fact that the materials sought are documentary does not in and of itself require a special showing beyond relevance and absence of privilege. The protective provisions are of course available, and if the party from whom production is sought raises a special issue of privacy (as with respect to income tax returns or grand jury minutes) or points to evidence primarily impeaching, or can show serious burden or expense, the court will exercise its traditional power to decide whether to issue a protective order. On the other hand, the requirement of a special showing for discovery of trial preparation materials reflects the view that each side's informal evaluation of its case should be protected, that each side should be encouraged to prepare independently, and that one side should not automatically have the benefit of the detailed preparatory work of the other side. See Field and McKusick, Maine Civil Practice 264 (1959).

Elimination of a "good cause" requirement from Rule 34 and the establishment of a requirement of a special showing in this subdivision will eliminate the confusion caused by having two verbally distinct requirements of justification that the courts have been unable to distinguish clearly. Moreover, the lanugage of the subdivision suggests the factors which the courts should consider in determining whether the requisite showing has been made. The importance of the materials sought to the party seeking them in preparation of his case and the difficulty he will have obtaining them by other means are factors noted in the *Hickman* case. The courts should also consider the likelihood that the party, even if he obtains the information by independent means, will not have the substantial equivalent of the documents the production of which he seeks.

Consideration of these factors may well lead the court to distinguish between witness statements taken by an investigator, on the one hand, and other parts of the investigative file, on the other. The court in *Southern Ry. v. Lanham*, 403 F.2d 119 (5th Cir.1968), while it naturally addressed itself to the "good cause" requirements of Rule 34, set forth as controlling considerations the factors contained in the language of this subdivision. The analysis of the court suggests circumstances under which witness statements will be discoverable. The witness may have given a fresh and contemporaneous account in a written statement while he is available to the party seeking discovery only a substantial time thereafter. *Lanham*, supra at 127–128; *Guilford*, supra at 926. Or he may be reluctant or hostile. *Lanham*, supra at 128–129; *Brookshire v. Pennsylvania RR*, 14 F.R.D. 154 (N.D.Ohio 1953); *Diamond v. Mohawk Rubber Co.*, 33 F.R.D. 264 (D.Colo.1963). Or he may have a lapse of memory. *Tannenbaum v. Walker*, 16 F.R.D. 570 (E.D.Pa.1954). Or he may probably be deviating from his prior statement. Cf. *Hauger v. Chicago, R.I. & Pac. RR*, 216 F.2d 501 (7th Cir.1954). On the other hand, a much stronger showing is needed to obtain evaluative materials in an investigator's reports. *Lanham*, supra at 131–133; *Pickett v. L.R. Ryan, Inc.*, 237 F.Supp. 198 (E.D.S.C.1965).

Materials assembled in the ordinary course of business, or pursuant to public requirements unrelated to litigation, or for other nonlitigation purposes are not under the qualified immunity provided by this subdivision. *Goosman v. A. Duie Pyle, Inc.*, 320 F.2d 45 (4th Cir. 1963); *cf. United States v. New York Foreign Trade Zone Operators, Inc.*, 304 F.2d 792 (2d Cir. 1962). No change is made in the existing doctrine, noted in the *Hickman* case, that one party may discover relevant facts known or available to the other party, even though such facts are contained in a document which is not itself discoverable.

Treatment of Lawyers; Special Protection of Mental Impressions, Conclusions, Opinions, and Legal Theories Concerning the Litigation.—The courts are divided as to whether the work-product doctrine extends to the preparatory work only of lawyers. The *Hickman* case left this issue open since the statements in that case were taken by a lawyer. As to courts of appeals compare *Alltmont v. United States*, 177 F.2d 971, 976 (3d Cir. 1949), *cert. denied*, 339 U.S. 967 (1950) (*Hickman* applied to statements obtained by FBI agents on theory it should apply to "all statements of prospective witnesses which a party has obtained for his trial counsel's use"), with *Southern Ry. v. Campbell*, 309 F.2d 569 (5th Cir. 1962) (statements taken by claim agents not work-product), and *Guilford Nat'l Bank v. Southern Ry.*, 297 F.2d 921 (4th Cir. 1962) (avoiding issue of work-product as to claim agents, deciding case instead under Rule 34 "good cause"). Similarly, the district courts are divided on statements obtained by claim agents, compare, *e.g.*, *Brown v. New York, N. H. & H. R. R.*, 17 F.R.D. 324 (S.D.N.Y.1955) with *Hanke v. Milwaukee Electric Ry. & Transp. Co.*, 7 F.R.D. 540 (E.D.Wis.1947); Investigators, compare *Burke v. United States*, 32 F.R.D. 213 (E.D.N.Y.1963) with *Snyder v. United States*, 20 F.R.D. 7 (E.D.N.Y.1956); and Insurers, compare *Gottlieb v. Bresler*, 24 F.R.D. 371 (D.D.C.1959) with *Burns v. Mulder*, 20 F.R.D. 605 (E.D.Pa.1957). See 4 Moore's Federal Practice ¶ 26.23[8.1] (2d ed. 1966); 2A Barron & Holtzoff, Federal Practice and Procedure § 652.2 (Wright ed. 1961).

A complication is introduced by the use made by courts of the "good cause" requirement of Rule 34, as described above. A court may conclude that trial preparation materials are not work-product because not the result of lawyer's work and yet hold that they are not producible because "good cause" has not been shown. Cf. *Guilford Nat'l Bank v. Southern Ry.*, 297 F.2d 921 (4th Cir. 1962), cited and described above. When the decisions on "good cause" are taken into account, the weight of authority affords protection of the preparatory work of both lawyers and nonlawyers (though not necessarily to the same extent) by requiring more than a showing of relevance to secure production.

Subdivision (b)(3) reflects the trend of the cases by requiring a special showing, not merely as to materials prepared by an attorney, but also as to materials prepared in anticipation of litigation or preparation for trial by or for a party or any representative acting on his behalf. The subdivision then goes on to protect against disclosure the mental impressions, conclusions, opinions, or legal theories concerning the litigation of an attorney or other representative of a party. The *Hickman* opinion drew special

478

attention to the need for protecting an attorney against discovery of memoranda prepared from recollection of oral interviews. The courts have steadfastly safeguarded against disclosure of lawyers' mental impressions and legal theories, as well as mental impressions and subjective evaluations of investigators and claim-agents. In enforcing this provision of the subdivision, the courts will sometimes find it necessary to order disclosure of a document but with portions deleted.

Rules 33 and 36 have been revised in order to permit discovery calling for opinions, contentions, and admissions relating not only to fact but also to the application of law to fact. Under those rules, a party and his attorney or other representative may be required to disclose, to some extent, mental impressions, opinions, or conclusions. But documents or parts of documents containing these matters are protected against discovery by this subdivision. Even though a party may ultimately have to disclose in response to interrogatories or requests to admit, he is entitled to keep confidential documents containing such matters prepared for internal use.

* * *

Subdivision (e)—Supplementation of Responses. The rules do not now state whether interrogatories (and questions at deposition as well as requests for inspection and admissions) impose a "continuing burden" on the responding party to supplement his answers if he obtains new information. The issue is acute when new information renders substantially incomplete or inaccurate an answer which was complete and accurate when made. It is essential that the rules provide an answer to this question. The parties can adjust to a rule either way, once they know what it is. See 4 Moore's Federal Practice ¶ 33.25[4] (2d ed. 1966).

Arguments can be made both ways. Imposition of a continuing burden reduces the proliferation of additional sets of interrogatories. Some courts have adopted local rules establishing such a burden. E.g., E.D.Pa.R. 20(f), quoted in *Taggart v. Vermont Transp. Co.*, 32 F.R.D. 587 (E.D.Pa.1963); D.Me.R. 15(c). Others have imposed the burden by decision. *E.g., Chenault v. Nebraska Farm Products, Inc.*, 9 F.R.D. 529, 533 (D.Nebr.1949). On the other hand, there are serious objections to the burden, especially in protracted cases. Although the party signs the answers, it is his lawyer who understands their significance and bears the responsibility to bring answers up to date. In a complex case all sorts of information reaches the party, who little understands its bearing on answers previously given to interrogatories. In practice, therefore, the lawyer under a continuing burden must periodically recheck all interrogatories and canvass all new information. But a full set of new answers may no longer be needed by the interrogating party. Some issues will have been dropped from the case, some questions are now seen as unimportant, and other questions must in any event be reformulated. See *Novick v. Pennsylvania R. R.*, 18 F.R.D. 296, 298 (W.D.Pa.1955).

Subdivision (e) provides that a party is not under a continuing burden except as expressly provided. Cf. Note, 68 Harv.L.Rev. 673, 677 (1955). An exception is made as to the identity of persons having knowledge of discoverable matters, because of the obvious importance to each side of knowing all witnesses and because information about witnesses routinely comes to each lawyer's attention. Many of the decisions on the issue of a continuing burden have in fact concerned the identity of witnesses. An exception is also made as to expert trial witnesses in order to carry out the provisions of Rule 26(b)(4). See *Diversified Products Corp. v. Sports Center Co.*, 42 F.R.D. 3 (D.Md.1967).

Another exception is made for the situation in which a party, or more frequently his lawyer, obtains actual knowledge that a prior response is incorrect. This exception does not impose a duty to check the accuracy of prior responses, but it prevents knowing concealment by a party or attorney. Finally, a duty to supplement may be imposed by order of the court in a particular case (including an order resulting from a pretrial conference) or by agreement of the parties. A party may of course make a new discovery request which requires supplementation of prior responses.

The duty will normally be enforced, in those limited instances where it is imposed, through sanctions imposed by the trial court, including exclusion of evidence, continuance, or other action, as the court may deem appropriate.

1980 Amendment

Subdivision (f). This subdivision is new. There has been widespread criticism of abuse of discovery. The Committee has considered a number of proposals to eliminate abuse, including a change in Rule 26(b)(1) with respect to the scope of discovery and a change in Rule 33(a) to limit the number of questions that can be asked by interrogatories to parties.

The Committee believes that abuse of discovery, while very serious in certain cases, is not so general as to require such basic changes in the rules that govern discovery in all cases. A very recent study of discovery in selected metropolitan districts tends to support its belief. P. Connolly, E. Holleman, & M. Kuhlman, *Judicial Controls and the Civil Litigative Process: Discovery* (Federal Judicial Center, 1978). In the judgment of the Committee abuse can best be prevented by intervention by the court as soon as abuse is threatened.

To this end this subdivision provides that counsel who has attempted without success to effect with opposing counsel a reasonable program or plan for discovery is entitled to the assistance of the court.

It is not contemplated that requests for discovery conferences will be made routinely. A relatively narrow discovery dispute should be resolved by resort to Rules 26(c) or 37(a), and if it appears that a request for a conference is in fact grounded in such a dispute, the court may refer counsel to those rules. If the court is persuaded that a request is frivolous or vexatious, it can strike it. See Rules 11 and 7(b)(2).

A number of courts routinely consider discovery matters in preliminary pretrial conferences held shortly after the pleadings are closed. This subdivision does not interfere with such a practice. It authorizes the court to combine a discovery conference with a pretrial conference under Rule 16 if a pretrial conference is held sufficiently early to prevent or curb abuse.

1983 Amendment

Excessive discovery and evasion or resistance to reasonable discovery requests pose significant problems. Recent studies have made some attempt to determine the sources and extent of the difficulties. See Brazil, *Civil Discovery: Lawyers' Views of its Effectiveness, Principal Problems and Abuses,* American Bar Foundation (1980); Connolly, Holleman & Kuhlman, *Judicial Controls and the Civil Litigative Process: Discovery,* Federal Judicial Center (1978); Ellington, *A Study of Sanctions for Discovery Abuse,* Department of Justice (1979); Schroeder & Frank, *The Proposed Changes in the Discovery Rules,* 1978 Ariz. St. L.J. 475.

The purpose of discovery is to provide a mechanism for making relevant information available to the litigants. "Mutual knowledge of all the relevant facts gathered by both parties is essential to proper litigation." *Hickman v. Taylor,* 329 U.S. 495, 507 (1947). Thus the spirit of the rules is violated when advocates attempt to use discovery tools as tactical weapons rather than to expose the facts and illuminate the issues by overuse of discovery or unnecessary use of defensive weapons or evasive responses. All of this results in excessively costly and time-consuming activities that are disproportionate to the nature of the case, the amount involved, or the issues or values at stake.

Given our adversary tradition and the current discovery rules, it is not surprising that there are many opportunities if not incentives, for attorneys to engage in discovery that, although authorized by the broad, permissive terms of the rules, nevertheless results in delay. See Brazil, *The Adversary Character of Civil Discovery: A Critique and Proposals for Change,* 31 Vand.L.Rev. 1259 (1978). As a result, it has been said that the rules have "not infrequently [been] exploited to the disadvantage of justice." *Herbert v. Lando,* 441 U.S. 153, 179 (1979) (Powell, J., concurring). These practices impose costs on an already overburdened system and impede the fundamental goal of the "just, speedy, and inexpensive determination of every action." Fed.R.Civ.P. 1.

Subdivision (a); Discovery Methods. The deletion of the last sentence of Rule 26(a)(1), which provided that unless the court ordered otherwise under Rule 26(c) "the frequency of use" of the various discovery methods was not to be limited, is an attempt to address the problem of duplicative, redundant, and excessive discovery and to reduce it. The amendment, in conjunction with the changes in Rule 26(b)(1), is designed to encourage district judges to identify instances of needless discovery and to limit the use of the various discovery devices accordingly. The question may be raised by one of the parties, typically on a motion for a protective order, or by the court on its own initiative. It is entirely appropriate to consider a limitation on the frequency of use of discovery at a discovery conference under Rule 26(f) or at any other pretrial conference authorized by these rules. In considering the discovery needs of a particular case, the court should consider the factors described in Rule 26(b)(1).

Subdivision (b); Discovery Scope and Limits. Rule 26(b)(1) has been amended to add a sentence to deal with the problem of over-discovery. The objective is to guard against redundant or disproportionate discovery by giving the court authority to reduce the amount of discovery that may be directed to matters that are otherwise proper subjects of inquiry. The new sentence is intended to encourage judges to be more aggressive in identifying and discouraging discovery overuse. The grounds mentioned in the amended rule for limiting discovery reflect the existing practice of many courts in issuing protective orders under Rule 26(c). See, *e.g., Carlson Cos. v. Sperry & Hutchinson Co.,* 374 F.Supp. 1080 (D.Minn.1973); *Dolgow v. Anderson,* 53 F.R.D. 661 (E.D.N.Y.1971); *Mitchell v. American Tobacco Co.,* 33 F.R.D. 262 (M.D.Pa.1963); *Welty v. Clute,* 1 F.R.D. 446 (W.D.N.Y.1941). On the whole, however, district judges have been reluctant to limit the use of the discovery devices. See, *e.g., Apco Oil Co. v. Certified Transp., Inc.,* 46 F.R.D. 428 (W.D.Mo.1969). See generally 8 Wright & Miller, *Federal Practice and Procedure: Civil* §§ 2036, 2037, 2039, 2040 (1970).

The first element of the standard, Rule 26(b)(1)(i), is designed to minimize redundancy in discovery and encourage attorneys to be sensitive to the comparative costs of different methods of securing information. Subdivision (b)(1)(ii) also seeks to reduce repetitiveness and to oblige lawyers to think through their discovery activities in advance so that full utilization is made of each deposition, document request, or set of interrogatories. The elements of Rule 26(b)(1)(iii) address the problem of discovery that is disproportionate to the individual lawsuit as measured by such matters as its nature and complexity, the importance of the issues at stake in a case seeking damages, the limitations on a financially weak litigant to withstand extensive opposition to a discovery program or to respond to discovery requests, and the significance of the substantive issues, as measured in philosophic, social, or institutional terms. Thus the rule recognizes that many cases in public policy spheres, such as employment practices, free speech, and other matters, may have importance far beyond the monetary amount involved. The court must apply the standards in an even-handed manner that will prevent use of discovery to wage a war of attrition or as a device to coerce a party, whether financially weak or affluent.

The rule contemplates greater judicial involvement in the discovery process and thus acknowledges the reality that it cannot always operate on a self-regulating basis. See Connolly, Holleman & Kuhlman, *Judicial Controls and the Civil Litigative Process: Discovery* 77, Federal Judicial Center (1978). In an appropriate case the court could restrict the number of depositions, interrogatories, or the scope of a production request. But the court must be careful not to deprive a party of discovery that is reasonably necessary to afford a fair opportunity to develop and prepare the case.

The court may act on motion, or its own initiative. It is entirely appropriate to resort to the amended rule in conjunction with a discovery conference under Rule 26(f) or one of the other pretrial conferences authorized by the rules.

Subdivision (g); Signing of Discovery Requests, Responses, and Objections. Rule 26(g) imposes an affirmative duty to engage in pretrial discovery in a responsible manner that is consistent with the spirit and purposes of Rules 26 through 37. In addition, Rule 26(g) is designed to curb discovery abuse by explicitly encouraging the imposition of sanctions. The subdivision provides a deterrent to both excessive discovery and evasion by imposing a certification requirement that obliges each attorney to stop and think about the legitimacy of a discovery request, a response thereto, or an objection. The term "response" includes answers to interrogatories and to requests to admit as well as responses to production requests.

If primary responsibility for conducting discovery is to continue to rest with the litigants, they must be obliged to act responsibly and avoid abuse. With this in mind, Rule 26(g), which parallels the amendments to Rule 11, requires an attorney or unrepresented party to sign each discovery request, response, or objection. Motions relating to discovery are governed by Rule 11. However, since a discovery request, response, or objection usually deals with more specific subject matter than motions or papers, the elements that must be certified in connection with the former are spelled out more completely. The signature is a certification of the elements set forth in Rule 26(g).

Although the certification duty requires the lawyer to pause and consider the reasonableness of his request, response, or objection, it is not meant to discourage or restrict necessary and legitimate discovery. The rule simply requires that the attorney make a reasonable inquiry into the factual basis of his response, request, or objection.

The duty to make a "reasonable inquiry" is satisfied if the investigation undertaken by the attorney and the conclusions drawn therefrom are reasonable under the circumstances. It is an objective standard similar to the one imposed by Rule 11. See the Advisory Committee Note to Rule 11. See also *Kinee v. Abraham Lincoln Fed. Sav. & Loan Ass'n,* 365 F.Supp. 975 (E.D.Pa.1973). In making the inquiry, the attorney may rely on assertions by the client and on communications with other counsel in the case as long as that reliance is appropriate under the circumstances. Ultimately what is reasonable is a matter for the court to decide on the totality of the circumstances.

Rule 26(g) does not require the signing attorney to certify the truthfulness of the client's factual responses to a discovery request. Rather, the signature certifies that the lawyer has made a reasonable effort to assure that the client has provided all the information and documents available to him that are responsive to the discovery demand. Thus, the lawyer's certification under Rule 26(g) should be distinguished from other signature requirements in the rules, such as those in Rules 30(e) and 33.

Nor does the rule require a party or an attorney to disclose privileged communications or work product in order to show that a discovery request, response, or objection is substantially justified. The provisions of Rule 26(c), including appropriate orders after *in camera* inspection by the court, remain available to protect a party claiming privilege or work product protection.

The signing requirement means that every discovery request, response, or objection should be grounded on a theory that is reasonable under the precedents or a good faith belief as to what should be the law. This standard is heavily dependent on the circumstances of each case. The certification speaks as of the time it is made. The duty to supplement discovery responses continues to be governed by Rule 26(e).

Concern about discovery abuse has led to widespread recognition that there is a need for more aggressive judicial control and supervision. *ACF Industries, Inc. v. EEOC,* 439 U.S. 1081 (1979) (certiorari denied) (Powell, J., dissenting). Sanctions to deter discovery abuse would be more effective if they were diligently applied "not merely to penalize those whose conduct may be deemed to warrant such a sanction, but to deter those who might be tempted to such conduct in the absence of such a deterrent." *National Hockey League v. Metropolitan Hockey Club,* 427 U.S. 639, 643 (1976). See also Note, *The Emerging Deterrence Orientation in the Imposition of Discovery Sanctions,* 91 Harv.L.Rev. 1033 (1978). Thus the premise of Rule 26(g) is that imposing sanctions on attorneys who fail to meet the rule's standards will significantly reduce abuse by imposing disadvantages therefor.

Because of the asserted reluctance to impose sanctions on attorneys who abuse the discovery rules, see Brazil, *Civil Discovery: Lawyers' Views of its Effectiveness, Principal Problems and Abuses,* American Bar Foundation (1980); Ellington, *A Study of Sanctions for Discovery Abuse,* Department of Justice (1979), Rule 26(g) makes explicit the authority judges now have to impose appropriate sanctions and requires them to use it. This authority derives from Rule 37, 28 U.S.C. § 1927, and the court's inherent power. See *Roadway Express, Inc. v. Piper,* 447 U.S. 752 (1980); *Martin v. Bell Helicopter Co.,* 85 F.R.D. 654, 661–62 (D.Col.1980); Note, *Sanctions Imposed by Courts on Attorneys Who Abuse the Judicial Process,* 44 U.Chi.L.Rev. 619 (1977). The new rule mandates that sanctions be imposed on attorneys who fail to meet the standards established in the first portion of Rule 26(g). The nature of the sanction is a matter of judicial discretion to be exercised in light of the particular circumstances. The court may take into account any failure by the party seeking sanctions to invoke protection under Rule 26(c) at an early stage in the litigation.

The sanctioning process must comport with due process requirements. The kind of notice and hearing required will depend on the facts of the case and the severity of the sanction being considered. To prevent the proliferation of the sanction procedure and to avoid multiple hearings, discovery in any sanction proceeding normally should be permitted only when it is clearly required by the interests of justice. In most cases the court will be aware of the circumstances and only a brief hearing should be necessary.

Rule 37. Failure to Make or Cooperate in Discovery: Sanctions

(a) Motion for Order Compelling Discovery. A party, upon reasonable notice to other parties and all persons affected thereby, may apply for an order compelling discovery as follows:

(1) Appropriate Court. An application for an order to a party may be made to the court in which the action is pending, or, on matters relating to a deposition, to the court in the district where the deposition is being taken. An application for an order to a deponent who is not a party shall be made to the court in the district where the deposition is being taken.

(2) Motion. If a deponent fails to answer a question propounded or submitted under Rules 30 or 31, or a corporation or other entity fails to make a designation under Rule 30(b)(6) or 31(a), or a party fails to answer an interrogatory submitted under Rule 33, or if a party, in response to a request for inspection submitted under Rule 34, fails to respond that inspection will be permitted as requested or fails to permit inspection as requested, the discovering party may move for an order compelling an answer, or a designation, or an order compelling inspection in accordance with the request. When taking a deposition on oral examination, the proponent of the question may complete or adjourn the examination before applying for an order.

If the court denies the motion in whole or in part, it may make such protective order as it would have been empowered to make on a motion made pursuant to Rule 26(c).

(3) Evasive or Incomplete Answer. For purposes of this subdivision an evasive or incomplete answer is to be treated as a failure to answer.

(4) Award of Expenses of Motion. If the motion is granted, the court shall, after opportunity for hearing, require the party or deponent whose conduct necessitated the motion or the party or attorney advising such conduct or both of them to pay to the moving party the reasonable expenses incurred in obtaining the order, including attorney's fees, unless the court finds that the opposition to the motion was substantially justified or that other circumstances make an award of expenses unjust.

If the motion is denied, the court shall, after opportunity for hearing, require the moving party or the attorney advising the motion or both of them to pay to the party or deponent who opposed the motion the reasonable expenses incurred in opposing the motion, including attorney's fees, unless the court finds that the making of the motion was substantially justified or that other circumstances make an award of expenses unjust.

If the motion is granted in part and denied in part, the court may apportion the reasonable expenses incurred in relation to the motion among the parties and persons in a just manner.

(b) Failure to Comply with Order.

(1) Sanctions by Court in District Where Deposition is Taken. If a deponent fails to be sworn or to answer a question after being directed to do so by the court in the district in which the deposition is being taken, the failure may be considered a contempt of that court.

(2) Sanctions by Court in Which Action Is Pending. If a party or an officer, director, or managing agent of a party or a person designated under Rule 30(b)(6) or 31(a) to testify on behalf of a party fails to obey an order to provide or permit discovery, including an order made under subdivision (a) of this rule or Rule 35, or if a party fails to obey an order entered under Rule 26(f), the court in which the action is pending may make such orders in regard to the failure as are just, and among others the following:

(A) An order that the matters regarding which the order was made or any other designated facts shall be taken to be established for the purposes of the action in accordance with the claim of the party obtaining the order;

(B) An order refusing to allow the disobedient party to support or oppose designated claims or defenses, or prohibiting that party from introducing designated matters in evidence;

(C) An order striking out pleadings or parts thereof, or staying further proceedings until the order is obeyed, or dismissing the action or proceeding or any part thereof, or rendering a judgment by default against the disobedient party;

(D) In lieu of any of the foregoing orders or in addition thereto, an order treating as a contempt of court the failure to obey any orders except an order to submit to a physical or mental examination;

(E) Where a party has failed to comply with an order under Rule 35(a) requiring that party to produce another for examination, such orders as are listed in paragraphs (A), (B), and (C) of this subdivision, unless the party failing to comply shows that that party is unable to produce such person for examination.

In lieu of any of the foregoing orders or in addition thereto, the court shall require the party failing to obey the order or the attorney advising that party or both to pay the reasonable expenses, including attorney's fees, caused by the failure, unless the court finds that the failure was substantially justified or that other circumstances make an award of expenses unjust.

(c) **Expenses on Failure to Admit.** If a party fails to admit the genuineness of any document or the truth of any matter as requested under Rule 36, and if the party requesting the admissions thereafter proves the genuineness of the document or the truth of the matter, the requesting party may apply to the court for an order requiring the other party to pay the reasonable expenses incurred in making that proof, including reasonable attorney's fees. The court shall make the order unless it finds that (1) the request was held objectionable pursuant to Rule 36(a), or (2) the admission sought was of no substantial importance, or (3) the party failing to admit had reasonable ground to believe that the party might prevail on the matter, or (4) there was other good reason for the failure to admit.

(d) **Failure of Party to Attend at Own Deposition or Serve Answers to Interrogatories or Respond to Request for Inspection.** If a party or an officer, director, or managing agent of a party or a person designated under Rule 30(b)(6) or 31(a) to testify on behalf of a party fails (1) to appear before the officer who is to take the deposition, after being served with a proper notice, or (2) to serve answers or objections to interrogatories submitted under Rule 33, after proper service of the interrogatories, or (3) to serve a written response to a request for inspection submitted under Rule 34, after proper service of the request, the court in which the action is pending on motion may make such orders in regard to the failure as are just, and among others it may take any action authorized under paragraphs (A), (B), and (C) of subdivision (b)(2) of this rule. In lieu of any order or in addition thereto, the court shall require the party failing to act or the attorney advising that party or both to pay the reasonable expenses, including attorney's fees, caused by the failure, unless the court finds that the failure was substantially justified or that other circumstances make an award of expenses unjust.

The failure to act described in this subdivision may not be excused on the ground that the discovery sought is objectionable unless the party failing to act has applied for a protective order as provided by Rule 26(c).

(e) [Abrogated].

(f) [Repealed. Pub.L. 96–481, Title II, § 205(a), Oct. 21, 1980, 94 Stat. 2330.]

(g) **Failure to Participate in the Framing of a Discovery Plan.** If a party or a party's attorney fails to participate in good faith in the framing of a discovery plan by agreement as is required by Rule 26(f), the court may, after opportunity for hearing, require such party or attorney to pay to any other party the reasonable expenses, including attorney's fees, caused by the failure.

(As amended Dec. 29, 1948, eff. Oct. 20, 1949; Mar. 30, 1970, eff. July 1, 1970; Apr. 29, 1980, eff. Aug. 1, 1980; Pub.L. 96–481, Title II, § 205(a), Oct. 21, 1980, 94 Stat. 2330; Mar. 2, 1987, eff. Aug. 1, 1987.)

Notes of Advisory Committee on Rules

The provisions of this rule authorizing orders establishing facts or excluding evidence or striking pleadings, or authorizing judgments of dismissal or default, for refusal to answer questions or permit inspection or otherwise make discovery, are in accord with *Hammond Packing Co. v. Arkansas*, 1909, 29 S.Ct. 370, 212 U.S. 322, 53 L.Ed. 530, 15 Ann.Cas. 645, which distinguishes between the justifiable use of such measures as a means of compelling the production of evidence, and their unjustifiable use, as in *Hovey v. Elliott*, 1897, 17 S.Ct. 841, 167 U.S. 409, 42 L.Ed. 215, for the mere purpose of punishing for contempt.

1970 Amendment

Rule 37 provides generally for sanctions against parties or persons unjustifiably resisting discovery. Experience has brought to light a number of defects in the language of the rule as well as instances in which it is not serving the purposes for which it was designed. See Rosenberg, *Sanctions to Effectuate Pretrial Discovery*, 58 Col.L.Rev. 480 (1958). In addition, changes being made in other discovery rules require conforming amendments to Rule 37.

Rule 37 sometimes refers to a "failure" to afford discovery and at other times to a "refusal" to do so. Taking note of this dual terminology, courts have imported into "refusal" a requirement of "willfulness." See *Roth v. Paramount Pictures Corp.*, 8 F.R.D. 31 (W.D.Pa.1948); *Campbell v. Johnson*, 101 F.Supp. 705, 707 (S.D.N.Y.1951). In *Societe Internationale v. Rogers*, 357 U.S. 197 (1958), the Supreme Court concluded that the rather random use of these two terms in Rule 37 showed no design to use them with consistently distinctive meanings, that "refused" in Rule 37(b)(2) meant simply a failure to comply, and that willfulness was relevant only to the selection of sanctions, if any, to be imposed. Nevertheless, after the decision in *Societe*, the court in *Hinson v. Michigan Mutual Liability Co.*, 275 F.2d 537 (5th Cir.1960) once again ruled that "refusal" required willfulness. Substitution of "failure" for "refusal" throughout Rule 37 should eliminate this confusion and bring the rule into harmony with the *Societe Internationale* decision. See Rosenberg, supra, 58 Col.L.Rev. 480, 489–490 (1958).

Subdivision (a). Rule 37(a) provides relief to a party seeking discovery against one who, with or without stated objections, fails to afford the discovery sought. It has always fully served this function in relation to depositions, but the amendments being made to Rules 33 and 34 give Rule 37(a) added scope and importance. Under existing Rule 33, a party objecting to interrogatories must make a motion for court hearing on his objections. The changes now made in Rules 33 and 37(a) make it clear that the interrogating party must move to compel answers, and the motion is provided for in Rule 37(a). Existing Rule 34, since it requires a court order prior to production of documents or things or permission to enter on land, has no relation to Rule 37(a). Amendments of Rules 34 and 37(a) create a procedure similar to that provided for Rule 33.

Subdivision (a)(1). This is a new provision making clear to which court a party may apply for an order compelling discovery. Existing Rule 37(a) refers only to the court in which the deposition is being taken; nevertheless, it has been held that the court where the action is pending has "inherent power" to compel a party deponent to answer. *Lincoln Laboratories, Inc. v. Savage Laboratories, Inc.*, 27 F.R.D. 476 (D.Del.1961). In relation to Rule 33 interrogatories and Rule 34 requests for inspection, the court where the action is pending is the appropriate enforcing tribunal. The new provision eliminates the need to resort to inherent power by spelling out the respective roles of the court where the action is pending and the court where the deposition is taken. In some instances, two courts are available to a party seeking to compel answers from a party deponent. The party seeking discovery may choose the court to which he will apply, but the court has power to remit the party to the other court as a more appropriate forum.

Subdivision (a)(2). This subdivision contains the substance of existing provisions of Rule 37(a) authorizing motions to compel answers to questions put at depositions and to interrogatories. New provisions authorizing motions for orders compelling designation under Rules 30(b)(6) and 31(a) and compelling inspection in accordance with a request made under Rule 34. If the court denies a motion, in whole or part, it may accompany the denial with issuance of a protective order. Compare the converse provision in Rule 26(c).

Subdivision (a)(3). This new provision makes clear that an evasive or incomplete answer is to be considered, for purposes of subdivision (a), a failure to answer. The courts have consistently held that they have the power to compel adequate answers. E.g., *Cone Mills Corp. v. Joseph Bancroft & Sons Co.*, 33 F.R.D. 318 (D.Del.1963). This power is recognized and incorporated into the rule.

Subdivision (a)(4). This subdivision amends the provisions for award of expenses, including reasonable attorney's fees, to the prevailing party or person when a motion is made for an order compelling discovery. At present, an award of expenses is made only if the losing party or person is found to have acted without substantial justification. The change requires that expenses be awarded unless the conduct of the losing party or person is found to have been substantially justified. The test of "substantial justification" remains, but the change in language is intended to encourage judges to be more alert to abuses occurring in the discovery process.

On many occasions, to be sure, the dispute over discovery between the parties is genuine, though ultimately resolved one way or the other by the court. In such cases, the losing party is substantially justified in carrying the matter to court. But the rules should deter the abuse implicit in carrying or forcing a discovery dispute to court when no genuine dispute exists. And the potential or actual imposition of expenses is virtually the sole formal sanction in the rules to deter a party from pressing to a court hearing frivolous requests for or objections to discovery.

The present provision of Rule 37(a) that the court shall require payment if it finds that the defeated party acted without "substantial justification" may appear adequate, but in fact it has been little used. Only a handful of reported cases include an award of expenses, and the Columbia Survey found that in only one instance out of about 50 motions decided under Rule 37(a) did the court award expenses. It appears that the courts do not utilize the most important available sanction to deter abusive resort to the judiciary.

The proposed change provides in effect that expenses should ordinarily be awarded unless a court finds that the losing party acted justifiably in carrying his point to court. At the same time, a necessary flexibility is maintained, since the court retains the power to find that other circumstances make an award of expenses unjust—as where the prevailing party also acted unjustifiably. The amendment does not significantly narrow the discretion of the court, but rather presses the court to address itself to abusive practices. The present provision that expenses may be imposed upon either the party or his attorney or both is unchanged. But it is not contemplated that expenses will be imposed upon the attorney merely because the party is indigent.

Subdivision (b). This subdivision deals with sanctions for failure to comply with a court order. The present captions for subsections (1) and (2) entitled, "Contempt" and "Other Consequences," respectively, are confusing. One of the consequences listed in (2) is the arrest of the party, representing the exercise of the contempt power. The contents of the subsections show that the first authorizes the sanction of contempt (and no other) by the court in which the deposition is taken, whereas the second subsection authorizes a variety of sanctions, including contempt, which may be imposed by the court in which the action is pending. The captions of the subsections are changed to reflect their contents.

The scope of Rule 37(b)(2) is broadened by extending it to include any order "to provide or permit discovery," including orders issued under Rules 37(a) and 35. Various rules authorize orders for discovery—e.g., Rule 35(b)(1), Rule 26(c) as revised, Rule 37(d). See Rosenberg, supra, 58 Col.L.Rev. 480, 484–486. Rule 37(b)(2) should provide comprehensively for enforcement of all these orders. Cf. *Societe Internationale v. Rogers*, 357 U.S. 197, 207 (1958). On the other hand, the reference to Rule 34 is deleted to conform to the changed procedure in that rule.

A new subsection (E) provides that sanctions which have been available against a party for failure to comply with an order under Rule 35(a) to submit to examination will now be available against him for his failure to comply with a Rule 35(a) order to produce a third person for examination, unless he shows that he is unable to produce the person. In this context, "unable" means in effect "unable in good faith." See *Societe Internationale v. Rogers*, 357 U.S. 197 (1958).

Subdivision (b)(2) is amplified to provide for payment of reasonable expenses caused by the failure to obey the order. Although Rules 37(b)(2) and 37(d) have been silent as to award of expenses, courts have nevertheless ordered them on occasion. E.g., *United*

Sheeplined Clothing Co. v. Arctic Fur Cap Corp., 165 F.Supp. 193 (S.D.N.Y.1958); *Austin Theatre, Inc. v. Warner Bros. Pictures, Inc.,* 22 F.R.D. 302 (S.D.N.Y.1958). The provision places the burden on the disobedient party to avoid expenses by showing that his failure is justified or that special circumstances make an award of expenses unjust. Allocating the burden in this way conforms to the changed provisions as to expenses in Rule 37(a), and is particularly appropriate when a court order is disobeyed.

An added reference to directors of a party is similar to a change made in subdivision (d) and is explained in the note to that subdivision. The added reference to persons designated by a party under Rules 30(b)(6) or 31(a) to testify on behalf of the party carries out the new procedure in those rules for taking a deposition of a corporation or other organization.

Subdivision (c). Rule 37(c) provides a sanction for the enforcement of Rule 36 dealing with requests for admission. Rule 36 provides the mechanism whereby a party may obtain from another party in appropriate instances either (1) an admission, or (2) a sworn and specific denial or (3) a sworn statement "setting forth in detail the reasons why he cannot truthfully admit or deny." If the party obtains the second or third of these responses, in proper form, Rule 36 does not provide for a pretrial hearing on whether the response is warranted by the evidence thus far accumulated. Instead, Rule 37(c) is intended to provide posttrial relief in the form of a requirement that the party improperly refusing the admission pay the expenses of the other side in making the necessary proof at trial.

Rule 37(c), as now written, addresses itself in terms only to the sworn denial and is silent with respect to the statement of reasons for an inability to admit or deny. There is no apparent basis for this distinction, since the sanction provided in Rule 37(c) should deter all unjustified failures to admit. This omission in the rule has caused confused and diverse treatment in the courts. One court has held that if a party give inadequate reasons, he should be treated before trial as having denied the request, so that Rule 37(c) may apply. *Bertha Bldg. Corp. v. National Theatres Corp.,* 15 F.R.D. 339 (E.D.N.Y.1954). Another has held that the party should be treated as having admitted the request. *Heng Hsin Co. v. Stern, Morgenthau & Co.,* 20 Fed.Rules Serv. 36a.52, Case 1 (S.D.N.Y. Dec. 10, 1954). Still another has ordered a new response, without indicating what the outcome should be if the new response were inadequate. *United States Plywood Corp. v. Hudson Lumber Co.,* 127 F.Supp. 489, 497–498 (S.D.N.Y.1954). See generally Finman, *The Request for Admissions in Federal Civil Procedure,* 71 Yale L.J. 371, 426–430 (1962). The amendment eliminates this defect in Rule 37(c) by bringing within its scope all failures to admit.

Additional provisions in Rule 37(c) protect a party from having to pay expenses if the request for admission was held objectionable under Rule 36(a) or if the party failing to admit had reasonable ground to believe that he might prevail on the matter. The latter provision emphasizes that the true test under Rule 37(c) is not whether a party prevailed at trial but whether he acted reasonably in believing that he might prevail.

Subdivision (d). The scope of subdivision (d) is broadened to include responses to requests for inspection under Rule 34, thereby conforming to the new procedures of Rule 34.

Two related changes are made in subdivision (d): the permissible sanctions are broadened to include such orders "as are just"; and the requirement that the failure to appear or respond be "wilful" is eliminated. Although Rule 37(d) in terms provides for only three sanctions, all rather severe, the courts have interpreted it as permitting softer sanctions than those which it sets forth. E.g., *Gill v. Stolow,* 240 F.2d 669 (2d Cir.1957); *Saltzman v. Birrell,* 156 F.Supp. 538 (S.D.N.Y.1957); 2A Barron & Holtzoff, *Federal Practice and Procedure* 554–557 (Wright ed. 1961). The rule is changed to provide the greater flexibility as to sanctions which the cases show is needed.

The resulting flexibility as to sanctions eliminates any need to retain the requirement that the failure to appear or respond be "wilful." The concept of "wilful failure" is at best subtle and difficult, and the cases do not supply a bright line. Many courts have imposed sanctions without referring to willfulness. E.g., *Milewski v. Schneider Transportation Co.,* 238 F.2d 397 (6th Cir.1956); *Dictograph Products, Inc. v. Kentworth Corp.,* 7 F.R.D. 543 (W.D.Ky.1947). In addition, in view of the possibility of light sanctions, even a negligent failure should come within Rule 37(d). If default is caused by counsel's ignorance of Federal practice, cf. *Dunn v. Pa. R.R.,* 96 F.Supp. 597 (N.D.Ohio 1951), or by his preoccupation with another aspect of the case, cf. *Maurer-Neuer, Inc. v. United Packinghouse Workers,* 26 F.R.D. 139 (D.Kan.1960), dismissal of the action and default judgment are not justified, but the imposition of expenses and fees may well be. "Willfulness" continues to play a role, along with various other factors, in the choice of sanctions. Thus, the scheme conforms to Rule 37(b) as construed by the Supreme Court in *Societe Internationale v. Rogers,* 357 U.S. 197, 208 (1958).

A provision is added to make clear that a party may not properly remain completely silent even when he regards a notice to take his deposition or a set of interrogatories or requests to inspect as improper and objectionable. If he desires not to appear or not to respond, he must apply for a protective order. The cases are divided on whether a protective order must be sought. Compare *Collins v. Wayland,* 139 F.2d 677 (9th Cir.1944), *cert. den.* 322 U.S. 744; *Bourgeois v. El Paso Natural Gas Co.,* 20 F.R.D. 358 (S.D.N.Y.1957); *Loosley v. Stone,* 15 F.R.D. 373 (S.D.Ill.1954), with *Scarlatos v. Kulukundis,* 21 F.R.D. 185 (S.D.N.Y.1957); *Ross v. True Temper Corp.,* 11 F.R.D. 307 (N.D.Ohio 1951). Compare also Rosenberg, *supra,* 58 Col.L.Rev. 480, 496 (1958) with 2A Barron & Holtzoff, Federal Practice and Procedure 530–531 (Wright ed. 1961). The party from whom discovery is sought is afforded, through Rule 26(c), a fair and effective procedure whereby he can challenge the request made. At the same time, the total noncompliance with which Rule 37(d) is concerned may impose severe inconvenience or hardship on the discovering party and substantially delay the discovery process. Cf. 2B Barron & Holtzoff, Federal Practice and Procedure 306–307 (Wright ed. 1961) (response to a subpoena).

The failure of an officer or managing agent of a party to make discovery as required by present Rule 37(d) is treated as the failure of the party. The rule as revised provides similar treatment for a director of a party. There is slight warrant for the present distinction between officers and managing agents on the one hand and directors on the other. Although the legal power over a director to compel his making discovery may not be as great as over officers or managing agents, *Campbell v. General Motors Corp.,* 13 F.R.D. 331 (S.D.N.Y.1952), the practical differences are negligible. That a director's interests are normally aligned with those of his corporation is shown by the provisions of old Rule 26(d)(2), transferred to 32(a)(2) (deposition of director of party may be used at trial by an adverse party for any purpose) and of Rule 43(b) (director of party may be treated at trial as a hostile witness on direct examination by any adverse party). Moreover, in those rare instances when a corporation is unable through good faith efforts to compel a director to make discovery, it is unlikely that the court will impose sanctions. Cf. *Societe Internationale v. Rogers,* 357 U.S. 197 (1958).

Subdivision (e). The change in the caption conforms to the language of 28 U.S.C. § 1783, as amended in 1964.

Subdivision (f). Until recently, costs of a civil action could be awarded against the United States only when expressly provided by Act of Congress, and such provision was rarely made. See H.R.Rep.No. 1535, 89th Cong., 2d Sess., 2–3 (1966). To avoid any conflict with this doctrine, Rule 37(f) has provided that expenses and attorney's fees may not be imposed upon the United States under Rule 37. See 2A Barron & Holtzoff, Federal Practice and Procedure 857 (Wright ed. 1961).

A major change in the law was made in 1966, 80 Stat. 308, 28 U.S.C. § 2412 (1966), whereby a judgment for costs may ordinarily be awarded to the prevailing party in any civil action brought by or against the United States. Costs are not to include the fees and expenses of attorneys. In light of this legislative development, Rule 37(f) is amended to permit the award of expenses and fees against the United States under Rule 37, but only to the extent permitted by statute. The amendment brings Rule 37(f) into line with present and future statutory provisions.

1980 Amendment

Subdivision (b)(2). New Rule 26(f) provides that if a discovery conference is held, at its close the court shall enter an order respecting the subsequent conduct of discovery. The amendment provides that the sanctions available for violation of other court orders respecting discovery are available for violation of the discovery conference order.

Subdivision (e). Subdivision (e) is stricken. Title 28, U.S.C. § 1783 no longer refers to sanctions. The subdivision otherwise duplicates Rule 45(e)(2).

Subdivision (g). New Rule 26(f) imposes a duty on parties to participate in good faith in the framing of a discovery plan by agreement upon the request of any party. This subdivision authorizes the court to award to parties who participate in good faith in an attempt to frame a discovery plan the expenses incurred in the attempt if any party or his attorney fails to participate in good faith and thereby causes additional expense.

Failure of United States to Participate in Good Faith in Discovery. Rule 37 authorizes the court to direct that parties or attorneys who fail to participate in good faith in the discovery process pay the expenses, including attorneys' fees, incurred by other parties as a result of that failure. Since attorneys' fees cannot ordinarily be awarded against the United States (28 U.S.C. § 2412), there is often no practical remedy for the misconduct of its officers and attorneys. However, in the case of a government attorney who fails to participate in good faith in discovery, nothing prevents a court in an appropriate case from giving written notification of that fact to the Attorney General of the United States and other appropriate heads of offices or agencies thereof.

Rule 60. Relief From Judgment or Order

(a) **Clerical Mistakes.** Clerical mistakes in judgments, orders or other parts of the record and errors therein arising from oversight or omission may be corrected by the court at any time of its own initiative or on the motion of any party and after such notice, if any, as the court orders. During the pendency of an appeal, such mistakes may be so corrected before the appeal is docketed in the appellate court, and thereafter while the appeal is pending may be so corrected with leave of the appellate court.

(b) **Mistakes; Inadvertence; Excusable Neglect; Newly Discovered Evidence; Fraud, etc.** On motion and upon such terms as are just, the court may relieve a party or a party's legal representative from a final judgment, order, or proceeding for the following reasons: (1) mistake, inadvertence, surprise, or excusable neglect; (2) newly discovered evidence which by due diligence could not have been discovered in time to move for a new trial under Rule 59(b); (3) fraud (whether heretofore denominated intrinsic or extrinsic), misrepresentation, or other misconduct of an adverse party; (4) the judgment is void; (5) the judgment has been satisfied, released, or discharged, or a prior judgment upon which it is based has been reversed or otherwise vacated, or it is no longer equitable that the judgment should have prospective application; or (6) any other reason justifying relief from the operation of the judgment. The motion shall be made within a reasonable time, and for reasons (1), (2), and (3) not more than one year after the judgment, order, or proceeding was entered or taken. A motion under this subdivision (b) does not affect the finality of a judgment or suspend its operation. This rule does not limit the power of a court to entertain an independent action to relieve a party from a judgment, order, or proceeding, or to grant relief to a defendant not actually personally notified as provided in Title 28, U.S.C. § 1655, or to set aside a judgment for fraud upon the court. Writs of coram nobis, coram vobis, audita querela, and bills of review and bills in the nature of a bill of review, are abolished, and the procedure for obtaining any relief from a judgment shall be by motion as prescribed in these rules or by an independent action.

(As amended Dec. 27, 1946, eff. Mar. 19, 1948; Dec. 29, 1948, eff. Oct. 20, 1949; Mar. 2, 1987, eff. Aug. 1, 1987.)

Notes of Advisory Committee on Rules

Note to Subdivision (b). When promulgated, the rules contained a number of provisions, including those found in Rule 60(b), describing the practice by a motion to obtain relief from judgments, and these rules, coupled with the reservation in Rule 60(b) of the right to entertain a new action to relieve a party from a judgment, were generally supposed to cover the field. Since the rules have been in force, decisions have been rendered that the use of bills of review, coram nobis, or audita querela, to obtain relief from final judgments is still proper, and that various remedies of this kind still exist although they are not mentioned in the rules and the practice is not prescribed in the rules. It is obvious that the rules should be complete in this respect and define the practice with respect to any existing rights or remedies to obtain relief from final judgments. For extended discussion of the old common law writs and equitable remedies, the interpretation of Rule 60, and proposals for change, see Moore and Rogers, Federal Relief from Civil Judgments, 1946, 55 Yale L.J. 623. See also 3 Moore's Federal Practice, 1938, 3254 et seq.; Commentary, Effect of Rule 60b on Other Methods of Relief From Judgment, 1941, 4 Fed.Rules Serv. 942, 945; *Wallace v. United States,* C.C.A.2, 1944, 142 F.2d 240, certiorari denied 65 S.Ct. 37, 323 U.S. 712, 89 L.Ed. 573.

The reconstruction of Rule 60(b) has for one of its purposes a clarification of this situation. Two types of procedure to obtain relief from judgments are specified in the rules as it is proposed to amend them. One procedure is by motion in the court and in the action in which the judgment was rendered. The other procedure is by a new or independent action to obtain relief from a judgment, which action may or may not be begun in the court which rendered the judgment. Various rules, such as the one dealing with a motion for new trial and for amendment of judgments, Rule 59, one for amended findings, Rule 52, and one for judgment notwithstanding the verdict, Rule 50(b), and including the provisions of Rule 60(b) as amended, prescribe the various types of cases in which the practice by motion is permitted. In each case there is a limit upon the time within which resort to a motion is permitted, and this time limit may not be enlarged under Rule 6(b). If the right to make a motion is lost by the expiration of the time limits fixed in these rules, the only other procedural remedy is by a new or independent action to set aside a judgment upon those principles which have heretofore been applied in such an action. Where the independent action is resorted to, the limitations of time are those of laches or statutes of limitations. The Committee has endeavored to ascertain all the remedies and types of relief heretofore available by coram nobis, coram vobis, audita querela, bill of review, or bill in the nature of a bill of review. See Moore and Rogers, Federal Relief from Civil Judgments, 1946, 55 Yale L.J. 623, 659–682. It endeavored then to amend the rules to permit, either by motion or by independent action, the granting of various kinds of relief from judgments which were permitted in the federal courts prior to the adoption of these rules, and the amendment concludes with a provision abolishing the use of bills of review and the other common law writs referred to, and requiring the practice to be by motion or by independent action.

To illustrate the operation of the amendment, it will be noted that under Rule 59(b) as it now stands, without amendment, a motion for new trial on the ground of newly discovered evidence is permitted within ten days after the entry of the judgment, or after that time upon leave of the court. It is proposed to amend Rule 59(b) by providing that under that rule a motion for new trial shall be served not later than ten days after the entry of the judgment, whatever the ground be for the motion, whether error by the court or newly discovered evidence. On the other hand, one of the purposes of the bill of review in equity was to afford relief on the ground of newly discovered evidence long after the entry of the judgment. Therefore, to permit relief by a motion similar to that heretofore obtained on bill of review, Rule 60(b) as amended permits an application for relief to be made by motion, on the ground of newly discovered evidence, within one year after judgment. Such a motion under Rule 60(b) does not affect the finality of the judgment, but a motion under Rule 59, made within 10 days, does affect finality and the running of the time for appeal.

If these various amendments, including principally those to Rule 60(b), accomplish the purpose for which they are intended, the federal rules will deal with the practice in every sort of case in which relief from final judgments is asked, and prescribe the practice. With reference to the question whether, as the rules now exist, relief by coram nobis, bills of review, and so forth, is permissible, the generally accepted view is that the remedies are still available, although the precise relief obtained in a particular case by use of these ancillary remedies is shrouded in ancient lore and mystery. * * *

The transposition of the words "the court" and the addition of the word "and" at the beginning of the first sentence are merely verbal changes. The addition of the qualifying word "final" emphasizes the character of the judgments, orders or proceedings from which Rule 60(b) affords relief; and hence interlocutory judgments are not brought within the restrictions of the rule, but rather they are left subject to the complete power of the court rendering them to afford such relief from them as justice requires.

The qualifying pronoun "his" has been eliminated on the basis that it is too restrictive, and that the subdivision should include the mistake or neglect of others which may be just as material and call just as much for supervisory jurisdiction as where the judgment is taken against the party through *his* mistake, inadvertence, etc.

Fraud, whether intrinsic or extrinsic, misrepresentation, or other misconduct of an adverse party are express grounds for relief by motion under amended subdivision (b). There is no sound reason for their exclusion. The incorporation of fraud and the like within the scope of the rule also removes confusion as to the proper procedure. It has been held that relief from a judgment obtained by extrinsic fraud could be secured by motion within a "reasonable time," which might be after the time stated in the rule had run. *Fiske v. Buder,* C.C.A.8, 1942, 125 F.2d 841; see also inferentially *Bucy v. Nevada Construction Co.,* C.C.A.9, 1942, 125 F.2d 213. On the other hand, it has been suggested that in view of the fact that fraud was omitted from original Rule 60(b) as a ground for relief, an independent action was the only proper remedy. Commentary, Effect of Rule 60b on Other Methods of Relief From Judgment, 1941, 4 Fed.Rules Serv. 942, 945. The amendment settles this problem by making fraud an express ground for relief by motion; and under the saving clause, fraud may be urged as a basis for relief by independent action insofar as established doctrine permits. See Moore and Rogers, Federal Relief from Civil Judgments, 1946, 55 Yale L.J. 623, 653–659; 3 Moore's Federal Practice, 1938, 3267 et seq. And the rule expressly does not limit the power of the court, when fraud has been perpetrated upon it, to give relief under the saving clause. As an illustration of this situation, see *Hazel-Atlas Glass Co. v. Hartford Empire Co.,* 1944, 64 S.Ct. 997, 322 U.S. 238, 88 L.Ed. 1250.

The time limit for relief by motion in the court and in the action in which the judgment was rendered has been enlarged from six months to one year.

It should be noted that Rule 60(b) does not assume to define substantive law as to the grounds for vacating judgments, but merely prescribes the practice in proceedings to obtain relief. It should also be noted that under § 200(4) of the Soldiers' and Sailors' Civil Relief Act of 1940, 50 U.S.C., Appendix, § 501 et seq. [§ 520(4)], a judgment rendered in any action or proceeding governed by the section may be vacated under certain specified circumstances upon proper application to the court.

Rule 63. Disability of a Judge

If by reason of death, sickness, or other disability, a judge before whom an action has been tried is unable to perform the duties to be performed by the court under these rules after a verdict is returned or findings of fact and conclusions of law are filed, then any other judge regularly sitting in or assigned to the court in which the action was tried may perform those duties; but if such other judge is satisfied that such other judge cannot perform those duties because such other judge did not preside at the trial or for any other reason, such other judge may in such other judge's discretion grant a new trial.

(As amended Mar. 2, 1987, eff. Aug. 1, 1987.)

Rule 68. Offer of Judgment

At any time more than 10 days before the trial begins, a party defending against a claim may serve upon the adverse party an offer to allow judgment to be taken against the defending party for the money or property or to the effect specified in the offer, with costs then accrued. If within 10 days after the service of the offer the adverse party serves written notice that the offer is accepted, either party may then file the offer and notice of acceptance together with proof of service thereof and thereupon the clerk shall enter judgment. An offer not accepted shall be deemed withdrawn and evidence thereof is not admissible except in a proceeding to determine costs. If the judgment finally obtained by the offeree is not more favorable than the offer, the offeree must pay the costs incurred after the making of the offer. The fact that an offer is made but not accepted does not preclude a subsequent offer. When the liability of one party to another has been determined by verdict or order or judgment, but the amount or extent of the liability remains to be determined by further proceedings, the party adjudged liable may make an offer of judgment, which shall have the same effect as an offer made before trial if it is served within a reasonable time not less than 10 days prior to the commencement of hearings to determine the amount or extent of liability.

(As amended Dec. 27, 1946, eff. Mar. 19, 1948; Feb. 28, 1966, eff. July 1, 1966; Mar. 2, 1987, eff. Aug. 1, 1987.)

FEDERAL RULES OF CRIMINAL PROCEDURE

Rule 44. Right to and Assignment of Counsel

(a) **Right to Assigned Counsel.** Every defendant who is unable to obtain counsel shall be entitled to have counsel assigned to represent that defendant at every stage of the proceedings from initial appearance before the federal magistrate or the court through appeal, unless that defendant waives such appointment.

(b) **Assignment Procedure.** The procedures for implementing the right set out in subdivision (a) shall be those provided by law and by local rules of court established pursuant thereto.

(c) **Joint Representation.** Whenever two or more defendants have been jointly charged pursuant to Rule 8(b) or have been joined for trial pursuant to Rule 13, and are represented by the same retained or assigned counsel or by retained or assigned counsel who are associated in the practice of law, the court shall promptly inquire with respect to such joint representation and shall personally advise each defendant of the right to the effective assistance of counsel, including separate representation. Unless it appears that there is good cause to believe no conflict of interest is likely to arise, the court shall take such measures as may be appropriate to protect each defendant's right to counsel.

Notes of Advisory Committee on Rules

1. This rule is a restatement of existing law in regard to the defendant's constitutional right of counsel as defined in recent judicial decisions. The Sixth Amendment provides:

"In all criminal prosecutions, the accused shall enjoy the right . . . to have the Assistance of Counsel for his defense."

28 U.S.C. former § 394 (now § 1654) provides:

"In all the courts of the United States the parties may plead and manage their own causes personally, or by the assistance of such counsel or attorneys at law as, by the rules of the said courts, respectively, are permitted to manage and conduct causes therein."

18 U.S.C. former § 563 (now § 3005), which is derived from the act of April 30, 1790 (1 Stat. 118), provides:

"Every person who is indicted of treason or other capital crime shall be allowed to make his full defense by counsel learned in the law; and the court before which he is tried or some judge thereof, shall immediately, upon his request, assign to him such counsel, not exceeding two, as he may desire, and they shall have free access to him at all seasonable hours."

The present extent of the right of counsel has been defined recently in *Johnson v. Zerbst,* 304 U.S. 458, 58 S.Ct. 1019, 82 L.Ed. 1461; *Walker v. Johnston,* 312 U.S. 275, 61 S.Ct. 574, 85 L.Ed. 830; and *Glasser v. United States,* 315 U.S. 60, 62 S.Ct. 457, 86 L.Ed. 680, rehearing denied 315 U.S. 827, 62 S.Ct. 629, 637, two cases, 86 L.Ed. 1222. The rule is a restatement of the principles enunciated in these decisions. See, also, Holtzoff, 20 N.Y.U.L.Q.R. 1.

2. The rule is intended to indicate that the right of the defendant to have counsel assigned by the court relates only to proceedings in court and, therefore, does not include preliminary proceedings before a committing magistrate. Although the defendant is not entitled to have counsel assigned to him in connection with preliminary proceedings, he is entitled to be represented by counsel retained by him, if he so chooses, Rule 5(b) (Proceedings before the Commissioner; Statement by the Commissioner) and Rule 40(b)(2) (Commitment to Another District; Removal—Arrest in Distant District—Statement by Commissioner or Judge). As to defendant's right of counsel in connection with the taking of depositions, see Rule 15(c) (Depositions—Defendant's Counsel and Payment of Expenses).

1966 Amendment

A new rule is provided as a substitute for the old to provide for the assignment of counsel to defendants unable to obtain counsel during all stages of the proceeding. The Supreme Court has recently made clear the importance of providing counsel both at the earliest possible time after arrest and on appeal. See *Crooker v. California,* 357 U.S. 433 (1958); *Cicenia v. LaGay,* 357 U.S. 504 (1958); *White v. Maryland,* 373 U.S. 59 (1963); *Gideon v. Wainwright,* 372 U.S. 335 (1963); *Douglas v. California,* 372 U.S. 353 (1963). See also Association of the Bar of the City of New York, Special Committee to Study the Defender System, Equal Justice for the Accused (1959); Report of the Attorney General's Committee on Poverty and the Administration of Justice (1963); Beaney, Right to Counsel Before Arraignment, 45 Minn.L.Rev. 771 (1961); Boskey, The Right to Counsel in Appellate Proceedings, 45 Minn.L.Rev. 783 (1961); Douglas, The Right to Counsel—A Foreword, 45 Minn.L.Rev. 693 (1961); Kamisar, The Right to Counsel and the Fourteenth Amendment; A Dialogue on "The Most Pervasive Right" of an Accused, 30 U.Chi.L.Rev. 1 (1962); Kamisar, Betts v. Brady Twenty Years Later: The Right to Counsel and Due Process Values, 61 Mich.L.Rev. 219 (1962); Symposium, The Right to Counsel, 22 Legal Aid Briefcase 4–48 (1963). Provision has been made by law for a Legal Aid Agency in the District of Columbia which is charged with the duty of providing counsel and courts are admonished to assign such counsel "as early in the proceeding as practicable." D.C.Code § 2–2202. Congress has now made provision for assignment of counsel and their compensation in all of the districts. Criminal Justice Act of 1964 (78 Stat. 552).

Like the original rule the amended rule provides a right to counsel which is broader in two respects than that for which compensation is provided in the Criminal Justice Act of 1964: (1) the right extends to petty offenses to be tried in the district courts, and (2) the right extends to defendants unable to obtain counsel for reasons other than financial. These rules do not cover procedures other than those in the courts of the United States and before United States commissioners. See Rule 1. Hence, the problems relating to the providing of counsel, prior to the initial appearance before a court or commissioner are not dealt with in this rule. Cf. *Escobedo v. United States*, 378 U.S. 478 (1964); Enker and Elsen, Counsel for the Suspect: *Massiah v. United States* and *Escobedo v. Illinois*, 49 Minn.L.Rev. 47 (1964).

Subdivision (a). This subdivision expresses the right of the defendant unable to obtain counsel to have such counsel assigned at any stage of the proceedings from his initial appearance before the commissioner or court through the appeal, unless he waives such right. The phrase "from his initial appearance before the commissioner or court" is intended to require the assignment of counsel as promptly as possible after it appears that the defendant is unable to obtain counsel. The right to assignment of counsel is not limited to those financially unable to obtain counsel. If a defendant is able to compensate counsel but still cannot obtain counsel, he is entitled to the assignment of counsel even though not to free counsel.

Subdivision (b). This new subdivision reflects the adoption of the Criminal Justice Act of 1964. See Report of the Judicial Conference of the United States on the Criminal Justice Act of 1964, 36 F.R.D. 277 (1964).

1972 Amendment

Subdivision (a) is amended to reflect the Federal Magistrates Act of 1968. The phrase "federal magistrate" is defined in rule 54.

1979 Amendment

Rule 44(c) establishes a procedure for avoiding the occurrence of events which might otherwise give rise to a plausible post-conviction claim that because of joint representation the defendants in a criminal case were deprived of their Sixth Amendment right to the effective assistance of counsel. Although "courts have differed with respect to the scope and nature of the affirmative duty of the trial judge to assure that criminal defendants are not deprived of their right to the effective assistance of counsel by joint representation of conflicting interests." *Holloway v. Arkansas*, 98 S.Ct. 1173 (1978) (where the Court found it unnecessary to reach this issue), this amendment is generally consistent with the current state of the law in several circuits. As held in *United States v. Carrigan*, 543 F.2d 1053 (2d Cir.1976):

> When a potential conflict of interest arises, either where a court has assigned the same counsel to represent several defendants or where the same counsel has been retained by co-defendants in a criminal case, the proper course of action for the trial judge is to conduct a hearing to determine whether a conflict exists to the degree that a defendant may be prevented from receiving advice and assistance sufficient to afford him the quality of representation guaranteed by the Sixth Amendment. The defendant should be fully advised by the trial court of the facts underlying the potential conflict and be given the opportunity to express his views.

See also *United States v. Lawriw*, 568 F.2d 98 (8th Cir.1977) (duty on trial judge to make inquiry where joint representation by appointed or retained counsel, and "without such an inquiry a finding of knowing and intelligent waiver will seldom, if ever, be sustained by this Court"); *Abraham v. United States*, 549 F.2d 236 (2d Cir.1977); *United States v. Mari*, 526 F.2d 117 (2d Cir.1975); *United States v. Truglio*, 493 F.2d 574 (4th Cir.1974) (joint representation should cause trial judge "to inquire whether the defenses to be presented in any way conflict"); *United States v. DeBerry*, 487 F.2d 488 (2d Cir.1973); *United States ex rel. Hart v. Davenport*, 478 F.2d 203 (3d Cir.1973) (noting there "is much to be said for the rule . . . which assumes prejudice and nonwaiver if there has been no on-the-record inquiry by the court as to the hazards to defendants from joint representation"); *United States v. Alberti*, 470 F.2d 878 (2d Cir.1973); *United States v. Foster*, 469 F.2d 1 (1st Cir.1972) (lack of sufficient inquiry shifts the burden of proof on the question of prejudice to the government); *Campbell v. United States*, 352 F.2d 359 (D.C.Cir.1965) (where joint representation, court "has a duty to ascertain whether each defendant has an awareness of the potential risks of that course and nevertheless has knowingly chosen it"). Some states have taken a like position; see, e.g., *State v. Olsen*, Minn.1977, 258 N.W.2d 898.

This procedure is also consistent with that recommended in the ABA Standards Relating to the Function of the Trial Judge (Approved Draft, 1972), which provide in § 3.4(b):

> Whenever two or more defendants who have been jointly charged, or whose cases have been consolidated, are represented by the same attorney, the trial judge should inquire into potential conflicts with may jeopardize the right of each defendant to the fidelity of his counsel.

Avoiding a conflict-of-interest situation is in the first instance a responsibility of the attorney. If a lawyer represents "multiple clients having potentially differing interests, he must weigh carefully the possibility that his judgment may be impaired or his loyalty divided if he accepts or continues the employment," and he is to "resolve all doubts against the propriety of the representation." Code of Professional Responsibility, Ethical Consideration 5-15. See also ABA Standards Relating to the Defense Function § 3.5(b) (Approved Draft, 1971) concluding that the "potential for conflict of interest in representing multiple defendants is so grave that ordinarily a lawyer should decline to act for more than one of several co-defendants except in unusual situations when, after careful investigation, it is clear that no conflict is likely to develop and when the several defendants give an informed consent to such multiple representation."

It by no means follows that the inquiry provided for by rule 44(c) is unnecessary. For one thing, even the most diligent attorney may be unaware of facts giving rise to a potential conflict. Often "counsel must operate somewhat in the dark and feel their way uncertainly to an understanding of what their clients may be called upon to meet upon a trial" and consequently "are frequently unable to foresee developments which may require changes in strategy." *United States v. Carrigan,* supra (concurring opinion). "Because the conflicts are often subtle it is not enough to rely upon counsel, who may not be totally disinterested, to make sure that each of his joint clients has made an effective waiver." *United States v. Lawriw,* supra.

Moreover, it is important that the trial judge ascertain whether the effective and fair administration of justice would be adversely affected by continued joint representation, even when an actual conflict is not then apparent. As noted in *United States v. Mari,* supra (concurring opinion):

> Trial court insistence that, except in extraordinary circumstances, codefendants retain separate counsel will in the long run . . . prove salutary not only to the administration of justice and the appearance of justice but the cost of justice; habeas corpus petitions, petitions for new trials, appeals and occasionally retrials . . . can be avoided. Issues as to whether there is an actual conflict of interest, whether the conflict has resulted in prejudice, whether there has been a waiver, whether the waiver is intelligent and knowledgeable, for example, can all be avoided. Where a conflict that first did not appear subsequently arises in or before trial, . . . continuances or mistrials can be saved. Essentially by the time a case . . . gets to the appellate level the harm to the appearance of justice has already been done, whether or not reversal occurs; at the trial level it is a matter which is so easy to avoid.

A rule 44(c) inquiry is required whether counsel is assigned or retained. It "makes no difference whether counsel is appointed by the court or selected by the defendants; even where selected by the defendants the same dangers of potential conflict exist, and it is also possible that the rights of the public to the proper administration of justice may be affected adversely." *United States v. Mari,* supra (concurring opinion). See also *United States v. Lawriw,* supra. When there has been "no discussion as to possible conflict initiated by the court," it cannot be assumed that the choice of counsel by the defendants "was intelligently made with knowledge of any possible conflict." *United States v. Carrigan,* supra. As for assigned counsel, it is provided by statute that "the court shall appoint separate counsel for defendants having interests that cannot properly be represented by the same counsel, or when other good cause is shown." 18 U.S.C. § 3006(A)(b). Rule 44(c) is not intended to prohibit the automatic appointment of separate counsel in the first instance, see *Ford v. United States,* 379 F.2d 123 (D.C.Cir.1967); *Lollar v. United States,* 376 F.2d 243 (D.C.Cir.1967), which would obviate the necessity for an inquiry.

Under rule 44(c), an inquiry is called for when the joined defendants are represented by the same attorney and also when they are represented by attorneys "associated in the practice of law." This is consistent with Code of Professional Responsibility, Disciplinary

Rule 5–105(D) (providing that if "a lawyer is required to decline employment or to withdraw from employment" because of a potential conflict, "no partner or associate of his or his firm may accept or continue such employment"); and ABA Standards Relating to the Defense Function § 3.5(b) (Approved Draft, 1971) (applicable to "a lawyer or lawyers who are associated in practice"). Attorneys representing joined defendants should so advise the court if they are associated in the practice of law.

The rule 44(c) procedure is not limited to cases expected to go to trial. Although the more dramatic conflict situations, such as when the question arises as to whether the several defendants should take the stand, *Morgan v. United States,* 396 F.2d 110 (2d Cir.1968), tend to occur in a trial context, serious conflicts may also arise when one or more of the jointly represented defendants pleads guilty.

> The problem is that even where as here both codefendants pleaded guilty there are frequently potential conflicts of interest . . . [T]he prosecutor may be inclined to accept a guilty plea from one codefendant which may harm the interests of the other. The contrast in the dispositions of the cases may have a harmful impact on the codefendant who does not initially plead guilty; he may be pressured into pleading guilty himself rather than face his codefendant's bargained-for testimony at a trial. And it will be his own counsel's recommendation to the initially pleading codefendant which will have contributed to this harmful impact upon him. . . . [I]n a given instance it would be at least conceivable that the prosecutor would be willing to accept pleas to lesser offenses from two defendants in preference to a plea of guilty by one defendant to a greater offense.

United States v. Mari, supra (concurring opinion). To the same effect is ABA Standards Relating to the Defense Function at 213–14.

It is contemplated that under rule 44(c) the court will make appropriate inquiry of the defendants and of counsel regarding the possibility of a conflict of interest developing. Whenever it is necessary to make a more particularized inquiry into the nature of the contemplated defense, the court should "pursue the inquiry with defendants and their counsel on the record but in chambers" so as "to avoid the possibility of prejudicial disclosures to the prosecution." *United States v. Foster,* supra. It is important that each defendant be "fully advised of the facts underlying the potential conflict and is given an opportunity to express his or her views." *United States v. Alberti,* supra. The rule specifically requires that the court personally advise each defendant of his right to effective assistance of counsel, including separate representation. See *United States v. Foster,* supra, requiring that the court make a determination that jointly represented defendants "understand that they may retain separate counsel, or if qualified, may have such counsel appointed by the court and paid for by the government."

Under rule 44(c), the court is to take appropriate measures to protect each defendant's right to counsel unless it appears "there is good cause to believe no conflict of interest is likely to arise" as a consequence of the continuation of such joint representation. A less demanding standard would not adequately protect the Sixth Amendment right to effective assistance of counsel or the effective administration of criminal justice. Although joint representation "is not per se violative of constitutional guarantees of effective assistance of counsel, *Holloway v. Arkansas,* supra, it would not suffice to require the court to act only when a conflict of interest is then apparent, for it is not possible to "anticipate with complete accuracy the course that a criminal trial may take." *Fryar v. United States,* 404 F.2d 1071 (10th Cir.1968). This is particularly so in light of the fact that if a conflict later arises and a defendant thereafter raises a Sixth Amendment objection, a court must grant relief without indulging "in nice calculations as to the amount of prejudice arising from its denial." *Glasser v. United States,* 315 U.S. 60 (1942). This is because, as the Supreme Court more recently noted in *Holloway v. Arkansas,* supra, "in a case of joint representation of conflicting interests the evil . . . is in what the advocate finds himself compelled to refrain from doing," and this makes it "virtually impossible" to assess the impact of the conflict.

Rule 44(c) does not specify what particular measures must be taken. It is appropriate to leave this within the court's discretion, for the measures which will best protect each defendant's right to counsel may well vary from case to case. One possible course of action is for the court to obtain a knowing, intelligent and voluntary waiver of the right to separate representation, for, as noted in *Holloway v. Arkansas,* supra, "a defendant may waive his right to the assistance of an attorney unhindered by a conflict of interests." See *United States v. DeBerry,* supra, holding that defendants should be jointly represented only if "the court has ascertained that . . . each understands clearly the possibilities of a conflict of interest and waives any rights in connection with it." It must be emphasized that a "waiver of the right to separate representation should not be accepted by the court unless the defendants have each been informed of the probable hazards; and the voluntary character of their waiver is apparent." ABA Standards Relating to the Function of the Trial Judge at 45. *United States v. Garcia*, supra, spells out in significant detail what should be done to assure an adequate waiver:

> As in Rule 11 procedures, the district court should address each defendant personally and forthrightly advise him of the potential dangers of representation by counsel with a conflict of interest. The defendant must be at liberty to question the district court as to the nature and consequences of his legal representation. Most significantly, the court should seek to elicit a narrative response from each defendant that he has been advised of his right to effective representation, that he understands the details of his attorney's possible conflict of interest and the potential perils of such a conflict, that he has discussed the matter with his attorney or if he wishes with outside counsel, and that he voluntarily waives his Sixth Amendment protections. It is, of course, vital that the waiver be established by "clear, unequivocal, and unambiguous language." . . . Mere assent in response to a series of questions from the bench may in some circumstances constitute an adequate waiver, but the court should nonetheless endeavor to have each defendant personally articulate in detail his intent to forego this significant constitutional protection. Recordation of the waiver colloque between defendant and judge, will also serve the government's interest by assisting in shielding any potential conviction from collateral attack, either on Sixth Amendment grounds or on a Fifth or Fourteenth Amendment "fundamental fairness" basis.

See also Hyman, Joint Representation of Multiple Defendants in a Criminal Trial: The Court's Headache, 5 Hofstra L.Rev. 315, 334 (1977).

Another possibility is that the court will order that the defendants be separately represented in subsequent proceedings in the case.

Though the court must remain alert to and take account of the fact that "certain advantages might accrue from joint representation," *Holloway v. Arkansas,* supra, it need not permit the joint representation to continue merely because the defendants express a willingness to so proceed. That is, there will be cases where the court should require separate counsel to represent certain defendants despite the expressed wishes of such defendants. Indeed, failure of the trial court to require separate representation may . . . require a new trial, even though the defendants have expressed a desire to continue with the same counsel. The right to effective representation by counsel whose loyalty is undivided is so paramount in the proper administration of criminal justice that it must in some cases take precedence over all other considerations, including the expressed preference of the defendants concerned and their attorney.

United States v. Carrigan, supra (concurring opinion). See also *United States v. Lawriw,* supra; *Abraham v. United States,* supra; ABA Standards Relating to the Defense Function at 213, concluding that in some circumstances "even full disclosure and consent of the client may not be an adequate protection." As noted in *United States v. Dolan,* 570 F.2d 1177 (3d Cir.1978), such an order may be necessary where the trial judge is

> not satisfied that the waiver is proper. For example, a defendant may be competent enough to stand trial, but not competent enough to understand the complex, subtle, and sometimes unforeseeable dangers inherent in multiple representation. More importantly, the judge may find that the waiver cannot be intelligently made simply because he is not in a position to inform the defendant of the foreseeable prejudices multiple representation might entail for him.

As concluded in *Dolan,* "exercise of the court's supervisory powers by disqualifying an attorney representing multiple criminal defendants in spite of the defendants' express desire to retain that attorney does not necessarily abrogate defendant's sixth amendment rights". It does not follow from the absolute right of self-representation recognized in *Faretta v. California,* 422 U.S. 806 (1975), that there is an *absolute* right to counsel of one's own choice. Thus,

> when a trial court finds an actual conflict of interest which impairs the ability of a criminal defendant's chosen counsel to conform with the ABA Code of Professional

Responsibility, the court should not be required to tolerate an inadequate representation of a defendant. Such representation not only constitutes a breach of professional ethics and invites disrespect for the integrity of the court, but it is also detrimental to the independent interest of the trial judge to be free from future attacks over the adequacy of the waiver or the fairness of the proceedings in his own court and the subtle problems implicating the defendant's comprehension of the waiver. Under such circumstances, the court can elect to exercise its supervisory authority over members of the bar to enforce the ethical standard requiring an attorney to decline multiple representation.

United States v. Dolan, supra. See also Geer, Conflict of Interest and Multiple Defendants in a Criminal Case: Professional Responsibilities of the Defense Attorney, 62 Minn.L.Rev. 119 (1978); Note, Conflict of Interests in Multiple Representation of Criminal Co-Defendants, 68 J.Crim.L. & C. 226 (1977).

The failure in a particular case to conduct a rule 44(c) inquiry would not, standing alone, necessitate the reversal of a conviction of a jointly represented defendant. However, as is currently the case, a reviewing court is more likely to assume a conflict resulted from the joint representation when no inquiry or an inadequate inquiry was conducted. *United States v. Carrigan,* supra; *United States v. DeBerry,* supra. On the other hand, the mere fact that a rule 44(c) inquiry was conducted in the early stages of the case does not relieve the court of all responsibility in this regard thereafter. The obligation placed upon the court by rule 44(c) is a continuing one, and thus in a particular case further inquiry may be necessary on a later occasion because of new developments suggesting a potential conflict of interest.

FEDERAL RULES OF APPELLATE PROCEDURE

Rule 38. Damages for Delay

If a court of appeals shall determine that an appeal is frivolous, it may award just damages and single or double costs to the appellee.

Notes of Advisory Committee on Appellate Rules

Compare 28 U.S.C. § 1912. While both the statute and the usual rule on the subject by courts of appeals (Fourth Circuit Rule 20 is a typical rule) speak of "damages for delay," the courts of appeals quite properly allow damages, attorney's fees and other expenses incurred by an appellee if the appeal is frivolous without requiring a showing that the appeal resulted in delay. See *Dunscombe v. Sayle,* 340 F.2d 311 (5th Cir.1965), *cert. den.,* 382 U.S. 814, 86 S.Ct. 32, 15 L.Ed.2d 62 (1965); *Lowe v. Willacy,* 239 F.2d 179 (9th Cir. 1956); *Griffith Wellpoint Corp. v. Munro-Langstroth, Inc.,* 269 F.2d 64 (1st Cir.1959); *Ginsburg v. Stern,* 295 F.2d 698 (3d Cir.1961). The subjects of interest and damages are separately regulated, contrary to the present practice of combining the two (see Fourth Circuit Rule 20) to make it clear that the awards are distinct and independent. Interest is provided for by law; damages are awarded by the court in its discretion in the case of a frivolous appeal as a matter of justice to the appellee and as a penalty against the appellant.

Rule 46. Attorneys

(a) Admission to the Bar of a Court of Appeals; Eligibility; Procedure for Admission. An attorney who has been admitted to practice before the Supreme Court of the United States, or the highest court of a state, or another United States court of appeals, or a United States district court (including the district courts for the Canal Zone, Guam and the Virgin Islands), and who is of good moral and professional character, is eligible for admission to the bar of a court of appeals.

An applicant shall file with the clerk of the court of appeals, on a form approved by the court and furnished by the clerk, an application for admission containing the applicant's personal statement showing eligibility for membership. At the foot of the application the applicant shall take and subscribe to the following oath or affirmation:

I, _____, do solemnly swear (or affirm) that I will demean myself as an attorney and counselor of this court, uprightly and according to law; and that I will support the Constitution of the United States.

Thereafter, upon written or oral motion of a member of the bar of the court, the court will act upon the application. An applicant may be admitted by oral motion in open court, but it is not necessary that the applicant appear before the court for the purpose of being admitted, unless the court shall otherwise order. An applicant shall upon admission pay to the clerk the fee prescribed by rule or order of the court.

(b) Suspension or Disbarment. When it is shown to the court that any member of its bar has been suspended or disbarred from practice in any other court of record, or has been guilty of conduct unbecoming a member of the bar of the court, the member will be subject to suspension or disbarment by the court. The member shall be afforded an opportunity to show good cause, within such time as the court shall prescribe, why the member should not be suspended or disbarred. Upon the member's response to the rule to show cause, and after hearing, if requested, or upon expiration of the time prescribed for a response if no response is made, the court shall enter an appropriate order.

(c) Disciplinary Power of the Court over Attorneys. A court of appeals may, after reasonable notice and an opportunity to show cause to the contrary, and after hearing, if requested, take any appropriate disciplinary action against any attorney who practices before it for conduct unbecoming a member of the bar or for failure to comply with these rules or any rule of the court.

(As amended Mar. 10, 1986, eff. July 1, 1986.)

Notes of Advisory Committee on Appellate Rules

Subdivision (a). The basic requirement of membership in the bar of the Supreme Court, or of the highest court of a state, or in another court of appeals or a district court is found, with minor variations, in the rules of ten circuits. The only other requirement in those circuits is that the applicant be of good moral and professional character. In the District of Columbia Circuit applicants other than members of the District of Columbia District bar or the Supreme Court bar must claim membership in the bar of the highest court of a state, territory or possession for three years prior to application for admission (D.C.Cir. Rule 7). Members of the District of Columbia District bar and the Supreme Court bar again excepted, applicants for admission to the District of Columbia Circuit bar must meet precisely defined prelaw and law school study requirements (D.C.Cir. Rule 7½).

A few circuits now require that application for admission be made by oral motion by a sponsor member in open court. The proposed rule permits both the application and the motion by the sponsor member to be in writing, and permits action on the motion without the appearance of the applicant or the sponsor, unless the court otherwise orders.

Subdivision (b). The provision respecting suspension or disbarment is uniform. Third Circuit Rule 8(3) is typical.

Subdivision (c). At present only Fourth Circuit Rule 36 contains an equivalent provision. The purpose of this provision is to make explicit the power of a court of appeals to impose sanctions less serious than suspension or disbarment for the breach of rules. It also affords some measure of control over attorneys who are not members of the bar of the court. Several circuits permit a non-member attorney to file briefs and motions, membership being required only at the time of oral argument. And several circuits permit argument pro hac vice by non-member attorneys.

RULES OF THE SUPREME COURT OF THE UNITED STATES

Rule 5. Admission to the Bar

1. It shall be requisite to the admission to practice in this Court that the applicant shall have been admitted to practice in the highest court of a State, Territory, District, Commonwealth, or Possession for the three years immediately preceding the date of application, and that the applicant appears to the Court to be of good moral and professional character.

2. Each applicant shall file with the Clerk (1) a certificate from the presiding judge, clerk, or other duly authorized official of the proper court evidencing the applicant's admission to practice there and present good standing, and (2) an executed copy of the form approved by the Court and furnished by the Clerk containing (i) the applicant's personal statement and (ii) the statement of two sponsors (who must be members of the Bar of this Court and must personally know, but not be related to, the applicant) endorsing the correctness of the applicant's statement, stating that the applicant possesses all the qualifications required for admission, and affirming that the applicant is of good moral and professional character.

3. If the documents submitted by the applicant demonstrate that the applicant possesses the necessary qualifications, the Clerk shall so notify the applicant. Upon the applicant's signing the oath or affirmation and paying the fee required under Rule 45(e), the Clerk shall issue a certificate of admission. If the applicant desires, however, the applicant may be admitted in open court on oral motion by a member of the Bar, provided that the requirements for admission have been satisfied.

4. Each applicant shall take or subscribe the following oath or affirmation:

I, _____, do solemnly swear (or affirm) that as an attorney and as a counselor of this Court I will conduct myself uprightly and according to law, and that I will support the Constitution of the United States.

. . .

Rule 6. Argument Pro Hac Vice

1. An attorney not admitted to practice in the highest court of a State, Commonwealth, Territory or Possession, or of the District of Columbia for the requisite three years, but who is otherwise eligible for admission to practice in this Court under Rule 5.1, may be permitted to argue *pro hac vice*.

2. An attorney, barrister, or advocate who is qualified to practice in the courts of a foreign state may be permitted to argue *pro hac vice*.

3. Oral argument *pro hac vice* will be allowed only on motion of the attorney of record for the party on whose behalf leave is requested. The motion must briefly and distinctly state the appropriate qualifications of the attorney who is to argue *pro hac vice*. It must be filed with the Clerk, in the form prescribed by Rule 21, no later than the date on which the respondent's or appellee's brief on the merits is due to be filed and must be accompanied by proof of service pursuant to Rule 29.

Rule 7. Prohibition Against Practice

1. The Clerk shall not practice as an attorney or counselor while holding office.

2. No law clerk, secretary to a Justice, or other employee of this Court shall practice as an attorney or counselor in any court or before any agency of government while employed at the Court; nor shall any person after leaving employment in this Court participate, by way of any form of professional consultation or assistance, in any case pending before this Court or in any case being considered for filing in this Court, until two years have elapsed after separation; nor shall a former employee ever participate, by way of any form of professional consultation or assistance, in any case that was pending in this Court during the employee's tenure.

Rule 8. Disbarment and Disciplinary Action

1. Whenever it is shown to the Court that a member of the Bar of this Court has been disbarred or suspended from practice in any court of record, or has engaged in conduct unbecoming a member of the Bar of this Court, that member will be suspended from practice before this Court forthwith and will be afforded the opportunity to show cause, within 40 days, why a disbarment order should not be entered. Upon response, or upon the expiration of the 40 days if no response is made, the Court will enter an appropriate order.

2. The Court may, after reasonable notice and an opportunity to show cause why disciplinary action should not be taken, and after a hearing if material facts are in dispute, take any appropriate disciplinary action against any attorney who practices before it for conduct unbecoming a member of the Bar or for failure to comply with these Rules or any Rule of the Court.

PART THREE

STANDARDS FOR SPECIALIZED
AREAS OF PRACTICE

Table of Contents

Introduction

Although the ABA has sought to regulate all lawyers' conduct through one general code of conduct, certain groups of lawyers who practice in a specialized area have sought to promulgate their own codes of conduct. On one level, such efforts have been justified on the grounds that their specific area of practice needs its own code of conduct because of unique characteristics that cannot be taken into account in the general code. On another level, such efforts may be viewed as a struggle between the general governing group of the bar and the governing groups of certain specialized areas of practice. By promulgating a special code for an area of practice, lawyers can control conduct and entry in a small area of practice. Although the future of such codes is not entirely clear, one can gain an appreciation for the different attempts to draft rules for a specialized area of practice. Thus, this part examines several standards for specialized areas of practice.

The first two standards, one dealing with criminal law and the other with family law, were drafted by groups within the ABA and are intended as supplements to the general codes of conduct. The third standard represents an effect by the Federal Bar Association to provide rules of conduct for federal lawyers. The fourth standard illustrates the regulation of one area of practice by a governmental agency, the Treasury of the United States. All lawyers who practice before the Internal Revenue Service must comply with these regulations. The fourth set of standards collects several examples of efforts to control abuse in litigation practice. These codes of professionalism and courtesy in litigation seek to temper the traditional view of the lawyer as a zealous advocate for the client.

AMERICAN BAR ASSOCIATION STANDARDS RELATING TO THE ADMINISTRATION OF CRIMINAL JUSTICE

The Prosecution Function (Chapter 3) is reprinted from "Prosecution and Defense Function," Chapter 3 of *Standards Relating to the Administration of Criminal Justice,* 2d Edition, Tentative Draft Approved February 12, 1979. Copyright © 1982 by American Bar Association. Reprinted with permission. The Defense Function (Chapter 4) was amended in 1991 and is reprinted as approved by the House of Delegates. Copyright © 1991 by American Bar Association. Reprinted with permission. These changes are part of a complete revision of the Standards Relating to the Administration of Criminal Justice, which will be completed over the next several years.

Chapter 3. The Prosecution Function

Chapter 4. The Defense Function

THE PROSECUTION FUNCTION

PART I.   GENERAL STANDARDS

Standard 3–1.1   The Function of the Prosecutor

(a) The office of prosecutor is charged with responsibility for prosecutions in its jurisdiction.

(b) The prosecutor is both an administrator of justice and an advocate. The prosecutor must exercise sound discretion in the performance of his or her functions.

(c) The duty of the prosecutor is to seek justice, not merely to convict.

(d) It is the duty of the prosecutor to know and be guided by the standards of professional conduct as defined in the codes and canons of the legal profession, and in this chapter. The prosecutor should make use of the guidance afforded by an advisory council of the kind described in standard 4–1.4.

(e) As used in this chapter, the term "unprofessional conduct" denotes conduct which, in either identical or similar language, is or should be made subject to disciplinary sanctions pursuant to codes of professional responsibility in force in each jurisdiction. Where other terms are used, the standard is intended as a guide to honorable professional conduct and performance. These standards are not intended as criteria for the judicial evaluation of alleged misconduct of the prosecutor to determine the validity of a conviction. They may or may not be relevant in such judicial evaluation, depending upon all the circumstances.

Standard 3–1.2   Conflicts of Interest

A prosecutor should avoid the appearance or reality of a conflict of interest with respect to official duties. In some instances, as defined in codes of professional responsibility, failure to do so will constitute unprofessional conduct.

Standard 3–1.3   Public Statements

(a) The prosecutor should not exploit the office by means of personal publicity connected with a case before trial, during trial, or thereafter.

(b) The prosecutor should comply with the chapter on fair trial and free press in these standards. In some instances, as defined in codes of professional responsibility, failure to do so will constitute unprofessional conduct.

(c) In order to assure a fair trial for the accused, the prosecutor and police should cooperate in achieving compliance with the chapter on Fair Trial and Free Press of these standards and codes of professional responsibility.

Standard 3–1.4   Duty to Improve the Law

It is an important function of the prosecutor to seek to reform and improve the administration of criminal justice. When inadequacies or injustices in the substantive or procedural law come to the prosecutor's attention, he or she should stimulate efforts for remedial action.

PART II.   ORGANIZATION OF THE PROSECUTION FUNCTION

Standard 3–2.1   Prosecution Authority to Be Vested in a Public Official

The prosecution function should be performed by a public prosecutor who is a lawyer subject to the standards of professional conduct and discipline.

Standard 3–2.2   Interrelationship of Prosecution Offices Within a State

(a) Local authority and responsibility for prosecution is properly vested in a district, county, or city attorney. Wherever possible, a unit of prosecution should be designed on the basis of population, caseload, and other relevant factors sufficient to warrant at least one full-time prosecutor and the supporting staff necessary to effective prosecution.

(b) In some states, conditions such as geographical area and population may make it appropriate to create a statewide system of prosecution in which the state attorney general is the chief prosecutor and the local prosecutors are deputies.

(c) In all states, there should be coordination of the prosecution policies of local prosecution offices to improve the administration of justice and assure the maximum practicable uniformity in the enforcement of the criminal law throughout the state. A state council of prosecutors should be established in each state.

(d) In cases where questions of law of statewide interest or concern arise which may create important precedents, the prosecutor should consult and advise with the attorney general of the state.

(e) A central pool of supporting resources and manpower, including laboratories, investigators, accountants, special counsel, and other experts to the extent needed, should be maintained by the state government and should be available to all local prosecutors.

Standard 3-2.3 Assuring High Standards of Professional Skill

(a) The function of public prosecution requires highly developed professional skills. This objective can best be achieved by promoting continuity of service and broad experience in all phases of the prosecution function.

(b) Wherever feasible, the offices of chief prosecutor and staff should be full-time occupations.

(c) Professional competence should be the only basis for selection for prosecutorial office. Prosecutors should select their staffs on the basis of professional competence without regard to partisan political influence.

(d) In order to achieve the objective of professionalism and to encourage competent lawyers to accept such offices, compensation for prosecutors and their staffs should be commensurate with the high responsibilities of the office and comparable to the compensation of their peers in the private sector.

Standard 3-2.4 Special Assistants, Investigative Resources, Experts

(a) Funds should be provided to enable a prosecutor to appoint special assistants from among the trial bar experienced in criminal cases, as needed for the prosecution of a particular case or to assist generally.

(b) Funds should be provided to the prosecutor for the employment of a regular staff of professional investigative personnel and other necessary supporting personnel, under the prosecutor's direct control, to the extent warranted by the responsibilities and scope of the office. The prosecutor should also be provided with funds for the employment of qualified experts as needed for particular cases.

509

Standard 3-2.5   Prosecutor's Handbook; Policy Guidelines and Procedures

(a) Each prosecutor's office should develop a statement of:

(i) general policies to guide the exercise of prosecutorial discretion, and

(ii) procedures of the office.

The objectives of these policies as to discretion and procedures should be to achieve a fair, efficient, and effective enforcement of the criminal law.

(b) In the interest of continuity and clarity, such statement of policies and procedures should be maintained in an office handbook. This handbook should be available to the public, except for subject matters declared "confidential," when it is reasonably believed that public access to their contents would adversely affect the prosecution function.

Standard 3-2.6   Training Programs

Training programs should be established within the prosecutor's office for new personnel and for continuing education of the staff. Continuing education programs for prosecutors should be substantially expanded and public funds should be provided to enable prosecutors to attend such programs.

Standard 3-2.7   Relations With Police

(a) The prosecutor should provide legal advice to the police concerning police functions and duties in criminal matters.

(b) The prosecutor should cooperate with police in providing the services of the prosecutor's staff to aid in training police in the performance of their function in accordance with law.

Standard 3-2.8   Relations With the Courts and Bar

(a) It is unprofessional conduct for a prosecutor intentionally to misrepresent matters of fact or law to the court.

(b) A prosecutor's duties necessarily involve frequent and regular official contacts with the judge or judges of the prosecutor's jurisdiction. In such contacts the prosecutor should carefully strive to preserve the appearance as well as the reality of the correct relationship which professional traditions and canons require between advocates and judges.

(c) It is unprofessional conduct for a prosecutor to engage in unauthorized ex parte discussions with or submission of material to a judge relating to a particular case which is or may come before the judge.

(d) In the prosecutor's necessarily frequent contacts with other members of the bar, the prosecutor should strive to avoid the appearance as well as the reality of any relationship which would tend to cast doubt on the independence and integrity of the office.

Standard 3–2.9 Prompt Disposition of Criminal Charges

(a) A prosecutor should not intentionally use procedural devices for delay for which there is no legitimate basis.

(b) The prosecution function should be so organized and supported with staff and facilities as to enable it to dispose of all criminal charges promptly. The prosecutor should be punctual in attendance in court and in the submission of all motions, briefs, and other papers. The prosecutor should emphasize to all witnesses the importance of punctuality in attendance in court.

(c) It is unprofessional conduct intentionally to misrepresent facts or otherwise mislead the court in order to obtain a continuance.

Standard 3–2.10 Supersession and Substitution of Prosecutor

(a) Procedures should be established by appropriate legislation to the end that the governor or other elected state official is empowered by law to suspend and supersede a local prosecutor upon making a public finding, after reasonable notice and hearing, that the prosecutor is incapable of fulfilling the duties of office.

(b) The governor or other elected official should be empowered by law to substitute special counsel in the place of the local prosecutor in a particular case, or category of cases, upon making a public finding that this is required for the protection of the public interest.

PART III. INVESTIGATION FOR PROSECUTION DECISION

Standard 3–3.1 Investigative Function of Prosecutor

(a) A prosecutor ordinarily relies on police and other investigative agencies for investigation of alleged criminal acts, but the prosecutor has an affirmative responsibility to investigate suspected illegal activity when it is not adequately dealt with by other agencies.

(b) It is unprofessional conduct for a prosecutor knowingly to use illegal means to obtain evidence or to employ or instruct or encourage others to use such means.

(c) A prosecutor should not discourage or obstruct communication between prospective witnesses and defense counsel. It is unprofessional conduct for the prosecutor to advise any person or cause any person to be advised to decline to give to the defense information which such person has the right to give.

(d) It is unprofessional conduct for a prosecutor to secure the attendance of persons for interviews by use of any communication which has the appearance or color of a subpoena or similar judicial process unless the prosecutor is authorized by law to do so.

(e) It is unprofessional conduct for a prosecutor to promise not to prosecute for prospective criminal activity, except where such activity is part of an officially supervised investigative and enforcement program.

(f) Unless a prosecutor is prepared to forgo impeachment of a witness by the prosecutor's own testimony as to what the witness stated in an interview or to seek leave to withdraw from the case in order to present the impeaching testimony, a prosecutor should avoid interviewing a prospective witness except in the presence of a third person.

Standard 3–3.2 Relations With Prospective Witnesses

(a) It is unprofessional conduct to compensate a witness, other than an expert, for giving testimony, but it is not improper to reimburse an ordinary witness for the reasonable expenses of attendance upon court, attendance for depositions pursuant to statute or court rule, or attendance for pretrial interviews. Payments to a witness may be for transportation and loss of income, provided there is no attempt to conceal the fact of reimbursement.

(b) Whenever a prosecutor knows or has reason to believe that the conduct of a witness to be interviewed may be the subject of a criminal prosecution, the prosecutor or the prosecutor's investigator should advise the witness concerning possible self-incrimination and the possible need for counsel.

Standard 3–3.3 Relations With Expert Witnesses

(a) A prosecutor who engages an expert for an opinion should respect the independence of the expert and should not seek to dictate the formation of the expert's opinion on the subject. To the extent necessary, the prosecutor should explain to the expert his or her role in the trial as an impartial expert called to aid the fact finders and the manner in which the examination of witnesses is conducted.

(b) It is unprofessional conduct for a prosecutor to pay an excessive fee for the purpose of influencing the expert's testimony or to fix the amount of the fee contingent upon the testimony the expert will give or the result in the case.

Standard 3–3.4 Decision to Charge

(a) The decision to institute criminal proceedings should be initially and primarily the responsibility of the prosecutor.

(b) Absent exceptional circumstances, no arrest warrant or search warrant should issue without the approval of the prosecutor.

(c) The prosecutor should establish standards and procedures for evaluating complaints to determine whether criminal proceedings should be instituted.

(d) Where the law permits a citizen to complain directly to a judicial officer or the grand jury, the citizen complainant should be required to present the complaint for prior approval to the prosecutor, and the prosecutor's action or recommendation thereon should be communicated to the judicial officer or grand jury.

Standard 3–3.5 Relations With Grand Jury

(a) Where the prosecutor is authorized to act as legal adviser to the grand jury, the prosecutor may appropriately explain the law and express an opinion on the legal significance of the evidence but should give due deference to its status as an independent legal body.

(b) The prosecutor should not make statements or arguments in an effort to influence grand jury action in a manner which would be impermissible at trial before a petit jury.

(c) The prosecutor's communications and presentations to the grand jury should be on the record.

Standard 3–3.6 Quality and Scope of Evidence Before Grand Jury

(a) A prosecutor should present to the grand jury only evidence which the prosecutor believes would be admissible at trial. However, in appropriate cases, the prosecutor may present witnesses to summarize admissible evidence available to the prosecutor which the prosecutor believes he or she will be able to present at trial.

(b) No prosecutor should knowingly fail to disclose to the grand jury evidence which will tend substantially to negate guilt.

(c) A prosecutor should recommend that the grand jury not indict if it is believed the evidence presented does not warrant an indictment under governing law.

(d) If the prosecutor believes that a witness is a potential defendant, the prosecutor should not seek to compel the witness's testimony before the grand jury without informing the witness that he or she may be charged and that the witness should seek independent legal advice concerning his or her rights.

(e) The prosecutor should not compel the appearance of a witness before the grand jury whose activities are the subject of the inquiry if the witness states in advance that if called he or she will exercise the constitutional privilege not to testify, unless the prosecutor intends to seek a grant of immunity according to the law.

Standard 3-3.7 Quality and Scope of Evidence for Information

Where the prosecutor is empowered to charge by information, the prosecutor's decisions should be governed by the principles embodied in standards 3-3.6 and 3-3.9.

Standard 3-3.8 Discretion as to Noncriminal Disposition

(a) The prosecutor should explore the availability of noncriminal disposition, including programs of rehabilitation, formal or informal, in deciding whether to press criminal charges. Especially in the case of a first offender, the nature of the offense may warrant noncriminal disposition.

(b) Prosecutors should be familiar with the resources of social agencies which can assist in the evaluation of cases for diversion from the criminal process.

Standard 3-3.9 Discretion in the Charging Decision

(a) It is unprofessional conduct for a prosecutor to institute, or cause to be instituted, or to permit the continued pendency of criminal charges when it is known that the charges are not supported by probable cause. A prosecutor should not institute, cause to be instituted, or permit the continued pendency of criminal charges in the absence of sufficient admissible evidence to support a conviction.

(b) The prosecutor is not obliged to present all charges which the evidence might support. The prosecutor may in some circumstances and for good cause consistent with the public interest decline to prosecute, notwithstanding that sufficient evidence may exist which would support a conviction. Illustrative of the factors which the prosecutor may properly consider in exercising his or her discretion are:

(i) the prosecutor's reasonable doubt that the accused is in fact guilty;

(ii) the extent of the harm caused by the offense;

(iii) the disproportion of the authorized punishment in relation to the particular offense or the offender;

(iv) possible improper motives of a complainant;

(v) reluctance of the victim to testify;

(vi) cooperation of the accused in the apprehension or conviction of others; and

(vii) availability and likelihood of prosecution by another jurisdiction.

(c) In making the decision to prosecute, the prosecutor should give no weight to the personal or political advantages or disadvantages which might be involved or to a desire to enhance his or her record of convictions.

(d) In cases which involve a serious threat to the community, the prosecutor should not be deterred from prosecution by the fact that in the jurisdiction juries have tended to acquit persons accused of the particular kind of criminal act in question.

(e) The prosecutor should not bring or seek charges greater in number or degree than can reasonably be supported with evidence at trial.

Standard 3–3.10   Role in First Appearance and Preliminary Hearing

(a) A prosecutor who is present at the first appearance (however denominated) of the accused before a judicial officer should not communicate with the accused unless a waiver of counsel has been entered, except for the purpose of aiding in obtaining counsel or in arranging for the pretrial release of the accused.

(b) The prosecutor should cooperate in good faith in arrangements for release under the prevailing system for pretrial release.

(c) The prosecutor should not encourage an uncounseled accused to waive preliminary hearing.

(d) The prosecutor should not seek a continuance solely for the purpose of mooting the preliminary hearing by securing an indictment.

(e) Except for good cause, the prosecutor should not seek delay in the preliminary hearing after an arrest has been made if the accused is in custody.

(f) The prosecutor should ordinarily be present at a preliminary hearing where such hearing is required by law.

Standard 3–3.11   Disclosure of Evidence by the Prosecutor

(a) It is unprofessional conduct for a prosecutor intentionally to fail to make disclosure to the defense, at the earliest feasible opportunity, of the existence of evidence which tends to negate the guilt of the accused as to the offense charged or which would tend to reduce the punishment of the accused.

(b) The prosecutor should comply in good faith with discovery procedures under the applicable law.

(c) It is unprofessional conduct for a prosecutor intentionally to avoid pursuit of evidence because he or she believes it will damage the prosecution's case or aid the accused.

PART IV. PLEA DISCUSSIONS

Standard 3–4.1   Availability for Plea Discussions

(a) The prosecutor should made known a general policy or willingness to consult with defense counsel concerning disposition of charges by plea.

(b) It is unprofessional conduct for a prosecutor to engage in plea discussions directly with an accused who is represented by counsel, except with counsel's approval. Where the defendant has properly waived counsel, the prosecuting attorney may engage in plea discussions with the defendant, although ordinarily a verbatim record of such discussions should be made and preserved.

(c) It is unprofessional conduct for a prosecutor knowingly to make false statements or representations in the course of plea discussions with defense counsel or the accused.

Standard 3–4.2 Fulfillment of Plea Discussions

(a) It is unprofessional conduct for a prosecutor to make any promise or commitment concerning the sentence which will be imposed or concerning a suspension of sentence. A prosecutor may properly advise the defense what position will be taken concerning disposition.

(b) It is unprofessional conduct for a prosecutor to imply a greater power to influence the disposition of a case than is actually possessed.

(c) It is unprofessional conduct for a prosecutor to fail to comply with a plea agreement, unless a defendant fails to comply with a plea agreement or other extenuating circumstances are present.

Standard 3–4.3 Record of Reasons for Nolle Prosequi Disposition

Whenever felony criminal charges are dismissed by way of nolle prosequi (or its equivalent), the prosecutor should make a record of the reasons for the action.

PART V. THE TRIAL

Standard 3–5.1 Calendar Control

Control over the trial calendar should be vested in the court. The prosecuting attorney should be required to file with the court as a public record periodic reports setting forth the reasons for delay as to each case for which the prosecuting attorney has not requested trial within a prescribed time following charging. The prosecuting attorney should also advise the court of facts relevant in determining the order of cases on the calendar.

Standard 3–5.2 Courtroom Decorum

(a) The prosecutor should support the authority of the court and the dignity of the trial courtroom by strict adherence to the rules of decorum and by manifesting an attitude of professional respect toward the judge, opposing counsel, witnesses, defendants, jurors, and others in the courtroom.

(b) When court is in session the prosecutor should address the court, not opposing counsel, on all matters relating to the case.

(c) It is unprofessional conduct for a prosecutor to engage in behavior or tactics purposefully calculated to irritate or annoy the court or opposing counsel.

(d) A prosecutor should comply promptly with all orders and directives of the court, but the prosecutor has a duty to have the record reflect adverse rulings or judicial conduct which the prosecutor considers prejudicial. The prosecutor has a right to make respectful requests for reconsideration of adverse rulings.

(e) A prosecutor should be punctual in all court appearances and in the submission of all motions, briefs, and other papers.

(f) Prosecutors should cooperate with courts and the organized bar in developing codes of decorum and professional etiquette for each jurisdiction.

Standard 3–5.3 Selection of Jurors

(a) The prosecutor should prepare himself or herself prior to trial to discharge effectively the prosecution function in the selection of the jury and the exercise of challenges for cause and peremptory challenges.

(b) In those cases where it appears necessary to conduct a pretrial investigation of the background of jurors, investigatory methods of the prosecutor should neither harass nor unduly embarrass potential jurors or invade their privacy and, whenever possible, should be restricted to an investigation of records and sources of information already in existence.

(c) The opportunity to question jurors personally should be used solely to obtain information for the intelligent exercise of challenges. A prosecutor should not intentionally use the voir dire to present factual matter which the prosecutor knows will not be admissible at trial or to argue the prosecution's case to the jury.

Standard 3–5.4 Relations With Jury

(a) It is unprofessional conduct for a prosecutor to communicate privately with persons summoned for jury duty or impaneled as jurors concerning a case prior to or during trial. The prosecutor should avoid the reality or appearance of any such improper communications.

(b) The prosecutor should treat jurors with deference and respect, avoiding the reality or appearance of currying favor by a show of undue solicitude for their comfort or convenience.

(c) After discharge of the jury from further consideration of a case, it is unprofessional conduct for the prosecutor to intentionally make comments to or ask questions of a juror for the purpose of harassing or embarrassing the juror in any way which will tend to influence judgment in future jury service.

517

Standard 3–5.5 Opening Statement

The prosecutor's opening statement should be confined to a brief statement of the issues in the case and to remarks on evidence the prosecutor intends to offer which the prosecutor believes in good faith will be available and admissible. It is unprofessional conduct to allude to any evidence unless there is a good faith and reasonable basis for believing that such evidence will be tendered and admitted in evidence.

Standard 3–5.6 Presentation of Evidence

(a) It is unprofessional conduct for a prosecutor knowingly to offer false evidence, whether by documents, tangible evidence, or the testimony of witnesses, or fail to seek withdrawal thereof upon discovery of its falsity.

(b) It is unprofessional conduct for a prosecutor knowingly and for the purpose of bringing inadmissible matter to the attention of the judge or jury to offer inadmissible evidence, ask legally objectionable questions, or make other impermissible comments or arguments in the presence of the judge or jury.

(c) It is unprofessional conduct for a prosecutor to permit any tangible evidence to be displayed in the view of the judge or jury which would tend to prejudice fair consideration by the judge or jury until such time as a good faith tender of such evidence is made.

(d) It is unprofessional conduct to tender tangible evidence in the view of the judge or jury if it would tend to prejudice fair consideration by the judge or jury unless there is a reasonable basis for its admission in evidence. When there is any substantial doubt about the admissibility of such evidence, it should be tendered by an offer of proof and a ruling obtained.

Standard 3–5.7 Examination of Witnesses

(a) The interrogation of all witnesses should be conducted fairly, objectively, and with due regard for the dignity and legitimate privacy of the witness, and without seeking to intimidate or humiliate the witness unnecessarily. Proper cross-examination can be conducted without violating rules of decorum.

(b) The prosecutor's brief that the witness is telling the truth does not preclude cross-examination, but may affect the method and scope of cross-examination. A prosecutor should not use the power of cross-examination to discredit or undermine a witness if the prosecutor knows the witness is testifying truthfully.

(c) A prosecutor should not call a witness who the prosecutor knows will claim a valid privilege not to testify for the purpose of impressing upon the jury the fact of the claim of privilege. In some instances, as defined in codes of professional responsibility, doing so will constitute unprofessional conduct.

(d) It is unprofessional conduct for a prosecutor to ask a question which implies the existence of a factual predicate for which a good faith belief is lacking.

Standard 3–5.8 Argument to the Jury

(a) The prosecutor may argue all reasonable inferences from evidence in the record. It is unprofessional conduct for the prosecutor intentionally to misstate the evidence or mislead the jury as to the inferences it may draw.

(b) It is unprofessional conduct for the prosecutor to express his or her personal belief or opinion as to the truth or falsity of any testimony or evidence or the guilt of the defendant.

(c) The prosecutor should not use arguments calculated to inflame the passions or prejudices of the jury.

(d) The prosecutor should refrain from argument which would divert the jury from its duty to decide the case on the evidence, by injecting issues broader than the guilt or innocence of the accused under the controlling law, or by making predictions of the consequences of the jury's verdict.

(e) It is the responsibility of the court to ensure that final argument to the jury is kept within proper, accepted bounds.

Standard 3–5.9 Facts Outside the Record

It is unprofessional conduct for the prosecutor intentionally to refer to or argue on the basis of facts outside the record whether at trial or on appeal, unless such facts are matters of common public knowledge based on ordinary human experience or matters of which the court may take judicial notice.

Standard 3–5.10 Comments by Prosecutor After Verdict

The prosecutor should not make public comments critical of a verdict, whether rendered by judge or jury.

PART VI. SENTENCING

Standard 3–6.1 Role in Sentencing

(a) The prosecutor should not make the severity of sentences the index of his or her effectiveness. To the extent that the prosecutor becomes involved in the sentencing process, he or she should seek to assure that a fair and informed judgment is made on the sentence and to avoid unfair sentence disparities.

(b) Where sentence is fixed by the court without jury participation, the prosecutor should be afforded the opportunity to address the court at sentencing and to offer a sentencing recommendation. When requested by the court to furnish a sentencing recommendation, the prosecutor should have the obligation to do so.

(c) Where sentence is fixed by the jury, the prosecutor should present evidence on the issue within the limits permitted in the jurisdiction, but the prosecutor should avoid introducing evidence bearing on sentence which will prejudice the jury's determination of the issue of guilt.

Standard 3–6.2   Information Relevant to Sentencing

(a) The prosecutor should assist the court in basing its sentence on complete and accurate information for use in the presentence report. The prosecutor should disclose to the court any information in the prosecutor's files relevant to the sentence. If incompleteness or inaccurateness in the presentence report comes to the prosecutor's attention, the prosecutor should take steps to present the complete and correct information to the court and to defense counsel.

(b) The prosecutor should disclose to the defense and to the court at or prior to the sentencing proceeding all information in the prosecutor's files which is relevant to the sentencing issue.

THE DEFENSE FUNCTION

PART I. GENERAL STANDARDS

Standard 4–1.1   The Function of the Standards

These standards are intended to be used as a guide to professional conduct and performance. They are not intended to be used as criteria for the judicial evaluation of alleged misconduct of defense counsel to determine the validity of a conviction. They may or may not be relevant in such judicial evaluation, depending upon all the circumstances.

Standard 4–1.2   The Function of Defense Counsel

(a) Counsel for the accused is an essential component of the administration of criminal justice. A court properly constituted to hear a criminal case must be viewed as a tripartite entity consisting of the judge (and jury, where appropriate), counsel for the prosecution, and counsel for the accused.

(b) The basic duty defense counsel owes to the administration of justice and as an officer of the court is to serve as the accused's counselor and advocate with courage and devotion and to render effective, quality representation.

(c) Since the death penalty differs from other criminal penalties in its finality, defense counsel in a capital case should respond to this difference by making extraordinary efforts on behalf of the accused.

Defense counsel should comply with the ABA Guidelines for the Appointment and Performance of Counsel in Death Penalty Cases.

(d) Defense counsel should seek to reform and improve the administration of criminal justice. When inadequacies or injustices in the substantive or procedural law come to defense counsel's attention, he or she should stimulate efforts for remedial action.

(e) Defense counsel, in common with all members of the bar, is subject to standards of conduct stated in statutes, rules, decisions of courts, and codes, canons, or other standards of professional conduct. Defense counsel has no duty to execute any directive of the accused which does not comport with law or such standards. Defense counsel is the professional representative of the accused, not the accused's alter ego.

(f) Defense counsel should not intentionally misrepresent matters of fact or law to the court.

(g) Defense counsel should disclose to the tribunal legal authority in the controlling jurisdiction known to defense counsel to be directly adverse to the position of the accused and not disclosed by the prosecutor.

(h) It is the duty of defense counsel to know and be guided by the standards of professional conduct as defined in codes and canons of the legal profession applicable in defense counsel's jurisdiction. Once representation has been undertaken, the functions and duties of defense counsel are the same whether defense counsel is assigned, privately retained, or serving in a legal aid or defender program.

Standard 4–1.3 Delays; Punctuality; Workload

(a) Defense counsel should act with reasonable diligence and promptness in representing a client.

(b) Defense counsel should avoid unnecessary delay in the disposition of cases. Defense counsel should be punctual in attendance upon court and in the submission of all motions, briefs, and other papers. Defense counsel should emphasize to the client and all witnesses the importance of punctuality in attendance in court.

(c) Defense counsel should not intentionally misrepresent facts or otherwise mislead the court in order to obtain a continuance.

(d) Defense counsel should not intentionally use procedural devices for delay for which there is no legitimate basis.

(e) Defense counsel should not carry a workload that, by reason of its excessive size, interferes with the rendering of quality representation, endangers the client's interest in the speedy disposition of charges, or may lead to the breach of professional obligations. Defense counsel should not accept employment for the purpose of delaying trial.

Standard 4–1.4 Public Statements

Defense counsel should not make or authorize the making of an extrajudicial statement that a reasonable person would expect to be disseminated by means of public communication if defense counsel knows or reasonably should know that it will have a substantial likelihood of prejudicing a criminal proceeding.

Standard 4–1.5 Advisory Councils on Professional Conduct

(a) In every jurisdiction, an advisory body of lawyers selected for their experience, integrity, and standing at the trial bar should be established as an advisory council on problems of professional conduct in criminal cases. This council should provide prompt and confidential guidance and advice to lawyers seeking assistance in the application of standards of professional conduct in criminal cases.

(b) Communications between an inquiring lawyer and an advisory council member have the same attorney-client privilege for protection of the client's confidences as ordinarily exists between any other lawyer and client. The council member should be bound by statute or rule of court in the same manner as a lawyer is ordinarily bound in that jurisdiction not to reveal any disclosure of the client. Confidences may also be revealed, however, to the extent necessary:

(i) if the inquiring lawyer's client challenges the effectiveness of the lawyer's conduct of the case and the lawyer relies on the guidance received from the council member, or

(ii) if the inquiring lawyer's conduct is called into question in an authoritative disciplinary inquiry or proceeding.

Standard 4–1.6 Trial Lawyer's Duty to Administration of Justice

(a) The bar should encourage through every available means the widest possible participation in the defense of criminal cases by lawyers. Lawyers should be encouraged to qualify themselves for participation in criminal cases both by formal training and through experience as associate counsel.

(b) All such qualified lawyers should stand ready to undertake the defense of an accused regardless of public hostility toward the accused or personal distaste for the offense charged or the person of the defendant.

(c) Such Qualified lawyers should not assert or announce a general unwillingness to appear in criminal cases. Law firms should encourage partners and associates to become qualified and to appear in criminal cases.

(d) Such qualified lawyers should not seek to avoid appointment by a tribunal to represent an accused except for good cause, such as: representing the accused is likely to result in violation of applicable ethical codes or other law, representing the accused is likely to result in an unreasonable financial burden on the lawyer, or the client or crime is so repugnant to the lawyer as to be likely to impair the client-lawyer relationship or the lawyer's ability to represent the client.

PART II. ACCESS TO COUNSEL

Standard 4–2.1 Communication

Every jurisdiction should guarantee by statute or rule of court the right of an accused person to prompt and effective communication with a lawyer and should require that reasonable access to a telephone or other facilities be provided for that purpose.

Standard 4–2.2 Referral Service for Criminal Cases

(a) To assist persons who wish to retain defense counsel privately and who do not know a lawyer or how to engage one, every jurisdiction should have a referral service for criminal cases. The referral service should maintain a list of defense counsel willing and qualified to undertake the defense of a criminal case; it should be so organized that it can provide prompt service at all times.

(b) The availability of the referral service should be publicized. In addition, notices containing the essential information about the referral service and how to contact it should be posted conspicuously in police stations, jails, and wherever else it is likely to give effective notice.

Standard 4–2.3 Prohibited Referrals

(a) Defense counsel should not give anything of value to a person for recommending the lawyer's services.

(b) Defense counsel should not accept a referral from any source, including prosecutors, law enforcement personnel, victims, bondsmen, or court personnel where the acceptance of such a referral is likely to create a conflict of interest.

PART III. LAWYER–CLIENT RELATIONSHIP

Standard 4–3.1 Establishment of Relationship

(a) Defense counsel should seek to establish a relationship of trust and confidence with the accused and should discuss the objectives of the representation and whether defense counsel will continue to represent the accused if there is an appeal. Defense counsel should explain the necessity of full disclosure of all facts known to the client for an effective defense, and defense counsel should explain the extent to which counsel's obligation of confidentiality makes privileged the accused's disclosures.

(b) To ensure the privacy essential for confidential communication between defense counsel and client, adequate facilities should be available for private discussions between counsel and accused in jails, prisons, courthouses, and other places where accused persons must confer with counsel.

(c) Personnel of jails, prisons, and custodial institutions should be prohibited by law or administrative regulations from examining or otherwise interfering with any communication or correspondence between client and defense counsel relating to legal action arising out of charges or incarceration.

Standard 4–3.2 Interviewing the Client

(a) As soon as practicable, defense counsel should seek to determine all relevant facts known to the accused. In so doing, defense counsel should probe for all legally relevant information without seeking to influence the direction of the client's responses.

(b) Defense counsel should not instruct the client or intimate to the client in any way that the client should not be candid in revealing facts so as to afford defense counsel free rein to take action which would be precluded by counsel's knowing of such facts.

Standard 4–3.3 Fees

(a) Defense counsel should not enter into an agreement for, charge, or collect an illegal or unreasonable fee.

(b) In determining the amount of the fee in a criminal case, it is proper to consider the time and effort required, the responsibility assumed by counsel, the novelty and difficulty of the questions involved, the skill requisite to proper representation, the likelihood that other employment will be precluded, the fee customarily charged in the locality for similar services, the gravity of the charge, the experience, reputation, and ability of defense counsel, and the capacity of the client to pay the fee.

(c) Defense counsel should not imply that his or her compensation is for anything other than professional services rendered by defense counsel or by others for defense counsel.

(d) Defense counsel should not divide a fee with a nonlawyer, except as permitted by applicable ethical codes of conduct.

(e) Defense counsel not in the same firm should not divide fees unless the division is in proportion to the services performed by each counsel or, by written agreement with the client, each counsel assumes joint responsibility for the representation, the client is advised of and does not object to the participation of all counsel involved, and the total fee is reasonable.

(f) Defense counsel should not enter into an arrangement for, charge, or collect a contingent fee for representing a defendant in a criminal case.

(g) When defense counsel has not regularly represented the client, defense counsel should communicate the basis or rate of the fee to the client, preferably in writing, before or within a reasonable time after commencing the representation.

Standard 4–3.4 Obtaining Literary or Media Rights From the Accused

Defense counsel, prior to conclusion of all aspects of the matter giving rise to his or her employment, should not enter into any agreement or understanding with a client or a prospective client by which defense counsel acquires an interest in literary or media rights to a portrayal or account based in substantial part on information relating to the employment or proposed employment.

Standard 4–3.5 Conflicts of Interest

(a) Defense counsel should not permit his or her professional judgment or obligations to be affected by his or her own political, financial, business, property, or personal interests.

(b) Defense counsel should disclose to the defendant at the earliest feasible opportunity any interest in or connection with the case or any other matter that might be relevant to the defendant's selection of counsel to represent him or her or counsel's continuing representation. Such disclosure should include communication of information reasonably sufficient to permit the client to appreciate the significance of any conflict or potential conflict of interest.

(c) Except for preliminary matters such as initial hearings or applications for bail, defense counsel who are associated in practice should not undertake to defend more than one defendant in the same criminal case if the duty to one of the defendants may conflict with the duty to another. The potential for conflict of interest in representing multiple defendants is so grave that ordinarily defense counsel should decline to act for more than one of several codefendants except in unusual situations when, after careful investigation, it is clear either that no conflict is likely to develop at trial, sentencing, or at any other time in the proceeding or that common representation will be advantageous to each of the codefendants represented and, in either case, that:

(i) the several defendants give an informed consent to such multiple representation; and

(ii) the consent of the defendants is made a matter of judicial record. In determining the presence of consent by the defendants, the trial judge should make appropriate inquiries respecting actual or potential conflicts of interest of counsel and whether the defendants fully comprehend the difficulties that defense counsel sometimes encounters in defending multiple clients.

(d) Defense counsel who has formerly represented a defendant should not thereafter use information related to the former representation to the disadvantage of the former client unless the information has become generally known or the ethical obligation of confidentiality otherwise does not apply.

(e) In accepting payment of fees by one person for the defense of another, defense counsel should be careful to determine that he or she will not be confronted with a conflict of loyalty since defense counsel's entire loyalty is due the accused. Defense counsel should not accept such compensation unless:

    (i) the accused consents after disclosure;

    (ii) there is no interference with defense counsel's independence of professional judgment or with the client-lawyer relationship; and

    (iii) information relating to the representation of the accused is protected from disclosure as required by defense counsel's ethical obligation of confidentiality.

Defense counsel should not permit a person who recommends, employs, or pays defense counsel to render legal services for another to direct or regulate counsel's professional judgment in rendering such legal services.

(f) Defense counsel should not defend a criminal case in which counsel's partner or other professional associate is or has been the prosecutor in the same case.

(g) Defense counsel should not represent a criminal defendant in a jurisdiction in which he or she is also a prosecutor.

(h) Defense counsel who formerly participated personally and substantially in the prosecution of a defendant should not thereafter represent any person in the same or a substantially related matter. Defense counsel who was formerly a prosecutor should not use confidential information about a person acquired when defense counsel was a prosecutor in the representation of a client whose interests are adverse to that person in a matter.

(i) Defense counsel who is related to a prosecutor as parent, child, sibling or spouse should not represent a client in a criminal matter where defense counsel knows the government is represented in the matter by such prosecutor. Nor should defense counsel who has a significant personal or financial relationship with a prosecutor represent a client in a criminal matter where defense counsel knows the government is represented in the matter by such prosecutor, except upon consent by the client after consultation regarding the relationship.

(j) Defense counsel should not act as surety on a bond either for the accused represented by counsel or for any other accused in the same or a related case.

(k) Except as law may otherwise expressly permit, defense counsel should not negotiate to employ any person who is significantly involved as an attorney or employee of the government in a matter in which defense counsel is participating personally and substantially.

Standard 4–3.6 Prompt Action to Protect the Accused

Many important rights of the accused can be protected and preserved only by prompt legal action. Defense counsel should inform the accused of his or her rights at the earliest opportunity and take all necessary action to vindicate such rights. Defense counsel should consider all procedural steps which in good faith may be taken, including, for example, motions seeking pretrial release of the accused, obtaining psychiatric examination of the accused when a need appears, moving for change of venue or continuance, moving to suppress illegally obtained evidence, moving for severance from jointly charged defendants, and seeking dismissal of the charges.

Standard 4–3.7 Advice and Service on Anticipated Unlawful Conduct

(a) It is defense counsel's duty to advise a client to comply with the law, but counsel may advise concerning the meaning, scope, and validity of a law.

(b) Defense counsel should not counsel a client in or knowingly assist a client to engage in conduct which defense counsel knows to be illegal or fraudulent but defense counsel may discuss the legal consequences of any proposed course of conduct with a client.

(c) Defense counsel should not agree in advance of the commission of a crime that he or she will serve as counsel for the defendant, except as part of a bona fide effort to determine the validity, scope, meaning, or application of the law, or where the defense is incident to a general retainer for legal services to a person or enterprise engaged in legitimate activity.

(d) Defense counsel should not reveal information relating to representation of a client unless the client consents after consultation, except for disclosures that are impliedly authorized in order to carry out the representation and except that defense counsel may reveal such information to the extent he or she reasonably believes necessary to prevent the client from committing a criminal act that defense counsel believes is likely to result in imminent death or substantial bodily harm.

Standard 4–3.8 Duty to Keep Client Informed

(a) Defense counsel should keep the client informed of the developments in the case and the progress of preparing the defense and should promptly comply with reasonable requests for information.

(b) Defense counsel should explain developments in the case to the extent reasonably necessary to permit the client to make informed decisions regarding the representation.

527

Standard 4–3.9 Obligations of Hybrid, Standby, and Replacement Counsel

(a) Defense counsel whose duty is to actively assist a pro se accused should permit the accused to make the final decisions on all matters, including strategic and tactical matters relating to the conduct of the case.

(b) Defense counsel whose duty is to assist a pro se accused only when the accused requests assistance may bring to the attention of the accused matters beneficial to him or her, but should not actively participate in the conduct of the defense unless requested by the accused or insofar as directed to do so by the court.

(c) Defense counsel whose duty is to serve as a replacement for the pro se accused when and if the court so orders may bring to the attention of the accused matters beneficial to him or her, but should not actively participate in the conduct of the defense.

PART IV. INVESTIGATION AND PREPARATION

Standard 4–4.1 Duty to Investigate

(a) Defense counsel should conduct a prompt investigation of the circumstances of the case and to explore all avenues leading to facts relevant to the merits of the case and the penalty in the event of conviction. The investigation should include efforts to secure information in the possession of the prosecution and law enforcement authorities. The duty to investigate exists regardless of the accused's admissions or statements to defense counsel of facts constituting guilt or the accused's stated desire to plead guilty.

(b) Defense counsel should not seek to acquire possession of physical evidence personally or through use of an investigator where defense counsel's sole purpose is to obstruct access to such evidence.

Standard 4–4.2 Illegal Investigation

Defense counsel should not knowingly use illegal means to obtain evidence or information or to employ, instruct, or encourage others to do so.

Standard 4–4.3 Relations With Prospective Witnesses

(a) Defense counsel, in representing an accused, should not use means that have no substantial purpose other than to embarrass, delay, or burden a third person, or use methods of obtaining evidence that violate the legal rights of such a person.

(b) Defense counsel should not compensate a witness, other than an expert, for giving testimony, but it is not improper to reimburse a witness for the reasonable expenses of attendance upon court, including transportation and loss of income, attendance for depositions pursuant to statute or court rule, or attendance for pretrial interviews, provided there is no attempt to conceal the fact of reimbursement.

(c) It is not necessary for defense counsel or defense counsel's investigator, in interviewing a prospective witness, to caution the witness concerning possible self-incrimination and the need for counsel.

(d) Defense counsel should not discourage or obstruct communication between prospective witnesses and the prosecutor. It is unprofessional conduct to advise any person other than a client, or cause such person to be advised to decline to give to the prosecutor or defense counsel for codefendants information which such person has a right to give.

(e) Unless defense counsel is prepared to forgo impeachment of a witness by counsel's own testimony as to what the witness stated in an interview or to seek leave to withdraw from the case in order to present such impeaching testimony, defense counsel should avoid interviewing a prospective witness except in the presence of a third person.

Standard 4-4.4   Relations With Expert Witnesses

(a) Defense counsel who engages an expert for an opinion should respect the independence of the expert and should not seek to dictate the formation of the expert's opinion on the subject. To the extent necessary, defense counsel should explain to the expert his or her role in the trial as an impartial witness called to aid the fact finders and the manner in which the examination of witnesses is conducted.

(b) Defense counsel should not pay an excessive fee for the purpose of influencing an expert's testimony or fix the amount of the fee contingent upon the testimony an expert will give or the result in the case.

Standard 4-4.5   Compliance With Discovery Procedure

Defense counsel should make a reasonably diligent effort to comply with a legally proper discovery request.

Standard 4-4.6   Physical Evidence

(a) Defense counsel who receives a physical item under circumstances implicating a client in criminal conduct should disclose the location of or should deliver that item to law enforcement authorities only: (1) if required by law or court order, or (2) as provided in paragraph (d).

(b) Unless required to disclose, defense counsel should return the item to the source from whom defense counsel received it, except as provided in paragraphs (c) and (d). In returning the item to the source, defense counsel should advise the source of the legal consequences pertaining to possession or destruction of the item. Defense counsel should also prepare a written record of these events for his or her file, but should not give the source a copy of such record.

(c) Defense counsel may receive the item for a reasonable period of time during which defense counsel: (1) intends to return it to the owner; (2) reasonably fears that return of the item to the source will result in destruction of the item; (3) reasonably fears that return of the item to the source will result in physical harm to anyone; (4) intends to test, examine, inspect, or use the item in any way as part of defense counsel's representation of the client; or (5) cannot return it to the source. If defense counsel tests or examines the item, he or she should thereafter return it to the source unless there is reason to believe that the evidence might be altered or destroyed or used to harm another or return is otherwise impossible. If defense counsel retains the item, he or she should retain it in his or her law office in a manner that does not impede the lawful ability of law enforcement authorities to obtain the item.

(d) If the item received is contraband, i.e. an item, possession of which is in and of itself a crime, such as narcotics, defense counsel may destroy it where there is no pending case or investigation relating to this evidence and where such destruction is clearly not in violation of any criminal statute. If such destruction is not permitted by law or if in defense counsel's judgment he or she cannot retain the item, whether or not it is contraband, in a way that does not pose an unreasonable risk of physical harm to anyone, defense counsel should disclose the location of or should deliver the item to law enforcement authorities.

(e) If defense counsel discloses the location of or delivers the item to law enforcement authorities under paragraphs (a) or (d), or to a third party under paragraph (c)(1), he or she should do so in the way best designed to protect the client's interests.

PART V. CONTROL AND DIRECTION OF LITIGATION

Standard 4–5.1 Advising the Accused

(a) After informing himself or herself fully on the facts and the law, defense counsel should advise the accused with complete candor concerning all aspects of the case, including a candid estimate of the probable outcome.

(b) Defense counsel should not intentionally understate or overstate the risks, hazards, or prospects of the case to exert undue influence on the accused's decision as to his or her plea.

(c) Defense counsel should caution the client to avoid communication about the case with witnesses, except with the approval of counsel, to avoid any contact with jurors or prospective jurors, and to avoid either the reality or the appearance of any other improper activity.

Standard 4–5.2 Control and Direction of the Case

(a) Certain decisions relating to the conduct of the case are ultimately for the accused and others are ultimately for defense counsel. The decisions which are to be made by the accused after full consultation with counsel include:

(i) what pleas to enter;

(ii) whether to accept a plea agreement;

(iii) whether to waive jury trial;

(iv) whether to testify in his or her own behalf; and

(v) whether to appeal.

(b) Strategic and tactical decisions should be made by defense counsel after consultation with the client where feasible and appropriate. Such decisions include what witnesses to call, whether and how to conduct cross-examination, what jurors to accept or strike, what trial motions should be made, and what evidence should be introduced.

(c) If a disagreement on significant matters of tactics or strategy arises between defense counsel and the client, defense counsel should make a record of the circumstances, counsel's advice and reasons, and the conclusion reached. The record should be made in a manner which protects the confidentiality of the lawyer-client relationship.

PART VI. DISPOSITION WITHOUT TRIAL

Standard 4–6.1 Duty to Explore Disposition Without Trial

(a) Whenever the law, nature, and circumstances of the case permit, defense counsel should explore the possibility of an early diversion of the case from the criminal process through the use of other community agencies.

(b) Defense counsel may engage in plea discussions with the prosecutor. Under no circumstances should defense counsel recommend to a defendant acceptance of a plea unless appropriate investigation and study of the case has been completed, including an analysis of controlling law and the evidence likely to be introduced at trial.

Standard 4–6.2 Plea Discussions

(a) Defense counsel should keep the accused advised of developments arising out of plea discussions conducted with the prosecutor.

(b) Defense counsel should promptly communicate and explain to the accused all significant plea proposals made by the prosecutor.

(c) Defense counsel should not knowingly make false statements concerning the evidence in the course of plea discussions with the prosecutor.

(d) Defense counsel should not seek concessions favorable to one client by any agreement which is detrimental to the legitimate interests of a client in another case.

(e) Defense counsel representing two or more clients in the same or related cases should not participate in making an aggregated agreement as to guilty or nolo contendere pleas, unless each client consents after consultation, including disclosure of the existence and nature of all the claims or pleas involved.

PART VII.   TRIAL

Standard 4–7.1   Courtroom Professionalism

(a) As an officer of the court, defense counsel should support the authority of the court and the dignity of the trial courtroom by strict adherence to codes of professionalism and by manifesting a professional attitude toward the judge, opposing counsel, witnesses, jurors, and others in the courtroom.

(b) Defense counsel should not engage in unauthorized ex parte discussions with or submission of material to a judge relating to a particular case which is or may come before the judge.

(c) When court is in session, defense counsel should address the court and should not address the prosecutor directly on all matters relating to the case.

(d) Defense counsel should comply promptly with all orders and directives of the court, but defense counsel has a duty to have the record reflect adverse rulings or judicial conduct which counsel considers prejudicial to his or her client's legitimate interests.   Defense counsel has a right to make respectful requests for reconsiderations of adverse rulings.

(e) Defense counsel should cooperate with courts and the organized bar in developing codes of professionalism for each jurisdiction.

Standard 4–7.2   Selection of Jurors

(a) Defense counsel should prepare himself or herself prior to trial to discharge effectively his or her function in the selection of the jury, including the raising of any appropriate issues concerning the method by which the jury panel was selected and the exercise of both challenges for cause and peremptory challenges.

(b) In those cases where it appears necessary to conduct a pretrial investigation of the background of jurors, investigatory methods of defense counsel should neither harass nor unduly embarrass potential jurors or invade their privacy and, whenever possible, should be restricted to an investigation of records and sources of information already in existence.

(c) The opportunity to question jurors personally should be used solely to obtain information for the intelligent exercise of challenges. Defense counsel should not intentionally use the voir dire to present factual matter which defense counsel knows will not be admissible at trial or to argue counsel's case to the jury.

Standard 4–7.3 Relations With Jury

(a) Defense counsel should not intentionally communicate privately with persons summoned for jury duty or impaneled as jurors prior to or during the trial. Defense counsel should avoid the reality or appearance of any such communications.

(b) Defense counsel should treat jurors with deference and respect, avoiding the reality or appearance of currying favor by a show of undue solicitude for their comfort or convenience.

(c) After discharge of the jury from further consideration of a case, defense counsel should not intentionally make comments to or ask questions of a juror for the purpose of harassing or embarrassing the juror in any way which will tend to influence judgment in future jury service. If defense counsel believes that the verdict may be subject to legal challenge, he or she may properly, if no statute or rule prohibits such course, communicate with jurors to determine whether such challenge may be available.

Standard 4–7.4 Opening Statement

Defense counsel's opening statement should be confined to a statement of the issues in the case and the evidence defense counsel believes in good faith will be available and admissible. Defense counsel should not allude to any evidence unless there is a good faith and reasonable basis for believing such evidence will be tendered and admitted in evidence.

Standard 4–7.5 Presentation of Evidence

(a) Defense counsel should not knowingly offer false evidence, whether by documents, tangible evidence, or the testimony of witnesses, or fail to take reasonable remedial measures upon discovery of its falsity.

(b) Defense counsel should not knowingly and for the purpose of bringing inadmissible matter to the attention of the judge or jury to offer inadmissible evidence, ask legally objectionable questions, or make other impermissible comments or arguments in the presence of the judge or jury.

(c) Defense counsel should not permit any tangible evidence to be displayed in the view of the judge or jury which would tend to prejudice fair consideration of the case by the judge or jury until such time as a good faith tender of such evidence is made.

(d) Defense counsel should not tender tangible evidence in the presence of the judge or jury if it would tend to prejudice fair consideration of the case unless there is a reasonable basis for its admission in evidence. When there is any substantial doubt about the admissibility of such evidence, it should be tendered by an offer of proof and a ruling obtained.

Standard 4–7.6 Examination of Witnesses

(a) The interrogation of all witnesses should be conducted fairly, objectively, and with due regard for the dignity and legitimate privacy of the witness, and without seeking to intimidate or humiliate the witness unnecessarily.

(b) Defense counsel's belief or knowledge that the witness is telling the truth does not preclude cross-examination.

(c) Defense counsel should not call a witness in the presence of the jury who the lawyer knows will claim a valid privilege not to testify.

(d) Defense counsel should not ask a question which implies the existence of a factual predicate for which a good faith belief is lacking.

Standard 4–7.7 Argument to the Jury

(a) In closing argument to the jury, defense counsel may argue all reasonable inferences from the evidence in the record. Defense counsel should not intentionally misstate the evidence or mislead the jury as to the inferences it may draw.

(b) Defense counsel should not express a personal belief or opinion in his or her client's innocence or personal belief or opinion in the truth or falsity of any testimony or evidence.

(c) Defense counsel should not make arguments calculated to appeal to the prejudices of the jury.

(d) Defense counsel should refrain from argument which would divert the jury from its duty to decide the case on the evidence.

Standard 4–7.8 Facts Outside the Record

Defense counsel should not intentionally refer to or argue on the basis of facts outside the record whether at trial or on appeal, unless such facts are matters of common public knowledge based on ordinary human experience or matters of which the court can take judicial notice.

Standard 4–7.9 Posttrial Motions

Defense counsel's responsibility includes presenting appropriate posttrial motions to protect the defendant's rights.

PART VIII. AFTER CONVICTION

Standard 4–8.1 Sentencing

(a) Defense counsel should, at the earliest possible time, be or become familiar with all of the sentencing alternatives available to the court and with community and other facilities which may be of assistance in a plan for meeting the accused's needs. Defense counsel's preparation should also include familiarization with the court's practices in exercising sentencing discretion, the practical consequences of different sentences, and the normal pattern of sentences for the offense involved, including any guidelines applicable at either the sentencing or parole stages. The consequences of the various dispositions available should be explained fully by defense counsel to the accused.

(b) Defense counsel should present to the court any ground which will assist in reaching a proper disposition favorable to the accused. If a presentence report or summary is made available to defense counsel, he or she should seek to verify the information contained in it and should be prepared to supplement or challenge it if necessary. If there is no presentence report or if it is not disclosed, defense counsel should submit to the court and the prosecutor all favorable information relevant to sentencing and in an appropriate case, with the consent of the accused, be prepared to suggest a program of rehabilitation based on defense counsel's exploration of employment, educational, and other opportunities made available by community services.

(c) Defense counsel should also insure that the accused understands the nature of the presentence investigation process, and in particular the significance of statements made by the accused to probation officers and related personnel. Where appropriate, defense counsel should attend the probation officer's interview with the accused.

(d) Defense counsel should alert the accused to the right of allocution, if any, and to the possible dangers of making a statement that might tend to prejudice an appeal.

Standard 4–8.2 Appeal

(a) After conviction, defense counsel should explain to the defendant the meaning and consequences of the court's judgment and defendant's right of appeal. Defense counsel should give the defendant his or her professional judgment as to whether there are meritorious grounds for appeal and as to the probable results of an appeal. Defense counsel should also explain to the defendant the advantages and disadvantages of an appeal. The decision whether to appeal must be the defendant's own choice.

(b) Defense counsel should take whatever steps are necessary to protect the defendant's rights of appeal.

Standard 4–8.3 Counsel on Appeal

(a) Appellate counsel should not seek to withdraw from a case solely on the basis of his or her own determination that the appeal lacks merit.

(b) Appellate counsel should give a client his or her best professional evaluation of the questions that might be presented on appeal. Counsel, when inquiring into the case, should consider all issues that might affect the validity of the judgment of conviction and sentence, including any that might require initial presentation in a postconviction proceeding. Counsel should advise on the probable outcome of a challenge to the conviction or sentence. Counsel should endeavor to persuade the client to abandon a wholly frivolous appeal or to eliminate contentions lacking in substance.

(c) If the client chooses to proceed with an appeal against the advice of counsel, counsel should present the case, so long as such advocacy does not involve deception of the court. When counsel cannot continue without misleading the court, counsel may request permission to withdraw.

(d) Appellate counsel has the ultimate authority to decide which arguments to make on appeal. When appellate counsel decides not to argue all of the issues that his or her client desires to be argued, appellate counsel should inform the client of his or her pro se briefing rights.

(e) In a jurisdiction with an intermediate appellate court, counsel for a defendant-appellant or a defendant-appellee should continue to represent the client if the prosecution seeks review in the highest court, unless new counsel is substituted or unless the court permits counsel to withdraw. Similarly, in any jurisdiction, such appellate counsel should continue to represent the client if the prosecution seeks review in the Supreme Court of the United States.

Standard 4–8.4 Conduct of Appeal

(a) Appellate counsel should be diligent in perfecting appeals and expediting their prompt submission to appellate courts.

(b) Appellate counsel should be accurate in referring to the record and the authorities upon which counsel relies in the presentation to the court of briefs and oral argument.

(c) Appellate counsel should not intentionally refer to or argue on the basis of facts outside the record on appeal, unless such facts are matters of common public knowledge based on ordinary human experience or matters of which the court may take judicial notice.

Standard 4–8.5 Post-conviction Remedies

After a conviction is affirmed on appeal, appellate counsel should determine whether there is any ground for relief under other post-conviction remedies. If there is a reasonable prospect of a favorable result, counsel should explain to the defendant the advantages and disadvantages of taking such action. Appellate counsel is not obligated to represent the defendant in a post-conviction proceeding unless counsel has agreed to do so. In other respects, the responsibility of a lawyer in a post-conviction proceeding should be guided generally by the standards governing the conduct of lawyers in criminal cases.

Standard 4–8.6 Challenges to the Effectiveness of Counsel

(a) If defense counsel, after investigation, is satisfied that another defense counsel who served in an earlier phase of the case did not provide effective assistance, he or she should not hesitate to seek relief for the defendant on that ground.

(b) If defense counsel, after investigation, is satisfied that another defense counsel who served in an earlier phase of the case provided effective assistance, he or she should so advise the client and may decline to proceed further.

(c) If defense counsel concludes that he or she did not provide effective assistance in an earlier phase of the case, defense counsel should explain this conclusion to the defendant and seek to withdraw from representation with an explanation to the court of the reason therefor.

(d) Defense counsel whose conduct of a criminal case is drawn into question is entitled to testify concerning the matters charged and is not precluded from disclosing the truth concerning the accusation to the extent defense counsel reasonably believes necessary, even though this involves revealing matters which were given in confidence.

MODEL RULES OF PROFESSIONAL CONDUCT FOR FEDERAL LAWYERS

This code of conduct was adopted by the Federal Bar Association in 1990

[The Federal Bar Association has promulgated these rules, which are patterned after the ABA Model Rules, as guidelines for lawyers involved in federal practice of law. These rules are reprinted in full with the exception of the cross reference sections that appear after the comments to most of the rules. Ed.]

Table of Contents

CLIENT–LAWYER RELATIONSHIP

Rule

1.1 Competence.
1.2 Scope of Representation.
1.3 Diligence.
1.4 Communication.
1.5 Fees.
1.6 Confidentiality of Information.
1.7 Conflict of Interest: General Rule.
1.8 Conflict of Interest: Prohibited Transactions.
1.9 Conflict of Interest: Former Client.
1.10 Imputed Disqualification: General Rule.
1.11 Successive Government and Private Employment.
1.12 Former Judge or Arbitrator.
1.13 The Federal Agency as the Client.
1.14 Client Under a Disability.
1.15 Safekeeping Property.
1.16 Declining or Terminating Representation.

COUNSELOR

2.1 Advisor.
2.2 Intermediary.
2.3 Evaluation for Use by Third Persons.

ADVOCATE

TRANSACTION WITH PERSONS OTHER THAN CLIENTS

LEGAL OFFICES

PUBLIC SERVICE

INFORMATION ABOUT LEGAL SERVICES

MAINTAINING THE INTEGRITY OF THE PROFESSION

PREAMBLE: A FEDERAL LAWYER'S RESPONSIBILITIES

A Federal lawyer is a representative of clients, an officer of the legal system, and a public citizen having special responsibility for the quality of justice. The Federal lawyer should demonstrate the highest standards of ethical conduct, personal dignity, truthfulness, honesty, fortitude, and professional integrity. The Federal lawyer should also promote public service.

As a representative of clients, a Federal lawyer performs various functions. As an advisor, a Federal lawyer provides a client with informed understanding of the client's rights and obligations and explains their practical implications. As an advocate, a Federal lawyer zealously asserts the client's position under the law and the ethical rules of the adversary system. As negotiator, a Federal lawyer seeks results advantageous to the client, but consistent with the requirement of honest dealing with others. As a mediator between clients, a Federal lawyer seeks to reconcile their divergent interests as an advisor and, to a limited extent, as a spokesperson for each client. A Federal lawyer acts as evaluator by examining client's legal affairs and reporting about them to the client or to others.

In all professional functions a Federal lawyer should be competent, prompt, diligent, and honest. A Federal lawyer should maintain communication with a client concerning the representation. A Federal lawyer should keep in confidence information relating to representation of a client, except insofar as disclosure is required or permitted by these Rules or other law.

A Federal lawyer's conduct should conform to the requirements of the law, both in professional service to clients and in the Federal lawyer's personal affairs. A Federal lawyer should use legal procedures only for their lawfully intended purposes and not to harass or intimidate others. A Federal lawyer should demonstrate respect for the legal system and for those who serve it, including judges, other Federal lawyers, and public officials. To the Federal Agency, the Federal lawyer owes the duties of professional dignity and integrity. While it is a Federal lawyer's duty, when necessary, to challenge the rectitude of official action, it is also a Federal lawyer's duty to uphold legal process.

As a public citizen, a Federal lawyer should seek improvement of the law, the administration of justice, and the quality of service rendered by the legal profession. Federal lawyers should strive at all times to uphold the honor and dignity of the Federal legal profession and to improve the administration of justice. As a member of a learned profession, a Federal lawyer should cultivate knowledge of the law beyond its use for clients, employ that knowledge in reform of the law where needed, and work to strengthen legal education.

Many of a Federal lawyer's professional responsibilities are prescribed in these Rules, as well as in substantive and procedural law. However, a Federal lawyer is also guided by personal conscience and the approbation of professional peers. A Federal lawyer should strive to attain the highest level of skill, to improve the law and the legal profession, to exemplify the legal profession's ideals of public service, and to respect the truth finding role of the courts.

A Federal lawyer's responsibilities as a representative of clients, an officer of the legal system, and a public citizen are usually harmonious. Thus, when an opposing party is well represented, a Federal lawyer can be zealous in advocating the interests of a client and justice will be served. A Federal lawyer also can be sure that preserving client confidence ordinarily serves the public interest because people are more likely to ask legal advice, and thereby heed their legal obligations, when they know their communications will be private.

A Federal lawyer should always uphold and promote the highest standards for the practice of law within the Federal sector. A Federal lawyer should seek to advance the development of sound Federal laws and the establishment and maintenance of an efficient Federal legal and judicial system. A Federal lawyer should promote the public's confidence in the Federal legal system. A Federal lawyer also should promote the highest professional standards for and the professional well being of all Federal lawyers. A Federal lawyer should seek to encourage outstanding lawyers to enter the Federal service.

In addition to the high standards of conduct expected of all Federal lawyers, the Government lawyer has a specific responsibility to strive to promote the public interest. The Government lawyer should not realize personal gain from the performance of official duties and should avoid any interest or activity that is in conflict with the Government lawyer's official duties. The Government lawyer should strive for personal professional excellence and encourage the professional development of other staff members and those seeking to enter the field of Government law practice.

Due to the nature of legal practice, however, Federal lawyers encounter conflicting responsibilities. Virtually all difficult ethical problems arise from conflicts between a Federal lawyer's responsibilities to clients, to the legal system, and to the Federal lawyer's own interest in remaining an upright person. These Rules prescribe terms for resolving such conflicts. Within the framework of these Rules many difficult issues of professional discretion can arise. Such issues must be resolved through the exercise of sensitive professional and moral judgment guided by the basic principles underlying these Rules.

SCOPE

These Rules, in conjunction with laws and regulations that control the practice of Federal lawyers, are intended to govern the ethical conduct of Federal lawyers.

They have been adopted by the National Council of the Federal Bar Association. The Federal Bar Association is not empowered to discipline members or enforce these Rules. As such, these Rules regulate professional conduct of Federal lawyers and impose certain duties only to the extent to which they are adopted by a Federal Agency. The Federal Bar Association encourages Federal agencies to adopt rules of professional responsibility based, in whole or in part, on these Rules. If so adopted, failure to comply with an obligation or prohibition imposed by a Rule may be the basis for invoking administrative or disciplinary action. The Rules presuppose that disciplinary assessment of a Federal lawyer's conduct will be made on the basis of the facts and circumstances as they existed at the time of the conduct in question and in recognition of the fact that a Federal lawyer often has to act upon uncertain or incomplete evidence of the situation. Moreover, these Rules presuppose that whether or not discipline should be imposed for a violation, and severity of a sanction, depend on all of the circumstances, such as the willfulness and seriousness of the violation, extenuating factors, and whether there have been previous violations. Violations of a Rule should not give rise to a cause of action nor should they create a presumption that a legal duty has been breached. These Rules are designed to provide guidance to Federal lawyers and to provide a structure for regulating conduct. They are not designed to be a basis for civil liability.

Furthermore, the purpose of these Rules can be subverted when they are invoked by opposing parties as procedural weapons. The fact that a Rule is a just basis for a Federal lawyer's self-assessment, or for sanctioning a Federal lawyer under the administration of a disciplinary authority, does not imply that an antagonist in a collateral proceeding or transaction has standing to seek enforcement of the Rule. Accordingly, nothing in these Rules should be deemed to augment any substantive legal duty of Federal lawyers or the extra-disciplinary consequences of violating such duty.

They are to be used in conjunction with laws and regulation that control the practice of Federal lawyers. Although not punitive in nature, the Rules establish the minimum standards of ethical conduct demanded of Federal lawyers.

The ethical conduct of lawyers specially retained by the Government is also intended to be governed by these Rules of Professional Conduct.

These Rules presuppose a larger legal context shaping the Federal lawyer's role. That context includes statutes and court rules relating to matters of licensing, laws defining specific obligations of Federal lawyers, and substantive and procedural law in general. Compliance with these Rules, as with all laws in an open society, depends primarily upon understanding and voluntary compliance, secondarily upon reinforcement by peer and public opinion, and finally, when applicable and necessary, upon enforcement through disciplinary proceedings. These Rules do not, however, exhaust the moral and ethical considerations that should inform a Federal lawyer, for no worthwhile human activity can be completely defined by legal rules. These Rules simply provide a framework for the ethical practice of law.

Furthermore, for purposes of determining the Federal lawyer's authority and responsibility, principles of substantive law external to these Rules determine whether a client-lawyer relationship exists. Whether a client-lawyer relationship exists for any specific purpose can depend on the circumstances and may be a question of fact.

Moreover, these Rules are not intended to govern or affect judicial application of either the attorney-client or work product privilege. Those privileges were developed to promote compliance with law and fairness in litigation. In reliance on the attorney-client privilege, clients are entitled to expect that communications within the scope of the privilege will be protected against compelled disclosure. The attorney-client privilege is that of the client and not of the Federal lawyer. The fact that in exceptional situations the Federal lawyer under these Rules is required or permitted to disclose client confidence does not vitiate the proposition that, as a general matter, the client has a reasonable expectation that information relating to the client will not be voluntarily disclosed and that disclosure of such information may be compelled only in accordance with recognized exceptions to the attorney-client and work product privileges.

The Federal lawyer's exercise of discretion not to disclose information under Rule 1.6(c) should not be subject to reexamination. Permitting such reexamination would be incompatible with the general policy of promoting compliance with law through assurances that communications will be protected against disclosure.

These Rules of Professional Conduct are rules of reason. They should be interpreted with reference to the purposes of legal representation and of the law itself. Some of these Rules are imperative, cast in the terms "shall" or "shall not." These define proper conduct for purposes of professional discipline. Others, generally cast in the term "may" are permissive and define areas under these Rules in which the Federal lawyer has professional discretion. No disciplinary action should be taken when the Federal lawyer chooses not to act or acts within the bounds of such discretion. Other Rules define the nature of relationships between the Federal lawyer and others. These Rules are thus partly obligatory and partly descriptive in that they define a Federal lawyer's professional role. Many of the comments use the term "should". Comments do not add obligations to these Rules, but provide guidance for practicing in compliance with these Rules. The comments are interpretative, while the text of each Rule is authoritative.

The Preamble and this note on Scope provide general orientation.

DEFINITIONS

Within the scope of these Rules:

"Attorney-client" is the term used to describe the evidentiary privilege against disclosure of communications between a Federal lawyer's client and the Federal lawyer. It is not used to describe the relationship between a Federal lawyer and the lawyer's client.

"Belief" or "believes" mean that the individual involved actually concludes the fact in question to be true. An individual's belief may be inferred from circumstances.

"Client-lawyer" is used to express the professional relationship between a Federal lawyer and the lawyer's client. The term is not used to reference any evidentiary privileges, such as the "attorney-client" privilege.

"Consult" or "consultation" means communication of information reasonably sufficient to permit the client to appreciate the significance of the matter in question.

"Federal Agency" means: (1) An Executive agency, including an Executive department, military department, Government corporation, Government controlled corporation, and an independent establishment; (2) The Congress, committees of Congress, members of Congress who employ lawyers, and Congressional agencies; (3) The courts of the United States and agencies of the Judiciary; (4) The Governments of the territories and possessions of the United States; or (5) The Government of the District of Columbia.

"Federal lawyer" means a Government lawyer or a Non–Government lawyer, as hereinafter defined.

"Firm" means the organizational entity through which Non–Government lawyers transact business. The term includes private law firms, the legal departments of corporations and other business entities that hire lawyers as employees, and legal service organizations. The term does not include a Federal Agency.

"Government employee" means an officer or employee of a Federal Agency. The term includes members of the Armed Forces.

"Government lawyer" means a Government employee who holds a position as an attorney with a Federal Agency or serves as a judge advocate in one of the Armed Forces, but only while performing official duties. The term includes a lawyer in private practice who has contracted with or been specially retained by a Federal Agency to represent the Agency or another person while engaged in the performance of the contractual obligation.

"Fraud" or "fraudulent" means conduct having deceit as its purpose and does not encompass merely negligent misrepresentation or failure to apprise another of relevant information.

"Individual" is used to describe a single human being.

"Knowingly," "known," or "knows" means actual knowledge of the fact in question. A person's knowledge may be inferred from circumstances.

"Law" as used in these Rules includes statutes, treaties and international agreements, legal precedents, Federal Agency regulations, directives, and orders.

"Non–Government lawyer" means an individual who is a member of the bar of a Federal court or the highest court of a State or Territory, who represents persons before a Federal Agency. When a Government lawyer is engaged in the private practice of law or pro bono representation not related to the Government lawyer's official duties, the lawyer is considered a Non–Government lawyer.

"Person" means an individual, a corporation, a company, an association, a firm, a partnership, a society, a joint stock company, or any other legal entity.

"Reasonable" or "reasonably" when used in relation to conduct by Federal lawyer means the conduct of a reasonably prudent and competent lawyer.

"Reasonable belief" or "reasonably believes" when used in reference to a Federal lawyer means that the lawyer believes the matter in question and that the circumstances are such that the belief is reasonable.

"Reasonably should know" when used in reference to a Federal lawyer means that a lawyer of reasonable prudence and competence would ascertain the matter in question.

"Substantial" when used in reference to degree or extent means a material matter of clear and weighty importance.

"Supervisory lawyer" means a Federal lawyer within an office or organization with authority over or responsibility for the direction, coordination, evaluation, or assignment of responsibilities and work of subordinate lawyers, contract legal representation, nonlawyer assistants (e.g., paralegals), and clerical personnel.

"Tribunal" means a court, board, hearing officer, investigating officer, judge, jury, panel, or other body or official that receives evidence and makes a ruling or determination.

CLIENT–LAWYER RELATIONSHIP

RULE 1.1 Competence

A Federal lawyer shall provide competent representation to a client. Competent representation requires the legal knowledge, skill thoroughness, and preparation reasonably necessary for the representation.

COMMENT:

Legal Knowledge and Skill

In determining whether a Federal lawyer employs the requisite knowledge and skill in a particular matter, relevant factors include the relative complexity and specialized nature of the matter, the lawyer's general experience, the lawyer's training and experience in the field in question, the preparation and study the lawyer is able to give the matter, and whether it is feasible to refer the matter to, or consult with, a lawyer of established competence in the field in question. In most instances, the required proficiency is that generally afforded to clients by other lawyers in similar matters. Expertise in a particular field of law may be required in some circumstances.

Initial determinations as to the competence of a Government lawyer for a particular assignment will be made by a supervisory lawyer prior to case or issue assignments. However, once assigned, a Government lawyer may consult with the supervisory lawyer concerning competence to continue handling a particular case or issue. See Rules 5.1 and 5.2.

A Federal lawyer need not necessarily have special training or prior experience to handle legal problems of a type with which the Federal lawyer is unfamiliar. A newly admitted Federal lawyer can be as competent as a practitioner with long experience. Some important legal skills, such as the analysis of precedent, the evaluation of evidence, and legal drafting, are required in all legal problems. Perhaps the most fundamental legal skill consists of determining what kind of legal problems a situation may involve, a skill that necessarily transcends any particular specialized knowledge. A Federal lawyer can provide adequate representation in a wholly novel field through necessary study or consultation with a Federal lawyer of established competence in the field in question.

A Federal lawyer may become involved in representing a client whose needs exceed either the lawyer's competence or authority to act in the client's behalf. In such a situation, the Federal lawyer should refer the matter to another Federal lawyer who has the requisite competence or authority to meet the client's needs. For Non–Government lawyers practicing before Federal agencies, competent representation may also be provided through the association of a Non-government lawyer of established competence in the field in question.

A Federal lawyer may give advice or assistance in a matter in which the Federal lawyer does not have the skill ordinarily required where referral to or consultation with another Federal lawyer would be impractical. However, assistance should be limited to that reasonably necessary in the circumstances, for ill-considered action can jeopardize the client's interest.

Thoroughness and Preparation

Competent handling of a particular matter includes inquiry into and analysis of the factual and legal elements of the problem, and use of methods and procedures meeting the standards of competent practitioners. It also includes adequate preparation. The attention and preparation required are determined in part by what is at stake; major litigation and complex transactions ordinarily require more elaborate treatment than matters of lesser consequence.

Maintaining Competence

To maintain the requisite knowledge and skill, a Federal lawyer should engage in continuing study and education.

RULE 1.2 Scope of Representation

(a) A Federal lawyer shall abide by a client's decisions concerning the objectives of representation, subject to paragraphs (c), (d), (e), and (f), and shall consult with the client as to the means by which these decisions are to be pursued. A Federal lawyer shall abide by a client's decision whether to accept an offer of settlement of a matter. In a criminal case, and to the extent applicable in civil cases and administrative hearings, the Federal lawyer shall abide by the client's decision, after consultation with the Federal lawyer, as to choice of counsel (as provided by law), a plea to be entered, selection of trial forum, whether to enter into a pretrial agreement, and whether the client will testify.

(b) A Federal lawyer's representation of a client, including representation by appointment, does not constitute an endorsement of the client's political, economic, social, or moral views or activities.

(c) A Federal lawyer may limit the objectives of the representation if the client consents after consultation or as required by law and communicated to the client.

(d) A Federal lawyer shall not counsel a client to engage, or assist a client, in conduct that the lawyer knows is criminal or fraudulent, but a Federal lawyer may discuss the legal and moral consequences of any proposed course of conduct with a client and may counsel or assist a client to make a good faith effort to determine the validity, scope, meaning, or application of the law.

(e) When a Federal lawyer knows that a client expects assistance not permitted by these Rules of Professional Conduct or other law, the lawyer shall advise the client of the relevant limitations on the lawyer's conduct.

(f) A Government lawyer's authority and control over decisions concerning the representation may, by law, be expanded beyond the limits imposed by paragraphs (a) and (c).

547

COMMENT:

General

In many cases, straightforward application of Rule 1.2 is possible. However, in other cases, primarily in the litigation context, the scope of representation is necessarily altered and set out by law. For example, a Government lawyer representing an individual may have significant control over the litigation decisions. Similarly, except as otherwise provided by law, the Department of Justice, under 28 U.S.C. § 516, is given the authority to represent certain Federal agencies in litigation. Procedures for resolving inter-agency disputes should be followed in cases of conflict between a position recommended by the litigating attorney and the Federal Agency being represented.

Scope of Representation

Both Federal lawyer and client have authority and responsibility in the objectives and means of representation. The client has ultimate authority to determine the purposes to be served by legal representation, within the limits imposed by law and the Federal lawyer's professional obligations. Within those limits, a client also has a right to consult with the Federal lawyer about the means to be used in pursuing those objectives. At the same time, a Federal lawyer is not required to pursue objectives or employ means simply because a client may wish that the Federal lawyer do so. A clear distinction between objectives and means sometimes cannot be drawn, and in many cases the client-lawyer relationship becomes a joint undertaking. In questions of means, the Federal lawyer should assume responsibility for technical and legal tactical issues, such as what witnesses to call, whether and how to conduct cross-examination, what court members to challenge, and what options to make. Except where precluded by Rule 4.4, the Federal lawyer should defer to the client regarding such questions as expenses to be incurred and concern for third persons who might be affected adversely.

When the client appears to be suffering mental disability, the Federal lawyer's duty to abide by the client's decisions is to be guided by Rule 1.14.

Service Limited in Objectives or Means

The objectives or scope of services provided by a Federal lawyer may be limited by agreement with the client or by the law governing the conditions under which the Federal lawyer's services are made available to the client. Formation of client-lawyer relationships and representation of clients by a Government lawyer is permissible only when authorized by competent authority. When the objectives or scope of services provided by a Federal lawyer are limited by law, the Federal lawyer should inform the client of such limitations at the earliest opportunity.

If a Government lawyer is uncertain of the scope of services permitted by the law governing the conditions under which the Federal lawyer's services are made available to a client, the Government lawyer should consult with the Government lawyer's supervisory lawyer concerning the matter. See Rule 5.2.

An agreement concerning the scope of representation must accord with these Rules of Professional Conduct and other law. Thus, the client shall not be asked to agree to representation so limited in scope as to violate Rule 1.1, to surrender the right to terminate the Federal lawyer's services, or to conclude a matter that the Federal lawyer might wish to continue.

Criminal, Fraudulent, and Prohibited Transactions

A Federal lawyer is required to give an honest opinion about the consequences likely to result from a client's conduct. Simply because a client uses advice in a course of action that is criminal or fraudulent does not, of itself, make a Federal lawyer a party to the course of action. However, a Federal lawyer shall not knowingly assist a client in criminal or fraudulent conduct. A critical distinction exists between presenting an analysis of legal aspects of questionable conduct and recommending the means by which a crime or fraud might be committed with impunity.

When the client's course of action has already begun and is continuing, the Federal lawyer's responsibility is especially delicate. The Federal lawyer is not permitted to reveal the client's wrongdoing, except where required or permitted by Rule 1.6 or Rule 3.3. However, the Federal lawyer is required to avoid furthering an illegal purpose, for example, by suggesting how it might be concealed. A Federal lawyer shall not continue assisting a client in conduct that the Federal lawyer originally supposes is legally proper but then discovers is criminal or fraudulent. Seeking to withdraw from the representation, therefore, may be appropriate.

Paragraph (d) applies whether or not the defrauded party is a party to the transaction. Hence, a Federal lawyer should not participate in a sham transaction; for example, a transaction to effectuate criminal or fraudulent escape of tax liability. The last clause of paragraph (d) recognizes that determining the validity or interpretation of a statute or regulation may include a course of action contrary to the terms of the statute or regulation or of the interpretation placed upon it by governmental authorities.

RULE 1.3 Diligence

A Federal lawyer shall act with reasonable diligence and promptness in representing a client.

COMMENT:

A Federal lawyer should pursue a matter on behalf of a client despite opposition, obstruction, or personal inconvenience to the Federal lawyer, and may take whatever lawful and ethical measures are required to vindicate a client's cause or endeavor. A Federal lawyer should act with commitment and dedication to the interests of the client and with morality in advocating the client's position. However, a Federal lawyer is not bound to press for every advantage that might be realized for a client. Although a Federal lawyer may be bound by court precedent to pursue certain matters on behalf of a client, a Federal lawyer has professional discretion in determining the means by which a matter should be pursued. See Rules 1.2 and 1.4(b). A Federal lawyer's work load should be managed by both the Federal lawyer and a supervisory lawyer so that each matter can be handled adequately. See Rule 5.1.

Perhaps no professional shortcoming is more widely resented than procrastination. A client's interest often can be adversely affected by the passage of time or the chance of condition; in extreme instances, as when a Federal lawyer overlooks a statute of limitation, the client's legal position may be destroyed. Even when the client's interests are not affected in substance, however, unreasonable delay can cause a client needless anxiety and undermine confidence in the Federal lawyer's trustworthiness.

Unless the relationship is terminated as provided in Rule 1.16, and to the extent permitted by law, a Federal lawyer should carry through to conclusion all matters undertaken for a client. If a Federal lawyer's representation is limited to a specific matter, the relationship terminates when the matter has been resolved. Doubt about whether a client-lawyer relationship exists should be clarified by the Federal lawyer, preferably in writing, so that the client will not mistakenly suppose the Federal lawyer is looking after the client's affairs when the Federal lawyer has ceased to do so. For example, a Federal lawyer who has handled a judicial or administrative proceeding that produced a result adverse to the client should advise the client of the possibility of appeal before relinquishing responsibility for the matter.

RULE 1.4 Communication

(a) A Federal lawyer shall keep a client reasonably informed about the status of a matter and promptly comply with reasonable requests for information.

(b) A Federal lawyer shall explain a matter to the extent reasonably necessary to permit the client to make informed decisions regarding the representation.

COMMENT:

A client should have sufficient information to participate intelligently in decisions concerning the objectives of the representation and the means by which they are to be pursued, to the extent a client is willing and able to do so. For example, a Federal lawyer negotiating a pretrial agreement on behalf of a client should provide the client with facts relevant to the matter, inform the client of communications from the Government, and take other reasonable steps that permit the client to make a decision regarding the feasibility of further negotiation with the Government. A Federal lawyer representing the Government who receives from the defendant an offer for a pretrial agreement must communicate that offer, and should provide advice as to that offer, to the appropriate authority.

Adequacy of communications depends in part on the kind of advice or assistance involved. For example, in negotiations where there is time to explain a proposal, a Federal lawyer should review all important provisions with the client before proceeding to an agreement. In litigation, a Federal lawyer should explain the general strategy and prospects of success and ordinarily should consult the client on tactics that might injure or coerce another. On the other hand, a Federal lawyer ordinarily cannot be expected to describe trial or negotiation strategy in detail. The guiding principle is that a Federal lawyer should fulfill reasonable client expectations for information consistent with the duty to act in the client's best interests, taking into account client's overall requirements as to the character of representation.

When the client is the Federal Agency, it is often impossible or inappropriate to inform all of its members about its legal affairs. Ordinarily, a Government lawyer should address communications to the appropriate officials of the Federal Agency. See Rule 1.13.

When the representation involves many routine matters, a system of limited or occasional reporting may be arranged with the client. Practical exigencies may limit the opportunity for consultation and also require a Federal lawyer to act for a client without prior consultation.

In some circumstances, a Federal lawyer may be required to withhold information from a client. For example, classified information shall not be disclosed without proper authority. In other circumstances, a Federal lawyer may be justified in delaying transmission of information when the client would be likely to react imprudently to an immediate communication. Thus, a Federal lawyer might withhold a psychiatric diagnosis of a client when the examining psychiatrist indicates that disclosure would harm the client. A Federal lawyer shall not withhold information to serve the Federal lawyer's own interest or convenience, or where disclosure would be favorable to the defense of a criminal defendant. Rules or court orders governing litigation may provide that information supplied to a Federal lawyer shall not be disclosed to the client.   Rule 3.4(c) directs compliance with such rules or orders.

RULE 1.5   Fees

(a) A Federal lawyer shall be regulated by the Rules of Professional Conduct or other applicable rules of the jurisdictions in which the Federal lawyer is licensed or is practicing law, and otherwise by law in regard to matters concerning fees.

(b) A Government lawyer, in connection with the Government lawyer's official duties, may not request or accept any compensation from client other than that provided by the United States for the performance of duties.

COMMENT:

Non–Government Lawyers

Rather than adopting a rule based on Rule 1.5 of the ABA Model Rule of Professional Conduct that would apply only to Non–Government lawyers practicing before Federal agencies, the Federal Agency defers on this matter to the rules of the jurisdictions in which these Non–Government lawyers are licensed, and otherwise by law.

Government Lawyers

Government lawyers are prohibited by statute from accepting, as compensation for services as a Government employee any salary or contribution to or supplementation of salary from any source other than the Government of the United States.   See, for example, 18 U.S.C. § 203 and § 209.

A Government lawyer shall not request or accept any gratuity, salary, or other compensation from a client, other than the Federal Agency that employs the Government lawyer, incident to the performance of duties as a Government employee.   However, to the extent permitted by applicable laws, a Government lawyer who is active in a non-Government organization or who delivers a speech to an organization may accept reimbursement from the organization for the Government lawyer's costs incurred as a result of the Government lawyer's participation, on the Government lawyer's own time, in that organization's activities.

While a Government lawyer may be able to represent clients in a private or pro bono capacity, the Rule prohibits the Government lawyer from using the Government lawyer's official position to solicit or obtain clients for the Government lawyer's private practice.

RULE 1.6   Confidentiality of Information

(a) A Federal lawyer shall not reveal information relating to the representation of a client unless the client consents after consultation, except for disclosures that are impliedly authorized

in order to carry out the representation, and except as stated in paragraphs (b), (c), and (d).

(b) A Federal lawyer shall reveal such information to the extent the Federal lawyer reasonably believes necessary to prevent the client from committing a criminal act that the Federal lawyer believes is likely to result in imminent death or substantial bodily harm, or imminent and significant impairment of national security or defense.

(c) A Federal lawyer may reveal such information to the extent the Federal lawyer reasonably believes necessary to establish a claim or defense on behalf of the Federal lawyer in a controversy between the Federal lawyer and the client, to establish a defense to a criminal charge or civil claim against the Federal lawyer based upon conduct in which the client was involved, or to respond to allegations in any proceeding concerning the Federal lawyer's representation of the client.

(d) A Government lawyer may reveal such information when required or authorized by law.

COMMENT:

The Federal lawyer is part of a judicial system charged with upholding the law. One of the Federal lawyer's functions is to advise clients so that they avoid any violation of the law in the proper exercise of their rights.

The observance of the ethical obligation of a Federal lawyer to hold inviolate confidential information of the client not only facilitates the full development of facts essential to proper representation of the client but also encourages people to seek early legal assistance.

Almost without exception, clients come to Federal lawyers in order to determine what their rights are and what, in the maze of laws and regulations, is deemed to be legal and correct. The common law recognizes that the client's confidences must be protected from disclosure. Based upon experience, Federal lawyers know that most clients follow the advice given, and the law is upheld.

A fundamental principle in the client-lawyer relationship is that the Federal lawyer maintains confidentiality of information relating to the representation. The client is thereby encouraged to communicate fully and frankly with the Federal lawyer even as to embarrassing or legally damaging matters.

The principle of confidentiality is given effect in two related bodies of law—the attorney-client privilege (which includes the work product doctrine) in the law of evidence and the rule of confidentiality established in professional ethics. The attorney-client privilege applies in judicial and other proceedings in which a Federal lawyer may be called as a witness or otherwise required to produce evidence concerning a client. The rule of client-lawyer confidentiality applies in situations other than those where evidence is sought from the Federal lawyer through compulsion of law. The confidentiality rule applies not merely to matters communicated in confidence by the client but also to all information relating to the representation, whatever its source. A Federal lawyer shall not disclose such information except as authorized or required by these Rules of Professional Conduct or other lawful order, directive, regulation, or statute. See also Scope.

The requirement of maintaining confidentiality of information relating to representation applies to Government lawyers, even those who may disagree with the policy goals that their representation is designed to advance.

Authorized Disclosure

A Federal lawyer is impliedly authorized to make disclosures about a client when appropriate in carrying out the representation, except to the extent that the client's instructions or special circumstances limit that authority. For example, a Federal lawyer may disclose information in litigation by admitting a fact that cannot properly be disputed, or in negotiation by making a disclosure that facilitates a satisfactory conclusion.

Federal lawyers may disclose to supervisory lawyers within the office and to nonlawyer assistants subject to the direction and control of the lawyer or the lawyer's supervisory lawyer information relating to a client, unless the client has instructed that particular information be confined to specified lawyers, or unless otherwise prohibited by these Rules of Professional Conduct or by law.

Disclosure Adverse to Client

The confidentiality rule is subject to limited exceptions. In becoming privy to information about a client, a Federal lawyer may foresee that the client intends serious harm to another person. However, to the extent a Federal lawyer is required or permitted to disclose a client's purposes, the client will be inhibited from revealing facts which would enable the Federal lawyer to counsel against a wrongful course of action. The public is better protected if full and open communication by the client is encouraged than if it is inhibited.

Several Situations Must be Distinguished

First, the Federal lawyer shall not counsel or assist a client in conduct that is criminal or fraudulent. See Rule 1.2(d). Similarly, a Federal lawyer owes a duty of candor to the court and has a duty under Rule 3.3(a)(3) not to use false evidence. These duties are essentially special instances of the duty prescribed in Rule 1.2(d) to avoid assisting a client in criminal or fraudulent conduct.

Second, the Federal lawyer may have been innocently involved in past conduct by the client that was criminal or fraudulent. In such a situation the Federal lawyer has not violated Rule 1.2(d), because to "counsel or assist" criminal or fraudulent conduct requires knowing that the conduct is of that character.

Third, the Federal lawyer may learn that a client intends prospective conduct that is criminal and likely to result in imminent death or substantial bodily harm, or imminent and significant impairment of national security or defense. As stated in paragraph (b), the Federal lawyer has a professional obligation to reveal the information to the extent that Federal lawyer reasonably believes necessary to prevent such consequences.

In any case, a disclosure adverse to the client's interest should be no greater than the Federal lawyer reasonably believes necessary to the purpose giving rise to the disclosure.

Withdrawal

If a Federal lawyer's services will be used by a client in materially furthering a course of criminal or fraudulent conduct, the Federal lawyer must seek to withdraw, as stated in Rule 1.16(a)(1).

After withdrawal the Federal lawyer is required to refrain from making disclosure of the client's confidence, except as otherwise provided in this Rule. Nothing in this Rule, Rule 1.8(b), or Rule 1.16(d) prevents the Federal lawyer from giving notice of the fact of withdrawal, and the Federal lawyer may also withdraw or disaffirm any opinion, document, affirmation, or the like.

When the client is a Federal Agency, the Federal lawyer may doubt whether contemplated conduct will actually be carried out. When necessary to guide conduct in connection with the Rule, the Federal lawyer may make inquiry within the Federal Agency as indicated in Rule 1.13(b).

Dispute Concerning a Federal Lawyer's Conduct

When a legal claim or disciplinary charge alleges complicity of the Federal lawyer in a client's conduct, or other misconduct of the Federal lawyer involving representation of the client, the Federal lawyer may respond to the extent the Federal lawyer reasonably believes necessary to establish a defense. The same is true with respect to a claim involving the conduct or representation of a former client. The Federal lawyer's right to respond arises when an assertion of such complicity has been made. Paragraph (c) does not require the Federal lawyer to await the commencement of an action or proceeding that charges such complicity. The defense may be established by responding directly to a third party who has made such an assertion. The right to defend, of course, applies where a proceeding has been commenced. Where practicable and not prejudicial to the Federal lawyer's ability to establish the defense, the Federal lawyer should advise the client of the third party's assertion and request that the client respond appropriately. In any event, disclosure should be no greater than the Federal lawyer reasonably believes is necessary to vindicate innocence; the disclosure should be made in a manner which limits access to the information to the tribunal or other persons having a need to know it; and appropriate protective orders or other arrangements should be sought by the Federal lawyer to the fullest extent practicable.

If a Federal lawyer is charged with wrongdoing in which the client's conduct is implicated, the rule of confidentiality should not prevent the Federal lawyer from defending against the charge. Such a charge can arise in a civil, criminal, or professional disciplinary proceeding, and can be based on a wrong allegedly committed by the Federal lawyer against the client, or a wrong alleged by a third person; for example, a person claiming to have been defrauded by the Federal lawyer and client acting together. A Non–Government lawyer entitled to a fee is permitted by paragraph (c) to prove the services rendered in an action to collect it. This aspect of the Rule expresses the principle that the beneficiary of a fiduciary relationship shall not exploit it to the detriment of the fiduciary. As stated above, the Federal lawyer must make every effort practicable to avoid unnecessary disclosure of information relating to a representation, to limit disclosure to those having the need to know it, and to obtain protective orders or make other arrangements to minimize the risk of disclosure.

Disclosure Otherwise Required or Authorized

If a Federal lawyer is called as a witness to give testimony concerning a client, absent waiver by the client, paragraph (a) requires the Federal lawyer to invoke the attorney-client privilege when it is applicable. The Federal lawyer must comply with the final orders of a court or other tribunal of competent jurisdiction requiring the Federal lawyer to give information about the client.

These Rules of Professional Conduct in various circumstances permit or require a Federal lawyer to disclose information relating to the representation. See Rules 2.2, 2.3, 3.3, and 4.1. In addition to these provisions, a Federal lawyer may be obligated or permitted by other provision of law to give information about a client. Whether another provision of law supersedes Rule 1.6 is a matter of interpretation beyond the scope of these Rules, but a presumption should exist against such a supersession.

Former Client

The duty of confidentiality continues after the client-lawyer relationship has terminated.

Government Lawyers

The identification of the client, for purposes of the Government lawyer, is critical to the application of this Rule. Generally, a Federal Agency is the Government lawyer's client for the purposes of this Rule. Communications by the Government lawyer, both outside and within the Federal Agency, may or may not be considered breaches of this Rule. There are numerous statutes, regulations, and directives that may affect the Government lawyer's obligations under this Rule. A secondary issue concerns statutory protections against reprisal for Government employees who disclose violations or abuses—the "whistleblower statutes." However, in such situations there may be a conflict with attorney-client privileges.

Government lawyers are often formally employed by a Federal Agency but assigned to an organizational element within the Federal Agency. Unless otherwise specifically provided, the Federal Agency, not the organizational element, is ordinarily considered the client.

Paragraph (d) permits disclosures that the Government authorizes its lawyers to make in connection with their professional services to the Government. Such disclosures may be authorized or required by statute, Executive Order, regulation, or directive, depending on the constitutional or statutory powers of the authorizing entity. This paragraph also clarifies that, under 28 U.S.C. § 516, Government lawyers may disclose all information relevant to representation by the Department of Justice to the Department's assigned attorney, and authorizes such information to be further disclosed by the assigned attorney to other Department of Justice lawyers concerned with the representation.

There are circumstances in which a Government lawyer may be assigned to provide an individual with counsel or representation in which it is clear that an obligation of confidentiality runs directly to that individual and not to the Federal Agency. Examples of such representation include a Government lawyer representing a defendant sued for damages arising out of the performance of the defendant's Government employment, a judge advocate representing an accused in a court-martial, or representation by a public defender.

The relevant circumstances may indicate the extent to which the individual client will be deemed to have granted or denied consent to disclosures by the Government lawyer to the Government lawyer's employing Agency under paragraph (d).

While the general thrust of this Rule may serve as guidance for the Government attorney, the Government lawyer's actions are defined and circumscribed by various Federal laws and these Rules. As a practical matter, in addition to determining the extent to which Rule 1.6 applies to a given situation, it is always advisable for Government lawyers to review the applicable Federal law that may govern their conduct under the circumstances, and to consult with their supervisors.

For example, Government employees are prohibited from using, for financial gain or other improper purposes, non-public information obtained by reason of their status as an employee. See 5 CFR 735.206. See also 28 CFR Part 17, which sets out regulations protecting confidential information relating to national security; 28 CFR 50.2, which establishes policy regarding the release of information relating to criminal and civil proceedings; 28 CFR 50.15(a)(3), which regulates the treatment of confidential attorney-client information in the context of Department of Justice representation of individual Government employees. The Privacy Act and other laws also prohibit the disclosure of certain types of confidential Government information. See 5 U.S.C. § 552a (personal information), 18 U.S.C. § 1905 (trade secrets), 18 U.S.C. § 798 (classified information), and 50 U.S.C. § 783(b) (classified information). Unique Government privileges also play a role in shaping a Government lawyer's duties and responsibilities regarding confidential Government information. Thus, for example, the law recognizes a deliberative process privilege, which protects from public disclosure predecisional communications that are part of the decision making processes of government agencies. See NLRB v. Sears, Roebuck & Co., 421 U.S. 132, 149, 150–51 (1975). See also 5 U.S.C. § 552(b) (5).

RULE 1.7 Conflict of Interest: General Rule

(a) A Federal lawyer shall not represent a client if the representation of that client will be directly adverse to another client, unless:

(1) The Federal lawyer reasonably believes the representation will not adversely affect the relationship with the other client; and

(2) Each client consents after consultation.

(b) A Federal lawyer shall not represent a client if the representation of that client may be materially limited by the lawyer's responsibilities to another client or to a third person, or by the Federal lawyer's own interests, unless:

(1) The Federal lawyer reasonably believes the representation will not be adversely affected; and

(2) The client consents after consultation. When representation of multiple clients in a single matter is undertaken, the consultation shall include explanation of the implications of the common representation and the advantages and risks involved.

COMMENT:

Loyalty is an essential element in the Federal lawyer's relationship to a client. If an impermissible conflict of interest exists before representation, the Federal lawyer should decline to represent the client. If such a conflict arises after representation has been undertaken, the Federal lawyer should seek to withdraw from representation of the subsequent client. See Rule 1.16. When more than one client is involved and the Federal lawyer is permitted to withdraw because a conflict arises after the representation has begun, the Federal lawyer's ethical ability to continue to represent any of the clients is determined by Rule 1.9. See also Rule 2.2(c). As to whether a client-lawyer relationship exists or, having once been established, is continuing, see Comment to Rule 1.3.

As a general proposition, loyalty to a client prohibits undertaking representation directly adverse to that client without that client's consent. Paragraph (a) expresses that general rule. Thus, a Federal lawyer ordinarily shall not act as advocate against a person the Federal lawyer represents in some other matter, even if it is wholly unrelated. On the other hand, simultaneous representation in unrelated matters of clients whose interests are only generally adverse, does not require consent of either client. Paragraph (a) applies only when the representation of one client would be directly adverse to the other.

Loyalty to a client is also impaired when a Federal lawyer cannot consider, recommend, or carry out an appropriate course of action for the client because of the Federal lawyer's other responsibilities or interests. This type of conflict effectively forecloses alternatives that would otherwise be available to the client. Paragraph (b) addresses such situations. A possible conflict does not itself preclude the representation. The critical questions are—the likelihood that a conflict will eventuate and, if it does, whether it will materially interfere with the Federal lawyer's independent professional judgment in considering alternatives or foreclose courses of action that reasonably should be pursued on behalf of the client. Consideration should be given to whether the client wishes to accommodate the other interest involved.

Consultation and Consent

A client, including an organization (see Rule 1.13(b)), may consent to representation notwithstanding a conflict. However, as indicated in paragraph (a)(1) with respect to representation directly adverse to a client, and paragraph (b)(1) with respect to material limitations on representation of a client, when a disinterested Federal lawyer would conclude that the client should not agree to the representation under the circumstances, the Federal lawyer involved cannot properly ask for such agreement to provide representation on the basis of the client's consent. When more than one client is involved, the question of conflict must be resolved as to each client. Moreover, there may be circumstances where it is impossible to make the disclosure necessary to obtain consent.

Federal Lawyer's Interests

The Federal lawyer's own interests should not be permitted to have an adverse effect on representation of a client. (See, e.g., 18 U.S.C. 208.) If the probity of a Federal lawyer's own conduct in a transaction is in serious question, it may be difficult or impossible for the Federal lawyer to give a client detached advice. A Federal lawyer shall not allow related business interests to affect representation, for example, by referring clients to an enterprise in which the Federal lawyer has an undisclosed interest.

Conflict of Litigation

Paragraph (a) prohibits representation of opposing parties in litigation. Simultaneous representation of parties whose interest in litigation may conflict, such as co-plaintiffs or co-defendants, is governed by paragraph (b). An impermissible conflict may exist by reason of substantial discrepancy in the parties' testimony, incompatibility in position in relation to an opposing party, or the fact that there are substantially different possibilities of settlement of the claims or liabilities in question. Such conflicts can arise in criminal cases, as well as civil matters. The potential for a conflict of interest in representing multiple defendants in a criminal case is so grave that ordinarily a Federal lawyer should not represent more than one co-defendant. On the other hand, common representation of persons having similar interests is proper if the risk of adverse effect is minimal and the requirements of paragraph (b) are met. Compare Rule 2.2 involving intermediation between clients.

Ordinarily, a Federal lawyer shall not act as advocate against a client the Federal lawyer represents in some other matter, even if the other matter is wholly unrelated. However, there are circumstances in which a Government lawyer may act as advocate against the Government lawyer's Federal Agency. For example, Government lawyers in some circumstances may represent another Government employee in proceedings (e.g., courts-martial or adverse personnel action proceedings) in which a Federal Agency is the opposing party. The propriety of concurrent representation can depend on the nature of the litigation. For example, a suit charging fraud entails conflict to a degree not involved in a suit for declaratory judgment concerning statutory interpretation.

A Federal lawyer may represent parties having antagonistic positions on a legal question that has arisen in different cases, unless representation of either client would be adversely affected. Thus, it is ordinarily proper to assert such positions in cases pending in different trial courts, but it may be improper to do so in cases pending in an appellate court.

Interest of a Person Paying for a Federal Lawyer's Service

A Non–Government lawyer may be paid from a source other than the client, if the client is informed of that fact, consents, and the arrangement does not compromise the Federal lawyer's duty of loyalty to the client. See Rule 1.8(f). For example, a defendant's family may pay a Non–Government lawyer to represent a defendant at trial.

Other Conflict Situations

Conflicts of interest in contexts other than litigation sometimes may be difficult to assess. Relevant factors in determining whether there is potential for adverse effect include the duration and intimacy of the Federal lawyer's relationship with the client or clients involved, the functions being performed by the Federal lawyer, the likelihood that actual conflict will arise and the likely prejudice to the client from the conflict if it does arise. The question is often one of the proximity and degree.

Although the Federal lawyer must be careful to avoid conflict of interest situations, resolving questions of conflict of interest is primarily the responsibility of the supervisory lawyer or the judge. See also Rule 5.1.

Conflict Charged by an Opposing Party

In litigation, courts raise conflict of interest issues when reason exists to believe that a Federal lawyer may have neglected his or her responsibilities. In a criminal case, inquiry by the court is generally required when a Federal lawyer represents multiple defendants. When an apparent conflict calls into question the fair or efficient administration of justice, opposing counsel may properly raise the issue. Such objections should be viewed with caution, however, for they can be misused as a technique of harassment. See Scope.

Government Lawyers

This Rule is not intended to apply to conflicts between Federal agencies or components of government (Federal, State or local), where the resolution of such conflicts has been entrusted by law to a specific individual or entity. Thus, for example, 28 U.S.C. § 516 authorizes the Attorney General and the Government lawyers of the Justice Department to resolve conflicts between certain Government agencies for purposes of litigation and even to assert positions in litigation that might be adverse to positions urged upon the Department of Justice by a client Agency. (See also Executive Order 12146, sections 1–4, which directs Executive agencies that are unable to resolve a legal dispute to submit the dispute to the Attorney General). Moreover, this rule is not intended to supersede Government regulations, such as 28 CFR 50.15, et seq., governing the resolution of conflicts in the context of representation of Government employees sued in their individual or personal capacities.

RULE 1.8 Conflict of Interest: Prohibited Transactions

(a) A Federal lawyer shall not enter into a business transaction with a client or knowingly acquire an ownership, possessory, security, or other pecuniary interest adverse to a client unless:

(1) The transaction and terms on which the Federal lawyer requires the interest are fair and reasonable to the client and are fully disclosed and transmitted in writing to the client in a manner which can be reasonably understood by the client;

(2) The client is given a reasonable opportunity to seek the advice of independent counsel in the transaction; and

(3) The client consents in writing thereto.

(b) A Federal lawyer shall not use information relating to representation of a client to the disadvantage of the client unless the client consents after consultation.

(c) A Federal lawyer shall not prepare an instrument giving the lawyer or an individual related to the lawyer as parent, child, sibling, or spouse any substantial gift from a client, including a testamentary gift, except where the client is related to the donee.

(d) While representing a client, a Federal lawyer shall not make or negotiate an agreement giving the lawyer literary or edit rights to a portrayal or account based in substantial part on information relating to the representation.

(e) A Federal lawyer shall not provide financial assistance to a client in connection with pending or contemplated litigation, except that:

(1) A Non-Government lawyer practicing before a Federal Agency may advance court costs and expenses of litigation, the repayment of which may be contingent on the outcome of the matter; and

(2) A Non-Government lawyer practicing before a Federal Agency representing an indigent client may pay court costs and expenses of litigation on behalf of the client.

(f) A Federal lawyer shall not accept compensation for representing a client from one other than the client unless:

(1) The client consents after consultation;

(2) There is no interference with the Federal lawyer's independence of professional judgment or with the Federal lawyer-client relationship; and

(3) Information relative to representation of a client is protected as required by Rule 1.6.

562

(g) A Federal lawyer who represents two or more clients shall not participate in making an aggregate settlement of the claims of or against the clients, or in a criminal case an aggregate agreement as to guilty pleas or nolo contendere pleas, unless each client consents after consultation, including disclosure of the existence and nature of all the claims or pleas involved and of the participation of each person in the settlement.

(h) A Federal lawyer shall not:

(1) Make an agreement prospectively limiting the lawyer's liability to a client for malpractice unless permitted by law and the client is independently represented in making the agreement.

(2) Settle a claim for liability due to allegations of malpractice with an unrepresented client or former client without first advising that person in writing that independent representation is appropriate in connection therewith.

(i) A Federal lawyer related to another lawyer as parent, child, sibling, or spouse shall not represent a client if the client's interest is directly adverse to a person who the Federal lawyer knows is represented by the other lawyer, except with the consent of the client after consultation regarding the relationship.

(j) A Non–Government lawyer shall not acquire a proprietary interest in the cause of action or subject matter of litigation the lawyer is conducting for a client, except that the lawyer may:

(1) Acquire a lien granted by law to secure the Non–Government lawyer's fee or expenses; and

(2) Contract with a client for a reasonable contingent fee in a civil case.

COMMENT:

Government Lawyers

Government lawyers shall strictly adhere to Federal Agency standards of conduct regulations and applicable laws in all dealings with individual clients. (See generally 18 U.S.C. § 202–211.) Such laws generally prohibit entering into business transactions with clients, deriving financial benefit from representations of clients, and accepting gifts from clients or other entities for the performance of official duties. This Rule does not authorize conduct otherwise prohibited by such regulations. A Government lawyer shall not refer legal or other business to any private Non–Government lawyer or enterprise with whom the Government lawyer has any present or expected direct or indirect personal interest. Special care will be taken to avoid giving preferential treatment to other Government lawyers in their private capacities.

A Government lawyer shall not request or accept any gratuity, salary, or other compensation from a client incident to the performance of duties as a Government employee.

Transactions Between Client and Federal Lawyer

As a general principle, all business transactions between client and Federal lawyer should be fair and reasonable to the client. In such transactions, a review by independent counsel on behalf of the client is often advisable. Furthermore, a Federal lawyer shall not exploit information relating to the representation to the client's disadvantage. For example, a Federal lawyer who has learned that the client is investing in specific real estate shall not, without the client's consent, seek to acquire nearby property where doing so would adversely affect the client's plan for investment. Paragraph (a) does not apply to standard commercial transactions between the Federal lawyer and the client for products or services that the client generally markets to others, for example, banking or brokerage services, medical services, products manufactured or distributed by the client, and utility services. In such transactions, the lawyer has no advantage in dealing with the client, and the restrictions in paragraph (a) are unnecessary and impracticable. All transactions must comply with promulgated standards of conduct and other laws. See also Rule 1.5.

Literary Rights

An agreement by which a Federal lawyer acquires literary or media rights concerning the conduct of the representation creates a conflict between the interests of the client and the personal interests of the Federal lawyer. Measures suitable in the representation of the client may detract from the publication value of an account of that representation.

Person Paying for a Federal Lawyer's Services

Paragraph (f) requires the Federal lawyer to disclose the fact that the Federal lawyer's services are being paid for by a third party. Such an arrangement must also conform to the requirements of Rule 1.6 concerning confidentiality and Rule 1.7 concerning conflict of interest.

Family Relationships Between Federal Lawyers

Paragraph (i) applies to related Federal lawyers who are in the same or different Federal Agency. Related Federal lawyers in the same office also are governed by Rules 1.7, 1.9, and 1.10. The disqualification stated in paragraph (i) is personal and is not imputed to other Federal lawyers in the offices with whom the Federal lawyer performs duty.

Acquisition of Interest in Litigation

Paragraph (j) states the traditional general rule that Federal lawyers are prohibited from acquiring a proprietary interest in litigation. This general rule, which has its basis in common law champerty and maintenance, is subject to specific exceptions developed in decisional law and continued in these Rules, such as the exception for reasonable contingent fees set forth in Rule 1.5 of the ABA Model Rules of Professional Conduct and the exception for certain advances of the costs of litigation set forth in paragraph (e).

The Rule is not intended to apply to customary qualifications and limitations in legal opinions and memoranda.

RULE 1.9 Conflict of Interest: Former Client

(a) A Federal lawyer who has formerly represented a client in a matter shall not thereafter represent another person in the same or a substantially related matter in which the person's interests are materially adverse to the interests of the client unless the former client consents after consultation.

(b) A Federal lawyer shall not knowingly represent a person in the same or a substantially related matter in which a firm with which the lawyer formerly was associated had previously represented a client:

(1) Whose interests are materially adverse to that person; and

(2) About whom the lawyer had acquired information protected by Rules 1.6 and 1.9(c) that is material to the matter; unless the former client consents after consultation.

(c) A Federal lawyer who has formerly represented a client in a matter or whose present or former firm has formerly represented a client in a matter shall not thereafter:

(1) Use information relating to the representation to the disadvantage of the former client except as Rule 1.6 would permit with respect to a client or when the information has become generally known.

(2) Reveal information relating to the representation except as Rule 1.6 or Rule 3.3. would permit or require with respect to a client.

COMMENT:

After termination of a client-lawyer relationship, a Federal lawyer shall not represent another client except in conformity with this Rule. The principles in Rule 1.7 determine whether the interests of the present and former client are adverse. The principles in Rule 1.11 govern successive Government and private employment.

The scope of a "matter" for purposes of paragraph (a) may depend on the facts of a particular situation or transaction. The Federal lawyer's involvement in a matter can also be a question of degree. When a Federal lawyer has been directly involved in a specific transaction, subsequent representation of other clients with materially adverse interest clearly is prohibited. On the other hand, a Federal lawyer who recurrently handled a type of problem for a former client is not precluded from later representing another client in a wholly distinct problem of that type, even though the subsequent representation involves a position adverse to the prior client. Thus, the reassignment of judge advocates between defense, prosecution, review, claim, and legal assistance functions within the same legal office is not precluded by this Rule.

Lawyers Moving Between Firms

When Non–Government lawyers have been associated within a firm, but then end their association, the question of whether the Non–Government lawyer should undertake representation is more complicated. There are several competing considerations. First, the client previously represented by the former firm must be reasonably assured that the principle of loyalty to the client is not compromised. Second, the rule should not be so broadly cast as to preclude other persons from having reasonable choice of legal counsel. Third, the rule should not unreasonably hamper lawyers from forming new associations and taking on new clients after having left a previous association. In this connection, it should be recognized that today many lawyers practice in firms, that many lawyers to some degree limit their practice to one field or another, and that many move from one association to another several times in their careers. If the concept of imputation were applied with unqualified rigor, the result would be radical curtailment of the opportunity of lawyers to move from one practice setting to another and of the opportunity of clients to change counsel.

Reconciliation of these competing principles in the past has been attempted under two rubrics. One approach has been to seek per se rules of disqualification. For example, it has been held that a partner in a law firm is conclusively presumed to have access to all confidences concerning all clients of the firm. Under this analysis, if a lawyer has been a partner in one law firm and then becomes a partner in another law firm, there may be a presumption that all confidences known by the partner in the first firm are known to all partners in the second firm. This presumption might properly be applied in some circumstances, especially where the client has been extensively represented, but may be unrealistic where the client was represented only for limited purposes. Furthermore, such a rigid rule exaggerates the difference between a partner and an associate in modern law firms.

The other rubric formerly used for dealing with disqualification is the appearance of impropriety proscribed in Canon 9 of the ABA Model

Code of Professional Responsibility. This rubric has a twofold problem. First, the appearance of impropriety can be taken to include any new client-lawyer relationship that might make a former client feel less anxious. If that meaning were adopted, disqualification would become little more than a question of subjective judgment by the former client. Second, since "impropriety" is undefined, the term "appearance of impropriety" is question-begging. It therefore has to be recognized that the problem of disqualification cannot be properly resolved either by simple analogy to a lawyer practicing alone or by the very general concept of appearance of impropriety.

Confidentiality

Preserving confidentiality is a question of access to information. Access to information, in turn, is essentially a question of fact in particular circumstances, aided by inferences, deductions, or working presumptions that reasonably may be made about the way in which lawyers work together. A lawyer may have general access to files of all clients of a law firm and may regularly participate in discussions of their affairs; it should be inferred that such a lawyer in fact is privy to all information about all of the firm's clients. In contrast, another lawyer may have access to the files of only a limited number of clients and participate in discussions of the affairs of no other clients; in the absence of information to the contrary, it should be inferred that such a lawyer in fact is privy to information about the clients actually served but not those of other clients.

Application of paragraph (b) depends on a situation's particular facts. In such an inquiry, the burden of proof should rest upon the lawyer whose disqualification is sought.

Paragraph (b) operates to disqualify the lawyer only when the lawyer involved has actual knowledge of information protected by Rules 1.6 and 1.9(c). Thus, if a lawyer while with one firm acquired no knowledge or information relating to a particular client of the firm, and that lawyer later joins another firm, neither the lawyer individually nor the second firm is disqualified from representing another client in the same or a related matter even though the interests of the two clients conflict. See Rule 1.10(b) for the restrictions on a firm once a lawyer has terminated association with the firm.

Independent of the question of disqualification of a firm, a lawyer changing professional association has a continuing duty to preserve confidentiality of information about a client formerly represented. See Rules 1.6 and 1.9.

Adverse Positions

The underlying question is whether the Federal lawyer was so involved in a particular matter that the subsequent representation can be justly regarded as a changing of sides in the matter in question.

Information acquired by the Federal lawyer in the course of representing a client shall not later be used by the Federal lawyer to the disadvantage of the client. However, just because a Federal lawyer once represented a client does not preclude the Federal lawyer from using generally known information about that client when later representing another client.

Disqualification from subsequent representation is for the protection of clients and can be waived by them. A waiver is effective only if it is preceded by full disclosure of the circumstances, including the Federal lawyer's role in behalf of the new client.

With regard to an opposing party's raising a question of conflict of interest, see Comment to Rule 1.7.

RULE 1.10 Imputed Disqualification: General Rule

(a) Government lawyers working in the same Federal Agency are not automatically disqualified from representing a client because any of them practicing alone would be prohibited from doing so by Rules 1.7, 1.8(c), 1.9, or 2.2.

(b) When a Federal lawyer has terminated an association with a firm, the firm is not prohibited from thereafter representing a person with interests materially adverse to those of a client represented by the formerly associated lawyer and not currently represented by the firm, unless:

(1) The matter is the same or substantially related to that in which the formerly associated lawyer represented the client; and

(2) Any Federal lawyer remaining in the firm has information protected by Rules 1.6 and 1.9(c) that is material to the matter.

(c) A disqualification under this Rule may be waived by the affected client under the conditions stated in Rule 1.7.

COMMENT:

Government Federal Agency Practice

The circumstances of Government service may require representation of opposing sides by Government lawyers working in the same Federal Agency. Such representation is permissible so long as conflicts of interest are avoided and independent judgment, zealous representation, and protection of confidences are not compromised. Thus, the principle of imputed disqualification is not automatically controlling for Government lawyers. The knowledge, action, and conflicts of interest of one Government lawyer are not to be imputed to another simply because they operate from the same office. For example, a number of

568

military defense counsels or public defenders operating from one office under a common supervisory lawyer and sharing clerical assistance are not prohibited from representing co-defendants at trial.

While it is permissible under this rule for a Government lawyer to represent an individual client in a military justice or an administrative proceeding that is under the control of a superior of the Government lawyer, particular care and attention is required when potential conflicts of interest exist between the organizational client of a supervisory lawyer and the individual clients of the Government lawyer being supervised.

Preserving confidentiality is a question of access to information. Access to information, in turn, is essentially a question of fact in particular circumstance, aided by inferences, deductions, or working presumptions that reasonably may be made about the way in which Government lawyers work together. A Government lawyer may have general access to files of all clients of a Federal Agency legal staff and may regularly participate in discussions of their affairs. It may be inferred that such a Government lawyer in fact is privy to all information about all the office's clients. In contrast, another Government lawyer may have access only to the files of his or her clients and does not participate in discussion of the affairs of other clients. In the absence of information to the contrary, it should be inferred that such a Government lawyer in fact is privy to information about the clients actually served, but not to information of other clients.

General

Whether a Federal lawyer is disqualified requires a functional analysis of the facts in a specific situation. The analysis should include consideration of whether the following will be compromised: preserving attorney-client confidentiality; maintaining independence of judgment; and avoiding positions adverse to a client.

Additionally, a Federal lawyer changing jobs has a continuing duty to preserve confidentiality of information about a client formerly represented. See Rules 1.6 and 1.9.

Maintaining independent judgment allows a Federal lawyer to consider, recommend, and carry out any appropriate course of action for a client without regard to the Federal lawyer's personal interests or the interests of another. When such independence is lacking or unlikely, representation cannot be zealous.

Another aspect of loyalty to a client is the Federal lawyer's obligation to decline subsequent representation involving positions adverse to a former client in substantially related matters. This obligation requires abstention from adverse representation by the individual Federal lawyer involved, but does not properly entail abstention of other Federal lawyers through imputed disqualification. Hence this aspect of the problem is governed by Rule 1.9(a).

RULE 1.11 Successive Government and Private Employment

(a) Except as law may otherwise expressly permit, a Federal lawyer shall not represent a private client in connection with a matter in which the Federal lawyer participated personally and substantially as a Government employee unless the appropriate Government Agency consents after consultation. No lawyer in a firm with which that lawyer is associated may knowingly undertake or continue representation in such matter unless:

(1) The disqualified Federal lawyer is screened from any participation in the matter and is apportioned no part of the fee therefrom; and

(2) Written notice is promptly given to the appropriate government Agency to enable it to ascertain compliance with the provisions of this Rule.

(b) Except as law may otherwise expressly permit, a Federal lawyer having information that the lawyer knows is confidential Government information about a person acquired when the lawyer was a Government employee shall not represent a private client whose interests are adverse to that person in a matter in which the information could be used to the material disadvantage of that person. A firm with which that lawyer is associated may undertake or continue representation in the matter only if the disqualified lawyer is screened from any participation in the matter and is apportioned no part of the fee therefrom.

(c) Except as law may otherwise expressly permit, a Federal lawyer serving as a Government employee shall not:

(1) Participate in a matter in which the Federal lawyer participated personally and substantially while in private practice or nongovernmental employment, unless under applicable law no one is, or by lawful delegation may be, authorized to act in the lawyer's stead in the matter.

(2) Negotiate for private employment with any person who is involved as a party or as attorney for a party in a matter in which the Federal lawyer is participating personally and substantially.

(d) As used in this Rule, the term "matter" includes:

(1) Any judicial or other proceeding, application, request for a ruling or other determination, contract, claim, controversy, investigation, charge, accusation, arrest, or other particular matter involving a specific party or parties.

(2) Any other matter covered by the conflict of interest rules of the appropriate Federal Agency.

(e) As used in this Rule, the term "confidential Governmental information" means information which has been obtained under

Governmental authority and that, at the time this Rule is applied, the Government is prohibited by law from disclosing to the public or has a legal privilege not to disclose, and which is not otherwise available to the public.

COMMENT:

This Rule prevents a Federal lawyer from exploiting public office for the advantage of a private client.

A Government lawyer representing a Federal Agency is subject to these Rules of Professional Conduct, including the prohibition against representing adverse interests stated in Rule 1.7 and the protections afforded former clients in Rule 1.9. In addition, such a Government lawyer is subject to Rule 1.11 and to laws regarding conflicts of interest, including 18 U.S.C. § 205 (prohibits Government employees from representing parties in actions against the United States), § 207 (restrictions on successive Government and private employment), § 208 (financial conflict of interest restrictions), and § 281 (restrictions on retired military officers); 5 CFR Part 2637 (regulations concerning post Government employment); and any Federal Agency regulations or directives. Such statutes and regulations may circumscribe the extent to which the Federal Agency may give consent under this Rule. If a Federal Agency has adopted rules governing practice before the agency by former federal lawyers, such issues (e.g., notice requirements) are governed by the Federal Agency rules and this Rule is not intended to displace such Agency requirements.

Where the successive clients are a Federal Agency and a private client, the risk exists that power or discretion vested in public authority might be used for the special benefit of a private client. A Federal lawyer should not be in a position in which benefit to a private client might affect performance of the Federal lawyer's professional functions on behalf of public authority. Also, unfair advantage could accrue to the private client by reason of access to confidential Government information about the client or by reason of access to confidential Government information about the client's adversary obtainable only through the Federal lawyer's government service. The rules governing Federal lawyers presently or formerly employed by a Federal Agency, however, should not be so restrictive as to inhibit transfer of employment to and from the Government. The Government has a legitimate need to attract qualified Federal lawyers as well as to maintain high ethical standards. The provisions for screening and waiver are necessary to prevent the disqualification rule from imposing too severe a deterrent against entering public service.

When the client is an agency of one government, that agency should be treated as a private client for purposes of this Rule if the Federal lawyer thereafter represents an agency of another government;

as when a Federal lawyer represents a city and subsequently is employed by a Federal Agency.

Paragraphs (a)(1) and (b) do not prohibit a Federal lawyer from receiving salary or partnership income where established by prior independent agreement. They prohibit directly relating the Federal lawyer's compensation to the fee in the matter in which the Federal lawyer is disqualified.

Paragraph (a)(2) does not require that a Federal lawyer give notice to the Federal Agency at a time when premature disclosure would injure the client; a requirement for premature disclosure might preclude engagement of the Federal lawyer. Such notice is, however, required to be given as soon as practicable to give the Federal Agency a reasonable opportunity to determine if the Federal lawyer is complying with Rule 1.11 and to take appropriate action if it believes the Federal lawyer is not complying.

Paragraph (b) operates only when the Federal lawyer in question has knowledge of the information. This means actual knowledge. Paragraph (b) does not operate with respect to information that merely could be imputed to the Federal lawyer.

RULE 1.12 Former Judge or Arbitrator

(a) Except as stated in paragraph (d), a Federal lawyer shall not represent anyone in connection with a matter in which the lawyer participated personally and substantially as a judge or other adjudicative officer, arbitrator, or law clerk to such a person, unless all parties to the proceeding consent after disclosure.

(b) A Federal lawyer shall not negotiate for employment with any person who is involved as a party or as attorney for a party in a matter in which the lawyer is participating personally and substantially as a judge or other adjudicative officer, or arbitrator.

(c) If a Federal lawyer is disqualified by paragraph (a), no Federal lawyer in a firm with which the lawyer is associated may knowingly undertake or continue representation in the matter unless:

(1) The disqualified Federal lawyer is screened from any participation in the matter and is apportioned no part of the fee therefrom.

(2) Written notice is promptly given to the appropriate tribunal to enable it to ascertain compliance with the provisions of this Rule.

(d) An arbitrator selected as a partisan of a party in a multi-member arbitration panel is not prohibited from subsequently representing that party.

572

COMMENT:

This Rule generally parallels Rule 1.11. The term "personally and substantially" means that a judge who was a member of a multi-member court, and thereafter left judicial office, is not prohibited from representing a client in a matter pending in the court, so long as it is a matter in which the former judge did not participate. Likewise, a former judge's exercise of administrative responsibility in a court or judiciary office does not prevent the former judge from acting as a Federal lawyer in a matter in which the judge had previously exercised remote or incidental administrative responsibility that did not affect the merits. Compare the Comment to Rule 1.11. The term "adjudicative officer" includes such officials as hearing officers, legal advisors to administrative boards, and investigating officers.

RULE 1.13 The Federal Agency as the Client

(a) **Except when representing another client pursuant to paragraphs (e), (f) and (g), a Government lawyer represents the Federal Agency that employs the Government lawyer. Government lawyers are often formally employed by a Federal Agency but assigned to an organizational element within the Federal Agency. Unless otherwise specifically provided, the Federal Agency, not the organizational element, is ordinarily considered the client. The Federal Agency acts through its authorized officials. These officials include the heads of organizational elements within the Federal Agency. When a Government lawyer is assigned to an organizational element and designated to provide legal services and advice to the head of that organization, the client-lawyer relationship exists between the Government lawyer and the Federal agency, as represented by the head of the organization, as to matters within the scope of the official business of the organization. The head of the organization may only invoke the attorney-client privilege or the rule of confidentiality for the benefit of the Federal Agency. In so invoking, either the attorney-client privilege or attorney-client confidentiality on behalf of the Federal Agency, the head of the organization is subject to being overruled by higher agency authority.**

(b) **If a Government lawyer knows that a Government employee is acting, intending to act, or refusing to act in a matter related to the representation in a manner such that either a violation of a legal obligation to the Federal Agency or a violation of law reasonably might be imputed to the Federal Agency, the Government lawyer shall proceed as is reasonably necessary in the best interest of the Federal Agency. In determining how to proceed, the Government lawyer shall give due consideration to the seriousness of the violation and its consequences, the scope and nature of the Government lawyer's representation, the re-**

sponsibility in the Federal Agency, the apparent motivation of the person involved, the policies of the Federal Agency concerning such matters, and any other relevant considerations. Any measures taken shall be designed to minimize disruption of the Federal Agency and the risk of revealing information relating to the representation to persons outside the Federal Agency. Such measures may include, among others:

(1) Advising the person that, in the Government lawyer's opinion, the action, planned action, or refusal to act is contrary to law; advising the person of the Federal Agency's policy on the matter concerned; advising the person that his or her personal legal interests are at risk and that he or she should consult independent counsel, because there may be a conflict of interest with the Government lawyer's responsibility to the organization; and asking the person to reconsider the matter.

(2) Advising the person that a separate legal opinion on the matter be sought for presentation to appropriate authority in Federal Agency.

(3) Advising the person that the lawyer is ethically obligated to preserve the interests of the Federal Agency and, as a result, must consider discussing the matter with supervisory lawyers within the Government lawyer's office or at a higher level within the Federal Agency.

(4) Referring the matter to or seeking guidance from higher authority in the Federal Agency, including, if warranted by the seriousness of the matter, referral to the highest authority that can act on behalf of the Federal Agency.

(c) If, despite the Government lawyer's efforts in accordance with paragraph (b), the highest authority that can act concerning the matter insists upon action, or refusal to act, that is clearly a violation of law, the Government lawyer shall terminate representation with respect to the matter in question. In no event may the Government lawyer participate or assist in the illegal activity.

(d) In dealing with the Government employee, a Government lawyer shall explain the identity of the client when it is apparent that the Federal Agency's interests are adverse to those of the Government employee.

(e) A Government lawyer shall not form a client-lawyer relationship or represent a client other than the Federal Agency unless specifically assigned or authorized by competent authority.

(f) A Government lawyer representing the Federal Agency may also represent any of its Government employees subject to the provisions of paragraph (f), Rule 1.7, and other applicable authority. If the Federal Agency's consent to dual representation

574

is required by Rule 1.7, the consent shall be given by an appropriate official of the Federal Agency, other than the individual to be represented.

(g) A Government lawyer who has been duly assigned or authorized to represent an individual who is subject to disciplinary action or administrative proceedings, or to provide civil legal assistance to an individual, has, for those purposes, a lawyer-client relationship with that individual.

COMMENT:

The Comment to the ABA Model Rule acknowledges the applicability of this Rule to governmental organizations; the balance between maintaining confidentiality and assuring that wrongful official acts are prevented or rectified; and the difficulty in defining precisely the identity of the client (and prescribing the resulting obligations of such lawyers) in the government context.

Except when a Government lawyer is assigned to represent the interest of another client, the Federal Agency that employs the Government lawyer is the client. This principle is critical to the application of these Rules, since the identity of the client affects significant confidentiality and conflict issues.

Because the Federal Agency is the Government lawyer's client, the Government lawyer represents the Federal Agency acting through its duly authorized constituents. Any application of Rule 1.13 to Government lawyers must, however, take into account the differences between Federal agencies and other organizations. These exceptions include, but are not limited to, Government lawyers assigned to represent individuals under subsection (g); prosecutors who represent the Government of the United States; Government lawyers authorized to represent several Federal agencies in intragovernmental legal controversies; and counsel assigned to perform special duties, such as assignment to other Federal agencies or subagencies.

In most cases, the Federal Agency will be a discrete entity with identifiable lines of authority. Federal Agency regulations and directives provide clear benchmarks for assessing conduct. In some situations, the Government lawyer may represent a branch of Government rather than a Federal Agency. Although arguments have been made that the Government lawyer's ultimate obligation is to serve the public interest or the "government as a whole", for practical purposes, these may be unworkable ethical guidelines, particularly with regard to client control and confidentiality.

A Federal Agency may, of course, establish different client-lawyer obligations by Executive or court order, regulation, or statute. See e.g., 5 U.S.C. 2302.

Nevertheless, the conclusion that the government lawyer's client is the lawyer's employing agency does not answer every ethical question. There are special considerations that affect the ethical responsibilities of the Government lawyer. For example, the Government lawyer has a responsibility to question the conduct of agency officials more extensively than a lawyer for a private organization would in similar circumstances. Government lawyers, in many situations, are asked to represent diverse client interests. For example, Government lawyers in the Executive branch also represent other branches of Government in a number of different situations. Here it becomes especially clear that the Government attorney's responsibilities are affected by the attorney's more general obligations to the United States, as for example, when it is necessary to refuse to defend an unconstitutional statute or regulation or to resist the encroachment by one branch on another's sphere of power. The client-lawyer obligations of Government lawyers in other branches of Government raise still different considerations. For example, lawyers engaged by the Senate or the House of Representatives, by Congressional committees, or on the staffs of individual members of Congress may develop client-lawyer relationships with those bodies, committees or individuals. Yet these relationships must themselves be viewed in the context of the Government lawyer's broader obligations to the Congress as a whole and ultimately to the United States.

Relation to Other Rules

The authority and responsibility provided in paragraph (b) are concurrent with the authority and responsibility provided in other Rules. In particular, this Rule does not limit or expand the Government lawyer's responsibility under Rules 1.6, 1.8, 1.16, 3.3, or 4.1. If the Government lawyer's services are being used by an organization to further a crime or fraud by the organization, Rule 1.2(d) may be applicable.

Termination of Representation

Paragraph (c) recognizes that the Government lawyer is not always free to withdraw from representation. Specific facts will govern each case.

Clarifying the Government Lawyer's Role

When the Federal Agency's interests are adverse to those of one or more of its Government employees, the Government lawyer should advise the Government employee that the Government lawyer cannot continue to advise that person and that person may wish to obtain independent representation. Care must be taken to ensure that the individual understands that, when there is such adversity of interest, the Government lawyer can no longer provide legal advice to that person on those matters in which the person's interests are adverse, and that discussions between the Government lawyer and the individual are not confidential or privileged.

Whether such a warning should be given by the Government lawyer to any Government employee may turn on the facts of each case.

Dual Representation

Paragraph (e) recognizes that a Government lawyer may only enter into a client-lawyer relationship and represent persons when specifically authorized by a Federal Agency directive or an authorized superior. Unless authorized and assigned to represent a specific person or class of persons, the Government lawyer shall not establish a client-lawyer relationship. If a Government lawyer is uncertain as to the scope of representation authorized, the Government lawyer shall consult the supervisory lawyer. Recognition is given to the Government lawyer representing a Government employee of the Federal Agency.

Paragraph (f) recognizes that a Government lawyer may also represent a Government employee of the Federal Agency.

Paragraph (g) recognizes that the Government lawyer who is designated to represent another individual in Federal Government service against whom disciplinary or administrative proceedings have been brought, establishes a client-lawyer relationship with its privilege and professional responsibility to protect and defend the interest of the individual represented. This is also true for Federal lawyers providing legal assistance. But See Rule 1.2. Representation of members of the Federal Agency, other Government employees, and other individuals in accordance with paragraph (g) and the assumption of the traditional client-lawyer relationship with such individuals is not inconsistent with the Government lawyer's duties to the Federal Agency.

RULE 1.14 Client Under a Disability

(a) When a client's ability to make adequately considered decisions in connection with the representation is impaired, whether because of minority, mental disability, or for some other reason, the Federal lawyer shall, as far as reasonably possible, maintain a normal client-lawyer relationship with the client.

(b) A Federal lawyer may seek the appointment of a guardian or take other protective action with respect to a client, only when the Federal lawyer reasonably believes the client cannot adequately act in the client's own interest.

COMMENT:

The normal client-lawyer relationship is based on the assumption that the client, when properly advised and assisted, is capable of making decisions about important matters. When the client is a minor or suffers from a mental disorder or disability, however, maintaining the ordinary client-lawyer relationship shall not be possible in all respects. In particular, an incapacitated person may have no power to make legally binding decisions. Nevertheless, a client lacking legal competence often has the ability to understand, deliberate upon, and reach conclusions about the matters affecting the client's own well-being. Furthermore, to an increasing extent, the law recognizes intermediate degrees of competence. For example, children as young as five or six years of age, and certainly those of ten or twelve, are regarded as having opinions that are entitled to weight in legal proceedings concerning their custody. Also, some persons of advanced age can be quite capable of handling routine financial matters while needing special legal protection concerning major transactions.

Simply because a client is under a disability does not diminish the Federal lawyer's obligation to treat the client with attention and respect. If the person has no guardian or legal representative, the Federal lawyer should take action so that procedures are initiated for the appointment of a guardian by the person's relatives, civil authorities, or the Veterans Administration. Even if the person does have a legal representative, the Federal lawyer should as far as possible accord the represented person the status of client, particularly in maintaining communication.

If a legal representative already has been appointed for the client, the Federal lawyer ordinarily should look to the representative for decisions on behalf of the client. If a legal representative has not been appointed, the Federal lawyer should consider recommending such an appointment when it would serve the client's best interests.

Disclosure of the Client's Conditions

Rules of procedure in civil litigation generally provide that minors or persons suffering mental disability shall be represented by a guardian or next friend if they do not have a general guardian. Disclosure of the client's disability, however, can adversely affect the client's interests. For example, raising the question of disability could, in some circumstances, lead to proceedings for involuntary commitment or to disclosure of information that would be detrimental to a client. The Federal lawyer's position in such cases is an unavoidably difficult one. The Federal lawyer may seek guidance from an appropriate diagnostician but military law does not recognize a physician-patient privilege.

RULE 1.15 Safekeeping Property

(a) A Federal lawyer shall hold property of clients or third persons that is in the lawyer's possession in connection with a representation separate from the lawyer's own property. Funds shall be kept in a separate account maintained in the state in which the Federal lawyer's office is situated, or elsewhere with the consent of the client or third person. Other property shall be identified as belonging to the client and safeguarded appropriately. Complete records of such account funds and other property shall be kept by the lawyer and shall be preserved for a period of five years after termination of the representation.

(b) Upon receiving funds or other property in which a client or third person has an interest, a Federal lawyer shall promptly notify the client or the third person. Except as stated in this Rule or as otherwise permitted by law or by agreement with the client, the lawyer shall promptly deliver to the client or third person any funds or other property that the client or third person is entitled to receive and, upon request by the client or third person, shall promptly render full accounting regarding such property.

(c) When in the course of representation a Federal lawyer is in possession of property in which both the lawyer and another person claim interests, the property shall be kept separate by the lawyer until an accounting is made and their respective interests are severed. If a dispute arises concerning their respective interests, the portion in dispute shall be kept separate by the lawyer until the dispute is resolved.

(d) When property of a client or third party is admitted into evidence or otherwise included in the record of a proceeding, the Federal lawyer should take reasonable action to ensure its prompt return.

COMMENT:

Government lawyers normally will not hold property of clients or third persons. Should a Government lawyer find it necessary to hold such property, care must be taken to ensure the United States Government does not become responsible for any claims for the property. This rule does not authorize a Government lawyer to hold property of clients or third persons when otherwise prohibited from doing so.

A Federal lawyer should hold property of others with the care required of a professional fiduciary. Securities should be kept in safe deposit boxes, except when some other form of safekeeping is warranted by special circumstances. All property that belongs to clients or third persons should be kept separate from the Federal lawyer's business and personal property and, if money, in one or more trust accounts. Separate trust accounts may be warranted when administering estate monies or acting in a similar fiduciary capacity.

When it is necessary to use a client's property as evidence, a Federal lawyer should seek to obtain court permission to withdraw the property as an exhibit and to substitute a description or photograph after trial. If a Federal lawyer is offered contraband property, the Federal lawyer should refer to Rule 3.4 and its accompanying Comment for guidance.

Federal lawyers often receive funds from third parties from which the Federal lawyer's fee will be paid. If a risk exists that the client may divert the funds without paying the fee, the Federal lawyer is not required to remit the portion from which the fee is to be paid. A Federal lawyer shall not hold funds to coerce a client into accepting the Federal lawyer's contention, however. The disputed portion of the funds should be kept in trust and the Federal lawyer should suggest means such as arbitration for prompt resolution of the dispute. The undisputed portion of the funds shall be distributed promptly.

Third parties, such as a client's creditors, may have just claims against funds or other property in a Federal lawyer's custody. A Federal lawyer may have a duty under applicable law to protect such third-party claims against wrongful interference by the client, and accordingly may refuse to surrender the property to the client. A Federal lawyer should not unilaterally assume to arbitrate a dispute between the client and the third party, however.

The obligations of a Federal lawyer under this Rule are independent of those arising from activity other than rendering legal services. For example, a Federal lawyer who serves as an escrow agent is governed by the applicable law relating to fiduciaries even though the Federal lawyer does not render legal services in the transaction.

A Federal attorney who holds the property of others that was admitted into evidence or otherwise included in the record of a proceeding should take reasonable steps to secure the return of the property to its rightful owner or proper custodian. Where possible, copies, descriptions, or photographs should be substituted for the original item in the record.

RULE 1.16 Declining or Terminating Representation

(a) Except as stated in paragraph (c), a Federal lawyer shall not represent a client, or, once representation has commenced, shall seek to withdraw from the representation of a client, if:

(1) The representation will result in violation of these Rules of Professional Conduct or law.

(2) The Federal lawyer's physical or mental condition materially impairs the lawyer's ability to represent the client.

(3) The Federal lawyer is dismissed by the client.

(b) Except as stated in paragraph (c), a Federal lawyer may seek to withdraw from representing a client if withdrawal can be accomplished without material adverse effect on the interests of the client, or if:

(1) The client persists in a course of action involving the Federal lawyer's services that the lawyer reasonably believes is criminal or fraudulent.

(2) The client has used the Federal lawyer's services to perpetrate a crime or fraud.

(3) A client insists upon pursuing an objective that the Federal lawyer considers repugnant or imprudent.

(4) The client fails substantially to fulfill an obligation to the Federal lawyer regarding the lawyer's services and has been given reasonable warning that the Federal lawyer will seek to withdraw unless the obligation is fulfilled.

(5) The representation will result in an unreasonable financial burden on the Federal lawyer or has been rendered unreasonable by the client.

(6) Other good cause for withdrawal exists.

(c) When properly ordered to do so by a tribunal or other competent authority, a Federal lawyer shall continue representation notwithstanding good cause for terminating the representation.

(d) Upon termination of representation, a Federal lawyer shall take steps to the extent reasonably practicable to protect a client's interests, such as giving reasonable notice to the client, allowing time for employment of other counsel, surrendering papers and property to which the client is entitled, and refunding any advance payment of fees that has not been earned. The Federal lawyer may retain papers relating to the client to the extent permitted by law.

COMMENT:

A Federal lawyer should not represent a client in a matter unless it can be performed competently, promptly, without improper conflict of interest, and to completion.

Mandatory Withdrawal

A Federal lawyer ordinarily must seek to withdraw from representation if the client demands that the Federal lawyer engage in conduct that is illegal or violates these Rules of Professional Conduct or other law. The Federal lawyer is not obliged to seek to withdraw simply because the client suggests such a course of conduct; a client may make such a suggestion in the hope that a Federal lawyer will not be constrained by a professional obligation.

Continued Representation Notwithstanding Good Cause

Notwithstanding the existence of good cause for terminating representation, a Federal lawyer appointed to represent a client shall continue such representation until relieved by competent authority. Who is competent authority will differ with the circumstances. A Government lawyer representing the Federal Agency may be authorized to withdraw from the representation by the Federal Agency's chief legal official or the Federal lawyer's supervisory lawyer. Difficulty may be encountered where competent authority requires an explanation for the termination and such explanation would necessitate the revelation of confidential facts. When necessary and practicable, a Federal lawyer should seek the advice of a supervisory lawyer. The decision by one authority to continue representation does not prevent the Federal lawyer from seeking withdrawal from other competent authority.

Discharge by the Client

A client has a right to discharge a Federal lawyer with or without cause. Where future disputes about the withdrawal are anticipated, it may be advisable to prepare a written statement reciting the circumstances leading to withdrawal.

Whether a client can release appointed counsel may depend on applicable law. A client seeking to release appointed counsel must be given a full explanation of the consequences. Those consequences may include a decision by the appointing authority that appointment of successor counsel is unjustified, thus requiring the client to represent himself or herself.

If the client is mentally incompetent, the client may lack the legal capacity to discharge the Federal lawyer, and in any event, the discharge may be seriously adverse to the client's interests. See Rule 1.14.

Optional Withdrawal

A Federal lawyer may seek to withdraw from representation in some circumstances. The Federal lawyer has the option of seeking to withdraw if it can be accomplished without material adverse effect to the client's interests. Seeking to withdraw is also justified if the client persists in a course of action that the Federal lawyer reasonably believes is criminal or fraudulent, for a Federal lawyer is not required to be associated with such conduct even if the Federal lawyer does not further it. Seeking to withdraw also is permitted if the Federal lawyer's services were misused in the past, even if that would materially prejudice the client. The Federal lawyer also may seek to withdraw when the client insists on a repugnant or imprudent objective.

As the scope of a Federal lawyer's representation may be limited by the law under which the Federal lawyer's services are made available to the client, see Comment to Rule 1.2, good cause to seek withdrawal may exist when a Federal lawyer changes duty stations or duties within an office. For example, a legal assistance Federal lawyer has good cause to seek withdrawal when the Federal lawyer is reassigned within the office to duties as prosecutor. In such a circumstance, the legal assistance Federal lawyer has been granted permission to withdraw from representation of legal assistance clients by virtue of the reassignment to prosecutor duties. If a question arises as to whether a Federal lawyer has permission to withdraw from a particular representation, the Federal lawyer should consult with the supervisory lawyer who has the authority to grant permission to withdraw from the representation.

Assisting the Client upon Withdrawal

A Federal lawyer who has withdrawn from representation must take all reasonable steps to mitigate adverse consequences to the client. Such steps may include referring of the client to another Federal lawyer who is able to represent the client further. A Federal lawyer making such a referral should ensure that these Rules and any agency policy governing referral of clients is followed. If a Federal lawyer must refer a client to another Federal lawyer due to a conflict of interest, the referring Federal lawyer should be careful not to disclose confidential information relating to representation of another client.

Government Lawyers

Paragraph (c) recognizes that the Government lawyer is not always free to withdraw from representation. Competent authority may be the Government lawyer's supervisory lawyers or, in some cases, other Federal Agency officials in the Government lawyer's chain of command. Specific facts will govern each case.

Whether a Government lawyer may, under certain unusual circumstances, have a legal obligation to the Federal Agency after withdrawing or being released by the Federal Agency's highest authority is beyond the scope of these Rules.

COUNSELOR

RULE 2.1 Advisor

In representing a client, a Federal lawyer shall exercise independent professional judgment and render candid advise. In rendering advice, a Federal lawyer may refer not only to law but to other considerations, such as moral, social, and political factors, that may be relevant to the client's situation, but not in conflict with the law.

COMMENT:

Scope of Advice

A client is entitled to straightforward advice expressing the Federal lawyer's honest assessment. Legal advice often involves unpleasant facts and alternatives that a client may be reluctant to confront. In presenting advice, a Federal lawyer endeavors to sustain the client's morale and may put advice in as acceptable a form as honesty permits. Nevertheless, a Federal lawyer should not be deterred from giving candid advice by the prospect that the advice will be unpalatable to the client.

Advice couched in narrowly legal terms may be of little value to a client, especially where practical considerations, such as cost or effects

on other people, are predominant. Purely technical legal advice, therefore, can sometimes be inadequate. It is proper for a Federal lawyer to
refer to other relevant considerations in giving advice. Such considerations impinge upon most legal questions and may decisively influence
how the law will be applied.

A client may expressly or impliedly ask the Federal lawyer for
purely technical advice. When such a request is made by a client
experienced in legal matters, the Federal lawyer may accept it at face
value. When such a request is made by a client inexperienced in legal
matters, however, the Federal lawyer's responsibility as advisor may
include indicating more may be involved than strictly legal considerations.

Matters that go beyond strictly legal questions may also be in the
domain of another profession. Family matters can involve problems
within the professional competence of psychiatry, clinical psychology,
or social work; business matters can involve problems within the
competence of the accounting profession or of financial specialists.
When consultation with a professional in another field is itself something a competent Federal lawyer would recommend, the Federal
lawyer should make such a recommendation. At the same time, a
Federal lawyer's best advice often consists of recommending a course of
action in the face of conflicting recommendations of experts.

Offering Advice

When a Non–Government lawyer knows that a client proposes a
course of action that is likely to result in substantial adverse legal
consequences to the client, however, duty to the client under Rule 1.4
may require that the Non–Government lawyer act if the client's course
of action is related to the representation. A Non–Government lawyer
ordinarily has no duty to initiate investigation of a client's affairs or to
give advice the client has indicated is unwanted, but a Non–Government lawyer should initiate advice to a client when doing so appears to
be in the client's interest.

A Government lawyer has an affirmative duty to offer advice to a
Government employee of the Federal Agency that employs the Government lawyer, if the Government lawyer knows that the Government
employee is engaging in or about to engage in a course of conduct that
would be a violation of law or that may result in substantial adverse
legal consequences to the Federal Agency. A Government lawyer has
the duty to provide the advice, even if the advice is unwanted.

RULE 2.2 Intermediary

(a) A Federal lawyer may act as an intermediary between
individuals if:

(1) The Federal lawyer consults with each client concerning the implications of common representation, including the

advantages and risks involved and the effect on the attorney-client confidentiality, and obtains each client's consent to the common representation;

(2) The Federal lawyer reasonably believes that the matter can be resolved on terms compatible with each client's best interest, that each client will be able to make adequately informed decisions in the matter, and that there is little risk of material prejudice to the interests of any of the clients if the contemplated resolution is unsuccessful; and

(3) The Federal lawyer reasonably believes that the common representation can be undertaken impartially and without improper effect on other responsibilities the lawyer has to any of the clients.

(b) While acting as an intermediary, the Federal lawyer shall consult with each client concerning the decisions to be made and the considerations relevant in making them, so each client can make adequately informed decisions.

(c) A Federal lawyer shall withdraw as an intermediary if any of the clients so requests or if any of the conditions stated in paragraph (a) is no longer satisfied. Upon withdrawal, the lawyer shall not represent any of the clients in the matter that was the subject of the common representation unless each client consents.

COMMENT:

A Federal lawyer acts as an intermediary under this Rule when the Federal lawyer represents two or more clients with potentially conflicting interests. Because confusion can arise as to the Federal lawyer's role when each client is not separately represented, it is important that the Federal lawyer make clear the relationship.

A Federal lawyer acts as an intermediary in seeking to establish or adjust a relationship between clients on an amicable and mutually advantageous basis. The Federal lawyer seeks to resolve potentially conflicting interests by developing the clients' mutual interests. The alternative can be that each client may have to obtain separate representation, with the possibility in some situations of incurring additional cost, complications, or even litigation. Given these and other relevant factors, all the clients may prefer the Federal lawyer to act as intermediary.

In considering whether to act as an intermediary, a Federal lawyer should remember that if the common representation fails, the result can be additional cost, embarrassment, and recrimination. In some situations the risk of failure is so great that common representation is plainly impossible. For example, a Federal lawyer cannot undertake mediation among clients when contentious litigation is imminent or when contentious negotiations are contemplated. More generally, if the relationship between the clients has already assumed definite antagonism, the possibility that the clients' interests can be adjusted by common representation ordinarily is not very good.

The appropriateness of intermediation can depend on its form. One form may be appropriate in circumstances in which another would not. Other relevant factors include whether the Federal lawyer subsequently will represent either client on a continuing basis and whether the situation involves creating or terminating a relationship between the clients.

Confidentiality and Privilege

A particularly important factor in determining the appropriateness of common representation is the effect on attorney-client confidentiality of information relating to the common representation. See Rules 1.4 and 1.6. As the Federal lawyer represents neither individual in the intermediation there is neither attorney-client privilege nor attorney-client confidentiality.

Since the Federal lawyer is required to be impartial between commonly represented clients, intermediation is improper when that impartiality cannot be maintained. For example, a Federal lawyer who has represented one of the clients for a long period and in a variety of matters might have difficulty being impartial between that client and one to whom the Federal lawyer has only recently been introduced.

Consultation

In acting as an intermediary between clients, the Federal lawyer is required to consult with the clients on the implications of doing so, and proceed only upon consent based on such a consultation. The consultation should make clear that the Federal lawyer's role is not that of partisanship normally expected in other circumstances.

Where the Federal lawyer is an intermediary, the clients ordinarily must assume greater responsibility for decisions than when each client is represented by a Federal lawyer.

Withdrawal

Common representation does not diminish the rights of each client in the client-lawyer relationship. Each client has the right to loyal and diligent representation. Any of the clients may discharge the Federal lawyer as stated in Rule 1.16 and gain the protection of Rule 1.9 concerning obligations to former clients.

RULE 2.3 Evaluation for Use by Third Persons

(a) A Federal lawyer may undertake an evaluation of a matter affecting a client for the use of someone other than the client if:

(1) The Federal lawyer reasonably believes that making the evaluation is compatible with other aspects of the lawyer's relationship with the client, and

(2) The client consents after sufficient consultation.

(b) Except when a disclosure is required in connection with a report of an evaluation, information relating to the evaluation is otherwise protected by Rule 1.6.

COMMENT:

Definition

An evaluation may be performed at the client's direction but for the primary purpose of establishing information for the benefit of third parties; for example, a Government lawyer is asked to prepare a brief setting forth the Federal Agency's position on a situation for use by another Federal Agency or the Congress.

A Government lawyer may be called upon to give a formal opinion on the legality of action contemplated by the Federal Agency. In making such an evaluation, the Government lawyer acts at the behest of the Federal Agency as the client, but for the purpose of establishing the limits of the Federal Agency's authorized activity. Such an opinion may be confidential legal advice, depending on whether the Federal Agency intended it to be confidential.

If a Federal lawyer believes that making an evaluation is incompatible with other aspects of the Federal lawyer's relationship with the client, the Federal lawyer should consult with a supervisory lawyer for advice and guidance.

A legal evaluation should be distinguished from an investigation of a person with whom the Federal lawyer does not have a Federal lawyer-client relationship. For example, a Government lawyer assigned to conduct an investigation of a traffic accident between a private citizen and a Government employee in accordance with applicable Federal Agency regulations and directives does not have a client-lawyer relationship with the Government employee. So also, an investigation into a person's affairs by a Government lawyer is not an evaluation as that term is used in this rule.

The question is whether the Government lawyer represents the person whose affairs are being examined. When the Government lawyer does represent the person, the general rules concerning loyalty to client and preservation of confidences apply. For this reason, the client must be identified. The identity of the client should be made clear not only to the person under examination, but also to others to whom the results are to be made available.

Duty to Third Person

When the evaluation is intended for the information or use of a third person, a legal duty to that person may or shall not arise. That legal question is beyond the scope of this rule. However, since such an evaluation involves a departure from the normal client-lawyer relationship, careful analysis of the situation is required. The Federal lawyer must be satisfied as a matter of professional judgment that making the evaluation is compatible with other functions undertaken on behalf of the client. For example, if the Federal lawyer is acting as advocate in defending the client against charges of fraud, it would normally be incompatible with that responsibility for the Federal lawyer to perform an evaluation for others concerning the same or a related transaction. Assuming no such impediment is apparent, however, the Federal lawyer should advise the client of the implications of the evaluation, particularly the Federal lawyer's responsibilities to third persons and the duty to disseminate the findings.

ADVOCATE

RULE 3.1 Meritorious Claims and Contentions

A Federal lawyer shall not bring or defend a proceeding, or assert or controvert an issue therein, unless there is a basis for doing so that is not frivolous. This basis may include a good faith argument for extending, modifying, or reversing existing law. A Federal lawyer for the defendant in a criminal proceeding, or the respondent in a proceeding that could result in incarceration or other adverse action, may nevertheless so defend the proceeding as to require that every element of the case be established.

COMMENT:

The advocate has a duty to use legal procedure for the fullest benefit of the client's cause, but also a duty not to abuse legal procedure. The law, both procedural and substantive, establishes the limits within which an advocate may proceed. Nevertheless, the law is not always clear and is never static. Accordingly, in determining the proper scope of advocacy, account must be taken of the law's ambiguities and potential for change.

The filing of a cause of action, defense, or similar act taken on behalf of a client is not frivolous merely because the facts have not first been fully substantiated or because the Federal lawyer expects vital evidence to develop only through discovery. Such action is not frivolous even though the Federal lawyer believes the client's position ultimately will not prevail. Merely because an issue has never been raised before, or because it may have been raised and resolved under different circumstances, does not make revisiting the issue frivolous. The action is frivolous, however, if the client desires to have the action taken solely for the purpose of harassing or maliciously injuring a person, or if the Federal lawyer is unable either to make a good faith argument on the merits of the action taken or to support the action taken by a good faith argument for an extending, modifying, or reversing of existing law.

A Federal lawyer does not violate this Rule by raising issues in good faith compliance with court precedent.

RULE 3.2 Expediting Litigation

A Federal lawyer shall make reasonable efforts to expedite litigation and other proceedings consistent with the interests of the client and the lawyer's responsibilities to the tribunal to avoid unwarranted delay.

COMMENT:

Dilatory practices bring the administration of justice into disrepute. The legitimate interests of the client are rarely well-served by such tactics. Delay exacts a toll upon a litigant in uncertainty, frustration, and apprehension. Expediting litigation, in contrast, often can directly benefit the client's interest in obtaining bargaining concessions and in obtaining an early resolution of the matter. Delay should not be indulged merely for the convenience of the advocates, or for the purpose of frustrating an opposing party's attempt to obtain rightful redress or repose. It is not a justification that similar conduct is often tolerated by the bench and bar. The question is whether a comptent Federal lawyer acting in good faith would regard the course of action as having some substantial purpose other than delay. Realizing financial or other benefit from otherwise improper delay in litigation is not a legitimate interest of the client.

RULE 3.3 Candor Toward the Tribunal

(a) A Federal lawyer shall not knowingly:

(1) Make a false statement of material fact or law to a tribunal.

(2) Fail to disclose a material fact to a tribunal when disclosure is necessary to avoid assisting a criminal or fraudulent act by the client.

(3) Fail to disclose to the tribunal legal authority in the controlling jurisdiction known to the Federal lawyer to be directly adverse to the position of the client and not disclosed by opposing counsel.

589

(4) Offer evidence that the lawyer knows to be false. If a Federal lawyer has offered material evidence and comes to know of its falsity, the lawyer shall take reasonable remedial measures.

(5) Disobey an obligation or order imposed by a tribunal, unless done openly before the tribunal in a good faith assertion that no valid obligation or order should exist.

(b) The duties stated in paragraph (a) continue to the conclusion of the proceeding, and apply even if compliance requires disclosure of information otherwise protected by Rule 1.6.

(c) A Federal lawyer may refuse to offer evidence that the lawyer reasonably believes to be false.

(d) In an ex parte proceeding, a Federal lawyer shall disclose to the tribunal all material facts known to the lawyer that are reasonably necessary to enable the tribunal to make an informed decision, whether or not the facts are adverse.

COMMENT:

The advocate's task is to present the client's case with persuasive force. Performance of that duty while maintaining confidences of the client is qualified by the advocate's duty of candor to the tribunal. An advocate does not vouch for the evidence submitted in a cause, however. The tribunal is responsible for assessing its probative value.

Relationship with Rule 1.6

The conflicting duties to reveal fraud and to preserve confidences have existed side-by-side for some time. A Federal lawyer should not be confronted with the necessity of either breaching the client's privilege or breaching a disciplinary Rule. This Rule recognizes that the policies underlying Rule 1.6 take precedence over Rule 3.3 in all but the most serious cases. When Rule 1.6 either permits or mandates disclosure of otherwise confidential information, Rule 3.3 requires that the Federal lawyer reveal criminal or fraudulent acts by the client. When Rule 1.6 requires confidentiality of information, Rule 3.3 does not permit the Federal lawyer to disclose such information to a tribunal, even if the disclosure would be necessary to avoid assisting a criminal or fraudulent act by the client. A Federal lawyer who follows the guidance in the Perjury by a Criminal Client section of this comment is not assisting a criminal or fraudulent act by a client for purposes of these Rules. See Rule 1.2(d) and Comment.

Representations by a Federal Lawyer

An advocate is responsible for pleadings and other documents prepared for litigation, but is usually not required to have personal knowledge of matters asserted therein, for litigation documents ordinarily present assertions by the client, or by someone on the client's behalf, not assertions by the Federal lawyer. Compare Rule 3.1. An assertion purporting to be on the Federal lawyer's own knowledge (as in an affidavit by the Federal lawyer or in a statement in open court), however, may properly be made only when the Federal lawyer knows the assertion is true or believes it to be true on the basis of a reasonably diligent inquiry. Circumstances can arise in which failure to make a disclosure is the equivalent of an affirmative misrepresentation. The obligation prescribed in Rule 1.2(d) not to counsel a client to commit or to assist the client in committing a fraud applies in litigation. Regarding compliance with this Rule, see Rule 11 of the Federal Rules of Civil Procedure. Regarding compliance with Rule 1.2(d), see the Comment to that Rule. See also the Comment to Rule 8.4(b).

Misleading Legal Argument

Legal argument based on a knowingly false representation of law constitutes dishonesty toward the tribunal. A Federal lawyer is not required to make a disinterested exposition of the law, but must recognize the existence of pertinent legal authorities. Furthermore, as stated in paragraph (a)(3), an advocate has a duty to disclose directly adverse authority in the controlling jurisdiction that has not been disclosed by the opposing party. The underlying concept is that legal argument is a discussion seeking to determine the legal premises properly applicable to the case. A Federal lawyer also should disclose to the tribunal legal authority from a non-controlling jurisdiction, directly adverse to the position of the client and not disclosed by opposing counsel, if the issue being litigated has not been decided by a controlling jurisdiction and the judge would reasonably consider it important to resolving the issue.

False Evidence

When evidence a Federal lawyer knows to be false is provided by a person who is not the client, the Federal lawyer must refuse to offer it regardless of the client's wishes.

When false evidence is offered by the client, however, a conflict may arise between the Federal lawyer's duty to keep revelations of the client confidential and the duty of candor to the tribunal. Upon discovering that material evidence is false, the Federal lawyer should try to persuade the client not to offer it. If the client has already offered the false evidence, the Federal lawyer should try to persuade the client to withdraw it.

If the client cannot be persuaded to withdraw the already offered false evidence, the Federal lawyer generally must disclose the client's deception to the tribunal or to the other party. This disclosure may result in grave consequences to the client, including not only a sense of betrayal, but also loss of the case and perhaps prosecution for perjury. The alternative, however, would be the Federal lawyer's participation in deceiving the tribunal, which would subvert the truth-finding process the adversary system is designed to implement. See Rule 1.2(d). Consequently, in seeking to persuade the client to withdraw false evidence, the Federal lawyer's intention to disclose the falsity if the client does not withdraw it must be made clear. Otherwise the client could simply reject the advice and insist upon the Federal lawyer's silence, thus effectively coercing the Federal lawyer into becoming a party to a fraud on the tribunal.

Perjury by a Criminal Defendant

A criminal case where the defendant insists on offering testimony the Federal lawyer knows is perjurious is the most difficult situation a Federal lawyer faces. The Federal lawyer's effort to rectify the situation can increase the likelihood of the client's being convicted, as well as, opening the possibility of a prosecution for perjury. On the other hand, if the Federal lawyer does not exercise control over the proof, the Federal lawyer participates, although passively, in deception of the tribunal.

If the defendant has admitted to the Federal lawyer facts that establish guilt and the Federal lawyer's independent investigation establishes the truth of the admissions, but the defendant insists on exercising the right to testify, the Federal lawyer must advise the client against taking the witness stand to testify falsely. If before trial the defendant insists on testifying falsely, the Federal lawyer shall seek to withdraw from representation. See Rule 1.16. If that is not permitted or if the situation arises during the trial or other proceedings and the defendant insists upon testifying falsely, it is unprofessional conduct for the Federal lawyer to lend aid to the client in presenting perjured testimony.

A criminal defendant has a right to the assistance of an advocate, a right to testify, and a right to communicate confidentially with counsel. A defendant does not have a right to the assistance of counsel in committing perjury, and an advocate has an obligation, not only in professional ethics but under the law, to avoid implication in the commission of perjury or other falsification of evidence. See Rule 1.2(d).

Remedial Measures

If perjured testimony or false evidence has been offered, the advocate's proper course ordinarily is to remonstrate with the client confidentially. If that effort fails, the advocate should seek to withdraw if that will remedy the situation. If withdrawal will not remedy the situation or is impossible, the advocate should make disclosure to the tribunal, subject to Rule 1.6.

Duration of Obligation

A practical time limit on the obligation to rectify the presentation of false evidence has to be established. The conclusion of the proceeding is a reasonably definite point for the termination of this obligation.

Refusing to Offer Proof Believed to be False

Generally speaking, a Federal lawyer has authority to refuse to offer testimony or other proof the Federal lawyer believes is untrustworthy. Offering such proof may reflect adversely on the Federal lawyer's ability to discriminate in the quality of evidence and thus impair the Federal lawyer's effectiveness as an advocate.

Ex Parte Proceedings

Ordinarily, an advocate has the limited responsibility of presenting one side of the matters that a tribunal should consider in reaching a decision; the conflicting position is expected to be presented by the opposing party. In an ex parte proceeding, however, such as in application for a temporary restraining order, there is no balance of presentation by opposing advocates. The object of an ex parte proceeding is, nevertheless, to yield a substantially just result. The judge, magistrate, or other official has an affirmative responsibility to accord the absent party just consideration. The Federal lawyer for the represented party has the correlative duty to disclose material facts known to the Federal lawyer and reasonably believed to be necessary to an informed decision.

RULE 3.4 Fairness to Opposing Party and Counsel

A Federal lawyer shall not:

(a) Unlawfully obstruct another party's access to evidence or unlawfully alter, destroy, or conceal a document or other material having potential evidentiary value. A Federal lawyer shall not counsel or assist another person to do any such act.

(b) Falsify evidence, counsel, or assist a witness to testify falsely, or offer an inducement to a witness that is prohibited by law.

(c) Knowingly disobey an obligation to an opposing party and counsel under the rules of a tribunal, except for an open refusal based on an assertion that no valid obligation exists.

(d) In pretrial procedure, make a frivolous discovery request or fail to make reasonably diligent efforts to comply with a legally proper discovery request by an opposing party.

(e) In trial, allude to any matter that the lawyer does not reasonably believe is relevant or that will not be supported by admissible evidence, assert personal knowledge of facts in issue except when testifying as a witness, or state a personal opinion as to the justness of a cause, the credibility of a witness, the culpability of a civil litigant, or the guilt or innocence of a defendant.

(f) Request a person other than a client to refrain from voluntarily giving relevant information to another party unless:

(1) The person is a relative or an employee or other agent of a client; and

(2) The Federal lawyer reasonably believes the person's interests will not be adversely affected by refraining from giving such information.

COMMENT:

The procedure of the adversary system contemplates that the evidence in a case is to be marshalled competitively by the contending parties. Fair competition in the adversary system is secured by prohibitions against destruction or concealment of evidence, improperly influencing witnesses, obstructive tactics in discovery procedure, and the like.

Documents and other items of evidence are often essential to establish a claim or defense. Subject to evidentiary privileges, the right of an opposing party, including the Government, to obtain evidence through discovery or subpoena is an important procedural right. The exercise of that right can be frustrated if relevant material is altered, concealed, or destroyed. Most criminal codes, including the Uniform Code of Military Justice, proscribe the destruction of material in an attempt to preclude its availability in a pending proceeding or reasonably foreseeable proceeding. Falsifying evidence is also a criminal offense. Paragraph (a) applies to evidentiary material generally, including computerized information.

A Federal lawyer who receives (i.e., has in the Federal lawyer's possession) an item of physical evidence implicating the client in criminal conduct shall disclose the location of or shall deliver that item to proper authorities when required by law or court order. Thus, if a Federal lawyer receives contraband, the Federal lawyer has no legal right to possess it and must always surrender it to lawful authorities. If a Federal lawyer receives stolen property, the Federal lawyer must surrender it to the owner or lawful authority to avoid violating the law. The appropriate disposition of such physical evidence is a proper subject to discuss confidentially with a supervisory lawyer. When a client informs the Federal lawyer about the existence of material having potential evidentiary value adverse to the client or when the client presents, but does not relinquish possession of such material to the Federal lawyer, the Federal lawyer should inform the client of the Federal lawyer's legal and ethical obligations regarding evidence. Frequently, the best course for the Federal lawyer is to refrain from either taking possession of such material or advising the client as to what course of action should be taken regarding it. See Rules 1.6 and 1.7. If a Federal lawyer discloses the location of or delivers an item of physical evidence to proper authorities, it should be done in the way best designed to protect the client's interest. The Federal lawyer should consider methods of return or disclosure that best protect (a) the client's identity; (b) the client's words concerning the item; (c) other confidential information; and (d) the client's privilege against self-incrimination.

Neither a Federal lawyer when interviewing victims or witnesses not represented by counsel nor another person appointed by a Federal lawyer to act in such capacity unlawfully obstructs another party's access to evidence or to material having potential evidentiary value by performing those duties in accordance with Federal Agency regulations or directives. For example, a Federal lawyer, upon the request of a victim or witness, may require prosecutor and defense counsel to coordinate with another person for interviews of a victim of or witness to the crime that forms the basis of a court-martial.

With regard to paragraph (b), it is not improper to pay a witness expenses or to compensate an expert witness on terms permitted by law. The common law rule in most jurisdictions is that it is improper to pay an occurrence witness any fee for testifying and that it is improper to pay an expert witness a contingent fee.

With regard to paragraph (c), a "rule of a tribunal" includes Rule 6(e) of the Federal Rules of Criminal Procedure governing discussion of grand jury testimony.

Paragraph (f) permits a Federal lawyer to advise relatives, employees, or other agents of a client to refrain from giving information to another party, because such persons may identify their interests with those of the client. See also Rule 4.2.

RULE 3.5 Impartiality and Decorum of the Tribunal

A Federal lawyer shall not:

(a) Seek to influence a tribunal, a member of a tribunal, a prospective member of a tribunal, or other official by means prohibited by law.

(b) Communicate ex parte with such a person about the matter except as permitted by law.

(c) Engage in conduct intended to disrupt a tribunal.

COMMENT:

Many forms of improper influence upon a tribunal are proscribed by law. The ABA Model Code of Judicial Conduct sets standards for the conduct of judges and other members of a tribunal. An advocate should be familiar with that Code, in order to avoid contributing to a violation by a tribunal.

The advocate's function is to present evidence and argument so that the cause may be decided according to law. Refraining from abusive or obstreperous conduct is a corollary of the advocate's right to speak on behalf of litigants. A Federal lawyer may stand firm against abuse by a judge but should avoid reciprocation; the judge's default is no justification for similar dereliction by an advocate. An advocate can present the cause, protect the record for subsequent review, and preserve professional integrity no less effectively by patient firmness than by belligerence or theatrics.

Because many tribunals are permanent or semi-permanent bodies, it may be impossible for Federal lawyers in the same community to avoid all communications with the members of a tribunal in the course of normal business, social, and professional activities. What is forbidden is any discussion with the individuals regarding a particular case or issue that has been or is likely to be referred to that tribunal for ultimate decision. Any Federal attorney who inadvertently engages in any conversations concerning a prohibitive subject should immediately report the incident to his supervisory lawyer, opposing counsel, and to the tribunal.

However, a Federal lawyer should always strive to avoid contact with a member of a tribunal when such contact could be perceived by an opposing party or member of the public to be an attempt to improperly influence the tribunal.

RULE 3.6 Tribunal Publicity

(a) **A Federal lawyer shall not make an extrajudicial statement that a reasonable person would expect to be disseminated by means of public communication if the lawyer knows or reasonably should know that it will have a substantial likelihood of materially prejudicing an adjudicative proceeding or an official review process thereof.**

(b) **A statement referred to in paragraph (a) ordinarily is likely to have such an effect when it refers to a civil matter triable to a jury, a criminal matter, any other proceeding that could result in incarceration, or other adverse action and that statement relates to:**

(1) **The character, credibility, reputation, or criminal record of a party, suspect in a criminal investigation, or witness, the identity of a witness, or the expected testimony of a party or witness.**

(2) **The possibility of a plea of guilty to the offense or the existence or contents of any confession, admission, or statement given by a defendant or suspect, or that person's refusal or failure to make a statement.**

(3) The performance or results of any examination or test, the refusal or failure of a person to submit to an examination or test, or the identity or nature of physical evidence expected to be presented.

(4) Any opinion as to the guilt or innocence of a defendant or suspect in an original case or proceeding that could result in incarceration or other adverse action.

(5) Information the Federal lawyer knows or reasonably should know is likely to be inadmissible as evidence in a trial and that would, if disclosed, create a substantial risk of prejudicing an impartial trial.

(6) A defendant's having been charged with a crime, unless included therein, is a statement explaining that the charge is merely an accusation and the defendant is presumed innocent until and unless proven guilty.

(c) Notwithstanding paragraphs (a) and (b)(1–5), a Federal lawyer involved in the investigation or litigation of a matter may state without elaboration:

(1) The general nature of the claim or defense.

(2) Information contained in a public record.

(3) That an investigation of the matter is in progress, including the general scope of the investigation, the offense or claim or defense involved and, except when prohibited by law, the identity of the persons involved.

(4) The scheduling or result of any step in litigation.

(5) A request for assistance in obtaining evidence and information necessary in litigation.

(6) A warning of danger concerning the behavior of the person involved, when there is reason to believe the likelihood of substantial harm to an individual or to the public interest exists.

(7) In a criminal case:

(i) The identity, place of business, occupation, and family status of the defendant.

(ii) If the defendant has not been apprehended, information necessary to aid in apprehension of that person.

(iii) The fact, time, and place of apprehension.

(iv) The identity of investigating and apprehending officers or agencies and the length of the investigation.

(d) The protection and release of information in matters pertaining to the Government shall be consistent with law.

COMMENT:

It is difficult to strike a balance between protecting the right to a fair trial and safeguarding the right of free expression. Preserving the right to a fair trial necessarily entails some curtailment of the information that may be disseminated about a party prior to trial, particularly when trial by jury or members is involved. If there were no such limits, the result would be the practical nullification of the protective effect of the rules of forensic decorum and the exclusionary rules of evidence. On the other hand, there are vital social interests served by the free dissemination of information about events having legal consequences and about legal proceedings themselves. The public has a right to know about threats to its safety and measures aimed at assuring its security. It also has a legitimate interest in the conduct of judicial proceedings, particularly in matters of general public concern. Furthermore, the subject matter of legal proceedings is often of direct significance in debate and deliberation over questions of public policy.

No body of rules can simultaneously satisfy all interests of fair trial and all those of free expression. Special rules of confidentiality may validly govern proceedings involving classified material, juveniles, domestic relations, and mental disability proceedings, and perhaps other types of proceedings. Rule 3.4(c) requires compliance with such Rules.

Special rules of confidentiality may validly govern proceedings involving classified material, juveniles, domestic relations and mental disability proceedings, and perhaps other types of proceedings. Rule 3.4(c) requires compliance with such Rules.

Rule 3.6(d) acknowledges that a Government lawyer's release of information is governed not only by Rule 3.6 but also by law. Prior to releasing any information, a Government lawyer should consult the appropriate statute, directive, regulation, or policy guideline.

RULE 3.7   Federal Lawyer as Witness

(a) A Federal lawyer shall not act as advocate at a trial in which the lawyer is likely to be a necessary witness except when:

(1) The testimony relates to an uncontested issue.

(2) The testimony relates to the nature, value, and quality of legal services rendered in the case.

(3) Disqualification of the Federal lawyer would work substantial hardship on the client.

(b) A Federal lawyer may act as advocate in a matter in which another lawyer in the Federal lawyer's agency or firm is likely to be called as a witness unless precluded from doing so by Rule 1.7 or Rule 1.9.

COMMENT:

Combining the roles of advocate and witness can prejudice the opposing party and involve a conflict of interest between the Federal lawyer and client.

The opposing party has a proper objection when the combination of roles may prejudice that party's rights in the litigation. A witness is required to testify on the basis of personal knowledge, while an advocate is expected to explain and comment on evidence given by others. It shall not be clear whether a statement by an advocate-witness should be taken as proof or as an analysis of the proof.

Rule 3.7(a)(1) recognizes that if the testimony will be uncontested, the ambiguities in the dual role are purely theoretical. Rule 3.7(a)(2) recognizes that, if the testimony concerns the value and quality of legal services rendered in the action in which the testimony is offered, permitting the Federal lawyer to testify avoids the need for a second trial with new counsel to resolve that issue. Moreover, in such a situation the judge has firsthand knowledge of the matter in issue; hence, there is less dependence on the adversary process to test the credibility of the testimony.

Apart from these two exceptions, Rule 3.7(a)(3) recognizes that a balancing is required between the interests of the client and those of the opposing party. Whether the opposing party is likely to suffer prejudice depends on the nature of the case, the importance and probable tenor of the Federal lawyer's testimony, and the probability that the Federal lawyer's testimony will conflict with that of other witnesses. Even if there is risk of such prejudice, in determining whether the Federal lawyer should be disqualified, due regard must be given to the effect of disqualification on the Federal lawyer's client. That one or both parties could reasonably have foreseen the probability that the Federal lawyer would be a witness is relevant to this determination.

Whether the combination of roles involves an improper conflict of interest with respect to the client is determined by Rule 1.7 or 1.9. For example, if substantial conflict is likely between the testimony of the client and that of the Federal lawyer the representation is improper. The problem can arise whether the Federal lawyer is called as a witness on behalf of the client or is called by the opposing party. Determining whether such a conflict exists is primarily the responsibility of the Federal lawyer involved. See Comment to Rule 1.7.

RULE 3.8 Special Responsibilities of a Prosecutor

A prosecutor shall:

(a) **Refrain from prosecuting a charge that the prosecutor knows is not supported by probable cause, or if not authorized to decline the prosecution of a charge to recommend to the appro-**

priate authority that any charge not warranted by the evidence be withdrawn;

(b) Make reasonable efforts to ensure that the defendant has been advised of the right to and the procedure for obtaining counsel and has been given reasonable opportunity to obtain counsel;

(c) Not seek to obtain from an unrepresented defendant a waiver of important pretrial rights;

(d) Make timely disclosure to the defense of all evidence or information known to the Federal lawyer that tends to negate the guilt of the defendant or mitigates the offense, and, in connection with sentencing, disclose to the defense all unprivileged mitigating information known to the Federal lawyer, except when the Federal lawyer is relieved of this responsibility by a protective order or regulation; and

(e) Exercise reasonable care to prevent investigators, law enforcement personnel, employees, or other persons assisting or associated with the Federal lawyer in a criminal case from making extrajudicial statements that the prosecutor would be prohibited from making under Rule 3.6.

(f) Respect the attorney-client privilege of defendants and not diminish the privilege through investigative or judicial processes.

COMMENT:

A prosecutor is not simply an advocate but is responsible for seeing that the defendant is accorded procedural justice and that guilt is decided upon the basis of sufficient evidence. See also Rule 3.3(d), governing ex parte proceedings. Applicable law may require other measures by the prosecutor and knowing disregard of those obligations or a systematic abuse of prosecutorial discretion could constitute a violation of Rule 8.4.

The exception in Rule 3.8(d) recognizes that a prosecutor may seek an appropriate protective order from the tribunal if disclosures of information to the defense could result in substantial harm to an individual or organization or to the public interest. This exception also recognizes that applicable regulations may proscribe the disclosure of certain information without proper authorization.

A prosecutor may comply with Rule 3.8(e) in a number of ways. These include personally informing others of the Federal lawyer's obligations under Rule 3.6, promulgating guidelines, conducting training of law enforcement personnel, and appropriately supervising the activities of personnel assisting the prosecutor.

RULE 3.9 Advocate in Nonadjudicative Proceedings

A Federal lawyer representing a client before a legislative or administrative tribunal in a nonadjudicative proceeding shall disclose that the appearance is in a representative capacity and shall conform to the provisions of Rules 3.3(a)–(c), 3.4(a)–(c), and 3.5.

COMMENT:

In representation before bodies such as legislatures, municipal councils, and executive and administrative agencies acting in a rulemaking or policy-making capacity, Federal lawyers present facts, formulate issues, and advance argument in the matters under consideration. The decision-making body, like a court, should be able to rely on the integrity of the submissions made it. A Federal lawyer appearing before such a body should deal with the tribunal honestly and in conformity with applicable rules of procedure.

Federal lawyers have no exclusive right to appear before nonadjudicative bodies. The requirements of this Rule, therefore, may subject Federal lawyers to regulations inapplicable to advocates who are not lawyers. Legislatures and administrative agencies, however, have a right to expect Federal lawyers to deal with them in the same manner as Federal lawyers deal with courts.

TRANSACTIONS WITH PERSONS OTHER THAN CLIENTS

RULE 4.1 Truthfulness in Statements to Others

In the course of representing a client a Federal lawyer shall not knowingly:

(a) Make a false statement of material fact or law to a third person.

(b) Fail to disclose a material fact to a third person when disclosure is necessary to avoid assisting a criminal or fraudulent act by a client, unless disclosure is prohibited by Rule 1.6.

COMMENT:

Misrepresentation

A Federal lawyer is required to be truthful when dealing with others on a client's behalf, but generally has no affirmative duty to inform an opposing party of relevant facts. A misrepresentation can occur if the Federal lawyer incorporates or affirms statements of another person the Federal lawyer knows to be false. Misrepresentations also can occur by failing to act.

Statements of Fact

This Rule refers to statements of fact. Whether a particular statement should be regarded as one of fact depends on the circumstances. Under generally accepted conventions in negotiation, certain types of statements ordinarily are not taken as statements of material fact. Estimates of price or value are placed in this category.

Fraud by a Client

Paragraph (b) recognizes that substantive law may require a Federal lawyer to disclose certain information to avoid being deemed to have assisted the client's crime or fraud. The requirement of disclosure created by this paragraph, however, is subject to the obligations created by Rule 1.6.

RULE 4.2 Communication With Persons Represented by Counsel

(a) In representing a client, a Federal lawyer shall not communicate about the subject of the representation with a party the lawyer knows to be represented by another lawyer in the matter, unless the Federal lawyer has the consent of the other lawyer; in a criminal matter, the individual initiates the communication with the Government lawyer and voluntarily and knowingly waives the right to counsel for the purposes of that communication; or the Federal lawyer otherwise is authorized by law to do so.

(b) This Rule does not prohibit communications by a Non-Government lawyer with Federal Agency officials who have the authority to resolve a matter affecting the lawyer's client, whether or not the lawyer's communications relate to matters that are the subject of the representation, provided that the lawyer discloses the lawyer's identity; the fact that the lawyer represents a client in a matter involving the official's Federal Agency; and that the matter is being handled for the Federal Agency by a Government lawyer.

COMMENT:

This Rule does not prohibit communication with a party, or an employee or agent of a party, concerning matters outside the representation. For example, the existence of a controversy between a Federal Agency and private party does not prohibit a Federal lawyer from either party from communicating with nonlawyer representatives of the other regarding a separate matter. Also, parties to a matter may communicate directly with each other and a Federal lawyer having independent justification for communicating with the other party is permitted to do so. Communications authorized by law include, for example, the right of a party to a controversy with a Federal Agency to speak with Federal Agency officials about the matter.

In the case of an organization, other than a Federal Agency, this Rule prohibits communications by a lawyer for one party concerning the matter in representation with individuals that have a managerial responsibility on behalf of the organization, and with any other person whose act or omission in connection with that matter may be imputed to the organization for purposes of civil or criminal liability or whose statement may constitute an admission on the part of the organization. If an agent or employee of the organization is represented in the matter by his or her own counsel, the consent by that counsel to a communication will be sufficient for purposes of this Rule. Compare Rule 3.4(f).

Paragraph (b) permits communications with those in government having the authority to resolve matters without the prior consent of the lawyer representing the government in such cases. A non-government lawyer making such a communication without the prior consent of the lawyer representing the government must make certain disclosures. If known, the lawyer should advise the Federal Agency official of the name of the Government lawyer handling the matter. This paragraph does not permit a lawyer to bypass counsel representing the Federal Agency on every issue which may arise in the course of disputes with the Federal Agency. It is intended to provide lawyers access to decisionmakers in government with respect to genuine grievances and not intended to provide direct access on routine disputes or routine aspects of the resolution of disputes.

This Rule also covers any person, even if not a party to a formal proceeding, who is represented by counsel concerning the matter in question.

In a criminal case there may be times when communications between a defendant and a Federal Agency without notice to defense counsel is in the interest of the defendant. Some communications will serve to protect the defendant and to identify sham representations. For example, in certain criminal enterprises, such as organized crime or drug rings, a defendant may wish to cooperate with a Federal Agency, but the counsel may also be the counsel of others involved in the enterprise. To ensure that in such instances there is no abuse, this rule would permit communications by the defendant with the Government lawyer, as long as the defendant voluntarily and knowingly waives the right to counsel.

RULE 4.3   Dealing With Unrepresented Persons

In dealing on behalf of a client with a person who is not represented by counsel, a Federal lawyer shall not state or imply that the lawyer is disinterested. When the Federal lawyer knows or reasonably should know that the unrepresented person misunderstands the lawyer's role in the matter, the lawyer shall make reasonable efforts to correct the misunderstanding.

COMMENT:

An unrepresented person, particularly one not experienced in dealing with legal matters, might assume a Federal lawyer is disinterested

603

in loyalties or is a disinterested authority on the law even when the lawyer represents a client. During the course of a Federal lawyer's representation of a client, the lawyer should not give advice to an unrepresented person other than the advice to obtain counsel.

RULE 4.4　Respect for Rights of Third Persons

In representing a client, a Federal lawyer shall not use means that have no substantial purpose other than to embarrass, delay, or burden a third person, or use methods of obtaining evidence that violate the legal rights of such a person.

COMMENT:

Responsibility to a client requires a Federal lawyer to subordinate the interests of others to those of the client. That responsibility does not imply that a Federal lawyer may disregard the rights of third persons. The duty of a Federal lawyer to represent the client with zeal does not mitigate against his concurrent obligation to treat with consideration all persons involved in the legal process and to avoid the infliction of needless harm. It is impractical to catalogue all such rights, but they include legal restrictions on methods of obtaining evidence from third persons.

LEGAL OFFICES

RULE 5.1　Responsibilities of a Supervisory Lawyer

(a) A supervisory lawyer shall make reasonable efforts to ensure that all Federal lawyers conform to these Rules of Professional Conduct.

(b) A Federal lawyer shall be responsible for another Federal lawyer's violation of these Rules of Professional Conduct if:

(1) The Federal lawyer orders or, with knowledge of the specific conduct, ratifies the conduct involved; or

(2) The Federal lawyer has direct supervisory authority over the other Federal lawyer and knows of the conduct at a time when its consequences can be avoided or mitigated, but fails to take reasonable remedial action.

(c) A Federal lawyer, who is a supervisory lawyer, is responsible for ensuring that the subordinate lawyer is properly trained and is competent to perform the duties to which the subordinate lawyer is assigned.

(d) A Government lawyer, who is a supervisory lawyer, should encourage subordinate lawyers to participate in pro bono publico service activities and the activities of bar associations and law reform organizations.

COMMENT:

Paragraph 5.1(a) recognizes the responsibilities of the supervisory lawyers to effect and ultimately to enforce these Rules. The measures required to fulfill the responsibility prescribed in Rule 5.1(a) can depend on the office's structure and the nature of its practice. In a small office, informal supervision and occasional admonition ordinarily might be sufficient. In a large office, or in practice situations in which intensely difficult ethical problems frequently arise, more elaborate procedures may be necessary. In some offices, for example, junior lawyers can make confidential referral of ethical problems directly to a senior lawyer. See Rules 1.13 and 5.2. Offices may also rely on continuing legal education in professional ethics. In any event, the ethical atmosphere of an office can influence the conduct of all its members and a Federal lawyer having authority over the work of another shall not assume the subordinate lawyer will inevitably conform to these Rules.

Supervisory lawyers must be careful to avoid conflicts of interest in providing advice to subordinate lawyers. Depending on the circumstances, the supervisory lawyer may advise one subordinate Federal lawyer and refer the other subordinate Federal lawyer to another supervisory lawyer in a different office. Alternatively, the supervisory lawyer may refer both subordinate Federal lawyers to separate supervisory lawyers in the same or another office.

Paragraph 5.1(b)(1) expresses a general principle of supervisory responsibility for acts of another. See also Rule 8.4(a). Ratification as used in paragraph 5.1(b)(1) means approval of or consent to another Federal lawyer's conduct.

Paragraph 5.1(b)(2) defines the duty of a Federal lawyer having direct supervisory authority over the performance of specific legal work by another Federal lawyer. Whether a Federal lawyer has such supervisory authority in particular circumstances is a question of fact. Appropriate remedial action would depend on the immediacy of the supervisor's involvement and the seriousness of the misconduct. Apart from the responsibility that may be incurred for ordering or ratifying another Federal lawyer's conduct under paragraph 5.1(b)(1), the supervisor is required to intervene to prevent avoidable consequences of misconduct if the supervisor knows the misconduct occurred. Thus, if a supervisory lawyer knows that a subordinate misrepresented a matter to an opposing party in negotiation, the supervisor, as well as the subordinate, has a duty to correct the resulting misapprehension.

Professional misconduct by a Federal lawyer under supervision could reveal a violation of paragraph 5.1(a) on the part of the supervisory lawyer even though it does not entail a violation of paragraph 5.1(b) because there was no direction, ratification, or knowledge of the violation.

Apart from this Rule and Rule 8.4(a), a Federal lawyer does not have disciplinary liability for the conduct of subordinate Federal lawyers. Whether a Federal lawyer may be liable civilly or criminally for another Federal lawyer's conduct is a question of law beyond the scope of these Rules.

RULE 5.2 Responsibilities of a Subordinate Federal Lawyer

(a) A Federal lawyer is bound by these Rules of Professional Conduct notwithstanding the Federal lawyer's acting at the direction of another person.

(b) A subordinate Federal lawyer does not violate these Rules of Professional Conduct if that lawyer acts in accordance with a supervisory lawyer's reasonable resolution of an arguable question of professional duty.

COMMENT:

Although a Federal lawyer is not relieved of responsibility for a violation by the fact that the Federal lawyer acted at the direction of a supervisor, that fact may be relevant in determining whether a Federal lawyer had the knowledge required to render conduct a violation of these Rules. For example, if a subordinate filed a frivolous motion at the direction of a supervisor, the subordinate would not be guilty of a professional violation, unless the subordinate knew of the document's frivolous character.

When Federal lawyers in a supervisor-subordinate relationship encounter a matter involving professional judgment as to ethical duty, the supervisor may assume responsibility for making the judgment. Otherwise a consistent course of action or position could not be taken. If the question can reasonably be answered only one way, the duty of both Federal lawyers is clear and they are equally responsible for fulfilling it. If the question is reasonably arguable, however, someone has to decide upon the course of action. That authority and responsibility ordinarily reposes in the supervisor, and a subordinate may be guided accordingly. For example, if a question arises whether the interests of two clients conflict under Rule 1.7, the supervisor's reasonable resolution of the question should protect the subordinate professionally if the resolution is subsequently challenged.

RULE 5.3 Responsibilities Regarding Nonlawyer Assistants

With respect to a nonlawyer under the authority, supervision, or direction of a Federal lawyer:

(a) A supervisory lawyer shall make reasonable efforts to ensure that the office has in effect measures giving reasonable assurance that the person's conduct is compatible with the professional obligations of the Federal lawyer.

(b) A Federal lawyer having direct supervisory authority over the nonlawyer shall make reasonable efforts to ensure that the nonlawyer's conduct is compatible with the professional obligations of the Federal lawyer.

(c) A Federal lawyer shall be responsible for conduct of the nonlawyer that would be a violation of these Rules if engaged in by the Federal lawyer if:

(1) The Federal lawyer orders or, with the knowledge of the specific conduct, ratifies the conduct involved; or

(2) The Federal lawyer has direct supervisory authority over the nonlawyer, and knows of the conduct at a time when its consequences can be avoided or mitigated but fails to take reasonable remedial action.

COMMENT:

Various nonlawyer assistants are employed by federal lawyers in their practices, including paralegals, legal technicians, secretaries, clerks, investigators, law student interns, and others. Such assistants act for the Federal lawyer in rendition of the Federal lawyer's professional services. A Federal lawyer should give such assistants appropriate instruction and supervision concerning the ethical aspects of their performance, particularly regarding the obligation not to disclose information relating to representation of the client, and should be responsible for their work product. The measures employed in supervising nonlawyers should take account of their lack of legal training and their not being subject to professional discipline.

RULE 5.4 Professional Independence of a Federal Lawyer

(a) A Federal lawyer is expected to exercise professional independence of judgment during the representation of a client, consistent with these Rules.

(b) Notwithstanding a Government lawyer's status as a Government employee, a Government lawyer detailed or assigned to represent an individual Government employee or another person as the client is expected to exercise loyalty and professional independence during the representation, consistent with these Rules and to the same extent as required by a Non–Government lawyer in private practice.

(c) A Supervisory Government lawyer may not base an adverse evaluation or other prejudicial action against a Subordinate Government lawyer on the Subordinate Government lawyer's exercise of professional independence under (b) above.

(d) A Government lawyer shall obey the lawful orders of superiors when representing the United States and individual clients, but a Government lawyer shall not permit a nonlawyer to direct or regulate the Government lawyer's professional judgment in rendering legal services.

(e) A Non–Government lawyer shall not permit a nonlawyer who recommends, employs, or pays the Non–Government lawyer to render legal services for another to direct or regulate the Non–Government lawyer's professional judgment in rendering legal services.

(f) A Non–Government lawyer shall comply with the Rules of Professional Conduct or other applicable laws of the jurisdiction in which the Non–Government lawyer is licensed or is practicing law concerning the limitations on sharing fees and the organizational form of their practice.

COMMENT:

Federal lawyers

A Federal lawyer subjected to outside pressures that might impair or give the appearance of impairing the effectiveness of the representation should make full disclosure of the pressures to the client. If the Federal lawyer or the client believes the effectiveness of the representation has been or will be impaired thereby, the lawyer should take proper steps to withdraw from representation of the client.

Government Lawyers

This Rule recognizes that a Government lawyer is a Government employee required by law to obey the lawful orders of superiors. Nevertheless, the practice of law requires the exercise of judgment solely for the benefit of the client and free of compromising influences and loyalties. Thus, when a Government lawyer is assigned to represent an individual client, neither the lawyer's personal interests, the interests of other clients, nor the interests of third persons should affect loyalty to the individual client.

Non–Government Lawyers

Rather than adopting specific rules on the sharing of fees or the organizational makeup of law practices that would apply only to Non-government lawyers practicing before the Federal Agency, the Federal Agency defers on this matter to the rules and applicable laws of the jurisdictions in which these Non–Government lawyers are licensed.

RULE 5.5   Unauthorized Practice of Law

A Federal lawyer shall not:

(a) Except as authorized by law, practice law in a jurisdiction where doing so violates the regulation of the legal profession in that jurisdiction; or

(b) Assist a person who is not a member of the bar in the performance of activity that constitutes the unauthorized practice of law.

COMMENT:

Limiting the practice of law to members of the bar protects the public against rendition of legal services by unqualified persons. A Government lawyer's performance of legal duties for a Federal Agency, however, is considered a Federal function and not subject to regulation by the states. Paragraph (b) does not prohibit a Federal lawyer from employing the services of nonlawyers and delegating functions to them, so long as the Federal lawyer supervises the delegated work and retains responsibility for their work. See Rule 5.3. Likewise, it does not prohibit Federal lawyers from providing professional advice and instruction to nonlawyers whose employment requires knowledge of law; for example, claims adjusters, social workers, accountants, and persons employed in Government agencies. In addition, a Federal lawyer may counsel nonlawyers who wish to proceed pro se, or nonlawyers authorized by law to practice in military proceedings.

The sole admission to practice requirement is applicable to Government lawyers. As such, admission in any of the several states should preclude the imposition of additional requirements on behalf of the U.S. Government.

PUBLIC SERVICE

RULE 6.1   Pro Bono Publico Service

(a) A Federal lawyer should render public interest legal service. A Federal lawyer may discharge this responsibility by providing professional services at no fee or a reduced fee to persons of limited means or to public service or charitable groups or organizations, by service in activities for improving the law, the legal system or the legal profession, and by financial support for organizations that provide legal service to persons of limited means.

(b) A Government lawyer should provide pro bono legal services consistent with applicable law.

COMMENT:

Each Federal lawyer has a basic responsibility to provide public interest legal services without fee, or at a substantially reduced fee, in one or more of the following areas: poverty law, civil rights law, public rights law, charitable organization representation, and the administration of justice. This Rule expresses that policy but is not intended to be enforced through disciplinary process.

The rights and responsibilities of individuals and organizations in the United States are increasingly defined in legal terms As a consequence, legal assistance in coping with the web of laws is imperative for persons of modest and limited means, as well as for the relatively well-to-do.

The basic responsibility for providing legal services for those unable to pay ultimately rests upon the individual lawyer, and personal involvement in the problems of the disadvantaged can be one of the most rewarding experiences in the life of a Federal lawyer. Every Federal lawyer, regardless of professional prominence or professional work load, should find time to participate in or otherwise support the provision of legal services to the disadvantaged. The provision of free legal services to those unable to pay reasonable fees continues to be an obligation of each Federal lawyer as well as the profession generally, but the efforts of individual Federal lawyers are often not enough to meet the need. Thus, it has been necessary for the profession and government to institute additional programs to provide legal services. Accordingly, legal aid offices, lawyer referral services, and other related programs have been developed, and others will be developed by the profession and government. Every Federal lawyer should support all proper efforts to meet this need for legal services.

18 U.S.C. § 205 and § 209 and other laws, including those governing off-duty employment by members of the Armed Forces, may regulate a Government lawyer's ability to provide legal services on a pro bono basis outside the scope of the Government lawyer's official duties.

RULE 6.2   Accepting Appointments

A Federal lawyer shall not seek to avoid appointment by a tribunal to represent a person except for good cause, such as:

(a) Representing the client is contrary to law or in violation of these Rules.

(b) Representing the client is likely to result in an unreasonable financial burden on the Federal lawyer.

(c) The client or the cause is so repugnant to the lawyer as to be likely to impair the client-lawyer relationship or the lawyer's ability to represent the client.

COMMENT:

A Federal lawyer ordinarily is not obliged to accept a client whose character or cause the Federal lawyer regards as repugnant. The Federal lawyer's freedom to select clients is, however, qualified. All lawyers have a responsibility to assist in providing pro bono publico service. See Rule 6.1. An individual Federal lawyer fulfills this responsibility by accepting a fair share of unpopular matters or indigent or unpopular clients. A Federal lawyer may also be subject to appointment by a court to serve unpopular clients or persons unable to afford legal services.

Appointed Counsel

For good cause a Federal lawyer may seek to decline an appointment to represent a person who cannot afford to retain counsel or whose cause is unpopular. Good cause exists if the Federal lawyer could not handle the matter competently, see Rule 1.1, or if undertaking the representation would result in an improper conflict of interest, for example, when the client or the cause is so repugnant to the Federal lawyer as to be likely to impair the client-lawyer relationship or the Federal lawyer's ability to represent the client. A Federal lawyer may also seek to decline an appointment if acceptance would be unreasonably burdensome, for example, when it would impose a financial sacrifice so great as to be unjust.

An appointed Federal lawyer has the same obligations to the client as retained counsel, including the obligations of loyalty and confidentiality, and is subject to the same limitations on the client-lawyer relationship, such as the obligation to refrain from assisting the client in violation of the Rules.

18 U.S.C. § 205 and other laws, including those governing off-duty employment, may prevent or restrict the types of cases that a Government lawyer may accept appointment to by a tribunal outside the scope of the Government lawyer's official duties.

RULE 6.3 Membership in Legal Services Organization

A Federal lawyer may serve as a director, officer, or member of a legal services organization, apart from the law firm or Federal Agency in which the lawyer practices, notwithstanding that the organization serves persons having interests adverse to a client of the Federal lawyer. The Federal lawyer shall not knowingly participate in a decision or action of the organization:

(a) If participating in the decision or action would be incompatible with the Federal lawyer's obligations to a client under Rule 1.7; or

(b) Where the decision or action could have a material adverse effect on the representation of a client of the organization whose interests are adverse to a client of the Federal lawyer.

COMMENT:

Federal lawyers should be encouraged to support and participate in legal service organizations. A Federal lawyer who is an officer or a member of such an organization does not thereby have a client-lawyer relationship with persons served by the organization. However, there is potential conflict between the interests of such persons and the interests of the Federal lawyer's clients. If the possibility of such conflict disqualified a Federal lawyer from serving on the board of a legal services organization, the profession's involvement in such organizations would be severely curtailed.

It may be necessary in appropriate cases to reassure a client of the organization that the representation will not be affected by conflicting loyalties of a member of the board. Established written policies in this respect can enhance the credibility of such assurances.

18 U.S.C. § 205 and § 208 and other laws may prevent or restrict a Government lawyer's participation in a legal services organization.

RULE 6.4 Membership in Bar Associations and Law Reform Activities Affecting Client Interests

A Federal lawyer may serve as a member, director, or officer of a bar association or an organization involved in reform of the law or its administration, notwithstanding that the reform may affect the interests of a client. The Federal lawyer shall not knowingly participate in a decision or action of the organization if participating in the decision would be incompatible with the Federal lawyer's obligations to the client under Rule 1.7. When the Federal lawyer knows the interests of the client may be materially benefitted by a decision in which the Federal lawyer participates, the Federal lawyer shall disclose that fact, but need not identify the client.

COMMENT:

Federal lawyers involved in organizations seeking law reform generally do not have a client-lawyer relationship with the organization. Otherwise, it might follow that a Government lawyer could not be involved in a bar association law reform program that might indirectly affect the United States. See also Rule 1.2(b). For example, a Government lawyer might be disqualified from participating in drafting proposed regulations. In determining the nature and scope of participation in such activities, a Federal lawyer should be mindful of obligations to clients under other Rules, particularly Rule 1.7. A Federal lawyer is professionally obligated to protect the integrity of the program by making an appropriate disclosure within the organization when the Federal lawyer knows that a client might be materially benefitted.

A Government lawyer who is active in bar association activities or who makes a presentation to a bar association in the lawyer's personal capacity, and not as a representative of the Government lawyer's Federal Agency, may accept reimbursement, subject to the provisions of applicable laws, for the Government lawyer's expenses in attending a meeting of the bar association on the Government lawyer's own time.

INFORMATION ABOUT LEGAL SERVICES

RULE 7.1 Communications Concerning a Federal Agency's Legal Services

A Government lawyer may advertise the Federal Agency's legal services through the public media, such as a telephone directory, newspaper, or other periodicals, outdoor sign, radio, television, or through written communications.

COMMENT:

To assist members of the public, Government employees, and dependents of Government employees, a Government lawyer may advertise or otherwise conduct information campaigns regarding the legal services that a Federal Agency makes available to the public, Government employees, and dependents of Government employees.

MAINTAINING THE INTEGRITY OF THE PROFESSION

RULE 8.1 Bar Admission and Disciplinary Matters

An applicant for admission to a bar or employment as a lawyer with a Federal Agency, a Federal lawyer seeking the right to practice before a Federal Agency, or a Federal lawyer in connection with a disciplinary matter, shall not:

(a) Knowingly make a false statement of material fact.

(b) Fail to disclose a fact necessary to correct a misapprehension known by the person to have arisen in the matter, or knowingly fail to respond to a lawful demand for information from an admission or disciplinary authority, except that the Rule does not require disclosure of information otherwise protected by Rule 1.6.

COMMENT:

The duty imposed by this Rule extends to applicants seeking admission to the bar or employment with a Federal Agency as well as to Federal lawyers. Hence, if a person makes a material false statement in connection with an application for admission, employment, or certification, it may form the basis for subsequent disciplinary action if the person is admitted or employed, and in any event may be relevant in a subsequent admission application. The duty imposed by this Rule applies to a Federal lawyer's own admission or discipline, as well as to that of others. Thus, it is a separate professional offense for a Federal lawyer to knowingly make a misrepresentation or omission in connection with a disciplinary investigation of the Federal lawyer's own conduct. This Rule also requires affirmative clarification of any misunderstanding on the part of the admission or disciplinary authority of which the person involved becomes aware.

A Federal lawyer representing an applicant for admission to the bar, or representing a Federal lawyer who is the subject of a disciplinary inquiry or proceeding, is governed by the Rules applicable to the client-lawyer relationship.

RULE 8.2   Judicial and Legal Officials

A Federal lawyer shall not make a statement the lawyer knows to be false or with reckless disregard as to its truth or falsity concerning the qualifications or integrity of a tribunal or of a candidate for election or appointment to judicial or legal office.

COMMENT:

Assessments by Federal lawyers are relied on in evaluating the professional or personal fitness of persons performing legal duties. Expressing honest and candid opinions on such matters contributes to improving the administration of justice. Conversely, false statements by a Federal lawyer can unfairly undermine confidence in the administration of justice.

To maintain the fair and independent administration of justice, Federal lawyers are encouraged to continue traditional efforts to defend judges and courts criticized unjustly.

RULE 8.3   Reporting Professional Misconduct

(a) A Federal lawyer having knowledge that another Federal lawyer has committed a violation of these Rules of Professional Conduct that raises a substantial question as to that lawyer's honesty, trustworthiness, or fitness as a Federal lawyer in other respects, shall report such a violation to the appropriate official as provided by law.

(b) A Federal lawyer having knowledge that a judge has committed a violation of applicable rules of judicial conduct that raises a substantial question as to the judge's fitness for office shall report such a violation to the appropriate official as provided by law.

(c) This Rule does not require disclosure of information otherwise protected by Rule 1.6.

COMMENT:

Self-regulation of the legal profession requires members of the profession to initiate disciplinary investigations when they know of violations of these Rules of Professional Conduct or other such rules. Federal lawyers have a similar obligation with respect to judicial misconduct. An apparently isolated violation may indicate a pattern of misconduct that only a disciplinary investigation can uncover. Reporting a violation is especially important if the victim is unlikely to discover the offense.

A report about misconduct is not required if it would involve violation of Rule 1.6. A Federal lawyer should, however, encourage a client to consent to disclosure when prosecution would not substantially prejudice the client's interests.

This Rule limits the reporting obligation to those offenses that a self-regulating profession must vigorously endeavor to prevent. A measure of judgment, therefore, is required in complying with this Rule. The term "substantial" refers to the seriousness of the possible offense and not the quantum of evidence of which the Federal lawyer is aware. Any report should be made to the appropriate official under the applicable law.

RULE 8.4 Misconduct

It is professional misconduct for a Federal lawyer to:

(a) Violate or attempt to violate these Rules of Professional Conduct, knowingly assist or induce another to do so, or do so through the acts of another.

(b) Commit a criminal act that reflects adversely on the Federal lawyer's honesty, trustworthiness, or fitness as a Federal lawyer in other respects.

(c) Engage in conduct involving dishonesty, fraud, deceit, or misrepresentation.

(d) Engage in conduct prejudicial to the administration of justice.

(e) State or imply an ability to influence improperly a government Federal Agency or official.

(f) Knowingly assist a judge or judicial officer in conduct that violates applicable rules of judicial conduct or other law.

COMMENT:

Many kinds of illegal conduct reflect adversely on fitness to practice law, such as offenses involving fraud and the offense of willful failure to file an income tax return. However, some kinds of offenses carry no such implication. Traditionally, the distinction was drawn in terms of offenses involving "moral turpitude." That concept can be construed to include offenses concerning some matters of personal morality, such as adultery and comparable offenses, which have no specific connection to fitness for the practice of law. Although a Federal lawyer is personally answerable under law, a Federal lawyer should be professionally answerable only for offenses that indicate lack of those characteristics relevant to law practice. Offenses involving violence, dishonesty, breach of truth, or serious interference with the administration of justice are in that category. One example of such conduct is the unlawful, unauthorized, or nonconsensual obtaining of confidential files, including confidential working paper files, of Federal lawyers who are known or reasonably should be known to be representing a client. Such conduct includes the solicitation or prompting of another person, not bound by these Rules, to engage in such activities. A pattern of repeated offenses, even ones of minor significance when considered separately, can indicate indifference to ethical obligations.

A Federal lawyer may refuse to comply with an obligation imposed by law upon a good faith belief that no valid obligation exists. The provision of Rule 1.2(d) concerning a good faith challenge to the validity, scope, meaning or application of the law applies to challenges of legal regulation of the practice of law.

A Government lawyer assumes legal responsibilities beyond those of other citizens. A Government lawyer's abuse of such status can suggest an inability to fulfill the professional role of Government lawyer and Federal lawyer.

RULE 8.5 Jurisdiction

(a) **A Federal lawyer shall comply with the rules of professional conduct applicable to the Federal Agency that employs the Government lawyer or the Federal Agency before which the Federal lawyer practices.**

(b) **If the Federal Agency has not adopted or promulgated rules of professional conduct, the Federal lawyer shall comply with the rules of professional conduct of the state bars in which the Federal lawyer is admitted to practice.**

COMMENT:

Many Federal lawyers practicing before Federal Agency tribunals practice outside the territorial limits of the jurisdiction in which they are licensed.

While the Federal lawyer may remain subject to the governing authority of their licensing jurisdiction, the Federal lawyer is also subject to these Rules. However, when a Government lawyer is engaged in the conduct of Federal Agency legal functions, whether servicing the Federal Agency as a client or serving an individual client in the course of official duties, these Rules are regarded as superseding any conflicting rules applicable in the jurisdictions in which the Government lawyer may be licensed.

When a Government lawyer is practicing before a Federal Agency whose rules conflict with these Rules, the Government lawyer shall comply with the rules of that Federal Agency.

A Non–Government lawyer practicing before a Federal Agency tribunal who violates these Rules may be suspended from practice before such tribunals.

AMERICAN BAR ASSOCIATION STANDARDS OF PRACTICE FOR LAWYER MEDIATORS IN FAMILY DISPUTES

Preamble

For the purposes of these standards, family mediation is defined as a process in which a lawyer helps family members resolve their disputes in an informative and consensual manner. This process requires that the mediator be qualified by training, experience, and temperament; that the mediator be impartial; that the participants reach decisions voluntarily; that their decisions be based on sufficient factual data; and that each participant understands the information upon which decisions are reached. While family mediation may be viewed as an alternative means of conflict resolution, it is not a substitute for the benefit of independent legal advice.

I. The Mediator Has a Duty to Define and Describe the Process of Mediation and Its Cost Before the Parties Reach an Agreement to Mediate

Specific Considerations

Before the actual mediation sessions begin, the mediator shall conduct an orientation session to give an overview of the process and to assess the appropriateness of mediation for the participants. Among the topics covered, the mediator shall discuss the following:

A. The mediator shall define the process in context so that the participants understand the differences between mediation and other means of conflict resolution available to them. In defining the process, the mediator shall also distinguish it from therapy or marriage counselling.

B. The mediator shall obtain sufficient information from the participants so they can mutually define the issues to be resolved in mediation.

C. It should be emphasized that the mediator may make suggestions for the participants to consider, such as alternative ways of resolving problems and may draft proposals for the participants' consideration, but that all decisions are to be made voluntarily by the participants themselves, and the mediator's views are to be given no independent weight or credence.

D. The duties and responsibilities that the mediator and the participants accept in the mediation process shall be agreed upon. The mediator shall instruct the participants that either of them or the mediator has the right to suspend or terminate the process at any time.

E. The mediator shall assess the ability and willingness of the participants to mediate. The mediator has a continuing duty to assess his or her own ability and willingness to undertake mediation with the particular participants and the issues to be mediated. The mediator shall not continue and shall terminate the process, if in his or her judgment, one of the parties is not able or willing to participate in good faith.

F. The mediator shall explain the fees for mediation. It is inappropriate for a mediator to charge a contingency fee or to base the fee on the outcome of the mediation process.

G. The mediator shall inform the participants of the need to employ independent legal counsel for advice throughout the mediation process. The mediator shall inform the participants that the mediator cannot represent either or both of them in a marital dissolution or in any legal action.

H. The mediator shall discuss the issue of separate sessions. The mediator shall reach an understanding with the participants as to whether and under what circumstances the mediator may meet alone with either of them or with any third party. *Commentary:* The mediator cannot act as lawyer for either party or for them jointly and should make that clear to both parties.

I. It should be brought to the participants' attention that emotions play a part in the decision-making process. The mediator shall attempt to elicit from each of the participants a confirmation that each understands the connection between one's own emotions and the bargaining process.

II. The Mediator Shall Not Voluntarily Disclose Information Obtained Through the Mediation Process Without the Prior Consent of Both Participants

Specific Considerations

A. At the outset of mediation, the parties should agree in writing not to require the mediator to disclose to any third party any statements made in the course of mediation. The mediator shall inform the participants that the mediator will not voluntarily disclose to any third party any of the information obtained through the mediation process, unless such disclosure is required by law, without the prior consent of the participants. The mediator also shall inform the parties of the limitations of confidentiality such as statutory or judicially mandated reporting.

B. If subpoenaed or otherwise noticed to testify, the mediator shall inform the participants immediately so as to afford them an opportunity to quash the process.

C. The mediator shall inform the participants of the mediator's inability to bind third parties to an agreement not to disclose information furnished during the mediation in the absence of any absolute privilege.

III. The Mediator Has a Duty to Be Impartial

Specific Considerations

A. The mediator shall not represent either party during or after the mediation process in any legal matters. In the event the mediator has represented one of the parties beforehand, the mediator shall not undertake the mediation.

B. The mediator shall disclose to the participants any biases or strong views relating to the issues to be mediated, both in the orientation session, and also before these issues are discussed in mediation.

C. The mediator must be impartial as between the mediation participants. The mediator's task is to facilitate the ability of the participants to negotiate their own agreement, while raising questions as to the fairness, equity and feasibility of proposed options for settlement.

D. The mediator has a duty to ensure that the participants consider fully the best interests of the children, that they understand the consequences of any decision they reach concerning the children. The mediator also has a duty to assist parents to examine the separate and individual needs of their children and to consider those needs apart from their own desires for any particular parenting formula. If the mediator believes that any proposed agreement of the parents does not protect the best interests of the children, the mediator has a duty to inform them of this belief and its basis.

E. The mediator shall not communicate with either party alone or with any third party to discuss mediation issues without the prior consent of the mediation participants. The mediator shall obtain an agreement from the participants during the orientation session as to whether and under what circumstances the mediator may speak directly and separately with each of their lawyers during the mediation process.

IV. The Mediator Has a Duty to Assure That the Mediation Participants Make Decisions Based upon Sufficient Information and Knowledge

Specific Considerations

A. The mediator shall assure that there is full financial disclosure, evaluation and development of relevant factual information in the mediation process, such as each would reasonably receive in the discovery process, or that the parties have sufficient information to intelligently waive the right to such disclosure.

B. In addition to requiring this disclosure, evaluation and development of information, the mediator shall promote the equal understanding of such information before any agreement is reached. This consideration may require the mediator to recommend that either or both obtain expert consultation in the event that it appears that additional knowledge or understanding is necessary for balanced negotiations.

C. The mediator may define the legal issues, but shall not direct the decision of the mediation participants based upon the mediator's interpretation of the law as applied to the facts of the situation. The mediator shall endeavor to assure that the participants have a sufficient understanding of appropriate statutory and case law as well as local judicial tradition, before reaching an agreement by recommending to the participants that they obtain independent legal representation during the process.

V. The Mediator Has a Duty to Suspend or Terminate Mediation Whenever Continuation of the Process Would Harm One or More of the Participants

Specific Considerations

A. If the mediator believes that the participants are unable or unwilling to meaningfully participate in the process or that reasonable agreement is unlikely the mediator may suspend or terminate mediation and should encourage the parties to seek appropriate professional help. The mediator shall recognize that the decisions are to be made by the parties on the basis of adequate information. The mediator shall not, however, participate in a process that the mediator believes will result in harm to a participant.

B. The mediator shall assure that each person has had the opportunity to understand fully the implications and ramifications of all options available.

C. The mediator has a duty to assure a balanced dialogue and must attempt to diffuse any manipulative or intimidating negotiation techniques utilized by either of the participants.

D. If the mediator has suspended or terminated the process, the mediator should suggest that the participants obtain additional professional services as may be appropriate.

VI. The Mediator Has a Continuing Duty to Advise Each of the Mediation Participants to Obtain Legal Review Prior to Reaching Any Agreement

Specific Considerations

A. Each of the mediation participants should have independent legal counsel before reaching final agreement. At the beginning of the mediation process, the mediator should inform the participants that each should employ independent legal counsel for advice at the beginning of the process and that the independent legal counsel should be utilized throughout the process and before the participants have reached any accord to which they have made an emotional commitment. In order to promote the integrity of the process, the mediator shall not refer either of the participants to any particular lawyers. When an attorney referral is requested, the parties should be referred to a Bar Association list if available. In the absence of such a list, the mediator may only provide a list of qualified family law attorneys in the community.

B. The mediator shall inform the participants that the mediator cannot represent either or both of them in a marital dissolution.

C. The mediator shall obtain an agreement from the husband and the wife that each lawyer, upon request, shall be entitled to review all the factual documentation provided by the participants in the mediation process.

D. Any memo of understanding or proposed agreement which is prepared in the mediation process should be separately reviewed by independent counsel for each participant before it is signed. While a mediator cannot insist that each participant have separate counsel, they should be discouraged from signing any agreement which has not been so reviewed. If the participants, or either of them, choose to proceed without independent counsel, the mediator shall warn them of any risk involved in not being represented, including where appropriate, the possibility that the agreement they submit to a court may be rejected as unreasonable in light of both parties' legal rights or may not be binding on them.

CIRCULAR 230 REGULATING PRACTICE BEFORE THE TREASURY

31 C.F.R. §§ 10.0–10.97 (1990)

Contents

PART 10. PRACTICE BEFORE THE INTERNAL REVENUE SERVICE

---

* Sections 10.1, 10.2, 10.5, 10.6, 10.7 and 10.8 have been omitted. Ed.

PART 10. PRACTICE BEFORE THE INTERNAL REVENUE SERVICE

Subpart A. Rules Governing Authority to Practice

§ 10.3 Who May Practice

(a) *Attorneys.* Any attorney who is not currently under suspension or disbarment from practice before the Internal Revenue Service may practice before the Service upon filing with the Service a written declaration that he is currently qualified as an attorney and is authorized to represent the particular party on whose behalf he acts. An enrollment card issued to such person before the effective date of this regulation shall be invalid and may not be used in lieu of such written declaration.[1]

(b) *Certified public accountants.* Any certified public accountant who is not currently under suspension or disbarment from practice before the Internal Revenue Service may practice before the Service upon filing with the Service a written declaration that he is currently qualified as a certified public accountant and is authorized to represent the particular party on whose behalf he acts. An enrollment card issued to such person before the effective date of this regulation shall be invalid and may not be used in lieu of such written declaration.

(c) *Enrolled agents.* Any person enrolled as an agent pursuant to this part may practice before the Internal Revenue Service.

(d) *Enrolled Actuaries.* (1) Any individual who is enrolled as an actuary by the Joint Board for the Enrollment of Actuaries pursuant to 29 U.S.C. 1242 may practice before the Internal Revenue Service upon filing with the Service a written declaration that he/she is currently qualified as an enrolled actuary and is authorized to represent the particular party on whose behalf he/she acts. Practice as an enrolled actuary is limited to representation with respect to issues involving the following statutory provisions.

Internal Revenue Code (Title 26 U.S.C.) sections: 401 (qualification of employee plans), 403(a) (relating to whether an annuity plan meets the requirements of section 404(a)(2)), 404 (deductibility of employer contributions), 405 (qualification of bond purchase plans), 412 (funding requirements for certain employee plans), 413 (application of qualification requirements to collectively bargained plans and to plans maintained by more than one employer), 414 (containing definitions and special rules relating to the employee plan area), 4971 (relating to excise taxes payable as a result of an accumulated funding deficiency

1. This supersedes the provision contained in a notice of interim course of action published in the FEDERAL REGISTER, Nov. 16, 1965 (30 FR 14331) which permitted attorneys and certified public accountants, who were enrolled as of Nov. 8, 1965, to continue to use their enrollment cards as evidence of authority to practice before the Service.

under section 412), 6057 (annual registration of plans), 6058 (information required in connection with certain plans of deferred compensation), 6059 (periodic report of actuary), 6652(e) (failure to file annual registration and other notifications by pension plan), 6652(f) (failure to file information required in connection with certain plans of deferred compensation), 6692 (failure to file acuarial report), 7805(b) (relating to the extent, if any, to which an Internal Revenue Service ruling or determination letter coming under the herein listed statutory provisions shall be applied without retroactive effect); and 29 U.S.C. 1083 (relating to waiver of funding for nonqualified plans).

(2) An individual who practices before the Internal Revenue Service pursuant to this subsection shall be subject to the provisions of this part in the same manner as attorneys, certified public accountants and enrolled agents.

(e) *Others.* Any person qualifying under § 10.7 or § 10.5(c) may practice before Internal Revenue Service.

(f) *Government officers and employees; others.* No officer or employee of the United States in the executive, legislative, or judicial branch of the Government, or in any agency of the United States, including the District of Columbia, may practice before the Service, except that such officer or employee may, subject to the conditions and requirements of these regulations and of 18 U.S.C. 205, represent a member of his immediate family or any other person or estate for which he serves as guardian, executor, administrator, trustee, or other personal fiduciary. No Member of Congress or Resident Commissioner (elect or serving) may practice before the Service in connection with any matter for which he directly or indirectly receives, agrees to receive, or seeks any compensation. 18 U.S.C. 203, 205. Nothing herein shall be construed as prohibiting an officer or employee of the United States as aforesaid, who is otherwise eligible to practice under the provision of this part, from representing others before the Internal Revenue Service when doing so in the proper discharge of his official duties.

(g) *State officers and employees.* No officer or employee of any State, or subdivision thereof, whose duties require him to pass upon, investigate, or deal with tax matters of such State or subdivision, may practice before the Service, if such State employment may disclose facts or information applicable to Federal tax matters.

§ 10.4 Eligibility for Enrollment

(a) *Enrollment upon examination.* The Director of Practice may grant enrollment to an applicant who demonstrates special competence in tax matters by written examination administered by the Internal Revenue Service and who has not engaged in any conduct which would justify the suspension or disbarment of any attorney, certified public accountant, or enrolled agent under the provisions of this part.

(b) *Enrollment of former Internal Revenue Service employees.* The Director of Practice may grant enrollment to an applicant who has not engaged in any conduct which would justify the suspension or disbarment of any attorney, certified public accountant, or enrolled agent under the provisions of this part and who, by virtue of his past service and technical experience in the Internal Revenue Service has qualified for such enrollment, as follows:

(1) Application for enrollment on account of former employment in the Internal Revenue Service shall be made to the Director of Practice. Each applicant will be supplied a form by the Director of Practice, which shall indicate the information required respecting the applicant's qualifications. In addition to the applicant's name, address, citizenship, age, educational experience, etc., such information shall specifically include a detailed account of the applicant's employment in the Internal Revenue Service, which account shall show (i) positions held, (ii) date of each appointment and termination thereof, (iii) nature of services rendered in each position, with particular reference to the degree of technical experience involved, and (iv) name of supervisor in such positions, together with such other information regarding the experience and training of the applicant as may be relevant.

(2) Upon receipt of each such application, it shall be transmitted to the appropriate officer of the Internal Revenue Service with the request that a detailed report of the nature and rating of the applicant's services in the Internal Revenue Service, accompanied by the recommendation of the superior officer in the particular unit or division of the Internal Revenue Service that such employment does or does not qualify the applicant technically or otherwise for the desired authorization, be furnished to the Director of Practice.

(3) In examining the qualification of an applicant for enrollment on account of employment in the Internal Revenue Service, the Director of Practice will be governed by the following policies:

(i) Enrollment on account of such employment may be of unlimited scope or may be limited to permit the presentation of matters only of the particular class or only before the particular unit or division of the Internal Revenue Service for which his former employment in the Internal Revenue Service has qualified the applicant.

(ii) Application for enrollment on account of employment in the Internal Revenue Service must be made within 3 years from the date of separation from such employment.

(iii) It shall be requisite for enrollment on account of such employment that the applicant shall have had a minimum of 5 years continuous employment in the Service during which he shall have been regularly engaged in applying and interpreting the provisions of the Internal Revenue Code and the regulations thereunder relating to income, estate, gift, employment, or excise taxes.

(iv) For the purposes of paragraph (b)(3)(iii) of this section an aggregate of 10 or more years of employment, at least 3 of which occurred within the 5 years preceding the date of application, shall be deemed the equivalent of 5 years continuous employment.

(c) *Natural persons.* Enrollment to practice may be granted only to natural persons.

(d) *Attorneys; certified public accountants.* Enrollment is not available to persons who qualify to practice under § 10.3(a) or (b).

Subpart B. Duties and Restrictions Relating to Practice Before the Internal Revenue Service

§ 10.20 Information to Be Furnished

(a) *To the Internal Revenue Service.* No attorney, certified public accountant, or enrolled agent shall neglect or refuse promptly to submit records or information in any matter before the Internal Revenue Service, upon proper and lawful request by a duly authorized officer or employee of the Internal Revenue Service, or shall interfere, or attempt to interfere, with any proper and lawful effort by the Internal Revenue Service or its officers or employees to obtain any such record or information, unless he believes in good faith and on reasonable grounds that such record or information is privileged or that the request for, or effort to obtain, such record or information is of doubtful legality.

(b) *To the Director of Practice.* It shall be the duty of an attorney or certified public accountant, who practices before the Internal Revenue Service, or enrolled agent, when requested by the Director of Practice, to provide the Director with any information he may have concerning violation of the regulations in this part by any person, and to testify thereto in any proceeding instituted under this part for the disbarment or suspension of an attorney, certified public accountant, or enrolled agent, unless he believes in good faith and on reasonable grounds that such information is privileged or that the request therefor is of doubtful legality.

§ 10.21 Knowledge of Client's Omission

Each attorney, certified public accountant, or enrolled agent who, having been retained by a client with respect to a matter administered by the Internal Revenue Service, knows that the client has not complied with the revenue laws of the United States or has made an error in or omission from any return, document, affidavit, or other paper which the client is required by the revenue laws of the United States to execute, shall advise the client promptly of the fact of such noncompliance, error, or omission.

§ 10.22 Diligent as to Accuracy

Each attorney, certified public accountant, or enrolled agent shall exercise due diligence:

(a) In preparing or assisting in the preparation of, approving, and filing returns, documents, affidavits, and other papers relating to Internal Revenue Service matters;

(b) In determining the correctness of oral or written representations made by him to the Department of the Treasury; and

(c) In determining the correctness of oral or written representations made by him to clients with reference to any matter administered by the Internal Revenue Service.

§ 10.23 Prompt Disposition of Pending Matters

No attorney, certified public accountant, or enrolled agent shall unreasonably delay the prompt disposition of any matter before the Internal Revenue Service.

§ 10.24 Assistance From Disbarred or Suspended Persons and Former Internal Revenue Service Employees

No attorney, certified public accountant or enrolled agent shall, in practice before the Internal Revenue Service, knowingly and directly or indirectly:

(a) Employ or accept assistance from any person who is under disbarment or suspension from practice before the Internal Revenue Service.

(b) Accept employment as associate, correspondent, or subagent from, or share fees with, any such person.

(c) Accept assistance from any former government employee where the provisions of § 10.26 of these regulations or any Federal law would be violated.

§ 10.25 Practice by Partners of Government Employees

No partner of an officer or employee of the executive branch of the U.S. Government, of any independent agency of the United States, or of the District of Columbia, shall represent anyone in any matter administered by the Internal Revenue Service in which such officer or employee of the Government participates or has participated personally and substantially as a Government employee or which is the subject of his official responsibility.

§ 10.26   Practice by Former Government Employees, Their Partners and Their Associates

(a) *Definitions.* For purposes of § 10.26: (1) "Assist" means to act in such a way as to advise, furnish information to or otherwise aid another person, directly or indirectly.

(2) "Government employee" is an officer or employee of the United States or any agency of the United States, including a "special government employee" as defined in 18 U.S.C. 202(a), or of the District of Columbia, or of any State, or a member of Congress or of any State legislature.

(3) "Member of a firm" is a sole practioner or an employee or associate thereof, or a partner, stockholder, associate, affiliate or employee of a partnership, joint venture, corporation, professional association or other affiliation of two or more practitioners who represent non-Government parties.

(4) "Practitioner" is an attorney, certified public accountant, enrolled agent or any other person authorized to practice before the Internal Revenue Service.

(5) "Official responsibility" means the direct administrative or operating authority, whether intermediate or final, and either exercisable alone or with others, and either personally or through subordinates, to approve, disapprove, or otherwise direct Government action, with or without knowledge of the action.

(6) "Participate" or "participation" means substantial involvement as a Government employee by making decisions, or preparing or reviewing documents with or without the right to exercise a judgment of approval or disapproval, or participating in conferences or investigations, or rendering advice of a substantial nature.

(7) "Rule" includes Treasury Regulations, whether issued or under preparation for issuance as Notices of Proposed Rule Making or as Treasury Decisions, and revenue rulings and revenue procedures published in the Internal Revenue bulletin. "Rule" shall not include a "transaction" as defined in paragraph (a)(9) of this section.

(8) "Transaction" means any decision, determination, finding, letter ruling, technical advice, contract or approval or disapproval thereof, relating to a particular factual situation or situations involving a specific party or parties whose rights, privileges, or liabilities under laws or regulations administered by the Internal Revenue Service, or other legal rights, are determined or immediately affected therein and to which the United States is a party or in which it has a direct and substantial interest, whether or not the same taxable periods are involved. "Transaction" does not include "rule" as defined in paragraph (a)(7) of this section.

(b) *General rules.* (1) No former Government employee shall, subsequent to his Government employment, represent anyone in any matter administered by the Internal Revenue Service if the representation would violate 18 U.S.C. 207(a) or (b) or any other laws of the United States.

(2) No former Government employee who participated in a transaction shall, subsequent to his Government employment, represent or knowingly assist, in that transaction, any person who is or was a specific party to that transaction.

(3) No former Government employee who within a period of one year prior to the termination of his Government employment had official responsibility for a transaction shall, within one year after his Government employment is ended, represent or knowingly assist in that transaction any person who is or was a specific party to that transaction.

(4) No former Government employee shall, within one year after his Government employment is ended, appear before any employee of the Treasury Department in connection with the publication, withdrawal, amendment, modification, or interpretation of a rule in the development of which the former Government employee participated or for which, within a period of one year prior to the termination of his Government employment, he had official responsibility. However, this subparagraph does not preclude such former employee for appearing on his own behalf or from representing a taxpayer before the Internal Revenue Service in connection with a transaction involving the application or interpretation of such a rule with respect to that transaction: *Provided,* That such former employee shall not utilize or disclose any confidential information acquired by the former employee in the development of the rule, and shall not contend that the rule is invalid or illegal. In addition, this subparagraph does not preclude such former employee from otherwise advising or acting for any person.

(c) *Firm representation.* (1) No member of a firm of which a former Government employee is a member may represent or knowingly assist a person who was or is a specific party in any transaction with respect to which the restrictions of paragraph (b)(1) (other than 18 U.S.C. 207(b)) or (b)(2) of this section apply to the former Government employee, in that transaction, unless:

(i) No member of the firm who had knowledge of the participation by the Government employee in the transaction initiated discussions with the Government employee concerning his becoming a member of the firm until his Government employment is ended or six months after the termination of his participation in the transaction, whichever is earlier;

(ii) The former Government employee did not initiate any discussions concerning becoming a member of the firm while participating in the transaction or, if such discussions were initiated, they conformed with the requirements of 18 U.S.C. 208(b); and

629

(iii) The firm isolates the former Government employee in such a way that he does not assist in the representation.

(2) No member of a firm of which a former Government employee is a member may represent or knowingly assist a person who was or is a specific party in any transaction with respect to which the restrictions of paragraph (b)(3) of this section apply to the former employee, in that transaction unless the firm isolates the former Government employee in such a way that he does not assist in the representation.

(3) When isolation of the former Government employee is required under paragraph (c)(1) or (c)(2) of this section, a statement affirming the fact of such isolation shall be executed under oath by the former Government employee and by a member of the firm acting on behalf of the firm, and shall be filed with the Director of Practice and in such other place and in the manner prescribed by regulation. This statement shall clearly identify the firm, the former Government employee, and the transaction or transactions requiring such isolation.

(d) *Pending representation.* Practice by former Government employees, their partners and associates with respect to representation in specific matters where actual representation commenced before publication of this regulation is governed by the regulations set forth in the June 1972 amendments to the regulations of this part (published at 37 FR 11676): *Provided,* That the burden of showing that representation commenced before publication is with the former Government employees, their partners and associates.

§ 10.27 Notaries

No attorney, certified public accountant, or enrolled agent as notary public shall with respect to any matter administered by the Internal Revenue Service take acknowledgments, administer oaths, certify papers, or perform any official act in connection with matters in which he is employed as counsel, attorney, or agent, or in which he may be in any way interested before the Internal Revenue Service (26 Op. Atty.Gen. 236).

§ 10.28 Fees

No attorney, certified public accountant, or enrolled agent shall charge an unconscionable fee for representation of a client in any matter before the Internal Revenue Service.

§ 10.29 Conflicting Interests

No attorney, certified public accountant, or enrolled agent shall represent conflicting interests in his practice before the Internal Revenue Service, except by express consent of all directly interested parties after full disclosure has been made.

§ 10.30 Solicitation

(a) *Advertising and solicitation restrictions.* (1) No attorney, certified public accountant, enrolled agent, or other individual eligible to practice before the Internal Revenue Service shall, with respect to any Internal Revenue Service matter, in any way use or participate in the use of any form of public communication containing a false, fraudulent, misleading, deceptive, unduly influencing, coercive or unfair statement or claim. For the purposes of this subsection, the prohibition includes, but is not limited to, statements pertaining to the quality of services rendered unless subject to factual verification, claims of specialized expertise not authorized by State or Federal agencies having jurisdiction over the practioner, and statements or suggestions that the ingenuity and/or prior record of a representative rather than the merit of the matter are principal factors likely to determine the result of the matter.

(2) No attorney, certified public accountant, enrolled agent or other individual eligible to practice before the Internal Revenue Service shall make, directly or indirectly, an uninvited solicitation of employment, in matters related to the Internal Revenue Service. Solicitation includes, but is not limited to, in-person contacts, telephone communications, and personal mailings directed to the specific circumstances unique to the recipient. This restriction does not apply to: (i) Seeking new business from an existing or former client in a related matter; (ii) solicitation by mailings, the contents of which are designed for the general public; or (iii) non-coercive in-person solicitation by those eligible to practice before the Internal Revenue Service while acting as an employee, member, or officer of an exempt organization listed in sections 501(c)(3) or (4) of the Internal Revenue Code of 1954 (26 U.S.C.).

(b) *Permissible advertising.* (1) Attorneys, certified public accountants, enrolled agents and other individuals eligible to practice before the Internal Revenue Service, may publish, broadcast, or use in a dignified manner through any means of communication set forth in paragraph (d) of this section:

(i) The name, address, telephone number, and office hours of the practitioner or firm.

(ii) The names of individuals associated with the firm.

(iii) A factual description of the services offered.

(iv) Acceptable credit cards and other credit arrangements.

(v) Foreign language ability.

(vi) Membership in pertinent, professional organizations.

(vii) Pertinent professional licenses.

(viii) A statement that an individual's or firm's practice is limited to certain areas.

(ix) In the case of an enrolled agent, the phrase "enrolled to represent taxpayers before the Internal Revenue Service" or "enrolled to practice before the Internal Revenue Service."

(x) Other facts relevant to the selection of a practitioner in matters related to the Internal Revenue Service which are not prohibited by these regulations.

(2) Attorneys, certified public accountants, enrolled agents and other individuals eligible to practice before the Internal Revenue Service may use, to the extent they are consistent with the regulations in this section, customary biographical insertions in approved law lists and reputable professional journals and directories, as well as professional cards, letterheads and announcements: *Provided,* That: (i) Attorneys do not violate applicable standards of ethical conduct adopted by the American Bar Association, (ii) certified public accountants do not violate applicable standards of ethical conduct adopted by the American Institute of Certified Public Accountants, and (iii) enrolled agents do not violate applicable standards of ethical conduct adopted by either the National Society of Public Accountants or the National Association of Enrolled Agents.

(c) *Fee information.* (1) Attorneys, certified public accountants, enrolled agents and other individuals eligible to practice before the Internal Revenue Service may disseminate the following fee information:

(i) Fixed fees for specific routine services.

(ii) Hourly rates.

(iii) Range of fees for particular services.

(iv) Fee charged for an initial consultation.

(2) Attorneys, certified public accountants, enrolled agents and other individuals eligible to practice before the Internal Revenue Service may also publish the availability of a written schedule of fees.

(3) Attorneys, certified public accountants, enrolled agents and other individuals eligible to practice before the Internal Revenue Service shall be bound to charge the hourly rate, the fixed fee for specific routine services, the range of fees for particular services, or the fee for an initial consultation published for a reasonable period of time, but no less than thirty days from the last publication of such hourly rate or fees.

(d) *Communications.* Communications, including fee information, shall be limited to professional lists, telephone directories, print media, permissible mailings as provided in these regulations, radio and television. In the case of radio and television broadcasting, the broadcast shall be pre-recorded and the practitioner shall retain a recording of the actual audio transmission.

(e) *Improper associations.* An attorney, certified public accountant or enrolled agent may, in matters related to the Internal Revenue Service, employ or accept employment or assistance as an associate, correspondent, or sub-agent from, or share fees with, any person or entity who, to the knowledge of the practitioner, obtains clients or otherwise practices in a manner forbidden under this section: *Provided,* That a practitioner does not, directly or indirectly, act or hold himself out as an Internal Revenue Service practitioner in connection with that relationship. Nothing herein shall prohibit an attorney, certified public accountant, or enrolled agent from practice before the Internal Revenue Service in a capacity other than that described above.

§ 10.31 Negotiation of Taxpayer Refund Checks

No attorney, certified public accountant or enrolled agent who is an income tax return preparer shall endorse or otherwise negotiate any check made in respect of income taxes which is issued to a taxpayer other than the attorney, certified public accountant or enrolled agent.

§ 10.32 Practice of Law

Nothing in the regulations in this part shall be construed as authorizing persons not members of the bar to practice law.

§ 10.33 Tax Shelter Opinions

(a) *Tax shelter opinions and offering materials.* A practitioner who provides a tax shelter opinion analyzing the Federal tax effects of a tax shelter investment shall comply with each of the following requirements:

(1) *Factual matters.* (i) The practitioner must make inquiry as to all relevant facts, be satisfied that the material facts are accurately and completely described in the offering materials, and assure that any representations as to future activities are clearly identified, reasonable and complete.

(ii) A practitioner may not accept as true asserted facts pertaining to the tax shelter which he/she should not, based on his/her background and knowledge, reasonably believe to be true. However, a practitioner need not conduct an audit or independent verification of the asserted facts, or assume that a client's statement of the facts cannot be relied upon, unless he/she has reason to believe that any relevant facts asserted to him/her are untrue.

(iii) If the fair market value of property or the expected financial performance of an investment is relevant to the tax shelter, a practitioner may not accept an appraisal or financial projection as support for the matters claimed therein unless:

(A) The appraisal or financial projection makes sense on its face;

(B) The practitioner reasonably believes that the person making the appraisal or financial projection is competent to do so and is not of dubious reputation; and

(C) The appraisal is based on the definition of fair market value prescribed under the relevant Federal tax provisions.

(iv) If the fair market value of purchased property is to be established by reference to its stated purchase price, the practitioner must examine the terms and conditions upon which the property was (or is to be) purchased to determine whether the stated purchase price reasonably may be considered to be its fair market value.

(2) *Relate law to facts.* The practitioner must relate the law to the actual facts and, when addressing issues based on future activities, clearly identify what facts are assumed.

(3) *Identification of material issues.* The practitioner must ascertain that all material Federal tax issues have been considered, and that all of those issues which involve the reasonable possibility of a challenge by the Internal Revenue Service have been fully and fairly addressed in the offering materials.

(4) *Opinion on each material issue.* Where possible, the practitioner must provide an opinion whether it is more likely than not that an investor will prevail on the merits of each material tax issue presented by the offering which involves a reasonable possibility of a challenge by the Internal Revenue Service. Where such an opinion cannot be given with respect to any material tax issue, the opinion should fully describe the reasons for the practitioner's inability to opine as to the likely outcome.

(5) *Overall evaluation.* (i) Where possible, the practitioner must provide an overall evaluation whether the material tax benefits in the aggregate more likely than not will be realized. Where such an overall evaluation cannot be given, the opinion should fully describe the reasons for the practitioner's inability to make an overall evaluation. Opinions concluding that an overall evaluation cannot be provided will be given special scrutiny to determine if the stated reasons are adequate.

(ii) A favorable overall evaluation may not be rendered unless it is based on a conclusion that substantially more than half of the material tax benefits, in terms of their financial impact on a typical investor, more likely than not will be realized if challenged by the Internal Revenue Service.

(iii) If it is not possible to give an overall evaluation, or if the overall evaluation is that the material tax benefits in the aggregate will not be realized, the fact that the practitioner's opinion does not constitute a favorable overall evaluation, or that it is an unfavorable overall evaluation, must be clearly and prominently disclosed in the offering materials.

(iv) The following examples illustrate the principles of this paragraph:

Example (1). A limited partnership acquires real property in a sale-leaseback transaction. The principal tax benefits offered to investing partners consist of depreciation and interest deductions. Lesser tax benefits are offered to investors by reason of several deductions under Internal Revenue Code section 162 (ordinary and necessary business expenses). If a practitioner concludes that it is more likely than not that the partnership will not be treated as the owner of the property for tax purposes (which is required to allow the interest and depreciation deductions), then he/she may not opine to the effect that it is more likely than not that the material tax benefits in the aggregate will be realized, regardless of whether favorable opinions may be given with respect to the deductions claimed under Code section 162.

Example (2). A corporation electing under subchapter S of the Internal Revenue Code is formed to engage in research and development activities. The offering materials forecast that deductions for research and experimental expenditures equal to 75% of the total investment in the corporation will be available during the first two years of the corporation's operations, other expenses will account for another 15% of the total investment, and that little or no gross income will be received by the corporation during this period. The practitioner concludes that it is more likely than not that deductions for research and experimental expenditures will be allowable. The practitioner may render an opinion to the effect that based on this conclusion, it is more likely than not that the material tax benefits in the aggregate will be realized, regardless of whether he/she can opine that it is more likely than not that any of the other tax benefits will be achieved.

Example (3). An investment program is established to acquire offsetting positions in commodities contracts. The objective of the program is to close the loss positions in year one and to close the profit positions in year two. The principal tax benefit offered by the program is a loss in the first year, coupled with the deferral of offsetting gain until the following year. The practitioner concludes that the losses will not be deductible in year one. Accordingly, he/she may not render an opinion to the effect that it is more likely than not that the material tax benefits in the aggregate will be realized, regardless of the fact that he/she is of the opinion that losses not allowable in year one will be allowable in year two, because the principal tax benefit offered is a one-year deferral of income.

    Example (4). A limited partnership is formed to acquire, own and operate residential rental real estate. The offering material forecasts gross income of $2,000,000 and total deductions of $10,000,000, resulting in net losses of $8,000,000 over the first six taxable years. Of the total deductions, depreciation and interest are projected to be $7,000,000, and other deductions $3,000,000. The practitioner concludes that it is more likely than not that all of the depreciation and interest deductions will be allowable, and that it is more likely than not that the other deductions will not be allowed. The practitioner may render an opinion to the effect that it is more likely than not that the material tax benefits in the aggregate will be realized.

    (6) *Description of opinion*. The practitioner must assure that the offering materials correctly and fairly represent the nature and extent of the tax shelter opinion.

    (b) *Reliance on other opinions*—(1) *In general*. A practitioner may provide an opinion on less than all of the material tax issues only if:

    (i) At least one other competent practitioner provides an opinion on the likely outcome with respect to all of the other material tax issues which involve a reasonable possibility of challenge by the Internal Revenue Service, and an overall evaluation whether the material tax benefits in the aggregate more likely than not will be realized, which is disseminated in the same manner as the practitioner's opinion; and

    (ii) The practitioner, upon reviewing such other opinions and any offering materials, has no reason to believe that the standards of paragraph (a) of this section have not been complied with.

Notwithstanding the foregoing, a practitioner who has not been retained to provide an overall evaluation whether the material tax benefits in the aggregate more likely than not will be realized may issue an opinion on less than all the material tax issues only if he/she has no reason to believe, based on his/her knowledge and experience, that the overall evaluation given by the practitioner who furnishes the overall evaluation is incorrect on its face.

    (2) *Forecasts and projections*. A practitioner who is associated with forecasts or projections relating to or based upon the tax consequences of the tax shelter offering that are included in the offering materials, or are disseminated to potential investors other than the practitioner's clients, may rely on the opinion of another practitioner as to any or all material tax issues, provided that the practitioner who desires to rely on the other opinion has no reason to believe that the standards of paragraph (a) of this section have not been complied with by the

practitioner rendering such other opinion, and the requirements of paragraph (b)(1) of this section are satisfied. The practitioner's report shall disclose any material tax issue not covered by, or incorrectly opined upon, by the other opinion, and shall set forth his/her opinion with respect to each such issue in a manner that satisfies the requirements of paragraph (a) of this section.

(c) *Definitions.* For purposes of this section:

(1) "Practitioner" is any person authorized under § 10.3 of this part to practice before the Internal Revenue Service.

(2) A "tax shelter," as the term is used in this section, is an investment which has as a significant and intended feature for Federal income or excise tax purposes either of the following attributes:

(i) Deductions in excess of income from the investment being available in any year to reduce income from other sources in that year, or

(ii) Credits in excess of the tax attributable to the income from the investment being available in any year to offset taxes on income from other sources in that year. Excluded from the term are municipal bonds; annuities; family trusts (but not including schemes or arrangements that are marketed to the public other than in a direct practitioner-client relationship); qualified retirement plans; individual retirement accounts; stock option plans; securities issued in a corporate reorganization; mineral development ventures, if the only tax benefit would be percentage depletion; and real estate where it is anticipated that in no year is it likely that deductions will exceed gross income from the investment in that year, or that tax credits will exceed the tax attributable to gross income from the investment in that year. Whether an investment is intended to have tax shelter features depends on the objective facts and circumstances of each case. Significant weight will be given to the features described in the offering materials to determine whether the investment is a tax shelter.

(3) A "tax shelter opinion," as the term is used in this section, is advice by a practitioner concerning the Federal tax aspects of a tax shelter either appearing or referred to in the offering materials, or used or referred to in connection with sales promotion efforts, and directed to persons other than the client who engaged the practitioner to give the advice. The term includes the tax aspects or tax risks portion of the offering materials prepared by or at the direction of a practitioner, whether or not a separate opinion letter is issued or whether or not the practitioner's name is referred to in the offering materials or in connection with the sales promotion efforts. In addition, a financial forecast or projection

prepared by a practitioner is a tax shelter opinion if it is predicated on assumptions regarding Federal tax aspects of the investment, and it meets the other requirements of the first sentence of this paragraph. The term does not, however, include rendering advice solely to the offeror or reviewing parts of the offering materials, so long as neither the name of the practitioner, nor the fact that a practitioner has rendered advice concerning the tax aspects, is referred to in the offering materials or in connection with the sales promotion efforts.

(4) A "material" tax issue as the term is used in this section is

(i) Any Federal income or excise tax issue relating to a tax shelter that would make a significant contribution toward sheltering from Federal taxes income from other sources by providing deductions in excess of the income from the tax shelter investment in any year, or tax credits available to offset tax liabilities in excess of the tax attributable to the tax shelter investment in any year;

(ii) Any other Federal income or excise tax issue relating to a tax shelter that could have a significant impact (either beneficial or adverse) on a tax shelter investor under any reasonably foreseeable circumstances (e.g., depreciation or investment tax credit recapture, availability of long-term capital gain treatment, or realization of taxable income in excess of cash flow, upon sale or other disposition of the tax shelter investment); and

(iii) The potential applicability of penalties, additions to tax, or interest charges that reasonably could be asserted against a tax shelter investor by the Internal Revenue Service with respect to the tax shelter. The determination of what is material is to be made in good faith by the practitioner, based on information available at the time the offering materials are circulated.

Subpart C. Rules Applicable to Disciplinary Proceedings

§ 10.50 Authority to Disbar or Suspend

Pursuant to section 3 of the Act of July 7, 1984, 23 Stat. 258 (31 U.S.C. 1026), the Secretary of the Treasury, after due notice and opportunity for hearing, may suspend or disbar from practice before the Internal Revenue Service any attorney, certified public accountant, or enrolled agent shown to be incompetent, disreputable or who refuses to comply with the rules and regulations in this part or who shall, with intent to defraud, in any manner willfully and knowingly deceive, mislead, or threaten any claimant or prospective claimant, by word, circular, letter, or by advertisement.

§ 10.51 Disreputable Conduct

Disreputable conduct for which an attorney, certified public accountant, or enrolled agent may be disbarred or suspended from practice before the Internal Revenue Service includes, but is not limited to:

(a) Conviction of any criminal offense under the revenue laws of the United States, or of any offense involving dishonesty, or breach of trust.

(b) Giving false or misleading information, or participating in any way in the giving of false or misleading information to the Department of the Treasury or any officer or employee thereof, or to any tribunal authorized to pass upon Federal tax matters, in connection with any matter pending or likely to be pending before them, knowing such information to be false or misleading. Facts or other matters contained in testimony, Federal tax returns, financial statements, applications for enrollment, affidavits, declarations, or any other document or statement, written or oral, are included in the term "information."

(c) Solicitation of employment as prohibited under § 10.30, the use of false or misleading representations with intent to deceive a client or prospective client in order to procure employment, or intimating that the practitioner is able improperly to obtain special consideration or action from the Internal Revenue Service or officer or employee thereof.

(d) Willfully failing to make Federal tax return in violation of the revenue laws of the United States, or evading, attempting to evade, or participating in any way in evading or attempting to evade any Federal tax or payment thereof, knowingly counseling or suggesting to a client or prospective client an illegal plan to evade Federal taxes or payment thereof, or concealing assets of himself or another to evade Federal taxes or payment thereof.

(e) Misappropriation of, or failure properly and promptly to remit funds received from a client for the purpose of payment of taxes or other obligations due the United States.

(f) Directly or indirectly attempting to influence, or offering or agreeing to attempt to influence, the official action of any officer or employee of the Internal Revenue Service by the use of threats, false accusations, duress or coercion, by the offer of any special inducement or promise of advantage or by the bestowing of any gift, favor or thing of value.

(g) Disbarment or suspension from practice as an attorney, certified public accountant, public accountant, or actuary by any duly constituted authority of any State, possession, territory, Commonwealth, the District of Columbia, any Federal court of record or any Federal agency, body or board.

(h) Knowingly aiding and abetting another person to practice before the Internal Revenue Service during a period of suspension, disbarment, or ineligibility of such other person. Maintaining a partnership for the practice of law, accountancy, or other related professional service with a person who is under disbarment from practice before the Service shall be presumed to be a violation of this provision.

(i) Contemptuous conduct in connection with practice before the Internal Revenue Service, including the use of abusive language, making false accusations and statements knowing them to be false, or circulating or publishing malicious or libelous matter.

(j) Giving a false opinion, knowingly, recklessly, or through gross incompetence, including an opinion which is intentionally or recklessly misleading, or a pattern of providing incompetent opinions on questions arising under the Federal tax laws. False opinions described in this paragraph include those which reflect or result from a knowing misstatement of fact or law; from an assertion of a position known to be unwarranted under existing law; from counseling or assisting in conduct known to be illegal or fraudulent; from concealment of matters required by law to be revealed; or from conscious disregard of information indicating that material facts expressed in the tax opinion or offering material are false or misleading. For the purpose of this paragraph, reckless conduct is a highly unreasonable omission or misrepresentation, involving not merely simple or inexcusable negligence, but an extreme departure from the standards of ordinary care that is either known or is so obvious that the competent practitioner must or should have been aware of it. Gross incompetence includes conduct that reflects gross indifference, preparation which is grossly inadequate under the circumstances, and a consistent failure to perform obligations to the client.

§ 10.52   Violation of Regulations

(a) *In general.* Any attorney, certified public accountant, or enrolled agent may be disbarred or suspended from practice before the Internal Revenue Service for willful violation of any of the regulations contained in this part.

(b) *Tax shelter opinions.* An attorney, certified public accountant, enrolled agent or enrolled actuary may be disbarred or suspended from practice before the Internal Revenue Service for violating any part of § 10.33 of this part, if such violation is willfull, reckless or through gross incompetence (within the meaning of § 10.51(j) of this part); or if the violation is part of a pattern of providing tax shelter opinions that fail to comply with § 10.33 of this part.

§ 10.53   Receipt of Information Concerning Attorneys, Certified Public Accountants and Enrolled Agents

If an officer or employee of the Internal Revenue Service has reason to believe that an attorney, certified public accountant, or enrolled agent has violated any provision of this part, or if any such officer or employee receives information to that effect, he shall promptly make a written report thereof, which report or a copy thereof shall be forwarded to the Director of Practice. If any other person has information of such violations, he may make a report thereof to the Director of Practice or to any officer or employee of the Internal Revenue Service.

§ 10.54 Institution of Proceeding

Whenever the Director of Practice has reason to believe that any attorney, certified public accountant, or enrolled agent has violated any provision of the laws or regulations governing practice before the Internal Revenue Service, he may reprimand such person or institute a proceeding for disbarment or suspension of such person. The proceeding shall be instituted by a complaint which names the respondent and is signed by the Director of Practice and filed in his office. Except in cases of willfulness, or where time, the nature of the proceeding, or the public interest does not permit, a proceeding will not be instituted under this section until facts or conduct which may warrant such action have been called to the attention of the proposed respondent in writing and he has been accorded opportunity to demonstrate or achieve compliance with all lawful requirements.

[The remaining sections of Circular 230 which deal with the disciplinary process are omitted. Ed.]

SELECTED STANDARDS FOR
PROFESSIONALISM AND COURTESY
IN LITIGATION

PROFESSIONALISM STANDARDS IN THE NORTHERN
DISTRICT OF TEXAS

121 F.R.D. 287, 88 (N.D.Tex.1988) (en banc)

* * *

B.

We next set out the standards to which we expect litigation counsel to adhere.

The Dallas Bar Association recently adopted "Guidelines of Professional Courtesy" and a "Lawyer's Creed" that are both sensible and pertinent to the problems we address here. From them we adopt the following as standards of practice [8] to be observed by attorneys appearing in civil actions in this district:

(A) In fulfilling his or her primary duty to the client, a lawyer must be ever conscious of the broader duty to the judicial system that serves both attorney and client.

(B) A lawyer owes, to the judiciary, candor, diligence and utmost respect.

(C) A lawyer owes, to opposing counsel, a duty of courtesy and cooperation, the observance of which is necessary for the efficient administration of our system of justice and the respect of the public it serves.

(D) A lawyer unquestionably owes, to the administration of justice, the fundamental duties of personal dignity and professional integrity.

(E) Lawyers should treat each other, the opposing party, the court, and members of the court staff with courtesy and civility and conduct themselves in a professional manner at all times.

(F) A client has no right to demand that counsel abuse the opposite party or indulge in offensive conduct. A lawyer shall always treat adverse witnesses and suitors with fairness and due consideration.

(G) In adversary proceedings, clients are litigants and though ill feeling may exist between clients, such ill feeling should not

8. We also commend to counsel the American College of Trial Lawyers' Code of Trial Conduct (rev. 1987). Those portions of the Code that are applicable to our decision today are set out in the appendix.

influence a lawyer's conduct, attitude, or demeanor towards opposing lawyers.

(H) A lawyer should not use any form of discovery, or the scheduling of discovery, as a means of harassing opposing counsel or counsel's client.

(I) Lawyers will be punctual in communications with others and in honoring scheduled appearances, and will recognize that neglect and tardiness are demeaning to the lawyer and to the judicial system.

(J) If a fellow member of the Bar makes a just request for cooperation, or seeks scheduling accommodation, a lawyer will not arbitrarily or unreasonably withhold consent.

(K) Effective advocacy does not require antagonistic or obnoxious behavior and members of the Bar will adhere to the higher standard of conduct which judges, lawyers, clients, and the public may rightfully expect.

Attorneys who abide faithfully by the standards we adopt should have little difficulty conducting themselves as members of a learned profession whose unswerving duty is to the public they serve and to the system of justice in which they practice. Those litigators who persist in viewing themselves solely as combatants, or who perceive that they are retained to win at all costs without regard to fundamental principles of justice, will find that their conduct does not square with the practices we expect of them. Malfeasant counsel can expect instead that their conduct will prompt an appropriate response from the court, including the range of sanctions the Fifth Circuit suggests in the Rule 11 context: "a warm friendly discussion on the record, a hard-nosed reprimand in open court, compulsory legal education, monetary sanctions, or other measures appropriate to the circumstances." *Thomas*, 836 F.2d at 878.

A PROPOSED CODE OF LITIGATION CONDUCT

By THE COMMITTEE ON FEDERAL COURTS

Reprinted from The Record of the Association of the Bar of the City of New York, Vol. 43, No. 6, pp. 738–750, © 1988. Reprinted with permission.

There is an emerging debate, in the pages of legal periodicals, in ABA committee reports, and elsewhere, over the conduct of lawyers. On one side of this debate are the many highly respected trial lawyers who believe that lawyers should play "hardball;" they contend that a lawyer has a duty to go "right to the limits of zealous advocacy" in representing his clients, and if he does not, he is somehow doing them a disservice. The views of many of the adherents of this position can be found in "Playing Hardball," *ABA Journal*, July 1987. Proponents of this view tend to describe their tactics in colorful, often militaristic, terminology: "When I go into the courtroom, I come in to do battle. I am not there to do a minuet. . . ." Another lawyer made the point that "you're really not in this to be liked," and added that although she generally cared about what people thought of her, in the context of litigation, she really did not care. A prominent law professor took the view that civility in litigation can be "a euphemism for the old boy network, or covering up for one another."

The opposing view was expressed in "Rambo Litigation—Why Hardball Tactics Don't Work," *ABA Journal*, March 1988. The author, also a prominent trial lawyer, argued that "hardball" litigation was bad advocacy: bad for a client's position, and bad for a lawyer's longevity and his or her standing at the bar. He also argued that "hardball" litigation was ineffective, and that lawyers who resorted to such tactics harmed their clients' cause more often than they helped.

While the Federal Courts Committee supports that [sic.] views of those who oppose "hardball" litigation tactics, it believes that there is more to be said in opposition. For one thing, it is simply not true that "hardball" litigation always constitutes bad or ineffective lawyering. Many clients do crumble in the face of an opposing counsel's campaign of harassment, and those lawyers who set out to make life unremittingly unpleasant for their adversaries often do succeed in wearing those adversaries down. We doubt that there could ever be any meaningful statistical evidence on whether "hardball" litigation tactics are ultimately effective or ineffective. Moreover, the argument against such tactics should not merely be utilitarian; that argument is too easily met by those who can demonstrate that "hardball" tactics often work.

The purpose of this report is to address the way lawyers treat one another. This is not simply an issue of interpersonal relations at the bar; the way lawyers treat each other inevitably affects how they treat each other's clients as well. Hence, clients, and thus the public at large, have a clear stake in how lawyers behave. The profession's own stake in this issue is too obvious to require extended discussion.

We start with a premise that some will challenge: the level of civility among lawyers is not what it should be. This conclusion does not apply with equal force to all segments of the bar; those parts of the bar that are smaller and more closely knit, such as the admiralty or patent bars, tend to be more civil. But in the environment in which most of us practice, the New York City commercial bar, the conclusion is certainly valid. We do not propose to explore the causes, but rather to suggest some solutions.

The kind of conduct that is the subject of this report is not the sort that is proscribed, for the most part, by the canons of ethics or even by judicial interpretations of Rule 11. We are interested more in conduct that is legal, ethical, and usually beyond the reach of sanctions, but is nevertheless, in our view, improper. Such conduct, although both legal and ethical, tends to violate the appropriate relationships among lawyers. It is the kind of conduct that makes life at the bar more difficult for lawyers and clients, and unnecessarily so. We hope that by suggesting rules of conduct, we will provide some guidance to the bar and initiate a debate about where proper lines should be drawn.

In what follows we shall address certain areas of conduct that we have identified as particularly subject to abuse. The list is not meant to be exhaustive, and we certainly invite others to contribute to the discussion we hope will ensue.

1. *Adjournments and Extensions of Time*

a. Upon request coupled with a simple representation by counsel that more time is required, first requests for extensions to respond to pleadings should be granted as a matter of courtesy unless time is of the essence.

b. After an extension comparable in length to the original time period, any additional requests for time should be dealt with by balancing the need for expedition against the time actually needed for the task and/or the opponent's scheduled engagements.

c. An opponent's schedule of professional and personal engagements should be accommodated to the extent reasonably possible in scheduling and rescheduling notice dates for depositions, motions and hearings.

d. A lawyer has the responsibility to advise clients against the strategy of "granting no adjournments for the sake of appearing tough."

e. A lawyer should not seek extensions and adjournments for the purpose of prolonging litigation.

f. A lawyer should not attach to extensions unfair and extraneous conditions of waiver of substantive rights or seek to use such extensions for tactical advantage. A lawyer is entitled to impose conditions such as preserving rights that an extension might otherwise jeopardize or seeking reciprocal scheduling concessions. A lawyer may not, by granting extensions, seek to preclude an opponent's substantive rights, such as his or her right to move against a complaint or to waive certain objections.

COMMENT:

This is an area in which there is much haggling among counsel, but there should be none. Judges do not want to be bothered with such disputes, and lawyers should rarely be bothered with them either. All counsel share the obligation to conduct litigation in an expeditious manner and to act within the time limits provided by the rules when no extension is needed. Expedition, however, is often best achieved by cooperation among counsel with respect to scheduling matters. In this regard, the granting of requests for extensions and adjournments of reasonable length beyond the minimum time period provided by the rules is a courtesy that both lawyers and clients should observe and be able to rely on.

2. *Service of Papers*

a. The timing and manner of service of papers should not be used to the disadvantage of the party receiving the papers.

b. Opposing counsel should be provided with papers in no less expeditious a manner than service made upon the court; for example, when the court is served by hand, opposing counsel should not be served by mail. See ABA Code of Professional Responsibility ("ABA Code"), EC 7–35; DR 7–110(B)(2).

c. Papers should not be served sufficiently close to a court appearance so as to inhibit the ability of opposing counsel to prepare for that appearance or respond to the papers.

d. Papers should not be served in order to take advantage of an opponent's known absence from the office.

e. Papers should not be served at a time or in a manner designed to inconvenience an adversary, such as late on Friday afternoon or the day preceding a secular or religious holiday.

COMMENT:

It is the Committee's view that service of papers should never, under any circumstances, be used as a litigation tactic. Stratagems involving service too often take advantage of disparities in the size and resources of lawyers and litigants. We believe that courts are entitled to hear from counsel fully prepared to address an opponent's arguments, not disadvantaged by tricks of service.

3. *Written Submissions to a Court, Including, But Not Limited to, Briefs, Memoranda, and Affidavits*

a. Written submissions should not rely on materials that are not part of, or that will not be part of, the record. A litigant may, however, present historical, economic, or sociological data if such data appears in or is derived from generally available sources.

b. Written submissions should avoid *ad hominem* arguments.

c. Written submissions should not, as a general rule, disparage the intelligence, ethics, morals, integrity or personal behavior of one's adversaries. Exceptions to this rule can be made when adversaries' conduct is an issue in the litigation as, for example, in an application for sanctions pursuant to Rule 11. See ABA Code DR 7–106(C)(6).

COMMENT:

Ad hominem arguments do not belong in briefs. Courts are not interested in seeing lawyers exchange insults, and are rarely, if ever, persuaded by this type of argumentation. The principal effects of *ad hominem* arguments are: (a) eliciting a comparable response; (b) poisoning, sometimes permanently, relationships among counsel; and (c) as a consequence of (a) and (b), increasing the expense of litigation for the clients.

4. *Sur–Reply Papers*

Such papers, unless permitted by rule, should not be served without leave of the court.

COMMENT:

Too many lawyers are unable to resist the last word. They will keep submitting briefs, letters, or affidavits until the last word is theirs, no matter how long it takes. The Committee believes that lawyers should follow the rules, and that if sur-reply briefs are not explicitly authorized by the applicable rules, they should not be served without leave of court.

5. *Communications with Adversaries*

a. In both written and oral communications, counsel should at all times be both civil and courteous.

b. Letters should not be written to ascribe to one's adversary a position he has not taken.

c. Letters should not be designed to create "a record" of events that have not occurred.

d. Letters between counsel should not be sent to judges unless the correspondence concerns matters before the court for adjudication or the judge has requested it.

COMMENT:

Some lawyers believe it acceptable—and, indeed, regard it as a sign of the requisite "toughness"—to be uncivil or abusive to one's adversaries, either orally or in writing. The Committee believes that such conduct is not now, and never has been, appropriate behavior for members of the bar.

Acrimonious letter writing is one manifestation of this incivility. Such letters largely serve to make the writer feel good, and let the client think that something is being accomplished where nothing really is. They are a major contributing factor to the disintegration of relationships among counsel.

6. *Depositions*

a. Depositions should be taken only where actually needed to ascertain facts or information or to perpetuate testimony. They should never be used as a means of harassment or to generate expenses.

b. In scheduling depositions, reasonable consideration should be given to accommodating schedules of opposing counsel and of the opponent, where it is possible to do so without prejudicing the client's rights.

c. Counsel should attempt to delay a deposition only if necessary to meet real scheduling problems, and not for dilatory purposes.

d. In defending a deposition, counsel for the deponent should refrain from all objections to questions except objections which are waived unless made relating to the form of the questions, privileged matters, or objections to questions calculated to harass or manifestly irrelevant to the subject matter of the examination.

e. At no time should counsel, through objections or otherwise, coach the deponent or suggest answers. See E.D.N.Y. Standing Order 12. Counsel should not direct the deponent to refuse to answer questions except those which seek privileged information or are manifestly irrelevant or calculated to harass.

f. Deponent's counsel should not attempt to confer with the deponent while a question is pending and should limit any private discussions with the deponent during the deposition to circumstances in which it is necessary to determine whether a privilege should be asserted or otherwise necessary to protect the rights of the witness or party.

g. Counsel should not inquire into a deponent's personal affairs or question a deponent's integrity where such inquiry is irrelevant to the subject matter of the deposition. See ABA Code DR 7–106(C)(2). Counsel should also refrain from other types of questions asked solely for purposes of harassment and from self-serving speeches designed to make a "record" of his or her own statements.

COMMENT:

The principal problems in the conduct of lawyers at depositions are symmetrical: abusive and unnecessarily intrusive or prolonged questioning on the one hand, and excessive interference with questioning by way of objection or instructions not to answer on the other. Among the causes of such behavior are inexperience; the desire to appear tough to one's client; the desire to use the deposition as an instrument of harassment rather than as a discovery tool; attempts to take advantage of a less experienced adversary through intimidation. Most such antics would not take place in the presence of a judicial officer, and the Committee believes that any conduct in which a lawyer would not engage in the presence of a judge is equally inappropriate in the judge's absence.

7. *Document Demands*

a. Demands for production of documents should be limited to documents actually and reasonably believed to be needed for the prosecution or defense of an action and not made to harass or embarrass a party or witness.

b. In responding to document demands, counsel should not strain to interpret the request in an artificially restricted manner in order to avoid disclosure, but instead should seek to comply with the purpose, spirit and intent of the demand.

c. Documents should be withheld on the grounds of privilege only where appropriate and then only when the privileged documents are enumerated and described by category, author, recipient, and date.

d. F.R.Civ.P. 34(b) permits a party responding to a document request to produce documents either "as they are kept in the usual course of business" or organized and labeled to correspond to the categories in the request. Counsel should follow one of these procedures, but in so doing should not produce documents in a disorganized or unintelligible fashion, or by means calculated to hide or obscure the existence of particular documents.

e. Document production should not be delayed to prevent opposing counsel from inspecting documents prior to scheduled depositions or for any other tactical reason.

COMMENT:

The abuses in document discovery are too well known to require detailed elaboration here. Here too, excesses exist on both sides—overly broad document demands, and unduly narrow responses to such demands. The Committee believes that it is the responsibility of counsel to see to it that document production becomes more than a game in which the proponent seeks to discover the universe, and the recipient hides behind unacceptably narrow interpretations of terms whose plain meaning is all too obvious.

8. *Interrogatories*

a. Interrogatories should be used sparingly, and form interrogatories should be avoided. See E.D.N.Y. Standing Order 15; S.D.N.Y. Civil Rule 46.

b. Interrogatories should be read by the recipient with the recognition that the attorney who prepared them did not have the information being sought; hence they should not be read in a technical or artificial manner designed to assure that the responses are technically in compliance with the inquiry, but not truly responsive. See E.D.N.Y. Standing Order 16.

COMMENT:

Much of the abuse formerly associated with the preparation of, and response to, interrogatories has been dealt with by local rule. See S.D. N.Y. Civil Rule 46. Such rules have severely limited the length, timing and number of interrogatories. We believe that interrogatory abuse is one example of a behaviorial problem that has been successfully addressed by rule making.

9. *Motion Practice*

a. More than a mere *pro forma* discussion should occur between counsel prior to the making of any motion, unless it is patently clear that such a discussion will be useless.

b. When an attorney believes his or her position is not sustainable, he or she should not force his or her adversary to make a motion and then not oppose it.

COMMENT:

Motion practice is expensive for clients and burdensome for the court. The Committee's proposals should cut down on two kinds of motions: those that can be resolved through negotiation among counsel, and those that are uncontested but which lawyers force their adversaries to make anyway.

10. *Dealing with Non-party Witnesses*

a. Counsel should not issue subpoenas to non-party witnesses except in connection with their appearance at trial or at a deposition.

b. Deposition subpoenas should be accompanied by notices of deposition with copies to all counsel.

c. Where an attorney obtains documents pursuant to a deposition subpoena, copies of the documents should be made available to the adversary even if the deposition is cancelled or adjourned.

d. Counsel may speak to any non-party witness who is willing to speak to them. Counsel should not use any threats or promises to secure or prevent such witnesses' cooperation, appearance or nonappearance. See ABA Code DR 7–109.

COMMENT:

When attorneys involve the processes of the court to obtain information from third-party witnesses, notice should always be given to one's adversary. Attorneys should not use the processes of the court to take advantage of non-party witnesses. *See Matter of Bein v. Wynyard,* 133 A.D.2d 37 (1st Dept.1987).

11. *Ex Parte Communications with the Court*

a. A lawyer should avoid *ex parte* communication on the subject of a pending case with a judge before whom such case is pending.

b. Even where applicable laws or rules permit an *ex parte* application or communication to the court, before making such an application or communication, a lawyer should make diligent efforts to notify the opposing party or a lawyer known to represent or likely to represent the opposing party and shall make reasonable efforts to accommodate the schedule of such lawyer to permit the opposing party to be represented on the application.

c. Where the rules permit an *ex parte* application or communication to the court in an emergency situation, a lawyer should make such an application or communication (including an application to shorten an otherwise applicable time period) only where there is a *bona fide* emergency such that the lawyer's client will be seriously prejudiced by a failure to make the application or communication on regular notice.

COMMENT:

In our adversary system, *ex parte* communications create a serious danger of prejudice to the rights of the unrepresented party as well as a substantial appearance of impropriety. *Ex parte* application on routine matters, such as bringing on a motion by order to show cause where there is no true emergency, constitutes another form of abuse. Such applications should be avoided. Even where it is necessary to proceed by order to show cause and where existing rules or practices permit such applications to be made *ex parte*, opposing counsel should be notified in advance.

Where the lawyer has reason to believe that a party is or is likely to be represented on a particular matter, no *ex parte* communication should be undertaken without reasonable efforts to notify such lawyer even if the lawyer has not formally appeared. The reality is that a lawyer frequently knows who is likely to represent the opposing party and should not hide behind the technicality that the lawyer has not yet appeared in order to legitimize an otherwise inappropriate *ex parte* communication or application.

12. *Settlement Practices*

a. Except where there are strong and overriding issues of principle, an attorney should raise and explore the issue of settlement in every case, preferably at the outset, so long as enough is known about the case to make settlement discussions meaningful.

b. In jury cases, attorneys should not hesitate to seek the assistance of the court in aid of settlement.

c. In non-jury cases, attorneys should use either the court or another third-party intermediary, where appropriate.

d. Attorneys should not falsely hold out the possibility of settlements as a means for adjourning discovery or delaying trial.

COMMENT:

Attorneys have an affirmative obligation to encourage settlement of litigation, except where (a) the litigation involves a question of principle that cannot be readily resolved by a financial settlement or (b) the position of the other side is totally lacking in merit. Attorneys should recognize the strength of the litigant's settlement posture as independent of who initiates settlement discussions or when such discussions are initiated.

June, 1988

*

PART FOUR

STANDARDS FOR THE ORGANIZED REGULATION OF LAWYERS

Table of Contents

Introduction

Although the legal profession has sought to exercise self regulation over its members through the promulgation of codes of conduct, true self regulation will not result unless the profession has implemented a mechanism for enforcing the codes. In other words, violations of the codes of conduct must in some manner be identified and prosecuted with some degree of effectiveness and fairness. Sanctions must be assessed against violators to deter others from violating the rules and to ensure that the violating lawyer does not commit future violations.

Until recently, the ABA had not focused its efforts on the disciplinary mechanism and sanctions; instead, its efforts were placed in defining the substantive aspect of the codes of conduct. In 1970, former Justice Tom Clark chaired a commission on evaluating disciplinary enforcement. The Commission's Report concluded that state bars needed model standards on which to base their systems of discipline. In 1979, the ABA adopted Standards for Lawyer Discipline and Disability Proceedings. In 1985, the ABA adopted the Model Rules for Lawyer Disciplinary Enforcement. These early codes for developing disciplinary systems proved to be inadequate and they have been replaced in 1986 by the Standards for Imposing Lawyer Standards and in 1989 by the Model Rules of Disciplinary Enforcement. In 1992, the ABA House of Delegates adopted 21 recommendations for the evaluation of a system of disciplinary enforcement. These standards are reproduced in this part.

ABA RECOMMENDATIONS FOR THE EVALUATION OF DISCIPLINARY ENFORCEMENT

[In 1992, the ABA House of Delegates adopted 21 recommendations with respect to the evaluation of systems of disciplinary enforcement. The recommendations were adopted only as suggestions to the various jurisdictions and the determination of whether a suggestion was to be accepted was left up to the individual jurisdictions. Ed.]

Recommendation 1: Regulation of the Profession by the Judiciary

Regulation of the legal profession should remain under the authority of the judicial branch of government.

Recommendation 2: Supporting Judicial Regulation and Professional Responsibility

2.1 The American Bar Association should continue to place the highest priority on promoting, developing, and supporting judicial regulation of the legal profession and professional responsibility.

2.2 The Association should continue to provide adequate funding and staffing for activities to support judicial regulation and professional responsibility.

2.3 To promote the most efficient allocation of resources, the Association should establish written policies to insure that all of its judicial regulation and professional responsibility activities are coordinate, regardless of the Association entity conducting the activity.

Recommendation 3: Expanding the Scope of Public Protection

The Court should establish a system of regulation of the legal profession that consists of:

3.1 component agencies, including but not limited to:

    (a) lawyer discipline,

    (b) a client protection fund,

    (c) mandatory arbitration of fee disputes,

    (d) voluntary arbitration of lawyer malpractice claims and other disputes,

654

(e) mediation,

(f) lawyer practice assistance,

(g) lawyer substance abuse counseling; and

3.2 a central intake office for the receipt of all complaints about lawyers, whose functions should include: (a) providing assistance to complainants in stating their complaints; (b) making a preliminary determination as to the validity of the complaint; (c) dismissing the complaint or determining the appropriate component agency or agencies to which the complaint should be directed and forwarding the complaint; (d) providing information to complainants about available remedies, operations and procedures, and the status of their complaints; and (e) coordinating among agencies and tracking the handling and disposition of each complaint.

Recommendation 4: Lawyer Practice Assistance Committee

4.1 The Court should establish a Lawyer Practice Assistance Committee. At least one third of the members should be nonlawyers. The Lawyer Assistance Committee should consider cases referred to it by the disciplinary counsel and the Court and should assist lawyers voluntarily seeking assistance. The Committee should provide guidance to the lawyer including, when appropriate: (a) review of the lawyer's office and case management practices and recommendations for improvement; and (b) review of the lawyer's substantive knowledge of the law and recommendations for further study.

4.2 In cases in which the lawyer has agreed with disciplinary counsel to submit to practice assistance, the Committee may require the lawyer to attend continuing legal education classes, to attend and successfully complete law school courses or office management courses, to participate in substance abuse recovery programs or in psychological counseling, or to take other actions necessary to improve the lawyer's fitness to practice law.

Recommendation 5: Independence of Disciplinary Officials

All jurisdictions should structure their lawyer disciplinary systems so that disciplinary officials are appointed by the highest court of the jurisdiction or by other disciplinary officials who are appointed by the Court. Disciplinary officials should possess sufficient independent authority to conduct the lawyer discipline function impartially:

5.1 Elected bar officials, their appointees and employees should provide only administrative and other services for the disciplinary system that support the operation of the system without impairing the independence of disciplinary officials.

5.2 Elected bar officials, their appointees and employees should have no investigative, prosecutorial, or adjudicative functions in the disciplinary process.

5.3 The budget for the office of disciplinary counsel should be formulated by disciplinary counsel. The budget for the state-wide disciplinary board should be formulated by the board. Disciplinary budgets should be approved or modified directly by the Court or by an administrative agency of the Court. Disciplinary counsel and the disciplinary board should be accountable for the expenditure of funds only to the Court, except that bar associations may provide accounting and other financial services that do not impair the independence of disciplinary officials.

5.4 Disciplinary counsel and staff, disciplinary adjudicators and staff, and other disciplinary agency personnel should be absolutely immune from civil liability for all actions performed within the scope of their duties, consistent with the American Bar Association's Model Rules for Lawyer Disciplinary Enforcement 12A.

Recommendation 6: Independence of Disciplinary Counsel

6.1 The Court alone should appoint and remove disciplinary counsel and should provide sufficient authority for prosecutorial independence and discretion.

The Court should also promulgate rules providing that disciplinary counsel shall:

(a) have authority to employ and terminate staff, formulate a budget and approve expenditures subject only to the authority of the Court;

(b) have authority, in cases involving allegations of minor incompetence, neglect, or misconduct, to resolve a matter with the consent of the respondent by administrative procedures established by the Court;

(c) have authority to appeal a decision of a hearing committee or the disciplinary board;

(d) be compensated sufficiently to attract competent counsel and retain experienced counsel; and

(e) be prohibited from providing advisory ethics opinions, either orally or in writing.

6.2 The Court should adopt a rule providing that no disciplinary adjudicative official (including hearing committee members, disciplinary board members, or members of the Court) shall communicate ex parte with disciplinary counsel regarding an ongoing investigation or disciplinary matter, except about administrative matters or to report information alleging the misconduct of a lawyer.

Recommendation 7: Access to Disciplinary Information

All records of the lawyer disciplinary agency except the work product of disciplinary counsel should be available to the public after a determination has been made that probable cause exists to believe misconduct occurred, unless the complainant or respondent obtains a protective order from the highest court or its designee for specific testimony, documents or records. All proceedings except adjudicative deliberations should be public after a determination that probable cause exists to believe that misconduct occurred.

Recommendation 8: Complainant's Rights

8.1 Complainants should receive notice of the status of disciplinary proceedings. In general, a complainant should receive, contemporaneously, the same notices and orders the respondent receives as well as copies of respondent's communications to the agency, except information that is subject to another client's privilege.

8.2 Complainants should be permitted a reasonable opportunity to rebut statements of the respondent before a complaint is summarily dismissed.

8.3 Complainants should be notified in writing when the complaint has been dismissed. The notice should include a concise recitation of the specific facts and reasoning upon which the decision to dismiss was made.

8.4 Disciplinary counsel should issue written guidelines for determining which cases will be dismissed for failure to allege facts that, if true, would constitute grounds for disciplinary action. These guidelines should be sent to complainants whose cases are dismissed.

8.5 Complainants should be notified of the date, time, and location of the hearing. Complainants should have the right to personally appear and testify at the hearing.

8.6 All jurisdictions should afford a right of review to complainants whose complaints are dismissed prior to a full hearing on the merits, consistent with the American Bar Association's Model Rules for Lawyer Disciplinary Enforcement 11B(3) and 31.

Recommendation 9: Procedures in Lieu of Discipline for Minor Misconduct

All jurisdictions should adopt procedures in lieu of discipline for matters in which a lawyer's actions constitute minor misconduct, minor incompetence, or minor neglect. The procedures should provide:

657

9.1 The Court shall define criteria for matters involving minor misconduct, minor incompetence, or minor neglect that may be resolved by non-disciplinary proceedings or dismissal.

9.2 If disciplinary counsel determines that a matter meets the criteria established by the Court, disciplinary counsel may reach agreement with the respondent to submit the matter to non-disciplinary proceedings. Such proceedings may consist of fee arbitration, mediation, lawyer practice assistance, substance abuse recovery programs, psychological counseling, or any other non-disciplinary proceedings authorized by the Court. Disciplinary counsel shall then refer the matter to the agency or agencies authorized by the Court to conduct the proceedings.

9.3 If the lawyer does not comply with the terms of the agreement, disciplinary counsel may resume disciplinary proceedings.

9.4 If the lawyer fulfills the terms of the agreement, the disciplinary counsel shall dismiss the disciplinary proceeding.

Recommendation 10: Expedited Procedures for Minor Misconduct

All jurisdictions should adopt simplified, expedited procedures to adjudicate cases in which the alleged misconduct warrants less than suspension or disbarment or other restriction on the right to practice. Expedited procedures should provide:

10.1 The Court shall define minor violations of the rules of professional conduct that shall subject the respondent to sanctions not constituting restrictions on the right to practice law, consistent with the ABA Standards for Imposing Lawyer Sanctions.

10.2 A hearing shall be held by a single adjudicator (member of a hearing committee).

10.3 The adjudicator shall make concise, written findings of fact and conclusions of law and shall either dismiss the case or impose a sanction that does not constitute a restriction on the respondent's right to practice.

10.4 Respondent and Disciplinary counsel shall have the right to appeal the decision to a second adjudicator (member of the statewide disciplinary board), who shall either adopt the decision below or make written findings. The appellate adjudicator shall either dismiss the case or impose a sanction that does not constitute a restriction on the respondent's right to practice.

10.5 The decision of the appellate adjudicator may be reviewed at the discretion of the Court upon application by respondent or Disciplinary counsel. The Court shall grant review only in cases involving significant issues of law or upon a showing that the decision below constituted an abuse of discretion. The Court shall either adopt the decision below or make written findings. The Court shall either dismiss the case or impose a sanction that does not constitute a restriction on the respondent's right to practice.

10.6 Upon final disposition of the case, the written findings of the final adjudicator shall be published in an appropriate journal or reporter and a copy shall be mailed to the respondent and the complainant and to the ABA National Discipline Data Bank.

Recommendation 11: Disposition of Cases by a Hearing Committee, the Board, or Court

The statewide disciplinary board should not review a determination of the hearing committee except upon a request for review by the disciplinary counsel or respondent or upon the vote of a majority of the Board. The Court should not review a matter except: (a) within its discretion upon a request for review of the determination of the Board by the disciplinary counsel or respondent; or (b) upon the vote of a majority of the Court to review a determination of the hearing committee or Board. Except in unusual cases requiring a de novo hearing by the Court, the Court should exercise its jurisdiction in the capacity of appellate review. The Court should issue and publish full written opinions in all disciplinary cases. In any matter finally determined by a hearing committee or the Board, the Court should, by per curiam order, adopt and publish the findings and conclusions contained in the written report of the committee or Board.

Recommendation 12: Interim Suspension for Threat of Harm

The immediate interim suspension of a lawyer should be ordered upon a finding that the lawyer poses a substantial threat of serious harm to the public.

Recommendation 13: Funding and Staffing

The Court should insure that adequate funding and staffing is provided for the disciplinary agency so that: (a) disciplinary cases are screened, investigated, prosecuted and adjudicated promptly; (b) the work load per staff person permits careful and thorough performance of duties; (c) professional and support staff are compensated at a level sufficient to attract and retain competent personnel; (d) sufficient office and data processing equipment exist to efficiently and quickly process the work load and manage the agency; (e) adequate office space exists to provide a productive working environment; and (f) staff and volunteers are adequately trained in disciplinary law and procedure.

Recommendation 14: Standards for Resources

14.1 Each jurisdiction should keep case load and time statistics to assist in determining the need for additional staff and resources. Case load and time statistics should include, at the minimum:

(a) time records for all counsel and investigators, tracked by case or other task including time spent on non-disciplinary functions;

(b) the number of pending cases at each stage in the disciplinary process for each counsel and for the whole agency;

(c) the number of new cases assigned to each counsel during the year and the total for the agency;

(d) the number of cases carried over from the prior year for each counsel and the total for the agency;

(e) the number of cases closed by each counsel during the year and the total for the agency;

(f) the number of cases of special difficulty or complexity at each stage in the proceedings; and

(g) the ratio of staff turnover.

14.2 The American Bar Association, National Organization of Bar Counsel, and disciplinary agencies in each jurisdiction should cooperate to develop standards for: (a) staffing levels and case load per professional and support staff member; (b) case processing time at all stages of disciplinary proceedings; and (c) compensation of professional and support staff.

Recommendation 15: Field Investigations

Disciplinary counsel should have sufficient staff and resources to: (1) fully investigate complaints, by such means as sending investigators into the field to interview witnesses and examine records and evidence; and (2) regularly monitor sources of public information such as news reports and court decisions likely to contain information about lawyer misconduct.

Recommendation 16: Random Audit of Trust Accounts

The Court should adopt a rule providing that lawyer trust accounts selected at random may be audited without having grounds to believe misconduct has occurred and also providing for appropriate procedural safeguards.

Recommendation 17: Burden of Proof in Arbitration of Fee Disputes

The Court should adopt a rule for fee arbitration proceedings to provide that, except where the fee agreement otherwise has been established in a continuing relationship, if there is no written agreement between the lawyer and the client, the lawyer shall bear the burden of proof of all facts, and the lawyer shall be entitled to no more than the reasonable value of services for the work completed or, if the failure to complete the work was caused by the client, for the work performed.

Recommendation 18: Mandatory Malpractice Insurance Study

The American Bar Association should continue studies to determine whether a model program and model rule should be created to: (a) make appropriate levels of malpractice insurance coverage available at a reasonable price; and (b) make coverage mandatory for all lawyers who have clients.

Recommendation 19: Effective Date of Disbarment and Suspension Orders

The Court should adopt a rule providing that orders of disbarment and suspension shall be effective on a date (15) days after the date of the order except where the Court finds that immediate disbarment or suspension is necessary to protect the public, contrary to the provisions of the Model Rules for Lawyer Disciplinary Enforcement 27E.

Recommendation 20: National Discipline Data Bank

The American Bar Association should provide or seek adequate funding to automate the dissemination of reciprocal discipline information by means of electronic data processing and telecommunications, so that:

20.1 appropriate discipline, bar admissions, and other officials in each jurisdiction can directly access and query the National Discipline Data Bank via a computer telecommunications network;

20.2 a uniform data format and software are developed permitting automated cross-checking of jurisdictions' rosters of licensed lawyers against the National Discipline Data Bank's contents;

20.3 a listing of the contents of the National Discipline Data Bank is disseminated to discipline officials quarterly or semi-annually on an electronic data processing medium suitable for automated comparison with a jurisdiction's roster of lawyers.

Recommendation 21: Coordinating Interstate Identification

21.1 The American Bar Association and the appropriate officials in each jurisdiction should establish a system of assigning a universal identification number to each lawyer licensed to practice law.

21.2 The highest court in each jurisdiction should require all lawyers licensed in the jurisdiction to (a) register annually with

661

the agency designated by the Court stating all other jurisdictions in which they are licensed to practice law, and (b) immediately report to the agency designated by the Court changes of law license status in other jurisdictions such as admission to practice, discipline imposed, or resignation.

AMERICAN BAR ASSOCIATION MODEL RULES FOR LAWYER DISCIPLINARY ENFORCEMENT

[The Model Rules for Lawyer Disciplinary Enforcement, adopted by the ABA House of Delegates at its Annual Meeting in August 1989, replace the Standards for Lawyer Discipline and Disability Proceedings (adopted in February 1979) and the Model Rules for Lawyer Disciplinary Enforcement (adopted in July 1985). The new Model Rules for Lawyer Disciplinary Enforcement combine into a single policy document the contents of these two documents which, though formatted in different styles, concerned the same subject matter, i.e., model operating procedures for lawyer disciplinary matters. The Rules are reprinted in full; however, we have omitted some of the commentary due to space considerations. Ed.]

Table of Contents

MODEL RULES

PREAMBLE: AUTHORITY OF THE COURT

This court declares that it has exclusive responsibility within this state for the structure and administration of the lawyer discipline and disability system and that it has inherent power to maintain appropriate standards of professional conduct and to dispose of individual cases of lawyer discipline and disability in a manner that does not discriminate by race, creed, color, sex, sexual orientation or national origin. In order to effectuate this declaration, the following rules for lawyer discipline and disability proceedings are hereby promulgated.

I. STRUCTURE AND SCOPE

RULE 1. [Disciplinary Districts

Disciplinary jurisdiction in this state shall be divided into the following districts: If necessary, provisions dividing the state into two or more disciplinary districts].

RULE 2. The Disciplinary Board of the Supreme Court [*State Bar*] of [*State Name*]

A. *Agency.* There is hereby established one permanent statewide agency to administer the lawyer discipline and disability system. The agency consists of a statewide board as provided in this Rule 2, hearing committees as provided for in Rule 3, disciplinary counsel as provided for in Rule 4, and staff appointed by the board and counsel. The agency is a unitary entity. While it performs both prosecutorial and adjudicative functions, these functions shall be separated within the agency insofar as practicable in order to avoid unfairness. The prosecutorial functions shall be directed by a lawyer employed full-time by the agency and performed, insofar as practicable, by employees of the agency. The adjudicative functions shall be performed by practicing lawyers and public members.

B. *Appointment.* A board shall be appointed which shall consist of [nine] members to serve for fixed, staggered terms, and to be referred to as the "board," which shall consist of:

    (1) [Two] members of the bar of this state and [one] public member appointed for an initial term of three years;

    (2) [Two] members of the bar of this state and [one] public member appointed for an initial term of two years; and

    (3) [Two] members of the bar of this state and [one] public member appointed for an initial term of one year.

Subsequent terms of all members shall be for three years. No member shall serve more than two consecutive three-year terms. The members of the board shall not be subject to removal by the court during their terms of office except for cause.

C. *Election of Officers.* The members of the board shall annually elect [the Court shall annually appoint] lawyer members as chair and vice-chair. The chair, and in the chair's absence the vice-chair, shall perform the duties normally associated with that office and shall preside over all meetings of the full board, ruling on all motions, objections, and evidence.

D. *Quorum.* [Five] members shall constitute a quorum. The board shall act only with the concurrence of a majority of the whole board except as to administrative matters, which shall only require a majority of those present and voting.

E. *Compensation and Expenses.* Members shall receive no compensation for their services, but may be reimbursed for travel and other expenses incidental to the performance of their duties.

F. *Abstention of Board Members [; Alternate Members].* Board members shall refrain from taking part in any proceeding in which a judge, similarly situated, would be required to abstain. [The court shall maintain current rosters of lawyer and nonlawyer alternates. If a board member becomes incapacitated or disqualified, the next alternate on the appropriate roster shall take the place of the board member in the matter.]

G. *Powers and Duties.* The board shall have the following powers and duties:

    (1) To propose rules of procedure for lawyer discipline and disability proceedings for promulgation by the court, and to comment on the enforceability of existing and proposed [Rules of Professional Conduct];

    (2) To review periodically the operation of the system with the court;

    (3) To appoint a chief disciplinary counsel, hereinafter referred to as "counsel" or "disciplinary counsel," to perform prosecutorial functions;

(4) To appoint three or more hearing committees [within each disciplinary district] and

    (i) establish the rotation by which they will be assigned formal hearings,

    (ii) designate the chair for each, and

    (iii) assign the chair to review in rotation recommendations of counsel for disposition of disciplinary matters and petitions for transfer to and from disability inactive status pursuant to Rule 3(E)(1); [1]

(5) To perform appellate review functions, consisting of review of the findings of fact, conclusions of law and recommendations of hearing committees with respect to formal charges, petitions for transfer to and from disability inactive status, and petitions for reinstatement, and prepare and forward to the court its own findings, if any, and recommendations, together with the record of the proceedings before the hearing committee; [1]

(6) To administer reprimands;

(7) To impose probation for a specified period with the consent of the respondent;

(8) To appoint and supervise its staff, separate from the prosecutorial staff, to assist the board in its functions;

(9) To inform the public about the existence and operation of the system and the disposition of each matter in which public discipline has been imposed, a lawyer has been transferred to or from disability inactive status, or a lawyer has been reinstated or readmitted;

(10) To delegate, in its discretion, to the chair or vice-chair the power to act for the board on administrative and procedural matters.

Commentary

With more than 700,000 lawyers licensed to practice in the United States, the highest courts of the states cannot handle discipline and disability matters directly by themselves. The agency assists the court in the exercise of its inherent power to supervise the bar, inquiring into all matters assigned to its jurisdiction by the court's rules of disciplinary enforcement. The agency performs prosecutorial and adjudicative functions, and reports its findings and recommendations to the court.

A statewide system provides the greatest degree of structural impartiality since it minimizes the adverse effects of local bias. Moreover, a statewide structure provides uniformity, since only a single statewide court and a single statewide agency are involved in the process. In a decentralized structure, complaints in one community

1. See Appendix for alternative provisions.

may be governed by one set of standards and those in a different community by another. Consequently, lawyers admitted to practice in the same state may receive radically different discipline for the same misconduct.

A single statewide agency avoids these problems by imposing a single standard of conduct throughout the state.

In a unitary system, both prosecution and adjudication are the responsibility of a single agency. Nevertheless, prosecutorial and adjudicative functions should be separated as much as possible within the unitary system to avoid unfairness and any appearance of unfairness. Persons who perform prosecutorial functions should neither perform nor supervise persons who perform adjudicative functions, and vice versa. In addition, persons who perform adjudicative functions in a particular matter at a preliminary stage should not thereafter perform nor have control over persons who must later perform ultimate adjudicative functions in the same matter.

It is of course desirable, and in the larger states essential, for the board to have available the assistance of staff to carry out its functions. Staff responsible directly to the board, totally separate from counsel, should be hired for that purpose to further the separation of the prosecutorial and adjudicative functions within the unitary agency.

A combination of lawyers and nonlawyers on the board results in a more balanced evaluation of complaints. Currently more than two-thirds of all jurisdictions involve public members in their disciplinary structure. Participation by nonlawyers increases the credibility of the discipline and disability process in the eyes of the public. There is a human tendency to suspect the objectivity of a discipline body composed solely of members of the respondent's professional colleagues. Involving public members helps allay that suspicion.

* * *

RULE 3. Hearing Committees [2]

A. *Appointment.* The board shall appoint three or more hearing committees [within each disciplinary district]. Each hearing committee shall consist of two members of the bar of this state and one public member. A lawyer member of each hearing committee shall be appointed chair by the board.

B. *Terms of Office.* The chair and other members of the hearing committee shall serve for fixed, staggered terms. One member shall be appointed for an initial term of one year, another member for an initial term of two years and the third member for an initial term of three years. Thereafter all regular terms shall be three years and no member shall serve for more than two consecutive three-year terms. A

2. See Appendix for alternative provisions.

670

member whose term has expired may continue to serve on any case that was commenced before the expiration of the member's term. A member who has served two consecutive three-year terms may not be reappointed before the expiration of at least one year. The members shall not be subject to removal by the board during their terms of office except for cause.

C. *Quorum.* Three members shall constitute a quorum. The committee shall act only with the concurrence of two. The chair of the board may appoint alternate members to a hearing committee as necessary to meet the requirements of this subsection.

D. *Powers and Duties.* Hearing committees shall have the following powers and duties:

(1) To conduct hearings into formal charges of misconduct, petitions for reinstatement or readmission, and petitions for transfer to and from disability inactive status upon assignment; and

(2) To submit to the board written findings of fact, conclusions of law, and recommendations, together with the record of the hearing.

E. *Powers and Duties of Hearing Committee Chair.* Each hearing committee chair shall have the following powers and duties:

(1) To review recommendations of disciplinary counsel following investigation for disposition of disciplinary matters, dismissals by disciplinary counsel upon a request for review by complainant, and petitions for transfer to and from disability inactive status. The hearing committee chair may approve, modify, or disapprove the recommendations of disciplinary counsel, or direct that the matter be investigated further. If the hearing committee chair modifies or disapproves the recommendation, or directs that the matter be investigated further, disciplinary counsel may appeal that action to the chair of another hearing committee designated by the board, who shall approve either disciplinary counsel's recommendation or the action of the first hearing committee chair. The decision of the second hearing committee chair shall be final within the agency.

(2) To conduct prehearing conferences regarding formal charges of misconduct, petitions for reinstatement or readmission, and petitions for transfer to and from disability inactive status; and

(3) To consider and decide prehearing motions.

Commentary

If any member of a hearing committee has a conflict of interest, the entire committee is disqualified and another committee must be appointed in its place. If that is not practicable, the individual member of the committee should be replaced for that particular matter only.

The creation of hearing committees for specific cases should be avoided. Hearing committees should have fixed membership. The committees should sit on a pre-established rotating schedule and cases should be assigned on the basis of which is the next committee to sit. Each committee should have one alternate member scheduled to sit in case of illness, emergency, or conflicts of interest.

* * *

RULE 4. Disciplinary Counsel

A. *Appointment.* The board shall appoint a lawyer admitted to practice in the state to serve as disciplinary counsel. Neither the chief disciplinary counsel nor full-time staff disciplinary counsel shall engage in private practice.

B. *Powers and Duties.* Disciplinary counsel shall perform all prosecutorial functions and have the following powers and duties:

(1) To screen all information coming to the attention of the agency to determine whether it concerns a lawyer subject to the jurisdiction of the agency because it relates to misconduct by the lawyer or to the incapacity of the lawyer;

(2) To investigate all information coming to the attention of the agency which, if true, would be grounds for discipline or transfer to disability inactive status and investigate all facts pertaining to petitions for reinstatement or readmission;

(3) To dismiss or recommend probation, informal admonition, a stay, the filing of formal charges, or the petitioning for transfer to disability inactive status with respect to each matter brought to the attention of the agency;

(4) To prosecute before hearing committees, the board, and the court discipline, reinstatement and readmission proceedings, and proceedings for transfer to or from disability inactive status;

(5) To employ and supervise staff needed for the performance of prosecutorial functions [and, when circumstances necessitate their use, appoint and supervise volunteer assistant counsel];

(6) To notify promptly the complainant and the respondent of the disposition of each matter;

(7) To notify each jurisdiction in which a lawyer is admitted of a transfer to or from disability inactive status, reinstatement, readmission, or any public discipline imposed in this state;

(8) To seek reciprocal discipline when informed of any public discipline imposed in any other jurisdiction;

(9) To forward a certified copy of the judgment of conviction to the disciplinary agency in each jurisdiction in which a lawyer is admitted when the lawyer is convicted of a serious crime (as hereinafter defined) in this state;

(10) To maintain permanent records of discipline and disability matters, subject to the expunction requirements of Rule 4(B)(11), and compile statistics to aid in the administration of the system, including but not limited to a single log of all complaints received, investigative files, statistical summaries of docket processing and case dispositions, transcripts of all proceedings (or the reporter's notes if not transcribed), and other records as the board or court requires to be maintained;

(11) To expunge (i.e. destroy) after [three] years all records or other evidence of the existence of complaints terminated by dismissals, except that upon disciplinary counsel's application, notice to respondent, and a showing of good cause, the board may permit disciplinary counsel to retain such records for one additional period of time not to exceed [three] years.

(i) Notice to Respondent. If the respondent was contacted by the agency concerning the complaint, or the agency otherwise knows that the respondent is aware of the existence of the complaint, the respondent shall be given prompt written notice of the expunction.

(ii) Effect of Expunction. After a file has been expunged, any agency response to an inquiry requiring a reference to the matter shall state that there is no record of such matter. The respondent may answer any inquiry requiring a reference to an expunged matter by stating that no complaint was made.

(12) To undertake, pursuant to directions from the board, whatever investigations are assigned to disciplinary counsel.

Commentary

The board should appoint a permanent, full-time disciplinary counsel whenever possible. In some jurisdictions, small caseloads or inadequate funding make that impossible. In those situations part-time counsel may be used.

Volunteers should be avoided if possible. They cannot devote the same time and attention to processing complaints as paid counsel, nor can they investigate complicated matters as thoroughly as one professionally trained to do so.

Disciplinary counsel may be allowed a reasonable amount of time for transition from private practice following appointment to phase out his or her private practice.

Since the board has the responsibility for the efficient operation of the agency, the board should appoint those who must carry out the duties of the agency, including disciplinary counsel. The court should not allow itself to become involved in the internal personnel management of the agency.

Vesting all prosecutorial responsibility in disciplinary counsel is necessary if there is to be a separation of prosecutorial and adjudicative functions within a unitary agency.

Disciplinary counsel has the responsibility for investigating and prosecuting all matters. Disciplinary counsel must therefore have the authority to hire, compensate, and fire the staff necessary to carry out that responsibility in conformity with the applicable limits established by the board in the budget it has approved for the operation of the agency. All personnel assigned prosecutorial functions, whether lawyer or nonlawyer, full-time, part-time, or volunteer, should be appointed by and responsible to counsel. Full-time lawyer personnel hired by counsel should not be permitted to engage in the private practice of law.

Members of the public who come to the agency seeking its services are entitled to be advised of the disposition of their complaints. Fairness requires that no recommendation adverse to the respondent be made without providing an opportunity to be heard.

The clerk of the court in which the lawyer is convicted should send a certified copy of the judgment of conviction to counsel for the agency of the state in which the lawyer is admitted to practice. The certified copy of the judgment should be filed with the court to support the proposed order for immediate interim suspension.

Meaningful statistics can most effectively be recorded by using uniform terminology. The following terms are adopted to identify available sanctions in disciplinary matters: disbarment, suspension, reprimand, admonition, probation, and discipline by consent. The term adopted to indicate removal from practice on grounds of disability is transfer to disability inactive status.

* * *

RULE 5. Expenses

The salaries of disciplinary counsel and staff, their expenses, administrative costs, and the expenses of the members of the board and of hearing committees shall be paid by the board [out of the funds collected under the provisions of Rule 8]. The board shall annually obtain an independent audit by a certified public accountant of the funds entrusted to it and their disposition and shall file a copy of the audit with this court.

RULE 6. Jurisdiction

A. *Lawyers Admitted to Practice.* Any lawyer admitted to practice law in this state, including any formerly admitted lawyer with respect to acts committed prior to resignation, suspension, disbarment, or transfer to inactive status, or with respect to acts subsequent thereto which amount to the practice of law or constitute a violation of these Rules or of the Rules of Professional Conduct [Code of Professional

Responsibility] or any Rules or Code subsequently adopted by the court in lieu thereof, and any lawyer specially admitted by a court of this state for a particular proceeding[, and any lawyer not admitted in this state who practices law or renders or offers to render any legal services in this state] is subject to the disciplinary jurisdiction of this court and the board.

B. *Former Judges.* A former judge who has resumed the status of a lawyer is subject to the jurisdiction of the board not only for conduct as a lawyer but also for misconduct that occurred while the lawyer was a judge and would have been grounds for lawyer discipline, provided that the misconduct was not the subject of a judicial disciplinary proceeding as to which there has been a final determination by the court. Misconduct by a judge that is not finally adjudicated before the judge leaves office falls within the jurisdiction of the lawyer disciplinary agency.

C. *Incumbent Judges.* Incumbent judges shall not be subject to the jurisdiction of the agency; however, if an incumbent judge is to be removed from office in the course of a judicial discipline or disability proceeding, the court shall first afford the board and the respondent an opportunity to submit a recommendation whether lawyer discipline should be imposed, and if so, the extent thereof.

D. *Powers Not Assumed.* These rules shall not be construed to deny to any court the powers necessary to maintain control over its proceedings.

Commentary

Admission to practice triggers the jurisdiction of the disciplinary authority, regardless of the location of the lawyer, the place where the act occurred, or whether the lawyer is qualified to practice; the court has the right and the obligation to inquire into any facts bearing upon the lawyer's fitness to practice.

A lawyer specially admitted in a state has a license for that limited appearance and is subject to the disciplinary authority of that jurisdiction. In the same way that the motorist has given his implied consent to be bound by the traffic laws of the states he travels, the lawyer admitted for a limited purpose subjects himself or herself to the rules of conduct in the jurisdiction.

It is inappropriate for the state in which the lawyer is specially admitted to rely exclusively upon the lawyer's home jurisdiction to enforce ethical standards. The witnesses and other evidence of misconduct are likely to be located in the adopted jurisdiction. Moreover, the jurisdiction in which the misconduct occurred will be far more interested in pursuing the matter. Finally, misconduct should in the first instance be judged by the ethical standards of the jurisdiction where it occurred.

If at the time a judge leaves office the entity responsible for bringing judicial disciplinary proceedings has an investigation in progress against him or her, the matter should be immediately transferred to the lawyer disciplinary agency. The only issue in that circumstance is the lawyer's fitness to continue to practice in light of the alleged misconduct. Since a judge may be subject to discipline as a judge for conduct that does not constitute misconduct as a lawyer, the allegations giving rise to the jurisdiction of the agency under paragraph B must cite conduct violating the Code of Judicial Conduct which also constitutes grounds for lawyer discipline.

The judicial discipline and disability retirement commission has special expertise to evaluate the conduct of sitting judges and to determine how that conduct reflects upon their continued ability to hold office. The status of a judge as a judge and discipline to be imposed during the judge's tenure should be determined by judicial discipline and disability retirement proceedings.

Consequently, even if the misconduct occurred prior to the judge's assumption of office, the commission should have jurisdiction since the judge's status as a judge is at issue. If a lawyer disciplinary agency has an investigation in progress against a judge at the time the judge takes office, it should immediately transfer the file to the commission. If the judge is to be removed from office and thus returned to the practice of law, the court should afford the lawyer disciplinary agency the opportunity to be heard on the issue of what lawyer discipline, if any, should be imposed. The agency has the special expertise to determine how conduct reflects upon a lawyer's continued qualification to practice law.

Affording the agency an opportunity to be heard on the subject of lawyer discipline protects the right of the profession to preserve the high standards of conduct that it maintains in the public interest.

RULE 7. Roster of Lawyers

Disciplinary counsel shall maintain or have ready access to current information relating to all lawyers subject to the jurisdiction of the board including:

(a) full name and all names under which the lawyer has been admitted or practiced;

(b) date of birth;

(c) current law office address and telephone number;

(d) current residence address;

(e) date of admission in the state;

(f) date of any transfer to or from inactive status;

(g) all specialties in which certified;

(h) other jurisdictions in which the lawyer is admitted and date of admission;

(i) location and account numbers in which clients' funds are held by the lawyer;

(j) nature, date, and place of any discipline imposed and any reinstatements in any other jurisdiction;

(k) date of death; and

(*l*) [social security number, if provided by the lawyer].

Commentary

A permanent registration system should be established from which the agency can determine whether an individual is licensed to practice in the state, is living or deceased, and where the individual is located. The registration records may be maintained by the court, a court-designated agency, or in unified bar states by the state bar. Disciplinary counsel should have ready access to the records.

The individual lawyer has the responsibility of keeping his or her registration information current, and should be required to promptly inform the registration agency of any change. Generally, the address listed in the roster is the lawyer's legal address for purposes of service of process and any other notices. See Rule 13.

* * *

RULE 8. Periodic Assessment of Lawyers

A. *Requirement.* Every lawyer admitted to practice before this court shall pay to the clerk of this court [*state bar*] an annual fee for each fiscal year beginning [*date*] to be set by the court [*state bar*] from time to time. The fee shall be used to defray the costs of disciplinary administration and enforcement under these rules, and for those other purposes the board shall from time to time designate with the approval of this court. The annual fee until further order of the court shall be:

After Date of Admission to Practice Law	Annual fee
Up to five years:	$
Five years or more:	$

B. *Exemption of Judges.* Full-time judges shall be exempt from the payment of the fee during the time they serve in office.

C. *Suspension for Nonpayment.* Unless excused on grounds of financial hardship pursuant to procedures to be established by the board, any lawyer who fails to timely pay the fee required under paragraph A shall be summarily suspended, provided that a notice of delinquency, addressed to the lawyer's last known business address, has been forwarded to the lawyer by certified mail, return receipt requested, at least [thirty] days prior to such suspension.

D. *Reinstatement After Payment.* Any lawyer suspended under paragraph C shall be reinstated without further order if, within five years of the effective date of the suspension for nonpayment, the lawyer makes payment of all arrears and a penalty of 20% of the amount due from the date of the last payment to the date of the request for reinstatement. Any lawyer who fails to make these complete payments within five years of the effective date of the suspension for nonpayment may, in the discretion of the court, be required to petition for reinstatement under Rule 25.

E. *Registration Statement.* To facilitate the collection of the annual fee provided for in paragraph A, each lawyer required by this rule to pay an annual fee shall, on or before [date] of every year, commencing [date] file with the clerk of this court a registration statement, on a form prescribed by this court, setting forth the lawyer's residence and office addresses, other jurisdictions in which the lawyer is admitted to practice, and such other information as this court may from time to time direct. Each lawyer shall file with the clerk of this court a supplemental statement of any change in the information previously submitted within [thirty] days of the change. All persons first becoming subject to these rules by admission to the practice of law before the courts of this state after [date] shall file the statement required by this rule at the time of admission, but no annual fee shall be payable until [date] next following such date of admission.

F. *Receipt Demonstrating Filing of Registration Statement.* Within [thirty] days of the receipt of a statement or supplement thereto filed by the lawyer in accordance with paragraph E, the clerk of this court shall acknowledge receipt on a form prescribed by the court in order to enable the lawyer on request to demonstrate compliance with the requirements of paragraphs A and E.

G. *Suspension for Failure to File Registration Statements.* Any lawyer who fails to file the statement or supplement in accordance with paragraph E shall be summarily suspended, provided a notice of delinquency has been forwarded to the lawyer by certified mail, return receipt requested, addressed to the lawyer's last known business address at least [thirty] days prior to the suspension. The lawyer shall remain suspended until compliance is demonstrated, whereupon the lawyer shall be reinstated without further order.

H. *Application for Transfer to Inactive Status.* A lawyer who has retired or is not engaged in practice shall advise the clerk of this court in writing that the lawyer desires to assume inactive status and discontinue the practice of law. Upon the filing of the notice, the lawyer shall no longer be eligible to practice law. A lawyer who is retired or on inactive status shall not be obligated to pay the annual fee imposed by this rule upon active practitioners. A lawyer on inactive status shall be removed from the roll of those classified as active until and unless the lawyer requests and is granted reinstatement to the active rolls.

I. *Reinstatement From Inactive Status.* Any lawyer on inactive status under paragraph H shall be reinstated without further order if the lawyer makes application within five years of the effective date of transfer to inactive status. Any lawyer who fails to make application for reinstatement within five years of the effective date of transfer to inactive status may, in the discretion of the court, be required to petition for reinstatement under Rule 25.

J. *Reinstatement While Under Disciplinary Order.* Any lawyer who is under an order of discipline in any jurisdiction shall be required to petition for reinstatement under Rule 25.

Commentary

Inadequate funding is the major cause of inadequate enforcement. The availability of adequate funds for personnel and expenses will enable an agency to perform all essential duties and not just unavoidable tasks.

The profession recognizes that the creation and maintenance of an effective structure for discipline and disability proceedings is one of its primary responsibilities.

The level of funding for the agency will determine whether it can hire experienced, full-time lawyers as counsel, or whether it can rely upon volunteers, part-time participants and clerks. Adequate funding will enable the agency to unravel a complex or obscure fact situation with which it might not otherwise be able to cope. The level of funding will determine how promptly allegations can be resolved, thereby affecting the length of time the lawyer remains uncertain about his future, the extent to which clients are exposed to further harm, and the amount of public confidence in the system.

Adequate funding is also necessary to ensure trained staff. Adequate personnel means not only sufficient numbers, but also sufficient training. There is a significant need for constant updating with respect to enforcement practices, procedure, and disciplinary law.

The court, pursuant to its power to regulate lawyers and the practice of law, may impose a fee to support the discipline and disability system. Assessments by the court to enable it to fulfill its obligation to the public are constitutional and appropriate.

The establishment of an adequate structure for lawyer discipline and disability proceedings is one of the principal obligations of the legal profession. It is likely therefore that the funding of the system will come primarily from lawyers admitted to practice in the state. It should be noted, however, that there is also a strong public interest in effective disciplinary enforcement. It is for that reason not inappropriate for public funds to be used toward financing the system. Public funds, if used, should always be channeled through the court as part of the budget allocation for the state's judicial system in order to insulate the discipline and disability structure from any attempted interference by either the legislative or executive branches of government.

RULE 9. Grounds for Discipline

It shall be a ground for discipline for a lawyer to:

(a) violate or attempt to violate the [State Rules of Professional Conduct], or any other rules of this jurisdiction regarding professional conduct of lawyers;

(b) engage in conduct violating applicable rules of professional conduct of another jurisdiction;

(c) willfully violate a valid order of the court or the board imposing discipline, willfully fail to appear before disciplinary counsel for admonition pursuant to Rule 10(A)(5), or knowingly fail to respond to a lawful demand from a disciplinary authority, except that this rule does not require disclosure of information otherwise protected by applicable rules relating to confidentiality.

Commentary

When a lawyer is admitted to practice he or she becomes subject to rules of conduct in effect in that jurisdiction. A violation of those rules triggers the jurisdiction of the agency. This does not mean that every violation necessarily requires the imposition of a sanction, but merely that the agency can investigate the matter.

The agency's jurisdiction to investigate and to take whatever action is deemed to be appropriate is triggered by discipline imposed in another state. The imposition of discipline in one jurisdiction does not mean that every other jurisdiction in which the lawyer is admitted must necessarily impose discipline, but the burden is on the respondent to demonstrate that the imposition of the same discipline is inappropriate. See Rule 22.

All lawyers have an affirmative duty to cooperate, including keeping disciplinary counsel advised of current address for service of process, cooperating with disciplinary investigations, and appearing at disciplinary hearings.

This rule establishes the proper policy for the relationship of the disciplinary system to the bar. Respondents are entitled to due process in disciplinary proceedings and are protected by fifth amendment rights against self-incrimination. However, disciplinary proceedings are not criminal proceedings; respondents are not entitled to "stonewall."

RULE 10. Sanctions

A. *Types of Sanctions.* Misconduct shall be grounds for one or more of the following sanctions:

(1) Disbarment by the court.

(2) Suspension by the court for an appropriate fixed period of time not in excess of three years.

(3) Probation imposed by the court not in excess of two years, or imposed by the board or counsel with the consent of the

respondent not in excess of two years; provided, however, that probation may be renewed for an additional [two year] period by consent or after a hearing to determine if there is a continued need for supervision. If the respondent objects to the board or counsel's imposition of probation, the misconduct must either be made the subject of formal charges or a recommendation that probation be imposed must be filed with the court. The conditions of probation should be stated in writing. Probation shall be used only in cases where there is little likelihood that the respondent will harm the public during the period of rehabilitation and the conditions of probation can be adequately supervised.

(4) Reprimand by the court or the board. A reprimand shall be in writing and either imposed in person or served upon the respondent by certified mail. A reprimand issued by the court shall be published in the official reports for the guidance of other lawyers. A reprimand imposed by the board shall be published in the journal of the state bar and in a newspaper of general circulation in each judicial district in which the lawyer maintained an office for the practice of law.

(5) Admonition by disciplinary counsel imposed with the consent of the respondent and the approval of the chair of a hearing committee. An admonition cannot be imposed after formal charges have been issued. Admonitions shall be in writing and served upon the respondent. They constitute private discipline since they are imposed before the filing of formal charges. Only in cases of minor misconduct, when there is little or no injury to a client, the public, the legal system, or the profession, and when there is little likelihood of repetition by the lawyer, should an admonition be imposed. A summary of the conduct for which an admonition was imposed may be published in a bar publication for the education of the profession, but the lawyer shall not be identified. An admonition may be used in subsequent proceedings in which the respondent has been found guilty of misconduct as evidence of prior misconduct bearing upon the issue of the sanction to be imposed in the subsequent proceeding.

(6) Upon order of the court or the board, or upon stipulation, restitution to persons financially injured and reimbursement to the client security fund.

(7) Upon order of the court or the board, or upon stipulation, assessment of the costs of the proceedings, including the costs of investigations, service of process, witness fees, and a court reporter's services, in any case where discipline is imposed or there is a transfer to disability inactive status.

(8) Limitation by the court on the nature or extent of the respondent's future practice.

B. *Conditions.* Written conditions may be attached to an admonition or a reprimand. Failure to comply with such conditions shall be grounds for reconsideration of the matter and prosecution of formal charges against the respondent.

C. *Factors to Be Considered in Imposing Sanctions.* In imposing a sanction after a finding of lawyer misconduct, the court or board shall consider the following factors:

(1) whether the lawyer has violated a duty owed to a client, to the public, to the legal system, or to the profession;

(2) whether the lawyer acted intentionally, knowingly, or negligently;

(3) the amount of the actual or potential injury caused by the lawyer's misconduct; and

(4) the existence of any aggravating or mitigating factors.

D. *Public Nature of Sanctions.* Disposition of lawyer discipline shall be public in cases of disbarment, suspension, probation, and reprimand. In all cases of public discipline by the court, the court shall issue a written opinion setting forth its justification for imposing the sanction in that particular case.

Commentary

* * *

The *Standards for Imposing Lawyer Sanctions* were adopted by the ABA in 1986. These standards provide a framework to guide the courts in imposing sanctions, thereby giving the courts the flexibility to select the appropriate sanction in each particular case of lawyer misconduct. * * * The *Standards for Imposing Lawyer Sanctions* set forth a comprehensive system for determining sanctions, permitting flexibility and creativity in assigning sanctions in particular cases of lawyer misconduct. Use of the *Standards* will help achieve the degree of consistency in the imposition of lawyer discipline necessary for fairness to the public and the bar.

II. PROCEDURE FOR DISCIPLINARY PROCEEDINGS

RULE 11. Generally

A. *Screening.* The disciplinary counsel shall evaluate all information coming to his or her attention by complaint or from other sources alleging lawyer misconduct or incapacity. If the lawyer is not subject to the jurisdiction of the court, the matter shall be referred to the appropriate entity in any jurisdiction in which the lawyer is admitted. If the information, if true, would not constitute misconduct or incapacity, the matter shall be dismissed. If the lawyer is subject to the jurisdiction of the court and the information alleges facts which, if true, would constitute misconduct or incapacity, counsel shall conduct an investigation.

B. *Investigation.*

(1) All investigations shall be conducted by disciplinary counsel. Upon the conclusion of an investigation, disciplinary counsel may dismiss or may recommend probation, admonition, the filing of formal charges, the petitioning for transfer to disability inactive status, or a stay.

(2) Notice to Respondent. Disciplinary counsel shall not recommend a disposition other than dismissal or stay without first notifying the respondent in writing of the substance of the matter and affording him or her an opportunity to be heard. Notice to the respondent at his or her last known address is sufficient.

(3) Disciplinary counsel's recommended disposition other than a dismissal shall be reviewed by the chair of a hearing committee selected in order from the roster established by the board. The complainant shall be notified of the disposition of a matter following investigation. The complainant may file a written request for review of counsel's dismissal within [thirty] days of receipt of notice of disposition pursuant to Rule 4(B)(6). Disciplinary counsel's dismissal shall be reviewed by the chair upon the complainant's request for review. The chair may approve, disapprove, or modify the recommendation or appealed dismissal. Disciplinary counsel may appeal a decision to disapprove or modify his or her recommendation to a reviewing chair of a second hearing committee also selected in order from the roster established by the board who shall approve either disciplinary counsel's recommendation or the action of the first reviewer. Any hearing committee whose chair reviews a recommendation of disciplinary counsel is disqualified from participating in further consideration of the matter.

C. *Admonition or Probation—Imposition.*

(1) If a matter is recommended to be concluded by admonition or by probation, disciplinary counsel shall notify the respondent in writing of the proposed disposition and of the right to demand in writing within [fourteen] days that the matter be disposed of by a formal proceeding. Failure of the respondent to so demand within [fourteen] days after written notice of the proposed admonition or probation constitutes consent to the admonition or probation.

(2) If the respondent within [fourteen] days demands a formal hearing, formal charges may be instituted.

D. *Formal Charges.* If a matter is to be resolved by a formal proceeding, disciplinary counsel shall prepare formal charges in writing that give fair and adequate notice of the nature of the alleged misconduct.

(1) Disciplinary counsel shall file the charges with the board.

683

(2) Disciplinary counsel shall cause a copy of the formal charges to be served upon the respondent and proof of service to be filed with the board.

(3) The respondent shall file a written answer with the board and serve a copy on disciplinary counsel within [twenty] days after service of the formal charges, unless the time is extended by the chair of the hearing committee. In the event the respondent fails to answer within the prescribed time, or the time as extended, the charges shall be deemed admitted.

(4) If there are any material issues of fact raised by the pleadings or if the respondent requests the opportunity to be heard in mitigation, the [hearing committee] [board] shall serve a notice of hearing upon disciplinary counsel and the respondent, stating the date and place of hearing at least [twenty-five] days in advance thereof. The notice of hearing shall advise the respondent of the right to be represented by a lawyer, to cross-examine witnesses and to present evidence. The hearing shall be recorded.

E. *Review by Board.* Review by the board shall be limited to a review of the report from the hearing committee and the record below. The respondent and disciplinary counsel should be afforded an opportunity to file briefs and present oral argument during the review by the board. The board shall adopt rules establishing a timetable and procedure for the filing of briefs and presentation of argument.

(1) Decision by Board. Following its review, the board may approve, modify, or disapprove the recommendation of the hearing committee.

(2) During its review, the board shall not receive or consider any evidence that was not presented to the hearing committee, except upon notice to the respondent and disciplinary counsel and opportunity to respond. The hearing committee is the initial trier of fact; the board serves an appellate review function. If new evidence warranting a reopening of the proceeding is discovered, the case should be remanded to the hearing committee.

F. *Review by the Court.* The board shall promptly submit to the court a report containing its findings and recommendations on each matter heard other than those that have been remanded, dismissed and not appealed, or concluded by probation or a reprimand that is not appealed. A copy of the report shall be served on disciplinary counsel and the respondent.

(1) The respondent and disciplinary counsel may file objections to the report within [twenty] days from the date of service. Within [sixty] days after the filing of the report and the filing of objections, if any, the respondent and disciplinary counsel may file briefs and present oral arguments pursuant to the rules governing civil appeals. Upon conclusion of the proceedings, the court shall prompt-

ly enter an appropriate order. The decision of the court shall be in writing and state the reasons for the decision.

(2) During its review, the court shall not receive or consider any evidence that was not presented to the hearing committee, except upon notice to the respondent and disciplinary counsel and opportunity to respond.

(3) If new evidence warranting a reopening of the proceeding is discovered, the case shall be remanded to the hearing committee.

Commentary

The screening process eliminates those matters over which the agency has no jurisdiction. It precedes investigation, which is reserved for those matters determined to involve a lawyer subject to the jurisdiction of the agency and allegations which, if true, would constitute misconduct.

If the matter is terminated at this screening stage because the matter does not involve allegations of misconduct, disciplinary counsel should notify the complainant and refer him or her to any other agencies or remedies available to assist, e.g., fee arbitration panels and lawyer referral agencies.

Matters terminated at the screening stage because they concern a lawyer not admitted to practice in the jurisdiction should be forwarded by disciplinary counsel to the agency for the jurisdiction in which the lawyer is admitted. The complainant should be notified of the disposition if a matter is concluded at the screening stage.

A stay is appropriate only in extraordinary circumstances. Disciplinary counsel must determine whether the complainant or the respondent will suffer prejudice in the pending proceeding should the disciplinary action proceed immediately. In some cases, witnesses and evidence pertinent to both cases might not be obtainable at a later date; in other cases, the disciplinary action may be expedited by waiting for evidence to be adduced in another proceeding.

Fairness requires that no recommendation adverse to the respondent be made without providing him or her an opportunity to be heard. This does not mean that the respondent is entitled to notice immediately upon receipt of a complaint. In some instances, early notice would be harmful to the investigation. It does mean that the respondent has a right to be heard before the investigation is concluded and an adverse disposition formulated.

The review process preserves elements of bifurcation within the unitary system, because the recommendation of disciplinary counsel is subject to review and approval by a representative of the adjudicative body. The approval of counsel's recommendation to file formal charges by the reviewing member amounts to a finding of probable cause to proceed.

In order to prevent any possibility of forum shopping by disciplinary counsel, the hearing committee chairperson should be designated by the board. The hearing committee of which the reviewing chair is a member should be disqualified from any future consideration of the matter, in order to avoid being placed in the position of passing upon the correctness of his or her approval of the recommendation to prosecute formal charges.

The board supervises the operations of the agency. Any person dissatisfied with the action of the agency may complain to the board. The complaint should be submitted to a panel of the board, rather than the entire board, so that those members not serving on the panel will be available to participate in any future proceedings involving the matter.

If the first reviewing chairperson does not approve the recommendation, disciplinary counsel may submit the matter to a second reviewing chairperson who shall decide the issue by approving either the recommendation of disciplinary counsel or the modification thereon made by the first reviewer.

The court, the board, or disciplinary counsel may impose probation. If probation is imposed by the board or by counsel, the consent of the respondent is required. The terms of the probation should specify periodic review of the order of probation, and provide a means to supervise the progress of the respondent.

Admonitions should be in writing and served upon the respondent. If the respondent does not consent to the admonition or probation, formal charges are instituted. The procedure is similar to the rejection of a settlement offer in a civil case or a plea bargain in a criminal case, which results in a trial.

The fact that refusal to consent to the admonition or probation subjects the respondent to formal charges and potentially more serious discipline does not violate due process any more than does the fact that a person charged with a crime is subject to conviction of a more serious offense when he or she refuses to plead to a lesser crime.

The hearing may be recorded by any method authorized in the jurisdiction. The record will assist the hearing committee in the preparation and presentation of its report.

If the matter ultimately results in a recommendation for discipline, the record should be forwarded with the findings and recommendation. The recording should be available to the respondent upon request, and a transcript provided at cost.

The hearing committee is the initial trier of fact; the board serves an appellate review function. If new evidence warranting a reopening of the proceeding is discovered, the case should be remanded to the hearing committee.

The report and recommendation of the board is advisory only. The court may modify the findings and may increase or decrease the discipline recommended. If new evidence warranting a reopening of the proceeding is discovered, the case should be remanded to the hearing committee.

Written opinions of the court not only serve to educate members of the profession about ethical behavior, but also provide precedent for subsequent cases. Moreover, this requirement is manageable; the courts in the jurisdictions with the heaviest caseloads currently write opinions in every contested disciplinary case they decide.

RULE 12. Immunity

A. *From Civil Suits.* Communications to the board, hearing committees, or disciplinary counsel relating to lawyer misconduct or disability and testimony given in the proceedings shall be absolutely privileged, and no lawsuit predicated thereon may be instituted against any complainant or witness. Members of the board, members of hearing committees, disciplinary counsel, and staff shall be immune from suit for any conduct in the course of their official duties.

B. *From Criminal Prosecution.* Upon application by disciplinary counsel and notice to [appropriate prosecuting authority], the court may grant immunity from criminal prosecution to a witness in a discipline or disability proceeding.

Commentary

Agency personnel are an integral part of the judicial process and are entitled to the same immunity which is afforded to prosecuting lawyers. Immunity protects the independent judgment of the agency and avoids diverting the attention of its personnel as well as its resources toward resisting collateral attack and harassment.

The Rule recommends absolute privilege rather than qualified privilege; qualified privilege may not protect against harassment made possible by simply alleging malice in a lawsuit. Conduct on the part of agency personnel which is not authorized or exceeds assigned duties is not protected.

* * * *

RULE 13. Service

A. *Service of Petition.* Service upon the respondent of the petition in any disciplinary or disability proceeding shall be made by personal service, by any person authorized by the chair of the board, or by registered or certified mail at an address shown in the current information roster filed by respondent pursuant to Rule 7 or other last known address.

B. *Service of Other Papers.* Service of any other papers or notices required by these rules may be made upon respondent or respondent's counsel and shall, unless otherwise provided by these rules, be made in accordance with Rule _____ of the [*state rules of civil procedure*].

RULE 14. Subpoena Power

A. *Oaths.* Any member of the board or of a hearing committee in matters before it, disciplinary counsel in matters under investigation by him or her, and any person authorized by law may administer oaths and affirmations.

B. *Investigatory Subpoenas.* Before formal charges have been filed, disciplinary counsel may, with the approval of the chairperson of a hearing committee, compel by subpoena the attendance of witnesses, and the production of pertinent books, papers, and documents, in accordance with [appropriate state rule of civil procedure].

C. *Subpoenas for Deposition or Hearing.* After formal charges are filed, disciplinary counsel or respondent may, in accordance with [appropriate state rule of civil procedure], compel by subpoena the attendance of witnesses and the production of pertinent books, papers, and documents at a deposition or hearing under these rules.

D. *Enforcement of Subpoenas.* The [appropriate court of general jurisdiction of the circuit, county, or city] in which the attendance or production is required may, upon proper application, enforce the attendance and testimony of any witnesses and the production of any documents subpoenaed.

E. *Quashing Subpoena.* Any attack on the validity of a subpoena so issued shall be heard and determined by the chair of the hearing committee before which the matter is pending or by the court wherein enforcement of the subpoena is being sought. Any resulting order is not appealable prior to entry of a final order in the proceeding.

F. *Witnesses and Fees.* Subpoena and witness fees and mileage shall be the same as those provided for proceedings in the [appropriate state court of general jurisdiction].

G. *Subpoena Pursuant to Law of Another Jurisdiction.* Whenever a subpoena is sought in this state pursuant to the law of another jurisdiction for use in lawyer discipline or disability proceedings, the chair of the board, upon petition for good cause, may issue a subpoena as provided in this section to compel the attendance of witnesses and production of documents.

Commentary

If the complainant cannot furnish adequate evidence to substantiate his or her allegations and the respondent will not cooperate, counsel must seek independent evidence. If this evidence consists of testimony of a potential witness who does not want to get involved or the records of a third party, such as a bank that will not disclose the transcripts of its depositors' accounts voluntarily, disciplinary counsel without subpoena power will be unable to dispose of the complaint on the merits. Disciplinary counsel thus denied an indispensable investigatory tool can neither be effective nor command public confidence.

RULE 15.   Discovery

A.   *Scope.*   Within [twenty] days following the filing of an answer, disciplinary counsel and respondent shall exchange the names and addresses of all persons having knowledge of relevant facts.   Within [sixty] days following the filing of an answer, disciplinary counsel and the respondent may take depositions in accordance with [appropriate state rule of civil procedure], and shall comply with reasonable requests for (1) non-privileged information and evidence relevant to the charges or the respondent, and (2) other material upon good cause shown to the chair of the hearing committee [board].

B.   *Resolution of Disputes.*   Disputes concerning discovery shall be determined by the chair of the hearing committee [board] before which the matter is pending.   All discovery orders by the chair are interlocutory and may not be appealed prior to the entry of the final order.

C.   *Civil Rules Not Applicable.*   Proceedings under these rules are not subject to the [state rules of civil procedure] regarding discovery except those relating to depositions and subpoenas.

Commentary

Liberal exchanges of non-privileged information should be encouraged, since they facilitate the trial of the charges.   However, because a skillful advocate can convert unlimited discovery into a tool for delay, the time for discovery should be limited.   An order regarding discovery should be interlocutory and should not be appealable prior to entry of a final order in the proceeding.

RULE 16.   Access to Disciplinary Information

A.   *Confidentiality.*   Prior to the filing and service of formal charges in a discipline matter, the proceeding is confidential, except that the pendency, subject matter, and status of an investigation may be disclosed by disciplinary counsel if:

(1) the respondent has waived confidentiality;

(2) the proceeding is based upon allegations that include either the conviction of a crime or reciprocal discipline;

(3) the proceeding is based upon allegations that have become generally known to the public; or

(4) there is a need to notify another person or organization, including the clients' security fund, in order to protect the public, the administration of justice, or the legal profession.

B.   *Public Proceedings.*   Upon filing and service of formal charges in a discipline matter, or filing of a petition for reinstatement, the proceeding is public, except for:

(1) deliberations of the hearing committee, board, or court; or

(2) information with respect to which the hearing committee has issued a protective order.

689

C. *Proceedings Alleging Disability.* Proceedings for transfer to or from disability inactive status are confidential. All orders transferring a lawyer to or from disability inactive status are public.

D. *Protective Orders.* In order to protect the interests of a complainant, witness, third party, or respondent, the [hearing committee to which a matter is assigned] [board] may, upon application of any person and for good cause shown, issue a protective order prohibiting the disclosure of specific information otherwise privileged or confidential and direct that the proceedings be conducted so as to implement the order, including requiring that the hearing be conducted in such a way as to preserve the confidentiality of the information that is the subject of the application.

E. *Request for Nonpublic Information.* A request for nonpublic information other than that authorized for disclosure under paragraph A above shall be denied unless the request is from one of the following agencies:

    (1) [*names of agencies authorized to investigate qualifications for admission to practice;*]

    (2) lawyer disciplinary enforcement agencies;

    (3) [*other agencies, if any, designated by the court.*]

F. *Notice to Lawyer.* Except as provided in paragraph G, if the board or counsel decides to provide nonpublic information requested, and if the lawyer has not signed a waiver permitting the requesting agency to obtain nonpublic information, the lawyer shall be notified in writing at his or her last known address of that information which has been requested and by whom, together with a copy of the information proposed to be released to the requesting agency. The notice shall advise the lawyer that the information shall be released at the end of [twenty-one] days following mailing of the notice unless the lawyer objects to the disclosure. If the lawyer timely objects to the disclosure, the information shall remain confidential unless the requesting agency obtains a court order requiring its release.

G. *Release Without Notice.* If an otherwise authorized requesting agency has not obtained a waiver from the lawyer to obtain nonpublic information, and requests that the information be released without giving notice to the lawyer, the requesting agency shall certify that:

    (1) the request is made in furtherance of an ongoing investigation into misconduct by the lawyer;

    (2) the information is essential to that investigation; and

    (3) disclosure of the existence of the investigation to the lawyer would seriously prejudice that investigation.

H. *Notice to National Discipline Data Bank.* The board shall transmit notice of all public discipline imposed against a lawyer, transfers to or from disability inactive status, and reinstatements to the

National Discipline Data Bank maintained by the American Bar Association.

I. *Duty of Participants*. All participants in a proceeding under these rules shall conduct themselves so as to maintain the confidentiality mandated by this rule.

Commentary

The confidentiality that attaches prior to a finding of probable cause and the filing of formal charges is primarily for the benefit of the respondent, and protects against publicity predicated upon unfounded accusations.

If the respondent waives confidentiality or if the nature of the accusation is already known to the public, the basis for confidentiality no longer exists. Where information has become widely known, interested individuals and particularly the media often seek comment from the disciplinary agency involved. The existence of privacy requirements places the disciplinary agency in the awkward position of being unable to acknowledge the existence of an investigation. This could lead to a mistaken notion that the agency is unaware of or uninterested in allegations of misconduct, without in any way protecting the reputation of the lawyer.

Once a finding of probable cause has been made, there is no longer a danger that the allegations against the respondent are frivolous. The need to assure the integrity of the disciplinary process in the eyes of the public requires that at this point further proceedings be open to the public. An announcement that a lawyer accused of serious misconduct has been exonerated after a hearing behind closed doors will be suspect. The same disposition will command respect if the public has had access to the evidence.

Disability proceedings remain confidential until the final order of the court, because medical evidence or other peculiarly personal information relating to the lawyer is often involved. An order of the court transferring the lawyer to disability inactive status is public. When a lawyer's license to practice has been limited in any way, public disclosure is necessary. Failure to reveal the fact of transfer to disability inactive status would mislead the public and others likely to come into contact with the lawyer into believing that he or she remains eligible to practice.

The order transferring the lawyer to disability inactive status should clearly state the conditions that must be met for the lawyer to be reinstated to active status. Orders of reinstatement to active status should be published in the journal of the state bar and in a newspaper of general circulation in each judicial district in which the lawyer maintained an office for the practice of law.

In most instances, requests to the agency for nonpublic information relating to a specific lawyer should be denied. The court in its

691

discretion may direct that the agency cooperate with specific entities by providing them with nonpublic information. These will usually be entities charged with a public responsibility requiring that they investigate specific individuals, such as bar admissions committees, committees on judicial appointments, or law enforcement agencies.

Many of these agencies require the lawyer to sign a waiver authorizing the release of information. If the lawyer does not know what the file contains, he or she cannot knowingly authorize the disclosure of its contents. Therefore, if the lawyer requests it, a copy of any information which the agency proposes to disclose to the requesting entity should be furnished before a waiver is signed.

If the agency is asked to release information without a waiver from the lawyer, and is prepared to do so, it should first notify the lawyer of the request and furnish the lawyer with a copy of the information it proposes to release. This should be done sufficiently in advance of the release of the information to the requesting party to permit the lawyer to object to the release. The lawyer's timely objection places upon the requesting agency the burden of seeking a court order to release the information involved.

The requirement of notice to the lawyer prior to release does not apply to requests for information about a lawyer which are made in furtherance of an ongoing investigation into alleged misconduct on the part of the lawyer by an entity authorized to engage in such investigation. Before the agency releases information to an authorized entity without notice to the lawyer, the entity must provide the certification required by the rule.

Exchange of public information between agencies contributes to more effective enforcement. It is absurd for one agency to struggle with a substantive or procedural problem completely unaware that the same problem has been faced and resolved by an agency in another state. Nor should cases involving fundamental questions in disciplinary enforcement be litigated through the courts in the state in which they arise without agencies in other states which are likely to be vitally affected by the outcome being made aware of the existence of the proceeding until the Supreme Court of the United States renders a decision disposing of the issue.

The ABA Center for Professional Responsibility has full-time legal and administrative staff trained and educated in the discipline and disability field available to provide research information and consulting services. The Center maintains a file of the current rules of disciplinary enforcement of each jurisdiction, periodically updates an Index of case law, and operates the National Discipline Data Bank. Current information relating to the handling of particular problems or approaches to specific situations throughout the country is available.

RULE 17. Dissemination of Disciplinary Information

A. *Notice to Disciplinary Agencies.* Disciplinary counsel shall transmit notice of public discipline, transfers to or from disability inactive status, reinstatements, readmissions, and certified copies of judgments of conviction to the disciplinary enforcement agency of every other jurisdiction in which the respondent is admitted.

B. *Public Notice of Discipline Imposed.* Disciplinary counsel shall cause notices of suspension, disbarment, reinstatement, readmission, and transfers to or from disability inactive status to be published in the journal of the state bar and in a newspaper of general circulation in each judicial district in which the lawyer maintained an office for the practice of law.

C. *Notice to the Courts.* Disciplinary counsel shall promptly transmit a certified copy of the order of suspension, disbarment, reinstatement, and transfer to or from disability inactive status to all courts in this state. In addition, disciplinary counsel shall request the presiding judge of the court of the judicial district in which a respondent transferred to disability inactive status or otherwise unable to comply with the requirement of Rule 27 maintained an office for the practice of law to take such action under the provision of Rule 28 as may be indicated in order to protect the interests of the respondent and the respondent's clients.

Commentary

Broad dissemination of information concerning public discipline serves several important purposes. Notification to disciplinary agencies outside the jurisdiction where a sanction has been imposed facilitates appropriate action, such as reciprocal discipline, in jurisdictions where the lawyer is admitted or is seeking admission to practice. Transmittal of notice concerning criminal convictions provides disciplinary agencies with information that may form the basis of a petition for interim suspension. Publication in state bar journals and newspapers of general circulation helps protect the public and the legal community from being misled concerning the lawyer's eligibility to provide representation. In addition, public awareness of sanctions also enhances confidence in the disciplinary system as an effective means of responding to lawyer misconduct.

When a limitation on a lawyer's license has been removed through reinstatement, readmission or transfer to active status, publication and notification help the lawyer avoid a potential burden involved in correcting misunderstandings concerning his or her eligibility to practice. It is fair and reasonable to give notice of reinstatements, readmissions, and transfers to active status in the same manner as notice of public sanctions.

RULE 18. Additional Rules of Procedure

A. *Nature of Proceedings.* Disciplinary proceedings are neither civil nor criminal but are *sui generis.*

B. *Proceedings Governed by Rules of Civil Procedure and Evidence.* Except as otherwise provided in these rules, the [state rules of civil procedure] and the [state rules of evidence in civil matters] apply in discipline and disability cases.

C. *Standard of Proof.* Formal charges of misconduct, petitions for reinstatement and readmission, and petitions for transfer to and from disability inactive status shall be established by clear and convincing evidence.

D. *Burden of Proof.* The burden of proof in proceedings seeking discipline or transfer to disability inactive status is on disciplinary counsel. The burden of proof in proceedings seeking reinstatement, readmission, or transfer from disability inactive status is on the respondent.

E. *Prehearing Conference.* At the discretion of the [hearing committee] [board] or upon request of either party, a conference may be ordered for the purpose of obtaining admissions or otherwise narrowing the issues presented by the pleadings. The conference shall be held before the chair of the [hearing committee] [board] or another member of the [committee] [board] designated by the chair.

F. *Hearings Recorded.* The hearing should be recorded. Upon respondent's request, disciplinary counsel shall make the record of a hearing available to the respondent at the respondent's expense.

G. *Related Pending Litigation.* Upon a showing of good cause to the board, the processing of a disciplinary matter may be stayed because of substantial similarity to the material allegations of pending criminal or civil litigation or disciplinary action.

H. *Delay Caused by Complainant.* Neither unwillingness or neglect of the complainant to sign a complaint or prosecute a charge or settlement or compromise between the complainant and the lawyer or restitution by the lawyer, shall, in itself, justify abatement of the processing of any complaint.

I. *Effect of Time Limitations.* Except as is otherwise provided in these rules, time is directory and not jurisdictional. Failure to observe prescribed time intervals may result in sanctions against the violator but does not justify abatement of any discipline or disability investigation or proceeding.

J. *Complaints Against Disciplinary Agency Members.* If a complaint is filed against disciplinary counsel or disciplinary counsel's staff, a member of a hearing committee, or a member of the board, the matter shall proceed in accordance with these rules except that:

(1) If the respondent is disciplinary counsel or a member of the staff, the board shall appoint a special counsel to present the case;

(2) If the respondent is a member of a hearing committee, the chair of the board shall appoint a special hearing committee for the case; or

(3) If the respondent is a member of the board, the chief justice shall appoint a special board for the case.

Commentary

The holder of a license to practice law is subject to discipline for breaches of the standards of professional conduct; the license must not be arbitrarily taken away and the holder is entitled to procedural due process in any proceeding relating to such conduct. Such due process rights include fair notice of the charges, right to counsel, right to cross-examine witnesses, right to present arguments to the adjudicators, right of appeal (Rule 11); and right to subpoena and discovery (Rules 14 and 15).

The standard of proof is higher than "preponderance of the weight of credible evidence" which is usually deemed sufficient in civil proceedings, yet not as stringent as "beyond a reasonable doubt" required in criminal cases.

A prehearing conference may be held by the chairman *sua sponte,* or upon request of counsel, the respondent (or respondent's counsel), or another hearing committee member.

The hearing may be recorded by any method authorized in the jurisdiction. The record will assist the hearing committee in the preparation and presentation of its report. If the matter ultimately results in a recommendation for discipline, the record should be forwarded with the findings and recommendation. The recording should be available to the respondent upon request, and a transcript provided at cost.

Statutes of limitation are wholly inappropriate in lawyer disciplinary proceedings. Conduct of a lawyer, no matter when it has occurred, is always relevant to the question of fitness to practice. The time between the commission of the alleged misconduct and the filing of a complaint predicated thereon may be pertinent to whether and to what extent discipline should be imposed, but should not limit the agency's power to investigate.

This rule provides a rational basis for appointment of special counsel, special hearing committee, or special board by the next higher entity in the adjudicative process.

RULE 19. Lawyers Convicted of a Crime

A. *Transmittal of Certificate of Conviction by Clerk of Trial Court.* The clerk of any court in this state in which a lawyer is convicted of a crime shall within [ten] days after the conviction transmit a certified copy of the judgment of conviction to counsel for the lawyer disciplinary agency of every state in which the lawyer is admitted to practice.

B. *Determination of "Serious Crime."* Upon being advised that a lawyer subject to the disciplinary jurisdiction of this court has been convicted of a crime, disciplinary counsel shall determine whether the crime constitutes a "serious crime" warranting immediate interim suspension. If the crime is a "serious crime," disciplinary counsel shall prepare an order for interim suspension and forward it to the court and the respondent with a certificate of the conviction. Disciplinary counsel shall in addition file formal charges against the respondent predicated upon the conviction. On or before the date established for the entry of the order of interim suspension the lawyer may assert any jurisdictional deficiency that establishes that the suspension may not properly be ordered, such as that the crime did not constitute a "serious crime" or that the lawyer is not the individual convicted. If the crime is not a "serious crime," counsel shall process the matter in the same manner as any other information coming to the attention of the agency.

C. *Definition of "Serious Crime."* A "serious crime" is any felony and any lesser crime a necessary element of which, as determined by the statutory or common law definition of the crime, involves interference with the administration of justice, false swearing, misrepresentation, fraud, deceit, bribery, extortion, misappropriation, theft, or an attempt, conspiracy or solicitation of another to commit a "serious crime."

D. *Immediate Interim Suspension.* The court has exclusive power to place a lawyer on interim suspension.

(1) Imposition. The court shall place a lawyer on interim suspension immediately upon proof that the lawyer has been convicted of a serious crime regardless of the pendency of any appeal.

(2) Termination. The court has exclusive power to terminate an interim suspension. In the interest of justice, the court may terminate an interim suspension at any time upon a showing of extraordinary circumstances, after affording disciplinary counsel notice and an opportunity to be heard.

E. *Conviction as Conclusive Evidence.* A certified copy of a judgment of conviction constitutes conclusive evidence that the lawyer committed the crime, and the sole issue in any hearing regarding the conviction shall be the nature and extent of the discipline to be imposed.

F. *Automatic Reinstatement From Interim Suspension Upon Reversal of Conviction.* If a lawyer suspended solely under the provisions of paragraph D demonstrates that the underlying conviction has been reversed or vacated, the order for interim suspension shall be vacated and the lawyer placed on active status. The vacating of the interim suspension will not automatically terminate any formal proceeding then pending against the lawyer, the disposition of which shall be determined by the hearing committee and the board on the basis of the available evidence other than conviction.

G. *Notice to Clients and Others on Interim Suspension.* An interim suspension under this rule shall constitute a suspension of the lawyer for the purpose of Rule 27.

Commentary

Interim suspension is necessary both to protect members of the public and to maintain public confidence in the legal profession. The interim suspension not only removes any danger to clients and the public which the respondent may pose, but also serves to protect the profession and the administration of justice from the specter created where an individual convicted of a "serious crime" continues to serve as an officer of the court in good standing.

Interim suspension is not final discipline; therefore counsel must proceed to file formal charges based upon the conviction. Formal proceedings should not be conducted until all appeals from the conviction have been exhausted, unless the respondent requests that the hearing not be deferred.

Continued practice by a lawyer convicted of a "serious crime" undermines the public confidence in the profession and the administration of justice. It is difficult to understand why a lawyer convicted of stealing funds from a client can continue to handle client funds, why a lawyer convicted of securities fraud can continue to prepare and certify registration statements, or why a lawyer convicted of conspiracy to suborn perjury can continue to try cases and present witnesses. Immediate suspension of a lawyer so convicted, regardless of the pendency of any appeal, is essential to preserve public confidence.

* * *

RULE 20. Interim Suspension for Threat of Harm

A. *Transmittal of Evidence.* Upon receipt of sufficient evidence demonstrating that a lawyer subject to the disciplinary jurisdiction of this court has committed a violation of the [state Rules of Professional Conduct] or is under a disability as herein defined and poses a substantial threat of irreparable harm to the public, disciplinary counsel shall:

(i) transmit the evidence to the court together with a proposed order for interim suspension; and

(ii) contemporaneously make a reasonable attempt to provide the lawyer with notice, which may include notice by telephone, that a proposed order for immediate interim suspension has been transmitted to the court.

B. *Immediate Interim Suspension.* Upon examination of the evidence transmitted to the court by disciplinary counsel and of rebuttal evidence, if any, which the lawyer has transmitted to the court prior to the court's ruling, the court may enter an order immediately suspending the lawyer, pending final disposition of a disciplinary proceeding predicated upon the conduct causing the harm, or may order such other action as it deems appropriate. In the event the order is entered, the court may appoint a trustee pursuant to Rule 28 to protect clients' interests.

C. *Notice to Clients.* A lawyer suspended pursuant to paragraph B shall comply with the notice requirements in Rule 27.

D. *Motion for Dissolution of Interim Suspension.* On [two] days notice to disciplinary counsel, a lawyer suspended pursuant to paragraph B may appear and move for dissolution or modification of the order of suspension, and in that event the motion shall be heard and determined as expeditiously as the ends of justice require.

Commentary

Certain misconduct poses such an immediate threat to the public and the administration of justice that the lawyer should be suspended from the practice of law immediately pending a final determination of the ultimate discipline to be imposed. Interim suspension is also appropriate when the lawyer's continuing conduct is causing or is likely to cause serious injury to a client or the public, as, for example, where a lawyer abandons the practice of law or is engaged in an ongoing conversion of trust funds.

The procedures set forth in Rule 20 are similar to those applicable to civil temporary restraining orders, except that an immediate interim suspension order does not expire automatically, but requires a motion for dissolution or modification. Since immediate interim suspension may be imposed *ex parte* following reasonable efforts to notify the lawyer, a lawyer suspended without a hearing should be afforded an opportunity to seek dissolution or modification of the suspension order on an expedited basis.

RULE 21. Discipline by Consent

A. *Board Approval of Tendered Admission.* A lawyer against whom formal charges have been made may tender a conditional admission to the petition or to a particular count thereof in exchange for a stated form of discipline. The tendered admission shall be submitted to disciplinary counsel and approved or rejected by the board [considering the recommendation of the hearing committee if the matter has already been assigned for hearing, and] subject to final approval or rejection by the court if the stated form of discipline includes disbarment, suspension or transfer to disability inactive status. If the stated form of discipline is rejected by the [adjudicative body] [board], the admission shall be withdrawn and cannot be used against the respondent in any subsequent proceedings.

B. *Review of Discipline by Consent.* The extent of discipline to be imposed is subject to review. If an agreement providing for admonition or probation is reached prior to the filing of formal charges, the agreement must be approved by the chair of a hearing committee [board].

C. *Discontinuance of Jurisdiction.* Approval of the discipline proposed by the board and, if required, by the court, shall divest the hearing committee of further jurisdiction and no report need be prepared in such cases. The final order of discipline shall be predicated upon the petition and the conditional admission tendered.

D. *Affidavit of Consent.* A lawyer who consents to a stated form of discipline shall present to the board an affidavit stating that he or she consents to the discipline and that:

(1) The consent is freely and voluntarily rendered; the lawyer is not being subjected to coercion or duress; the lawyer is fully aware of the implications of submitting the consent;

(2) The lawyer is aware that there is presently pending an investigation into, or proceeding involving, allegations that there exist grounds for discipline, the nature of which shall be specifically set forth;

(3) The lawyer acknowledges that the material facts so alleged are true; and

(4) The lawyer consents because the lawyer knows that if charges predicated upon the matters under investigation were filed, or if the pending proceeding were prosecuted, the lawyer could not successfully defend against them.

E. *Order of Discipline.* The board shall file the affidavit with the court. If the discipline by consent is a reprimand, the board shall enter the order. In all other instances in which proposed discipline has been approved the court shall enter the order disciplining the lawyer on consent. The affidavit shall be sealed and shall not be disclosed or made available for use in any other proceeding except upon order of the court.

Commentary

If an agreement provides for reprimand, suspension or disbarment, or if any agreement is reached after formal charges have been filed, the agreement must be approved by a panel of the board. Members of the panel are disqualified from any future consideration of the matter in the event the stipulated discipline is for any reason not imposed. If the stipulated discipline provides for suspension or disbarment, it must also be approved by the court.

Acceptance of stipulated discipline by a lawyer who has been guilty of misconduct and desires to avoid the trauma and expense of a proceeding is in the interest of the public and the agency. The public is immediately protected from further misconduct by the lawyer, who otherwise might continue to practice until a formal proceeding is concluded. The agency is relieved of the time-consuming and expensive necessity of prosecuting a formal proceeding.

The respondent should be required to admit the charges before discipline is stipulated, so that evidence of guilt will be available if the respondent later claims that he or she was not, in fact, guilty. Petitions for reinstatement are often filed years after discipline has been imposed, and if there is no admission it may be difficult for the agency to establish the misconduct because relevant evidence and witnesses may no longer be available.

Discipline by consent which results in the lawyer withdrawing from the practice of law should be recorded and treated as disbarment, not as resignation. An agreement made when the charges are before the board shall be reviewed by the court. In the event that proposed stipulated discipline is disapproved by the reviewing entity, or the matter is returned to formal proceedings for any reason, the respondent's admission of the charges cannot be used against the respondent.

RULE 22. Reciprocal Discipline

A. *Disciplinary Counsel Duty to Obtain Order of Discipline From Other Jurisdiction.* Upon being disciplined in another jurisdiction, a lawyer admitted to practice in [name of state] shall promptly inform disciplinary counsel of the discipline. Upon notification from any source that a lawyer within the jurisdiction of the agency has been disciplined in another jurisdiction, disciplinary counsel shall obtain a certified copy of the disciplinary order and file it with the board and with the court.

B. *Notice Served Upon Respondent.* Upon receipt of a certified copy of an order demonstrating that a lawyer admitted to practice in [name of state] has been disciplined in another jurisdiction, the court shall forthwith issue a notice directed to the lawyer and to disciplinary counsel containing:

(1) A copy of the order from the other jurisdiction; and

(2) An order directing that the lawyer or disciplinary counsel inform the court, within [thirty] days from service of the notice, of any claim by the lawyer or disciplinary counsel predicated upon the grounds set forth in paragraph D, that the imposition of the identical discipline in this state would be unwarranted and the reasons for that claim.

C. *Effect of Stay of Discipline in Other Jurisdiction.* In the event the discipline imposed in the other jurisdiction has been stayed there, any reciprocal discipline imposed in this state shall be deferred until the stay expires.

D. *Discipline to Be Imposed.* Upon the expiration of [thirty] days from service of the notice pursuant to the provisions of paragraph B, this court shall impose the identical discipline unless disciplinary counsel or the lawyer demonstrates, or this court finds that it clearly appears upon the face of the record from which the discipline is predicated, that:

(1) The procedure was so lacking in notice or opportunity to be heard as to constitute a deprivation of due process; or

(2) There was such infirmity of proof establishing the misconduct as to give rise to the clear conviction that the court could not, consistent with its duty, accept as final the conclusion on that subject; or

(3) The imposition of the same discipline by the court would result in grave injustice; or

(4) The misconduct established warrants substantially different discipline in this state.

If this court determines that any of those elements exists, this court shall enter such other order as it deems appropriate. The burden is on the party seeking different discipline in this jurisdiction to demonstrate that the imposition of the same discipline is not appropriate.

E. *Conclusiveness of Adjudication in Other Jurisdictions.* In all other aspects, a final adjudication in another jurisdiction that a lawyer has been guilty of misconduct shall establish conclusively the misconduct for purposes of a disciplinary proceeding in this state.

Commentary

If a lawyer suspended or disbarred in one jurisdiction is also admitted in another jurisdiction and no action can be taken against the lawyer until a new disciplinary proceeding is instituted, tried, and concluded, the public in the second jurisdiction is left unprotected against a lawyer who has been judicially determined to be unfit. Any procedure which so exposes innocent clients to harm cannot be justified. The spectacle of a lawyer disbarred in one jurisdiction yet permitted to practice elsewhere exposes the profession to criticism and undermines public confidence in the administration of justice.

Disciplinary counsel in the forum jurisdiction should be notified by disciplinary counsel of the jurisdiction where the original discipline was imposed. Upon receipt of such information, disciplinary counsel should promptly obtain and serve upon the lawyer an order to show cause why identical discipline should not be imposed in the forum state. The certified copy of the order in the original jurisdiction should be incorporated into the order to show cause.

The imposition of discipline in one jurisdiction does not mean that every other jurisdiction in which the lawyer is admitted must necessarily impose discipline. The agency has jurisdiction to recommend reciprocal discipline on the basis of public discipline imposed by a state in which the respondent is licensed.

A judicial determination of misconduct by the respondent in another jurisdiction is conclusive, and not subject to relitigation in the forum state. The court should impose identical discipline unless it determines, after review limited to the record of the proceedings in the foreign jurisdiction, that one of the grounds specified in paragraph D exists.

RULE 23. Proceedings in Which Lawyer Is Declared to Be Incompetent or Alleged to Be Incapacitated

A. *Involuntary Commitment or Adjudication of Incompetency.* If a lawyer has been judicially declared incompetent or is involuntarily committed on the grounds of incompetency or disability, the court, upon proper proof of the fact, shall enter an order immediately transferring the lawyer to disability inactive status for an indefinite period until the further order of the court. A copy of the order shall be served, in the manner the court may direct, upon the lawyer, his or her guardian, or the director of the institution to which the lawyer has been committed.

B. *Inability to Properly Defend.* If a respondent alleges in the course of a disciplinary proceeding an inability to assist in the defense due to mental or physical incapacity, the court shall immediately transfer the lawyer to disability inactive status pending determination of the incapacity.

(1) If the court determines the claim of inability to defend is valid, the disciplinary proceeding shall be deferred and the respondent retained on disability inactive status until the court subsequently considers a petition for transfer of the respondent to active status. If the court considering the petition for transfer to active status determines the petition shall be granted, the court shall also determine the disposition of the interrupted disciplinary proceedings.

(2) If the court determines the claim of incapacity to defend to be invalid, the disciplinary proceeding shall resume and the respondent shall immediately be placed on interim suspension pending the final disposition of the matter.

C. *Proceedings to Determine Incapacity.* Information relating to a lawyer's physical or mental condition which adversely affects the lawyer's ability to practice law shall be investigated, and where warranted, shall be the subject of formal proceedings to determine whether the lawyer shall be transferred to disability inactive status. The hearings shall be conducted in the same manner as disciplinary proceedings, except that all of the proceedings shall be confidential. The court shall provide for such notice to the respondent of proceedings in the matter as it deems proper and advisable and may appoint a lawyer to represent the respondent if the respondent is without adequate representation. The court may take or direct whatever action it deems necessary or proper to determine whether the respondent is so incapacitated, including the examination of the respondent by qualified medical experts designated by the court. If, upon due consideration of the matter, the court concludes that the respondent is incapacitated from continuing to practice law, it shall enter an order transferring the respondent to disability inactive status for an indefinite period and until the further order of the court. Any pending disciplinary proceedings against the respondent shall be held in abeyance.

D. *Public Notice of Transfer to Disability Inactive Status.* The board shall cause a notice of transfer to disability inactive status to be published in the journal of the state bar and in a newspaper of general circulation in each judicial district in which the lawyer maintained an office for the practice of law.

E. *Reinstatement From Disability Inactive Status.*

(1) Generally. No respondent transferred to disability inactive status may resume active status except by order of this court.

(2) Petition. Any respondent transferred to disability inactive status shall be entitled to petition for transfer to active status once a year, or at whatever shorter intervals the court may direct in the order transferring the respondent to disability inactive status or any modifications thereof.

(3) Examination. Upon the filing of a petition for transfer to active status, the court may take or direct whatever action it deems necessary or proper to determine whether the disability has been removed, including a direction for an examination of the respondent by qualified medical experts designated by the court. In its discretion, the court may direct that the expense of the examination be paid by the respondent.

(4) Waiver of Doctor–Patient Privilege. With the filing of a petition for reinstatement to active status, the respondent shall be required to disclose the name of each psychiatrist, psychologist, physician and hospital or other institution by whom or in which the respondent has been examined or treated since the transfer to disability inactive status. The respondent shall furnish to this court written consent to the release of information and records relating to the disability if requested by the court or court-appointed medical experts.

(5) Learning in Law; Bar Examination. The court may also direct that the respondent establish proof of competence and learning in law, which proof may include certification by the bar examiners of successful completion of an examination for admission to practice.

(6) Granting Petition for Transfer to Active Status. The court shall grant the petition for transfer to active status upon a showing by clear and convincing evidence that the disability has been removed.

(7) Judicial Declaration of Competence. If a respondent transferred to disability inactive status on the basis of a judicial determination of incompetence has been judicially declared to be competent, the court may dispense with further evidence that his disability has been removed and may immediately direct his reinstatement to active status upon terms as are deemed proper and advisable.

Commentary

Since the principal responsibility of the agency is to protect the public, it must concern itself with disabled lawyers who endanger the interests of clients, even if no misconduct has been committed. It is important that incapacity not be treated as misconduct, and to clearly distinguish willful conduct from conduct beyond the control of the lawyer.

* * *

RULE 24. Reinstatement Following a Suspension of Six Months or Less

A lawyer who has been suspended for six months or less pursuant to disciplinary proceedings shall be reinstated at the end of the period of suspension by filing with the court and serving upon disciplinary counsel an affidavit stating that he or she has fully complied with the requirements of the suspension order and has paid any required fees and costs.

Commentary

Reinstatement proceedings may take months to complete. Requiring a proceeding before a lawyer can be reinstated after a suspension of six months or less would unfairly prolong the period of suspension. Consequently, reinstatement following a suspension for six months or less should be automatic upon the expiration of the prescribed period of time, a filing of an affidavit alleging compliance with the terms of the order of suspension and the payment of fees and costs.

RULE 25. Reinstatement After Suspension for More Than Six Months and Readmission

A. *Generally.* A lawyer suspended for more than six months or a disbarred lawyer shall be reinstated or readmitted only upon order of the court. No lawyer may petition for reinstatement until [six months before] the period of suspension has expired. No lawyer may petition for readmission until [five] years after the effective date of disbarment. A lawyer who has been placed on interim suspension and is then disbarred for the same misconduct that was the ground for the interim suspension may petition for readmission at the expiration of [five] years from the time of the effective date of the interim suspension.

B. *Petition.* A petition for reinstatement or readmission must be under oath or affirmation under penalty of perjury and shall specify with particularity the manner in which the lawyer meets each of the criteria specified in paragraph E or, if not, why there is good and sufficient reason for reinstatement or readmission. [Unless abated under Rule 26] the petition must be accompanied by an advance cost deposit in the amount set from time to time by the board to cover anticipated costs of the proceeding.

C. *Service of Petition.* The lawyer shall file a copy of the petition with disciplinary counsel and disciplinary counsel shall serve a copy of the petition upon each complainant in the disciplinary proceeding that led to the suspension or disbarment.

D. *Publication of Notice of Petition.* At the same time that a lawyer files a petition for reinstatement or readmission, the lawyer shall also publish a notice of the petition in the journal of the state bar and in a newspaper of general circulation in each judicial district in which the lawyer maintained an office for the practice of law when the lawyer was suspended or disbarred. The notice shall inform members of the bar and the public about the application for reinstatement or readmission, and shall request that any individuals file notice of their opposition or concurrence with the board within [sixty] days. In addition, the lawyer shall notify the complainant(s) in the disciplinary proceeding that led to the lawyer's suspension or disbarment that the lawyer is applying for reinstatement or readmission, and shall inform each complainant that he or she has [sixty] days to raise objections to or to support the lawyer's petition.

E. *Criteria for Reinstatement and Readmission.* A lawyer may be reinstated or readmitted only if the lawyer meets each of the following criteria, or, if not, presents good and sufficient reason why the lawyer should nevertheless be reinstated or readmitted:

(1) The lawyer has fully complied with the terms and conditions of all prior disciplinary orders except to the extent that they are abated under Rule 26.

(2) The lawyer has not engaged nor attempted to engage in the unauthorized practice of law during the period of suspension or disbarment.

(3) If the lawyer was suffering under a physical or mental disability or infirmity at the time of suspension or disbarment, including alcohol or other drug abuse, the disability or infirmity has been removed. Where alcohol or other drug abuse was a causative factor in the lawyer's misconduct, the lawyer shall not be reinstated or readmitted unless:

705

(a) the lawyer has pursued appropriate rehabilitative treatment;

(b) the lawyer has abstained from the use of alcohol or other drugs for at least [one year]; and

(c) the lawyer is likely to continue to abstain from alcohol or other drugs.

(4) The lawyer recognizes the wrongfulness and seriousness of the misconduct for which the lawyer was suspended or disbarred.

(5) The lawyer has not engaged in any other professional misconduct since suspension or disbarment.

(6) Notwithstanding the conduct for which the lawyer was disciplined, the lawyer has the requisite honesty and integrity to practice law.

(7) The lawyer has kept informed about recent developments in the law and is competent to practice.

F. *Review of Petition.* Within [ninety] days after receiving a lawyer's petition for reinstatement or readmission, disciplinary counsel shall either: (1) advise the lawyer and the [board] court that disciplinary counsel will stipulate to the lawyer's reinstatement or readmission, or (2) advise the lawyer and the [board] court that disciplinary counsel opposes reinstatement or readmission and request the [board] court to set a hearing.

G. *Hearing; Report.* Upon receipt of disciplinary counsel's request for a hearing, the [board] court shall promptly refer the matter to a hearing committee. Within [ninety] days of the request, the hearing committee shall conduct a hearing at which the lawyer shall have the burden of demonstrating by clear and convincing evidence that he or she has met each of the criteria in paragraph E or, if not, that there is good and sufficient reason why the lawyer should nevertheless be reinstated or readmitted. The hearing committee shall file a report with the [board] court containing its findings and recommendations. [The board shall promptly review the report of the hearing committee and the record and shall file its own findings and recommendations with the court.]

H. *Decision as to Reinstatement or Readmission.* The court shall review the report filed by the [hearing committee] [board] or any stipulation agreed to by the lawyer and disciplinary counsel. If the court finds that the lawyer has complied with each of the criteria of paragraph E, or has presented good and sufficient reason for failure to comply, the court shall reinstate or readmit the lawyer. If the court reinstates or readmits the lawyer, the court shall issue a written opinion setting forth the grounds for its decision; if the court denies reinstatement or readmission, the court shall issue a written opinion setting forth the ground for its decision and shall identify the period after which the lawyer may reapply. Generally, no lawyer should be permitted to reapply for reinstatement or readmission within one year following an adverse judgment upon a petition for reinstatement or readmission.

I. *Conditions of Reinstatement or Readmission.* The court may impose conditions on a lawyer's reinstatement or readmission. The conditions shall be imposed in cases where the lawyer has met the burden of proof justifying reinstatement or readmission, but the court reasonably believes that further precautions should be taken to insure that the public will be protected upon the lawyer's return to practice.

The court may impose any conditions that are reasonably related to the grounds for the lawyer's original suspension or disbarment, or to evidence presented at the hearing regarding the lawyer's failure to meet the criteria for reinstatement or readmission. The conditions may include any of the following: passing the bar examination as a condition to readmission following disbarment; limitation upon practice (to one area of law or through association with an experienced supervising lawyer); participation in continuing legal education courses; monitoring of the lawyer's practice (for compliance with trust account rules, accounting procedures, or office management procedures); abstention from the use of drugs or alcohol; active participation in Alcoholics Anonymous or other alcohol or drug rehabilitation program; monitoring of the lawyer's compliance with any other orders (such as abstinence from alcohol or drugs, or participation in alcohol or drug rehabilitation programs). If the monitoring lawyer determines that the reinstated or readmitted lawyer's compliance with any condition of reinstatement or readmission is unsatisfactory and that there exists a potential for harm to the public, the monitoring lawyer shall notify the court and, where necessary to protect the public, the lawyer may be suspended from practice under Rule 20(B).

J. *Reciprocal Reinstatement or Readmission.* Where the court has imposed a suspension or disbarment solely on the basis of imposition of discipline in another jurisdiction, and where the lawyer gives notice to the court that he or she has been reinstated or readmitted in the other jurisdiction, the court shall determine whether the lawyer should be reinstated or readmitted. Unless disciplinary counsel presents evidence demonstrating procedural irregularities in the other jurisdiction's proceeding or presents other compelling reasons, the court shall reinstate or readmit a lawyer who has been reinstated or readmitted in the jurisdiction where the misconduct occurred.

Commentary

Readmission occurs when a disbarred lawyer is returned to practice. Since the purpose of lawyer discipline is not to punish, readmission may be appropriate; the presumption, though, should be against readmission. In no event should a lawyer be considered for readmission until at least five years after the effective date of disbarment.

Reinstatement occurs when a suspended lawyer is returned to practice. Reinstatement is appropriate when a lawyer shows rehabilitation. Application for reinstatement should be permitted at the expiration of the ordered period of suspension. While reinstatement should not be ordered prior to the expiration of the ordered period of suspension, application for reinstatement may be allowed up to six months preceding the expiration so that the time required for a decision on the application does not unfairly prolong the suspension.

As a condition of readmission or reinstatement, a disbarred or suspended lawyer is usually required to establish rehabilitation, fitness to practice and competence, and may be required to pay the costs of the disciplinary proceedings, to make restitution, to pass an examination in professional responsibility, and to comply with court orders.

There is a compelling reason not to grant reciprocal reinstatement under paragraph J if the forum jurisdiction imposed a longer suspension than the original jurisdiction or if there was a delay between the imposition of the original discipline and the imposition of the reciprocal discipline.

[RULE 26. Abatement or Modification of Conditions of Discipline, Reinstatement, or Readmission

Where the court has imposed conditions in an order of discipline or in an order of reinstatement or readmission, the lawyer may request of the court an order of abatement discharging the lawyer from the obligation to comply with the conditions, or an order modifying the conditions. The lawyer may so request either prior to or as part of lawyer's petition for reinstatement or readmission. The court may grant the request if the lawyer shows by clear and convincing evidence that the lawyer has made a timely, good faith effort to meet the condition(s) but it is impossible to fulfill the condition(s).]

Commentary

A jurisdiction adopting this Rule should also adopt the bracketed language in Rule 25(B).

RULE 27. Notice to Clients, Adverse Parties, and Other Counsel

A. *Recipients of Notice; Contents.* Within [ten] days after the date of the court order imposing discipline or transfer to disability inactive status, a respondent disbarred, transferred to disability inactive status, placed on interim suspension, or suspended for more than [six months] shall notify or cause to be notified by registered or certified mail, return receipt requested,

(1) all clients being represented in pending matters;

(2) any co-counsel in pending matters; and

(3) any opposing counsel in pending matters, or in the absence of opposing counsel, the adverse parties, of the order of the court

and that the lawyer is therefore disqualified to act as lawyer after the effective date of the order.

The notice to be given to the lawyer(s) for an adverse party, or, in the absence of opposing counsel, the adverse parties, shall state the place of residence of the client of the respondent.

B. *Special Notice.* The court may direct the issuance of notice to such financial institutions or others as may be necessary to protect the interests of clients or other members of the public.

C. *Duty to Maintain Records.* The respondent shall keep and maintain records of the steps taken to accomplish the requirements of paragraphs A and B, and shall make those records available to the disciplinary counsel on request.

D. *Return of Client Property.* The respondent shall deliver to all clients being represented in pending matters any papers or other property to which they are entitled and shall notify them and any counsel representing them of a suitable time and place where the papers and other property may be obtained, calling attention to any urgency for obtaining the papers or other property.

E. *Effective Date of Order; Refund of Fees.* Orders imposing disbarment, suspension, or transfers to disability inactive status are effective immediately, unless otherwise ordered by the court. The respondent shall refund within [ten] days after entry of the order any part of any fees paid in advance that has not been earned.

F. *Withdrawal From Representation.* In the event the client does not obtain another lawyer before the effective date of the disbarment or suspension, it shall be the responsibility of the respondent to move in the court or agency in which the proceeding is pending for leave to withdraw. The respondent shall in that event file with the court, agency or tribunal before which the litigation is pending a copy of the notice to opposing counsel or adverse parties.

G. *New Representation Prohibited.* Prior to the effective date of the order, if not immediate, the respondent shall not agree to under-take any new legal matters between service of the order and the effective date of the discipline.

H. *Affidavit Filed With Court.* Within [ten] days after the effective date of the disbarment or suspension order, or order of transfer to disability inactive status, the respondent shall file with this court an affidavit showing:

(1) Compliance with the provisions of the order and with these rules;

(2) All other state, federal and administrative jurisdictions to which the lawyer is admitted to practice;

(3) Residence or other addresses where communications may thereafter be directed; and

709

(4) Service of a copy of the affidavit upon disciplinary counsel.

Commentary

These notice provisions are necessary to ensure that the respondent's inability to practice does not prejudice the rights of existing clients or other parties, and that those who might otherwise have occasion to deal with the lawyer are made aware of the lawyer's suspension or disbarment. Compliance with the notice provision is an absolute precondition for reinstatement or readmission, and failure to comply may be grounds for further discipline.

Usually the effective date of discipline or transfer to disability inactive status should be the end of the period during which the final order may be appealed. The interval between the entry of the order and its effective date permits the respondent to wind up his or her practice in an orderly manner. The respondent should not accept new retainers during this period since it is unlikely he or she can adequately represent new clients before the effective date when practice must be discontinued.

RULE 28. Appointment of Counsel to Protect Clients' Interests When Respondent Is Transferred to Disability Inactive Status, Suspended, Disbarred, Disappears, or Dies

A. *Inventory of Lawyer Files.* If a respondent has been transferred to disability inactive status, or has disappeared or died, or has been suspended or disbarred and there is evidence that he or she has not complied with Rule 27, and no partner, executor or other responsible party capable of conducting the respondent's affairs is known to exist, the presiding judge in the judicial district in which the respondent maintained a practice, upon proper proof of the fact, shall appoint a lawyer or lawyers to inventory the files of the respondent, and to take such action as seems indicated to protect the interests of the respondent and his or her clients.

B. *Protection for Records Subject to Inventory.* Any lawyer so appointed shall not be permitted to disclose any information contained in any files inventoried without the consent of the client to whom the file relates, except as necessary to carry out the order of the court which appointed the lawyer to make the inventory.

Commentary

In any situation in which the lawyer is not available to protect clients, the agency has an obligation to protect them. When such information comes to the attention of the agency, it need not await the determination that misconduct has occurred before acting.

The cost of the inventory may be paid from the fees owing to the lawyer whose files are inventoried. The cost may also be paid by funds made available for that purpose by state and local bar associations.

Often the lawyer appointed as trustee will waive all or part of his or her fee as a public service.

The trustee is appointed to inventory the files of the lawyer's clients, not to represent them. The trustee should review each file and recommend to the judge who appointed him or her a proposed disposition. The trustee may take only such action with respect to each client's file as is authorized by the judge who appointed him or her.

The lawyer-client privilege must be extended so that review of the file by the trustee is not deemed to be disclosure to a third party, which would waive the privilege.

RULE 29. Maintenance of Trust Funds in Approved Financial Institutions; Overdraft Notification

A. *Clearly Identified Trust Accounts in Approved Financial Institutions Required.*

(1) Lawyers who practice law in [name of state] shall deposit all funds held in trust in this jurisdiction [in accordance with Rule 1.15(a) of the Model Rules of Professional Conduct] in accounts clearly identified as "trust" or "escrow" accounts, referred to herein as "trust accounts," and shall take all steps necessary to inform the depository institution of the purpose and identity of the accounts. Funds held in trust include funds held in any fiduciary capacity in connection with a representation, whether as trustee, agent, guardian, executor or otherwise. Lawyer trust accounts shall be maintained only in financial institutions approved by the court [the board].

(2) Every lawyer engaged in the practice of law in [name of state] shall maintain and preserve for a period of at least five years, after final disposition of the underlying matter, the records of the accounts, including checkbooks, cancelled checks, check stubs, vouchers, ledgers, journals, closing statements, accountings or other statements of disbursements rendered to clients or other parties with regard to trust funds or similar equivalent records clearly and expressly reflecting the date, amount, source, and explanation for all receipts, withdrawals, deliveries and disbursements of the funds or other property of a client.

B. *Overdraft Notification Agreement Required.* A financial institution shall be approved as a depository for lawyer trust accounts if it files with the court an agreement, in a form provided by the court [board] to report to the disciplinary agency whenever any properly payable instrument is presented against a lawyer trust account containing insufficient funds, irrespective of whether or not the instrument is honored. The court [board] shall establish rules governing approval and termination of approved status for financial institutions, and shall annually publish a list of approved financial institutions. No trust account shall be maintained in any financial institution that does not agree to so report. Any such agreement shall apply to all branches of the financial institution and shall not be cancelled except upon [thirty] days notice in writing to the court [board].

C. *Overdraft Reports.* The overdraft notification agreement shall provide that all reports made by the financial institution shall be in the following format:

(1) In the case of a dishonored instrument, the report shall be identical to the overdraft notice customarily forwarded to the depositor, and should include a copy of the dishonored instrument, if such a copy is normally provided to depositors;

(2) In the case of instruments that are presented against insufficient funds but which instruments are honored, the report shall identify the financial institution, the lawyer or law firm, the account number, the date of presentation for payment, and the date paid, as well as the amount of overdraft created thereby.

D. *Timing of Reports.* Reports under paragraph C shall be made simultaneously with, and within the time provided by law for notice of dishonor, if any. If an instrument presented against insufficient funds is honored, then the report shall be made within [five] banking days of the date of presentation for payment against insufficient funds.

E. *Consent by Lawyers.* Every lawyer practicing or admitted to practice in this jurisdiction shall, as a condition thereof, be conclusively deemed to have consented to the reporting and production requirements mandated by this rule.

F. *Costs.* Nothing herein shall preclude a financial institution from charging a particular lawyer or law firm for the reasonable cost of producing the reports and records required by this rule.

G. *Definitions.* For purposes of this Rule:

(1) "Financial institution" includes a bank, savings and loan association, credit union, savings bank, and any other business or person that accepts for deposit funds held in trust by lawyers.

(2) "Properly payable" refers to an instrument which, if presented in the normal course of business, is in a form requiring payment under the laws of this jurisdiction.

(3) "Notice of dishonor" refers to the notice that a financial institution is required to give, under the laws of this jurisdiction, upon presentation of an instrument that the institution dishonors.

Commentary

Paragraph A sets forth the requirements for deposit of trust funds in clearly identified trust accounts in approved financial institutions. Funds held not in connection with a representation, such as a trust fund for a lawyer's own spouse or minor child, do not fall under the rule. The rule also does not concern a lawyer's own funds properly held in a non-fiduciary capacity, such as funds in a business or personal account.

Under Rule 1.15(a) of the Model Rules of Professional Conduct, trust property may be held outside the lawyer's home jurisdiction upon consent of the client. The overdraft notification rule governs funds held within the adopting state. A lawyer's obligation to deposit trust funds in an approved institution will arise upon adoption of the over-draft notification rule in a state where the lawyer deposits trust funds, whether that state is the state wherein the lawyer's office is situated or some other state.

The overdraft notification agreement requires that all overdrafts be reported, irrespective of whether the instrument is honored. In light of the purposes of Rule 29, and in view of ethical proscriptions concerning the preservation of client funds and commingling of client and lawyer funds, it would be improper for a lawyer to accept overdraft privileges or any other arrangement for a personal loan on a client trust account in exchange for the institution's promise to delay or not to report an overdraft.

Absence of discretion makes notification by a financial institution an administratively simple matter. An institution which receives an instrument for payment against insufficient funds need not evaluate whether circumstances require that notification be given; it merely provides notice. It then becomes the responsibility of the disciplinary agency to determine whether further action is necessary. In cases where an overdraft is a result of an accounting error (caused by either the lawyer or the institution), but notification has already been sent to the state agency, the institution should provide the lawyer with a written explanation (preferably, an affidavit from an officer of the institution) that the lawyer can then submit to the agency to verify the error.

The rule provides the proper format for overdraft reports. In so doing, the rule distinguishes between dishonored instruments and in-struments that are presented against insufficient funds but honored. Where instruments are presented against insufficient funds but paid, the rule specifies the information that the institution should provide.

Ordinarily, within 24 hours of dishonor an institution gives notice of an overdraft to a depositor whose account is charged. See Uniform Commercial Code, Section 3–508. This is the same time period in which overdraft notification is given to the state disciplinary agency.

Where an instrument presented against insufficient funds is honored, the financial institution should send overdraft notification to the agency within five days of the date of presentation.

Upon receipt of an overdraft notification, Rule 29 contemplates that the state agency will contact the lawyer or firm by telephone and request an explanation for the overdraft. A letter requesting a documented explanation may also be sent. If the overdraft is an accounting error, the lawyer or firm submits a written explanation, including any documents to substantiate the claim. Where the lawyer or firm cannot supply an adequate or complete explanation for the overdraft, other action may be generated, including an audit or a demand for production of the lawyer's books and records.

The rule establishes that consent to the reporting and production requirements mandated by the rule is a condition of the privilege to practice law in a jurisdiction that has adopted the rule. This condition is intended to protect financial institutions from claims by lawyer-depositors based on disclosures made by financial institutions, provided that the disclosures are in accordance with the rule. Parties to an overdraft notification agreement are the court and a financial institution. The consent provision in the rule avoids the necessity for financial institutions to draft separate agreements with lawyers to establish consent to overdraft notification.

In addition to normal monthly maintenance fees on each account, a lawyer or firm can anticipate additional fees to be charged by the financial institutions for reporting overdrafts in accordance with this rule. However, because financial institutions already flag overdrafts and returned checks, it appears only slightly more burdensome for the institution to forward a copy to the local disciplinary agency. As a result, the additional cost to the lawyer should not be exorbitant.

Paragraph F should not be interpreted to allow a lawyer to permit trust account funds to be reduced through deductions made by a financial institution to cover costs of overdraft notification. Such costs should not be borne by clients.

Under the laws of most jurisdictions, the definition of "properly payable" will be contained in section 4–104 of the Uniform Commercial Code.

Under the laws of most jurisdictions, the definition of "notice of dishonor" will be determined by reference to section 3–508 of the Uniform Commercial Code, under which notice must be given by a bank before its midnight deadline and by any other person or institution before midnight on the third business day after dishonor or receipt of notice of dishonor.

RULE 30. Verification of Bank Accounts

A. *Generally.* Whenever disciplinary counsel has probable cause to believe that bank accounts of a lawyer that contain, should contain or have contained funds belonging to clients have not been properly maintained or that the funds have not been properly handled, disciplinary counsel shall request the approval of the chair of a hearing committee selected in order from the roster established by the board to initiate an investigation for the purpose of verifying the accuracy and integrity of all bank accounts maintained by the lawyer. If the

714

reviewing member approves, counsel shall proceed to verify the accuracy of the bank accounts. If the reviewing member denies approval, counsel may submit the request for approval to one other chair of a hearing committee selected in order from the roster established by the board.

B. *Confidentiality.* Investigations, examinations, and verifications shall be conducted so as to preserve the private and confidential nature of the lawyer's records insofar as is consistent with these rules and the lawyer-client privilege.

Commentary

Evidence that one account of a lawyer has not been properly maintained or that funds of one client have not been properly handled should constitute cause for verifying the accuracy of all accounts containing the funds of any client maintained by the lawyer.

Examples of cause warranting audit include a check drawn on a client trust account returned for insufficient funds, failure to timely distribute funds to a client, or failure to file a certificate of compliance with the jurisdiction's audit rule.

RULE 31. Appeal by Complainant

A. *To Board Panel.* If the complainant is not satisfied with the disposition of the matter following investigation and review by a committee chair, the complainant may appeal, within [thirty] days of receipt of notice pursuant to Rule 4(B)(6) of the disposition by the committee chair, to a panel of the board, which may approve, modify or disapprove the disposition, or direct that the matter be investigated further.

B. *To Court.* The determination of the board may be the subject of a petition for leave to appeal to the court, but leave shall not be granted unless the complainant shows that the board acted arbitrarily, capriciously, or unreasonably.

Commentary

It is very important that the disciplinary system be structured not only to actually protect the public, but also to inspire confidence in the public that the profession is acting to regulate itself. Thus it is important that complainants have the right to appeal a dismissal of their complaints.

It is important that complainants feel they have had their day in court on the basis for their complaint. Disciplinary hearings are neither civil nor criminal but *sui generis.* It is incorrect to assume that, as in a criminal proceeding, the complainant has no rights in regard to case disposition. It is also incorrect to assume that, as in a civil proceeding, a complainant has full participation in the litigation.

Without a limited right of appeal, complainants may feel that their grievances were not given sufficient consideration by the disciplinary system as a whole. Public sentiments of "lawyers protecting their own" can stem from this misunderstanding.

* * *

RULE 32. Statute of Limitations

Proceedings under these rules shall be exempt from all statutes of limitations.

Commentary

Statutes of limitation are wholly inappropriate in lawyer disciplinary proceedings. Conduct of a lawyer, no matter when it has occurred, is always relevant to the question of fitness to practice. The time between the commission of the alleged misconduct and the filing of a complaint predicated thereon may be pertinent to whether and to what extent discipline should be imposed, but should not limit the agency's power to investigate.

Discipline and disability proceedings serve to protect the public from lawyers who are unfit to practice; they measure the lawyer's qualifications in light of certain conduct, rather than punish for specific transgressions. Misconduct by a lawyer whenever it occurs reflects upon the lawyer's fitness.

EFFECTIVE DATE

These rules shall become effective on [*date*], and any discipline or disability investigation pending on that date shall be transferred to the board. Any matter then pending with respect to which a formal hearing has been commenced shall be concluded under the procedure existing prior to the effective date of these rules.

APPENDIX

A system in which inquiry officers, rather than hearing committees, are used may be established by adoption of the following two alternative provisions in place of Rules 2(G)(4), 2(G)(5), and 3:

AS AN ALTERNATIVE TO RULES 2(G)(4) AND (5), THE FOLLOWING SUBPARAGRAPH MAY BE ADOPTED:

(4) To conduct hearings into formal charges of misconduct, petitions for reinstatement, and petitions for transfer to and from disability inactive status, and prepare and forward to the court its own findings, if any, and recommendations together with the record of the hearing;

AS AN ALTERNATIVE TO RULE 3, THE FOLLOWING MAY BE ADOPTED: RULE 3. INQUIRY OFFICERS.

A. *Appointment*. The board shall appoint three or more inquiry officers [within each disciplinary district].

B. *Terms of Office.* All terms shall be three years and no inquiry officer shall serve for more than two consecutive three-year terms. An inquiry officer who has served two consecutive three-year terms may not be reappointed before the expiration of at least one year.

C. *Powers and Duties.* Inquiry officers shall review recommendations of counsel following investigation for disposition of disciplinary matters and petitions for transfer to and from disability inactive status.

AMERICAN BAR ASSOCIATION STANDARDS FOR IMPOSING LAWYER SANCTIONS

Approved February 1986. Copyright © 1986 by the American Bar Association. All rights reserved. Reprinted with permission.

[In 1970, an ABA Report chaired by former Supreme Court Justice Tom Clark recognized that lawyers and judges needed standards for the enforcement of professional discipline. This report prompted the ABA to create a special commission to draft Standards for Lawyer Discipline and Disability Proceedings (1979). These standards, however, did not provide much guidance on the particular sanction that should be imposed upon a lawyer in a disciplinary proceeding. In 1980, the ABA commissioned another committee to study lawyer sanctions and to draft guidelines for imposing sanctions so that variations in punishment for the same offenses could be avoided. This committee studied all published disciplinary cases between 1980 and 1984 and developed Standards for Imposing Lawyer Sanctions. The ABA adopted these standards in 1986. They were amended in 1992. Ed.]

Contents

718

I. PREFACE

A. BACKGROUND

In 1979, the American Bar Association published the Standards for Lawyer Discipline and Disability Proceedings.[1] That book was a result of work by the Joint Committee on Professional Discipline of the American Bar Association. The Joint Committee was composed of members of the Judicial Administration Division and the Standing Committee on Professional Discipline of the American Bar Association. The task of the Joint Committee was to prepare standards for enforcement of discipline in the legal community.

---

1. Standards for Lawyer Discipline and Disability Proceedings (Chicago: Joint Committee of Professional Discipline of the Appellate Judges' Conference and the American Bar Association Standing Committee on Professional Discipline, 1979).

ABA STANDARDS

The 1979 standards have been most helpful, and have been used by numerous jurisdictions as a frame of reference against which to compare their own disciplinary systems. Many jurisdictions have modified their procedures to comport with these suggested standards, and the Standing Committee on Professional Discipline of the American Bar Association has assisted state disciplinary systems in evaluating their programs in light of the approved standards.

It became evident that additional analysis was necessary in one important area—that of *appropriate sanctions* for lawyer misconduct. The American Bar Association Standards for Lawyer Discipline and Disability Proceedings (hereinafter "Standards for Lawyer Discipline") do not attempt to recommend the type of discipline to be imposed in any particular case. The Standards merely state that the discipline to be imposed "should depend upon the facts and circumstances of the case, should be fashioned in light of the purpose of lawyer discipline, and may take into account aggravating or mitigating circumstances" (Standard 7.1).

For lawyer discipline to be truly effective, sanctions must be based on clearly developed standards. Inappropriate sanctions can undermine the goals of lawyer discipline: sanctions which are too lenient fail to adequately deter misconduct and thus lower public confidence in the profession; sanctions which are too onerous may impair confidence in the system and deter lawyers from reporting ethical violations on the part of other lawyers. Inconsistent sanctions, either within a jurisdiction or among jurisdictions, cast doubt on the efficiency and the basic fairness of all disciplinary systems.

As an example of this problem of inconsistent sanctions, consider the range in levels of sanctions imposed for a conviction for failure to file federal income taxes. In one jurisdiction, in 1979, a lawyer who failed to file income tax returns for one year was suspended for one year,[2] while, in 1980, a lawyer who failed to file income tax returns for two years was merely censured.[3] Within a two-year period, the sanctions imposed on lawyers who converted their clients' funds included disbarment,[4] suspension,[5] and censure.[6] The inconsistency of sanctions imposed by different jurisdictions for the same misconduct is even greater.

An examination of these cases illustrates the need for a comprehensive system of sanctions. In many cases, different sanctions are imposed for the same acts of misconduct, and the courts rarely provide any explanation for the selection of sanctions. In other cases, the

2. *In re* Gold, 77 Ill.2d 224, 396 N.E.2d 25 (1979).

3. *In re* Oliver, M.R. 2454, 79–CH–6 (1980).

4. *In re* Smith, 63 Ill.2d 250, 347 N.E.2d 133 (1976).

5. *In re* DiBella, 58 Ill.2d 5, 316 N.E.2d 771 (1974).

6. *In re* Sherman, 60 Ill.2d 590, 328 N.E.2d 553 (1975).

courts may give reasons for their decisions, but their statements are too general to be useful. In still other cases, the courts may list specific factors to support a certain result, but they do not state whether these factors *must* be considered in every discipline case, nor do they explain whether these factors are entitled to equal weight.

The Joint Committee on Professional Sanctions (hereinafter "Sanctions Committee") was formed to address these problems by formulating standards to be used in imposing sanctions for lawyer misconduct. The Sanctions Committee was composed of members from the Judicial Administration Division and the Standing Committee on Professional Discipline. The mandate given was ambitious: the Committee was to examine the current range of sanctions imposed and to formulate standards for the imposition of appropriate sanctions.

In addressing this task, the Sanctions Committee recognized that any proposed standards should serve as a *model* which sets forth a comprehensive system of sanctions, but which leaves room for flexibility and creativity in assigning sanctions in particular cases of lawyer misconduct. These standards are designed to promote thorough, rational consideration of all factors relevant to imposing a sanction in an individual case. The standards attempt to ensure that such factors are given appropriate weight in light of the stated goals of lawyer discipline, and that only relevant aggravating and mitigating circumstances are considered at the appropriate time. Finally, the standards should help achieve the degree of consistency in the imposition of lawyer discipline necessary for fairness to the public and the bar.

While these standards will improve the operation of lawyer discipline systems, there is an additional factor which, though not the focus of this report, cannot be overlooked. In discussing sanctions for lawyer misconduct, this report assumes that all instances of unethical conduct will be brought to the attention of the disciplinary system. Experience indicates that such is not the case. In 1970, the ABA Special Committee on Evaluation of Disciplinary Enforcement (the Clark Committee), was charged with the responsibility for evaluating the effectiveness of disciplinary enforcement systems. The Clark Committee concluded that one of the most significant problems in lawyer discipline was the reluctance of lawyers and judges to report misconduct.[7] That same problem exists today. It cannot be emphasized strongly enough that lawyers and judges must report unethical conduct to the appropriate disciplinary agency.[8] Failure to render such reports is a disservice to the public and the legal profession.

---

7. Problems and Recommendations in Disciplinary Enforcement (Chicago: American Bar Association, Special Committee on Evaluation of Disciplinary Enforcement, 1970), at 167.

8. Lawyers have a duty to report ethical misconduct of other lawyers under Rule 8.3 of the Model Rules of Professional Conduct (American Bar Association, 1983) and under DR1–103 of the Code of Professional Responsibility (American Bar Association,

Judges in particular should be reminded of their obligation to report unethical conduct to the disciplinary agencies. Under the ABA Code of Judicial Conduct, a judge is obligated to "take or initiate appropriate disciplinary measures against a judge or lawyer for unprofessional conduct of which the judge may become aware." [9] Frequently, judges take the position that there is no such need and that errant behavior of lawyers can be remedied solely by use of contempt proceedings and other alternative means. It must be emphasized that the goals of lawyer discipline are not properly and fully served if the judge who observes unethical conduct simply deals with it on an *ad hoc* basis. It may be proper and wise for a judge to use contempt powers in order to assure that the court maintains control of the proceeding and punishes a lawyer for abusive or obstreperous conduct in the court's presence. However, the lawyer discipline system is in addition to and serves purposes different from contempt powers and other mechanisms available to the judge. Only if all lawyer misconduct is in fact reported to the appropriate disciplinary agency can the legal profession have confidence that consistent sanctions are imposed for similar misconduct.

Consistency of sanctions depends on reporting of other types as well. The American Bar Association Center for Professional Responsibility has established a "National Discipline Data Bank" which collects statistics on the nature of ethical violations and sanctions imposed in lawyer discipline cases in all jurisdictions. The information available from the data bank is only as good as the reports which reach it. It is vital that the data bank promptly receive complete, accurate and detailed information with regard to all discipline cases.

Finally, the purposes of lawyer sanctions can best be served, and the consistency of those sanctions enhanced, if courts and disciplinary agencies throughout the country articulate the reasons for sanctions imposed. Courts of record that impose lawyer discipline do a valuable service to the legal profession and the public when they issue opinions in lawyer discipline cases that explain the imposition of a specific sanction. The effort of the Sanctions Committee was made easier by the well-reasoned judicial opinions that were available. At the same time, the Sanctions Committee was frustrated by the fact that many jurisdictions do not publish lawyer discipline decisions, and that even published decisions are often summary in nature, failing to articulate the justification for the sanctions imposed.

B. METHODOLOGY

The Standards for Lawyer Sanctions have been developed after an examination of all reported lawyer discipline cases from 1980 to June,

1981). Judges have a similar duty under the Code of Judicial Conduct, Canon 3(B)(3) (American Bar Association, 1972).

9. *Id.,* Code of Judicial Conduct.

1984, where public discipline was imposed.[10] In addition, eight jurisdictions, which represent a variety of disciplinary systems as well as diversity in geography and population size, were examined in depth. In these jurisdictions—Arizona, California, the District of Columbia, Florida, Illinois, New Jersey, North Dakota, and Utah—all published disciplinary cases from January 1974 through June 1984 were analyzed. In each case, data were collected concerning the type of offense, the sanction imposed, the policy considerations identified, and aggravating or mitigating circumstances noted by the court.[11]

These data were examined to identify the patterns that currently exist among courts imposing sanctions and the policy considerations that guide the courts. In general, the courts were consistent in identifying the following policy considerations: protecting the public, ensuring the administration of justice, and maintaining the integrity of the profession. In the words of the California Supreme Court: "The purpose of a disciplinary proceeding is not punitive but to inquire into the fitness of the lawyer to continue in that capacity for the protection of the public, the courts, and the legal profession." [12] However, the courts failed to articulate any theoretical framework for use in imposing sanctions.

In attempting to develop such a framework, the Sanctions Committee considered a number of options. The Committee considered the obvious possibility of identifying each and every type of misconduct in which a lawyer could engage, then suggesting either a recommended sanction or a range of recommended sanctions to deal with that

10. See Appendix 3 for a listing of the actual number of reported cases from each jurisdiction. The differences in the number of reported cases among the jurisdictions is a function not only of the differences in lawyer populations, but in the operation of the state discipline systems. States differ dramatically in the sophistication of their disciplinary systems; most importantly for this study, states vary in the extent to which disciplinary orders are published. In those jurisdictions where disciplinary decisions are not published in the regional reporters, summaries in state bar publications or unreported cases (supplied by bar counsel) were examined. (To obtain copies of unreported decisions, contact the ABA Center for Professional Responsibility.) The states in which only reported cases were examined were: Alabama, Alaska, Arkansas, Colorado, Connecticut, Delaware, Georgia, Hawaii, Idaho, Indiana, Iowa, Kansas, Louisiana, Maryland, Minnesota, Mississippi, Missouri, Montana, Nebraska, Nevada, New

Jersey, New Mexico, North Carolina, South Dakota, Ohio, Oklahoma, Oregon, Rhode Island, South Carolina, South Dakota, Utah, Vermont, Washington, West Virginia, and Wisconsin. In the following jurisdictions both reported and unreported cases were examined: Arizona, California, District of Columbia, Florida, Illinois, Kentucky, Massachusetts, New York, Pennsylvania, Tennessee, Virginia, and Wyoming. In the following jurisdictions, all data were collected from unreported decisions (supplied by bar counsel or taken from case summaries in bar publications): Maine, Michigan, New Hampshire, and Texas.

11. Because of the difficulty in getting complete factual statements, the report does not include cases which were the result of consent orders, or cases in which reciprocal discipline was imposed.

12. Ballard v. State Bar of California, 35 Cal.3d 274, 673 P.2d 226, 197 Cal.Rptr. 556 (1983).

particular misconduct. The Sanctions Committee unanimously rejected that option as being both theoretically simplistic and administratively cumbersome.[13]

The Sanctions Committee next considered an approach that dealt with general categories of lawyer misconduct and applied recommended sanctions to those types of misconduct depending on whether or not—and to what extent—the misconduct resulted from intentional or malicious acts of the lawyer. There is some merit in that approach; certainly, the intentional or unintentional conduct of the lawyer is a relevant factor. Nonetheless, that approach was also abandoned after the Sanctions Committee carefully reviewed the purposes of lawyer sanctions. Solely focusing on the intent of the lawyer is not sufficient, and proposed standards must also consider the damage which the lawyer's misconduct causes to the client, the public, the legal system, and the profession. An approach which looked only at the extent of injury was also rejected as being too narrow.

The Committee adopted a model that looks first at the ethical duty and to whom it is owed, and then at the lawyer's mental state and the amount of injury caused by the lawyer's misconduct. (See Theoretical Framework, p. 5, for a detailed discussion of this approach.) Thus, one will look in vain for a section of this report which recommends a specific sanction for, say, improper contact with opposing parties who are represented by counsel [Rule 4.2/DR 7–104(A)(1)],[14] or for any other specific misconduct. What one will find, however, is an organizational framework that provides recommendations as to the type of sanction that should be imposed based on violations of duties owed to clients, the public, the legal system, and the profession.

To provide support for this approach, the Sanctions Committee has offered as much specific data and guidance as possible from reported

13. An example of the problems which would be encountered in such an approach will suffice to demonstrate why that approach was rejected. It is improper for a lawyer to neglect a legal matter entrusted to him (Rule 1.3/DR 6–101(A)(3)). Sanctions which are imposed for violations of this ethical rule vary dramatically. Such conduct may be an intentional violation of the rule (as where a lawyer takes a client's money never intending to perform the services requested), or it may result from negligence (as where an overworked or inexperienced lawyer does not meet a deadline relating to some aspect of the representation). The Sanctions Committee felt that a listing of sanctions based merely on the type of lawyer misconduct would not adequately differentiate between conduct which has an extremely deleterious effect on the client, the public, the legal system, and the profession, and conduct which has only a minimal effect. In short, the Sanctions Committee concluded that an approach that reviewed each type of misconduct would result in nothing more than a general statement that the individual circumstances of a case dictate the type of sanction which ought to be imposed.

14. Although the House of Delegates of the American Bar Association adopted the Model Rules of Professional Conduct on August 2, 1983, as the ethical standards for the legal profession, references to the Code of Professional Responsibility are included here because most states' ethical standards still follow the Code in both form and substance.

cases.[15] Thus, with regard to each category of misconduct, the report provides the following:

— discussion of what types of sanctions have been imposed for similar misconduct in reported cases;

— discussion of policy reasons which are articulated in reported cases to support such sanctions; and,

— finally, a recommendation as to the level of sanction imposed for the given misconduct, absent aggravating or mitigating circumstances.

While it is recognized that any individual case may present aggravating or mitigating factors which would lead to the imposition of a sanction different from that recommended, these standards present a model which can be used initially to categorize misconduct and to identify the appropriate sanction. The decision as to the effect of any aggravating or mitigating factors should come only after this initial determination of the sanction.

The Sanctions Committee also recognized that the imposition of a sanction of suspension or disbarment does not conclude the matter. Typically, disciplined lawyers will request reinstatement or readmission. While this report does not include an in-depth study of reinstatement and readmission cases, a general recommendation concerning standards for reinstatement and readmission appears as Standard 2.10.

II. THEORETICAL FRAMEWORK

These standards are based on an analysis of the nature of the professional relationship. Historically, being a member of a profession has meant that an individual is some type of expert, possessing knowledge of high instrumental value such that the members of the community give the professional the power to make decisions for them. In the legal profession, the community has allowed the profession the right of self-regulation. As stated in the Preamble to the ABA Model Rules of Professional Conduct (hereinafter "Model Rules"), "[t]he legal profession's relative autonomy carries with it special responsibilities of self-government. The profession has a responsibility to assure that its regulations are conceived in the public interest and not in furtherance of parochial or self-interested concerns of the bar."[16]

This view of the professional relationship requires lawyers to observe the ethical requirements that are set out in the Model Rules (or applicable standard in the jurisdiction where the lawyer is licensed). While the Model Rules define the ethical guidelines for lawyers, they do not provide any method for assigning sanctions for ethical violations.

15. While it is not possible to discuss in detail each of the 2,991 cases which have been examined in preparing this report, statistical summaries are available from the American Bar Association Center for Professional Responsibility.

16. Preamble to Model rules, paragraph 11, *supra* note 8.

The Committee developed a model which requires a court imposing sanctions to answer each of the following questions:

(1) What ethical duty did the lawyer violate? (A duty to a client, the public, the legal system, or the profession?)

(2) What was the lawyer's mental state? (Did the lawyer act intentionally, knowingly, or negligently?)

(3) What was the extent of the actual or potential injury caused by the lawyer's misconduct? (Was there a serious or potentially serious injury?) and

(4) Are there any aggravating or mitigating circumstances?

In determining the nature of the ethical duty violated, the standards assume that the most important ethical duties are those obligations which a laywer owes to *clients*. These include:

(a) the duty of *loyalty* which (in the terms of the Model Rules and Code of Professional Responsibility) includes the duties to:

(i) preserve the property of a client [Rule 1.15/DR9–102],

(ii) maintain client confidences [Rule 1.6/DR4–101], and

(iii) avoid conflicts of interest [Rules 1.7 through 1.13, 2.2, 3.7, 5.4(c) and 6.3/DR5–101 through DR5–105, DR9–101];

(b) the duty of *diligence* [Rules 1.2, 1.3, 1.4/DR6–101(A)(3)];

(c) the duty of *competence* [Rule 1.1/DR6–101(A)(1) & (2)]; and

(d) the duty of *candor* [Rule 8.4(c)/DR1–102(A)(4) & DR7–101(A)(3)].

In addition to duties owed to clients, the lawyer also owes duties to the *general public*. Members of the public are entitled to be able to trust lawyers to protect their property, liberty, and their lives. The community expects lawyers to exhibit the highest standards of honesty and integrity, and lawyers have a duty not to engage in conduct involving dishonesty, fraud, or interference with the administration of justice [Rules 8.2, 8.4(b) & (c)/DR1–102(A)(3)(4) & (5), DR8–101 through DR8–103, DR9–101(c)].

Lawyers also owe duties to the *legal system*. Lawyers are officers of the court, and must abide by the rules of substance and procedure which shape the administration of justice. Lawyers must always operate within the bounds of the law, and cannot create or use false evidence, or engage in any other illegal or improper conduct [Rules 3.1 through 3.6, 3.9, 4.1 through 4.4, 8.2, 8.4(d)(e) & (f)/DR7–102 through DR7–110].

Finally, lawyers owe duties to the *legal profession*. Unlike the obligations mentioned above, these duties are not inherent in the relationship between the professional and the community. These duties do not concern the lawyer's basic responsibilities in representing clients, serving as an officer of the court, or maintaining the public trust, but include other duties relating to the profession. These ethical rules concern:

(a) *restrictions on advertising and recommending employment* [Rules 7.1 through 7.5/DR2–101 through 2–104];

(b) *fees* [Rules 1.5, 5.4 and 5.6/DR2–106, DR2–107, and DR3–102];

(c) *assisting unauthorized practice* [Rule 5.5/DR3–101 through DR3–103];

(d) *accepting, declining, or terminating representation* [Rules 1.2, 1.14, 1.16/DR2–110]; and

(e) *maintaining the integrity of the profession* [Rules 8.1 & 8.3/ DR1–101 and DR1–103].

The *mental states* used in this model are defined as follows. The most culpable mental state is that of intent, when the lawyer acts with the conscious objective or purpose to accomplish a particular result. The next most culpable mental state is that of knowledge, when the lawyer acts with conscious awareness of the nature or attendant circumstances of his or her conduct both without the conscious objective or purpose to accomplish a particular result. The least culpable mental state is negligence, when a lawyer fails to be aware of a substantial risk that circumstances exist or that a result will follow, which failure is a deviation from the standard of care that a reasonable lawyer would exercise in the situation.

The extent of the *injury* is defined by the type of duty violated and the extent of actual or potential harm. For example, in a conversion case, the injury is determined by examining the extent of the client's actual or potential loss. In a case where a lawyer tampers with a witness, the injury is measured by evaluating the level of interference or potential interference with the legal proceeding. In this model, the standards refer to various levels of injury: "serious injury," "injury," and "little or no injury." A reference to "injury" alone indicates any level of injury greater than "little or no" injury.

As an example of how this model works, consider two cases of conversion of a client's property. After concluding that the lawyers engaged in ethical misconduct, it is necessary to determine what duties were breached. In these cases, each lawyer breached the duty of loyalty owed to clients. To assign a sanction, however, it is necessary to go further, and to examine each lawyer's mental state and the extent of the injuries caused by the lawyers' actions.

In the first case, assume that the client gave the lawyer $100 as an advance against the costs of investigation. The lawyer took the money, deposited it in a personal checking account, and used it for personal expenses. In this case, where the lawyer acted intentionally and the client actually suffered an injury, the most severe sanction—disbarment—would be appropriate.

Contrast this with the case of a second lawyer, whose client delivered $100 to be held in a trust account. The lawyer, in a hurry to get to court, neglected to inform the secretary what to do with these funds and they were erroneously deposited into the lawyer's general office account. When the lawyer needed additional funds he drew against the general account. The lawyer discovered the mistake, and immediately replaced the money. In this case, where there was no actual injury and a potential for only minor injury, and where the lawyer was merely negligent, a less serious sanction should be imposed. The appropriate sanction would be either reprimand or admonition.

In each case, after making the initial determination as to the appropriate sanction, the court would then consider any relevant *aggravating or mitigating factors* (Standard 9). For example, the presence of aggravating factors, such as vulnerability of the victim or refusal to comply with an order to appear before the disciplinary agency, could increase the appropriate sanction. The presence of mitigating factors, such as absence of prior discipline or inexperience in the practice of law, could make a lesser sanction appropriate.

While there may be particular cases of lawyer misconduct that are not easily categorized, the standards are not designed to propose a specific sanction for each of the myriad of fact patterns in cases of lawyer misconduct. Rather, the standards provide a theoretical framework to guide the courts in imposing sanctions. The ultimate sanction imposed will depend on the presence of any aggravating or mitigating factors in that particular situation. The standards thus are not analogous to criminal determinate sentences, but are guidelines which give courts the flexibility to select the appropriate sanction in each particular case of lawyer misconduct.

The standards do not account for multiple charges of misconduct. The ultimate sanction imposed should at least be consistent with the sanction for the most serious instance of misconduct among a number of violations; it might well be and generally should be greater than the sanction for the most serious misconduct. Either a pattern of misconduct or multiple instances of misconduct should be considered as aggravating factors (see Standard 9.22).

IV. STANDARDS FOR IMPOSING SANCTIONS: BLACK LETTER RULES AND COMMENTARY

Definitions

"Injury" is harm to a client, the public, the legal system, or the profession which results from a lawyer's misconduct. The level of injury can range from "serious" injury to "little or no" injury; a reference to "injury" alone indicates any level of injury greater than "little or no" injury.

"Intent" is the conscious objective or purpose to accomplish a particular result.

"Knowledge" is the conscious awareness of the nature or attendant circumstances of the conduct but without the conscious objective or purpose to accomplish a particular result.

"Negligence" is the failure of a lawyer to heed a substantial risk that circumstances exist or that a result will follow, which failure is a deviation from the standard of care that a reasonable lawyer would exercise in the situation.

"Potential injury" is the harm to a client, the public, the legal system or the profession that is reasonably foreseeable at the time of the lawyer's misconduct, and which, but for some intervening factor or event, would probably have resulted from the lawyer's misconduct.

A. PURPOSE AND NATURE OF SANCTIONS

1.1 Purpose of Lawyer Discipline Proceedings

The purpose of lawyer discipline proceedings is to protect the public and the administration of justice from lawyers who have not discharged, will not discharge, or are unlikely properly to discharge their professional duties to clients, the public, the legal system, and the legal profession.

Commentary

A similar statement of purpose appears as Standard 1.1 of the Standards for Lawyer Discipline. While courts express their views on the purpose of lawyer sanctions somewhat differently, an examination of reported cases reveals surprising accord as to the basic purpose of discipline. As identified by the courts, the primary purpose is to protect the public.[17] Second, the courts cite the need to protect the integrity of the legal system, and to insure the administration of justice.[18] Another purpose is to deter further unethical conduct and, where appropriate, to rehabilitate the lawyer.[19] A final purpose of imposing sanctions is to educate other lawyers and the public, thereby deterring unethical behavior among all members of the profession.[20] As the courts have noted, while sanctions imposed on a lawyer obviously have a punitive aspect, nonetheless, it is not the purpose to impose such sanctions for punishment.[21]

17. *In re* Stout, 75 N.J. 321, 382 A.2d 630 (1978); Matter of Rubi, 133 Ariz. 491, 652 P.2d 1014 (1982).

18. *In re* Zderic, 92 Wash.2d 777, 600 P.2d 1297 (1979); *In re* Nadler, 91 Ill.2d 326, 438 N.E.2d 198 (1982).

19. Matter of McInerney, 389 Mass. 528, 451 N.E.2d 401 (1983).

20. Matter of Carroll, 124 Ariz. 80, 602 P.2d 461 (1979); Committee on Professional Ethics v. Gross, 326 N.W.2d 272 (Iowa 1982); The Florida Bar v. Lord, 433 So.2d 983 (Fla.1983).

21. Matter of Maragos, 285 N.W.2d 541 (N.D.1979); Matter of Grimes, 414 Mich. 483, 326 N.W.2d 380 (1982).

To achieve these purposes, sanctions for misconduct must apply to all licensed lawyers. Lawyers who are not actively practicing law, but who are serving in such roles as corporate officers, public officials, or law professors, do not lose their association with the legal profession because of their primary occupation. The public quite properly expects that anyone who is admitted to the practice of law, regardless of daily occupational activities, will conform to the minimum ethical standards of the legal profession. If the lawyer fails to meet these standards, appropriate sanctions should be imposed.

1.2 Public Nature of Lawyer Discipline Proceedings

Upon the filing and service of formal charges, lawyer discipline proceedings should be public, and disposition of lawyer discipline should be public in cases of disbarment, suspension, and reprimand. Only in cases of minor misconduct, when there is little or no injury to a client, the public, the legal system, or the profession, and when there is little likelihood of repetition by the lawyer, should private discipline be imposed.

Commentary

Standard 8.25 of the Standards for Lawyer Discipline states that "upon the filing and service of formal charges [against a lawyer] the proceeding should be public. . . ."[22] Although the majority of jurisdictions still do not follow this procedure,[23] a combination of public proceedings, after probable cause is found, and public sanctions is the better approach. Individual lawyers may prefer to avoid the embarrassment and stigma associated with a public sanction, but the profession as a whole will benefit. The more the public knows about how effectively the disciplinary system works, the more confidence they will have in that system. If there is approval of the system, it is hoped that public confidence in the profession's ability to discipline itself will be assured. In the words of one court, ". . . the purpose of bar disciplinary proceedings is not to punish the respondent lawyer but to vindicate in the eyes of the public the overall reputation of the bar."[24] Public discipline accompanied by written opinions setting forth the court's rationale for imposing a particular sanction can enhance that reputation.

Public identification of a lawyer who has been sanctioned serves other purposes as well. Where only some of the misconduct is known and more than one lawyer appears to be involved, announcement of the

22. Lawyer Standards, *supra* note 1.

23. Only 19 jurisdictions currently follow the provision of Standard 8.25 (1983 Survey of Lawyer Disciplinary Procedures in the United States, American Bar Association Center for Professional Responsibility): Arkansas, Connecticut, Florida, Geor-gia, Idaho, Indiana, Kansas, Louisiana, Maryland, Michigan, Minnesota, Nebraska, New Hampshire, North Carolina, Oregon, Texas, Utah, Washington, and Wisconsin.

24. Levi and Denham v. Mississippi State Bar, 436 So.2d 781, 786 (Miss.1983).

names of those who are sanctioned permits others' names to be cleared. Where the lawyer sanctioned is particularly prominent, public identification demonstrates that the system does not play favorites. Where the lawyer sanctioned may have caused injury to others who did not know they could complain, identification enables other victims to make themselves known.

Public sanctions also serve other members of the legal profession. When all sanctions are public, lawyers themselves can observe whether the system is operating fairly, treating consistently lawyers who are disciplined for similar misconduct. Public sanctions also educate other lawyers, and help deter misconduct by others in the profession. The preventive aspect of discipline cannot be overlooked.

Even while recognizing these interests of the public and the profession, however, it is important to note that there are certain situations in which it may be appropriate to impose private discipline. In cases of minor misconduct, when there is little or no injury to a client, the public, the legal system, or the profession, and when there is little or no likelihood of repetition, the court or disciplinary counsel should consider imposing an admonition. A private sanction in such cases informs the lawyer that his or her actions are unethical, but does not unnecessarily stigmatize a lawyer from whom the public needs no protection. To deter other lawyers, the court can still issue a public report describing the facts in cases where admonitions are imposed, but omitting the names of the disciplined lawyers.

Finally, in discussing private discipline, it is important to examine cases of discipline "by consent" in cases of disbarment, suspension, and reprimand. While sanctions imposed after a consent agreement can be public, the process by which the sanction decision is reached is private. The respondent lawyer and disciplinary counsel stipulate as to the facts, and that private interpretation of the facts then becomes the basis for imposing a public sanction. While there are many practical reasons why this disciplinary "plea bargaining" occurs, it is inconsistent with the policies described above. At a minimum, where discipline by consent is imposed in cases of disbarment, suspension, or reprimand, the court should require that a statement of the facts be made public.

In cases of both public and private discipline, the court should state clearly and unambiguously what sanction or sanctions are to be imposed. The purposes of lawyer discipline are not served if the sanction is unclear or is conditioned on unnamed factors. Even when a private sanction is imposed, a disciplined lawyer is entitled to know exactly what is expected of him or her.

1.3 Purpose of These Standards

These standards are designed for use in imposing a sanction or sanctions following a determination by clear and convincing evidence that a member of the legal profession has violated a provision of the Model Rules of Professional Conduct (or applicable standard under the laws of the jurisdiction where the proceeding is brought). Descriptions in these standards of substantive disciplinary offenses are not intended to create grounds for determining culpability independent of the Model Rules. The Standards constitute a model, setting forth a comprehensive system for determining sanctions, permitting flexibility and creativity in assigning sanctions in particular cases of lawyer misconduct. They are designed to promote: (1) consideration of all factors relevant to imposing the appropriate level of sanction in an individual case; (2) consideration of the appropriate weight of such factors in light of the stated goals of lawyer discipline; (3) consistency in the imposition of disciplinary sanctions for the same or similar offenses within and among jurisdictions.

Commentary

The Model Rules of Professional Conduct (or other standard under the laws of the particular jurisdiction) establish the ethical standards for lawyers, and lawyers who violate these standards are subject to discipline. When disciplinary proceedings are brought against lawyers alleged to have engaged in ethical misconduct, disciplinary counsel have the burden of proving misconduct by clear and convincing evidence (see Standards for Lawyer Discipline, Standard 8.40). Following such a finding, the court or disciplinary agency should impose a sanction.

The Standards for Imposing Lawyer Sanctions are guidelines which are to be used by courts or disciplinary agencies in imposing sanctions *following* a finding of lawyer misconduct. These standards are not grounds for discipline, but, rather, constitute a model for the courts to follow in deciding what sanction to impose for proven lawyer misconduct. While these standards set forth a comprehensive model to be used in imposing sanctions, they also recognize that sanctions imposed must reflect the circumstances of each individual lawyer, and therefore provide for consideration of aggravating and mitigating circumstances in each case.

The Standards for Imposing Lawyer Sanctions are designed to promote consistency in the imposition of sanctions by identifying the relevant factors that courts should consider (see Standard 3.0) and then applying these factors to situations where lawyers have engaged in various types of misconduct (see Standards 4.0 through 8.0). Because the Model Rules of Professional Conduct have been adopted by the American Bar Association as the ethical standards for the legal profession, the language of the Model Rules is used herein. However, because only a minority of jurisdictions have actually adopted the Model Rules, these Standards are phrased in terms of the fundamental duties owed to clients, the public, the legal system, and the profession. This general language should make these standards applicable in all jurisdictions regardless of whether the jurisdiction chooses to adopt the Model Rules, the former Code of Professional Responsibility, or some combination of these standards.

B. SANCTIONS

2.1 Scope

A disciplinary sanction is imposed on a lawyer upon a finding or acknowledgement that the lawyer has engaged in professional misconduct.

Commentary

Sanctions in disciplinary matters are neither criminal nor civil but *sui generis* and imposed under authority of the state's highest court.[25] Disciplinary sanctions are separate and apart from penalties which may be imposed solely for civil or criminal conduct, or contempt of court.[26] Disciplinary sanctions do not include restrictions upon a lawyer's practice which may be imposed solely as a result of a lawyer's disability. For example, a lawyer who has not engaged in professional misconduct, but whose ability to practice law is impaired, as by alcoholism or mental illness, should be helped to limit his practice or transferred to inactive status; disciplinary sanctions should not be imposed (see Standards for Lawyer Discipline, Standard 12). Disciplinary sanctions do not include penalties that may be imposed on lawyers who violate administrative rules or regulations applicable to members of the bar, such as by failing to pay dues or to attend mandatory continuing legal education programs.

2.2 Disbarment

Disbarment terminates the individual's status as a lawyer. Where disbarment is not permanent, procedures should be established for a lawyer who has been disbarred to apply for readmission, provided that:

    (1) no application should be considered for five years from the effective date of disbarment; and

    (2) the petitioner must show by clear and convincing evidence:

        (a) successful completion of the bar examination,

        (b) compliance with all applicable discipline or disability orders or rules; and

        (c) rehabilitation and fitness to practice law.

25. Some states, for example, delegate this power to other agencies. See Standards for Lawyer Discipline, Standards 1.2, 2.1.

26. Attorney Grievance Commission v. Velasquez, 301 Md. 450, 483 A.2d 354 (1984); *In re* McDaniel, 470 N.E.2d 1327 (Ind.1984).

Commentary

Disbarment is the most severe sanction, terminating the lawyer's ability to practice law. Disbarment enforces the purpose of discipline in that the public is protected from further practice by the lawyer; the reputation of the legal profession is protected by the action of the bench and bar in taking appropriate actions against unethical lawyers. Even though disbarment is reserved for the most serious cases, the majority of jurisdictions allow application for readmission after a period of time. For the protection of the public, however, the presumption should be against readmission, and, in order to insure that disbarment is in reality a more serious sanction than suspension, in no event should a lawyer even be considered for readmission until at least five years after the effective date of disbarment. After that time, a lawyer seeking to be readmitted to practice must show by clear and convincing evidence: successful completion of the bar examination, compliance with all applicable discipline or disability orders or rules, and rehabilitation and fitness to practice law (see Standards for Lawyer Discipline, Standards 6.1 and 6.2).

Disbarment includes disbarment by consent, resignation in lieu of disbarment, and reciprocal disbarment. Although a lawyer who has been disbarred on consent or who has resigned in lieu of disbarment may not be readmitted any earlier than any other lawyer who has been disbarred, the fact that the lawyer resigned or was disbarred on consent is a factor that can be considered if the lawyer applies for readmission.

2.3 Suspension

Suspension is the removal of a lawyer from the practice of law for a specified minimum period of time. Generally, suspension should be for a period of time equal to or greater than six months, but in no event should the time period prior to application for reinstatement be more than three years. Procedures should be established to allow a suspended lawyer to apply for reinstatement, but a lawyer who has been suspended should not be permitted to return to practice until he has completed a reinstatement process demonstrating rehabilitation, compliance with all applicable discipline or disability orders and rules, and fitness to practice law.

Commentary

Suspension includes suspension by consent, resignation in lieu of suspension and reciprocal suspension. Although jurisdictions impose suspensions for various time periods, the Standards for Lawyer Discipline recommend that suspension be for a definite period of time not to exceed three years. If the conduct is so egregious that a longer suspension seems warranted, the sanction of disbarment should be imposed.

In addition, the Standards draw a distinction between suspensions for six months or less, and suspensions for more than six months. Standard 6.4 states that a lawyer who has been suspended for six months or less should be reinstated automatically (i.e., without establishing rehabilitation). However, a lawyer who has been suspended for more than six months should *not* be reinstated without being required to show by clear and convincing evidence: rehabilitation, compliance with all applicable discipline or disability orders or rules, and fitness to practice law.

While the Standards for Lawyer Discipline currently provide for suspensions of less than six months, short-term suspensions with automatic reinstatement are not an effective means of protecting the public. If a lawyer's misconduct is serious enough to warrant a suspension from practice, the lawyer should not be reinstated until rehabilitation can be established. While it may be possible in some cases for a lawyer to show rehabilitation in less than six months, it is preferable to suspend a lawyer for at least six months in order to insure effective demonstration of rehabilitation. In order to insure that administrative procedures do not extend the period of actual suspension beyond that imposed, however, expedited procedures should be established to reinstate immediately lawyers who show rehabilitation, compliance with rules, and fitness to practice.

A six-month suspension is also necessary to protect clients. When shorter suspensions are imposed, lawyers can merely delay performing the requested services. If the lawyer eventually completes the work for the client and receives a fee, the suspension has only served to inconvenience the client. In reality, a short-term suspension functions as a fine on the lawyer, and fines are prohibited by the Lawyer Standards (see Standard 6.14).

The amount of time for which a lawyer should be suspended, then, should generally be for a minimum of six months. In no case should the time period prior to application for reinstatement be more than three years. The specific period of time for the suspension should be determined after examining any aggravating or mitigating factors in the case. At the end of this time period the lawyer may apply for reinstatement, and the lawyer must show: rehabilitation, compliance with all applicable discipline or disability orders and rules, and fitness to practice law (see Standard 6.4).

2.4 Interim Suspension

Interim suspension is the temporary suspension of a lawyer from the practice of law pending imposition of final discipline. Interim suspension includes:

(a) **suspension upon conviction of a "serious crime" or,**

(b) **suspension when the lawyer's continuing conduct is or is likely to cause immediate and serious injury to a client or the public.**

Commentary

Standard 6.5 of the Standards for Lawyer Discipline states that the court should place a lawyer on interim suspension immediately upon proof that the lawyer has been convicted of a "serious crime" or is causing great harm to the public. A "serious crime" is defined as any felony or any lesser crime a necessary element of which, as determined by the statutory or common law definition of such crime, involves interference with the administration of justice, false swearing, misrepresentation, fraud, extortion, misappropriation, theft; or an attempt or a conspiracy or solicitation of another to commit a "serious crime."[27] Interim suspension is necessary in such cases both to protect members of the public and to maintain public confidence in the legal profession. As explained in the commentary to Standard 6.5, it is difficult for members of the public to understand why a lawyer who has been convicted of stealing funds from a client can continue to handle client funds. Public confidence in the profession is strengthened when expedited procedures are available in such instances of lawyer misconduct.

Although due process does not require a hearing prior to imposing an interim suspension following a criminal conviction, an opportunity to show cause as to why it should not be imposed should be available. An interim suspension remains in effect until it is lifted by the court, or until the court imposes a final disciplinary sanction after compliance with relevant procedural rules.

Interim suspension is also appropriate when the lawyer's continuing conduct is causing or is likely to cause immediate and serious injury to a client or the public. The commentary to Standard 6.5 cites the example of a lawyer who has displayed a pattern of misconduct, such as ongoing conversion of trust funds, as warranting interim suspension. Interim suspension is also appropriate where a lawyer abandons the practice of law.

(As explained above in Section 2.1, cases of lawyer disability are not included in the scope of this report. See Standard 12.1 in the Standards for Lawyer Discipline for a discussion of transfer to disability inactive status.)

27. See Definitions, Standards for Lawyer Discipline.

2.5 Reprimand

Reprimand, also known as censure or public censure, is a form of public discipline which declares the conduct of the lawyer improper, but does not limit the lawyer's right to practice.

Commentary

Publicity enhances the effect of the discipline and emphasizes the concern of the court with all lawyer misconduct, not only serious ethical violations. A reprimand is appropriate in cases where the lawyer's conduct, although violating ethical standards, is not serious enough to warrant suspension or disbarment. (See Definitions, Standards for Lawyer Discipline.) A reprimand serves the useful purpose of identifying lawyers who have violated ethical standards, and, if accompanied by a published opinion, educates members of the bar as to these standards.

A reprimand is not always sufficient to protect the public; it may also be appropriate to attach additional conditions to a reprimand. When a lawyer lacks competence in one area of practice, for example, the court could impose a reprimand and also require the lawyer to attend continuing education courses. In a case of neglect, the court could impose reprimand and probation, during which period of time the lawyer's diligence in handling client matters could be monitored.

2.6 Admonition

Admonition, also known as private reprimand, is a form of non-public discipline which declares the conduct of the lawyer improper, but does not limit the lawyer's right to practice.

Commentary

Admonition is the least serious of the formal disciplinary sanctions, and is the only private sanction. (See Definitions, Standards for Lawyer Discipline.) Because imposing an admonition will not inform members of the public about the lawyer's misconduct, admonition should be used only when the lawyer is negligent, when the ethical violation results in little or no injury to a client, the public, the legal system, or the profession, and when there is little or no likelihood of repetition. Relying on these criteria should help protect the public while, at the same time, avoid damage to a lawyer's reputation when future ethical violations seem unlikely. To enhance the preventive nature of lawyer discipline, the court or disciplinary agency should publish a fact description in admonition cases without disclosing the lawyer's name.

2.7 Probation

Probation is a sanction that allows a lawyer to practice law under specified conditions. Probation can be imposed alone or in conjunction with a reprimand, an admonition or immediately

following a suspension. Probation can also be imposed as a condition of readmission or reinstatement.

Commentary

Probation is a sanction that should be imposed when a lawyer's right to practice law needs to be monitored or limited rather than suspended or revoked. The need for probation can arise under a variety of situations, and it can be imposed either alone or along with a sanction of reprimand or admonition. If probation is imposed with a reprimand, it would be a public sanction; if probation is imposed with an admonition, it would be a private sanction. If probation is the sole sanction imposed, it can be either public or private, but the sanction should be public in any case in which the lawyer has violated a duty owed to a client, the public, or the legal system. Probation can also be imposed as a condition of readmission following disbarment or as a condition of reinstatement following a period of suspension from practice.

By imposing probation, the court allows a lawyer to continue to practice, but also requires the lawyer to meet certain conditions that will protect the public and will assist the lawyer to meet ethical obligations. Conditions of probation can include:

    (a) quarterly or semi-annual reports of caseload status, especially appropriate in neglect cases, see *Florida Bar v. Neale*, 432 So. 2d 50 (Fla.1980);

    (b) supervision by a local disciplinary committee member, see *In re Maragos*, 285 N.W.2d 541 (N.D.1979) and *In re Hessberger*, 96 Ill.2d 423, 451 N.E.2d 821 (1983);

    (c) periodic audits of trust accounts, especially appropriate in cases where lawyers improperly handle client funds, see *Florida Bar v. Montgomery*, 418 So.2d 267 (Fla.1982);

    (d) attendance at continuing education programs, especially appropriate in cases of incompetence, see *Florida Bar v. Glick*, 383 So.2d 642 (Fla.1980);

    (e) participation in alcohol or drug abuse programs, especially appropriate where the lawyer's abuse of alcohol or drugs was a significant cause of his misconduct, see *Tenner v. State Bar*, 28 Cal.3d 202, 617 P.2d 486, 168 Cal.Rptr. 333 (1980) and *In re Heath*, 296 Or. 683, 678 P.2d 736 (1984);

    (f) periodic physical or mental examinations, appropriate where the lawyer's physical or mental condition was a significant cause of his misconduct, see *In re McCallum*, 289 N.W.2d 146 (Minn.1980) and *In re Mudge*, 33 Cal.3d 152, 654 P.2d 1307, 187 Cal.Rptr. 779 (1982);

    (g) passing the bar examination or the appropriate professional responsibility examination, see *Florida Bar v. Peterson*, 418 So.

2d 246 (Fla.1982) and *In re Morales,* 35 Cal.3d 1, 671 P.2d 857, 196 Cal.Rptr. 353 (1983);

(h) limitations on practice, see *Florida Bar v. Neely,* 417 So.2d 957 (Fla.1983); or

(i) such other conditions as are appropriate for the misconduct.

Probation may be terminated by the court after the respondent has filed an affidavit of compliance with all conditions of probation and the court is satisfied that the need for probation no longer exists. In the event that a lawyer is charged with violating the conditions of probation, a hearing is needed to determine whether a violation has occurred. The disciplinary authority has the burden of establishing any such violation by clear and convincing evidence. Upon a finding that a lawyer has violated probation conditions, the court may extend the probation, impose a more severe sanction, or otherwise handle the matter.

2.8 Other Sanctions and Remedies

Other sanctions and remedies which may be imposed include:

(a) **restitution,**

(b) **assessment of costs,**

(c) **limitation upon practice,**

(d) **appointment of a receiver,**

(e) **requirement that the lawyer take the bar examination or professional responsibility examination,**

(f) **requirement that the lawyer attend continuing education courses, and**

(g) **other requirements that the state's highest court or disciplinary board deems consistent with the purposes of lawyer sanctions.**

Commentary

These other sanctions and remedies are those that the court or the board may impose when it is deemed necessary to carry out the goals of the disciplinary system. The court should be creative and flexible in approaching those cases where there is some misconduct but where a severe sanction is not required. In less serious cases of incompetence, for example, a sanction requiring the lawyer to attend continuing legal education courses or to limit the lawyer's practice to handling certain types of cases may better protect the public than a period of suspension from practice. Fines are not an appropriate sanction (see Standard 6.14, Lawyer Standards).

2.9 Reciprocal Discipline

Reciprocal discipline is the imposition of a disciplinary sanction for conduct for which a lawyer has been disciplined in another jurisdiction.

Commentary

Public confidence in the profession is enhanced when lawyers who are admitted in more than one jurisdiction are prevented from avoiding the effect of discipline in one jurisdiction by practicing in another. Standard 10.2 of the Standards for Lawyer Discipline provides that a certified copy of the findings of fact in the disciplinary proceeding in the other jurisdiction should constitute conclusive evidence that the respondent committed the misconduct. Reciprocal discipline can be imposed without a hearing, but the court should provide the lawyer with an opportunity to raise a due process challenge or to show that a sanction different from the sanction imposed in the other jurisdiction is warranted. In order to facilitate the imposition of reciprocal discipline, bar counsel or other appropriate authority in each state should report all cases of public discipline to the ABA National Discipline Data Bank.[28]

2.10 Readmission and Reinstatement

In jurisdictions where disbarment is not permanent, procedures should be established to allow a disbarred lawyer to apply for readmission. Procedures should be established to allow a suspended lawyer to apply for reinstatement.

Commentary

Readmission occurs when a disbarred lawyer is returned to practice. Since the purpose of lawyer discipline is not punishment, readmission may be appropriate; the presumption, however, should be against readmission. In no event should a lawyer even be considered for readmission until at least five years after the effective date of disbarment. After that time, a lawyer seeking to be readmitted to practice must show by clear and convincing evidence: rehabilitation, compliance with all applicable discipline or disability orders or rules, and fitness to practice law.

Reinstatement occurs when a suspended lawyer is returned to practice. Since the purpose of lawyer discipline is not punishment, reinstatement is appropriate when a lawyer can show rehabilitation. Application for reinstatement should not be permitted until expiration of the ordered period of suspension and generally not until at least six

28. The National Discipline Data Bank is operated by the American Bar Association Center for Professional Responsibility. For further information on how to report or to receive current statistical data, contact the Center for Professional Responsibility at the American Bar Association, 750 N. Lake Shore Drive, Chicago, Illinois, 60611, or call (312) 988-5000.

months after the effective date of suspension. A lawyer should not be reinstated unless he can show by clear and convincing evidence: rehabilitation, compliance with all applicable discipline or disability orders and rules and fitness to practice law (see Standard 6.4).

Conditional readmission and conditional reinstatement can occur when appropriate. Conditions that can be imposed include probation (see Standard 2.7) or other sanctions or remedies (see Standard 2.8).

C. FACTORS TO BE CONSIDERED IN IMPOSING SANCTIONS

3.0 Generally

In imposing a sanction after a finding of lawyer misconduct, a court should consider the following factors:

(a) the duty violated;

(b) the lawyer's mental state; and

(c) the actual or potential injury caused by the lawyer's misconduct; and

(d) the existence of aggravating or mitigating factors.

Commentary

This system for determining an initial sanction upon a finding of lawyer misconduct requires courts to examine four factors: the nature of the duty violated, the lawyer's mental state, the actual or potential injury resulting from the lawyer's misconduct, and the existence of aggravating or mitigating factors. As explained above (see Theoretical Framework, p. 5), a lawyer's misconduct may be a violation of a duty owed to a client, the public, the legal system, or the profession. The lawyer's mental state may be one of intent, knowledge, or negligence. The injury resulting from the lawyer's misconduct need not be actually realized; in order to protect the public, the court should also examine the potential for injury caused by the lawyer's misconduct. In a case where a lawyer intentionally converts client funds, for example, disbarment can be imposed even where there is no actual injury to any client (see 4.11). In other situations, the standards make distinctions between various levels of actual or potential injury; disbarment may be reserved for cases of serious or potentially serious injury, while admonition may be imposed only in cases where there is little or no actual or potential injury. In any case, however, the court may then take account of any particular aggravating or mitigating factors (see Standard 9.0 for a list of these factors).

4.0 Violations of Duties Owed to Clients

Introduction

This duty arises out of the nature of the basic relationship between the lawyer and the client. The lawyer is not required to accept all clients,[29] but, having agreed to perform services for a client, the lawyer has duties that arise under ethical rules, agency law, and under the terms of the contractual relationship with the individual client. The lawyer must preserve the property of a client [Rule 1.15/DR 9–102], maintain client confidences [Rule 1.6/DR 4–101] and avoid conflicts which will impair the lawyer's independent judgment [Rules 1.7 through 1.13, 2.2, 3.7, 5.4(c), and 6.3/DR 5–101 through 5–105, DR 9–102]. In addition, the lawyer must be competent to perform the services requested by the client [Rule 1.1/DR 6–101(A)(1) and (2)] and be diligent in performing those services [Rules 1.2, 1.3, 1.4/DR 6–101(A)(3)]. The lawyer must also be candid with the client during the course of the professional relationship [Rule 8.4/DR 1–102(A)(4) and DR 7–101(A)(3)].

4.1 Failure to Preserve the Client's Property

Absent aggravating or mitigating circumstances, upon application of the factors set out in 3.0, the following sanctions are generally appropriate in cases involving the failure to preserve client property:

> **4.11 Disbarment is generally appropriate when a lawyer knowingly converts client property and causes injury or potential injury to a client.**

Commentary

Some courts have held that disbarment is always the appropriate discipline when a lawyer knowingly converts client funds. For example, in the case of *In re Wilson*, 81 N.J. 451, 409 A.2d 1153 (1979), the Supreme Court of New Jersey discussed the rationale for imposing disbarment as a sanction on lawyers who misappropriate client funds:

> Like many rules governing the behavior of lawyers, this one has its roots in the confidence and trust which clients place in their attorneys. Having sought his advice and relying on his expertise, the client entrusts the lawyer with the transaction—including the handling of the client's funds. Whether it be a real estate closing, the establishment of a trust, the purchase of a business, the investment of funds, the receipt of proceeds of litigation, or any one of a multitude of other situations, it is common-place that the work of lawyers involves possession of their client's funds. . . . Whatever the need may be for the lawyer's handling of client's money,

---

29. Comment to Rule 6.2, paragraph 1, Model Rules, *supra* note 8; EC 2–26, Code of Professional Responsibility, *supra* note 8.

the client permits it because he trusts the lawyer. . . . [T]here are few more egregious acts of professional misconduct of which an attorney can be guilty than the misappropriation of a client's funds held in trust. [citing *In re Beckman,* 79 N.J. 402, 404–05, 400 A.2d 792, 793 (1979)]. . . . Recognition of the nature and gravity of the offense suggests only one result—disbarment (81 N.J. at 454–55, 409 A.2d at 1154–55).

California has held that disbarment is appropriate even absent knowing conversion when a lawyer is grossly negligent in dealing with client property. As the California Supreme Court observed, "[e]ven if [the attorney's] conduct were not wilful and dishonest, gross careless-ness and negligence constitute a violation of an attorney's oath faithful-ly to discharge his duties and involve moral turpitude." (*Chefsky v. State Bar,* 36 Cal.3d 116, at 123, 680 P.2d 82 (1984).)

Most courts, however, reserve disbarment for cases in which the lawyer uses the client's funds for the lawyer's own benefit. In *Carter v. Ross,* 461 A.2d 675 (R.I.1983), for example, the lawyer took money from an estate and used it to pay office and personal expenses. The Rhode Island Supreme Court cited the *Wilson* case and imposed disbarment: "We, like our New Jersey colleagues, are convinced that continuing public confidence in the judicial system and the bar as a whole requires that the strictest discipline be imposed in misappropriation cases" (461 A.2d at 676). Similarly, in *In re Freeman,* 647 P.2d 820 (Kan.App.1982), a lawyer was disbarred who caused checks from an insurance company to be issued to fictitious payees, and then converted that money for his own use. In these types of cases, where the lawyer's lack of integrity is clear, only the most compelling mitigating circumstances should justify a lesser sanction than disbarment.

In such cases, it may not even seem necessary to consider whether there is any injury to a client. Even though there will always be a potential injury to a client in such cases, the injury factor should still be considered. First, consideration of the extent of actual or potential injury can be important when it is especially serious: injury should be proved up at the disciplinary proceeding in order to make a record in the event that a lawyer applies for readmission. Second, even in jurisdictions where disbarment is permanent, consideration of injury reinforces the concept that a basic purpose of lawyer discipline is protection of the public. As the New York Supreme Court explained in a case where it imposed disbarment on a lawyer who misappropriated more than $31,000 from a client-descendent's estate by forging the administratrix's signature on checks: "This result is called for by the duty to protect the public and to vindicate the public's trust in lawyers as custodians of clients' funds" (*In re Marks,* 72 A.D.2d 399, 401, 424 N.Y.S.2d 229, 230 (1980)). (Note: Lawyers who convert the property of persons other than their clients are covered by Standard 5.11.)

4.12 Suspension is generally appropriate when a lawyer knows or should know that he is dealing improperly with client property and causes injury or potential injury to a client.

Commentary

Suspension should be reserved for lawyers who engage in misconduct that does not amount to misappropriation or conversion. The most common cases involve lawyers who commingle client funds with their own, or fail to remit client funds promptly. While the court in *In re Wilson,* 81 N.J. 451, 409 A.2d 1153 (1979), defined misappropriation to include "any unauthorized use by the lawyer of clients' funds entrusted to him, ... whether or not he derives any personal gain or benefit therefrom" (81 N.J. at 455, n. 1, 409 A.2d at 1155, n. 1), most courts do not impose disbarment on lawyers who merely commingle funds. As the Washington Supreme Court recently concluded, "We do not now nor have we ever held that trust account violations per se result in disbarment" (*In re Salvesen,* 94 Wash.2d 73, 79, 614 P.2d 1264, 1266 (1980)).

For example, in *State v. Chartier,* 234 Kan. 834, 676 P.2d 740 (1984), the lawyer commingled a client's funds, and failed to notify a client of receipt of garnishment proceeds. The court imposed an indefinite suspension, stating that the lawyer "knew, or should have known though the exercise of reasonable diligence" that the garnishment funds collected exceeded the amounts actually due (234 Kan. at 836, 676 P.2d at 742). Similarly, in *Disciplinary Board of the Supreme Court v. Banks,* 641 S.W.2d 501 (Tenn.1982), the court imposed a one-year suspension where the lawyer took the client's money to invest but did not pay her interest on a regular basis or pay over the client's money upon her demand. The court noted that the lawyer did not intend to convert the client's funds to his own use: "At all times he acknowledged his responsibility for them and his indebtedness to her" (641 S.W.2d at 504). Because lawyers who commingle client's funds with their own subject the client's funds to the claims of creditors, commingling is a serious violation for which a period of suspension is appropriate even in cases when the client does not suffer a loss. As explained by the Illinois Supreme Court: "It is the risk of the loss of the funds while they are in the attorney's possession, and not only their actual loss, which the rule is designed to eliminate. . . ." *In re Bizar,* 97 Ill.2d 127, 454 N.E.2d 271 (1983).

4.13 Reprimand is generally appropriate when a lawyer is negligent in dealing with client property and causes injury or potential injury to a client.

Commentary

Reprimand should be reserved for lawyers who are merely negligent in dealing with client property, and who cause injury or potential injury to a client. Suspension or disbarment as applicable under Standards 4.11 and 4.12 and the commentary thereto is appropriate for lawyers who are grossly negligent. For example, lawyers who are grossly negligent in failing to establish proper accounting procedures should be suspended; reprimand is appropriate for lawyers who simply fail to follow their established procedures. Reprimand is also appropriate when a lawyer is negligent in training or supervising his or her office staff concerning proper procedures in handling client funds.

The courts have typically imposed reprimands in cases when lawyers fail to maintain adequate trust accounting procedures, or neglect to return the client's property promptly. In *The Florida Bar v. Golden*, 401 So.2d 1340 (Fla.1981), a public reprimand was imposed on a lawyer who failed to repay a loan made to him by a client for two years and who failed to keep adequate records of his trust accounting procedures. Similarly, in *Carter v. Gallucci*, 457 A.2d 269 (R.I.1983), because of inadequate records, a lawyer failed to pay real estate taxes out of funds disbursed to him. He did subsequently pay the taxes, and the court imposed a reprimand.

4.14 Admonition is generally appropriate when a lawyer is negligent in dealing with client property and causes little or no actual or potential injury to a client.

Commentary

Admonition should be reserved for cases where the lawyer's negligence poses little or no risk of injury to a client. An admonition would be appropriate, for example, when a lawyer's sloppy bookkeeping practices make it difficult to determine the state of a client trust account, but where all client funds are actually properly maintained. Imposing an admonition in such a case should serve as a warning to the lawyer to improve his or her accounting procedures, thus preventing any actual injury to any client.

4.2 Failure to Preserve the Client's Confidences

Absent aggravating or mitigating circumstances, upon application of the factors set out in 3.0, the following sanctions are generally appropriate in cases involving the failure to preserve client property:

4.21 Disbarment is generally appropriate when a lawyer, with the intent to benefit the lawyer or another, knowingly reveals information relating to representation of a client not otherwise lawfully permitted to be disclosed, and this disclosure causes injury or potential injury to a client.

Commentary

Disbarment is warranted in situations when a lawyer intentionally abuses the client's trust by using the professional relationship to gain information which benefits the lawyer or another, and which causes injury or potential injury to a client. Because the violation of a client's confidence poses such a serious threat to the lawyer-client relationship, disbarment should be imposed whenever the lawyer acts with the intent to benefit the lawyer or another. Neither a "serious" injury nor a "potentially serious" injury to a client need be proved; any injury to a client will be sufficient to impose disbarment. An example of a case where disbarment is appropriate occurred in *In re Pool,* No. 83–37 BD, Sup.J.Ct., Suff.Cty., Mass. (1984), where a defendant's lawyer gave a federal prosecutor information about the location of a safety deposit box containing incriminating evidence in order to gain access to obtain funds to cover the costs of investigation. In the words of the court, "[t]he disclosure of confidential information by a defense attorney to a prosecutor, without the client's consent, is a serious violation of the defense attorney's obligations" (*Id.* at 4). (Note: This situation should be distinguished from the situation where a lawyer is acting under a good faith belief that there is no choice but to reveal a client's confidence, as in a case where a lawyer is called to testify as to the whereabouts of the client in a divorce proceeding and the lawyer's answer involves facts learned in the lawyer-client relationship. Here, the lawyer's good faith belief that the law requires disclosure of the information would be a mitigating factor, see Standard 9.32(b).)

4.22 Suspension is generally appropriate when a lawyer knowingly reveals information relating to the representation of a client not otherwise lawfully permitted to be disclosed, and this disclosure causes injury or potential injury to a client.

Commentary

Suspension is appropriate when the lawyer is not intentionally using the professional relationship to benefit himself or another, but nevertheless knowingly breaches a client's confidence such that the client suffers injury or potential injury. An appropriate case for a suspension would involve a lawyer who knowingly revealed confidential information to the opposing party in litigation, with the result that the client's position was weakened.

4.23 Reprimand is generally appropriate when a lawyer negligently reveals information relating to representation of a client not otherwise lawfully permitted to be disclosed and this disclosure causes injury or potential injury to a client.

Commentary

Reprimand should be imposed when a lawyer negligently breaches a client's confidence. Even when the client is not actually harmed, the potential for harm to the client and damage to the professional relationship is so significant that a public sanction should be imposed. In the words of one court: "This element of trust is the very essence of the attorney-client relationship" [*Matter of Roache,* 446 N.E.2d 1302, 1303 (Ind.1983)]. An appropriate case for a reprimand would involve a lawyer who negligently leaves a client's documents in a conference room following a meeting, or who discusses a client matter in a public place.

4.24 Admonition is generally appropriate when a lawyer negligently reveals information relating to representation of a client not otherwise lawfully permitted to be disclosed and this disclosure causes little or no actual or potential injury to a client.

Commentary

Maintaining a client's confidence is so fundamental to the professional relationship that generally it is inappropriate to impose a private sanction. At a minimum, a reprimand should be imposed (see Standard 4.23).

4.3 Failure to Avoid Conflicts of Interest

Absent aggravating or mitigating circumstances, upon application of the factors set out in Standard 3.0, the following sanctions are generally appropriate in cases involving conflicts of interest:

4.31 Disbarment is generally appropriate when a lawyer, without the informed consent of client(s):

(a) **engages in representation of a client knowing that the lawyer's interests are adverse to the client's with the intent to benefit the lawyer or another, and causes serious or potentially serious injury to the client; or**

(b) **simultaneously represents clients that the lawyer knows have adverse interests with the intent to benefit the lawyer or another, and causes serious or potentially serious injury to a client; or**

747

   (c) **represents a client in a matter substantially related to a matter in which the interests of a present or former client are materially adverse, and knowingly uses information relating to the representation of a client with the intent to benefit the lawyer or another, and causes serious or potentially serious injury to a client.**

Commentary

The courts generally disbar lawyers who intentionally exploit the lawyer-client relationship by acquiring an ownership, possessory, security or other pecuniary interest adverse to a client without the client's understanding or consent. For example, in *Matter of Easler,* 269 S.E.2d 765 (S.C.1980), a lawyer who engaged in a fraudulent scheme to obtain the client's property at a price well below market value was disbarred. The court noted that "in his attempt to acquire their property for his personal gain," the lawyer falsely notarized one of the clients' signature, and took advantage of the "domestic and financial difficulties the McFarlins [the clients] were undergoing" (269 S.E.2d at 766). In *In re Wolf,* 82 N.J. 326, 413 A.2d 317 (1980), a widow retained the lawyer who had represented her husband during his lifetime to handle her husband's estate. When she asked the lawyer to suggest an investment for a portion of her inheritance, he suggested that she invest in property which was owned by a company in which he was a stockholder and officer. Knowing that his client was naive and inexperienced in business matters, he directed her to invest her money in property worth only half of what he represented to her, and did not inform her as to the status of the mortgage, the title, or unpaid real estate taxes. Later on, he failed to notify her of a foreclosure action on the property or to defend the action on her behalf. In the words of the court, "It is clear that he exploited his client for his own financial benefit. It was unthinkable in the first place for respondent to have suggested such an investment, but, having done so, it was unconscionable for him to have continued to represent the widow. He should have insisted that she retain independent counsel or refused to consummate the transaction. Undoubtedly, independent counsel would never have allowed the widow to make this investment" (413 A.2d at 321). (Note: the lawyer, who was disbarred, also attempted to commit fraud on the court in order to secure a larger fee.) Similarily, in *In re Hills,* 296 Or. 526, 678 P.2d 262 (1984), the lawyer entered into a loan transaction with clients in which he intentionally misrepresented that funds were available to pay the note. He also entered into a partnership agreement with another client in which he misrepresented that the client would be a limited partner but, in fact, made the client a general partner. In neither of these cases did the lawyer advise the clients to seek independent legal counsel.

   Disbarment is also appropriate in cases of multiple representation when a lawyer knowingly engages in conduct with the intent to benefit the lawyer or another. As one court has explained, "Although many ingredients go into the recipe for a successful lawyer-client relationship, one ingredient is indispensable: individual loyalty. The relationship cannot properly exist absent the laywer's uncompromised commitment to the client's cause. DR 5–105 aims to insure undivided loyalty; in its absence, the lawyer cannot serve. The rule also seeks to maintain or increase public confidence in public institutions, for the appearance of impropriety tht sometimes exists when a lawyer represents multiple clients . . . erodes public confidence in the legal profession." *In re Jans,* 295 Or. 289, 666 P.2d 830, 832 (1983). In *In re Keast,* 497 P.2d 103 (Mont.1972), a lawyer represented a client charged with procuring girls for immoral purposes. Although the lawyer was named as one of the individuals for whom the girls were procured, he served as defense counsel in his client's criminal case. While this case was pending, the lawyer also filed an action for divorce against the client on behalf of the client's wife. The court imposed disbarment. In *Stanley v. Board of Professional Responsibility,* 640 S.W.2d 210 (Tenn.1982), a lawyer was disbarred who represented both the victim and the defendant in a criminal matter. After learning about the crime from the victim, the lawyer misled the defendant into employing him when the lawyer knew that the victim no longer wished to prosecute. In the words of the court, "Stanley [the lawyer] deceived an immature youth and his naive parents. He compounded the deception with his lack of understanding of the proper role of a lawyer—which does not include a self-appointed role as a paraclete, comforter, helper, or hand-holder, under the guise of legal services and at a lawyer's compensation rate" (640 S.W.2d at 213). (Note: the lawyer also was involved in another conflict of interest by entering into usurious loan transactions with two other clients.)

Finally, disbarment is appropriate when a lawyer knowingly uses information relating to representation of a former client with the intent to benefit the lawyer or another, and causes serious or potentially serious injury to a client. Although such cases are rare, disbarment is warranted when there is such an intentional abuse of the lawyer-client relationship.

4.32 Suspension is generally appropriate when a lawyer knows of a conflict of interest and does not fully disclose to a client the possible effect of that conflict, and causes injury or potential injury to a client.

Commentary

Conflicts can take the form of a conflict between the lawyer and his or her client, between current clients, or between a former client and a present client. In the case of conflicts between a lawyer and a present client, suspension is appropriate when the lawyer knows that his or her interests may be or are likely to be adverse to that of the client, but does not fully disclose the conflict, and causes injury or potential injury to a client. For example, in *In re Boyer,* 295 Or. 624, 669 P.2d 326 (1983), the lawyer represented a client for a number of years, rendering both financial and legal advice. When another of his clients wanted to borrow money, the lawyer arranged for the first client to make a loan, and he prepared the note and a mortgage to secure the note, but the lawyer did not tell the first client either that such a loan might be usurious, and thus unenforceable, or that he had received a finder's fee from the second client for his efforts. The Oregon Supreme Court found that the lawyer violated DR 5–101(A) in his representation of the first client, and suspended him for seven months. [Note: the court also found a violation of DR 5–105(B).] Similarly, in *Joseph E. Chabat,* DP–161/80, DP 74/81 (Michigan Attorney Discipline Board, 1980), a lawyer in a divorce action was suspended for nine months when he lent hmself money from the sale of a client's house and failed to advise the client to seek independent representation in regard to the loan.

Suspension is also appropriate when a lawyer knows of a conflict among several clients, but does not fully disclose the possible effect of the multiple representation, and causes injury or potential injury to one or more of the clients. For example, in *State v. Callahan,* 232 Kan. 136, 652 P.2d 708 (1982), the lawyer represented both the vendors and the purchaser in a land sale transaction. The lawyer failed to warn the vendors that they did not have a perfected security interest and failed to make full disclosure to the vendors of his close business and professional associations with the purchaser. The Supreme Court of Kansas imposed an indefinite suspension. Similarly, in *Matter of Krakauer,* 81 N.J. 32, 404 A.2d 1137 (1979), the New Jersey Supreme Court imposed a one-year suspension on a lawyer who represented both sides in a real estate transaction (and who also attempted to retain an unearned commission and called for a title search which was not ordered by the client).

Finally, suspension is appropriate when a lawyer knows or should know that the interests of a client are materially adverse to the interests of a former client in a substantially related matter, and causes injury or potential injury to the former or the subsequent client. For example, in *In re LaPinska,* 72 Ill.2d 461, 381 N.E.2d 700 (1978), the lawyer represented a contractor to secure title papers for a residence being sold. The lawyer, a city attorney, then represented the city in a suit brought by the purchasers of the residence against the contractor regarding a zoning violation of the property. When the purchasers complained about the leniency of the fine imposed on the contractor, the lawyer agreed to represent them in a civil suit against the contractor. Despite the fact that the lawyer had acted openly, and all the affected parties were aware of the dual representation, the Illinois Supreme Court suspended the lawyer for one year. Similarly, *In re Odendahl,* M.R. 2787 (Ill.1982), the Illinois Supreme Court suspended a lawyer for one year when, while a state's attorney, he represented individuals in nine divorce proceedings in which support payments were due. In one case, he represented the wife to obtain the divorce, and then the husband, in a petition to reduce the support payments. In another case, he prosecuted a defendant for disorderly conduct and then filed an answer for him in a divorce suit by his wife. The court noted that four of these cases occurred after motions to disqualify had been filed against the lawyer and that he knew or should have known of the impropriety of his conduct.

> **4.33 Reprimand is generally appropriate when a lawyer is negligent in determining whether the representation of a client may be materially affected by the lawyer's own interests, or whether the representation will adversely affect another client, and causes injury or potential injury to a client.**

Commentary

The courts generally impose a reprimand when a lawyer engages in a single instance of misconduct involving a conflict of interest when the lawyer has merely been negligent and there is no overreaching or serious injury to a client. For example, in *State v. Swoyer,* 228 Kan. 799, 619 P.2d 1166 (1980), a public censure was imposed on a lawyer who was representing a client who owned his own business, and who also advised the client's former employee to sue the client for back wages. Although the lawyer stated that he was simply carrying out his client's wishes by attempting to secure payment for the employee, and that he merely advised her to file suit herself, the court found an ethical violation worthy of censure (reprimand) since her petition was actually typed in the lawyer's office and filed by the lawyer. In a multiple representation situation, the court in *Gendron v. State Bar of California,* 35 Cal.3d 409, 673 P.2d 260, 197 Cal.Rptr. 590 (1983), imposed a public reprimand on a public defender who neglected to obtain written waiver of conflict forms from three defendants who were jointly charged with robbery. In *Matter of Palmieri,* 76 N.J. 51, 385 A.2d 856 (1978), a public reprimand was imposed on a lawyer who represented the seller of a supermarket when, with the buyers unable to hire a lawyer and upon the insistence of the seller, he also represented the buyers. Although the lawyer made full disclosure of the relevant facts and pitfalls of multiple representation, he later filed suit against the buyers and eventually had to withdraw when he was required to be a witness concerning the nature of the agreement between the parties.

Courts also impose reprimands in cases of subsequent representation. For example, in *In re Drendel,* M.R. 1708 (Ill.1975), a lawyer represented a client in a divorce suit against his wife, but the parties reconciled before the hearing and the case was dismissed. About 18 months later, he represented the wife in a divorce action against the husband, but this suit was also dismissed. Similarly, in *In re Lewis,* M.R. 2766 (Ill.1982), the lawyer represented the executor of a will and later, while employed in another office, represented a client who was the devisee of the residence property who filed a petition alleging misconduct by the executor. The court ordered the lawyer censured [reprimanded], noting no evidence of secrecy, fraud, or financial benefit to the lawyer.

> **4.34** **Admonition is generally appropriate when a lawyer engages in an isolated instance of negligence in determining whether the representation of a client may be materially affected by the lawyer's own interests, or whether the representation will adversely affect another client, and causes little or no actual or potential injury to a client.**

4.4 Lack of Diligence

Absent aggravating or mitigating circumstances, upon application of the factors set out in Standard 3.0, the following sanctions are generally appropriate in cases involving a failure to act with reasonable diligence and promptness in representing a client:

> **4.41** **Disbarment is generally appropriate when:**
>
>   **(a)** **a lawyer abandons the practice and causes serious or potentially serious injury to a client; or**
>
>   **(b)** **a lawyer knowingly fails to perform services for a client and causes serious or potentially serious injury to a client; or**
>
>   **(c)** **a lawyer engages in a pattern of neglect with respect to client matters and causes serious or potentially serious injury to a client.**

Commentary

Lack of diligence can take a variety of forms. Some lawyers simply abandon their practices, leaving clients completely unaware that they have no legal representation and often leaving clients without any legal remedy. Other lawyers knowingly fail to perform services for a client, or engage in a pattern of misconduct, demonstrating by their behavior that they either cannot or will not conform to the required ethical standards.

Disbarment is appropriate in each of these situations. For example, in *The Florida Bar v. Lehman,* 417 So.2d 648 (Fla.1982), a lawyer abandoned his practice and kept approximately 450 pending client matters. The clients suffered serious injuries; one client's statute of limitations ran, and many of the clients never recovered money paid to the lawyer as fees. See also: *In re Cullinam,* M.R. 2963 (Ill.1983) (with other charges). In a case demonstrating a pattern of neglect, *State v. Dixon,* 233 Kan. 465, 664 P.2d 286, (1983), a lawyer was disbarred after having been disciplined for 13 counts of neglect of probate cases, with each case involving a long period of neglect (16 years, 28 years, etc.). The court noted that, although there was no evidence of dishonesty on the part of the lawyer, disbarment was appropriate because "the extent of the neglect is extreme and had reached proportions never before considered by this court" (233 Kan. at 470, 644 P.2d at 289). See also: *The Florida Bar v. Mitchell,* 285 So.2d 96 (Fla.1980).

4.42 Suspension is generally appropriate when:

(a) a lawyer knowingly fails to perform services for a client and causes injury or potential injury to a client; or

(b) a lawyer engages in a pattern of neglect and causes injury or potential injury to a client.

Commentary

Suspension should be imposed when a lawyer knows that he is not performing the services requested by the client, but does nothing to remedy the situation, or when a lawyer engages in a pattern of neglect, with the result that the lawyer causes injury or potential injury to a client. Most cases involve lawyers who do not communicate with their clients. For example, in *In re Earl J. Taylor,* 666 Ill.2d 567, 363 N.E.2d 845 (1977), a lawyer was suspended for one year when he failed to appear at a criminal hearing, failed to file a divorce action, and failed to prosecute a civil case. In the third case, the lawyer told the client that "he'd take care of everything," yet did not contact her or return her telephone calls. This last client suffered a default judgment, which forced her to settle and pay a second lawyer; the first two clients suffered the loss of the fee. See also: *Hunt v. Disciplinary Board of the Alabama State Bar,* 381 So.2d 52 (Ala.1980); *People v. Dixon,* 616 P.2d 103 (Colo.1980).

4.43 Reprimand is generally appropriate when a lawyer is negligent and does not act with reasonable diligence in representing a client, and causes injury or potential injury to a client.

Commentary

Most courts impose a reprimand when the lawyer is negligent. For example, in *In re Logan,* 70 N.J. 222, 358 A.2d 787 (1976), a lawyer who neglected a client matter was reprimanded when, knowing that a motion for reduction of alimony was dependent on the court's examination of his client's tax return, he failed to file a copy of the tax return with the court. See also: *In re Donohue,* 77 A.D.2d 112, 432 N.Y.S.2d

498 (1980), where a lawyer neglected an estate matter, but where the estate was eventually closed to the satisfaction of all parties and with no financial loss, and *Louis Lan,* DP–194180 (Mich.Atty.Dis. Board 1980), where the lawyer attempted to transfer cases to other lawyers without adequately communicating with his clients.

> **4.44** **Admonition is generally appropriate when a lawyer is negligent and does not act with reasonable diligence in representing a client, and causes little or no actual or potential injury to a client.**

4.5 Lack of Competence

Absent aggravating or mitigating circumstances, upon application of the factors set out in Standard 3.0, the following sanctions are generally appropriate in cases involving failure to provide competent representation to a client:

> **4.51** **Disbarment is generally appropriate when a lawyer's course of conduct demonstrates that the lawyer does not understand the most fundamental legal doctrines or procedures, and the lawyer's conduct causes injury or potential injury to a client.**

Commentary

Disbarment should be imposed on lawyers who are found to have engaged in multiple instances of incompetent behavior. Since disbarment is such a serious sanction, it should rarely be imposed on a lawyer who has demonstrated only a single instance of incompetence; rather, disbarment should be imposed on lawyers whose course of conduct demonstrates that they cannot or will not master the knowledge and skills necessary for minimally competent practice. For example, in *The Florida Bar v. Blaha,* 366 So.2d 443 (Fla.1978), the court disbarred a lawyer who totally mishandled a guardianship and real estate transaction, and also filed a complaint for another client in the wrong court, such that relief was denied. In representing a third client, the lawyer mishandled a replevin action, filing replevin under old rules at a time when his client had not yet perfected a security interest necessary to support the action. As a result of this incompetence, the lawyer was eventually held in contempt and fined $3,000.

> **4.52** **Suspension is generally appropriate when a lawyer engages in an area of practice in which the lawyer knows he or she is not competent, and causes injury or potential injury to a client.**

Commentary

In order to protect the public, a suspension should be imposed in cases when a lawyer engages in practice in areas in which a lawyer knows that he or she is not competent. In such cases, it may also be appropriate to attach certain conditions to the suspension, such as a requirement that the lawyer pass the bar examination or limit his or her practice to certain areas.

Such a situation arose in the case of *Office of Disciplinary Counsel v. Henry,* 664 S.W.2d 62 (Tenn.1983), where the lawyer mishandled four cases in a relatively short period of time. In one case, the lawyer attempted to represent a client charged with murder. The lawyer had never handled any felony case before, and yet did not associate any lawyer with him. He made little investigation of the crime, and filed motions based on statutes which had been superceded. Further, he severely damaged his client's case by filing an "amended answer" to the indictment, following the form which would be filed in a civil action, which set forth his client's version of the homicide. The court imposed a two-year suspension with reinstatement conditioned "upon a showing that he has obtained a level of competence adequate to justify the issuance of a license" (664 S.W.2d at 64).

4.53 Reprimand is generally appropriate when a lawyer:

    (a) demonstrates failure to understand relevant legal doctrines or procedures and causes injury or potential injury to a client; or

    (b) is negligent in determining whether he or she is competent to handle a legal matter and causes injury or potential injury to a client.

Commentary

Most courts impose reprimands on lawyers who are incompetent. For example, in *The Florida Bar v. Gray,* 380 So.2d 1292 (Fla.1980), the lawyer agreed to represent a client in a claim of violation of the truth in lending laws, but, although the evidence showed that he expected to become qualified in this area, he did not engage in sufficient study and investigation to become competent (only securing a number of laymen's publications). The court imposed a public reprimand. Similarly, in *State ex rel. Nebraska State Bar Association v. Holscher,* 193 Neb. 729, 230 N.W.2d 75 (1975), a county lawyer who filed a claim for services he rendered in foreclosing tax sale certificates without familiarizing himself with the statute prescribing the fee for such services received a reprimand.

While reprimand alone can be appropriate, a combination of reprimand and probation is often a more productive approach. Probation can be very effective in assisting lawyers to improve their legal skills. The court can use probation creatively, imposing whatever conditions are necessary to assist that particular lawyer. It may be appropriate, for example, to require an inexperienced lawyer to associate with co-counsel. In *Florida Bar v. Glick,* 383 So.2d 642 (Fla.1980), the court imposed a reprimand and one-year probation on a lawyer who mishandled a quiet title action. The court imposed the following conditions of probation: that the lawyer refrain from representing clients in real estate matters and that he complete 30 hours of approved continuing education courses in real property.

4.54 **Admonition is generally appropriate when a lawyer engages in an isolated instance of negligence in determining whether he or she is competent to handle a legal matter, and causes little or no actual or potential injury to a client.**

4.6 Lack of Candor

Absent aggravating or mitigating circumstances, upon application of the factors set out in Standard 3.0, the following sanctions are generally appropriate in cases where the lawyer engages in fraud, deceit, or misrepresentation directed toward a client:

4.61 **Disbarment is generally appropriate when a lawyer knowingly deceives a client with the intent to benefit the lawyer or another, and causes serious injury or potentially serious injury to a client.**

Commentary

Disbarment is appropriate when a lawyer intentionally abuses the fiduciary relationship, making misrepresentations to a client in order to benefit himself or another and causing serious injury or potentially serious injury to a client. (For a discussion of lack of candor before a court, see Standard 6.1). For example, in *Matter of Wolfson*, 313 N.W.2d 596 (Minn.1981), the court disbarred a lawyer who asked a client to help him arrange for a loan, and who misrepresented that the loan was for medical treatment for his daughter, when the loan was actually used in his wife's business. The client personally guaranteed payment of the loan and, when the lawyer failed to repay it, the client had to institute legal action against the lawyer to obtain an $832.61 judgment. In imposing disbarment, the court stated that the lawyer had not "hesitated to use his knowledge and skill as a lawyer for improper purposes" (313 N.W.2d at 602). (Note: The lawyer had also engaged in acts of neglect and abuse of the legal process.) Similarly, in (anonymous) 49 Cal.State Bar J. 73 (1974), a lawyer was disbarred after he borrowed money from two clients, falsely leading them to believe that he was solvent, with the result that the clients received an unsecured promissory note. In *Virginia State Bar ex rel. Eighth District Committee v. Fred W. Bender, Jr.*, No. 50228 (Va.App.Ct.1981), the court revoked the license of a lawyer who intentionally overstated the number of hours he worked on a client's estate to make it appear that he was entitled to $9,500.

4.62 Suspension is generally appropriate when a lawyer knowingly deceives a client, and causes injury or potential injury to the client.

Commentary

Suspension is appropriate when a lawyer knowingly deceives a client, although not necessarily for his own direct benefit, and the client is injured. The most common cases are those in which a lawyer misrepresents the nature or the extent of services performed. For example, in *Kentucky Bar Association v. Reed,* 623 S.W.2d 228 (Ky. 1981), the court suspended a lawyer for one year when he misrepresented the status of three different cases and all three clients suffered injury (two clients suffered a summary judgment against them and another client was denied a settlement payment for an extensive period of time).

4.63 Reprimand is generally appropriate when a lawyer negligently fails to provide a client with accurate or complete information, and causes injury or potential injury to the client.

Commentary

Reprimand is justified when the lawyer is merely negligent and there is injury or potential injury to a client. In *Hawkins v. State Bar,* 23 Cal.3d 622, 591 P.2d 524, 153 Cal.Rptr. 234 (1979), a lawyer received a public reproval (reprimand) when he failed to fully explain to his clients the nature of a contigency interest which he possessed in insurance proceeds used to satisfy an adverse judgment against the clients in a personal injury action.

4.64 Admonition is generally appropriate when a lawyer engages in an isolated instance of negligence in failing to provide a client with accurate or complete information, and causes little or no actual or potential injury to the client.

5.0 Violations of Duties Owed to the Public

Introduction

The most fundamental duty which a lawyer owes the public is the duty to maintain the standards of personal integrity upon which the community relies. The public expects the lawyer to be honest and to abide by the law; public confidence in the integrity of officers of the court is undermined when lawyers engage in illegal conduct [Rules 8.4(b) and (c)/DR 1–102(A)(3)(4)) and (5)]. In addition, a lawyer who serves as a public official has the duty to avoid using his public position to obtain any special advantage for himself or a client, or to influence a tribunal to act in favor of himself or a client [Rules 3.5(a), 8.4(e) and (f)/ DR 8–101 through DR 8–103, DR 9–101(c)]. Finally, prosecutors have a special obligation to protect the public interest by insuring that charges are brought only after a finding of probable cause, and that exculpatory evidence is turned over to the accused (Rule 3.8(a)/DR 7–103).

It is important to note that the ABA Standards for Lawyer Discipline provide that the court should place a lawyer on interim suspension immediately and without reference to the pendency of an appeal upon proof that the lawyer has been convicted of a "serious crime" or is causing great harm to the public (Standard 6.5). A "serious crime" is defined as any felony and any lesser crime a necessary element of which involves interference with the administration of justice, false swearing, misrepresentation, fraud, extortion, misappropriation, theft, or an attempt or a conspiracy to commit a "serious crime." The sanctions which are set out below are those which should be imposed as final discipline, at which time the interim suspension should be terminated (Standard 6.6).

5.1 Failure to Maintain Personal Integrity

Absent aggravating or mitigating circumstances, upon application of the factors set out in Standard 3.0, the following sanctions are generally appropriate in cases involving commission of a criminal act that reflects adversely on the lawyer's honesty, trustworthiness, or fitness as a lawyer in other respects, or in cases with conduct involving dishonesty, fraud, deceit, or misrepresentation:

5.11 Disbarment is generally appropriate when:

(a) a lawyer engages in serious criminal conduct, a necessary element of which includes intentional interference with the administration of justice, false swearing, misrepresentation, fraud, extortion, misappropriation, or theft; or the sale, distribution or importation of controlled substances; or the intentional killing of another; or an attempt or conspiracy or solicitation of another to commit any of these offenses; or

(b) a lawyer engages in any other intentional conduct involving dishonesty, fraud, deceit, or misrepresentation that seriously adversely reflects on the lawyer's fitness to practice.

Commentary

A lawyer who engages in any of the illegal acts listed above has violated one of the most basic professional obligations to the public, the pledge to maintain personal honesty and integrity. This duty to the public is breached regardless of whether a criminal charge has been brought against the lawyer. In fact, this type of misconduct is so closely related to practice and poses such an immediate threat to the public that the lawyer should be suspended from the practice of law immediately pending a final determination of the ultimate discipline to be imposed (see Standards for Lawyer Discipline, Standard 6.5).

In imposing final discipline in such cases, most courts impose disbarment on lawyers who are convicted of serious felonies. As the court noted in a case where a lawyer was convicted of two counts of federal income tax evasion and one count of subornation of perjury, "we cannot ask the public to voluntarily comply with the legal system if we, as lawyers, reject its fairness and application to ourselves." *In the Matter of Grimes*, 414 Mich. 483, 326 N.W.2d 380 (1982). See also: *In re Fry*, 251 Ga. 247, 305 S.E.2d 590 (Ga.1983), conviction of murder; *Sixth District Committee of the Virginia State Bar v. Albert C. Hodgson*, No. 80–18 (Va.Disciplinary Board, 1981), where a lawyer advised a client that he could make arrangements to have her husband killed in lieu of bringing a child custody suit.

5.12 Suspension is generally appropriate when a lawyer knowingly engages in criminal conduct which does not contain the elements listed in Standard 5.11 and that seriously adversely reflects on the lawyer's fitness to practice.

Commentary

Lawyers who engage in criminal conduct other than that described above in Standard 5.11 should be suspended in cases where their conduct seriously adversely reflects on their fitness to practice. As in the case of disbarment, a suspension can be imposed even where no criminal charges have been filed against the lawyer. Not every lawyer who commits a criminal act should be suspended, however. As pointed out in the Model Rules of Professional Conduct:

Although a lawyer is personally answerable to the entire criminal law, a lawyer should be professionally answerable only for offenses that indicate lack of those characteristics relevant to law practice. Offenses involving violence, dishonesty, or breach of trust, or serious interference with the administration of justice are in that category. A pattern of repeated offenses, even ones of minor significance when considered separately, can indicate indifference to legal obligation.[30]

The most common cases involved lawyers who commit felonies other than those listed above, such as the possession of narcotics or sexual assault. See: *In re Robideau*, 102 Wis.2d 16, 306 N.W.2d 1

---

30. Comment to Rule 8.4, Model Rules, *Id.*

(1981), suspension for three years for contributing to the delinquency of a minor and possession of a controlled substance; *In re Lanier*, 309 S.E.2d 754 (S.C.1983), indefinite suspension for possession of marijuana; *In re Safran*, 18 Cal.3d 134, 554 P.2d 329, 133 Cal.Rprtr. 9 (1976), suspension for three years for conviction of two counts of child molesting.

> **5.13 Reprimand is generally appropriate when a lawyer knowingly engages in any other conduct that involves dishonesty, fraud, deceit, or misrepresentation and that adversely reflects on the lawyer's fitness to practice law.**

Commentary

There are few situations not involving fraud or dishonesty which are sufficiently related to the practice of law to subject a lawyer to discipline. The Arizona Supreme Court applied this standard in *In re Johnson*, 106 Ariz. 73, 471 P.2d 269 (1970), a case where a lawyer was charged with assault, stating that "isolated, trivial incidents of this kind not involving a fixed pattern of misbehavior find ample redress in the criminal and civil laws. They have none of the elements of moral turpitude, arising more out of the infirmities of human nature. They are not the appropriate subject matter of a solemn reprimand by this court" (471 P.2d at 271). However, a pattern of repeated offenses, even ones of minor significance when considered separately, can indicate such indifference to legal obligation as to justify a reprimand.

There can be situations, however, in which the lawyer's conduct is not even criminal, but, because it is directly related to his or her professional role, discipline is required. For example, in *In re Lamberis*, 93 Ill.2d 222, 443 N.E.2d 549 (1982), the court imposed a censure [reprimand] on a lawyer who knowingly plagiarized two published works in a thesis submitted in satisfaction of the requirements for a master's degree. The court noted that although the lawyer's conduct might appear to be "fairly distant from the practice of law," discipline was "appropriate and required because both the extent of the appropriated material and the purpose for which it was used evidence the respondent's complete disregard for values that are most fundamental in the legal profession" (443 N.E.2d at 551). Specifically, the lawyer's plagiarism displayed "an extreme cynicism toward the property rights of others," and a "lack of honesty which cannot go undisciplined, especially because honesty is so fundamental to the functioning of the legal profession" (443 N.E.2d at 551–52).

5.14 Admonition is generally appropriate when a lawyer engages in any other conduct that reflects adversely on the lawyer's fitness to practice law.

5.2 Failure to Maintain the Public Trust

Absent aggravating or mitigating circumstances, upon application of the factors set out in Standard 3.0, the following sanctions are generally appropriate in cases involving public officials who engage in conduct that is prejudicial to the administration of justice or who state or imply an ability to influence improperly a government agency or official:

5.21 Disbarment is generally appropriate when a lawyer in an official or governmental position knowingly misuses the position with the intent to obtain a significant benefit or advantage for himself or another, or with the intent to cause serious or potentially serious injury to a party or to the integrity of the legal process.

Commentary

The public officials who are subject to disbarment generally engage in conduct involving fraud and deceit, and are generally subject to criminal sanctions as well. For example, in *In re Rosenthal*, 73 Ill.2d 46, 382 N.E.2d 257 (1978), two lawyers were disbarred who participated in an extortion scheme to benefit their client as part of a zoning request. One of the lawyers was an assistant Attorney General, a fact which the court emphasized as significant in imposing disbarment: "Despite his obligations as a law officer, he knowingly participated and furthered conduct which he knew to be illegal, and then, further, deliberately misled federal agents" (382 N.E.2d at 262). The court concluded, "corruption within government could not, in most instances, thrive but for those few attorneys, who, like respondents, are willing to tolerate such illegal activity if it will benefit their client. The practice of law is a privilege and demands a greater acceptance of responsibility and adherence to ethical standards than respondents have demonstrated" (382 N.E.2d at 261).

5.22 Suspension is generally appropriate when a lawyer in an official or governmental position knowingly fails to follow proper procedures or rules, and causes injury or potential injury to a party or to the integrity of the legal process.

Commentary

Suspension is an appropriate sanction when lawyers who are public officials knowingly act improperly, but not necessarily for their own benefit. For example, in *In re DeLucia*, 76 N.J. 329, 387 A.2d 362

(1978), a judge fixed a traffic ticket by entering a not guilty judgment when no hearing had been held. He later attempted to cover up his wrongdoing by preparing an affidavit with a backdated acknowledgment. Disciplinary proceedings were instituted after the lawyer had resigned from his part-time judgeship. The court imposed a one-year suspension, noting that he did not personally benefit. Similarly, in *In re Weishoff,* 75 N.J. 326, 382 A.2d 632 (1978), the court held that a municipal prosecutor's knowing participation in an improper disposition of a traffic ticket warranted a one-year suspension. In *In re Vasser,* 75 N.J. 357, 382 A.2d 1114 (1978), the court imposed a six-month suspension on a lawyer/part-time judge who improperly practiced law and also interceded in another court to obtain a postponement of a trial to give his client an advantage in an unrelated civil matter. The lawyer also used official court stationery with respect to a transaction relating solely to his private law practice. The court noted that "the instances of proved misconduct did not assume egregious proportions. His improper intercession in the neighboring municipal court apparently did not result in any tangible or lasting distortion of justice" (382 A.2d at 1117).

> **5.23   Reprimand is generally appropriate when a lawyer in an official or governmental position negligently fails to follow proper procedures or rules, and causes injury or potential injury to a party or to the integrity of the legal process.**

Commentary

In *In re Shafir,* 92 N.J. 138, 455 A.2d 1114 (1983), the court imposed a public reprimand on a county prosecutor who improperly placed his supervisor's signature on forms filed in plea bargaining cases. The lawyer stated that he believed he had explicit or implicit authority to sign what he thought were internal records and the disciplinary committee found that the lawyer "was not motivated by personal gain but only by a desire to move cases on his trial list" (455 A.2d at 1116). Similarly, in *State v. Socolofsky,* 233 Kan. 1020, 666 P.2d 725 (1983), the court imposed a public censure [reprimand] on a county attorney who anonymously mailed to discharged members of a jury a copy of a newspaper article describing that the acquitted defendant had subsequently pled guilty to a misdemeanor charge of delivery of L.S.D. in an unrelated case. Some of the jurors who received the mailing were called for service only a month later. The lawyer testified that he would not have mailed the article had he realized that the jurors were to be called for further service, and, that in his experience as a prosecutor, "he had never seen jurors called back for further duty so soon" (666 P.2d at 726).

5.24 **Admonition is generally appropriate when a lawyer in an official or governmental position engages in an isolated instance of negligence in not following proper procedures or rules, and causes little or no actual or potential injury to a party or to the integrity of the legal process.**

6.0 Violations of Duties Owed to the Legal System

Introduction

Lawyers are officers of the court, and the public expects lawyers to abide by the legal rules of substance and procedure which affect the administration of justice. Lawyers must always operate within the bounds of the law, and cannot create or use false evidence, or make false statement of material fact [Rules 3.3, 3.4, and 4.1/DR 7–102(A)]. Ethical standards require that a lawyer refrain from filing frivolous suits (Rule 3.1/DR 7–102), delaying a trial (Rule 3.2/DR 7–102), improperly communicating with a party, juror, witness, or judge (Rules 3.5, 4.2, 4.3/DR 7–104, DR 7–108 through DR 7–110), threatening criminal prosecution (DR 7–105), or otherwise interfering with a legal process (Rules 3.4, 3.6, 4.1, 4.4/DR 7–106 and DR 7–107).

6.1 False Statements, Fraud, and Misrepresentation

Absent aggravating or mitigating circumstances, upon application of the factors set out in Standard 3.0, the following sanctions are generally appropriate in cases involving conduct that is prejudicial to the administration of justice or that involves dishonesty, fraud, deceit, or misrepresentation to a court:

6.11 **Disbarment is generally appropriate when a lawyer, with the intent to deceive the court, makes a false statement, submits a false document, or improperly withholds material information, and causes serious or potentially serious injury to a party, or causes a significant or potentially significant adverse effect on the legal proceeding.**

Commentary

The lawyers who engage in these practices violate the most fundamental duty of an officer of the court. As the court noted in a case in which a criminal defense lawyer was disbarred for putting a client on the stand to testify falsely, "A lawyer's participation in the presentation of knowing false evidence is the clearest kind of ethical breach" [*Board of Overseers of the Bar v. James Dineen*, No. 83–46 (Maine 1983) at 4]. In *Office of Disciplinary Counsel v. Grigsby*, 493 Pa. 194, 425 A.2d 730 (1981), a lawyer was disbarred where he filed a false sworn pleading in connection with a pending garnishment proceeding. The pleading stated that the funds in the lawyer's checking account be-

763

longed to clients and could not be reached. The lawyer's action to save his money from garnishment was both intentional and damaging to his creditors. Similarly, in *Matter of Discipline of Agnew,* 311 N.W.2d 869 (Minn.1981), the court disbarred a lawyer who refused to return a client's documents after an initial consultation and, without the client's knowledge or consent, then instituted a suit on his behalf in which he made false allegations that the client had been harmed by the defendant. Because of the lawyer's actions, the client incurred legal bills of $8,000 and lost time appearing in court to obtain his own documents.

> **6.12 Suspension is generally appropriate when a lawyer knows that false statements or documents are being submitted to the court or that material information is improperly being withheld, and takes no remedial action, and causes injury or potential injury to a party to the legal proceeding, or causes an adverse or potentially adverse effect on the legal proceeding.**

Commentary

Suspension is appropriate when a lawyer has not acted with intent to deceive the court, but when he knows that material information is being withheld and does not inform the court, with the result that there is injury or potential injury to a party, or an adverse or potentially adverse effect on the legal proceeding. For example, in *In re Nigohosian,* 88 N.J. 308, 442 A.2d 1007 (1982), the court suspended a lawyer for six months when he failed to disclose to the court or to opposing counsel the fact that he had previously conveyed property that was the subject of a settlement to someone else. The court noted that, while a lawyer does not have a continuing obligation to inform the court of the state of a client's assets, he "has a duty of disclosure of any significant fact" touching upon the status of an asset which is the subject matter of a stipulation before the court (442 A.2d at 1009).

> **6.13 Reprimand is generally appropriate when a lawyer is negligent either in determining whether statements or documents are false or in taking remedial action when material information is being withheld, and causes injury or potential injury to a party to the legal proceeding, or causes an adverse or potentially adverse effect on the legal proceeding.**

Commentary

Reprimand is appropriate when a lawyer is merely negligent. For example, in *Gilbert E. Meltry,* D.P. 144/81 (Mich.Atty.Dis.Brd.1981), the lawyer was publicly reprimanded where he accidentally filed a motion for a bond which contained inaccurate statements. Similarly, in *In re Coughlin,* 91 N.J. 374, 450 A.2d 1326 (1982), the court held that a public reprimand should be imposed on a lawyer who did not follow proper procedures in acknowledging a deed (neglecting to secure the grantor's acknowledgement in his presence). The court noted that "his actions were not grounded on any intent of self-benefit, nor was any one harmed as a result of his actions" (450 A.2d at 1327). In *Davidson v. State Bar,* 17 Cal.3d 570, 551 P.2d 1211, 131 Cal.Rptr. 379 (1976), the court imposed a public reprimand on a lawyer who failed to disclose to the court the location of his client in a child custody case when his conduct occurred in confused circumstances caused by contradictory *ex parte* custody orders.

> **6.14 Admonition is generally appropriate when a lawyer engages in an isolated instance of neglect in determining whether submitted statements or documents are false or in failing to disclose material information upon learning of its falsity, and causes little or no actual or potential injury to a party, or causes little or no adverse or potentially adverse effect on the legal proceeding.**

6.2 Abuse of the Legal Process

Absent aggravating or mitigating circumstances, upon application of the factors set out in Standard 3.0, the following sanctions are generally appropriate in cases involving failure to expedite litigation or bring a meritorious claim, or failure to obey any obligation under the rules of a tribunal except for an open refusal based on an assertion that no valid obligation exists:

> **6.21 Disbarment is generally appropriate when a lawyer knowingly violates a court order or rule with the intent to obtain a benefit for the lawyer or another, and causes serious injury or potentially serious injury to a party, or causes serious or potentially serious interference with a legal proceeding.**

Commentary

Lawyers should be disbarred for intentionally misusing the judicial process to benefit the lawyer or another when the lawyer's conduct causes injury or potentially serious injury to a party, or serious or potentially serious interference with a legal proceeding. For example, in *In the Matter of Daniel Friedland,* 416 N.E.2d 433 (Ind.1981), the lawyer filed charges against members of the Disciplinary Committee and witnesses in the lawyer disciplinary hearing. The lawyer attempted to use the lawsuit to intimidate and discredit those who administered and prosecuted grievances against him. In holding that the lawyer was not protected by the First Amendment, the court recognized the harm to judicial integrity. "It is the Constitutional duty of this Court, on behalf of sovereign interest, to preserve, manage, and safeguard the adjudicatory system of this State. The adjudicatory process cannot function when its officers misconstrue the purpose of litigation. The respondent attempted to influence the process through the use of threats and intimidation against the participants involved. This type of conduct must be enjoined to preserve the integrity of the system. The adjudicatory process, including disciplinary proceedings, must permit the orderly resolution of issues; Respondent's conduct impeded the order of this process" (416 N.E.2d at 438). See also: *In re Crumpacker*, 269 Ind. 630, 383 N.E.2d 36 (1978), where the court disbarred a lawyer who had engaged in nineteen acts of misconduct, including shouting at and verbally abusing witnesses and opposing counsel, taking an action merely to harass another, and generally using offensive tactics. In the words of the court, his misconduct showed that he was "a vicious, sinister person, tunnel-visioned by personal pique, willing to forego all professional responsibilities which conflict with acts of preconceived vengeance on personal enemies" (383 N.E.2d at 52).

> **6.22 Suspension is appropriate when a lawyer knows that he is violating a court order or rule, and there is injury or potential injury to a client or a party, or interference or potential interference with a legal proceeding.**

Commentary

In many cases, lawyers are suspended when they knowingly violate court orders. Such knowing violations can occur when a lawyer fails to comply with a court order that applies directly to him or her, as in the case of lawyers who do not comply with a divorce decree ordering spousal maintenance or child support. Suspension is also appropriate where the lawyer interferes directly with the legal process. For example, in *In re Vincenti*, 92 N.J. 591, 458 A.2d 1268 (1983), the court imposed a suspension for one year and until further order of court where the lawyer made repeated discourteous, insulting and degrading verbal attacks on the judge and his rulings which substantially interfered with the orderly trial process. The court noted that it was not confronted with "an isolated example of loss of composure brought on by the emotion of the moment; rather, the numerous instances of impropriety pervaded the proceedings over a period of three months" (458 A.2d at 1274).

> **6.23 Reprimand is generally appropriate when a lawyer negligently fails to comply with a court order or rule, and causes injury or potential injury to a client or other party, or causes interference or potential interference with a legal proceeding.**

Commentary

Most courts impose a reprimand on lawyers who engage in misconduct at trial or who violate a court order or rule that causes injury or potential injury to a client or other party, or who cause interference or potential interference with a legal proceeding. For example, in *McDaniel v. State of Arkansas,* 640 S.W.2d 442 (Ark.1982), a lawyer who failed to file briefs in a timely manner after having been given extensions received a reprimand. In *Florida Bar v. Rosenberg,* 387 So.2d 935 (Fla.1980), the court imposed a reprimand on a lawyer who used harassing delay tactics at trial and who also refused to send copies of documents to opposing counsel. Courts also impose reprimands when lawyers neglect to respond to orders of the disciplinary agency. For example, in *In re Minor,* 658 P.2d 781 (Alaska 1983), the court imposed a public censure [reprimand] on a lawyer who, because of poor office procedures, neglected to respond to a letter from the Alaska Bar Association.

    6.24 Admonition is generally appropriate when a lawyer engages in an isolated instance of negligence in complying with a court order or rule, and causes little or no actual or potential injury to a party, or causes little or no actual or potential interference with a legal proceeding.

6.3 Improper Communications With Individuals in the Legal System

Absent aggravating or mitigating circumstances, upon application of the factors set out in Standard 3.0, the following sanctions are generally appropriate in cases involving attempts to influence a judge, juror, prospective juror or other official by means prohibited by law:

    6.31 Disbarment is generally appropriate when a lawyer:

       (a) intentionally tampers with a witness and causes serious or potentially serious injury to a party, or causes significant or potentially significant interference with the outcome of the legal proceeding; or

       (b) makes an ex parte communication with a judge or juror with intent to affect the outcome of the proceeding, and causes serious or potentially serious injury to a party, or causes significant or potentially significant interference with the outcome of the legal proceeding; or

       (c) improperly communicates with someone in the legal system other than a witness, judge, or juror with the intent to influence or affect the outcome of the proceeding, and causes significant or potentially significant interference with the outcome of the legal proceeding.

Commentary

Disbarment is warranted in cases where the lawyer uses fraud or undue influence to injure a party or to affect the outcome of a legal proceeding. For example, in *In the Matter of Stroh,* 97 Wash.2d 289, 644 P.2d 1161 (1982), a lawyer was disbarred when he was convicted of tampering with a witness. The court justified imposing disbarment on the following basis: "First, the crime of tampering with a witness strikes at the very core of the judicial system and therefore necessarily involves moral turpitude. . . . An attorney presents his case almost entirely through the testimony of witnesses. Although an occasional witness may perjure him/herself, the presentation of the opponent's other witnesses and effective cross-examination frequently reveals the falsehood before a fraud has been perpetrated upon the court. A witness, tampered by an attorney, however, becomes much more destructive to the search for truth. That witness, privy to the testimony of other witnesses, can avoid the pitfalls of contradiction and refutation by judicious fabrication. Vigorous cross-examination may become ineffective as the coached witness would know both the questions and the proper answers. In sum, the legal system is virtually defenseless against the united forces of a corrupt attorney and a perjured witness" (644 P.2d at 1165). Similarly, in *Matter of Holman,* 286 S.E.2d 148 (S.C.1982), a lawyer was disbarred who was convicted of contempt of court based on a communication with a member of a jury selected for trial.

6.32 Suspension is generally appropriate when a lawyer engages in communication with an individual in the legal system when the lawyer knows that such communication is improper, and causes injury or potential injury to a party or causes interference or potential interference with the outcome of the legal proceeding.

Commentary

In the case of *John Arnold Fitzgerald* (Tenn.1980) (unpublished decision), a lawyer was suspended for one year for threats to an opposing party. Similarly, in *The Florida Bar v. Lopez,* 406 So.2d 1100 (Fla.1982), a lawyer was suspended for one year where he urged two parties he was suing on behalf of his client to change their testimony in exchange for general releases from prosecution. In imposing this sanction, the court rejected a referee's recommendation of a three-month suspension with automatic reinstatement, stating, "we feel that a three-month suspension is insufficient to impress upon respondent, the bar, and the public our dissatisfaction with and distress over his conduct. If Mr. Lopez had been convicted in a court of this state of tampering with a witness, he would have been subject to a one-year term of imprisonment. Using the witness-tampering statute as a guideline, we find a one-year suspension appropriate in this case" (406

So.2d at 1102). In *The Florida Bar v. Mason*, 334 So.2d 1 (Fla.1976), the court imposed a reprimand and suspension for one year and until proof of rehabilitation when a lawyer engaged in ex parte communications with justices of the Florida Supreme Court concerning the merits of a pending case and subsequently concealed his actions from opposing counsel.

> **6.33 Reprimand is generally appropriate when a lawyer is negligent in determining whether it is proper to engage in communication with an individual in the legal system, and causes injury or potential injury to a party or interference or potential interference with the outcome of the legal proceeding.**

Commentary

Most courts impose reprimands on lawyers who engage in improper communications. For example, in *In re McCaffrey*, 549 P.2d 666 (Or. 1976), the court imposed a reprimand on a lawyer who unknowingly improperly communicated with a party represented by a lawyer. Even though the lawyer claimed that he thought the party, the husband in a dispute of visitation, was representing himself, the court stated that discipline could be imposed in cases of misconduct that the rule is designed to prevent, and it is "immaterial whether the communication is an intentional or a negligent violation of the rule" (549 P.2d at 668).

> **6.34 Admonition is generally appropriate when a lawyer engages in an isolated instance of negligence in improperly communicating with an individual in the legal system, and causes little or no actual or potential injury to a party, or causes little or no actual or potential interference with the outcome of the legal proceeding.**

7.0 Violations of Duties Owed to the Profession

Introduction

The Model Rules include many ethical standards that are not fundamental to the professional relationship but which define certain standards of conduct. These standards concern restrictions on advertising (Rules 7.1, 7.2, 7.4, 7.5/DR 2–101, DR 2–102, DR 2–105), recommending employment (Rule 7.3/DR 2–103, DR 2–104), fees (Rules 1.5, 5.4 and 5.6/DR 2–106, DR 2–107 and DR 3–102), and assisting unauthorized practice (Rule 5.5/DR 3–101 and DR 3–103). Other such standards include the duty to comply with proper procedures for admission to the bar (Rule 8.1/DR 1–101), to report other lawyers who engage in unethical behavior (Rule 8.3/DR 1–103), and to properly withdraw from representation (Rule 1.16/DR 2–110).

While these standards have been developed out of a desire to protect the public, such as by restricting practice to those persons who have met appropriate educational requirements, a violation of these standards generally is less likely to cause injury to a client, the public, or the administration of justice than the other standards discussed above. In fact, in the area of advertising, the United States Supreme Court has ruled that lawyer advertising is protected by the First Amendment and has struck down certain ethical prohibitions on advertising [see *Bates v. State Bar of Arizona,* 433 U.S. 350, 97 S.Ct. 2691, 53 L.Ed.2d 810 (1977); *In re R.M.J.,* 455 U.S. 191, 102 S.Ct. 929, 71 L.Ed.2d 64 (1982); *Zauderer v. Office of Disciplinary Counsel of the Supreme Court of Ohio,* 53 U.S.L.W. 4587, decided May 28, 1985].

In general, then, a sanction of disbarment or suspension will rarely be required, and a sanction of reprimand, admonition or probation will be sufficient to insure that the public is protected and the bar is educated. While it will as a rule be inappropriate to impose a sanction of disbarment or suspension for six months or more, there are situations when a more severe sanction should be imposed. The standards set out below identify those exceptional situations.

Absent aggravating or mitigating circumstances, upon application of the factors set out in Standard 3.0, the following sanctions are generally appropriate in cases involving false or misleading communication about the lawyer or the lawyer's services, improper communication of fields of practice, improper solicitation of professional employment from a prospective client, unreasonable or improper fees, unauthorized practice of law, improper withdrawal from representation, or failure to report professional misconduct.

> 7.1 **Disbarment is generally appropriate when a lawyer knowingly engages in conduct that is a violation of a duty owed as a professional with the intent to obtain a benefit for the lawyer or another, and causes serious or potentially serious injury to a client, the public, or the legal system.**

Commentary

Disbarment should be imposed in cases when the lawyer knowingly engages in conduct that violates a duty owed to the profession with the intent to benefit the lawyer or another, and which causes serious injury or potentially serious injury to a client, the public or the legal system. For example, disbarment is appropriate when a lawyer intentionally makes false material statements in his application for admission to the bar. For example, in *In re W. Jason Mitan,* 75 Ill.2d 118, 387 N.E.2d 278 (1979), *cert. denied,* 444 U.S. 916 (1979), the respondent made false statements and deliberately failed to disclose certain information on his application for admission to the bar. These false statements and omissions included his failure to disclose at least four of his previous addresses, the wrong birth date, his change of name, a previous marriage, a subsequent divorce, other law schools attended, application for admission to another state's bar, previous employers and occupations, prior civil suits and arrests, and conviction of a felony. The court felt that these falsehoods and omissions had a direct effect on the ability to practice law and be a competent member of the profession, and imposed disbarment.

7.2 Suspension is generally appropriate when a lawyer knowingly engages in conduct that is a violation of a duty owed as a professional, and causes injury or potential injury to a client, the public, or the legal system.

Commentary

Suspension is appropriate when the lawyer knowingly violates a duty owed to the profession and causes injury or potential injury to a client, the public, or the legal system, even when a lawyer does not intentionally abuse the professional relationship by engaging in deceptive conduct. Suspension is appropriate, for example, when the lawyer did not mislead a client but engages in a pattern of charging excessive or improper fees. A suspension is also appropriate when a lawyer solicits employment knowing that the individual is in a vulnerable state. For example, in *In re Teichner*, 75 Ill.2d 88, 387 N.E.2d 265 (1979), the court suspended a lawyer for two years who was invited by a minister to speak to victims of a railway disaster, but who then contacted victims whom he knew were still in a vulnerable state as a result of the tragedy.

7.3 Reprimand is generally appropriate when a lawyer negligently engages in conduct that is a violation of a duty owed as a professional, and causes injury or potential injury to a client, the public, or the legal system.

Commentary

Reprimand is the appropriate sanction in most cases of a violation of a duty owed to the profession. Usually there is little or no injury to a client, the public, or the legal system, and the purposes of lawyer discipline will be best served by imposing a public sanction that helps educate the respondent lawyer and deter future violations. A public sanction also informs both the public and other members of the profession that this behavior is improper. For example, in *Carter v. Falcarelli*, 402 A.2d 1175 (R.I. 1979), the court imposed public censure (reprimand) on a lawyer who failed to divulge the identity of another lawyer when matters had been forwarded and subsequently neglected.

Courts typically impose reprimands when lawyers engage in a single instance of charging an excessive or improper fee. See *In the Matter of Donald L. Fasig*, 444 N.E.2d 849 (Ind.1983), where the court imposed a public reprimand when the lawyer entered into an agreement for a contingent fee in a criminal case; *Russell J. Perry*, DP 63 (Mich.Atty.Dis.Board, 1983), where a lawyer charged an excessive fee by improperly adding investigation costs; and *The Florida Bar v. Sagrans*, 388 So.2d 1040 (Fla.1980), where the lawyer improperly split fees with a chiropractor.

Courts also impose reprimands on lawyers who are negligent in supervising their employees. For example, in the case of *Donald Franklin Kotter*, 52 Calif.State Bar J. 552–3 (Cal.1977), the court imposed a public reproval (reprimand) on a lawyer who neglected properly to instruct his employees regarding what acts constitute solicitation.

> **7.4 Admonition is generally appropriate when a lawyer engages in an isolated instance of negligence that is a violation of a duty owed as a professional, and causes little or no actual or potential injury to a client, the public, or the legal system.**

8.0 Prior Discipline Orders

Introduction

Severe sanctions should be imposed on lawyers who violate the terms of prior disciplinary orders. While such lawyers may also demonstrate a pattern of misconduct that will serve as an aggravating factor (see Standard 9.22), these violations are so serious as to warrant special discussion.

Absent aggravating or mitigating circumstances, upon application of the factors set out in Standard 3.0, the following sanctions are generally appropriate in cases involving prior discipline.

> **8.1 Disbarment is generally appropriate when a lawyer:**
>
> **(a) intentionally or knowingly violates the terms of a prior disciplinary order and such violation causes injury or potential injury to a client, the public, the legal system, or the profession; or**
>
> **(b) has been suspended for the same or similar misconduct, and intentionally or knowingly engages in further acts of misconduct that cause injury or potential injury to a client, the public, the legal system, or the profession.**

Commentary

Disbarment is warranted when a lawyer who has previously been disciplined intentionally or knowingly violates the terms of that order and, as a result, causes injury or potential injury to a client, the public, the legal system, or the profession. The most common case is one where a lawyer has been suspended but, nevertheless, practices law. The courts are generally in agreement in imposing disbarment in such cases. As the court explained in *Matter of McInerney*, 389 Mass. 528, 451 N.E.2d 401, 405 (1983), when the record establishes a lawyer's willingness to violate the terms of his suspension order, disbarment is appropriate "as a prophylactic measure to prevent further misconduct by the offending individual." See also: *In re Reiser*, M.R. 2269 (Ill. 1980), where a lawyer was disbarred when he continued to practice law in violation of an order of suspension and caused serious injury to a client by neglecting her legal matter.

Disbarment is also appropriate when a lawyer intentionally or knowingly engages in the same or similar misconduct. For example, in *Benson v. State Bar*, 13 Cal.3d 581, 531 P.2d 1081, 119 Cal.Rptr. 297 (1975), the court disbarred a lawyer who induced a client to loan him money by making false representations and who then failed to repay the loan. The lawyer in that case had previously been suspended for one year (with a four-year probationary period) for misappropriation of client funds. See also: *Matter of Friedland*, 416 N.E.2d 433 (Ind.1981).

8.2   Suspension is generally appropriate when a lawyer has been reprimanded for the same or similar misconduct and engages in further acts of misconduct that cause injury or potential injury to a client, the public, the legal system, or the profession.

Commentary

Lawyers should be suspended when they engage in the same or similar misconduct for which they were previously disciplined when that misconduct causes injury or potential injury to a client, the public, the legal system, or the profession. As the court noted in *The Florida Bar v. Glick*, 397 So.2d 1140, 1141 (Fla.1981), "[W]e must deal more severely with an attorney who exhibits cumulative misconduct."

8.3   Reprimand is generally appropriate when a lawyer:

(a)   negligently violates the terms of a prior disciplinary order and such violation causes injury or potential injury to a client, the public, the legal system, or the profession; or

(b)   has received an admonition for the same or similar misconduct and engages in further acts of misconduct that cause injury or potential injury to a client, the public, the legal system, or the profession.

Commentary

Reprimands are most commonly imposed on lawyers who have been disciplined and engage in the same or similar acts of misconduct. For example, in *Shalant v. State Bar of California*, 33 Cal.3d 485, 658 P.2d 737, 189 Cal.Rptr. 374 (1983), the court imposed a public reproval [reprimand] on a lawyer who failed to communicate with a client and who had received a private reproval for the same misconduct. See also: *Matter of Davis,* 280 S.E.2d 644 (S.C.1981), where the court explained that a reprimand for neglect was necessary because prior warnings for similar behavior were "ignored" (280 S.E.2d at 647).

8.4 An admonition is generally not an appropriate sanction when a lawyer violates the terms of a prior disciplinary order or when a lawyer has engaged in the same or similar misconduct in the past.

Commentary

An admonition is a sanction which should only be imposed in cases of minor misconduct, where the lawyer's acts cause little or no injury to a client, the public, the legal system, or the profession, and where the lawyer is unlikely to engage in further misconduct. Lawyers who do engage in additional similar acts of misconduct, or who violate the terms of a prior disciplinary order, have obviously not been deterred, and a more severe sanction should be imposed.

9.0 Aggravation and Mitigation

9.1 Generally

After misconduct has been established, aggravating and mitigating circumstances may be considered in deciding what sanction to impose.

Commentary

Each disciplinary case involves unique facts and circumstances. In striving for fair disciplinary sanctions, consideration must necessarily be given to the facts pertaining to the professional misconduct and to any aggravating or mitigating factors (see Standards for Lawyer Discipline, Standard 7.1). Aggravating and mitigating circumstances generally relate to the offense at issue, matters independent of the specific offense but relevant to fitness to practice, or matters arising incident to the disciplinary proceeding.

9.2 Aggravation

9.21 *Definition.* Aggravation or aggravating circumstances are any considerations, or factors that may justify an increase in the degree of discipline to be imposed.

9.22 *Factors which may be considered in aggravation.* Aggravating factors include:

(a) **prior disciplinary offenses;**

(b) **dishonest or selfish motive;**

(c) **a pattern of misconduct;**

(d) **multiple offenses;**

774

(e) **bad faith obstruction of the disciplinary proceeding by intentionally failing to comply with rules or orders of the disciplinary agency;**

(f) **submission of false evidence, false statements, or other deceptive practices during the disciplinary process;**

(g) **refusal to acknowledge wrongful nature of conduct;**

(h) **vulnerability of victim;**

(i) **substantial experience in the practice of law;**

(j) **indifference to making restitution.**

(k) **illegal conduct, including that involving the case of controlled substances.**

Commentary

Cases citing each of the factors listed above include: (a) prior disciplinary offenses: *Matter of Walton*, 251 N.W.2d 762 (N.D.1977); *People v. Vernon*, 660 P.2d 879 (Colo.1982); (b) dishonest or selfish motive: *In re: James H. Dineen*, SJC–535 (Maine 1980); (c) pattern of misconduct: *The Florida Bar v. Mavrides*, 442 So.2d 220 (Fla.1983); *State v. Dixon*, 233 Kan. 465, 664 P.2d 286 (1983); (d) multiple offenses: *State ex rel. Oklahoma Bar Association v. Warzya*, 624 P.2d 1068 (Okla. 1981); *Ballard v. State Bar of California*, 35 Cal.3d 274, 673 P.2d 226, 197 Cal.Rptr. 556 (1983); (e) bad faith obstruction of disciplinary proceedings: *In re Brody*, 65 Ill.2d 152, 357 N.E.2d 498 (1976); *Committee on Prof. Ethics v. Brodsky*, 318 N.W.2d 180 (Iowa 1982); (f) lack of candor during the disciplinary process: *In re Stillo*, 68 Ill.2d 49, 368 N.E.2d 897 (1977); *Weir v. State Bar*, 23 Cal.3d 564, 591 P.2d 19, 152 Cal.Rptr. 921 (1979); (g) refusal to acknowledge wrongful nature of conduct: *Greenbaum v. State Bar*, 18 Cal.3d 893, 544 P.2d 921, 126 Cal. Rptr. 785 (1976); *H. Parker Stanley v. Bd. of Professional Responsibility*, 640 S.W.2d 210 (Tenn.1982); (h) vulnerability of victim: *People v. Lanza*, 613 P.2d 337 (Colo.1980); (i) substantial experience in the practice of law: *John F. Buckley*, 2 Mass.Atty.Dis.Rpt. 24 (1980); (j) indifference to making restitution: *The Florida Bar v. Zinzell*, 387 So. 2d 346 (Fla.1980); *Bate v. State Bar of California*, 34 Cal.3d 920, 671 P.2d 360, 196 Cal.Rptr. 209 (1983).

9.3 Mitigation

9.31 *Definition.* **Mitigation or mitigating circumstances are any considerations or factors that may justify a reduction in the degree of discipline to be imposed.**

9.32 *Factors which may be considered in mitigation.* **Mitigating factors include:**

(a) **absence of a prior disciplinary record;**

(b) **absence of a dishonest or selfish motive;**

775

(c) personal or emotional problems;

(d) timely good faith effort to make restitution or to rectify consequences of misconduct;

(e) full and free disclosure to disciplinary board or cooperative attitude toward proceedings;

(f) inexperience in the practice of law;

(g) character or reputation;

(h) physical disability;

(i) mental disability or chemical dependency including alcoholism or drug abuse when:

    (1) there is medical evidence that the respondent is affected by a chemical dependency or mental disability;

    (2) the chemical dependency or mental disability caused the misconduct;

    (3) the respondent's recovery from the chemical dependency or mental disability is demonstrated by a meaningful and sustained period of successful rehabilitation; and

    (4) the recovery arrested the misconduct and recurrence of that misconduct is unlikely.

(j) delay in disciplinary proceedings;

(k) imposition of other penalties or sanctions;

(l) remorse;

(m) remoteness of prior offenses.

Commentary

While the courts generally agree that each of these factors can be considered in mitigation, the courts differ on whether restitution is a mitigating factor. Some courts hold that restitution should not be considered. See *Ambrose v. State Bar,* 31 Cal.3d 184, 643 P.2d 486, 481 Cal.Rptr. 903 (1982); *Oklahoma Bar Association v. Lowe,* 640 P.2d 1361 (Okla.1982); *In re Galloway,* 300 S.E.2d 479 (S.C.1983). Other courts do consider restitution. See *People v. Luxford,* 626 P.2d 675 (Colo.1981); *The Florida Bar v. Pincket,* 398 So.2d 802 (Fla.1980); *In re Suernick,* 100 Wis.2d 427, 321 N.W.2d 298 (1982). While restitution should not be a complete defense to a charge of misconduct, the better policy is to allow a good faith effort to make restitution to be considered as a factor in mitigation. Such a policy will encourage lawyers to make restitution, reducing the degree of injury to the client and helping insure that the lawyer has recognized the wrongfulness of his conduct. Restitution which is made upon the lawyer's own initiative should be considered as mitigating; lawyers who make restitution prior to the initiation of disciplinary proceedings present the best case for mitigation, while lawyers who make restitution later in the proceedings present a weaker case.

Cases citing personal and emotional problems as mitigating factors include a wide range of difficulties, most often involving marital or financial problems. The factor which has been treated most inconsistently by the courts is (h): physical/mental disability or impairment. The cases include the following types of behaviors or conditions: alcoholism, *The Florida Bar v. Ullensvang,* 400 So.2d 969 (Fla.1981); mental disorders, *In re Weyrich,* 339 N.W.2d 274 (Minn. 1983); drug abuse, *In re Maragos,* 285 N.E.2d 541 (N.D.1979); and senility, *In re Hansen,* 318 N.W.2d 856 (Minn.1982). While most courts treat such disabilities or impairments as mitigating factors, it is important to note that the consideration of these factors does not completely excuse the lawyer's misconduct. In the words of the Illinois Supreme Court, "alcoholism is at most an extenuating circumstance, a mitigating fact, not an excuse." *In re Driscoll,* 85 Ill.2d 312, 423 N.E.2d 873, 874 (1981).

Cases citing each of the factors listed above include: (a) absence of a prior disciplinary record: *In re Battin,* 617 P.2d 1109, 168 Cal.Rptr. 477 (1980); *The Florida Bar v. Shannon,* 398 So.2d 453 (Fla.1981); (b) absence of selfish or dishonest motive: *People ex rel. Goldberg v. Gordon,* 607 P.2d 995 (Colo.1980); (c) personal/emotional problems: *In re Stout,* 75 N.J. 321, 382 A.2d 630 (1981); *Matter of Barron,* 246 Ga. 327, 271 S.E.2d 474 (1980); (d) timely good faith effort to make restitution or to rectify consequences of misconduct: *Matter of Byars,* 268 S.E.2d 155 (Ga.1980); *Matter of Rubi,* 133 Ariz. 491, 652 P.2d 1014 (1982); (e) full and free disclosure to disciplinary board/cooperative attitude toward proceedings: *Matter of Shaw,* 298 N.W.2d 133 (Minn. 1980); *In the Matter of Rhame,* 416 N.E.2d 823 (Ind.1981); (f) inexperience in the practice of law: *In re: James M. Pool,* No. 83–37 BD (Sup. Jud.Ct.Suffolk Cty., Mass.1984); *Matter of Price,* 429 N.E.2d 961 (Ind. 1982); (g) character/reputation: *Matter of Shaw,* 298 N.W.2d 133 (Minn.1980); *In re Bizar,* 97 Ill.2d 127, 454 N.E.2d 271 (1983); (h) physical/mental disability or impairment: *The Florida Bar v. Routh,* 414 So.2d 1023 (1982); *In re Hopper,* 85 Ill.2d 318, 423 N.E.2d 900 (1981); (i) delay in disciplinary proceedings: *Yokozeki v. State Bar,* 11 Cal.3d 436, 521 P.2d 858, 113 Cal.Rptr. 602 (1974); *The Florida Bar v. Thomson,* 429 So.2d 2 (Fla.1983); (j) interim rehabilitation: *In re Barry,* 90 N.J. 286, 447 A.2d 923 (1982); *Tenner v. State Bar of California,* 617 P.2d 486, 168 Cal.Rptr. 333 (1980); (k) imposition of other penalties or sanctions: *In re Lamberis,* 93 Ill.2d 222, 443 N.E.2d 549 (1982); *In re: John E. Walsh,* SJC—53.9 (Maine 1980); *Matter of Garrett,* 399 N.E.2d 369 (Ind.1980); (*l*) remorse: *In re Power,* 91 N.J. 408, 451 A.2d 666 (1982); *In re Nadler,* 91 Ill.2d 326, 438 N.E.2d 198 (1982); (m) remoteness of prior offenses: (no cases found).

9.4 Factors Which Are Neither Aggravating Nor Mitigating

The following factors should not be considered as either aggravating or mitigating:

(a) forced or compelled restitution;

(b) agreeing to the client's demand for certain improper behavior or result;

(c) withdrawal of complaint against the lawyer;

(d) resignation prior to completion of disciplinary proceedings;

(e) complainant's recommendation as to sanction;

(f) failure of injured client to complain.

Commentary

While courts have considered each of these factors, the purposes of lawyer discipline are best served by viewing them as irrelevant to the imposition of a sanction. Lawyers who make restitution voluntarily and on their own initiative demonstrate both a recognition of their ethical violation and their responsibility to the injured client or other party. Such conduct should be considered as mitigation (see Standard 8.32), even if the restitution is made in response to a complaint filed with the disciplinary agency. Lawyers who make restitution only after a disciplinary proceeding has been instituted against them, however, cannot be regarded as acting out of a sense of responsibility for their misconduct, but, instead, as attempting to circumvent the operation of the disciplinary system. Such conduct should not be considered in mitigation. See *Fitzpatrick v. State Bar of California,* 20 Cal.3d 73, 141 Cal.Rptr. 169, 569 P.2d 763 (1977); *In re O'Bryant,* 425 A.2d 1313 (D.C.1981).

Similarly, mitigation should not include a lawyer's claim that "the client made me do it". Each lawyer is reponsible for adhering to the ethical standards of the profession. Unethical conduct is much less likely to be deterred if lawyers can lessen or avoid the imposition of sanctions merely by blaming the client (see *In re Price,* 429 N.E.2d 961 (Ind.1982); *People v. Kennelly,* 648 P.2d 1065 (Colo.1982). In addition, neither the withdrawal of the complaint against the lawyer nor the lawyer's resignation prior to completion of disciplinary proceedings should mitigate the sanction imposed. In order for the public to be protected, sanctions must be imposed on lawyers who engage in unethical conduct. The mere fact that a complainant may have decided to withdraw a complaint should not result in a lesser sanction being imposed on a lawyer who has behaved unethically and from whom other members of the public need protection (see *In re McWhorter,* 405 Mich. 563, 275 N.W.2d 259 (1979), *on reh'g,* 407 Mich. 278, 284 N.W.2d 472 (1979)). Similarly, the lawyer's resignation is irrelevant; the purposes of deterrence and education can only be served if sanctions are imposed on all lawyers who violate ethical standards (see *In re Johnson,* 290 N.W.2d 604 (Minn.1980) and *In re Phillips,* 452 A.2d 345 (D.C.1982)).

The complainant's recommendation as to a sanction is a factor which should be neither aggravating nor mitigating. The consistency of sanctions cannot be assured if any individual's personal views concerning an appropriate sanction can either increase or decrease the severity of the sanction to be imposed by the court. Although the court should not consider the complainant's recommendation as to sanction, the complainant's feelings about the lawyer's misconduct need not be completely ignored. The complainant's views will be relevant and important in determining the amount of injury caused by the lawyer's misconduct, a factor which can be either aggravating [Standard 8.22(j)] or mitigating [Standard 8.32(i)].

Finally, the fact that an injured client has not complained should not serve as mitigation. The disciplinary system is designed to protect all members of the public. The fact that one injured person is willing to forgive and forget should not relieve or excuse the lawyer, who then has the capability of injuring others (see *In re Krakauer,* 81 N.J. 32, 404 A.2d 1137 (1979); *State ex rel. Oklahoma Bar Association v. Braswell,* 663 P.2d 1228 (Okla.1983)).

APPENDIX 1

Cross-Reference Table: ABA Model Rules of Professional Conduct and Standards for Imposing Sanctions

ABA Model Rules of Professional Conduct	Standards for Imposing Sanctions
Competence	
Rule 1.1	Standard 4.5
Scope of Representation	
Rule 1.2(a), (b), (c), (e)	Standard 4.4
Rule 1.2(d)	Standard 6.1
Diligence	
Rule 1.3	Standard 4.4
Communication	
Rule 1.4	Standard 4.4
Fees	
Rule 1.5	Standards 4.6 & 7.0
Confidentiality of Information	
Rule 1.6	Standard 4.2
Conflict of Interest	
Rule 1.7	Standard 4.3
Prohibited Transactions	
Rule 1.8	Standard 4.3
Former Client	
Rule 1.9	Standard 4.3
Imputed Disqualification	
Rule 1.10	Standard 4.3
Successive Government and Private Employment	
Rule 1.11	Standard 4.3
Former Judge or Arbitrator	
Rule 1.12	Standard 4.3
Organization as Client	
Rule 1.13	Standard 4.3
Disabled Client	
Rule 1.14	Standard 7.0
Safekeeping Property	
Rule 1.15	Standard 4.1
Declining or Terminating Representation	
Rule 1.16	Standard 7.0
Advisor	
Rule 2.1	Standard 7.0
Intermediary	
Rule 2.2	Standard 4.3

APPENDIX 1

ABA Model Rules of Professional Conduct	Standards for Imposing Sanctions
Evaluation for Use by Third Persons	
Rule 2.3	Standard 7.0
Meritorious Claims and Contentions	
Rule 3.1	Standard 6.2
Expediting Litigation	
Rule 3.2	Standard 6.2
Candor Toward the Tribunal	
Rule 3.3	Standard 6.1
Fairness to Opposing Party and Counsel	
Rule 3.4	Standard 6.2
Impartiality and Decorum	
Rule 3.5	Standard 6.3
Trial Publicity	
Rule 3.6	Standard 6.2
Lawyer as Witness	
Rule 3.7	Standard 4.3
Special Responsibilities of a Prosecutor	
Rule 3.8	Standard 5.2
Advocate in Nonadjudicative Proceedings	
Rule 3.9	Standard 6.2
Truthfulness to Others	
Rule 4.1	Standard 6.1
Communication with Represented Persons	
Rule 4.2	Standard 6.3
Dealing with Unrepresented Persons	
Rule 4.3	Standard 6.3
Respect for Rights of Third Persons	
Rule 4.4	Standard 6.2
Responsibilities of a Partner or Supervisory Lawyer	
Rule 5.1	Standard 7.0
Responsibilities of a Subordinate Lawyer	
Rule 5.2	Standard 7.0
Responsibilities Regarding Nonlawyer Assistants	
Rule 5.3	Standard 7.0
Professional Independence of Lawyer	
Rule 5.4(a) & (b)	Standard 7.0
Rule 5.4(c)	Standard 4.3
Rule 5.4(d)	Standard 7.0
Unauthorized Practice of Law	
Rule 5.5	Standard 7.0
Restrictions on Right to Practice	
Rule 5.6	Standard 7.0

ABA Model Rules of Professional Conduct	*Standards for Imposing Sanctions*
Pro Bono Publico Service	
Rule 6.1	No Applicable Standard
Accepting Appointments	
Rule 6.2	Standard 7.0
Membership in Legal Services Organization	
Rule 6.3	Standard 4.3
Law Reform Activities Affecting Client Interests	
Rule 6.4	Standard 5.2
Communication Concerning Lawyer's Services	
Rule 7.1	Standard 7.0
Advertising	
Rule 7.2	Standard 7.0
Direct Contact with Prospective Clients	
Rule 7.3	Standard 7.0
Communication of Fields of Practice	
Rule 7.4	Standard 7.0
Firm Names and Letterheads	
Rule 7.5	Standard 7.0
Bar Admission and Disciplinary Matters	
Rule 8.1	Standards 5.1 & 7.0
Judges and Legal Officials	
Rule 8.2	Standard 6.1
Reporting Professional Misconduct	
Rule 8.3	Standard 7.0
Misconduct	
Rule 8.4(a)	Standards 4.0, 5.0, 6.0, & 7.0
Rule 8.4(b)	Standard 5.1
Rule 8.4(c)	Standards 4.6 & 5.1
Rule 8.4(d)	Standard 6.0
Rule 8.4(e) & (f)	Standard 6.2
Jurisdiction	
Rule 8.5	None

APPENDIX 2

Cross-Reference Table: ABA Code of Professional Responsibility and Standards for Imposing Sanctions

ABA Code of Professional Responsibility	*Standards for Imposing Sanctions*
Canon 1: Integrity of Profession	
DR 1–101	Standard 7.0
DR 1–102	Standards 4.6, 5.1, 6.2
DR 1–103	Standard 7.0
Canon 2: Making Counsel Available	
DR 2–101	Standard 7.0
DR 2–102	Standard 7.0
DR 2–103	Standard 7.0
DR 2–104	Standard 7.0
DR 2–105	Standard 7.0
DR 2–106	Standard 7.0
DR 2–107	Standard 7.0
DR 2–108	Standard 7.0
DR 2–109	Standard 7.0
DR 2–110	Standard 7.0
Canon 3: Unauthorized Practice	
DR 3–101(A)	Standard 7.0
DR 3–101(B)	Standard 8.0
DR 3–102	Standard 7.0
DR 3–103	Standard 7.0
Canon 4: Confidences and Secrets	
DR 4–101	Standard 4.2
Canon 5: Independent Judgment	
DR 5–101	Standard 4.3
DR 5–102	Standard 4.3
DR 5–103	Standard 4.3
DR 5–104	Standard 4.3
DR 5–105	Standard 4.3
DR 5–106	Standard 4.3
DR 5–107	Standard 4.3
Canon 6: Competence	
DR 6–101(A)(1) & (2)	Standard 4.5
DR 6–101(A)(3)	Standard 4.4
DR 6–102	Standard 4.3
Canon 7: Zealous Representation	
DR 7–101(A)(1) & (2)	Standard 4.4
DR 7–101(A)(3)	Standard 4.6

CROSS-REFERENCE TABLE

ABA Code of Professional Responsibility	Standards for Imposing Sanctions
DR 7–101(B)	Standard 7.0
DR 7–102	Standards 6.1 & 6.2
DR 7–103	Standard 5.2
DR 7–104	Standard 6.3
DR 7–105	Standard 6.2
DR 7–106	Standard 6.2
DR 7–107	Standard 6.2
DR 7–108	Standard 6.3
DR 7–109	Standard 6.3
DR 7–110	Standard 6.3

Canon 8: Improving the Legal System

DR 8–101	Standard 5.2
DR 8–102	Standard 5.2
DR 8–103	Standard 5.2

Canon 9: Appearance of Impropriety

DR 9–101(A) & (B)	Standard 4.3
DR 9–101(C)	Standard 5.2
DR 9–102	Standard 4.1

APPENDIX 3

Frequency Statistics

Jurisdiction	Total Number of Cases	Percentage of Total	Years
Alabama	13	.4%	1980–84
Alaska	8	.3%	1980–84
Arkansas	5	.2%	1980–84
Arizona	96	3.2%	1974–84
California	681	22.8%	1974–84
Colorado	56	1.9%	1980–84
Delaware	3	.1%	1980–84
D. of Columbia	126	4.2%	1974–84
Florida	347	11.6%	1974–84
Georgia	12	.4%	1980–84
Hawaii	4	.1%	1980–84
Idaho	10	.3%	1980–84
Illinois	198	6.6%	1974–84
Indiana	44	1.5%	1980–84
Iowa	39	1.3%	1980–84
Kansas	53	1.8%	1980–84
Kentucky	32	1.1%	1980–84
Louisiana	20	.7%	1980–84
Maine	17	.6%	1980–84
Maryland	3	.1%	1980–84
Massachusetts	92	3.1%	1980–84
Michigan	228	7.6%	1980–83
Minnesota	18	.6%	1980–84
Mississippi	4	.1%	1980–84
Missouri	1	0%	1980–84
Montana	3	.1%	1980–84
Nebraska	3	.1%	1980–84
Nevada	1	0%	1980–84
New Hampshire	0	0%	1980–84
New Jersey	69	2.3%	1974–84
New Mexico	4	.1%	1980–84
New York	243	8.1%	1979–82
North Carolina	1	0%	1980–84
North Dakota	16	.5%	1974–84
Ohio	16	.5%	1980–84
Oklahoma	15	.5%	1980–84
Oregon	47	1.6%	1980–84
Pennsylvania	4	.1%	1980–84
Rhode Island	6	.2%	1980–84

FREQUENCY STATISTICS

Jurisdiction	Total Number of Cases	Percentage of Total	Years
South Carolina	30	1.0%	1980–84
South Dakota	1	0%	1980–84
Tennessee	69	2.3%	1980–84
Texas	225	7.5%	1974–84
Utah	28	.9%	1980–84
Vermont	0	0%	1980–84
Virginia	56	1.9%	1980–84
Washington	24	.8%	1980–84
West Virginia	2	.1%	1980–84
Wisconsin	12	.4%	1980–84
Wyoming	1	0%	1980–84
(Missing cases)	(5)	(.2%)	
	2991	100%	

786

PART FIVE

CODES OF JUDICIAL CONDUCT

Table of Contents

Introduction

As in the case of regulating lawyers' conduct, the ABA has sought to provide standards for regulating judicial conduct. In 1924, the ABA adopted the Canons of Judicial Ethics. During the 1960s, the federal Judicial Conference of the United States developed standards for federal judges. Soon after the ABA adopted the Model Code of Professional Responsibility, the ABA appointed a commission to produce a revised code of conduct for judges. The resulting document is the 1972 Code of Judicial Conduct. In 1990, the ABA replaced the 1972 Code with a new Code of Judicial Conduct. Both the 1990 and the 1972 codes are reproduced in this part.

ABA MODEL CODE OF JUDICIAL CONDUCT (1990) †

Table of Contents

PREAMBLE

Our legal system is based on the principle that an independent, fair and competent judiciary will interpret and apply the laws that govern us. The role of the judiciary is central to American concepts of justice and the rule of law. Intrinsic to all sections of this Code are the precepts that judges, individually and collectively, must respect and honor the judicial office as a public trust and strive to enhance and maintain confidence in our legal system. The judge is an arbiter of facts and law for the resolution of disputes and a highly visible symbol of government under the rule of law.

The Code of Judicial Conduct is intended to establish standards for ethical conduct of judges. It consists of broad statements called Canons, specific rules set forth in Sections under each Canon, a Terminology Section, an Application Section and Commentary. The text of the Canons and the Sections, including the Terminology and Application Sections, is authoritative. The Commentary, by explanation and example, provides guidance with respect to the purpose and meaning of the Canons and Sections. The Commentary is not intended as a statement of additional rules. When the text uses "shall" or "shall not," it is intended to impose binding obligations the violation of which can result in disciplinary action. When "should" or "should not" is used, the text

† Model Code of Judicial Conduct (August 1990) was adopted by the House of Delegates of the American Bar Association on August 7, 1990.

is intended as hortatory and as a statement of what is or is not appropriate conduct but not as a binding rule under which a judge may be disciplined. When "may" is used, it denotes permissible discretion or, depending on the context, it refers to action that is not covered by specific proscriptions.

The Canons and Sections are rules of reason. They should be applied consistent with constitutional requirements, statutes, other court rules and decisional law and in the context of all relevant circumstances. The Code is to be construed so as not to impinge on the essential independence of judges in making judicial decisions.

The Code is designed to provide guidance to judges and candidates for judicial office and to provide a structure for regulating conduct through disciplinary agencies. It is not designed or intended as a basis for civil liability or criminal prosecution. Furthermore, the purpose of the Code would be subverted if the Code were invoked by lawyers for mere tactical advantage in a proceeding.

The text of the Canons and Sections is intended to govern conduct of judges and to be binding upon them. It is not intended, however, that every transgression will result in disciplinary action. Whether disciplinary action is appropriate, and the degree of discipline to be imposed, should be determined through a reasonable and reasoned application of the text and should depend on such factors as the seriousness of the transgression, whether there is a pattern of improper activity and the effect of the improper activity on others or on the judicial system. See ABA Standards Relating to Judicial Discipline and Disability Retirement.†

The Code of Judicial Conduct is not intended as an exhaustive guide for the conduct of judges. They should also be governed in their judicial and personal conduct by general ethical standards. The Code is intended, however, to state basic standards which should govern the conduct of all judges and to provide guidance to assist judges in establishing and maintaining high standards of judicial and personal conduct.

TERMINOLOGY

Terms explained below are noted with an asterisk (*) in the Sections where they appear. In addition, the Sections where terms appear are referred to after the explanation of each term below.

"Appropriate authority" denotes the authority with responsibility for initiation of disciplinary process with respect to the violation to be reported. See Sections 3D(1) and 3D(2).

† Judicial disciplinary procedures adopted in the jurisdictions should comport with the requirements of due process. The ABA Standards Relating to Judicial Discipline and Disability Retirement are cited as an example of how these due process requirements may be satisfied.

"Candidate." A candidate is a person seeking selection for or retention in judicial office by election or appointment. A person becomes a candidate for judicial office as soon as he or she makes a public announcement of candidacy, declares or files as a candidate with the election or appointment authority, or authorizes solicitation or acceptance of contributions or support. The term "candidate" has the same meaning when applied to a judge seeking election or appointment to non-judicial office. See Preamble and Sections 5A, 5B, 5C and 5E.

"Continuing part-time judge." A continuing part-time judge is a judge who serves repeatedly on a part-time basis by election or under a continuing appointment, including a retired judge subject to recall who is permitted to practice law. See Application Section C.

"Court personnel" does not include the lawyers in a proceeding before a judge. See Sections 3B(7)(c) and 3B(9).

"De minimis" denotes an insignificant interest that could not raise reasonable question as to a judge's impartiality. See Sections 3E(1)(c) and 3E(1)(d).

"Economic interest" denotes ownership of a more than de minimis legal or equitable interest, or a relationship as officer, director, advisor or other active participant in the affairs of a party, except that:

(i) ownership of an interest in a mutual or common investment fund that holds securities is not an economic interest in such securities unless the judge participates in the management of the fund or a proceeding pending or impending before the judge could substantially affect the value of the interest;

(ii) service by a judge as an officer, director, advisor or other active participant in an educational, religious, charitable, fraternal or civic organization, or service by a judge's spouse, parent or child as an officer, director, advisor or other active participant in any organization does not create an economic interest in securities held by that organization;

(iii) a deposit in a financial institution, the proprietary interest of a policy holder in a mutual insurance company, of a depositor in a mutual savings association or of a member in a credit union, or a similar proprietary interest, is not an economic interest in the organization unless a proceeding pending or impending before the judge could substantially affect the value of the interest;

(iv) ownership of government securities is not an economic interest in the issuer unless a proceeding pending or impending before the judge could substantially affect the value of the securities.

See Sections 3E(1)(c) and 3E(2).

"Fiduciary" includes such relationships as executor, administrator, trustee, and guardian. See Sections 3E(2) and 4E.

"Knowingly," "knowledge," "known" or "knows" denotes actual knowledge of the fact in question. A person's knowledge may be inferred from circumstances. See Sections 3D, 3E(1), and 5A(3).

"Law" denotes court rules as well as statutes, constitutional provisions and decisional law. See Sections 2A, 3A, 3B(2), 3B(6), 4B, 4C, 4D(5), 4F, 4I, 5A(2), 5A(3), 5B(2), 5C(1), 5C(3) and 5D.

"Member of the candidate's family" denotes a spouse, child, grandchild, parent, grandparent or other relative or person with whom the candidate maintains a close familial relationship. See Section 5A(3)(a).

"Member of the judge's family" denotes a spouse, child, grandchild, parent, grandparent, or other relative or person with whom the judge maintains a close familial relationship. See Sections 4D(3), 4E and 4G.

"Member of the judge's family residing in the judge's household" denotes any relative of a judge by blood or marriage, or a person treated by a judge as a member of the judge's family, who resides in the judge's household. See Sections 3E(1) and 4D(5).

"Nonpublic information" denotes information that, by law, is not available to the public. Nonpublic information may include but is not limited to: information that is sealed by statute or court order, impounded or communicated in camera; and information offered in grand jury proceedings, presentencing reports, dependency cases or psychiatric reports. See Section 3B(11).

"Periodic part-time judge." A periodic part-time judge is a judge who serves or expects to serve repeatedly on a part-time basis but under a separate appointment for each limited period of service or for each matter. See Application Section D.

"Political organization" denotes a political party or other group, the principal purpose of which is to further the election or appointment of candidates to political office. See Sections 5A(1), 5B(2) and 5C(1).

"Pro tempore part-time judge." A pro tempore part-time judge is a judge who serves or expects to serve once or only sporadically on a part-time basis under a separate appointment for each period of service or for each case heard. See Application Section E.

"Public election." This term includes primary and general elections; it includes partisan elections, nonpartisan elections and retention elections. See Section 5C.

"Require." The rules prescribing that a judge "require" certain conduct of others are, like all of the rules in this Code, rules of reason. The use of the term "require" in that context means a judge is to exercise reasonable direction and control over the conduct of those persons subject to the judge's direction and control. See Sections 3B(3), 3B(4), 3B(6), 3B(9) and 3C(2).

"Third degree of relationship." The following persons are relatives within the third degree of relationship: great-grandparent, grandparent, parent, uncle, aunt, brother, sister, child, grandchild, great-grandchild, nephew or niece. See Section 3E(1)(d).

CANON 1

A Judge Shall Uphold the Integrity and Independence of the Judiciary

A. An independent and honorable judiciary is indispensable to justice in our society. A judge should participate in establishing, maintaining and enforcing high standards of conduct, and shall personally observe those standards so that the integrity and independence of the judiciary will be preserved. The provisions of this Code are to be construed and applied to further that objective.

Commentary

Deference to the judgments and rulings of courts depends upon public confidence in the integrity and independence of judges. The integrity and independence of judges depends in turn upon their acting without fear or favor. Although judges should be independent, they must comply with the law, including the provisions of this Code. Public confidence in the impartiality of the judiciary is maintained by the adherence of each judge to this responsibility. Conversely, violation of this Code diminishes public confidence in the judiciary and thereby does injury to the system of government under law.

CANON 2

A Judge Shall Avoid Impropriety and the Appearance of Impropriety in All of the Judge's Activities

A. A judge shall respect and comply with the law * and shall act at all times in a manner that promotes public confidence in the integrity and impartiality of the judiciary.

* See Terminology, "law."

Commentary

Public confidence in the judiciary is eroded by irresponsible or improper conduct by judges. A judge must avoid all impropriety and appearance of impropriety. A judge must expect to be the subject of constant public scrutiny. A judge must therefore accept restrictions on the judge's conduct that might be viewed as burdensome by the ordinary citizen and should do so freely and willingly.

The prohibition against behaving with impropriety or the appearance of impropriety applies to both the professional and personal conduct of a judge. Because it is not practicable to list all prohibited acts, the proscription is necessarily cast in general terms that extend to conduct by judges that is harmful although not specifically mentioned in the Code. Actual improprieties under this standard include violations of law, court rules or other specific provisions of this Code. The test for appearance of impropriety is whether the conduct would create in reasonable minds a perception that the judge's ability to carry out judicial responsibilities with integrity, impartiality and competence is impaired.

See also Commentary under Section 2C.

B. A judge shall not allow family, social, political or other relationships to influence the judge's judicial conduct or judgment. A judge shall not lend the prestige of judicial office to advance the private interests of the judge or others; nor shall a judge convey or permit others to convey the impression that they are in a special position to influence the judge. A judge shall not testify voluntarily as a character witness.

Commentary

Maintaining the prestige of judicial office is essential to a system of government in which the judiciary functions independently of the executive and legislative branches. Respect for the judicial office facilitates the orderly conduct of legitimate judicial functions. Judges should distinguish between proper and improper use of the prestige of office in all of their activities. For example, it would be improper for a judge to allude to his or her judgeship to gain a personal advantage such as deferential treatment when stopped by a police officer for a traffic offense. Similarly, judicial letterhead must not be used for conducting a judge's personal business.

A judge must avoid lending the prestige of judicial office for the advancement of the private interests of others. For example, a judge must not use the judge's judicial position to gain advantage in a civil suit involving a member of the judge's family. In contracts for publication of a judge's writings, a judge should retain control over the advertising to avoid exploitation of the judge's office. As to the acceptance of awards, see Section 4D(5)(a) and Commentary.

Although a judge should be sensitive to possible abuse of the prestige of office, a judge may, based on the judge's personal knowledge, serve as a reference or provide a letter of recommendation. However, a judge must not initiate the communication of information to a sentencing judge or a probation or corrections officer but may provide to such persons information for the record in response to a formal request.

Judges may participate in the process of judicial selection by cooperating with appointing authorities and screening committees seeking names for consideration, and by responding to official inquiries concerning a person being considered for a judgeship. See also Canon 5 regarding use of a judge's name in political activities.

A judge must not testify voluntarily as a character witness because to do so may lend the prestige of the judicial office in support of the party for whom the judge testifies. Moreover, when a judge testifies as a witness, a lawyer who regularly appears before the judge may be placed in the awkward position of cross-examining the judge. A judge may, however, testify when properly summoned. Except in unusual circumstances where the demands of justice require, a judge should discourage a party from requiring the judge to testify as a character witness.

C. A judge shall not hold membership in any organization that practices invidious discrimination on the basis of race, sex, religion or national origin.

Commentary

Membership of a judge in an organization that practices invidious discrimination gives rise to perceptions that the judge's impartiality is impaired. Section 2C refers to the current practices of the organization. Whether an organization practices invidious discrimination is often a complex question to which judges should be sensitive. The answer cannot be determined from a mere examination of an organization's current membership rolls but rather depends on how the organization selects members and other relevant factors, such as that the organization is dedicated to the preservation of religious, ethnic or cultural values of legitimate common interest to its members, or that it is in fact and effect an intimate, purely private organization whose membership limitations could not be constitutionally prohibited. Absent such factors, an organization is generally said to discriminate invidiously if it arbitrarily excludes from membership on the basis of race, religion, sex or national origin persons who would otherwise be admitted to membership. *See New York State Club Ass'n. Inc. v. City of New York,* 108 S.Ct. 2225, 101 L.Ed.2d 1 (1988); *Board of Directors of Rotary International v. Rotary Club of Duarte,* 481 U.S. 537, 107 S.Ct. 1940, 95 L.Ed.2d 474 (1987); *Roberts v. United States Jaycees,* 468 U.S. 609, 104 S.Ct. 3244, 82 L.Ed.2d 462 (1984).

Although Section 2C relates only to membership in organizations that invidiously discriminate on the basis of race, sex, religion or national origin, a judge's membership in an organization that engages in any discriminatory membership practices prohibited by the law of the jurisdiction also violates Canon 2 and Section 2A and gives the appearance of impropriety. In addition, it would be a violation of Canon 2 and Section 2A for a judge to arrange a meeting at a club that the judge knows practices invidious discrimination on the basis of race, sex, religion or national origin in its membership or other policies, or for the judge to regularly use such a club. Moreover, public manifestation by a judge of the judge's knowing approval of invidious discrimination on any basis gives the appearance of impropriety under Canon 2 and diminishes public confidence in the integrity and impartiality of the judiciary, in violation of Section 2A.

When a person who is a judge on the date this Code becomes effective [in the jurisdiction in which the person is a judge] [1] learns that an organization to which the judge belongs engages in invidious discrimination that would preclude membership under Section 2C or under Canon 2 and Section 2A, the judge is permitted, in lieu of resigning, to make immediate efforts to have the organization discontinue its invidiously discriminatory practices, but is required to suspend participation in any other activities of the organization. If the organization fails to discontinue its invidiously discriminatory practices as promptly as possible (and in all events within a year of the judge's first learning of the practices), the judge is required to resign immediately from the organization.

CANON 3

A Judge Shall Perform the Duties of Judicial Office Impartially and Diligently

A. Judicial Duties in General. The judicial duties of a judge take precedence over all the judge's other activities. The judge's judicial duties include all the duties of the judge's office prescribed by law.* In the performance of these duties, the following standards apply.

B. Adjudicative Responsibilities.

(1) A judge shall hear and decide matters assigned to the judge except those in which disqualification is required.

(2) A judge shall be faithful to the law * and maintain professional competence in it. A judge shall not be swayed by partisan interests, public clamor or fear of criticism.

1. The language within the brackets should be deleted when the jurisdiction adopts this provision.

* See Terminology, "law."

795

(3) A judge shall require * order and decorum in proceedings before the judge.

(4) A judge shall be patient, dignified and courteous to litigants, jurors, witnesses, lawyers and others with whom the judge deals in an official capacity, and shall require * similar conduct of lawyers, and of staff, court officials and others subject to the judge's direction and control.

Commentary

The duty to hear all proceedings fairly and with patience is not inconsistent with the duty to dispose promptly of the business of the court. Judges can be efficient and businesslike while being patient and deliberate.

(5) A judge shall perform judicial duties without bias or prejudice. A judge shall not, in the performance of judicial duties, by words or conduct manifest bias or prejudice, including but not limited to bias or prejudice based upon race, sex, religion, national origin, disability, age, sexual orientation or socioeconomic status, and shall not permit staff, court officials and others subject to the judge's direction and control to do so.

Commentary

A judge must refrain from speech, gestures or other conduct that could reasonably be perceived as sexual harassment and must require the same standard of conduct of others subject to the judge's direction and control.

A judge must perform judicial duties impartially and fairly. A judge who manifests bias on any basis in a proceeding impairs the fairness of the proceeding and brings the judiciary into disrepute. Facial expression and body language, in addition to oral communication, can give to parties or lawyers in the proceeding, jurors, the media and others an appearance of judicial bias. A judge must be alert to avoid behavior that may be perceived as prejudicial.

(6) A judge shall require * lawyers in proceedings before the judge to refrain from manifesting, by words or conduct, bias or prejudice based upon race, sex, religion, national origin, disability, age, sexual orientation or socioeconomic status, against parties, witnesses, counsel or others. This Section 3B(6) does not preclude legitimate advocacy when race, sex, religion, national origin, disability, age, sexual orientation or socioeconomic status, or other similar factors, are issues in the proceeding.

(7) A judge shall accord to every person who has a legal interest in a proceeding, or that person's lawyer, the right to be heard according to law.† A judge shall not initiate, permit, or

* See Terminology, "require."   † See Terminology, "law."

consider ex parte communications, or consider other communications made to the judge outside the presence of the parties concerning a pending or impending proceeding except that:

(a) Where circumstances require, ex parte communications for scheduling, administrative purposes or emergencies that do not deal with substantive matters or issues on the merits are authorized; provided:

(i) the judge reasonably believes that no party will gain a procedural or tactical advantage as a result of the ex parte communication, and

(ii) the judge makes provision promptly to notify all other parties of the substance of the ex parte communication and allows an opportunity to respond.

(b) A judge may obtain the advice of a disinterested expert on the law * applicable to a proceeding before the judge if the judge gives notice to the parties of the person consulted and the substance of the advice, and affords the parties reasonable opportunity to respond.

(c) A judge may consult with court personnel † whose function is to aid the judge in carrying out the judge's adjudicative responsibilities or with other judges.

(d) A judge may, with the consent of the parties, confer separately with the parties and their lawyers in an effort to mediate or settle matters pending before the judge.

(e) A judge may initiate or consider any ex parte communications when expressly authorized by law * to do so.

Commentary

The proscription against communications concerning a proceeding includes communications from lawyers, law teachers, and other persons who are not participants in the proceeding, except to the limited extent permitted.

To the extent reasonably possible, all parties or their lawyers shall be included in communications with a judge.

Whenever presence of a party or notice to a party is required by Section 3B(7), it is the party's lawyer, or if the party is unrepresented the party, who is to be present or to whom notice is to be given.

An appropriate and often desirable procedure for a court to obtain the advice of a disinterested expert on legal issues is to invite the expert to file a brief amicus curiae.

Certain ex parte communication is approved by Section 3B(7) to facilitate scheduling and other administrative purposes and to accommodate emergencies. In general, however, a judge must discourage ex

* See Terminology, "law."   † See Terminology, "court personnel."

parte communication and allow it only if all the criteria stated in Section 3B(7) are clearly met. A judge must disclose to all parties all ex parte communications described in Sections 3B(7)(a) and 3B(7)(b) regarding a proceeding pending or impending before the judge.

A judge must not independently investigate facts in a case and must consider only the evidence presented.

A judge may request a party to submit proposed findings of fact and conclusions of law, so long as the other parties are apprised of the request and are given an opportunity to respond to the proposed findings and conclusions.

A judge must make reasonable efforts, including the provision of appropriate supervision, to ensure that Section 3B(7) is not violated through law clerks or other personnel on the judge's staff.

If communication between the trial judge and the appellate court with respect to a proceeding is permitted, a copy of any written communication or the substance of any oral communication should be provided to all parties.

(8) A judge shall dispose of all judicial matters promptly, efficiently and fairly.

Commentary

In disposing of matters promptly, efficiently and fairly, a judge must demonstrate due regard for the rights of the parties to be heard and to have issues resolved without unnecessary cost or delay. Containing costs while preserving fundamental rights of parties also protects the interests of witnesses and the general public. A judge should monitor and supervise cases so as to reduce or eliminate dilatory practices, avoidable delays and unnecessary costs. A judge should encourage and seek to facilitate settlement, but parties should not feel coerced into surrendering the right to have their controversy resolved by the courts.

Prompt disposition of the court's business requires a judge to devote adequate time to judicial duties, to be punctual in attending court and expeditious in determining matters under submission, and to insist that court officials, litigants and their lawyers cooperate with the judge to that end.

(9) A judge shall not, while a proceeding is pending or impending in any court, make any public comment that might reasonably be expected to affect its outcome or impair its fairness or make any nonpublic comment that might substantially interfere with a fair trial or hearing. The judge shall require * similar abstention on the part of court personnel † subject to the judge's direction and control. This Section does not prohibit judges from making public statements in the course of their official duties or

* See Terminology, "require."   † See Terminology, "court personnel."

from explaining for public information the procedures of the court. This Section does not apply to proceedings in which the judge is a litigant in a personal capacity.

Commentary

The requirement that judges abstain from public comment regarding a pending or impending proceeding continues during any appellate process and until final disposition. This Section does not prohibit a judge from commenting on proceedings in which the judge is a litigant in a personal capacity, but in cases such as a writ of mandamus where the judge is a litigant in an official capacity, the judge must not comment publicly. The conduct of lawyers relating to trial publicity is governed by [Rule 3.6 of the ABA Model Rules of Professional Conduct]. (Each jurisdiction should substitute an appropriate reference to its rule.)

(10) A judge shall not commend or criticize jurors for their verdict other than in a court order or opinion in a proceeding, but may express appreciation to jurors for their service to the judicial system and the community.

Commentary

Commending or criticizing jurors for their verdict may imply a judicial expectation in future cases and may impair a juror's ability to be fair and impartial in a subsequent case.

(11) A judge shall not disclose or use, for any purpose unrelated to judicial duties, nonpublic information * acquired in a judicial capacity.

C. Administrative Responsibilities.

(1) A judge shall diligently discharge the judge's administrative responsibilities without bias or prejudice and maintain professional competence in judicial administration, and should cooperate with other judges and court officials in the administration of court business.

(2) A judge shall require † staff, court officials and others subject to the judge's direction and control to observe the standards of fidelity and diligence that apply to the judge and to refrain from manifesting bias or prejudice in the performance of their official duties.

(3) A judge with supervisory authority for the judicial performance of other judges shall take reasonable measures to assure the prompt disposition of matters before them and the proper performance of their other judicial responsibilities.

* See Terminology, "nonpublic information."   † See Terminology, "require."

(4) A judge shall not make unnecessary appointments. A judge shall exercise the power of appointment impartially and on the basis of merit. A judge shall avoid nepotism and favoritism. A judge shall not approve compensation of appointees beyond the fair value of services rendered.

Commentary

Appointees of a judge include assigned counsel, officials such as referees, commissioners, special masters, receivers and guardians and personnel such as clerks, secretaries and bailiffs. Consent by the parties to an appointment or an award of compensation does not relieve the judge of the obligation prescribed by Section 3C(4).

D. Disciplinary Responsibilities.

(1) A judge who receives information indicating a substantial likelihood that another judge has committed a violation of this Code should take appropriate action. A judge having knowledge * that another judge has committed a violation of this Code that raises a substantial question as to the other judge's fitness for office shall inform the appropriate authority.†

(2) A judge who receives information indicating a substantial likelihood that a lawyer has committed a violation of the Rules of Professional Conduct [substitute correct title if the applicable rules of lawyer conduct have a different title] should take appropriate action. A judge having knowledge * that a lawyer has committed a violation of the Rules of Professional Conduct [substitute correct title if the applicable rules of lawyer conduct have a different title] that raises a substantial question as to the lawyer's honesty, trustworthiness or fitness as a lawyer in other respects shall inform the appropriate authority.†

(3) Acts of a judge, in the discharge of disciplinary responsibilities, required or permitted by Sections 3D(1) and 3D(2) are part of a judge's judicial duties and shall be absolutely privileged, and no civil action predicated thereon may be instituted against the judge.

Commentary

Appropriate action may include direct communication with the judge or lawyer who has committed the violation, other direct action if available, and reporting the violation to the appropriate authority or other agency or body.

* See Terminology, "knowingly," "knowledge," "known" and "knows."

† See Terminology, "appropriate authority."

E. Disqualification.

(1) A judge shall disqualify himself or herself in a proceeding in which the judge's impartiality might reasonably be questioned, including but not limited to instances where:

Commentary

Under this rule, a judge is disqualified whenever the judge's impartiality might reasonably be questioned, regardless whether any of the specific rules in Section 3E(1) apply. For example, if a judge were in the process of negotiating for employment with a law firm, the judge would be disqualified from any matters in which that law firm appeared, unless the disqualification was waived by the parties after disclosure by the judge.

A judge should disclose on the record information that the judge believes the parties or their lawyers might consider relevant to the question of disqualification, even if the judge believes there is no real basis for disqualification.

By decisional law, the rule of necessity may override the rule of disqualification. For example, a judge might be required to participate in judicial review of a judicial salary statute, or might be the only judge available in a matter requiring immediate judicial action, such as a hearing on probable cause or a temporary restraining order. In the latter case, the judge must disclose on the record the basis for possible disqualification and use reasonable efforts to transfer the matter to another judge as soon as practicable.

(a) the judge has a personal bias or prejudice concerning a party or a party's lawyer, or personal knowledge * of disputed evidentiary facts concerning the proceeding;

(b) the judge served as a lawyer in the matter in controversy, or a lawyer with whom the judge previously practiced law served during such association as a lawyer concerning the matter, or the judge has been a material witness concerning it;

Commentary

A lawyer in a government agency does not ordinarily have an association with other lawyers employed by that agency within the meaning of Section 3E(1)(b); a judge formerly employed by a government agency, however, should disqualify himself or herself in a proceeding if the judge's impartiality might reasonably be questioned because of such association.

(c) the judge knows * that he or she, individually or as a fiduciary, or the judge's spouse, parent or child wherever

* See Terminology, "knowingly," "knowledge," "known" and "knows."

801

residing, or any other member of the judge's family residing in the judge's household,* has an economic interest † in the subject matter in controversy or in a party to the proceeding or has any other more than de minimis ** interest that could be substantially affected by the proceeding;

(d) the judge or the judge's spouse, or a person within the third degree of relationship †† to either of them, or the spouse of such a person:

(i) is a party to the proceeding, or an officer, director or trustee of a party;

(ii) is acting as a lawyer in the proceeding;

(iii) is known *** by the judge to have a more than de minimis ** interest that could be substantially affected by the proceeding;

(iv) is to the judge's knowledge *** likely to be a material witness in the proceeding.

Commentary

The fact that a lawyer in a proceeding is affiliated with a law firm with which a relative of the judge is affiliated does not of itself disqualify the judge. Under appropriate circumstances, the fact that "the judge's impartiality might reasonably be questioned" under Section 3E(1), or that the relative is known by the judge to have an interest in the law firm that could be "substantially affected by the outcome of the proceeding" under Section 3E(1)(d)(iii) may require the judge's disqualification.

(2) A judge shall keep informed about the judge's personal and fiduciary ††† economic interests,† and make a reasonable effort to keep informed about the personal economic interests of the judge's spouse and minor children residing in the judge's household.

F. Remittal of Disqualification. A judge disqualified by the terms of Section 3E may disclose on the record the basis of the judge's disqualification and may ask the parties and their lawyers to consider, out of the presence of the judge, whether to waive disqualification. If following disclosure of any basis for disqualification other than personal bias or prejudice concerning a party, the parties and lawyers, without participation by the judge, all agree that the judge should not be disqualified, and the judge is then willing to participate, the judge may participate in the

* See Terminology, "member of the judge's family residing in the judge's household."

† See Terminology, "economic interest."

** See Terminology, "de minimis."

†† See Terminology, "third degree of relationship."

*** See Terminology, "knowingly," "knowledge," "known" and "knows."

††† See Terminology, "fiduciary."

proceeding. The agreement shall be incorporated in the record of the proceeding.

Commentary

A remittal procedure provides the parties an opportunity to proceed without delay if they wish to waive the disqualification. To assure that consideration of the question of remittal is made independently of the judge, a judge must not solicit, seek or hear comment on possible remittal or waiver of the disqualification unless the lawyers jointly propose remittal after consultation as provided in the rule. A party may act through counsel if counsel represents on the record that the party has been consulted and consents. As a practical matter, a judge may wish to have all parties and their lawyers sign the remittal agreement.

CANON 4

A Judge Shall So Conduct the Judge's Extra–Judicial Activities as to Minimize the Risk of Conflict With Judicial Obligations

A. Extra-judicial Activities in General. A judge shall conduct all of the judge's extra-judicial activities so that they do not:

(1) cast reasonable doubt on the judge's capacity to act impartially as a judge;

(2) demean the judicial office; or

(3) interfere with the proper performance of judicial duties.

Commentary

Complete separation of a judge from extra-judicial activities is neither possible nor wise; a judge should not become isolated from the community in which the judge lives.

Expressions of bias or prejudice by a judge, even outside the judge's judicial activities, may cast reasonable doubt on the judge's capacity to act impartially as a judge. Expressions which may do so include jokes or other remarks demeaning individuals on the basis of their race, sex, religion, national origin, disability, age, sexual orientation or socioeconomic status. See Section 2C and accompanying Commentary.

B. Avocational Activities. A judge may speak, write, lecture, teach and participate in other extra-judicial activities concerning the law,* the legal system, the administration of justice and non-legal subjects, subject to the requirements of this Code.

* See Terminology, "law."

Commentary

As a judicial officer and person specially learned in the law, a judge is in a unique position to contribute to the improvement of the law, the legal system, and the administration of justice, including revision of substantive and procedural law and improvement of criminal and juvenile justice. To the extent that time permits, a judge is encouraged to do so, either independently or through a bar association, judicial conference or other organization dedicated to the improvement of the law. Judges may participate in efforts to promote the fair administration of justice, the independence of the judiciary and the integrity of the legal profession and may express opposition to the persecution of lawyers and judges in other countries because of their professional activities.

In this and other Sections of Canon 4, the phrase "subject to the requirements of this Code" is used, notably in connection with a judge's governmental, civic or charitable activities. This phrase is included to remind judges that the use of permissive language in various Sections of the Code does not relieve a judge from the other requirements of the Code that apply to the specific conduct.

C. Governmental, Civic or Charitable Activities.

(1) A judge shall not appear at a public hearing before, or otherwise consult with, an executive or legislative body or official except on matters concerning the law,* the legal system or the administration of justice or except when acting pro se in a matter involving the judge or the judge's interests.

Commentary

See Section 2B regarding the obligation to avoid improper influence.

(2) A judge shall not accept appointment to a governmental committee or commission or other governmental position that is concerned with issues of fact or policy on matters other than the improvement of the law,* the legal system or the administration of justice. A judge may, however, represent a country, state or locality on ceremonial occasions or in connection with historical, educational or cultural activities.

Commentary

Section 4C(2) prohibits a judge from accepting any governmental position except one relating to the law, legal system or administration of justice as authorized by Section 4C(3). The appropriateness of accepting extra-judicial assignments must be assessed in light of the demands on judicial resources created by crowded dockets and the need to protect the courts from involvement in extra-judicial matters that

* See Terminology, "law."

may prove to be controversial. Judges should not accept governmental appointments that are likely to interfere with the effectiveness and independence of the judiciary.

Section 4C(2) does not govern a judge's service in a nongovernmental position. See Section 4C(3) permitting service by a judge with organizations devoted to the improvement of the law, the legal system or the administration of justice and with educational, religious, charitable, fraternal or civic organizations not conducted for profit. For example, service on the board of a public educational institution, unless it were a law school, would be prohibited under Section 4C(2), but service on the board of a public law school or any private educational institution would generally be permitted under Section 4C(3).

(3) A judge may serve as an officer, director, trustee or non-legal advisor of an organization or governmental agency devoted to the improvement of the law,* the legal system or the administration of justice or of an educational, religious, charitable, fraternal or civic organization not conducted for profit, subject to the following limitations and the other requirements of this Code.

Commentary

Section 4C(3) does not apply to a judge's service in a governmental position unconnected with the improvement of the law, the legal system or the administration of justice; see Section 4C(2).

See Commentary to Section 4B regarding use of the phrase "subject to the following limitations and the other requirements of this Code." As an example of the meaning of the phrase, a judge permitted by Section 4C(3) to serve on the board of a fraternal institution may be prohibited from such service by Sections 2C or 4A if the institution practices invidious discrimination or if service on the board otherwise casts reasonable doubt on the judge's capacity to act impartially as a judge.

Service by a judge on behalf of a civic or charitable organization may be governed by other provisions of Canon 4 in addition to Section 4C. For example, a judge is prohibited by Section 4G from serving as a legal advisor to a civic or charitable organization.

(a) A judge shall not serve as an officer, director, trustee or non-legal advisor if it is likely that the organization

(i) will be engaged in proceedings that would ordinarily come before the judge, or

(ii) will be engaged frequently in adversary proceedings in the court of which the judge is a member or in any court subject to the appellate jurisdiction of the court of which the judge is a member.

* See Terminology, "law."

Commentary

The changing nature of some organizations and of their relationship to the law makes it necessary for a judge regularly to reexamine the activities of each organization with which the judge is affiliated to determine if it is proper for the judge to continue the affiliation. For example, in many jurisdictions charitable hospitals are now more frequently in court than in the past. Similarly, the boards of some legal aid organizations now make policy decisions that may have political significance or imply commitment to causes that may come before the courts for adjudication.

(b) A judge as an officer, director, trustee or non-legal advisor, or as a member or otherwise:

(i) may assist such an organization in planning fund-raising and may participate in the management and investment of the organization's funds, but shall not personally participate in the solicitation of funds or other fund-raising activities, except that a judge may solicit funds from other judges over whom the judge does not exercise supervisory or appellate authority;

(ii) may make recommendations to public and private fund-granting organizations on projects and programs concerning the law,* the legal system or the administration of justice;

(iii) shall not personally participate in membership solicitation if the solicitation might reasonably be perceived as coercive or, except as permitted in Section 4C(3)(b)(i), if the membership solicitation is essentially a fund-raising mechanism;

(iv) shall not use or permit the use of the prestige of judicial office for fund-raising or membership solicitation.

Commentary

A judge may solicit membership or endorse or encourage membership efforts for an organization devoted to the improvement of the law, the legal system or the administration of justice or a nonprofit educational, religious, charitable, fraternal or civic organization as long as the solicitation cannot reasonably be perceived as coercive and is not essentially a fund-raising mechanism. Solicitation of funds for an organization and solicitation of memberships similarly involve the danger that the person solicited will feel obligated to respond favorably to the solicitor if the solicitor is in a position of influence or control. A

* See Terminology, "law."

judge must not engage in direct, individual solicitation of funds or memberships in person, in writing or by telephone except in the following cases: 1) a judge may solicit for funds or memberships other judges over whom the judge does not exercise supervisory or appellate authority, 2) a judge may solicit other persons for membership in the organizations described above if neither those persons nor persons with whom they are affiliated are likely ever to appear before the court on which the judge serves and 3) a judge who is an officer of such an organization may send a general membership solicitation mailing over the judge's signature.

Use of an organization letterhead for fund-raising or membership solicitation does not violate Section 4C(3)(b) provided the letterhead lists only the judge's name and office or other position in the organization, and, if comparable designations are listed for other persons, the judge's judicial designation. In addition, a judge must also make reasonable efforts to ensure that the judge's staff, court officials and others subject to the judge's direction and control do not solicit funds on the judge's behalf for any purpose, charitable or otherwise.

A judge must not be a speaker or guest of honor at an organization's fund-raising event, but mere attendance at such an event is permissible if otherwise consistent with this Code.

D. Financial Activities.

(1) A judge shall not engage in financial and business dealings that:

    (a) may reasonably be perceived to exploit the judge's judicial position, or

    (b) involve the judge in frequent transactions or continuing business relationships with those lawyers or other persons likely to come before the court on which the judge serves.

Commentary

The Time for Compliance provision of this Code (Application, Section F) postpones the time for compliance with certain provisions of this Section in some cases.

When a judge acquires in a judicial capacity information, such as material contained in filings with the court, that is not yet generally known, the judge must not use the information for private gain. See Section 2B; see also Section 3B(11).

A judge must avoid financial and business dealings that involve the judge in frequent transactions or continuing business relationships with persons likely to come either before the judge personally or before other judges on the judge's court. In addition, a judge should discourage members of the judge's family from engaging in dealings that would reasonably appear to exploit the judge's judicial position. This rule is necessary to avoid creating an appearance of exploitation of office or favoritism and to minimize the potential for disqualification. With respect to affiliation of relatives of judge with law firms appearing before the judge, see Commentary to Section 3E(1) relating to disqualification.

Participation by a judge in financial and business dealings is subject to the general prohibitions in Section 4A against activities that tend to reflect adversely on impartiality, demean the judicial office, or interfere with the proper performance of judicial duties. Such participation is also subject to the general prohibition in Canon 2 against activities involving impropriety or the appearance of impropriety and the prohibition in Section 2B against the misuse of the prestige of judicial office. In addition, a judge must maintain high standards of conduct in all of the judge's activities, as set forth in Canon 1. See Commentary for Section 4B regarding use of the phrase "subject to the requirements of this Code."

(2) A judge may, subject to the requirements of this Code, hold and manage investments of the judge and members of the judge's family,* including real estate, and engage in other remunerative activity.

Commentary

This Section provides that, subject to the requirements of this Code, a judge may hold and manage investments owned solely by the judge, investments owned solely by a member or members of the judge's family, and investments owned jointly by the judge and members of the judge's family.

(3) A judge shall not serve as an officer, director, manager, general partner, advisor or employee of any business entity except that a judge may, subject to the requirements of this Code, manage and participate in:

(a) a business closely held by the judge or members of the judge's family,* or

(b) a business entity primarily engaged in investment of the financial resources of the judge or members of the judge's family.

Commentary

Subject to the requirements of this Code, a judge may participate in a business that is closely held either by the judge alone, by members of the judge's family, or by the judge and members of the judge's family.

* See Terminology, "member[s] of the judge's family."

808

Although participation by a judge in a closely-held family business might otherwise be permitted by Section 4D(3), a judge may be prohibited from participation by other provisions of this Code when, for example, the business entity frequently appears before the judge's court or the participation requires significant time away from judicial duties. Similarly, a judge must avoid participating in a closely-held family business if the judge's participation would involve misuse of the prestige of judicial office.

(4) A judge shall manage the judge's investments and other financial interests to minimize the number of cases in which the judge is disqualified. As soon as the judge can do so without serious financial detriment, the judge shall divest himself or herself of investments and other financial interests that might require frequent disqualification.

(5) A judge shall not accept, and shall urge members of the judge's family residing in the judge's household,* not to accept, a gift, bequest, favor or loan from anyone except for:

Commentary

Section 4D(5) does not apply to contributions to a judge's campaign for judicial office, a matter governed by Canon 5.

Because a gift, bequest, favor or loan to a member of the judge's family residing in the judge's household might be viewed as intended to influence the judge, a judge must inform those family members of the relevant ethical constraints upon the judge in this regard and discourage those family members from violating them. A judge cannot, however, reasonably be expected to know or control all of the financial or business activities of all family members residing in the judge's household.

(a) a gift incident to a public testimonial, books, tapes and other resource materials supplied by publishers on a complimentary basis for official use, or an invitation to the judge and the judge's spouse or guest to attend a bar-related function or an activity devoted to the improvement of the law,† the legal system or the administration of justice;

Commentary

Acceptance of an invitation to a law-related function is governed by Section 4D(5)(a); acceptance of an invitation paid for by an individual lawyer or group of lawyers is governed by Section 4D(5)(h).

A judge may accept a public testimonial or a gift incident thereto only if the donor organization is not an organization whose members

---

* See Terminology, "member of the judge's family residing in the judge's household."

† See Terminology, "law."

comprise or frequently represent the same side in litigation, and the testimonial and gift are otherwise in compliance with other provisions of this Code. See Sections 4A(1) and 2B.

(b) **a gift, award or benefit incident to the business, profession or other separate activity of a spouse or other family member of a judge residing in the judge's household, including gifts, awards and benefits for the use of both the spouse or other family member and the judge (as spouse or family member), provided the gift, award or benefit could not reasonably be perceived as intended to influence the judge in the performance of judicial duties;**

(c) **ordinary social hospitality;**

(d) **a gift from a relative or friend, for a special occasion, such as a wedding, anniversary or birthday, if the gift is fairly commensurate with the occasion and the relationship;**

Commentary

A gift to a judge, or to a member of the judge's family living in the judge's household, that is excessive in value raises questions about the judge's impartiality and the integrity of the judicial office and might require disqualification of the judge where disqualification would not otherwise be required. See, however, Section 4D(5)(e).

(e) **a gift, bequest, favor or loan from a relative or close personal friend whose appearance or interest in a case would in any event require disqualification under Section 3E;**

(f) **a loan from a lending institution in its regular course of business on the same terms generally available to persons who are not judges;**

(g) **a scholarship or fellowship awarded on the same terms and based on the same criteria applied to other applicants; or**

(h) **any other gift, bequest, favor or loan, only if: the donor is not a party or other person who has come or is likely to come or whose interests have come or are likely to come before the judge; and, if its value exceeds $150.00, the judge reports it in the same manner as the judge reports compensation in Section 4H.**

Commentary

Section 4D(5)(h) prohibits judges from accepting gifts, favors, bequests or loans from lawyers or their firms if they have come or are likely to come before the judge; it also prohibits gifts, favors, bequests or loans from clients of lawyers or their firms when the clients' interests have come or are likely to come before the judge.

E. Fiduciary Activities.

(1) A judge shall not serve as executor, administrator or other personal representative, trustee, guardian, attorney in fact or other fiduciary,* except for the estate, trust or person of a member of the judge's family,† and then only if such service will not interfere with the proper performance of judicial duties.

(2) A judge shall not serve as a fiduciary * if it is likely that the judge as a fiduciary will be engaged in proceedings that would ordinarily come before the judge, or if the estate, trust or ward becomes involved in adversary proceedings in the court on which the judge serves or one under its appellate jurisdiction.

(3) The same restrictions on financial activities that apply to a judge personally also apply to the judge while acting in a fiduciary * capacity.

Commentary

The Time for Compliance provision of this Code (Application, Section F) postpones the time for compliance with certain provisions of this Section in some cases.

The restrictions imposed by this Canon may conflict with the judge's obligation as a fiduciary. For example, a judge should resign as trustee if detriment to the trust would result from divestiture of holdings the retention of which would place the judge in violation of Section 4D(4).

F. Service as Arbitrator or Mediator. A judge shall not act as an arbitrator or mediator or otherwise perform judicial functions in a private capacity unless expressly authorized by law.**

Commentary

Section 4F does not prohibit a judge from participating in arbitration, mediation or settlement conferences performed as part of judicial duties.

G. Practice of Law. A judge shall not practice law. Notwithstanding this prohibition, a judge may act pro se and may, without compensation, give legal advice to and draft or review documents for a member of the judge's family.†

Commentary

This prohibition refers to the practice of law in a representative capacity and not in a pro se capacity. A judge may act for himself or herself in all legal matters, including matters involving litigation and

* See Terminology, "fiduciary."   ** See Terminology, "law."

† See Terminology, "member of the judge's family."

matters involving appearances before or other dealings with legislative and other governmental bodies. However, in so doing, a judge must not abuse the prestige of office to advance the interests of the judge or the judge's family. See Section 2(B).

The Code allows a judge to give legal advice to and draft legal documents for members of the judge's family, so long as the judge receives no compensation. A judge must not, however, act as an advocate or negotiator for a member of the judge's family in a legal matter.

* * *

Canon 6, new in the 1972 Code, reflected concerns about conflicts of interest and appearances of impropriety arising from compensation for off-the-bench activities. Since 1972, however, reporting requirements that are much more comprehensive with respect to what must be reported and with whom reports must be filed have been adopted by many jurisdictions. The Committee believes that although reports of compensation for extra-judicial activities should be required, reporting requirements preferably should be developed to suit the respective jurisdictions, not simply adopted as set forth in a national model code of judicial conduct. Because of the Committee's concern that deletion of this Canon might lead to the misconception that reporting compensation for extra-judicial activities is no longer important, the substance of Canon 6 is carried forward as Section 4H in this Code for adoption in those jurisdictions that do not have other reporting requirements. In jurisdictions that have separately established reporting requirements, Section 4H(2) (Public Reporting) may be deleted and the caption for Section 4H modified appropriately.

* * *

H.   Compensation, Reimbursement and Reporting.

(1) Compensation and Reimbursement. A judge may receive compensation and reimbursement of expenses for the extra-judicial activities permitted by this Code, if the source of such payments does not give the appearance of influencing the judge's performance of judicial duties or otherwise give the appearance of impropriety.

(a) Compensation shall not exceed a reasonable amount nor shall it exceed what a person who is not a judge would receive for the same activity.

(b) Expense reimbursement shall be limited to the actual cost of travel, food and lodging reasonably incurred by the judge and, where appropriate to the occasion, by the judge's spouse or guest. Any payment in excess of such an amount is compensation.

(2) Public Reports. A judge shall report the date, place and nature of any activity for which the judge received compensation,

and the name of the payor and the amount of compensation so received. Compensation or income of a spouse attributed to the judge by operation of a community property law is not extra-judicial compensation to the judge. The judge's report shall be made at least annually and shall be filed as a public document in the office of the clerk of the court on which the judge serves or other office designated by law.*

Commentary

See Section 4D(5) regarding reporting of gifts, bequests and loans.

The Code does not prohibit a judge from accepting honoraria or speaking fees provided that the compensation is reasonable and commensurate with the task performed. A judge should ensure, however, that no conflicts are created by the arrangement. A judge must not appear to trade on the judicial position for personal advantage. Nor should a judge spend significant time away from court duties to meet speaking or writing commitments for compensation. In addition, the source of the payment must not raise any question of undue influence or the judge's ability or willingness to be impartial.

I.   Disclosure of a judge's income, debts, investments or other assets is required only to the extent provided in this Canon and in Sections 3E and 3F, or as otherwise required by law.*

Commentary

Section 3E requires a judge to disqualify himself or herself in any proceeding in which the judge has an economic interest. See "economic interest" as explained in the Terminology Section. Section 4D requires a judge to refrain from engaging in business and from financial activities that might interfere with the impartial performance of judicial duties; Section 4H requires a judge to report all compensation the judge received for activities outside judicial office. A judge has the rights of any other citizen, including the right to privacy of the judge's financial affairs, except to the extent that limitations established by law are required to safeguard the proper performance of the judge's duties.

* See Terminology, "law."

CANON 5 [2]

A Judge or Judicial Candidate Shall Refrain From Inappropriate Political Activity

A. All Judges and Candidates.

(1) Except as authorized in Sections 5B(2), 5C(1) and 5C(3), a judge or a candidate * for election or appointment to judicial office shall not:

(a) act as a leader or hold an office in a political organization †;

(b) publicly endorse or publicly oppose another candidate for public office;

(c) make speeches on behalf of a political organization;

(d) attend political gatherings; or

(e) solicit funds for, pay an assessment to or make a contribution to a political organization or candidate, or purchase tickets for political party dinners or other functions.

Commentary

A judge or candidate for judicial office retains the right to participate in the political process as a voter.

2. Introductory Note to Canon 5: There is wide variation in the methods of judicial selection used, both among jurisdictions and within the jurisdictions themselves. In a given state, judges may be selected by one method initially, retained by a different method, and selected by still another method to fill interim vacancies.

According to figures compiled in 1987 by the National Center for State Courts, 32 states and the District of Columbia use a merit selection method (in which an executive such as a governor appoints a judge from a group of nominees selected by a judicial nominating commission) to select judges in the state either initially or to fill an interim vacancy. Of those 33 jurisdictions, a merit selection method is used in 18 jurisdictions to choose judges of courts of last resort, in 13 jurisdictions to choose judges of intermediate appellate courts, in 12 jurisdictions to choose judges of general jurisdiction courts and in 5 jurisdictions to choose judges of limited jurisdiction courts.

Methods of judicial selection other than merit selection include nonpartisan election (10 states use it for initial selection at all court levels, another 10 states use it for initial selection for at least one court level) and partisan election (8 states use it for initial selection at all court levels, another 7 states use it for initial selection for at least one level). In a small minority of the states, judicial selection methods include executive or legislative appointment (without nomination of a group of potential appointees by a judicial nominating commission) and court selection. In addition, the federal judicial system utilizes an executive appointment method. See State Court Organization 1987 (National Center for State Courts, 1988).

* See Terminology, "candidate."

† See Terminology, "political organization."

Where false information concerning a judicial candidate is made public, a judge or another judicial candidate having knowledge of the facts is not prohibited by Section 5A(1) from making the facts public.

Section 5A(1)(a) does not prohibit a candidate for elective judicial office from retaining during candidacy a public office such as county prosecutor, which is not "an office in a political organization."

Section 5A(1)(b) does not prohibit a judge or judicial candidate from privately expressing his or her views on judicial candidates or other candidates for public office.

A candidate does not publicly endorse another candidate for public office by having that candidate's name on the same ticket.

(2) A judge shall resign from judicial office upon becoming a candidate * for a non-judicial office either in a primary or in a general election, except that the judge may continue to hold judicial office while being a candidate for election to or serving as a delegate in a state constitutional convention if the judge is otherwise permitted by law † to do so.

(3) A candidate * for a judicial office:

(a) shall maintain the dignity appropriate to judicial office and act in a manner consistent with the integrity and independence of the judiciary, and shall encourage members of the candidate's family ** to adhere to the same standards of political conduct in support of the candidate as apply to the candidate;

Commentary

Although a judicial candidate must encourage members of his or her family to adhere to the same standards of political conduct in support of the candidate that apply to the candidate, family members are free to participate in other political activity.

(b) shall prohibit employees and officials who serve at the pleasure of the candidate,* and shall discourage other employees and officials subject to the candidate's direction and control from doing on the candidate's behalf what the candidate is prohibited from doing under the Sections of this Canon;

(c) except to the extent permitted by Section 5C(2), shall not authorize or knowingly †† permit any other person to do for the candidate * what the candidate is prohibited from doing under the Sections of this Canon;

---

* See Terminology, "candidate."
† See Terminology, "law."

** See Terminology, "member of the candidate's family."

†† See Terminology, "knowingly."

815

(d) shall not:

(i) make pledges or promises of conduct in office other than the faithful and impartial performance of the duties of the office;

(ii) make statements that commit or appear to commit the candidate with respect to cases, controversies or issues that are likely to come before the court; or

(iii) knowingly * misrepresent the identity, qualifications, present position or other fact concerning the candidate or an opponent;

Commentary

Section 5A(3)(d) prohibits a candidate for judicial office from making statements that appear to commit the candidate regarding cases, controversies or issues likely to come before the court. As a corollary, a candidate should emphasize in any public statement the candidate's duty to uphold the law regardless of his or her personal views. See also Section 3B(9), the general rule on public comment by judges. Section 5A(3)(d) does not prohibit a candidate from making pledges or promises respecting improvements in court administration. Nor does this Section prohibit an incumbent judge from making private statements to other judges or court personnel in the performance of judicial duties. This Section applies to any statement made in the process of securing judicial office, such as statements to commissions charged with judicial selection and tenure and legislative bodies confirming appointment. See also Rule 8.2 of the ABA Model Rules of Professional Conduct.

(e) may respond to personal attacks or attacks on the candidate's record as long as the response does not violate Section 5A(3)(d).

B. Candidates Seeking Appointment to Judicial or Other Governmental Office.

(1) A candidate † for appointment to judicial office or a judge seeking other governmental office shall not solicit or accept funds, personally or through a committee or otherwise, to support his or her candidacy.

(2) A candidate † for appointment to judicial office or a judge seeking other governmental office shall not engage in any political activity to secure the appointment except that:

(a) such persons may:

(i) communicate with the appointing authority, including any selection or nominating commission or other agency designated to screen candidates;

---

* See Terminology, "knowingly."   † See Terminology, "candidate."

(ii) **seek support or endorsement for the appointment from organizations that regularly make recommendations for reappointment or appointment to the office, and from individuals to the extent requested or required by those specified in Section 5B(2)(a); and**

(iii) **provide to those specified in Sections 5B(2)(a)(i) and 5B(2)(a)(ii) information as to his or her qualifications for the office;**

(b) **a non-judge candidate * for appointment to judicial office may, in addition, unless otherwise prohibited by law †;**

(i) **retain an office in a political oganization,****

(ii) **attend political gatherings, and**

(iii) **continue to pay ordinary assessments and ordinary contributions to a political organization or candidate and purchase tickets for political party dinners or other functions.**

Commentary

Section 5B(2) provides a limited exception to the restrictions imposed by Sections 5A(1) and 5D. Under Section 5B(2), candidates seeking reappointment to the same judicial office or appointment to another judicial office or other governmental office may apply for the appointment and seek appropriate support.

Although under Section 5B(2) non-judge candidates seeking appointment to judicial office are permitted during candidacy to retain office in a political organization, attend political gatherings and pay ordinary dues and assessments, they remain subject to other provisions of this Code during candidacy. See Sections 5B(1), 5B(2)(a), 5E and Application Section.

C. Judges and Candidates Subject to Public Election.

(1) **A judge or a candidate * subject to public election †† may, except as prohibited by law †:**

(a) **at any time**

(i) **purchase tickets for and attend political gatherings;**

(ii) **identify himself or herself as a member of a political party; and**

(iii) **contribute to a political organization **;**

* See Terminology, "candidate."   ** See Terminology, "political organiza-
† See Terminology, "law."   tion."

†† See Terminology, "public election."

(b) when a candidate for election

    (i) speak to gatherings on his or her own behalf;

    (ii) appear in newspaper, television and other media advertisements supporting his or her candidacy;

    (iii) distribute pamphlets and other promotional campaign literature supporting his or her candidacy; and

    (iv) publicly endorse or publicly oppose other candidates for the same judicial office in a public election in which the judge or judicial candidate is running.

Commentary

Section 5C(1) permits judges subject to election at any time to be involved in limited political activity. Section 5D, applicable solely to incumbent judges, would otherwise bar this activity.

(2) A candidate * shall not personally solicit or accept campaign contributions or personally solicit publicly stated support. A candidate may, however, establish committees of responsible persons to conduct campaigns for the candidate through media advertisements, brochures, mailings, candidate forums and other means not prohibited by law. Such committees may solicit and accept reasonable campaign contributions, manage the expenditure of funds for the candidate's campaign and obtain public statements of support for his or her candidacy. Such committees are not prohibited from soliciting and accepting reasonable campaign contributions and public support from lawyers. A candidate's committees may solicit contributions and public support for the candidate's campaign no earlier than [one year] before an election and no later than [90] days after the last election in which the candidate participates during the election year. A candidate shall not use or permit the use of campaign contributions for the private benefit of the candidate or others.

Commentary

Section 5C(2) permits a candidate, other than a candidate for appointment, to establish campaign committees to solicit and accept public support and reasonable financial contributions. At the start of the campaign, the candidate must instruct his or her campaign committees to solicit or accept only contributions that are reasonable under the circumstances. Though not prohibited, campaign contributions of which a judge has knowledge, made by lawyers or others who appear before the judge, may be relevant to disqualification under Section 3E.

Campaign committees established under Section 5C(2) should manage campaign finances responsibly, avoiding deficits that might necessitate post-election fund-raising, to the extent possible.

* See Terminology, "candidate."

Section 5C(2) does not prohibit a candidate from initiating an evaluation by a judicial selection commission or bar association, or, subject to the requirements of this Code, from responding to a request for information from any organization.

(3) **Except as prohibited by law,† a candidate † for judicial office in a public election ** may permit the candidate's name: (a) to be listed on election materials along with the names of other candidates for elective public office, and (b) to appear in promotions of the ticket.**

Commentary

Section 5C(3) provides a limited exception to the restrictions imposed by Section 5A(1).

D. Incumbent Judges. A judge shall not engage in any political activity except (i) as authorized under any other Section of this Code, (ii) on behalf of measures to improve the law,* the legal system or the administration of justice, or (iii) as expressly authorized by law.

Commentary

Neither Section 5D nor any other section of the Code prohibits a judge in the exercise of administrative functions from engaging in planning and other official activities with members of the executive and legislative branches of government. With respect to a judge's activity on behalf of measures to improve the law, the legal system and the administration of justice, see Commentary to Section 4B and Section 4C(1) and its Commentary.

E. Applicability. Canon 5 generally applies to all incumbent judges and judicial candidates.† A successful candidate, whether or not an incumbent, is subject to judicial discipline for his or her campaign conduct; an unsuccessful candidate who is a lawyer is subject to lawyer discipline for his or her campaign conduct. A lawyer who is a candidate for judicial office is subject to [Rule 8.2(b) of the ABA Model Rules of Professional Conduct]. (An adopting jurisdiction should substitute a reference to its applicable rule.)

APPLICATION OF THE CODE OF JUDICIAL CONDUCT

A. Anyone, whether or not a lawyer, who is an officer of a judicial system [3] and who performs judicial functions, including

---

* See Terminology, "law."

† See Terminology, "candidate."

** See Terminology, "public election."

3. Applicability of this Code to administrative law judges should be determined by each adopting jurisdiction. Administrative law judges generally are affiliated with the executive branch of government rather than the judicial branch and each adopting jurisdiction should consider the unique characteristics of particular administrative law judge positions in adopting and adapt-

an officer such as a magistrate, court commissioner, special master or referee, is a judge within the meaning of this Code. All judges shall comply with this Code except as provided below.

Commentary

The four categories of judicial service in other than a full-time capacity are necessarily defined in general terms because of the widely varying forms of judicial service. For the purposes of this Section, as long as a retired judge is subject to recall the judge is considered to "perform judicial functions." The determination of which category and, accordingly, which specific Code provisions apply to an individual judicial officer, depend upon the facts of the particular judicial service.

B. Retired Judge Subject to Recall. A retired judge subject to recall who by law is not permitted to practice law is not required to comply:

(1) except while serving as a judge, with Section 4F; and

(2) at any time with Section 4E.

C. Continuing Part-time Judge. A continuing part-time judge *:

(1) is not required to comply:

(a) except while serving as a judge, with Section 3B(9); and

(b) at any time with Sections 4C(2), 4D(3), 4E(1), 4F, 4G, 4H, 5A(1), 5B(2) and 5D.

(2) shall not practice law in the court on which the judge serves or in any court subject to the appellate jurisdiction of the court on which the judge serves, and shall not act as a lawyer in a proceeding in which the judge has served as a judge or in any other proceeding related thereto.

Commentary

When a person who has been a continuing part-time judge is no longer a continuing part-time judge, including a retired judge no longer subject to recall, that person may act as a lawyer in a proceeding in which he or she has served as a judge or in any other proceeding related thereto only with the express consent of all parties pursuant to [Rule 1.12(a) of the ABA Model Rules of Professional Conduct]. (An adopting jurisdiction should substitute a reference to its applicable rule).

ing the Code for administrative law judges. See, e.g., Model Code of Judicial Conduct for Federal Administrative Law Judges, endorsed by the National Conference of Administrative Law Judges in February 1989.

* See Terminology, "continuing part-time judge."

D. Periodic Part-time Judge. A periodic part-time judge *:

(1) is not required to comply

(a) **except while serving as a judge, with Section 3B(9);**

(b) **at any time, with Sections 4C(2), 4C(3)(a), 4D(1)(b), 4D(3), 4D(4), 4D(5), 4E, 4F, 4G, 4H, 5A(1), 5B(2) and 5D.**

(2) shall not practice law in the court on which the judge serves or in any court subject to the appellate jurisdiction of the court on which the judge serves, and shall not act as a lawyer in a proceeding in which the judge has served as a judge or in any other proceeding related thereto.

Commentary

When a person who has been a periodic part-time judge is no longer a periodic part-time judge (no longer accepts appointments), that person may act as a lawyer in a proceeding in which he or she has served as a judge or in any other proceeding related thereto only with the express consent of all parties pursuant to [Rule 1.12(a) of the ABA Model Rules of Professional Conduct]. (An adopting jurisdiction should substitute a reference to its applicable rule).

E. Pro Tempore Part–Time Judge. A pro tempore part-time judge †:

(1) is not required to comply:

(a) **except while serving as a judge, with Sections 2A, 2B, 3B(9) and 4C(1);**

(b) **at any time with Sections 2C, 4C(2), 4C(3)(a), 4C(3)(b), 4D(1)(b), 4D(3), 4D(4), 4D(5), 4E, 4F, 4G, 4H, 5A(1), 5A(2), 5B(2) and 5D.**

(2) A person who has been a pro tempore part-time judge † shall not act as a lawyer in a proceeding in which the judge has served as a judge or in any other proceeding related thereto except as otherwise permitted by [Rule 1.12(a) of the ABA Model Rules of Professional Conduct]. (An adopting jurisdiction should substitute a reference to its applicable rule.)

F. Time for Compliance. A person to whom this Code becomes applicable shall comply immediately with all provisions of this Code except Sections 4D(2), 4D(3) and 4E and shall comply with these Sections as soon as reasonably possible and shall do so in any event within the period of one year.

Commentary

If serving as a fiduciary when selected as judge, a new judge may, notwithstanding the prohibitions in Section 4E, continue to serve as

---

* See Terminology, "periodic part-time judge."

† See Terminology, "pro tempore part-time judge."

fiduciary but only for that period of time necessary to avoid serious adverse consequences to the beneficiary of the fiduciary relationship and in no event longer than one year. Similarly, if engaged at the time of judicial selection in a business activity, a new judge may, notwithstanding the prohibitions in Section 4D(3), continue in that activity for a reasonable period but in no event longer than one year.

AMERICAN BAR ASSOCIATION CODE OF JUDICIAL CONDUCT (1972)

As amended until 1989.

[In 1969, the ABA created a commission chaired by California Supreme Court Justice Traynor to draft a code of conduct for judges. The new code of conduct was to replace the Canons of Judicial Ethics, which had been adopted by the ABA in 1924. This committee produced the Code of Judicial Conduct and this document was adopted by the ABA in 1972. Most state courts have adopted codes based largely upon the 1972 Code of Judicial Conduct. Note, however, that the ABA replaced the 1972 Code with a 1990 Code of Judicial Conduct. Ed.]

Contents

INTRODUCTION

Almost fifty years ago the American Bar Association formulated the original *Canons of Judicial Ethics*. Those Canons, occasionally amended, have been adopted in most states. In 1969 the Association determined that current needs and problems required revision of the Canons. In the revision process, the Association has sought and considered the views of the Bench and Bar and other interested persons. In

ABA CODE

the judgment of the Association this Code, consisting of statements of norms denominated canons, the accompanying text setting forth specific rules, and the commentary, states the standards that judges should observe. The canons and text establish mandatory standards unless otherwise indicated. It is hoped that all jurisdictions will adopt this Code and establish effective disciplinary procedures for its enforcement.

CANON 1

A Judge Should Uphold the Integrity and Independence of the Judiciary

An independent and honorable judiciary is indispensable to justice in our society. A judge should participate in establishing, maintaining, and enforcing, and should himself observe, high standards of conduct so that the integrity and independence of the judiciary may be preserved. The provisions of this Code should be construed and applied to further that objective.

CANON 2

A Judge Should Avoid Impropriety and the Appearance of Impropriety in All His Activities

A. A judge should respect and comply with the law and should conduct himself at all times in a manner that promotes public confidence in the integrity and impartiality of the judiciary.

B. A judge should not allow his family, social, or other relationships to influence his judicial conduct or judgment. He should not lend the prestige of his office to advance the private interests of others; nor should he convey or permit others to convey the impression that they are in a special position to influence him. He should not testify voluntarily as a character witness.

Commentary

Public confidence in the judiciary is eroded by irresponsible or improper conduct by judges. A judge must avoid all impropriety and appearance of impropriety. He must expect to be the subject of constant public scrutiny. He must therefore accept restrictions on his conduct that might be viewed as burdensome by the ordinary citizen and should do so freely and willingly.

The testimony of a judge as a character witness injects the prestige of his office into the proceeding in which he testifies and may be misunderstood to be an official testimonial. This Canon, however, does not afford him a privilege against testifying in response to an official summons.

824

It is inappropriate for a judge to hold membership in any organization that practices invidious discrimination on the basis of race, sex, religion, or national origin. Membership of a judge in an organization that practices invidious discrimination may give rise to perceptions by minorities, women, and others, that the judge's impartiality is impaired. Whether an organization practices invidious discrimination is often a complex question to which judges should be sensitive. The answer cannot be determined by a mere examination of an organization's current membership rolls but rather depends upon the history of the organization's selection of members and other relevant factors. Ultimately, each judge must determine in the judge's own conscience whether an organization of which the judge is a member practices invidious discrimination.[1]

CANON 3

A Judge Should Perform the Duties of His Office Impartially and Diligently

The judicial duties of a judge take precedence over all his other activities. His judicial duties include all the duties of his office prescribed by law. In the performance of these duties, the following standards apply:

A. Adjudicative Responsibilities.

    (1) A judge should be faithful to the law and maintain professional competence in it. He should be unswayed by partisan interests, public clamor, or fear of criticism.

    (2) A judge should maintain order and decorum in proceedings before him.

    (3) A judge should be patient, dignified, and courteous to litigants, jurors, witnesses, lawyers, and others with whom he deals in his official capacity, and should require similar conduct of lawyers, and of his staff, court officials, and others subject to his direction and control.

Commentary

The duty to hear all proceedings fairly and with patience is not inconsistent with the duty to dispose promptly of the business of the court. Courts can be efficient and business-like while being patient and deliberate.

    (4) A judge should accord to every person who is legally interested in a proceeding, or his lawyer, full right to be heard according to law, and, except as authorized by law, neither initiate nor consider *ex parte* or other communica-

1. This paragraph was added on August 7, 1984, by the American Bar Association House of Delegates meeting in Chicago.

tions concerning a pending or impending proceeding. A judge, however, may obtain the advice of a disinterested expert on the law applicable to a proceeding before him if he gives notice to the parties of the person consulted and the substance of the advice, and affords the parties reasonable opportunity to respond.

Commentary

The proscription against communications concerning a proceeding includes communications from lawyers, law teachers, and other persons who are not participants in the proceeding, except to the limited extent permitted. It does not preclude a judge from consulting with other judges, or with court personnel whose function is to aid the judge in carrying out his adjudicative responsibilities.

An appropriate and often desirable procedure for a court to obtain the advice of a disinterested expert on legal issues is to invite him to file a brief *amicus curiae*.

(5) **A judge should dispose promptly of the business of the court.**

Commentary

Prompt disposition of the court's business requires a judge to devote adequate time to his duties, to be punctual in attending court and expeditious in determining matters under submission, and to insist that court officials, litigants and their lawyers cooperate with him to that end.

(6) **A judge should abstain from public comment about a pending or impending proceeding in any court, and should require similar abstention on the part of court personnel subject to his direction and control. This subsection does not prohibit judges from making public statements in the course of their official duties or from explaining for public information the procedures of the court.**

Commentary

"Court personnel" does not include the lawyers in a proceeding before a judge. The conduct of lawyers is governed by DR7–107 of the *Code of Professional Responsibility*.

(7) **A judge should prohibit broadcasting, televising, recording or photographing in courtrooms and areas immediately adjacent thereto during sessions of court, or recesses between sessions, except that under rules prescribed by a supervising appellate court or other appropriate authority, a judge may authorize broadcasting, televising, recording and photographing of judicial proceedings in courtrooms and areas immediately adjacent thereto consistent**

with the right of the parties to a fair trial and subject to express conditions, limitations, and guidelines which allow such coverage in a manner that will be unobtrusive, will not distract the trial participants, and will not otherwise interfere with the administration of justice.[2]

B. Administrative Responsibilities.

(1) A judge should diligently discharge his administrative responsibilities, maintain professional competence in judicial administration, and facilitate the performance of the administrative responsibilities of other judges and court officials.

(2) A judge should require his staff and court officials subject to his direction and control to observe the standards of fidelity and diligence that apply to him.

(3) A judge should take or initiate appropriate disciplinary measures against a judge or lawyer for unprofessional conduct of which the judge may become aware.

Commentary

Disciplinary measures may include reporting a lawyer's misconduct to an appropriate disciplinary body.

(4) A judge should not make unnecessary appointments. He should exercise his power of appointment only on the basis of merit, avoiding nepotism and favoritism. He should not approve compensation of appointees beyond the fair value of services rendered.

Commentary

Appointees of the judge include officials such as referees, commissioners, special masters, receivers, guardians and personnel such as clerks, secretaries, and bailiffs. Consent by the parties to an appointment or an award of compensation does not relieve the judge of the obligation prescribed by this subsection.

C. Disqualification.

(1) A judge should disqualify himself in a proceeding in which his impartiality might reasonably be questioned, including but not limited to instances where:

(a) he has a personal bias or prejudice concerning a party, or personal knowledge of disputed evidentiary facts concerning the proceeding;

(b) he served as lawyer in the matter in controversy, or a lawyer with whom he previously practiced law served

2. As amended August 11, 1982, American Bar Association House of Delegates, San Francisco, per Report 107.

during such association as a lawyer concerning the matter, or the judge or such lawyer has been a material witness concerning it;

Commentary

A lawyer in a governmental agency does not necessarily have an association with other lawyers employed by that agency within the meaning of this subsection; a judge formerly employed by a governmental agency, however, should disqualify himself in a proceeding if his impartiality might reasonably be questioned because of such association.

    (c) he knows that he, individually or as a fiduciary, or his spouse or minor child residing in his household, has a financial interest in the subject matter in controversy or in a party to the proceeding, or any other interest that could be substantially affected by the outcome of the proceeding;

    (d) he or his spouse, or a person within the third degree of relationship to either of them, or the spouse of such a person:

        (i) is a party to the proceeding, or an officer, director, or trustee of a party;

        (ii) is acting as a lawyer in the proceeding;

Commentary

The fact that a lawyer in a proceeding is affiliated with a law firm with which a lawyer-relative of the judge is affiliated does not of itself disqualify the judge. Under appropriate circumstances, the fact that "his impartiality might reasonably be questioned" under Canon 3C(1), or that the lawyer-relative is known by the judge to have an interest in the law firm that could be "substantially affected by the outcome of the proceeding" under Canon 3C(1)(d)(iii) may require his disqualification.

        (iii) is known by the judge to have an interest that could be substantially affected by the outcome of the proceeding;

        (iv) is to the judge's knowledge likely to be a material witness in the proceeding;

    (2) A judge should inform himself about his personal and fiduciary financial interests, and make a reasonable effort to inform himself about the personal financial interests of his spouse and minor children residing in his household.

    (3) For the purposes of this section:

    (a) the degree of relationship is calculated according to the civil law system;

Commentary

According to the civil law system, the third degree of relationship test would, for example, disqualify the judge if his or his spouse's father, grandfather, uncle, brother, or niece's husband were a party or lawyer in the proceeding, but would not disqualify him if a cousin were a party or lawyer in the proceeding.

(b) "fiduciary" includes such relationships an executor, administrator, trustee, and guardian;

(c) "financial interest" means ownership of a legal or equitable interest, however small, or a relationship as director, advisor, or other active participant in the affairs of a party, except that:

    (i) ownership in a mutual or common investment fund that holds securities is not a "financial interest" in such securities unless the judge participates in the management of the fund;

    (ii) an office in an educational, religious, charitable, fraternal, or civic organization is not a "financial interest" in securities held by the organization;

    (iii) the proprietary interest of a policy holder in a mutual insurance company, of a depositor in a mutual savings association, or a similar proprietary interest, is a "financial interest" in the organization only if the outcome of the proceeding could substantially affect the value of the interest;

    (iv) ownership of government securities is a "financial interest" in the issuer only if the outcome of the proceeding could substantially affect the value of the securities.

D. **Remittal of Disqualification.** A judge disqualified by the terms of Canon 3C(1)(c) or Canon 3C(1)(d) may, instead of withdrawing from the proceeding, disclose on the record the basis of his disqualification. If, based on such disclosure, the parties and lawyers, independently of the judge's participation, all agree in writing that the judge's relationship is immaterial or that his financial interest is insubstantial, the judge is no longer disqualified, and may participate in the proceeding. The agreement, signed by all parties and lawyers, shall be incorporated in the record of the proceeding.

Commentary

This procedure is designed to minimize the chance that a party or lawyer will feel coerced into an agreement. When a party is not immediately available, the judge without violating this section may proceed on the written assurance of the lawyer that his party's consent will be subsequently filed.

CANON 4

A Judge May Engage in Activities to Improve the Law, the Legal System, and the Administration of Justice

A judge, subject to the proper performance of his judicial duties, may engage in the following quasi-judicial activities, if in doing so he does not cast doubt on his capacity to decide impartially any issue that may come before him:

A. He may speak, write, lecture, teach, and participate in other activities concerning the law, the legal system, and the administration of justice.

B. He may appear at a public hearing before an executive or legislative body or official on matters concerning the law, the legal system, and the administration of justice, and he may otherwise consult with an executive or legislative body or official, but only on matters concerning the administration of justice.

C. He may serve as a member, officer, or director of an organization or governmental agency devoted to the improvement of the law, the legal system, or the administration of justice. He may assist such an organization in raising funds and may participate in their management and investment, but should not personally participate in public fund raising activities. He may make recommendations to public and private fund-granting agencies on projects and programs concerning the law, the legal system, and the administration of justice.

Commentary

As a judicial officer and person specially learned in the law, a judge is in a unique position to contribute to the improvement of the law, the legal system, and the administration of justice, including revision of substantive and procedural law and improvement of criminal and juvenile justice. To the extent that his time permits, he is encouraged to do so, either independently or through a bar association, judicial conference, or other organization dedicated to the improvement of the law.

Extra-judicial activities are governed by Canon 5.

CANON 5

A Judge Should Regulate His Extra-Judicial Activities to Minimize the Risk of Conflict with His Judicial Duties

A. Avocational Activities. A judge may write, lecture, teach, and speak on non-legal subjects, and engage in the arts, sports, and other social and recreational activities, if such avocational activities do not detract from the dignity of his office or interfere with the performance of his judicial duties.

Commentary

Complete separation of a judge from extra judicial activities is neither possible nor wise; he should not become isolated from the society in which he lives.

B. Civic and Charitable Activities. A judge may participate in civic and charitable activities that do not reflect adversely upon his impartiality or interfere with the performance of his judicial duties. A judge may serve as an officer, director, trustee, or non-legal advisor of an educational, religious, charitable, fraternal, or civic organization not conducted for the economic or political advantage of its members, subject to the following limitations:

(1) A judge should not serve if it is likely that the organization will be engaged in proceedings that would ordinarily come before him or will be regularly engaged in adversary proceedings in any court.

Commentary

The changing nature of some organizations and of their relationship to the law makes it necessary for a judge regularly to reexamine the activities of each organization with which he is affiliated to determine if it is proper for him to continue his relationship with it. For example, in many jurisdictions charitable hospitals are now more frequently in court than in the past. Similarly, the boards of some legal aid organizations now make policy decisions that may have political significance or imply commitment to causes that may come before the courts for adjudication.

(2) A judge should not solicit funds for any educational, religious, charitable, fraternal, or civic organization, or use or permit the use of the prestige of his office for that purpose, but he may be listed as an officer, director, or trustee of such an organization. He should not be a speaker or the guest of honor at an organization's fund raising events, but he may attend such events.

(3) A judge should not give investment advice to such an organization, but he may serve on its board of directors or trustees even though it has the responsibility for approving investment decisions.

Commentary

A judge's participation in an organization devoted to quasi-judicial activities is governed by Canon 4.

C. **Financial Activities.**

    (1) A judge should refrain from financial and business deal-
ings that tend to reflect adversely on his impartiality,
interfere with the proper performance of his judicial duties, exploit his judicial position, or involve him in frequent transactions with lawyers or persons likely to come
before the court on which he serves.

    (2) Subject to the requirements of subsection (1), a judge may
hold and manage investments, including real estate, and
engage in other remunerative activity, but should not
serve as an officer, director, manager, advisor, or employee of any business.

Commentary

The Effective Date of Compliance provision of this Code qualifies
this subsection with regard to a judge engaged in a family business at
the time this Code becomes effective.

Canon 5 may cause temporary hardship in jurisdictions where
judicial salaries are inadequate and judges are presently supplementing
their income through commercial activities. The remedy, however, is
to secure adequate judicial salaries.

[Canon 5C(2) sets the minimum standard to which a full-time
judge should adhere. Jurisdictions that do not provide adequate judicial salaries but are willing to allow full-time judges
to supplement their incomes through commercial activities
may adopt the following substitute until such time as adequate salaries are provided:

* (2) Subject to the requirement of subsection (1), a judge may
hold and manage investments, including real estate, and engage in other remunerative activity including the operation
of a business.

Jurisdictions adopting the foregoing substitute may also wish
to prohibit a judge from engaging in certain types of businesses such as that of banks, public utilities, insurance companies, and other businesses affected with a public interest.

    (3) A judge should manage his investments and other finan-
cial interests to minimize the number of cases in which he
is disqualified. As soon as he can do so without serious
financial detriment, he should divest himself of investments and other financial interests that might require
frequent disqualification.

    (4) Neither a judge nor a member of his family residing in his
household should accept a gift, bequest, favor, or loan
from anyone except as follows:

(a) a judge may accept a gift incident to public testimonial to him; books supplied by publishers on a complimentary basis for official use; or an invitation to the judge and his spouse to attend a bar-related function or activity devoted to the improvement of the law, the legal system, or the administration of justice;

(b) a judge or a member of his family residing in his household may accept ordinary social hospitality; a gift, bequest, favor, or loan from a relative; a wedding or engagement gift; a loan from a lending institution in its regular course of business on the same terms generally available to persons who are not judges; or a scholarship or fellowship awarded on the same terms applied to other applicants;

(c) a judge or a member of his family residing in his household may accept any other gift, bequest, favor, or loan only if the donor is not a party or other person whose interests have come or are likely to come before him, and, if its value exceeds $100, the judge reports it in the same manner as he reports compensation in Canon 6C.

Commentary

This subsection does not apply to contributions to a judge's campaign for judicial office, a matter governed by Canon 7.

(5) For the purposes of this section "member of his family residing in his household" means any relative of a judge by blood or marriage, or a person treated by a judge as a member of his family, who resides in his household.

(6) A judge is not required by this Code to disclose his income, debts, or investments, except as provided in this Canon and Canons 3 and 6.

Commentary

Canon 3 requires a judge to disqualify himself in any proceeding in which he has a financial interest, however small; Canon 5 requires a judge to refrain from engaging in business and from financial activities that might interfere with the impartial performance of his judicial duties; Canon 6 requires him to report all compensation he receives for activities outside his judicial office. A judge has the rights of an ordinary citizen, including the right to privacy of his financial affairs, except to the extent that limitations thereon are required to safeguard the proper performance of his duties. Owning and receiving income from investments do not as such affect the performance of a judge's duties.

(7) Information acquired by a judge in his judicial capacity should not be used or disclosed by him in financial deal-

ings or for any other purpose not related to his judicial duties.

D. **Fiduciary Activities.** A judge should not serve as the executor, administrator, trustee, guardian, or other fiduciary, except for the estate, trust, or person of a member of his family, and then only if such service will not interfere with the proper performance of his judicial duties. "Member of his family" includes a spouse, child, grandchild, parent, grandparent, or other relative or person with whom the judge maintains a close familial relationship. As a family fiduciary a judge is subject to the following restrictions:

(1) He should not serve if it is likely that as a fiduciary he will be engaged in proceedings that would ordinarily come before him, or if the estate, trust, or ward becomes involved in adversary proceedings in the court on which he serves or one under its appellate jurisdiction.

Commentary

The Effective Date of Compliance provision of this Code qualifies this subsection with regard to a judge who is an executor, administrator, trustee, or other fiduciary at the time this Code becomes effective.

(2) While acting as a fiduciary a judge is subject to the same restrictions on financial activities that apply to him in his personal capacity.

Commentary

A judge's obligation under this Canon and his obligation as a fiduciary may come into conflict. For example, a judge should resign as trustee if it would result in detriment to the trust to divest it of holdings whose retention would place the judge in violation of Canon 5C(3).

E. **Arbitration.** A judge should not act as an arbitrator or mediator.

F. **Practice of Law.** A judge should not practice law.

G. **Extra-judicial Appointments.** A judge should not accept appointment to a governmental committee, commission, or other position that is concerned with issues of fact or policy on matters other than the improvement of the law, the legal system, or the administration of justice. A judge, however, may represent his country, state, or locality on ceremonial occasions or in connection with historical, educational, and cultural activities.

Commentary

Valuable services have been rendered in the past to the states and the nation by judges appointed by the executive to undertake important extra-judicial assignments. The appropriateness of conferring these assignments on judges must be reassessed, however, in light of the demands on judicial manpower created by today's crowded dockets and the need to protect the courts from involvement in extra-judicial matters that may prove to be controversial. Judges should not be expected or permitted to accept governmental appointments that could interfere with the effectiveness and independence of the judiciary.

CANON 6

A Judge Should Regularly File Reports of Compensation Received for Quasi-Judicial and Extra-Judicial Activities

A judge may receive compensation and reimbursement of expenses for the quasi-judicial and extra-judicial activities permitted by this Code, if the source of such payments does not give the appearance of influencing the judge in his judicial duties or otherwise give the appearance of impropriety, subject to the following restrictions:

A. **Compensation.** Compensation should not exceed a reasonable amount nor should it exceed what a person who is not a judge would receive for the same activity.

B. **Expense Reimbursement.** Expense reimbursement should be limited to the actual cost of travel, food, and lodging reasonably incurred by the judge and, where appropriate to the occasion by his spouse. Any payment in excess of such an amount is compensation.

C. **Public Reports.** A judge should report the date, place, and nature of any activity for which he received compensation, and the name of the payor and the amount of compensation so received. Compensation or income of a spouse attributed to the judge by operation of a community property law is not extra-judicial compensation to the judge. His report should be made at least annually and should be filed as a public document in the office of the clerk of the court on which he serves or other office designated by rule of court.

CANON 7

A Judge Should Refrain From Political Activity Inappropriate to His Judicial Office

A. **Political Conduct in General.**

(1) A judge or a candidate for election to judicial office should not:

(a) act as a leader or hold any office in a political organization;

835

(b) **make speeches for a political organization or candidate or publicly endorse a candidate for public office;**

Commentary

A candidate does not publicly endorse another candidate for public office by having his name on the same ticket.

(c) **solicit funds for or pay an assessment or make a contribution to a political organization or candidate, attend political gatherings, or purchase tickets for political party dinners, or other functions, except as authorized in subsection A(2);**

(2) **A judge holding an office filled by public election between competing candidates, or a candidate for such office, may, only insofar as permitted by law, attend political gatherings, speak to such gatherings on his own behalf when he is a candidate for election or re-election, identify himself as a member of a political party, and contribute to a political party or organization.**

(3) **A judge should resign his office when he becomes a candidate either in a party primary or in a general election for a nonjudicial office, except that he may continue to hold his judicial office while being a candidate for election to or serving as a delegate in a state constitutional convention, if he is otherwise permitted by law to do so.**

(4) **A judge should not engage in any other political activity except on behalf of measures to improve the law, the legal system, or the administration of justice.**

B. **Campaign Conduct.**

(1) **A candidate, including an incumbent judge, for a judicial office that is filled either by public election between competing candidates or on the basis of a merit system election:**

(a) **should maintain the dignity appropriate to judicial office, and should encourage members of his family to adhere to the same standards of political conduct that apply to him;**

(b) **should prohibit public officials or employees subject to his direction or control from doing for him what he is prohibited from doing under this Canon; and except to the extent authorized under subsection B(2) or B(3), he should not allow any other person to do for him what he is prohibited from doing under this Canon;**

836

(c) should not make pledges or promises of conduct in office other than the faithful and impartial performance of the duties of the office; announce his views on disputed legal or political issues; or misrepresent his identity, qualifications, present position, or other fact.

(2) A candidate, including an incumbent judge, for a judicial office that is filled by public election between competing candidates should not himself solicit or accept campaign funds, or solicit publicly stated support, but he may establish committees of responsible persons to secure and manage the expenditure of funds for his campaign and to obtain public statements of support for his candidacy. Such committees are not prohibited from soliciting campaign contributions and public support from lawyers. A candidate's committees may solicit funds for his campaign no earlier than [90] days before a primary election and no later than [90] days after the last election in which he participates during the election year. A candidate should not use or permit the use of campaign contributions for the private benefit of himself or members of his family.

Commentary

Unless the candidate is required by law to file a list of his campaign contributors, their names should not be revealed to the candidate.

[Each jurisdiction adopting this Code should prescribe a time limit on soliciting campaign funds that is appropriate to the elective process therein.]

(3) An incumbent judge who is a candidate for retention in or re-election to office without a competing candidate, and whose candidacy has drawn active opposition, may campaign in response thereto and may obtain publicly stated support and campaign funds in the manner provided in subsection B(2).

Compliance With the Code of Judicial Conduct

Anyone, whether or not a lawyer, who is an officer of a judicial system performing judicial functions, including an officer such as a referee in bankruptcy, special master, court commissioner, or magistrate, is a judge for the purpose of this Code. All judges should comply with this Code except as provided below.

A. **Part-time Judge.** A part-time judge is a judge who serves on a continuing or periodic basis, but is permitted by law to devote time to some other profession or occupation and whose compensation for that reason is less than that of a full-time judge. A part-time judge:

   (1) is not required to comply with Canon 5C(2), D, E, F, and G, and Canon 6C;

   (2) should not practice law in the court on which he serves or in any court subject to the appellate jurisdiction of the court on which he serves, or act as a lawyer in a proceeding in which he has served as a judge in any other proceeding related thereto.

B. **Judge Pro Tempore.** A judge <u>pro tempore</u> is a person who is appointed to act temporarily as a judge.

   (1) While acting as such, a judge <u>pro tempore</u> is not required to comply with Canon 5C(2), (3), D, E, F, and G, and Canon 6C.

   (2) A person who has been a judge <u>pro tempore</u> should not act as a lawyer in a proceeding in which he has served as a judge or in any other proceeding related thereto.

C. **Retired Judge.** A retired judge who receives the same compensation as a full-time judge on the court from which he retired and is eligible for recall to judicial service should comply with all the provisions of this Code except Canon 5G, but he should refrain from judicial service during the period of an extra-judicial appointment not sanctioned by Canon 5G. All other retired judges eligible for recall to judicial service should comply with the provisions of this Code governing part-time judges.

Effective Date of Compliance

A person to whom this Code becomes applicable should arrange his affairs as soon as reasonably possible to comply with it. If, however, the demands on his time and the possibility of conflicts of interest are not substantial, a person who holds judicial office on the date this Code becomes effective may:

   (a) continue to act as an officer, director, or non-legal advisor of a family business;

   (b) continue to act as an executor, administrator, trustee, or other fiduciary for the estate or person of one who is not a member of his family.

CORRELATION TABLES

The Correlation Tables identify 1990 Code rules that relate to the same subject matter as the corresponding rules of the 1972 Code. The substance of the rules cited is not necessarily identical, and in many instances varies considerably. Although the Commentary is not cross-referenced, the subject matter of certain rules of the 1990 Code may have been addressed by the Commentary in the 1972 Code.

CORRELATION TABLE A

1990 CODE	1972 CODE
Preamble	None
Terminology	Canons 3C(3)(a), (b), (c); 5C(5); 5D
Canon 1	Canon 1
Section 1A	Paragraph to Canon 1
Canon 2	Canon 2
Section 2A	Canon 2A
Section 2B	Canon 2B
Section 2C	None
Canon 3	Canon 3
Section 3A	Paragraph to Canon 3
Section 3B(1)	None
Section 3B(2)	Canon 3A(1)
Section 3B(3)	Canon 3A(2)
Section 3B(4)	Canon 3A(3)
Section 3B(5)	None
Section 3B(6)	None
Section 3B(7)	Canon 3A(4)
Section 3B(7)(a)	None
Section 3B(7)(a)(i)	None
Section 3B(7)(a)(ii)	None
Section 3B(7)(b)	Canon 3A(4)
Section 3B(7)(c)	None
Section 3B(7)(d)	None
Section 3B(7)(e)	None
Section 3B(8)	Canon 3A(5)
Section 3B(9)	Canon 3A(6)
Section 3B(10)	None
Section 3B(11)	Canon 5C(7)
Section 3C(1)	Canon 3B(1)
Section 3C(2)	Canon 3B(2)
Section 3C(3)	None
Section 3C(4)	Canon 3B(4)
Section 3D(1)	Canon 3B(3)
Section 3D(2)	Canon 3B(3)
Section 3D(3)	None
Section 3E(1)	Canon 3C(1)
Section 3E(1)(a)	Canon 3C(1)(a)
Section 3E(1)(b)	Canon 3C(1)(b)
Section 3E(1)(c)	Canon 3C(1)(c)
Section 3E(1)(d)	Canon 3C(1)(d)
Section 3E(1)(d)(i)	Canon 3C(1)(d)(i)
Section 3E(1)(d)(ii)	Canon 3C(1)(d)(ii)
Section 3E(1)(d)(iii)	Canon 3C(1)(d)(iii)
Section 3E(1)(d)(iv)	Canon 3C(1)(d)(iv)

CORRELATION TABLES

CORRELATION TABLES

CORRELATION TABLES

*

PART SIX

SELECTED STATE STANDARDS, RULES, AND STATUTES

Table of Contents

Introduction

This part presents a more in depth perspective on how two states have chosen to regulate lawyers. The California Rules of Professional Conduct for governing lawyers' conduct differ substantially from the ABA codes of ethics. The California approach to regulating lawyer must also consider the legislature's control over lawyers. This form of regulation is contained in the California Business and Professions Code. Selected sections are reproduced below. We have also added the Disciplinary Rules of the New York Code of Professional Responsibility as a state that continues to retain a code based upon the ABA Model Code of Professional Responsibility.

CALIFORNIA RULES OF
PROFESSIONAL CONDUCT

Approved by Supreme Court November 28, 1988

Effective May 27, 1989

CHAPTER 1. PROFESSIONAL INTEGRITY IN GENERAL

CHAPTER 2. RELATIONSHIPS AMONG MEMBERS

CHAPTER 3. PROFESSIONAL RELATIONSHIP WITH CLIENTS

CHAPTER 4. FINANCIAL RELATIONSHIP WITH CLIENTS

CHAPTER 5.   ADVOCACY AND REPRESENTATION

CHAPTER 1.   PROFESSIONAL INTEGRITY IN GENERAL

Rule 1-100.   Rules of Professional Conduct, in General

(A) Purpose and Function.

The following rules are intended to regulate professional conduct of members of the State Bar through discipline. They have been adopted by the Board of Governors of the State Bar of California and approved by the Supreme Court of California pursuant to Business and Professions Code sections 6076 and 6077 to protect the public and to promote respect and confidence in the legal profession. These rules together with any standards adopted by the Board of Governors pursuant to these rules shall be binding upon all members of the State Bar.

For a willful breach of any of these rules, the Board of Governors has the power to discipline members as provided by law.

The prohibition of certain conduct in these rules is not exclusive. Members are also bound by applicable law including the State Bar Act (Bus. & Prof. Code, § 6000 et seq.) and opinions of California courts. Although not binding, opinions of ethics committees in California should be consulted by members for guidance on proper professional conduct. Ethics opinions and rules and standards promulgated by other jurisdictions and bar associations may also be considered.

These rules are not intended to create new civil causes of action. Nothing in these rules shall be deemed to create, augment, diminish, or eliminate any substantive legal duty of lawyers or the non-disciplinary consequences of violating such a duty.

(B) Definitions.

   (1) "Law Firm" means:

      (a) two or more lawyers whose activities constitute the practice of law, and who share its profits, expenses, and liabilities; or

    (b) a law corporation which employs more than one member; or

    (c) a division, department, office, or group within a business entity, which includes more than one lawyer who performs legal services for the business entity; or

    (d) a publicly funded entity which employs more than one lawyer to perform legal services.

    (2) "Member" means a member of the State Bar of California.

    (3) "Lawyer" means a member of the State Bar of California or a person who is admitted in good standing of and eligible to practice before the bar of any United States court or the highest court of the District of Columbia or any state, territory, or insular possession of the United States.

    (4) "Associate" means an employee or fellow employee who is employed as a lawyer.

    (5) "Shareholder" means a shareholder in a professional corporation pursuant to Business and Professions Code section 6160 et seq.

(C) Purpose of Discussions.

Because it is a practical impossibility to convey in black letter form all of the nuances of these disciplinary rules, the comments contained in the Discussions of the rules, while they do not add independent basis for imposing discipline, are intended to provide guidance for interpreting the rules and practicing in compliance with them.

(D) Geographic Scope of Rules.

    (1) As to members:

        These rules shall govern the activities of members in and outside this state, except as members lawfully practicing outside this state may be specifically required by a jurisdiction in which they are practicing to follow rules of professional conduct different from these rules.

    (2) As to lawyers from other jurisdictions:

        These rules shall also govern the activities of lawyers while engaged in the performance of lawyer functions in this state; but nothing contained in these rules shall be deemed to authorize the performance of such functions by such persons in this state except as otherwise permitted by law.

(E) These rules may be cited and referred to as "Rules of Professional Conduct of the State Bar of California."

<u>Discussion:</u>

The Rules of Professional Conduct are intended to establish the standards for members for purposes of discipline. (See *Ames v. State Bar* (1973) 8 Cal.3d 910 [106 Cal.Rptr. 489].) The fact that a member has engaged in conduct that may be contrary to these rules does not automatically give rise to a civil cause of action. (See *Noble v. Sears, Roebuck & Co.* (1973) 33 Cal.App.3d 654 [109 Cal.Rptr. 269]; *Wilhelm v. Pray, Price, Williams & Russell* (1986) 186 Cal.App.3d 1324 [231 Cal.Rptr. 355].) These rules are not intended to supercede existing law relating to members in non-disciplinary contexts. (See, e.g., *Klemm v. Superior Court* (1977) 75 Cal.App.3d 893 [142 Cal.Rptr. 509] (motion for disqualification of counsel due to a conflict of interest); *Academy of California Optometrists, Inc. v. Superior Court* (1975) 51 Cal.App.3d 999 [124 Cal.Rptr. 668] (duty to return client files); *Chronometrics, Inc. v. Sysgen, Inc.* (1980) 110 Cal.App.3d 597 [168 Cal.Rptr. 196] (disqualification of member appropriate remedy for improper communication with adverse party).

Law firm, as defined by subparagraph (B)(1), is not intended to include an association of members who do not share profits, expenses, and liabilities. The subparagraph is not intended to imply that a law firm may include a person who is not a member in violation of the law governing the unauthorized practice of law.

Rule 1-110. Disciplinary Authority of the State Bar

A member shall comply with conditions attached to public or private reprovals or other discipline administered by the State Bar pursuant to Business and Professions Code sections 6077 and 6078 and rule 956, California Rules of Court.

Rule 1-120. Assisting, Soliciting, or Inducing Violations

A member shall not knowingly assist in, solicit, or induce any violation of these rules or the State Bar Act.

Rule 1-200. False Statement Regarding Admission to the State Bar

(A) A member shall not knowingly make a false statement regarding a material fact or knowingly fail to disclose a material fact in connection with an application for admission to the State Bar.

(B) A member shall not further an application for admission to the State Bar of a person whom the member knows to be unqualified in respect to character, education, or other relevant attributes.

(C) This rule shall not prevent a member from serving as counsel of record for an applicant for admission to practice in proceedings related to such admission.

Discussion:

For purposes of rule 1-200 "admission" includes readmission.

Rule 1-300. Unauthorized Practice of Law

(A) A member shall not aid any person or entity in the unauthorized practice of law.

(B) A member shall not practice law in a jurisdiction where to do so would be in violation of regulations of the profession in that jurisdiction.

Rule 1-310. Forming a Partnership With a Non-lawyer

A member shall not form a partnership with a person not licensed to practice law if any of the activities of that partnership consist of the practice of law.

Discussion:

Rule 1-310 is not intended to govern members' activities which cannot be considered to constitute the practice of law. It is intended solely to preclude a member from being involved in the practice of law with a person not licensed to practice law.

Rule 1-320. Financial Arrangements With Non-lawyers

(A) Neither a member nor a law firm shall directly or indirectly share legal fees with a person or entity not licensed to practice law, except that:

(1) An agreement between a member and a law firm, partner, or associate may provide for the payment of money after the member's death to the member's estate or to one or more specified persons over a reasonable period of time; or

(2) A member or law firm undertaking to complete unfinished legal business of a deceased member may pay to the estate of the deceased member or other person legally entitled thereto that proportion of the total compensation which fairly represents the services rendered by the deceased member;

(3) A member or law firm may include non-member employees in a compensation, profit-sharing, or retirement plan even though the plan is based in whole or in part on a profit-sharing arrangement, if such plan does not circumvent these rules or Business and Professions Code section 6000 et seq.; or

(4) A member may pay a prescribed registration, referral, or participation fee to a lawyer referral service established, sponsored, and operated in accordance with the State Bar of California's Minimum Standards for a Lawyer Referral Service in California.

(B) A member shall not compensate, give, or promise anything of value to any person or entity for the purpose of recommending or securing employment of the member or the member's law firm by a client, or as a reward for having made a recommendation resulting in employment of the member or the member's law firm by a client. A member's offering of or giving a gift or gratuity to any person or entity having made a recommendation resulting in the employment of the member or the member's law firm shall not of itself violate this rule, provided that the gift or gratuity was not offered or given in consideration of any promise, agreement, or understanding that such a gift or gratuity would be forthcoming or that referrals would be made or encouraged in the future.

(C) A member shall not compensate, give, or promise anything of value to any representative of the press, radio, television, or other communication medium in anticipation of or in return for publicity of the member, the law firm, or any other member as such in a news item, but the incidental provision of food or beverage shall not of itself violate this rule.

Discussion:

Rule 1-320(C) is not intended to preclude compensation to the communications media in exchange for advertising the member's or law firm's availability for professional employment.

Rule 1-400. Advertising and Solicitation

(A) For purposes of this rule, "communication" means any message or offer made by or on behalf of a member concerning the availability for professional employment of a member or a law firm directed to any former, present, or prospective client, including but not limited to the following:

(1) Any use of firm name, trade name, fictitious name, or other professional designation of such member or law firm; or

(2) Any stationery, letterhead, business card, sign, brochure, or other comparable written material describing such member, law firm, or lawyers; or

(3) Any advertisement (regardless of medium) of such member or law firm directed to the general public or any substantial portion thereof; or

(4) Any unsolicited correspondence from a member or law firm directed to any person or entity.

(B) For purposes of this rule, a "solicitation" means any communication:

(1) Concerning the availability for professional employment of a member or a law firm in which a significant motive is pecuniary gain; and

851

(2) Which is;

    (a) delivered in person or by telephone, or

    (b) directed by any means to a person known to the sender to be represented by counsel in a matter which is a subject of the communication.

(C) A solicitation shall not be made by or on behalf of a member or law firm to a prospective client with whom the member or law firm has no family or prior professional relationship, unless the solicitation is protected from abridgment by the Constitution of the United States or by the Constitution of the State of California. A solicitation to a former or present client in the discharge of a member's or law firm's professional duties is not prohibited.

(D) A communication or a solicitation (as defined herein) shall not:

    (1) Contain any untrue statement; or

    (2) Contain any matter, or present or arrange any matter in a manner or format which is false, deceptive, or which tends to confuse, deceive, or mislead the public; or

    (3) Omit to state any fact necessary to make the statements made, in the light of circumstances under which they are made, not misleading to the public; or

    (4) Fail to indicate clearly, expressly, or by context, that it is a communication or solicitation, as the case may be; or

    (5) Be transmitted in any manner which involves intrusion, coercion, duress, compulsion, intimidation, threats, or vexatious or harassing conduct; or

    (6) State that a member is a "certified specialist" unless the member holds a current certificate as a specialist issued by the California Board of Legal Specialization pursuant to a plan for specialization approved by the Supreme Court.

(E) The Board of Governors of the State Bar shall formulate and adopt standards as to communications which will be presumed to violate this rule 1-400. The standards shall only be used as presumptions affecting the burden of proof in disciplinary proceedings involving alleged violations of these rules. "Presumption affecting the burden of proof" means that presumption defined in Evidence Code sections 605 and 606. Such standards formulated and adopted by the Board, as from time to time amended, shall be effective and binding on all members.

(F) A member shall retain for two years a true and correct copy or recording of any communication made by written or electronic media. Upon written request, the member shall make any such copy or recording available to the State Bar, and, if requested, shall provide to the State Bar evidence to support any factual or objective claim contained in the communication.

Standards:

Pursuant to Rule 1–400(E) the Board of Governors of the State Bar has adopted the following standards effective _____ * as forms of "communication" defined in rule 1–400(A) which are presumed to be in violation of Rule 1–400:

(1) A "communication" which contains guarantees, warranties, or predictions regarding the result of the representation.

(2) A "communication" which contains testimonials about or endorsements of a member unless such communication also contains an express disclaimer such as "this testimonial or endorsement does not constitute a guarantee, warranty, or prediction regarding the outcome of your legal matter."

(3) A "communication" which is delivered to a potential client whom the member knows or should reasonably know is in such a physical, emotional, or mental state that he or she would not be expected to exercise reasonable judgment as to the retention of counsel.

(4) A "communication" which is transmitted at the scene of an accident or at or en route to a hospital, emergency care center, or other health care facility.

(5) A "communication," except professional announcements, seeking professional employment primarily for pecuniary gain which is transmitted by mail or equivalent means which does not clearly identify itself as an advertisement. If transmitted in an envelope, the envelope shall be identified as an advertisement on the outside thereof.

(6) A "communication" in the form of a firm name, trade name, fictitious name, or other professional designation which states or implies a relationship between any member in private practice and a government agency or instrumentality or a public or non-profit legal services organization.

(7) A "communication" in the form of a firm name, trade name, fictitious name, or other professional designation which states or implies that a member has a relationship to any other member or a law firm as a partner or associate, or officer or shareholder pursuant to Business and Professions Code sections 6160–6172 unless such relationship in fact exists.

(8) A "communication" which states or implies that a member or law firm is "of counsel" to another member or a law firm unless the former has a relationship with the latter (other than as a partner or associate, or officer or shareholder pursuant to

* **NOTE:** The Board of Governors has not yet acted upon these standards.

Business and Professions Code sections 6160–6172) which is close, personal, continuous, and regular.

(9) A "communication" in the form of a firm name, trade name, fictitious name, or other professional designation used by a member or law firm in private practice which differs materially from any other such designation used by such member or law firm at the same time in the same community.

(10) A "communication" which implies that the member or member's firm is participating in a lawyer referral service which has been certified by the State Bar of California or as having satisfied the Minimum Standards for Lawyer Referral Services in California, when that is not the case.

Rule 1-500. Agreements Restricting a Member's Practice

(A) A member shall not be a party to or participate in offering or making an agreement, whether in connection with the settlement of a lawsuit or otherwise, if the agreement restricts the right of a member to practice law.

(B) Nothing in paragraph (A) of this rule shall be construed as prohibiting such a restrictive agreement which:

(1) Is a part of an employment, shareholders' or partnership agreement among members provided the restrictive agreement does not survive the termination of the employment, shareholder, or partnership relationship; or

(2) Requires payments to a member upon the member's retirement from the practice of law.

(C) A member shall not be a party to or participate in offering or making an agreement which precludes the reporting of a violation of these rules.

Discussion:

Paragraph (A) makes it clear that the practice, in connection with settlement agreements, of proposing that a member refrain from representing other clients in similar litigation, is prohibited. Neither counsel may demand or suggest such provisions nor may opposing counsel accede or agree to such provisions.

Paragraph (B) permits a restrictive covenant in a law corporation, partnership, or employment agreement. The law corporation shareholder, partner, or associate may agree not to have a separate practice during the existence of the relationship; however, upon termination of the relationship (whether voluntary or involuntary), the member is free to practice law without any contractual restriction except in the case of retirement from the active practice of law.

Rule 1-600. Legal Service Programs

(A) A member shall not participate in a nongovernmental program activity, or organization furnishing, recommending, or paying for legal services, which allows any third person or organization to interfere with the member's independence of professional judgment, or with the client-lawyer relationship, or allows unlicensed persons to practice law, or allows any third person or organization to receive directly or indirectly any part of the consideration paid to the member except as permitted by these rules, or otherwise violates the State Bar Act or these rules.

(B) The Board of Governors of the State Bar shall formulate and adopt Minimum Standards for Lawyer Referral Services, which, as from time to time amended, shall be binding on members.

Discussion:

The participation of a member in a lawyer referral service established, sponsored, supervised, and operated in conformity with the Minimum Standards for a Lawyer Referral Service in California is encouraged and is not, of itself, a violation of these rules.

Rule 1-600 is not intended to override any contractual agreement or relationship between insurers and insureds regarding the provision of legal services.

Rule 1-600 is not intended to apply to the activities of a public agency responsible for providing legal services to a government or to the public.

For purposes of paragraph (A), "a nongovernmental program, activity, or organization" includes, but is not limited to group, prepaid, and voluntary legal service programs, activities, or organizations.

CHAPTER 2. RELATIONSHIP AMONG MEMBERS

Rule 2-100. Communication With a Represented Party

(A) While representing a client, a member shall not communicate directly or indirectly about the subject of the representation with a party the member knows to be represented by another lawyer in the matter, unless the member has the consent of the other lawyer.

(B) For purposes of this rule, a "party" includes:

(1) An officer, director, or managing agent of a corporation or association, and a partner or managing agent of a partnership; or

(2) An association member or an employee of an association, corporation, or partnership, if the subject of the communication is any act or omission of such person in connection with the matter which may be binding upon or imputed to the organization for purposes of civil or criminal liability or whose

statement may constitute an admission on the part of the organization.

(C) This rule shall not prohibit:

    (1) Communications with a public officer, board, committee, or body;

    (2) Communications initiated by a party seeking advice or representation from an independent lawyer of the party's choice; or

    (3) Communications otherwise authorized by law.

Discussion:

Rule 2-100 is intended to control communications between a member and persons the member knows to be represented by counsel unless a statutory scheme or case law will override the rule. There are a number of express statutory schemes which authorize communications between a member and person who would otherwise be subject to this rule. These statutes protect a variety of other rights such as the right of employees to organize and to engage in collective bargaining, employee health and safety, or equal employment opportunity. Other applicable law also includes the authority of government prosecutors and investigators to conduct criminal investigations, as limited by the relevant decisional law.

Rule 2-100 is not intended to prevent the parties themselves from communicating with respect to the subject matter of the representation, and nothing in the rule prevents a member from advising the client that such communication can be made. Moreover, the rule does not prohibit a member who is also a party to a legal matter from directly or indirectly communicating on his or her own behalf with a represented party. Such a member has independent rights as a party which should not be abrogated because of his or her professional status. To prevent any possible abuse in such situations, the counsel for the opposing party may advise that party (1) about the risks and benefits of communications with a lawyer-party, and (2) not to accept or engage in communications with the lawyer-party.

Rule 2-100 also addresses the situation in which member A is contacted by an opposing party who is represented and, because of dissatisfaction with that party's counsel, seeks A's independent advice. Since A is employed by the opposition, the member cannot give independent advice.

As used in paragraph (A), "the subject of the representation," "matter," and "party" are not limited to a litigation context.

Paragraph (B) is intended to apply only to persons employed at the time of the communication.

Subparagraph (C)(2) is intended to permit a member to communicate with an individual seeking to hire new counsel or to obtain a second opinion. A member contacted by such an individual continues to be bound by other Rules of Professional Conduct. (See, e.g., rules 1–400 and 3–310.)

Rule 2–200.   Financial Arrangements Among Lawyers

(A) A member shall not divide a fee for legal services with a lawyer who is not a partner of, associate of, or shareholder with the member unless:

   (1) The client has consented in writing thereto after a full disclosure has been made in writing that a division of fees will be made and the terms of such division; and

   (2) The total fee charged by all lawyers is not increased solely by reason of the provision for division of fees and is not unconscionable as that term is defined in rule 4–200.

(B) Except as permitted in paragraph (A) of this rule or rule 2–300, a member shall not compensate, give, or promise anything of value to any lawyer for the purpose of recommending or securing employment of the member or the member's law firm by a client, or as a reward for having made a recommendation resulting in employment of the member or the member's law firm by a client. A member's offering of or giving a gift or gratuity to any lawyer who has made a recommendation resulting in the employment of the member or the member's law firm shall not of itself violate this rule, provided that the gift or gratuity was not offered in consideration of any promise, agreement, or understanding that such a gift or gratuity would be forthcoming or that referrals would be made or encouraged in the future.

Rule 2–300.   Sale or Purchase of a Law Practice of a Member, Living or Deceased

All or substantially all of the law practice of a member, living or deceased, including goodwill, may be sold to another member or law firm subject to all the following conditions:

(A) Fees charged to clients shall not be increased solely by reason of such sale.

(B) If the sale contemplates the transfer of responsibility for work not yet completed or responsibility for client files or information protected by Business and Professions Code section 6068, subdivision (e), then;

   (1) if the seller is deceased, has a conservator or other person acting in a representative capacity, prior to the transfer;

     (a) the purchaser shall cause a written notice to be given to the client stating that the interest in the law practice is being transferred to the purchaser; that the client has the right to retain other counsel; that the client may take possession of any client papers and property, as required by rule 3–700(D); and that if no response is received to the notification within 90 days of the sending of such notice, or in the event the client's rights would be prejudiced by a failure to act during that time, the purchaser may act on behalf of the client until otherwise notified by the client. Such notice shall comply with the requirements as set forth in rule 1–400(D) and any provisions relating to attorney-client fee arrangements, and

(b) the purchaser shall obtain the written consent of the client provided that such consent shall be presumed until otherwise notified by the client if no response is received to the notification specified in subparagraph (a) within 90 days of the date of the sending of such notification to the client's last address as shown on the records of the seller, or the client's rights would be prejudiced by a failure to act during during such 90-day period.

(2) in all other circumstances, not less than 90 days prior to the transfer;

(a) the seller shall cause a written notice to be given to the client stating that the interest in the law practice is being transferred to the purchaser; that the client has the right to retain other counsel; that the client may take possession of any client papers and property, as required by rule 3–700(D); and that if no response is received to the notification within 90 days of the sending of such notice, the purchaser may act on behalf of the client until otherwise notified by the client. Such notice shall comply with the requirements as set forth in rule 1–400(D) and any provisions relating to attorney-client fee arrangements, and

(b) the seller shall obtain the written consent of the client prior to the transfer provided that such consent shall be presumed until otherwise notified by the client if no response is received to the notification specified in subparagraph (a) within 90 days of the date of the sending of such notification to the client's last address as shown on the records of the seller.

(C) If substitution is required by the rules of a tribunal in which a matter is pending, all steps necessary to substitute a member shall be taken.

(D) All activity of a purchaser or potential purchaser under this rule shall be subject to compliance with rules 3–300 and 3–310 where applicable.

(E) Confidential information shall not be disclosed to a nonmember in connection with a sale under this rule.

(F) Admission to or retirement from a law partnership or law corporation, retirement plans and similar arrangements, or sale of tangible assets of a law practice shall not be deemed a sale or purchase under this rule.

Discussion:

Paragraph (A) is intended to prohibit the purchaser from charging the former clients of the seller a higher fee than the purchaser is charging his or her existing clients.

"All or substantially all of the law practice of a member" means, for purposes of rule 2-300, that, for example, a member may retain one or two clients who have such a longstanding personal and professional relationship with the member that transfer of those clients' files is not feasible. Conversely, rule 2-300 is not intended to authorize the sale of a law practice in a piecemeal fashion except as may be required by subparagraph (B)(1)(a) or paragraph (D).

Transfer of individual client matters, where permitted, is governed by rule 2-200. Payment of a fee to a non-lawyer broker for arranging the sale or purchase of a law practice is governed by rule 1-320.

CHAPTER 3. PROFESSIONAL RELATIONSHIP WITH CLIENTS

Rule 3-110. Failing to Act Competently

(A) A member shall not intentionally, or with reckless disregard, or repeatedly fail to perform legal services competently.

(B) To perform legal services competently means diligently to apply the learning and skill necessary to perform the member's duties arising from employment or representation. If the member does not have sufficient learning and skills when the employment or representation is undertaken, or during the course of the employment or representation, the member may nonetheless perform such duties competently by associating or, where appropriate, professionally consulting another member reasonably believed to be competent, or by acquiring sufficient learning and skill before performance is required, if the member has sufficient time, resources, and ability to do so.

(C) As used in this rule, the term "ability" means a quality or state of having sufficient learning and skill and being mentally, emotionally, and physically able to perform legal services.

Discussion:

The duties set forth in rule 3-110 include the duty to supervise the work of subordinate attorney and non-attorney employees or agents. (See, e.g., *Waysman v. State Bar* (1986) 41 Cal.3d 452; *Trousil v. State Bar* (1985) 38 Cal.3d 337, 342 [211 Cal.Rptr. 525]; *Palomo v. State Bar* (1984) 36 Cal.3d 785 [205 Cal.Rptr. 834]; *Crane v. State Bar* (1981) 30

Cal.3d 117, 122; *Black v. State Bar* (1972) 7 Cal.3d 676, 692 [103 Cal.Rptr. 288; 499 P.2d 968]; *Vaughn v. State Bar* (1972) 6 Cal.3d 847, 857–858 [100 Cal.Rptr. 713; 494 P.2d 1257]; *Moore v. State Bar* (1964) 62 Cal.2d 74, 81 [41 Cal.Rptr. 161; 396 P.2d 577].)

Rule 3–200. Prohibited Objectives of Employment

A member shall not seek, accept, or continue employment if the member knows or should know that the objective of such employment is:

(A) To bring an action, conduct a defense, assert a position in litigation, or take an appeal, without probable cause and for the purpose of harassing or maliciously injuring any person; or

(B) To present a claim or defense in litigation that is not warranted under existing law, unless it can be supported by a good faith argument for an extension, modification, or reversal of such existing law.

Rule 3–210. Advising the Violation of Law

A member shall not advise the violation of any law, rule, or ruling of a tribunal unless the member believes in good faith that such law, rule, or ruling is invalid. A member may take appropriate steps in good faith to test the validity of any law, rule, or ruling of a tribunal.

Discussion:

Rule 3–210 is intended to apply not only to the prospective conduct of a client but also to the interaction between the member and client and to the specific legal service sought by the client from the member. An example of the former is the handling of physical evidence of a crime in the possession of the client and offered to the member. (See *People v. Meredith* (1981) 29 Cal.3d 682 [175 Cal.Rptr. 612].)   An example of the latter is a request that the member negotiate the return of stolen property in exchange for the owner's agreement not to report the theft to the police or prosecutorial authorities. (See *People v. Pic'l* (1982) 31 Cal.3d 731 [183 Cal.Rptr. 685].)

Rule 3–300. Avoiding Adverse Interests

A member shall not enter into a business transaction with a client; or knowingly acquire an ownership, possessory, security, or other pecuniary interest adverse to a client, unless each of the following requirements has been satisfied:

(A) The transaction or acquisition and its terms are fair and reasonable to the client and are fully disclosed and transmitted in writing to the client in a manner which should reasonably have been understood by the client; and

(B) The client is advised in writing that the client may seek the advice of an independent lawyer of the client's choice and is given a reasonable opportunity to seek that advice; and

(C) The client thereafter consents in writing to the terms of the transaction or the terms of the acquisition.

Discussion:

Rule 3–300 is not intended to apply to the agreement by which the member is retained by the client, unless the agreement confers on the member an ownership, possessory, security, or other pecuniary interest adverse to the client. Such an agreement is governed, in part, by rule 4–200.

Rule 3–300 is not intended to apply where the member and client each make an investment on terms offered to the general public or a significant portion thereof. For example, rule 3–300 is not intended to apply where A, a member, invests in a limited partnership syndicated by a third party. B, A's client, makes the same investment. Although A and B are each investing in the same business, A did not enter into the transaction "with" B for the purposes of the rule.

Rule 3–300 is intended to apply where the member wishes to obtain an interest in client's property in order to secure the amount of the member's past due or future fees.

Rule 3–310. Avoiding the Representation of Adverse Interests

(A) If a member has or had a relationship with another party interested in the representation, or has an interest in its subject matter, the member shall not accept or continue such representation without all affected clients' informed written consent.

(B) A member shall not concurrently represent clients whose interests conflict, except with their informed written consent.

(C) A member who represents two or more clients shall not enter into an aggregate settlement of the claims of or against the clients, except with their informed written consent.

(D) A member shall not accept employment adverse to a client or former client where, by reason of the representation of the client or former client, the member has obtained confidential information material to the employment except with the informed written consent of the client or former client.

(E) A member shall not accept compensation for representing a client from one other than the client unless:

(1) There is no interference with the member's independence of professional judgment or with the client-lawyer relationship; and

861

(2) Information relating to representation of a client is protected as required by Business and Professions Code section 6068, subdivision (e); and

(3) The client consents after disclosure, provided that no disclosure is required if;

   (a) such nondisclosure is otherwise authorized by law, or

   (b) the member is rendering legal services on behalf of any public agency which provides legal services to other public agencies or members of the public.

(F) As used in this rule "informed" means full disclosure to the client of the circumstances and advice to the client of any actual or reasonably foreseeable adverse effects of those circumstances upon the representation.

Discussion:

Rule 3-310 is not intended to prohibit a member from representing parties having antagonistic positions on the same legal question that has arisen in different cases, unless representation of either client would be adversely affected.

Paragraph (A) is intended to apply to all types of legal employment, including the representation of multiple parties in litigation or in a single transaction or other common enterprise or legal relationship. Examples of the latter include the formation of a partnership for several partners or a corporation for several shareholders, the preparation of an ante-nuptial agreement, or joint or reciprocal wills for a husband and wife, or the resolution of an "uncontested" marital dissolution. In such situations, for the sake of convenience or economy, the parties may well prefer to employ a single counsel, but a member must disclose the potential adverse aspects of such multiple representation (e.g., Evid. Code § 962) and must obtain the consent of the clients thereto. Moreover, if the potential adversity should become actual, the member must obtain the further consent of the clients pursuant to paragraph (B).

Paragraph (E) is not intended to abrogate existing relationships between insurers and insureds whereby the insurer has the contractual right to unilaterally select counsel for the insured, where there is no conflict of interest. (See *San Diego Navy Federal Credit Union v. Cumis Insurance Society* (1984) 162 Cal.App.3d 358 [208 Cal.Rptr. 494].)

Rule 3-320. Relationship With Other Party's Lawyer

A member shall not represent a client in a matter in which another party's lawyer is a spouse, parent, child, or sibling of the member, lives with the member, is a client of the member, or has an intimate personal relationship with the member, unless the member informs the client in writing of the relationship.

Discussion:

Rule 3–320 is not intended to apply to circumstances in which a member fails to advise the client of a relationship with another member who is merely a partner or associate in the same law firm as the adverse party's counsel, and who has no direct involvement in the matter.

Rule 3–400. Limiting Liability to Client

A member shall not:

(A) Contract with a client prospectively limiting the member's liability to the client for the member's professional malpractice; or

(B) Settle a claim or potential claim for such liability unless the client is informed in writing that the client may seek the advice of an independent lawyer of the client's choice regarding the settlement and is given a reasonable opportunity to seek that advice.

Discussion:

Rule 3–400 is not intended to apply to customary qualifications and limitations in legal opinions and memoranda, nor is it intended to prevent a member from reasonably limiting the scope of the member's employment or representation.

Rule 3–500. Communication

A member shall keep a client reasonably informed about significant developments relating to the employment or representation and promptly comply with reasonable requests for information.

Discussion:

Rule 3–500 is not intended to change a member's duties to his or her clients. It is intended to make clear that, while a client must be informed of significant developments in the matter, a member will not be disciplined for failing to communicate insignificant or irrelevant information. (See Bus. & Prof.Code, § 6068, subd. (m).)

Rule 3–510. Communication of Settlement Offer

(A) A member shall promptly communicate to the member's client:

(1) All terms and conditions of any offer made to the client in a criminal matter; and

(2) All amounts, terms, and conditions of any written offer of settlement made to the client in all other matters.

(B) As used in this rule, "client" includes a person who possesses the authority to accept an offer of settlement or plea, or, in a class action, all the named representatives of the class.

Discussion:

Rule 3–510 is intended to require that counsel in a criminal matter convey all offers, whether written or oral, to the client, as give and take negotiations are less common in criminal matters, and, even were they to occur, such negotiations should require the participation of the accused.

Any oral offers of settlement made to the client in a civil matter should also be communicated if they are "significant" for the purposes of rule 3–500.

Rule 3–600. Organization as Client

(A) In representing an organization, a member shall conform his or her representation to the concept that the client is the organization itself, acting through its highest authorized officer, employee, body, or constituent overseeing the particular engagement.

(B) If a member acting on behalf of an organization knows that an actual or apparent agent of the organization acts or intends or refuses to act in a manner that is or may be a violation of law reasonably imputable to the organization, or in a manner which is likely to result in substantial injury to the organization, the member shall not violate his or her duty of protecting all confidential information as provided in Business and Professions Code section 6068, subdivision (e). Subject to Business and Professions Code section 6068, subdivision (e), the member may take such actions as appear to the member to be in the best lawful interest of the organization. Such actions may include among others:

　(1) Urging reconsideration of the matter while explaining its likely consequences to the organization; or

　(2) Referring the matter to the next higher authority in the organization, including, if warranted by the seriousness of the matter, referral to the highest internal authority that can act on behalf of the organization.

(C) If, despite the member's actions in accordance with paragraph (B), the highest authority that can act on behalf of the organization insists upon action or a refusal to act that is a violation of law and is likely to result in substantial injury to the organization, the member's response is limited to the member's right, and, where appropriate, duty to resign in accordance with rule 3–700.

(D) In dealing with an organization's directors, officers, employees, members, shareholders, or other constituents, a member shall explain the identity of the client for whom the member acts, whenever it is or becomes apparent that the organization's interests are or may become adverse to those of the constituent(s) with whom the member is dealing. The member shall not mislead such a constituent into believing that the constituent may communicate confidential information to the member in a way that will not be used in the organization's interest if that is or becomes adverse to the constituent.

(E) A member representing an organization may also represent any of its directors, officers, employees, members, shareholders, or other constituents, subject to the provisions of rule 3–310. If the organization's consent to the dual representation is required by rule 3–310, the consent shall be given by an appropriate constituent of the organization other than the individual or constituent who is to be represented, or by the shareholder(s) or organization members.

Discussion:

Rule 3–600 is not intended to enmesh members in the intricacies of the entity and aggregate theories of partnership.

Rule 3–600 is not intended to prohibit members from representing both an organization and other parties connected with it, as for instance (as simply one example) in establishing employee benefit packages for closely held coprorations or professional partnerships.

Rule 3–600 is not intended to create or to validate artificial distinctions between entities and their officers, employees, or members, nor is it the purpose of the rule to deny the existence or importance of such formal distinctions. In dealing with a close corporation or small association, members commonly perform professional engagements for both the organization and its major constituents. When a change in control occurs or is threatened, members are faced with complex decisions involving personal and institutional relationships and loyalties and have frequently had difficulty in perceiving their correct duty. (See *People ex rel. Deukmejian v. Brown* (1981) 29 Cal.3d 150 [172 Cal.Rptr. 478]; *Goldstein v. Lees* (1975) 46 Cal.App.3d 614 [120 Cal.Rptr. 253]; *Woods v. Superior Court* (1983) 149 Cal.App.3d 931 [197 Cal.Rptr. 185]; *In re Banks* (1978) 283 Ore. 459 [584 P.2d 284]; 1 A.L.R.4th 1105.) In resolving such multiple relationships, members must rely on case law.

Rule 3–700. Termination of Employment

(A) In General.

(1) If permission for termination of employment is required by the rules of a tribunal, a member shall not withdraw from employment in a proceeding before that tribunal without its permission.

(2) A member shall not withdraw from employment until the member has taken reasonable steps to avoid reasonably foreseeable prejudice to the rights of the client, including giving due notice to the client, allowing time for employment of other counsel, complying with rule 3–700(D), and complying with applicable laws and rules.

(B) Mandatory Withdrawal.

A member representing a client before a tribunal shall withdraw from employment with the permission of the tribunal, if required by its rules, and a member representing a client in other matters shall withdraw from employment, if:

(1) The member knows or should know that the client is bringing an action, conducting a defense, asserting a position in litigation, or taking an appeal, without probable cause and for the purpose of harassing or maliciously injuring any person; or

(2) The member knows or should know that continued employment will result in violation of these rules or of the State Bar Act; or

(3) The member's mental or physical condition renders it unreasonably difficult to carry out the employment effectively.

(C) Permissive Withdrawal.

If rule 3–700(B) is not applicable, a member may not request permission to withdraw in matters pending before a tribunal, and may not withdraw in other matters, unless such request or such withdrawal is because:

(1) The client

    (a) insists upon presenting a claim or defense that is not warranted under existing law and cannot be supported by good faith argument for an extension, modification, or reversal of existing law, or

    (b) seeks to pursue an illegal course of conduct, or

    (c) insists that the member pursue a course of conduct that is illegal or that is prohibited under these rules or the State Bar Act, or

    (d) by other conduct renders it unreasonably difficult for the member to carry out the employment effectively, or

    (e) insists, in a matter not pending before a tribunal, that the member engage in conduct that is contrary to the judgment and advice of the member but not prohibited under these rules or the State Bar Act, or

    (f) breaches an agreement or obligation to the member as to expenses or fees.

(2) The continued employment is likely to result in a violation of these rules or of the State Bar Act; or

(3) The inability to work with co-counsel indicates that the best interests of the client likely will be served by withdrawal; or

(4) The member's mental or physical condition renders it difficult for the member to carry out the employment effectively; or

(5) The client knowingly and freely assents to termination of the employment; or

(6) The member believes in good faith, in a proceeding pending before a tribunal, that the tribunal will find the existence of other good cause for withdrawal.

(D) Papers, Property and Fees.

A member whose employment has terminated shall:

(1) Subject to any protective order or non-disclosure agreement, promptly release to the client, at the request of the client, all the client papers and property. "Client papers and property" includes correspondence, pleadings, deposition transcripts, exhibits, physical evidence, expert's reports, and other items reasonably necessary to the client's representation, whether the client has paid for them or not; and

(2) Promptly refund any part of a fee paid in advance that has not been earned. This provision is not applicable to a true retainer fee which is paid solely for the purpose of ensuring the availability of the member for the matter.

Discussion:

Subparagraph (A)(2) provides that "a member shall not withdraw from employment until the member has taken reasonable steps to avoid reasonably foreseeable prejudice to the rights of the clients." What such steps would include, of course, will vary according to the circumstances. Absent special circumstances, "reasonable steps" do not include providing additional services to the client once the successor counsel has been employed and rule 3–700(D) has been satisfied.

Paragraph (D) makes clear the member's duties in the recurring situation in which new counsel seeks to obtain client files from a member discharged by the client. It codifies existing case law. (See *Academy of California Optometrists v. Superior Court* (1975) 51 Cal.App.3d 999 [124 Cal.Rptr. 668]; *Weiss v. Marcus* (1975) 51 Cal.App.3d 590 [124 Cal.Rptr. 297].) Paragraph (D) also requires that the member "promptly" return unearned fees paid in advance. If a client disputes the amount to be returned, the member shall comply with rule 4–100(A)(2).

Paragraph (D) is not intended to prohibit a member from making, at the member's own expense, and retaining copies of papers released to the client, nor to prohibit a claim for the recovery of the member's expense in any subsequent legal proceeding.

CHAPTER 4. FINANCIAL RELATIONSHIP WITH CLIENTS

Rule 4-100. Preserving Identity of Funds and Property of a Client

(A) All funds received or held for the benefit of clients by a member or law firm, including advances for costs and expenses, shall be deposited in one or more identifiable bank accounts labelled "Trust Account," "Client's Funds Account" or words of similar import, maintained in the State of California, or, with written consent of the client, in any other jurisdiction where there is a substantial relationship between the client or the client's business and the other jurisdiction. No funds belonging to the member or the law firm shall be deposited therein or otherwise commingled therewith except as follows:

   (1) Funds reasonably sufficient to pay bank charges.

   (2) In the case of funds belonging in part to a client and in part presently or potentially to the member or the law firm, the portion belonging to the member or law firm must be withdrawn at the earliest reasonable time after the member's interest in that portion becomes fixed. However, when the right of the member or law firm to receive a portion of trust funds is disputed by the client, the disputed portion shall not be withdrawn until the dispute is finally resolved.

(B) A member shall:

   (1) Promptly notify a client of the receipt of the client's funds, securities, or other properties.

   (2) Identify and label securities and properties of a client promptly upon receipt and place them in a safe deposit box or other place of safekeeping as soon as practicable.

   (3) Maintain complete records of all funds, securities, and other properties of a client coming into the possession of the member or law firm and render appropriate accounts to the client regarding them; preserve such records for a period of no less than five years after final appropriate distribution of such funds or properties; and comply with any order for an audit of such records issued pursuant to the Rules of Procedure of the State Bar.

   (4) Promptly pay or deliver, as requested by the client, any funds, securities, or other properties in the possession of the member which the client is entitled to receive.

(C) The Board of Governors of the State Bar shall have the authority to formulate and adopt standards as to what "records" shall be maintained by members and law firms in accordance with subparagraph (B)(3). The standards formulated and adopted by the Board, as from time to time amended, shall be effective and binding on all members.

Rule 4-200. Fees for Legal Services

(A) A member shall not enter into an agreement for, charge, or collect an illegal or unconscionable fee.

(B) Unconscionability of a fee agreement shall be determined on the basis of all the facts and circumstances existing at the time the agreement is entered into except where the parties contemplate that the fee will be affected by later events. Among the factors to be considered, where appropriate, in determining the conscionability of a fee are the following:

 (1) The amount of the fee in proportion to the value of the services performed.

 (2) The relative sophistication of the member and the client.

 (3) The novelty and difficulty of the questions involved and the skill requisite to perform the legal service properly.

 (4) The likelihood, if apparent to the client, that the acceptance of the particular employment will preclude other employment by the member.

 (5) The amount involved and the results obtained.

 (6) The time limitations imposed by the client or by the circumstances.

 (7) The nature and length of the professional relationship with the client.

 (8) The experience, reputation, and ability of the member or members performing the services.

 (9) Whether the fee is fixed or contingent.

 (10) The time and labor required.

 (11) The informed consent of the client to the fee agreement.

Rule 4-210. Payment of Personal or Business Expenses Incurred by or for a Client

(A) A member shall not directly or indirectly pay or agree to pay, guarantee, represent, or sanction a representation that the member or member's law firm will pay the personal or business expenses of a prospective or existing client, except that this rule shall not prohibit a member:

 (1) With the consent of the client, from paying or agreeing to pay such expenses to third persons from funds collected or to be collected for the client as a result of the representation; or

869

(2) After employment, from lending money to the client upon the client's promise in writing to repay such loan; or

(3) From advancing the costs of prosecuting or defending a claim or action or otherwise protecting or promoting the client's interests, the repayment of which may be contingent on the outcome of the matter. Such costs within the meaning of this subparagraph (3) shall be limited to all reasonable expenses of litigation or reasonable expenses in preparation for litigation or in providing any legal services to the client.

(B) Nothing in rule 4-210 shall be deemed to limit rules 3-300, 3-310, and 4-300.

Rule 4-300. Purchasing Property at a Foreclosure or a Sale Subject to Judicial Review

A member shall not directly or indirectly purchase property at a probate, foreclosure, receiver's, trustee's or judicial sale in an action or proceeding in which such member or any member affiliated by reason of personal, business, or professional relationship with that member or with that member's law firm is an attorney for a party or is acting as executor, receiver, trustee, administrator, guardian, or conservator.

Rule 4-400. Gifts From Client

A member shall not induce a client to make a substantial gift, including a testamentary gift, to the member or to the member's parent, child, sibling, or spouse, except where the client is related to the member.

Discussion:

A member may accept a gift from a member's client, subject to general standards of fairness and absence of undue influence. The member who participates in the preparation of an instrument memorializing a gift which is otherwise permissible ought not to be subject to professional discipline. On the other hand, where impermissible influence occurred, discipline is appropriate. (See *Magee v. State Bar* (1962) 58 Cal.2d 423 [24 Cal.Rptr. 839].)

CHAPTER 5. ADVOCACY AND REPRESENTATION

Rule 5-100. Threatening Criminal, Administrative, or Disciplinary Charges

(A) A member shall not threaten to present criminal, administrative, or disciplinary charges to obtain an advantage in a civil dispute.

(B) As used in paragraph (A) of this rule, the term "administrative charges" means the filing or lodging of a complaint with a federal, state, or local governmental entity which may order or recommend the loss or suspension of a license, or may impose or recommend the imposition of a fine, pecuniary sanction, or other sanction of a quasi-criminal nature but does not include filing charges with an administrative entity required by law as a condition precedent to maintaining a civil action.

(C) As used in paragraph (A) of this rule, the term "civil dispute" means a controversy or potential controversy over the rights and duties of two or more parties under civil law, whether or not an action has been commenced, and includes an administrative proceeding of a quasi-civil nature pending before a federal, state, or local governmental entity.

Discussion:

Rule 5-100 is not intended to apply to a member's threatening to initiate contempt proceedings against a party for a failure to comply with a court order.

Paragraph (B) is intended to exempt the threat of filing an administrative charge which is a prerequisite to filing a civil complaint on the same transaction or occurrence.

For purposes of paragraph (C), the definition of "civil dispute" makes clear that the rule is applicable prior to the formal filing of a civil action.

Rule 5-110. Performing the Duty of Member in Government Service

A member in government service shall not institute or cause to be instituted criminal charges when the member knows or should know that the charges are not supported by probable cause. If, after the institution of criminal charges, the member in government service having responsibility for prosecuting the charges becomes aware that those charges are not supported by probable cause, the member shall promptly so advise the court in which the criminal matter is pending.

Rule 5-200. Trial Conduct

In presenting a matter to a tribunal, a member:

(A) Shall employ, for the purpose of maintaining the causes confided to the member such means only as are consistent with truth;

(B) Shall not seek to mislead the judge, judicial officer, or jury by an artifice or false statement of fact or law;

(C) Shall not intentionally misquote to a tribunal the language of a book, statute, or decision;

(D) Shall not, knowing its invalidity, cite as authority a decision that has been overruled or a statute that has been repealed or declared unconstitutional; and

(E) Shall not assert personal knowledge of the facts at issue, except when testifying as a witness.

Rule 5–210. Member as Witness

A member shall not act as an advocate before a jury which will hear testimony from the member unless:

(A) The testimony relates to an uncontested matter; or

(B) The testimony relates to the nature and value of legal services rendered in the case; or

(C) The member has the informed, written consent of the client. If the member represents the People or a governmental entity, the consent shall be obtained from the head of the office or a designee of the head of the office by which the member is employed and shall be consistent with principles of recusal.

Discussion:

Rule 5–210 is intended to apply to situations in which the member knows or should know that he or she ought to be called as a witness in litigation in which there is a jury. This rule is not intended to encompass situations in which the member is representing the client in an adversarial proceeding and is testifying before a judge. In non-adversarial proceedings, as where the lawyer testifies on behalf of the client, in a hearing before a legislative body, rule 5–210 is not applicable.

Rule 5–210 is not intended to apply to circumstances in which a partner or associate in an advocate's firm will be a witness.

Rule 5–220. Suppression of Evidence

A member shall not suppress any evidence that the member or the member's client has a legal obligation to reveal or to produce.

Rule 5–300. Contact With Officials

(A) A member shall not directly or indirectly give or lend anything of value to a judge, official, or employee of a tribunal unless the personal or family relationship between the member and the judge, official, or employee is such that gifts are customarily given and exchanged. Nothing contained in this rule shall prohibit a member from contributing to the campaign fund of a judge running for election or confirmation pursuant to applicable law pertaining to such contributions.

(B) A member shall not directly or indirectly communicate with or argue to a judge or judicial officer upon the merits of a contested matter pending before such judge or judicial officer, except:

(1) In open court; or

(2) With the consent of all other counsel in such matter; or

(3) In the presence of all other counsel in such matter; or

(4) In writing with a copy thereof furnished to such other counsel; or

(5) In ex parte matters.

(C) As used in this rule, the phrase "judge or judicial officer" shall include law clerks, research attorneys, or other court personnel who participate in the decision-making process.

Rule 5–310. Prohibited Contact With Witnesses

A member shall not:

(A) Advise or directly or indirectly cause a person to secrete himself or herself or to leave the jurisdiction of a tribunal for the purpose of making that person unavailable as a witness therein.

(B) Directly or indirectly pay, offer to pay, or acquiesce in the payment of compensation to a witness contingent upon the content of the witness's testimony or the outcome of the case. Except where prohibited by law, a member may advance, guarantee, or acquiesce in the payment of:

(1) Expenses reasonably incurred by a witness in attending or testifying.

(2) Reasonable compensation to a witness for loss of time in attending or testifying.

(3) A reasonable fee for the professional services of an expert witness.

Rule 5–320. Contact With Jurors

(A) A member connected with a case shall not communicate directly or indirectly with anyone the member knows to be a member of the venire from which the jury will be selected for trial of that case.

(B) During trial a member connected with the case shall not communicate directly or indirectly with any member of the jury.

(C) During trial a member who is not connected with the case shall not communicate directly or indirectly concerning the case with anyone a member knows is a juror in the case.

(D) After discharge of the jury from further consideration of a case a member shall not ask questions of or make comments to a member of that jury that are intended to harass or embarrass the juror or to influence the juror's actions in future jury service.

(E) A member shall not conduct directly or indirectly an out of court investigation of either a venireman or a juror of a type likely to influence the state of mind of such venireman or juror in present or future jury service.

(F) All restrictions imposed by rule 5–320 upon a member also apply to communications with or investigations of members of the family of a venireman or a juror.

(G) A member shall reveal promptly to the court improper conduct by a venireman or a juror, or by another toward a venireman or a juror or a member of his or her family, of which the member has knowledge.

(H) Rule 5–320 does not prohibit a member from communicating with veniremen or jurors as a part of the official proceedings.

CALIFORNIA BUSINESS AND PROFESSIONS CODE

(Selected Sections)

Table of Contents

CHAPTER 4. ATTORNEYS

ARTICLE 4. ADMISSION TO THE PRACTICE OF LAW

§ 6067. Oath

Every person on his admission shall take an oath to support the Constitution of the United States and the Constitution of the State of California, and faithfully to discharge the duties of any attorney at law to the best of his knowledge and ability. A certificate of the oath shall be indorsed upon his license.

§ 6068. Duties of attorney

It is the duty of an attorney:

(a) To support the Constitution and laws of the United States and of this State.

(b) To maintain the respect due to the courts of justice and judicial officers.

877

(c) To counsel or maintain such actions, proceedings or defenses only as appear to him legal or just, except the defense of a person charged with a public offense.

(d) To employ, for the purpose of maintaining the causes confided to him such means only as are consistent with truth, and never to seek to mislead the judge or any judicial officer by an artifice or false statement of fact or law.

(e) To maintain inviolate the confidence, and at every peril to himself to preserve the secrets, of his client.

(f) To abstain from all offensive personality, and to advance no fact prejudicial to the honor or reputation of a party or witness, unless required by the justice of the cause with which he is charged.

(g) Not to encourage either the commencement or the continuance of an action or proceeding from any corrupt motive of passion or interest.

(h) Never to reject, for any consideration personal to himself, the cause of the defenseless or the oppressed.

(i) To cooperate and participate in any disciplinary investigation or other regulatory or disciplinary proceeding pending against the attorney. However, this subdivision shall not be construed to deprive an attorney of any privilege guaranteed by the Fifth Amendment to the Constitution of the United States or any other constitutional or statutory privileges.

(j) To comply with the requirements of Section 6002.1.

(k) To comply with all conditions attached to any disciplinary probation, including a probation imposed with the concurrence of the attorney.

(*l*) To keep all agreements made in lieu of disciplinary prosecution with the agency charged with attorney discipline.

(m) To respond promptly to reasonable status inquiries of clients and to keep clients reasonably informed of significant developments in matters with regard to which the attorney has agreed to provide legal services.

(n) To provide copies to the client of certain documents under time limits and as prescribed in a rule of professional conduct which the board shall adopt.

(o) To report to the agency charged with attorney discipline, in writing, within 30 days of the time the attorney has knowledge of any of the following:

(1) The filing of three or more lawsuits in a 12-month period against the attorney for malpractice or other wrongful conduct committed in a professional capacity.

(2) The entry of judgment against the attorney in any civil action for fraud, misrepresentation, breach of fiduciary duty, or gross negligence committed in a professional capacity.

(3) The imposition of any juducial sanctions against the attorney, except for sanctions for failure to make discovery or monetary sanctions of less than one thousand dollars ($1,000).

(4) The bringing of an indictment or information charging a felony against the attorney.

(5) The conviction of the attorney, including any verdict of guilty, or plea of guilty or no contest, of any felony, or any misdemeanor committed in the course of the practice of law, or in any manner such that a client of the attorney was the victim, or a necessary element of which, as determined by the statutory or common law definition of the misdemeanor, involves improper conduct of an attorney, including dishonesty or other moral turpitude, or an attempt or a conspiracy or solicitation of another to commit a felony or any such misdemeanor.

(6) The imposition of discipline against the attorney by any professional or occupational disciplinary agency or licensing board, whether in California or elsewhere.

(7) Reversal of judgment in a proceeding based in whole or in part upon misconduct, grossly incompetent representation, or wilful misrepresentation by an attorney.

(8) As used in this subdivision, "against the attorney" includes claims and proceedings against any firm of attorneys for the practice of law in which the attorney was a partner at the time of the conduct complained of and any law corporation in which the attorney was a shareholder at the time of the conduct complained of unless the matter has to the attorney's knowledge already been reported by the law firm or corporation.

(9) The State Bar may develop a prescribed form for the making of reports required by this section, usage of which it may require by rule or regulation.

(10) This subdivision is only intended to provide that the failure to report as required herein may serve as a basis of discipline.

ARTICLE 6. DISCIPLINARY AUTHORITY OF THE COURTS

§ 6100. Disbarment or suspension

For any of the causes provided in this article, arising after an attorney's admission to practice, he or she may be disbarred or suspended by the Supreme Court. Nothing in this article limits the inherent power of the Supreme Court to discipline, including to summarily disbar, any attorney.

§ 6101. Conviction of crime; notice of pendency of action; record of conviction; proceedings

(a) Conviction of a felony or misdemeanor, involving moral turpitude, constitutes a cause for disbarment or suspension.

In any proceeding, whether under this article or otherwise, to disbar or suspend an attorney on account of that conviction, the record of conviction shall be conclusive evidence of guilt of the crime of which he or she has been convicted.

(b) The district attorney, city attorney, or other prosecuting agency shall notify the Office of the State Bar of the State of California of the pendency of an action against an attorney charging a felony or misdemeanor immediately upon obtaining information that the defendant is an attorney. The notice shall identify the attorney and describe the crimes charged and the alleged facts. The prosecuting agency shall also notify the clerk of the court in which the action is pending that the defendant is an attorney, and the clerk shall record prominently in the file that the defendant is an attorney.

(c) The clerk of the court in which an attorney is convicted of a crime shall, within 48 hours after the conviction, transmit a certified copy of the record of conviction to the Office of the State Bar. Within five days of receipt, the Office of the State Bar shall transmit the record of any conviction which involves or may involve moral turpitude to the Supreme Court with such other records and information as may be appropriate to establish the Supreme Court's jurisdiction. The State Bar of California may procure and transmit the record of conviction to the Supreme Court when the clerk has not done so or when the conviction was had in a court other than a court of this state.

(d) The proceedings to disbar or suspend an attorney on account of such a conviction shall be undertaken by the Supreme Court pursuant to the procedure provided in this section and Section 6102, upon the receipt of the certified copy of the record of conviction.

(e) A plea or verdict of guilty or a conviction after a plea of nolo contendere is deemed to be a conviction within the meaning of those sections.

§ 6102. Immediate suspension and subsequent disbarment upon conviction of crime; crimes involving moral turpitude or felonies; procedure

(a) Upon the receipt of the certified copy of the record of conviction, if it appears therefrom that the crime of which the attorney was convicted involved or that there is probable cause to believe that it involved moral turpitude or is a felony under the laws of California or of the United States, the Supreme Court shall suspend the attorney until the time for appeal has elapsed, if no appeal has been taken, or until the judgment of conviction has been affirmed on appeal, or has otherwise become final, and until the further order of the court. Upon its own motion or upon good cause shown the court may decline to impose, or may set aside, the suspension when it appears to be in the interest of justice to do so, with due regard being given to maintaining the integrity of and confidence in the profession.

(b) For the purposes of this section, a crime is a felony under the law of California if it is declared to be so specifically or by subdivision (a) of Section 17 of the Penal Code, unless it is charged as a misdemeanor pursuant to paragraph (4) or (5) of subdivision (b) of Section 17 of the Penal Code, irrespective of whether in a particular case the crime may be considered a misdemeanor as a result of postconviction proceedings, including proceedings resulting in punishment or probation set forth in paragraph (1) or (3) of subdivision (b) of Section 17 of the Penal Code.

(c) After the judgment of conviction of an offense specified in subdivision (a) has become final or, irrespective of any subsequent order under Section 1203.4 of the Penal Code, an order granting probation has been made suspending the imposition of sentence, the Supreme Court shall summarily disbar the attorney if the conviction is a felony under the laws of California or of the United States which meets both of the following criteria:

(1) An element of the offense is the specific intent to deceive, defraud, steal, or make or suborn a false statement.

(2) The offense was committed in the course of the practice of law or in any manner such that a client of the attorney was a victim.

(d) Except as provided in subdivision (c), if after adequate notice and opportunity to be heard (which hearing shall not be had until the judgment of conviction has become final or, irrespective of any subsequent order under Section 1203.4 of the Penal Code, an order granting probation has been made suspending the imposition of sentence), the court finds that the crime of which the attorney was convicted, or the circumstances of its commission, involved moral turpitude, it shall enter an order disbarring the attorney or suspending him or her from practice for a limited time, according to the gravity of the crime and the circumstances of the case; otherwise it shall dismiss the proceedings.   In determining the extent of the discipline to be imposed in a proceeding pursuant to this article any prior discipline imposed upon the attorney may be considered.

(e) The court may refer the proceedings or any part thereof or issue therein, including the nature or extent of discipline, to the State Bar for hearing, report, and recommendation.

(f) The record of the proceedings resulting in the conviction, including a transcript of the testimony therein, may be received in evidence.

(g) The Supreme Court shall prescribe rules for the practice and procedure in proceedings had pursuant to this section and Section 6101.

(h) The other provisions of this article providing a procedure for the disbarment or suspension of an attorney do not apply to proceedings pursuant to this section and Section 6101, unless expressly made applicable.

§ 6103. Disobedience of court order; violation of oath or attorney's duties

A wilful disobedience or violation of an order of the court requiring him to do or forbear an act connected with or in the course of his profession, which he ought in good faith to do or forbear, and any violation of the oath taken by him, or of his duties as such attorney, constitute causes for disbarment or suspension.

§ 6103.5 Written offers of settlement; required communication to client; discovery

(a) A member of the State Bar shall promptly communicate to the member's client all amounts, terms, and conditions of any written offer of settlement made by or on behalf of an opposing party. As used in this section, "client" includes any person employing the member of the State Bar who possesses the authority to accept an offer of settlement, or in a class action, who is a representative of the class.

(b) Any written offer of settlement or any required communication of a settlement offer, as described in subdivision (a), shall be discoverable by either party in any action in which the existence or communication of the offer of settlement is an issue before the trier of fact.

§ 6104. Unauthorized appearance

Corruptly or wilfully and without authority appearing as attorney for a party to an action or proceeding constitutes a cause for disbarment or suspension.

§ 6105. Permitting misuse of name

Lending his name to be used as attorney by another person who is not an attorney constitutes a cause for disbarment or suspension.

§ 6106. Moral turpitude, dishonesty or corruption irrespective of criminal conviction

The commission of any act involving moral turpitude, dishonesty or corruption, whether the act is committed in the course of his relations as an attorney or otherwise, and whether the act is a felony or misdemeanor or not, constitutes a cause for disbarment or suspension.

If the act constitutes a felony or misdemeanor, conviction thereof in a criminal proceeding is not a condition precedent to disbarment or suspension from practice therefor.

§ 6106.1 Advocacy of overthrow of government

Advocating the overthrow of the Government of the United States or of this State by force, violence, or other unconstitutional means, constitutes a cause for disbarment or suspension.

§ 6106.5 Insurance claims; fraud

It shall constitute cause for disbarment or suspension for an attorney to engage in any conduct prohibited under Section 1871.1 or 1871.4 of the Insurance Code.

§ 6106.7 Professional sport service contracts; violation of requirements

(a) It shall constitute cause for the imposition of discipline of an attorney within the meaning of this chapter for an attorney to negotiate a professional sport service contract, as defined by subdivision (d) of Section 1500 of the Labor Code, and in willful violation of subdivision (b) of Section 1531 of the Labor Code, to collect a fee that in any calendar year exceeds 10 percent of the compensation the athlete is receiving in that calendar year under the contract.

(b) Willful violation of Section 1530.5, subdivision (b) or (c) of Section 1531, or Section 1535.5, 1535.7, or 1539 of the Labor Code constitutes cause for the imposition of discipline of an attorney within the meaning of this chapter.

§ 6106.8 Sexual involvement between lawyers and clients; rule of professional conduct

(a) The Legislature hereby finds and declares that there is no rule that governs propriety of sexual relationships between lawyers and clients. The Legislature further finds and declares that it is difficult to separate sound judgment from emotion or bias which may result from sexual involvement between a lawyer and his or her client during the period that an attorney-client relationship exists, and that emotional detachment is essential to the lawyer's ability to render competent legal services. Therefore, in order to ensure that a lawyer acts in the best interest of his or her client, a rule of professional conduct governing sexual relations between attorneys and their clients shall be adopted.

(b) With the approval of the Supreme Court, the State Bar shall adopt a rule of professional conduct governing sexual relations between attorneys and their clients in cases involving, but not limited to, probate matters and domestic relations, including dissolution proceedings, child custody cases, and settlement proceedings.

(c) The State Bar shall submit the proposed rule to the Supreme Court for approval no later than January 1, 1991.

(d) Intentional violation of this rule shall constitute a cause for suspension or disbarment.

§ 6107. Proceedings upon court's own knowledge or upon information

The proceedings to disbar or suspend an attorney, on grounds other than the conviction of a felony or misdemeanor, involving moral turpitude, may be taken by the court for the matters within its knowledge, or may be taken upon the information of another.

§ 6108. Accusation

If the proceedings are upon the information of another, the accusation shall be in writing and shall state the matters charged, and be verified by the oath of some person, to the effect that the charges therein contained are true.

The verification may be made upon information and belief when the accusation is presented by an organized bar association.

§ 6109. Order to appear and answer; service

Upon receiving the accusation, the court shall make an order requiring the accused to appear and answer it at a specified time, and shall cause a copy of the order and of the accusation to be served upon the accused at least five days before the day appointed in the order.

§ 6110. Citation

The court or judge may direct the service of a citation to the accused, requiring him to appear and answer the accusation, to be made by publication for thirty days in a newspaper of general circulation published in the county in which the proceeding is pending, if it appears by affidavit to the satisfaction of the court or judge that the accused either:

(a) Resides out of the State.

(b) Has departed from the State.

(c) Can not, after due diligence, be found within the State.

(d) Conceals himself to avoid the service of the order to show cause.

The citation shall be:

(a) Directed to the accused.

(b) Recite the date of the filing of the accusation, the name of the accuser, and the general nature of the charges against him.

(c) Require him to appear and answer the accusation at a specified time.

On proof of the publication of the citation as herein required, the court has jurisdiction to proceed to hear the accusation and render judgment with like effect as if an order to show cause and a copy of the accusation had been personally served on the accused.

§ 6111. Appearance; determination upon default

The accused shall appear at the time appointed in the order, and answer the accusation, unless, for sufficient cause, the court assigns another day for that purpose. If he does not appear, the court may proceed and determine the accusation in his absence.

§ 6112. Answer

The accused may answer to the accusation either by objecting to its sufficiency or by denying it.

If he objects to the sufficiency of the accusation, the objection shall be in writing, but need not be in any specific form. It is sufficient if it presents intelligibly the grounds of the objection.

If he denies the accusation, the denial may be oral and without oath, and shall be entered upon the minutes.

§ 6113. Time for answer after objection

If an objection to the sufficiency of the accusation is not sustained, the accused shall answer within the time designated by the court.

§ 6114. Judgment upon plea of guilty or failure to answer; trial upon denial of charges

If the accused pleads guilty, or refuses to answer the accusation, the court shall proceed to judgment of disbarment or suspension.

If he denies the matters charged, the court shall, at such time as it may appoint, proceed to try the accusation.

§ 6115. Reference to take depositions

The court may, in its discretion, order a reference to a committee to take depositions in the matter.

§ 6116. Judgment

When an attorney has been found guilty of the charges made in proceedings not based upon a record of conviction, judgment shall be rendered disbarring the attorney or suspending him from practice for a limited time, according to the gravity of the offense charged.

§ 6117. Effect of disbarment or suspension

During such disbarment or suspension, the attorney shall be precluded from practicing law.

When disbarred, his name shall be stricken from the roll of attorneys.

ARTICLE 7. UNLAWFUL PRACTICE OF LAW

§ 6125. Necessity of active membership in state bar

No person shall practice law in California unless the person is an active member of the State Bar.

§ 6126. Unauthorized practice, advertising or holding out; penalties

(a) Any person advertising or holding himself or herself out as practicing or entitled to practice law or otherwise practicing law who is not an active member of the State Bar, is guilty of a misdemeanor.

(b) Any person who has been involuntarily enrolled as an inactive member of the State Bar, or has been suspended from membership from the State Bar, or has been disbarred, or has resigned from the State Bar with charges pending, and thereafter advertises or holds himself or herself out as practicing or otherwise entitled to practice law, is guilty of a crime punishable by imprisonment in the state prison or county jail. However, any person who has been involuntarily enrolled as an inactive member of the State Bar pursuant to paragraph (1) of subdivision (e) of Section 6007 and who knowingly thereafter advertises or holds himself or herself out as practicing or otherwise entitled to practice law, is guilty of a crime punishable by imprisonment in the state prison or county jail.

(c) The willful failure of a member of the State Bar, or one who has resigned or been disbarred, to comply with an order of the Supreme Court to comply with Rule 955, constitutes a crime punishable by imprisonment in the state prison or county jail.

§ 6127. Contempt of court

The following acts or omissions in respect to the practice of law are contempts of the authority of the courts:

(a) Assuming to be an officer or attorney of a court and acting as such, without authority.

(b) Advertising or holding oneself out as practicing or as entitled to practice law or otherwise practicing law in any court, without being an active member of the State Bar.

Proceedings to adjudge a person in contempt of court under this section are to be taken in accordance with the provisions of Title V of Part III of the Code of Civil Procedure.

§ 6127.5 Law corporation under professional corporation act

Nothing in Sections 6125, 6126 and 6127 shall be deemed to apply to the acts and practices of a law corporation duly certificated pursuant to the Professional Corporation Act, as contained in Part 4 (commencing with Section 13400) of Division 3 of Title 1 of the Corporations Code, and pursuant to Article 10 (commencing with Section 6160) of Chapter 4 of Division 3 of this code, when the law corporation is in compliance with the requirements of (a) the Professional Corporation Act; (b) Article 10 (commencing with Section 6160) of Chapter 4 of Division 3 of this code; and (c) all other statutes and all rules and regulations now or hereafter enacted or adopted pertaining to such corporation and the conduct of its affairs.

§ 6128. Deceit, collusion, delay of suit and improper receipt of money as misdemeanors

Every attorney is guilty of a misdemeanor who either:

(a) Is guilty of any deceit or collusion, or consents to any deceit or collusion, with intent to deceive the court or any party.

(b) Wilfully delays his client's suit with a view to his own gain.

(c) Wilfully receives any money or allowance for or on account of any money which he has not laid out or become answerable for.

Any violation of the provisions of this section is punishable by imprisonment in the county jail not exceeding six months, or by a fine not exceeding two thousand five hundred dollars ($2,500), or by both.

§ 6129. Buying claim as misdemeanor

Every attorney who, either directly or indirectly, buys or is interested in buying any evidence of debt or thing in action, with intent to bring suit thereon, is guilty of a misdemeanor.

Any violation of the provisions of this section is punished by imprisonment in the county jail not exceeding six months, or by a fine not exceeding two thousand five hundred dollars ($2,500), or by both.

§ 6130. Disbarred or suspended attorney suing as assignee

No person, who has been an attorney, shall while a judgment of disbarment or suspension is in force appear on his own behalf as plaintiff in the prosecution of any action where the subject of the action has been assigned to him subsequent to the entry of the judgment of disbarment or suspension and solely for purpose of collection.

§ 6131. Aiding defense where partner or self has acted as public prosecutor; misdemeanor and disbarment

Every attorney is guilty of a misdemeanor and, in addition to the punishment prescribed therefor, shall be disbarred:

(a) Who directly or indirectly advises in relation to, or aids, or promotes the defense of any action or proceeding in any court the prosecution of which is carried on, aided or promoted by any person as district attorney or other public prosecutor with whom such person is directly or indirectly connected as a partner.

(b) Who, having himself prosecuted or in any manner aided or promoted any action or proceeding in any court as district attorney or other public prosecutor, afterwards, directly or indirectly, advises in relation to or takes any part in the defense thereof, as attorney or otherwise, or who takes or receives any valuable consideration from or on behalf of any defendant in any such action upon any understanding or agreement whatever having relation to the defense thereof.

This section does not prohibit an attorney from defending himself in person, as attorney or counsel, when prosecuted, either civilly or criminally.

ARTICLE 8.5 CONTINGENCY FEE AGREEMENTS

§ 6146. Limitations; periodic payments

(a) An attorney shall not contract for or collect a contingency fee for representing any person seeking damages in connection with an action for injury or damage against a health care provider based upon such person's alleged professional negligence in excess of the following limits:

(1) Forty percent of the first fifty thousand dollars ($50,000) recovered.

(2) Thirty-three and one-third percent of the next fifty thousand dollars ($50,000) recovered.

(3) Twenty-five percent of the next five hundred thousand dollars ($500,000) recovered.

(4) Fifteen percent of any amount on which the recovery exceeds six hundred thousand dollars ($600,000).

The limitations shall apply regardless of whether the recovery is by settlement, arbitration, or judgment, or whether the person for whom the recovery is made is a responsible adult, an infant, or a person of unsound mind.

(b) If periodic payments are awarded to the plaintiff pursuant to Section 667.7 of the Code of Civil Procedure, the court shall place a total value on these payments based upon the projected life expectancy of the plaintiff and include this amount in computing the total award from which attorney's fees are calculated under this section.

(c) For purposes of this section:

(1) "Recovered" means the net sum recovered after deducting any disbursements or costs incurred in connection with prosecution or settlement of the claim. Costs of medical care incurred by the plaintiff and the attorney's office-overhead costs or charges are not deductible disbursements or costs for such purpose.

(2) "Health care provider" means any person licensed or certified pursuant to Division 2 (commencing with Section 500), or licensed pursuant to the Osteopathic Initiative Act, or the Chiropractic Initiative Act, or licensed pursuant to Chapter 2.5 (commencing with Section 1440) of Division 2 of the Health and Safety Code; and any clinic, health dispensary, or health facility, licensed pursuant to Division 2 (commencing with Section 1200) of the Health and Safety Code. "Health care provider" includes the legal representatives of a health care provider.

(3) "Professional negligence" is a negligent act or omission to act by a health care provider in the rendering of professional services, which act or omission is the proximate cause of a personal injury or wrongful death, provided that the services are within the scope of services for which the provider is licensed and which are not within any restriction imposed by the licensing agency or licensed hospital.

§ 6147. Contract; duplicate copies; contents; effect of noncompliance; application to contracts for recovery of workers' compensation benefits

(a) An attorney who contracts to represent a plaintiff on a contingency fee basis shall, at the time the contract is entered into, provide a duplicate copy of the contract, signed by both the attorney and the plaintiff, or his guardian or representative, to the plaintiff, or to the plaintiff's guardian or representative. The contract shall be in writing and shall include, but is not limited to, all of the following:

(1) A statement of the contingency fee rate which the client and attorney have agreed upon.

(2) A statement as to how disbursements and costs incurred in connection with the prosecution or settlement of the claim will affect the contingency fee and the client's recovery.

(3) A statement as to what extent, if any, the plaintiff could be required to pay any compensation to the attorney for related matters that arise out of their relationship not covered by their contingency fee contract. This may include any amounts collected for the plaintiff by the attorney.

(4) Unless the claim is subject to the provisions of Section 6146, a statement that the fee is not set by law but is negotiable between attorney and client.

(5) If the claim is subject to the provisions of Section 6146, a statement that the rates set forth in that section are the maximum limits for the contingency fee agreement, and that the attorney and client may negotiate a lower rate.

(b) Failure to comply with any provision of this section renders the agreement voidable at the option of the plaintiff, and the attorney shall thereupon be entitled to collect a reasonable fee.

(c) This section shall not apply to contingency fee contracts for the recovery of workers' compensation benefits.

§ 6147.5 Contingency fee contracts; recovery of claims between merchants

(a) Sections 6147 and 6148 shall not apply to contingency fee contracts for the recovery of claims between merchants as defined in Section 2104 of the Commercial Code, arising from the sale or lease of goods or services rendered, or money loaned for use, in the conduct of a business or profession if the merchant contracting for legal services employs 10 or more individuals.

(b)(1) In the instances in which no written contract for legal services exists as permitted by subdivision (a), an attorney shall not contract for or collect a contingency fee in excess of the following limits:

(A) Twenty percent of the first three hundred dollars ($300) collected.

(B) Eighteen percent of the next one thousand seven hundred dollars ($1,700) collected.

(C) Thirteen percent of sums collected in excess of two thousand dollars ($2,000).

(2) However, the following minimum charges may be charged and collected:

(A) Twenty-five dollars ($25) in collections of seventy-five dollars ($75) to one hundred twenty-five dollars ($125).

(B) Thirty-three and one-third percent of collections less than seventy-five dollars ($75).

§ 6148. Contracts for services in cases not coming within § 6147; bills for services rendered; contents; effect of noncompliance

(a) In any case not coming within Section 6147 in which it is reasonably foreseeable that total expense to a client, including attorney fees will exceed one thousand dollars ($1,000), the contract for services in the case shall be in writing and shall contain all of the following:

(1) The hourly rate and other standard rates, fees, and charges applicable to the case.

(2) The general nature of the legal services to be provided to the client.

(3) The respective responsibilities of the attorney and the client as to the performance of the contract.

(b) All bills rendered by an attorney to a client shall clearly state the basis thereof. Bills for the fee portion of the bill shall include the amount, rate, basis for calculation, or other method of determination of the attorney's fees and costs. Bills for the cost and expense portion of the bill shall clearly identify the costs and expenses incurred and the amount of the costs and expenses. Upon request by the client, the attorney shall provide a bill to the client no later than 10 days following the request unless the attorney has provided a bill to the client within 31 days prior to the request, in which case the attorney may provide a bill to the client no later than 31 days following the date the most recent bill was provided. The client is entitled to make similar requests at intervals of no less than 30 days following the initial request. In providing responses to client requests for billing information, the attorney may use billing data that is currently effective on the date of the request, or, if any fees or costs to that date cannot be accurately determined, they shall be described and estimated.

(c) Failure to comply with any provision of this section renders the agreement voidable at the option of the client, and the attorney shall, upon the agreement being voided, be entitled to collect a reasonable fee.

(d) This section shall not apply to any of the following:

(1) Services rendered in an emergency to avoid foreseeable prejudice to the rights or interests of the client or where a writing is otherwise impractical.

(2) An arrangement as to the fee implied by the fact that the attorney's services are of the same general kind as previously rendered to and paid for by the client.

(3) If the client knowingly states in writing, after full disclosure of this section, that a writing concerning fees is not required.

(4) If the client is a corporation.

(e) This section applies prospectively only to fee agreements following its operative date.

§ 6149. Written fee contract as confidential communication

A written fee contract shall be deemed to be a confidential communication within the meaning of subdivision (e) of Section 6068 and of Section 952 of the Evidence Code.

ARTICLE 9.   UNLAWFUL SOLICITATION

§ 6150.   Relation of article to chapter

This article is a part of Chapter 4 of this division of the Business and Professions Code, but the phrase "this chapter" as used in Chapter 4 does not apply to the provisions of this article unless expressly made applicable.

§ 6151.   Definitions

As used in this article:

(a) A runner or capper is any person, firm, association or corporation acting for consideration in any manner or in any capacity as an agent for an attorney at law or law firm, whether the attorney or any member of the law firm is admitted in California or any other jurisdiction, in the solicitation or procurement of business for the attorney at law or law firm as provided in this article.

(b) An agent is one who represents another in dealings with one or more third persons.

§ 6152.   Prohibition of solicitation

(a) It is unlawful for:

(1) Any person, in his individual capacity or in his capacity as a public or private employee, or for any firm, corporation, partnership or association to act as a runner or capper for any such attorneys or to solicit any business for any such attorneys in and about the state prisons, county jails, city jails, city prisons, or other places of detention of persons, city receiving hospitals, city and county receiving hospitals, county hospitals, justice courts, municipal courts, superior courts, or in any public institution or in any public place or upon any public street or highway or in and about private hospitals, sanitariums or in and about any private institution or upon private property of any character whatsoever.

(2) Any person to solicit another person to commit or join in the commission of a violation of subdivision (a).

(b) A general release from a liability claim obtained from any person during the period of the first physical confinement, whether as an inpatient or outpatient, in a clinic or health facility, as defined in Sections 1203 and 1250 of the Health and Safety Code, as a result of the injury alleged to have given rise to such claim and primarily of treatment of such injury, is presumed fraudulent if such release is executed within 15 days after the commencement of such confinement or prior to release from such confinement, which ever occurs first.

(c) Nothing in this section shall be construed to prevent the recommendation of professional employment where such recommendation is not prohibited by the Rules of Professional Conduct of the State Bar of California.

(d) Nothing in this section shall be construed to mean that a public defender or assigned counsel may not make known his or her services as a criminal defense attorney to persons unable to afford legal counsel whether such persons are in custody or otherwise.

§ 6153. Violation as misdemeanor; forfeiture of public office or employment

Any person, firm, partnership, association, or corporation violating subdivision (a) of Section 6152 is punishable, upon a first conviction by imprisonment in a county jail for not more than one year. Upon a second or subsequent conviction, a person, firm, partnership, association, or corporation is punishable by imprisonment in a county jail for not more than one year, or by imprisonment in the state prison for 16 months or 2 or 3 years, or by a fine up to ten thousand dollars ($10,000), or by both that imprisonment and fine.

Any person employed either as an officer, director, trustee, clerk, servant or agent of this State or of any county or other municipal corporation or subdivision thereof, who is found guilty of violating any of the provisions of this article, shall forfeit the right to his office and employment in addition to any other penalty provided in this article.

§ 6154. Invalidity of contract for services

Any contract for professional services secured by any attorney at law or law firm in this state through the services of a runner or capper is void. In any action against any attorney or law firm under the Unfair Practices Act, Chapter 4 (commencing with Section 17000) of Division 7, or Chapter 5 (commencing with Section 17200) of Division 7, any judgment shall include an order divesting the attorney or law firm of any fees and other compensation received pursuant to any such void contract. Those fees and compensation shall be recoverable as additional civil penalties under Chapter 4 (commencing with Section 17000) or Chapter 5 (commencing with Section 17200) of Division 7.

§ 6155. Referral services; conflicts of interest; enforcement; rules and regulations; duration of section

(a) An individual, partnership, corporation, association, or any other entity shall not use the term "referral service" or similar terms, if the purpose of the individual, partnership, corporation, association, or entity is to refer potential clients to attorneys, unless all of the following requirements are met:

(1) The service is registered with the State Bar of California and (a) on July 1, 1988, is operated in conformity with minimum standards for a lawyer referral service established by the State Bar, or (b) upon approval by the Supreme Court of minimum standards

for a lawyer referral service, is operated in conformity with those standards.

(2) The combined charges to the potential client by the referral service and the attorney to whom the potential client is referred do not exceed the total cost that the client would normally pay if no referral service were involved.

(b) A referral service shall not be owned or operated, in whole or in part, directly or indirectly, by those lawyers to whom, individually or collectively, more than 20 percent of referrals are made. For purposes of this subdivision, a referral service that is owned or operated by a bar association, as defined in the minimum standards, shall be deemed to be owned or operated by its governing committee so long as the governing committee is constituted and functions in the manner prescribed by the minimum standards.

(c) Neither of the following is a lawyer referral service:

(1) A plan of legal insurance as defined in Section 119.6 of the Insurance Code.

(2) A group or prepaid legal plan, whether operated by a union, trust, mutual benefit or aid association, public or private corporation, or other entity or person, which meets both of the following conditions:

(A) It recommends, furnishes, or pays for legal services to its members or beneficiaries.

(B) It provides telephone advice or personal consultation.

(d) The following are in the public interest and do not constitute an unlawful restraint of trade or commerce:

(1) An agreement between a referral service and a participating attorney to eliminate or restrict the attorney's fee for an initial office consultation for each potential client or to provide free or reduced fee services.

(2) Requirements by a referral service that attorneys meet reasonable participation requirements, including experience, education, and training requirements.

(3) Provisions of the minimum standards as approved by the Supreme Court.

(e) A violation or threatened violation of this section may be enjoined by any person.

(f) With the approval of the Supreme Court, the State Bar shall formulate and enforce rules and regulations for carrying out this section, including rules and regulations which do the following:

(1) Establish minimum standards for lawyer referral services. The minimum standards shall include provisions ensuring that panel membership shall be open to all attorneys practicing in the

geographical area served who are qualified by virtue of suitable experience, and limiting attorney registration and membership fees to reasonable sums which do not discourage widespread attorney membership.

(2) Require that an entity seeking to qualify as a lawyer referral service register with the State Bar and obtain from the State Bar a certificate of compliance with the minimum standards for lawyer referral services. A lawyer referral service that, on July 1, 1988, has been authorized by the State Bar shall have a reasonable period, not to exceed six months, after approval of the minimum standards by the Supreme Court to obtain a certificate of compliance.

(3) Require that the certificate may be obtained, maintained, suspended, or revoked pursuant to procedures set forth in the rules and regulations.

(4) Require the lawyer referral service to pay an application and renewal fee for the certificate in such reasonable amounts as may be determined by the State Bar. The State Bar shall adopt rules authorizing the waiver or reduction of the fees upon a demonstration of financial necessity.

(5) Require each lawyer who is a member of a certified lawyer referral service to possess a policy of errors and omissions insurance in an amount not less than one hundred thousand dollars ($100,000) for each occurrence and three hundred thousand dollars ($300,000) aggregate, per year. By rule, the State Bar may provide for alternative proof of financial responsibility to meet this requirement.

(g) The State Bar of California shall submit the proposed rules and regulations adopted pursuant to this section to the Supreme Court for approval no later than July 1, 1988.

(h) This section shall not be construed to prohibit attorneys from jointly advertising their services.

(i) This section shall become inoperative on July 1, 1993, and, as of January 1, 1994, is repealed, unless a later enacted statute, which becomes effective on or before January 1, 1994, deletes or extends the dates on which it becomes inoperative and is repealed.

ARTICLE 13. ARBITRATION OF ATTORNEYS' FEES

§ 6200. Establishment of System and Procedure; Applicability of Article; Voluntary or Mandatory Nature; Rules; Immunity of Arbitrator; Powers of Arbitrator

(a) The board of governors shall, by rule, establish, maintain, and administer a system and procedure for the arbitration of disputes concerning fees, costs, or both, charged for professional services by members of the State Bar or by members of the bar of other jurisdictions. The rules may include provision for a filing fee in such amount as the board may, from time to time, determine.

(b) This article shall not apply to any of the following:

(1) Disputes where a member of the State Bar of California is also admitted to practice in another jurisdiction or where an attorney is only admitted to practice in another jurisdiction, and he or she maintains no office in the State of California, and no material portion of the services were rendered in the State of California.

(2) Claims for affirmative relief against the attorney for damages or otherwise based upon alleged malpractice or professional misconduct, except as provided in subdivision (a) of Section 6203.

(3) Disputes where the fee or cost to be paid by the client or on his or her behalf has been determined pursuant to statute or court order.

(c) Arbitration under this article shall be voluntary for a client and shall be mandatory for an attorney if commenced by a client.

(d) The board of governors shall adopt rules to allow arbitration of attorney fee and cost disputes under this article to proceed under arbitration systems sponsored by local bar associations in this state. Rules of procedure promulgated by local bar associations are subject to review by the board to insure that they provide for a fair, impartial, and speedy hearing and award.

(e) In adopting or reviewing rules of arbitration under this section the board shall provide that the panel shall include one attorney member whose area of practice is either, at the option of the client, civil or criminal law, as follows:

(1) If the panel is composed of three members the panel shall include one attorney member whose area of practice is either, at the option of the client, civil or criminal law, and shall include one lay member.

(2) If the panel is composed of one member, that member shall be an attorney whose area of practice is either, at the option of the client, civil or criminal law.

(f) In any arbitration conducted pursuant to this article by the State Bar or by a local bar association, pursuant to rules of procedure approved by the board of governors, the arbitrator or arbitrators, as well as the arbitrating association and its directors, officers, and employees, shall have the same immunity which attaches in judicial proceedings.

(g) In the conduct of arbitrations under this article the arbitrator or arbitrators may do all of the following:

(1) Take and hear evidence pertaining to the proceeding.

(2) Administer oaths and affirmations.

(3) Compel, by subpoena, the attendance of witnesses and the production of books, papers, and documents pertaining to the proceeding.

§ 6201.   Notice to Client and State Bar; Stay of Action; Right to Arbitration; Waiver by Client

(a) The rules adopted by the board of governors shall provide that, except as to an action filed in small claims court, an attorney shall forward a written notice to the client prior to or at the time of service of summons in an action against the client for recovery of fees, costs, or both, covered by the provisions of this article. The written notice shall be in such form as the board of governors may prescribe, but shall include a statement of the client's right to arbitration under this article. Failure to give this notice shall be a ground for the dismissal of the action.

The rules adopted by the board of governors shall provide that the client's failure to request arbitration within 30 days after receipt of notice from the attorney shall be deemed a waiver of the client's right to arbitration under the provisions of this article.

(b) If an attorney, or the attorney's assignee, subject to the provisions of this article, commences an action in any court, other than a small claims court, and the dispute is not one to which subdivision (b) of Section 6200 applies, the client may stay the action by serving and filing a request for arbitration in accordance with the rules established by the board of governors pursuant to subdivision (a) of Section 6200. If the attorney files an action against the client in small claims court for recovery of fees, costs, or both, covered by the provisions of this article, and the client has not filed a request for arbitration, the small claims action, including any appeal, shall not be stayed under the provisions of this section, and the matter shall not be subject to arbitration under this article while the matter is pending in small claims court or after judgment is given in that court. A small claims court action shall not be filed by the attorney after the client has filed a request for arbitration while the arbitration is pending or after the award is issued. Any such action shall be dismissed without prejudice, and the pendency of the action shall not preclude the arbitration from going forward. The request for arbitration shall be served and filed prior to the filing of an answer in the action; failure to so request arbitration prior to the filing of an answer shall be deemed a waiver of the client's right to arbitration under the provisions of this article if notice of the client's right to arbitration was given pursuant to subdivision (a).

(c) Upon filing and service of the request for arbitration, the action shall be stayed, without the necessity of court order, until the award of the arbitrators is issued or the arbitration is otherwise terminated, and the time of the continuance of the stay shall not be part of the time limited for the commencement of the action. The stay may be vacated in whole or in part, after a hearing duly noticed by any party or the court, if the court finds that the matter, or any part of it, is not an appropriate one for arbitration under the provisions of this article. The action may thereafter proceed subject to the provisions of Section 6204.

(d) A client's right to request or maintain arbitration under the provisions of this article is waived by (1) the commencement of an action or the filing of any pleading by the client seeking judicial resolution of a dispute to which this article applies, or (2) seeking affirmative relief against the attorney for damages or otherwise based upon alleged malpractice or professional misconduct.

§ 6203. Award; Contents; Damages and Offset; Fees and Costs; Finality of Award; Appellate Fees and Costs

(a) The award shall be in writing and signed by the arbitrators concurring therein. It shall include a determination of all the questions submitted to the arbitrators, the decision of which is necessary in order to determine the controversy. The award shall not include any award to either party for attorney's fees incurred, notwithstanding any contract between the parties providing for such an award or attorney's fees. However, this section shall not preclude an award of attorney's fees to either party by a court pursuant to subdivision (c) of this section or of subdivision (d) of Section 6204. The State Bar, or the local bar association delegated by the State Bar to conduct the arbitration, shall deliver to each of the parties with the award, an original declaration of service of the award.

The arbitrators may receive evidence relating to claims of malpractice and professional misconduct, but only to the extent that those claims bear upon the fees, costs, or both, to which the attorney is entitled. The arbitrators shall not award affirmative relief, in the form of damages or offset or otherwise, for injuries underlying any such claim. Nothing in this section shall be construed to prevent the arbitrators from awarding a refund of unearned prepaid fees.

(b) Even if the parties to the arbitration have not agreed in writing to be bound, the arbitration award shall become binding upon the passage of 30 days after mailing of notice of the award, unless a party has, within the 30 days, sought a trial after arbitration pursuant to Section 6204. If an action has previously been filed in any court, any petition to confirm, correct, or vacate the award shall be to the court in which the action is pending, and may be served by mail on any party who has appeared, as provided in Chapter 4 (commencing with Section

1003) of Title 14 of Part 2 of the Code of Civil Procedure; otherwise it shall be in the same manner as provided in Chapter 4 (commencing with Section 1285) of Title 9 of Part 3 of the Code of Civil Procedure. If no action is pending in any court, the award may be confirmed, corrected, or vacated by petition to the court having jurisdiction over the amount of the arbitration award, but otherwise in the same manner as provided in Chapter 4 (commencing with Section 1285) of Title 9 of Part 3 of the Code of Civil Procedure.

(c) A court confirming, correcting, or vacating an award under this section may award to the prevailing party reasonable fees and costs including, if applicable, fees or costs on appeal, incurred in obtaining confirmation, correction, or vacation of the award. The party obtaining judgment confirming, correcting, or vacating the award shall be the prevailing party except that, without regard to consideration of who the prevailing party may be, if a party did not appear at the arbitration hearing in the manner provided by the rules adopted by the board of governors, that party shall not be entitled to attorney's fees or costs upon confirmation, correction, or vacation of the award.

ARTICLE 14. FUNDS FOR THE PROVISION OF LEGAL SERVICES TO INDIGENT PERSONS

§ 6210. Legislative findings; purpose

The Legislature finds that, due to insufficient funding, existing programs providing free legal services in civil matters to indigent persons, especially underserved client groups, such as the elderly, the disabled, juveniles, and non-English-speaking persons, do not adequately meet the needs of these persons. It is the purpose of this article to expand the availability and improve the quality of existing free legal services in civil matters to indigent persons, and to initiate new programs that will provide services to them. The Legislature finds that the use of funds collected by the State Bar pursuant to this article for these purposes is in the public interest, is a proper use of the funds, and is consistent with essential public and governmental purposes in the judicial branch of government. The Legislature further finds that the expansion, improvement, and initiation of legal services to indigent persons will aid in the advancement of the science of jurisprudence and the improvement of the administration of justice.

§ 6211. Establishment by attorney of demand trust account; interest earned to be paid to state bar; other accounts not prohibited; rules of professional conduct, authority of supreme court or state bar not affected

(a) An attorney or law firm, which in the course of the practice of law receives or disburses trust funds, shall establish and maintain an interest bearing demand trust account and shall deposit therein all client deposits that are nominal in amount or are on deposit for a short period of time. All such client funds may be deposited in a single unsegregated account. The interest earned on all such accounts shall be paid to the State Bar of California to be used for the purposes set forth in this article.

(b) Nothing in this article shall be construed to prohibit an attorney or law firm from establishing one or more interest bearing bank accounts or other trust investments as may be permitted by the Supreme Court, with the interest or dividends earned on the accounts payable to clients for trust funds not deposited in accordance with subdivision (a).

(c) With the approval of the Supreme Court, the State Bar may formulate and enforce rules of professional conduct pertaining to the use by attorneys or law firms of interest bearing trust accounts for unsegregated client funds pursuant to this article.

(d) Nothing in this article shall be construed as affecting or impairing the disciplinary powers and authority of the Supreme Court or of the State Bar or as modifying the statutes and rules governing the conduct of members of the State Bar.

§ 6212. Establishment by attorney of demand trust account; amount of interest; remittance to state bar; statements and reports

An attorney who, or a law firm which, establishes an interest bearing demand trust account pursuant to subdivision (a) of Section 6211 shall comply with all of the following provisions:

(a) The interest bearing trust account shall be established with a bank or such other financial institution as are authorized by the Supreme Court.

(b) The rate of interest payable on any interest bearing demand trust account shall not be less than the rate paid by the depository institution to regular, nonattorney depositors. Higher rates offered by the institution to customers whose deposits exceed certain time or quantity qualifications, such as those offered in the form of certificates of deposit, may be obtained by an attorney or law firm so long as there is no impairment of the right to withdraw or transfer principal immediately (except as accounts generally may be subject to statutory notification requirements), even though interest may be sacrificed thereby.

(c) The depository institution shall be directed to do all of the following:

(1) To remit interest on the average daily balance in the account, less reasonable service charges, to the State Bar, at least quarterly.

(2) To transmit to the State Bar with each remittance a statement showing the name of the attorney or law firm for

whom the remittance is sent, the rate of interest applied, and the amount of service charges deducted, if any.

(3) To transmit to the depositing attorney or law firm at the same time a report showing the amount paid to the State Bar for that period, the rate of interest applied, the amount of service charges deducted, if any, and the average daily account balance for each month of the period for which the report is made.

§ 6213. Definitions

As used in this article:

(a) "Qualified legal services project" means either of the following:

(1) A nonprofit project incorporated and operated exclusively in California which provides as its primary purpose and function legal services without charge to indigent persons and which has quality control procedures approved by the State Bar of California.

(2) A program operated exclusively in California by a nonprofit law school accredited by the State Bar of California which meets the requirements of subparagraphs (A) and (B).

(A) The program shall have operated for at least two years at a cost of at least twenty thousand dollars ($20,000) per year as an identifiable law school unit with a primary purpose and function of providing legal services without charge to indigent persons.

(B) The program shall have quality control procedures approved by the State Bar of California.

(b) "Qualified support center" means an incorporated nonprofit legal services center, which has as its primary purpose and function the provision of legal training, legal technical assistance, or advocacy support without charge and which actually provides through an office in California a significant level of legal training, legal technical assistance, or advocacy support without charge to qualified legal services projects on a statewide basis in California.

(c) "Recipient" means a qualified legal services project or support center receiving financial assistance under this article.

(d) "Indigent person" means a person whose income is (1) 125 percent or less of the current poverty threshold established by the United States Office of Management and Budget, or (2) who is eligible for Supplemental Security Income or free services under the Older Americans Act or Developmentally Disabled Assistance Act. With regard to a project which provides free services of attorneys in private practice without compensation, "indigent person" also means a person whose income is 75 percent or less of the maximum levels of income for lower income households as defined in Section 50079.5 of the Health and Safety Code. For the purpose of this subdivision, the income of a person who is disabled shall be determined after deducting the costs of medical and other disability-related special expenses.

(e) "Fee generating case" means any case or matter which, if undertaken on behalf of an indigent person by an attorney in private practice, reasonably may be expected to result in payment of a fee for legal services from an award to a client, from public funds, or from the opposing party. A case shall not be considered fee generating if adequate representation is unavailable and any of the following circumstances exist:

(1) The recipient has determined that free referral is not possible because of any of the following reasons:

(A) The case has been rejected by the local lawyer referral service, or if there is no such service, by two attorneys in private practice who have experience in the subject matter of the case.

(B) Neither the referral service nor any attorney will consider the case without payment of a consultation fee.

(C) The case if of the type that attorneys in private practice in the area ordinarily do not accept, or do not accept without prepayment of a fee.

(D) Emergency circumstances compel immediate action before referral can be made, but the client is advised that, if appropriate and consistent with professional responsibility, referral will be attempted at a later time.

(2) Recovery of damages is not the principal object of the case and a request for damages is merely ancillary to an action for equitable or other nonpecuniary relief, or inclusion of a counterclaim requesting damages is necessary for effective defense or because of applicable rules governing joinder of counterclaims.

(3) A court has appointed a recipient or an employee of a recipient pursuant to a statute or a court rule or practice of equal applicability to all attorneys in the jurisdiction.

(4) The case involves the rights of a claimant under a publicly supported benefit program for which entitlement to benefit is based on need.

(f) "Legal Services Corporation" means the Legal Services Corporation established under the Legal Services Corporation Act of 1974, (Public Law 93–355; 42 U.S.C. Sec. 2996 et seq.).

(g) "Older Americans Act" means the Older Americans Act of 1965, as amended (Public Law 89–73; 42 U.S.C. Sec. 3001 et seq.).

(h) "Developmentally Disabled Assistance Act" means the Developmentally Disabled Assistance and Bill of Rights Act of 1975, as amended (Public Law 94–103; 42 U.S.C. Sec. 6001 et seq.).

(i) "Supplemental security income recipient" means an individual receiving or eligible to receive payments under Title XVI of the federal Social Security Act, or payments under Chapter 3 (commencing with Section 12000) of Part 3 of Division 9 of the Welfare and Institutions Code.

§ 6214. Qualified legal service projects

(a) Projects meeting the requirements of subdivision (a) of Section 6213 which are funded either in whole or part by the Legal Services Corporation or with Older American Act funds shall be presumed qualified legal services projects for the purpose of this article.

(b) Projects meeting the requirements of subdivision (a) of Section 6213 but not qualifying under the presumption specified in subdivision (a) shall qualify for funds under this article if they meet all of the following additional criteria:

(1) They receive cash funds from other sources in the amount of at least twenty thousand dollars ($20,000) per year to support free legal representation to indigent persons.

(2) They have demonstrated community support for the operation of a viable ongoing program.

(3) They provide one or both of the following special services:

(A) The coordination of the recruitment of substantial numbers of attorneys in private practice to provide free legal representation to indigent persons or to qualified legal services projects in California.

(B) The provision of legal representation, training, or technical assistance on matters concerning special client groups, including the elderly, the disabled, juveniles, and non-English-speaking groups, or on matters of specialized substantive law important to the special client groups.

§ 6214.5 Qualified legal services projects; eligibility for distributions of funds

A law school program that meets the definition of a "qualified legal services project" as defined in paragraph (2) of subdivision (a) of Section 6213, and that applied to the State Bar for funding under this article not later than February 17, 1984, shall be deemed eligible for all distributions of funds made under Section 6216.

§ 6215. Qualified support centers

(a) Support centers satisfying the qualifications specified in subdivision (b) of Section 6213 which were operating an office and providing services in California on December 31, 1980, shall be presumed to be qualified support centers for the purposes of this article.

(b) Support centers not qualifying under the presumption specified in subdivision (a) may qualify as a support center by meeting both of the following additional criteria:

(1) Meeting quality control standards established by the State Bar.

(2) Being deemed to be of special need by a majority of the qualified legal services projects.

§ 6216. Distribution of funds

The State Bar shall distribute all moneys received under the program established by this article for the provision of civil legal services to indigent persons. The funds first shall be distributed 18 months from the effective date of this article, or upon such a date, as shall be determined by the State Bar, that adequate funds are available to initiate the program. Thereafter, the funds shall be distributed on an annual basis. All distributions of funds shall be made in the following order and in the following manner:

(a) To pay the actual administrative costs of the program, including any costs incurred after the adoption of this article and a reasonable reserve therefor.

(b) Eighty-five percent of the funds remaining after payment of administrative costs allocated pursuant to this article shall be distributed to qualified legal services projects. Distribution shall be by a pro rata county-by-county formula based upon the number of persons whose income is 125 percent or less of the current poverty threshold per county. For the purposes of this section, the source of data identifying the number of persons per county shall be the latest available figures from the United States Department of Commerce, Bureau of the Census. Projects from more than one county may pool their funds to operate a joint, multicounty legal services project serving each of their respective counties.

(1)(A) In any county which is served by more than one qualified legal services project, the State Bar shall distribute funds for the county to those projects which apply on a pro rata basis, based upon the amount of their total budget expended in the prior year for legal services in that county as compared to the total expended in the prior year for legal services by all qualified legal services projects applying therefor in the county. In determining the amount of funds to be allocated to a qualified legal services project specified in paragraph (2) of subdivision (a) of Section 6213, the State Bar shall recognize only expenditures attributable to the representation of indigent persons as constituting the budget of the program.

(B) The State Bar shall reserve 10 percent of the funds allocated to the county for distribution to programs meeting the standards of subparagraph (A) of paragraph (3) and paragraphs (1) and (2) of subdivision (b) of Section 6214 and which perform the services described in subparagraph (A) of paragraph (3) of Section 6214 as their principal means of delivering legal services. The State Bar shall distribute the funds for that county to those programs which apply on a pro rata basis, based upon the amount of their total budget expended for free legal services in that county as compared to the total expended for free legal services by all programs meeting the standards of subparagraph (A) of paragraph (3) and paragraphs (1) and (2) of subdivision (b) of Section 6214 in that county. The State Bar shall distribute any funds for which no program has qualified pursuant hereto, in accordance with the provisions of subparagraph (A) of paragraph (1) of this subdivision.

(2) In any county in which there is no qualified legal services projects providing services, the State Bar shall reserve for the remainder of the fiscal year for distribution the pro rata share of funds as provided for by this article. Upon application of a qualified legal services project proposing to provide legal services to the indigent of the county, the State Bar shall distribute the funds to the project. Any funds not so distributed shall be added to the funds to be distributed the following year.

(c) Fifteen percent of the funds remaining after payment of administrative costs allocated for the purposes of this article shall be distributed equally by the State Bar to qualified support centers which apply for the funds. The funds provided to support centers shall be used only for the provision of legal services within California. Qualified support centers that receive funds to provide services to qualified legal services projects from sources other than this article, shall submit and shall have approved by the State Bar a plan assuring that the services funded under this article are in addition to those already funded for qualified legal services projects by other sources.

§ 6217. Maintenance of quality services, professional standards, attorney-client privilege; funds to be expended in accordance with article; interference with attorney prohibited

With respect to the provision of legal assistance under this article, each recipient shall ensure all of the following:

(a) The maintenance of quality service and professional standards.

(b) The expenditure of funds received in accordance with the provisions of this article.

(c) The preservation of the attorney-client privilege in any case, and the protection of the integrity of the adversary process from any impairment in furnishing legal assistance to indigent persons.

(d) That no one shall interfere with any attorney funded in whole or in part by this article in carrying out his or her professional responsibility to his or her client as established by the rules of professional responsibility and this chapter.

§ 6218. Eligibility for services; establishment of guidelines; funds to be expended in accordance with article

All legal services projects and support centers receiving funds pursuant to this article shall adopt financial eligibility guidelines for indigent persons.

(a) Qualified legal services programs shall ensure that funds appropriated pursuant to this article shall be used solely to defray the costs of providing legal services to indigent persons or for such other purposes as set forth in this article.

(b) Funds received pursuant to this article by support centers shall only be used to provide services to qualified legal services projects as defined in subdivision (a) of Section 6213 which are used pursuant to a plan as required by subdivision (c) of Section 6216, or as permitted by Section 6219.

§ 6219. Provision of work opportunities and scholarships for disadvantaged law students

Qualified legal services projects and support centers may use funds provided under this article to provide work opportunities with pay, and where feasible, scholarships for disadvantaged law students to help defray their law school expenses.

§ 6220. Private attorneys providing legal services without charge; support center services

Attorneys in private practice who are providing legal services without charge to indigent persons shall not be disqualified from receiving the services of the qualified support centers.

§ 6221. Services for indigent members of disadvantaged and underserved groups

Qualified legal services projects shall make significant efforts to utilize 20 percent of the funds allocated under this article for increasing the availability of services to the elderly, the disabled, juveniles, or other indigent persons who are members of disadvantaged and underserved groups within their service area.

§ 6222.   Financial statements; submission to state bar; state bar report

A recipient of funds allocated pursuant to this article annually shall submit a financial statement to the State Bar, including an audit of the funds by a certified public accountant or a fiscal review approved by the State Bar, a report demonstrating the programs on which they were expended, a report on the recipient's compliance with the requirements of Section 6217, and progress in meeting the service expansion requirements of Section 6221.

The Board of Governors of the State Bar shall include a report of receipts of funds under this article, expenditures for administrative costs, and disbursements of the funds, on a county-by-county basis, in the annual report of State Bar receipts and expenditures required pursuant to Section 6145.

§ 6223.   Expenditure of funds; prohibitions

No funds allocated by the State Bar pursuant to this article shall be used for any of the following purposes:

(a) The provision of legal assistance with respect to any fee generating case, except in accordance with guidelines which shall be promulgated by the State Bar.

(b) The provision of legal assistance with respect to any criminal proceeding.

(c) The provision of legal assistance, except to indigent persons or except to provide support services to qualified legal services projects as defined by this article.

§ 6224.   State bar; powers; determination of qualifications to receive funds; denial of funds; termination; procedures

The State Bar shall have the power to determine that an applicant for funding is not qualified to receive funding, to deny future funding, or to terminate existing funding because the recipient is not operating in compliance with the requirements or restrictions of this article.

A denial of an application for funding or for future funding or an action by the State Bar to terminate an existing grant of funds under this article shall not become final until the applicant or recipient has been afforded reasonable notice and an opportunity for a timely and fair hearing. Pending final determination of any hearing held with reference to termination of funding, financial assistance shall be continued at its existing level on a month-to-month basis. Hearings for denial shall be conducted by an impartial hearing officer whose decision shall be final. The hearing officer shall render a decision no later than 30 days after the conclusion of the hearing. Specific procedures governing the conduct of the hearings of this section shall be determined by the State Bar pursuant to Section 6225.

§ 6225. Implementation of article; adoption of rules and regulations; procedures

The Board of Governors of the State Bar shall adopt the regulations and procedures necessary to implement this article and to ensure that the funds allocated herein are utilized to provide civil legal services to indigent persons, especially underserved client groups such as but not limited to the elderly, the disabled, juveniles, and non-English-speaking persons.

In adopting the regulations the Board of Governors shall comply with the following procedures:

(a) The board shall publish a preliminary draft of the regulations and procedures, which shall be distributed, together with notice of the hearings required by subdivision (b), to commercial banking institutions, to members of the State Bar, and to potential recipients of funds.

(b) The board shall hold at least two public hearings, one in southern California and one in northern California where affected and interested parties shall be afforded an opportunity to present oral and written testimony regarding the proposed regulations and procedures.

§ 6226. Implementation of article; resolution

The program authorized by this article shall become operative only upon the adoption of a resolution by the Board of Governors of the State Bar stating that regulations have been adopted pursuant to Section 6225 which conform the program to all applicable tax and banking statutes, regulations, and rulings.

§ 6227. Credit of state not pledged

Nothing in this article shall create an obligation or pledge of the credit of the State of California or of the State Bar of California. Claims arising by reason of acts done pursuant to this article shall be limited to the moneys generated hereunder.

§ 6228. Severability

If any provision of this article or the application thereof to any group or circumstances is held invalid, such invalidity shall not affect the other provisions or applications of this article which can be given effect without the invalid provision or application, and to this end the provisions of this article are severable.

NEW YORK CODE OF PROFESSIONAL RESPONSIBILITY: CANONS AND DISCIPLINARY RULES

[In 1990, the Appellate Divisions of the Supreme Court promulgated the following Code of Professional Responsibility. The New York Code continues to retain the Canons and the Ethical Considerations; however, the ethical considerations are not reprinted below. Ed.]

Table of Contents

DEFINITIONS

As used in the Disciplinary Rules of the Code of Professional Responsibility [1]:

1. "Differing interests" include every interest that will adversely affect either the judgment or the loyalty of a lawyer to a client, whether it be a conflicting, inconsistent, diverse, or other interest.

1 "Confidence" and "Secret" are defined in DR 4–101(A).

2. "Law firm" includes, but is not limited to, a professional legal corporation, the legal department of a corporation or other organization and a legal services organization.

3. "Person" includes a corporation, an association, a trust, a partnership, and any other organization or legal entity.

4. "Professional legal corporation" means a corporation, or an association treated as a corporation, authorized by law to practice law for profit.

5. "State" includes the District of Columbia, Puerto Rico, and other federal territories and possessions.

6. "Tribunal" includes all courts and all other adjudicatory bodies. A tribunal shall be deemed "available" when it would have jurisdiction to hear a complaint, if timely brought.

7. "Bar association" includes a bar association of specialists as referred to in DR 2–105(B).

8. "Qualified legal assistance organization" means an office or organization of one of the four types listed in DR 2–103(D)(1) through (4), inclusive, that meets all the requirements thereof.

9. "Fraud" does not include conduct, although characterized as fraudulent by statute or administrative rule, which lacks an element of scienter deceit, intent to mislead, or knowing failure to correct misrepresentations which can be reasonably expected to induce detrimental reliance by another.

CANON 1

A Lawyer Should Assist in Maintaining the Integrity and Competence of the Legal Profession

DISCIPLINARY RULES

DR 1–101. Maintaining Integrity and Competence of the Legal Profession

A. A lawyer is subject to discipline if the lawyer has made a materially false statement in, or has deliberately failed to disclose a material fact requested in connection with, the lawyer's application for admission to the bar.

B. A lawyer shall not further the application for admission to the bar of another person that the lawyer knows to be unqualified in respect to character, education, or other relevant attribute.

DR 1-102. Misconduct

A.[1] A lawyer shall not:

1. Violate a Disciplinary Rule.

2. Circumvent a Disciplinary Rule through actions of another.

3. Engage in illegal conduct involving moral turpitude.

4. Engage in conduct involving dishonesty, fraud, deceit, or misrepresentation.

5. Engage in conduct that is prejudicial to the administration of justice.

6. Unlawfully discriminate in the practice of law, including in hiring, promoting or otherwise determining conditions of employment, on the basis of age, race, creed, color, national origin, sex, disability, or marital status.

Where there is available a tribunal of competent jurisdiction, other than a Departmental Disciplinary Committee, a complaint of professional misconduct based on unlawful discrimination shall be brought before such tribunal in the first instance. A certified copy of a determination by such a tribunal, which has become final and enforceable, and as to which the right to judicial or appellate review has been exhausted, finding that the lawyer has engaged in an unlawful discriminatory practice shall constitute *prima facie* evidence of professional misconduct in a disciplinary proceeding.

7. Engage in any other conduct that adversely reflects on the lawyer's fitness to practice law.

DR 1-103. Disclosure of Information to Authorities

A. A lawyer possessing knowledge, not protected as a confidence or secret, of a violation of DR 1-102 that raises a substantial question as to another lawyer's honesty, trustworthiness or fitness in other respects as a lawyer shall report such knowledge to a tribunal or other authority empowered to investigate or act upon such violation.

B. A lawyer possessing knowledge or evidence, not protected as a confidence or secret, concerning another lawyer or a judge shall reveal fully such knowledge or evidence upon proper request of a tribunal or other authority empowered to investigate or act upon the conduct of lawyers or judges.

DR 1-104. Responsibilities of a Supervisory Lawyer

A.[1] A lawyer shall be responsible for a violation of the Disciplinary Rules by another lawyer or for conduct of a non-lawyer employed or

1. So in original. No par. B has been enacted.

retained by or associated with the lawyer that would be a violation of the Disciplinary Rules if engaged in by a lawyer if:

1. The lawyer orders the conduct; or

2. The lawyer has supervisory authority over the other lawyer or the non-lawyer, and knows or should have known of the conduct at a time when its consequences can be avoided or mitigated but fails to take reasonable remedial action.

CANON 2

A Lawyer Should Assist the Legal Profession in Fulfilling Its Duty to Make Legal Counsel Available

DR 2–101. Publicity and Advertising

A. A lawyer on behalf of himself or herself or partners or associates, shall not use or disseminate or participate in the preparation or dissemination of any public communication containing statements or claims that are false, deceptive, misleading or cast reflection on the legal profession as a whole.

B. Advertising or other publicity by lawyers, including participation in public functions, shall not contain puffery, self-laudation, claims regarding the quality of the lawyers' legal services, or claims that cannot be measured or verified.

C. It is proper to include information, provided its dissemination does not violate the provisions of subdivisions (A) and (B) of this section, as to:

1. education, degrees and other scholastic distinctions, dates of admission to any bar; areas of the law in which the lawyer or law firm practices, as authorized by the Code of Professional Responsibility; public offices and teaching positions held; memberships in bar associations or other professional societies or organizations, including offices and committee assignments therein; foreign language fluency;

2. names of clients regularly represented, provided that the client has given prior written consent;

3. bank references; credit arrangements accepted; prepaid or group legal services programs in which the attorney or firm participates; and

4. legal fees for initial consultation; contingent fee rates in civil matters when accompanied by a statement disclosing whether percentages are computed before or after deduction of costs and disbursements; range of fees for services, provided that there be available to the public free of charge a written statement clearly describing the scope of each advertised service; hourly rates; and fixed fees for specified legal services.

D. Advertising and publicity shall be designed to educate the public to an awareness of legal needs and to provide information relevant to the selection of the most appropriate counsel. Information other than that specifically authorized in subdivision (C) of this section that is consistent with these purposes may be disseminated providing that it does not violate any other provisions of this Rule.

E. A lawyer or law firm advertising any fixed fee for specified legal services shall, at the time of fee publication, have available to the public a written statement clearly describing the scope of each advertised service, which statement shall be delivered to the client at the time of retainer for any such service. Such legal services shall include all those services which are recognized as reasonable and necessary under local custom in the area of practice in the community where the services are performed.

F. If the advertisement is broadcast, it shall be prerecorded or taped and approved for broadcast by the lawyer, and a recording or videotape of the actual transmission shall be retained by the lawyer for a period of not less than one year following such transmission. All advertisements of legal services that are mailed, or are distributed other than by radio, television, directory, newspaper, magazine or other periodical, by a lawyer or law firm with an office for the practice of law in this state, shall also be subject to the following provisions:

    1. A copy of each advertisement shall at the time of its initial mailing or distribution be filed with the Departmental Disciplinary Committee of the appropriate judicial department.

    2. Such advertisement shall contain no reference to the fact of filing.

    3. If such advertisement is directed to a predetermined addressee, a list, containing the names and addresses of all persons to whom the advertisement is being or will thereafter be mailed or distributed, shall be retained by the lawyer or law firm for a period of not less than one year following the last date of mailing or distribution.

    4. The advertisements filed pursuant to this subdivision shall be open to public inspection.

    5. The requirements of this subdivision shall not apply to such professional cards or other announcements the distribution of which is authorized by DR 2–102(A).

G. If a lawyer or law firm advertises a range of fees or an hourly rate for services, the lawyer or law firm may not charge more than the fee advertised for such services. If a lawyer or law firm advertises a fixed fee for specified legal services, or performs services described in a fee schedule, the lawyer or law firm may not charge more than the fixed fee for such stated legal service as set forth in the advertisement or fee schedule, unless the client agrees in writing that the services performed or to be performed were not legal services referred to or implied in the advertisement or in the fee schedule and, further, that a different fee arrangement shall apply to the transaction.

H. Unless otherwise specified in the advertisement, if a lawyer publishes any fee information authorized under this Disciplinary Rule in a publication which is published more frequently than once per month, the lawyer shall be bound by any representation made therein for a period of not less than 30 days after such publication. If a lawyer publishes any fee information authorized under this Rule in a publication which is published once per month or less frequently, the lawyer shall be bound by any representation made therein until the publication of the succeeding issue. If a lawyer publishes any fee information authorized under this Rule in a publication which has no fixed date for publication of a succeeding issue, the lawyer shall be bound by any representation made therein for a reasonable period of time after publication, but in no event less than 90 days.

1. Unless otherwise specified, if a lawyer broadcasts any fee information authorized under this Rule, the lawyer shall be bound by any representation made therein for a period of not less than 30 days after such broadcast.

J. A lawyer shall not compensate or give any thing of value to representatives of the press, radio, television or other communication medium in anticipation of or in return for professional publicity in a news item.

K. All advertisements of legal services shall include the name, office address and telephone number of the attorney or law firm whose services are being offered.

DR 2–102. Professional Notices, Letterheads, and Signs

A. A lawyer or law firm may use professional cards, professional announcement cards, office signs, letterheads or similar professional notices or devices, provided the same do not violate any statute or court rule, and are in accordance with DR 2–101, including the following:

1. A professional card of a lawyer identifying the lawyer by name and as a lawyer, and giving addresses, telephone numbers, the name of the law firm, and any information permitted under DR 2–105. A professional card of a law firm may also give the names of members and associates.

2. A professional announcement card stating new or changed associations or addresses, change of firm name, or similar matters pertaining to the professional offices of a lawyer or law firm. It may state biographical data, the names of members of the firm and associates and the names and dates of predecessor firms in a continuing line of succession. It shall not state the nature of the practice except as permitted under DR 2–105.

3. A sign in or near the office and in the building directory identifying the law office. The sign shall not state the nature of the practice, except as permitted under DR 2-105.

4. A letterhead identifying the lawyer by name and as a lawyer, and giving addresses, telephone numbers, the name of the law firm, associates and any information permitted under DR 2-105. A letterhead of a law firm may also give the names of members and associates, and names and dates relating to deceased and retired members. A lawyer may be designated "Of Counsel" on a letterhead if there is a continuing relationship with a lawyer or law firm, other than as a partner or associate. A lawyer or law firm may be designated as "General Counsel" or by similar professional reference on stationery of a client if the lawyer or the firm devotes a substantial amount of professional time in the representation of that client. The letterhead of a law firm may give the names and dates of predecessor firms in a continuing line of succession.

B. A lawyer in private practice shall not practice under a trade name, a name that is misleading as to the identity of the lawyer or lawyers practicing under such name, or a firm name containing names other than those of one or more of the lawyers in the firm, except that the name of a professional corporation may contain "P.C." or such symbols permitted by law, and, if otherwise lawful, a firm may use as, or continue to include in its name the name or names of one or more deceased or retired members of the firm or of a predecessor firm in a continuing line of succession. Such terms as "legal clinic", "legal aid", "legal service office", "legal assistance office", "defender office" and the like, may be used only by qualified legal assistance organizations described in DR 2-103(D), except that the term "legal clinic" may be used by any lawyer or law firm provided the name of a participating lawyer or firm is incorporated therein. A lawyer who assumes a judicial, legislative or public executive or administrative post or office shall not permit his or her name to remain in the name of the law firm or be used in professional notices of the firm during any significant period in which the lawyer is not actively and regularly practicing law as a member of the firm and, during such period, other members of the firm shall not use the lawyer's name in the firm name or in professional notices of the firm.

C. A lawyer shall not hold himself or herself out as having a partnership with one or more other lawyers unless they are in fact partners.

D. A partnership shall not be formed or continued between or among lawyers licensed in different jurisdictions unless all enumerations of the members and associates of the firm on its letterhead and in other permissible listings make clear the jurisdictional limitations on those members and associates of the firm not licensed to practice in all listed jurisdictions; however, the same firm name may be used in each jurisdiction.

DR 2–103.   Solicitation and Recommendation of Professional Employment

A.   A lawyer shall not, directly or indirectly, seek professional employment for the lawyer or a partner or associate of the lawyer from a person who has not sought advice regarding employment of the lawyer in violation of any statute or existing court rule in the judicial department in which the lawyer practices.

B.   A lawyer shall not compensate or give anything of value to a person or organization to recommend or obtain employment by a client, or as a reward for having made a recommendation resulting in employment by a client, except by any of the organizations listed in DR 2–103(D).

C.   A lawyer shall not request a person or organization to recommend or promote the use of the lawyer's services or those of the lawyer's partner or associate, or any other affiliated lawyer as a private practitioner, other than by advertising or publicity not proscribed by DR 2–101, except that:

1.   The lawyer may request referrals from a lawyer referral service operated, sponsored or approved by a bar association and may pay its fees incident thereto.

2.   The lawyer may cooperate with the legal service activities of any of the offices or organizations enumerated in DR 2–103(D)(1) through (4) and may perform legal services for those to whom the lawyer was recommended by such an office or organization to do such work if:

a.   The person to whom the recommendation is made is a member or beneficiary of such office or organization; and

b.   The lawyer remains free to exercise independent professional judgment on behalf of the client.

3.   The lawyer may request such a recommendation from another lawyer or an organization performing legal services.

D.   A lawyer or the lawyer's partner or associate or any other affiliated lawyer may be recommended, employed or paid by, or may cooperate with one of the following offices or organizations which promote the use of the lawyer's services or those of a partner or associate or any other affiliated lawyer if there is no interference with the exercise of independent professional judgment on behalf of the client:

1.   A legal aid office or public defender office:

a.   Operated or sponsored by a duly accredited law school;

b. Operated or sponsored by a bona fide, non-profit community organization;

c. Operated or sponsored by a governmental agency; or

d. Operated, sponsored, or approved by a bar association;

2. A military legal assistance office;

3. A lawyer referral service operated, sponsored or approved by a bar association;

4. Any bona fide organization which recommends, furnishes or pays for legal services to its members or beneficiaries provided the following conditions are satisfied:

a. Neither the lawyer, nor the lawyer's partner, nor associate, nor any other affiliated lawyer nor any non-lawyer, shall have initiated or promoted such organization for the primary purpose of providing financial or other benefit to such lawyer, partner, associate or affiliated lawyer.

b. Such organization is not operated for the purpose of procuring legal work or financial benefit for any lawyer as a private practitioner outside of the legal services program of the organization.

c. The member or beneficiary to whom the legal services are furnished, and not such organization, is recognized as the client of the lawyer in the matter.

d. Any member or beneficiary who is entitled to have legal services furnished or paid for by the organization may, if such member or beneficiary so desires, select counsel other than that furnished, selected or approved by the organization for the particular matter involved; and the legal service plan of such organization provides appropriate relief for any member or beneficiary who asserts a claim that representation by counsel furnished, selected or approved would be unethical, improper or inadequate under the circumstances of the matter involved; and the plan provides an appropriate procedure for seeking such relief.

e. The lawyer does not know or have cause to know that such organization is in violation of applicable laws, rules of court or other legal requirements that govern its legal service operations.

f. Such organization has filed with the appropriate disciplinary authority, to the extent required by such authority, at least annually a report with respect to its legal service plan, if any, showing its terms, its schedule of benefits, its subscription charges, agreements with counsel and financial results of its legal service activities or, if it has failed to do so, the lawyer does not know or have cause to know of such failure.

E. A lawyer shall not accept employment when the lawyer knows or it is obvious that the person who seeks services does so as a result of conduct prohibited under this Disciplinary Rule.

F. Advertising not proscribed under DR 2–101 shall not be deemed in violation of any provision of this Disciplinary Rule.

DR 2–104. Suggestion of Need of Legal Services

A. A lawyer who has given unsolicited advice to an individual to obtain counsel or take legal action shall not accept employment resulting from that advice, in violation of any statute or court rule.

B. A lawyer may accept employment by a close friend, relative, former client (if the advice is germane to the former employment) or one whom the lawyer reasonably believes to be a client.

C. A lawyer may accept employment which results from participation in activities designed to educate the public to recognize legal problems, to make intelligent selection of counsel or to utilize available legal services.

D. A lawyer who is recommended, furnished or paid by a qualified legal assistance organization enumerated in DR 2–103(D)(1) through (4) may represent a member or beneficiary thereof, to the extent and under the conditions prescribed therein.

E. Without affecting the right to accept employment, a lawyer may speak publicly or write for publication on legal topics so long as the lawyer does not undertake to give individual advice.

F. Subject to compliance with the provisions of DR 2–103(A), if success in asserting rights or defenses of a client in litigation in the nature of a class action is dependent upon the joinder of others, a lawyer may accept employment from those contacted for the purpose of obtaining their joinder.

DR 2–105. Identification of Practice and Specialty

A. A lawyer or law firm may publicly identify one or more areas of law in which the lawyer or the law firm practices, or may state that the practice of the lawyer or law firm is limited to one or more areas of law.

B. A lawyer who is certified as a specialist in a particular area of law or law practice by the authority having jurisdiction under the laws of this state over the subject of specialization by lawyers may hold himself or herself out as a specialist, but only in accordance with the rules prescribed by that authority.

DR 2–106. Fee for Legal Services

A. A lawyer shall not enter into an agreement for, charge or collect an illegal or excessive fee.

B.   A fee is excessive when, after a review of the facts, a lawyer of ordinary prudence would be left with a definite and firm conviction that the fee is in excess of a reasonable fee. Factors to be considered as guides in determining the reasonableness of a fee include the following:

1.   The time and labor required, the novelty and difficulty of the questions involved and the skill requisite to perform the legal service properly.

2.   The likelihood, if apparent or made known to the client, that the acceptance of the particular employment will preclude other employment by the lawyer.

3.   The fee customarily charged in the locality for similar legal services.

4.   The amount involved and the results obtained.

5.   The time limitations imposed by the client or by circumstances.

6.   The nature and length of the professional relationship with the client.

7.   The experience, reputation and ability of the lawyer or lawyers performing the services.

8.   Whether the fee is fixed or contingent.

C.   A lawyer shall not enter into an arrangement for, charge or collect:

1.   A contingent fee for representing a defendant in a criminal case; or

2.   Any fee in a domestic relations matter, the payment or amount of which is contingent upon the securing of a divorce or upon the amount of maintenance, support, equitable distribution, or property settlement; or

3.   A fee proscribed by law or rule of court.

D.   Promptly after a lawyer has been employed in a contingent fee matter, the lawyer shall provide the client with a writing stating the method by which the fee is to be determined, including the percentage or percentages that shall accrue to the lawyer in the event of settlement, trial or appeal, litigation and other expenses to be deducted from the recovery and whether such expenses are to be deducted before or after the contingent fee is calculated. Upon conclusion of a contingent fee matter, the lawyer shall provide the client with a written statement stating the outcome of the matter, and if there is a recovery, showing the remittance to the client and the method of its determination.

DR 2–107.   Division of Fees Among Lawyers

A.   A lawyer shall not divide a fee for legal services with another lawyer who is not a partner in or associate of the lawyer's law firm or law office, unless:

1. The client consents to employment of the other lawyer after a full disclosure that a division of fees will be made.

2. The division is in proportion to the services performed by each lawyer or, by a writing given to the client, each lawyer assumes joint responsibility for the representation.

3. The total fee of the lawyers does not exceed reasonable compensation for all legal services they rendered the client.

B. This Disciplinary Rule does not prohibit payment to a former partner or associate pursuant to a separation or retirement agreement.

DR 2–108. Agreements Restricting the Practice of a Lawyer

A. A lawyer shall not be a party to or participate in a partnership or employment agreement with another lawyer that restricts the right of a lawyer to practice law after the termination of a relationship created by the agreement, except as a condition to payment of retirement benefits.

B. In connection with the settlement of a controversy or suit, a lawyer shall not enter into an agreement that restricts the right of a lawyer to practice law.

DR 2–109. Acceptance of Employment

A.[1] A lawyer shall not accept employment on behalf of a person if the lawyer knows or it is obvious that such person wishes to:

1. Bring a legal action, conduct a defense, or assert a position in litigation, or otherwise have steps taken for such person merely for the purpose of harassing or maliciously injuring any person.

2. Present a claim or defense in litigation that is not warranted under existing law, unless it can be supported by good faith argument for an extension, modification, or reversal of existing law.

DR 2–110. Withdrawal From Employment

A. **In general.** 1. If permission for withdrawal from employment is required by the rules of a tribunal, a lawyer shall not withdraw from employment in a proceeding before that tribunal without its permission.

2. Even when withdrawal is otherwise permitted or required under DR 2–110(A)(1), (B) or (C), a lawyer shall not withdraw from employment until the lawyer has taken steps to the extent reasonably practicable to avoid foreseeable prejudice to the rights of the client, including giving due notice to the client, allowing time for employment of other counsel, delivering to the client all papers and

1. So in original. No par. B has been enacted.

921

property to which the client is entitled and complying with applicable laws and rules.

3.   A lawyer who withdraws from employment shall refund promptly any part of a fee paid in advance that has not been earned.

B.   Mandatory withdrawal. A lawyer representing a client before a tribunal, with its permission if required by its rules, shall withdraw from employment, and a lawyer representing a client in other matters shall withdraw from employment, if:

1.   The lawyer knows or it is obvious that the client is bringing the legal action, conducting the defense, or asserting a position in the litigation, or is otherwise having steps taken, merely for the purpose of harassing or maliciously injuring any person.

2.   The lawyer knows or it is obvious that continued employment will result in violation of a Disciplinary Rule.

3.   The lawyer's mental or physical condition renders it unreasonably difficult to carry out the employment effectively.

4.   The lawyer is discharged by his or her client.

C.   Permissive withdrawal. Except as stated in DR 2–110(A), a lawyer may withdraw from representing a client if withdrawal can be accomplished without material adverse effect on the interests of the client, or if:

1.   The client:

a.   Insists upon presenting a claim or defense that is not warranted under existing law and cannot be supported by good faith argument for an extension, modification, or reversal of existing law.

b.   Persists in a course of action involving the lawyer's services that the lawyer reasonably believes is criminal or fraudulent.

c.   Insists that the lawyer pursue a course of conduct which is illegal or prohibited under the Disciplinary Rules.

d.   By other conduct renders it unreasonably difficult for the lawyer to carry out employment effectively.

e.   Insists, in a matter not pending before a tribunal, that the lawyer engage in conduct which is contrary to the judgment and advice of the lawyer but not prohibited under the Disciplinary Rules.

f.   Deliberately disregards an agreement or obligation to the lawyer as to expenses or fees.

g.   Has used the lawyer's services to perpetrate a crime or fraud.

2. The lawyer's continued employment is likely to result in a violation of a Disciplinary Rule.

3. The lawyer's inability to work with co-counsel indicates that the best interests of the client likely will be served by withdrawal.

4. The lawyer's mental or physical condition renders it difficult for the lawyer to carry out the employment effectively.

5. The lawyer's client knowingly and freely assents to termination of the employment.

6. The lawyer believes in good faith, in a proceeding pending before a tribunal, that the tribunal will find the existence of other good cause for withdrawal.

CANON 3

A Lawyer Should Assist in Preventing the Unauthorized Practice of Law

DR 3-101. Aiding Unauthorized Practice of Law

A. A lawyer shall not aid a non-lawyer in the unauthorized practice of law.

B. A lawyer shall not practice law in a jurisdiction where to do so would be in violation of regulations of the profession in that jurisdiction.

DR 3-102. Dividing Legal Fees With a Non-lawyer

A.[1] A lawyer or law firm shall not share legal fees with a non-lawyer, except that:

1. An agreement by a lawyer with his or her firm, partner, or associate may provide for the payment of money, over a reasonable period of time after the lawyer's death, to the lawyer's estate or to one or more specified persons.

2. A lawyer who undertakes to complete unfinished legal business of a deceased lawyer may pay to the estate of the deceased lawyer that proportion of the total compensation which fairly represents the services rendered by the deceased lawyer.

3. A lawyer or law firm may include non-lawyer employees in a retirement plan, even though the plan is based in whole or in part on a profit-sharing arrangement.

DR 3-103. Forming a Partnership With a Non-lawyer

A.[1] A lawyer shall not form a partnership with a non-lawyer if any of the activities of the partnership consist of the practice law.

1. So in original. No par. B has been enacted.

CANON 4

A Lawyer Should Preserve the Confidences and Secrets of a Client

DR 4–101.　Preservation of Confidences and Secrets of a Client

A.　"Confidence" refers to information protected by the attorney-client privilege under applicable law, and "secret" refers to other information gained in the professional relationship that the client has requested be held inviolate or the disclosure of which would be embarrassing or would be likely to be detrimental to the client.

B.　Except when permitted under DR 4–101(C), a lawyer shall not knowingly:

1.　Reveal a confidence or secret of a client.

2.　Use a confidence or secret of a client to the disadvantage of the client.

3.　Use a confidence or secret of a client for the advantage of the lawyer or of a third person, unless the client consents after full disclosure.

C.　A lawyer may reveal:

1.　Confidences or secrets with the consent of the client or clients affected, but only after a full disclosure to them.

2.　Confidences or secrets when permitted under Disciplinary Rules or required by law or court order.

3.　The intention of a client to commit a crime and the information necessary to prevent the crime.

4.　Confidences or secrets necessary to establish or collect the lawyer's fee or to defend the lawyer or his or her employees or associates against an accusation of wrongful conduct.

5.　Confidences or secrets to the extent implicit in withdrawing a written or oral opinion or representation previously given by the lawyer and believed by the lawyer still to be relied upon by a third person where the lawyer has discovered that the opinion or representation was based on materially inaccurate information or is being used to further a crime or fraud.

D.　A lawyer shall exercise reasonable care to prevent his or her employees, associates, and others whose services are utilized by the lawyer from disclosing or using confidences or secrets of a client, except that a lawyer may reveal the information allowed by DR 4–101(C) through an employee.

CANON 5

A Lawyer Should Exercise Independent Professional Judgment on Behalf of a Client

DR 5-101. Refusing Employment When the Interest of the Lawyer May Impair Independent Professional Judgment

A. Except with the consent of the client after full disclosure, a lawyer shall not accept employment if the exercise of professional judgment on behalf of the client will be or reasonably may be affected by the lawyer's own financial, business, property, or personal interests.

B. A lawyer shall not act, or accept employment that contemplates the lawyer's acting, as an advocate before any tribunal if the lawyer knows or it is obvious that the lawyer ought to be called as a witness on behalf of the client, except that the lawyer may act as an advocate and also testify:

1. If the testimony will relate solely to an uncontested issue.

2. If the testimony will relate solely to a matter of formality and there is no reason to believe that substantial evidence will be offered in opposition to the testimony.

3. If the testimony will relate solely to the nature and value of legal services rendered in the case by the lawyer or the lawyer's firm to the client.

4. As to any matter, if disqualification as an advocate would work a substantial hardship on the client because of the distinctive value of the lawyer as counsel in the particular case.

C. Neither a lawyer nor the lawyer's firm shall accept employment in contemplated or pending litigation if the lawyer knows or it is obvious that the lawyer or another lawyer in the lawyer's firm may be called as a witness other than on behalf of the client, and it is apparent that the testimony would or might be prejudicial to the client.

DR 5-102. Withdrawal as Counsel When the Lawyer Becomes a Witness

A. If, after undertaking employment in contemplated or pending litigation, a lawyer learns or it is obvious that the lawyer ought to be called as a witness on behalf of the client, the lawyer shall withdraw as an advocate before the tribunal, except that the lawyer may continue as an advocate and may testify in the circumstances enumerated in DR 5-101(B)(1) through (4).

B. If, after undertaking employment in contemplated or pending litigation, a lawyer learns or it is obvious that the lawyer or a lawyer in his or her firm may be called as a witness other than on behalf of the client, the lawyer may continue the representation until it is apparent that the testimony is or may be prejudicial to the client at which point the lawyer and the firm must withdraw from acting as an advocate before the tribunal.

DR 5–103. Avoiding Acquisition of Interest in Litigation

A. A lawyer shall not acquire a proprietary interest in the cause of action or subject matter of litigation he or she is conducting for a client, except that the lawyer may:

1. Acquire a lien granted by law to secure the lawyer's fee or expenses.

2. Except as provided in DR 2–106(C)(2) or (3), contract with a client for a reasonable contingent fee in a civil case.

B. While representing a client in connection with contemplated or pending litigation, a lawyer shall not advance or guarantee financial assistance to the client, except that:

1. A lawyer may advance or guarantee the expenses of litigation, including court costs, expenses of investigation, expenses of medical examination, and costs of obtaining and presenting evidence, provided the client remains ultimately liable for such expenses.

2. Unless prohibited by law or rule of court, a lawyer representing an indigent client on a pro bono basis may pay court costs and reasonable expenses of litigation on behalf of the client.

DR 5–104. Limiting Business Relations With a Client

A. A lawyer shall not enter into a business transaction with a client if they have differing interests therein and if the client expects the lawyer to exercise professional judgment therein for the protection of the client, unless the client has consented after full disclosure.

B. Prior to conclusion of all aspects of the matter giving rise to employment, a lawyer shall not enter into any arrangement or understanding with a client or a prospective client by which the lawyer acquires an interest in literary or media rights with respect to the subject matter of the employment or proposed employment.

DR 5–105. Refusing to Accept or Continue Employment if the Interests of Another Client May Impair the Independent Professional Judgment of the Lawyer

A. A lawyer shall decline proffered employment if the exercise of independent professional judgment in behalf of a client will be or is likely to be adversely affected by the acceptance of the proffered employment, or if it would be likely to involve the lawyer in representing differing interests, except to the extent permitted under DR 5–105(C).

B. A lawyer shall not continue multiple employment if the exercise of independent professional judgment in behalf of a client will be or is likely to be adversely affected by the lawyer's representation of another client, or if it would be likely to involve the lawyer in representing differing interests, except to the extent permitted under DR 5–105(C).

C. In the situations covered by DR 5–105(A) and (B), a lawyer may represent multiple clients if it is obvious that the lawyer can adequately represent the interest of each and if each consents to the representation after full disclosure of the possible effect of such representation on the exercise of the lawyer's independent professional judgment on behalf of each.

D. While lawyers are associated in a law firm, none of them shall knowingly accept or continue employment when any one of them practicing alone would be prohibited from doing so under DR 5–101(A), DR 5–105(A), (B) or (C), DR 5–108, or DR 9–101(B) except as otherwise provided therein.

DR 5–106. Settling Similar Claims of Clients

A.[1] A lawyer who represents two or more clients shall not make or participate in the making of an aggregate settlement of the claims of or against the clients, unless each client has consented to the settlement after being advised of the existence and nature of all the claims involved in the proposed settlement, of the total amount of the settlement, and of the participation of each person in the settlement.

DR 5–107. Avoiding Influence by Others Than the Client

A. Except with the consent of the client after full disclosure a lawyer shall not:

1. Accept compensation for legal services from one other than the client.

2. Accept from one other than the client any thing of value related to his or her representation of or employment by the client.

B. A lawyer shall not permit a person who recommends, employs, or pays the lawyer to render legal service for another to direct or regulate his or her professional judgment in rendering such legal services.

C. A lawyer shall not practice with or in the form of a professional corporation or association authorized to practice law for a profit, if:

1. A non-lawyer owns any interest therein, except that a fiduciary representative of the estate of a lawyer may hold the stock or interest of the lawyer for a reasonable time during administration;

1. So in original. No par. B has been enacted.

2. A non-lawyer is a corporate director or officer thereof; or

3. A non-lawyer has the right to direct or control the professional judgment of a lawyer.

DR 5–108. Conflict of Interest—Former Client

A.[1] Except with the consent of a former client after full disclosure a lawyer who has represented the former client in a matter shall not:

1. Thereafter represent another person in the same or a substantially related matter in which that person's interests are materially adverse to the interests of the former client.

2. Use any confidences or secrets of the former client except as permitted by DR 4–101(C) or when the confidence or secret has become generally known.

DR 5–109. Conflict of Interest—Organization as Client

A.[1] When a lawyer employed or retained by an organization is dealing with the organization's directors, officers, employees, members, shareholders or other constituents, and it appears that the organization's interests may differ from those of the constituents with whom the lawyer is dealing, the lawyer shall explain that the lawyer is the lawyer for the organization and not for any of the constituents.

DR 5–110. Membership in Legal Services Organization

A.[1] A lawyer may serve as a director, officer or member of a not-for-profit legal services organization, apart from the law firm in which the lawyer practices, notwithstanding that the organization serves persons having interests that differ from those of a client of the lawyer or the lawyer's firm, provided that the lawyer shall not knowingly participate in a decision or action of the organization.

1. If participating in the decision or action would be incompatible with the lawyer's duty of loyalty to a client under Canon 5; or

2. Where the decision or action could have a material adverse effect on the representation of a client of the organization whose interests differ from those of a client of the lawyer or the lawyer's firm.

1. So in original. No par. B has been enacted.

CANON 6

A Lawyer Should Represent a Client Competently

DISCIPLINARY RULES

DR 6-101. Failing to Act Competently

A.[1] A lawyer shall not:

1. Handle a legal matter which the lawyer knows or should know that he or she is not competent to handle, without associating with a lawyer who is competent to handle it.

2. Handle a legal matter without preparation adequate in the circumstances.

3. Neglect a legal matter entrusted to the lawyer.

DR 6-102. Limiting Liability to Client

A.[1] A lawyer shall not seek, by contract or other means, to limit prospectively the lawyer's individual liability to a client for malpractice, or, without first advising that person that independent representation is appropriate in connection therewith, to settle a claim for such liability with an unrepresented client or former client.

CANON 7

A Lawyer Should Represent a Client Zealously Within the Bounds of the Law

DR 7-101. Representing a Client Zealously

A. A lawyer shall not intentionally:

1. Fail to seek the lawful objectives of the client through reasonably available means permitted by law and the Disciplinary Rules, except as provided by DR 7-101(B). A lawyer does not violate this Disciplinary Rule, however, by acceding to reasonable requests of opposing counsel which do not prejudice the rights of the client, by being punctual in fulfilling all professional commitments, by avoiding offensive tactics, or by treating with courtesy and consideration all persons involved in the legal process.

2. Fail to carry out a contract of employment entered into with a client for professional services, but the lawyer may withdraw as permitted under DR 2-110, DR 5-102, and DR 5-105.

3. Prejudice or damage the client during the course of the professional relationship, except as required under DR 7-102(B).

1. So in original. No par. B has been enacted.

B. In the representation of a client, a lawyer may:

1. Where permissible, exercise professional judgment to waive or fail to assert a right or position of the client.

2. Refuse to aid or participate in conduct that the lawyer believes to be unlawful, even though there is some support for an argument that the conduct is legal.

DR 7-102. Representing a Client Within the Bounds of the Law

A. In the representation of a client, a lawyer shall not:

1. File a suit, assert a position, conduct a defense, delay a trial, or take other action on behalf of the client when the lawyer knows or when it is obvious that such action would serve merely to harass or maliciously injure another.

2. Knowingly advance a claim or defense that is unwarranted under existing law, except that the lawyer may advance such claim or defense if it can be supported by good faith argument for an extension, modification, or reversal of existing law.

3. Conceal or knowingly fail to disclose that which the lawyer is required by law to reveal.

4. Knowingly use perjured testimony or false evidence.

5. Knowingly make a false statement of law or fact.

6. Participate in the creation or preservation of evidence when the lawyer knows or it is obvious that the evidence is false.

7. Counsel or assist the client in conduct that the lawyer knows to be illegal or fraudulent.

8. Knowingly engage in other illegal conduct or conduct contrary to a Disciplinary Rule.

B. A lawyer who receives information clearly establishing that:

1. The client has, in the course of the representation, perpetrated a fraud upon a person or tribunal shall promptly call upon the client to rectify the same, and if the client refuses or is unable to do so, the lawyer shall reveal the fraud to the affected person or tribunal, except when the information is protected as a confidence or secret.

2. A person other than the client has perpetrated a fraud upon a tribunal shall promptly reveal the fraud to the tribunal.

DR 7-103. Performing the Duty of Public Prosecutor or Other Government Lawyer

A. A public prosecutor or other government lawyer shall not institute or cause to be instituted criminal charges when he or she knows or it is obvious that the charges are not supported by probable cause.

B. A public prosecutor or other government lawyer in criminal litigation shall make timely disclosure to counsel for the defendant, or to a defendant who has no counsel, of the existence of evidence, known to the prosecutor or other government lawyer, that tends to negate the guilt of the accused, mitigate the degree of the offense or reduce the punishment.

DR 7-104. Communicating with One of Adverse Interest

A.[1] During the course of the representation of a client a lawyer shall not:

1. Communicate or cause another to communicate on the subject of the representation with a party the lawyer knows to be represented by a lawyer in that matter unless the lawyer has the prior consent of the lawyer representing such other party or is authorized by law to do so.

2. Give advice to a person who is not represented by a lawyer, other than the advice to secure counsel, if the interests of such person are or have a reasonable possibility of being in conflict with the interests of the lawyer's client.

DR 7-105. Threatening Criminal Prosecution

A.[1] A lawyer shall not present, participate in presenting, or threaten to present criminal charges solely to obtain an advantage in a civil matter.

DR 7-106. Trial Conduct

A. A lawyer shall not disregard or advise the client to disregard a standing rule of a tribunal or a ruling of a tribunal made in the course of a proceeding, but the lawyer may take appropriate steps in good faith to test the validity of such rule or ruling.

B. In presenting a matter to a tribunal, a lawyer shall disclose:

1. Controlling legal authority known to the lawyer to be directly adverse to the position of the client and which is not disclosed by opposing counsel.

2. Unless privileged or irrelevant, the identities of the clients the lawyer represents and of the persons who employed the lawyer.

C. In appearing as a lawyer before a tribunal, a lawyer shall not:

1. State or allude to any matter that he or she has no reasonable basis to believe is relevant to the case or that will not be supported by admissible evidence.

1. So in original. No par. B has been enacted.

2.   Ask any question that he or she has no reasonable basis to believe is relevant to the case and that is intended to degrade a witness or other person.

3.   Assert personal knowledge of the facts in issue, except when testifying as a witness.

4.   Assert a personal opinion as to the justness of a cause, as to the credibility of a witness, as to the culpability of a civil litigant, or as to the guilt or innocence of an accused; but the lawyer may argue, upon analysis of the evidence, for any position or conclusion with respect to the matters stated herein.

5.   Fail to comply with known local customs of courtesy or practice of the bar or a particular tribunal without giving to opposing counsel timely notice of the intent not to comply.

6.   Engage in undignified or discourteous conduct which is degrading to a tribunal.

7.   Intentionally or habitually violate any established rule of procedure or of evidence.

DR 7–107. Trial Publicity

A.   A lawyer participating in or associated with a criminal or civil matter shall not make an extrajudicial statement that a reasonable person would expect to be disseminated by means of public communication if the lawyer knows or reasonably should know that it will have a substantial likelihood of materially prejudicing an adjudicative proceeding.

B.   A statement ordinarily is likely to prejudice materially an adjudicative proceeding when it refers to a civil matter triable to a jury, a criminal matter, or any other proceeding that could result in incarceration, and the statement relates to:

1.   The character, credibility, reputation or criminal record of a party, suspect in a criminal investigation or witness, or the identity of a witness, or the expected testimony of a party or witness.

2.   In a criminal case or proceeding that could result in incarceration, the possibility of a plea of guilty to the offense or the existence or contents of any confession, admission, or statement given by a defendant or suspect or that person's refusal or failure to make a statement.

3.   The performance or results of any examination or test or the refusal or failure of a person to submit to an examination or test, or the identity or nature of physical evidence expected to be presented.

4. Any opinion as to the guilt or innocence of a defendant or suspect in a criminal case or proceeding that could result in incarceration.

5. Information the lawyer knows or reasonably should know is likely to be inadmissible as evidence in a trial and would if disclosed create a substantial risk of prejudicing an impartial trial.

6. The fact that a defendant has been charged with a crime, unless there is included therein a statement explaining that the charge is merely an accusation and that the defendant is presumed innocent until and unless proven guilty.

C. Provided that the statement complies with DR 7-107(A), a lawyer involved with the investigation or litigation of a matter may state the following without elaboration:

1. The general nature of the claim or defense.

2. The information contained in a public record.

3. That an investigation of the matter is in progress.

4. The scheduling or result of any step in litigation.

5. A request for assistance in obtaining evidence and information necessary thereto.

6. A warning of danger concerning the behavior of a person involved, when there is reason to believe that there exists the likelihood of substantial harm to an individual or to the public interest.

7. In a criminal case:

    a. The identity, age, residence, occupation and family status of the accused.

    b. If the accused has not been apprehended, information necessary to aid in apprehension of that person.

    c. The fact, time and place of arrest, resistance, pursuit, use of weapons, and a description of physical evidence seized, other than as contained only in a confession, admission, or statement.

    d. The identity of investigating and arresting officers or agencies and the length of the investigation.

DR 7-108. Communication With or Investigation of Jurors

A. Before the trial of a case a lawyer connected therewith shall not communicate with or cause another to communicate with anyone the lawyer knows to be a member of the venire from which the jury will be selected for the trial of the case.

B. During the trial of a case:

1. A lawyer connected therewith shall not communicate with or cause another to communicate with any member of the jury.

2.   A lawyer who is not connected therewith shall not communicate with or cause another to communicate with a juror concerning the case.

C.   DR 7–108(A) and (B) do not prohibit a lawyer from communicating with members of the venire or jurors in the course of official proceedings.

D.   After discharge of the jury from further consideration of a case with which the lawyer was connected, the lawyer shall not ask questions of or make comments to a member of that jury that are calculated merely to harass or embarrass the juror or to influence the juror's actions in future jury service.

E.   A lawyer shall not conduct or cause, by financial support or otherwise, another to conduct a vexatious or harassing investigation of either a member of the venire or a juror.

F.   All restrictions imposed by DR 7–108 upon a lawyer also apply to communications with or investigations of members of a family of a member of the venire or a juror.

G.   A lawyer shall reveal promptly to the court improper conduct by a member of the venire or a juror, or by another toward a member of the venire or a juror or a member of his or her family of which the lawyer has knowledge.

DR 7–109.   Contact With Witnesses

A.   A lawyer shall not suppress any evidence that the lawyer or the client has a legal obligation to reveal or produce.

B.   A lawyer shall not advise or cause a person to hide or to leave the jurisdiction of a tribunal for the purpose of making the person unavailable as a witness therein.

C.   A lawyer shall not pay, offer to pay, or acquiesce in the payment of compensation to a witness contingent upon the content of his or her testimony or the outcome of the case.   But a lawyer may advance, guarantee, or acquiesce in the payment of:

1.   Expenses reasonably incurred by a witness in attending or testifying.

2.   Reasonable compensation to a witness for the loss of time in attending or testifying.

3.   A reasonable fee for the professional services of an expert witness.

DR 7–110.   Contact With Officials

A.   A lawyer shall not give or lend anything of value to a judge, official, or employee of a tribunal except as permitted by Section C(4) of Canon 5 of the Code of Judicial Conduct, but a lawyer may make a contribution to the campaign fund of a candidate for judicial office in conformity with Section B(2) under Canon 7 of the Code of Judicial Conduct.

B. In an adversary proceeding, a lawyer shall not communicate, or cause another to communicate, as to the merits of the cause with a judge or an official before whom the proceeding is pending, except:

1. In the course of official proceedings in the cause.

2. In writing if the lawyer promptly delivers a copy of the writing to opposing counsel or to an adverse party who is not represented by a lawyer.

3. Orally upon adequate notice to opposing counsel or to an adverse party who is not represented by a lawyer.

4. As otherwise authorized by law, or by Section A(4) under Canon 3 of the Code of Judicial Conduct.

CANON 8
A Lawyer Should Assist in Improving the Legal System

DR 8-101. Action as a Public Official

A.[1] A lawyer who holds public office shall not:

1. Use the public position to obtain, or attempt to obtain, a special advantage in legislative matters for the lawyer or for a client under circumstances where the lawyer knows or it is obvious that such action is not in the public interest.

2. Use the public position to influence, or attempt to influence, a tribunal to act in favor of the lawyer or of a client.

3. Accept any thing of value from any person when the lawyer knows or it is obvious that the offer is for the purpose of influencing the lawyer's action as a public official.

DR 8-102. Statements Concerning Judges and Other Adjudicatory Officers

A. A lawyer shall not knowingly make false statements of fact concerning the qualifications of a candidate for election or appointment to a judicial office.

B. A lawyer shall not knowingly make false accusations against a judge or other adjudicatory officer.

DR 8-103. Lawyer Candidate for Judicial Office

A.[1] A lawyer who is a candidate for judicial office shall comply with the applicable provisions of Canon 7 of the Code of Judicial Conduct.

1. So in original. No par. B has been enacted.

CANON 9

A Lawyer Should Avoid Even the Appearance of Professional Impropriety

DR 9–101. Avoiding Even the Appearance of Impropriety

A. A lawyer shall not accept private employment in a matter upon the merits of which the lawyer has acted in a judicial capacity.

B. Except as law may otherwise expressly permit:

1. A lawyer shall not represent a private client in connection with a matter in which the lawyer participated personally and substantially as a public officer or employee, and no lawyer in a firm with which that lawyer is associated may knowingly undertake or continue representation in such a matter unless:

a. The disqualified lawyer is effectively screened from any participation, direct or indirect, including discussion, in the matter and is apportioned no part of the fee therefrom; and

b. There are no other circumstances in the particular representation that create an appearance of impropriety.

2. A lawyer having information that the lawyer knows is confidential government information about a person, acquired when the lawyer was a public officer or employee, may not represent a private client whose interests are adverse to that person in a matter in which the information could be used to the material disadvantage of that person. A firm with which that lawyer is associated may knowingly undertake or continue representation in the matter only if the disqualified lawyer is effectively screened from any participation, direct or indirect, including discussion, in the matter and is apportioned no part of the fee therefrom.

3. A lawyer serving as a public officer or employee shall not:

a. Participate in a matter in which the lawyer participated personally and substantially while in private practice or nongovernmental employment, unless under applicable law no one is, or by lawful delegation may be, authorized to act in the lawyer's stead in the matter; or

b. Negotiate for private employment with any person who is involved as a party or as attorney for a party in a matter in which the lawyer is participating personally and substantially.

C. A lawyer shall not state or imply that the lawyer is able to influence improperly or upon irrelevant grounds any tribunal, legislative body, or public official.

936

D. A lawyer related to another lawyer as parent, child, sibling or spouse shall not represent in any matter a client whose interests differ from those of another party to the matter who the lawyer knows is represented by the other lawyer unless the client consents to the representation after full disclosure and the lawyer concludes that the lawyer can adequately represent the interests of the client.

DR 9-102. Preserving Identity of Funds and Property of Others; Fiduciary Responsibility; Maintenance of Bank Accounts; Recordkeeping; Examination of Records

A. Prohibition Against Commingling. A lawyer in possession of any funds or other property belonging to another person, where such possession is incident to his or her practice of law, is a fiduciary, and must not commingle such property with his or her own.

B. Separate Accounts. 1. A lawyer who is in possession of funds belonging to another person incident to the lawyer's practice of law, shall maintain in a bank or trust company within the State of New York in the lawyer's own name, or in the name of a firm of lawyers of which he or she is a member, or in the name of the lawyer or firm of lawyers by whom he or she is employed, a special account or accounts, separate from any business or personal accounts of the lawyer or lawyer's firm, and separate from any accounts which the lawyer may maintain as executor, guardian, trustee or receiver, or in any other fiduciary capacity, into which special account or accounts all funds held in escrow or otherwise entrusted to the lawyer or firm shall be deposited; provided, however, that such funds may be maintained in a bank or trust company located outside the State of New York with the prior written approval of the person to whom such funds belong specifying the name and address of the bank or trust company where such funds are to be maintained.

2. Other than accounts maintained by a lawyer as executor, guardian, trustee or receiver, or in any other such fiduciary capacity, all special accounts as well as all deposit slips relating to and checks drawn upon such special accounts, shall be designated in a manner sufficient to distinguish them from all other bank accounts maintained by the lawyer or the lawyer's firm.

3. Funds reasonably sufficient to maintain the account or to pay account charges may be deposited therein.

4. Funds belonging in part to a client or third person and in part presently or potentially to the lawyer or law firm shall be kept in such special account or accounts, but the portion belonging to the lawyer or law firm may be withdrawn when due unless the right of the lawyer or law firm to receive it is disputed by the client or third person, in which event the disputed portion shall not be withdrawn until the dispute is finally resolved.

C. Notification of Receipt of Property; Safekeeping; Rendering Accounts; Payment or Delivery of Property. A lawyer shall:

1. Promptly notify a client or third person of the receipt of funds, securities, or other properties in which the client or third person has an interest.

2. Identify and label securities and properties of a client or third person promptly upon receipt and place them in a safe deposit box or other place of safekeeping as soon as practicable.

3. Maintain complete records of all funds, securities, and other properties of a client or third person coming into the possession of the lawyer and render appropriate accounts to the client or third person regarding them.

4. Promptly pay or deliver to the client or third person as requested by the client or third person the funds, securities, or other properties in the possession of the lawyer which the client or third person is entitled to receive.

D. Required Bookkeeping Records. A lawyer shall maintain for seven years after the events which they record:

1. The records of all deposits in and withdrawals from special accounts specified in DR 9–102(B) and of any other bank account which records the operations of the lawyer's practice of law. These records shall specifically identify the date, source and description of each item deposited, as well as the date, payee and purpose of each withdrawal or disbursement.

2. A record for special accounts, showing the source of all funds deposited in such accounts, the names of all persons for whom the funds are or were held, the amount of such funds, the description and amounts, and the names of all persons to whom such funds were disbursed.

3. Copies of all retainer and compensation agreements with clients.

4. Copies of all statements to clients or other persons showing the disbursement of funds to them or on their behalf.

5. Copies of all bills rendered to clients.

6. Copies of all records showing payments to lawyers, investigators or other persons, not in the lawyer's regular employ, for services rendered or performed.

7. Copies of all retainer and closing statements filed with the Office of Court Administration.

8. All checkbooks and checkstubs, bank statements, prenumbered cancelled checks and duplicate deposit slips with respect to the special accounts specified in DR 9–102(B) and any

other bank account which records the operations of the lawyer's practice of law.

Lawyers shall make accurate entries of all financial transactions in their records of receipts and disbursements, in their special accounts, in their ledger books or similar records, and in any other books of account kept by them in the regular course of their practice, which entries shall be made at or near the time of the act, condition or event recorded.

E. Authorized Signatories. All special account withdrawals shall be made only to a named payee and not to cash. Such withdrawals shall be made by check or, with the prior written approval of the party entitled to the proceeds, by bank transfer. Only an attorney admitted to practice law in New York State shall be an authorized signatory of a special account.

F. Missing Clients. Whenever any sum of money is payable to a client and the lawyer is unable to locate the client, the lawyer shall apply to the court in which the action was brought, or, if no action was commenced, to the Supreme Court in the county in which the lawyer has his or her office, for an order directing payment to the lawyer of his or her fee and disbursements and to the clerk of the court of the balance due to the client.

G. Dissolution of a Firm. Upon the dissolution of any firm of lawyers, the former partners or members shall make appropriate arrangements for the maintenance by one of them or by a successor firm of the records specified in DR 9-102(D). In the absence of agreement on such arrangements, any partner or former partner or member of a firm in dissolution may apply to the Appellate Division in which the principal office of the law firm is located or its designee for direction and such direction shall be binding upon all partners, former partners or members.

H. Availability of Bookkeeping Records; Records Subject to Production in Disciplinary Investigations and Proceedings. The financial records required by this Disciplinary Rule shall be located, or made available, at the principal New York State office of the lawyers subject hereto and any such records shall be produced in response to a notice or subpoena duces tecum issued in connection with a complaint before or any investigation by the appropriate grievance or departmental disciplinary committee, or shall be produced at the direction of the appropriate Appellate Division before any person designated by it. All books and records produced pursuant to this subdivision shall be kept confidential, except for the purpose of the particular proceeding, and their contents shall not be disclosed by anyone in violation of the lawyer-client privilege.

I. Disciplinary Action. A lawyer who does not maintain and keep the accounts and records as specified and required by this Disciplinary Rule, or who does not produce any such records pursuant to this Rule, shall be deemed in violation of these Rules and shall be subject to disciplinary proceedings.

†